Management

A Faith-Based Perspective

Management

A Faith-Based Perspective

MICHAEL E. CAFFERKY *Southern Adventist University*

PEARSON

Boston Columbus Indianapolis New York San Francisco Upper Saddle River
Amsterdam Cape Town Dubai London Madrid Milan Munich Paris Montréal Toronto
Delhi Mexico City São Paulo Sydney Hong Kong Seoul Singapore Taipei Tokyo

Editorial Director: Sally Yagan
Senior Acquisitions Editor: Kim Norbuta
Editorial Project Manager: Claudia Fernandes
Editorial Assistant: Carter Anderson
Director of Marketing: Patrice Lumumba Jones
Senior Marketing Manager: Nikki Ayana Jones
Marketing Assistant: Ian Gold
Senior Managing Editor: Judy Leale
Production Project Manager: Becca Groves
Senior Operations Supervisor: Arnold Vila
Operations Specialist: Cathleen Petersen
Creative Director: Christy Mahon
Senior Art Director: Janet Slowik
Art Director: Steve Frim
Text and Cover Designer: Jill Lehan
Cover Photo: Martin Kawalski/iStockphoto
Media Project Manager, Editorial: Denise Vaughn
Media Project Manager, Production: Lisa Rinaldi
Full-Service Project Management: BookMasters, Inc.
Composition: Integra Software Services, Inc.
Printer/Binder: Courier/Kendalville
Cover Printer: Lehigh-Phoenix/Hagerstown
Text Font: 10/12, Times

Credits and acknowledgments borrowed from other sources and reproduced, with permission, in this textbook appear on the appropriate page within text.

Library of Congress Cataloging-in-Publication Data

Cafferky, Michael E.
Management : a faith based perspective / Michael E. Cafferky.
p. cm.
Includes bibliographical references and index.
ISBN 978-0-13-605834-2 (pbk. : alk. paper)
1. Management—Religious aspects—Christianity. I. Title.
HD31.C25 2011
658—dc22
2011016900

10 9 8 7 6 5 4 3 2

PEARSON

ISBN 10: 0-13-605834-5
ISBN 13: 978-0-13-605834-2

Dedication

To Marlene . . .

My loving wife and partner, a faithful source of strength and encouragement and the model of the virtuous woman described in Proverbs 31:

> *An excellent wife, who can find? For her worth is far above jewels. The heart of her husband trusts in her. . . . She rises also while it is still night, and gives food to her household. . . . She extends her hand to the poor; she stretches out her hands to the needy. . . . Strength and dignity are her clothing, and she smiles at the future. She opens her mouth in wisdom, and the teaching of kindness is on her tongue. She looks well to the ways of her household, and does not eat the bread of idleness. Her children rise up and bless her.*
>
> *Proverbs 31*

Brief Table of Contents

Contents

Preface

Managerial work ranges far beyond the technical level such as the mathematics of measuring productivity, calculating net present value, formatting the written proposal for a new strategic initiative, or the use of technical planning tools. Managerial work quickly delves into the larger questions of life at work related to relationships, values, significance, and meaning. Because of this the particular perspective one has can make a difference when considering managerial work and its impact on global commerce.

An assumption in this book is that it matters to be aware of your perspective, particularly when the issues one must deal with touch on things in life and work that have meaning and where values are key influencing elements. Also, it is assumed that it matters that you intentionally examine the reasons why you view management issues in a particular way. This amounts to examination of the scholarship in the discipline as much as it is a self-examination. It is assumed that over time self-examination will contribute to your emergence as an integrated leader who is growing in effectiveness.

This book further assumes that the perspective of religious faith is a valid perspective with which to approach the issues suggested here, including self-examination and managerial work. Belief that a connection exists between religious faith and business management is not new. If we take the ancient Judeo-Christian holy writings as evidence we must say that for thousands of years many adherents to these two world religions have shared this assumption.[i]

Through the years theologians, religious leaders, and business writers have encouraged people to live their religious faith regardless of their occupation. No large leap of logic is required to see that such a call applies equally to managers as to other occupations. Here are a few examples from the last 800 years. St. Thomas Aquinas, one of the giant intellects of the Christian faith, wrote in his *Summa Theologica* on several topics related to business management. An interesting example is his treatise on prudence. In his 1524 essay on trade Martin Luther discussed tensions that the Christian experiences while managing pricing policies. Daniel Defoe included in his 1727 book *The Complete English Tradesman* ideas about how a person's faith should be integrated with business management. Half a century later Adam Smith offered his approach to integrating religious faith and explanations for human economic behavior in his book on moral philosophy. In 1852 Edwin Freedley published *Common Sense in Business,* a small portion of which was devoted to the issues of religious faith and management. About the same time Cambridge economist Alfred Marshall recognized the connection between economics and spirituality in his influential microeconomics textbook. After studying the phenomenon of business in society, German sociologist Max Weber claimed in his somewhat controversial book *The Protestant Ethic and the Spirit of Capitalism* that religion is one of the more influential forces in the conduct of business.[ii] In 1912 Frank W. Crane wrote in *Business and Kingdom Come*, his book about the National Cash Register Company, that religion consists of how a person makes money rather than in what he does with his money after it is made. In his 1920 book *Religion and Business* Roger Babson argued that religion is the strongest influence in achieving efficiency. In a 1924 letter to the editor of the *New York Times* Harrington Emerson, a proponent of scientific management, made a similar connection between religious faith and efficiency.[iii] We may or may not agree with the specific counsel provided by these and other authors. But the Christian manager interested in exploring how religious faith might guide managerial behavior will be willing to consider the issues they raise.

A growing choir of voices from more than one world religion such as Judaism, Christianity, and Islam support the desire to live a life of faith. Authors representing the Christian faith have produced dozens of trade books over the last quarter century, each with the purpose of encouraging further exploration of the implications of this assumption in business. Contributors to the *Journal of Biblical Integration in Business*, *Christian Scholar's Review*, and other journals have collectively grown the stream of thought regarding spirituality, religion, and management. The Management, Spirituality, and Religion Interest Group of the *Academy of Management* has for many years explored the implications of integrating spirituality in managerial study and practice.

Christian business professors have for decades been challenging their students to consider the claims of the Christian faith as applied to business and management. For most this has meant that they must bring supplemental material to the classroom not found in traditional so-called "secular" textbooks. Now the time has come for scholars in Christian colleges and universities to have an additional resource that encourages them to examine how their own religious beliefs influence their thinking about management theory and practice and vice versa. A resource such as this text may support the belief that the Christian higher education classroom is an appropriate place to consider the issues of religious faith as they relate to the discipline of management.

This brings me to the mission of this project. The purpose of this book is to be a distinctive management text that encourages the integration of a faith-based perspective founded on values and teachings that are common to most Christian denominations. To accomplish this the book presents the biblical record on the major management issues as well as the findings of contemporary management scholarship.

This book is a pedagogical tool. This text will attempt to deal with selected big questions and core issues of management from a faith-based perspective. It is not a devotional or inspirational book, though some readers may find new foundations here for devotion and inspiration and thereby deepen their worship. Some readers may find issues raised here that should be debated and through such intellectual exercises contribute to the richness of their worship experiences.[iv]

I assume a plurality of Christian perspectives. Because of this I have resisted presenting a monolithic, normative statement of how I personally believe all Christians ought to think and act as managers on every issue. Instead I have attempted to present the biblical record on the issues that guide how many practicing managers think and act relevant to the significant issues in managerial work when using a Christian worldview as their foundation.[v] I also present some of the challenging questions that Christians must face as they follow their faith recognizing that well-meaning Christians may differ in what they believe and practice. This is neither a book on comparative religion, nor a book that will resolve the differences between Protestants and Catholics or between Muslims and Jews and Christians on matters related to management.[vi] Readers will see gaps between what I present here and the distinctive beliefs they hold.

For those scholars who wish to supplement classroom discussions of the issues raised here with material peculiar to their own faith tradition, this text will provide a context from which to launch such explorations. For example, I encourage the Nazarene reader to take the foundation I have laid out and build on it to explore how the Nazarene perspective on the Bible will guide the Christian manager. Likewise, the Baptist, Lutheran, Presbyterian, Reformed, Mennonite, Anglican, Wesleyan, Roman Catholic, Seventh-day Adventist, and the reader who is an adherent to another faith will be able to engage the material guided by their particular interpretation of the Bible.

Because of space limitations some trade-off choices were made in selecting the content for this book. I do not represent all management theories and theorists. There is not space to review all scholarly contributions to management thought that has come to shape the discipline over the last century. There is not space here to biblically and theologically "test" every contemporary management theory. Scholars familiar with the discipline will agree or disagree with the choices I've made.

I assume that many if not most of the readers of this book will come from a Christian religious background or are studying business at Christian colleges and universities, and because of this they are generally aware of the Christian influences present and assumed to be valid by members of the faculty and administration in these institutions. This book offers to the person of Christian faith an opportunity to explore management issues from the perspective of that faith.[vii] Such an approach is not intended to foist on the reader particular religious beliefs of one denomination or another or, put in more crass terms, to be an irresponsible attempt to proselytize under the guise of scholarship. Rather it is designed to offer for consideration claims of the Christian religion as they affect Christians who are managers. Such an approach may be perceived by some readers to be more confessional than scholarly. Christianity, after all, is a confessional religion, and not merely an intellectual exercise.

Nothing in this book is intended to portray the assumption that a Christian perspective on issues related to management is complete. For those who believe that a Christian faith perspective should wrap up all the loose ends, provide definitive answers to all questions, comment on every difficult passage of the Bible, resolve every unsavory dilemma, and remove every unsettling paradox, this declaration might be disappointing. Instead of tying up loose ends, this book will offer an opportunity for the reader to explore them. It will offer an opportunity to celebrate the complex tensions that Christian managers face.

Though there are differences of opinion on how to interpret specific passages of the Bible, most Christians consider the Bible to be the authoritative rule of faith and practice. As you review the hundreds of chapter endnotes you will see that I make use of the Bible without apology. Of necessity particular Bible references and Christian theological themes must be explored. But this process raises a tension point for any scholar wishing to understand the biblical worldview on this or any other topic. On the one hand, specific Bible passages must be addressed since collectively these comprise the Bible's message for managers. On the other hand, I have tried to avoid cherry-picking a verse here and a verse there (a.k.a. "proof-texting") or employing biblical phrases without considering the larger theological themes that represent the whole of biblical truth. Even so, some readers may disagree with some interpretations of particular Scripture passages in this book. Others may not disagree but may have a slightly different perspective to offer on such passages.[viii]

Developing this book has raised my awareness of the need to dig deeper into the biblical record on the various management issues than heretofore has been done. For some management topics a few scholarly resources exist from which to draw for expressing the biblical worldview on management. Much more work in this area is needed. This suggests that the biblical worldview is not yet completely developed for the business disciplines such as management. For example, when conducting biblical word studies, concept studies, and reading various Bible narratives for the various chapters of this book, I identified many words in the original Hebrew and Greek that have received little scholarly attention among Christian business scholars as these apply to the world of business. Over 20 Hebrew words used in the Old Testament refer to or identify specific types of managers and leaders. Many words in the Greek New Testament describe managers and leaders. To conduct a thorough study of the concepts of motivation and organizing scores of Hebrew and Greek words need to be explored. While this book does not offer a complete study of the words at the level of the original Hebrew and Greek, it identifies these terms and specific examples of where they are used. I have gathered this material together, placing it conveniently into an appendix for use by scholars who share an interest in digging deeper.

In addition to biblical studies and theological studies I considered several other streams of thought depicted in the following illustration.

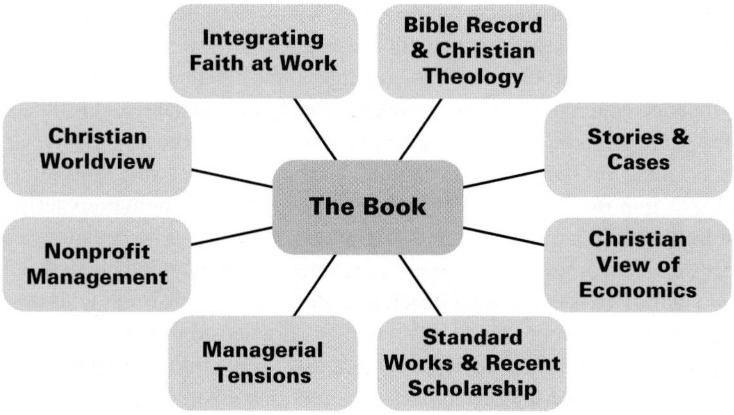

A major part of the literature reviewed for this book includes not only the standard, influential works from past management scholarship but also current contributions by management researchers and theorists. This should not be taken to mean that a comprehensive review has been accomplished. This is an introductory textbook. Offering a comprehensive review would be overwhelming to most undergraduate students.

Also, I searched for cases and stories illustrating the issues that surface in the study of a Christian worldview on management. I read from the literature representing Christian views on economics. This is important since managers cannot isolate their work from the economic dimension of their work. Along the way I identified dozens of managerial tensions that scholars consider to be universal. This collection of tensions is important since the Christian manager must manage these as well as the tensions that are peculiar to the Christian. Some of the readers of this book are already working as or will later work as managers in nonprofit organizations. Exploring the literature on management issues from this perspective became important as the project progressed. In developing this book I also surveyed the literature on Christian worldview and the literature on the faith at work movement.

General reading in the standard, influential works of management created an awareness of the big issues that the discipline has traditionally considered important for each chapter of the book. This reading informed my reading of the Bible and Christian scholars who have presented their understanding of the Christian perspective. I began the development of each chapter by considering the theological themes that run through the Bible that *prima facie* seem relevant to the big questions of the field. These themes also informed me regarding the applicability of particular Bible passages. This phase of the process required 4 to 6 weeks for each chapter. With the theological themes and particular Bible passages in mind I have evaluated the work of other Christian scholars and evaluated particular contributions to contemporary management scholarship that are considered normative in the discipline.

From this process emerged the recurring conceptual model called here the Management Pyramid: Management is about who we are and who we are becoming, how we think and feel in management situations, and faith-informed faith-inspired managerial action. The Management Pyramid model is intended to lead the reader to see how Christian faith is integrated with each management concept introduced. Another element that emerged which contributes to faith integration is a cluster of recurring biblical themes, introduced in Chapter 1, that run through the entire text, providing the larger biblical perspective with which to understand particular Bible verses as well as the management issues. A chapter devoted to exploring spirituality and faith integration as well as a few appendices related to the biblical record and Bible study on the topic also came out of this process. As a result, I developed two distinct but closely related sections for the main body of each chapter: a section representing the biblical record on the topic and a section on contemporary management scholarship on the topic. This raises an important question regarding the book's structure as it relates to the goals of faith integration.

Five basic structural choices seemed to be available to encourage the integration of a faith-based perspective founded on values and teachings that are common to most Christian denominations.[ix] The first and the last choices shown in the following table were unacceptable. For example, writing a management book that does not consider the Bible would jeopardize the accomplishment of the book's purpose. Also, in economic terms such an approach would place this book in direct competition with the many standard college textbooks present in a saturated market. Without a clear basis for differentiation, such a book would find the road to getting established difficult if not impossible to achieve. The other unacceptable choice is to write a management text that attempts to consider only the Bible record on management issues and not contemporary management scholarship. While the Bible has much to say to managers and leaders, it is not a comprehensive, unambiguous management handbook. Its purpose is theological in nature. On some specific managerial issues the Bible provides clear and direct guidance. On the core issues, it has a lot to say. On other issues it is silent. As humans have gone about the process of subduing the earth scientific investigations into important social phenomena imbedded in the human experience have contributed to our understanding of management and organizations. This book assumes that Christians should evaluate the findings from such research for therein they may find elements of truth that are not necessarily contrary to specific Bible teachings, that may be consistent with the broad biblical themes, and very well might represent God's will that Christians aspire to understand.

Another structural option is to divide the book as a whole into two sections: one devoted to what the Bible says about the management issues and one devoted to surveying contemporary management theory, research, and practice. It seemed that most colleges and universities would find such a structure unfamiliar and impractical for use in undergraduate classroom instruction.

Another structural choice is to attempt a so-called seamless integration throughout for each management issue of theory and practice. Some may consider this to be the ideal approach to faith integration. This structural choice appears to contain an inherent contradiction. Calling for a seamless integration requires that we assume first of all that it is possible to create a single expression of the biblical worldview that takes into consideration the many debatable issues in management, the issues related to economics, as well as the plurality of views on the Bible prevalent among Christians. Given the complexity of the issues in management and economics and the variety of Christian perspectives, one must question the validity of such an assumption. An alternative assumption seems more reasonable, namely that a seamless approach would require advancing faith integration scholarship to a level of specificity that does not honor the plurality of Christian perspectives. If an author attempts to filter all the issues through his or her particular denominational perspective, it might very well reflect how such a perspective seamlessly integrates the biblical worldview with many, though perhaps not all, management issues to the satisfaction of some but not all management scholars. But this would come at a trade-off: The product created would decrease in usefulness for scholars who hold a different interpretation of what constitutes the normative biblical worldview.

Structural Choices	
Management Scholarship only: No attempt to integrate the Christian perspective.	Unacceptable. This approach fails to achieve the purpose of the book; it fails to establish a clear basis of differentiation from substitute products present in the market.
Integration at the **BOOK** level by presenting two perspectives in side-by-side fashion in separate sections of the book.	One section of the book to address the Biblical perspective on various management issues and another section to address contemporary management scholarship. Such an approach would be unfamiliar to most textbook users. It might be impractical from the point of view of a reader. This approach may not advance faith integration far enough.
Integration at the level of each **CHAPTER** by presenting two perspectives in side-by-side fashion in separate sections of the chapter.	Part of each chapter devoted to addressing the biblical record and part devoted to contemporary management scholarship. This approach carries some benefits and weaknesses. This is the alternative chosen.
Integration **THROUGHOUT** each subsection of each chapter; no attempt to separate the biblical record from contemporary management scholarship.	This would attempt to present a so-called "seamless" treatment of the issues through the lens of one author's perspective. This would require advancing faith integration scholarship to a level of specificity that does not honor the plurality of Christian perspectives.
Bible only with no attempt to integrate the findings of contemporary management scholarship.	Unacceptable. The Bible is incomplete or ambiguous on some management issues. This approach does not consider current scholarship that the Christian may find helpful in fulfilling God's will.

Testing each management principle or theory by the Bible would require, in my opinion, a book more complex and advanced to read than can be expected of a work that attempts to be accessible to undergraduate students. An advanced treatment of the topic will require the work of multiple volumes, multiple years, and multiple authors—a worthy project no doubt. The product created by such an effort may be better suited for graduate education. To achieve such a worthy goal the volume and intensity of Christian business scholarship will need to increase over what it has been the last quarter century. And, even if this type of scholarship were to be produced during the next 5 to 10 years, creating a seamless approach that is acceptable to many scholars would still remain a challenge.

I offer for consideration the many attempts by scholars to create systematic theologies of the Christian religion over the past two thousand years. No single seamless approach to theology has successfully captured the minds of all Christians everywhere. Further, most of these works on theology do not consider theories from economics, organization studies, sociology, or psychology. On what basis do we believe that a seamless approach to faith integration in management, commonly accepted by a majority of Christian management scholars and practitioners, would be possible to accomplish over the next decade?

For this edition of a faith-based management text I am content to encourage readers to develop more advanced, detailed biblical/theological reviews of management theories in the context of their own study, in discussions with others, and in the pages of academic journals that come in the future. Out of such dialogue we may indeed see some commonly accepted formulations emerge that approach seamlessness. I predict that even with such an effort (which I heartily support and encourage), debatable issues will remain, making it extremely difficult to rally wide support for a commonly accepted seamless approach.

The structural option that I selected is to integrate faith and learning about management at the chapter level, namely to offer in each chapter a specialized section on the Bible record and a second section on contemporary management scholarship. The reasons for this are as follows. I assume that some readers are curious and will want to know what just the Bible alone says on various management topics. Some readers, even if they attend a Christian church on a regular basis, may be unfamiliar with some details contained in the Bible, especially as these relate to management issues. Similar to the role that specialization plays in organizations such a division helps prevent confusion as to which ideas come from the Bible and which ideas come from contemporary management scholarship. Making the biblical record prominent in each chapter honors the Bible's place in the life of the Christian. One can argue that these two types of information sources are quite different from each other by nature. It is responsible scholarship to separate the main body of each chapter into these two sections. Doing so allows readers to evaluate separately each section on its own merits. Such evaluation is a valuable exercise in its own right. By specializing the chapter content the biblical perspective will become an obvious prominent feature of each chapter, something that I believe many readers will appreciate. The biblical perspective is at the foundation of what makes this book different from all other management texts currently on the market. Making the biblical record prominent will strengthen the product's differentiation. Seamless integration might provide an opportunity for meeting the theological needs of a small group of readers who relate easily to the words I choose or to the emphasis that I might place on the issues. The result is that such an approach would surely increase the risk that the theological needs of others may be unmet because of the potentially insurmountable intellectual barriers thrown up through particular words chosen and the degree of emphasis made. Specialization does not necessarily prevent the process of integration from taking place in the experience of the reader. Rather, it encourages contemplation of the claims of faith in terms of the managerial experience. It encourages intellectual and spiritual honesty with one's theological assumptions in moving from the portrayal of the biblical record to an integrated understanding of God's will for a manager's life. Specialization allows for asking some difficult and, in some cases, debatable questions that get at the heart of how a person integrates his or her faith in the world of management thinking and practice. Examples of some of these questions are offered in the end-of-chapter material.

In spite of these benefits, such an approach is not perfect. I will address two weaknesses though I'm sure there are others. One weakness in this structural choice may be that for some readers the process of intellectual-spiritual integration of faith and learning about management does not go far enough. I will accept this criticism in hopes that readers will be open to becoming participants in the integration process as they read, discuss with others, contemplate the material in the book, and then practice managerial actions in real-life settings. To this weakness I offer the following considerations. A single book, regardless of the degree to which the concepts are intellectually integrated, cannot of its own accord do the entire work of integration *for* a person. Even if this book were a perfect representation of God's will for the manager's life, a reader can experience the progression of faith integration only so far through reading alone. Ultimately faith integration occurs in the head, heart, and hand of the *practicing* manager. A book can raise the substantive questions and issues that must become the grist for the ongoing process of faith integration at work. Thus, while I believe that this book will contribute to faith integration, I am under no illusion that it or any other book or lecture has the power to both start and finish the integration process for any given person. Like the work of sanctification, faith integration is a lifelong work and not the result of reading one book.

Another potential weakness is that some readers may believe the structure of the book might communicate the opposite of what the book stands for, namely faith fragmentation. I will accept this criticism but with the following considerations. The fact that information of a religious nature is included so prominently in the book may counteract this weakness to a large degree, minimizing the chances that a reader will get the wrong idea. Producing a book that leaves out the biblical record might encourage faith fragmentation or at least not encourage faith integration, but specializing information in each chapter for scholarship purposes does not by nature automatically require or cause faith fragmentation. One can also argue that specialization for academic purposes supports the process of learning for improved discernment. Information sources in life are often fragmented while life itself is integrated. Practicing managers and management scholars continually receive information on which we must perform critical thinking as we integrate such information into or reject the information from our knowledge and religious value structures. This is the nature of reality. Specializing a portion of each chapter has the potential of raising awareness for readers that critical thinking is their job after they close the book and live the life of a manager. Each chapter offers the reader the two perspectives by saying, "Here's what the Bible says on the issue, and here's what contemporary management scholars say on the issue. How does your religious faith lead you to think and act as a manager?"

The findings of management research do not come neatly packaged by authors who have tested the findings for alignment with biblical teaching. This book acknowledges that there are two quite distinct, though not necessarily separate or automatically opposing, sources of information: The Bible and science.[x] These two perspectives are presented openly while the reader is encouraged to employ biblically grounded discernment when considering both.

This book's structure, this discussion on what it means to integrate faith in the context of a product such as a textbook, as well as this book's contents may spark more debate—something that few textbook authors might naturally aspire to achieve. Some Christian scholars will have a worldview that leads them to take exception to some of the structural rationale presented here or the assumptions I present regarding faith integration.[xi]

Regardless of the extent to which one book promises an integrated viewpoint of management thought and practice, in life management problems do not come with prepackaged faith-integrated solutions awaiting the manager to pull it off the shelf and use. Christian managers must continually engage in critical thinking and pursue the ongoing work of faith integration by making faith-informed choices from among different ways of thinking and action for the particular and often changing situations they face.

A few additional cautions to the reader are in order. Not everything presented in this text is unique to the Christian religion. Since both Testaments of the Bible are considered here, there is bound to be some overlap with the teachings of Judaism. On some points of Christian belief the reader may find points of commonality with other religions such as Islam. There is no requirement here that a faith-perspective is unique in everything in the practice of management. This will be disappointing to some Christian scholars who believe that literally everything about a biblical worldview on management must be markedly different from the so-called "worldly" perspective if it is to be truly biblical. In this volume I assume that if a secular scholar agrees with a Christian scholar (or vice versa) on a particular point, this does not make one scholar's position any less (or more) valid than the other. Not every example and illustration will be drawn from solely Christian organizations, Christian managerial experiences, or from the Bible. Certainly, much managerial knowledge and action that Christians prize will be in close alignment with the views common to other religions as well as with nonreligious perspectives. It does mean that by design there is an attempt to view the management scholarship represented through the lens of Christian principles. This book offers an opportunity for Christians to consider the choices they make when considering which management theories to embrace and integrate into their work life and which ones to question or outright reject. The book offers the scholar working in a religious college or university the opportunity to put on the table for classroom discussion the perspective of religious faith. I hope the book will make more accessible to business students the questions and issues that they will likely consider for the rest of their career, encouraging them to deal honestly with them.

The effort to bring a Christian perspective to the discipline, by necessity, must be seen as a work in progress for two reasons. First, this is the product of one person who has attempted to wrap the mind around the major issues of managerial thought and practice. Such a work was not done in isolation from what other Christian scholars believe; I have attempted to listen carefully to what others say on the topics. Even so, given the human limitations of accomplishing this, such a work will be ongoing in nature and will be refined by the feedback received from readers. This suggests that later editions of this book, should they be required, are likely to do a progressively better job in fulfilling the purpose of the book.

Second, this work in progress is a work that is occurring in the mind of readers whether they are professors, students, or practicing managers. In other words, the "work in progress" will require on the part of readers an intentional self-examination of the issues from the perspective of their own particular faith tradition or philosophical beliefs. It suggests the value of constantly asking the question, *Given my religious beliefs, what do I believe about management on this issue and how should I practice management?* As such, this book may be of some use for those who are connected with other faith communities outside Christianity, including Judaism, Islam, or Hinduism, who have their own particular beliefs that form the foundation for their thinking about management. Seeing one religious faith perspective presented here will provide a ready-made framework for comparison and self-examination regardless of the reader's personal perspective.

Because of the nature of the subject some readers will be interested in the particular religious faith of the author. If you accept the premise that the perspective one has can make a difference, it is only natural to be curious about the author's perspective on a work that claims to represent a Christian perspective. My own faith tradition in the Seventh-day Adventist denomination stems from the Protestant Christian experience with its historical roots in the Methodist/Wesleyan movements of the 19th century. During the third decade of my life I studied English Baptist (Reformed) theology. In addition to its distinctive teachings such as those related to worship, eschatology, and the conservative lifestyle expected of members of this faith community, my faith tradition holds to traditional Protestant theology including the three central pillars of *sola scriptura* (the Bible alone), *sola fide* (salvation by faith alone), and *sola gratia* (salvation by Divine grace alone), as well as the centrality of the person and work of Jesus Christ for salvation. My faith tradition respects each Testament of the Bible and resists making a "canon within a canon" where one Testament is held superior to the other. Instead, the unity of Scripture is assumed and respected. For the management issues addressed here, I find much in common between my own theological tradition and other Christian perspectives. It is the common beliefs and themes I have attempted to draw out for review here rather than those distinctive to one denomination or another.

As Christians we have developed a finely-tuned ability to disagree with each other with a high degree of emotional intensity. This is especially true among representatives of the various Protestant denominations. Sad, but true, the intensity of our differences has isolated Protestants from each other and from the larger world of Christendom—each of us believing that our particular interpretation of Scripture is right and all others are either wrong or highly suspect until ultimately proven to be wrong. Yet, ironically, differences in perspective even among Christians are a source of positive creative energy. For those readers who use this product in the context of a college or university course, such differences may fuel many vigorous discussions and debates something that most professors welcome. This is an important part of the university experience. Such use will provide the Christian professor of business the opportunity to reflect with students regarding how the particular faith tradition of the college either agrees or disagrees with what is portrayed here.

In addition to influences of my own religious faith tradition, I acknowledge the biases of my own personality, temperament, personal interests, and the 20-some years of experience as a practicing mid-level and senior-level manager. These all played a part in the development of this product. Also, I have had the opportunity to develop friendships with scholars from a variety of other religious backgrounds. This has enriched my work and challenged my thinking. My study at Anderson University Falls School of Business has given me the privilege of working closely with several giants of faith from other faith traditions (Roman Catholic, Reformed, Nazarene, Church of God, Baptist, Presbyterian, Lutheran, Wesleyan, Mennonite, etc.) who also are business scholars and whom I deeply respect. Some of these scholars are farther down the road than I am in terms of thinking about faith integration with respect to specific topics of business or specific Bible passages that relate to the practice of business. In addition, my exposure to the scholarly work of those with similar faith-integration interests in the *Christian Business Faculty Association*, contributors to the *Christian Scholar's Review*, publications of the *Academy of Management* (Management, Spirituality, and Religion Interest Group), and other publications cited in this text have widened my perspective on how religious faith influences managerial being, thinking, and action. These relationships and resources continue to challenge my thinking on the subject.

The spelling style guide for this project is the *Chicago Manual of Style.* This will be of interest to some readers who have particular expectations for spelling of words related to religious belief. For example, words that refer directly to God and Jesus are always capitalized, but pronouns that refer to God or Jesus are not. This is consistent with the convention used by most English translations of the Bible. The word Bible is always capitalized but the word biblical is not.

Supplements

At the Instructor Resource Center, www.pearsonhighered.com/irc, instructors can access a variety of print, digital, and presentation resources available with this text in downloadable format. Registration is simple and gives you immediate access to new titles and new editions. As a registered faculty member, you can download resource files and receive immediate access to and instructions for installing course management content on your campus server. In case you ever need assistance, our dedicated technical support team is ready to help with the media supplements that accompany this text. Visit http://247.pearsoned.com for answers to frequently asked questions and toll-free user support phone numbers.

The following supplements are available for download to adopting instructors:

- Instructor's Resource Manual
- Test Item File
- TestGen® Computerized Test Bank
- PowerPoint Slides

Videos on DVD

Exciting and high-quality video clips help deliver engaging topics to the classroom to help students better understand the concepts explained in the textbook. Please contact your local representative to receive a copy of the DVD.

CourseSmart

CourseSmart eTextbooks were developed for students looking to save on required or recommended textbooks. Students simply select their eText by title or author and purchase immediate access to the content for the duration of the course using any major credit card. With a CourseSmart eText, students can search for specific keywords or page numbers, take notes online, print out reading assignments that incorporate lecture notes, and bookmark important passages for later review. For more information or to purchase a CourseSmart eTextbook, visit www.coursesmart.com.

Acknowledgments

Several people deserve acknowledgments. There were 30-some peer reviewers, most from different religious faith backgrounds than mine, who provided valuable suggestions for how to improve the manuscript. Several took the time to write personal encouragements to continue working on this project in their feedback reports. I appreciate these!

Clarence Anderson, Blue Mountain Credit Union

Ken Armstrong, Anderson University

Emil Berendt, Friends University

Monty Bohrer, East Texas Baptist University

Jonathan Bradshaw, Houghton College

Mary Jane Byrd, University of Mobile

Jeffrey Decker, Whittier College

Ray Eldridge, Lipscomb University

William Fennema, University of Indianapolis

John Frazier, Southern Wesleyan University

Ron Galloway, Northwest Nazarene University

Franco Gandolfi, Regent University

Kimberly Hadley, John Brown University

Brian Hoekstra, Dordt College

Karen Jacobs, LeTourneau University

Sharon Johnson, Charleston Southern University

Karen Jones, Northwest Nazarene University

Steven J. Krause, Concordia University–Portland OR
Steve Little, InfoWorks, Inc.
Larry Locke, University of Mary Hardin Baylor
Doyle Lucas, Anderson University
Monty Lynn, Abilene Christian University
Richard Martinez, Charleston Southern University
Jeanne McNett, Assumption College
Stanley Patterson, Andrews University
Prudence Pollard, La Sierra University
Janis Prewitt-Auner, Drury University
Scott Quatro, Covenant College
Harriet Rojas, Indiana Wesleyan University
Jean Sampson, McKendree University
Bruce Schooling, Point Loma Nazarene University
Kent W. Seibert, Gordon College
Ervin Starr, Roberts Wesleyan College
Gregory Stephens, Texas Christian University

There were also several scholars who contributed original pieces in "The Christian Mind on . . ." features of the text. These contributors included:

Corné J. Bekker, Regent University
Monty Bohrer, East Texas Baptist University
Kathleen M. Fisher, Assumption College
Franco Gandolfi, Regent University
Brian Hoekstra, Dordt College
Karen Jacobs, LeTourneau University
Sharon Johnson, Charleston Southern University
Larry Locke, University of Mary Hardin-Baylor
Doyle Lucas, Anderson University
Jeanne McNett, Assumption College
Stanley Patterson, Andrews University
Scott Quatro, Covenant College
Ervin Starr, Roberts Wesleyan College
Harriet Rojas, Indiana Wesleyan University
Jean Scheller-Sampson, McKendree University

The other contributions to this feature came from published works authored by Richard C. Chewning, John W. Eby, Ralph Klein, Steven J. Musser, and Shirley J. Roels.

The development editor Lori Cerreto who collaborated on this project deserves special mention. She made the manuscript much easier to read. It was a joy to work with her. Finally, my wife Marlene, who was unfailing in her encouragement and support during this project, deserves an award for putting up with me as I devoted myself to the intensity of the project. In deep gratitude: Thank you!

Michael E. Cafferky
Collegedale, TN

Endnotes

i. Many scholars and authors of trade books agree with this assumption. Indeed many of those referenced in this book support it.

ii. Weber, M. (1930/1972). *The Protestant ethic and the spirit of capitalism.* New York: Routledge. p. 27.

iii. Aquinas, T. (1947). *Summa Theologica: First complete American edition in three volumes.* Volume 2. New York: Benziger Brothers, Inc. pp. 1389–1412; Luther, M. (1524/1962). Trade and usury. In Brandt, W. I. (Ed.). *Luther's works. Volume 45 The Christian in Society II.* Philadelphia, PA: Fortress Press. pp. 233–310; Defoe, D. (1727/1969). *The complete English tradesman in familiar letters.* Volume 1. New York: Augustus M. Kelley; Smith, A. (1759/2010). The theory of moral sentiments. New York: Cosimo Classics; Freedley, E. T. (1853). *A practical treatise on business: Or how to get, save, spend, give, lend and bequeath money.* Philadelphia, PA: Lippincott, Grambo & Company; Marshall, A. (1890/1949). *Principles of economics: An introductory volume.* New York: The Macmillan Company; Crane, F. (1912). *Business and kingdom come.* Chicago, IL: Forbes and Company; Babson, R. W. (1920). *Religion and business.* New York: The Macmillan Company; Emerson, H. (1924). The essence of efficiency: Letter to the editor. *New York Times.* December 7, p. X19.

iv. Deuteronomy 6:5, 10:12, 30:6; Matthew 22:37; Mark 12:30; Luke 10:27.

v. Here I am following on to that offered by Marsden, G. M. (1998). What difference might Christian perspectives make? In Wells, R. A. (Ed.). *History and the Christian historian.* Grand Rapids, MI: William B. Eerdmans Publishing Company. pp. 11–22; Marsden, G. M. (2005). Faith-informed scholarship. In Henderson, J. W., & Pisciotta, J. (Eds.). *Faithful economics: The moral worlds of a neutral science.* Waco, TX: Baylor University Press. pp. 15–24. The sources referenced in the book represent what Christian scholars suggest as appropriate ways of thinking and action for some management issues. A great need exists for empirical research that describes how Christian practicing managers actually think, feel, and act in terms of particular management issues they face on a daily basis. An example of such research is Agle, B. R., & Van Buren III, H. J. (1979). God and mammon: The modern relationship. *Business Ethics Quarterly.* 9(4), 563–582.

vi. "There is no 'Christian' theory of management. But there are principles, which when integrated with other theories, do suggest how Christians should carry out their management responsibilities." Chewning, R. C., Eby, J. W., & Roels, S. J. (1990). *Business through the eyes of faith.* San Francisco, CA: HarperSanFrancisco. p. 90.

vii. Other books on the topic of management have contributed to this including (but not limited to) Rush, M. (1983). *Management: A biblical approach.* Wheaton, IL: Victor Books; Johnson, S. (1988). *Values driven people: A Christian approach to management.* Dallas, TX: Probe Books; College of Administration and Management. (1989). *The word on management: A topical index of Scriptures for managers and employees.* Virginia Beach, VA: Regent University Press; Chewning, R. C. (Ed.). (1990). *Biblical principles and business: The practice.* Colorado Springs, CO: NavPress; Chewning, R. C., Eby, J. W., & Roels, S. J. (1990). *Business through the eyes of faith.* San Francisco, CA: HarperSanFrancisco; Higginson, R. (1996). *Transforming leadership: A Christian approach to management.* London: SPCK; Alford, H. J., & Naughton, M. J. (2001). *Managing as if faith mattered: Christian social principles in the modern organization.* South Bend, IN: University of Notre Dame Press.

viii. I humbly acknowledge that this edition of the book does not pay as much attention to the Eastern Orthodox perspective as it might have.

ix. These five are the ones that *prima facie* offered the clearest possibilities. There may be other structural possibilities, too.

x. The reader may appreciate the perspective of Barbour who outlines four possible interactions between science and religion. See Barbour, I. G. (1997). *Religion and science: Historical and contemporary issues.* New York: HarperCollins; Barbour, I. G. (2000). *When science meets religion.* New York: HarperCollins.

xi. An example of the differences of opinion among Christians in the field of leadership is the following: Beadles II, N. A. (2000). Stewardship-leadership: A biblical refinement of servant-leadership. *Journal of Biblical Integration in Business.* Fall, 25–37; Porter, B. (2000). A response to "Stewardship-leadership: A biblical refinement of servant-leadership." *Journal of Biblical Integration in Business.* Fall, 38–42; Smith, V. (2000). Response to "Stewardship-leadership: A biblical refinement of servant-leadership." *Journal of Biblical Integration in Business.* Fall, 43–47. The topic of servant leadership will be addressed later in this book. Likewise an example of differences of opinion among Christians in the field of economics is the following: Leightner, J. E. (2003). Utility versus self-sacrificing love. *Christian Scholar's Review*, 32(3), 317–328; Rose, J. T. (2004). Reflection: Utility versus self-sacrificing love. *Christian Scholar's Review*, 34(1), 11–15; Leightner, J. E. (2004). Response: "Not my will . . . ": Further thoughts on utility versus self-sacrificing love. *Christian Scholar's Review*, 34(1), 17–20. Several Christian scholars have written books and articles evaluating the morality of capitalism. Some are in support; others are critical. Likewise, various Christian scholars have written on the topic of faith integration. Not all of them agree with each other on every point.

About the Author

Michael E. Cafferky is an award-winning Professor of Business & Management at Southern Adventist University. In 2011 he received the Southern Adventist University President's Award for Excellence in Scholarship. Prior to his career as a university professor he served in a variety of organizations and at different levels of leadership including entry-level positions of janitor and construction worker, church pastor, middle and senior manager in the healthcare industry as marketing director, medical clinic administrator, hospital chief operating officer, chief financial officer, and an interim chief executive officer.

Michael holds advanced degrees in theology, public health, and business. He earned the Doctor of Business Administration (DBA) from Anderson University, Falls School of Business, Anderson, IN. He teaches graduate and undergraduate management courses in *Principles of Management, Business Strategy, Organizational Behavior, Leadership in Organizations, Ethical, Legal and Social Environment of Business, Integrating Faith and Business, Organization Theory,* and *Strategic Decision Making.* He has lectured in Canada, Australia, Romania, Ghana, France, Mexico, and The Russian Federation.

Michael is a *Fellow* in the *American College of Healthcare Executives,* a member of the *Academy of Management,* and a member of the *Christian Business Faculty Association.* For 3 years he served as a volunteer examiner for the Malcolm Baldrige National Quality Award Program. His hobbies include travel, film, "making stuff from scratch," and writing for publication. He is the author of hundreds of published articles and five other books.

Michael and his wife Marlene have two grown sons, Bryan and Nolan.

Management

A Faith-Based Perspective

CHAPTER 1

Introduction to Management

LEARNING OBJECTIVES

- Understand the three dimensions of being, thinking, and action in management.
- Be aware of the big issues in the field of management from both the secular and religious perspectives, and explain how a Christian worldview influences management thinking and action.
- Contrast the traditional definitions of management with a definition representing the perspective of spiritual meaning that embraces a Christian worldview.
- Contrast the selected perspectives that are used to understand management.
- Understand the four types of managerial tensions and why they are important in management.

"Much management theory and education has lost sight of the fundamental reasons for which we go into business . . ."[1]

"There is no 'Christian' theory of management. But there are principles, which when integrated with other theories, do suggest how Christians should carry out their management responsibilities."[2]

WHY WAIT UNTIL RETIREMENT TO MAKE A DIFFERENCE?

On June 28, 2007, Bruce R. Kennedy, "longtime CEO of Alaska Airlines, whose hand continued to gently guide the airline following his retirement in 1991, died when his Cessna plane crashed."[3] Early in his career Kennedy became known as someone who made a difference. He is remembered for his willingness to infuse his religious faith into his work and into his company, Alaska Airlines.

In 1979, Kennedy became CEO of a small regional air carrier in Alaska with annual revenues of $100 million. Under his leadership, the company grew to 38 routes flying to destinations in three countries, grossing over $10 billion per year.

At his retirement, he reportedly said that it was time to trade *success* for *significance*. Those who worked for and with Kennedy realize that while he was working full-time his life wasn't just about success from the bottom line. Significance also mattered. Kennedy was known for his openness about his religious faith. For example, Alaska Airlines became famous for including hope-filled Scripture verses on its in-flight napkins.

Source: AP Photo/Jim Davidson.

Following Kennedy's death, Alaska Airlines Chairman and CEO Bill Ayer commented that Bruce Kennedy's "most valuable contributions were not inked on financial statements. They were inscribed in the hearts and minds of the airline's employees."[4] We often think about a company's founder as having the most significant impact on company culture. But managers who succeed the founders can also have enormous influence. In Kennedy's case, his impact was in terms of employees living the values of integrity, caring, resourcefulness, spirit, and professionalism. These values were a part of who Kennedy was long before the corporation formally adopted them as company values.

Though he continued to guide the airline following his retirement, Kennedy devoted his retirement years to teaching English in China, opening a home for refugees from Cambodia, and developing an air service to support Christian missionary work and humanitarian aid worldwide.

Volunteering after retirement is a growing trend. Some serve individually, following their personal passion in leadership capacities. Others join organized volunteer efforts and take minor, though no less significant, roles in service. Some seek to live their religious faith through volunteer service. Thousands of retired executives who had worked their way up the corporate ladder to success serve as volunteer counselors with SCORE (Service Corps of Retired Executives), a free business advice consulting service of the U.S. Small Business Administration. Just as volunteering after retirement is growing in popularity, so is the quest shared by many to make a difference before retirement by infusing religious faith into their work.[5]

The personal questions that Bruce Kennedy's experience naturally calls to mind are: What legacy will you leave behind at your death? What values will you be remembered for? In what way will you, as a manager, find significance? Will you wait until your retirement to find significance through volunteer service, or will you find significance within your work as a manager? Anyone with any job description can make a difference now.

As we will explore in this book, work does not have to be separate from spirituality. Working as a manager offers an unusually exciting way to infuse spirituality into work while taking care of the sometimes mundane details of getting work done.

Who Cares About Management?

So you are sitting down to read the first chapter in this book because you know you need to get started sometime. You know that your professor is going to test you sooner or later and you might as well start preparing. And you are thinking to yourself, what can this book possibly add to my learning? Besides, Bruce Kennedy was able to have so much impact because he was a chief executive officer (CEO). Not everyone becomes a CEO.

Or maybe you believe that someday you will be a manager and you are thinking, "Why should I spend my time reading about this when I could be doing this?" This book will introduce you to the work of a manager from a Christian faith perspective. On the one hand, there is a limit to how much you can learn about management from reading a book. On the other hand, this book can provide a solid foundation for you to build on in your career. A lot that you will learn will come from practical management experience throughout your life. You can also learn a lot about management by watching others manage.

Some readers don't expect to become a manager of any kind under any circumstance. But things don't always turn out as you expect them to. Take, for example, Elizabeth,[6] a management student. She was an accounting major who planned to get an accounting job and leave managing to other people. Why, she wondered, should she be required to take a course in management, as she would never use it after graduation? Sure enough, today she is a supervisor in an accounting department.

Use this book as a mirror for self-understanding, which is vital to becoming an effective leader. Think about your roles and responsibilities as a student. Are students managers? Of course! Every student gets experience managing. See Exhibit 1-1.

Management relationships exist everywhere there are people, organizations, and communities. Managers are the frontline supervisors at Whirlpool. They are the middle managers at 20th Century Fox who coordinate the production of feature films. They are the store managers for A&W Root Beer and the top-level executives at DKNY. Managers are department directors at county government organizations such as the Orange County Children and Family services department. They are the managing partners of law practices and medical groups. They manage nonprofit organizations such as Human Rights Watch. In the United States nonprofit organizations are exempt from paying taxes on the net revenue that is earned. Many **nonprofit organizations** are focused on a social service, philanthropic, educational, healthcare, or religious mission to provide services to members of society. They are the project managers in thousands of organizations that are in transition. In virtually all of our work and volunteer relationships, we are either managing or interacting with a

EXHIBIT 1-1
Management in a Student's Experience

Being a student = being a manager:

- Registering for classes each semester
- Moving into or out of your dorm room
- Finding a job
- Leading a student club or organization
- Starting and managing a prayer group or Bible study group
- Serving as a team leader in athletics, musical groups, or drama teams
- Preparing for, going on, and following up on a date
- Arranging for pizza delivery
- Making arrangements for and completing your trip home for the holidays
- Organizing and executing a community service project
- Organizing an informal weekend campout
- Leading in a small group discussion
- Working as a Residence Hall Assistant or Floor Monitor
- Selecting and working with classmates for participation on team projects
- Anytime you make a commitment to someone to get something done and then follow through with that commitment, you are acting as a manager—even self-management often involves working with others to get something done
- Any time you take responsibility for what other people do

manager. Reading this book will help you understand the job of managers and, thereby, how you can be more effective in working for them.

Some readers of this book are interested in finding a way to integrate their Christian faith with their learning about business, and, in doing so, better discern God's will for their life. One way to understand the integration of faith and work is through the Management Pyramid.

Management Pyramid

To get to the foundation of things from a Christian faith perspective, let's look at an example. Consider Julie, an accounts receivable supervisor in an accounting department of a manufacturing company. Julie has three junior accounting clerks who report to her, and Julie reports to the controller. Her management activities include delegating tasks to subordinates, monitoring her work unit's progress, setting the agenda for team meetings, hiring and training new accountants, working with auditors, and solving operational problems related to internal control of cash and inventory. As a manager, she needs to plan, communicate, and make decisions.

However, managers like Julie need not only the ability to perform all of these tasks but also a source of values that goes deeper than just what they do in their work.[7] Three dimensions of Julie and her work are continually present: (1) who she is and who she is becoming as a Christian, (2) how she thinks and feels as a Christian manager, and (3) what she does and how she acts as a Christian. In all three dimensions, Christian *faith integration* is occurring in her life and work.

Faith integration is the process of combining Christian faith and religious experience with the rest of our lives into a combined whole where Christian beliefs and actions become consistent in the work life of a manager. In the context of managerial work, the opposite of integration is fragmentation, in which a Christian acts or believes one way at church but acts in another way as a manager. Faith integration may not always be easy, but it is a goal to which many Christian managers aspire.[8]

Think of these three dimensions operating at three levels simultaneously: the individual level inside Julie herself, the organizational level of where she works or volunteers, and the larger community level. **Organizational level** refers to the degree of discretionary decision-making authority in the organization. The three dimensions form a model called the Management Pyramid.[9] See Exhibit 1-2.

We use models in many places in our lives. Human models at a fashion show and photographs of models in magazines or on billboard advertisements help potential buyers see and consider new products. A basketball coach draws Xs, Os, and arrows on a clipboard showing where he thinks the players should move for an inbound pass with 3 seconds to go before the final buzzer. The drawing is a model of how the coach wants the play to unfold so that the designated shooter can make the final shot. Environmental scientists create models of the ecological impact of different ways to dispose of garbage. Architects create physical models of the buildings they envision. Economists create models that show the relationship between supply and demand or scarcity and bargaining power. We use models in the field of management to illustrate managerial ideas and principles. We call these **conceptual models**.

Conceptual models are not perfect. They can't explain everything about managing. A coach's drawing on a clipboard is a conceptual model illustrating how he intends his team to manage a particular situation. It does not show the players' motivation and skills or what the competing team will do. These are assumed. An architect's model does not show the surrounding noise in the neighborhood

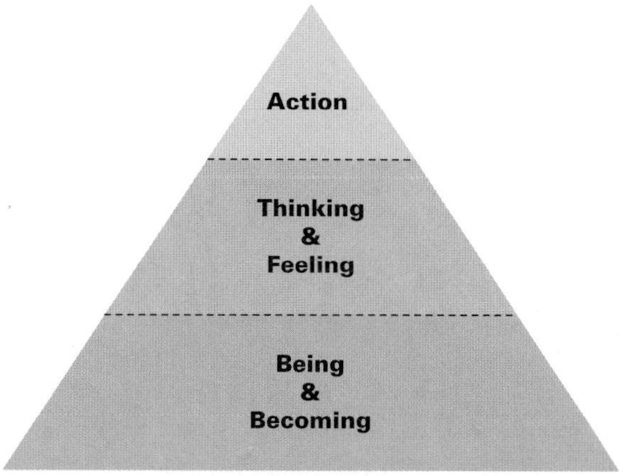

EXHIBIT 1-2
The Management Pyramid Model

Source: Courtesy of Michael E. Cafferky, © Michael E. Cafferky 2011.

in which the building will be built or the feeling workers get when they walk into the building every day. But it does provide a visual of the overall effect that the building will have in its location.

The **Management Pyramid** is a conceptual model that can help you think about the dynamic relationship between who we are as persons, how we think and feel, and our actions as Christian managers.

Being and Becoming

The epicenter of Christian effectiveness ultimately resides in who we are as individuals and how we are connected with a larger community. While there are many factors that influence our actions, who we are greatly influences how we think and feel. In turn, how we think and feel influences our actions. In the long run, our actions can change how we think and who we are.[10] The somewhat artificial distinction between being and thinking should not be taken too strongly. The point is not to identify a specific place where one stops and the other begins.

As humans, like the organizations we manage, we are never in a single, static state of being for very long. We are constantly changing as a result of our cumulative experiences.[11] In addition, the shared values of the organizations we work for can change our behaviors, our thinking patterns, and who we are.[12]

At a deep level, we can think of this connection between being, thinking, and action in terms of the spiritual and religious changes taking place in the heart of the person who wants to follow God's will. For the person of Christian faith, personal identity is rooted in a relationship with God. This awareness begins with the knowledge that God entrusts to humans the role of serving in ways that respect everything that God created. Such awareness is the foundation for taking responsibility as a steward of what God has given us. This identity provides the vision, motivation, and direction for action. In addition, the Christian manager will likely view being and becoming as an example of the religious process known as sanctification—the process of making holy.[13] The elements of the Management Pyramid model are found in the Bible. See Exhibit 1-3, The Management Pyramid Represented in the Bible.

Who we are is the foundation for everything else in our lives.[14] Although all three dimensions are important, some believe that of the three who we are is the most important because it is from this that action springs.[15] Who we are includes our spiritual experience, values, beliefs, moral standards, character traits, virtues,[16] personality, and perceptions of self and of others. **Character traits** are the moral and mental qualities that distinguish one person from another in terms of moral values and habitual behavior.[17] These elements encompass both religious and nonreligious influences.[18]

Another way of seeing this is that all management is value driven.[19] Personal values, shared organizational values, our biases, and our dispositions influence the kinds of information we seek, our interpretation of this information, and our reactions to it.[20]

Popular interest in business virtues such as integrity and faithfulness speaks loudly about how important these ideas have become in the marketplace.[21] Bill Pollard, CEO of ServiceMaster, is quoted as saying, "Before asking someone to do something, you have to help them be something."[22] Another way to think of this is in terms of character. Peter Drucker, one of the popular management consultants of the second half of the 20th century, described the importance of character: "There is one quality that cannot be learned, one qualification that the manager cannot acquire but must bring with him. It is not genius; it is character."[23]

Another element of who we are is the set of presuppositions, or assumptions, that make up our view of the world. Assumptions are our point of view, which, like colored lenses, work as filters through which we understand the world. These assumptions are the basis of all management theory and action.[24]

Thinking and Feeling

Management is as much about how we think and feel as it is about our actions. Intuitively it might be easy to see that thinking precedes action. Thinking includes the patterns of thinking, awareness of our own abilities to succeed, and the way we engage in social situations. Because of this, management work is characterized by a lot of mental work.

Managerial behaviors such as decision making, talking, reading reports, writing letters, and delegating work to others are either inputs or outputs to the hidden mental work going on inside the manager.[25] Managers at Tony Hawk's Birdhouse skateboard company, for example, think about the needs of the organization and compare the needs with what they are getting done. When managers at Vans, Inc. debate with each other regarding what the company should do in

Find out what the Bible says! Using the Bible references in this table, synthesize the main ideas presented in these passages in terms of the three elements of the Management Pyramid model.

Action	Deuteronomy 5:13–14	Matthew 26:41
	Deuteronomy 31:6	Luke 12:48
	Proverbs 6:6	Luke 16:10
	Proverbs 10:4–5, 26	Romans 7:15–19, 22–23
	Proverbs 12:22	Romans 8:28
	Proverbs 16:3	Romans 15:1
	Proverbs 19:15	1 Corinthians 10:31
	Proverbs 20:11	Galatians 5:13–14
	Proverbs 21:3	Ephesians 2:10
	Proverbs 23:4	Philippians 2:3–4
	Ecclesiastes 3:12–13	Colossians 3:23
	Ecclesiastes 5:18–20	James 1:22
	Matthew 5:16; 6:1	1 Peter 1:15
	Matthew 7:12	1 Peter 4:9–11
Thinking & Feeling	Isaiah 26:3	2 Corinthians 10:5
	Proverbs 23:6–7	Ephesians 4:22–24
	Proverbs 27:19	Philippians 2:5
	Ecclesiastes 7:14	Philippians 4:8–11
	Matthew 6:34	Colossians 3:2
	Luke 3:14	1 Timothy 6:6
	Romans 12:3	1 Peter 1:13
	1 Corinthians 2:16	Hebrews 13:5
Being & Becoming	Proverbs 4:23	1 Corinthians 12:7–11
	Proverbs 25:28	1 Corinthians 13:11
	Jeremiah 17:9	Galatians 2:16–20
	Matthew 12:34–35	Galatians 5:22–23
	Mark 7:20–23	Ephesians 4:15
	Luke 6:45	Colossians 3:12–15
	Romans 3:20–24	2 Peter 1:5–6
	Romans 12:2	2 Peter 3:18

EXHIBIT 1-3
The Management Pyramid Represented in the Bible

the future to maintain relationships with the skateboarding culture or discuss this month's productivity, most of their work is mental.

But the mental work goes far deeper. As managers, we are limited in our ability to predict how others such as employees, customers, or suppliers will act. Because of this limitation in information we create theories about how we assume they will act.[26] We also develop certain beliefs regarding what it means to be a good manager.

Thinking involves determining what will work and comparing the practical options with past experiences and values. Management thinking also involves day-to-day problem solving. It is an important foundation for coordinating efforts of workers across the whole company.

The mental work of a manager requires a great deal of agility. We must be close enough to a work situation to understand it and interact with the people in it, yet at the same time remain at enough of a mental and emotional distance to see what else is going on around the situation and to anticipate what is coming up. This mental agility is similar to that of a soccer player who must simultaneously focus on what is happening with the ball as well as what is happening in the entire field of play away from the ball. The shifting positions of offensive and defensive players, the time on the clock, the developing opportunities that lie within what the opposing team is allowing, and the current mix of players with their abilities all influence how the successful player thinks and acts.

Action

Managerial action is the most visible part of managing. Managers make decisions. They implement decisions by taking actions such as directing employees, suppliers, or customers to accomplish tasks. When we consider the action dimension of management, we often think about roles, functions, practices, and skills. Managerial action involves several sets of skills including technical skills, human relationship skills, conceptual skills, and self-regulation skills[27]—taking action to adjust our own behavior as managers.[28]

Who we are is important, and thinking is necessary but not sufficient. Ultimately, it is managerial actions that move an organization toward its goals. If managers at Apple had not acted, their great idea for the iPhone project would have remained just a great idea. Emphasis on great execution of management ideas highlights the importance of getting things done.[29]

While some managers may be more adept at thinking about business problems, to be effective today's manager also needs to have the strength and conviction to take thoughtful action even in the face of resistance. For example, Jeffrey Swartz of Timberland shoes had the conviction that every Timberland employee should have the opportunity to get involved in community service on company time. He also established literacy training for factory workers in the Dominican Republic. For these actions, he faced tough questions from investors.

A few observations about the being–thinking–action model are in order. First, to manage in an organization in an effective manner, the starting place is in managing yourself.[30] Often this means being open to change how you act, how you think, and ultimately who you are.

Second, some books on management emphasize the action dimension. But to consider the action dimension of management without the thinking and being dimensions oversimplifies life's experience.

Third, the pyramid model applies to both the organizational level and the larger community level.[31] Herbert Simon, Nobel Prize winner in Economics and expert in decision making, taught that organizational culture is a set of premises that resides in the minds of the organizational leaders.[32] If Simon is correct, the organizational culture is founded on the assumptions of the organization's leaders, but it is lived out every day in the being, thinking, and actions of all employees—including the managers. Collectively, these values, thought patterns, and action patterns in an organization affect the rest of society and even the global community.[33] See Exhibit 1-4.

EXHIBIT 1-4

How Being, Thinking, and Action Affect All Levels

DIMENSION	LEVEL		
	Individual	**Organizational**	**Community**
Action	What we do; Taking actions or making decisions that affect self, other individuals, the organization, and the larger communities in society.	What the organization does; Getting work done; Taking collective action that affects the market, the industry, or society; Collectively, individual and organizational actions shape society.	What society does; Enacting and administering public policy that affects society, the nation, and other nations.
Thinking & Feeling	How we think and feel; Individual mental awareness of self, of others, and of the situation; Emotions, patterns of thinking, perception, worldview; Individual thinking influences thinking in the organization.	How the organization as a whole thinks and feels; Strategic and operational thinking; Collective ways of thinking about how problems are solved; Individual and organizational thinking influences thinking in the larger community.	How society thinks and feels; Collective ways of thinking about how social and political problems should be solved; National thinking influences global thinking.
Being & Becoming	Who we are as individuals; Our identity, spirituality, values, character, moral standards, worldview, assumptions, virtues, purpose, and calling; Individual identity shapes individual and organizational thinking.	Who we are as an organization; The organization's identity, values, organizational assumptions, organizational culture, climate, and purpose (mission); Organizational identity shapes organizational and societal thinking and action.	Who we are as a society; National or regional identity, values, culture, and shared purposes; Who we are as a society shapes regional, national, and international thinking and action.

Fourth, this doesn't mean that religious beliefs, thoughts, and actions are always consistent once a person becomes a Christian. It means that the Christian attempts to live a consistent life. Research into human behavior has confirmed that we are not always consistent. Psychologists call our inconsistencies **cognitive dissonance**.[34] Research shows that the more stable our attitudes are over time and the more direct experience we have with the objects of our attitudes, the more likely our behavior will be consistent with our beliefs. The more confident we are in our attitudes and the more we can see how our behavior is linked to our attitudes, the more we should expect to experience consistency. The Christian would add to this research the belief that as we maintain a close relationship with God, our actions become increasingly consistent with our beliefs in God's will for our life.

Faith Perspective on Management

In this book, we will explore management from the points of view of business scholarship and practical experience, as well as from a Christian faith perspective. This is not a book about the Bible per se, although many passages in the Bible help us learn about some dimensions of management and leadership. Each chapter presents a summary of the biblical record on the major management issues covered in that chapter.

Religious faith continues to be a strong but subtle influence in the workplace. In many countries the Christian religion is still the most popular faith tradition, but this is changing as religious diversity in the population is increasing. Religious teachings form an important basis of morality that workers and their managers bring to work with them. Interest in integrating faith at work is growing among many denominations. Yet religion continues to be a sensitive subject of conversation in most organizations. Legal and cultural constraints limit the degree to which religion can be openly discussed in many organizations. The goal of this book is to help Christian managers develop a better understanding of how their religious faith influences their management thought and action and how they can be more effective as a Christian manager.

The Big Questions

To illustrate the faith perspective on management, let's consider some of the most important questions that practicing managers and management scholars alike have been fascinated with for many years:

- What do effective managers do differently compared with ineffective managers?
- How can managers improve their own efficiency and effectiveness as they seek to improve the efficiency and effectiveness of the organization for which they work?
- Why do workers produce at different levels of efficiency?
- How do effective managers motivate and lead others?
- What are the special challenges of managing in a global business environment?
- How does a manager balance the economic needs of the organization and the needs of the wider community of stakeholders served by the organization?
- How do managers contribute to strategic thinking and decision making in their organizations?
- What are the most effective ways to communicate?
- How do managers ensure a good fit between the organization and prospective employees?
- How can managers effectively influence the process of innovation and change in their organization?

Now consider some of the questions about management from the point of view of the shared values of the Christian community:[35]

- Why do Christians serve in the marketplace? What is the purpose of business?
- How does business affect the world?
- How can managers who are interested in being faithful to their religious beliefs be effective in business without compromising faith?
- How does the person of religious faith manage the paradoxes of faith and work?
- Should a manager keep a unified vision of life where economics is subordinate to religion?
- How does the manager measure career success?
- What does it actually look like when a manager integrates work and religious faith?

Notice how this last group of questions differs from the first group, and how these questions spotlight deeper issues. This is not to say that the first set of questions is unimportant. It just means that, for the Christian, asking the second set of questions is important as well. These additional questions are asked because of something we call the Christian worldview.[36]

The Concept of Worldview

For decades, society viewed religion and business as separate aspects of life. But that has been changing since the 1970s. As we will explore in this book, people today are much more interested in integrating their spirituality and faith with their work than in the past. People, including managers at all levels, desire to live consistent, authentic lives. One reason is that life is more than the abundance of economic things.[37] Some scholars now recognize that people steeped in religious traditions, nurtured by their church, synagogue, or mosque, bring this shaped sense of reality into the corporate world.[38] The religious faith perspective forms the manager's worldview.

Worldview is "a set of presuppositions—assumptions which may be true, partially true, or entirely false—which we hold—consciously or subconsciously, consistently or inconsistently—about the basic makeup of our world."[39] For the Christian, worldview is built on a set of core beliefs:

1. Worldview attempts to see every area of life and thought as an integrated whole.
2. Worldview is exploratory. It probes faith's relationship with every dimension of life including leisure time, family life, the world of work, and culture.
3. Worldview is pluralistic. For example, Christians share much in common with each other, but each Christian sees business issues from a slightly different perspective.
4. Worldview guides social behavior.

There is no single Christian worldview. It is diverse.[40] In addition, a worldview is always a work in progress.

> Worldview is "something you are aware of only in moments of crisis or contemplation. In ordinary time, it is like a pair of glasses or contact lenses. You are so accustomed to looking *through* it that you barely notice it's there."[41]

Elements of a Christian worldview that are common to many Christian traditions include the following fundamental beliefs:

- Spiritual and material dimensions of life cannot be separated. Life is an integrated whole.
- The standard (norms) of conduct in the spiritual and material dimensions of life is guided by the faith community's interpretation of the Bible.

We might say that for the Christian, paying attention to your own worldview and making adjustments is an act of worship.[42] As you explore the complex world of management, you will sometimes be challenged to test and even change your thinking, as a Christian, about the work of a manager. Even when there seem to be more questions than answers, worshiping God with your mind means that you learn with an attitude of humility, recognizing whom you serve and that there are limits to how much you know. Out of this process comes wisdom.

Use of the Bible and Biblical Teachings

One of the ways this book is different from other introductory management textbooks is its explicit reference to specific Bible passages and broader biblical teachings common to most Christian denominations and their connections to modern-day management.

Interpreting the Bible to draw conclusions regarding any aspect of life requires the Bible reader to carefully weigh the entire biblical record, taking into consideration the original historical context.[43] It requires considering the broad, guiding themes of the Bible when attempting to understand particular passages. Management issues are embedded in narratives, wisdom literature, the teachings of Jesus, counsel to the churches, and even prophetic writings. Although the Bible does offer the Christian faith perspective on management, it does not deal with every contemporary management idea. However, readers can draw guidance from the Bible on these issues by using prayerful judgment. This means that there may be disagreements among well-meaning Christians regarding specific passages or how the Christian worldview will look at particular management ideas.

Source: hunta/Shutterstock.

The Bible has a lot of guidance for managers and leaders.

Some Bible passages address the work of managers and leaders directly. We can take these at face value when searching for biblical guidance. Other Bible passages apply generally to all people under every circumstance regardless of whether the person is a manager or leader. Such passages can provide a rich background within which to consider managerial work.

The fact that a certain managerial behavior is mentioned in the Bible does not, by itself, mean that God condones such behavior. Some Bible passages are clear illustrations of managerial behavior that goes against God's will. For example, King Ahab steals the vineyard of Naboth. We should not deduce from this story that because stealing is one of the most efficient ways to build wealth, the Bible condones it. Implicit in the Ahab-Naboth story is the utter wrongness of the king's actions.[44] Another example is that of King David's son Absalom who undermines his father's authority.[45] This story is not biblical evidence that managers should use underhanded, dirty politics to get what they want. Instead, it is a good illustration of inappropriate political behavior in an organization.

Some Bible passages appear to implicitly accept the validity of the management ideas and practices that were current during the time of the Bible writers. The Bible reader must make a judgment whether the reported ideas and practices are consistent with the rest of the Bible as an expression of God's will or whether the references are simply part of the context of the narrative and do not, in themselves, form the basis of biblical teaching. For example, in Jesus' parable of the farmer who needed his crops harvested, the farmer paid all the workers the same day-wage regardless of how many hours they worked.[46] Some workers complained to the farmer that those who had been hired at the end of the day were paid just as much as those who had worked all day. Of course the point of the parable is not fair pay scales and human resource practices. The student of the Bible needs to make a judgment informed by the rest of the Bible whether this represents a specific command that some workers be paid more on a per-hour basis than other workers. In another parable, Jesus tells about the owner of assets who entrusted the job of building his wealth to three managers while he was away.[47] When the owner returned, he praised the managers who had accomplished positive net cash flow but harshly scolded the one manager who was afraid to try. Many Christian business scholars see in this story an implicit understanding in Jesus' day that, all things being equal, managers were expected to employ ethical means to build wealth for owners. We can also see in this story the harshness of the owner and, in light of other biblical teachings, determine that we should not emulate this element of the parable. The point of the parable is not economic efficiency but rather the significance of the final judgment.

In addition to specific Bible passages, we need to consider the broader themes of Christian teaching when attempting to understand what the Bible has to say to managers. Even when the Bible does not comment on every contemporary management idea, these broad themes provide a deep foundation for understanding the Christian faith perspective on management and leadership. The following themes naturally emerge out of the biblical record relating to management topics.

- **The Character of God.** The Bible portrays God's character as an expression of his will for humans to follow as an example. His character is the foundation for all his thinking and action. The Bible portrays God, in his relationship to his created beings, as setting goals;[48]

leading by example;[49] communicating vision and purpose;[50] organizing;[51] making decisions and acting in faithfulness to carry out his plans and promises;[52] establishing policies;[53] using all his legitimate, sovereign power to get things done;[54] maintaining relationships based on justice and mercy;[55] and seeking to reveal truth.[56]

- **The Creation narrative.** God gave humans the responsibility to work, subdue and care for the earth, and care for each other.[57] Created in the image of God, humans participate in the ongoing process of creation by creating new things, solving problems, and innovating in the physical, social, and spiritual or moral dimensions of life.[58] Together we create a culture of shared values. All these fundamental ideas have direct implications for the work of a manager.
- **Creation–Fall–Redemption narrative.** The Bible recognizes that God created humans in his image. But we have all fallen into sin. Because of his love for us, God set in motion a plan of redemption to save us. In addition, he gave humans, including managers, a part to play in his ongoing creative, sustaining, and redemptive work.
- **Community.** The Bible recognizes that managers work on behalf of the greater human community. Not only does an organization serve communities, but the organization itself is a community.[59] Business relationships are communal by nature. What one business does impacts others in the community. Unless businesses watch out for the interests of others, the whole community can be at risk of loss. When it is in our power to do good by preventing loss and we withhold this, we increase the risks for everyone.[60] We conclude that one purpose of business is to foster community interdependencies from which everyone benefits. To undermine these interdependencies is to undermine the basis of the fundamental relationships that are part of the structure of human society.
- **Covenant.** Covenant is a way of thinking about and caring for relationships in the community in which each party watches out for the interests of the other party. Compared with traditional managerial thinking in the marketplace culture, covenantal thinking is radical! This alone can make the Christian worldview different from other worldviews. Similarly, from a faith perspective, shalom—peace—is a deep guiding principle for all of business. Covenant and shalom relate directly to the work of managers and leaders who have a responsibility to help the community achieve its goals. Covenant is related to the concept of the Sabbath-relationship that God intends to have with humans built on trust, rest, hope, blessing, belonging, and setting apart as holy those we serve, the time we spend, and the work we do for and with each other.[61]
- **Calling.** Each person is called by God into a relationship with him. This calling extends to our entire life, including managerial work, and not just our experience in church.[62]

We will connect to these six themes throughout the rest of the book to illustrate how they apply to today's Christian managers.

The Christian Mind on Management

The "OUDA Loop" describes the thinking process as an interactive cycle of OBSERVATIONS (what we see), UNDERSTANDINGS (what we make of what we see), DECISIONS (what we determine to do about what we see and what we make of what we see), and ACTIONS (how we behave). This thinking process occurs within some context of presuppositions and principles—fundamental assumptions about how the world works (reality) and what rules of right and wrong should govern that work (values). The Christian faith provides the foundational presuppositions (for example, God exists and has expressed His moral will in Scripture), and principles (for example, application of the Ten Commandments) that help guide and support the Christian manager's journey through the "OUDA Loop" of the choices and commitments they face and make.

Dr. Sharon G. Johnson
Charleston Southern University

Contemporary Management Thought and Practice

We have been using the words *management* and *manager*, but what do they actually mean? Let's look at a few perspectives on their definitions.

Definitions of Management

Our English word *manage* came to us borrowed from the French verb *manége,* meaning to train or direct a horse in its exercises. Before that time, the Latin word for *hand* seems to be the root word for this idea common to several European languages. Early uses of the English word *manage* refer to a skillful handling of a sword or other weapon, conducting business affairs, giving direction, or maintaining control.[63]

Business definitions of management traditionally focus on the major tasks of management, achieving organizational goals, and the concept of effectiveness and efficiency.[64] Other popular definitions focus on the social, political, and interpersonal relationships between people: For example, *management involves using a set of pragmatic skills to get things done through or with other people*, or as an older slogan put it: the manager "does his work by getting other people to do theirs."[65]

These definitions sound straightforward and appear to present management as something you could easily reduce to a science, develop a set of formulae to apply to different situations, and, with proper training, be successful. This is not to criticize these definitions or their authors. Definitions, by nature, tend to simplify things that are complicated. This is one of the strengths of a definition for individuals who are new to the topic. But it is also a weakness. As a result, alternative definitions are sometimes developed to bring a different perspective into view.

In practice, attempting to apply a simple formula in a management situation can be futile. Unlike other business studies such as accounting in which there are more well-defined rules for achieving the right answer, in any given management situation there may be 10 different approaches, and all of them could be right, or all of them could be wrong. Exhibit 1-5 illustrates the complexity of management from a Christian faith perspective.

EXHIBIT 1-5
On Management Complexity

Multiple categories are needed to properly consider the complexity of management from a Christian faith perspective:[66]

- Relationships
  - with God
    - Expectations
    - Guiding principles
  - with self
    - Managing perception and perceptual biases
    - Self-awareness of abilities
    - Personality
    - Character, values, purpose
  - between people within the organization
  - between people and the organization as a whole
  - between people in the organization and people outside the organization
- Resources
  - Material
  - Technological
  - Financial
- Changing situations: both business and moral
  - Paradoxes
  - Ambiguities
  - Dilemmas
  - Trade-offs
- Systems and processes

An Alternative Perspective

Take a moment to picture yourself in terms of a whole career as a manager: meeting goals, meeting deadlines, maintaining efficiency targets, achieving organizational effectiveness, performing tasks or functions, and using your influence. All these and more are leveraged to get things done. Is this all there is to managerial work life? For an individual seeking to find spiritual meaning in managerial work or bring spiritual meaning to the work, there is more to management.

Consider another definition of management that encompasses the moral fabric, religious beliefs, and the potential for spiritual calling:

> **Management** is accepting the trust that others have placed in you as a manager and taking responsibility for who you are, how you think and feel, and what you do in serving a community of people, helping them collectively to create meaningful value for society by serving higher spiritual goals.

This definition is not in competition with other popular definitions. For some it will be supplementary. For others, however, this definition will be central to what it means to serve as a manager in the context of religious beliefs.

Several components are included in this definition, so let's look more closely at each one. Effective management is about trust. Managers are entrusted to watch out for the needs of the organization and for the people who report to them. **Trust** is confidence in or reliance on people in terms of what they say and do when working with others. Management is also about taking **responsibility**—part of the trust that the manager accepts to accomplish the larger organizational purpose. For example, managers who work for Deloitte accept the responsibility to achieve sales and service goals and at the same time maintain positive working relationships with employees. Taking responsibility in itself distinguishes management work from non-management work. See Exhibit 1-6.

From this point of view, a manager who is focused solely on spiritual meaning apart from getting things done would quickly be replaced. The successful Christian manager sees the work of achieving effectiveness and efficiency as ultimately serving God through managerial work and serving others in the organization and in society for the glory of God.

The context of management is service to a community. Whether the manager supervises one small work unit or is a senior executive responsible for an entire division, management is always performed within and on behalf of a community of workers and the larger community of the market place.

Managers and their subordinates all want to see that what they do makes a difference in terms of creating value for customers and employees. Management is about creating meaningful value for both the organization and those the organization serves.

To further illustrate the complexity of management, let's look at two concepts that are commonly associated with the definition of management: effectiveness and efficiency. Each concept raises important questions for the Christian manager to consider.

Effectiveness

Effectiveness is the degree to which the organization accomplishes what it sets out to do. The focus of effectiveness is to reach outcomes that are aligned with an organization's goal or agreed-upon standard[67]—in other words, "to do the right things." It is the manager's

EXHIBIT 1-6
Management vs. Non-Management Work

What distinguishes management work from non-management work?

- Taking responsibility for actions and decisions (yours and others)
- Coordinating the work of other people (individuals, work teams, or groups of departments)
- Being oriented toward the future but at the same time focusing on what is needed now and remembering where the organization has come from

responsibility to monitor whether the part of the organization he or she oversees is being effective and, if not, to make changes. Rooted in values, effectiveness is sometimes difficult to measure in quantitative terms.[68] Effectiveness will be defined in different ways by different people in the same organization.[69]

To illustrate, consider that in the for-profit world, things like stock price, return on investment (ROI), profit, and market share can be used as measures of effectiveness.[70] Two organizations can obtain a profit by doing completely different things in the same market. ROI is based on past experience but says little or nothing about the changes that will take place in the marketplace in the future.

Further, if every organization had just one goal that everyone agreed on, then it would be easier to determine effectiveness. In reality, an organization has multiple goals, and sometimes these goals conflict with each other.[71] **Goal conflict** is a situation in which one goal seems to be incompatible with other goals. A classic example of goal conflict is the balancing of long-term goals and short-term goals.[72] Managers must consider the work that needs to be done today, and, at the same time, keep in mind the long-term goals of the organization.

Another example of goal conflict is the set of conflicting expectations that organizations often face from *stakeholders*. **Stakeholders** are the individuals and groups inside and outside the organization that have expectations of the organization. For example, the government expects one thing, such as safety, from an organization, while customers expect something else, such as speed, and stockholders expect yet something else—cash flow. Safety, speed, and cash flow can easily conflict and create challenges for the managers who are trying to effectively meet all of these expectations, and many more, simultaneously.

Goal conflict also occurs when the goal of one department is at odds with the goal of another department in the same company.[73] An assembly department is focused on efficiency, managing the use of materials, and meeting daily or weekly production quotas. The materials management department is also focused on efficiency, but it has an additional goal of ordering sufficient quantities to receive the benefits of price discounts. Volume-discount purchases can result in receiving materials in quantities greater than the assembly department can deal with without additional attention by managers.

Conflicts between goals arise with more frequency and intensity in nonprofit organizations (NPOs) than in for-profit firms.[74] In the nonprofit world, the idea of effectiveness is even more subjective, making the task of defining it more difficult.[75] In any organization, the "right things" are defined by the key decision makers in the organization. But many nonprofit organizations have multiple sets of stakeholders, each of which expects a different goal to be achieved. When money is scarce, the organization may face difficult trade-offs when allocating budgets among many worthy programs.

Integrating the issues of spirituality and religion in this discussion creates even more complexity.[76] Christian managers face two layers of issues in terms of managerial effectiveness:

- being effective in achieving the practical, material purpose of the organization they work for, and
- being effective in living religious faith consistent with their worldview.[77]

Fortunately for the Christian, these goals are often in good alignment with each other. One reason for this is that the marketplace in free enterprise is founded on the Judeo-Christian values of honesty, faithfulness to commitments, and respect for the ownership of private property. Once in a while, however, they can be incompatible. When this happens, the manager's job is to attempt to bring clarity out of confusion or to attempt reconciliation.

Managers must have an understanding of the *purpose*, or mission, of their particular department in its relationship to other work units and the rest of the organization, and must coordinate workers to accomplish that mission. **Purpose** is why an organization exists. For most organizations the purpose is bigger than "to make a profit." It involves a description of how the organization is making a difference in its industry or in society. Exhibit 1-7 describes purpose at the individual, work-unit, and organization level and its link to effectiveness. You can apply the idea of purpose at any of these levels. For example, as an individual worker, you have a cluster of responsibilities, things that you do that help the organization and your work unit do its work. Maybe you spray paint parts that are then

EXHIBIT 1-7
Effectiveness Is Linked with Purpose

Purpose = your reason for working in a particular organization; your mission

Individual	Work Unit or Department	Organization
Personal mission; the purpose of your assigned tasks in the organization.	The purpose or mission of the department in the organization.	The overall purpose or mission of the organization in its relationship with the market, and ultimately with society.

Effectiveness = faithfulness in achieving your **Purpose** and living your **Values**

delivered to the assembly department. Maybe you create the financial statements every month for the chief accountant to review. Or maybe you manage a team of workers who clean the corporate headquarters' offices. In all of these cases, your work means something important for the organization's ability to achieve its goals. Each work team has one or more reasons for existing in the organization. And each organization has an overall reason why it exists in the marketplace.

The Christian Mind on Effectiveness

Being an effective Christian manager includes choosing and accomplishing organizational goals, but that's not all. Managers model and reflect God's wisdom in how they set controls, set benchmarks, and assign responsibilities to accomplish each goal. An effective manager achieves goals through resources, most notably through the work of other people. But both managers and employees are broken image bearers of God who make mistakes and fail (sometimes deliberately). Ultimately, the purpose of a Christian manager is to serve the best interests of others (Matthew 20:26–28).

The Christian manager's challenge is to set and accomplish goals that are consistent with Biblical values. Scripture has much to say about God's claim on your heart and your expected attitude, motives, desires, and values, which are often in direct opposition to the world's values. Christian managers have many opportunities to reflect God's wisdom through the activities they do.

Brian Hoekstra
Assistant Professor of Business
Dordt College

Efficiency

Another important concept in management is **efficiency**, which means achieving the economic performance necessary for the organization's survival. A key element of efficiency is comparing the level of work output with the resources provided for doing the work.[78] **Performance** means accomplishing a set of goals in a way that uses the optimal level of resources while generating the optimal level of output. Exhibit 1-8 describes efficiency and performance at the individual, work-unit, and organization level.

We might first think of efficiency as applying to just an individual, a work unit, or a company. But efficiency can also affect an entire market—in achieving fair prices, in determining which goods and services are distributed, and in weeding out weak and inefficient companies from the marketplace.

Rooted in economics, efficiency is about using the fewest amount of resources (inputs) to achieve the greatest amount of output during a specific period of time—in other words, "doing

Performance = how well you have used the resources available

Individual	Work Unit	Organization
Personal performance given the resources you have available: your time, materials, equipment, knowledge, and skills.	Performance of the work unit or department given the limited resources available.	Overall performance of the entire organization given the resources available.

Efficiency = faithfulness in economic **Performance** with the resources entrusted to you

EXHIBIT 1-8
Efficiency Is Linked with Performance

things right" in terms of economic outcomes. We can think of efficiency in terms of improving practical usefulness. Efficiency can also be defined as the ratio of what an organization actually produces divided by what it could feasibly produce given its existing resources, knowledge, and ability.[79]

As with effectiveness, attention to efficiency is required of all managers. From a faith perspective, this is none other than being entrusted with stewardship over resources. Exhibit 1-9 illustrates the differences and relationship between effectiveness and efficiency, both of which are vital in any organization.

As important as efficiency is, moral issues can arise if the drive for efficiency is unconstrained. By itself, efficiency says very little about how a manager should act.[80] Stripped of moral boundaries, almost anything might be allowed as long as that behavior does not violate the law or the managers don't get caught. Striving for efficiency at the expense of values such as integrity, respect, and dignity for humans is dangerous because unchecked it will inevitably destroy morale, cohesiveness, and organizational effectiveness. In an extreme example, between 1992 and 2008, Bernard Madoff operated Bernard L. Madoff Investment Securities, a scheme to defraud investors and hide information from investigators. Eventually, after many complaints

EXHIBIT 1-9
Effectiveness vs. Efficiency

Effectiveness	Efficiency
Evaluating how well or to what degree the organization (or a work unit) is achieving its purpose	Measuring how well resources are used in fulfilling the organization's purpose
The ends (purpose, mission)	The means to achieve the purpose
The foundation for long-term success	The foundation for survival
How well the overall goals of the organization are being achieved	What the organization produces ÷ by what it can potentially produce; Output ÷ Input
Doing the right things	Doing things right
What the organization and the value it provides means for employees, suppliers, customers, and society.	The technical (minimize waste) and economic (optimal allocation; optimal operating performance) details of offering value to customers and other stakeholders
Major spiritual challenge: Being vigilant to maintain a purpose for the organization (or work unit) that is in alignment with moral values.	**Major spiritual challenge:** Having the courage to apply moral constraints on actions, keeping them in alignment with core values and beliefs; knowing when moral restraint is necessary; working vigorously for productivity but not at the expense of integrity or people.

were investigated, his actions brought the entire organization down. Madoff confessed to his unethical behavior and went to prison.[81]

Unrestrained drive for efficiency will likely create a conflict with fundamental Christian beliefs. As a manager, you can do all the right economic things to achieve high performance and be wildly successful economically while at the same time fail to follow your religious beliefs. For example, pushing for increased efficiency raises questions about the appropriate use of humans to get work done and how much work should be expected of individual workers. Efficiency also raises questions about how much employees should be paid, what it means to be honest, and how to talk honestly with top-level executives regarding the need for resources.

Unfortunately there is no religious teaching that answers the question: At what point does the drive for efficiency in a particular situation violate religious faith? The Christian manager must use judgment that is informed by both economics and the Bible to fulfill the stewardship responsibility to the organization for organizational success and, at the same time, fulfill a God-given stewardship responsibility for moral and spiritual success.

The Christian Mind on Efficiency

Our creator God calls each of us to be stewards of His creation (Genesis 1:28). As the parable of the talents (Matthew 25) displays, our charge is to use those resources productively. This parable shows idleness is frowned upon and frankly, scolded. Being a good steward mandates performance from the resources entrusted to the manager.

There are improper shortcuts to efficiency. For example, managers may fail to maintain equipment (Ecclesiastes 10:10), choose to not pay bills on time (Proverbs 3:27–28) and the list goes on. While these practices may appear to be somewhat harmless on the surface, they reveal a manager's motives and lack of stewardship. Managers need to carefully monitor their motives to ensure God remains in His rightful place as Lord over all their life.

Christian managers have many opportunities to reflect God's character through the activities they do, and also in the way they do them.

Brian Hoekstra
Assistant Professor of Business
Dordt College

Other Perspectives on Management

We have covered Christian worldview and the being–thinking–action Management Pyramid as perspectives through which to think about management. We have also introduced the broad biblical themes that provide a spiritual perspective on the work of a manager. Next we look at a few other perspectives that have traditionally been used to understand management. Each perspective offers something slightly different but helpful for understanding the nature of management work.

MANAGERIAL FUNCTIONS.[82] For a century the most popular perspective on management has been on the functions or tasks that managers perform. Based on his observations in France a hundred years ago, Henri Fayol, a mining engineer who worked his way up to become the top manager of his company, identified five generic management functions: planning, organizing, coordinating, commanding, and controlling. Over time these five functions have been condensed into four: *planning* (anticipating what needs to be done in the future), *organizing* (dividing up and coordinating the work), *leading* (communicating a vision for where the workers are headed in the future), and *controlling* (monitoring results and making adjustments as needed for future improvements). Other functions have been added to Fayol's list such as staffing (hiring, training), decision making, evaluating (work performance, output), negotiating, and representing (communicating). We will address many of these in this book. See Exhibit 1-10.

EXHIBIT 1-10
Managerial Functions

Planning
Organizing
Leading
Controlling

A **management function** is a category of activities performed by managers of all types. A **management role** is a set of behavior patterns that is expected of someone who has a specific position in a social unit.[83] Both functions and roles are the means by which a manager completes the job. The means are used to accomplish the purpose of the manager's job, in other words, to see that meaningful value is created for someone.

MANAGEMENT ROLES.[84] Management is more than just functions. In the late 1960s, Henry Mintzberg, a management researcher, raised the question, "You can talk about managerial functions all you want, but what do managers actually do during their day?" He asserted that when we say that a manager engages in planning, we are not saying much, if anything, about what the manager actually does. In Mintzberg's observations of detailed activities of managers, he grouped the activities into three categories of work that he described in terms of managerial roles:

- **Interpersonal role:**
  - Figurehead—participating in symbolic activities representing the organization
  - Leader—motivating subordinates
  - Liaison—maintaining relationships with individuals outside the organization (or work unit)
- **Informational role:**
  - Monitoring—obtaining and interpreting information that describes how well the organization is doing
  - Disseminating—transmitting information to others inside the organization
  - Spokesperson—transmitting information to others outside the organization
- **Decisional role:**
  - Entrepreneur—seeking new opportunities to advance the organization's goals
  - Disturbance-handler—solving problems and giving direction to adapt to unexpected situations that create inefficiencies
  - Resource allocator—making decisions regarding the allocation of resources
  - Negotiator—representing the organization during negotiations with employees or with outside entities

Some of the role categories popularized by Mintzberg are themselves ambiguous in terms of what a manager actually does for any specific role. Such ambiguity has led some to look at managerial jobs from the point of view of demands of superiors and from the nature of the work itself, constraints or limitations, and choices that managers have in how work gets done and what work gets done.

SKILLS.[85] It is natural to think that if management is about tasks and roles, then there must be certain skills involved. A **management skill** is the ability to perform a management activity well. Notice how three types of managerial skill encompass both the thinking and action dimensions of the Management Pyramid. Technical skills are skills that include knowledge of and proficiency in specialized activities. Many of these skills are learned on the job and are specific to the particular company for which you work. Human relationship skills include the ability to work well with other people and build cooperative behavior among workers. Conceptual skills enable the manager to think about the organization as a system. They include the ability to think about business situations, seeing the organization as a whole, and understanding the interdependencies among the various stakeholders.

Since the 1970s, scholars have debated the bare minimum skills and competencies needed for managers.[86] Likewise, companies themselves use a variety of approaches to describe managerial competencies. One unresolved difficulty involves the complexity and ambiguity of management. Some believe that managerial competency can be developed only in the context of specific management jobs at specific companies and the particular problems they face in their marketplaces. Others believe that some generic competencies apply to most managers under most conditions. For example, suppose that Manager A supervises a group of 10 workers on an assembly line who are making bicycles, and Manager B supervises a group of 10 housekeepers in a hotel who are preparing rooms for guests. Are the skills that Manager A needs the same as the skills that Manager B needs?

DIFFERENCES IN ORGANIZATIONAL LEVEL.[87] Managers come in all different types and organizational levels. The organizational level in which you work will shape your managerial thinking and

Source: Digital Vision/Thinkstock.

The manager of a hotel has different ways of thinking, feeling and acting than the supervisor in the housekeeping department.

action. There are four organizational levels: non-management workers who help with managerial tasks, frontline supervisors, middle managers, and senior managers. Some elements of the work of managers in the same organization will be different depending on their level of decision-making authority and whether the manager is in charge of production (line management) or a support department (staff management) such as purchasing, maintenance, or accounting. For example, in the U.S. Food and Drug Administration we see all levels of management.[88]

Individual non-management workers who don't have formal management responsibilities are sometimes called on to help with management duties. In addition to managing themselves, their time, and their work materials, these workers may be asked to manage a project or a problem-solving team. They may be asked to help on an ongoing basis with supervisory tasks such as planning a work schedule, planning and carrying out a move of the work team from one location to another, or preparing a production report.

Frontline supervisors and team leaders work one-on-one with individuals who are getting the day-to-day technical work done. Here the focus is on managing individual performance and teamwork. Because of this, their work tends to pull their thinking toward dealing with specific events or projects that occur. The frontline supervisor may perform some technical work in addition to management work. Becoming a frontline supervisor or team leader is often your first opportunity to be a manager.

Middle managers and project managers connect interdependent groups of workers and manage the performance of work teams and departments. This work pulls their thinking toward watching for patterns of behaviors among the individuals and the work teams. Their focus is primarily on the means of getting the work done.[89] In the Food and Drug Administration, one example of a middle manager is a physician who is in charge of the staff members who work with new regulations and revisions to existing regulations. This person reports to the director in charge of the office of communication, education, and radiation programs.

When you accept a position in middle management, you are stepping into a role that is both exciting and challenging.[90] Let's consider both the upside and the downside of being a middle manager. The upside:[91] Middle managers are an important source of innovation. Middle managers participate in strategic decision making. Their involvement in the actual day-to-day work gives them a perspective that senior-level managers need to craft and adjust strategy during implementation. They guide frontline workers in understanding and applying strategy to their day-to-day work. More than anyone else in the organization, it is the middle manager who is in the position to compliment those who make the most difference for the success of the organization.

There is also a downside to middle management.[92] Depending on how long they have worked for the organization, middle managers may lack the historical perspective of the company that senior managers typically have. Their authority is sometimes uncertain. Some have multiple reporting relationships and task assignments that overlap with other employees.

- Senior managers believe conventional stereotypes of middle managers in terms of resistance to change.
- Senior managers pretend to listen.
- Middle managers know they are not listened to.
- Middle managers take the role of a compliant child:
  - They hide their efforts to introduce change believing that if they fail, they will be punished.
  - They don't push senior managers to pay attention.
  - They withhold information.
  - If consultants are brought in, they often provide the same suggestions that are being made by middle managers. The consultant is listened to but not the middle manager. This perpetuates the cycle.

EXHIBIT 1-11
The Vicious Cycle[93]

This can create confusion and frustration. They try to solve contradictions between what top management hopes to create and what is realistic to create. They sometimes find themselves in the middle of a vicious cycle of negative perception by their supervisors. See Exhibit 1-11.

Middle managers can get pressure from above and resentment from below. For these and other reasons middle managers may experience frustration as they are literally caught in the middle. As difficult as this role can be, it also can be very rewarding.

Middle managers should keep in mind what it takes to be effective in their role. See Exhibit 1-12.

Senior (top-level) **managers** are responsible for thinking about the organization as a whole as it responds to changes in the outside environment. In the FDA, senior managers include the Deputy Commissioner for the Office of Foods, the Chief Scientist and Deputy Commissioner for Science and Public Health, the Chief Financial Officer and Deputy Commissioner for the Office of Administration, and the Opportunity and Diversity Management Director.[94] Their viewpoints encompass all the work processes and how they interrelate, as well as systems both inside and outside the organization. Because of this, they must focus on the interrelated organizational

EXHIBIT 1-12
How to Be an Effective Middle Manager[95]

- When bringing reports of potential changes in consumer behavior, supplier behavior, or competitor behavior, be aware of your own biases: How will such a change affect your department and in what ways do you feel compelled to protect your interests over the interests of the company? How you frame your report can close the ears of senior leaders.
- Practice taking the big picture of the whole company into consideration when interpreting signals from the marketplace.
- Be a change agent in your own sphere of influence. As the old saying goes: Bloom where you are planted. If something needs to be changed in your work unit and no one is leading, take the lead and learn from your experience.
- Be a positive critical thinking middle manager who critically evaluates senior leaders' proposals and then gives constructive feedback along with alternatives.
- Take on projects that build your versatility and flexibility.
- Be trustworthy and loyal. When you are tempted in a group setting to criticize the bosses when they are not around, instead say, "Their strategy has merit. What we need to do is find the best way to implement the strategy or to make recommendations for adjustments if our implementation doesn't work."
- Become known as a person who reports the brutal facts but with diplomacy.
- Build a network of supporters who trust you. Some middle managers are able to develop influence beyond the limits of their formal authority.
- Build your own self-awareness and talent for emotional intelligence.

Thinking Patterns	Management Level	Skills	Knowledge
Events that affect themselves and their work team	Non-management workers who help with management tasks	Technical skills; human relationship skills	Specialized
Events that affect individual workers on a day-to-day basis	Frontline supervisors	Technical skills; human relationship skills	Specialized
Behavior patterns of work units and work processes	Middle managers	Human relationship skills; conceptual skills	Specialized; general
Internal and external **systemic structures** that influence behavior patterns and work processes	Senior managers	Conceptual skills; human relationship skills	General

EXHIBIT 1-13
Thinking Patterns of Management

issues that the company faces now and in the future. With experience, they develop the skill of tolerating ambiguous situations while setting the strategic agenda for the future of the entire organization.

Managers of all levels need to change their thinking patterns from looking at mere events in their day-to-day work to observing the behavioral patterns across the organization over time.[96] But more important, effective managers will move their thinking toward understanding the relationships between the firm and companies that supply it with materials and other resources, its customers, and other organizations that have an effect on how the firm serves society. These are the underlying but larger influences on employee behavior patterns and day-to-day events. We call these systemic structures. See Exhibit 1-13.

MANAGEMENT PROCESSES.[97] Another way to look at management is from the viewpoint of management processes. Management itself can be construed as a process. A process is nothing more than a series of sequential tasks or steps that are performed to accomplish a goal. The **management process** involves the planning, organizing, leading, and controlling work using resources to produce products and services. But the management process can be broken down into smaller subprocesses. Here are some of the subprocesses that managers participate in or for which they are responsible:

- Operational and capital budget processes
- Strategic management process
- Managerial decision-making process
- Knowledge management process
- Human resource management process
- Communications process
- Organizational development process
- Management control process

Other management processes include operations process (creating products and services of value), quality improvement process (improving product quality, service quality, and process quality), and the project management process (planning and carrying out projects). For the Christian manager, we might add to this list the process of integrating religious faith with work.

DIFFERENCES BETWEEN THE ECONOMIC SECTORS.[98] Considering management from the point of view of the economic sector in which a manager works adds something new to our understanding. Most people think in terms of three sectors of the free-market economy:

- the commercial sector, sometimes referred to as the private, for-profit, corporate, business enterprise, or simply business sector
- the nonprofit sector, sometimes identified as the not-for-profit, voluntary, or not for gain sector
- the public sector, sometimes referred to as the government sector

Each of these sectors relies on managers to get work done. But does the manager who works in a manufacturing company go about the business of managing in the same way as the manager who works for a United Way agency? Actually, some similarities exist and some important differences exist, too. Knowledge of managerial competencies effective in the for-profit world continues to be imported into the government and nonprofit sectors. But knowing when it is appropriate to copy business practices into the nonprofit sector is still a problem for some managers. Simply taking some management concepts from the for-profit world and applying them straight across to the nonprofit sector or public can cause the manager problems.[99]

The size, scope, and economic significance of the nonprofit sector have increased since 1970. In 2010, tax-exempt organizations employed over 9 million individuals, or a little more than 7 percent of nonfarm workers in the economy. Government employment represented 17 percent of the workforce,[100] and the commercial sector still employs the majority of workers in the United States at 75 percent of the workforce.

Earlier in this chapter we considered two of the differences between for-profit firms and nonprofit organizations (the ambiguity and complexity of goals and the difficulty in measuring effectiveness). Exhibit 1-14 highlights other differences.

DIFFERENCES IN NATIONAL CULTURES.[101] Given the mobility of people and organizations, managing organizations requires an awareness of the cross-cultural dynamics that managers will face in their work. Not all management principles apply equally well in all countries and in all cultures. Employees come to the workplace representing a variety of national cultural and religious perspectives that the manager must consider.

The Transition to Becoming a Manager

Researchers studying first-time managers discovered that they experience a transformational identity.[102] For the first few months on the job, new managers viewed their role in terms of responsibilities, not relationships. They were focused on the new rights and privileges that came with their increased authority. It was this that had attracted them to the managerial work. They relied on past experiences as doers to make sense out of their new role. They tended to be cynical about managing their relationships with peers or dealing with organizational politics.

It took several months for the new managers in the study to move beyond their personal interests to begin seeing their job from their boss's point of view. They had expected their boss's interest to be focused solely on production. Surprisingly, they found that their supervisors were more interested than they had expected in how well they were doing in developing their subordinates as people. This transformation of personal identity can take up to a year to accomplish in the role of a first-time manager. See Exhibit 1-15.

EXHIBIT 1-14
Differences Between For-Profit and Nonprofit Organizations[103]

Issue	For-Profit	Nonprofit
Rewards and punishments	Used more	Used less
Focus of planning	Results	Resources
Goals	Profit	Goals are often ambiguous
Measure of organizational effectiveness	Financial	Tend to consider everything that is done as worthwhile
Degree of executive control	Much higher degree of autocratic control	Lower degree of control
Economic bottom line	Profitability	Prosperity
Resource availability	Limited	Scarce
The route to leadership	Through the ownership of capital	Through ideas, personality, and character

EXHIBIT 1-15

Transformation of a Non-Management Worker to a First-Time Manager

Source: Based on Katz, R. L. (1955). Skills of an effective administrator. *Harvard Business Review*. 33(1), 33–42; Kochanski, J. (1997). Competency-based management. *Training & Development*. 51(10), 40–44; Senge, P. M. (1990). *The fifth discipline*. New York: Doubleday; Hill, L. (1992). *Becoming a manager*. Boston, MA: Harvard Business School Press.

NON-MANAGEMENT WORKER

- **Responsible for accomplishing individually assigned tasks**
- **Technical skills**
- **Thinks about events that affect self**
- **Specialist**
- **Collaborates with other workers as directed by supervisor**
- **Identity is associated with specific tasks or work team**
- **Emphasis is on self and independence**

→

FIRST-TIME MANAGER

- **Responsible for many different tasks and for the work that subordinates do**
- **Technical skills and human relations skills**
- **Thinks about patterns of events that affect a team of workers**
- **Generalist and specialist**
- **Collaborates with subordinates and with other managers**
- **Identity is associated with the organization or the profession**
- **Emphasis is on developing subordinates and on interdependence**

Managerial Tensions

Managers experience a high volume of activities during their day. They often face time pressures to get jobs done. Managers work at a fast pace, but their work is rarely complete.[104]

More than this, managers are often put in difficult positions where they can easily be criticized no matter what they do. Or they are given expectations by both subordinates and superiors who have contradictory needs and desires. Managers are sometimes given problems that cannot be solved—only managed. The drive for greater and greater organizational flexibility has required managers to learn how to be chameleons (and yet act with integrity!) in terms of how they think and act when dealing with temporary workers, part-time workers, flexible schedules, and quick changes between production runs.[105] In spite of these challenges, success can give a manager a clear sense of fulfillment and satisfaction in a job well done. Not everyone is cut out to do this work.

You don't hear even seasoned managers say, "It's never been about the increased pay. The reason I got into management in the first place was that the work is confusing and the situations I face are ambiguous. I love the way that information that you *really* need always comes in too late. I get so excited when I am the last to know something important that is going on in my organization. Besides that, I clawed my way up to middle management because I really want to make choices that require gut-wrenching trade-offs in which no matter what I choose, someone is going to be unhappy. Oh, and I almost forgot to mention the sheer joy that comes from muddling through dilemmas and paradoxes. And to think that they pay me to have this much fun!"

The reality is that not everyone who becomes a manager expects to work under these challenging types of circumstances. When you are a non-manager, you have a certain amount of freedom from having to make decisions in ambiguous situations. The more complex the issue, the more likely it will be passed to higher levels of management authority. Many managers, even the ones with experience, feel ill-equipped for their role. See Exhibit 1-16.

The complexity of management defies simple answers for some of what managers do. One characteristic of this book is that it respects, even celebrates, this complexity. We can think of this complexity in terms of four categories of cognitive tension that every manager faces: ambiguities, trade-offs, dilemmas, and paradoxes.

EXHIBIT 1-16

Nine Out of 10 Managers Feel Ill-Equipped

"Nine out of 10 managers feel ill-equipped for their role as leaders, doubting their own judgment and feeling 'dispirited when facing new and challenging situations,' according to a survey of 1,000 managers published today [April 11, 2005]. The study by Common Purpose, a leadership development organisation, found that dealing with difficult personalities—including customers, workers or employers, giving and receiving criticism, making judgments under time pressure and communicating bad news were among the biggest challenges faced by managers."[106]

One of the truly exciting dimensions of being a manager is the opportunity to help an organization when what needs to be done is ambiguous or when the context is so rapidly changing that the organization needs to quickly adapt in ways that are not clearly understood.[107] **Ambiguities** are situations that are not clearly defined, are complicated, or are changing rapidly. Certainly the broader your responsibility becomes as a manager, the more likely you will face ambiguous situations. But even frontline supervisors face ambiguous problems.

A second category of management complexity is that some management problems are rooted in the trade-offs inherent in business. To use a football analogy, you can develop your team around speed but in so doing you will likely have to sacrifice some size. A **trade-off** is a giving up of one thing in order to get something else.

The challenge for managers in making these decisions is that not all trade-offs can be measured with ease or precision. Plus, sometimes you are given a mandate to avoid the trade-off when, for all practical purposes, the trade-off can't be avoided. You may be called upon to make a decision without having complete information about the trade-offs. Add to this the fact that some stakeholders will view the trade-off one way and others will view it another way.

A third challenging type of management tension is a **dilemma**, which is the position of deciding between two things that offer the strong potential for expected unpleasant outcomes. You are probably familiar with two phrases that refer to a dilemma: "pick your poison" and "choose the lesser of two evils." Organizational managers may face a dilemma when deciding what to do when setting up the company's relational database. One option is to create a simple, easy-to-use database. It will save money up front, but it won't be truly satisfying in the long run because managers may not be able to easily generate and access key reports that they need. Another option is to create a more expensive, complex database, but this will take more time and may increase the risk that the database will be more difficult to use.

Not all managerial problems are dilemmas. To use a sports analogy, suppose you are a football linebacker defending against the league's top-rated passing quarterback. The quarterback is skilled at reading defensive alignment and personnel and at making split-second decisions to adjust his passing attack. He can pick your defense apart with his arm like a cannon. It is extremely difficult to defend against him. This is a management problem. A dilemma is when, as a linebacker, you face a quarterback who is equally skilled at running the ball and passing the ball. If you stay back and cover the receivers expecting a pass, the quarterback will run with the ball. If you rush the quarterback expecting him to run, this leaves a receiver open, and he will throw the ball.

Unlike problems, which can be solved with the right resources and timeframe, dilemmas appear to be unsolvable (at least until the play unfolds) with the timeframe or the resources that are available. Sometimes dilemmas are like mechanical puzzles and they require taking a whole new perspective to see the problem in a different light.

The fourth type of tension is when you must do two seemingly opposite things at the same time to pursue goals that appear to be in direct conflict with each other. We call this a **paradox**. Some situations in business require you to attempt to "have your cake and eat it too."[108] For example, managers are called on to make decisions that take care of current needs but at the same

Source: Glen Jones/Shutterstock.

Management dilemmas, as in team sports, sometimes require the manager to make decisions that minimize the risk of unpleasant outcomes.

EXHIBIT 1-17
Paradoxical Management Proverbs

Slow and steady wins the race.	Time waits for no one.
Look before you leap.	Strike while the iron is hot.
Silence is golden.	The squeaky wheel gets the grease.
A miss is as good as a mile.	Something is better than nothing.
A good beginning makes a good ending.	It's not over till it's over.
There's safety in numbers.	Better be alone than in bad company.
If at first you don't succeed, try, try again.	Don't beat a dead horse.

time take care of the organization's long-run needs. You need to hire one more employee to help a work team get its work done. The work needs to be done as soon as possible and the pressure is on to hire someone quickly. But you also need to hire someone who will be a good match for the company in the long run and must look past the work that needs to be done tomorrow and select the person who will be the best long-term match. See Exhibit 1-17.

If you are looking for a way to find spiritual meaning in your work as a manager, get as much practice as you can managing paradoxes and dilemmas. It is the "extreme sport" equivalent in management and the place where your character will be tested and shaped. Some managers find personal and professional fulfillment in managing paradoxes such as one where you must walk the tightrope between changing how work gets done while preserving continuity of the organization's core values.[109]

In this book we will devote a small section at the end of each chapter to some of these tension points.[110] The reason for this is twofold:

1. To minimize the element of surprise for those who go into management.
2. To raise the awareness of others who work for managers who are asked to lead during these challenging situations.

Chapter Summary

1. Faith integration is the process of combining Christian faith and religious experience with the rest of our lives into a combined whole where Christian beliefs and actions become consistent in the work life of a manager. The Management Pyramid illustrates three dimensions of Christian faith integration: the dynamic relationship between who we are, how we think and feel, and our actions. Who we are influences how we think and feel. How we think and feel about things at work affects our behavior. Over time, our behavior affects how we think and feel in our work. Eventually changes in how we think and feel have an influence in who we are. This model applies to three levels simultaneously: individual, organizational, and society as a whole.
2. The Christian faith perspective on management is based on a particular worldview. Worldview is the set of assumptions and beliefs regarding the makeup of the world. A Christian worldview includes a belief in the existence of God, the authority of the Bible, that the spiritual and material dimensions of life cannot be separated, and that the Bible is the authoritative standard of conduct in the spiritual and material dimensions of life. The Christian must use judgment in how to interpret the Bible in terms of management issues. The fact that a certain managerial behavior is mentioned in the Bible does not, by itself, mean that God condones such behavior.
3. Even when the Bible does not comment on every contemporary management idea, it contains broad themes that provide a deep foundation for understanding the Christian faith perspective on management and leadership. These themes include the character of God, creation, creation–fall–redemption, community, covenant, and calling.
4. Traditional definitions of management usually focus on getting things done through other people in an efficient and effective manner. While this emphasis is important an alternative definition is considered in this book: Management is accepting the trust that others have placed in you as a manager and taking responsibility for who you are, how you think and feel, and what you do in serving a community of people, helping them collectively to create meaningful value for society by serving higher spiritual goals.
5. Effectiveness is the degree to which the organization accomplishes what it sets out to do. The focus of effectiveness is to reach outcomes that are aligned with an organization's goal or agreed-upon standard. Efficiency is achieving the economic performance necessary for the organization's survival while using the least amount of resources. Each of these concepts comes with a spiritual challenge for the manager. For effectiveness, the challenge is in being vigilant to maintain

a purpose for the organization (or work unit) that is in alignment with moral values. For Christian managers it includes being effective in living religious faith consistent with their worldview. For efficiency, the challenge means having the courage to apply moral constraints on actions, keeping them in alignment with core values and beliefs such as working vigorously for productivity but not at the expense of integrity or people. Unrestrained drive for efficiency will likely create a conflict with fundamental Christian beliefs.

6. Besides the worldview perspective, management can be seen from several other perspectives. Each perspective reveals a slightly different dimension and set of issues related to managerial work. These perspectives including the following:
   - Functions: planning, organizing, leading, and controlling
   - Roles: interpersonal roles, informational roles, decisional roles
   - Skills: technical, human relations, conceptual thinking
   - Organizational level: individual non-management workers, frontline supervisor, middle management, top-level management. Middle managers are in an interesting situation facing pressures from subordinates as well as top-level managers.
   - Management processes such as budgeting, planning, communication, and decision making.
   - Differences in economic sectors: for-profit, non-profit, public (government). Some managerial practices might be different depending on the sector in which a manager works.
   - Differences in national cultures: Not all management principles apply equally well in all countries and in all cultures.
7. Managers face tensions in their work including: ambiguities, trade-offs, dilemmas, and paradoxes. One reason why organizations hire managers is to help them manage these tensions effectively.

Key Terms

Ambiguity 25
Calling 12
Character of God 11
Character traits 6
Cognitive dissonance 9
Conceptual models 5
Covenant 12
Creation narrative 12
Creation–fall–redemption narrative 12
Dilemma 25
Effectiveness 14
Efficiency 16
Faith integration 5
Frontline supervisor 20
Goal conflict 15
Management 14
Management process 22
Management Pyramid 6
Management function 18
Management role 18
Management skill 19
Middle manager 20
Nonprofit organization 4
Organizational level 5
Paradox 25
Performance 16
Purpose 15
Responsibility 14
Senior manager 21
Stakeholders 15
Trade-off 25
Trust 14
Worldview 10

Discussion Questions

1. What is the difference between non-Christian managers who understand their responsibilities to superiors, to workers, and to society and managers with a Christian worldview?
2. Do you think that managers who are actively involved with a faith community should get better performance out of their organizations than managers who are not actively involved? Why or why not? Will their performance be different or will their experience be different?
3. As a middle manager what would you do to break "the vicious cycle" described in this chapter?
4. In terms of how you think as a manager, contrast the difference between "behavior patterns" and "systemic structures."
5. What are the weaknesses of the being–thinking–action model? What does it leave out? Does it fairly characterize life's experience as you see it?
6. When you read the description of dilemmas and paradoxes, what situations came to mind that you have experienced in your life?
7. Why is thinking so important to a manager?
8. If being drives thinking, which in turn drives behavior, how can action change who you are?
9. Why is it important to immerse yourself in management work in order to learn what it really means to be a manager? In other words, why is it so difficult to teach management through a book?
10. Contrast managers at different levels of authority. Which level of management authority is the most attractive to you? Why?
11. If you had $100 to spend on your entire management education, how much would you spend, and why, on the following items?
    a. Theory and principles
    b. Practice
12. What are the potential downside risks of each of the following?
    a. Learning management on the job rather than in school
    b. Learning management in school rather than on the job
13. Reflect on a personal experience you have had with a manager. Was this manager successful? To what degree

did each of the following contribute to the manager's success (or lack of it): human relations skills, technical skills, conceptual skills?

14. What important management perspectives can we learn from Ephesians 4:1–16 (Unity in the Body of Christ)?
15. What important management perspectives can we learn from Luke 16:1–13 (Parable of the Shrewd Manager)?
16. What responsibility do humans have for those persons who are unable to contribute productive labor in society?

STUDENT EXERCISES

1. See Exhibit 1-3, The Management Pyramid Represented in the Bible, and check out the Bible verses listed. Read some of the verses in each part of the pyramid and write a summary of what you see the Bible teaching regarding each element of the Management Pyramid. Select a favorite Bible verse from each of the three sections. Reflect: Why is that verse a favorite?
2. Use an Internet search engine and look for websites that contain information about "managerial competencies." Find an organization that lists managerial competencies. Which competencies are things you can learn quickly? Which ones might take years to learn?
3. Find a family member or acquaintance who works in an organization that is faith-based. Is effectiveness valued more than efficiency in such an organization? Interview this person.
4. Pair up with another person. Interview each other, and, if need be, talk with a supportive friend. Find out how the person is making a difference in someone else's life right now. (The goal is for each student to have something written about them that reflects how they are making a difference in someone's life now.)
5. Review the "big questions" of management from a Christian worldview perspective. Select one of these questions and write a paragraph (or more) describing why this is an important question for the Christian.
6. Interview a middle manager and attempt to confirm or challenge how this chapter portrays the work experience of the middle manager for that person.
7. Pair up with another student. The members of each pair decide what questions to ask of practicing managers about which they are curious. Have one member of each pair interview a manager who works for a nonprofit organization regarding management activities and experience. The other member of the pair interviews a manager who works in a for-profit organization. The pair then should compare notes and attempt to describe the similarities and differences between the experience of the two types of managers.

IN-CLASS EXERCISES

In-Class Debate

Divide the class into small groups of five to six people each. Hand out a sheet of paper containing the following quotations. Assign half of the groups to develop a rationale for why the first quotation is valid and the other half to develop a rationale for why the second quotation is valid. Give the groups 5 minutes to discuss. Then call for groups to give a summary of the rationale they developed. Discussion can follow for a few minutes.

Discussion Topic #1: Should management theories be taught and learned at the undergraduate level?

A. "The driving force behind our quest for theory is the need to impose order on unordered experiences, and thereby solve real-world problems that require collective effort. Grounding our theories in everyday problems is all important because it is the logical relation to a problem situation which makes a theory interesting and meaningful, and gives it power to solve existing problems and to illuminate new ones."[111]

B. "Professors should not spend time teaching undergraduate business students theory. Instead, they should teach us practical things that we can do when we get out of school. Theory is boring and not very practical. Theory is not what I came to learn in business school."[112]

Discussion Topic #2: The Bible speaks of God in human terms. One reason for this is that while we realize that God is beyond complete human understanding right now, human concepts help us understand the important elements of God and His Work.

A. One way to think about management is in the following terms:
   - **Efficiency** is getting the most output from the least amount of inputs, the goal of which is to minimize resource costs. Efficiency is sometimes described as "doing things right."
   - **Effectiveness** is completing activities of various work groups so that organizational goals are attained; it is often described as "doing the right things."

   If you were to describe God in terms of efficiency and effectiveness, what ideas come to mind?

B. We might think about God and his work in terms of the classical management functions (Henri Fayol):
   - Planning
   - Organizing
   - Leading
   - Controlling

   If you were to describe God in terms of these four functions, what ideas come to mind?

Discussion Topic #3: Regarding the faith integration issue of consistency of behavior between personal life and business life: Should the Christian manager be expected to apply the Golden Rule (Matthew 7:12) in exactly the same way at work as with family and personal friends?

A. **No.** By nature the world of commerce is impersonal. It is impossible for a manager to know everything about everyone in a particular business situation. What you think is doing good to someone may actually be doing bad to someone else. This imperfect knowledge makes it impossible for a manager to know how to live out the Golden Rule in the world of business like he can do at home. The Golden Rule assumes a certain type of community where everyone knows each other and where relative transparency exists in terms of needs. In the world of work and commerce we must deal with people whom we don't know very well. Thus, we should focus on a "Silver Rule": "Don't do to others what you would consider unfair or unjust if they did it to you."[113] Following such a principle does not mean that the person is living a spiritually fragmented life. Rather, the Christian is living a faith-integrated life within a context that is more complicated than life at home or among close friends.

B. **Yes.** Jesus' counsel to do unto others what you would have them do unto you applies equally well in the world of work and management as it does in our personal life. Jesus does not condone doing one thing at church and another thing in the marketplace. Holding to two different standards of behavior requires the Christian to live a fragmented life. This undermines faith integration.

Discussion Topic #4: Is the constant drive for improvement in efficiency contrary to the teachings of the Bible?

A. **Yes.** Constant focus on efficiency makes efficiency the value rather than serving God and fellow humans. Efficiency leads to idolatry. Economics has become essentially a religion. The gospel of efficiency has replaced the gospel of Christ. Humans have come to worship abundance rather than worship God. Efficiency is a method of control and exploitation which is antithetical to the notion of God-created human freedom. The economic orientation toward efficiency leads managers to neglect other elements of the employer-employee relationship. We should be content with a certain level of productivity but not desire an excessive degree of efficiency. The Bible counsels us to rest from our labor one day per week.[114]

B. **No.** Efficient, productive labor is part of God's original plan for humans. The promises inherent in the biblical ideas of covenant, shalom, and blessing all point to enjoying the results of productive labor. When humans work efficiently, they imitate God's work. Productivity is a spiritual obligation to God and to each other. God's call for us to be good stewards requires us to be efficient. God approves of being useful and fruitful. The Bible presents higher agricultural yield as better than lower yield. The Bible speaks about unproductive resources and unfruitfulness in strong disapproving tones.[115]

Endnotes

1. Alford, H. J., & Naughton, Michael (2001). *Managing as if faith mattered: Christian social principles in the modern organization.* Notre Dame, IN: University of Notre Dame Press. p. 1.
2. Chewning, R. C., Eby, J. W., & Roels, S. J. (1990). *Business through the eyes of faith.* San Francisco, CA: HarperSanFrancisco. p. 90.
3. Ayer, B. (2007). Farewell, Bruce. *Alaska Airlines Magazine.* 31(8), 7.
4. Ayer, B. (2007). Farewell, Bruce. *Alaska Airlines Magazine.* 31(8), 7.
5. Folger, M. (2007). From corporation to inspiration. *Alaska Airlines Magazine.* 31(8), 115–128.
6. Her name has been changed to disguise her identity.
7. Gooden, W. E. (2000). Confidence under pressure: How faith supports risk taking. In Banks, R., & Powell, K. (Eds.). (2000). *Faith in leadership: How leaders live out their faith in their work—and why it matters.* San Francisco, CA: Jossey-Bass. p. 48.
8. For an interesting collection of stories and wisdom regarding faith integration offered by seasoned executives see Darden, R., & Richardson, P. J. (2002). *Corporate giants: Personal stories of faith and finance.* Grand Rapids, MI: Fleming H. Revell.
9. The three-part model of being–thinking–action is simple and because of this there is a risk that thinking about the concepts and the interrelationships represented by the model can, without constraint, become *simplistic.* A simplistic use of the model is rejected and should be guarded against.
10. Myers, D. G., & Jeeves, M. A. (2003). *Psychology through the eyes of faith.* San Francisco, CA: HarperSanFrancisco. pp. 83, 193–198.
11. One of the early business scholars to recognize this interactive nature of business and character was Marshall: ". . . very often the influence [from experience in business] exerted on a person's character by the amount of his income is hardly less, if it is less, than that exerted by the way in which it is earned." ". . . the business by which a person earns his livelihood generally fills his thoughts during by far the greater part of those hours in which his mind is at its best; during them his character is being formed by the way in which he uses his faculties in his work, by the thoughts and the feelings which it suggests, and by his relations to his associates in work, his employers or his employees." Marshall, A. (1890). *Principles of economics*, Book 1, Chapter 1. New York: Macmillan. pp. 1–2. Peter Drucker would have agreed with Marshall. Drucker claimed that vision and values are formed while the manager performs functional tasks. Drucker, Peter F. (1954). *The practice of management.* New York: Harper & Row. See also the discussion regarding the reciprocal relationship between thinking and action in Faw, H. W. (1995). *Psychology in Christian perspective: An analysis of key issues.* Grand Rapids, MI: Baker Books. pp. 182–185; Philipchalk, R. P. (1988).

Psychology and Christianity: An introduction to controversial issues. (Rev. Ed.). Lanham, MD: University Press of America. pp. 92–95.

12. Ramsey, R. D. (2004). Understanding the culture of your workplace. *Supervision.* 65(8), 3. See also Perrow, C. (1986). *Complex organizations: A critical essay.* (3rd ed.). New York: McGraw-Hill, Inc. p. 116.
13. Sire, J. W. (1990). *Discipleship of the mind: Learning to love God in the ways we think.* Downers Grove, IL: InterVarsity Press. pp. 97–98, 106; Williams, B. D. (2000). Humility and vision in the life of the effective leader. In Banks, R., & Powell, K. (Eds.). (2000). *Faith in leadership: How leaders live out their faith in their work—and why it matters.* San Francisco, CA: Jossey-Bass. p. 69. See also Proverbs 4:23.
14. Johnson, S. (1988). *Values-driven people: A Christian approach to management.* Dallas, TX: Probe Books. pp. 3–4, 26, 31; Bennis, W. (1989). *On becoming a leader.* Reading, MA: Addison-Wesley Publishing Company; Banks, R. (2000). Moving from faith to faithfulness. In Banks, R., & Powell, K. (Eds.). (2000). *Faith in leadership: How leaders live out their faith in their work—and why it matters.* San Francisco, CA: Jossey-Bass. p. 14; Kraft, C. H. (1996). *Anthropology for Christian witness.* Maryknoll, NY: Orbis Books. p. 59. For an early expression of this see Babson, R. W. (1920). *Religion and business.* New York: The Macmillan Company. pp. 77–80.
15. See for examples Matthew 7:17–19; Luke 6:43–44; John 15:2–8; Galatians 5:22–23.
16. For a discussion of Christianity's perspective on virtues see Lewis, C. S. (1952). *Mere Christianity.* San Francisco, CA: HarperSanFrancisco. pp. 76–150.
17. See the Oxford English Dictionary.
18. As an example of marketplace beliefs influencing strategic choices see Adamides, E. D., Stamboulis, Y., & Kanellopoulos, V. (2003). Economic integration and strategic change: The role of managers' mental models. *Strategic Change.* 12(2), 69–82.
19. Johnson, S. (1988). *Values-driven people: A Christian approach to management.* Dallas, TX: Probe Books. p. 5.
20. Hambrick, D. C. (2007). Upper echelons theory: An update. *Academy of Management Review.* 32(2), 334. See also Lencioni, P. M. (2002). Make your values mean something. *Harvard Business Review.* 80(7), 113–117; Boyatzis, R., McKee, A., & Goleman, D. (2002). Reawakening your passion for work. *Harvard Business Review.* 80(4), 86–94; Nonis, S., & Swift, C. O. (2001). Personal value profiles and ethical business decisions. *Journal of Education for Business.* 76(5), 251–256.
21. Zinaich Jr., S. (2004). Returning to virtue theory: Some problems and challenges. *Global Virtue Ethics Review.* 5(4), 50–89; Blackburn, M., & McGhee, P. (2004). Talking virtue: Professionalism in business and virtue ethics. *Global Virtue Ethics Review.* 5(4), 90–122; Shanahan, K. J., & Hyman, M. R. (2003). The development of a virtue ethics scale. *Journal of Business Ethics.* 42(2), 197–208; Banks, R., & Powell, K. (Eds.). (2000). *Faith in leadership: How leaders live out their faith in their work—and why it matters.* San Francisco, CA: Jossey-Bass. pp. 3–76; Whetstone, J. T. (2001). How virtue fits within business ethics. *Journal of Business Ethics.* 33(2), 101–114; Marcic, D. (1997). *Managing with the wisdom of love: Uncovering virtue in people and organizations.* San Francisco, CA: Jossey-Bass; Godin, S. (1995). *Wisdom, Inc.: 26 business virtues that turn ordinary people into extraordinary leaders.* New York: Collins; Solomon, R. C. (2003). *A better way to think about business: How personal integrity leads to corporate success.* New York: Oxford University Press; Bennett, W. J. (1996). *The book of virtues.* New York: Simon & Schuster.
22. Nash, L. L. (1994). *Believers in business.* Nashville, TN: Thomas Nelson Publishers. p. 102. Emphasis added.
23. Drucker, P. F. (1954). *The practice of management.* New York: Harper & Brothers. p. 349.
24. Dixon, J., & Dogan, R. (2003). A philosophical analysis of management: Improving praxis. *The Journal of Management Development.* 22(5/6), 458–482. See also comments by Pattison, S. (2000). Recognizing leaders' hidden beliefs. In Banks, R., & Powell, K. (Eds.). (2000). *Faith in leadership: How leaders live out their faith in their work—and why it matters.* San Francisco, CA: Jossey-Bass. p. 174: "All kinds of human activity, behavior, and practices express fundamental views and beliefs, or assumptions, about the nature of the world. These assumptions often remain implicit, for they constitute everyday reality; they are essentially invisible and unquestionable." Also see Simon, H. A. (1997). *Administrative behavior.* (4th ed.). New York: The Free Press; Schein, E. H. (2004). *Organizational culture and leadership.* (3rd ed.). San Francisco: John Wiley & Sons; Hosmer, L. T. (2004). *The ethics of management.* Boston, MA: McGraw-Hill; Werhane, P. (1999). *Moral imagination and management decision-making.* Oxford: Oxford University Press.
25. Senge, P. M. (1990). *The fifth discipline.* New York: Doubleday; Wood, R., & Bandura, A. (1989). Social cognitive theory of organizational management. *The Academy of Management Review.* 14(3), 361–384; Bandura, A. (1986). *Social foundations of thought and action: A social cognitive theory.* Engelwood Cliffs, NJ: Prentice-Hall; Goleman, D. (1998). *Working with emotional intelligence.* New York: Bantam Books; Carroll, S. J., & Gillen, D. J. (1987). Are the classical management functions useful in describing managerial work? *The Academy of Management Review.* 12(1), 38–51.
26. Drucker, P. F. (1994). The theory of business. *Harvard Business Review.* 72(5), 95–104.
27. See the article by Drucker, P. F. (2005). Managing oneself. *Harvard Business Review.* 83(1), 100–109. See also Drucker, P. F. (1954). *The practice of management.* New York: Harper & Row. pp. 130–133.
28. Wood, R., & Bandura, A. (1989). Social cognitive theory of organizational management. *The Academy of Management Review.* 14(3), 361–384.
29. Collins, J. (2001). *Good to great.* New York: HarperBusiness; Bossidy, L., & Charan, R. (2002). *Execution: The discipline of getting things done.* New York: Crown Business.
30. Drucker, P. F. (2005). Managing oneself. *Harvard Business Review.* 83(1), 100–109.
31. See the article on organizational identity by Brickson, S. L. (2007). Organizational identity orientation: The genesis of the role of the firm and distinct forms of social value. *Academy of Management Review.* 32(3): 864–888;

Drucker, P. F. (2005). Managing oneself. *Harvard Business Review*. 83(1), 105; Miller, J., & Bedford, B. (2003). How to re-establish trust with core values. *People Management*. 9(25), 44–45; Banks, R. (2000). Moving from faith to faithfulness. In Banks, R., & Powell, K. (Eds.). (2000). *Faith in leadership: How leaders live out their faith in their work—and why it matters*. San Francisco, CA: Jossey-Bass. p. 10.

32. Simon, H. A. (1993). Strategy and organizational evolution. *Strategic Management Journal*. 14, 131–142.
33. The idea that there are three levels (individual, group, societal) that are interconnected and interdependent is not new. Kurt Lewin proposed this in 1941. See Lewin, K. (1951). *Field theory in social science*. New York: Harper & Brothers. pp. 188–237.
34. Festinger, L. (1957). *A theory of cognitive dissonance*. Stanford, CA: Stanford University Press. See Glasman, L. R., & Albarracin, D. (2006). Forming attitudes that predict future behavior: A meta-analysis of the attitude-behavior relation. *Psychological Bulletin*. 132(5), 778–822. See also the Bible passage Romans 7:19–21.
35. To extend into the world of business the thought of one scholar who commented on the work of historians, the perspective we take on managerial issues related to values, meaning, and significance "will influence the questions we ask about the subject." Marsden, G. M. (1998). What difference might Christian perspectives make? In Wells, R. A. (Ed.). *History and the Christian historian*. Grand Rapids, MI: William B. Eerdmans Publishing Company. p. 15. See also the questions posed in Steingard, D. S. (2005). Spiritually-informed management theory: Toward profound possibilities for inquiry and transformation. *Journal of Management Inquiry*. 14(3), 227–241; Johnson, S. (1988). *Values-driven people: A Christian approach to management*. Dallas, TX: Probe Books; Williams, O. F., & Houck, J. W. (1982). *The Judeo-Christian vision and the modern corporation*. Notre Dame, IN: University of Notre Dame Press; Beckett, J. D. (2006). *Mastering Monday: A guide to integrating faith and work*. Downers Grove, IL: InterVarsity Press; Tawney, R. H. (1958). *Religion and the rise of capitalism*. New York: New American Library. p. 227; Nash, L. L. (1994). *Believers in business*. Nashville, TN: Thomas Nelson Publishers.
36. Some readers may prefer the term "biblical worldview." I acknowledge that a distinction can be made between these two terms.
37. See Matthew 6:25; Luke 12:21–23.
38. Williams, O. F., & Houck, J. W. (1982). *The Judeo-Christian vision and the modern corporation*. Notre Dame, IN: University of Notre Dame Press. p. 18.
39. Sire, J. W. (1990). *Discipleship of the mind: Learning to love God in the ways we think*. Downers Grove, IL: InterVarsity Press. p. 30. See also the discussion in Blamires, H. (1963). *The Christian mind: How should a Christian think?* Ann Arbor, MI: Servant Books; Walsh, B. J., & Middleton, J. R. (1984). *The transforming vision: Shaping a Christian world view*. Downers Grove, IL: InterVarsity Press; Holmes, A. (1985). *The making of a Christian mind, a Christian world view & the academic enterprise*. Downers Grove, IL: InterVarsity Press; Meadors, G. T. (2003). *Decision making God's way: A new model for knowing God's will*. Grand Rapids, MI: Baker Books. pp. 51–61; Bertrand, J. M. (2007). *Rethinking worldview: Learning to think, live, and speak in this world*. Wheaton, IL: Crossway Books; Marsden, G. M. (1998). What difference might Christian perspectives make? In Wells, R. A. (Ed.). *History and the Christian historian*. Grand Rapids, MI: William B. Eerdmans Publishing Company. pp. 11–22; Miller, W. R., & Delaney, H. D. (2005). *Judeo-Christian perspectives on psychology: Human nature, motivation and change*. Washington, DC: American Psychological Association. pp. 145–164; Daniels, D., Franz, R. S., & Wong, K. (2000). A classroom with a worldview: Making spiritual assumptions explicit in management education. *Journal of Management Education*. 24(5), 540–561; Marsden, G. M. (2005). Faith-informed scholarship. In Henderson, J. W., & Pisciotta, J. (Eds.). *Faithful economics: The moral worlds of a neutral science*. Waco, TX: Baylor University Press. pp. 15–24; Chewning, R. C., Eby, J. W., & Roels, S. J. (1990). *Business through the eyes of faith*. San Francisco, CA: HarperSanFrancisco; Farinaccio, J. R. (2002). *Faith with reason: Why Christianity is true*. Pennsville, NJ: BookSpecs Publishing. pp. 9–36. Following on Marsden's point, this management textbook does not attempt to present a single, definitive example of how Christian managers ought to think but rather how they might think differently about some things in managerial work when using a Christian worldview.
40. Palmer, M. D. (1998). *Elements of a Christian worldview*. Springfield, MO: Gospel Publishing House. pp. 74–76. See also the discussion of worldview in Beed, C., & Beed, C. (2006). *Alternatives to economics: Christian socio-economic perspectives*. Lanham, MD: University Press of America. pp. 134–153; Hollinger, D. P. (2002). A Christian world view foundation for ethics. In *Choosing the good: Christian ethics in a complex world*. Grand Rapids, MI: Baker Academic. pp. 61–88.
41. Bertrand, J. M. (2007). *Rethinking worldview: Learning to think, live, and speak in this world*. Wheaton, IL: Crossway Books. p. 26.
42. Matt. 22:37; Mark 12:30; Luke 10:27; Rom. 12:2.
43. See comments from other authors on this issue in Higginson, R. (1993). *Called to account—Adding value in God's world: Integrating Christianity and business effectively*. Guildford, Surrey: Eagle. pp. 26–35; Preston, R. H. (1993). *Religion and the ambiguities of capitalism*. Cleveland, OH: The Pilgrim Press. pp. 95–109; Boersema, J. M. (2002). *The use of Scripture in the integration of faith in business*. Paper presented to the Christian Business Faculty Association. Nampa, ID. October 17–20; Dockery, D. S. (1995). *Christian scripture: An evangelical perspective on inspiration, authority and interpretation*. Nashville, TN: Broadman & Holman Publishers; Maier, G. (1994). *Biblical hermeneutics*. Wheaton, IL: Crossway Books.
44. 1 Kings 21.
45. 2 Samuel 13–19.
46. Matthew 20.
47. Matthew 25.
48. See Genesis 3:15, 6:13; Isaiah 1:18; John 2:19–20, 14:1–3.

49. See Genesis 1:26–27; Leviticus 11:44, 19:2; Matthew 5:48; Luke 6:36; Ephesians 5:1–2; 1 Peter 1:15–16; 1 John 3:3, 4:7–21.
50. At times he communicated directly and at times through his appointed spokespersons such as Moses, Joshua, Ezekiel, Daniel, Isaiah, Jeremiah, Jesus, Paul, and others.
51. He appoints, delegates, gives instructions for specific tasks, and coordinates. See Genesis 6:13–22, 12:1; Matthew 9:8; John 10:18, 14:26; Romans 13:1–3.
52. Deuteronomy 7:9; Psalm 36:5, 100:5, 146:6; Lamentations 3:23; Matthew 24:35; Luke 19:40; 1 Corinthians 1:9, 10:13; 1 Thessalonians 5:24; 2 Thessalonians 3:3; 2 Timothy 2:13; Titus 1:2; Hebrews 10:23; 1 John 1:9.
53. Exodus 20:1–17; Leviticus 19:18; Deuteronomy 27–29; Psalm 19:7, 119:97; Nehemiah 9:13; Matthew 5:17, 19:19, 22:38–40; Romans 13:8–9; Galatians 5:14; James 2:8.
54. Numbers 11:23; Deuteronomy 4:37, 8:18; Psalm 33:6, 77:15, 148:4–5; Jeremiah 10:12, 27:5; Mark 2:10–11; John 1:3, 3:16, 5:27; Acts 1:7; Colossians 1:16.
55. Genesis 9:17, 15:18, 17:2–4; Exodus 2:24, 6:4–5, 19:5, 25:17; Deuteronomy 4:13, 5:2–3, 10:18; Psalm 25:14, 86:15, 97:2, 101:1; Daniel 4:37; Romans 11:27; Ephesians 2:4; Hebrews 8; 1 Peter 1:3.
56. 1 Kings 2:4, 3:6; 2 Kings 20:3; Psalm 25:10, 26:3, 31:5, 45:4, 51:6, 57:3, 57:10, 85:10, 86:11, 89:14, 117:2, 119:43, 119:142, 119:151; Proverbs 20:28, 23:23; Isaiah 8:3; John 17:17; Galatians 2:14; 2 John 4; 3 John 3-4.
57. Genesis 1–3; Psalm 8.
58. For passages describing the importance of creativity now and in the future see Psalm 33:3, 51:10, 96:1, 98:1, 144:9, 149:1; Matthew 13:52; Mark 1:27; Romans 6:4, 7:6, 12:2; 1 Corinthians 15:51–52; 2 Corinthians 3:18; 5:17; Ephesians 4:23–24; Colossians 3:10.
59. See for example, Romans 12:4–5; 1 Peter 4:10. Higginson, R. (1993). *Called to account—Adding value in God's world: Integrating Christianity and business effectively*. Guildford, Surrey: Eagle. pp. 49–51; Goldingay, J. (2006). *Old testament theology. Vol. 1: Israel's faith*. Downers Grove, IL: IVP Academic. pp. 527–537, 564–567; Tiemstra, J. P., Graham, W. F., Monsma, G. N., Sinke, C. J., Storkey, A., & Ebels, D. M. (1990). *Reforming economics: Calvinist studies on methods and institutions*. Lewiston, NY: The Edwin Mellen Press. p. 167.
60. Proverbs 3:27.
61. Genesis 3:15, 3:6–9, 3:12–18; Exodus 19:5, 20:8–11; Deuteronomy 4:31, 5:12–15, 8:18; Hebrews 4:9. Stendebach, F. J. (2006). Shalom. In Botterweck, G. J., Ringren, H., & Fabry, H. J. (Eds.). *Theological dictionary of the Old Testament*. Volume 15. Grand Rapids, MI: William B. Eerdmans Publishing Company. pp. 13–49; Yoder, P. B. (1987). Shalom: The Bible's peace. In *Shalom: The Bible's word for salvation, justice, & peace*. Nappanee, IN: Evangel Publishing House. pp. 10–23.
62. Romans 1:6, 8:28, 9:24, 11:29; 1 Corinthians 1:26; Ephesians 1:18, 4:1-4; 2 Thessalonians 2:13–14.
63. See the etymology of *manage* and related words in *The Oxford English Dictionary* (1933). Manage. Vol. VI. Oxford: The Clarendon Press. pp. 104–107. The Latin word *manus* (hand) seems to be the common ancestor word for the French, Italian, and Spanish and through translation from the French for the related English words. There are other Latin root words that have meanings related to management. Also, see the etymology of the word *administer* and related terms. Administer, and its cognate words, is a synonym of manage that originally had several related meanings: to minister to others, to supply, to give, to serve and the performance of a duty. *The Oxford English Dictionary* (1933). Manage. Vol. I. Oxford: The Clarendon Press. p. 117.
64. As examples: Richard Daft defines management as "the attainment of organizational goals in an effective and efficient manner through planning, organizing, leading, and controlling organizational resources." Daft, R. L. (2008). *Management*. (8th ed.). Mason, OH: Thomson South-Western. p. 7. Kreitner defines management as "the process of working with and through others to achieve organizational objectives in a changing environment." Kreitner, R. (2003). *Management*. (8th ed.). Boston, MA: Houghton Mifflin Company. p. 5. Stephen Robbins and Mary Coulter say that "management involves coordinating and overseeing the work activities of others so that their activities are completed efficiently and effectively." Robbins, S. P., & Coulter, M. (2009). *Management*. (10th ed.). Upper Saddle River, NJ: Prentice Hall. p. 6.
65. Drucker, P. F. (1954). *The practice of management*. New York: Harper & Row. p. 6. See also the definition "getting things done through other people" in Urwick, L. F. (1956). *The pattern of management*. Minneapolis, MN: University of Minnesota Press. p. 27.
66. Johnson, S. (1988). *Values-driven people: A Christian approach to management*. Dallas, TX: Probe Books. p. 3.
67. Neal, A., & Hesketh, B. (2001). Productivity in organizations. In Anderson, N., Ones, D. S., Sinangil, H. K., & Viswesvaran, C. (Eds.). *Handbook of industrial, work and organizational psychology. Volume 2 Organizational Psychology*. Thousand Oaks, CA: Sage Publications. p. 8.
68. See the discussion on the challenges in measuring organizational effectiveness in Cameron, K. (2005). Organizational effectiveness: Its demise and re-emergence through positive organizational scholarship. In Smith, K. G., & Hitt, M. A. (Eds.). *Great minds in management: The process of theory development*. New York: Oxford University Press. pp. 304–330; Katz, D., & Kahn, R. L. (1978). *The social psychology of organizations*. (2nd ed.). New York: John Wiley & Sons. pp. 759–760; Simon H. A. (1997). *Administrative behavior*. (4th ed.). New York: The Free Press. pp. 154–155.
69. Barnard, C. I. (1938). *The functions of the executive*. Cambridge, MA: Harvard University Press; Thompson, J. D. (1967/2004). *Organizations in action: Social science bases of administrative theory*. New Brunswick: Transaction Publishers. pp. 127–128. Pfeffer, J., & Salancik, G. R. (2003). *The external control of organizations: A resource dependence perspective*. Stanford, CA: Stanford Business Books. pp. 11, 32–36.
70. Some of these quantitative measures also are used as measures of efficiency.
71. See the discussion on this in Hall, R. H., & Tolbert, P. S. (2005). *Organizations: Structures, processes and outcomes*. Upper Saddle River, NJ: Pearson Prentice-Hall. pp. 222–244.

72. Drucker, P. F. (1959). Long-range planning: Challenge to management science. *Management Science*. 5(3), 238–249; Chandler, A. (1962). *Strategy and structure*. Cambridge, MA: The MIT Press. p. 309; Hamel, G., & Prahalad, C. K. (1994). *Competing for the future*. Boston, MA: Harvard Business School Press; Doz, Y., Santos, J., & Williamson, P. (2001). *From global to metanational: How companies win in the knowledge economy*. Boston, MA: Harvard Business School Press.
73. Jones, G. R. (2007). *Organizational theory, design and change*. Upper Saddle River, NJ: Pearson Prentice-Hall. pp. 32–33, 397.
74. Newman, W. H., & Wallender III, H. W. (1978). Managing not-for-profit enterprises. *Academy of Management Review*. January, 24–31; James, E. (1983). How nonprofits grow: A model. *Journal of Policy Analysis and Management*. 2(3), 350–366; Knoke, D., & Prensky, D. (1984). What relevance do organization theories have for voluntary organizations? *Social Science Quarterly*. 65, 3–20; Nutt, P. C., & Backoff, R. W. (1987). A strategic management process for public and third-sector organizations. *Journal of the American Planning Association*. 53(1), 44–57; Euske, K. J. (2003). Public, private, not-for-profit: Everybody is unique? *Measuring Business Excellence*. 7(4), 5–11; Stone, M. M., Begelow, B., & Crittenden, W. (1999). Research on strategic management in nonprofit organizations: Synthesis, analysis, and future directions. *Administration & Society*. 31(3), 378–423.
75. Murray, V., & Tassie, B. (1994). Evaluating the effectiveness of nonprofit organizations. In Herman, R. D. (Ed.). *The Jossey-Bass handbook of nonprofit leadership and management*. San Francisco, CA: Jossey-Bass Publishers.
76. Johnson, S. (1988). *Values-driven people: A Christian approach to management*. Dallas, TX: Probe Books. p. 16.
77. See the discussion on worldview in Walsh, B. J., & Middleton, J. R. (1984). *The transforming vision: Shaping a Christian world view*. Downers Grove, IL: InterVarsity Press; Blamires, H. (1978). *The Christian mind: How should a Christian think?* Ann Arbor, MI: Servant Books.
78. Peter Drucker claimed that the first function of management is economic performance. "Management must always, in every decision and action, put economic performance first. It can only justify its existence and its authority by the economic results it produces." "In this management is unique." Drucker, P. F. (1954). *The practice of management*. New York: Harper & Row. p. 8. Drucker also claimed that the first duty of business is to survive. (p. 46) What does this mean for the manager? "The first responsibility of a manager is upward: to the enterprise whose organ he is." (p. 349) See also Barnard, C. I. (1938). *The functions of the executive*. Cambridge, MA: Harvard University Press; Thompson, J. D. (1967/2004). *Organizations in action: Social science bases of administrative theory*. New Brunswick: Transaction Publishers. pp. 127–128. Pfeffer, J., & Salancik, G. R. (1978/2003). *The external control of organizations: A resource dependence perspective*. Stanford, CA: Stanford Business Books. pp. 11, 32–36; Simon, H. (1997). *Administrative behavior*. (4th ed.). New York: The Free Press. pp. 250–277; Neal, A., & Hesketh, B. (2001). Productivity in organizations. In Anderson, N., Ones, D. S., Sinangil, H. K., & Viswesvaran, C. (Eds.). *Handbook of industrial, work and organizational psychology. Volume 2 Organizational Psychology*. Thousand Oaks, CA: Sage Publications. pp. 7–24; Alexander, J. K. (2008). *The mantra of efficiency: From waterwheel to social control*. Baltimore, MD: The Johns Hopkins University Press; Neal, A., & Hesketh, B. (2001). Productivity in organizations. In Anderson, N., Ones, D. S., Sinangil, H. K., & Viswesvaran, C. (Eds). *Handbook of industrial, work and organizational psychology. Volume 2 Organizational Psychology*. Thousand Oaks, CA: Sage Publications. pp. 7–24; Putterman, L. (1990). *Division of labor and welfare: An introduction to economic systems*. New York: Oxford University Press; Tiemstra, J. P., Graham, W. F., Monsma, G. N., Sinke, C. J., Storkey, A., & Ebels, D. M. (1990). *Reforming economics: Calvinist studies on methods and institutions*. Lewiston, NY: The Edwin Mellen Press. pp. 44–45, 169–170.
79. Maital, S. (1994). *Executive economics: Ten essential tools for managers*. New York: The Free Press.
80. Boatright, J. R. (1988). Ethics and the role of the manager. *Journal of Business Ethics*. 7(4), 303–312.
81. Office of Inspector General. (2009). Report of Investigation. United States Securities and Exchange Commission, Case Number OIG-509.
82. Fayol, H. (1949). *General and industrial management*. London: Pitman; Barnard, Chester I. (1938). *The functions of the executive*. Cambridge, MA: Harvard University Press; Carroll, S. J., & Gillen, D. (1987). Are the classical management functions useful in describing managerial work? *The Academy of Management Review*. 12(1), 38–51. For a brief review of four management functions from a Christian perspective see Creighton, A., Arendall, C. W., & Pray, B. B. (1995). Biblical managers and the functions of management: Do today's management principles apply? *Journal of Biblical Integration in Business*. Fall, 9–13.
83. Robbins, S. P. (1998). *Organizational behavior: Concepts, controversies, applications*. London: Prentice-Hall.
84. Mintzberg, H. (1973). *The nature of managerial work*. New York: Harper & Row; Stewart, R. (1982). A model for understanding managerial jobs and behavior. *The Academy of Management Review*. 7(1), 7–13.
85. Katz, R. L. (1955). Skills of an effective administrator. *Harvard Business Review*. 33(1), 33–42; Kochanski, J. (1997). Competency-based management. *Training & Development*. 51(10), 40–44; Mann, F. C. (1965). Toward an understanding of the leadership role in formal organizations. In Dubin, R., Homans, G. C., Mann, F. C., & Miller, D. C. (Eds.). *Leadership and productivity*. San Francisco, CA: Chandler Publishing Company. pp. 68–103.
86. Gentry, W. A., Harris, L. W., Baker, B. A., & Leslie, J. B. (2008). Managerial skills: What has changed since the late 1980s. *Leadership & Organization Development Journal*. 29(2), 167–181; Grzeda, M. M. (2005). In competence we trust? Addressing conceptual ambiguity. *The Journal of Management Development*. 24(5/6), 530–545; Burgoyne, J. G. (1993). The competence movement: Issues, stakeholders and prospects. *Personnel Review*. 22(6), 6–13.
87. Kraut, A. I., Pedigo, P. R., McKenna, D. D., & Dunnette, M. D. (2005). The role of the manager: What's really

important in different management jobs? *Academy of Management Executive*. 19(4), 122–129; Isenberg, D. J. (1984). How senior managers think. *Harvard Business Review*. 62(6), 81–90; Hambrick, D. C., & Mason, P. A. (1984). Upper echelons: The organization as a reflection of its top managers. *The Academy of Management Review*. 9(2), 193–206; Kotter, J. P. (1982). *The general managers*. New York: The Free Press; Andrews, K. R. (1971). *The concept of corporate strategy*. Homewood, IL: Dow Jones-Irwin, Inc.; Leighton, D. S. R., & Thain, D. H. (1990). The role of the corporate director. *Business Quarterly*. 55(2), 20–24; Strategizing throughout the organization: Managing role conflict in strategic renewal. *Academy of Management Review*. 25(1), 154–177.

88. http://www.fda.gov/AboutFDA/CentersOffices/OrganizationCharts/default.htm.
89. Etzioni, A. (1961). *A comparative analysis of complex organizations*. New York: Free Press.
90. In addition to the references for contributions to this discussion shown below the following additional contributors should be noted: Argyris, C. (1957). *Personality and organization: The conflict between system and the individual*. New York: Harper & Row, Publishers. pp. 163–174; Skrabec Jr., Q. R. (2001). The lost grail of middle management. *Industrial Management*. 43(3), 19–22; Balogun, J. (2003). From blaming the middle to harnessing its potential: Creating change intermediaries. *British Journal of Management*. 14(1), 69–83; Thomas, R., & Dunkerley, D. (1999). Careering downwards? Middle managers' experiences in the downsized organization. *British Journal of Management*. 10(2), 157–169; Antonioni, D. (1999). What motivates middle managers. *Industrial Management*. 41(6), 27–30; Giangreco, A., & Peccei, R. (2005). The nature and antecedents of middle manager resistance to change: Evidence from an Italian context. *International Journal of Human Resource management*. 16(10), 1812–1829; King, A. W., Fowler, S. W., & Zeithaml, C. P. (2001). Managing organizational competencies for competitive advantage: The middle management edge. *Academy of Management Executive*. 15(2), 95–106; Sethi, D. (1999). Leading from the middle. *Human Resource Planning*. 22(3), 9–10; Turnbull, S. (2001). Corporate ideology—Meanings and contradictions for middle managers. *British Journal of Management*. 12(3), 231–242; Janczak, S. (2004). Middle management: The phoenix phenomenon. *Canadian Manager*. 29(3), 22–23; Valentino, C. L. (2004). The role of middle managers in the transmission and integration of organizational culture. *Journal of Healthcare Management*. 49(6), 393–404. For a Christian perspective on middle managers see Klay, R., Lunn, J., & TenHaken, V. (2004). Middle management as a calling. *Journal of Biblical Integration in Business*. Fall, 118–137.
91. Henricks, M. (2007). Go-betweens. *Entrepreneur*. 35(3), 91–92; Kanter, R. M. (2004). The middle manager as innovator. *Harvard Business Review*. 82(7/8), 150–161; Floyd, S. W., & Wooldridge, B. (1994). Dinosaurs or dynamos? Recognizing middle management's strategic role. *Academy of Management Executive*. 8(4), 48–49; Huy, Q. N. (2001). In praise of middle managers. *Harvard Business Review*. 79(8), 72–79; Ireland, R. D. (1992). Corporate culture best conveyed by mid-level managers. *Baylor Business Review*. 10, 18–19; Novak, M. (1996). *Business as a calling: Work and the examined life*. New York: The Free Press. pp. 28–30.
92. Abels, M. (2004). The middle manager, leadership and the public interest. *PA Times*. 27(3), 4; Fenton-O'Creevy, M. (1996). Middle manager: Friend or foe of employee involvement. *Journal of Applied Management Studies*. 5(1), 47–62; Floyd, S. W., & Wooldridge, B. (1994). Dinosaurs or dynamos? Recognizing middle management's strategic role. *Academy of Management Executive*. 8(4), 47–53; Scharmer, C. O. (2002). Managers in the middle. *Training*. 39(3), 16; Huy, Q. N. (2001). In praise of middle managers. *Harvard Business Review*. 79(8), 72–79; Wetlaufer, S. (2001). Right in the middle. *Harvard Business Review*. 79(8), 12; Samuelson, R. J. (1999). Why I am not a manager. *Newsweek*. 133(12), 47; Laff, M. (2007). Middle managers feel squeezed. *Training and Development*. 61(6), 20; Priestland, A., & Hanig, R. (2005). Developing first-level leaders. *Harvard Business Review*. 83(6), 112–120; Floyd, S. W., & Lane, P. J. (2000). Strategizing throughout the organization: Managing role conflict in strategic renewal. *Academy of Management Review*. 25(1), 154–177; Chandler Jr., A. D., McCraw, T. K., McDonald, A. L., Tedlow, R. S., Vietor, R. H. K., & Kantrow, A. M. (Eds.). (1986). Why history matters to managers. *Harvard Business Review*. 64(1), 81–88.
93. Huy, Q. N. (2001). In praise of middle managers. *Harvard Business Review*. 79(8), 74.
94. http://www.fda.gov/downloads/AboutFDA/CentersOffices/OrganizationCharts/UCM181391.pdf.
95. Some of these suggestions come as a logical extension of the article by Huy, Q. N. (2001). In praise of middle managers. *Harvard Business Review*. 79(8), 75.
96. Senge, P. M. (1990). *The fifth discipline*. New York: Doubleday.
97. Mintzberg, H., & Lampel, J. (1999). Reflecting on the strategy process. *Sloan Management Review*. 40(3), 21–30; Deming, W. E. (1986). *Out of the crisis*. Cambridge, MA: MIT; Juran, J. M. (1995). *Managerial breakthrough*. New York: McGraw-Hill; Simon, H. A. (1997). *Administrative behavior*. (4th ed.). New York: The Free Press; Hamel, G. (2007). *The future of management*. Boston, MA: Harvard Business School Press. pp. 20–21.
98. Fottler, M. D. (1981). Is management really generic? *The Academy of Management Review*. 6(1), 1–12; Lau, A. W., & Pavett, C. M. (1980). The nature of managerial work: A comparison of public- and private-sector managers. *Group & Organization Studies*. 5(4), 453–466; Coase, R. H. (1937). The nature of the firm. *Economica*. November, 386–405; Jensen, M. C., & Meckling, W. H. (1976). Theory of the firm: Managerial behavior, agency costs and ownership structure. *Journal of Financial Economics*. 3(4), 305–360.
99. Liao, M., Foreman, S., & Sargeant, A. (2001). Market versus societal orientation in the nonprofit context. *International Journal of Nonprofit and Voluntary Sector Marketing*. 6(3), 254–268. See also Crittenden, W. F., & Crittenden, V. L. (1997). Strategic planning in third-sector organizations. *Journal of Managerial Issues*. 9(1), 86–104.
100. U.S. Department of Labaor. Bureau of Labor Statistics (2010). ftp://ftp.bls.gov/pub/suppl/empsit.ceseeb1.txt. Accessed March 11, 2010. Data also reviewed

from: Sherlock, M. F. & Gravelle, J. G. (2009). *An overview of the nonprofit and charitable sector*. CRS Report for Congress 7-5700 R40919. Congressional Research Service. November 17. http://www.fas.org/sgp/crs/misc/R40919.pdf.

101. For examples see Hofstede, G. (1980). Do American theories apply abroad? *Organizational Dynamics*. 5(1), 23–45; Hofstede, G. (1993). Cultural constraints in management theories. *The Academy of Management Executive*. 7(1), 81–94; Triandis, H. C., Bontempo, R., Villareal, M. J., Asai, M., & Lucca, N. (1988). Individualism and collectivism: Cross-cultural perspectives on self-ingroup relationships. *Journal of Personality and Social Psychology*. 54(2), 323–338.
102. Hill, L. (1992). *Becoming a manager*. Boston, MA: Harvard Business School Press. See also the research reported in Gabarro, J. J. (1985). When a new manager takes charge. *Harvard Business Review*. 63(3), 110–123.
103. Newman, W. H., & Wallender III, H. W. (1978). Managing not-for-profit enterprises. *Academy of Management Review*. January, 24–31; Nutt, P. C., & Backoff, R. W. (1987). A strategic management process for public and third-sector organizations. *Journal of the American Planning Association*. 53(1), 44–57; Drucker, P. F. (1992). *Managing the non-profit organization: Principles and practices*. New York: HarperBusiness; Euske, K. J. (2003). Public, private, not-for-profit: Everybody is unique? *Measuring Business Excellence*. 7(4), 5–11; Phills Jr., J. A. (2005). *Integrating mission and strategy for nonprofit organizations*. Oxford: Oxford University Press; McLaughlin, T. A. (2006). *Nonprofit strategic positioning: Decide where to be, plan what to do*. San Francisco, CA: John Wiley.
104. Mintzberg, H. (1975). The manager's job: Folklore and fact. *Harvard Business Review*. 53(4), 49–53.
105. Johnson, J. (2004). Flexible working: Changing the manager's role. *Management Decision*. 42(5/6), 721–737.
106. Taylor, A. (2005). Most managers feel ill-equipped for new role. *Financial Times*. April 11, p. 4.
107. See the insightful article Heifetz, R. A., & Laurie, D. L. (2001). The work of leadership. *Harvard Business Review*. 79(11), 131–141.
108. Several scholars have explored paradoxes of management and leadership. Here are a few examples: Quinn, R. E., Faerman, S. R., Thompson, M. P., & McGrath, M. R. (1996). *Becoming a master manager: A competency framework*. (2nd ed.). New York: John Wiley & Sons, Inc.; Handy, C. (1994). *The age of paradox*, Cambridge, MA: Harvard Business School Press; Clegg, S. (2002). *Management and organization paradoxes* (Advances in organization studies, 9). Amsterdam: John Benjamins Publishing Company; Keidel, R. W. (1995). *Seeing organizational patterns: A new theory and language of organizational design*. San Francisco, CA: Berrett-Koehler; Lewis, M. W. (2000). Exploring paradox: Toward a more comprehensive guide. *Academy of Management Review*. 25(4), 760–776; Poole, M. S., & Van de Ven, A. H. (1989). Using paradox to build management and organization theories. *Academy of Management Review*. 14(4), 562–578; Quinn, R. E. (1988). *Mastering the paradoxes and competing demands of high performance*. San Francisco: Jossey-Bass; Smith, K. K., & Berg, D. N. (1997). *Paradoxes of group life: Understanding conflict, paralysis and movement in group dynamics*. San Francisco: The New Lexington Press; Wacker, W., Taylor, J., & Means, H. (2000). *The visionary's handbook: Nine paradoxes that will shape the future of your business*. New York: HarperBusiness; Barrett, D. (1998). *The paradox process: Creative business solutions—where you least expect to find them*. New York: AMACOM.
109. Huy, Q. N. (2001). In praise of middle managers. *Harvard Business Review*. 79(8), 78–79.
110. Support for including the idea of paradox in management education has come from many authors. One article should be noted here in particular: Lips-Wiersma, M. (2004). Furthering management and spirituality education through the use of paradox. *Journal of Management Education*. 28(1), 119–133.
111. Fry, L. W., & Smith, D. A. (1987). Congruence, contingency, and theory building. *Academy of Management Review*. 12(1), 129–130.
112. Comments of an undergraduate business student.
113. Heyne, P. T. (1998). Moral misunderstanding and the justification of markets. *The Region*. 12(4), 32. Paul Heyne is a Lutheran scholar who, following his seminary training, studied economics.
114. Sider, R. J. (2005). *Rich Christians in an age of hunger*. (New Ed.). Nashville, TN: Thomas Nelson Publishers. p. 102; Nelson, R. H. (2005). The theology of economics. In Henderson, J. W., & Pisciotta, J. L. (Eds.). *Faithful economics: The moral worlds of a neutral science*. Waco, TX: Baylor University Press. pp. 89–107; Rempel, H. (2003). *A high price for abundant living: The story of capitalism*. Scottdale, PA: Herald Press. p. 51; Alexander, J. K. (2008). *The mantra of efficiency: From waterwheel to social control*. Baltimore, MD: The Johns Hopkins University Press. p. 1; Tiemstra, J. P., Graham, W. F., Monsma, G. N., Sinke, C. J., Storkey, A., & Ebels, D. M. (1990). *Reforming economics: Calvinist studies on methods and institutions*. Lewiston, NY: The Edwin Mellen Press. p. 189. See also: Exodus 20:8–11, 23:10–12; Leviticus 23:3–5; Ecclesiastes 4:6; Matthew 6:28; Mark 6:31.
115. Sproul Jr., R. C. (2008). *Biblical economics: A commonsense guide to our daily bread*. White Hall, WV: Tolle Lege Press. p. 47; Grudem, W. (2003). *Business for the glory of God: The Bible's teaching on the moral goodness of business*. Wheaton, IL: Crossway Books. pp. 25–29; Boersema, J. M. (2005). *The use of scripture in the integration of faith in business*. Paper presented to the Christian Business Faculty Association Annual Conference. San Diego, CA. October. p. 11; Chewning, R. C., Eby, J. W., & Roels, S. J. (1990). *Business through the eyes of faith*. San Francisco, CA: HarperSanFrancisco. p. 173. See also: Deuteronomy 29:23; 1 Kings 7:37; Nehemiah 2:17; Psalm 144:13–15; Proverbs 18:9, 24:27, 27:23–27; Ecclesiastes 3:2, 10:9–10, 15; Matthew 3:10; Luke 3:9, 13:6–7; 2 Timothy 2:21, 4:11; Hebrews 6:7–8.

CHAPTER 2

Management History

LEARNING OBJECTIVES

- Understand the importance of history making and storytelling for managers and leaders.
- Explain the biblical teachings related to managerial behavior.
- Understand that the basic managerial principles were developed in ancient times.
- Explore the contributions of selected management thinkers during the 19th and 20th centuries, and understand the influence that technology and world events have had on management in history.
- Explore why some management ideas have declined in popularity.
- Consider the paradox of memory.

"Whether he knows it or not every person is to some degree a historian because history is the study of the past and everyone has some sense of the past, even if only the recent past. The human mind habitually moves in familiar tracks. People constantly think of the past, argue in terms of it, and try to justify or discredit present modes by references to the past . . . history is simply accumulated experience."[1]

"When you have eaten and are satisfied, you shall bless the LORD your God for the good land which He has given you. Beware that you do not forget the LORD your God . . . and when your herds and your flocks multiply, and your silver and gold multiply, and all that you have multiplies . . . for it is He who is giving you power to make wealth . . . "[2]

THE SNACK CAKE KING

Between 1930 and 1939 the United States experienced "The Great Depression." Thousands of banks went out of business. Tens of thousands of businesses failed. Thousands of people lost their savings and their jobs. Economic depressions are not the best times to go into a business that is dependent on consumer discretionary income. Or are they?

It was 1934. Ruth McKee was not excited about her husband's idea to buy a struggling bakery named Jack's Cookies on Main Street in downtown Chattanooga, Tennessee. They had lived in Chattanooga for less than a year. Although her husband was a successful salesman, he had just landed a steady job. The idea of risking family security was something she resisted.

Her husband, Oather D. McKee (O.D.), saw it differently. Never mind that to buy the bakery he had to pawn the family's 1928 classic Whippet touring car. Never mind that he had just a few months of experience selling bakery products. Never mind that running the business would take the combined efforts of Ruth, O.D., and their children. Into business he went.

Source: PRNewsFoto/McKee Foods.

O.D. McKee was born in 1905 and adopted by his mother's first cousin after his mother died of pneumonia that same year. O.D.'s adoptive father, Finis McKee, was a man of principles of Scottish Presbyterian descent who raised his children to be God-fearing, hard working, and entrepreneurial.

In school, O.D. excelled at math and at analyzing and solving practical problems. But he struggled to learn to read, and had to repeat the first and fourth grades. It was not until 60 years later that he discovered he suffered from a learning disorder known as dyslexia.

When O.D. was 16 he had the opportunity to prove to himself and to his family that he could be successful. In the spring of 1921, a man who made his living selling religious books boarded for several weeks with the McKee family. In the evenings he told anecdotes about his book-selling experiences. These stories thrilled O.D. so much that he made it his mission to sell the very product he couldn't use himself, the product that had given him so much grief during school—books. Although he was not an instant success at selling, he was persistent.

The depression hit hard for the McKee family, as it did for so many families. O.D.'s father lost his farm. After he married Ruth, O.D. moved from job to job trying to find steady work. One day O.D. leveraged his book-selling experience by convincing the sales manager of Becker's Bakery, located in Spartanburg, South Carolina, to give him a try. At that time Becker's Bakery had a distributorship in Chattanooga that needed someone in charge of sales. They hired him on the spot.

In October 1933, O.D. began selling six kinds of 5-cent Virginia Dare snack cakes to grocery stores and restaurants. He learned quickly how to sell to the retail market. Within a year McKee realized that if he had a broader product line, his sales efforts would be far more efficient. He obtained permission from Becker's Bakery to begin selling bakery products that Becker's did not produce. They agreed as long as he kept selling their products, too. A few months after obtaining their permission, he decided to risk it all and put $200 down on the $5,000 needed to purchase Jack's Cookies.

O.D.'s $200 investment, plus strong faith in God and an enormous amount of commitment from his family, turned into one of the most successful privately owned companies in the United States. It become the nation's number one snack cake brand most people know as Little Debbie®.[3] And the rest, as the cliché goes, is history.[4]

Who Cares About the History of Management?

One of the most important aspects of a manager's job is to lead the process of remembering how an organization got to where it is now while looking forward to where the organization should be in the future. Managers also help members of organizations interpret events from the past in ways that shed light on present decisions and issues as well as on those in the future.

Every organization has a story that begins with the personal story of its founders overcoming obstacles, making key decisions, and giving everything they have for the organization's success. Over time, the personal stories of managers and employees who work for the company, together with the founders' stories, become an important part of the bigger story that is told by the company's brand name. The company's brand story becomes an important backdrop against which the company makes major decisions. This story holds the present shared values that have resulted from past experiences and carries them into the future.

Whether recorded in Scripture, in the annals of history, or in a business executive's correspondence file, the history of business and management is the collection of stories about people and the consequences of their decisions. It is the record of how managers have come to think and act as they do. Being aware of these stories, especially the ones involving your organization, can help you become a wiser manager.

A company's story is about valuing and interpreting memories of past events: individually, organizationally, and in the larger community that the organization serves. Workers remember former managers and the strange situations they got themselves into. They compare new managers with the former ones. They tell stories about what it was like during difficult times and good times. Suppliers and customers tell stories to illustrate what it is like to deal with the organization. Marketing and public relations professionals are in the business of telling stories to build brand strength. Managers tell and retell stories to keep alive the shared values important for future organizational performance. Your ability to understand your company's stories and why certain management ideas are in use now will help you become a better organizational leader.

The Christian Mind on the Importance of History

History is important. Our identity comes in part from our memory of past social experiences. Accurate memory of the past helps us maintain integrity for dealing with today's problems. The spiritual experiences of hope for the future and faith in God's promises are anchored in our awareness of what God has done in the past. The Bible encourages us to remember the great things he has done.[5] Seeking the truth about God's will in our life requires us to be open to understand experiences of humans from the past who faced similar situations. While we cannot predict the future with 100 percent categorical certainly, we can come to know a lot about the future consequences of our actions by studying the recurring patterns of what happens to people who were in similar social situations.

Leadership in the past has created the organization as it is today. Knowledge of a company's history can also help a manager avoid embarrassment. For example, managers sometimes make bad decisions that they would not have made if they had simply understood prior events and what these events meant to members of the organization. No manager wants to announce a long-awaited new management solution only to find out that previous managers had already tried that idea. Exhibit 2-1 highlights the personal and organizational value of storytelling for managers.

Personal stories help us

- Make sense of our own past and make changes for the future.
- Develop a sense of meaning in our work.
- Remain humble.
- Have courage.
- Learn from the consequences of our choices.
- Evaluate our priorities.
- See the commonness with and the differences from others.
- Develop a heart to move beyond our own self-interests to serve others.

Organizational stories help managers

- Test the validity of their theories about the marketplace.
- Frame better questions to ask of current situations.
- Develop strategic thinking abilities.
- Make sense of the organization and what it stands for.
- Develop leadership abilities.
- Avoid the embarrassment that comes from making uneducated decisions.
- Improve their ability to communicate the company's vision of the future.

EXHIBIT 2-1
The Value of Storytelling for Managers[6]

Management Pyramid

In terms of the being–thinking–action model in this book, stories illuminate the character of individuals who made decisions. We can learn much about how they thought through problems. Some well-known leaders of industry such as Ford, Rockefeller, Carnegie, Wedgewood, Disney, Eastman, Firestone, Getty, and Kaiser in the 19th and 20th centuries created large, successful organizations that traded internationally. Some did a lot of good economically; some treated their workers with patronizing contempt. Some were benevolent; others were unnecessarily cruel to their competitors. Their attitudes regarding democracy and the free market shaped their thinking on contemporary social issues of their day. In turn, their thinking influenced the actions they took, whether it was to influence the domestic government, foreign governments, their workers, labor unions, customers, or competitors. Sometimes they faced political or judicial consequences for their actions. See Exhibit 2-2.

The same processes are at work today. Sometimes it is only in retrospect that we can see the complete connection between attitudes and beliefs, the thinking and feeling that result, the actions that follow, and the consequences. Some managers may believe that they can do just

Effect of managerial actions on the community that the organization serves **Managerial actions today become the legacy for what comes in the future**	**Action**
Interpreting events from the past in the organization and in the industry **Making sense of the present based on past actions of employees, customers, and competitors**	**Thinking & Feeling**
Perceptions about the company, the industry, and the market **Beliefs** **Values** **Assumptions**	**Being & Becoming**

EXHIBIT 2-2
The Management Pyramid and Management History

Source: Courtesy of Michael E. Cafferky, © Michael E. Cafferky 2011.

about anything they want and get away with it. It is only later, after the consequences of their actions are clear, that they realize how they must change. For some, like Ivar Krueger, Robert Vesco, Bernard Madoff, Kenneth Lay, and Dennis Kozlowski, the wider political, social, and economic damage from their misguided being–thinking–action can be so great, they have little if any opportunity to make amends.[7] Moral scandal will forever, perhaps, be tied to our memory of them. Lest the Christian manager point an accusing, self-righteous finger, remember that Christians, too, have been caught in organizational scandals.

As we set out to explore management ideas that have developed over time, we will begin by considering the biblical record on management. We start with the Christian faith perspective because it is an important part of the Christian's personal beliefs and values (the "being and becoming" part of the Management Pyramid). In addition, some of the management ideas contained in the Bible are still widely respected today.

Faith Perspective on Management History

For the Christian, the story of business is the story of the human response to God's call to bear his image as we subdue the earth and fill it. It is the story of how humans exercise our power over and care for creation to create cultural forms and institutions that help us serve each other. The choices we make reveal our way of looking at the earth and society, as well as our willingness to be obedient to God.

In this part of the chapter we will explore a few of the many biblical stories of managers. See Exhibit 2-3.

Joseph

From an early age Joseph exhibited an ability to see the big picture of organizations.[8] At the age of 17, Joseph's brothers kidnapped him and sold him to an Egypt-bound caravan of Ishmaelite traders for 20 pieces of silver. Potiphar, the captain of Pharaoh's body guard, purchased Joseph. Soon Potiphar promoted Joseph as overseer of his entire household of servants. When Potiphar's wife made sexual advances toward Joseph he refused, citing that Potiphar had entrusted to him the safekeeping of the entire household. He could not in good conscience break that trust. In addition, breaching this trust also was against his commitment to his God.

When he was thrown in jail based on false charges of rape, it appeared that for all practical purposes Joseph's life had come to an end. But while in jail Joseph used his management talents, and the jailor appointed Joseph overseer of the other prisoners.

EXHIBIT 2-3
Managers in the Bible[9]

Noah manages the first major multi-year construction project mentioned in the Bible; later he becomes a vineyard entrepreneur.	Daniel is promoted to top-level manager for Belshazzar.
Joseph is promoted to overseer of Potiphar's household and later to the job of prime minister of all of Egypt.	Ezra is a manager for King Cyrus.
Obadiah is the head of King Ahab and Queen Jezebel's household.	Nehemiah, the cup-bearer for King Cyrus, becomes an important project manager and community leader.
Abraham, Isaac, and Jacob are entrepreneurial managers.	King Solomon becomes the wealthiest public manager in the Bible.
Josiah the young king manages the temple rebuilding.	Joshua is chosen to be the assistant manager for Moses for many years.
Peter becomes one of the early church's managers.	Moses, Aaron, and Miriam manage the emerging nation of Israel.
Paul manages several missionary trips.	Jesus manages a full-time ministry team for 3 1/2 years.
Jesus tells stories about managers.	The Centurion is a military manager.

Then one day Pharaoh had a dream. On the recommendation of one of Joseph's former cellmates, Pharaoh called for Joseph to interpret the dream. In response to Pharaoh's dream, Joseph formulated a plan designed to help the nation. The plan led to Pharaoh appointing Joseph as prime minister. Under his leadership, the Egyptian empire survived a terrible famine by spending years harvesting and storing grain and then carefully rationing it out during the lean years. This required political savvy, knowledge of Egyptian economics, and human resources management.

Joseph's experience provides important contributions to the Christian worldview on management. Besides his commitment to stand firm on moral principles, Joseph was keenly aware that a manager is given a trust for the greater good of the organization. His trustworthiness may have been what set him apart from all the others in Pharaoh's court. His faithfulness in managing small details contributed to his trustworthiness for managing matters of international importance. He used strategic thinking employed for the common good of those for whom he worked, whether a single household, the jail, or the entire nation. As a leader he learned to forgive one of the most hated acts—family disloyalty. In his work, Joseph saved from extinction not only thousands of Egyptians but also his own family, preserving the ancestral line that eventually led to the birth of Jesus.

Moses

When he was still a child, Moses went to live in the court of Pharaoh and studied the ways of the Egyptians.[10] We might assume that he had some firsthand knowledge about Egyptian politics and management of the empire from watching his new family in action.

As a young man, Moses went out from Pharaoh's court and observed the heavy burdens that the Hebrews were under. Enraged by the cruelty under which his people suffered, Moses murdered an Egyptian taskmaster who had been beating a Hebrew slave. Fearing that Pharaoh would find out, Moses fled to the land of Midian. There he married the daughter of Jethro, a Midianite priest, and lived a pastoral life for 40 years.

Many years later he received the call of God to return to Egypt on a mission to set the Hebrew people free. For the next 40 years, Moses led the Israelites through the wilderness on their arduous journey to their Promised Land. From their experiences recorded in Scripture we learn a lot about the leadership and management that Moses employed. For example, we observe the principle of division of labor based on artisan and craftsman skills in constructing the Sanctuary.[11] We see the division of authority by setting aside the sons of Aaron to be priests and the Levites to care for the Sanctuary.

One takeaway from Moses' experience is that as an organization grows in size, more diversity of opinion exists regarding what the group's goals should be and how the goals should be pursued. In difficult times, these differences come to the surface and can threaten the viability of the organization. Power struggles like that which occurred among Aaron, Miriam, and Moses undermine the influence of the top leader.

We also see from the experience of Moses how important organizing is to accomplishing the shared goals of a group. One of the first lessons in organizing that Moses learned came through the advice of his father-in-law Jethro. Moses had so many day-to-day problems to deal with that he was wearing himself out on the operational issues while neglecting the strategic issues.[12] Jethro counseled Moses to do three things: (1) establish the rule of law to guide social behavior, (2) set up a justice system organized in the form of a hierarchical chain of command, and (3) carefully select mid-level leaders. This hierarchical chain of command followed the **rule of ten**—one supervisor appointed for every 10 workers—observed in Egyptian management.[13] The difficult cases that could not be handled by mid-level leaders with delegated authority were to be brought to Moses.[14] We refer to this today as **managing by exception**.

The interaction with Jethro shows us that sometimes a leader becomes too embroiled in the details of a situation to be able to step back and lead. It's not that Moses lacked exposure to how a large organization should be operated. He spent many years in the court of the Pharaoh observing a top-level leader in action. When you are actually in the middle of a management situation, the operational details can easily overwhelm the strategic picture.[15] When this happens, the wise counsel of someone removed from the day-to-day situation can be invaluable.

Having a close relationship with God does not prevent a leader from making mistakes. On more than one occasion Moses lost his temper with the people. Even seasoned leaders experience frustrations from their work. But we can see from the experience of Moses that he never lost sight of the essential purpose of the organization: escape from bondage and establish a new homeland under God's guidance.

Although a leader may be effective in portraying the vision of the future, the realities of the hard work needed to actually accomplish the vision can be discouraging to everyone including the leader.

When collective opinion becomes focused on a common purpose (such as escape from the bondage of Egypt), rhetoric alone will not help the group accomplish the goal. Someone needs to step forward to organize the group; establish the ground rules; plan, direct, and coordinate efforts; and communicate with the outside environment. In other words, leaders need to be able to be managers as well or to get help from managers to get things done.

Solomon

The nation of Israel achieved its greatest global influence under King Solomon's reign.[16] Of all the kings of Israel and Judah, Solomon may have been the preeminent organizer. His organizational abilities spanned state, military, scientific, and commercial ventures. He also has been acclaimed as the wisest man in the Hebrew narratives.

As young Solomon began his reign after the death of his father David, he prayed for wisdom. The Hebrew narratives tell the story of how this prayer was answered. After consolidating his power, Solomon began building a strategic alliance with Hiram, King of Tyre, a region near Israel, for the production of materials with which to build the Temple. One of his first actions was to appoint over 3,600 managers to oversee the work.

For 7 years, hundreds of thousands of workers focused on the goal of building the temple. Following this, Solomon spent 13 years building the royal palace. His strategic trading alliances extended far and wide. He built cities for Israel. He built a fleet of ships on the shore of the Red Sea and sent seamen and miners out in search of valuable products such as gold, silver, and cedar, which, because of his ventures, became as plentiful as commodities. Solomon's fame and the fame of Israel spread throughout the Middle East.

Unfortunately it was at the height of Israel's power that this power corrupted Solomon. The Hebrew narrative tells how following the first 20 years of spiritual and material success, Solomon spent the next 20 years selling the soul of the Israelite nation. Following his reign, the nation crumbled.

The Hebrew narratives about Solomon and his leadership raise interesting issues for our consideration. Certainly Solomon was a complex individual. On the one hand, Solomon committed his work to serving what he believed to be right in terms of worship of God. On the other hand, to accomplish this, he followed the principles observed in other nations such as Egypt, including the use of hundreds of thousands of slave laborers. Solomon's experience as a leader raises the question of what success means. His experience shows that it is possible to be successful from an economic perspective while at the same time feel spiritually shallow.

One of Solomon's legacies is that he recorded in writing some of the best managerial wisdom that he learned from his own experiences as king.[17] We turn next to this wisdom and the wisdom of others recorded in the Old Testament.

Management Wisdom in the Hebrew Bible

Hebrew understanding of leadership and management is grounded in the creation event. Through the creation narrative we learn that human life is directly dependent on the relationship with God.[18] The Hebrew Bible known as "The Old Testament" in Christian terminology sometimes describes humans as having dominion over all creation. At other times, it describes humans as being an insignificant creature in the larger universe. These two views are sometimes expressed in the same passage, implying that both are to be kept in mind.[19] These two points of view provide a tension that, if followed, will protect humans from the two extremes of idolatry and ecological abuse.

If management is grounded in the relationship a person has with God because of creation, then it is the gifts of God that make it possible for managers to succeed. In fact, the opportunity to manage itself is a gift from God.[20] And the chief gift and the greatest need for managers is wisdom.

Wisdom for all of life, but especially the wisdom needed for successful business ventures, is a gift from God received by listening. It is one of the most highly prized of all virtues because it

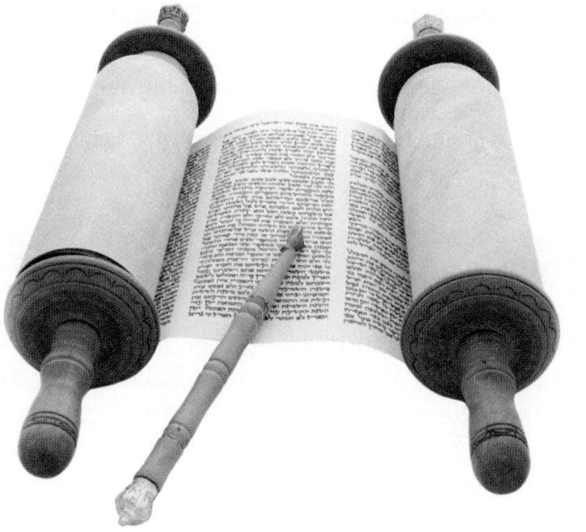

Source: Luba/Shutterstock.

The Hebrew Scriptures contain wisdom that is practical for managers today.

leads not only to material success but to successful living all around.[21] The Hebrews emphasized the importance of listening to wise counsel as the act of intelligence:

- The seat of intelligence lies in the ears.[22]
- Wisdom comes from God's law but also is spoken by God-fearing people who are experienced.[23]
- However, humans should be careful to whom they listen for if they listen to the ungodly or only to themselves, they can easily go astray.[24]
- If the ears are the seat of the ability to gain wisdom, then the lips produce what others hear, and the wise manager is someone who speaks with care so that those who hear will receive benefit.[25]

The human heart is another vital center for managers and leaders. As a person thinks in his heart, so is he. The heart is to be guarded carefully for it is the heart that is the foundation for self-awareness, for all moral action, and for the person's entire relationship with God. It is the heart that becomes the basis for self-deception.[26]

The human hand is one of the root ideas for what it means to be a manager. When someone in ancient Hebrew times was appointed as a manager, his subordinates were placed under his hand.[27] The word hand is often used in the sense of someone's power to achieve, as well as his skill in workmanship.[28] When someone needs to be helped or guided, it is often another person's hand that is the connecting link between the one who needs the help and the one helping.[29] But it also is used to refer to authority, control, or responsibility. The phrase "under the hand" means to be under the rule, control, or power of another.[30]

All of the emphasis on authority and dominion over others might imply that managers were expected to "lord it over" their subordinates. Here the Hebrew Scriptures present another tension point for God-fearing managers. On the one hand the Scriptures expect managers to look out for the interests of the organization they serve. They have a job to do. On the other hand, managers have a disproportionate amount of power compared with subordinates. The Scriptures emphasize that because of this, managers must use their power responsibly:

- Managers must not forget that, like themselves, subordinates were created in the image of God.
- The goal for managers is to follow God's character of loving kindness and faithfulness as they exercise their authority, just as God exercises his authority over the whole earth.[31]
- Managers will destroy their own soul if they are cruel to their subordinates. But if they are good, their soul will be nourished.[32]
- When it is in the manager's power to do good to a worker who deserves it, the manager must not withhold this.[33]
- In everything that is done as a manager, it is honor to God and obedience to Him that is paramount.[34] If a manager expects to enjoy the honor of being placed over others, he must also learn humility, for it is in humility that wisdom is obtained.[35]

- Managers should act with integrity and justice.[36] They should not act rashly but instead be quick to seek advice.[37]
- The wise manager will not speak in anger but will control his or her emotions.[38]

Together, these principles of management portray a worthy ideal to which Christian managers should strive.

The Biblical Story of Abraham

Read the story of Abraham found in Genesis 11–25 in the Bible. Based on his experience, grasp the significance of the accomplishments that occurred under the leadership of Abraham. Make a mental note of the leadership strengths and weaknesses of Abraham. What leadership principles can we gain from the experience of Abraham that are applicable today?

Management Wisdom in the New Testament

The Hebrew Bible provides an important foundation for understanding the manager's relationship to God and to others. This foundation is assumed by the writers of the New Testament who tell the story of the life and work of Jesus of Nazareth.

Christians point to Jesus as the clearest example in all of Scripture of what it means to be a leader.[39] His teachings provide guidance for successful Christian living in all walks of life, including managing and leading. The New Testament also tells the story of the early beginnings of the Christian church as a movement and as an organization. Letters from the apostles written to the early churches give more guidance to all church members, including their leaders.

Jesus

For the first 30 years of his life, Jesus focused his ministry on his family's carpentry business in Nazareth.[40] In terms of his work as a manager, nothing is known about this period of his life. The fact that he was a carpenter may have added to the surprise that people felt when they heard Jesus teach. Other than this, what Jesus did was of little consequence to the gospel writers in terms of understanding his religious work.

It is in his public ministry of teaching, healing, and preaching that we see evidence of Jesus' management and leadership. One of his first activities was the recruitment of 12 disciples who were volunteers. For the next 3 1/2 years, he spent many hours teaching them.

One of the central tenets of his message is that the Kingdom of God had come. The kingdom is a reality that has begun, but, at the same time, has not been fully completed.[41] While kingdom living applies to all followers of God, Jesus' prescriptions for living have particular application to managers. Living in the kingdom (such as described in the Sermon on the Mount) is about living a transforming life.

The relationship between Jesus and his disciples quickly resulted in the establishment of his authority as a teacher.[42] Although the twelve apostles were organized informally, they became more organized when the situation required it. At times Jesus planned ahead and used a great amount of organization.[43] Jesus delegated specific assignments to the apostles for special missions.[44] Later when he recruited a larger number of disciples, he delegated specific mission-oriented assignments to them, too.[45]

The teachings of Jesus apply to all his followers regardless of what role they have in society. Some of his teachings portray the characteristics of a manager quite differently from what people were used to.[46] For example, Jesus was aware that the separation between manager and subordinate results in the subordinate not understanding what the manager does.[47] His relationship with his disciples was different.

Some of his teachings were intended to make a point about our relationship with God, but in these, Jesus drew on wisdom commonly accepted in his day that was applicable to managers. For example:[48]

- Subordinates are expected to be loyal to legitimate authority.[49]
- Subordinates cannot serve more than one manager.[50]

- Managers should practice the Golden Rule.[51]
- To whom much is given much will be required.[52]
- Wisdom comes from hearing and following wise counsel, especially counsel from God.[53]
- Whoever desires to be a great leader among others will become so by becoming a servant to them.[54]

For many Christians, Jesus' teachings and example offer special guidance of how we are to follow God's will. Managerial behavior is guided by two great commands: Love God supremely and love humans unselfishly. In addition to these two great commands, the Ten Commandments reflect the Divine standard of behavior.[55] Service and Love mean Integrity and Justice: Some of Jesus' strongest criticisms of leaders of his day were directed toward injustice and lack of integrity. Followers of God have a responsibility to serve those in need, to correct injustices, and to serve with integrity.[56]

Management of the Early Church

Initially, the Christian church was informally organized, but as the number of Christians grew, it became increasingly difficult to care for the needs of the followers without some management. Greek-speaking Jews who had become followers of Jesus began to complain that their needs were not being met. In response to this, the twelve apostles convened a meeting with all the disciples and began organizing the church. The first step was to appoint seven men to manage the distribution of resources to those followers in need.[57]

In the early years, the twelve apostles managed the church. After listening to the needs of the Jerusalem church, they made decisions as a group. When a dispute arose regarding belief and practice as applied to the non-Jews who were coming to faith, the apostles convened a conference of leaders from other local congregations to resolve the issue. What was once just one church was becoming a Church on a larger scale with many congregations spread over a wide geographic area.[58] See Exhibit 2-4.

As the Christian movement grew geographically, individual apostles traveled to different cities to help establish new congregations. Decentralized authority allowed the church to grow quickly. But this also opened the door for differences of opinion to develop regarding theology. Soon the apostles saw the need for centralized guidance regarding belief and practice. Because they could not be in every congregation at once, some of the apostles resorted to writing letters to

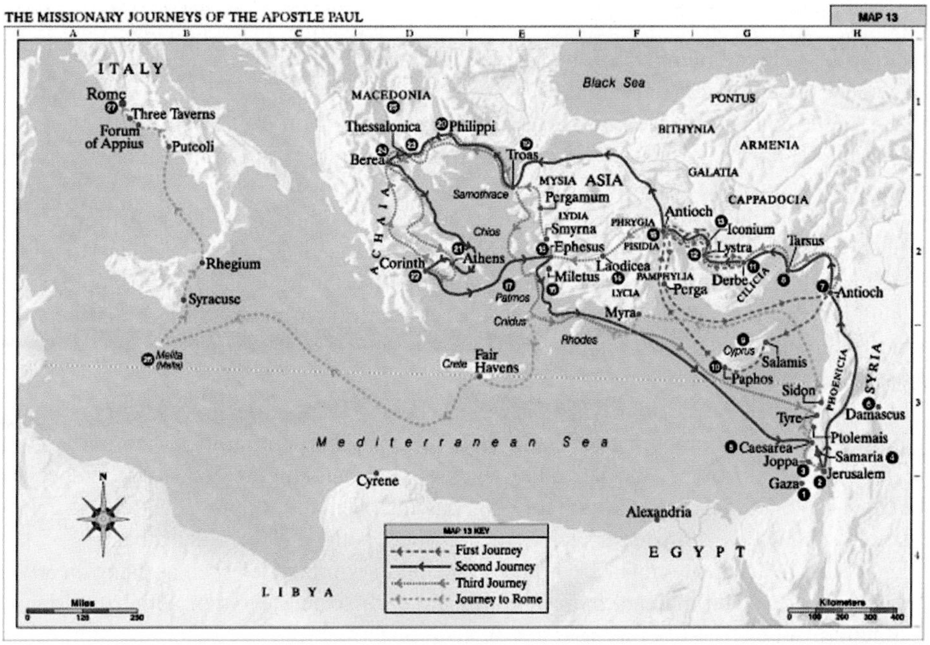

EXHIBIT 2-4

Map of the Near East During New Testament Times

the congregations. The teachings of the apostles related to leadership in the church include the following:

- Selection of leaders should be done with care based primarily on character traits as evidenced from their behaviors. Because a person's weaknesses can be hidden, the selection should not be hasty.[59]
- Every city where there are Christians should have one or more leaders appointed to serve the congregations.[60]
- Leaders should be humble servants acting like gentle shepherds. They should avoid serving for the purpose of dishonest personal gain. True leadership means that leaders and followers submit to each other. Subordinates should provide service with a good will as if serving God directly. Managers should serve their subordinates with the same approach, not threatening them into service but treating them impartially. The reason: leaders know "that he who is both their Master and yours is in heaven and that there is no partiality with him [God]."[61]
- Leadership is shared among many people in the community. It is not only the elders and deacons who serve. Many others have been given gifts that are useful for the faith community. Each one can be used by the community in some leadership capacity.[62]
- Service to others should be modeled after the Incarnation of Christ. Look out for the interests of others and not only for your self-interest. Esteem others better than yourself. Let nothing be done through selfish ambition.[63]

Notice the consistency between these principles and those found in other places in the Bible. As you consider specific dimensions of management and leadership, keep these fundamental principles in mind.

It was during these early years that ideas on church authority and the role of official church leaders (bishops) began to develop. After New Testament times, church leaders periodically convened official church councils to make decisions about belief and practice. The impact of these church councils is still felt today in how the Christian denominations structure reporting relationships and make decisions regarding authority.

Management History in Ancient Times

The history of management practices of Western countries in North America and Western Europe can be traced back to Ancient Egyptian, Greek, and Roman cultures. Some management ideas that we think are commonplace today actually were used thousands of years ago. For as long as there have been organizations, there have been managers serving these organizations. Even relatively simple cultures (by today's standards) that were organized along tribal or clan lines needed management to achieve the goals of the clan. In this we see two fundamental connections between management and organization. First, management is a service provided to a community as a whole. When managers help one small part of the community (an organization), they are helping members of the entire community to serve each other's needs. Second, management is needed for the pursuit of commonly held values and goals. As clans banded together for the common purposes of food production, protection from enemies, transportation, trade with neighboring groups, religious worship, construction of buildings, and equipment, management became more important.

Ancient Egyptian pottery, tomb writings, and other artifacts give us an awareness of the significant management issues this advanced civilization faced. Known for golden tomb treasures, fast chariots, the great pyramids, and the giant sphinx, the Egyptian empire would not have been built if managers had not marshaled the collective efforts from thousands of laborers. What may not be common knowledge is that Egypt produced one of the first books of management advice ever written.[64]

Egypt developed the idea of **division of labor** where workers were divided based on the tasks they performed. It used this principle in the state religion, the state military, and in the government. Governmental workers specialized by function. For building projects, workers specialized in the functions of cutting, measuring, sculpting, hauling over land, shipping, and fitting. Workers also specialized by type of material such as metal, wood, pottery, cloth, and leather.

Egyptian management emphasized other contemporary principles such as using an advisory staff and operating with a clear chain of command with scaled levels of authority. Managers were encouraged to listen before reacting to the concerns brought to them by subordinates.

Supervisors (in Egypt called *viziers*) at all levels were required to exercise managerial controls by obtaining reports from subordinates.[65] The span of control (how many people one manager should supervise) in Egypt followed the rule of ten: one supervisor appointed for every 10 workers.[66]

Top leaders of the Egyptian empire learned the principles of what we know today as centralization and decentralization. Decentralized government offered the most flexibility for each of the territories to operate under the authority of and with complete loyalty to the Pharaoh. The trade-off was that the king was less able to generate funds needed to field an organized military force for protection. Over time, the Egyptian kings took steps to centralize controls by the government using the military, while leaving much of the authority for local matters in the hands of the Pharaoh-appointed territorial governors.[67]

Management in several ancient empires reflects the basic ideas of planning, organizing, division of labor, decision-making authority, and control. While Egypt was building its wonders of the world, leaders in China and India were developing approaches to management that were similar to those found in other regions.[68] In Greece, writers such as Socrates, Aristotle, and Xenophon wrote about various facets of management. We can observe from their writings the advantages of division of labor and functional specialization in society.[69] Experimentation with division of labor within a business organization came much later.[70] As in Egypt, the massive public works projects in Rome required a high degree of organization. Roman military organizations depended on the rule of ten used in Egypt and among the Hebrews.[71] The organization of the empire, coupled with the development of Roman roads, enabled the empire to extend its boundaries farther than any previous empire had achieved.

The ancient principles of management might be summarized by the following:

- Establish respect for, authority over, and obedience from subordinates.
- Respect and be loyal to your superiors.
- Divide the work among workers to be more efficient.
- Pursue the larger goals of the organization (or the nation) for the common good.
- Organize workers based on skills and functions; match the job with the person.
- Give clear delegation of tasks and authority.
- Plan ahead.
- Employ managerial control systems to make sure goals are achieved efficiently.

In the Judeo-Christian tradition additional principles were developed: Managers are appointed to positions of authority, but they are called to serve their fellow human beings, including subordinates, under God's authority. Pursue the goals of the organization but not at the expense of other goals such as respect for God's creation. Treat subordinates with respect. Moral conduct of managers and subordinates alike is guided by the two great commands, love God and love one another.

Management History in Modern Times

During the 19th century, although machines were used in many businesses such as the textile industry, physical labor still dominated most types of work. Most persons were employed in agriculture.[72] By 1880, fewer than 3,000,000 people were employed in manufacturing in the United States. A generation later, over 8,000,000 would be working in factories.[73] The largest companies (measured by the number of employees) were the railroads, the steel mills, and the textile factories. These large organizations experienced significant management problems related to their drive for improved productivity—problems that smaller organizations had not experienced because they were less complicated and owners generally had more direct control over many aspects of the work. The solutions to these problems, many of which are still in place today, came from careful thinking about management.

Frederick W. Taylor and the Scientific Management Movement

One of the strongest influences on management thinking emerged from an increased need for economic efficiency. Frederick W. Taylor, who worked in the steel industry, was an important promoter of efficiency and became known as "The Father of Scientific Management." The seeds of **scientific management**, which is the formal, rational attempt to improve efficiency of individual workers and teams of workers, had been sown long before Taylor championed this cause in the late 19th century. In the process, he formed an entire approach to management.[74]

Frederick W. Taylor is known as the "Father of Scientific Management."

It was not just Taylor's books and articles promoting scientific management that made his influence so strong in business but also his personal impact through consulting, public speaking, and mentoring business executives.[75] Taylor was an engineer, but his contributions to management lie in his understanding of microeconomics.

Taylor was born into a successful Quaker family in Germantown, Pennsylvania.[76] Instead of enrolling in Harvard Law School to follow in his father's footsteps as an attorney, Taylor volunteered as an apprentice to learn mechanics at the Enterprise Hydraulic Works of Philadelphia. At the completion of his apprenticeship in 1878, he took a job as a common laborer at Midvale Steel Company. Within 6 years he advanced in responsibility, serving in various roles including machinist, gang boss and supervisor of the machine shop, master mechanic, chief draftsman, auditor, chief engineer, head of the sales department, and general manager. To improve his technical skills during these 6 years, Taylor trained himself in mechanical engineering through a home study course from the Stevens Institute of Technology of Hoboken, New Jersey.

During this period of history, many machine shop owners allowed workers to determine the machining methods to employ. Workers kept technical knowledge to themselves to help maintain the company's dependence on them, but they trained each other as best they could. Managers used imprecise rules of thumb to monitor productivity.

One of Taylor's early accomplishments as a mid-level manager was the doubling of productivity by his work group. His superiors rewarded him for this, but his subordinates resented his efforts to make them work faster. They were being paid on a piece-rate system and thought that if they worked harder, management would only cut their pay. Workers had developed an unwritten code of how much output they were willing to create and resisted increasing output beyond this. Taylor referred to this resistance as **soldiering** and used a technique called the *time and motion study* to analyze the wasted energy and time that workers were expending. **Time and motion studies** involve someone observing specific motions that workers use to perform tasks and then using a stopwatch to record how much time is spent on various motions. With this information, Taylor attempted to show the workers more labor-saving ways to use their tools and machinery.

When the machinists refused to follow his instructions, Taylor hired unskilled laborers and trained them in what he considered the best methods. Unfortunately the social pressures from the other workers were too great, and even the new workers failed to respond to Taylor's ideas. So, Taylor cut their pay rates to create an incentive to work harder. Angered by this, workers undermined his efforts by jamming and breaking their machines. Taylor responded by fining the workers if their machine jammed or broke.

Taylor believed in the principle that there should be a clear distinction between the tasks of labor and those of management. For Taylor, everything in the shop can be broken down into single tasks. It was the development of the individual task as a unit of study that proved to be the key for Taylor in applying science to improve productivity. He used the term **task management** as a synonym of scientific management.[77] Another significant contribution was in using quantitative techniques for management controls. He advocated setting specific work goals or targets for employees to accomplish.[78]

Scientific management was more than applying a few techniques such as time and motion study and task analysis. It was a whole philosophy of management that guided everything that managers and workers do. In Taylor's mind, it was the best way to resolve the age-old conflicts between workers and their managers. His thoughts encompassed employee selection, motivation, performance improvement, organization, planning, change management, accounting, employee safety, and corporate citizenship. Taylor's philosophy of management included four principles, which he applied not only to companies but, in theory, to society as a whole:

1. Develop a science for each element of each individual's work. The scientific knowledge gained from analysis and time study should replace the old rule of thumb method. Every worker, including managers, must surrender to the findings of science.
2. Scientifically select, train, and develop each worker. Workers should be carefully selected for tasks they are best suited for. For example, menial tasks involving heavy physical labor are best suited for individuals who have physical strength and stamina. Such individuals, when performing at the highest possible level, should be considered first-class workers. But they should not be relied on for great ideas on how to improve productivity.
3. Managers should cooperate with the workers to ensure that all work is done in accordance with the principles of the science that has been developed.
4. Divide work and responsibility fairly between management and workers. Management's role is to scientifically analyze and set the production quotas for workers. Workers must accept these quotas and commit to vigorous labor.

See Exhibit 2-5, Frederick Taylor Defines Management.

Taylor and others believed that the traditional shop foreman, by himself, was unable to properly monitor workers under conditions of increased productivity. In place of the shop foreman, Taylor established a cluster of eight supervisors, each of which had specific functional authority over workers. Under this system the individual machinist had an inspector, a gang boss, speed boss, and repair boss to report to in the production side of the business. On the planning side of the business, each employee reported to an instruction card clerk, time and cost clerk, order routing clerk, and a disciplinarian.

For years the issue of wages had been a constant source of irritation for both management and labor. Taylor came to believe that management needed to take charge of the information about how work was performed, the procedures used, and the quantity of production expected for each task. Using this information, scientifically gathered using time studies, fair wages could be established and production standards could be set and monitored.

Worker motivation was vital to the success of scientific management. Taylor had learned that scientific management can work only when workers cooperate with management. Employees should be given specific and realistic, though challenging, goals to accomplish. The more difficult the goal, the better, as long as the goal does not exceed the individual's actual abilities. Workers should then be rewarded for performance at a rate that provides a fair living. Piecework rates should not be reduced as a means of motivation. Working conditions should be analyzed because these also affect productivity. Shop floors should be safe, sanitary, and healthful.

Despite his efforts in scientific management to resolve conflicts between subordinates and managers, Taylor became the focal point of criticism. His methods, sometimes referred to as

EXHIBIT 2-5
Frederick Taylor Defines Management

Frederick W. Taylor defined management as follows: "The art of management has been defined . . . 'as knowing exactly what you want men to do, and then seeing that they do it in the best and cheapest way.' No concise definition can fully describe an art, but the relations between employers and men form without question the most important part of this art."[79]

"Taylorism," have been criticized by some theologians and others as being an extreme form of division of labor that has negative effects on human workers.[80] Some blamed Taylor for the monotonous, dehumanizing work that resulted from scientific analysis. The scientific method undermined the influence that workers had over managers because their hold on knowledge of productivity had been broken. Although Taylor advocated for workers to provide suggestions for how work might be improved, some workers felt that they were not being heard by management. Scientifically established work quotas were unrealistic for some workers. Cynical workers thought this approach was merely a means to get more out of them to line the pockets of owners with more cash. Managers criticized Taylor because his approach required them to change their methods of supervision and increased the conflicts with workers rather than resolving them. Years after Taylor died, a few scholars criticized Taylor for not being truthful on all details of some of the stories he told regarding his scientific experiments.[81] Despite these criticisms, Taylor's reputation continues as one of the most influential management thinkers of the 20th century.

Taylor was not the only advocate of scientific management. (See Exhibit 2-6.) Among the other champions of the concept were Frank and Lillian Gilbreth, two efficiency experts who developed international reputations as management consultants. Later they were the inspiration for the book and original movie *Cheaper by the Dozen.*[82]

EXHIBIT 2-6

Harrington Emerson on the Essence of Efficiency[83]

In a November 24, 1924, letter to the editor of the *New York Times*, Harrington Emerson (1853–1931), an influential efficiency engineer and management consultant, reflected on the essence of efficiency. The contents of his letter might surprise you.

A dozen years before this when the prominent Boston attorney Louis D. Brandeis appeared at a hearing of the U.S. Interstate Commerce Commission in Washington, D.C., on November 23, 1910, to lobby against rail shipping rate increases, Harrington Emerson proved to be one of his star witnesses.

During his testimony Emerson claimed that if all railroad companies used scientific management, then collectively they could save up to $1,000,000 per day by tackling the inefficiency of labor (which in many companies was commonly estimated at 5 percent) and by improving engine fuel consumption from 261 pounds per ton of freight down to less than 80 pounds. If the railroads would become more efficient, he argued, there would be no need to increase shipping rates. Emerson published his cost savings estimates in the *New York Times*. Later he would claim that labor was as much as 33 percent inefficient and capital up to 70 percent inefficient.

From his vantage point of over 20 years' experience in efficiency consulting, he attempted to describe in his letter to the editor the essence of efficiency. To do this he turned to the Bible for support. He said that efficiency is the relationship "between what is and what ought to be."[84] But it is more than this. The goal of efficiency is to make us free. To illustrate his point Emerson pointed to the Bible for descriptions of efficiency. "It begins in the first verse of the first chapter of the first book." God's work was good and because it was good, the work was followed by rest. "It has been so ever since. The more noble the man the more efficient he has been, the better his work, the more he rests when it is completed." Emerson refers to Jethro who provided Moses with efficiency counsel. "The Commandments contain tremendous efficiency commands . . . The Proverbs are a collection of efficiency precepts . . . The feeding of the multitude is one of the greatest examples of efficiency that has ever been commemorated. The basic formula of efficiency is the reverent formula of the Deity. His efficiency is infinite, because without supplies and without equipment by an infinite personality, the infinite is accomplished." "Competence, another word for efficiency, is one of the seven great fundamental moralities. It is as much an obligation to be competent as to be good, or to be healthy, or to be educated."

The Christian Mind on the Importance of Science in Business

When God placed Adam and Eve on the earth, he commissioned them to subdue the earth and foster the flourishing. God values excellence and quality. This applies as much to cultural forms in creation such as organizations as it does to the natural world. Thus, the Bible expects us to study organizations for the purpose of better understanding how they can better be of service to society. God would have Christians become excellent in their work as leaders and managers so that they are respected by all. This means that studying the principles of management and leadership from a scientific point of view can help the believer become wise in ways that are respected by all.[85]

When Frank Gilbreth was a young man, he prepared to enter the Mechanical Institute (later renamed the Massachusetts Institute of Technology). At the last minute, he decided that attending college would be too much of a financial burden on his family. Instead, he looked for a trade to enter.

His Sunday School teacher helped Frank get started as an apprentice bricklayer. Soon Frank distinguished himself as an innovative, productive worker. Within a year he invented a moveable scaffold that made him the fastest bricklayer. With encouragement, he submitted the plans for the scaffold to the Mechanical Institute, and the plan won a prize.

Frank soon became foreman of a bricklaying crew. He noticed the inefficiency of the work, and he set about to change that problem. He reorganized the work flow, bringing the bricks closer to the masons and eliminating unneeded movements. This reduced the amount of bending and lifting. The result: The number of motions needed to lay one brick decreased from 18 to 6. Productivity was increased from 175 bricks per hour to 350 per hour with less fatigue. He and his crew achieved such astonishing speed in laying bricks that he was made superintendent.

Frank believed that reducing waste would decrease costs, increase productivity, and increase income. He broke work tasks down into specific motions (micro-motions) and then analyzed clusters and sequences of motions to determine the most efficient motion pattern.

Soon Frank founded his own construction company. Sometimes after a contract was finished his client would ask him to remain on the job to apply his motion study methods inside the factory itself. By the time he was 27, he had become a successful management consultant maintaining company offices in New York, Boston, and London.

In 1903 Frank's cousin introduced him to 25-year-old Lillian Moller, who was 10 years younger than Frank; their friendship blossomed immediately. After being together for less than 3 weeks, Frank proposed to Lillian, and they married the next year.

Frank and Lillian worked together in his growing consulting business. They both were interested in the technical aspects of worker efficiency, but Lillian took a special interest in the human dimension of work. This made for a great combination. They used timing devices, special effects lighting, and motion picture cameras to record work processes and analyze distances and timings, while looking for opportunities to reduce fatigue and make the entire process more efficient. They used this technology to improve efficiency in a variety of industries including filming professional baseball players in action, training soldiers for the U.S. military, and improving the efficiency of surgeons.

All during this time Lillian was a successful career woman, consultant, and mother to their 12 children. She earned a doctoral degree in psychology from Brown University in 1915.

When Frank Gilbreth died suddenly in 1924, Lillian continued offering consulting services. This was not easy because most of their clients were men. Virtually all of them terminated the Gilbreths' consulting agreements when Frank died. Undaunted, Lillian kept pursuing the bigger ideals for which she and Frank had stood. Gradually the consulting opportunities returned. She returned to school and earned advanced degrees in engineering. In 1926, she became the first woman member of the American Society of Mechanical Engineers. From 1930 to 1932 she headed the women's division of President Hoover's Organization on Unemployment Relief. She went to Purdue University in 1935 as a professor of management and was the first female professor in the engineering school. In 1938 Lillian was named one of 12 women "capable of holding the office of president of the United States." In 1965, she was the first woman ever to be elected to the National Academy of Engineering. She helped design modern kitchens to make housework more efficient. She also helped adapt her techniques for the disabled, developing devices to help them lead more normal lives.[86]

So completely had top leaders of American businesses bought into the concepts of scientific management that it was hailed as the next great "Industrial Revolution." Scientific management may be the most powerful and one of the most long-lasting contributions America has made to Western thought.[87] In France, another, complementary, revolution in management ideas was taking place that would influence management education for decades to follow.

Henri Fayol (1841–1925)

With the development of the railroad in France in the 19th century, it became possible to transport coal anywhere, including to ports for export. Coal was needed for the burgeoning factories powered by steam engines. Between 1850 and 1870, coal consumption in France tripled. This increased demand resulted in the growth of coal-mining companies. Coal-mining production expanded at a fast pace to keep up with demand. As these companies changed, the management issues changed, too.

At the age of 19, Henri Fayol, a graduate of the French National School of Mines, became an engineer at a coal mine. He applied his engineering knowledge not only to coal mining but also to management problems. From his observations of what worked for managers in the coal mine, Fayol developed a list of concepts that he put in writing later in his career. Henri Fayol was the first European manager to present a comprehensive discussion of general management, how it works in practice, and how we should train managers.

Fayol was the first to see that management is not just a recipe of rules but a process that encompasses the entire organization. He believed that everyone in the organization shares responsibilities for managing. He promoted the idea of organizational improvement, believing that organizations continually need improving. Although his observations were accurate, Fayol never believed that his ideas were the final word on management.

He understood the importance of the relationships between workers and their supervisors. He taught that workers should be treated with dignity and fairness. Fayol was one of the first to recognize that work teams are important and that some work teams in some situations can be self-directed. He taught, at the end of his life, that the highest level of the organization and how it is structured is more important than how the middle levels actually carry out their directions.[88]

From his observations, Fayol emphasized several management functions: planning, organizing materials and workers, commanding, coordinating, and controlling.[89] These functions became

Henri Fayol studied principles of management by carefully observing what happened in his own mining company.

Source: Courtesy of the Library of Congress, LC-USZ62-116688.

1. Division of labor is the most efficient way of organizing.
2. Authority with responsibility. When a manager is given the authority to make decisions, this person also should be held responsible for decisions that are made.
3. Workers should be expected to work with discipline.
4. Unity of command: Every worker should have just one supervisor who gives direction.
5. Unity of direction: All managers and workers should understand the objectives of the organization and of their immediate tasks so that together they can work toward achieving the organization's goals.
6. Subordination of individual interests to the interests of the organization and its goals.
7. Remuneration: workers should be paid fairly for their labor. Pay is a good motivator for good performance.
8. Centralization: Some decisions, especially financial ones, must be made by top-level leaders. Other decisions should be given to lower-level managers and workers to make (decentralization).
9. Scalar chain/line of authority: Every worker should know exactly who their supervisor is and who is above this person in decision-making authority.
10. Managers should organize workers and materials so that work is accomplished in an orderly manner.
11. Workers should be treated fairly.
12. Workers do better if they are not afraid they will be laid off and if they have opportunities to advance in responsibility.
13. Managers should encourage workers to take initiative to solve problems that are within their ability.
14. Esprit de corps (morale) among workers is an important component of productivity. Managers have an important role in maintaining workers' morale.

EXHIBIT 2-7
Fayol's 14 Principles of Management

the standard categories of managerial work. Modern scholars condensed them into four functions, as described in Chapter 1: planning, organizing, leading, and controlling.

Fayol also recorded 14 principles of management that he believed contribute to organizational success, as shown in Exhibit 2-7.[90] While these were not new ideas, Fayol is widely regarded as the one who organized these thoughts in terms that managers can understand and apply. One of the reasons why Fayol is such a strong influence on current management thinking a century later is that his ideas are a fully integrated whole view of management in its entirety rather than just a collection of disjointed ideas.

Others have criticized his writings as misguided and mechanistic.[91] Despite these criticisms, Fayol's observations have formed the foundations for a general theory of management on which others have built. Fayol set a precedent of evaluating the type of education that managers need (practical skills versus theory)—an issue that continues to ignite debate even today.[92]

While the proponents of scientific management focused their thinking on the tasks of individual workers, Fayol made his mark in management by focusing on the work of higher level managers and their responsibilities in serving employees of the entire organization.[93]

Max Weber (1864–1920)

Another European thought leader who influenced thinking about management in large bureaucracies such as government organizations was Max Weber, a German sociologist. At the time that Weber observed society and economics, large government and commercial organizations were inefficient, sometimes chaotic places to work. Based on his observations, Weber taught that to bring order out of chaos, large organizations must follow a few simple, rational rules, which became known as **bureaucracy**. Some now associate the idea of bureaucracy with negative feelings that come from all the "red tape" involved in decision making in large, complex organizations. But in Weber's day, the idea of bureaucracy came as a welcome relief to management problems. Weber helps us understand the value that bureaucratic management principles bring to organizations.

According to Weber, the ideal bureaucracy is built on several principles.[94] Efficient organizations have a hierarchical authority structure with multiple levels of supervision sometimes called a **scalar chain of command.** Managers should be trained professionals. Work should be divided allowing individuals to become experts at particular tasks. This should guide the selection of workers based on their technical qualifications for the tasks. Formal rules of behavior and procedures for work should guide employee behavior. Rules applied impartially and uniformly across the entire organization promote fairness. Pay rates should be based on how long a worker has worked for the organization and the different tasks the worker performs.

Like other observers of management experience, Weber analyzed the issue of authority of bureaucratic administrators. Another one of Weber's contributions that continues to be debated today is his assessment of the effect of the Protestant Reformation on business. Weber contended that religious beliefs establish a certain "spirit" among Protestants related to work and wealth. Christians in business work hard to serve God. The by-product of this effort is the accumulation of wealth. But Christians in business avoid making wealth an idol. They save their wealth rather than spend it wastefully on themselves. The result: Christians in business accumulate large amounts of capital that can then be used to build larger, more efficient enterprises with which to serve God. Weber said, "When the limitation of consumption is combined with this release of acquisitive activity, the inevitable practical result is obvious: accumulation of capital through ascetic compulsion to save."[95]

Chester I. Barnard (1886–1961)

Another sociologist who had a major influence on thinking about organizations was Chester I. Barnard.[96] Barnard gained his management experience working for American Telephone & Telegraph (AT&T), first as an engineer and then as general manager when he became president of Jersey Bell. He studied economics at Harvard University.[97] Barnard's legacy for management thinking is in how he viewed organizations as part of dynamic, open systems. According to Barnard, organizations need consciously coordinated activities in order to be effective in relating to other organizations in their environment. And it is the high-level manager who plays the key role in these activities.

Barnard is well known because of his book *The Functions of the Executive*, which presents his understanding of executive authority, decision making, and organizing.[98] Any time you have a group of two or more people who are focused on achieving an agreed-upon goal, someone needs to take charge and oversee the effort. This involves executive thought and action. Executives have the task of deciding what needs to be done; securing the needed resources of people, materials, equipment, and property; and then organizing these resources to accomplish the organization's mission.

For centuries division of labor had been understood as one of the fundamental management roles to achieve economic efficiency. Barnard[99] showed how important coordination of effort is to achieving effectiveness. While Taylor and others taught that efficiency of task is important, Barnard built on the work of Fayol by focusing on the larger forces at work in an organization as a whole, showing the interconnections between individual tasks, coordination of effort, and executive functions.

One of the reasons Barnard's thinking has endured the test of time is that he addressed the fundamental never-ending issues that managers face. One such issue is that of authority.[100] The traditional view was that authority flows from the chief executive (who has the most authority) downward to the frontline workers (who have the least authority). Barnard surprised the management world by saying that the ultimate proof of whether a manager has authority to issue commands to workers lies with the subordinates and not with the person issuing commands. The consent of subordinates to follow commands from their superiors is influenced by four key elements: (1) Subordinates must understand the executive's communication. Without their understanding, authority is meaningless. (2) Subordinates must believe that the communication is consistent with organizational goals. If workers perceive inconsistency, they will question the authority of the command giver. (3) Subordinates must consider work assignments consistent with their own goals. If they don't, they will undermine authority. (4) Last, subordinates must be physically and mentally able to perform the tasks they are given.

Based on these assertions, Bernard claimed that authority really flows upward when subordinates consent to the authority of their bosses. Because authority flows upward, executives must win the cooperation of subordinates and establish the company systems that support workers in their will to work with each other.

For most administrative orders that flow downward, employees accept the authority of their bosses. For these common situations Barnard explained that employees are operating in a **zone of indifference** within which administrative orders are not questioned. To maintain an efficient coordinating system, however, every worker needs to report to a supervisor and the lines of communication need to be as short as possible. When messages are passed down from the top levels, it should be clear to frontline workers that the message is official. And, managers must show respect and dignity to workers.

Barnard was one of the first to identify that an informal organization exists in and around the formal organization where conscious coordination of activity takes place along the chain of command. The informal organization, dominated by word-of-mouth communication, spontaneously develops along the shifting lines of power and influence. It is natural for employees to form informal relationships around their common interests. Their communication with each other is not the official communication from supervisor to subordinate. They don't write memos to each other. They just talk about what is going on at work, what needs to get done, and how they will get their work done.

The Human Relations Movement

The experiences of managers using the principles of scientific management showed the enormous economic potential of eliminating waste and, in general, improving productivity. The heavy emphasis on the economics of managerial decision making during the first quarter of the 20th century resulted in an unintended consequence—a growing interest in the human side of enterprise. This emphasis is called the **human relations movement**, or the *behavioral movement*, in management thought.

The human side of enterprise didn't gain widespread attention until the 1920s or 1930s, but there were advocates of it long before then. Robert Owen, an entrepreneur and social activist, lived and worked as a manager for Piccadilly textile mill. Later he started his own cotton-spinning business to produce yarns for the textile mills. When he converted mule power to steam power, he soon developed a reputation for spinning fine yarns. In 1816, Owen wrote that if managers of industrial enterprises care for inanimate machines of industry, even more good can be accomplished if managers would "devote equal attention to your vital machines [human beings], which are far more wonderfully constructed."[101] The good expected from caring for workers was not only human welfare improvement but also economic improvement for the company. Owen estimated that spending money on the workers might in many cases bring a 50 or even 100 percent economic payback to the company. Despite his claims of increasing worker welfare and productivity, Owens's welfare policies were initially not well accepted by workers who saw his initiatives as an attempt to control their lives.

Source: Courtesy of Library of Congress Prints and Photographs Division Washington, D.C. 20540 USA, LC-DIG-nclc-02315.

The Human Relations Movement highlighted the fact that, after all, work is a social experience. Treating workers as people who deserve respect and dignity has a positive impact on work performance.

Two generations later, Henri Fayol recognized the importance of treating workers with respect and care. But Owen and Fayol did not represent the majority of general managers. Their wisdom was all but lost among factory superintendents, many of whom believed that common laborers were lazy, undisciplined, and untrustworthy.

When labor unions rebelled at what they considered excessive interest in productivity, the backlash caused some to consider more deeply the human side of enterprise. And, when the scientific management movement showed what can be accomplished by paying attention to tasks and work processes, managers began to ask how the organization might improve productivity even more. Studying worker physiology and motivation seemed to be a natural next step.

In the 1920s, Harvard University was awarded a grant to study human physiology and motivation in the work setting. Researchers set up a series of experiments at the Western Electric Hawthorne plant in Cicero, Illinois. For 5 years the research team studied the effects of various dimensions of working conditions, small group dynamics, and individual differences. The Hawthorne studies surprised the researchers by revealing the importance of small group dynamics. They also revealed how important a worker's sense of belonging is to the community of workers. Researchers observed how employee attitudes toward the work and fellow workers play a role in productivity. The significance of events at work influence how workers respond to what is happening around them.[102]

Managers who learned from the Hawthorne plant researchers began to approach their work as parents might deal with children, expending just enough personal interest to increase productivity. The idea was that morale, and consequently productivity, could be improved if managers made even a marginal increase in their attention to workers.

Another voice advocating on behalf of humans at work came from an energetic social worker, Mary Parker Follett, during the 1920s until her death in 1933. Follett claimed that people are central to enterprise.[103] She was particularly interested in how conflict emerges and is managed and the effect of managers interacting with their workers. In her view, workers will improve the chances of an enterprise's success if they are given more responsibility for decision making. Leadership emerges naturally out of the nature of the work to be done and the common purpose that the workers and their managers work toward.

Some of Follett's ideas were so radical in her day that she was largely ignored for two generations. For example, in her view, leadership must be shared with followers. Likewise, followership must be shared with leaders. At that time, most of the leaders of business and government were white males who had been socialized into their roles believing that leaders and followers have distinctly different roles that should not be exchanged. Leaders lead and followers follow, and that's that.

One of the legacies from the start of the human relations movement was an increased realization that human organizations are far more complex than we thought them to be in previous centuries. Humans do have a key role to play in organizational productivity. In addition, humans have particular needs related to their experiences at work. The interest in studying the behavior and motivation of individual workers and small groups of workers in organizations that began in the 1920s has continued to this day.

The effects of modern economics on management can be traced back for over two hundred years. The human relations perspective on management had early champions but developed more fully during the decades between 1930 and 1960. Later in the 20th century, management thinkers began to integrate both the economic and the human relations perspectives. (See Exhibit 2-8.) One of the most influential of these thinkers was Peter Drucker.

Peter Drucker (1909–2005)

Peter Drucker was a management consultant, writer, and scholar whose career spanned over half a century. His 1954 book *The Practice of Management* is ranked third among the most influential management books of the 20th century.[104] It is considered the first management book that addresses every aspect of management, not just isolated topics. In 1968, Drucker saw the effect that computers were beginning to have on management when he introduced the idea of the *knowledge society* and *knowledge worker.* One of Drucker's lasting contributions is his view of business's connection with society. Drucker thought deeply about the problems that managers face. He encouraged many to have a realistic understanding of management. See Exhibit 2-9, The Person Who Should Not Be a Manager.

EXHIBIT 2-8
Timeline of Selected Influences on Western Management Ideas[105]

2500 BC	The ancient Egyptian book of management is one of the first to provide guidance to future leaders.
2200 BC	Joseph, Prime Minister of Egypt, institutes economic reforms in preparation for famine.
1500 BC	With Jethro's advice Moses restructures the leadership of Israel.
970–931 BC	Reign of Solomon and the expansion of government bureaucracy; Wisdom regarding leadership is written in the book of *Proverbs.*
ca. 600 BC	Sun Tzu writes ancient Chinese book *The Art of War,* in which he explains how to manage using military strategy.
360 BC	Aristotle writes regarding leadership of the state.
ca. 300 BC	The ancient Indian book *Arthaśāstra* is written to provide advice on managing military and political organizations.
30 AD	Jesus teaches about leadership in the Kingdom of God.
1776	Adam Smith publishes his book *The Wealth of Nations,* in which he discusses division of labor.
1832	Charles Babbage writes *On the Economy of Machinery and Manufacturers,* in which he discusses management principles for factories.
1911	Frederick Taylor popularizes the scientific management movement and publishes his book *The Principles of Scientific Management.*
1916	Henri Fayol in France publishes his book *General and Industrial Management.*
1922	Max Weber puts forth his ideas on managing bureaucracies in his book *Economy and Society.*
1926	Mary Parker Follett begins promoting her ideas on leadership and authority.
1933	Elton Mayo publishes his book *The Human Problems of an Industrial Civilization,* which is a major contribution to the human relations movement.
1938	Chester Barnard publishes his book *The Function of the Executive,* in which he analyzes organizations and leadership.
1943	Abraham Maslow's hierarchy of needs article is published in the magazine *Psychological Review.*
1954	Peter Drucker's book *The Practice of Management* is published.
1965	Joan Woodward publishes her research on technology and organizations in her book *Industrial Organization: Theory and Practice.*
1966	Katz and Kahn publish their book *The Social Psychology of Organizations,* building awareness regarding motivation.
1980	Michael Porter publishes his book *Competitive Strategy,* in which he discusses ideas about strategic thinking.
1985	Edgar Schein publishes his book *Organizational Culture and Leadership,* raising awareness regarding the importance of organizational culture.
1994	Hamel and Prahalad publish the book *Competing for the Future,* popularizing the idea of organizational core competencies.

EXHIBIT 2-9
The Person Who Should Not Be a Manager

In his book *The Practice of Management*, Peter Drucker said that the person who should *not* be appointed as a manager is the person who is more interested in the question "*Who* is right?" than in the question "*What* is right?" The question *Who* is right? teaches subordinates to play it safe or to play politics. The question *What* is right? focuses on the most important fundamental value on which all of business stands: integrity.[106]

Drucker was one of the first to focus on the moral responsibility of the manager. In his view, profit is not the primary reason for business activity; it is a result. Business is a social institution embedded in society and affected by public interest for the common good. Thus the overriding goal common to every business is to strive to make whatever is productive to our society and whatever strengthens and advances the common good to also be the source of strength, prosperity, and profit for the business.

Drucker gleaned much of his ideas on management from his connections with top-level executives of large corporations. From his observations and consulting work, he came to believe that managers have three areas they must manage. First, they must manage the major functions of business—the central purpose of which is to create customers. Managers also must manage other managers. Some of the approaches needed here include management by objectives, executive leadership, governance, and organizational structure. Last, managers must manage the frontline workers. In this regard, personnel management, employee motivation, and effective supervision all are important.

Drucker is perhaps best known for his *management by objectives* concept, based on his observations at General Electric.[107] **Management by objectives (MBO)** is a planning process based on setting objectives, developing action plans, and then determining how close to the desired goals the organization is performing. Organizations of all types have applied MBO. We will explore MBO in more detail in Chapter 6, Planning and Decision Making.

Many individuals have contributed to management thinking over time. Exhibit 2-10 lists some of the most important contributors we have not covered in this chapter. We will revisit many of them and their specific areas of focus in corresponding chapters throughout this book.

EXHIBIT 2-10

Others Who Have Influenced Management Thinking

Individual	Contribution to Management Thinking
Alfred P. Sloan (1875–1966)[108]	• Multi-divisional form of organization • Blending centralized financial controls with decentralized operational decisions • The professional manager serves the organization as his client
Elton Mayo (1880–1949)[109]	• Publicist of the Hawthorne experiments at Western Electric • The interconnections between morale and productivity • Importance of individual needs and social processes
Alfred D. Chandler Jr. (1918–2007)[110]	• The relationship between a company's strategy and its structure: Structure follows strategy • Use of in-depth historical analysis to develop business theory
Abraham Maslow (1908–1970)[111]	• The "Hierarchy of needs" • Human motivation • Eupsychian management
W. Edwards Deming (1900–1993)[112]	• 14 points of management • Process management • Continuous quality improvement • Breaking down barriers between departments • Employee training
Joseph Juran (1904–2008)[113]	• Quality improvement • Statistical process control
H. Igor Ansoff (1918–2002)[114]	• Strategic planning and analysis • Product-market strategy matrix
Frederick Herzberg (1923–2000)[115]	• Employee motivation • Job satisfaction • Job enrichment

Douglas McGregor (1906–1964)[116]	• The impact of managerial assumptions about workers: Theory X, Theory Y • Employee motivation
William Ouchi (1943–)[117]	• Theory Z management • Japanese management theory
Charles Handy (1932–)[118]	• The future of work • Implications of virtual organizations
Geert Hofstede (1928–)[119]	• Cultural differences in work-related values
Henry Mintzberg (1939–)[120]	• The nature of managerial work • Strategic thinking • Managerial decision making • Organizational design
Michael Porter (1947–)[121]	• The economics of strategy • Industry structure • The value chain • Generic strategies
Edgar Schein (1928–)[122]	• Organizational culture • Organizational learning

EXHIBIT 2-10
Continued

Management and the Consequences of History

Management always takes place within the context of broader historical influences. Looking back over the long history of business, we see a connection between social influences on organizations and the issues that managers faced.[123] Some of the management issues came in response to unintended consequences of business implementing previous management ideas. Others came as a result of specific historical situations (such as World Wars I and II) that required major commitments by business leaders as well as new ways of thinking about management. Still others arose as a result of the emergence of new technology, the general advances in knowledge, or the affect of broader forces at work such as globalization.

In the 15th and 16th centuries the technology of ocean navigation changed the approaches to business management. Few technological advances had as direct an influence on changes in management as did the invention of the steam engine in the early 18th century. Prior to the steam engine, small manufacturing companies relied on power from a water wheel and a system of interconnecting pulleys and drive belts. Before the steam engine was applied to manufacturing, it was used for pumping water and blowing air into blast furnaces. But once the power of steam was harnessed for driving machinery such as weaving looms, the size of factories increased.

Two other technological developments that affected managerial practices were the railroad and the telegraph.[124] With the application of the steam engine, railroads increased the speed of land travel for both passengers and goods, creating a revolution in transportation. The railroad industry spawned other technical developments which then spread into other industries. Although it was not immediately embraced by commerce, the invention of the telegraph started a revolution in communication. The telegraph allowed for virtually instant communication of basic business information that could be used in coordinating shipments of goods. A quick telegraph could alert managers of changes taking place with needed key resources. As corporations grew in size and began spreading over larger geographic areas, the telegraph helped corporate managers coordinate with business unit managers.

Transportation by rail meant that the surplus of productivity generated in many regions could be brought to faraway markets. The development of rapid transportation increased the importance of each commercial organization coordinating its work with other entities in the marketplace. National commodity markets began to emerge where competition was based primarily on market price. Railroads made possible (and sometimes required) the development of very large

EXHIBIT 2-11
Changing Situations Result in Changing Management Ideas

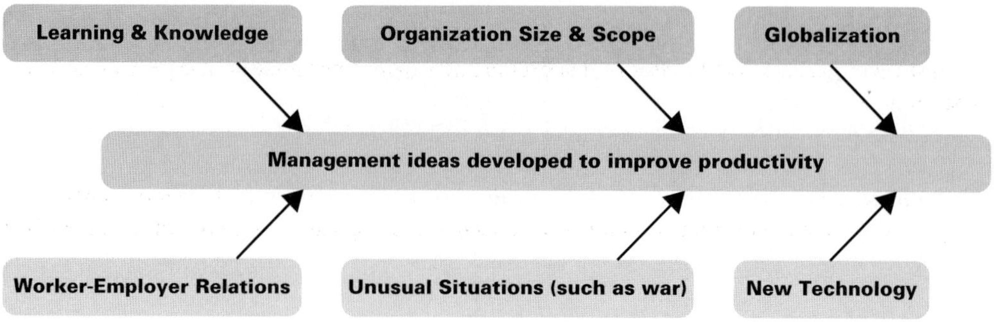

but geographically dispersed commercial organizations. Organizations that operated the railroads and steel production became larger.

As scientific knowledge increased, other technological improvements and inventions such as the telephone, automobile, and airplane all contributed to changes in the way businesses operated. These new technologies, many of them used for market coordination and increased productivity, required a sharper focus on management as stockholders came to believe that increased profits could be generated only through the use of managerial skills. See Exhibit 2-11. Changing Situations Result in Changing Management Ideas.

We are still experiencing the full effects of the development of electronic communication systems, computers, and the Internet. One thing we know is that managers have never had so much data at their disposal for use in making decisions as they do today. The extensive use of machines and information systems controlled by computers has resulted in a shift from a manufacturing-based economy to an information-based economy. Mobile computer-driven communication devices have made it possible for managers to communicate with anyone "on the go." This has further increased the pace of doing business.

Some believe that computers have increased efficiency. Others worry that these devices, which enable managers to wring every ounce of value out of every moment in time, are having unintended consequences of increased stress and managerial burnout that are bringing to some a crisis of meaning in life.

The phenomenon of the networked organization has increased the importance of trust in all business relationships. Sophisticated information systems have been used for both good and ill in business, putting the issues of trust and integrity at the forefront of management. Because of the moral lapses that have been so prominent in business in recent years, organizations will likely increasingly expect managers to demonstrate solid integrity and help other managers and their subordinates maintain a high level of trustworthiness. If being–thinking–acting as a way of looking at management was important in the past, there is an unparalleled need for it now.

Networking and electronic communications systems have continued to transform the work of managers.

Source: © Nruboc/Dreamstime.com.

The Rise and Fall of Management Ideas

The history of management teaches us that exciting new management ideas emerge with each new generation. These new ideas often sweep through the marketplace in the form of popular books and videos or in the brief cases of management consultants hired to bring solutions to problems that frustrate companies. Some of the new management ideas are substantive innovations or improvements on old ideas. Others sometimes turn out to be nothing more than **management fads**, management ideas that are exciting at first but then decrease in popularity or go out of use altogether. Some ideas prove to be far more difficult to actually use in practice than their promoters like to think. However, many contain a kernel of truth that deserves to be considered. Some popular management ideas that have risen and fallen in popularity over the years include the following.[125]

MULTIPLE CHAINS OF COMMAND. Frederick Taylor and a few others advocated that each worker should have more than one boss, each one focusing on a different function. Employees who worked under this system could have as many as eight bosses. What Taylor evidently failed to consider is that with multiple supervisors, each worker will likely receive conflicting commands. Fortunately Taylor's idea was short-lived. While some organizations do have situations in which two individuals have decision-making authority over one worker, we know that such reporting relationships can become complicated and highly political.

MANAGEMENT BY OBJECTIVES (MBO). Made popular by Peter Drucker, MBO became the rage in many organizations in the 1970s, but by the mid-1990s its popularity had declined. Even so, MBO is still in use, sometimes under new terminology. A kernel of truth in MBO has remained: the belief that organizations are more productive when specific goals are set, when managers follow up to ensure that the goals are being reached, and when decisions make specific corrections as needed.

SENSITIVITY TRAINING (T-GROUPS). Dating back to the 1940s and becoming popular during the 1960s, **sensitivity training (T-Groups)** involved a focus on interpersonal dynamics among the participants in a controlled environment. T-groups faded away during the 1970s. But a kernel of management truth became the legacy of T-groups, namely that in highly complex organizations, it is not technical skill alone that is needed for coordination of effort. Employees at all levels must learn how to relate with each other.

QUALITY CIRCLES (QCS). Becoming popular in the 1970s, quality circles came to the United States from Japan where industrial leaders had integrated into their management systems the teachings of W. Edwards Deming and Joseph Juran—two of the management thinkers described in Exhibit 2-11. **Quality circles (QCs)** are small groups of employees who meet on a regular basis to solve quality or production problems. After 1983, QCs declined in popularity as newer approaches to product and service quality improvement became popular. The successor to QCs was total quality management (TQM) when it became increasingly evident that American firms were not catching up to the quality that Japanese firms were attaining. **Total quality management (TQM)** is a company-wide systematic approach to continuously making improvements to quality and efficiency. It would be wrong to classify TQM as a fad because its basic ideas enjoy as much popularity as ever. While quality improvement continues to be a high priority with companies, TQM as a particular method declined in the 1990s as, once again, newer quality initiatives became popular such as Six Sigma and lean manufacturing. We will discuss these newer initiatives in Chapter 14, Managerial Control and Accountability.

SELF-MANAGED TEAMS (SMT). Also known as self-managed work teams and self-directed teams, **self-managed teams (SMT)** is an approach to management that emphasizes worker participation in team leadership. Employees who participate in self-managed teams develop a new sense of self-efficacy and power to make a difference in their organizations. SMT eventually began to decline as more organizations reported mixed results. While the idea of worker participation has remained as the kernel of truth in SMT, some organizations have found that other methods are more effective than SMT for some management problems.

Business culture in a free market economy is susceptible to management fads partly because of the national belief that with a little ingenuity, just about anything can be improved. Some new ideas provide a false sense of comfort even though they fail to address the underlying organic problems of an organization, its industry, or the economy. Many management ideas offer the promise of progress, especially when managers sense a performance gap between their firm and competitors. Such a performance gap creates an urgent need to close the gap as quickly as possible.[126]

Consider the following five myths that reveal the weaknesses of so-called *new* management ideas that sometimes turn into fads.

NEWNESS. Few management ideas that are promoted as new are truly new. Although management approaches have changed over the years, the fundamental issues of management have not changed much. This doesn't mean there is nothing more to learn. It could very well be that in the coming years we will find new breakthrough ideas that make the work of a manager more effective.

UNIVERSALITY. Some popular management ideas, though successful in some organizations at certain times and places, are promoted as if they can be successful anywhere at any time. The historical context and current situation for every company is different.

SIMPLICITY. Proponents of popular management ideas often present them as relatively simple solutions to management needs. In reality, management problems are rarely as easy to solve as overly simplistic solutions suggest.

THE PANACEA. Single management ideas or programs rarely, if ever, solve the complex problems that contemporary organizations face. Beware of hot new management ideas that claim they can solve all of the complicated issues that you as a manager face every day. No single management idea has ever been a permanent panacea for complex management problems.

NO TRADE-OFFS. This myth is probably the most harmful because it gives the false impression that there are no downsides or trade-offs to using a particular management idea. New management ideas are especially prone to this myth but even solid, time-tested ideas, when taken alone or to the extreme, can create the same impression. Some management ideas, when used exclusively or in excess, cause as many problems as they solve. Other management ideas reveal deeper layers of unresolved organizational problems when they are applied.

Using an Organization's History to Learn

Learning about management ideas that have emerged over time is one thing. Knowing the history of management ideas in the organization in which you work is another. Earlier in this chapter we discussed the importance of knowing an organization's stories, especially for managers. But can playing amateur company historian actually help a busy manager be more effective? Perhaps so.

In 1997, the butane production team at an oil refinery decided to intentionally learn from their successes and failures.[127] They designed an interactive board game based on real events at the plant. As the team played, they learned to think together about the most difficult problems that both managers and frontline employees shared in common.

Their exercise resulted in renewed commitments to work together to create innovative solutions. The spontaneous quality improvement projects that developed ended up saving the company millions of dollars. So successful was the team that others in the corporation began asking for more information. The team members discovered that describing how improvements came about was more difficult than they had expected.

Corporate leaders realized how important the information that they held in their brains—tacit knowledge—might be for others. To help extract this tacit knowledge and make it available to others, the company hired oral historians to interview managers and frontline workers to record the stories of their improvement efforts—problems, failures, and successes. The outcome was a 20-page "learning history" document that told the company's stories in the words of the people who made that history.

Recording a contemporary history of how an organization makes changes offers a tangible and useful way for the company's managers and employees alike to learn from each other.

Using the Case Study Method to Learn

For decades business students have learned to evaluate management situations using stories of particular organizations in their environments. Originally used in law schools to illustrate how the courts interpreted law and the constitution, the case study approach became a favorite way to demonstrate how businesses reap the consequences of their decisions. Thus, one of the popular ways to study business is by using case studies.

A **case study** contains a short story of a particular organization or its industry at a particular time and place. Case studies are challenging to new students of business because they require the integration of all types of information: financial, marketing, operational, environmental, competitive, and so forth. Case studies offer a window into the inner workings of organizations and help bring to life the principles and theories of business.

But case studies are not without their problems. Some recurring weaknesses are that they are brief, highly refined into relatively simple accounts that often simplify complex situations, and selective in terms of which facts are included and excluded. Most organizations are more complicated than one case study can fairly represent. Case studies, if used superficially, can give the false impression that management decisions are straightforward and easily implemented, which, in reality, is rarely true.

Focus on an Organization

International Christian Chamber of Commerce (ICCC)

Many organizations have formed to encourage Christians to integrate their faith with their work on a daily basis. One such organization is the International Christian Chamber of Commerce (ICCC). The ICCC was founded by Gunnar Olson in Sweden in 1984 and has grown into a worldwide network. The ICCC's mission "is to serve as a vehicle in extending the operation and principles of wisdom, love and rule of God Almighty into the marketplaces of the world."

The ICCC is a worldwide network of committed businesspeople who wish to exchange ideas, products, and services as they serve as a support net for one another. The assumption is that there is a difference between a person who professes to be a Christian and a person who actually brings the Kingdom of God into the marketplace through his or her business activity.

The founders and current leaders of ICCC recognize that true spiritual leadership begins with people of character who pursue a life of faith, obedience to God, and humble service toward others. Such leaders seek to learn and practice wisdom not only for business success but also for "releasing business people into the walk of God's Kingdom." For more information, visit the ICCC's website: http://www.iccc.net/.

Paradoxes of Memory

As we began exploring in Chapter 1, managers face a variety of tension points. One interesting tension point regarding the history of an organization is that all organizational members must at the same time believe and doubt their past experiences.[128] If past experiences are automatically believed to be valid for today, the organization will likely miss marketplace signals about changes, and the organization could become rigid. But if past experiences are doubted too frequently, the organization will constantly be changing but without roots that are necessary for stability. In this way, organizational memory is both friend and foe to managers. When the organization is able to both believe and doubt, it is able to maintain stability and flexibility.

An individual's personal memory and religious faith also contain a paradox. Religious faith is anchored in the belief that some things do not change, and at the same time, that people can and do change. Faith allows you to look forward and backward at the same time, drawing on the lessons learned from the past while looking to the future with hope and assurance. If we are to find meaning in our lives, then we must remember. However, we cannot afford to get stuck dwelling on the mistakes we made in the past. If we want to avoid this type of self-destructive behavior, we must also learn to forget and move on with our lives.[129]

Chapter Summary

1. For the Christian, the story of business is the story of the human response to God's call to bear his image as we subdue the earth and fill it. The Bible contains many examples of managers who were responsible for serving a community of people, helping them collectively to create meaningful value. Their experiences provide valuable lessons for managers today. Three examples of leaders include Joseph, Moses, and Solomon:
   a. Because of Joseph's integrity and strategic thinking, he was appointed to a top position in the Egyptian government and through his policies the empire was saved from famine.

b. Accepting counsel from his father-in-law Moses reorganized the people of Israel, appointing leaders with different levels of authority. Moses, though not perfect as a leader, never lost sight of the essential purpose of the organization: Escape from bondage and establish a new homeland under God's guidance.

c. Solomon, the wisest and richest king described in the Scriptures, showed organizational abilities that spanned state, military, scientific, and commercial ventures. He recorded in writing some of the best managerial wisdom that he learned from his own experiences as king. His experience shows the tragedy of what can happen when a powerful person compromises what he believes to be right.

2. The Bible also contains many guidelines for managers and leaders. The Hebrew Bible teaches that managerial wisdom comes from God and includes the principles of serving others with fairness, prudence, diligence, and integrity. Managers are expected to care for the needs of the organization (community) as well as the needs of subordinates. In the New Testament the teachings and example of Jesus apply directly to the work of managers and leaders. Among other things Jesus taught that leaders become great by being faithful stewards and servants of the community. The experiences of the early Christian church provide additional examples and teachings that help a manager.
3. We can learn from the experiences of the Egyptians, Romans, and Greeks. Some of the principles that were true for the ancient civilizations are still true today: respect for authority, pursuing the larger goals of the organization, organizing workers based on skill and function, and giving clear delegation of tasks and authority.
4. In modern times management ideas were built on ancient ideas but also gradually became more sophisticated. Scientific management (Frederick Taylor) became one of the most influential movements of the 20th century. Thinking about management as a profession began to take shape when Henri Fayol wrote his observations about managerial work. Management thinkers such as Max Weber, Chester Barnard, Peter Drucker, and many others have contributed to the development of the body of knowledge that contemporary managers still practice.
5. Ideas about management always take place within the context of broader historical influences. Technological developments and major events affect the development of managerial practices. Some of the new ideas about management persist over many years while a few ideas turn out to be management fads that last just a few years.
6. Managers can learn a lot by reflecting on the history of events in their organizations and professions. The stories that organizational members tell to each other carry important points that should be remembered when making decisions about the future.
7. The case study method is a popular device to learn about management of organizations. A case study contains the stories of people, events, and decisions that have been made which bring the organization to its present situation.

Key Terms

Bureaucracy 53
Case study 62
Division of labor 46
Human relations movement 55
Managing by exception 41
Management by objectives (MBO) 58
Management fads 61
Quality circles (QCs) 61
Rule of ten 41
Scalar chain of command 54
Scientific management 47
Self-managed teams (SMT) 61
Sensitivity training (T-Groups) 61
Soldiering 48
Task management 49
Time and motion studies 48
Total quality management (TQM) 61
Wisdom 42
Zone of indifference 55

Discussion Questions

1. Why have some management ideas such as chain of command or division of labor stood the test of time from ancient days until now, while other ideas have declined in usefulness or simply disappeared altogether?
2. On what basis can we say that Solomon was the best manager to have lived before the time of Christ? In what ways might he also have been the worst manager?
3. Thinking about the future generation of workers, which older management ideas might be at risk of declining in popularity? Why?
4. If you lived during Frederick W. Taylor's time, what advice would you have given him to improve the approach he took regarding scientific management?
5. Are the contributions from the human relations movement more important than the contributions from the scientific management movement? Why?
6. Do you agree or disagree with Chester Barnard that authority flows upward rather than downward?
7. If Barnard is correct regarding authority flowing upward, how much authority does the chief executive actually have?

8. Are the principles of scientific management inherently in conflict with Judeo-Christian teachings of respect for human beings created in the image of God?
9. If sin had not entered the human experience, how might the history of business been different?
10. In the New Jerusalem as a city (Revelation 21), what economic organizations might exist?
11. What kinds of things must people remember if they are to find meaning in their lives? What kinds of things should they forget to avoid self-destruction?
12. Of all the historical management ideas reviewed in this chapter, which seem to be the most important? Why?

STUDENT EXERCISES

1. Type a one-page (single-spaced) story of your experiences in management. What have you learned about management? What insights do you have about yourself as a manager?
2. Write your "Resume of Failures" describing things you wanted to accomplish but didn't, and mistakes you made. For each "failure" describe what you learned from it. Next write a "Resume of Successes" describing things that you have accomplished. For each success, what part did other people around you play in your success? Describe what you learned about yourself from each success.
3. Interview a company manager. Ask the manager to tell you the company story, and to tell you the three top company values that have stood the test of time. How knowledgeable about the company's story and history does the manager seem to be?
4. Choose one person mentioned in this chapter who contributed to the development of management ideas. Find more information about this person in other books and articles. Write a short paper describing to what degree their ideas are still useful today.
5. The history of management ideas in China and India are not well known in Europe and the Western Hemisphere. Using resources available to you through your library and on the Internet research and write a short paper comparing the management ideas that emerged in China or India with the management ideas that emerged in Europe and the United States.
6. Joseph, Moses, Solomon, and Jesus are examples of managers whose experiences are described in the Bible. Using Bible study reference books and your Bible select one person from the following list and write a summary of the management and leadership principles that this person exhibited. Describe the lessons we can learn today from the experiences of the person you study.
   - Noah
   - Abraham
   - Jacob
   - David
   - Ahab
   - Esther
   - Paul
   - Peter

IN-CLASS EXERCISES

Issue Debate/Discussion

Divide the class into small groups of five to six people each. Hand out a sheet of paper containing the quotations that follow. Assign half of the groups to defend the first quotation as a valid definition/description of a leader's humility and the other half to defend the second quotation as valid. Give the groups 5 minutes to discuss. Then call for groups to give a summary of the rationale they developed. Discussion can follow.

Discussion Topic #1: What is the value of history? Which of the following two perspectives reflect what you think the next generation of business leaders will value more? Applying these quotations to the level of the firm, which perspective will lead to the path of success?

A. **Studying history is a valuable use of our time.** "Progress, far from consisting in change, depends on retentiveness. Those who cannot remember the past are condemned to repeat it."[130] The past is never completely separated from the present. It constantly influences the future.

B. **Studying history is a waste of time.** "History is more or less bunk. It's tradition. We don't want tradition. We want to live in the present and the only history that is worth a tinker's damn is the history we made today."[131] Managers should focus on the future performance of the organization. Clinging to the past is harmful. The future will bring new challenges and new opportunities for which the past does not prepare us.

Discussion Topic #2: What is God's role in business history?

A. **Transcendence of God.** If God exists, he is transcendent (distant) from humans and does not interact with humans during the course of business history. Business history is simply the economic actions of human beings making choices and interacting with each other in the marketplaces of the earth.

B. **Immanence and omnipresence of God.** God is personal, interacting with humans on a regular basis as they interact in the marketplace. God is a spiritual being and has the capacity to interact with spiritual beings he has created.[132]

His interaction with humans may be by special revelation or through his Providence worked out through the actions of humans.

Discussion Topic #3: What is the connection between religion and efficiency? Efficiency became a popular theme throughout the culture of the United States by the 1920s. Some found a connection between spiritual values and efficiency. In his book *Religion and Business,* Roger Babson[133] wrote that "religion is the greatest factor in developing real efficiency. The four qualities of faith, industry, initiative, and courage, which make men efficient, are spiritual qualities." On what biblical basis can Babson's statement be supported?

Discussion Topic #4: One of the most popular passages of Scripture is called The Lord's Prayer. Christians have used it for centuries as a model for praying. This prayer is found in Matthew 6:9–13 (also in Luke 11:1–4):

> **Matthew 6:9–13**[9] Pray, then, in this way: "Our Father who art in heaven, Hallowed be Thy name.[10] Thy kingdom come. Thy will be done, on earth as it is in heaven.[11] Give us this day our daily bread.[12] And forgive us our debts, as we also have forgiven our debtors.[13] And do not lead us into temptation, but deliver us from evil. *For Thine is the kingdom, and the power, and the glory, forever. Amen.*" (New American Standard Version)

A. What words and phrases seem especially relevant to the work of a manager?
B. What might verse 10 mean for the manager?

Discussion Topic #5: The Hebrew word for *hand* is one of the root metaphors for being a manager. See, for example, Genesis 49:8; Exodus 21:20; Numbers 4:28; Deuteronomy 8:17, 15:10; Job 31:25; Ecclesiastes 9:10; Psalm 73:3, 128:2, 139:10; Proverbs 3:27, 10:4, 12:14; Job 5:12; 1 Chronicles 29:5. Invite a small group of students to the front of the classroom. One of the students is appointed as the "manager." This student's task is to communicate without speaking to the small group in as many ways as possible using only hands. Each hand gesture should be something that a manager might do with subordinates. The rest of the class can guess what the manager is "doing" by gesturing with the hand. Discuss the many ways that just the manager's hand can be used in a positive or negative way to conduct managerial work.

Endnotes

1. Norling, B. (1960). *Towards a better understanding of history.* South Bend, IN: University of Notre Dame Press. p. 1.
2. Deuteronomy 8:10–18.
3. The Little Debbie product line was introduced by McKee Foods Corporation in 1960. Debra McKee, O.D. McKee's granddaughter, became the namesake of the product line.
4. Oliphant, C. A. (1994). *Sweet success: O. D. McKee America's snack cake king.* Cleveland, TN: Sundial Press.
5. Deuteronomy 4:10, 5:15, 7:18, 8:2, 9:7, 15:5, 16:3, 24:9, 24:18, 32:7; 1 Chronicles 16:12–16; Psalm 22:27; Ecclesiastes 12:1.
6. Neustadt, R. E., & May, E. R. (1986). *Thinking in time: The uses of history for decision makers.* New York: The Free Press; Norling, B. (1960). *Towards a better understanding of history.* South Bend, IN: University of Notre Dame Press; Chandler Jr., A. D.; McCraw, T. K.; McDonald, A. L.; Tedlow, R. S.; Vietor, R. H. K., & Kantrow, A. M. (Eds.). (1986). Why history matters to managers. *Harvard Business Review.* 64(1), 81–88; Lamond, D. (2005). On the value of management history. *Management Decision.* 43(10), 1273–1281; Down, S. (2001). Knowledge sharing review: The use of history in business and management, and some implications for management learning. *Management Learning.* 32(3), 393–410; Lerner, G. (1997). *Why history matters: Life and thought.* New York: Oxford University Press. pp. 199–211; Diller, L. C. (2007). *The value of history for business students.* Convocation lecture given to the Southern Adventist University School of Business & Management Convocation. Collegedale, TN. September 13; Barnard, Chester I. (1938). *The functions of the executive.* Cambridge, MA: Harvard University Press. p. 209; Perrow, C. (1986). *Complex organizations: A critical essay.* (3rd ed.). New York: McGraw-Hill, Inc. p. 158; Schein, E. H. (2004). *Organizational culture and leadership.* (3rd ed.). San Francisco, CA: John Wiley & Sons. p. 86.
7. For an interesting book cataloging some of the more notorious business scandals see The Editors of Fortune Magazine. (2009). *Scandal! Amazing tales of scandals that shocked the world and shaped modern business.* New York: Time Inc. Home Entertainment.
8. Joseph's story is told in Genesis 37–50.
9. Genesis 6, 37–50; Exodus; Numbers 27:18; 1 Kings 18; 2 Kings 21–22; Ezra; Nehemiah; Psalm 105:16–22; Daniel 5; Matthew 8; Luke 7, 16; Acts 10–15.
10. Acts 7:22.
11. Exodus 35:30–40:33.
12. Exodus 18:13–18.
13. Exodus 18:25–26.
14. Exodus 18:19–26; Deuteronomy 1:15–18. See also George Jr., C. S. (1972). *The history of management thought.* (2nd ed.). Englewood Cliffs, NJ: Prentice-Hall, Inc. p. 11.
15. See Chandler, A. (1962). *Strategy and structure.* Cambridge, MA: MIT Press. p. 309; Ansoff, H. I. (1987). The emerging paradigm of strategic behavior. *Strategic Management Journal.* 8(6), 501–515; Simon, H. A. (1993). Strategy and organizational evolution. *Strategic Management Journal.* 14, 131–142.
16. See 1 Kings 2–11; 2 Chronicles 2.
17. For a collection of texts from both the Old and New Testament see Regent University College of

Administration and Management Graduate School of Business (1989). *The Word on management: A topical index of Scriptures for managers and employees.* Regent University Press. See also Rush, M. (1983). *Management: A biblical approach.* Wheaton, IL: Victor Books; Dose, J. J. (2006). *Proverbs: Ancient wisdom for contemporary organizations.* Paper presented to the Christian Business Faculty Association Annual Conference. Dayton, OH. October; Zigarelli, M. A. (2004). *Management by proverbs.* Otsego, MI: PageFree Publishing.

18. Doukhan, J. B. (1993). *Hebrew for theologians: A textbook for the study of biblical Hebrew in relation to Hebrew thinking.* Lanham, MD: University Press of America. p. 208.
19. Genesis 1, 2; Psalm 8:3–4. See also Doukhan, J. B. (1993). *Hebrew for theologians: A textbook for the study of biblical Hebrew in relation to Hebrew thinking.* Lanham, MD: University Press of America. p. 197.
20. Proverbs 8:15, 8:16; Ecclesiastes 5:19.
21. Deuteronomy 8:17–18; Job 28:18; Proverbs 2:7, 3:21, 4:5–8, 16:16, 19:8, 29:26; Exodus 31:3; Ecclesiastes 7:12, 9:10; Ezekiel 28:4.
22. Doukhan, J. B. (1993). *Hebrew for theologians: A textbook for the study of biblical Hebrew in relation to Hebrew thinking.* Lanham, MD: University Press of America. p. 194. See also Isaiah 50:5; Job 12:11; Nehemiah 8:3; Jeremiah 6:10; Psalm 119:125, 119:144; Job 32:8; Proverbs 8:11, 15:31–32, 16:16, 18:15, 19:8.
23. Proverbs 9:9, 10:17, 12:1, 13:10, 18:15, 20:18, 23:12.
24. Psalm 1; Proverbs 12:15, 23:4; Ecclesiastes 7:5.
25. Proverbs 10:19, 10:21, 12:6, 12:18, 13:17, 14:3, 15:1–2.
26. 1 Samuel 16:7; Psalm 16:7; Proverbs 2:10, 4:23, 23:7, 27:19; Jeremiah 17:9.
27. Genesis 49:8; Proverbs 3:27; Exodus 21:20; Numbers 4:28. It is interesting that the miracles performed prior to the release of the Hebrews from Egyptian captivity involved Aaron stretching out his hand over the waters of Egypt (Exodus 7 and 8). A person is under self-responsibility, i.e., their own hand and because of this is expected to work diligently (Proverbs 10:4, 12:14, 12:24). A wise king will place his heart under the authority of the hand of God and by doing this will prosper spiritually and materially (Proverbs 21:1).
28. Deuteronomy 8:17; Job 31:25; Ecclesiastes 9:10; Psalm 128:2; Proverbs 10:4, 12:14; Job 5:12; 1 Chronicles 29:5; Deuteronomy 15:10.
29. Psalm 73:3, 139:10.
30. Genesis 37:21–22, 39:4; Exodus 2:19; Proverbs 3:27.
31. Proverbs 20:28.
32. Ecclesiastes 8:9; Proverbs 11:17. See also Exodus 21:20.
33. Proverbs 3:27.
34. Ecclesiastes 12:13–14.
35. Proverbs 11:2, 15:31–33, 16:18, 18:12, 22:4, 26:12, 29:23.
36. Deuteronomy 1:17; Proverbs 10:9–10, 11:1, 11:26, 12:17, 16:11–13, 17:23, 21:3, 23:24–25, 24:28, 25:13, 28:16, 29:4; Ecclesiastes 7:7; 2 Samuel 23:4ff.
37. Proverbs 12:15, 13:10, 15:12, 15:22, 20:18.
38. Proverbs 12:16, 14:29, 16:15, 16:32, 19:11, 19:19, 29:11.
39. See as examples Jones, L. B. (1995). *Jesus CEO: Using ancient wisdom for visionary leadership.* New York: Hyperion; Nouwen, H. J. M. (1989). *In the name of Jesus: Reflections on Christian leadership.* New York: The Crossroad Publishing Company; Blanchard, K. (2007). *Lead like Jesus: Lessons from the greatest leadership role model of all time.* Nashville: Thomas Nelson; Wilkes, C. G. (1998). *Jesus on leadership.* Carol Stream, IL: Tyndale House Publishers; Briner, B., & Prichard, R. (2001). *Leadership lessons of Jesus.* New York: Gramercy Publishing Company.
40. The gospels ignore most of the details from this phase of his life and work. The gospel of Luke simply says that Jesus was obedient to his parents and grew in wisdom and in favor with God and men (Luke 2:51– 2). When he was about 30 years of age he left his home and the family business and started preaching and teaching in public (Luke 3:23), depending upon the generosity of others for sustenance (Luke 8:3). During his public ministry he is referred to as "the carpenter's son" (Matthew 13:55; Mark 6:3) and as "Jesus of Nazareth" (e.g., John 1:45–46; Luke 18:37; Luke 24:19; Mark 1:9, 10:47; Acts 2:22, 6:14, 26:9). His early reputation was built around the belief of the people that he was a great teacher and worker of miracles. Although he is described as the Creator (John 1:1–4), nowhere in the New Testament is Jesus referred to as a manager *per se.* For a discussion of Jesus' work as a carpenter see Oakman, D. E. (1986). *Jesus and the economic questions of his day.* Lewiston, NY: The Edwin Mellen Press. pp. 175–220.
41. Gushee, D. P. (2005). The economic ethics of Jesus. In Henderson, J. W., & Pisciotta, J. (Eds.). *Faithful economics: The moral worlds of a neutral science.* Waco, TX: Baylor University Press. pp. 109–130.
42. Matthew 7:29, 9:6; Mark 1:22, 1:27; John 2:1–11.
43. Matthew 14:15–21.
44. Matthew 10, 21:1–7, 26:18–20; Mark 6:7–13.
45. Luke 10:1–22.
46. Matthew 20:25.
47. John 15:15.
48. Luke 12:41–48, 16:1–8; Matthew 25:14–46.
49. Matthew 10:24.
50. Luke 16:13; Matthew 6:24. The primary teaching point of these passages seems to be in the context of God's spiritual kingdom established by Jesus, i.e., we cannot serve God and mammon. Many scholars point to this passage as a recognition of the principle of "unity of command." As we will consider in a later chapter, ancient organizations were organized with vertical hierarchical command and control systems. Some modern organizations are designed for more horizontal collaboration. In some of these organizations some workers have two bosses.
51. Matthew 7:12, 22:39.
52. Luke 12:48.
53. Matthew 7:24–29. Here Jesus seems to be referring to his teachings recorded in Matthew 5:1 7:23.
54. Matthew 20:20–28, 23:11; Mark 9:35–37, 10:35–45; Luke 9:46–48, 22:24–27.
55. Leviticus 19:18; Exodus 20:1–17; Matthew 5:17, 22:36–40; Mark 12:29–31; John 15:12.
56. Matthew 8:1–3, 21:12–13, 23:13–29; Luke 11:42–52; Mark 2:15–17.
57. Acts 6:1–7.
58. Acts 15:1–21.

59. 1 Timothy 3:1–7; 5:22–25; Titus 1:5–11. See also Strauch, A. (1995). *Biblical eldership: An urgent call to restore biblical church leadership.* (Rev. Ed.). Colorado Springs, CO: Lewis and Roth Publishers.
60. Titus 1:5.
61. Ephesians 6:7–9. See also Galatians 5:13–14; Colossians 3:25; 1 Peter 5:1–10.
62. 1 Corinthians 12.
63. Philippians 2:1–11.
64. George Jr., C. S. (1972). *The history of management thought.* (2nd ed.). Englewood Cliffs, NJ: Prentice-Hall, Inc. pp. 5–6.
65. George Jr., C. S. (1972). *The history of management thought.* (2nd ed.). Englewood Cliffs, NJ: Prentice-Hall, Inc. p. 7.
66. Wren, D. A. (1994). *The evolution of management thought.* San Francisco, CA: John Wiley & Sons, Inc. p. 16.
67. George Jr., C. S. (1972). *The history of management thought.* (2nd ed.). Englewood Cliffs, NJ: Prentice-Hall, Inc. p. 8.
68. George Jr., C. S. (1972). *The history of management thought.* (2nd ed.). Englewood Cliffs, NJ: Prentice-Hall, Inc. pp. 11–14, 18–19.
69. Wren, D. A. (1994). *The evolution of management thought.* (4th ed.). San Francisco, CA: John Wiley & Sons, Inc. pp. 17–18.
70. Hosseini, H. (1998). Seeking the roots of Adam Smith's division of labor in medieval Persia. *History of Political Economy.* 39(4), 653–681.
71. Wren, D. A. (1994). *The evolution of management thought.* (4th ed.). San Francisco, CA: John Wiley & Sons, Inc. p. 19.
72. Appleby, J. (2010). *The relentless revolution: A history of capitalism.* New York: W. W. Norton & Company. pp. 1–86.
73. Sheldrake, J. (2003). *Management theory.* London: Thomson. p. 10.
74. Freeman, M. (1996). Scientific management: 100 years old; poised for the next century. *SAM Advanced Management Journal.* 61(2), 35–41.
75. Taylor's book on scientific management has been considered the single most influential book during the 20th century. Bedeian, A. G., & Wren, D. A. (2001). Most influential management books of the 20th century. *Organizational Dynamics.* 29(3), 221–225; Taylor, F. W. (1903). *Shop management.* New York: Harper & Brothers; Taylor, F. W. (1911). *The principles of scientific management.* New York: Harper & Brothers.
76. "Although Taylor was not deeply committed to any particular religious dogma, his family were members of the Unitarian Church." Wrege, C. D., & Greenwood, R. G. (1991). *Frederick W. Taylor the father of scientific management: Myth and reality.* Homewood, IL: Business One Irwin. p. 221.
77. Taylor, F. W. (1903). *Shop management.* New York: Harper & Brothers.
78. Wren, D. A., & Greenwood, R. G. (1998). *Management innovators: The people and ideas that have shaped modern business.* New York: Oxford University Press.
79. Taylor, F. W. (1903). *Shop management.* New York: Harper & Brothers. p. 21.
80. Volf, M. (1991). *Work in the spirit: Toward a theology of work.* Eugene, OR: Wipf and Stock Publishers. pp. 174–176; Jensen, D. H. (2006). *Responsive labor: A theology of work.* Louisville, KY: Westminster John Knox Press. p. 104; Braverman, H. (1998). *Labor and monopoly capital: The degradation of work in the twentieth century.* New York: Monthly Review Press. pp. 85–138.
81. Wrege, C. D., & Hodgetts, R. M. (2000). Frederick W. Taylor's 1899 pig iron observations: Examining fact, fiction, and lessons for the new millennium. *Academy of Management Journal.* 43(6), 1283–1291; Wrege, C. D., & Perroni, A. G. (1974). Taylor's pig-tale: A historical analysis of Frederick W. Taylor's pig-iron experiments. *Academy of Management Journal.* 17(1), 6–27.
82. Gilbreth Jr., F. B., & Gilbreth-Carey, E. (1948). *Cheaper by the dozen.* New York: Bantam Books. The original movie was produced in 1950 by Lamar Trotti and directed by Walter Lang.
83. Emerson, H. (1924). The essence of efficiency: Letter to the editor. *New York Times.* December 7, p. X19.
84. Emerson, H. (1924). The essence of efficiency: Letter to the editor. *New York Times.* December 7, p. X19. Other newspaper articles about Harrington Emerson and his influence on the scientific management movement include the following: Anonymous (1911). The colossal waste in our business methods. *New York Times.* February 19, p. SM7; Anonymous. (1910). Special to the New York Times. *New York Times.* November 24, p. 8; Emerson, H. (1911). Saving by scientific management. *New York Times.* January 8, p. AFR7; Anonymous. (1911). Say Brandeis plan proves effective. *New York Times.* March 28, p. 10; Anonymous. (1912). Efficiency society a waste preventer. *New York Times.* November 6, p. 18.
85. Some passages offered in support of these ideas include Proverbs 14:8, 17:7; Matthew 10:16; 2 Corinthians 8:20–21; Philippians 1:9–10, 1:27; Colossians 4:5; 1 Peter 2:12; James 3:13.
86. For accounts of their contributions see Gilbreth, F. B. (1911). *Motion study.* New York: D. Van Nostrand Company; Gilbreth, F. B., & Gilbreth-Carey, E. (1948). *Cheaper by the dozen.* New York: Bantam Books; Gotcher, J. M. (1992). Assisting the handicapped: The efforts of Frank & Lillian Gilbreth. *Journal of Management. 18*(1), 5–14; Gilbreth, L. (1973). *The psychology of management.* Easton: Hive Publishing; Gilbreth, F., & Gilbreth, L. (1973). *Applied motion study.* Easton: Hive Publishing; Wren, D. A., & Greenwood, R. G. (1998). *Management innovators: The people and ideas that have shaped modern business.* New York: Oxford University Press.
87. Drucker, P. F. (1954). *The practice of management.* New York: Harper & Row. p. 280.
88. Fayol, H. (1937). The administrative theory of the state. In Gulick, L., & Urwick, L. (Eds.). *Papers on the science of administration.* New York: Institute of Public Administration at Columbia University.
89. Fayol, Henri (1949). *General and industrial management.* London: Pitman & Sons, Ltd.
90. Fayol, Henri (1949). *General and industrial management.* London: Pitman & Sons, Ltd.
91. Mintzberg, H. (1973). *The nature of managerial work.* New York: Harper & Row; Argyris, C. (1957).

Personality and organizations; The conflict between system and the individual. New York: HarperCollins; Drucker, P. F. (1973). *Management: Tasks, responsibilities, practices.* New York: Harper & Row; March, J. G., & Simon, H. A. (1958). *Organizations.* New York: Wiley.

92. See as examples Korukonda, A. R. (1992). Managerial action skills in business education: Missing link or misplaced emphasis? *S.A.M. Advanced Management Journal* 57(3), 27–34; Abraham, S. E., & Karns, L. A. (2009). Do business schools value the competencies that businesses value? *Journal of Education for Business.* 84(6), 350–356; Berry, P. (2009). Redesign of the undergraduate business curriculum: The way forward, a paradigm shift. *American Journal of Business Education.* 2(8), 55–63; Jackson, D. (2009). Undergraduate management education: Its place, purpose and efforts to bridge the skills gap. *Journal of Management & Organization.* 15, 206–223; Clarke, M., & Butcher, D. (2006). Reconciling hierarchy and democracy: The value of management learning. *Management Learning.* 37(3), 313–333; Elmuti, D. (2004). Can management be taught? *Management Decision.* 42(3/4), 439–453.
93. George Jr., C. S. (1972). *The history of management thought.* (2nd ed.). Englewood Cliffs, NJ: Prentice-Hall, Inc. p. 115; Wren, D. A. (1994). *The evolution of management thought.* (4th ed.). San Francisco, CA: John Wiley & Sons, Inc. p. 193.
94. Weber, M. (1947). *The theory of social and economic organizations.* Glencoe, IL: The Free Press; Collins, R. (1986). *Max Weber: A skeleton key.* Newbury Park: Sage Publications; Sheldrake, John (2003). *Management theory.* (2nd ed.). London: Thomson; Wren, D. A. (1994). *The evolution of management thought.* San Francisco: John Wiley & Sons.
95. Weber, M. (1930/1972). *The Protestant work ethic and the spirit of capitalism.* London: Allen and Unwin. p. 172.
96. George, C. S. (1972). *The history of management thought.* (2nd ed.). Englewood Cliffs, NJ: Prentice Hall. pp. 140–141.
97. Though Barnard didn't graduate from Harvard since he lacked a course in laboratory science, his understanding of economics colored his understanding of organizations. See Wren, D. A. (1994*). The evolution of management thought.* (4th ed.). San Francisco, CA: John Wiley & Sons, Inc. pp. 265–273.
98. Barnard, C. I. (1938). *The functions of the executive.* Cambridge: Harvard University Press.
99. Barnard was not the first to highlight the importance of coordination. For example, see Marshall, A. (1890). *Principles of economics.* London: Macmillan and Company, Ltd. Book IV, Chapter 8; Mill, J. S. (1862). *Principles of political economy.* London: Parker, Son and Bourn. Book I, Chapter VIII. 1.8.1.; Church, A. H. (1914). *The science and practice of management.* New York: The Engineering Magazine Company. pp. 101–102; Mooney, J. D. (1937). In Gulick, L. & Urwick, L. (Eds.). *Papers on the science of administration.* Fairfield, NJ: Augustus M. Kelley Publishers.
100. Gazell, J. A. (1970). Authority-flow theory and the impact of Chester Barnard. *California Management Review.* 13(1), 68–74.
101. Owen, R. (1991/1816). *A new view of society and other writings.* New York: Penguin Classics. p. 5.
102. Roethlisberger, J. F. (1946). *Management and morale.* Cambridge, MA: Harvard University Press. pp. 7–26; Mayo, E. (1945). *The social problems of an industrial civilization*, Boston: Division of Research, Graduate School of Business Administration, Harvard University; Crainer, S. (2000). *The management century: A critical review of 20th century thought and practice.* San Francisco, CA: Jossey-Bass Publishers.
103. Sethi, N. K. (1962, December). Mary Parker Follett: Pioneer in management theory. *Academy of Management Journal, 5*, 214–221; Graham, P. (Ed.). (1995). *Mary Parker Follett—Prophet of management: A celebration of writings from the 1920s.* Boston, MA: Harvard Business School Press; Fox, E. M. (1968, Nov/Dec). Mary Parker Follett: The enduring contribution. *Public Administration Review, 28*, 250–260; Parker, L. D. (1984). Control in organizational life: The contribution of Mary Parker Follett. *Academy of Management Review, 9*, 734–745; Wren, D. A. (1994). *The evolution of management thought.* (4th ed.). New York: John Wiley & Sons, Inc.
104. Bedeian, A. G., & Wren, Daniel A. (2001). Most influential management books of the 20th century. *Organizational Dynamics.* 29(3), 221–225.
105. Some of these are included in Bedeian, A. G., & Wren, D. A. (2001). Most influential management books of the 20th century. *Organizational Dynamics.* 29(3), 221–225.
106. Drucker, P. F. (1954). *The practice of management.* New York: Harper & Row. pp. 157–158.
107. Wren, D. A. (1994). *The evolution of management thought.* San Francisco: John Wiley & Sons. pp. 365–367.
108. Greco, J. (1999, Sept/Oct). Alfred P. Sloan, Jr. (1875–1966): The original "organization" man. *The Journal of Business Strategy*, 29(5), 30–31; Sloan Jr., A. P. (1963). *My years with General Motors.* Garden City, NY: Doubleday; Sloan Jr., A. P. (1941). *Adventures of a white-collar man.* New York: Doubleday, Doran & Co.
109. Mayo, E. (1960). *The human problems of an industrial civilization.* New York: Viking Press; Mayo, E. (1977). *The social problems of an industrial civilization.* New York: Arno Press; O'Connor, E. S. (1999). Minding the workers: The meaning of "human" and "human relations" in Elton Mayo. *Organization.* 6(2), 233–246; Sarachek, B. (1968). Elton Mayo's social psychology and human relations. *Academy of Management Journal.* 11(2), 189–197; Smith, J. H. (1998). The enduring legacy of Elton Mayo. *Human Relations. 51*(3), 221–249.
110. Chandler, A. D. (1962). *Strategy and structure: Chapters in the history of the industrial enterprise.* Cambridge: MIT Press; Chandler, A. D. (1977). *The visible hand: The managerial revolution in American business.* Cambridge: The Belknap Press; Chandler, A. D. (1992, Summer). Organizational capabilities and the economic history of the industrial enterprise. *The Journal of Economic Perspectives.* 6, 79–100; Chandler, A. D. (1990). *Scale and scope: The dynamics of industrial capitalism.* Cambridge: The Belknap Press.
111. Maslow, A. H. (1943). A theory of human motivation. *Psychological Review.* 50, 370–396; Maslow, A. H. (1965). *Eupsychian management, A journal.* Homewood, IL: Richard D, Irwin & Dorsey; Heylighen, F. (1992).

A cognitive-systemic reconstruction of Maslow's theory of self-actualization. *Behavioral Science.* 37(1), 39–59; Maslow, A. (1954). *Motivation and personality.* New York: Harper and Row; Maslow, A. (1998). *Maslow on management.* New York: John Wiley.

112. Deming, W. E. (1986). *Out of the crisis.* Cambridge, MA: MIT Center for Advanced Engineering Study; Landesberg, P. (1999, Nov/Dec). In the beginning, there were Deming and Juran. *The Journal for Quality & Participation*, 59-60; Walton, M. (1986). *The Deming management method.* New York: Perigee Books; Gabor, A. (2000). Remembrance—W. Edwards Deming made America think about quality. *Fortune.* 142(10), 292; Gabor, A. (2000). *The capitalist philosophers: The geniuses of modern business—their lives, times, and ideas.* New York: Times Business.
113. Juran, J. M., & Godfrey, A. B. (Eds.) (1999). *Juran's quality handbook.* New York: McGraw-Hill; Juran, J. M. (1995). *Managerial breakthrough: The classic book on improving management performance.* New York: McGraw-Hill; Juran, J. M. (1989). *Juran on leadership for quality: An executive handbook.* New York: The Free Press.
114. Ansoff, H. I. (1957). Strategies for diversification. *Harvard Business Review.* 35(5), 113–124; Ansoff, H. I. (1965). *Corporate strategy.* New York: McGraw-Hill; Ansoff, H. I. (1988). *The new corporate strategy.* New York: John Wiley & Sons.
115. Herzberg, F. (1966). *Work and the nature of man.* New York: New World Publishing Co.; Herzberg, F. (1979). Motivation and innovation: Who are workers serving? *California Management Review.* 22(2), 60–70; Herzberg, F. (2003). One more time: How do you motivate employees? *Harvard Business Review.* 81(1), 87–96; Wall, T. D., & Stephenson, G. M. (1970). Herzberg's two-factor theory of job attitudes: A critical evaluation and some fresh evidence. *Industrial Relations Journal.* 1(3), 41–65.
116. McGregor, D. (1960). *The human side of enterprise.* New York: McGraw-Hill Co.; McGregor, D., McGregor, C., & Bennis, W. (Eds.). (1967). *The professional manager.* New York: McGraw-Hill, Inc.
117. Ouchi, W. (1981). *Theory Z: How American business can meet the Japanese challenge.* Reading, MA: Addison-Wesley.
118. Handy, C. (1989). *The age of unreason.* London: Arrow Books; Handy, C. (1999). *Understanding organizations.* (4th ed.). Harmondsworth: Penguin Books; Handy, C. (1994). *The age of paradox.* Cambridge, MA: Harvard Business School Press.
119. Hofstede, G. (1980). *Culture's consequences: International differences in work related values.* Beverly Hills, CA: Sage Publications; Hofstede, G. (1991). *Cultures and organizations: Software of the mind.* London: Harper Collins Business; Hofstede, G. (1993). Cultural constraints in management theories. *The Executive.* 7(1), 81–94.
120. Mintzberg, H. (1973). *The nature of managerial work.* New York: Harper & Row; Mintzberg, H. (1975). The manager's job: Folklore and fact. *Harvard Business Review, 53*(4), 49–61; Mintzberg, H. (2001). Decision making: It's not what you think. *MIT Sloan Management Review.* 42(3), 89–93; Mintzberg, H., & Lampel, J. (1999). Reflecting on the strategy process. *MIT Sloan Management Review.* 40(3), 21–30; Mintzberg, H. (1979) *The structuring of organizations: A synthesis of the research.* Englewood Cliffs, NJ: Prentice-Hall; Mintzberg, H. (1994). *The rise and fall of strategic planning: Reconceiving roles for planning, plans and planners.* New York: The Free Press; Mintzberg, H. (1990). The design school: Reconsidering the basic premises of strategic management. *Strategic Management Journal.* 11(3), 171–195.
121. Porter, M. E., & Kramer, M. R. (2006). Strategy and society: The link between competitive advantages and corporate social responsibility. *Harvard Business Review.* 84(12), 78–92; Porter, M. E., & Kramer, M. R. (2002). The competitive advantage of corporate philanthropy. *Harvard Business Review.* 80(12), 56–69; Porter, M. E. (2001). Strategy and the Internet. *Harvard Business Review.* 79(3), 62–78; Porter, M. E. (1980). *Competitive strategy.* New York: The Free Press; Porter, M. E. (1985). *Competitive advantage: Creating and sustaining superior performance.* New York: The Free Press; Porter, M. (1996). What is strategy? *Harvard Business Review.* 74(6), 61–78; Porter, M. E. (1990). *The competitive advantage of nations.* New York: The Free Press.
122. Schein, E. (1992). *Organizational culture and leadership.* San Francisco: Jossey-Bass; Schein, E. (1996). Three cultures of management: The key to organizational learning. *Sloan Management Review,* 38(1), 9–20; Schein, E. H. (1996). Culture: The missing concept in organizational studies. *Administrative Science Quarterly.* 41(2), 229–240; Schein, E. H. (1989). Reassessing the "Divine Rights" of managers. *Sloan Management Review.* 30(2), 63–68; Schein, E. H. (1988). Organizational socialization and the profession of management. *Sloan Management Review.* 30(1), 53–65.
123. Indeed the experience of society in terms of commercial activities has always been interrelated with social issues. On this assumption see Appleby, J. (2010). *The relentless revolution: A history of capitalism.* New York: W. W. Norton & Company. p. 118.
124. Yates, J. (1989). *Control through communication: The rise of system in American management.* Baltimore, MD: The Johns Hopkins University Press; Wren, Daniel A. (1994). *The evolution of management thought.* (4th ed.). San Francisco, CA: John Wiley & Sons, Inc. pp. 75–76.
125. Gibson, J. W., & Tesone, D. V. (2001). Management fads: Emergence, evolution, and implications for managers. *The Academy of Management Executive.* 15(4), 122–133.
126. Horton, T. R. (1988). That old management magic. *Management Review.* 77(4), 5–7; Stern, S. (2007). The next big thing. *Management Today.* April, 50–51; Stansfield, T., & Massey, R. (2007). A remedy to fad fatigue. *Industrial Management.* 49(2), 26–30; Hymowitz, C. (2006). Executives must stop jumping fad to fad and learn to manage. *Wall Street Journal* (Eastern Edition). May 15, B1; Hilmer F. G., & Donaldson, L. (1996). *Management redeemed: Debunking the fads that undermine our corporations.* New York: The Free Press; Williams, R. (2004). Management fashions and fads: Understanding the role of consultants and managers in the evolution of ideas. *Management Decision.* 42(5/6), 769–780; Gibson, J. W., & Tesone, D. V. (2001). Management fads: Emergence, evolution and

implications for managers. *The Academy of Management Executive.* 15(4), 122–133; Abrahamson, E. (1991). Managerial fads and fashions: The diffusion and rejection of innovations. *The Academy of Management Review.* 16(3), 586–611; Abrahamson, E. (1996). Management fashion. *The Academy of Management Review.* 21(1), 254–285; Carson, P. P., Lanier, P. A., Carson, K. D., & Berkenmeier, B. J. (1999). An historical perspective on fad adoption and abandonment: Developing theory from the management fad jungle. *Journal of Management History.* 5, 320–333.

127. This story is told and evaluated in Roth, G., & Kleiner, A. (1998). Developing organizational memory through learning histories. *Organizational Dynamics.* 27(2), 43–60.
128. Weick, K. E. (1979). *The social psychology of organizing.* Reading, MA: Addison-Wesley. p. 7.
129. Weldon, V. (1996). Faith and values in a corporate environment. *Vital Speeches of the Day.* 62(15), 461–462; Weick, Karl E. (1979). *The social psychology of organizing.* (2nd ed.). New York: McGraw-Hill, Inc. p. 205.
130. Santayana, G. (1905). *The life of reason: Or, the phases of human progress.* New York: C. Scribner's Sons. p. 284.
131. Interview with Henry Ford in: *Chicago Tribune.* May 25, 1916.
132. Widgery, A. G. (1967). *The meanings of history.* London: George Allen & Unwin, Ltd. p. 93.
133. Babson, R. W. (1920). *Religion and business.* New York: The Macmillan Company. p. 96.

CHAPTER 3

External and Internal Environment

LEARNING OBJECTIVES

- Understand the importance of developing systems thinking for managerial success.
- Consider a systems view from a Christian worldview perspective.
- Distinguish between the various elements of a system and how systems operate.
- Understand the major elements of an organization's external environment that the organization must adjust to in pursuing organizational goals.
- Understand what an organization's internal environment is and how organizational culture is embedded into the work lives of employees.
- Be aware of the cognitive tensions related to an organization as it interacts with the environment.

"A cloud masses, the sky darkens, leaves twist upward, and we know that it will rain. We also know that after the storm, the runoff will feed into the groundwater miles away, and the sky will grow clear by tomorrow. All these events are distant in time and space, and yet they are all connected within the same pattern. Each has an influence on the rest, an influence that is usually hidden from view. You can only understand the system of a rainstorm by contemplating the whole, not any individual part of the pattern. Business and other human endeavors are also systems."[1]

BAXTER BELAFONTE

Baxter Belafonte adjusted the ear piece from his MP3 player that he had accidently pulled loose when reaching into his file cabinet. He was looking for a written report that he had submitted last month to the company president requesting authorization to hire one more machine maintenance worker.

He allowed the music to clear his head from the stress that had mounted just before lunch. He began thinking about the organizational culture as it was impacting his departments. His first thought was that if his workers had just a few more resources, he might have prevented what happened earlier in the morning. But there may be a better solution than just hiring another worker.

Belafonte had been hired to oversee six support departments in a small manufacturing company: janitorial, maintenance, landscaping, telecommunications, security, and transportation. The maintenance workers performed preventive maintenance on production machines to minimize the risks of machines breaking down during production. Maintenance workers were stationed in the department, ready to provide immediate help. Sometimes preventive maintenance was only partially completed because a machine breakdown somewhere else required a maintenance worker to drop everything and tend to the broken machine. The production department depended on the expertise of the maintenance staff but they sometimes treated maintenance workers rudely, especially when the department was under pressure to reach the weekly production goals.

Source: Dmitry Kalinovsky/Shutterstock.

Landscaping services was largely isolated from the goings-on inside the plant. Transportation services provided vehicles for executives and middle managers to use for special purposes. As long as the transportation manager followed the priority protocols, the department encountered few disputes, since managers had learned that they must plan ahead to get access to equipment.

Telecommunications had a different set of issues to deal with, which usually involved maintaining continuous connections for telephone, broadband Internet, wireless, internal closed-circuit television monitoring used by security, and the electronic access system for doors and gates. Since becoming a manager, Baxter had proposed that the telecommunications and security departments be merged into one so they could work more closely together but the company president had flatly refused.

This morning, instead of asking maintenance to take machine parts to the designated clean-up area for processing, a machine operator decided to carry a pail of toxic solvent to his machine to clean the parts himself. He wanted to get his machine up and running as soon as possible and he knew it might be an hour before maintenance could do it for him. In his haste, he did not put a cover on the pail. Rounding the corner of one of the production machines, he bumped into a maintenance worker coming from the other direction. When the two collided, toxic liquid spilled under a production machine.

A flurry of shouts and phone calls brought together a small group of people to figure out what to do. Production on that machine had come to a halt because the worker operating the machine did not want to be breathing toxic fumes. One by one other machine operators in the vicinity shut down their machines, partly out of support for their coworker and partly out of anxiety over fumes. Within 2 minutes the company president had been notified. Baxter had been notified 2 minutes after that.

When the president saw Baxter arrive on scene, he lit into him with a tirade. "Why is it that when something goes haywire in this place, it is maintenance or janitorial that screwed things up? And where were you when this happened? How come you are the last to find out about this mess?"

Baxter started to say, "Let's find out what happened in the system before we lay blame . . . "

The president cut him off. "If your workers had been doing their job, production would not have had to carry uncovered pails of solvent around doing the work of your team. You need to get control of your people, Belafonte. I want to see a report on my desk by the end of today outlining how you are going to do this."

Baxter's thought to himself: *How can I explain to the boss that this is primarily a systems problem?*

Who Cares About Systems?

One reason organizations hire managers is to help them think clearly about relevant things happening inside and outside the organization. Managers are called to help organizational members practice **systemic thinking**, which means considering both the external and internal environments in which work takes place. Managers are important voices for what is happening outside of the organization. They play an important role in managing the culture on the inside of the organization.

If you could remove the roof of the Blistex® factory in Oakbrook, Illinois and place a video camera high enough in the sky so that every building, employee, doorway, and loading dock came into view, you would see similar activity across the factory. Blistex is one of the leading companies that makes and sells personal lip-care products.[2] It is in competition with companies such as Carmex, Clearasil, and Phisoderm. Lip-care products are a small subsegment of the larger toilet preparation manufacturing industry.[3]

With the aid of time-lapse photography, you would see delivery vehicles drive up to the outside physical boundaries of the organization and deliver their cargoes of chemicals and other materials. Other vehicles drive up to receive finished goods to take to the market.

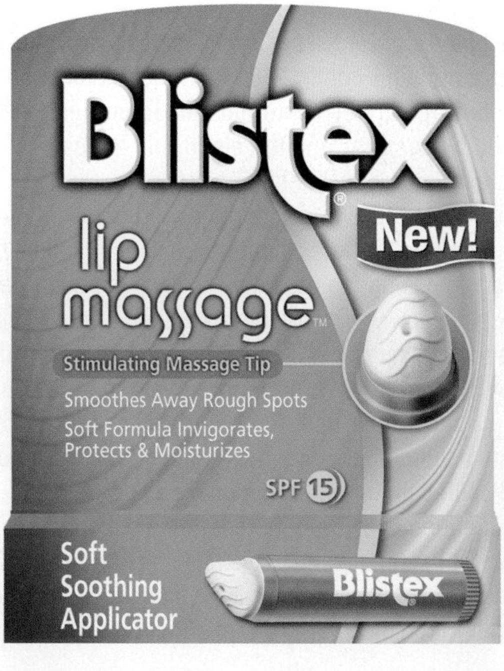

Source: PRNewsFoto/Blistex.

The Blistex factory is a good illustration of an organizational system at work within a larger external environment.

"It is widely held, this idea that there is some technique or system waiting round the corner and all the busy executive has got to do is to buy a yard or two of it and slap it on the affected part. It is, of course, nonsense. Every business enterprise is a living organism, with its own traditions, its own climate of opinion, its own special make-up. Every situation is different. And every kind of system has to be custom-built to the individual business. A method that is a gold mine for corporation A will be pure poison for corporation B."[4]

EXHIBIT 3-1
Organizations as Systems

Inside the organization you see patterned movements of materials and people as they go from room to room, tend the equipment, or conduct small group meetings. Workers talk with each other individually, in small groups, or on the telephone. Managers send and receive written and electronic communications with each other and with the outside world. Other managers and supervisors read indicators on machinery and computer reports on-screen or printed on paper. All this is taking place in ways that connect the organization with the larger context of society.

In essence you would see in action what we call a system.[5] A **system** is an organized arrangement of elements that are interdependent and interconnected to form a purposeful, organic whole.

Systemic thinking is vital to managers anytime they are expected to help make changes in the organization. The reason: Nothing ever operates in complete isolation from everything else. If you change one thing in your department, other changes will likely follow in other places in the organization. For example, at appliance manufacturer Whirlpool, if managers decide to separate the sheet metal fabrication team, which shapes the exterior body of washing machines, from the team that puts together subassemblies such as components, then someone must make sure that fabrication workers coordinate their efforts with subassembly workers. Likewise, an awareness of the organization's culture is vital to making changes. Less experienced managers sometimes forget how their organization is connected to the outside world or sometimes lose touch with the internal organizational culture. When implementing organizational changes, managers may be surprised at how much resistance to change subordinates and fellow managers might harbor. To be effective, managers must maintain an awareness that they are working within a whole system that is part of an even larger system in society.[6] Every manager who has attempted to copy a best practice from a competitor has learned how difficult it can be to take ideas from one company and use them effectively in another. What works well in one organization may not work nearly as well in your company. One reason this is true is that the two organizations are different as systems. The people, the procedures, and the shared values are all different. See Exhibit 3-1.

Management Pyramid: Systems Thinking

One interesting thing about organizations is that the people and departments can be closely interrelated to each other. Here's an example. When the market research team presents the results of their consumer behavior studies, the new product development department, production department, and the sales team may need to make adjustments. Or, take the example of the purchasing department that creates a new form for managers to use when placing orders for materials and supplies. The form requires managers to provide more information than they are accustomed to giving. This requires the managers to make subtle changes so that they can gather the information prior to ordering.

The point is that persons inside the organization are interrelated, forever connected to each other; persons inside the organization are also connected with elements of the outside environment. This means that one person truly can make a difference! It also means that a person can take an action without realizing the unwanted, unintended consequences that it has on other people or organizations. Sometimes the influence of just one person has ripple effects on other people who then work change in an entire industry or even for society as a

Actions in one section of the organization have a ripple effect throughout the organization and even beyond Changes in procedures in one department may require adjustments in procedures in other departments	Action
Thinking about events, behavior patterns, and systemic structures Making sense of the external environment Anticipating what might happen next	Thinking & Feeling
Beliefs Perceptions Moral values Organizational culture: Shared organizational values and assumptions Assumptions regarding the behavior of other employees or persons in the external environment	Being & Becoming

EXHIBIT 3-2

The Management Pyramid: Systems Thinking

Source: Courtesy of Michael E. Cafferky, © Michael E. Cafferky 2011.

whole. More commonly, it is the collective effect of managers, workers, and leaders in several industries that influences an entire industry or society. And the opposite is true, too. One change in the external environment such as a new regulation, the action of a competitor, or a change in consumer tastes will likely have ripple effects on many people inside the organization. See Exhibit 3-2.

Actions that have ripple effects normally begin at the level of assumptions and beliefs. For example, a new manager decides that instead of making a long list of announcements in the weekly staff meeting he will just post them on a bulletin board in the staff lounge. He assumes that since staff meeting time is not taken up with making announcements, employees will go to the lounge to read them. This seems like a reasonable assumption. Later he remembers that three staff members are out of the office a lot and do not frequent the staff lounge just to read the latest announcements. Because these three employees have contact with other departments and outside organizations they don't pass along important information to these stakeholders. It's not long before these other people are being left "out of the loop" and, as a result, not doing what the organization expects. After hours of delays and wasted time, the manager revises his assumption and changes his approach to communication.

In this chapter we focus on managerial thinking about systems both inside and outside the organization. We start with the Christian faith perspective because it is an important part of the Christian's personal beliefs and values (the "being and becoming" part of the Management Pyramid model).

Faith Perspective on Open Systems

An **open system** is a system that the outside environment has some influence on. For example, the performance of the accounts payable department of an organization depends on the accuracy of information contained on invoices, packing slips, and purchase orders—all of which are generated outside the accounts payable department.

Many principles of systems align with Christian teachings. That humans are part of a larger set of systems can be demonstrated in biology and ecology.[7] But how "high" do systems go? Are the only systems those that we can observe in human time and space?

The Bible teaches that a larger, broader system exists that encompasses realities accepted by faith and included in religious experience. However, humans are limited in their ability to view all dimensions of our time-and-space systems.[8] See Exhibit 3-3.

Hierarchical View of Open Systems

Christian teaching takes a hierarchical view to open systems that allows for a context larger than what is considered in the traditional humanistic approach to physical and social sciences.

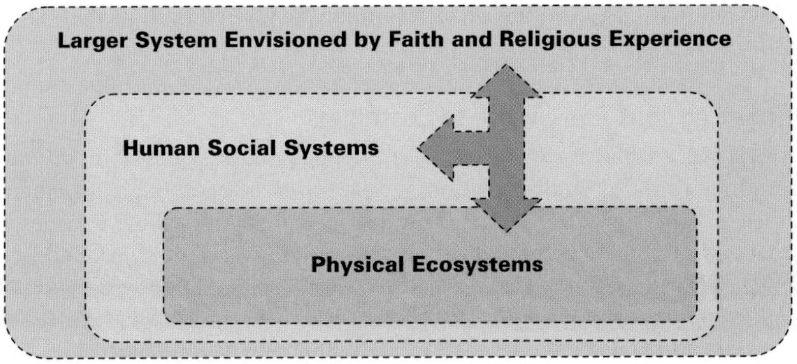

EXHIBIT 3-3
Three Levels of Systems in Human Experience

A Christian worldview includes the belief that life is lived within a divinely created system that encompasses all human and physical subsystems.[9] As such its parameter is not measured directly by empirical science but is believed to exist as demonstrated in the recurring patterns of religious experience across many cultures and times. Because of this, the Christian worldview assumes an open system, which embraces everything including the existence of God, a viewpoint that many people in North America agree with.[10]

We might not be able to observe God directly in a scientific manner but Christians believe that he observes us, the Earth, and everything in it.[11] Belief in his existence will be factored in when considering everything that happens on Earth.

System Elements Are Interrelated and Interdependent

God created social community for mutual service. Acting in his image, we create social organizations to serve each other's needs. We are part of an interdependent relational community forever linked with each other around the globe and with all other life forms on our planet. As members of this larger community, we have the responsibility to care for each other regardless of whether the other person is a member of the same community of faith.[12]

The Bible writers' perspectives are consistent with systems thinking. For example, when Paul describes the church, he uses the metaphor of the body, which contains interdependent and interrelated parts working together toward a common purpose. Spiritual gifts are seen in this context and are to be used in service to each other.[13]

A Christian worldview holds that managers achieve genuine meaning when they are open to the divine influences of the larger system and see their work in the larger context of all Creation in its relationship to God. This presents the Christian manager with an opportunity to be both a recipient of and a channel for redemption to encourage openness to spiritual and moral realities.

In practical terms for the Christian, systems include more than just the materials, personnel, equipment, and supplies required to make and deliver products and services. Inputs also include the moral and spiritual values that decision makers bring to their work, the attitude of community, and respect for the ecosystems.

The Natural Human Tendency

The natural tendency for humans is to avoid moral constraints because these place unwanted fetters on our desires. The Bible teaches that by nature humans are notoriously and quite destructively self-centered individuals who attempt to use the social community and the Earth's natural resources for selfish or unfair personal gain. For all the good that humans can do for each other, economic scarcity of resources tends to bring out the worst in people.[14] Some humans may attempt to shape their organizational systems to take advantage of others. If unrestrained, this tendency leads to human systems that become closed to moral and spiritual influences. As this happens moral or spiritual decay results in a crisis of meaning and purpose.[15]

Yet not all self-interested behavior is selfish. To survive humans cannot be completely self-centered; they must take into consideration the needs of others when pursuing their own legitimate interests. Humans can be extraordinarily unselfish, considering the needs of other people before their own. But collectively we need a rule of law that imposes moral constraints on individuals. And we need an impartial justice system that supports legal constraints.

Organizational Systems Carry Value to Customers

When we work, we transform raw materials into goods and services with an understanding that we are all stewards of God's creation and stewards of each other. In managing work processes, the Christian looks for ways that customers can get everything they deserve. It is in the core processes of value creation where service to others and glory to God is co-created. A Christian worldview will lead a manager not only toward quality improvement but also toward working to eliminate the underlying sources of potential distrust that customers may have.

It follows that Christians are interested in the moral values represented by what organizations produce as these values are the vehicles of interconnection with the community, carriers of value expected by the customer, and representative of the human response to God. The Christian manager will view these as more than mere value-laden carriers of the organization's brand. Organizational outputs are the result of human hands co-working with God in the ongoing work on behalf of others.

Necessary Conditions for Effective Systems

For this approach to work effectively, Christian managers need feedback based on integrity and truthfulness. Without an accurate understanding of the marketplace, our assumptions about customers, suppliers, and competitors will be flawed and will lead to mistakes.

Truth-telling also requires that the individual continually resist self-deception. The feedback that is generated through self reflection and religious experience helps a manager continue to make sense of human experience in light of religious beliefs. This feedback is a vital part of becoming transformed as a leader. Active in this process, a Christian leader will work to support individual responsibility, starting with personal responsibility.[16]

Interaction with the open social system provides opportunities to express deep values in action. Because of this, Christian managers will desire not to isolate moral principles from economic life but instead to find creative ways to infuse economic life with moral principles.[17] Christian managers will resist moral decay in social systems, and, when it is within their power and ability, they will try to heal broken relationships in these systems.

As you can see, the social systems environment is important to the Christian manager. To explore this further, we will consider contemporary views on the external and the internal environments. These comprise the context in which a manager is being and becoming, thinking and feeling, and acting. Let's start by considering systems thinking and the external environment.

The Biblical Story of Noah

Read the story of Noah recorded in Genesis 5–9 in the Bible. Grasp the significance of the accomplishments that occurred under the leadership of Noah. What strengths and weaknesses can you see in Noah's leadership experience? What leadership principles can we gain from the experience of Noah that are applicable today?

Systems Thinking

We've introduced the idea of systems and systems thinking from the Christian perspective. Now let's consider the nature of systems from a scientific point of view starting with the components of systems.

Components of Systems

Any system, however large and complex or small and simple, contains at minimum the following elements: the external environment, inputs, transformation processes, outputs, and feedback loops. Let's consider Blistex again.

EXHIBIT 3-4
Blistex as a System

The **external environment** is the larger system or context within which a company operates. For Blistex, for example, this includes the skin care industry, the wholesale and retail marketplace, suppliers and their industries, competitors like Carmex, the legal environment of the State of Illinois and the U.S. government, the social and cultural environment that continually shapes consumer tastes, the economic forces at work in society, as well as international organizations and their activities. See Exhibit 3-4.

Inputs provide the elements needed to accomplish the organization's goal. For example, inputs to the Blistex company, whose goal is to be a leader in lip care, include the following: recipes, ingredients,[18] packaging materials and supplies, employees, legal constraints, federal and state regulations, the organizational mission, personal values of leaders, information from the outside environment, information from internal feedback, personal influence of managers, agreements with suppliers and wholesalers or retailers, work schedules, work plans, quality control policies, and procedures. Because Blistex operates within an uncertain, changing environment, the inputs are neither constant nor guaranteed. They must be managed—which is one reason why an organization like Blistex hires people to be managers.

Transformation processes occur as work is performed in pursuit of the organization's core purpose in creating value in its products. Supporting work (accounting, purchasing, maintenance) helps those at the core of the organization do their work efficiently and effectively. Transformation of ingredients into lip-care products, for example, does not happen automatically. Managers must direct, organize, and monitor specific tasks throughout transformation processes.

Outputs are the things that organizations produce for use by others. For example, at Blistex, outputs are primarily the 18 different products that it releases into the marketing channels for distribution and retail sale in hundreds of thousands of stores worldwide. But outputs can also include things as diverse as waste products, innovative ideas that new product development teams create, information that one support department provides another department, and the influences that the company has in the local community.

Feedback loops are components of a system that provide information that is used to make corrections or improvements in transformation processes. At Blistex, feedback loops are managerial control systems, budget reports, operational reports, quality control reports, informal conversations between managers and subordinates, technical-mechanical-electrical control systems attached to machinery, and customer feedback.[19] Managers need to design feedback loops to move the company toward its goals and use them on a consistent basis in order for them to be effective.

Organizational systems operate along several observable parameters that have direct implications for managers and their day-to-day work.

- **Interconnectivity.** Every person in every organization and every organization within every community or industry is connected with another. This **interconnectivity** is so prevalent that we sometimes lose sight of how important it is.
- **Interdependency.** Every organization as a system is "dependent upon the larger stream of life in which it occurs."[20] Because one organization has business relationships with a host of other organizations, these organizations become dependent on each other. We call this mutual dependence **interdependence**. It is the manager's job to see that interdependency flourishes.
- **Boundaries.** Every organization has one or more boundaries that separate it from the larger society. Boundaries are more than the physical walls of buildings that separate workers

from the outside environment. **Boundaries** are anything that separates the organization from the outside world such as the legal boundaries that separate one firm from another, firewalls that protect information systems, physical security systems and personnel that prevent access to proprietary information, and differences in perceptions of value. The more closed an organization is to the outside environment the more protected it is. But the more closed it becomes, the more difficult it is for other organizations and individuals to do business with each other. It is the manager's job to ensure that boundaries are managed appropriately so that the company is open enough as a system to be effective in its mission as it looks out for the interests of others but also closed enough to be efficient as it protects its own interests.

- **Decay** (entropy). Of all the parameters listed here, decay is the most feared. Without attention by managers, many organizations will eventually begin to break down and fail. For example, if employees in the Blistex purchasing department stopped ordering ingredients, supplies, and materials, the whole operation would grind to a halt. Likewise, if the finished goods were not shipped out the door, Blistex would soon need to stop production, due to lack of room to store inventory.
- **Change.** Because they are connected to the outside environment, which changes, organizations are constantly changing, too. This requires departments, work units, and individuals to change their work processes and procedures from time to time. It is the manager's job to help manage change.
- **Limited variety.** Most systems are open and, over time, tend to reflect the variety that is present in the outside environment. Every different area of the environment that has a significant interaction with the organization represents variety. For example, there are many different types of consumers, each of which has a different set of needs and wants that may be filled by Blistex products. The government represents another source of variety in that many different regulations apply to the company and its operations. Managers need to be aware of the outside environment. They make judgments regarding the specialized tasks the organization needs to accomplish inside to meet the demands of the outside environment.
- **Purpose and meaning.** From one point of view, the whole work of a manager is to help systems achieve their overall organizational goals. This perspective is valid, but its sole focus on the inner workings of the organization as a system obscures an important parameter of the larger social systems that are rooted outside an organization in a community: namely *purpose* and *meaning*. Social systems such as business organizations that create value for society in particular ways gather particular inputs, transform these through specific work processes, and create particular outputs for their customers.[21] The overall purpose of the organization is what unifies it as a system to serve society.[22] A business does not exist merely for its own sake as an end in itself but rather for the sake of the greater good in society.[23] An organization's shared meaning is shaped by accomplishing the particular greater good defined by the organization's purpose. If an organization loses its sense of mission, decay begins to occur and managers must take corrective action. In part, it is the manager's calling to serve a work community by helping the organization's members collectively to create meaningful contributions of value to society. Through the manager's leadership, workers come to understand the contribution they are making to the specific community[24] value created by the organization. The meaning of their own work is connected with the meaning of the entire company.

To explore the external environment more completely, we will take a tour of Greyston Bakery in Yonkers, New York.[25] The day-to-day experiences of Greyston managers provide an illustration of the key elements of the external environment.

The External Environment

Managers at Greyston face an environment that is neither static nor completely certain. It is impossible for them to predict with certainty the demand for the company's products, what products customers will want next year, the availability of employees, changes that might take

Greyston Bakery has a reputation for its brownies.

place with suppliers, or future actions by competing bakeries. Because of these and other uncertainties, managers must do their best to manage the company's relationship with the external environment.

Greyston is known for its high-quality desserts, its company philosophy that encourages employment of local disadvantaged residents, and its support of other social causes. Greyston's profits, generated from the work of over 60 employees, are contributed to the Greyston Foundation, a nonprofit organization that helps individuals with medical care and social services.

Try baking one pan of chocolate brownies at home. If you follow the recipe, keep the oven temperature just right, and get the brownies out of the oven at just the right time, then you have a chance that they will come out tasting very good. Now imagine that you are the sole supplier of brownies for Ben & Jerry's Ice Cream, as Greyston has been. Try making a few thousand pans of brownies using efficient production line systems, large quantities of ingredients, and large mixing machines and ovens. Getting the right ingredients in one door and thousands of brownies to come out the other door tasting delicious is not easy.

To accomplish this, managers at Greyston must do more than make sure that employees follow large-scale recipes correctly. They must deal with the external environment on two levels. One level, which is closest to the company, is what we call the **task environment**—where an organization transacts business with customers, suppliers, and workers, and where competitors have a direct influence on customers. Most of the strategic and operational decisions are made in the task environment. The second level of the environment Greyston managers must be aware of is the larger *general environment*—the environment that influences all businesses and citizens. Let's explore the elements of the task environment first. See Exhibit 3-5.

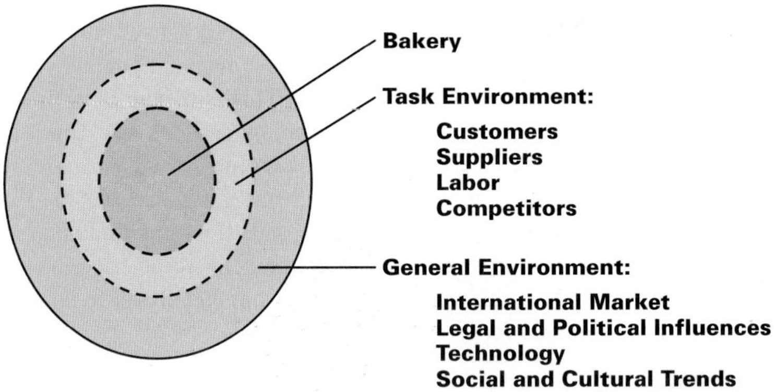

EXHIBIT 3-5

The Environment of a Commercial Bakery

Elements of the Task Environment

Much of what a manager does is focused on serving the needs of others outside the organization who have a stake in what the organization does. We will consider each major group.

CUSTOMERS. One of the elements of the task environment that managers at many companies must deal with is the moving target of customer expectations and preferences. Something as simple as changing customer preferences for more or less of one flavoring such as almond requires changes in the management of the task environment. Greyston supplies baked goods that other companies such as upscale restaurants and gourmet food stores resell. Some of these resellers promote these products under their own brand name. Greyston also sells products through the Internet. Other potential customer groups include supermarkets, institutional food services, coffee shops, and convenience stores. Organizations and individuals who want a custom cake for a special occasion can also buy directly from the bakery. To serve these companies and individuals, Greyston must have easy access for distributing fresh baked goods every day within their region.

This means that there are two dominant types of customers that Greyston must keep in view: the commercial buyers at other organizations (chefs, managers, purchasing agents) who resell the Greyston products and the end-user consumers who eat the desserts produced by Greyston. These two customer groups are the company's lifeblood for the future.

An important dimension of the outside environment is Greyston's relationships with customers. Individuals who order chocolate cake at restaurants may not realize that they are ordering a Greyston brand product. These dessert lovers probably have no need to develop a relationship with the bakery. But for the chef who serves perishable and fragile food items such as gourmet cakes and tarts, relationships are important.

Greyston depends on its commercial customers. Its commercial customers depend on Greyston. Because dependence is a two-way street in this case, interdependence is at work. To manage this interdependence, Greyston managers might prefer to have a small number of commercial customers who place large orders on a consistent basis. This is more efficient than selling small orders to many commercial customers. With fewer accounts, the company managers might be able to have a closer relationship with their customers—something that their customers might prefer, too. However, if one of the few large customers decides to switch to another bakery, this could cause a major internal disruption for bakery managers and workers. In reality, bakery managers must balance their interest in serving customers that help them achieve efficiencies against the risk that these same customers can switch to a competitor at any time.

SUPPLIERS. Every company has one or more tangible or intangible raw materials, ingredients, or supplies that are used to create value for customers on a daily basis. Service companies require materials and qualified service personnel. Greyston, for example, produces about 11,000 pounds of chocolate brownies every day. To meet Ben & Jerry's requirements on a daily basis, managers must ensure that the company has ready access to all the ingredients—flour, sugar, fat, milk, chocolate, vanilla, packaging, and so on—in sufficient quantities so that production does not stop.

Like the relationship with commercial customers, the interdependent relationship with suppliers is important. Suppliers such as Otto Brehm, Inc. depend on bakeries such as Greyston for their orders.[26] In turn, some of these ingredient distributors depend on manufacturers to supply them. Greyston depends on its suppliers to deliver the level of quality expected, on time and in quantities and packaging convenient for Greyston's production systems.

To improve efficiencies on the input side of the business, managers in many industries have experimented with having fewer suppliers to deal with. This can save both time and money. It can be a way to ensure consistency with quality, packaging, and delivery. But it also sets up a delicate balancing act for managers. Staying with one supplier for major ingredients such as flower, sugar, fat, eggs, and chocolate might mean lower prices for these items. But it can also mean that if the supplier makes a mistake with an order, sends flawed or stale ingredients, raises prices, or doesn't fill an order on time, then Greyston managers would have to scramble to get supplies in from other sources. This can strain the relationship and create frustration for bakery managers under pressure to produce for their customers.

Source: Ray Hub/Shutterstock.

The relationship with one or more flour mills is just one example of the dozens of supplier relationships that a company like Greyston must manage.

One of the fundamental reasons why organizations need managers is to manage the tension inherent in supplier relationships. Managers work hard at cultivating positive relationships with suppliers while seeking ways to minimize risks to the organization. When difficulties arise, managers at both organizations need to work things out.

LABOR. With the exception of companies that bake bread and snacks on a high-volume basis using automated equipment, bakeries are often labor-intensive businesses where workers move, mix, shape, bake, and package the ingredients. One of the key success factors in this type of business is the use of qualified workers and efficient work processes.

When Julius Walls, Jr. became an employee of Greyston in 1993, the company was already operating on the foundation of spiritual principles established by the company's founder.[27] Located in the middle of an urban blighted area of Yonkers north of the Bronx, Greyston managers had developed a tradition of hiring workers from low-income African American and Hispanic families. By the time Walls became CEO in 1997, he understood how this principle was consistent with his own background as a Roman Catholic.

Outside of work, company employees live in the midst of other social systems that affect their ability to successfully fulfill their roles as workers. When these larger social systems have systemic problems, it affects the organization's ability to retain good workers. For example, if workers and their families do not have access to healthcare services, this will have a negative effect on attendance at work. To manage this, Greyston maintains a three-person department that helps employees cope with the problems they experience in their personal lives. Not every company is willing to pay for support staff members to help employees get to the doctor or find child care services.

Wednesday is open hiring day at Greyston. Individuals looking for entry-level work gather outside the building early in the morning. If work is available, then they are taken on a first-come, first-served basis. If they work out well in the tedious production line that cranks out thousands of pounds of brownies each day, then they progress to other jobs. Greyston managers believe that everyone should be given a chance to prove themselves at work.[28] New employees are given a 12- or 16-week trial period. During this trial period, new hires receive on-the-job training plus an orientation to company values such as personal responsibility, self-sufficiency, listening, and cooperation. In other words, company values focus on teaching new employees two-way interdependence.

Managers must be aware of the larger outside influences on their workers that might affect the company's ability to retain qualified personnel. This awareness may lead them to propose activities in the community that serve the organization's needs as well as the needs of workers.

COMPETITORS. Successful managers pay attention to competitors. These organizations represent potential threats to attract employees and customers away. Competitors also may have new ideas that are worth considering. There is no shortage of competition in Greyston's task environment. The bakery goods industry in the United States generates $35 billion in sales annually.[29] As the population grows, this industry will grow. But products like bread, cakes, tarts, and pies have been around for hundreds of years. There are several national brands that operate regional bakeries. Hundreds of local and regional brands compete in Greyston's territory of New York, New Jersey, and Connecticut.

Some product categories, such as a commodity like bread, tend to be highly competitive on price. Greyston has chosen products where it can differentiate itself and tailor-make products for customers. Thus, even though its customers are price-sensitive for some of its products, Greyston has avoided competing solely on price. While price is important, the quality of the product is often more important when competing with other bakeries. Quality, one might say, is in the taste buds of the beholder. Fresh-baked desserts have a very short shelf life, so when a bakery uses the highest quality ingredients and minimizes staleness, consumers can usually tell the difference in taste, freshness, and texture.

Whether the company attempts to compete solely on price or on making its products and services different in terms of product features and benefits, what managers tend to look for is a competitive advantage over their competition.

In addition to the environment that is closest to Greyston and its operations, the larger, general environment also influences companies like Greyston. We turn to this next.

Elements of the General Environment

The **general environment** is comprised of various influences and forces at work that affect all industries and consumers. These influences include the international market in which most industries compete, advances in technology, the legal and political environment for commerce, cultural and social trends, economics, the physical environment, and cultural values such as religious beliefs. Let's consider these.

INTERNATIONAL MARKET. The international marketplace is part of both the general environment and the task environment in many industries. We truly are working in a global community. Companies in the United States compete head-to-head in an international task environment that includes producers of similar or substitute products from all around the world.

China and India, with their vast supplies of low-cost labor, growing use of technology, efficient manufacturing facilities, and natural resources, are becoming the two chief economic rivals of the United States. These countries represent vast numbers of consumers, many of whom are moving toward the middle classes with discretionary income to purchase their own products as well as products made around the world.

For the particular niche of the market that Greyston serves, it would be difficult for an international company to export products into the United States. This is especially true for fresh baked goods. Frozen desserts have a longer shelf life and can more easily be imported into the United States.

However, the international market is likely to affect Greyston's task environment. Sometimes ingredients that Greyston uses in its recipes such as sugar, chocolate, vanilla, and nuts are produced in other countries. Conditions in these countries can affect supplies and prices. Also, immigrants to the United States bring with them the desire for particular types of food. Over time, these shared values influence consumer preferences and tastes.

LEGAL AND POLITICAL INFLUENCES. Greyston Bakery, like all businesses, must comply with state and federal laws and regulations governing its particular industry. The Fair Packaging and Labeling Act of 1967 and the Federal Food, Drug, and Cosmetic Act are two examples of legislation that influence the operations of bakeries and other food manufacturing companies. Providing the consumer with a label indicating the date of perish helps prevent food poisoning. At the federal level, the **Food and Drug Administration (FDA)** is the U.S. government agency that is responsible for managing regulations related to food products. It guides companies like Greyston in what they must do to comply with federal law. County and state health departments regulate food handling requirements. Occupational safety is another important issue to managers at companies like Greyston. The **Occupational Safety and Health Administration (OSHA)** at the federal level and state occupational safety agencies regulate the kinds of safety equipment and procedures that companies must use to protect workers. The federal **Environmental Protection Agency (EPA)** enforces environmental issues related to water and air pollution control. See Exhibit 3-6.

EXHIBIT 3-6
Logos from EPA, OSHA, and FDA

Compared with the waste products at Greyston, the waste products of other industries are far more serious, and because of this, these companies face more stringent regulations regarding how solid, liquid, and gaseous waste can be disposed of safely.

To help them maintain positive relationships with regulatory and legislative bodies, company managers participate in one or more professional trade associations. A **trade association** is an organization comprised of individuals and companies in a particular industry or type of company who join together to promote their common interests. For Greyston, this might mean joining a local food manufacturers' association or the national group known as the American Bakers Association. This national association represents the interests of the commercial baking industry. When federal or state legislation is introduced that is unfavorable to bakeries, the association staff members or their hired lobbyists contact legislators and regulators to argue their position. The association also conducts an annual convention to help association members learn about new technology, new products and services, and new regulations that will affect them in the future.

ADVANCES IN TECHNOLOGY. Advances in technology are affecting every industry and transforming how companies do business. Handheld devices, special-function computers, robotics, and wireless communication have made it possible for computers to be in the field, on the factory floor, and in a manager's pocket. Successful managers are willing to learn new ways of managing workers and production systems that these advances bring. For example, at a company like Greyston, computer devices aid in the receiving of ingredients and materials, computing hours and wages for workers, monitoring and controlling production equipment, ordering materials, sending out invoices for finished goods, and managing the output logistics for delivery. Technologies like these can also be linked for more efficient creation of managerial reports such as daily, weekly, and monthly production reports and financial statements used in decision making.

The future of technology at work is exciting for managers. Many of the predictions about the future of work in the early 1990s are still true today.[30] New technologies will continue to improve efficiencies. Research and development will play an increasing role in the future as the rate of change doubles every 10 years. Robotics will proliferate into more and more industries. Nanotechnology has the potential to completely transform not only the products that are created but also the processes used in creating them.

Along with the benefits that technology brings, managers need to understand the challenges it creates. For example, at a company like Greyston, which produces a combination of one-of-a kind custom products and high-volume products, coordinating low-tech, labor-intensive technologies with advanced technologies can be a challenge. Also, as technology increasingly dominates society and the economy,[31] information is available more and more quickly. The lines between work and leisure are blurring, and it is increasingly difficult to get away from the job. Managers are working longer hours, and taking a true vacation is becoming more and more difficult. Every spare minute is being filled to the brim with computing and communication.

Since the Industrial Revolution in the 18th century, workers and managers have had to contend with continual advances in technology. Some technologies completely reshape the way work is done. This can be unsettling for workers accustomed to existing technology. Learning new technology requires both managers and workers to move outside of their comfort zone. Managers need to be aware that this can be traumatic for some workers.

SOCIAL AND CULTURAL TRENDS. The **social and cultural influences** are some of the fundamental forces that are constantly reshaping society and its preferences. In turn, these forces influence organizations and the industries in which they operate. For example, some of the social and cultural trends that affect Greyston's general environment are consumers' changing health concerns and lifestyles, diet trends, holidays, seasonal celebrations, and the ethnic mix of the population.

Demographic trends reshape work and consumer behaviors. Workers are retiring later in life than ever before. This means that there are more older workers available to organizations. More women are taking leadership roles in organizations. Their experiences will provide important role models to younger workers who desire to move up the ranks of responsibility. Geographic shifts in the population are occurring within the United States and between the United States and other countries. This will make it difficult for some organizations to recruit workers. It also makes it difficult for communities to attract new businesses. Since the 1950s, Americans have been moving out of congested cities into the suburbs. The ethnic mix of the population is also changing.[32] Hispanic Americans are now the largest minority group in the United States and are growing four times faster than the general population. Managers need to monitor and understand all of these trends and how they affect their own organization.

Labor unions are another social and cultural influence on companies. As measured by their membership, labor unions have been losing their influence since the last quarter of the 20th century as competitive pressures from international companies to take manufacturing jobs out of the United States make it more difficult for labor unions to demand pay increases.[33] However, many citizens still see the need for labor unions to protect worker rights. This is a social and a political factor. Politicians need to court the union vote but at the same time not alienate those who value unions less.

Yet another social trend is the ebb and flow of criticism of corporations and their executives. The values commonly shared in business often come under scrutiny following corporate scandals and alleged improprieties. Paradoxically there are increasing calls for improved business morality at the same time as there is increasing pressure on company managers to squeeze every ounce of performance out of employees.[34]

Exhibit 3-7 describes additional social and cultural influences that some researchers predict will affect organizations in the future. Some of these influences have international roots. Some are related to technology, and others are related to the thinking patterns of people.

ECONOMICS. Economic trends also affect businesses. For example, interest rates affect the ability of Greyston to obtain short-term and long-term cash on loan for expansion and renovation. Unemployment affects consumers' discretionary income. As consumer income drops, middle-class consumers are less willing to purchase nonessential products and services such as dining at upscale restaurants that sell gourmet bakery products. But upper-class consumers are able to continue their spending patterns, including the use of gourmet restaurants. For Greyston and other bakeries, a severe increase in general unemployment could cause such a decline in demand for desserts that bakery managers might face the gut-wrenching decision to lay off workers.

Other economic influences affect all industries. Some industries have labor shortages while others have labor surpluses as companies have downsized or moved operations to other countries. These shortages and surpluses cause career shifts as individuals return to school or otherwise retrain for new jobs.

PHYSICAL ENVIRONMENT. Some industries are vulnerable to climate changes and geological events such as earthquakes, storms, fires, hurricanes, freezing temperatures, and droughts. A tornado that destroys grain elevators in a wheat-producing county in the Midwest might not affect a bakery like Greyston because wheat is produced in many states and countries. A massive winter storm in the New York City area could disrupt the operations of the bakery and its customers for several days, making it more difficult for Greyston to manage its inventory of baked goods. A power failure in the heat of the summer can also have a similar short-term impact. A severe drought in several states that produce the soft wheat used to produce cake flour would affect ingredient suppliers such as Otto Brehm and, in turn, would affect bakeries and the restaurants that depend on them to provide desserts. The cost of wheat flour would increase, causing the price of cakes, brownies, and tarts to rise. Demand would start to fall.

Exceptional physical circumstances can create marketing opportunities for companies like Greyston to help their communities deal with the situation. For example, supplying emergency workers with fresh brownies can go a long way to build goodwill regardless of whether the

Some of the most important environmental influences on business that managers will contend with in the future are:

1. **Microsegmentation of the market.** When you couple the great diversity of lifestyles, values, and interests among consumers along with the ability to create customized commercial messages with electronic communication devices, the market can be segmented down to the individual.
2. **Value targeting.** Companies that are seeking to build brand loyalty are attempting to develop ways to aim "for whatever matters most to individual consumers."
3. **Chinese economy.** As a nation, China is one of the biggest collections of middle-class consumers worldwide. China produces more than 70 percent of the world's toys, 60 percent of the world's bicycles, one-third of the world's television sets and air conditioners, and half of all microwaves sold around the world.
4. **Information to knowledge.** Information is fast becoming a profitless commodity while knowledge is what gives companies power to offer a competitive edge. The world is more highly connected now than at any previous time in history. Yet the gap between the technology "haves" and "have-nots" is a problem.
5. **Cyber politics.** The emergence of the Internet as a personal communication device has spawned the ability of swarms of consumers to form temporary political alliances in the form of small advocacy groups to present their case to politicians.
6. **Dumb and sensational pop culture.** Competition for attention by marketers who promote products central to culture has resulted in dumbing down entertainment and news content while emphasizing the sensational. Another result is the growing differences in worldview between consumers who enjoy "junk food" entertainment and news and a smaller number of citizens who want to distance themselves from pop culture.
7. **Knowledge warfare.** As companies become more dependent on knowledge-intensive technologies for their competitive advantage, commercial knowledge warfare will increase. Protecting proprietary knowledge will become more and more difficult.
8. **Counter-Americanism.** America is still a dominant economic and political force around the world. Yet some citizens of other countries are increasingly viewing American influence as unilateral and imperialistic. This perception is seen as a threat, and some who feel threatened are pushing back politically. Extremist groups use this anti-American bias to promote their own political agendas of violence.

EXHIBIT 3-7
Eight Supertrends Shaping the Future of Business[35]

bakery gains any media publicity. Some bakeries experiment with creating specialty desserts designed to commemorate an event such as a storm using a recipe and presentation style that consumers can enjoy with their friends.

RELIGIOUS BELIEFS AND VALUES. The majority of Americans practice religion and espouse a belief in God. Interest in spirituality in the United States has increased since the 1970s. Yet participation in religious practices such as attendance at church has remained relatively stable over the years. Individuals are finding ways outside of church to meet their spiritual needs. Religious beliefs guide consumption patterns as well as work values. For example, in some religions, dietary practices influence food shopping behaviors. As we will see in Chapter 9, Human Resource Management, and Chapter 15, Spirituality, Faith, and Management, deeply held spiritual values shape the activities of workers while they are on the job. Some workers may want to structure their workday around their formal prayer life.

We've looked at the external environment that affects organizations such as Greyston. Next we will explore the internal environment and its influence on the company's ability to carry out its mission.

The Internal Environment and Organizational Culture

As organizations adapt to their external environments a certain internal environment is created. The **internal environment** is the system inside an organization comprised of the shared values among leaders and employees regarding behaviors and processes. While successful managers are always aware of the external environment, for many middle managers and frontline supervisors the majority of their mental, emotional, and physical energy is spent with what is going on inside the company.[36] It is the internal environment that is the closest to their day-to-day work and demands their immediate attention.

The internal environment is comprised of several interrelated elements:

- the underlying values and morals of leaders and employees
- the norms of group behavior such as the implicit standards of dress, decorum, and protocols
- how employees think about the external environment and about their own capabilities to succeed in that environment
- how decisions are made
- how workers are organized
- how new workers are chosen and trained
- communication patterns
- what motivates workers
- how leaders behave
- how influence is used to get work done
- how organizational leaders help the organization stay focused on its goals
- the spiritual dynamics present in the organization

These elements of the internal environment form an organization's *culture*.

Borrowing study techniques from cultural anthropologists, organizational scholars since the 1940s have studied the idea that organizations have cultures similar to the way that larger society has cultures.[37] But it was the work of scholars during the early 1980s that brought the concept of corporate culture into the mainstream.[38]

The word culture is sometimes used to indicate that a person shows a high level of sophistication, as when we say that someone is very "cultured." In business its use, for example, "the right kind of culture" or "a culture of quality," usually refers to certain values that managers are trying to build and maintain in the organization.

Some see organizational culture as "the organizational equivalent of a person's character."[39] We will return to organizational character later in this chapter. See Exhibit 3-8.

Organizational culture is the set of commonly held and deeply embedded values and assumptions within an organization. It forms as an organization adapts to its external environment and integrates various internal ways of thinking and behaving. **External adaptation tasks** are the actions that help the organization fulfill its fundamental purpose when it responds to the needs of customers, suppliers, and other entities in the outside environment. **Internal integration tasks** are the actions that facilitate the completion of work processes. See Exhibit 3-9.

To illustrate culture and its links to external adaptation tasks and internal integration tasks, let's consider another organization: St. Teriza Valley Medical Center,[40] a religious nonprofit hospital located in a small American town. St. Teriza competes with two other hospitals and offers a moderate range of general hospital services.

Like other hospitals, St. Teriza faces several challenges in the external environment. One challenge is that hospitals must collaborate with other players in the healthcare industry such as

EXHIBIT 3-8
Organizational Culture and Values

Organizational Culture
Commonly held and deeply embedded values and assumptions within an organization.
Part of the being and becoming dimension of the Management Pyramid at the organizational level.

External Adaptation Tasks	Internal Integration Tasks
Establish organizational mission, purpose, goals, and tasks	Use a common language that helps members understand and communicate with each other
Establish or adjust organizational structure; assign specific tasks and responsibilities	Establish both the separations and the linkages between work groups and individuals
Determine the preferred means to accomplish goals	Determine criteria for allocating social status
Establish how results will be measured and how corrections will be made when necessary	Determine criteria for friendship and rewards

EXHIBIT 3-9

Internal and External Tasks that All Organizations Face[41]

physicians, pharmacists, insurance companies, state and federal health agencies, and even other hospitals. Hospitals need to maintain open and frequent communication channels among all of these groups on a daily basis.

Another challenge is that patients who need hospital care come with a vast array of health problems. Hospitals must be ready to provide patients with a corresponding vast array of diagnostic and treatment services. Healthcare is a personal, even intimate service that involves many people with different professional backgrounds. If the only service that a hospital provided was knee surgery, then the personnel in collaboration with the physicians and surgeons could establish set routines for care that would make them the most efficient and effective at providing that one service. But when hospitals provide hundreds, even thousands of different kinds of services, there are scores of policies and procedures to follow. Add to this the fact that care must be customized for each patient's particular condition and you have a recipe for inefficiency.

Businesses in other industries have their own sets of challenges. As they find solutions to these problems their organizational cultures take shape in ways that are different from what happens in hospitals. If you had the opportunity to observe the organizational cultures of businesses from eight different industries all on one day, you would likely see eight different patterns of culture related to the eight different sets of challenges these companies face. But looking across all of these industries, you would see some things that organizations do in common as they develop their cultures. To these we turn next.

Cultural Leadership Tools

Like managers in other types of businesses who work hard to develop shared values, managers at St. Teriza have several tools at their disposal to strengthen and, when necessary, to change their organization's culture.[42] With these tools, leaders can "teach" their organization how to perceive, think, feel, and behave in solving the problems that are inherent in their work. We can think of these tools in two categories: *primary embedding mechanisms* and *secondary reinforcement mechanisms.*

PRIMARY EMBEDDING MECHANISMS. **Primary embedding mechanisms** are organizational activities that tend to support the acceptance of shared values by employees. What organizational leaders pay attention to is one of the most important ways that shared values get embedded in an organization. This will be one of your most important jobs as a manager: to identify for your subordinates the important issues that you care about.[43] What you care about is what you talk about, what you ask others to report on, what you measure, and what you focus on for making adjustments to efficiency and effectiveness. For example, in a hospital, managers pay attention to things such as the clinical indicators of patients' health status, whether there are too many or too few employees to care for the patients, how close to the expense budget a department is operating, whether best practice procedures are being followed, whether the hospital is getting support from and collaborating effectively with physicians, and whether the hospital is receiving timely payment for services provided.

Paying attention to particular issues and employee behaviors often involves showing employees how something is done, explaining why a procedure is important, and mentoring others who are still learning. This teaching and coaching work of the manager, coupled with showing by example, helps employees accept company values.

When a particularly difficult problem arises, how a manager reacts tells subordinates and others a lot about the ways of thinking the organization expects. As a manager you must be familiar with policies and procedures so that when an unusual event occurs, you can react in a calm, professional manner, know who else needs to be involved, act quickly to get them involved, and respond to the situation appropriately.

Learning how to solve problems is also communicated through the resource allocation decisions that leaders make. During the development of budgets, managers learn the resource priorities that the organization as a whole is emphasizing. Managers then pass this knowledge down either formally or informally to rank-and-file employees.

As a manager you will have some authority to reward workers for aligning their behavior with the preferred behavior patterns of the organization. You can show recognition, increase a worker's status, and, when authorized, increase a person's pay. All of these rewards encourage workers to accept organizational values.

When you recruit, select, hire, and orient new employees you strengthen organizational values. Likewise, when an employee needs correction, discipline, or even termination, these actions communicate louder than words what is believed to be important for the organization to continue to solve its problems with success. See Exhibit 3-10.

SECONDARY REINFORCING MECHANISMS. Once organizational shared values are established other things reinforce these values. **Secondary reinforcing mechanisms** are things and activities in and around the organization that maintain or strengthen company values. Several kinds of things in an organization reinforce the company culture if they are consistent with the primary embedding mechanisms. How work is divided among workers and what means are used for these workers to coordinate their efforts reinforces the limits of authority. Division of labor maintains a certain way of thinking about the company's challenges. For example, in hospitals nurses view the challenges of caring for patients through the eyes of providing 24-hour bedside care and carrying out treatment orders, all while coordinating the work of physicians and technical support staff. Technical support staff who are specialists in a narrow set of procedures such as taking X-rays or drawing blood do not have this wide perspective.

Another reinforcing mechanism is the physical layout of buildings and equipment. When work units are placed in close proximity to each other, this sometimes means that these units must work closely together in discussing and solving problems. Purchasing departments are often located toward the outside of building so they can receive shipments from suppliers. Surgery suites, in contrast, are located toward the center of hospital buildings, in part to keep these spaces isolated from casual contact for infection control.

Every group of workers assigned to specific tasks has a set of operational procedures and systems that it must use to get work done efficiently. **Operational procedures** are sets of sequenced, routine work tasks. They limit individual employee behaviors to those that are believed to be best for getting work done efficiently. These procedures, which cover the daily, weekly, monthly, and yearly routines, encompass a wide variety of activities from how to coordinate with another department to how to use specific pieces of equipment, when and how to

EXHIBIT 3-10
Primary Imbedding Mechanisms

What leaders pay attention to	What you ask others to report on
Teaching and coaching	How a manager reacts to difficult problems
Learning how to solve problems	Rewarding workers for desired behaviors
Recruiting, selecting, hiring, and orienting new employees	

How work is divided among workers	How workers coordinate with each other
Physical layout of buildings and equipment	Operational procedures and systems
Stories that managers tell	

EXHIBIT 3-11
Secondary Reinforcing Mechanisms

perform maintenance, and how to record and maintain information for later reference. Procedures increase predictability and, as a result, increase stability. When workers follow procedures consistently on a daily basis, these work habits reinforce the shared beliefs in the organization regarding how best to solve the organization's problems.

Hospitals operate on a 24-hour basis, which means that two or three times each day employees transfer the care of patients to the next shift of employees. In the nursing units, this shift change is accompanied by a daily ritual of the outgoing nurses reporting to the incoming nurses the status of patients, instructions, any unusual situations with equipment, and other resources that might affect patient care during the next shift. This is just one example of the hundreds of different rituals that companies of all types use to reinforce the expected ways of thinking and behaving in the company. Other examples include new-employee orientation programs, employee recognition programs, weekly or monthly staff meetings, and governing board meetings.

Stories that managers tell also reinforce the shared values that underlie expected behaviors. Every organization has stories of individuals who have performed heroically or who have made mistakes. Such narratives communicate how current leaders interpret these events. For example, a nurse tells a new employee about a situation involving one of the doctors, what happened when the hospital administrator got involved, and how it was resolved for the good of the patient only when a nurse stepped in and advocated on behalf of the patient. The employee listening to the story learns implicitly how important it is for nurses to be patient advocates and act with courage under difficult circumstances. See Exhibit 3-11.

The Christian Mind on Organizational Culture

One of the metaphors for corporate culture is that of social or normative glue that holds organizations together. This "glue" allows us to obtain a sense of identify and commitment to an entity or group or purpose other than our selves. The leadership style of the CEO or president often is a primary factor in determining what will be the "adhesive" of the corporate culture. In Matthew 20, Mark 9, and Luke 10 the same story is told about the Disciples' discussions regarding who among them would be the greatest in the Kingdom. All three gospel writers noted that Jesus' response to their discussion was that the greatest must first be the servant of all. For the Christian manager it would seem that a culture based on service to all would provide a viable glue to hold us together.

Doyle J. Lucas, Ph.D.
Professor of Management
Falls School of Business
Anderson University
Anderson, IN

Levels of Culture

Organizational culture has three levels. The first is a visible layer of cultural artifacts, which are things that can be observed such as the stories, rituals, and physical objects at work. The second layer is invisible and takes the form of the interpretation of the stories, the meaning behind the rituals, the shared beliefs about how best to accomplish tasks, and the justification

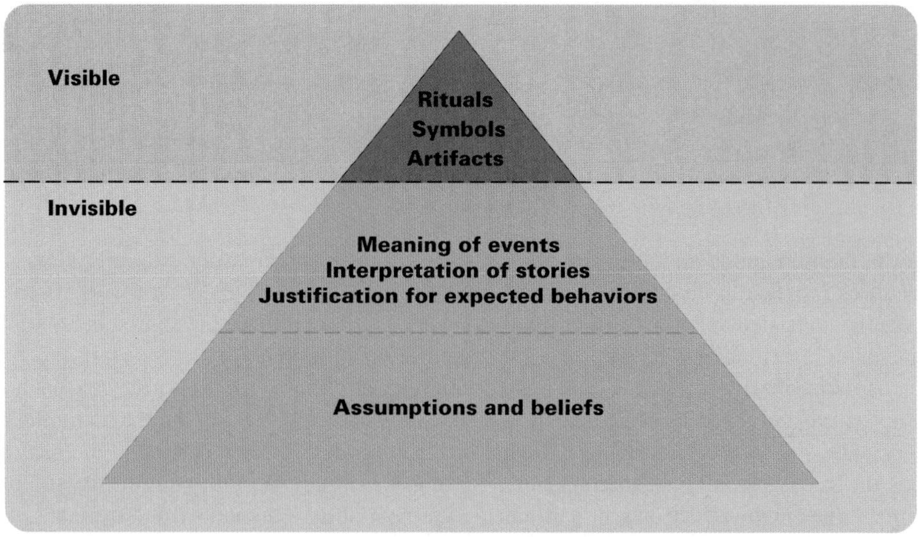

EXHIBIT 3-12
Visible and Invisible Culture

Source: Based on the discussion in Schein, E. H. (2004). *Organizational culture and leadership.* (3rd ed.). San Francisco, CA: John Wiley & Sons. pp. 25–37.

of certain expectations. A third, deeper invisible level is the underlying assumptions the organization shares regarding what is good, how people should be treated, and what goals are most important. These are the seldom-discussed and sometimes nonnegotiable beliefs. See Exhibit 3-12.

Perspective Matters

Culture can be an elusive idea, and perspective makes a difference in understanding the culture of a particular organization. For example, think about the organizational culture of a college or university from the perspectives of students and school officials. Students see the procedures and rules as they affect their ability to accomplish their goals. School officials view culture from the perspective of attempting to balance the school's traditional values, the commitments the school has made in deploying its assets and allocating other resources, and the expectations of alumni and students. Because of their perspective, students miss some of the important elements of the organizational culture that are experienced by school administrators. Likewise, school administrators miss some important elements of the organization that are experienced by students.

Individuals are biased in how they view their organization because they have a narrow perspective and because they do not know completely the minds of others in the organization. They can mistake their personal perception of what occurs among other members, at all levels, as fact.[44] This can make getting at the absolute truth about an organization's culture difficult. There will be differences in the assumptions that each individual begins with, in interpretation of the facts, and in the meaning that these facts give. But these differences do not negate the importance of organizational culture. Successful managers attempt to view culture from their own perspective as well as from the perspectives and assumptions of other stakeholders both inside and outside the organization.

Organizational Subcultures

This leads us to consider **organizational subcultures**, which are collections of mental orientations among groups or teams of workers in the company.[45]

Back at St. Teriza Valley Medical Center several subcultures have developed. Administrators view the challenges of the external environment in terms of the competing hospital, the government regulations, the demands of the health insurance companies, and the expectations of the community. Physicians and surgeons view the problems of the hospital from the perspective of interrelated and complex technical and scientific problems. Nurses are the core of why a hospital exists. They view the hospital's problems from the perspective of patient care processes that require collaboration with support staff and physicians. Secretaries, administrative assistants, and other administrative support personnel are important links in the collaboration between the top-level leaders and many individuals both inside and outside the organization.

Staff support personnel (marketing, planning, purchasing, accounting, human resources) act as internal consultants to the organization, providing information and services to other departments that promote the business functions. Some of these departments such as marketing and purchasing will be situated at the external boundaries of the organization, watching the trends. Periodically, they will bring information and opinions to organizational managers encouraging the organizational leaders to adjust their perceptions of the environment.

One challenge for organizations is that these subcultures related to the major occupational communities have differences in tasks and decision-making authority that are not always aligned with each other. Each has a slightly different sense of identity. Each views the environment through a slightly different though valid set of assumptions. Each has a slightly different set of values.

Subcultures also develop among those who work at different levels of decision-making authority. For example, over time, frontline supervisors develop similar assumptions about how to deal with workers and work groups. Their focus is always on today and tomorrow. Middle managers have a special set of shared problems and solutions focused on groups of workers and the processes that these groups have in common. This leads to similar ways of thinking about subordinates and superiors and the company as a whole. Senior leaders such as vice presidents and the chief executive have another, different, orientation because of their level of responsibility looking out for the organization's financial success and effectiveness in pursuing its mission. They become aware of the economic forces at work in their industry.

Sometimes one or more of the subcultures will not get its needs met or will somehow be blocked from fulfilling its expectations. When subcultures collide because of conflicting goals, dysfunctional behaviors emerge: inaction, actions that are ineffective or inefficient, and actions that undermine others in the organization. Managers have the responsibility to open functional lines of communication and collaboration to resolve these issues. Otherwise, the organization will become bound by the goal conflicts that occur among its various subcultures.

Cultural Similarity Within Industries

Shared assumptions in a given industry lead to similar but not identical organizational cultures among organizations in that industry.[46] Over time, organizations in the same industry may mimic each other. They have similar problems. They borrow ideas from each other through professional meetings, trade publications, trade association meetings, and the use of consultants. Leaders in an industry have similar sets of technologies, work processes, and other means by which they generate solutions. For example, the organizational culture at a hospital such as St. Teriza is quite different from the culture found in a food-processing plant operated by ConAgra Foods, but it is probably quite similar to a local competing hospital.

Despite their similarities, all firms in the same industry do not have identical organizational cultures. There are individual differences that are influenced by the local differences in values, organizational structure, and the personal value preferences of organizational leaders.

Dimensions of Culture

Organizational culture is difficult to measure directly. Some researchers have identified several **dimensions of organizational culture** common to many organizations. These dimensions can be used to create an overall description of an organization in terms of culture:[47]

- Innovation
- Stability
- Respect for people
- Outcome orientation
- Detail orientation
- Team orientation
- Aggressiveness

Researchers have identified four clusters of shared values common in effective organizations.[48] First, effective organizations get employees involved by empowering workers, organizing around

EXHIBIT 3-13
Sociability and Solidarity in an Organization

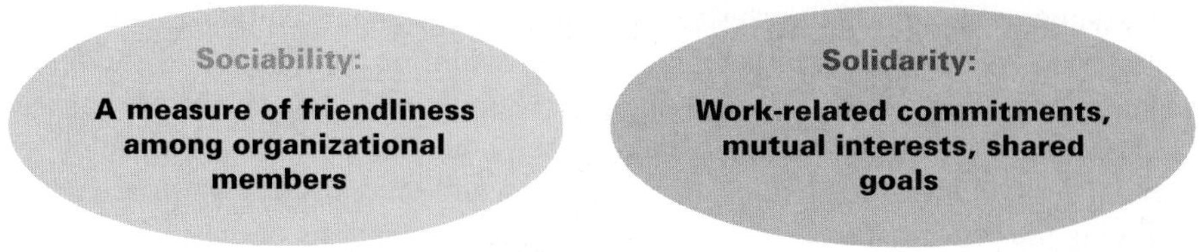

teams, and developing both team and individual capabilities. Workers in these organizations develop a sense of shared ownership in the work processes for which they are responsible. Second, effective organizations develop an integrated system of shared values that are consistently reinforced so much that the culture becomes strong or thick around the organization. So strong are the core values that guide behavior that workers with divergent views are able to reach agreement for the good of the organization. Third, effective organizations also work at being adaptive to changes in their environment. This can be difficult for organizations in which behaviors are aligned for efficiency and routine. Fourth, organizations that are effective have a clear, shared sense of purpose.

Other scholars suggest that the character of a corporate culture can be illuminated by identifying the degree of *sociability* and *solidarity* among the members of the organizational community (employees, volunteers, etc.).[49] We can observe the character of the organizational culture in terms of sociability and solidarity by looking at communication patterns, how physical space is used, how time is spent, and how personal identity is achieved.

Sociability is a measure of friendliness among members of the organizational community. When sociability is high, the line of distinction between work and personal life becomes murky. Sociability spurs creativity and fosters company loyalty. But a high degree of sociability can also enable some dysfunction at work if friendships prevent supervisors from holding the line on accountability. In the extreme, high sociability can result in decreased fairness as small groups of close friends with power make decisions that benefit each other.

Solidarity is based on common tasks, mutual interests because of work responsibilities, and shared work-related goals. Coworkers make commitments to each other and to the organization for getting work accomplished and fulfilling organizational goals. See Exhibit 3-13.

Strong vs. Weak Cultures

Organizational culture has been called the glue that holds an organization together.[50] The ability of an organization to effectively and efficiently pursue its goals is somewhat dependent on how strong the organizational culture is.

An organization's **cultural strength** is how much consistency in shared values exists among members of the organization.[51] The stronger the culture the more likely it is that more individuals in the entire organization share the basic assumptions and beliefs, and the more likely it is that these beliefs are firmly integrated into daily actions that are consistent. The stronger the organizational culture the more stable and predictable it becomes.

Organizations have tried many ways to strengthen their culture through the socialization of new employees.[52] New employees receive extensive training in how the organization works, the goals of the organization, the philosophy of business, and the history of the organization. This process lowers the ambiguity of the new employee's role and informs the new employee what is expected. Experienced employees who are thought to embody the best of prized organizational values are assigned to mentor new employees. Top-level leaders expect supervisors to observe behaviors of new employees and provide guidance when behaviors deviate from what is expected. Employee newsletters focus on stories of employees who exhibit the shared values desired by organizational leaders. Employee recognition programs focus on exemplary work behaviors. Standardizing the job of an employee limits the freedom of the worker to experiment with alternative ways of behaving. Standardization also promotes mastering the tasks of a job which, in turn, helps support the organizational drives toward coordination and efficiency.[53] Standardizing managerial controls on performance also shapes employee attitudes. See Exhibit 3-14.

Train employees	Tell employees the organizational goals
Tell the philosophy of the organization	Tell the history of the organization
Have experienced employees mentor new workers	Tell stories of model employees
Standardize the job tasks	Standardize managerial controls

EXHIBIT 3-14
How to Strengthen an Organizational Culture

High-level leaders take new managers through a careful socialization process to help ensure that their managerial decisions will be aligned with company goals.[54] The **socialization process** is the process by which the new manager learns the shared values of the organization, especially the ones that are high priority for managers in higher levels of authority. Socialization also includes learning to practice acceptable behaviors while avoiding unacceptable behaviors. New managers might receive training in how to use the company's progressive discipline process, how to manage employees who exhibit unsafe behaviors, how to manage time and attendance, how to deal with angry employees, how to work with the human resources department, and how to prepare budgets and read financial statements.

Not every organization is perfect in its ability to align shared values among all employees. Any one of the top leaders who is given a great amount of discretionary decision-making authority can have an enormous impact to strengthen or weaken the culture. Employees may exhibit passive resistance or even open disagreement with the values of top leaders.

Weakening the culture can result in creating a dysfunctional culture that is destructive. When cultural dysfunction occurs, it requires someone to take a leadership role to heal the dysfunction, realign priorities, and then work vigorously by selecting primary embedding mechanisms and secondary reinforcing mechanisms to change the organizational culture.[55]

Paradoxes in the Environment

Comprehending the tensions inherent in the managerial environment starts with contradictions. These are like two sides of the same coin. You need both sides to make a whole coin but each side represents an action or way of thinking that is in contradiction (or at least in opposition) to the other side.[56] The natural tendency for humans is to avoid contradictions. Unfortunately, the complexity of social systems is so great that we cannot avoid these tension points altogether. Here are a few examples of contradictions from the perspective of an organization's internal and external environment.

ENVIRONMENTAL INSULATION—ENVIRONMENTAL INVOLVEMENT.[57] To be effective, every organization must remain somewhat insulated from its larger environment and, at the same time, be involved with the environment. The risk of involvement is that it can bring in elements of the environment that are unintended or even undesirable in terms of the organizational culture. For example, a food-processing company such as J. M. Smucker cannot let just anyone come in and look around and touch equipment. The company must be diligent in protecting its trade secrets. However, the company must remain in contact with food growers, material suppliers, government regulators, and food retailers in order to operate.

STRENGTHEN THE CULTURE—CHANGE THE CULTURE TO PROMOTE ADAPTATION TO CHANGING CONDITIONS.[58] If you are constructing a building in an area known for earthquakes, the materials and construction methods that you use need to provide for both stability and flexibility at the same time. The same is true with organizational cultures. The stronger an organization's culture becomes, the more resistant to change it becomes. Members become attached to the status quo and less willing to question the validity of their assumptions about the market. It becomes more difficult for the organization to adapt to changing environmental conditions.

DEPENDENT—SELF-RELIANT.[59] Every organization is to a certain degree dependent on the outside environment. No single organization is absolutely self-sufficient. At the same time, organizations must also be self-reliant to prevent becoming vulnerable to environmental uncertainty.

Focus on an Organization

Boeing Employees Bible Fellowship[60]

As mentioned earlier in the chapter, religious belief is one of several influences in an organization's general environment. Some workers wish to incorporate their prayer life into their workday. At aerospace giant Boeing, the Boeing Employees Bible Fellowship (BEBF), a Boeing Recreation Club, offers an organized opportunity for employees to get involved with Christian lunchtime fellowship groups. Bible fellowship groups are offered weekly at many geographical locations and as a virtual Bible study group that meets online.

As a recognized company recreation club, BEBF's members agree to promote the Fellowship in ways consistent with Boeing company policies. For example, fliers announcing the meeting times and places of Fellowship groups may be posted on the BEBF website and on officially designated Boeing Employee Personal Notices Bulletin Boards. Notices may not be posted in elevators, in stairwells, or on other Boeing bulletin boards used for Boeing business purposes without specific permission of Boeing. New members joining the Fellowship must sign a Release and Indemnity Agreement releasing the club, its officers and members, and the Boeing company, its officers and employees, from all liability and claims that arise from participation in club activities. New members also sign a statement of faith.

If guests (such as clergy and guest speakers) are invited to facilitate discussions or share about their work in ministry at a BEBF-sponsored gathering, they must follow BEBF guidelines so that their presentations don't conflict with Boeing policies. For example, Fellowship group leaders must notify the BEBF Board one week in advance of a guest's participation. The Bible Fellowship group leader must preview the speaker's topic and provide the Board with an outline. Guests must be instructed regarding Boeing policies related to religious toleration of participants who might believe differently from the guest. Guests may not espouse a religious position or try to recruit followers. They must be careful not to speak condescendingly of non-biblical or non-religious viewpoints. The Fellowship group leader who invited the guest must closely monitor the guest speaker's presentation and notify the BEBF President if she observes something that the guest says or does that is in violation of the guidelines.

Chapter Summary

1. A system is an organized arrangement of elements that are interdependent and interconnected to form a purposeful, organic whole. Successful managers view their organization through the lens of systems thinking.
2. Christians hold a hierarchical view of open systems that includes the physical or natural environment, the social environment, and the larger spiritual environment that includes the existence of God. A Christian worldview holds that managers achieve genuine meaning when they are open to the divine influences of the larger system and see their work in the larger context of all Creation in its relationship to God. When humans act in selfish ways they become closed to the broader spiritual values. This takes a toll on meaning and significance in the organizational systems in which they work and live. From a Christian perspective organizational systems are the means by which value is created and delivered to stakeholders such as customers. In order for managers to work effectively in social systems they need feedback based on integrity and truthfulness.
3. Systems contain several components: the external environment, inputs, transformation processes, outputs, and feedback loops. These components allow the system to work as a functioning whole. Systems also can be described in terms of their operating parameters: interconnectivity, interdependency, boundaries that separate the system from larger systems, decay (entropy) when the system is not managed, change, limited variety influenced by the nature of the outside environment, and purpose and meaning.

4. Managers must do their best to manage the company's relationship with the external environment. The external environment can be divided into two categories. The task environment is where an organization transacts business with customers, suppliers, and workers, and where competitors have a direct influence on customers. The task environment includes customers, suppliers, labor, and competitors. The general environment is the environment that influences all businesses and citizens. This includes the international market, legal and political influences, technology, social and cultural trends, economics, the physical environment, and religious beliefs and values.
5. The internal environment is comprised of several interrelated elements: the underlying values and morals of leaders and employees, the norms of group behavior such as the implicit standards of dress, decorum, and protocols, how employees think about the external environment and about their own capabilities to succeed in that environment, how decisions are made, how workers are organized, how new workers are chosen and trained, communication patterns, what motivates workers, how leaders behave, how influence is used to get work done, how the organizational leaders help the organization stay focused on its goals, and the spiritual dynamics present in the organization. These elements of the internal environment form an organization's *culture.*
6. Managers employ cultural leadership tools to shape the organization's culture. Primary embedding mechanisms tend to support the acceptance of shared values by employees. Secondary reinforcing mechanisms are things and activities in and around the organization that maintain or strengthen company values.
7. Organizational cultures have three levels. The first is a visible layer of things that can be observed. The second layer is invisible and takes the form of the interpretation of the stories and the meaning behind shared beliefs. A third, deeper invisible level is the underlying assumptions the organization shares. Organizations typically develop one or more subcultures where groups of workers come to have similar values that are important to their work.
8. Scholars who have studied organizational cultures have identified categories of shared values that are common to many organizations. Each organization is different in terms of these dimensions: innovation, stability, respect for people, outcome orientation, detail orientation, team orientation, and aggressiveness.
9. Organizations can have either a strong or weak culture. Managers are often called upon to strengthen certain cultural values that are important for achieving organizational goals.
10. Organizations experience tensions in terms of their internal and external environment.

Key Terms

Discussion Questions

1. In the chapter-opening scenario, what could Baxter Belafonte have done differently to prevent the confrontation with his boss?
2. What place does a Christian manager at a company like Greyston Bakery have in being firm with a supplier regarding specific ingredients, conditions, quantities, and so forth? Does a Christian demanding certain things from suppliers (even if accomplished in a non-demanding manner) misrepresent the name of Christ in marketplace?
3. How would you describe the difference between self-interest and selfishness?
4. Is it unchristian to develop positive relationships with some suppliers at the same time as maintaining relationships with other suppliers "just in case" preferred suppliers cannot meet the company's needs?

5. Knowing that making a substantial change with a supplier can result in internal chaos for that supplier, what obligations does a Christian have to stay with a supplier once a relationship has been established? What if your company is the biggest customer of that supplier and changing suppliers might result in workers being laid off from their jobs?
6. For the Christian manager, do the relationships with customers take precedence over the relationships with suppliers?
7. How has the Internet changed the environment in which a commercial cake bakery like Greyston competes?
8. Go online and try to identify three companies that sell fresh cakes nationwide over the Internet.
9. What important perspectives regarding organizational culture can we learn from Acts 15:1–29 (The Council at Jerusalem)?
10. In what ways is the BEBF supporting the Boeing Company culture? What are the risks to the Boeing Company culture by allowing the BEBF fellowship groups to operate? Why are BEBF members required to sign the Release and Indemnity Agreement that other Recreation Club members sign? Why must BEBF leaders so closely monitor the activities of Bible Fellowship groups?
11. How can the successful manager hire new workers from the outside hoping they will bring new ideas for innovation while at the same time preserve the unchanging shared values of the organization?
12. Consider one of the most famous prayers recorded in the Bible, Matthew 6:9–13:

> 9 Pray, then, in this way: Our Father who art in heaven, Hallowed be Thy name. 10 Thy kingdom come. Thy will be done, On earth as it is in heaven. 11 Give us this day our daily bread. 12 And forgive us our debts, as we also have forgiven our debtors. 13 And do not lead us into temptation, but deliver us from evil. *For Thine is the kingdom, and the power, and the glory, forever. Amen.*

In what way does this prayer point to a larger system that Christian managers take into account when they manage an organization?

STUDENT EXERCISES

1. Use the following dimensions to evaluate the culture of a nonprofit organization with which you are familiar (your congregation, community service agency, etc.):
   - External adaptation focus vs. internal integration focus
   - Preserving tradition vs. changing
   - Centralized control vs. allowing individual discretion
   - Task-oriented vs. relationship-oriented
   - Uniformity vs. allowing for differentiation
   - Autocratic vs. democratic
   - Transaction vs. transformational
   - Directive vs. participative

   Do you see evidence that on some of these dimensions the organization exhibits *both* sides? What might account for this?
2. Choose a company within two miles of where you are located. Visit the company as any customer might. Record your observations based on the following questions:
   - How are employees dressed, and what might the significance of this attire be?
   - How similar are employees' behaviors?
   - Observe the physical setting in which work gets done. What objects do you see in this company that you don't see in other companies? What is the significance of these objects?
   - Listen to conversations between employees and customers. What themes, stories, or ideas are repeated? What terms have special meaning inside the company? Do the company employees use terms not commonly used in society?
   - Can you observe any ceremonies or rituals taking place that reflect company values?
   - If you worked in this company, what things should you never do (taboos)?
   - Overall, how would you characterize this company's culture?
   - What must this company *assume* to be true regarding customers?
   - What are the key external environmental challenges (customers, suppliers, competitors, government regulations, etc.) that may be influencing the shared values of this particular company? How has the company adapted "on the inside" to solve these external problems?

   Based on your observations, identify where this company is in terms of the following seven dimensions:[61]
   - Innovation and risk taking vs. avoiding risks
   - Tight attention to detail vs. loose attention to detail
   - Oriented to getting things done vs. oriented to the process
   - People orientation vs. task orientation
   - Focus on the individual worker vs. focus on the team effort
   - Aggressiveness in taking action vs. easygoing
   - Stability vs. openness to change
3. Go online and find an example of Rube Goldberg art in which Goldberg illustrates common "systems" from everyday life as he imagines how they could be. What makes these sketches humorous? How many elements of a system can you identify in the illustration you found?
4. Select just one part of an organization with which you are familiar. Describe this as if you were identifying the elements of a system. You can call it a subsystem. What is the "outside" environment of this subsystem? Is it outside the organization or simply the rest of the organization? What are the inputs? What are the transformational processes? What are the outputs? What feedback loops exist? With what other systems is this subsystem interdependent?

IN-CLASS EXERCISES

Issue Debate/Discussion

Divide the class into small groups of five to six people each. Hand out a sheet of paper containing the following quotations. Assign half of the groups to develop a rationale for why the first quotation is valid and the other half to develop a rationale for why the second quotation is valid. Give the groups 5 minutes to discuss. Then call for groups to give a summary of the rationale they developed. Discussion can follow.

Discussion Topic #1: In his book *Religion and the Workplace,* Douglas Hicks defines respectful religious pluralism in terms of the *presumption of inclusion*: "To the greatest extent, workplace organizations should allow employees to express their religious, spiritual, cultural, political, and other commitments at work, subject to the limiting norms of noncoercion, nondegradation, and nonestablishment, and in consideration of the reasonable instrumental demands of the for-profit enterprise."[62]

- Nondegredation prohibits workers from employing speech or symbols or otherwise conveying messages directed at particular individuals or groups of coworkers that show clear disrespect for them.
- Noncoercion means that employees must not use their position, power, or proximity illegitimately to influence coworkers or subordinates.
- Nonestablishment means that "it is not morally acceptable for a company to endorse, or in any way promote, one particular religious or spiritual worldview over others, even if that worldview is deemed 'generic' or is intended to apply to all employees."[63]

How can the Christian leader maintain an organizational culture that promotes respectful religious pluralism and still be true to the beliefs of his/her faith tradition? Do you think that if leaders of a privately-owned, for-profit company promote one particular religious worldview, this is an indirect way of establishing a state-supported religion and because of this a breach of the First Amendment of the Bill of Rights in the U.S. Constitution?

A. **Yes.**
B. **No.**

Discussion Topic #2: Recall the seven dimensions of culture described in this chapter:

- Innovation
- Stability
- Respect for people
- Outcome orientation
- Detail orientation
- Team orientation
- Aggressiveness

Based on what you know of biblical teachings, which of these dimensions seem to have the strongest support in the Bible? Can you give examples of biblical narratives, wisdom, and teachings for each of these?

Discussion Topic #3: If the principles of systems as presented in this chapter are a fair description of reality for organizations, we should expect to see for every organization inputs, transformation processes, outputs, and a feedback loop. If every organization is truly interdependent with its outside environment, how much control does an organization have over its environment?

A. The outside environment determines what happens inside an organization as it seeks to adapt to the needs of customers. If organizations truly operate in an open system, then that system must ultimately determine what the organization does. Customers are king. Their preferences and tastes dictate the types of products that organizations produce. Competitors' actions shape the organization, which reacts to these competitors. The legal and regulatory system sets the boundaries of organizational action. The availability of resources is controlled by organizations and influences outside the control of the organization.
B. The outside environment is malleable to the influences of the organization. If organizations truly operate in an open system, then they must affect every other element of that open system. Every organization can influence customers, suppliers, and competitors. Organizations can and do influence lawmakers and regulators.

Discussion Topic #4: Managers are expected to communicate the organization's vision, purpose, and strategic choices to employees in such a way that employees embrace these and integrate them into the organization's shared values. This requires leaders to give an interpretation of the data in alignment with what they believe are the values. Is this a good thing?

A. **Yes.** Leaders must help employees interpret the data in light of the organization's shared values. Further, leaders must help employees interpret the events and processes taking place in the larger outside environment because this will help employees understand the strategic choices that the organization is pursuing.
B. **No.** Spinning the interpretation of the facts can oversimplify a complicated situation, leaving out some interpretations that employees might have on their own. Oversimplification makes it more difficult for employees to embrace and integrate the vision, purpose, and strategic choices into their own experience because they have their own opinions about what is happening in the larger environment.

Discussion Topic #5: The Christian who believes in a larger system by faith in the existence of God faces some important choices with respect to managerial decision making. Which of the following is the Christian approach?

A. Believe in the existence of God but make decisions at work by considering only the human social systems and physical environmental systems present on the Earth.

B. Believe in the existence of God and make decisions by *quietly* considering not only the human social systems and physical environment but also God's will.

C. Believe in the existence of God and make decisions by *openly* considering not only the human social systems and physical environment but also God's will.

Endnotes

1. Senge, P. M. (1990). *The fifth discipline: The art and practice of the learning organization.* New York: Doubleday. pp. 6–7.
2. Blistex, Inc. is located in Oakbrook, IL. Gunther, M. (2001). God and business. *Fortune.* 144(1), 58–70. Blistex's website is http://www.blistex.com/home.htm.
3. See the North American Industry Classification System (NAICS) No. 32562. http://www.census.gov/epcd/www/naics.html. The NAICS is an organized way to consider the various industrial systems and subsystems in the economic sector of society.
4. Urwick, L. F. (1956). *The pattern of management.* Minneapolis, MN: University of Minnesota Press. p. 13.
5. Scholars who explored systems theory applied to organizations include the following: Mayo, E. (1933). *The human problems of an industrial civilization.* New York: The Macmillan Company; Barnard, C. I. (1938). *The functions of the executive.* Cambridge: Harvard University Press; Barnard, C. I. (1962). *Organization and management: Selected papers.* Cambridge, MA: Harvard University Press; Parsons, T. (1951). *The social system.* New York: The Free Press of Glencoe; Kast, F. E., & Rosenzweig, J. E. (1972). General systems theory: Applications for organization and management. *Academy of Management Journal.* 15(4), 447–465; Katz, D., & Kahn, R. L. (1966). *The social psychology of organizations.* New York: John Wiley; Koontz, H. (1980). The management theory jungle revisited. *The Academy of Management Review.* 5(2), 175–187; Scott, W. G. (1961). Organization theory: An overview and an appraisal. *Academy of Management Journal.* April, 7–26; Scott, W. R. (1987). *Organizations: Rational, natural and open systems.* Englewood Cliffs, NJ: Prentice Hall; Thompson, J. D. (1967). *Organizations in action.* New York: McGraw-Hill Book Company; Werhane, P. H. (2002). Moral imagination and systems thinking. *Journal of Business Ethics.* 38(1/2), 33–42.
6. Mitroff, I. I., & Linstone, H. (1993). *The unbounded mind.* New York: Oxford University Press; Senge, P. (1990). *The fifth discipline.* New York: Doubleday; Bolman, L. G., & Deal, T. E. (2003). *Reframing organizations: Artistry, choice and leadership.* (3rd ed.). San Francisco: Jossey-Bass.
7. Gottfried, R. R. (1995). *Economics, ecology, and the roots of western faith.* Lanham MD: Rowman & Littlefield Publishers, Inc.
8. Porter, B. E., Smith, T. M., & Vellenga, D. B. (2000). *The systems approach: A biblical integration.* Paper presented to the Annual Conference of the Christian Business Faculty Association. Buffalo, NJ. August 29; La Larive, A. (2004). *After Sunday: A theology of work.* New York: Continuum. pp. 93–100.
9. This concept of hierarchy to systems is not new though it has fallen into disuse and has never been a part of the mainstream of scholarly discussion of systems theory applied to organizations. When he proposed it in the 1950s as one classification of systems in a hierarchy, the economist Kenneth E. Boulding described this a "transcendental systems" that was at the pinnacle of all other systems. More recently others, using the frameworks of humanism, have attempted to show the connection between religious beliefs and the systems at work in human existence. See Niebuhr, R. (1954). The idea of covenant and American democracy. *Church History.* 27(4), 126–135; Boulding, K. E. (1956). General systems theory—the skeleton of a science. *Management Science.* April, 197–205; Scott, W. G. (1961). Organization theory: An overview and an appraisal. *Academy of Management Journal.* April, 7–26; de Raadt, J. D. R. (1997). Faith and the normative foundation of systems science. *Systems Practice.* 10(1), 13–35; de Raadt, J. D. R. (1996). What the prophet and the philosopher told their nations: A multi-modal systems view of norms and civilization. *World Futures.* 47, 53–67; de Raadt, J. D. R. (2005). Where there is no vision the people perish: Ethical vision and community sustainability. *Systems Research and Behavioral Science.* 22, 233–247; de Raadt, J. D. R. (2006). Samaritan ethics, systems science and society. *Systemic Practice and Action Research.* 19(5), 498–500; Eriksson, D. M. (2003). Identification of normative sources for systems thinking: An inquiry into religious ground-motives for systems thinking paradigms. *Systems Research and Behavioral Science.* 20(6), 475–487; Gottfried, R. R. (1995). *Economics, ecology, and the roots of western faith.* Lanham MD: Rowman & Littlefield Publishers, Inc.
10. Genesis 1:1; 1 Chronicles 16:26; Nehemiah 9:6; Psalm 8:3, 33:6–9, 89:11, 102:25, 104:24, 136:5; Proverbs 3:19, 16:4; Ecclesiastes 12:1; Isaiah 37:16; John 1:1–3; Acts 4:24, 17:24; Romans 1:19–20; 1 Corinthians 8:6; Ephesians 3:9; Colossians 1:16–17; Hebrews 1:10, 11:3; 1 John 1:1; Revelation 14:7. See also Pauchant, T. C. (2002). *Ethics and spirituality at work: Hopes and pitfalls of the search for meaning in organizations.* Westport, CT: Quorum Books. p. 8. Not everyone in the world of management scholarship agrees with this portrayal of a hierarchical view of systems which include the belief in the existence of God.
11. 2 Chronicles 16:9; Job 34:21–22; Psalm 22:28, 66:7, 103:19, 104:14, 145:14–15; Proverbs 5:21, 15:3; Jeremiah 16:17, 23:24, 32:19; Matthew 10:29–30;

Hebrews 4:13. See also Berkouwer, G. C. (1962). *Man: The image of God.* Grand Rapids, MI: William B. Eerdmans. pp. 68–73; Erickson, M. J. (1998). *Christian theology.* (2nd ed.). Grand Rapids, MI: Baker Books. pp. 177–370; Spykman, G. J. (1992). *Reformational theology: A new paradigm for doing dogmatics.* Grand Rapids, MI: William B. Eerdmans, pp. 245–249.

12. Exodus 23:9; Leviticus 19:10, 19:33–34, 25:35; Deuteronomy 10:19; Matthew 5:43–44, 22:39; Mark 12:31; Luke 6:35, 10:25–37; Romans 13:9–10; Galatians 5:13; James 2:8–10.
13. Romans 12; 1 Corinthians 12; 1 Peter 4:8–11.
14. Opitz, E. A. (1970). *Religion and capitalism: Allies, not enemies.* New Rochelle, NY: Arlington House. pp. 33, 47, 49–50, 61, 108–109.
15. Psalm 10:4, 14:1, 36:1–4, 53:1; Romans 1:21, 1:28; Titus 1:16.
16. In this context Patricia Werhane's comment is worth considering: "Each of us is at once byproducts of, characters in, and authors of, our own experiences. So each of us is responsible for examining, evaluating, critiquing and finding means to change organizations and systems in which we find ourselves." Werhane, P. (2002). Moral imagination and systems thinking. *Journal of Business Ethics.* 38(1/2): 33–42.
17. Rossouw, G. J. (1994). Business ethics: Where have all the Christians gone? *Journal of Business Ethics.* 13(7), 557–570.
18. These ingredients include such things as dimethicone, oxybenzone, padmiate, camphor, beeswax, and cacao seed butter.
19. Kast, F. E., & Rosenzweig, J. E. (1972). General systems theory: Applications for organization and management. *Academy of Management Journal.* 15(4), 447–465.
20. Katz, D., & Kahn, R. L. (1978). *The social psychology of organizations.* (2nd ed.). New York: John Wiley & Sons. p. 752.
21. Blau, P. M., & Scott, W. R. (2003). *Formal organizations: A comparative approach.* Stanford, CA: Stanford Business Books. pp. 38–39; Hall, R. H., & Tolbert P. S. (2005). *Organizations: Structures, processes and outcomes.* (9th ed.). Upper Saddle River, NJ: Pearson Prentice Hall. pp. 4–5, 229–237; Simon H. A. (1997). *Administrative behavior.* (4th ed.). New York: The Free Press. pp. 154–155; Thompson, J. D. (2004). *Organizations in action: Social science bases of administrative theory.* New Brunswick: Transaction Publishers. pp. 127–128.
22. Barnard, C. I. (1938). *The functions of the executive.* Cambridge, MA: Harvard University Press. pp. 137, 233.
23. Drucker, P. F. (1954). *The practice of management.* New York: Harper and Row. pp. 34–48; Drucker, P. F. (1974). *Management: Tasks, responsibilities, practices.* New York: HarperBusiness. pp. 58–94.
24. Here the term "community" is used in a generic sense. Depending on the type of business community might mean the town in which it operates. But community also can mean the industry or the marketplace served by the business whether or not that market is located in a particular town or city. The idea of community also applies to the organization itself as a collection of individuals organized around a common purpose.
25. Gunther, M. (2001). God and business. *Fortune.* 144(1), 58–70. See also the company website at http://www.greystonbakery.com/.
26. Otto Brehm, Inc. is located in Yonkers, NJ. It is unknown whether they are a supplier for Greyston. The Otto Brehm website is http://www.ottobrehm.com /.
27. Gunther, M. (2001). God & business. *Fortune.* 144(1), 58–70.
28. See the CBS News story at http://www.cbsnews.com/stories/2004/01/09/60minutes/main592382.shtml.
29. NAICS 31181: Bread and bakery product manufacturing in the US.
30. Coates, J. F., Jarratt, J., & Mahaffie, J. B. (1991). Future work. *The Futurist.* 25(3), 9–19; Coy, P. (Ed.). (2004/March 22). The future of work. *Business Week.* 3875, 50; Coy, P. (Ed.). (2007/August 20 & 27). The future of work. *Business Week.* 42–66; Colteryahn, K., & Davis, P. (2004). Trends you need to know. *Training & Development.* 58(1), 29–36.
31. Cetron, M. J., & Davies, O. (2005). Trends now shaping the future. *The Futurist.* 39(3), 37–50.
32. Stapinski, H. (1999). Generacion Latino. *American Demographics.* 21(7), 62–68. Navaer, L. E. V. (2004). *The rise of the Hispanic market in the United States.* Armonk, NH: M. E. Sharpe; Gardyn, R. & Fetto, J. (2003). Race, ethnicity and the way we shop. *American Demographics.* 25(1), 30–33.
33. Panagopoulos, C., & Francia, P. L. (2008). The polls-trends: Labor unions in the United States. *Public Opinion Quarterly.* 72(1), 134–159.
34. Thornton, E. (2007/November 5). Perform or perish. *Business Week.* 40576, 38–45; der Hovanesian, M. & Grow, B. (2007/August 20). Did big lenders cross the line? *Business Week.* 4047, 33; McLean, B., & Elkind, P. (2006). The guiltiest guys in the room. *Fortune.* 153(11), 26; Kelly, K. (2005/February). My slithery rivals. *Fortune Small Business.* 15(1), 27–28; Nocera, J., Kahn, J., Rynecki, D., & Leaf, C. (2002/June 24). System failure. *Fortune.* 145(13), 62–70.
35. Albrecht, K. (2006). Eight supertrends shaping the future of business. *The Futurist.* 40(5), 25–29.
36. Managers whose job is to connect the organization to the external environment (e.g., senior-level executives, sales managers, procurement managers, etc.) will spend a good portion of their mental, emotional, and physical energy focused on the external environment. But even these managers, if they are to be effective, will have a keen eye turned inward to their own organization and the how, what, and why their organization must be. Being completely focused on the external environment without much thought about the organization will cause the manager to be ineffective.
37. An example of the use of cultural anthropology to study organizations is: Jacques, E. (1951). *The changing culture of a factory.* London: Tavistock Institute.

38. Deal, T. E., & Kennedy, A. A. (1982). *Corporate cultures: The rites and rituals of corporate life.* Reading, MA: Addison-Wesley; Peters, T. J., & Waterman Jr., R. H. (1982). *In search of excellence: Lessons from America's best-run companies.* New York: Harper & Row; Ouchi, W. G. (1981). *Theory Z: How American business can meet the Japanese challenge.* New York: Avon.
39. Kouzes, J., & Posner, B. (2003). Character development: It's what leadership development is all about. *Executive Excellence.* 20(9), 3.
40. The organization's real name has been changed for this illustration.
41. Schein, E. H. (1990, February). Organizational culture. *American Psychologist.* 45, 109–119.
42. Schein, E. H. (2004). *Organizational culture and leadership.* (3rd ed.). San Francisco, CA: John Wiley & Sons.
43. Ireland, R. D. (1992). Corporate culture best conveyed by mid-level managers. *Baylor Business Review.* 10, 18–19.
44. For a discussion of the biases inherent in studying organizational culture see Rousseau, D. M. (1985). Issues of level in organizational research: Multi-level and cross-level perspectives. In Cummings, L. L., & Staw, B. M. (Eds.). *Research in organizational behavior.* (Vol. 7). Greenwich, CT: JAI Press. pp. 1–38; Ashkansasy, N. M., & Jackson, C. R. A. (2001). Organizational culture and climate. In Anderson, N., Ones, D. S., Sinangil, H. K., & Viswesvaran, C. (Eds.). *Handbook of industrial, work and organizational psychology.* (Vol. 2). Thousand Oaks, CA: Sage Publications. pp. 398–415.
45. For an example from a manufacturing organization see Schein, E. H. (1996). Three cultures of management: The key to organizational learning. *Sloan Management Review.* 38(1), 9–20.
46. Chatman, J. A., & Jehn, K A. (1994). Assessing the relationship between industry characteristics and organizational culture: How different can you be? *The Academy of Management Journal.* 37(3), 522–553; Gordon, G. (1991). Industry determinants of organizational culture. *Academy of Management Review.* 16, 396–415.
47. O'Reilly, C., Chatman, J., & Caldwell, D. (1991). People and organizational culture: A Q-sort approach to assessing person-organization fit. *Academy of Management Journal.* 34, 487–516; Dennison, D. R. (1990). *Corporate culture and effectiveness.* New York: Wiley; Rousseau, D. (1990). Quantitative assessment of organizational culture: The case for multiple measures. In B. Schneider (Ed.). *Frontiers in industrial and organizational psychology.* Vol. 3, pp. 153–192. San Francisco, CA: Jossey-Bass; Chatman, J. A., & Jehn, K A. (1994). Assessing the relationship between industry characteristics and organizational culture: How different can you be? *The Academy of Management Journal.* 37(3), 522–553.
48. Denison, D. R., & Mishra, A. K. (1995). Toward a theory of organizational culture and effectiveness. *Organizational Science.* 6(2), 204–223; Fey, C. F., & Denison, D. R. (2003). Organizational culture and effectiveness: Can American theory be applied in Russia? *Organizational Science.* 14(6), 686–706.
49. Gofee, R., & Jones, G. (1998). *The character of a corporation.* New York: HarperBusiness.
50. Bolman, L. G., & Deal, T. E. (2003). *Reframing organizations: Artistry, choice and leadership.* (3rd ed.). San Francisco, CA: Jossey-Bass. p. 243.
51. Meglino, B. M., Ravlin, C. E., & Adkins, C. L. (1991). Value congruence and satisfaction with a leader: An examination of the role of interaction. *Human Relations.* 44, 481–495.
52. Cooper-Thomas, H., & Anderson, N. (2006). Organizational socialization: A new theoretical and recommendations for future research and HRM practices in organizations. *Journal of Managerial Psychology.* 21(5), 492–516.
53. Tung, L. H., & An, T. H. (2003). Newcomer socialization: The role of job standardization. *Public Personnel Management.* 32(4), 579–689.
54. Goodstein, L. D. (1979). Maintaining the organizational culture: An experiential strategy for socializing new managers. *Group & Organization Studies.* 4(3): 287–293; Yosup, L., & Larwood, L. (1983). The socialization of expatriate managers in multinational firms. *Academy of Management Journal.* 26(4), 657–665.
55. Higgins, J. M., & McAllaster, C. (2004). If you want strategic change, don't forget to change your cultural artifacts. *Journal of Change Management.* 4(1), 63–73; Childers, P. (2005). Organizational culture affects the bottom line. *HR Magazine.* 50(9), 104–110.
56. Lewis, M. W., & Dehler, G. E. (2000). Learning through paradox: A pedagogical strategy for exploring contradictions and complexity. *Journal of Management Education.* 24(6), 708–725.
57. Scott, W. R. (1987). *Organizations: Rational, natural and open systems.* Englewood Cliffs, NJ: Prentice Hall.
58. Wendt, R. F. (1998). The sound of one hand clapping: Counterintuitive lessons extracted from paradoxes and double blinds in participative organizations. *Management Communication Quarterly.* 11(3), 323–371; Lowy, A., & Hood, P. (2004). *The power of the 2×2 matrix: Using 2×2 thinking to solve business problems and make better decisions.* San Francisco, CA: Jossey-Bass; Besanko, D., Dranove, D., Shanley, M., & Schaefer, S. (2004). *Economics of strategy.* (3rd ed.). New York: John Wiley & Sons. p. 99; Denison, D. R., Haaland, S, & Goelzer, P. (2004). Corporate culture and organizational effectiveness: Is Asia different from the rest of the world? *Organizational Dynamics.* 33(1), 98–109; Hall, R. H., & Tolbert, P. S. (2005). *Organizations: Structures, processes and outcomes.* (9th ed.). Upper Saddle River, NJ: Pearson Prentice Hall; Overholt, M. H. (1997). Flexible organizations: Using organizational design as a competitive advantage. *HR. Human Resource Planning.* 21(1), 22–33; Fiol, C. M. (2002). Capitalizing on paradox: The role of language

in transforming organizational identities. *Organization Science.* 13(6), 653–667; Trice, H., & Beyer, J. (1993). *The cultures of work organizations.* Englewood Cliffs, NJ: Prentice Hall; Collins, J. C., & Porras, J. I. (1994). *Built to last: Successful habits of visionary companies.* New York: HarperBusiness.

59. Smith, K. K., & Berg, D. N. (1997). *Paradoxes of group life: Understanding conflict, paralysis and movement in group dynamics.* San Francisco: The New Lexington Press; Pascale, R. T. (1990). *Managing on the edge: How the smartest companies use conflict to stay ahead.* New York: Simon and Schuster.
60. Information from the Boeing Employees Bible Fellowship website: http://www.bebf.org.
61. O'Reilly, C., Chatman, J., & Caldwell, D. (1991). People and organizational culture: A profile comparison approach to assessing person-organization fit. *Academy of Management Journal.* 34, 487–516.
62. Hicks, D. A. (2003). *Religion and the workplace: Pluralism, spirituality, leadership.* New York: Cambridge University Press. p. 173.
63. Hicks, D. A. (2003). *Religion and the workplace: Pluralism, spirituality, leadership.* New York: Cambridge University Press. p. 174.

CHAPTER 4

Cross-Cultural Management

LEARNING OBJECTIVES

- Gain an increased awareness of the complexity and importance of cross-cultural management.
- Explain the management pyramid in the context of cross-cultural management.
- Understand the faith perspective on cross-cultural management.
- Describe the concept of cultural intelligence and how it is developed.
- Distinguish between the various dimensions and dilemmas of cross-cultural management.
- Understand the moral issues that emerge in global business.
- Describe selected paradoxes of cross-cultural management.

"Christians have a worldview that differs from others, but Christians cannot claim to have greater technological or intellectual competency. We must nurture the abilities of those who are not Christians with the same respect and dedication that we would want for ourselves, for all people bear God's image."[1]

"After these things he [Paul] left Athens and went to Corinth. And he found a Jew named Aquila, a native of Pontus, having recently come from Italy with his wife Priscilla, because Claudius had commanded all the Jews to leave Rome. He came to them. And because he was of the same trade, he stayed with them and they were working, for by trade they were tent-makers. And he was reasoning in the synagogue every Sabbath and trying to persuade Jews and Greeks."[2]

JON AND BRITTANY THAYER

Jon Thayer was getting moody. He tried to feel better by taking weekend excursions from Bangkok to Hong Kong or Singapore with his wife Brittany. But soon both Jon and Brittany grew tired of hotel rooms, lugging around travel bags, and eating restaurant food. Brittany missed her friends back in the United States. She found it pleasant but a bit curious that complete strangers would smile at her for no apparent reason.[3] But other things irritated her, for example, having to "tip" the driver's license bureau agent to get a driver's license.[4] Jon and Brittany also became concerned when a group of protesters took over and shut down the Bangkok Airport.[5]

What surprised Jon at first was how much more complicated managing in an international arena was than he expected. For Jon, the greatest challenge of working in Asia for an American pharmaceutical company was communication. Jon, already fluent in French and English, now realized that he needed to relate with people who spoke Mandarin. Jon soon tired of asking work associates to translate into English and decided to enroll in a Mandarin language training program at night. Also, in America, Jon was used to quick, brief messages sent by email, text, or telephone. Many of his Asian colleagues expected to see him face to face when he needed to give them a message. In addition, he had a difficult time accepting that females were, compared to North American standards, treated as second-class citizens.

Source: Jupiterimages/Thinkstock.

Jon observed that other Americans who had moved to Thailand a year or two before were way ahead of him in their experience. While he was cautious, they were adventurous. They reminded him that he was not in America, and advised him to relax and learn from the Asians.

During his first 18 months in Bangkok, Jon learned the many differences between working in Thailand and working in the United States: communication and control systems, the importance of currency exchange, the role of government in commerce, the political and financial risks of doing business, and cultural expectations on a variety of issues including scheduling meetings and protocols for communication. He learned the importance of understanding the organizational structure (reporting relationships), and how his corporation attempted to coordinate the efforts of divisions across multiple Asian cultures. He learned to appreciate many of the Asian cultural values and communication styles. See Exhibit 4-1 on Western Views Versus Asian Views.

Jon and Brittany learned that what was right and wrong was more often ambiguous compared with what they had experienced in the United States. Jon's religious beliefs were tested during his time working in Bangkok. Back in North America, Jon was able to stay connected with his faith community by attending church services each week and participating in church fellowship activities. But here, Jon's religious values were quite different from those of his coworkers. He didn't understand their religious beliefs. For a long time, Jon and his family felt out of place.

There was something else that was different about working in the new environment. It took Jon a few years of experience and his eventual return to the United States before he could explain it completely. The point of view regarding work and prosperity was different for many he had contact with compared with those in business in North America. Many Thai believe that economic prosperity results from the collective effect of humans who have

EXHIBIT 4-1
Western Views Versus Asian Views

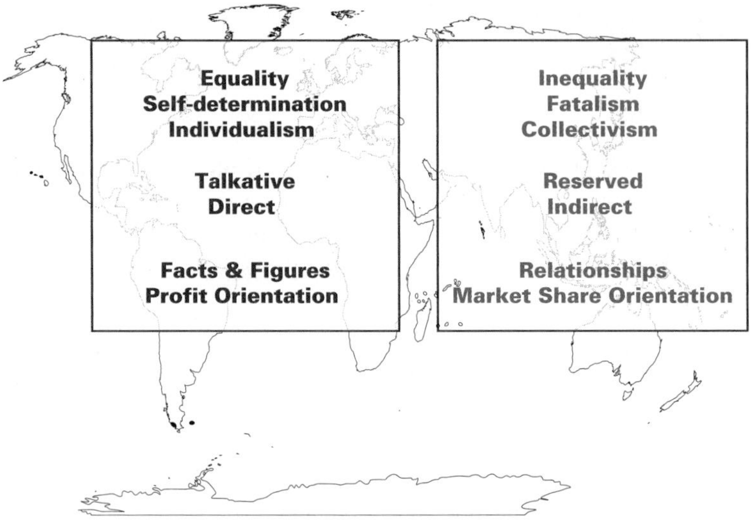

Source: Based on Lewis, R. D. (2003). Cultural orientations affecting leadership styles. In *The cultural imperative*. Boston, MA: Nicholas Brealy/Intercultural Press. Shown in Moran, R. T., Harris, P. R., & Moran, S. V. (2007). *Managing cultural differences: Global leadership strategies for the 21st century.* New York: Elsevier. p. 121.

developed four virtues: kindness, sympathetic joy, compassion, and impartiality. In North America, many believe that prosperity comes from hard work, capitalizing on opportunities, and resourcefulness. Their worldview, just like his, was the thread that connected everything that they did making it coherent and completely understandable from their perspective.[6]

Jon and Brittany eventually returned to North America from Thailand. Jon's new knowledge of Asian business gave him an important perspective to share with others in his company.

Even though humans around the world share many similarities, every national culture is different. From one perspective, Jon and Brittany Thayer's experience says more about them than it does about the people of Thailand. Their experiences illustrate the complexities of taking management ideas from one culture to another and the personal impact of these complexities. Working cross culturally as a manager affects you and your family down to the very core of who you are, how you think and feel, and ultimately your actions.

Who Cares About Cross-Cultural Management?

One of the reasons organizations need managers is to help employees understand and communicate with people from cultures other than their own.

Cross-cultural management is becoming more prevalent as companies increasingly expand their reach globally. Corporations ask quick-learning managers to transfer to new locations where they can work closely with local managers. Also, the decrease in costs of global communication has opened up some industries to new competitors who are eager to exploit the opportunities the global marketplace provides.[7] For example, Cemex from Mexico now sells cement globally. Some of these organizations span multiple industries and serve multiple countries. For example, General Electric operates a variety of businesses worldwide in power generation, healthcare equipment, oil and gas, consumer products, aviation, business finance, and consumer finance. Its competitor, Siemens, operates in some of the same industries as General Electric.

Cultures in other countries are not arbitrarily different from your home culture. What is important to people in other countries might be different from what is important to you. What might seem strange to you about the behavior of people in another culture makes perfect sense to them.[8] Learning to understand these differences is vital for managers who want to help their companies succeed in the global economy. Even managers who never travel from their home country find that to be successful they must know how to work with employees, customers, or suppliers that come from or work in cultures different from their own.

Management Pyramid at the Cross-Cultural Level

We have seen that the Management Pyramid of being and becoming, thinking and feeling, and action applies at both the individual and the organizational level. The Management Pyramid also applies at the society level in terms of culture, as Exhibit 4-2 illustrates.

Actions taken with organizations and individuals from another culture		**Action**
Wondering why people in another culture behave differently from how you behave **Feelings that arise from experiencing a different culture** **Culture shock**		**Thinking & Feeling**
Home Culture + **Beliefs** **Perceptions** **Moral values** **Shared values** **Assumptions**	**Host Culture** **Beliefs** **Perceptions** **Moral values** **Shared values** **Assumptions**	**Being & Becoming**

EXHIBIT 4-2

The Management Pyramid: Cross-Cultural Management

Source: Courtesy of Michael E. Cafferky, © Michael E. Cafferky 2011.

While the most visible differences between cultures are found at the action level, more significant differences lie at the deeper levels of thinking, feeling, and worldview.

Even the simplest of actions carry deep-rooted thoughts, beliefs, and assumptions. In North America and Europe, the simple action of a handshake can be critical in business. The handshake signifies openness to having a working connection with the person. It is a sign of courtesy and respect even if you do not like the other person. To refuse a handshake that is offered is offensive. But the handshake can be so quick and perfunctory that its meaning is lost in the conversational context in which it occurs. "Get the handshake out of the way so we can get to the core of why we are here" can be the essence of the action in a fast-paced, time-sensitive culture of efficient business.

Greetings take on different forms as you travel from culture to culture. In Asia, bowing has a meaning that is deeper than simply being a sign of respect and courtesy. Bowing to greet a person is a physical expression of a mental attitude of openness and paying attention to the other person who is external to you. It expresses awareness that the external environment (such as the person you are bowing to) is an important contributor to the virtues that guide your actions. It signifies an expectancy that something may be offered to the one bowing that may be incorporated into future actions.[9]

Expatriate managers will find it relatively easy to adapt to simple behaviors such as introducing themselves to others. (**Expatriates** are people who leave their home country to work in another country.) Copying the action of the Asian respectful bow, for example, is relatively easy, but copying the whole mindset that is integrated with and is the meaning behind the respectful bow is much more difficult to understand, much less to copy. It is usually more difficult to adapt to differences in thinking styles and emotional reactions to situations. It is at the deepest level of assumptions, beliefs, values, and worldview where the most difficult challenges await the manager who works in a cross-cultural environment.

Faith Perspective on Cross-Cultural Management

The question before us is what elements of the Christian faith perspective are important when we think about management in a cross-cultural environment? We start with the Christian faith perspective because it is an important part of the Christian's personal beliefs and values (the "being and becoming" part of the Management Pyramid model).

Christian faith is founded on a basic belief in what is called monotheism, the belief that there is just one Supreme Being we call God. For the Christian faith, God is the God of all creation, of every culture, every nation, and every time.[10] This is significant for the Christian, the Jew, and the Muslim, all of whom believe that God's will for creatures spans the entire globe, not just the locale where believers in God currently reside. To the person of faith, God's will spans not only private life but also the public life in the marketplace. This means that the life of human beings is never outside the sovereignty of God. All actions, regardless of where we are on earth, must be put into alignment with God's will. This includes all of our actions in the world marketplaces. The assumption embedded in this belief is that God's will is the unerring, absolute, and objective authority on faith and living.

Cross-Cultural Exchange

The Bible accepts cross-cultural exchange as valid social activity. Long before companies such as Kimberly-Clark (producers of the Kleenex brand products) and Coca-Cola (the number one global brand) existed,[11] Bible writers were aware of differences in language[12] and national or regional culture.[13] They were aware that when encountering unfamiliar nations, fear is a natural reaction.[14] We read about several Bible characters who either spoke a second language or depended on interpreters to help them communicate with people of other cultures: Abraham, Joseph, Moses, David, Solomon, Daniel, and the Apostle Paul. Those who could speak more than one language were valuable, especially in border territories and merchant cities where trading occurred.

International trade was accepted as part of life in biblical times.[15] It even played an important role in God's Providence of saving the family and descendants of Jacob who became the Israeli nation, culminating in the birth of the Messiah.[16] Joseph's brothers sold him into slavery to Midianite traders, who then resold him after they arrived in Egypt. Joseph eventually became the prime minister of Egypt and secured Pharaoh's permission for his family to settle in an area where they had access to food. This preserved the family during the famine.

While most products were produced and distributed locally, some regions had already developed brand strength—for example, Lebanon became known for its cedar tree products.[17] Most international trade involved transporting goods by land using pack animals or by sea using ships.[18] Certain cities became centers of international trade. Babylon, Jerusalem, and the Phoenician seaport of Tyre all became wealthy trading centers.[19]

In Scripture we see examples of remarkable cross-cultural exchange. Joseph was sold to Midianite traders and ended up as the head of Egyptian international and domestic commerce.[20] Solomon became very wealthy, in part, because of his international trading. Despite his later unfaithfulness to God, his ability to move from the Israeli culture to other cultures was phenomenal and should not be minimized.

During his ministry, Jesus easily interacted with people from other cultures.[21] It is interesting that Jesus judged his own culture more vehemently than the cultures of other nations. On occasion he violated the cultural values of his own people.[22] For example, he pointed out the hypocrisy of those who emphasized outward ceremonial cleansing while they neglected the cleansing of the heart.

The Apostle Paul was aware of his own cultural values.[23] A tent maker by trade, Paul traveled on a trading ship from Galilee and Judea to Greece and Rome.[24] He even selected some highly visible trading ports to be the centers of his evangelistic work.

In Bible times international trade became an important dimension for the work of spreading the Gospel.

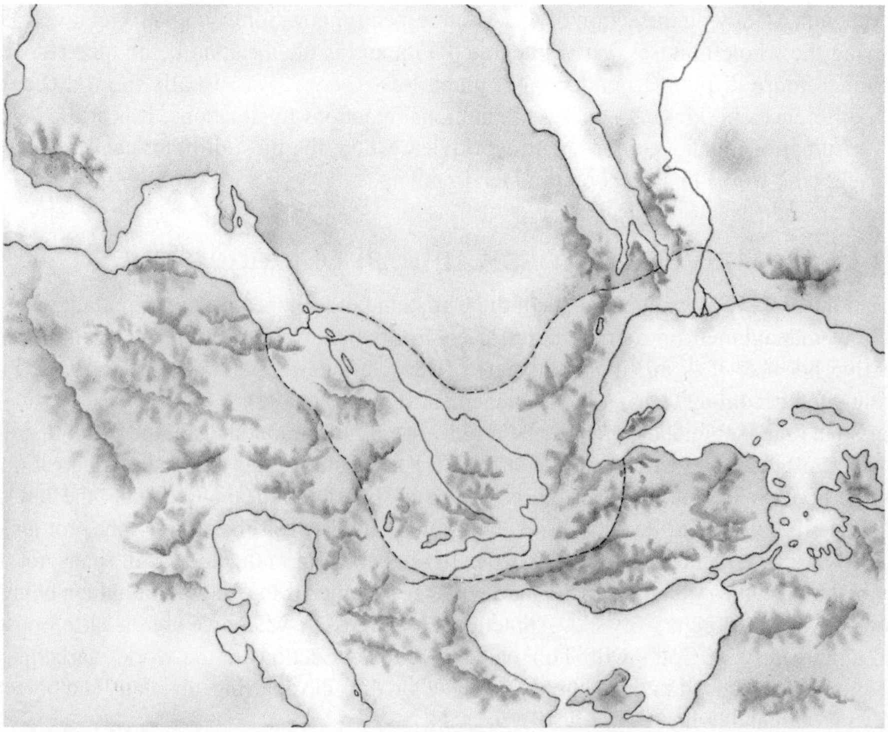

Source: Peter Dennis © Dorling Kindersley.

Covenant Relationships Are Global

God's covenants to Adam, Noah, Abraham, and Moses were all global covenants.[25] For example, Abraham's reputation would be great in the international arena.[26] His descendents were to become a great nation, and through such a nation, all families of the whole world would receive a blessing.[27] Believers were expected to live in nations whose cultures were different from their own so that they could spread this blessing.[28] Their superior virtuous character, health, intellect, economic prosperity, skill in craftsmanship, and agriculture would contribute to their international reputation. They were to live a life of faithful service to God that would result in such rich blessings that other nations would seek the same for themselves.

While the plan evidently did not include aggressive evangelism, it is difficult to see how God's plan could be accomplished without a significant amount of cross-cultural contact between Abraham's descendents and the rest of the world. Some of that contact would be as a result of ambassadors from other nations visiting Israel and then taking the good news back to their own countrymen. Other contacts would come from Israelites traveling and trading with other nations. Through all of this, Israel was destined to be a witness, a light to the Gentiles.[29]

We might conclude from Scripture that members of the faith community developed their self-identity and purpose within a global context. The identity of Israel began with God's covenant to Abraham.[30] It continued to be built through Israel's call out of Egypt.[31] The nation's international trading could not, without harmful consequences, be separated from its broader covenantal purpose on earth. Later, captivity added to the awareness that when believers were unfaithful to God they were to be scattered around the globe.[32] One of the punishments for not following the Law given by Moses included being displaced from the comforts of their own culture and forced to live in cultures that were foreign to them.[33] Yet, even the captivity, as an opportunity for witnessing, became a part of this self-consciousness.[34] Following God's law was one pathway to gaining international respect not only for believers but also for God.

Some of the nations around Israel were known for breaking treaties, enslaving captives, and using violence.[35] Some of these nations were comprised of the Israelites' distant relatives.[36] Israeli traders also engaged in immoral business practices.[37]

Covenant is based on establishing and maintaining an enduring relationship that considers not only your own interests, but also the interests of a particular person or organization with which you do business. It also considers the wider community of individuals or organizations that are affected, including those who are related to you and those who are related to the other party. In global commerce, this wider community affected by a management relationship may be spread across many countries, making it more difficult to maintain a covenant approach in all relationships.

Israel's Hope

The people of Israel hoped and expected that their nation would become the leader among nations to whom other nations would come to learn of God. Israel would share its faith in God by sharing the moral absolutes of God's law with other nations. It would also form relationships with people of other cultures to arouse curiosity and encourage conversations about the basis of their faith.[38]

When God's followers found themselves in other nations, they were not to follow the cultural practices that were inconsistent with God's law.[39] Unfortunately, many did not heed this instruction.[40] King Solomon began following some of the forbidden cultural practices, and the whole nation of Israel reaped a catastrophic result.[41]

God's original plan for Israel must have been conditioned on Israel remaining faithful to the covenant. We find evidence in Scripture that because of unbelief and the lowering of its own moral standards, its international influence was only partially successful. However, the idea that members of the faith community were to influence the world was not totally lost. The hope of Israel was fulfilled in Jesus Christ. As a result, there was still work for the spiritual descendents of Abraham to do in witnessing to the whole world—a belief that was embraced by the early Christians, many of whom were Jewish.[42]

The early Christian church also grew from a multicultural environment.[43] Christians sensed that their role in extending God's Kingdom was to be a global experience.[44] The Great Gospel

Commission of Jesus for his followers was to "go therefore and teach all nations" to spread the gospel. In this way, God's promise to Abraham that his descendents would bless the whole earth could be fulfilled.[45]

An Agent for Peace

Taking the biblical record as a whole, some scholars have concluded that business is to be an agent of shalom (peace).[46] The Bible does not condemn international business, but it does condemn the use of international trade to unjustly build wealth.[47]

Today, Christians engaged in world commerce will see their purpose in honoring God in all that they do. Under this view, a manager's work is a means of extending the kingdom of God in and through managerial work. Managers can attempt to keep business separate from mission, but this will be difficult if the manager wants to be true to the gospel's Great Commission.[48] Several possible ways that managers can be agents of peace through international business follow.[49]

- When they have legitimate authority to do so, Christian managers will make business decisions that are consistent with their understanding of biblical principles. The challenge is that reasonable Christians may likely disagree regarding how to apply biblical principles in complicated situations.
- Managers who have responsibility for making capital investment decisions will decide, in part, based on whether the investment is expected to contribute to an affirmation of life. Such consideration ranges far beyond discussions of return on investment.
- Some Christian managers will intentionally decide to seek employment in geographical areas of the world where social and economic problems exist. Working in these areas places the manager in a position to model faith behaviors while helping needy individuals.
- Other Christian managers will work in global commerce so that they can earn money to contribute to social service organizations who help or in other ways minister to those in need.[50]
- Still other managers will engage in global commerce to generate funds to donate to church evangelism. This is the model of business as the economic engine of church mission.
- Some managers intentionally use their positions to evangelize and plant congregations of believers in new areas of the globe.

Being an agent for peace is not always easy. It can be difficult for the person of faith to maintain a solid ethical anchor in a cross-cultural environment. Some practices that are illegal in the home country are legal in the host country. Standards of morality are different around the world, and the morality of some practices may be ambiguous. For the manager of faith this will raise the difficult question of whether to be effective the manager must adopt a double moral standard.[51] What was clearly right and wrong in one's home country can become ambiguous in another country. "Stay in a foreign culture long enough, some believe, and you will lose your ethical moorings and sink down into a swamp of relativism."[52]

The Biblical Story of Daniel

Read the story of Daniel recorded in the book of Daniel. Grasp the significance of the accomplishments that occurred under the leadership of Daniel after he moved from his land to the empire of Babylon. What leadership principles can we gain from the experience of Daniel that are applicable today?

Cultural Intelligence

The expansion of electronic information technologies, rapid world travel, and the movement of multilingual people and organizations worldwide are increasing. By comparison, cultures are slow to change. Similarly, business practices are changing rapidly, while the underlying cultural beliefs and practices of business are changing slowly.

- **Respect for others in your host country.** In some cultures, respect is the top priority when you are speaking with or about someone who is older or who is in a formal position.
- **Tolerating ambiguity.** You may not understand some elements of the host culture's way of life and viewpoint. The unpredictability of life in a new culture will gradually improve, but until it does, you will need toleration.
- **Relating to people.** Individuals from Western cultures value getting the job done as their top priority. Individuals in other cultures value relationships as their top priority.
- **Being nonjudgmental.** Keep your opinions to yourself when you observe actions that grate against your personal value system. If you make value differences a point of contention, the hosts will feel like you are judging them and will be offended.
- **Personalizing observations.** Recognize that you bring a different set of perceptions to social situations. Be cautious about drawing generalized conclusions from what you observe.
- **Empathy.** Practice putting yourself in the place of others in your host country. Even if you don't get every detail absolutely correct, your hosts will appreciate that you are interested in them.
- **Persistence.** Learning how and why a new culture works takes time. You will experience delays and failed attempts. Don't give up. Learn from each situation and experience.

EXHIBIT 4-3
Key Skills for Cross-Cultural Leadership[53]

This means that organizations increasingly need managers who possess a *cultural intelligence* that equips them to be leaders in a cross-cultural environment.[54] **Cultural intelligence** is "the capability to deal effectively with people from different cultural backgrounds."[55] See Exhibit 4-3.

Being culturally intelligent means that you have a cluster of competencies consisting of "cultural knowledge, the practice of mindfulness, and a repertoire of behavioral skills" that help you establish and maintain positive rapport with others.[56]

You can't gain these competencies with just one or two trips to another culture. Even living on the inside of another culture for a year may not fully develop your cultural intelligence, but it will help a lot. Learning another culture requires time and firsthand experience. See Exhibit 4-4. In some cases, building cultural intelligence requires participating in a focused learning and training program.[57] Being immersed in another culture for an extended period of time is the quickest way to learn.

As you enter a new culture to live and work, your experience will change as time passes.[58] At first you will simply be reacting to new, confusing situations. It is not uncommon for people to mindlessly adhere to their own cultural values without regard for the people in the new host country. What motivates other people is different from what motivates you. With experience, you will learn to accommodate these differences, even if you don't agree with everything. Your

You can develop your cultural intelligence by:

- Taking a job or an internship with an international company
- Studying in another country
- Traveling abroad
- Developing and maintaining friendships with people from other cultures
- Teaching English as a second language
- Working for the government in another country
- Serving in foreign mission
- Serving in the military

EXHIBIT 4-4
How to Develop Cultural Intelligence[59]

behaviors and your thinking will gradually change as you adjust to what you learn about the expectations of those around you.

As your cultural intelligence grows, you will be able to anticipate situations and the reactions of others to your behavior. This ability will allow you to be more proactive in adjusting your behavior in advance, rather than merely reacting to unfamiliar situations. At this level of development, you will begin to see past simplistic stereotypes and understand the history and broader context in which you are experiencing the culture.

Part of learning another culture is making mistakes. At first, you may misinterpret actions and misunderstand the point of view of individuals in the host country. To be successful you must watch closely, listen, and at times ask questions of those who are effective in that cross-cultural environment. Developing cultural intelligence is a humble process of being and becoming, thinking and feeling, and acting in ways that are consistent with your own values but that are also respectful of the values of your host culture.

The Christian Mind on Cultural Intelligence

I Chronicles 12:32 and Esther 1:13 encourage us to "understand the times" of the culture and context we find ourselves in. Managers working in or with people from other cultural contexts need to understand distinctions between their own cultural values and norms and the target (new) country. Hofstede's (http://www.geert-hofstede.com/) work is a great starting point. Understanding the importance of the group (collective) relative to the individual and the need for certainty or comfort with uncertainty are critical to managing persons and organizations in a cross-cultural context. Cultural intelligence is important for managers to acclimate to their new setting, and to understand how to work effectively. Managers who fail to acclimate to the new culture are often frustrated and return to their home country.

Dr. Ervin Starr
Associate Professor of Management & Entrepreneurship
Roberts Wesleyan College
Rochester, NY

Cross-Cultural Awareness for Managers

Your awareness of the dimensions of national culture and the differences between cultures will help you become a more effective manager. This awareness will affect your approaches to decision making, communication, and many other managerial activities. It will help you become more respectful of how others around the world think about work.

Dimensions of National Culture

Culture is defined as the set of deeply held values shared among members of a social group. We speak of values as being deeply held, meaning that they change very slowly over time; they are the fundamental ways of thinking that affect everything else that we think about in life. Because values are deeply held, they are an important driving force behind thinking, emotions, and behavior. Cultural context can explain a lot about why managers from different cultures behave differently.

Researchers have identified several **dimensions of culture**, which are the things that distinguish one cultural group from another and which can be used to compare cultural groups. We will briefly explore these next.[60] Exhibit 4-5 lists various dimensions of culture.

RELIGIOUS BELIEF AND PRACTICE. Of all the various dimensions of culture, this may be the most influential in some cultures. Religious beliefs are embedded at the deepest level of human consciousness. They keep alive a person's conscience, which in turn acts as an important guide to behavior. Religions usually provide some guidance regarding marketplace behaviors even if

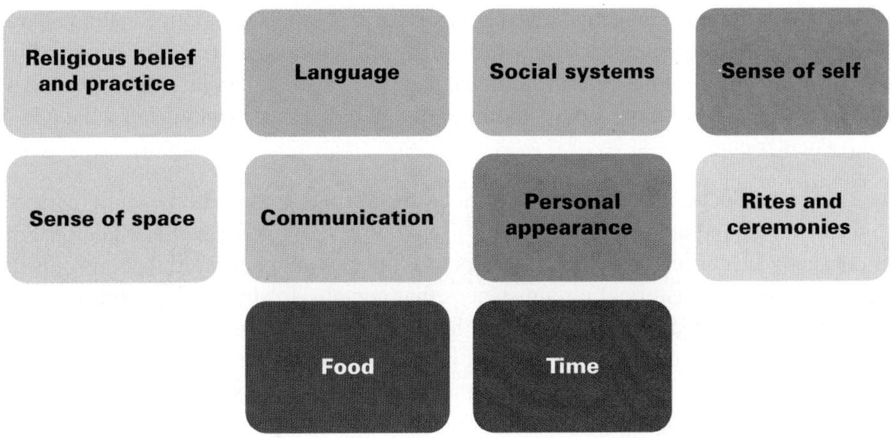

EXHIBIT 4-5
Dimensions of Culture

such guidance is not a comprehensive teaching on economics.[61] For example, Orthodox Jews and Seventh-day Adventists keep their businesses closed on Saturday. Some Protestant and Catholic believers close their businesses on Sunday, their day of worship. In both cases, the owners are willing to lose some revenue because it means remaining faithful to their belief and practice. See Exhibit 4-6.

EXHIBIT 4-6
Three Monotheistic World Religions and Business

Judaism[62]	In Judaism, all human actions have cosmic significance. All of life is sacred. Spiritual attainment is not about attempting to rise above the temporal and mundane but rather to live *within* the sanctified everyday in such a way that brings God into our world. It means being preoccupied with finding ways to serve others. While the Sabbath is sacred time set aside for worship, every portion of time we have during the rest of the week is considered sacred and unique, and the actions we take now (whether in the marketplace or in leisure) will surely affect what is to come in the future. The business of the marketplace is never separated from this. Economic activity is a reflection of the moral principles molded by the Torah, shared by communal practice and contemplated through prayer and meditation. "Accordingly, business activity, as are all aspects of human endeavor, is an inherently religious undertaking." [63]
Christianity[64]	In Christian belief, all of business life is experienced under God. Business is a calling to worship God through one's work. Worship is both the activities in religious services or programs as well as the activities of private personal devotions and the believer's life of service to others in the world. The marketplace is a place to preach Gospel; a place to serve others. Because of this, it is potentially a good place. At the same time, the marketplace can be a destructive place if the rich get richer at the expense of the poor. Competition can be good in that it spurs business owners to become more efficient stewards. Competition that is unchecked by moral constraints also can be destructive. Business imitates God's sovereignty by taking charge over things we own. It becomes a model of God's creative power by using human creativity in work to serve each other. Humans are expected to be wise stewards over resources that God has given them because, ultimately, everything belongs to God. The believer's role in business is not complete unless both persons and organizations become useful for redeeming the marketplace.
Islam[65]	In Islamic teaching, humans were created for the purpose of worshiping Allah and for serving each other. In this they are Allah's trustees. The metaphor of worship as a journey best depicts this spirituality in Islam. This journey is a difficult one that is achieved out of love and devotion to Allah. The goal of the journey is to unite with the Creator (in whom a part of Allah resides) in faith and, through this, unite with *all* Creation. Islam views action in day-to-day life as inseparable from faith. Humans are accountable to Allah for all their actions. Muhammad said, "Work for your worldly life as if you were going to live forever, but work for the life to come as if you were going to die tomorrow." [66]

LANGUAGE. Differences in language may be one of the first things you notice when you travel to another culture. Such differences affect the ability of individuals from different cultures to transact business and coordinate efforts. But language goes deeper than just alphabets and words. Embedded in language are more subtle idioms and even the deeper meanings of what it is like to live in a particular culture.

SOCIAL SYSTEMS. **Social systems** are the various social rules, expectations, and practices "that govern the behavior and customs of people."[67] If you were to work for Nokia, the global distributor of consumer electronics with headquarters in Finland, you would find that customs usually develop out of specific historical circumstances that contain, for those who experienced them, deep significance. Such significance is often hidden to the outsider. For example, the Finnish culture is known for courtesy in conversations. Interrupting someone is rude. The deeper cultural value at the basis of this expectation may be that members of Finnish society believe in human equality. Humility and modesty are virtues. Social systems shape what the people in the local culture think about things such as work behaviors, productivity, dating, marriage, family life, and entertainment.

SENSE OF SELF. Your **sense of self**, or self-identity, is shaped, to a large degree, by your perceptions of the social group around you. In one culture, individuals learn to think of themselves as humble servants of the group. In a contrasting culture, individuals learn to think of themselves as important in their own right regardless of what the group thinks.

SENSE OF SPACE. In some countries, individuals are expected to stand very close together when talking. In other countries, individuals need more space between them. These expectations about distances between individuals form a person's **sense of space**. The next time you have a conversation with someone ask that person to stand closer than normal. Or ask the person to stand a step or two farther away than normal. Notice your comfort level.

COMMUNICATION. Differences in language are an obvious way to compare one culture with another. But communication goes deeper than language. Nonverbal communication may represent the majority of "the message" that is communicated. While tone of voice and gestures are universal, the meaning of gestures can be vastly different across cultures.

PERSONAL APPEARANCE. How a person dresses and decorates his or her body (or not) tends to be culturally distinctive. This is as true for the world of business as it is in the rest of society. For example, with some exceptions in North America, the traditional business outfit for men is a suit and tie. In Asian and Latin countries, an open-collared shirt is acceptable for business settings.

Even the simplest of actions, such as the traditional bow in greeting, can have much deeper cultural meaning.

Source: Digital Vision/Thinkstock.

RITES AND CEREMONIES. Human beings have developed an almost unlimited ability to use symbols, metaphors, parables, stories, and other forms of narrative to capture the meaningful events in the human experience. Out of these narratives have come simple or elaborate ceremonies that elicit intense emotions. For the outsider, ceremonies can represent some of the great mysteries of a new culture, yet they represent some of the most important keys to understanding national consciousness.

FOOD. Food carries forward many memories of past events. The ingredients, the preparation, the presentation, the social occasions, and how the food is consumed (or in other ways used) are culturally significant. For example, the North America practice of grabbing a quick bite to eat from a drive-through restaurant would be offensive to some from cultures that require a more leisurely pace, as well as the presence of close family members, when consuming food. In contrast, an American may feel impatient regarding the "waste of time" during the meal in another culture.

TIME. In business, time can be one of the more important dimensions to be aware of when moving from one culture to another. Some cultures consider the present primarily in terms of the past. Events of today can be understood only in the context of past events. Further, today's events are really a continuation of past events. Another, more practical, issue with respect to time is the concept of punctuality. In some cultures when you say you will arrive at 7:00 in the evening for dinner, you will arrive right at 7:00 or a little earlier. In other cultures, 7:00 is more of an indicator of the approximate time ("we will come for dinner sometime during the evening").

You can see from this list of cultural dimensions that some of the items are highly visible (such as personal appearance and food) and other items are less visible or completely hidden from view (such as beliefs and historical memories). We can think of the dimensions of culture as being either explicit or implicit. Strangely enough, some of the more visible elements of culture are some of the more difficult to interpret because their deeper meanings are hidden from view.

This observation leads us to think about culture as if it were an iceberg. The part of the iceberg that we can see is just the visible portion of culture. But the values that are shared among members of a social group go far deeper. This is also why some visible cultural expressions are difficult for the outsider to interpret. See Exhibit 4-7.

Value Dimensions

The depth of culture is one thing that makes managing in a cross-cultural environment a challenge. Why? First, differences likely exist when comparing value sets of differing cultures. For example, managers who work for Nescafe beverages based in Switzerland must simultaneously relate to their own set of values, the Swiss values, company values, and the values of the host country.

Second, most cultures are in transition. Coming to understand a foreign culture is like trying to catch a moving target. This is especially true in business as commerce continues to become a global experience. Thus, the world of business is a curious blend of old and new, East and West. For example, some French managers carry the ways of thinking that were passed down from medieval feudal times when an autocratic male head of household ran the business. Other French managers who have had more international experience may have picked up different cultural values from the host countries in which they were stationed.[68]

Third, there are thousands of variations in shared values around the world. But some types of variations have a bigger effect on managers than others. Business scholars have identified a few values that are universally experienced. Consider the following scenario. You are a manager at HSBC financial services, a well-known worldwide bank, and one of your employees asks the company to reimburse part of her tuition for her MBA degree. Your company's policy is that reimbursement will be authorized only on certain conditions: Eligible employees must have been employed by the firm for at least one year, and the employee must make a commitment to work for the firm for a specified period of time following the completion of the degree program. This employee has been working for the company for only nine months, but the MBA degree program starts before the employee completes a full year of work. Should you make an exception to the policy so that the employee can start the MBA program? Or

OBSERVABLE DIMENSIONS OF CULTURE

fine arts literature religious ceremonies food
drama music tools and machinery designs and styles
dance games artifacts cooking processes clothing
facial expressions arrangement of physical space
body language eye behavior bodily decorations
hairstyles courtship practices tone of voice
conversational patterns in various social contexts

HIDDEN DIMENSIONS OF CULTURE

notions of modesty conceptions of beauty
rules of acceptance and belonging
ideals child raising rules of descent
perceptions of outsiders definition of loyalty and disloyalty
concept of justice
patterns of handling emotions
incentives to work notions of leadership tempo of work
patterns of group decision making concept of cleanliness
attitudes toward dependents
approaches to problem solving concept of status mobility
beliefs concept of past and future
roles in relation to status by age, gender, class, occupation, kinship
definition of insanity nature of friendship
ordering of time definition of reciprocity
concept of self patterns of visual perception
preference for competition or cooperation
social interaction rate notions of adolescence
values concepts of aging, maturation, development
notions about logic and validity

EXHIBIT 4-7
The Depth of Culture

should you support the policy and tell the employee that she can start the MBA degree on her own and once she has completed her full year of employment, she can apply for tuition reimbursement?

Researchers have found that a manager in the United States will view this differently from a manager who grew up in Venezuela. The Venezuelan manager is more likely to make an exception to the rule if there is a good reason for the exception. The manager from North America is more likely to hold the line on policy, wanting to apply the policy fairly to all employees. So what happens when the manager from North America moves to Venezuela to take a management job? Now you can see the dilemma that this manager will face. If he reacts like his Venezuelan counterparts react, he will feel an inner tension that he is going against a deeply held value of applying rules fairly to all. If he attempts to hold the line on the policy, he risks undermining his relationships with his employees.

This is just one example. Researchers have identified several dimensions of values that can create dilemmas for the manager when working cross culturally.[69] Exhibit 4-8 lists the most common cross-cultural value dimensions found worldwide. These dimensions look at culture from a broad point of view. They help us to understand ourselves in our own culture as well as to respect the people we do business with who come from other cultures.

Value Dimension	Description	
Universalism—Particularism	**Universalism** Applying morals, rules, and laws to everyone in society in the same way	**Particularism** Making exceptions and taking into consideration special circumstances or unique relationships when applying morals, rules, and laws
Individualism—Communitarianism	**Individualism** Emphasizing personal freedom, human rights, and competitiveness	**Communitarianism** Emphasizing social responsibility, solidarity with community and family, and cooperation
Specificity—Diffusion	**Specificity** Breaking things down into their basic elements; analytic, objective	**Diffusion** Seeing the whole and the relations between elements; synthetic, intuitive
Achieved Status—Ascribed Status	**Achieved Status** Social status is based on individual performance and accomplishments	**Ascribed Status** Social status is based on who you are, your social connections, and your potential
Inner Direction—Outer Direction	**Inner Direction** Moral guidance based on internalized values and convictions of the heart	**Outer Direction** Moral guidance based on the situation and influences from outside the person
Sequential Time—Synchronous Time	**Sequential Time** Time is linear with a beginning and an end; past, present, and future are distinctly discrete periods	**Synchronous Time** Past, present, and future overlap and are intertwined

EXHIBIT 4-8
Common Cross-Cultural Value Dimensions[70]

UNIVERSALISM—PARTICULARISM. Recall the example earlier comparing native North American and Venezuelan managers. North American managers are likely to think that rules should be applied fairly to everyone under all circumstances and that it is wrong to make exceptions based on family connections. If policies, rules, and laws are not applied generally to everyone, the whole idea of rules, policies, and laws becomes meaningless. This thinking is called *universalism.*

Universalism offers fairness regardless of social rank or situation. Taken to an extreme, however, universalism will ignore the particular circumstances of a situation. Moral principles may tend to become overly simplistic, depicting issues as black and white when they may be more complicated. Without flexibility, company policies applied without regard to circumstances will cause problems for the manager and the organization because exceptions to the rule do occur.

By contrast, managers who were raised in Venezuela, Korea, or Russia, for example, might believe that there may be rules, but there are just as many exceptions as there are rules. Any particular event or situation may be outside the scope of a rule and require an exception. This type of thinking is called *particularism.*

Particularism searches for the differences or for exceptional circumstances that might require "bending the rules" to accommodate the unusual. Particularism respects what is different about situations and people. But when there are so many exceptions to the rules, the rules cease to hold meaning. Company policies degenerate into company politics: If you can convince the boss that your situation is unique, then you can gain an exception to the policy and "get off." Taken to an extreme, a particularist culture "becomes hostile to human rights and universalizing claims of equality."[71] If rules, laws, and policies have no general application, then power struggles and coercion using intimidation result. "Much Particularism in the world is a protest against rules imposed from the outside by cultures seen as foreign."[72]

INDIVIDUALISM—COLLECTIVISM. Exhibit 4-9 shows a comparison of an individualist culture (such as in Western nations like the United States or Canada) versus a collectivist culture (such as Thailand, China, and Vietnam).

Individualist	Collectivist
Nonconformity occurs more frequently than conformity.	Conformity occurs more frequently than nonconformity (with occasional anticonformity erupting).
Cooperation is high when forming new groups and getting along with new people.	Cooperation is high within groups; cooperation is low with persons outside of the groups.
The most important relationships tend to be horizontal (spouse–spouse, friend–friend).	The most important relationships are with individuals in a vertical hierarchical authority position (parent–child, supervisor–subordinate).
Emphasis at work tends to be more on the task.	Emphasis at work tends to be more on relationships.
Individuals are more likely to bring conflict into the open.	Individuals are more likely to mask or hide conflict within the group.
Individuals have many rights and few obligations to groups; groups provide less social support, resources, and security to individuals.	Individuals suppress personal interests and adopt group goals; groups provide more social support, resources, and security.
Individuals may have greater skills for making new friends easily, but such friendships may be superficial; they appear more sociable to outsiders.	Individuals may have fewer skills in making new friends, but "friend" in the collectivist culture is a lifelong bond; they appear less sociable to outsiders.
Competition is between individuals.	Competition is between groups.
Achievement is accomplished by individuals.	Achievement is accomplished by the group.

EXHIBIT 4-9
Individualist Cultures vs. Collectivist Cultures[73]

Individualism emphasizes personal freedom, human rights, and competitiveness. Individualists value self-reliance and self-interest and encourage self-development. An individualist has no problem with competition and accepts risk taking as part of attempting to better oneself. Being first is highly valued. Not everyone who tries to improve their own economic situation succeeds, but individualism places a premium on equal opportunity for all who are willing to work hard. Individualism spawns creativity, innovation, and inventions. Individualists view morality in terms of individual behavior and see acts as immoral or moral in their own right regardless of whether the action has public consequences.[74]

Extreme individualism breeds unrestrained greed and destructive competition. Individualism can encourage a short-term view of business that is detrimental in the long-run. Individualists tend to view the organization as a tool to get things done and to make money. Work teams are the owners' instruments to build wealth. Highly individualist societies have higher rates of violent crimes and discrimination. Some blame the rampant acquisitiveness of the American consumers on extreme individualism.

Communitarianism, or **collectivism**, emphasizes social responsibility, solidarity with community and family, and cooperation. Collectivists highly value altruism and seek to have the community equally share human burdens. An individual who needs to make a decision considers first what the family or community would say. When a member of the community needs a job, others in the community will step forward to help the person find a job. When implementation of a decision fails, the communitarian seeks ways to "save face" with the family and community.

Communitarians learn to think about the next generation that is to come. While they don't ignore the short-run impact, their actions are constrained by an awareness of the long-term impact. Communitarians don't have to be first. They are content to follow others. In business, communitarian industries find ways to encourage collaboration between businesses, suppliers, educators, finance, labor, and government. When one of the businesses suffers, the community of businesses and its leaders help restore the ailing business back to financial health.

Extreme collectivism can breed complacency and mediocre performance. It can also benefit the few in power at the expense of those with less influence. When individuals attempt to improve the organization or their personal life, others in the community can undermine their efforts. In a communitarian society, it matters whether you are an insider in a community or an outsider. Outsiders are sometimes taken advantage of.

The essential dilemma here is should the manager "pay heed to individual convictions and dissenting ideas, even when these appear to undermine hard-won agreements, or should the welfare of the wider group, corporation, and society, consisting as these do of multiple persons, be our principle concern?"[75]

The individualism—communitarian category is one example in which these two ideas are present in every culture but in varying degrees. We all have the capability to emphasize individual interests and needs. And we all have some cohesiveness to a larger social group.

The Christian Mind on Individualism—Collectivism

A fundamental tenet of Christianity is the responsibility of the individual. In Christ's parable of the sheep and the goats, each man is evaluated on the basis of his own relationship with God (Matthew 25:31–46). Scripture also celebrates individual accomplishments, particularly individual acts of courage and faithfulness. (See, e.g., Hebrews 11.) At the same time, God is acknowledged as the author of community. He created family units, tribes, and nations, distinguished them from one another, and holds individuals accountable for the acts of their community. In the tension between the needs of the individual and those of the group, Christianity calls for a relationship of love, often defined in terms of self-sacrifice. (See, e.g., John 15:13.) It is particularly in a sacrificial relationship to the community that Christian individuality reaches its highest form and people universally acknowledge the value of this relationship. The loving manager who sacrifices her own needs for those of her business unit may find that she not only expresses the highest Christian ideal but also engenders the respect and devotion of her subordinates.

Larry G. Locke, JD, MBA, MATh
Assistant Professor of Management, Entrepreneurship & Marketing
University of Mary Hardin-Baylor
Belton, TX

SPECIFICITY—DIFFUSENESS. The value of **specificity** is the breaking down of things into their basic elements. It leads a manager to view the organization as a system of practical tasks that need to be performed as efficiently as possible. Managers in such a system are expected to gather data and debate the implications when making decisions. Through debate and analysis, organizational leaders expect to gain a clear understanding of the reality of the market. In such a system, feedback regarding performance is vital for success. For-profit organizations watch profits earned from customers and capital obtained from investors. Obtaining commitments from individuals and expecting follow-through in such a business environment encourage parties to honor commitments. If a mistake is made, workers expect that an individual will be identified as the responsible party, and after appropriate correction, will be monitored to prevent the same mistake from being made again. In the same way, quality improvement efforts become a search for the specific root cause of a performance problem.

Extreme specificity can lead to inaction when the truth about the reality of the market cannot easily be obtained. Individuals with highly trained analytical skills sometimes can kill an otherwise good idea simply by shooting holes in the logic of the decision makers. If upper management is unsure what to do, it hires another consultant or analyst to give another perspective on "the truth." In such an extreme environment, hiring a new employee becomes a highly detailed, laborious task in which the job is analyzed, and the job description is broken down, analyzed, and revised. The candidates are tested and subjected to a battery of analysis in terms of individual personality traits, individual performance history, and specific competencies.

In contrast, employees with a style of thinking based on *diffuseness* see work as a cluster of interlocking processes. The value of **diffuseness** is seeing the whole and the relations between elements. It leads a manager to view the organization as a group of people collaborating and coordinating their efforts together. Social relations are very important in diffuseness. In such a system, social feedback is vital for successful performance. When a mistake is made, responsibility is assigned throughout the group and everyone shares responsibility.[76]

Quality improvement in such a system is less about finding the single cause of performance problems. Rather it is a continual awareness of the whole product, the whole process of making the product, and the whole team of employees who are working on the product. Remote consequences and causes are just as important as one specific cause. A manager with a diffuse thinking style will be keenly aware of the network of other individuals in the community of the work environment as well as those outside the organization who play important roles in the organization.

Extreme diffuseness causes the loss of important details in the broader historical and social context of work. As the broader purposes of an organization take on increased importance, specific actions that harm an individual are more easily justified in light of the broader purposes.

Diffuseness tends to emphasize the harmony of a situation and relationships with the bigger historical picture. The less experienced, subordinate worker gets caught in such a close personal relationship with the more experienced, senior employee that individual ideas are stifled. The junior employee is aware of the disproportionate amount of power the supervisor has. Employees may see their work as paying a debt of gratitude to the supervisor. Loyalty to the supervisor and to the organization trumps personal interests. Individuality, when expressed, is seen as disrespectful and insensitive to senior leaders. Dissenters are marginalized by being assigned to tasks with no influence.

The essential dilemma in this value dimension is how precisely should the manager view the problems and issues in business? Would the manager do well by breaking down the problems into their easy-to-define elements, or should the manager attempt to view a situation and its environment as a whole?[77]

ACHIEVED STATUS—ASCRIBED STATUS. Some cultures, such as found in the United States, are more achievement-oriented than others. **Achieved-status** thinking asserts that social status is based on individual performance and accomplishments. Achievement-oriented people believe that performance is the way to achieve economic progress and esteem from society. Achievement-oriented managers set goals for themselves and their workers and expect workers to use their personal judgment to make decisions. When they succeed, individuals are likely to receive commendations and praise for their hard work. But if they overextend themselves or their organization, or overstep their authority and fail to achieve the desired results, their superiors can easily hold them personally accountable.

Taken to the extreme, achieved-status thinking glamorizes the winners, leaving in the shadows those who did not come in first. When winning is honored to the extreme, some of the spiritual values of life are marginalized, if not drowned out.

Ascribed-status thinking asserts that social status is based on who you are, your social connections, and your potential. It emphasizes making sure that what you accomplish brings honor and harmony to your group. For example, workers in this type of culture defer to the opinion of the older, wiser workers and leaders. The individual may not commit the organization without first checking with the persons in authority. Those who remain connected to the trust relationships in the group gain status.

Taken to the extreme, ascribed-status thinking places senior leaders on such a pedestal that performance is about who can provide the humblest deference rather than about achieving the goals of the organization. Organizational leaders receiving such devoted loyalty can come to believe the myth of their own power and, as a result, abuse their authority.

The essential dilemma here is should the rewards that come from social status be tied to a person's reputation based on performance and work track record (achieved status) or based on who the person is and who his family is (ascribed status)?[78]

INNER DIRECTION—OUTER DIRECTION. **Inner direction** is moral guidance based on internalized values and convictions of the heart. The inner-directed person assumes that virtue derives from inside each individual's character and will. **Outer direction** is moral guidance based on the situation and influences from outside the person. The outer-directed person assumes that virtue comes from the larger environment of nature and human relationships.

In inner-directed cultures, individuals are expected to quickly evaluate a situation and express their virtues to openly take charge of a situation. In so doing, they are expected to influence those around them to take appropriate action. Inner-directed persons look for the winning idea that emerges from the minds of leaders. Also, if inner-directed individuals find themselves in an untenable situation, they are expected to dissent out of conscience even if it means risking one's economic stability. Inner-directed cultures hold high regard for those who brave risking life and reputation in support of big, bold ideas.

Taken too far, however, inner-directed persons can be driven to success regardless of the means used to achieve it. This can result in subordinates working under someone they perceive as an insensitive tyrant. Inner-directed persons easily become adversaries, each promoting their own great ideas as being right or best.

Outer-directed cultures emphasize the importance of staying in tune with one's environment (including nature and the organization in which one works). Harmony in the world outside the self is important because virtues come to the person from the environment.

Those in business in an outer-directed culture become exceptional at identifying opportunities and technologies that have been tried in other countries. Entrepreneurs in Asia are content to allow Western entrepreneurs to get the glory for inventing the newest technology. Their ability lies in their use of the momentum of the good ideas that are developed by competitors. Outer-directed cultures do invent new products, but they are more likely than inner-directed cultures to encourage the use of cross-disciplinary teams that include professionals outside their organization. It is through interacting with the outside environment that a person comes to improve oneself.

Taken too far, however, the outer-directed mind will submit to outside authority even if it means endangering life and limb. Giving the social environment precedence over individual self-direction can cause other problems such as minimizing or even eliminating moral standards.

SEQUENTIAL TIME—SYNCHRONOUS TIME. The essential dilemma represented here is whether we think of time as **sequential**, characterized by a beginning, a direction, and an end with discrete differences between past, present, and future, or as **synchronous**, meaning that the past, present, and future overlap and are intertwined.[79]

Sequential-time thinkers have made prominent fundamental economic ideas such as present value (the time-value of money) and opportunity cost. To this type of mind, time is fleeting and cannot be recovered once it is gone. To the sequential thinker, time is precise and unbending.

Time-sensitive managers are interested in studying productivity. Focusing on one activity at a time, they engage in time and motion studies, making ever more efficient the work until the whole time-sensitive process is humming along in perfection. If such work processes can be computer controlled, so much the better, as computer programming can remove the last seconds of wasted time from any mechanical process. For example, managers at a plant that assembles baseball gloves will be interested in breaking down the work tasks into the various components of activities such as die cutting leather parts, sewing the parts, inserting a lining, inserting a reinforcement pad and support materials, lacing the web, and stitching the edges. Each step can then be studied for potential improvements in productivity.

Taken to the extreme, sequential-time and efficiency-engineer thinking can take a person into a never-ending race with time that waits for no one. The sequential thinker ends up being chased by a constant unease that more can be done to squeeze even more inefficiency out of a system. Human beings are treated like machines to be controlled with engineering and science. Such a mentality will purchase marginal economic improvements at the cost of social relationships.

Synchronous thinkers are aware of the march of time, but their focus is on the recurring patterns of events that occur throughout all of time. They are concerned with keeping with the rhythms of life. To the synchronous thinker, time is flexible. Opportunities will come and go, and to succeed, one must be in tune with the patterns of events in order to identify an opportunity. To the sequential-time thinker, synchronous cultures will appear chaotic and distracting. Managers in a synchronous culture may be expected to handle multiple conversations at the same time.

Extreme synchronous thinking leads to some unintended consequences. For example, instead of forming a line, people will crowd around an entrance and push forward even if only one person can fit through the door at one time. Traffic intersections, in comparison to those in sequential-thinking cultures, are more chaotic with autos, bicyclists, pedestrians, trucks, and buses all competing for a space in the intersection. Traffic signals at such intersections are relatively useless. Traffic injuries and fatalities are far higher in synchronous cultures than in sequential cultures where each driver and pedestrian takes a turn at busy intersections or on crowded roads.

In addition to these value dimensions and the dilemmas they can create, some researchers believe other tension points exist. Geert Hofstede, a respected researcher on cultural differences in business, identified five categories of values that he called *cultural dimensions*: power distance, uncertainty avoidance, individualism, time orientation, and masculinity—femininity.[80] We have covered individualism and time orientation. Let's briefly explore the other three categories.

POWER DISTANCE. Power is distributed unequally in virtually all societies. But in some cultures, some individuals have a disproportionate amount of power compared with other citizens. Cultures can differ in how easily people accept this disproportionate distribution of power in society. **High power distance** means that people with less power willingly accept that power is unequally distributed. **Low power distance** means that citizens expect to have power more equally distributed in society. High power distance employees implicitly accept and are less inclined to challenge managerial authority than low power distance employees.

UNCERTAINTY AVOIDANCE. In some cultures, citizens feel uncomfortable in ambiguous or unstructured situations. The untested, unknown can be dangerous. They have a low tolerance of uncertainty. They may prefer that their leaders announce plans rather than struggle to develop a plan as the situation unfolds. They tend to avoid taking risks. Laws, regulations, and formal rules at work help improve predictability. The more a society tends to avoid uncertainty, the more it will appear to outsiders as rigid or inflexible. In other cultures, citizens are comfortable with ambiguous or unstructured situations. They are more willing to take risks, seeing potential opportunities in the uncertainty.

MASCULINITY—FEMININITY. In many societies, males are expected to perform certain traditional roles characterized by assertiveness, competition, and results-oriented performance. Females, in contrast, are expected to foster warm social relationships, care for the weak, and provide service. Hofstede observed that some national cultures tend to emphasize traditional masculine traits and others tend to emphasize traditional feminine traits.

Researchers believe that forces in society that come from the value dimensions influence organizational practices of managers and leaders. In a comprehensive study involving over 60 countries and thousands of managers working in almost 1,000 organizations, researchers have begun building on the work of previous scholars.[81] Known as the GLOBE (Global Leadership and Organizational Behavior Effectiveness) research program, this study is developing a framework that explores nine attributes:

1. future orientation
2. gender egalitarianism
3. assertiveness
4. humane orientation (the degree to which society rewards fairness, altruism, and caring)
5. in-group collectivism (the degree to which individuals express loyalty to societal groups)
6. institutional collectivism (the degree to which groups reward collective distribution of resources)
7. performance orientation (the degree to which society rewards group members for performance)
8. power concentration versus decentralization (power distance)
9. uncertainty avoidance

Differences between cultures can be seen along these nine attribute categories. Researchers have also observed differences between the espoused values and actual practices of managers. They compared the average scores, called cultural dimension scores, for various regions using a scale of 1 to 7. For example, as shown in Exhibit 4-10, Asian countries influenced by Confucianism exhibit a higher collectivism in both values and practice compared with the United States, which is just as

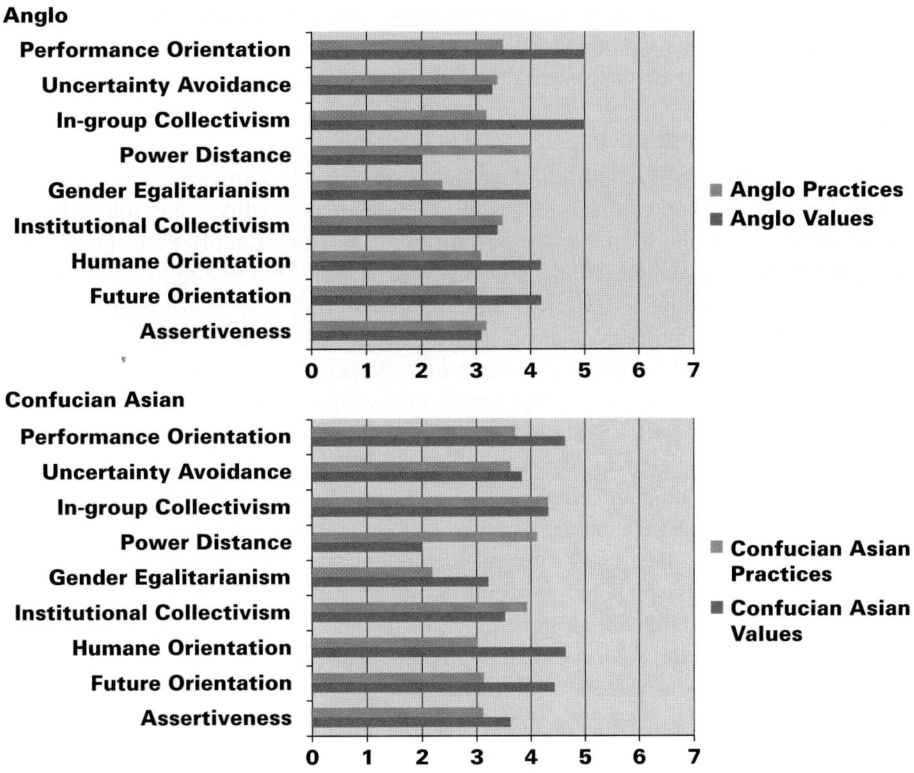

EXHIBIT 4-10
Cultural Dimension Scores—A Comparison

Source: Based on House, R. J., Hanges, P. J., Javidan, M., Dorfman, P. W., & Gupta, V. (Eds.). (2004). *Culture, leadership, and organizations: The GLOBE study of 62 societies.* Thousand Oaks, CA: Sage Publications. pp. 32–33.

high in terms of espoused values but is much lower in terms of actual practice. Exhibit 4-11 illustrates some of the other country differences.

You may be starting to see how complicated it is to come from one culture and learn the ways of another culture. It requires learning not only the language but also how to interpret the culture.

One of the positive outcomes from working in a cross-cultural environment is how much you learn about your own culture. American culture has been characterized as being universalistic, highly individualistic, specific, achievement-oriented, inner-directed, and sequential.[82] Hofstede believes that in comparison with other nations, America is average in terms of power distance and uncertainty avoidance. Americans tend to be more masculine and short-term oriented than their counterparts in some other nations. Also, the American culture places more emphasis on managers and management processes than on workers.

EXHIBIT 4-11
Rankings from the GLOBE Research Project

Value Attribute	Lowest	Highest
Power distance	Denmark, Netherlands, Costa Rica, Israel	Thailand, Spain, Russia
Uncertainty avoidance	Russia, Hungary, Bolivia, Greece	Switzerland, Sweden, Denmark, Austria
Institutional collectivism	Greece, Hungary, Argentina, Italy	Sweden, South Korea, Japan, Singapore, Denmark
In-group collectivism	Denmark, New Zealand, Sweden, Finland	Iran, India, Morocco, China, Egypt
Gender egalitarianism	South Korea, Egypt, China, Morocco	Hungary, Poland, Denmark, Sweden
Assertiveness	Sweden, New Zealand, Switzerland, Japan	Austria, Greece, USA, Spain
Future orientation	Russia, Argentina, Poland, Italy	Singapore, Switzerland, Netherlands, Denmark
Performance orientation	Russia, Argentina, Greece, Italy	Singapore, Hong Kong, New Zealand, USA
Humane orientation	Spain, France, Singapore, Brazil	Philippines, Ireland, Malaysia, Egypt, Indonesia

For managers who come from America (or other countries with a similar profile), these cultural characteristics can have important influences on their religious experience when moving from their home culture to another country. To this we turn next.

Effect on Religious Experience

One of the most challenging issues for the Christian manager is how to manage the cross-cultural dilemmas in a way that you can be true to your religious beliefs while being tolerant of others who have different beliefs. Your particular faith tradition (for example Protestant or Roman Catholic) may influence which values are important to you. For example, Protestantism is associated with individualism while Roman Catholicism may emphasize community needs. Also, Protestantism may have been an important influence on the development of science and engineering in which breaking down a problem into its specific elements for analysis is highly prized. Roman Catholicism may encourage a more diffuse approach to seeing the whole of life as integrated.[83] Depending on which religious tradition you come from, the new host country may pose more or less of a challenge to you.

The inner-directed Christian believer who comes face to face with someone who is outer-directed will have the urge to be an emissary for economic truth—carrying "the good news" of the best way of solving a business problem. Such a situation presents an opportunity for the believer to openly express personal spiritual values as well. But such an approach may be offensive to outer-directed individuals in your new host country, who may prefer a solution to the business problem among the community of key people who have the most relevant experience. To the outer-directed person, the one with the best way of solving the problem may very likely come across as arrogant or insensitive to the opinions of those in and around the organization who have wisdom.

Sequential thinkers approach the Christian gospel with the "time is fleeting" mentality. "Now is the day to make a decision about salvation." "There may never be a tomorrow." Sharing their faith in terms of these time sensitivities may be seen as pushy or arrogant by someone from a synchronous-thinking culture.

Examples: Russian Managers and Chinese Managers

Most of the information covered in this book is from the perspective of North American culture. Given what we now know about the vast differences in cultures, can we assume that management ideas from America will "fly" in other cultures? Not necessarily. As Geert Hofstede and other scholars point out, management is a human set of thinking and behaving patterns. It follows that the fundamental ideas we have about management are socially influenced.[84]

While each culture around the world has its own notion of management, we'll focus on two countries here to get an in-depth look at what it might be like to become a manager in a different culture. These two examples illustrate that people in some nations do not think of their bosses in the same way as workers do in North America. The Russian Federation and China are becoming increasingly important in the world trade. They illustrate some of the complexity of managing in a cultural environment where their economy is changing. Let's consider the possibility that you work with managers from either country. What ways of thinking might you expect to encounter in your work?

RUSSIAN MANAGERS. Each country has unique cultural characteristics that defy blanket application of models that might have validity elsewhere. When models of management or leadership emerge from one cultural context such as the United States, the idiosyncrasies of that culture will, naturally, be present in those models. Research of management and leadership as experienced in the Russian Federation since its emergence from the Soviet Union has validated this.

Each country has a unique historical context out of which particular ways of thinking and behaving in the marketplace have evolved.[85] The Russian Federation, the largest country in the world as measured by land mass, opened its markets to foreign direct investment in 1991 and, as a result, began to reshape its economy toward a form of free-market capitalism. This caused an interesting mix of traditional Russian ways of thinking and new ideas imported through organizations from Western nations.

Russia is still in transition,[86] so it is difficult to generalize about its management practices. As the Russian Federation continues to develop its market economy, some cities are experiencing job dislocation and rising unemployment. Systems we take for granted in North America such as an independent court system, investment banking, and transportation are not as stable in Russia. Consumers are beginning to expect higher quality and more diversity in goods. Corruption, bribery, and commercial crime are present in the economy to a greater extent than in other countries.

Although the younger generation in Russia is changing its views, strong, centralized leadership is still prized in society. Power and control are expected to come from the top of the organization. Traditional organizational leaders centrally control activities of subordinates, maintain clear hierarchical authority, and impose bureaucratic rules. Management in traditional organizations is characterized by "obedience to authority, a distrust of outsiders, the use of coercive power and an emphasis on rank and status."[87] Newer organizations that have frequent contact with organizations in the West are changing in this regard.

Russia is a nation whose people have a huge capacity for endurance under hardship. Over the centuries, the Russian people have had to survive multiple attacks on their homeland from foreigners, as well as abuses of authority from their own leaders. These historical experiences have resulted in an ambivalence toward suffering. Russians have a great ability to restrain their emotions. Paradoxically, they easily wear their emotions on their shirtsleeves. Someone from a western country meeting a Russian in business for the first time might misinterpret the Russian's body language as a lack of interest or expression. But the reality is quite different. Russians, in more private settings, are highly expressive. At the same time, many Russians who are used to a more formal relationship in business may be put off by the informality of an American or other westerner.

International consultant Daniel Bollinger tested four cultural dimensions in the experience of Russian managers and found that Russian management culture is characterized by high power distance, low tolerance for uncertainty, and a high value placed on collectivism.[88] Compared with Americans they experience roughly equal emphasis on assertiveness and competition with emphasis on quality of life and personal relationships. American managers, in comparison to their Russian counterparts, tend to score lower on uncertainty avoidance, higher on individualism, and lower on power distance.[89]

In one study, researchers observed that decision making among Russian managers tends to be collectivistic by including other managers in decisions.[90] However, these managers tended not to include subordinates in decision making. Complicating our understanding of managerial decision making is the observation that many managers make important decisions individually without consulting others.

The mentality of the agricultural village commune carried over into succeeding generations even as cities grew in population. "In all realms of human endeavor, they favour the collectivist orientation" that is at the heart of the village life.[91] Individual Russians highly value belonging to a group. In a collectivist orientation, individuals sacrifice self-interests for those of the group. But the group can be relied on for support and security. These values were reinforced by the Russian Orthodox Church.[92]

When the village experiences hardships together, individuals choose to make self-sacrifices for the sake of the community. A mentality of such community support, when added to the commitment to national economic policies, has created the preoccupation with egalitarianism and maintaining the status quo. Paradoxically, organizational leaders modeling their behavior after the national leaders are allowed to live above this law of egalitarianism and to personally benefit from their position. During times of transition, defense of traditional values, conformity to expectations of those in authority, and fear of change compete for psychic energy with the knowledge that new ways of leading may be necessary.

Public conformity is another study in contrasts. The dual expectation exists that when in public, the individual is expected to avoid engaging in creative thinking, but in the privacy of home, freedom to innovate is allowed as long as it does not disrupt the integrity of this primary ingroup. Despite the social conditioning toward conformity, many Russians have learned to survive by passively resisting the inertia of authoritarian rule. More than this, they seem to share a hidden desire to throw off the behavioral constraints imposed. Applying this to the workplace environment, managers need to understand that while Russian employees may appear to be accepting of a change at work, they may be hesitant to express their ideas to their superiors.

Another result of the collectivist mentality is the supremacy of friendship.[93] While business leaders in Western nations tend to be more task-oriented, their Russian counterparts are more likely to desire to develop relationships to accomplish tasks. "Whatever Russians do, friends come first."[94]

Bureaucratic rules in traditional Russian organizations act as a defense against influences over which workers and managers alike have no control. Ironically, bureaucratic routines also make it difficult to get anything accomplished. Leaders who get things done outwardly obey and submit to authority and bureaucratic rules, but inwardly disobey. Thus, leaders who see the need for major changes in their organization may resist attempts at radical change (for fear that the floodgates of chaos will be opened), preferring instead to simply work around the unwieldy system. This can result in pressuring subordinates at the last minute to step up productivity to present a favorable report for superiors.

Russian workers "have established cohesion, solidarity, and camaraderie over the years. Russian factory workers tend to be fiercely loyal to one another" and to their leaders.[95] The strong sense of subordination to authority is paradoxically coupled with the more hidden mentality of periodically needing to throw off the bounds that constrain independent thinking and acting.

A Russian historian describes the typical Russian work behavior that includes resourcefulness, patience under adversity, deprivation, and spurts of energy, combined with a tendency to conceal an inconsistency in seeing things through. This historian found that Russians are circumspect, cautious, and ambiguous with a preference for looking back instead of forward. They prefer to work in groups and tend to monitor results rather than set goals.[96]

The traditional Russian mindset that workers work and managers know everything still exists in many organizations as does the high regard for centralized authority. The tendency to respond only to centralized authority means "that most Russian workers and managers place little value on responsiveness, the goals of the firm, the shared responsibility of employees, or the mechanisms by which unresolved problems" are addressed by managers.[97] The concept of time will likely vary from firm to firm. Those firms with contact with western nations or who are in highly competitive industries tend to view time as workers in the West do.

Compared with their counterparts in the United States, Russian managers value less participative management on the part of workers. Participative intervention may even have a negative effect on Russian workers' performance. Even though workers may have the opportunity to express opinions to management in some organizations, rarely do they expect superiors to take action as a result.[98] By not participating in redesigning their jobs or in job enrichment, workers "could avoid the frustration of being rejected or ignored."[99] By not offering opinions about how to make improvements, they avoid indirectly complaining about coworkers.

As Russia emerged from decades of communist rule into a free-market capitalist system, it lacked some of the features of the American version of capitalism believed to be important for maintaining high ethical values. In the United States, fundamental moral values are supported by a comprehensive code of law and an impartial justice system for enforcement. Such a system provides a high level of stability and certainty when compared with experiences in other countries.[100]

Russia's situation is different. Its history of organizations surviving under oppressive political regimes created conflicting moral standards. This has resulted in some ambiguity about what constitutes moral behavior.[101] In both Russia and the United States, keeping one's word, maintaining trust, and giving rewards based on performance are considered moral. Price gouging, refusing to pay debts, and extortion are considered immoral. However, in the United States, layoffs and wide differences in salary among managers are considered moral. In Russia, many people would consider these immoral. In Russia, price fixing, showing personal favoritism, paying bribes, and manipulating information are considered by many to be moral. These are considered immoral in the United States.

CHINESE MANAGERS. More managers and workers work for organizations in China than in any other country on earth. China represents approximately one-fourth of the world's population. As China grows as a world economic power, more and more American companies are either doing business with China or considering it. Thus American managers need to develop some awareness of how managers think and work in China.[102]

Leadership and management styles in American culture are different from leadership styles in China. In China, as in other countries, the expectations of followers are affected by political and ideological factors. China differs from America (where most of the management and organizational theories were developed) on so many elements that we must be careful about applying our management ideas to China.

Like Russia, the socialist country of the People's Republic of China is in transition. China's market reform policies that began in the late 1970s picked up momentum in the early 1990s.

Source: markrhiggins/Shutterstock.

Hong Kong is an important city for world trade.

Market reforms resulted in a dramatic increase in privately owned businesses, entrepreneurial ventures, and international joint ventures.

By 2001, China entered the World Trade Organization as the fastest growing economy in the world. There are 170 cities in China with populations greater than one million. Compared with most other nations on earth, China has an insatiable need for importing raw materials to use as it builds its economic, transportation, telecommunication, educational, and other system infrastructures.[103]

China is the prototypical collectivist culture in which harmony within groups (family, community, company, and nation) is a high priority. The tendency toward collectivism is slow to change. As ancient thinking taught: "Do not ignore your own relatives and treat others as if they were your kin; do not let what you hear from servants and slaves cause you to turn against your relatives and friends."[104] For many Chinese, individualism is selfishness because it places an individual's self-interest above the needs of the group. Collectivism supports the group. For example, when a person is choosing a career, collectivism encourages the person to decide based on what is best for the community or the political party.

The legacy of Confucian values of kindness and benevolence continue to influence the Chinese. Personal integrity, the willingness to search for truth, fairness, and humility are core values that have been passed down to contemporary Chinese after 2,500 years.[105] Such values encourage individuals to recede into the fabric of the community and not stick out socially. Chinese prefer to receive praise indirectly so as not to stand out as an example to others.[106] For leaders, this means that to gain support of followers they must be humble and relate openly to the common person. Pompous speeches generate dislike and distrust among workers.[107]

Under the state-controlled economy that was patterned after the Soviet economic model since 1949, socialist leaders decided fixed wage scales, market prices, production quotas, human resource allocation, operational control, and economic dependence of the firm on the state. This system was tied to the state-operated general welfare system. Few people ever worried whether they would have a job. Ineffective managers were simply transferred to another company to save face. With fixed prices, production controlled by the state, and ineffective management, many of the state-owned enterprises lost money.[108]

Perhaps because of the increased contact with individualist cultures and the increase in foreign direct investment in China by Western companies, certain individualist traits are emerging in China. Performance evaluations are used in some organizations. Incentive bonuses are tied to performance. Ineffective managers are now more likely to be given warnings that if they do not change, they will not be guaranteed a job.[109] Competition between teams may be encouraged in some organizations when teams are rewarded based on team performance relative to other teams.[110] Strangely enough, the distinction between intrinsic reward inherent in the work itself and extrinsic rewards of pay is questionable in the Chinese context.[111] In the city of Xuzhou the mayor announced that if companies did not improve, they would be demoted or removed. Within 6 months, four unprofitable companies completed a financial turnaround from a $4.7 million dollar loss to a $12.3 million dollar profit.[112]

Several changes have taken place for Chinese managers who work in private firms. Paradoxically companies in China are experiencing surpluses and shortages of workers. Some firms must make the difficult decision to lay workers off to improve efficiency and make a profit. This has resulted in the displacement of hundreds of thousands of people and their families. Some firms have the opposite problem: recruiting and retaining the best workers. With increased opportunities for advancement, the most effective leaders can apply for more lucrative positions.

Chinese managers are interested in self-development just like managers in Western nations—only for slightly different reasons. They are even willing to take a job for less pay if the job offers opportunity for learning. In China, self-development is achieved for the good of the company and its needs. Self-improvement will help Chinese managers enhance their ability to serve their superiors.[113]

China is a curious mix of top-down authority and organic management style in which technical specialization is deemphasized, regulations are opposed, and nonmaterial incentives are higher in importance than material incentives.[114] Although private enterprise is growing in China, some elements of the traditional relationships between employer and employee continue. Employees are still expected to commit themselves to total immersion into the firm. For many organizations, employees live in neighborhoods close to the company. After work, employees and their families socialize with the families of fellow workers. In the Chinese culture, children and adults do most activities as a family.[115] The company managers affect not only the work life of workers but also leisure activities. Child care is managed by the firm. Healthcare is provided by the company. If certain foods or other products are to be rationed during times of shortage, the firm is in control of distribution of ration cards. Few things are outside the scope of supervision by managers. The traditional great divide between white-collar workers and blue-collar workers still exists.

Chinese workers tend to be synchronous thinkers. They tend to keep in mental view the relationship with superiors as much as or more than the relationship with subordinates. They accept that superiors have more power than subordinates. Avoiding uncertainty is important. Managers are expected to stay current on the technical aspects of the work being done in their work units and have the right answers when questions arise.

Harmony and hierarchy are two never-ending areas of social focus that both managers and their subordinates use as filters for decision making. Harmony is achieved, in part, as managers show they are willing to accept criticism (much of it coming indirectly). This guides both subordinates and mid-level managers to show deference and respect to their superiors. Because of their keen focus on responding to the wants of their superiors, Chinese managers are expected to work effectively through other people to achieve results. When facing conflict, Chinese managers use the warmth of relationships and respect for each other to cooperate to resolve, rather than avoid, the conflict.[116]

Morality of Global Business

Deciding whether to get involved in cross-cultural management can be pretty straightforward for someone who is eager to travel and experience other cultures. But working for a multinational corporation can be controversial.[117]

Most people recognize that humanity cannot get along very well without international trade. Nations are dependent on each other to provide needed goods and services. Companies from developed nations bring job opportunities for citizens of less developed nations. This improves the standard of living in the location. These companies often bring technical and management expertise that they teach to locals. These new jobs stimulate the local economies where the multinational businesses locate. For example, Trico, a company that makes auto windshield wiper systems, set up a factory in Matamoros, Mexico. This facility became the largest wiper systems and blade manufacturing facility in North America.[118]

Large corporations that locate in developing countries can spawn the development of support businesses. This has a cumulative effect of helping the whole economy of the host nation. Products that are made in developing countries help producers keep prices low for a worldwide market. For example, Volkswagen decided to develop a new assembly plant located in Pune, India. The plant was designed to employee 2,500 people. But other businesses such as metal fabrication and welding were needed to support the building of the Volkswagen plant. In addition, some component suppliers needed to locate in Pune to give easy access to the Volkswagen assembly plant for ongoing operations.

As these developing countries gain the benefits of hosting new global businesses, they become more dependent on international relations. The businesses that locate in their country need a stable political environment. To keep a stable workforce, the company encourages government policies that promote human freedom. In essence what is being encouraged is a network of interdependencies on a local, regional, and national basis. Such interdependencies and increased standard of living help keep the peace in regions that may otherwise be at risk of political upheaval.

But some people criticize the continued expansion of global trade. Just as in domestic markets, corporations have not always covered themselves in glory. Large multinational corporations generate annual revenues that rival the gross domestic product of their host nation. This gives the firm an excessive amount of influence compared with other organizations in the country.

Global corporations are not always transparent about their business practices. Some have employed children and youth in factories that do not measure up to the standards for safety that are enjoyed in the developed nations. Others have been criticized for turning a blind eye toward other human rights violations. For example, Burmese villagers sued Unocal and Talisman Energy, alleging human rights violations arising from the companies' involvement in a gas pipeline construction project in Myanmar. The trial judge stated that Unocal was aware that forced labor was being used in the project.[119]

After developing some of the best citizens as managers or technical experts, the multinational corporation can more easily transfer such individuals to other countries. The resulting *brain drain* leaves the country impoverished. As a local economy becomes more dependent on the large multinational corporation, it is at an increased risk of being harmed should the corporation decide to move its factory to another country.

Some believe that such corporations place too much emphasis on profits at the expense of people. Others criticize multinational corporations when such firms can locate in other countries and avoid paying taxes in their home country. Because the environmental protection regulations in many developing countries are not as strict as in developed nations, large corporations can get away with more ecologically harmful activities that, at least in the short run, allow them to reduce their production costs compared with other firms.

Other criticisms stem from the concern that many of the multinational businesses are based in Western countries. The fear is that these firms are either directly or indirectly transferring Western cultural values into traditional cultures, creating an unwanted cultural upheaval.

Paradoxes of Cross-Cultural Management

Cross-cultural management is not immune to the challenges that come from paradox. Some of the same paradoxes and dilemmas that managers in a domestic business face are also present in multicultural management situations. If anything, international business adds another layer of complexity to the already complex process of leading and managing. Here are a few examples.

GLOBAL THINKING—LOCAL THINKING.[120] This is sometimes called the *consistency-adaptation* paradox or the tension between efficiency and flexibility. Some organizations attempt to get the benefits of both a **multidomestic strategy**, in which products and services are customized for each country, and a **global strategy**, in which products are standardized across as many countries or regions as possible. They try to simultaneously meet the needs of being global and local, big and small. But these goals sometimes conflict, making it more difficult to succeed. The more countries that a corporation enters to do business and the larger the corporation becomes, the more complicated this organizational tension becomes.

COLLABORATION—CONFLICT.[121] This tension is sometimes called *cooperative conflict.* There are many methods that company leaders can use to expand their business into the international market: exporting, licensing, building a new business from scratch, acquiring an existing company (if this is allowed by government regulations), long-term contracts, and joint ventures. Regardless of what method a business uses, the managers must collaborate with local managers in the new country. This collaboration can be challenging as the managers and local managers sometimes have different ideas about what success will mean, causing goal conflict. This is especially true for managers who work for an international joint venture.

PSYCHIC DISTANCE PARADOX.[122] Managers who work in a cross-cultural environment in a culture that is similar to their own may actually find it more difficult than they expect. The reason: Their assumptions regarding the similarity of the two cultures can prevent them from learning the subtle yet critical differences between the cultures. This is known as **close psychic distance.**

Focus on an Organization

Full Gospel Businessmens Fellowship International

From its beginning in 1951 at a dinner held at Knott's Berry Farm in Southern California, the Full Gospel Businessmens Fellowship International (FGBMFI) has grown into an international ministry to business professionals located in 160 countries, consisting of thousands of local chapters. The organization was founded by Demos Shakarian, an Armenian Pentecostal Christian.

The mission of the organization is to help men "find the reality of the Spirit-filled walk with Christ" and in so doing to reach men in all nations for Jesus. Local chapters offer opportunities for Christian fellowship and encouragement to share the gospel in the marketplace.

The FGBMFI claims to be the largest network of Christian businessmen in the world. It has retained its links to the Pentecostal Christian movement. Information about the organization can be obtained at its website: http://www.fgbmfi.org.

Chapter Summary

1. For the Christian faith, God is the God of all creation, of every culture, every nation, and every time. To the person of faith, God's will spans not only private life but also the public life in the marketplaces of the entire world. The Bible accepts cross-cultural exchange as valid social activity. International trade was accepted as part of life in biblical times. God's covenants to Adam, Noah, Abraham, and Moses were global covenants. The identity of believers was created with an awareness that God's purpose for his people is a global purpose. Taking the biblical record as a whole, some scholars have concluded that business is to be an agent of shalom (peace). The Bible does not condemn international business, but it does condemn the use of international trade to unjustly build wealth.
2. Organizations increasingly need managers who possess a cultural intelligence that equips them to be leaders in a cross-cultural environment. Cultural intelligence is the capability to deal effectively with people from different cultural backgrounds.
3. Researchers have identified several dimensions of culture, which are the things that distinguish one cultural group from another. These dimensions include religious belief and practice, language, social systems, sense of self, sense of space, communication, personal appearance, rites and ceremonies, food, and time.
4. Culture can be thought of in terms of its various levels. The visible level of cultural includes what can be observed such as food, clothing, and rites and ceremonies. The hidden level of culture involves the meanings behind what can be observed including beliefs and assumptions.
5. Several cross-cultural value dimensions have been identified that help us understand the deeper levels of cultural. These include:
   a. Universalism—Particularism
   b. Individualism—Communitarianism
   c. Specificity—Diffusion
   d. Achieved status—Acquired status
   e. Inner direction—Outer direction
   f. Sequential time—Synchronous time
   g. Power distance
   h. Uncertainty avoidance
   i. Masculinity—Femininity
6. One of the most challenging issues for the Christian manager is how to manage the cross-cultural dilemmas in a way that you can be true to your religious beliefs while being tolerant of others who have different beliefs.
7. Examples of management in the Russian Federation and in China are given.
8. The globalization of business is a controversial topic. On the one hand, most people recognize that humanity cannot get along very well without international trade. Nations are dependent on each other to provide needed goods and services. On the other hand, multinational corporations are sometimes criticized.
9. Global management is not immune to the challenges that come from paradox. Some of the same paradoxes and dilemmas that managers in a domestic business face are also present in multicultural management situations. Also, there are some particular tensions that are prevalent in cross-cultural management situations.

Key Terms

Achieved status 120
Ascribed status 120
Close psychic distance 130
Collectivism 118
Communitarianism 118
Cultural intelligence 111
Diffuseness 120
Dimensions of culture 112
Expatriates 107
Global strategy 129
High power distance 122
Individualism 118
Inner direction 120
Low power distance 122
Multidomestic strategy 129
Outer direction 121
Particularism 117
Sense of self 114
Sense of space 114
Sequential time 121
Social systems 114
Specificity 119
Synchronous time 121
Universalism 117

Discussion Questions

1. Is it possible for a manager from one culture to learn to see a situation through the eyes of both her own culture and another culture that she is currently working in?
2. If the world of global commerce continues to expand during the next 30 years, how will the cross-cultural experiences of managers then be different from what they are now?
3. Which set of skills is more important: (a) conflict negotiation skills or (b) learning how and why other cultures work?
4. How can a Christian working in a cross-cultural setting maintain a healthy spiritual life?
5. What role has religion played in the American culture becoming so
   a. Universalist?
   b. Individualistic?
   c. Specific?
   d. Achievement-oriented?
   e. Inner-directed?
   f. Sequential?
6. What important management perspectives can we learn from 1 Corinthians 9:19–23?
7. Discuss the difference between global consistency and local adaptation. What are the benefits and liabilities of each approach?
8. Discuss how the national culture can influence business practices of a foreign company.
9. Discuss the ways you should prepare for an international assignment.
10. How can a Christian manager accommodate the ways of doing business in another country when the fundamental values seem to be different from Christian values?
11. Is accommodation to another culture really a necessary step in developing cultural intelligence?
12. How does a manager develop humility when he thinks that the ways of doing business in the host culture are inferior to the methods used in his home culture?
13. What ceremony have you observed from another culture? What was unusual about the ceremony? Did you understand the meaning behind some of the actions of people during the ceremony?
14. What kind of training and experience would you need to obtain to become an effective and dependable cultural interpreter?
15. When working in a culture whose dominant values conflict with biblical principles, how can the Christian manager be nonjudgmental and yet be true to biblical values?
16. What clashes are likely to exist when a manager from a particularist culture transfers to work in a culture dominated by universalist values?

STUDENT EXERCISES

1. Consider the six universal value dimensions outlined in Exhibit 4-8. Based on your knowledge of the Bible, where does the Bible stand on each of these dichotomies? Draw a chart that describes what you believe the ideal biblical culture would be like.
2. In this chapter we have explored the complexities of managerial thinking and action in the Russian Federation and in China. Select another country in which you have an interest and research the managerial thinking and practices in that country.

IN-CLASS EXERCISES

Visualization

Some of the concepts in this chapter are abstract, yet they have practical value for practicing managers. One way to process abstract ideas is to visualize them. Assign small groups the task of illustrating visually on one piece of poster paper one key concept of their choice from the chapter. Allow some class time to start the posters, and, if needed, additional time outside of class to finish them. When the posters are complete, ask each group to present and explain its poster to the class.

Issue Debate/Discussion

Divide the class into small groups of five to six people each. Hand out a sheet of paper containing the following quotations. Assign half of the groups to defend the first quotation as a valid definition/description of a leader's humility and the other half to defend the second quotation as valid. Give the groups 5 minutes to discuss. Then call for groups to give a summary of the rationale they developed. Discussion can follow.

Discussion Topic #1: Is global business moral or immoral?

A. **Global business is moral.** "The global corporation provides a multitude of benefits to billions of people around the world: Jobs, goods, and income. Global firms hire local people, and provide them with training and sometimes education. Moreover, global firms have a vested interest in stability. Terrorism, wars, and revolutions disrupt business, even as they bring anguish, injury, and death to people. The global firm bridges nations, cultures, and peoples. Even when political institutions—individual countries and even the United Nations—are burdened by bureaucracy and nationalism, the global corporation is able to cross boundaries and deal with people where they live. From the standpoint of values, the global firm brings the great advantages of jobs, person-to-person contact of people of different cultures, and the necessity that one understand and work with people of another culture."[123]

B. **Global business is immoral.** "The main charge against multinational corporations is that they adopt a double standard, doing in less developed, Third World countries what would be regarded as wrong if done in the developed First World."[124] "Multinational corporations, by their nature, are largely independent of the social policies of the nation-states in which they operate . . . The independence of multinationals also allows them greater influence on the creation of local and national policy . . . Multinationals have been known to use this influence in ways that strain both legality and credulity."[125]

Discussion Topic #2: "Since individualists see performance as a personal quality, if the person has no ability or expends no effort, his performance is considered to be poor. Collectivists see performance as a group quality, and thus it is possible to succeed if one member of the group has ability and the others expend effort."[126]

Collectivist: Performance = Ability + Effort
Individualist: Performance = Ability × Effort

What will happen if a manager from an individualist culture takes a management job in a collectivist culture? How will this manager's attempts to deal with low-performing employees be accepted?

Discussion Topic #3: Are Christian character traits superior to all cultures, or are Christian character traits found in all cultures? The following table presents common character traits that are the ideal for the Christian to pursue.

Love	Joy	Faithfulness	Forgiveness
Peace	Patience	Truth	Thankfulness
Perseverance	Long-suffering	Compassion	Kindness
Courage	Faith	Humility	Steadfastness
Hope	Temperance	Gentleness	Honor

A. **Biblical character traits are above all cultures.** The principles of right living have been established by God and espoused by believers. These are above all cultures, times, and places. God judges all cultures based on the same set of principles. If character traits were culturally conditioned, then they would become no more than human character traits.

B. **Biblical character traits are embedded in all cultures.** Regardless of what we say about the biblical teaching on character traits and the ultimate source in God, ultimately such traits are, by necessity, embedded in human culture. Character traits are social behavior patterns. Because they are primarily social in nature, such behavior patterns are shaped by culturally shared values. What faithfulness is to a person in the United States may not be the same as faithfulness to a person in Vietnam. This does not mean that faithfulness in Vietnam is any less valid than faithfulness as expressed in the United States.

Discussion Topic #4: Refer to the table of character traits in Discussion Topic #3. Think of these as being the primary biblical values. Can biblical values be found in all cultures of the world or primarily in nations that have traditionally embraced Christianity?

A. **Biblical values can be found in all nations.** Most of the values in the table are consistent with the values of other major world religions. For example, love, compassion, faithfulness, and courage are encouraged by most, if not all, world religions. To say that these values can be found primarily in Christian nations is arrogance masquerading as righteousness. These are basic human values that are important because of how God created humans, regardless of the particular religion that some humans practice.

B. **Biblical values can be found primarily in nations that have traditionally embraced Christianity.** Biblical values go beyond human capabilities. Only the values espoused and lived by Jesus Christ are the true and valid values for humans. A non-Christian can demonstrate a certain kind of love, but it is not the true love that comes from God unless such a person has a vibrant relationship with Jesus. Likewise, humility can seem like true humility when a non-Christian demonstrates it, but true humility can be expressed only when the person is in a relationship with God.

Discussion Topic #5: Evaluate the dominant culture in a nation you are familiar with using the table of biblical character traits in Discussion Topic #3. Then compare the dominant culture of the United States with the dominant culture of that nation.

A. What character traits are well known and commonly seen in the United States? Which character traits are lacking in the United States?

B. What character traits are well known and commonly seen in the nation you chose to evaluate? Which character traits are lacking in that nation?

Endnotes

1. Chewning, R. C., Eby, J. W., & Roels, S. J. (1990). *Business through the eyes of faith.* San Francisco, CA: HarperSanFrancisco. p. 47.
2. Acts 18:1–4.
3. Martin, J. S., & Chaney, L. H. (2006). *Global business etiquette: A guide to international communication and customs.* Westport, CT: Praeger. p. 58.
4. Martin, J. S., & Chaney, L. H. (2006). *Global business etiquette: A guide to international communication and customs.* Westport, CT: Praeger. p. 7.
5. Events such as the one that occurred at the Bangkok airport in November 2008 illustrate the increased risk for managers working in countries that are politically unstable. See Beech, H. (2008). Briefing. *Time South Pacific.* December 15, p. 5.
6. Townsend, P., & Cairns, L. (2003). Developing the global manager using a capability framework. *Management Learning.* 34(3), 313–327.
7. Hamel, G. (2007). *The future of management.* Boston, MA: Harvard Business Review Press. pp. 10–11.
8. Hampden-Turner, C. M., & Trojmpenaars, F. (2000). *Building cross-cultural competence: How to create wealth from conflicting values.* New Haven, CT: Yale University Press.
9. Hampden-Turner, C. M., & Trojmpenaars, F. (2000). *Building cross-cultural competence: How to create wealth from conflicting values.* New Haven, CT: Yale University Press. p. 250.
10. Isaiah 2:4, 60:12; Jeremiah 12:17, 18:8; 1 Kings 18:10; Micah 4:3; Psalm 22:23–31, 33:12, 82:8.
11. Based on the 2009 rankings published by Interbrand available on the Internet: http://www.interbrand.com/best_global_brands.aspx. Accessed December 1, 2009.
12. Genesis 11:1–9; 2 Kings 18:26–28; Nehemiah 13:24; Esther 1:22, 8:9; Psalm 114:1; Ezekiel 3:5–6; Acts 2:6; 1 Corinthians 14:7–9.
13. Genesis 26:4; Leviticus 18:24, 18:28; Deuteronomy 4–12, 28–32; Joshua 23; 2 Kings 17–18; 2 Chronicles 32; Isaiah 14; Jeremiah 10, 25, 50–51; Ezekiel 5–6; Matthew 24, 28:19–20.
14. Numbers 13:21–25.
15. Genesis 42:34; Ezekiel 27, 1 Kings 10:15, 28; Proverbs 31:14; Isaiah 23:2-9.
16. Genesis 37:25–28; Matthew 1.
17. Psalm 104:16.
18. Genesis 49:13; 1 Kings 9:26–28; 2 Chronicles 9:21–23; Psalm 107:23–30; Proverbs 31:14; Isaiah 23:1–14; Ezekiel 27:9, 25; Revelation 18:17–19.
19. 1 Kings 9–10; Isaiah 23:8.
20. Genesis 37–50.
21. Matthew 4:24–25, 8:28, 15:21–28; Mark 7:26; John 4.
22. Matthew 15:2–6; Mark 7:3–13.
23. Acts 26:4–5; Galatians 1:13–24.
24. Acts 21:2, 27.
25. Genesis 3, 9, 12; Exodus 19–20. See also Scobie, C. H. H. (1992). Israel and the nations: An essay in Biblical theology. *Tyndale Bulletin.* 43(2), 283–305; Muilenburg, J. (1965). Abraham and the nations: Blessing and world history. *Interpretation.* 19(4), 387–398; Bright, J. (1959). *A history of Israel.* Philadelphia, PA: Westminster Press; Kaiser, W. C. (2000). *Mission in the Old Testament: Israel as a light to the nations.* Grand Rapids, MI: Baker Books.
26. Genesis 12:1–3, 18:18, 26:4, 35:9–15, 46:1–4.
27. Israel was to become a kingdom of priests to the whole world as a leader in spiritual worship to the one true God. Exodus 19:4–6; Psalm 96:3, 96:10; Isaiah 19:23–25; Jeremiah 3:1–4:4; Hosea 4:6; 1 Peter 2:9–10; Revelation 1:5–6.
28. Deuteronomy 7:1–22.
29. Exodus 15:26; Leviticus 19:2; Deuteronomy 4:6–7, 7:6–15, 8:17–18, 28:1–8; 1 Kings 8:41–43; Isaiah 2:2–4, 42:6–7, 43:10, 43:21, 44:8, 49:6, 61:9–10, 66:19; Jeremiah 33:9; Micah 4:1–5; Zechariah 8:21–23; Malachi 3:8–12. In Psalm 47 the psalmist realizes that God has become the God of the whole world, not just of Abraham. See also the allusion in Luke 1:72–79 and Luke 2:32 where the Messiah is viewed as the fulfillment of the Abrahamic promise. Walter Kaiser makes the point that Isaiah's preaching about the Servant of the Lord applied both to an individual (the Messiah) and to the nation of Israel as a whole. See the passages that apply the concept to the whole nation: Isaiah 41:8–10, 42:6, 43:8–13, 43:14–44:5, 44:6–8, 44:21–23, 44:24–45:13, 48:1–17, 51:4. Kaiser, W. C. (2000). *Mission in the Old Testament: Israel as a light to the nations.* Grand Rapids, MI: Baker Books. pp. 56–58.
30. Genesis 12:1–3.
31. Exodus 3.
32. Psalm 106:24–27.

33. Leviticus 26:34–38, 2 Chronicles 36:20–21; Jeremiah 25:11–12; 29:7–10.
34. Daniel 1–4.
35. Henry, C. F. (1991). Linking the Bible to public policy. In Chewning, R. C. (Ed.). *Biblical principles and public policy: The practice.* Colorado Springs, CO: NavPress. p. 19.
36. Genesis 19:37–38, 25:30, 36:43.
37. Deuteronomy 25:13–16; Micah 6.
38. Many Bible passages can be offered in support of this: Deuteronomy 4:6–7, 4:32–40, 7:6–11, 8:18, 28:1–10; Jeremiah 16:19–21, 22:6–9; Malachi 3:10–12; 1 Kings 8:41–43; Isaiah 19:18–25, 42:1–7, 45:20–25, 49:6–22, 55:3–4, 61:1–91; Micah 4:1–2; Zechariah 8:20–23; Acts 10:34–35, 14:16–17, 17:27; Romans 4:32, 9:6–8, 10:12–13; Galatians 3:8; Hebrews 3:16–19.
39. Leviticus 20:23; Philippians 2:15.
40. Psalm 106:34–36.
41. 1 Kings 11:1–11.
42. Romans 11:20; Luke 19:41–44; Matthew 8:10–12; Luke 1:54–75; Acts 3:17–26, 10:34–43, 13:26–43. For a discussion of the two theological perspectives see Kaiser Jr., W. C. (1977). The Davidic promise and the inclusion of the gentiles (Amos 9:9–15 and Acts 15:13–18): A test passage for theological systems. *Journal of the Evangelical Theological Society.* 20(2), 97–111.
43. Acts 2:5.
44. Matthew 5:14–16, 28:19–20; Mark 16:15; Acts 1:6–8.
45. Acts 10.
46. Chewning, R. C., Eby, J. W., & Roels, S. J. (1990). *Business through the eyes of faith.* San Francisco, CA: HarperSanFrancisco. pp. 194–195.
47. Ezekiel 28:1–8, 18.
48. Matthew 28:19–20.
49. Chewning, R. C., Eby, J. W., & Roels, S. J. (1990). *Business through the eyes of faith.* San Francisco, CA: HarperSanFrancisco. pp. 193–194; Johnson, C. N. (2009). *Business as mission: A comprehensive guide to theory and practice.* Downers Grove, IL: IVP Academic. pp. 27–57.
50. The Philippian congregation was one of the first to intentionally support the work of Paul the Apostle in ministering to other locations. See Acts 18:5; Philippians 4:12–20.
51. Robertson, C. J., & Crittenden, W. F. (2003). Mapping moral philosophies: Strategic implications for multinational firms. *Strategic Management Journal.* 24(4), 391.
52. Hampden-Turner, C. M., & Trojmpenaars, F. (2000). *Building cross-cultural competence: How to create wealth from conflicting values.* New Haven, CT: Yale University Press. p. 1.
53. Adapted from Moran, R. T., Harris, P. R., & Moran, S. V. (2007). *Managing cultural differences: Global leadership strategies for the 21st century.* New York: Elsevier. pp. 148–149.
54. Thomas, D. C., & Inkson, K. (2003). *Cultural intelligence: People skills for global business.* San Francisco, CA: Berrett-Koehler Publishers, Inc.; Earley, P. C., & Mosakowski, E. (2004). Cultural intelligence. *Harvard Business Review.* 82(10), 139–146.
55. Thomas, D. C., & Inkson, K. (2003). *Cultural intelligence: People skills for global business.* San Francisco, CA: Berrett-Koehler Publishers, Inc. p. 182.
56. Thomas, D. C., & Inkson, K. (2003). *Cultural intelligence: People skills for global business.* San Francisco, CA: Berrett-Koehler Publishers, Inc. p. 183.
57. Kohls, L. R. (1994). Intercultural training for overseas posting. In Tracey, W. R. (Ed.). *Human resources management & development handbook.* (2nd ed.). New York: AMACOM. pp. 1001–1013.
58. Thomas, D. C., & Inkson, K. (2003). *Cultural intelligence: People skills for global business.* San Francisco, CA: Berrett-Koehler Publishers, Inc. pp. 66–68.
59. Thomas, D. C., & Inkson, K. (2003). *Cultural intelligence: People skills for global business.* San Francisco, CA: Berrett-Koehler Publishers, Inc. p. 71.
60. Sanyal, R. N. (2001). *International management: A strategic perspective.* Upper Saddle River, NJ: Pearson Custom Publishing. pp. 46–48; Moran, R. T., Harris, P. R., & Moran, S. V. (2007). *Managing cultural differences: Global leadership strategies for the 21st century.* New York: Elsevier. pp. 7–10. The very process of breaking down cultures into variables for analysis is a Western cultural phenomenon. It might be recognized that the various models of culture have been developed by scholars who have been influenced by cultures in Western countries. Other scholars have put forward models of cultural elements or variables such as Schmitz, J. (2003). *Cultural orientations guide.* Princeton, NJ: Princeton Training Press; Kluckholn, F. R., & Strodtbeck, F. L. (1961). *Variations in value orientations.* Westport, CT: Greenwood Publishing; Hofstede, G. (1980). *Cultures consequences: International differences in work-related values.* Beverly Hills, CA: Sage Publications; Trompenaars, F., & Hampden-Turner, C. (1998). *Riding the waves of culture: Understanding diversity in global business.* (2nd ed.). New York: McGraw-Hill.
61. For an interesting discussion of the role of belief in economic thought see Rosser Jr., J. B. (1999). Belief: Its role in economic thought and action. *American Journal of Economics and Sociology.* 52(3), 355–368.
62. Jacobs, L. (1986). Judaism. In Jones, C., Wainwright, G., & Yarnold, E. (Eds.). *The study of spirituality.* New York: Oxford University Press. pp. 491–497; Melé, D. (2006). Religious foundations of business ethics. In Epstein, M. J., & Hanson, K. O. (Eds.). *The accountable corporation: Business ethics.* Vol. 2. Westport, CT: Praeger; Lapin, D. (2005). An explanation for Jewish business success. In Capaldi, N. (Ed.). *Business and religion: A clash of civilizations?* Salem, MA: M & M Scrivener Press. pp. 184–191; Thienhaus, O. J. (1999). Jewish time: Ancient practice, Hellenistic and modern habits, Freud's reclaiming. *Judaism.* 48(4), 442–449.
63. Epstein, E. M. (2003). Judaism's contribution to our understanding of business, religion, and spirituality: Reflections during a Jubilee Year. In Williams, O. F. (Ed.). *Business, religion and spirituality: A new synthesis.* Notre Dame, IN: University of Notre Dame Press. p. 116.

64. White, J. F. (1967). *The worldliness of worship.* New York: Oxford University Press; Stevens, R. P. (2006). *Dong God's business: Meaning and motivation for the marketplace.* Grand Rapids, MI: William B. Eerdmans Publishing Company; Novak, M. (1981). *Toward a theology of the corporation.* (Rev. ed.). Washington, DC: The AEI Press; Griffiths, B. (1984). *The creation of wealth: A Christian's case for capitalism.* Downers Grove, IL: InterVarsity Press; Grudem, W. (2003). *Business to the glory of God: The Bible's teaching on the moral goodness of business.* Wheaton IL: Crossway Books; Chewning, R. C., Eby, J. W., & Roels, S. J. (1990). *Business through the eyes of faith.* San Francisco, CA: HarperSanFrancisco; Arbogast, S. V. (2005). Disconnected at the roots: How gaps in Catholic social doctrine impede dialogue and action and economic justice. In Capaldi, N. (Ed.). *Business and religion: A clash of civilizations?* Salem, MA: M&M Scrivener Press. pp. 41–54; Hollis, C. (1961). *Christianity and economics.* New York: Hawthorn Books.
65. Farah, C. E. (2003). *Islam: Beliefs and observances.* (7th ed.). Hauppauge, NY: Barron's Educational Series, Inc.; Uddin, S. J. (2003). Understanding the framework of business in Islam in an era of globalization: A review. *Business Ethics: A European Review*, 12(1), 23–32; Graafland, J., Mazereeuw, C., & Yahia, A. (2006). Islam and socially responsible business conduct: An empirical study of Dutch entrepreneurs. *Business Ethics: A European Review*, 15(4), 390–406; Badawi, J. A. (2003). Islamic teaching and business. In Williams, O. F. (Ed.). *Business, religion and spirituality: A new synthesis.* Notre Dame, IN: University of Notre Dame Press: Notre Dame, IN. pp. 139–167; Badawi, J. A., & Beekun, R. I. (2005). Balancing ethical responsibility among multiple organizational stakeholders: The Islamic perspective. *Journal of Business Ethics.* 60(2), 131–145.
66. Quoted in Rice, G. (1999). Islamic ethics and the implications for business. *Journal of Business Ethics*, 18(4), 349.
67. Sanyal, R. N. (2001). *International management: A strategic perspective.* Upper Saddle River, NJ: Pearson Custom Publishing. p. 47.
68. Moran, R. T., Harris, P. R., & Moran, S. V. (2007). *Managing cultural differences: Global leadership strategies for the 21st century.* New York: Elsevier. p. 18.
69. Parsons, T., & Shils, E. A. (1962). *Toward a general theory of action: Theoretical foundations for the social sciences.* New York: Harper & Row. pp. 77–99; Trompenaars, F., & Hampden-Turner, C. (1998). *Riding the waves of culture: Understanding cultural diversity.* (2nd ed.). New York: McGraw-Hill.
70. Hampden-Turner, C. M., & Trompenaars, F. (2000). *Building cross-cultural competence: How to create wealth from conflicting values.* New Haven, CT: Yale University Press.
71. Hampden-Turner, C. M., & Trompenaars, F. (2000). *Building cross-cultural competence: How to create wealth from conflicting values.* New Haven, CT: Yale University Press. p. 24.
72. Hampden-Turner, C. M., & Trompenaars, F. (2000). *Building cross-cultural competence: How to create wealth from conflicting values.* New Haven, CT: Yale University Press. p. 24.
73. Adapted from the observations reported in Triandis, H. C., Bontempo, R., Villareal, M. J., Asai, M., & Lucca, N. (1988). Individualism and collectivism: Cross-cultural perspectives on self-ingroup relationships. *Journal of Personality and Social Psychology.* 54(2), 323–338.
74. Triandis, H. C. (1995). *Individualism and collectivism.* Boulder, CO: Westview Press. p. 32.
75. Hampden-Turner, C. M., & Trompenaars, F. (2000). *Building cross-cultural competence: How to create wealth from conflicting values.* New Haven, CT: Yale University Press. pp. 68–69.
76. Triandis, H. C. (1995). *Individualism and collectivism.* Boulder, CO: Westview Press. p. 78.
77. Hampden-Turner, C. M., & Trompenaars, F. (2000). *Building cross-cultural competence: How to create wealth from conflicting values.* New Haven, CT: Yale University Press. p. 123.
78. Hampden-Turner, C. M., & Trompenaars, F. (2000). *Building cross-cultural competence: How to create wealth from conflicting values.* New Haven, CT: Yale University Press. pp. 189–190.
79. Hampden-Turner, C. M., & Trompenaars, F. (2000). *Building cross-cultural competence: How to create wealth from conflicting values.* New Haven, CT: Yale University Press. p. 295.
80. Hofstede, G. (1993). Cultural constraints in management theories. *The Executive.* 7(1), 81–94.
81. Kluckhohn, F., & Strodtbeck, F. L. (1961). *Variations in value orientation.* Evanston, IL: Peterson; Triandis, H. C. (1995). *Individualism and collectivism.* Boulder, CO: Westview Press; House, R. J., Hanges, P. J., Javidan, M., Dorfman, P. W., & Gupta, V. (Eds.). (2004). *Culture, leadership, and organizations: The GLOBE study of 62 societies.* Thousand Oaks, CA: Sage Publications.
82. Hampden-Turner, C. M., & Trompenaars, F. (2000). *Building cross-cultural competence: How to create wealth from conflicting values.* New Haven, CT: Yale University Press. pp. 16–17, 73, 128, 192–193, 239–242, 299–301.
83. Hampden-Turner, C. M., & Trompenaars, F. (2000). *Building cross-cultural competence: How to create wealth from conflicting values.* New Haven, CT: Yale University Press. p. 123.
84. Jaeger, A. M. (1990). The applicability of western management techniques in developing countries: A cultural perspective. In Jeager, A. M., & Kanungo, R. N. (Eds.). *Management in developing countries.* New York: Routledge; Hofstede, G. (1993). Cultural constraints in management theories. *The Executive.* 7(1), 81–94; Trompenaars, F., & Hampden-Turner, C. (1998). *Riding the waves of culture: Understanding diversity in global business.* (2nd ed.). New York: McGraw-Hill; Hofstede, G. (1999). Problems remain, but theories will change: The universal and the specific in 21st-century global management. *Organizational Dynamics.* 28(1), 34–44; Gopalan, S., & Stahl, A. (1998). Application of American management theories and practices to the

Indian business environment: Understanding the impact of national culture. *American Business Review.* 16(2), 30–41; Scarborough, J. (2000). *The origins of cultural differences and their impact on management.* Westport, CT: Quorum.

85. Kets de Vries, M. F. R. (2001). The anarchist within: Clinical reflections on Russian character and leadership style. *Human Relations.* 54(5), 585–627.
86. Moran, R. T., Harris, P. R., & Moran, S. V. (2007). *Managing cultural differences: Global leadership strategies for the 21st century.* New York: Elsevier. pp. 582–590.
87. Kets de Vries, M. F. R. (2001). The anarchist within: Clinical reflections on Russian character and leadership style. *Human Relations.* 54(5), 617.
88. Bollinger, D. (1994). The four cornerstones and three pillars in the "House of Russia" management system. *Journal of Management Development.* 13(2), 49–65.
89. Fey, C. F., & Denison, D. R. (2003). Organizational culture and effectiveness: Can American theory be applied in Russia? *Organizational Science.* 14(6), 686–706.
90. Ardichvili, A., Cardozo, R. N., & Gasparishvili, A. (1998). Leadership styles and management practices of Russian entrepreneurs: Implications for transferability of Western HRD interventions. *Human Resource Development Quarterly.* 9(2), 145–155.
91. Kets de Vries, M. F. R. (2001). The anarchist within: Clinical reflections on Russian character and leadership style. *Human Relations.* 54(5), 599.
92. Puffer, S. M., & McCarthy, D. J. (1995). Finding the common ground in Russian and American business ethics. *California Management Review.* 37(2), 29–46.
93. Kets de Vries, M. F. R. (2001). The anarchist within: Clinical reflections on Russian character and leadership style. *Human Relations.* 54(5), 607.
94. Kets de Vries, M. F. R. (2001). The anarchist within: Clinical reflections on Russian character and leadership style. *Human Relations.* 54(5), 607.
95. Welsh, D. H. B., Luthans, F., & Sommer, S. M. (1993). Managing Russian factory workers: The impact of U.S.-based behavioral and participative techniques. *Academy of Management Journal.* 36(1), 63.
96. Fey, C. F., & Denison, D. R. (2003). Organizational culture and effectiveness: Can American theory be applied in Russia? *Organizational Science.* 14(6), 687–688.
97. Fey, C. F., & Denison, D. R. (2003). Organizational culture and effectiveness: Can American theory be applied in Russia? *Organizational Science.* 14(6), 700.
98. Welsh, D. H. B., Luthans, F., & Sommer, S. M. (1993). Managing Russian factory workers: The impact of U.S.-based behavioral and participative techniques. *Academy of Management Journal.* 36(1), 58–79.
99. Welsh, D. H. B., Luthans, F., & Sommer, S. M. (1993). Managing Russian factory workers: The impact of U.S.-based behavioral and participative techniques. *Academy of Management Journal.* 36(1), 74.
100. Puffer, S. M., & McCarthy, D. J. (1995). Finding the common ground in Russian and American business ethics. *California Management Review.* 37(2), 29–46.
101. Puffer, S. M., & McCarthy, D. J. (1995). Finding the common ground in Russian and American business ethics. *California Management Review.* 37(2), 29–46.
102. Ling, W., Chia, R. C., & Fang, L. (2000). Chinese implicit leadership theory. *The Journal of Social Psychology.* 140(6), 730.
103. Moran, R. T., Harris, P. R., & Moran, S. V. (2007). *Managing cultural differences: Global leadership strategies for the 21st century.* New York: Elsevier. pp. 410–423.
104. Triandis, H. C. (1995). *Individualism and collectivism.* Boulder, CO: Westview Press. p. 22.
105. Ling, W., Chia, R. C., & Fang, L. (2000). Chinese implicit leadership theory. *The Journal of Social Psychology.* 140(6), 729–739.
106. Triandis, H. C. (1995). *Individualism and collectivism.* Boulder, CO: Westview Press. p. 79.
107. Den Hartog, D. N., House, R. J., Hanges, P. J., Ruiz-Quintanilla, S. A., & Dorfman, P. W. (1999). Culture specific and cross-culturally generalizable implicit leadership theories: Are attributes of charismatic/transformational leadership universally endorsed? *Leadership Quarterly.* 10(2), 219–259.
108. Zhu, C. J., & Dowling, P. J. (1994). The impact of the economic system upon human resources management practices in China. *Human Resources Planning.* 17(4), 1–21.
109. Zhu, C. J., & Dowling, P. J. (1994). The impact of the economic system upon human resources management practices in China. *Human Resources Planning.* 17(4), 1–21.
110. Triandis, H. C. (1995). *Individualism and collectivism.* Boulder, CO: Westview Press. p. 90.
111. Shenkar, O., & von Glinow, M. A. (1994). Paradoxes of organizational theory and research: Using the case of China to illustrate national contingency. *Management Science.* 40(1), 56–71.
112. Zhu, C. J., & Dowling, P. J. (1994). The impact of the economic system upon human resources management practices in China. *Human Resources Planning.* 17(4), 1–21.
113. Triandis, H. C. (1995). *Individualism and collectivism.* Boulder, CO: Westview Press. p. 91.
114. Shenkar, O., & von Glinow, M. A. (1994). Paradoxes of organizational theory and research: Using the case of China to illustrate national contingency. *Management Science.* 40(1), 56–71.
115. Triandis, H. C. (1995). *Individualism and collectivism.* Boulder, CO: Westview Press. p. 64.
116. Tjosvold, D., Hui, C., & Law, K. S. (2001). Constructive conflict in China: Cooperative conflict as a bridge between east and west. *Journal of World Business.* 36(2), 166–183; Chen, Y., Tjosvold, D., & Fang, S. S. (2005). Working with foreign managers: Conflict management for effective leader relationships in China. *The International Journal of Conflict Management.* 16(3), 265–286.
117. This discussion based on Boatright, J. R. (2003). *Ethics and the conduct of business.* (4th ed.). Upper Saddle River, NJ: Prentice Hall. pp. 411–438. Weiss, J. W. (2003). *Business ethics: A stakeholder and issues*

management approach with cases. (5th ed.). Mason, OH: Thompson South-Western. pp. 417–465; de George, R. T. (2010). *Business ethics.* (7th ed.). Upper Saddle River, NJ: Prentice Hall. pp. 159–183, 480–505.

118. Information gleaned from the company's website: http://www.tricoproducts.com/Trico2/corporatecapabilities/manufacturing.aspx.
119. Bennett, J. (2002). Multinational corporations, social responsibility and conflict. *Journal of International Affairs.* 55(2), 393–410.
120. Doz, Y., Santos, J., & Williamson, P. (2001). *From global to metanational: How companies win in the knowledge economy.* Boston, MA: Harvard Business School Press. pp. 1–28; Trompenaars, F., & Hampden-Turner, C. (1998). *Riding the waves of culture: Understanding diversity in global business.* (2nd ed.). New York: McGraw-Hill. pp. 1–12.
121. Chen, Y., Tjosvold, D., & Fang, S. S. (2005). Working with foreign managers: Conflict management for effective leader relationships in China. *The International Journal of Conflict Management.* 16(3), 265–286.
122. O'Grady, S., & Lane, H. W. (1996). The psychic distance paradox. *Journal of International Business Studies.* 27(2), 309–333.
123. Cavanagh, G. F. (2006). *American business values: A global perspective.* (5th ed.). Upper Saddle River, NJ: Pearson Prentice Hall. p. 294.
124. Boatright, J. R. (2003). *Ethics and the conduct of business.* (4th ed.). Upper Saddle River, NJ: Prentice Hall. p. 413.
125. DesJardins, J. R., & McCall, J. J. (2005). *Contemporary issues in business ethics.* (5th ed.). Belmont, CA: Wadsorth/Thomson Learning. pp. 471–472.
126. Triandis, H. C. (1995). *Individualism and collectivism.* Boulder, CO: Westview Press. p. 73.

CHAPTER 5

The Manager and Moral and Social Responsibility

LEARNING OBJECTIVES

- Describe why considering moral and social responsibility is important in managerial work.
- Assess the Christian view on covenant relationships, ethical decision making, corporate social responsibility, and care for the environment.
- Distinguish between morality, ethics, and the law.
- Explain the factors that promote and restrain moral problems in organizations.
- Describe the concept of stakeholders and what is at stake in ethical dilemmas.
- Explain various approaches to ethical decision making: the social contract, egoism, moral relativism, utilitarianism, universalism, rights, justice, virtues, and the community process of ethical thinking.
- State the reasons for and against a broad view of corporate social responsibility.
- Understand the tension points that managers face as they engage in ethical thinking.

". . . each of us is at once byproducts of, characters in, and authors of, our own experiences. So each of us is responsible for examining, evaluating, critiquing and finding means to change organizations and systems in which we find ourselves."[1]

"Now for this very reason also, applying all diligence, in your faith supply moral excellence, and in your moral excellence, knowledge."[2]

RILEY JUSTICE

Riley Justice stood in front of the brightly colored front-loading washing machine as it reached its open door to her as if to say, "Take me home. I'm yours!" Riley thought of all the trips she and her husband had made to coin-operated laundromats to wash and dry their clothes. After researching the different brands and models, she had narrowed down the choice to one highly respected brand and popular deluxe model, AQR98DLX, which promised the highest energy savings. The deluxe model was more expensive than basic models, but Riley and her husband decided that they were willing to pay more for a washer that had more features. Now that she was in the presence of the answer to what she dreaded most on the weekends, she didn't want to leave without buying it. Only one question came between her and possessing it: Is this the best price for this washer right now?

The store sales associate sensed her desire and hesitation. He said, "Our policy is we will not be undersold on price. If you find a lower advertised price on the same model advertised by another retailer within 30 days of your purchase, we will refund you the difference plus 10 percent of the difference. The other retailer must be in our local market. Just bring us your receipt and our competitor's advertisement."

Source: Ryan McVay/Thinkstock.

Two weekends later Riley was back in the store carrying a competitor's advertisement and her receipt. She was looking for the sales associate and a $132 refund. The competitor, a much smaller store that specialized in household appliances, was advertising the same brand of washer. It had the same capacity, the same options for temperature settings, the same style of finish on the cabinet, the same options for load sizes, the same warranty, and the same choices for washing various types of fabrics. From what Riley could tell it was the same washer. It contained the same characteristics as the deluxe model that she had purchased. It was even described as the deluxe model. The price was $120 less than she had paid.

Riley had even visited the competing store to see the washer just to make sure it was the same as hers. She looked on the back to read the small label that listed the power rating of the motor and other technical details. It was identical to her new washer. She told all this to the sales associate.

The sales associate took a few minutes to study the competitor's advertisement, comparing it with the brochure that described the washer he had sold her. When he finished he said, "Your washer looks similar to theirs but your model number **AQ**R98DLX is different from their model number. See, here in their advertisement the model number they are advertising is a **BP**R98DLX." He pointed to the model number.

Riley protested. "But it is the same deluxe washer! It not only looks exactly the same; it is described the same way. It has the same capacity, the same settings on the switches, the same warranty, the same door handle, the same finish on the cabinet, even the same power rating on the motor. I saw it myself."

The sales associate said, "I'm sorry but there's nothing I can do about this. The competitor is selling a different model than the one we sell. The different model number means that the washer must be different in some way."

"You're telling me that since the first two letters of the model number are different, you will not honor your price-match offer. I'd like to talk with the store manager."

Riley was unsuccessful in persuading the store manager to give her a refund. Later she did more research on retail prices of deluxe models of the same brand of washer. She could not find any retailer in her market that sold a washer with the exact same model number as hers, even though there were several stores that sold washers that, as far as she could tell, had the same characteristics and specifications. She even asked one retailer if they ever sold the **AQ**R98DLX model. He told her that the manufacturer did not make available to him the washer sold under that particular model number but that the **BP**R98DLX seemed to be the same washer.

This story brings us to the heart of one of the most interesting and challenging dimensions of what it means to be a manager and leader these days—managing the complexities of moral and social responsibilities.

Management Pyramid: Moral Responsibility

The management pyramid is founded on a key assumption: Actions that individuals take in society affect other members of society. A second assumption is that moral actions come from patterns of thinking and feeling, which are connected with fundamental values and beliefs. See Exhibit 5-1.

Consider the request of two employees for additional safety equipment for their work station. These employees work in a laboratory where they are exposed to hazardous fumes and the risks from toxic liquids. But the small company is strapped for cash. At a minimum, additional safety equipment costs $10,000, and the best equipment costs $60,000. Managers must decide whether the company should invest in the additional equipment, and if so, how much.

To make a decision, the managers need to evaluate this situation from the perspective of standards of right and wrong.[3] Religious beliefs, cultural traditions, personal beliefs and values, and personal goals all play a part in evaluating what should be done.

The managers will think about their legal duties to employees and the economic effect on the company. While there may be no way to completely eliminate the risk of the materials the employees work with, managers need to consider the various actions, and their consequences, that could help reduce the risks. If the company decides not to provide any additional safety equipment, then it could be vulnerable to higher healthcare costs due to injuries, the cost of replacing a disgruntled employee who quits, or the costs of defending a lawsuit brought by employees. These are not the only unfavorable outcomes the managers will consider. For example, managers will consider the effect the decision has on morale and productivity. Several managers would likely be involved in a decision of this magnitude. In some organizations, a capital expense of even $10,000 might require the approval of top-level leaders.

The decisions that emerge from this ethical process lead to actions such as purchasing equipment and implementing additional safety measures such as training. The decision process

EXHIBIT 5-1

The Management Pyramid: Moral Responsibility

Source: Courtesy of Michael E. Cafferky, © Michael E. Cafferky 2011.

Actions that affect the environment Honoring contracts and commitments Managing confidentiality and privacy Handling conflicts of interest Following safety standards Structuring incentives to promote moral action Honesty in reports and disclosures Managing employee discipline Setting fair wages and benefits	Action
Approaches to ethical decision making Thinking about duties and consequences of actions Processing ethical tensions Discussion and debate with others on moral issues	Thinking & Feeling
Beliefs about what is right and wrong Moral values and standards Shared organizational values Assumptions regarding legal constraints	Being & Becoming

may even lead to taking no action. But even this is a result of values influencing thinking and decision making.

Who Cares About Moral Responsibility?

One reason why organizations need managers is to help guide the organization to stay within the boundaries of right and wrong behavior. Managers also guide the organization in terms of social expectations. For example, your firm hired several Cambodian refugees to work in your plant that manufactures chemicals used in industrial coatings.[4] These chemicals are highly toxic. The work is dirty and unpleasant. Mishandling raw materials can lead to serious injury and possibly permanent disability. The Cambodian refugees are willing to work for minimum wage and no health benefits. They seem grateful to have jobs. Beyond complying with minimum legal requirements, managers have the task of deciding fair compensation and working conditions.

Because moral standards are at the basis of all action, one primary task of a manager is to consider the moral implications of actions before making decisions.[5] When managers pay attention to moral issues, their organizations gain positive benefits.[6] Studies show that focusing on moral issues can improve employee morale and loyalty, customer loyalty and relationships, and the power of the brand. In addition, it can sway customer decision making.

Moral issues are an intrinsic part of management because both economic and social survival is at stake.[7] Managers who ignore the moral dimension of work are at risk of creating personal and organizational legal liability.[8] Defending lawsuits that result from moral lapses can cost hundreds of thousands of dollars, not to mention damage to the company's image and credibility. Unraveling the consequences of immoral behavior can be frustrating for managers and takes time away from pursuing organizational objectives. For example, sometimes it can take years to resolve issues that arise. In 1989, the *Exxon Valdez* oil tanker ran aground in Alaska's Prince William Sound, spilling millions of gallons of oil. Exxon was slow to accept responsibility. While the clean-up effort costing millions was still in progress, attention quickly focused on the actions of the ship's captain. Litigation began almost as quickly. Nineteen years later, in 2008, after spending thousands of hours and hundreds of millions of dollars to defend the company from lawsuits, paying costs associated with the oil spill cleanup, spending millions on an advertising campaign, and dealing with the distraction this event caused the company's top-level executives, the company appealed to the U.S. Supreme Court. The lower court had asked Exxon to pay $2.5 billion in punitive damages. In the end, the Supreme Court limited punitive damages to $507.5 million.[9] The total estimated cost of the event and the litigation that followed is over $1 billion.

Some problems encountered in the marketplace will be clear-cut, and, because of your values, you will know what you need to do as a manager. But some moral issues will not be so clear-cut, and thinking through these will be more difficult.

In this chapter we will review various perspectives that managers have as they consider what is right and wrong and what is socially responsible. We start with the Christian faith perspective because it is an important part of the Christian's personal beliefs and values (the "being and becoming" part of the Management Pyramid model).

Faith Perspective on Moral and Social Responsibility

It should be no surprise to a Christian working in a free-market democratic economy that business ethics comes from a foundation in the religious teachings of Judaism, and, because of this, Christianity.[10] The ancient teachings of Scripture provide a reasonable set of standards that guide behavior. The focus provided by religious beliefs and practices embraces key dimensions sometimes left out of other philosophical approaches to thinking about right and wrong actions.

For the Christian, God is not left at the door to the workplace. He is an important stakeholder in the decisions that a Christian manager makes.[11] To believers God's will is a legitimate, authoritative guide for behavior. For some Christians, the sovereignty of God has universal, primary claims on the behaviors of his created beings. Others emphasize that because of God's free offer of salvation, the believer will respond to God by being loyal to him and to his will. This is a covenant relationship described in the Bible.

Covenant Relationships

Business relationships are often more complicated than what can be put into a written agreement. Our expectations of each other are broader than what a formal agreement contains. For example, managers at Gucci, the maker of luxury consumer products, cannot stipulate in writing everything that they expect of their suppliers. There may be ambiguous elements of the agreement. Because of this, a supplier could choose to take advantage of Gucci in its dealings. For example, an unscrupulous supplier may agree to terms for the sale of thousands of pounds of high-quality leather used in the manufacture of stylish handbags but later ship slightly lower quality leather that is difficult to detect. Or the manufacturer might stipulate the types of animals from which the leather should be harvested. But there may be limitations on how well, within a reasonable cost, Gucci can verify from which animals the material came. What constrains suppliers from doing this regularly, other than fear that managers at Gucci will quickly catch on? Human beings in the marketplaces of the world operate at a level deeper than agreements and contracts. Some argue that the only way business works as well as it does is because of unwritten covenants that humans make with each other.

The ancient concept of *covenant* is gaining currency among some scholars and practicing managers as a valid way to understand managerial work. While contracts are still used extensively in business, some see the biblical covenants as a template that humans should model for all social relationships where a contract is unable to represent the entire relationship.[12] Covenant is a voluntary commitment to enter a relationship with one or more other parties and the obligations that the parties foster for each other. A covenant relationship is deeper than one that is based on obligations to perform tasks in exchange for payment. In a covenant relationship, both parties attempt to build trust and loyalty. This requires time.

In contractual relationships individuals pledge specific activity in exchange for specific responses such as payment of money. A contractual approach to management attempts to do no more than is required in an agreement. Contracts care for the needs of individual interests. Many contractual relationships, such as with employment where labor is provided in exchange for wages, can also include the logic of covenant where mutual commitments are emphasized. By contrast, in a covenant, the parties are partners in a long-term relationship. Both seek to do things that will enhance the relationship rather than merely fulfill a list of obligations in a contract. In a covenant, the relationship is paramount and needs faithfulness, nurturing, and loving kindness. See Exhibit 5-2.

Covenantal relationships are required in managerial work for several reasons.[13] First, those in a business relationship are in each other's presence continually over a long period of time. Some relationships in business must outlive particular business transactions. Employees

EXHIBIT 5-2
Contracts vs. Covenants[14]

Contracts	Covenants
Focused on carrying out specific activities	Focused on maintaining the relationship
An agreement made in suspicion	An agreement made in trust
Based on self-interest	Based on mutual interest
Based on laws/rules; built on fear, blame	Based on grace; built on trust, repair
Limits the parties	Nourishes the parties
Bond based on limited purposes and limited commitments	Bond based on unlimited promises, pledges, and commitments
Limited or episodic contact as needed	Continuous fellowship, faithfulness, and mercy
Punishment of wrongdoers	Reconciliation of wrongdoers
Entered into for mutual advantages	Promotes a cause to which all advantages are subject to being sacrificed for the sake of the cause
Limited to the parties involved in the contract	Extends to family and to the larger community who are affected by the relationship

are continually connected with their employer. A business usually has a long-term presence in a particular community and has an influence broader than buying and selling transactions. Companies are often in a long-term relationship with their customers. Second, each party in a business relationship has the power to choose behavior that supports or undermines the relationship. This creates uncertainty and vulnerability that one party may act in an untrustworthy manner toward the other. However, while a written contract cannot cover all possible actions to prevent untrustworthy behaviors, a covenant can. One party might try to impose its will on the other, but the ideal covenantal relationship leads both parties to restrain their own behavior and encourage the other party to internalize covenant values. Third, both parties in a business relationship continually depend on each other, which we call **interdependence.** The covenant is designed to promote life and prosperity for both parties and even for a broader community. Covenant recognizes the continued interdependence of those involved in the covenant. Interdependence means that each party is vulnerable to the actions of the other. A covenant is a continual test of trustworthiness. Each party will be thoughtful in moral action to avoid the risk of undermining the relationship of trust. Fourth, this interdependence requires cooperation, but there is always the potential for conflict, as the parties may disagree at times. Fifth, covenant forms the basis of a relationship that is too broad to put into a legal business contract. Because the relationship is long term and involves commitments beyond the performance of specific tasks in exchange for payment, it is difficult to put in writing all that is required for the relationship.

Organizations go beyond the requirements of business contracts in support of more fundamental covenantal relationships. For example, firms sometimes voluntarily retrain or relocate their workers instead of laying them off. Workers are not always required to tell their employer means by which lower costs can be achieved, but they do.[15]

The biblical pattern of covenants is an interesting model for managers to consider.[16] For example, when one party has more power than the other, the dominant party first takes action on behalf of the other party to show trustworthiness and to provide a basis of the relationship for the future. This radical principle of *others first* (while not completely forgetting self-interests and responsibilities) presents an interesting challenge for many managers. See Exhibit 5-3.

The Bible recognizes that in covenant relationships, one or both parties are capable of making and breaking the covenant. Freedom creates vulnerability. The Bible records the many times in which God's people made and broke covenants with God and with each other. Even though the Ten Commandments are explicit statements of expectations, as Jesus demonstrated, the covenantal principles at the basis of these commandments are more broad and complex than they appear on the surface.[17] The Bible portrays God as making provisions both for the human moral freedom to break the covenant and for his divine acceptance of this vulnerability. Biblical covenants include both conflict and cooperation as God and his people continually work to influence each other's behavior. Instead of letting go of each other when the relationship is undermined by human disobedience, they seek reconciliation.

EXHIBIT 5-3
The Significance of the Abrahamic Covenant[18]

In the typical ancient covenant, the less dominant party was expected to kill a ceremonial animal and then to walk between the split animal parts as a symbolic way of saying, "If I do not fulfill my obligations in this covenant, let me be as this animal and die." In his covenant with Abraham, God was the dominant party. Yet it was God that passed through the midst of the slain animals as if to say, "If I do not fulfill my promises, I will pay the price with my life." The covenant showed God's faithful, loving-kindness to humans with the expectation that Abraham and his family would reciprocate with love to God and love to each other (the two great commands).

For Christians an interesting connection exists between the Abrahamic covenant and the life and work of Jesus Christ. Because of covenantal violations, humans, as a race, were condemned to die. The New Testament teaches that "Christ took on himself the curses of the covenant and died in the place of the sinner. His death was covenantal . . .",[19] fulfilling the covenant made with Abraham when he passed through the midst of the slain animals.

A covenant relationship does not eliminate the need for specific agreements. Indeed, it would be impossible to have a covenant relationship without some specific agreements for expected behaviors. Without specific agreements the covenant relationship would soon become meaningless. In a business covenant relationship a contract still may be needed to explicitly address specific commitments.

Covenant relationships are not entered into lightly or formed instantly. An initial commitment is only the beginning of a covenant relationship. The firms may need to test the relationship before making a long-term commitment.

Covenant relations require a high degree of agreement on basic values and interests. The more different the two parties are in values and interests, the more difficult it will be to maintain a covenant relationship. Because of this there may be settings in which a covenant relationship is more likely to have a higher degree of success than other settings. For example, in an employment relationship where the employee and the managers of the firm are in close proximity on a daily basis the interests of the firm and the interests of the employee become integrated. This type of covenant relationship may have a higher probability of success. In contrast, two independent firms located in different parts of the world may have more divergent interests and cultural values and are not as close in proximity on a daily basis. In such a situation the covenant relationship may be more difficult to maintain.

A covenantal approach to management is a radical departure from traditional views of management that have developed in modern times. Managers who exhibit covenantal behavior will definitely be noticed in modern societies where many managers are in the marketplace to get what they can in the short term, even if that means taking advantage of others. This does not mean that covenantal managers will gain wide approval and acclaim. On the contrary, individuals who are interested in pursuing the bare minimum elements of legal contracts are likely to resist covenantal ethics. Nor does it mean that covenantal managers should allow others to take advantage of them. Covenantal managers can and do exhibit strength with diplomacy, just like anyone else.

Christian Ethics

Christian ethics begins with the belief in God's existence, God as the originator of life on Earth, and God's self-revelation to human beings. God himself is the foundation for standards of morality.[20] The principles of human conduct can be traced to the Creation event where human beings were created into a particular relationship with their Creator. All humans and all of creation are equally valued as created beings and, because of this, must be treated with the compassion, respect, and dignity that promote the full experience of their place in the community of God's creation. Though God revealed his character and divine will in nature and then to ancient prophets, the pinnacle of his revelation occurred in the person and work of Jesus Christ, the only Son of God incarnated into human flesh and believed by Christians to be the Messiah foretold of by the ancient prophets. These are the nonnegotiable elements of Christian faith that guide moral behavior.

Jesus' two commands are often described as centered on love in two dimensions: The *vertical* love to God and the *horizontal* love to others.[21] From these two moral principles all other duties can be derived. Love shows itself through obedience to eternal Divine law.[22] Christian teaching asserts that love takes the person past the moral minimum of "do no harm."[23] The first great commandment is the foundation for fulfilling the second commandment. Most Christians believe that the vertical dimension of love to God must be in place before the horizontal dimension can be truly experienced. In other words, it is only as we come to love God because he first loved us that we can truly love each other.[24]

Love is demonstrated in obedience to the Ten Commandments.[25] This moral law is eternal and universal.[26] When Jesus commented on the law and its true meaning, he went beyond the letter of the law and attempted to show the fundamental principles on which the law is based.[27] For example, one important principle in the Bible is that self-interest should not be promoted at the expense of others.[28] **Self-interest** is the desire to promote one's own well-being.[29] When applied to an organization, the desire is to promote the interests of the firm. While individuals who make a profit are spoken of in positive terms, Jesus warned his followers of being consumed by greed.[30] Profit-making must meet moral standards. Like Moses, Jesus taught the **Golden Rule** of behavior: Do unto others as you would have them do unto you.[31] The principles at work here are love and accountability to each other.

Love	Joy	Faithfulness	Forgiveness
Peace	Patience	Truth	Thankfulness
Perseverance	Long-suffering	Compassion	Kindness
Courage	Faith	Humility	Steadfastness
Hope	Temperance	Gentleness	Honor

EXHIBIT 5-4
Christian Virtues

The Bible establishes a behavior standard linked with personal character. For example, Jesus taught that the person who is faithful in small things will be faithful also in larger things. The Bible encourages Christians to integrate into their lives important fruit of the Spirit virtues that will guide their behavior.[32] See Exhibit 5-4.

According to the Bible, despite instances of altruism in society, humans tend to be selfish. We cannot rise above this by our own effort.[33] **Altruism** is the willingness to look out for others by taking actions that result in benefits to them. It is only the grace of God, received by faith in Jesus Christ, whereby the selfish person can become transformed by the renewing of his or her mind.[34] As this renewal process takes place, the person begins to desire to follow God's will by behaving in moral ways.

After the early centuries as Christians sought to more clearly interpret the teachings of Scripture regarding business activities, Christian scholars developed a progressive understanding of Scripture. An example of how teachings on ethics changed is the concern for taking advantage of others in financial matters through fraud, deceit, and unfair prices. In the Middle Ages, the practice of lending money was believed by church leaders to be sinful because of a misunderstanding about the time-value of money. As economic understanding improved, church theologians began to distinguish between fair interest rates and unfair or abusive interest rates, which are considered **usury**.[35]

Many Christians believe that economic activity can be carried out within moral limits. Ownership of private property is valued, and the stealing of private property is immoral. Also, when a person destroys or devalues another person's property, the other individual expects economic restitution.[36] Private property ownership is always in the context of the belief that God owns everything in creation, and because of this humans must be stewards to watch over and preserve the earth's natural resources.

Christians and Responsibility to Society

Many Christians believe that all organizations should exist to serve the greater good of society and not solely to earn economic profit. Just as individuals should live by the Golden Rule, so too should organizations follow this principle.

Social responsibility applied to organizations comes from four interlocking ideas.[37] First, because God is the Creator of everything in the universe, God owns everything that exists. Christians will want their organizations to show care for everyone and everything because they desire to honor God.[38] Second, organizations are not owners in the ultimate sense but rather are temporary stewards who have responsibilities.[39] Third, humans and their organizations must respect the physical environment of this earth because these are God's gifts to everyone.[40] Fourth, just as God is eternal and changeless, the biblical requirements related to social responsibility are timeless, everlasting principles that guide us in everything we do.[41]

Care for the Environment

Most people in most cultures agree that it is wrong to use another person for selfish purposes. For Christians, this principle applies equally to our relationship with the natural **environment** of the earth, air, and water.[42] God loves his creation. He continually sustains it. Therefore creation must have inherent divine value. We are called to worship the Creator. But worship includes not only our thoughts and emotions but also our actions toward that which God values.[43] Creation reveals God.[44] Defacing, abusing, or destroying the environment is an attack on the Creator. The environment is not just a natural resource for human exploitation. It is holy and must be cared for as loving stewards would care for their own families. The environment is God's handiwork, and it should enjoy its own natural integrity.

Sin has distorted our relationship with each other and with the natural environment. Humans have acted as tyrants with violence toward the earth, upsetting the ecological balances, greedily grabbing resources for economic gain, and leaving behind an earth that has a harder time healing itself. For example, lumber is a useful resource that provides materials for shelter and other beneficial purposes for society. In the 19th century, American companies engaged in clear-cutting vast forests in the Appalachian Mountains to get the lumber needed for buildings for the growing population without taking responsibility to plant new trees and do other things for the land to prevent erosion.

God's plan of salvation encompasses not only human beings but also the earth.[45] Humans participate with God in carrying out his plan of salvation by doing our part to redeem the earth. Humans are called to live in peace and justice toward each other and to live with respect for the natural environment such that the environment is self-renewing and sustainable. We have freedom to interact with the environment as long as we don't use that freedom as license to be destructive.[46]

This God-centered view of the environment results in six important interrelated dimensions of the human response to God.[47]

Humility: Humility is the cardinal virtue of a God-centered perspective. God, the Creator, is omnipotent and all knowing. In contrast, while humans know a lot about the environment, there is much that we don't know. Our power is limited.

Respect: Respect is required if we are to act in humility toward each other and the earth. The earth is not merely a thing without value beyond our economic estimates. It has divine value. The earth is not for humans alone but for humans and nature together.

Selflessness: Environmental problems result from the cumulative effects of many human actions over many years. God-centered environmentalism calls for a reduction in the impact we have on the earth. We must limit our desires and make sacrifices if we are to respect the earth and the God who created it.

Moderation: Taking from the earth without self-restraint is arrogance toward something that we do not own. Christians will move beyond seeking selfish satisfaction *from* nature toward finding satisfaction *in* nature.

Mindfulness: The Christian perspective therefore requires being mindful of every action we take in terms of the impact that these actions have on the earth. Mindfulness leads us to examine our practices such as product packaging and disposable products.

Responsibility: All this points to the responsibility that we have to be careful as we use the earth and then to heal the damage we do to the earth.

Having seen the Christian perspective on moral issues, we turn next to consider additional perspectives that you will encounter as a manager.

The Biblical Story of Elijah

Read the story of Elijah in 1 Kings 17–21 and 2 Kings 1–2 in the Bible. Based on his experience, grasp the significance of the accomplishments that occurred under the leadership of Elijah. Make a mental note of the leadership strengths and weaknesses of Elijah. What leadership principles can we gain from the experience of Elijah that are applicable today?

Definitions and Distinctions: Morality, Ethics, and the Law

After several highly publicized legal cases involving moral lapses on the part of high-level managers, managerial ethics is now far more important than in the past. Having explored the Christian perspective on ethics, we need to look at several related ideas, starting with the distinction among morality, ethics, and the law.

Defining Morality and Ethics

What is the difference, if any, between ethics and morality? Although these terms, and various forms of them, are often used interchangeably, there is an important distinction between them.[48]

Morality is concerned with standards of right and wrong behavior. Morality asks the question "What behaviors are right and wrong?" For example, we could ask, "Is it right for an employee to take a ream of paper home to use on a personal project?" In most, if not all, cultures stealing property is wrong. When we say that a behavior is immoral, we are saying that it is not consistent with or it does not conform to generally accepted moral standards of behavior.

Contemporary Western organizational cultures have a simplified moral system that is the foundation for the ability of the free market economy to work successfully: Don't steal, don't lie; follow through on your commitments. This does not mean that all people and organizations in a free market consistently avoid stealing, lying, and shirking their commitments. But the system as a whole cannot function unless these three principles of morality are generally accepted as being valid. As we have seen, the Christian moral system has been established by the Bible.

Ethics is the study of morality. It is also the process of thinking about the morality or immorality of particular behaviors. Ethics is like asking the question "Why is a particular behavior right or wrong?" Ethics applies to behaviors that affect individuals as well as to behaviors that affect groups or society as a whole. Ethics is not something that only scholars consider on a formal basis. We all do informal or formal ethical thinking from time to time. Whenever we attempt to think about right and wrong, we are engaging in ethics.

The capacity for ethical thinking begins developing at an early age, gradually becoming more sophisticated as mental capacities develop. When given a rule to follow in the household (e.g., "Pick up your toys before dinner.") the child asks, "Why?" When the high school principal announces a new student policy, a student asks, "Why?" These questions are an attempt to understand more clearly the thinking behind the rules, the fundamental assumptions and beliefs for policies and standards.

Morality ≠ Legality

Law is the collection of specific standards that describe behaviors that are either **proscribed**, meaning forbidden, or **prescribed**, meaning required. See Exhibit 5-5. For example, the laws of most states generally forbid misrepresentation (fraud) when entering into agreements. The law prohibits stealing tax revenue from the State treasury and many other specific behaviors that are detrimental to society. Laws also mandate certain behaviors that are considered beneficial to society. Administrators and employees of nursing homes must treat nursing home residents with respect and dignity, providing them with safety, nutritious meals, and proper care. Local laws related to land use prevent owners of a noisy manufacturing facility from locating their plant in a residential neighborhood. To reduce the risks of harm to themselves and to others in society, the law prohibits long-haul truck drivers from driving too many hours without getting rest.

EXHIBIT 5-5

Legal vs. Moral vs. Ethical Behavior

Legal	Moral	Ethical
Bare minimum standards of morality agreed to by society as written in the formal rule of laws and regulations; enforced by the justice system; founded on moral principles; addresses a particular set of specific required and forbidden behaviors.	The fundamental principles that embrace a wide range of behaviors; values implicitly or explicitly embraced by individuals in society; enforced by personal will, social-cultural expectations, or social pressure.	How a person or a group of people evaluate a specific situation and come to a decision of what to do; the study of moral principles; enforced by managerial decision-making policies and procedures or by personal will of integrity of mind and heart.
Example: Tell the truth when you report financial statements.	Example: Be honest; act with integrity toward investors.	Example: Conducting a discussion with top-level executives regarding what and how to report earned revenue in financial statements.

Law is a contractual obligation that citizens make to each other "in exchange for which every individual has resigned a part of his natural liberty."[49] It is a formal way to govern individual conduct: If a citizen disobeys the law, the citizen is subject to legal consequences.

Legal requirements, or the "letter of the law," are based on a *minimum* level of morality accepted by citizens; however, laws do not always specifically define what is moral, or all of the behaviors that should be included in the "spirit of the law." In other words, a particular behavior may be legal if the law doesn't explicitly forbid it, but the behavior still might lack a broader moral foundation.[50] For example, many states have enacted employment-at-will laws that permit employers to lay off an employee for no reason. But when an employer uses this law to fire an employee unfairly, the employer's behavior goes against fundamental moral principles of fairness, even though it might be within the provision of the law.[51] Also, some laws such as slavery were later shown to be immoral and as a result were changed. When making a management decision, a manager must consider both the law and its deeper, moral foundation.

Accountability

When we compare moral standards with legal codes, we can see some interesting similarities.[52] Both have rules with general applicability; both have special importance in our lives. Both give us reasons to act that can override other compelling reasons that arise from personal interest; both carry consequences for citizens who deviate from expected behaviors.

Both law and morality are based on fundamental **accountabilities**—responsibilities for our conduct in society.[53] Some accountabilities are inherent in human existence and in the need to care for each other in order to survive. Other obligations stem from being a part of a family or other social group. Some derive from religious or spiritual teachings. Still other responsibilities are acquired in formal positions, such as a manager, and in agreements that are made with others.

Obligations encompass more than just individual behaviors. See Exhibit 5-6. When individuals come together in groups to achieve common goals (organize), the individuals and the organizations they form have obligations. A commercial organization such as fashion megachain Forever 21 has obligations to stakeholders and to society as a whole. Governmental organizations have obligations to the citizens and to other governments.

All communities (including organizations) have developed ways to maintain accountability. For example, many organizations use employees and supervisors to ensure accountability throughout the organization. Individuals hold themselves accountable for their own work. Employees hold each other accountable for tasks they have been asked to perform. Frontline supervisors hold accountable their workers. Mid-level managers hold accountable the frontline supervisors. And senior executives hold accountable the mid-level managers. Governing boards hold accountable the senior executives. Customers hold the company accountable. Over time, society as a whole holds accountable the entire organization.

As they fulfill their obligations, managers deal with concrete problems such as deciding which tasks to assign to which employees, which resources to use, and which production methods to employ. But because managerial problems involve people, it is impossible for a manager to make a decision or take an action that is completely void of morals.[54] So the question is not *when*, but rather *how* will a manager integrate moral values in the performance of managerial work. Similarly, we ask not *whether*, but rather *to what extent do* individuals and organizations have responsibilities that go beyond the bare minimum legal compliance.[55]

EXHIBIT 5-6
Three Levels of Accountability

Accountability		
Personal	**Organizational/Systemic**	**Accountability to society**
Accountability for actions taken by an individual.	Accountability for systems, structures, policies, and procedures that set up expectations for or in other ways shape individual behaviors.	Responsibility that derives from the fact that we have organized systems for managing the needs of individuals and the needs of society as a whole. During our civic duties, we empower government and other societal organizations to take actions on our behalf.

Factors That Promote and Prevent Moral Problems in Organizations

In some organizations that have a strong company culture, maintaining accountability for the moral dimension of work is routine. But company culture is just one important factor that plays a part in promoting or preventing moral problems. In this section, we explore other factors.

Influences That Promote Moral Problems

Despite the moral and legal obligations individuals have to each other, some individuals make decisions that ignore these obligations. Mitsubishi Motors' former president and 10 other senior leaders were jailed on charges related to systematic suppression of widespread vehicle defects. Five of them were charged with negligence tied to a fatal accident caused by a known defect. Former Adelphia Communications CEO John Rigas and his son Timothy were convicted of hiding more than $2 billion in debt while embezzling cash. The Securities and Exchange Commission (SEC) charged Lucent Technologies with fraudulently and improperly recognizing more than $1 billion in revenues and $470 million in pre-tax income during fiscal year 2000. Richard Scrushy, former chairman and CEO of healthcare services provider HealthSouth Corporation, faced a trial in 2005 for $2.5 billion in accounting frauds. More than a dozen HealthSouth executives pleaded guilty.[56] What influences people in organizations to take these kinds of risks?

It's tempting for the Christian to oversimplify the problem of immoral behavior simply by blaming the problem on sin and assume that nothing can be done about that. Christians believe sin is the root of moral problems and brokenness in society. There are several factors that managers can pay attention to in order to counteract the effects of this brokenness. Let's consider the individual and organizational influences on moral problems in organizations.[57]

NARROWLY-FOCUSED AND UNRESTRAINED SELF-INTEREST.[58] A basic tenet of western thought is that humans are fallible and willing to go to great lengths to get what they want.[59] When stripped of moral values, striving for efficiency can become a moral disadvantage. Individuals can easily see moral standards as constraints that are optional. In our natural condition, humans prefer not to live under restraints placed on selfish desires.

AMBIGUOUS SITUATIONS. Morally ambiguous situations lend themselves to **reframing**, which is the interpretation of the facts to support a particular perspective. Individuals can use reframing to rationalize a situation to fit selfish desires or to mislead others.

CODE OF SILENCE.[60] In many organizations moral issues are not discussed. Openly weighing the moral implications of decisions can quickly be interpreted as dissent and even worse, lack of loyalty. People quickly learn to be silent about the things they know are illegal or immoral. By developing a **code of silence**, they protect themselves from being fired. But silence can be taken as consent. For example, the extreme aggressiveness and high economic rewards handed out to employees of the Enron Corporation encouraged a code of silence regarding the company's inappropriate actions in its accounting practices. Enron executives hid billions of dollars in debt, misled the board of directors, and pressured their public accounting firm Arthur Anderson to ignore accounting irregularities.

COMPETITIVE PRESSURES AND AGGRESSIVE PROFIT GOALS.[61] Few would question the assertion that the marketplace can be an efficient mechanism to drive costs down. Consumers are always looking for a better deal. The presence of competitors in the market, while good for efficiency, pressures companies to make moral decisions that give them an edge over the competition. This can bring the individual in direct conflict with personal standards of right and wrong.

ORGANIZATIONAL STRUCTURE.[62] Bureaucracies tend to distribute decision-making authority through the chain of command. However, managers may find themselves asking, "Is this my job to decide, or is it someone else's job?" As a result, some managers learn to let others make the difficult moral decisions. When committees make decisions, no one individual is left with the responsibility. Those who implement these decisions may be the ones most likely to experience the ethical conflicts and yet they have the least amount of authority to dissent. Financial incentive systems that are poorly designed, coupled with aggressive sales goals, are another structural element that can encourage moral problems.

TIME PRESSURES.[63] As we have already considered, many managers, especially middle managers, work under tight deadlines to complete projects. Managers often have little discretion over their own time at work because both subordinates and bosses demand their time. In terms of ethical decision making, this often means that managers do not have much time to evaluate the moral implications of their decisions.

ORGANIZATIONAL CULTURE.[64] When the culture of an organization such as World Vision supports the assumption of personal responsibility, it will likely encourage ethical behaviors toward donors, recipients, and organizations with which the organization collaborates. But if immoral behaviors go unpunished, the organizational culture emboldens individuals to make selfish decisions. Also, an organizational culture that supports the diffusion of responsibility increases the chances that individuals will knowingly behave in unethical ways or ignore unethical behavior observed in others.

One striking example of how organizational culture can affect ethical behavior is the problem known as groupthink. **Groupthink** is a process in organizations in which individual members of a group strive for consensus within the group in a way that overrides the motivation to realistically appraise a situation and its alternatives.[65] Maintaining the approval and avoiding the disapproval of group members becomes extremely important when groupthink occurs, leading individuals to do things they might not do under different circumstances. Exhibit 5-7 illustrates the danger that groupthink might encourage group members to agree with group decisions even when such decisions are misguided, risky, or unethical.

DIVERSE MORAL STANDARDS.[66] Commerce is filled with diversity in terms of the moral standards underlying economic behavior. For example, when we consider the idea of telling the truth, we find a variety of interpretations of what that means. If we add to this how workers learn to tell lies without concern for whether lying is right or wrong, we have a recipe for moral problems.[67] See Exhibit 5-8.

Influences That Prevent Moral Problems

Counteracting influences that promote moral problems in the marketplace are influences that restrain the emergence of moral problems.

THE RULE OF LAW AND AN IMPARTIAL JUSTICE SYSTEM.[68] Government acts as a stability-creating, evil-restraining force in society. In the United States, the Constitution is the legal foundation on which laws and regulations are founded. Laws consistent with the Constitution are based on fundamental moral principles that society (through its lawmakers) believes should prohibit some actions and require other actions. When managers at a company like Cloud Ten Pictures, a Christian film production firm, use legal contracts and agreements, they minimize the risks of misunderstandings and misrepresentations. Impartiality in applying the laws and regulations is crucial for a society to engage in marketplace exchanges that are just. This is not to suggest that the organized justice system acting in concert with the rule of law is perfect. But it does act as a deterrent to moral problems.

OWNERSHIP OF PRIVATE PROPERTY.[69] Owning possessions is the flip side to the biblical command "You shall not steal," a fundamental principle found in most cultures of the world.[70] Through

EXHIBIT 5-7
Danger of Groupthink

Group becomes cohesive
Group lacks procedures to evaluate alternatives
Group members seek agreement
Group develops the illusion of being invulnerable
Group members put pressure on each other to conform
Group members avoid speaking up to confront moral issues
Group members fail to examine risks
Group takes an action that is immoral

Influences That Promote Moral Problems	Influences That Restrain Moral Problems
Narrowly focused and unrestrained self-interest	The rule of law in society backed up by an impartial justice system
Ambiguous situations combined with reframing the interpretation	Ownership of private property
Code of silence and inaction coupled with penalties for dissent	Restrained and broadly focused self-interest
Competitive pressures mixed with aggressive profit-oriented goals	Organizational systems designed for interdependence with the external environment
Organizational structure that undermines accountability	Ethical review processes and impartial grievance procedures
Time pressures	Individuals committed to maintaining solid personal standards
Organizational culture that allows for moral ambiguity	Selection and orientation of new employees
Diversity and instability of personal standards of right and wrong	Consistent application of progressive disciplinary procedures
Double standards mixed with personal economic pressures	Clearly enunciated statements of values backed up by supportive top-level leader behaviors

EXHIBIT 5-8
Promoting and Restraining Influences on Moral Problems

ownership and care of things that we own, humans are fulfilling part of what it means to be created in God's image.[71] Property owners develop a sense of responsibility and accountability for the property over which they serve as stewards. This restrains their behavior.

RESTRAINED SELF-INTEREST.[72] Self-interest is as complex as individuals. Although people have the drive to compete, they also cooperate. While it is true that humans commit immoral acts, humans also are concerned about the future consequences of their decisions. Expecting to live in peace with others, we cannot completely disregard the interests of others in society. Thus, most people most of the time impose limits on self-interested behaviors.

ORGANIZATIONAL SYSTEMS DESIGNED FOR INTERDEPENDENCE.[73] Maintaining a vibrant interdependence with the outside environment is vital for an organization to fulfill its purpose. Thus internal control systems, clear chains of command, division of authority, policies and procedures, and work-coordinating systems all are examples of organizational structures that foster moral behaviors, which are needed to support interdependencies with other organizations. While organizational structure can unintentionally promote moral lapses, structure also acts as a deterrent to immorality.

ETHICAL REVIEW PROCESSES AND IMPARTIAL GRIEVANCE PROCEDURES. When employees know they can safely voice dissent based on their moral concerns about business practices, they are more likely to hold firm to personal moral standards. Likewise, if the ethical review process is an organizational learning process rather than a "witch hunt," employees are more likely to act according to what they believe is right. In alignment with these principles, moral problems are restrained when employees feel safe in discussing ethical dilemmas at work or when they feel free to report unethical behavior without fear of retaliation.

INDIVIDUAL COMMITMENT TO PERSONAL STANDARDS. When individuals decide to orient their work based on personal moral standards, whether from humanistic philosophy or from religious beliefs, this helps to prevent moral lapses. By following what we believe to be right and developing ways to clearly discuss the moral standards for behavior, we contribute to moral stability where we work.

SELECTION AND ORIENTATION OF NEW EMPLOYEES.[74] Careful attention to personal values that new employees bring to the organization can prevent a host of moral problems. Asking prospective employees to talk about situations where ethical dilemmas were present can give you a window

EXHIBIT 5-9
Five Ways to Promote Ethical Behavior in Business

- Live by example the standards of behavior.
- Set formal standards of behavior for the organization.
- Train employees in these standards.
- Reinforce behavior that aligns with the standards.
- Use influence to preserve the standards.

into their behavior patterns. Selecting an employee who is willing to compromise certain values that your company stands on raises the risk that the company will be less able to fulfill its purpose using these values.

CONSISTENT DISCIPLINE. When managers impose consequences to actions that go against agreed-upon moral standards, they are restraining immoral behavior as long as such disciplinary actions are consistently applied across the entire organization.

CLEARLY ENUNCIATED STATEMENTS OF ETHICAL VALUES BACKED UP BY TOP-LEVEL LEADER BEHAVIORS.[75] Many scholars and practitioners report that an organizational culture of moral behavior based on generally accepted positive values flows "downhill" from the upper echelons of company leadership out to the frontline workers. For example, when the company president or vice president tells employees that telling lies will not be tolerated and then engages in lying, the organization will never rise higher than how the top leaders are living out their moral standards. Lower-level employees take their behavior cues from superiors and, over time, model their behaviors after those of higher-level leaders. See Exhibit 5-9.

Stakeholders and What's at Stake

Many in society are challenging the traditional concept that business exists primarily for the interests of the owners. In large corporations the owners are many shareholders who are simply short-term speculators or long-term, loyal shareholders. While shareholders are owners and have rights, the capital they invest is simply one of many resources that the managers of the corporation need in order to achieve the organization's goals. There are other individuals and groups who have an interest in the affairs of the corporation, too.[76] Collectively we call all those to whom the organization has a moral obligation the **stakeholders**.

The concept of stakeholders can be defined both narrowly and broadly. A narrow definition includes groups who are vital to the economic survival of the company. For example, stockholders have a legal claim on the corporation's dividends. Donors are vital to the success of nonprofit organizations. Employees who expect wages, suppliers who expect payment, and customers who expect fair value from the products and services all are stakeholders who transact business and through these transactions have an economic claim to the firm. They are called *primary* or *market* stakeholders. Many people believe that the primary stakeholders should receive the primary consideration when company managers make decisions. Market stakeholders sometimes can use their bargaining power to influence the moral decisions of an organization. See Exhibit 5-10 for an illustration of a university's stakeholders.

A wide definition of the term includes any group or individual who can affect or is affected by the organization. The government, lawmakers, the media, businesses in related industries, the general public, and public interest groups all are examples of *secondary* or *non-market* stakeholders. Non-market stakeholders do not have primary economic bargaining power at their disposal, but they still may have influence. The government will have the force of law and regulations. The media has its own influence, and public interest groups often seek support from the media as they attempt to hold organizations accountable.[77] The general public can use the power of word of mouth to shape an organization's reputation. This wide definition of stakeholder does not deny that managers have an obligation to run the organization as efficiently as possible generating the best return on investment as possible.

The presence of diverse stakeholders presents managers with some interesting moral choices. For example, increasing the pension benefits of employees may result in higher prices to customers. A company that protects one community by keeping an unprofitable factory open might become uncompetitive and eventually be forced to close not only that factory but factories in other communities.

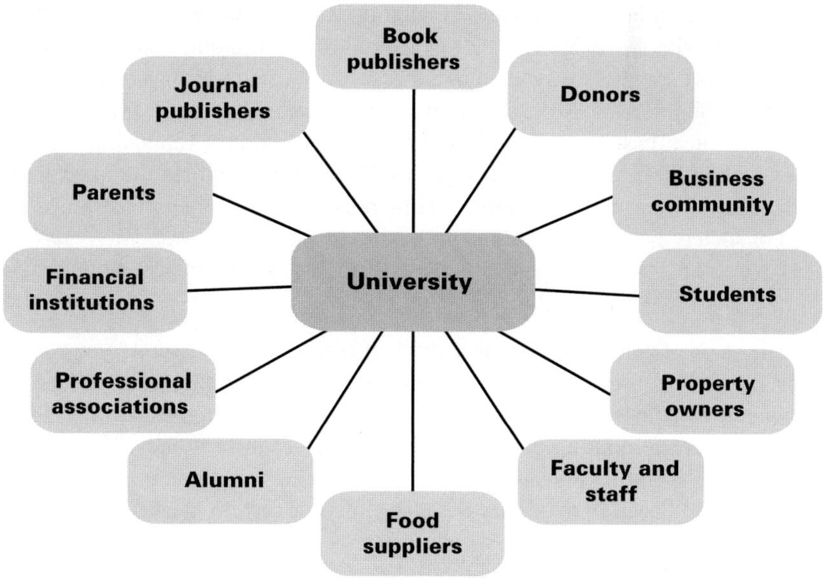

EXHIBIT 5-10
Stakeholders of a University

Approaches to Ethical Decision Making

Given what we know about the characteristics of moral problems, we come to the question of how managers think about moral issues. While religion is a strong influence on the ways in which people traditionally think about morality, for some people it is not the only influence. There are several approaches to ethical thinking. We will begin with the social contract.

The Social Contract

Sometimes the common interests of society conflict with the interests of an individual or the interests of a single company. The problem is how to find a way for individuals (or individual companies) to support the needs of society while at the same time preserving their freedom to choose behaviors that promote their own interests.[78] The solution to this problem is called the social contract.[79] A **social contract** is an unwritten set of general social expectations accepted by all citizens that is meant to constrain the behavior of the citizens who live in a state or country. It is one of the foundations for deciding what is right and wrong behavior and how far to go beyond the minimum requirements of the law. By contrast, a **business contract** is a written or unwritten set of specific expectations that is legally binding and that constrains the behavior of the parties that participate in the agreement.

In the social contract the interests of the individual and the common interests of others in society always are reciprocal, interdependent, and complementary. No individual can live as an island and survive long solely on the basis of self-interest. We all have mutual, interdependent obligations toward each other. For the social contract to work, individuals must live according to self-imposed restraints so that their self-interest is not acted out in a way that harms the freedom of others.

In business,[80] this social contract is between companies and their customers or between companies and the society as a whole.[81] Society gives the privilege of operating a business to investors by allowing the company to purchase land, obtain a business license, hire workers, and transact business with suppliers and customers. Customers allow the company the privilege of doing business by voluntarily patronizing its products and services. This gives the firm legitimacy based on the consent of society. We can think of this legitimacy as being offered on loan from society.

Embedded in the customs of society, these expectations are based on mutual trust. Consumers and communities trust the company to do no harm to them and to behave in ways that support minimum standards of right and wrong. Companies trust that workers they hire and customers they serve will not attempt to take advantage of them.

One important way that company managers retain and reinforce the public trust is by acting morally and showing concern for the greater good of society. As this occurs, the community gives a certain reputation to the company. Reputation is owned by society, not by the company who enjoys it.[82] Reputation is a value that is offered on conditional loan but held in trust by society. Reputation is society's way of allowing the firm to share in the society's hopes, fears, dreams, and common interests. If the conditions of the loan are breached, for example when the company acts unethically, society withdraws the reputation, and the reputation suffers.

As an ethical decision-making method, the social contract requires the manager to ask the question when faced by a moral dilemma, "How must our actions be constrained so that the greater good of society is considered along with our interests?"

Egoism

Consider the decision of whether to rent an apartment or purchase a house. As you work your way to a decision, you will consider the costs and benefits of both options. You will think about the short-term benefits and the long-term results. You also will consider the other things that you need such as food, transportation, and clothing—all of which require money. If you have a fixed amount of money to spend on housing each month and a certain amount to spend on food and transportation, you will need to maximize the utility of your cash to balance your multiple needs and wants. **Utility** is satisfaction that a person derives or goals achieved by making choices on how to spend time and money. We might call this a simplified form of self-interested utility maximization analysis.[83]

If a person made moral decisions based solely on the personal utility that can be achieved, this would lead to what ethics scholars have labeled *egoism*. **Egoism** is the approach to deciding what is right and wrong only in terms of selfish self-interest. While some individuals follow the path of egoism as a consistent guide to all of life's decisions, many more people are situational egoists, meaning that they will consider the interests of others as well as their own interests unless a situation comes up where they want only their own interests.

As an ethical decision-making approach, egoism asks the simple question, "What do I want to get out of this decision?" It ignores the interests of other stakeholders. The Christian faith perspective on egoism sees it as unbridled selfishness, which is sinful and destructive. If everyone followed this approach, the result would be social conflict, murder, and war followed by a general breakdown of human society. Closely related to egoism is moral relativism. To this we turn next.

Moral Relativism

Moral relativism is the belief that determining what is right and wrong can be accomplished only when considering the culture or group in which the action will take place.[84] Those who hold to this view believe that there are no absolute moral standards that cross all cultures, locations, situations, and times.

When considering this perspective it is important to note that there is a difference between describing that individuals in different cultures have different moral standards and prescribing that when two groups or cultures hold different moral standards, both can be right.

The Christian worldview rejects moral relativism as being completely contradictory to the moral absolutes given in the Bible. Moral relativism has been criticized on logical grounds, too. If moral relativism is correct, then there is no criterion independent of one's culture for determining right or wrong. Moral relativism is inconsistent with many of our fundamental moral standards, such as honesty, which would be utterly meaningless if moral relativism were true. Just because people believe differently on an issue doesn't mean that there is no objective means to determine that one person is right and the other person is wrong. Taken to its logical conclusion, if moral relativism became the norm, then there would be no reason to hold each other accountable for actions. As a result, without accountability, society would cease to exist. Whereas disagreements on the morality of specific behaviors might occur when comparing one culture with another, no disagreement can usually be found on fundamental moral ideas such as stealing and lying. Two cultures might agree on the fundamental moral principle and yet disagree on how the principle should be implemented.

Ethics scholar LaRue Hosmer believes that at least one moral principle exists across all groups, all cultures, and all times—the irreducible minimum common denominator that binds all humans together: Members of every social group have responsibility for the well-being of other group members. Because of the nature of being human, cooperation is necessary for our survival. Thus, some basic standards of behavior are required to ensure such cooperation.[85]

Utilitarianism

Because organizations are goal-oriented, managers must consider the practical outcomes of their decisions in terms of the organization's goals. Because many organizations have economic issues that are embedded in their activities, it is impossible to escape the pragmatic choices about what results will be generated in terms of revenue and expenses, costs and benefits, for short-term and long-term performance. But these managers cannot completely ignore the interests of others who are affected by their decisions: employees, suppliers, and customers. This inclusive approach is called *utilitarianism.*[86]

Utilitarianism is an approach to decision making that holds that an action is moral if it produces the greatest amount of good for the greatest number of people, including all those affected by the action.[87] John Stuart Mill, an economist and philosopher and one of the strongest proponents of utilitarianism, argued that because God is benevolent toward his creatures, he wishes them all to be happy. God commands behaviors that tend to produce the most happiness for the greatest number of his creatures.

Some Christian managers might reject utilitarianism as a way to decide what is moral. However, managers cannot ignore economic influences of their decisions. A Christian faith perspective suggests that making decisions based merely on the utility of an action, even if the analysis includes the impact on all the affected stakeholders, doesn't go far enough. Utilitarianism, if used alone, has other weaknesses.[88] For example, how can a person possibly foresee all consequences of any particular action? History teaches us that some consequences are unintentional. Humans might not anticipate the most important consequences. Proponents of utilitarianism argue that we can foresee a large number of expected consequences because we have the benefit of having learned from past experience. Utilitarianism requires that the benefits for the greatest number of people be traded off for the harms done to the small number of people. Another criticism from Christians is that if your moral direction is based on the principle "get more for less," then your moral sensitivities toward stealing are dulled. Stealing as a means of acquiring goods is one of the possible logical conclusions that can be drawn from utilitarian principles. It is one of the most efficient labor-saving devices.

The Christian Mind on Utilitarianism

Utilitarianism is a consequential approach to ethics that argues human beings ought to act in a way that brings about the best possible results from their actions. On the surface, for us as Christians, this widely accepted principle may seem to fit well to our fundamental Christian beliefs. However, as Christians, we must reject this concept for two reasons. First, adoption of this ethical principle violates the rights of the individual/minority for the benefit of the majority; and secondly, it violates the concept of justice which implies that everyone be treated fairly with reward and punishment based on their own merits. The Bible is quite clear in telling us that everyone has value and worth. God clearly wants us to love one another and to take care of one another.[89] Hence, as Christians we cannot adopt the utilitarian viewpoint as an ethical standard.

Dr. Monty Bohrer
Assistant Professor of Marketing
East Texas Baptist University
Marshall, TX

Universalism

Immanuel Kant (1724–1804), a German philosopher and committed Christian,[90] believed that humans are unique in the world because of their ability to use their reasoning powers. It is the God-given ability to reason that gives humans their true worth. After thinking about the complicated moral dilemmas that humans must deal with, he concluded that we have a duty to use pure reason alone as the basis for determining moral standards regardless of the consequences. He called this *the categorical imperative* (requirement).[91] This belief has come to be known as **universalism**.

Kant proposed three tests for right and wrong that are based on pure reason. He said that for an action to be moral, all three tests must be passed. His first test is that moral actions must not become logically self-contradictory when applied to everyone everywhere (universally). For example, if we say that telling lies is morally right and we apply this to everyone everywhere, suddenly lying and truth-telling become logically meaningless ideas. For this reason, telling lies must be wrong.

Second, human beings must be treated with respect and dignity, never using other people as mere means to an end but rather as ends in themselves. Thus, all moral actions will be free of coercion and deception. Kant's reason is that humans have been given the gift of reason and anything that prevents people from using their reason undermines this gift and is therefore wrong. For example, a person who steals is not giving the other party an opportunity to use reason in deciding whether he or she should have something that belongs to them. Therefore, stealing is always wrong.

Third, Kant said to put yourself in the shoes of both king and subject and then act in a way that is consistent for both. In business, this test would be to place yourself in the position of both business owner and employee or of business owner and a member of society. An action is moral if and only if the action would be acceptable to both parties as each freely uses reasoning power when deciding.

As an approach to making decisions about what is right and wrong, universalism is attractive in its appeal to reason. For some, the Christian perspective on morality agrees with Kant's view of humans created in the image of God. It promotes freedom to think and respects God's creation and God himself. Another attractive feature is the close relationship it has to the Golden Rule: "Do unto others as you would have them do unto you."[92]

As powerful as universalism is, some people have criticized it as an approach to moral decision making.[93] Built on pure reason alone, the categorical imperative is impossibly strict and rigid, requiring the assumption that there is little or no individuality. Circumstances in an imperfect world are not all the same in all contexts. In some situations equally valid imperatives are in conflict, and universalism offers no clear way to resolve these conflicts. It is not always clear when a person is treated as a means to an end rather than an end in itself. It is difficult to treat others as ends and not as means all of the time. What has moral value? Universalism does not define ultimate standards or priorities. Do we really want to say that giving money to famine relief has no moral worth if one is moved by emotion rather than moved by a sense of duty? Some Christians see in Kant's thinking that ultimate truth is subjective. By assuming that it is reason alone that can be used to determine what is right and wrong, it allows for the rejection of or attacks on Christianity through reason. Reason becomes a substitute for Christianity.

Rights

Rights are "important, normative, justifiable claims or entitlements."[94] The idea that individuals have certain inalienable rights such as the right to life, liberty, and the pursuit of happiness became the foundation of the United States government in the 18th century. But these ideas found currency long before the American Revolution, and they continue to be popular today.

Since the 1970s human rights have captivated the interest of many in western society, including as an approach to ethical decision making. Robert Nozick, one of the strongest proponents of this approach,[95] proposed a principle that we should never act in such a way that the liberties of others are interfered with. As we go about the business of exchanging goods and services with each other, what we gain ("holdings") comes from others in the exchange process. But to promote the rights of liberty, all exchanges must be voluntary.

Christians will be attracted to the rights approach to business ethics because the fundamental principle is in close alignment with Creation theology and the Gospel message. Human rights are universal. All persons should have equal access to the same degree of rights. Because rights are inherent in being human, they cannot be transferred, sold, or given up.[96]

Justice

Closely related to rights is justice. **Justice** is the ideal that humans acting morally will never take action that would harm the least advantaged person or group. This viewpoint is based on two fundamental ideas. First, all humans must have equal access to liberty. Second, if there is to be inequality, there must be some consideration given to those who have unequal access.

For example, using this approach, business managers will decide whether to lay off workers only after considering the lowest paid workers and the effect on their families.

John Rawls, one of the foremost proponents of what is known as distributive justice, proposed that in Western society, one of the fundamental problems that needs a solution is that there is a vast difference when you compare the poor and otherwise disadvantaged with the wealthy and advantaged.[97] Using an approach similar to that of Kant, Rawls argues that an inherent contradiction occurs in moral behavior unless you apply the principle of justice equally to everyone.

The Christian worldview will find much in common with the basic ideas of behaving in ways that promote justice. Justice is a theme that runs consistently throughout the Bible.[98]

Virtues

When we think about morals in the context of business, it is easy to concentrate on questions like, "What should I do?" or "How should I act?" After all is said and done, morality is concerned with norms of behavior. In seeking a norm, we are really seeking a rule or a principle that will guide our behavior and answer those questions. But there is another approach that de-emphasizes the importance of rules and principles and instead focuses on the character of the person. This is the perspective of virtues.

We can think of **virtues** as character traits.[99] The basis for virtues as the guiding principle in ethics is the assumption that there are certain character traits that most people in society consider valid regardless of the situation. Character traits form the foundation for all thought and action, which makes character one of the more popular selection criteria of executives who are seeking the next generation of organizational leaders.[100]

Ancient Greek scholars taught that the highest pursuit in life was the pursuit of the good in persons and in society. One of the aspirations of society was to improve the character of its citizens by helping members of society develop desirable character traits. Aristotle emphasized the point of pursuing excellence in all of life. This excellence included a number of dimensions that we call virtues: prudence, temperance, justice, fortitude, courage, compassion, and liberality. Virtues, as conceived by ancient Greek scholars such as Aristotle, are a kind of middle ground between the two extremes of excess of the virtue and deficiency or the opposite of the virtue. Exhibit 5-11 demonstrates this middle ground using three of the seven popular ancient virtues.[101]

Later when the Christian church scholars studied Aristotle in light of Scripture they adopted four of the ancient virtues as cardinal virtues: prudence, temperance, justice, and courage. They named them cardinal virtues because they are central to living an effective Christian life. In addition to these, three theological virtues also became recognized by Christians everywhere: faith, hope, and love.[102]

Some virtues are particularly relevant and basic for business.[103] Honesty, fairness, loyalty, compassion, and justice are important for social interactions of all types including business.

Christians will find a strong attraction to the principle of virtues. We see virtues taught in Scripture.[104] Virtues provide a different perspective to bring to moral dilemmas by emphasizing the character of the person who takes action. By itself, however, the principle of virtue seems unsatisfying when we consider the complexities of moral dilemmas in the world of work.[105] While the virtues approach emphasizes the formation of habits and character traits, some claim that virtues are dependent on the social conditioning that an individual experiences. But this seems to beg the question of how to know what is right. If someone finds himself in a community that is racist, is he to accept the "virtues" of that community as being valid? The Christian would answer a resounding, "No!"

In many work environments, it is considered inappropriate to discuss religion or religious beliefs. Considering the various approaches to ethical decision making, some Christian managers may employ more than one approach to prevent becoming branded at work as being "righteous" or "holier than thou." When presented with an ethical dilemma by a

EXHIBIT 5-11
Ancient Virtues

Excess	Virtue	Deficiency
Rashness	Courage	Cowardice
Patronizing pity	Compassion	Cold-heartedness
Prodigality	Liberality (Generosity)	Meanness

When debating the value of acting ethically in the marketplace, a manager might use the following arguments:

- Speaking to a boss when faced with a request to act unethically regarding a client: "Would you want to leave work today wondering if I am acting unethically regarding our company and its interests?"
- Speaking to a coworker who suggests acting unethically toward a client: "If our actions are discovered, we would be jeopardizing the fundamental company–client relationship. Is it worth that risk? It's not worth it to me."
- "Trust is the foundation of success in the marketplace. Acting in a way that undermines trust also undermines our ability to succeed."
- "If we simply choose the expedient, easy way out of this difficult situation, we don't allow for the creative, safer alternative to surface."
- "If we do this action, what are the principles that we are *un*willing to compromise?"
- "Our relationship with our marketplace is bigger and will last longer than this one transaction. If we don't treat our customer (or supplier, or employee) with integrity this time, we hurt our long-term relationship with this individual (or organization)."
- "Is this the kind of action we would want to be reported on the front page of the *Wall Street Journal*?"
- "What if we found out that this supplier (or customer, employee) was about to treat us this way; would we want to have this done to us?"

EXHIBIT 5-12
Arguments a Manager Might Use When Facing Unethical Requests

coworker or boss, managers may need to be creative in their responses. Exhibit 5-12 offers some suggested arguments.

Ethical Thinking Is a Community Process

With so many different approaches to ethical thinking available, the question becomes, how do we determine what should be the standards of right and wrong? Some ethical dilemmas in the marketplace are so difficult to deal with that it would be nice if we could just turn these problems over to a moral specialist. However, thinking about morality is a **community process** whereby individuals in a work team, an organization, or in the larger society participate together in discussions about what is right and wrong.[106] Four reasons support ethics as a community process.

First, the moral foundations that guide our behaviors are at the same time individual-focused and community-focused.[107] Individual behaviors almost always affect other people. The process of individuals becoming a community requires the development of a set of shared values. But for values to be shared across the community, the community members must participate in discussions regarding the moral basis for these values.

Second, marketplace exchanges involve many individuals, and because market exchanges are based on minimally accepted moral standards, all individuals who interact with the marketplace will be drawn into ethical thinking, especially when their own self-interests are threatened. Third, the rule of law requires consent of society to uphold the law. Such consent cannot be given except as members of society evaluate the moral rightness and wrongness of law. Fourth, this means that responsibility to fulfill moral expectations is shared among members of society.

Managers and entrepreneurs play an important role in this community dialogue about right and wrong. Their knowledge of specific contexts of economic situations can help others to think about right and wrong. For example, managers understand the economic pressures that their organizations are under to reduce costs. Making the decision to downsize a company's workforce will usually have an unfavorable effect on the community as some workers lose their jobs. Talking with employees, their families, and the media about the downsizing is an important part of the dialogue.

Some Christian managers believe that they have a responsibility to the rest of the community to discuss the moral issues that arise in organizations. They believe that choosing not to participate in such discussions neglects an important part of what it means to be a fully functioning member of society.

The Debate Over Corporate Social Responsibility (CSR)

The first cousin of the discussion about moral issues in business is the debate on corporate social responsibility.[108] **Corporate social responsibility (CSR)** is an awareness by company decision makers that the company has a responsibility to promote the good of society. But the question is how to define "the good of society."

Some people use the phrase "social responsibility" to contrast a business's "social" responsibilities from its ordinary business-related responsibilities.[109] Ordinary responsibilities are focused on managing the revenue and expenses in order to accomplish the core purpose of the organization. When an organization is for-profit, managers may be required by the owners to spend company resources to promote socially beneficial purposes when doing so will likely promote long-term profitability. When people use the phrase "social responsibility" in contrast to ordinary responsibilities, they sometimes mean that the business has responsibilities to support socially beneficial purposes even if doing so is not for accomplishing the purpose of the firm. This is an important point in the debate.

Over the years, business practitioners and scholars have developed two points of view on CSR. In the *narrow view*, corporate social responsibility is limited to pursuing profit within the constraints of the law. In the *broad view*, in addition to pursuing profit within the law, every firm also has a responsibility to serve the interests of the broader society in which it operates—a responsibility that goes beyond making profit and beyond the minimal requirements of law.

For example, following the broad view, an executive might refrain from increasing the price of a product to contribute to the social concern of preventing inflation even though a price increase would be in the best interests of the company. Or, out of altruism an executive might authorize capital expenses to reduce pollution beyond the amount that is in the best interest of the corporation or that required by law to contribute to efforts to improve the environment.[110] Another executive might decide to spend money to improve literacy in the community in which the company operates regardless of whether the community members who participate are employees of the company.

The debate over these two views arose when some companies were discovered acting irresponsibly. Growing public awareness that manufacturing company operations can result in unintended, harmful side effects for the environment intensified the discussion. This debate continues today.

Focus on an Organization

Recycline Preserve Socially Responsible Products

Companies like Recycline Inc., maker of eco-friendly products, are cashing in on the growing public awareness about protecting the environment. As customers demand more social accountability by firms, support companies are experimenting with ways to provide companies with products that are believed to be more socially responsible. Retailers such as Whole Foods and Target are stocking their shelves with socially responsible products like those made by Recycline in its Preserve line of kitchen and bathroom products made from 100 percent recycled materials.

Some companies find that they must respond to shifting consumer preferences related to social responsibility. For example, growing social discontent about the amount of plastic used for bottled water products eventually had an effect on managers at PepsiCo Inc.'s Aquafina brand. During the economic downturn of 2009, consumers became attracted to substitutes for bottled water, sparking a price war among the highly competitive brands. Sales of bottled water dropped 6 percent. In addition to slashing their prices, bottled-water companies ordered new bottles that used less plastic in response to social pressures.[111]

Arguments in Support of a Broad View of CSR

Let's review the arguments of those who support the idea that corporations should be socially responsible in ways that exceed lawful profit making. As we review these, think about which point of view you hold.

SOCIAL CONTRACT.[112] Proponents of the broad view point to the social contract between society and businesses. Permission to engage in enterprise is a privilege that comes with expectations to operate in a way that promotes freedom of others. Unless the business goes beyond the minimum legal requirements, its legitimacy as a social institution can become threatened.

COVENANT. Humans organize their efforts for the purpose of serving humans over the long term. Business is a social enterprise built on enduring social relationships that must be nurtured. Ownership of production property comes with both privileges and responsibilities.[113] One such responsibility is to watch out for the interests of individuals and groups outside the firm. Proponents argue that this covenantal basis of the broader business relationships is unavoidable.

THE GOLDEN RULE.[114] The Golden Rule has practical and Biblical dimensions: "Do unto others as you would have them do unto you." If we desire others to treat us in a manner that is right, just, and fair, then we should be concerned with how we treat them. This means that organizations will care about not only business issues but also the larger social issues.

LAW IS LIMITED.[115] It would be nice if the law was complete. It is not. Laws are insufficient as a guide because they do not cover all aspects or gray areas of a problem. Regulations are not complete either. A company must base its actions on principles that are broader than the bare minimum of the law.

CORPORATE POWER MUST BE BALANCED WITH RESPONSIBILITY.[116] Businesses have been given tremendous social power. With power comes responsibility to act in ways that use the power in a just manner. This is a principle that has come down to us from the Judeo-Christian tradition: "To whom much is given, of him will much be required."[117] Businesses have a role as one of the trustees of society's resources. Businesses operate in a two-way, open system with their environments. Businesses develop areas of competence that should be used for social involvement in places where the social needs can be met by these competencies. For example, if a business operates in an area where high rates of illiteracy exist, it should take actions to help eliminate this problem.

THE LONG RUN.[118] Here proponents sometimes follow the principle of "enlightened self-interest." Companies must meet their short-term obligations, but at the same time, they have a responsibility to sustain a viable future for the environment. Business is in an interdependent relationship with society. Successful businesses need a successful society. If a business makes decisions at the expense of society, its success will only be temporary. Ultimately such businesses will become weakened and less capable of serving society. Beyond reciprocity is the concern for the quality of our own lives and those of succeeding generations. A basic question is: Do we have an obligation to leave the world a little better than when we found it, or may we simply take what we want now and let other people, including the next generation, worry about making up for any shortfalls?

PREVENTS THE NEED FOR REGULATION.[119] When businesses take a proactive stance, society will not pressure lawmakers to set the minimum legal standard. It is only when companies act against the interests of society that lawmakers must step in and restrain business.

REPUTATION.[120] On the positive side, businesses should view altruistic behaviors as an investment in the future goodwill of society. Doing the right thing matters these days. Incorporating social responsibility concerns into business decision making has good public relations value. Damage to a company's reputation cannot be directly measured, but the deterioration of relationships; declining employee productivity, creativity, and loyalty; ineffective information flow through the organization; absenteeism; and difficulty recruiting and retaining the most competent employees are all costs of being uninterested in social responsibility at work. When businesses act in socially responsible ways, they build community cooperation and support. Socially responsible action provides the basis for the community to trust the business. Without trust, commitment cannot follow.

CORRECTS PROBLEMS.[121] Businesses that act responsibly will correct their mistakes and not leave them to another generation or to society as a whole (negative economic "externalities") to clean up.

REDUCES THE LONG-TERM COST OF DOING BUSINESS.[122] Acting legally and socially responsibly can save a company billions of dollars each year in lawsuits, settlements, and theft. This affects the income statement, balance sheet, and statement of cash flows. Managers can improve their future financial statements (estimated liability) by what they do today.

Arguments in Support of a Narrow View of CSR

Recall that the narrow view of CSR holds that the social obligation of business is the lawful pursuit of profit. Proponents of the narrow view of corporate social responsibility base their arguments on two pillars of a free-market economy: property rights and economic theory. Let's consider their point of view.

PRIMARY RESPONSIBILITY.[123] Managers have direct, legal responsibilities to the owners of the corporation. The manager has been hired as an *agent* of the owner. An **agent** is responsible for conducting business in accordance with the owner's desires, which generally means building economic performance in lawful ways and by conforming to the principles embodied in ethical custom. Correspondingly, management's first responsibility to society is to shareholders by working hard to generate economic performance. A business that does not show a profit that is at least equal to its cost of capital is socially irresponsible because this is a waste of society's resources.

PROPERTY RIGHTS. If the market system is expected to grow the wealth of society, owners of production property must be protected from illegitimate claims against that which they own. It is the manager's job to protect the production property of the owner. Taking actions that support social causes outside the business lowers economic efficiency and profits that rightfully belong to owners.

IMPOSES UNEQUAL COSTS AMONG COMPETITORS.[124] The more of the company's money that managers spend on social causes that are outside the company, the higher the production costs become compared with competitors. This gives competitors an unfair advantage.

IMPOSES HIDDEN COSTS PASSED ON TO STAKEHOLDERS.[125] Supporting social causes by spending the firm's capital is a form of discretionary altruism that becomes an illegitimate claim on (theft of) the property that belongs to owners. If such an action results in lowering wages, then the manager is stealing from employees. If the action results in higher prices, then the manager is stealing from customers.

PLACES RESPONSIBILITY ON BUSINESS RATHER THAN ON INDIVIDUALS.[126] A business is not a person. Only humans have moral responsibilities with respect to larger social issues in society.

MARKET MECHANISMS ARE THE ROUTE TO SOCIAL WELFARE.[127] **Market mechanisms** are the actions that buyers and sellers take to serve each other. For example, by generating economic growth for the shareholders, business improves the social welfare of society as a whole. More wealth means more investment and better-paying jobs for workers who can then donate personal income to social causes if they so choose. Company managers are individuals who can decide how to spend their personal earnings. As such, they are acting as an owner of the cash they earned and not an agent. But if the manager makes a decision to spend company money to alleviate a social problem outside the firm, this is tantamount to taxation without representation. Taxation is a government function that should not be taken over by business no matter how laudable the social goals might be.

THE MARKET PUNISHES CORPORATE WRONGDOERS.[128] When a company crosses the line to social irresponsibility, consumers will go away, people will lobby lawmakers, and aggrieved plaintiffs will bring lawsuits to force the firm to make changes. All of this will affect the organization's balance sheet and income statement. The company will incur liabilities. Legal expenses and potentially punitive fines will increase operating expenses, which in turn will create the incentive to avoid wrongdoing.

INAPPROPRIATE EXECUTIVE DILEMMA.[129] The executive role is inappropriate to handle the difficult dilemmas posed by social problems outside the company. On what basis would the corporate executive decide which social cause is better than another?

ACCOUNTABILITY.[130] Encouraging social responsibility actions in areas of society for which these individuals could not be held accountable would be socially irresponsible. Even more of a problem is that requiring managers to serve multiple goals, which can conflict, aggravates one of the central problems of organizations: managers not taking responsibility for the goods of the owners as seriously as they should. This results in reduced accountability.

BUSINESS POWER.[131] Businesses already have enough power in society. If we allow businesses to also get involved with repairing social problems outside the company, the political power of businesses will only increase.

The Christian Mind on Corporate Social Responsibility

All organizations have social responsibilities; this is not a uniquely Christian idea. But from a Christian perspective these commitments are rooted in the "covenant" that exists between a business and the larger community. In a covenant view, businesses are stewards of the world's resources. The goods and services they offer are simply part of the larger creation given by God to be shared and nurtured by all human beings. A business covenant emphasizes the interests of both parties, but it does not denounce profit or commercial success.

Profit is a legitimate "interest" of any business organization. Understood in the context of covenant principles, it is the result of good stewardship and social responsibility. An organization's wise use of the world's resources builds long-lasting relationships with customers and preserves a place for future companies and communities.

Jeanne M. McNett, PhD
Professor of Management
Assumption College

Kathleen M. Fisher, PhD
Associate Professor of Theology
Assumption College

The growing interest in the broad view of corporate social responsibility has encouraged entrepreneurs to start businesses or change the ways they go about doing business. For example, the traditional high-fat American diet is under increased scrutiny as concerned parents and citizens evaluate the healthfulness of food served in public schools. Kirsten Tobey and Kristin Groos Richmond, co-founders of Revolution Foods, hope to support growing social awareness about healthful diets by preparing and selling low-fat meals to schools.[132]

Another development that has strengthened worldwide interest in social responsibility is the **United Nations Global Compact**. The Compact is a commitment by global businesses to support 10 widely accepted principles related to human rights, labor standards, care for the environment, and prevention of corruption. The 10 principles are as follows:[133]

1. Support the protection of human rights.
2. Avoid being complicit in human rights abuses by third parties.
3. Uphold the freedom of association and the right to form labor unions.
4. Eliminate all forms of forced labor or slavery.
5. Abolish child labor.
6. Eliminate employment discrimination.
7. Take precautions when creating an impact on the natural environment.
8. Promote greater natural environmental responsibility.
9. Encourage the development and use of environmentally friendly technology.
10. Work against corruption in all its forms including bribery and extortion.

Source: Carmen Martinez Banús/IStockphoto.com.

The traditional high-fat American diet is under increased scrutiny as concerned parents and citizens evaluate the healthfulness of food served in public schools.

The United Nations desires to advance these 10 principles so that they become universally accepted worldwide. Businesses who are interested in supporting the Compact must do so on a voluntary basis.

Paradoxes

It has been said that the drivers of our deepest dilemmas "lie in the tensions between our most cherished values."[134] Nowhere is this better illustrated than when we consider some of the tensions managers face when thinking about what is right and wrong.

ROOTED IN A SPECIFIC CONTEXT—TRANSCENDENT FROM CONTEXT.[135] All behavior occurs in particular historical, social circumstances that cannot be ignored when thinking about what is right and wrong. But ethical thinking cannot be limited to specific situations. Ethical thinking also requires considering the timeless, universal standards of behavior that apply across many different contexts. In terms of the ethical process, this may be the most fundamental paradoxical tension that managers face.

INDIVIDUAL FREEDOM—GROUP RESPONSIBILITY.[136] A never-ending fundamental tension in all of life is between pursuing the satisfaction of individual needs and pursuing the satisfaction of needs common in the community. The economic dimension of life is not above this tension point. A degree of individual self-interest is allowed and even expected by a community. But when self-interested behaviors of individuals exceed community norms, the community responds by limiting self-interested behavior. Likewise, if community self-interest becomes too dominant, individuals respond by attempting to limit community behaviors through the enactment of laws and by changing the government.[137]

Consider the situation where one of your dependable employees requests days off to attend a special event important to the family such as the graduation from basic training in the U.S. Marines. Allowing the worker this opportunity will place a burden on you and the other workers to make adjustments while he is away. You are not authorized to hire a temporary worker to replace the employee. On the one hand you want to show concern for the employee's family situation, allowing the whole family to get the full benefit of attendance at the event. On the other hand, you need to watch out for the needs of the team who depend on this worker to achieve the production goals. At the heart of this tension is that individuals simultaneously have individual freedoms and group responsibilities. Freedom constrains responsibility and responsibility constrains freedom.

SOCIAL UNIFORMITY WITHOUT MANIPULATION.[138] For an organization to develop a strong culture, its leaders must encourage conformity to the shared values. At the same time, individuals are opposed to manipulation of individuals for organizational purposes. Most organizations value new employees who bring new ways of being–thinking–action that, if incorporated, could strengthen the organization. This dilemma is especially intense for the Christian manager who values human freedom—derived from the image of God at creation—but also values the stewardship responsibility of watching out for the interests of the organization and its goals.

Chapter Summary

1. For the Christian moral and social responsibility is grounded in belief in God. Human actions occur within a wider frame of reference than human social settings and the natural environment of the earth. All action takes place in the presence of God.
2. Some see the biblical covenants as a template that humans should model for all social relationships where a contract is unable to represent the entire relationship. Covenant is a voluntary commitment. A covenant relationship is deeper than one that is based on obligations to perform tasks in exchange for payment. Covenant can be distinguished from business contracts. A covenantal approach to management is a radical departure from traditional views of management that have developed in modern times.
3. Christian ethics is based on belief in God, awareness of the biblical record of God's character, and a religious faith experience related to Jesus Christ. These foundations extend to acceptance of the Bible as the rule of faith and practice for deciding what is right and wrong. This includes the Two Great Commands, the Ten Commandments, and the many principles of guidance found throughout the Bible.
4. Social responsibility applied to organizations comes from four interlocking ideas. God is the Creator/Owner of the universe. Organizations are temporary stewards who have responsibilities. Humans and their organizations must respect the physical environment of this earth. Just as God is eternal and changeless, so the biblical requirements related to social responsibility are timeless.
5. The Christian view of the environment includes the obligation to care for this earth. This view calls for several interrelated responses: humility, respect, selflessness, moderation, mindfulness, and responsibility.
6. Key distinctions should be made for key terms. Morality is the standards of right and wrong behavior. Law is the collection of specific standards that describe behaviors that are either proscribed or prescribed. Ethics is the study of morality. Both law and morality are based on fundamental accountabilities—responsibilities for our conduct in society.
7. Several influences are at present in society that promote and restrain moral problems.
8. Actions that managers take can have an impact on all stakeholders to whom the organization has a moral obligation. Primary (market) stakeholders are those who transact business and through these transactions have an economic claim to the firm. Non-market stakeholders do not have primary economic power at their disposal, but they still may have influence.
9. A variety of ethical decision making models exist in society. These include the social contract, egoism, moral relativism, utilitarianism, universalism, rights, justice, and virtues. Some experts in ethics suggest that ethical thinking is not just an individual mental activity but a community activity.
10. Corporate social responsibility (CSR) is a vigorously debated issue. Some believe that the social responsibility of business is to earn economic profits using lawful means and abiding by the basic moral standards of society. Others believe that businesses have obligations that go beyond profit making.

Key Terms

Accountabilities 148
Agent 161
Altruism 145
Business contract 153
Christian ethics 144
Code of silence 149
Community process 158
Corporate social responsibility (CSR) 159
Covenant 142
Egoism 154
Environment 145
Ethics 147
Golden Rule 144
Groupthink 150
Interdependence 143
Justice 156
Law 147
Market mechanisms 161
Morality 147
Moral relativism 154
Prescribed behavior 147
Proscribed behavior 147
Reframing 149
Rights 156
Self-interest 144
Social contract 153
Stakeholders 152
United Nations Global Compact 162
Universalism 155
Usury 145
Utility 154
Utilitarianism 155
Virtues 157

Discussion Questions

1. How do you define self-interest? Is self-interest, by nature, selfish?
2. Would society work well if everyone always acted with benevolent intentions?
3. What forms the basis of behavior for many people in society: law or morality? Why?
4. Who has the responsibility in society to do the difficult work of ethical thinking regarding what happens in business? Pastors? Professors? Politicians and lawmakers? Journalists? Stockholders? Company executives? Frontline workers? Managers?
5. What would happen in society if no one spent the time and mental and emotional energy to do the difficult work of ethics?
6. Select any two of the normative approaches to deciding what is right and wrong and compare how a person holding to each of these would describe a situation in which someone lied.
7. Describe a situation in which a particular behavior might be legal but not moral.
8. Would all the moral dilemmas and ethical problems of organizations be resolved if Christians ran the economy?
9. For the Christian, how can egoism be bad but maximizing utility good?
10. When business leaders lobby lawmakers and regulators in an attempt to undermine or skirt around laws and public policies that are in the public interest, are they acting in a socially irresponsible way?
11. Should managers give primacy to the primary stakeholders when making business decisions? Why?
12. What does it mean when a manager is said to be keeping in balance the needs of the various stakeholder groups?
13. Evaluate the arguments for and against corporate social responsibility. Which arguments seem to be the most significant? Why?
14. If a manager consistently exhibited a covenantal approach to business relationships, would the manager be consistently taken advantage of in the marketplace?
15. What important management perspectives can we learn from Matthew 25:31–46 (The Sheep and the Goats)?
16. What important management perspectives can we learn from Luke 6:31 (The Golden Rule)?

STUDENT EXERCISES

1. Assuming that Riley was telling the truth about the information she obtained regarding the competitor's washing machine offer, were the sales associate and his manager right or wrong in how they responded to Riley's claim for a price-matching refund? Go online and research retail companies that use price-matching policies. Read the text of one of these policies carefully. See if you can find customer complaints regarding retail price-matching. On what basis might disgruntled customers be justified in their reactions? On what basis are store managers justified in using price-matching policies? On what basis are manufacturers justified in selling the same product under two different model numbers to different retailers? In your opinion, should retail price-matching policies be made illegal? Why?
2. Using library resources such as magazine articles and the Internet identify at least three ways that organizations are being environmentally friendly and at the same time are benefiting economically.
3. Using library resources such as magazine articles and the Internet, research the corporate culture of Enron Corporation. What elements of the organizational culture contributed to the moral lapses that eventually took the company down?
4. Design a recreational game that is fun to play but that has no rules. How would the game work? In what way does a recreational game represent the larger society in which we live and work?
5. Read the article in the *Wall Street Journal* by Vanessa O'Connell from January 7, 2009, "Test for Dwindling Retail Jobs Spawns a Culture of Cheating." Do you think organizations should use online personality tests for hiring purposes? Explain your rationale for your answer.
6. Using library resources such as magazine articles and the Internet, research TOMS Shoes. What sets the corporate social responsibility program at TOMS apart from other companies that say they are engaged in social responsibility? How can TOMS support itself economically by giving away so many shoes? Are the owners foregoing some profit?
7. Using library resources such as magazine articles and the Internet, research the corporate social responsibility activities of Timberland Shoes. How is the corporate social responsibility actions of Timberland different from what other organizations do?
8. Using the Internet read about the companies that rank high in terms of their social responsibility activities. For example, look at http://www.csrwire.com/ for examples of companies promoting their CSR activities. Or look at http://inspiredeconomist.com/2010/10/12/the-2010-corporate-social-responsibility-index-who-made-the-top-10/. Write a two-page paper describing the criteria that a person should use to discern the validity of a particular company's CSR activities.

IN-CLASS EXERCISES

Issue Debates/Discussions

Divide the class into small groups of five to six people each. Hand out a sheet of paper containing the following debate statements. Assign half of the groups to develop a rationale why the first statement is valid and the other half to develop a rationale for why the second statement is valid. Members of groups do not have to agree with the perspective they are asked to present. Give the groups 5 minutes to discuss. Then call for groups to give a summary of the rationale they developed. Discussion can follow.

Discussion Topic #1: A company that makes and sells EPA-certified pesticides in the United States has received an inquiry from a farm supply distributor in another country. This distributor is interested in buying pesticides that have been banned in the United States but not in the other country. The U.S. company has the capability of manufacturing and packaging the banned pesticide. Is it moral for the company to produce and sell this banned pesticide to the distributor in the other country?

A. **Yes.**
B. **No.**

Discussion Topic #2: Does it matter to a Christian that the organization she works for "goes green," meaning adopts management practices that are environmentally socially responsible? In this chapter we considered the debate over corporate social responsibility. A related debate surrounds environmental social responsibility. In the August 2009 issue of the *Academy of Management Perspectives*, two articles present opposing viewpoints that are worth debating.

A. **Green management matters only if it adds green (cash) to the bottom line.**[139] Firms should adopt environmentally friendly management practices only if such activities complement the organization's business-level strategies and, ultimately, enhance profitability or shareholder wealth.
B. **Green management matters regardless of how much profit is earned.**[140] A growing number of citizens expect firms and their managers to consider the effect that their decisions will have on the larger environment regardless of whether profit is earned. Many of the resources on which businesses depend are shared in common (air, water, land, energy). Companies should recycle and reuse to the extent that they can rather than contributing to the depletion of the earth's resources. From a moral perspective, all managers have an obligation to pursue environmentally friendly actions. This obligation is unconditional.

Discussion Topic #3: If the Christian manager views management relationships as covenantal, is it ever appropriate to view bargaining and negotiation as a zero-sum situation in which for one party to get what they want, the other party must give up something—known as distributive bargaining?[141]

A. **Yes.** We cannot forget the economic limitations that organizations and their members face. Compared with what we want to have in organizations, resources are limited in their supply. It might sound "right" to say that in negotiations the covenant-minded manager will attempt to enlarge the pie and integrate the needs of both parties, but not all organizational resources can be enlarged to meet the needs of everyone. If the Christian manager believes that integrative bargaining is the only way to foster covenantal relationships, then such a manager is doomed to fail in achieving that ideal. Just because there are zero-sum situations in life doesn't mean that covenantal management is never possible. A single Christian manager does not have control over all the conditions necessary for integrative bargaining. In addition, the amount of time needed to engage in integrative bargaining will often exceed the practical amount of time in dynamic business situations when things need to get done and the organization needs to move forward. Managers who are firm in their desire to always be integrative in their approach will be seen as inflexible and blocking organizational progress.
B. **No.** The Christian manager who wishes to treat relationships as covenants will, over time, learn to be creative and innovative in finding ways that both parties can get their needs met. Integrative bargaining promotes collective ownership rather than winners and losers. Integrative bargaining promotes critical thinking on the issues. Both parties learn to be open to new alternatives. This is the way to foster long-term productive relationships. In distributive bargaining, one party is always the loser. In integrative bargaining, both parties win. In distributive bargaining, a solution emerges from a test of strength and bargaining power. In integrative bargaining, solutions emerge from a test of the assumptions, issues, and alternatives. The Christian manager who fosters covenantal relationships will also learn to overcome conditions that are barriers to integrative bargaining. They will foster trust so that both parties are open with each other with information and honest about their concerns. They will model sensitivity to the other party's needs, and over time this will be reciprocated in kind. Covenantal relationships foster trust and flexibility.
C. **Sometimes but not as a rule.** Christian managers will aspire to use integrative bargaining to meet the needs of both parties. This is the ideal. When resources are fixed and there is no way out of a zero-sum situation, the Christian manager will be open about this and may choose to engage in distributive bargaining. However, distributive bargaining should be the last resort.

Discussion Topic #4: A new federal law that took effect in February 2009 makes it illegal for anyone to sell children's toys, books, clothing, and jewelry if the products contain any lead or certain other chemicals.[142] A provision in the law requires all products on store shelves to be immediately recalled by manufacturers. Some businesses are concerned that while large companies will have the resources needed to recall, discard, and replace products that are out of compliance, the law will hurt small companies to take back their uncertified products. Is this law fair to small businesses?

A. **Yes.**
B. **No.**

What moral principles are at the basis of this law? Are these moral principles in conflict with other moral principles? Explain

Discussion Topic #5: Does the Bible support making a distinction between self-interest and selfishness? Provide biblical evidence in support of your position.

A. **Yes.**
B. **No.**

Endnotes

1. Werhane, P. H. (2002) Moral imagination and systems thinking. *Journal of Business Ethics.* 38(1/2), 33–42.
2. Peter 1:5.
3. Adapted from the process described in Hosmer, L. T. (2008). *The ethics of management.* (6th ed.). New York: McGraw-Hill/Irwin. pp. 3–15.
4. This example drawn from Chewning, R. C., Eby, J. W., & Roels, S. J. (1990). *Business through the eyes of faith.* San Francisco, CA: HarperSanFrancisco. pp. 26–28.
5. Adapted from Hosmer, L. T. (2008). *The ethics of management.* (6th ed.). New York: McGraw-Hill Irwin. pp. 127–128.
6. Verschoor, C. C. (2001). Ethical behavior brings tangible benefits to organizations. *Strategic Finance.* 82(11), 20–21.
7. Lozano, J. M. (1996). Ethics and management: A controversial issue. *Journal of Business Ethics.* 15(2), 227–236.
8. Paine, L. S. (1994). Managing for organizational integrity. *Harvard Business Review.* March/April, 106–117.
9. Anonymous. (2008). Supreme court overturns Exxon Valdez $2.5 billion punitive damages award. *Oil & Gas Journal.* 106(25), 39–40.
10. Melé, D. (2006). Religious foundations of business ethics. In Epstein, M. J., & Hanson, K. O. (Eds.). *The accountable corporation: Business ethics.* (Vol. 2). Westport, CT: Praeger. pp. 11–43; De George, R. T. (2006). *Business ethics.* (6th ed.). Upper Saddle River, NJ: Pearson Prentice Hall. pp. 78–80.
11. Schwartz, M. S. (2006). God as a managerial stakeholder? *Journal of Business Ethics.* 66, 291–306.
12. Niebuhr, R. (1954). The idea of covenant and American democracy. *Church History.* 27(4), 126–135; Walton, C. C. (1988). *The moral manager.* Cambridge, MA: Ballinger Publishing Company. pp. 209–211; Bromley, D. G., & Busching, B. C. (1988). Understanding the structure of contractual and covenantal social relations: Implications for the sociology of religion. *Sociological Analysis.* 49(Special Issue), 15–32; Nash, L. (1990). *Good intentions aside: A manager's guide to resolving ethical problems.* Cambridge, MA: Harvard Business School Press; Herman, S. W. (1992). The potential for building covenants in business corporations. *Annual of the Society of Christian Ethics.* 201–222; Childs Jr., J. M. (1995). *Ethics in business: Faith at work.* Minneapolis, MN: Fortress Press. pp. 66–70; Herman, S. W. (1997). *Durable goods: A covenantal ethic for management and employees.* Notre Dame, IN: University of Notre Dame Press; McCann, D. P. (1997). On moral business: A theological perspective. *Review of Business.* 19(1), 9–14; Spears, L. C. (1997). *Insights on leadership: Service, stewardship, spirit and servant-leadership.* New York: John Wiley. pp. 77–86; Pava, M. L. (2001). The many paths to covenantal leadership: Traditional resources for contemporary business. *Journal of Business Ethics.* 29(1/2), 85–93; Pava, M. (2003). *Leading with meaning: Using covenantal leadership to build a better organization.* New York: Palgrave Macmillan; Depree, M. (2004). *Leadership is an art.* New York: Doubleday Business. pp. 23–44; Moisan, L. J. (2007). *Leadership is a covenant.* Bloomington, IN: AuthorHouse; Hafemann, S. J. (2007). The covenant relationship. In Hafemann, S. J., & House, P. R. (Eds.). *Central themes in biblical theology: Mapping unity in diversity.* Grand Rapids, MI: Baker Academic. pp. 20–65; LaRondelle, H. K. (2005). *Our Creator Redeemer: An introduction to biblical covenant theology.* Berrien Springs, MI: Andrews University Press; Maston, T. B. (1965). Biblical bases for social concern. *Southwestern Journal of Theology.* 7(2), 5–16; Snape, E., & Redman, T. (2004). Exchange or covenant? The nature of the member-union relationship. *Industrial Relations.* 43(4), 855–873; Caldwell, C., & Karri, R. (2005). Organizational governance and ethical systems: A covenantal approach to building trust. *Journal of Business Ethics.* 58(3), 249–259; Barnett, T., & Schubert, E. (2002). Perceptions of the ethical work climate and covenantal relationships. *Journal of Business Ethics.* 36(3), 279–290; Graham, J. W., & Organ, D. W. (1993). Commitment and the covenantal organization. *Journal of Managerial Issues* 5, 483–502; Caldwell, C. (2005). Leading with meaning: Using covenantal leadership to build a better organization. *Business Ethics Quarterly.* 15(3), 499–505. See also 2 Corinthians 5:17–20.
13. Herman, S. W. (1997). *Durable goods: A covenantal ethic for management and employees.* Notre Dame, IN: University of Notre Dame Press.
14. Adapted from: Adkins, R. (2008). Client relationships: Covenant or contract. *Journal of Financial Planning.* 21(3), 28–29; Smith, M. H. (1978). The church and covenant theology. *Journal of the Evangelical Theological Society.* 21(1), 47–65; Niebuhr, R. (1954). The idea of covenant and American democracy. *Church History.* 27(4), 126–135.
15. Tiemstra, J. P., Graham, W. F., Monsma, G. N., Sinke, C. J., Storkey, A., & Ebels, D. M. (1990). *Reforming economics: Calvinist studies on methods and institutions.* Lewiston, NY: The Edwin Mellen Press. p. 191.

16. Dumbrell, W. J. (1984). *Covenant and creation: A theology of the Old Testament covenants.* Grand Rapids, MI: Baker Book House; Pink, A. W. (1973). *The divine covenants.* Grand Rapids, MI: Baker Book House; Robertson, O. P. (1980). *The Christ of the covenants.* Grand Rapids, MI: Baker Book House; Allen, J. L. (1984). *Love and conflict: A covenantal model of Christian ethics.* Nashville, TN: Abingdon Press; Pava, M. L. (2001). The many paths to covenantal leadership: Traditional resources for contemporary business. *Journal of Business Ethics.* 29(1/2), 85–93; McCann, D. P. (1997). On moral business: A theological perspective. *Review of Business.* 19(1), 9–14; Herman, S. W. (1997). *Durable goods: A covenantal ethic for management and employees.* Notre Dame, IN: University of Notre Dame Press; Weinfeld, M. (1977). Berith. In Botterweck, G. J., & Ringren, H. (Eds.). *Theological dictionary of the Old Testament.* Volume 2. (Revised edition). Grand Rapids, MI: William B. Eerdmans Publishing Company. pp. 253–279; Archer Jr., G. L. (1960). Covenant. In Harrison, E. F., Bromiley, G. W., & Henry, C. F. H. (Eds.) *Baker's dictionary of theology.* Grand Rapids, MI: Baker Book House. pp. 142–144; Stendebach, F. J. (2006). Shalom. In Botterweck, G. J., Ringren, H., & Fabry, H. J. (Eds.). *Theological dictionary of the Old Testament.* Volume 15. Grand Rapids, MI: William B. Eerdmans Publishing Company. pp. 13–49.
17. Matthew 5–7.
18. Robertson, O. P. (1980). *The Christ of the covenants.* Grand Rapids, MI: Baker Book House. See also Genesis 15.
19. Robertson, O. P. (1980). *The Christ of the covenants.* Grand Rapids, MI: Baker Book House. p. 12.
20. Hollinger, D. P. (2002). *Choosing the good: Christian ethics in a complex world.* Grand Rapids, MI: Baker Academic. p. 64.
21. Leviticus 19:18; Luke 10:27; Romans 13:9–10; Galatians 5:13–14; Ephesians 3:14–19.
22. Romans 13:8–11.
23. Childs Jr., J. M. (1995). *Ethics in business: Faith at work.* Minneapolis, MN: Fortress Press. pp. 58–66.
24. 1 John 4:19.
25. Matthew 5:17.
26. Hosmer, L. T. (2008). *The ethics of management.* (6th ed.). Boston, MA: McGraw-Hill Irwin. pp. 103–104.
27. Matthew 5–7; John 14:6, 15:9, 15:12; Luke 11:27.
28. Exodus 20, 21:33, 22:5, 22:14, 22:25, 23:4, 23:10; Leviticus 19:9–11, 25:23, 25:39–40; Deuteronomy 15:1–2, 15:7–11, 23:24, 24:6, 24:14–15, 24:19, 26:12; Malachi 3:5; Matthew 5:17–48; Romans 12:17; Hebrews 13:18.
29. An alternative definition of "self-interest" is the attempt to pursue things that are of interest to yourself. A person can be interested in selfish pursuits or altruistic endeavors. Thus, self-interest can be distinguished from selfishness. See: Heyne, P. T. (1998). Moral misunderstanding and the justification of markets. *The Region.* 12(4), 31–32; Richards, R. R. (2002). *God and business: Christianity's case for capitalism.* Fairfax, VA: Xulon Press. pp. 263–266; Beed, C. & Beed, C. (1999). A Christian perspective on neoclassical rational choice theory. *International Journal of Social Economics.* 35(4), 501–520; Putterman, L. (1990). *Division of labor and welfare: An introduction to economic systems.* New York: Oxford University Press. pp. 217–220; Novak, M. (1982). *The spirit of democratic capitalism.* New York: Simon & Schuster. pp. 92–95.
30. Matthew 25:14–30; Luke 12; Matthew 6:24.
31. Matthew 7:12. See also John 13:34, 15:12–17; Romans 12:10; 1 Corinthians 12:26–27, 13:4–7; Galatians 5:13–14, 6:2; 1 John 3:23; 2 John 1:5.
32. Luke 16:10; 1 Corinthians 13; Galatians 5:22; Ephesians 4:2, 5:9; Philippians 4:4–9; Colossians 3:10–17; 2 Timothy 3:10.
33. Mark 7:21–23; John 3:19; Romans 3: 10–12; Ephesians 2:3.
34. Romans 12:2.
35. Melé, D. (2006). Religious foundations of business ethics. In Epstein, M. J., & Hanson, K. O. (Eds.). *The accountable corporation: Business ethics.* (Vol. 2). Westport, CT: Praeger. p. 21; Higginson, R. (1993). *Called to account—Adding value in God's world: Integrating Christianity and business effectively.* Guildford, Surrey: Eagle. pp. 107–109; Kaiser, E. G. (1966). *Theology of work.* Westminster, MD: The Newman Press. pp. 173–175; Preston, R. H. (1993). *Religion and the ambiguities of capitalism.* Cleveland, OH: The Pilgrim Press. pp. 35–47, 135–152.
36. Exodus 20:15, 22:1–15; Leviticus 19:11–13; Deuteronomy 25:13–16; Proverbs 11:1; Ephesians 4:28; 1 Thessalonians 4:6.
37. Hui, L. T. (2008). Combining faith and CSR: A paradigm of corporate sustainability. *International Journal of Social Economics.* 35(6), 449–465. See also the discussion in Brammer, S., Williams, G., & Zinkin, J. (2007). Religion and attitudes to corporate social responsibility in a large cross-country sample. *Journal of Business Ethics.* 71(3), 229–243.
38. Genesis 1:1–2:3; Deuteronomy 6:5, 10:1; Psalm 22:23; Isaiah 42:12; Ezekiel 18:4; Luke 12:42–48; John 17:4; Romans 12:4–8; 1 Corinthians 10:31; Ephesians 4:28.
39. Leviticus 19:18; Matthew 22:36–40; Mark 9:35, 10:43; John 13:1–14:7; Romans 13:8–10; Philippians 2:6–8.
40. Matthew 25:14–23; 2 Peter 1:11.
41. Genesis 21:33; Psalm 90; Isaiah 57:15; John 1:1–14, 8:54–59; Colossians 1:13–19.
42. Hoffman, A. J., & Sandelands, L. E. (2005). Getting right with nature. *Organization & Environment.* 18(2), 141–161; Gottfried, R. R. (1995). Economics, ecology, and the roots of western faith. Lanham, MD: Roman & Littlefield Publishers, Inc.; Van Dyke, F., Mahan, D. C., Sheldon J. K., & Brand, R. H. (1996). *Redeeming creation: The biblical basis for environmental stewardship.* Downers Grove, IL: InterVarsity Press; Land, R. D., & Moore, L. A. (Eds.). (1992). *The earth is the Lord's: Christians and the environment.* Nashville, TN: Broadman Press; Acton Institute. (2007). *Environmental stewardship in the Judeo-Christian tradition.* Grand Rapids, MI: Acton Institute; Higginson, R. (1993). *Called to account—Adding value in God's world: Integrating Christianity and business effectively.* Guildford, Surrey: Eagle. pp. 69–73; Volf, M. (1991). *Work in the spirit: Toward a theology of work.* Eugene, OR: Wipf and Stock Publishers. pp. 141–148.
43. Psalm 102:25–27, 102:104; Colossians 1:17; Hebrews 1:3, 1:10–12.

44. Psalm 19:1–6; Romans 1:18–20.
45. Romans 8:19–22.
46. Galatians 5:13; 1 Peter 2:16.
47. Hoffman, A. J., & Sandelands, L. E. (2005). Getting right with nature. *Organization & Environment.* 18(2), 141–161.
48. Beauchamp, T. L., & Bowie, N. E. (Ed.). (2004). *Ethical theory and business.* (7th ed.). Upper Saddle River, NJ: Pearson Prentice Hall. pp. 1–10.
49. Blackstone, W. (1818). *Commentaries on the laws of England.* (Vols. 1–4). Boston, MA: T. B. Wait & Sons. p. 34.
50. Paine, L. S. (1994). Managing for organizational integrity. *Harvard Business Review.* March/April, 106–117; Beauchamp. T. L., & Bowie, N. E. (2004). *Ethical theory and business.* (7th ed.). Upper Saddle River, NJ: Pearson Prentice Hall. pp. 4–5; Milne, A. J. M. (1968). *Freedom and rights.* New York: Humanities Press, Inc. pp. 95–96, 235.
51. Beauchamp. T. L., & Bowie, N. E. (2004). *Ethical theory and business.* (7th ed.). Upper Saddle River, NJ: Pearson Prentice Hall. pp. 4–5.
52. Kar, R. B. (2006). The deep structure of law and morality. *Texas Law Review.* 84(4): 877–942.
53. Barnard, C. I. (1938). *The functions of the executive.* Cambridge, MA: Harvard University Press. p. 267; Windsor, D. (2006). Corporate social responsibility: Cases for and against. In Epstein, M. J., & Hanson, K. O. (Eds.). *The accountable corporation: Corporate social responsibility.* (Vol. 3). Westport, CT: Praeger. p. 31.
54. Toulouse, J. M. (2002). Values and ethics: One of the six most difficult questions of management. In Pauchant, T. C. (Ed.). *Ethics and spirituality at work: Hopes and pitfalls of the search for meaning in organizations.* Westport, CT: Quorum Books.
55. Windsor, D. (2006). Corporate social responsibility: Cases for and against. In Epstein, M. J., & Hanson, K. O. (Eds.). *The accountable corporation: Corporate social responsibility.* (Vol. 3). Westport, CT: Praeger. p. 32; Hasnas, J. (1998). The normative theories of business ethics: A guide for the perplexed. *Business Ethics Quarterly.* 8(1), 19–42.
56. Lennick, D., & Kiel, F. (2005). *Moral intelligence: Enhancing business performance and leadership* success. Upper Saddle River, NJ: Pearson Education, Inc. pp. 16–17.
57. Paine, L. S. (1994). Managing for organizational integrity. *Harvard Business Review.* March/April: 106–117; Ferrell, O. C., & Fraedrich, J. (1996). Understanding pressures that cause unethical behavior in business. In Rae, S. B., & Wong, K. L. (Eds.). *Beyond integrity: A Judeo-Christian approach to business ethics.* Grand Rapids, MI: Zondervan Publishing House. pp. 597–601; Treviño, L. K., & Brown, M. E. (2004). Managing to be ethical: debunking five business ethics myths. *Academy of Management Executive.* 18(2), 69–81.
58. Opitz, E. A. (1970). *Religion and capitalism: Allies, not enemies.* New Rochelle, NY: Arlington House.
59. Milne, A. J. M. (1968). *Freedom and rights.* New York: Humanities Press, Inc. pp. 265, 266.
60. Jackall, R. (1988). *Moral mazes: The world of corporate managers.* New York: Oxford University Press. pp. 17–74; Pfeffer, J. (1992). Understanding power in organizations. *California Management Review.* 34(2), 29–50.
61. Ferrell, O. C., & Fraedrich, J. (1996). Understanding pressures that cause unethical behavior in business. In Rae, S. B., & Wong, K. L. (Eds.). *Beyond integrity: A Judeo-Christian approach to business ethics.* Grand Rapids, MI: Zondervan Publishing House. pp. 597–601.
62. James Jr., H. S. (2000). Reinforcing ethical decision making through organizational structure. *Journal of Business Ethics.* 28(1), 43–58; Sauser Jr., W. I. (2005). Ethics in business: Answering the call. *Journal of Business Ethics.* 58, 345–357; Paine, L. S. (1994). Managing for organizational integrity. *Harvard Business Review.* March/April, 106–117; Ferrell, O. C., & Fraedrich, J. (1996). Understanding pressures that cause unethical behavior in business. In Rae, S. B., & Wong, K. L. (Eds.). *Beyond integrity: A Judeo-Christian approach to business ethics.* Grand Rapids, MI: Zondervan Publishing House. pp. 597–601.
63. Sauser Jr., W. I. (2005). Ethics in business: Answering the call. *Journal of Business Ethics.* 58, 345–357; Jackall, R. (1988). *Moral mazes: The world of corporate managers.* New York: Oxford University Press.
64. Sims, R. R. (1992). Linking groupthink to unethical behavior in organizations. *Journal of Business Ethics.* 11(9), 651–662.
65. Janis, I. L. (1972). *Victims of groupthink.* Boston, MA: Houghton-Mifflin. Janis, I. L. (1982). *Groupthink.* Boston, MA: Houghton-Mifflin.
66. Hosmer, L. T. (2008). *The ethics of management.* (6th ed.). New York: McGraw-Hill Irwin.
67. Schein, E. H. (2004). Learning when and how to lie: A neglected aspect of organizational and occupational socialization. *Human Relations.* 57(3), 260–273.
68. Hayek, F. A. (1944). *The road to serfdom.* Chicago, IL: The University of Chicago Press. pp. 80–96.
69. Sirico, F. R. (1996). The entrepreneurial vocation. In Rae, S. B., & Wong, K. L. (Eds.). *Beyond integrity: A Judeo-Christian approach to business ethics.* Grand Rapids, MI: Zondervan Publishing House. pp. 209–215; Schein, E. H. (2004). Learning when and how to lie: A neglected aspect of organizational and occupational socialization. *Human Relations.* 57(3), 260–273; de Soto, H. (2000). *The mystery of capital: Why capitalism triumphs in the West and fails everywhere else.* New York: Basic Books.
70. Exodus 20:15; Leviticus 19:11; Ephesians 4:28.
71. Grudem, W. (2003). *Business for the glory of God.* Wheaton, IL: Crossway Books. pp. 19–24.
72. Novak, M. (1991). *The spirit of democratic capitalism.* Lanham, MD: Madison Books/University Press of America. pp. 92–95; Friedman, M., & Friedman, R. (1980). *Free to choose.* New York: Harcourt Brace Jovanovich. p. 27; Freeman, R. E., Martin, K., & Parmar, B. (2006). Ethics and capitalism. In Epstein, M. J., & Hanson, K. O. (Eds.). *The accountable corporation: Business ethics.* (Vol. 2). Westport, CT: Praeger. p. 204; Hosmer, L. T. (2008). *The ethics of management.* (6th ed.). New York: McGraw-Hill Irwin. p. 101; Milne, A. J. M. (1968). *Freedom and rights.* New York: Humanities Press, Inc. pp. 251–252.
73. Treviño, L. K. (2006). Creating the ethical organization. In Epstein, M. J., & Hanson, K. O. (Eds.). *The accountable corporation: Business ethics.* (Vol. 2). Westport, CT: Praeger. pp. 157–168.

74. Stead, W. E., Worrell, D. L., & Stead, J. G. (1990). An integrative model for understanding and managing ethical behavior in business organizations. *Journal of Business Ethics.* 9(3), 233–242; Collins, J. (2001). *Good to great.* New York: HarperBusiness; Buckingham, M., & Coffman, C. C. (1999). *First, break all the rules.* New York: Simon & Schuster. pp. 71–108, 177–214.
75. Barnard, C. I. (1938). *The functions of the executive.* Cambridge, MA: Harvard University Press. pp. 200–211, 282–284.
76. Freeman, R. E. (2004). A stakeholder theory of the modern corporation. In Beauchamp, T. L., & Bowie, N. E. (Eds.). *Ethical theory and business.* (7th ed.). Upper Saddle River, NJ: Pearson Prentice Hall. pp. 55–64; Hosmer, L. T. (2008). *The ethics of management.* (6th ed.). New York: McGraw-Hill Irwin. pp. 126–128; Schwartz, M. S. (2006). God as a managerial stakeholder? *Journal of Business Ethics.* 66, 291–306.
77. Porter, M. E., & Kramer, M. R. (2006). Strategy and society: The link between competitive advantage and corporate social responsibility. *Harvard Business Review.* 84(12), 78–92.
78. Rousseau, J. J. (1762/1913). *The social contract & discourses.* New York: E. P. Dutton & Co. p. 14.
79. Yankelovich, D. (2007). Social contract. *Leadership Excellence.* 24(7), 9–10; Donaldson, T., & Dunfee, T. W. (1994). Toward a unified conception of business ethics: Integrative social contracts theory. *The Academy of Management Review.* 19(2), 252–284; Wempe, B. (2004). On the use of the social contract model in business ethics. *Business Ethics: A European Review.* 13(4), 332–341; Chewning, R. C., Eby, J. W., & Roels, S. J. (1990). *Business through the eyes of faith.* San Francisco, CA: HarperSanFrancisco. pp. 193–205.
80. The concept of the social contract also applies to the civic level of how we structure politics and government. See Locke, J. (1690/1823). Concerning the true original extent and end of civil government. In *The works of John Locke. The two treatises of government.* Vol. V. London: W. Sharpe and Son; Hobbes, T. (1660/1996). *The leviathan.* New York: Cambridge University Press; Rousseau, J. J. (1762/1913). *The social contract & discourses.* New York: E. P. Dutton & Co.
81. Donaldson, T. (1982), *Corporations and morality.* Englewood Cliffs, NJ: Prentice Hall; Keeley, M. (1988). *A social contract theory of organizations.* Notre Dame, IN: University of Notre Dame Press; Frederick, W. C. (1995). *Values, nature, and culture in the American corporation.* New York: Oxford University Press; Blau, J. R. (1993), *Social contracts and economic markets.* New York: Plenum Press.
82. This is an ancient concept first taught by the Hebrews. See Proverbs 22:1, 27:2.
83. For the economic description of this see Pindyck, R. S., & Rubinfeld, D. L. (2001). *Microeconomics.* (5th ed.). Upper Saddle River, NJ: Prentice Hall. pp. 72–75, 139–140. An interesting debate has occurred regarding the faith perspective on utility maximization. See Leightner, J. E. (2003). Utility versus self-sacrificing love. *Christian Scholar's Review.* 32(3), 317–328; Rose, J. T. (2004). Reflection: Utility versus self-sacrificing love. *Christian Scholar's Review.* 34(1), 11–15; Leightner, J. E. (2004). Response: "Not my will . . .": Further thoughts on utility versus self-sacrificing love. *Christian Scholar's Review.* 34(1), 17–20.
84. Hosmer, L. T. (2008). *The ethics of management.* (6th ed.). New York: McGraw-Hill Irwin. pp. 100–103; Kidder, R. M. (1996). *How good people make tough choices: Resolving the dilemmas of ethical living.* New York: Fireside Books. pp. 92–99; Beauchamp, T. L., & Bowie, N. E. (Eds.). (2004). *Ethical theory and business.* (7th ed.). Upper Saddle River, NJ: Pearson Prentice Hall. pp. 8–10.
85. Hosmer, L. T. (2008). *The ethics of management.* (6th ed.). New York: McGraw-Hill Irwin. pp. 100–101. Other scholars say that the value of freedom is shared in common across the world. See Sen, A. (1999). *Development as freedom.* New York: Alfred Knopf.
86. Bentham, J. (1789). *An introduction to the principles of morals and legislation.* Oxford: Clarendon Press; Mill, J. S. (1998/1861). *Utilitarianism.* New York: Oxford University Press. pp. 1–110; Sidgwick, H. (1874). *The methods of ethics.* London: Macmillan.
87. De George, R. T. (1999). *Business ethics.* (5th ed.). Upper Saddle River, NJ: Prentice Hall. pp. 56–77; Hosmer, L. T. (2008). *The ethics of management.* (6th ed.). New York: McGraw-Hill Irwin. pp. 106–107.
88. Hosmer, L.T. (2008). *The ethics of management.* (6th ed.). New York: McGraw-Hill Irwin. pp. 106–107; Kidder, R. M. (1996). *How good people make tough choices: Resolving the dilemmas of ethical living.* New York: Fireside Books. pp. 156–157; De George, R. T. (1999). *Business ethics.* (5th ed.). Upper Saddle River, NJ: Prentice Hall. pp. 56–77; Boatright, J. R. (1988). Ethics and the role of the manager. *Journal of Business Ethics.* 7(4), 303–312.
89. Matthew 18:10–14, 22:37–39; Luke 10:25–37; John 13:334, 15:12; Romans 12:10, 13:8; 1 Thessalonians 4:9; 1 John 3:11
90. This section based on: Kant, I. (1785/2002). *Groundwork for the metaphysics of morals.* Hill Jr., T. E., & Zweig, A. (Eds.). Arnulf Zweig (Translator). New York: Oxford University Press. pp. 7–27; Wolff, R. P. (Ed.). (1969). *Foundations of the metaphysics of morals, with critical essays.* Indianapolis, IN: Bobbs-Merrill Co.; Paton, H. J. (1948). *The categorical imperative.* Chicago, IL: University of Chicago Press.
91. De George, R. T. (1999). *Business ethics.* (5th ed.). Upper Saddle River, NJ: Prentice Hall. pp. 83–89; Hosmer, L.T. (2008). *The ethics of management.* (6th ed.). New York: McGraw-Hill Irwin. pp. 108–109; Beauchamp. T. L., & Bowie, N. E. (2004). *Ethical theory and business.* (7th ed.). Upper Saddle River, NJ: Pearson Prentice Hall. pp. 22–27.
92. Matthew 7:12.
93. Hosmer, L. T. (2008). *The ethics of management.* (6th ed.). New York: McGraw-Hill Irwin. pp. 108–109; Kidder, R. M. (1996). *How good people make tough choices: Resolving the dilemmas of ethical living.* New York: Fireside Books. pp. 157–158; Opitz, E. A. (1970). *Religion and capitalism: Allies, not enemies.* New Rochelle, NY: Arlington House.
94. De George, Richard T. (2006). *Business Ethics.* Upper Saddle River, NJ: Pearson Prentice Hall. p. 94.
95. Nozick, R. (1974). *Anarchy, state and utopia.* New York: Basic Books.

96. Shaw, W. H., & Barry, V. (2001). *Moral issues in business.* Belmont, CA: Thompson Learning. pp. 72–74.
97. Rawls, J. (1971). *A theory of justice.* Cambridge, MA: Harvard University Press.
98. Genesis 18:19; Exodus 23:2; Deuteronomy 16:19; Psalm 33:5; Proverbs 2:8–9; Micah 6:8.
99. Boatright, J. R. (2003). *Ethics and the conduct of business.* (4th ed.). Upper Saddle River, NJ: Prentice Hall. p. 62.
100. Zinaich Jr., S. (2004). Returning to virtue theory: Some problems and challenges. *Global Virtue Ethics Review.* 5(4), 50–89; Blackburn, M., & McGhee, P. (2004). Talking virtue: Professionalism in business and virtue ethics. *Global Virtue Ethics Review.* 5(4), 90–122; Shanahan, K. J., & Hyman, M. R. (2003). The development of a virtue ethics scale. *Journal of Business Ethics.* 42(2), 197–208; Banks, R., & Powell, K. (Eds.). (2000). *Faith in leadership: How leaders live out their faith in their work—and why it matters.* San Francisco, CA: Jossey-Bass. pp. 3–76; Whetstone, J. T. (2001). How virtue fits within business ethics. *Journal of Business Ethics.* 33(2), 101–114; Marcic, D. (1997). *Managing with the wisdom of love: Uncovering virtue in people and organizations.* San Francisco, CA: Jossey-Bass; Godin, S. (1995). *Wisdom, Inc.: 26 business virtues that turn ordinary people into extraordinary leaders.* New York: Collins; Solomon, R. C. (2003). *A better way to think about business: How personal integrity leads to corporate success.* New York: Oxford University Press; Bennett, W. J. (1996). *The book of virtues.* New York: Simon & Schuster.
101. DesJardins, J. R., & McCall, J. J. (2005). *Contemporary issues in business ethics.* Belmont, CA: Wadsworth/Thompson Learning. pp. 24–27; Hollinger, D. P. (2002). *Choosing the good: Christian ethics in a complex world.* Grand Rapids, MI: BakerAcademic. pp. 45–60; Hosmer, L. T. (2008). *The ethics of management.* (6th ed.). New York: McGraw-Hill Irwin. pp. 104–106; De George, R. T. (2006). *Business ethics.* Upper Saddle River, NJ: Pearson Prentice Hall. pp. 106–109; Shaw, W. H., & Barry, V. (2001). *Moral issues in business.* Belmont, CA: Thomson Learning. pp. 979–999; D'Souza, D. (2000). *The virtue of prosperity: Finding values in an age of techno-affluence.* New York: Simon & Schuster. p. 169.
102. See the discussion of the three theological virtues in Alford, H. J., & Naughton, M. J. (2001). *Managing as if faith mattered: Christian social principles in the modern organization.* Notre Dame, IN: University of Notre Dame Press. pp. 70–96, 207–228; Lewis, C. S. (1952). *Mere Christianity.* San Francisco, CA: HarperSanFrancisco. p. 76.
103. Cavanagh, G. F., & Bandsuch, M. R. (2002). Virtue as a benchmark for spirituality in business. *Journal of Business Ethics.* 38(1/2), 112.
104. Deuteronomy 6:4–9; Ezekiel 11:19–21; Jeremiah 17:9; Matthew 22:37; Mark 7:21; Luke 6:43–45; Romans 12:2; Galatians 5:22–23; Ephesians 6:5–6; Philippians 4:8; 2 Corinthians 3:18.
105. Hollinger, D. P. (2002). *Choosing the good: Christian ethics in a complex world.* Grand Rapids, MI: BakerAcademic. pp. 45–60.
106. Rossouw, G. J. (1994). Business ethics: Where have all the Christians gone? *Journal of Business Ethics.* 13(7), 557–570.
107. Treviño, L. K. (2006). Creating the ethical organization. In Epstein, M. J., & Hanson, K. O. (Eds.). *The accountable corporation: Business ethics.* (Vol. 2). Westport, CT: Praeger. pp. 155–158.
108. See for example Berle Jr., A. A. (1931). Corporate powers as powers in trust. *Harvard Law Review.* 44(7), 1049–1074; Dodd Jr., E. M. (1932). For whom are corporate managers trustees? *Harvard Law Review.* 45(7), 1144–1163; Carroll, A. B. (1979). A three-dimensional conceptual model of corporate performance. *The Academy of Management Review.* 4(4), 497–505; Carroll, A. B. (1991). The pyramid of corporate social responsibility: Toward a moral management of organizational stakeholders. *Business Horizons.* 34(4), 39–48; Carroll, A. B. (1999). Corporate social responsibility: Evolution of a definitional construct. *Business and Society.* 38(3), 268–295; Porter, M. E., & Kramer, M. R. (2006). Strategy and society: The link between competitive advantage and corporate social responsibility. *Harvard Business Review.* 84(12), 78–92.
109. Hasnas, J. (1998). The normative theories of business ethics: A guide for the perplexed. *Business Ethics Quarterly.* 8(1), 19–42.
110. These examples were posed by Milton Friedman in 1970: Friedman, M. (1970). The social responsibility of business is to increase its profits. *New York Times Sunday Magazine.* September 13.
111. Bauerlein, V. (2009). Bottled-water price war heats up as demand falls. *The Wall Street Journal.* August 31. B1.
112. Porter, M. E., & Kramer, M. R. (2006). Strategy and society: The link between competitive advantage and corporate social responsibility. *Harvard Business Review.* 84(12), 78–92; Drucker, P. E. (1954). *The practice of management.* New York: HarperBusiness. pp. 386–387; Also adapted from Hosmer, L. T. (2008). *The ethics of management.* (6th ed.). New York: McGraw-Hill Irwin, pp. 125–131.
113. See Matthew 12:36; Romans 14:12; 1 Peter 4:5.
114. Hosmer, L. T. (2008). *The ethics of management.* (6th ed.). New York: McGraw-Hill Irwin. pp. 103–104.
115. Weiss, J. W. (2003). *Business ethics: A stakeholder and issues management approach.* (3rd ed.). Mason, OH: South-Western.
116. Davis, K., & Blomstrom, R. (1966). *Business and its environment.* New York: McGraw-Hill; Drucker, P. F. (1973/1974). *Management: Tasks, responsibilities, practices.* New York: HarperBusiness. pp. 326–351; Windsor, D. (2006). Corporate social responsibility: Cases for and against. In Epstein, M. J., & Hanson, K. O. (Eds.). *The accountable corporation: Corporate social responsibility.* (Vol. 3). Westport, CT: Praeger. pp. 31–50; Lawrence, A. T., & Weber, J. (2008). *Business and society: Stakeholders, ethics, public policy.* New York: McGraw-Hill Irwin. p. 51; Porter, M. E., & Kramer, M. R. (2006). Strategy and society: The link between competitive advantage and corporate social responsibility. *Harvard Business Review.* 84(12), 78–92. Peter Drucker's comment is insightful on this point: "[The concentration of power in the private hands of enterprise] . . . imposes upon the business and its managers a responsibility which not only goes far beyond any traditional responsibility of private property but is altogether different. It can no longer be based on the assumption that the

self-interest of the owner of property will lead to the public good, or that self-interest and public good can be kept apart and considered to have nothing to do with each other. On the contrary, it requires of the manager that he assume responsibility for the public good, that he subordinate his actions to an ethical standard of conduct, and that he restrain his self-interest and his authority wherever their exercise would infringe upon the commonwealth and upon the freedom of the individual." Drucker, P. E. (1954). *The practice of management.* New York: HarperBusiness. pp. 382–283.

117. Luke 12:48.
118. Davis, K. (1973). The case for and against business assumption of social responsibilities. *Academy of Management Journal.* 16(2), 312–322; Windsor, D. (2006). Corporate social responsibility: Cases for and against. In Epstein, M. J., & Hanson, K. O. (Eds.). *The accountable corporation: Corporate social responsibility.* (Vol. 3). Westport, CT: Praeger. pp. 31–50; Porter, M. E., & Kramer, M. R. (2006). Strategy and society: The link between competitive advantage and corporate social responsibility. *Harvard Business Review.* 84(12), 78–92.
119. Lawrence, A. T., & Weber, J. (2008). *Business and society: Stakeholders, ethics, public policy.* New York: McGraw-Hill Irwin. p. 51; Davis, K. (1973). The case for and against business assumption of social responsibilities. *Academy of Management Journal.* 16(2), 312–322.
120. Lawrence, A. T., & Weber, J. (2008). *Business and society: Stakeholders, ethics, public policy.* New York: McGraw-Hill Irwin. p. 52; Windsor, D. (2006). Corporate social responsibility: Cases for and against. In Epstein, M. J., & Hanson, K. O. (Eds.). *The accountable corporation: Corporate social responsibility.* (Vol. 3). Westport, CT: Praeger. pp. 31–50; Porter, M. E., & Kramer, M. R. (2006). Strategy and society: The link between competitive advantage and corporate social responsibility. *Harvard Business Review.* 84(12), 78–92; Weiss, J. W. (2003). *Business ethics: A stakeholder and issues management approach.* (3rd ed.). Mason, OH: South-Western. pp. 157–158; Davis, K. (1973). The case for and against business assumption of social responsibilities. *Academy of Management Journal.* 16(2), 312–322.
121. Lawrence, A. T., & Weber, J. (2008). *Business and society: Stakeholders, ethics, public policy.* New York: McGraw-Hill Irwin. p. 52.
122. Weiss, J. W. (2003). *Business ethics: A stakeholder and issues management approach.* (3rd ed.). Mason, OH: South-Western. pp. 89–92, 157–162; Davis, K. (1973). The case for and against business assumption of social responsibilities. *Academy of Management Journal.* 16(2), 312–322.
123. Drucker, P. F. (1954). *The practice of management.* New York: HarperBusiness. p. 386; Friedman, M. (2002/1962). *Capitalism and freedom.* Chicago, IL: The University of Chicago Press, pp. 133–136; Friedman, M. (1970). The social responsibility of business is to increase its profits. *New York Times Sunday Magazine.* September 13; Windsor, D. (2006). Corporate social responsibility: Cases for and against. In Epstein, M. J., & Hanson, K. O. (Eds.). *The accountable corporation: Corporate social responsibility.* (Vol. 3). Westport, CT: Praeger. pp. 31–50; Lawrence, A. T., & Weber, J. (2008). *Business and society: Stakeholders, ethics, public policy.* New York: McGraw-Hill Irwin. p. 53; Davis, K. (1973). The case for and against business assumption of social responsibilities. *Academy of Management Journal.* 16(2), 312–322.
124. Lawrence, A. T., & Weber, J. (2008). *Business and society: Stakeholders, ethics, public policy.* New York: McGraw-Hill Irwin. p. 54.
125. Lawrence, A. T., & Weber, J. (2008). *Business and society: Stakeholders, ethics, public policy.* New York: McGraw-Hill Irwin. p. 54; Davis, K. (1973). The case for and against business assumption of social responsibilities. *Academy of Management Journal.* 16(2), 312–322.
126. Lawrence, A. T., & Weber, J. (2008). *Business and society: Stakeholders, ethics, public policy.* New York: McGraw-Hill Irwin. p. 55; Friedman, M. (1970). The social responsibility of business is to increase its profits. *New York Times Sunday Magazine.* September 13.
127. Windsor, D. (2006). Corporate social responsibility: Cases for and against. In Epstein, M. J., & Hanson, K. O. (Eds.). *The accountable corporation: Corporate social responsibility.* (Vol. 3). Westport, CT: Praeger. pp. 31–50.
128. Friedman, M. (1970). The social responsibility of business is to increase its profits. *New York Times Sunday Magazine.* September 13.
129. Friedman, M. (1970). The social responsibility of business is to increase its profits. *New York Times Sunday Magazine.* September 13.
130. Davis, K. (1973). The case for and against business assumption of social responsibilities. *Academy of Management Journal.* 16(2), 312–322; Bretsen, S. N. (2008). The creation, the Kingdom of God, and a theory of the faithful corporation. *Christian Scholar's Review.* 38(1), 115–154.
131. Davis, K. (1973). The case for and against business assumption of social responsibilities. *Academy of Management Journal.* 16(2), 312–322.
132. Perlroth, N. (2009). Health nuts. *Forbes.* 183(2), 42.
133. http://www.unglobalcompact.org/aboutthegc/thetenprinciples/index.html. United Nations Global Compact. Accessed November 23, 2010.
134. Kidder, R. M. (2006). Ethical decision-making and moral courage. In Epstein, M. J., & Hanson, K. O. (Eds.). *The accountable corporation: Business ethics.* (Vol. 2). Westport, CT: Praeger. p. 86.
135. Solomon, R. C. (1994). Business and the humanities: An Aristotelian approach to business ethics. In Donaldson, T. J., & Freeman, R. E. (Eds.). *Business as a humanity.* New York: Oxford University Press. pp. 45, 58; Nesteruk, J. (1996). The moral dynamics of law in business. *American Business Law Journal.* 34(2), 134. See also comments related to this in Lozano, J. M. (1996). Ethics and management: A controversial issue. *Journal of Business Ethics.* 15(2), 227–236. See also the comments on the issue of context in Hollinger, D. P. (2002). *Choosing the good: Christian ethics in a complex world.* Grand Rapids, MI: Baker Academic. p. 87; Warehane, P. H. (1994). Moral character and moral reasoning. In Donaldson, T. J., & Freeman, R. E. (Eds.). *Business as a humanity.* New York: Oxford University Press. pp. 98, 100; Hasnas, J. (1998). The normative theories of business ethics: A guide for the perplexed. *Business Ethics Quarterly.* 8(1), 19–42.

136. The issue of freedom and responsibility is implicit in discussions of political philosophy during the last 250 years. It also is a discussion relevant in commerce at the organizational level. See Rousseau, J. J. (1913). *The social contract & discourses.* New York: E. P. Dutton; Collins, J. (2001). *Good to great.* New York: HarperBusiness; Bouchikhi, H. (1998). Living with and building on complexity: A constructivist perspective on organizations. *Organization.* 2, 217–232; Milne, A. J. M. (1968). *Freedom and rights.* New York: Humanities Press, Inc.
137. Compare this with the U.S. Declaration of Independence. "We hold these truths to be self-evident, that all men are created equal, that they are endowed by their Creator with certain unalienable Rights, that among these are Life, Liberty and the pursuit of Happiness. — That to secure these rights, Governments are instituted among Men, deriving their just powers from the consent of the governed, — That whenever any Form of Government becomes destructive of these ends, it is the Right of the People to alter or to abolish it, and to institute new Government, laying its foundation on such principles and organizing its powers in such form, as to them shall seem most likely to effect their Safety and Happiness."
138. Pascale, R. T. (1985). The Paradox of "Corporate Culture": Reconciling ourselves to socialization. *California Management Review.* 27(2), 26–41.
139. Siegel, D. S. (2009). Green management matters only if it yields more green: An economic/strategic perspective. *Academy of Management Perspectives.* 23(3), 5–16.
140. Marcus, A. A., & Fremeth, A. R. (2009). Green management matters regardless. *Academy of Management Perspectives.* 23(3), 17–26.
141. Robbins, S. R., & Judge, T. A. (2010). *Essentials of organizational behavior.* (10th ed.). Upper Saddle River, NJ: Prentice Hall. pp. 201–204.
142. Anonymous. (2009). Pelosi's toy story. *The Wall Street Journal.* January 14. A12; O'Donnell, J., & Szabo, L. (2009). Safety rules on lead in kids' products perplex and polarize. *USA Today.* February 5. Found on the USAToday website: http://www.usatoday.com/money/industries/retail/2009-02-04-new-lead-safety-law_N.htm.

CHAPTER 6

Planning and Decision Making

LEARNING OBJECTIVES

- Explain why planning and decision making are important functions for managers.
- Understand how the Bible's view of planning and decision making influences contemporary Christian managers.
- Understand the fundamental ideas of planning.
- Identify the process, styles, and challenges in managerial decision making.
- Be aware of selected tension points that managers face as they fulfill their role as planners and decision makers.

"Discernment is the intentional practice by which a community or an individual seeks, recognizes, and intentionally takes part in the activity of God in concrete situations."[1]

"Planning represents management's attempt to anticipate the future and win some security against the menace of temporal change of which man's time sense makes him so urgently aware."[2]

DISASTER ON THE INDIAN OCEAN

Just two minutes before 8:00 a.m. local time on December 26, 2004, Philip Manuel was in church the morning after Christmas in his village of Trincomalee, Sri Lanka.[3] Thousands of miles away somewhere in the Indian Ocean one of Earth's massive tectonic crust plates crushed the edge of another, triggering an earthquake measuring 9.1 on the Richter scale. The horrific quake rocked Sumatra, Indonesia, for 10 minutes but caused the entire planet to quiver. Not long after the quake, a tsunami pounded 11 nations ringing the Indian Ocean. Hardest hit were Indonesia, Sri Lanka, India, Thailand, Myanmar, Somalia, and Madagascar. In the church where Philip and other worshipers had gathered panicked cries rang out, "The sea is coming!" Philip ran to a hillside to survey the situation in his village. The ocean receded before coming back with deadly vengeance. It took with it boats, houses, churches, businesses, and people, including 10 members of Philip's family. Like other villagers, Philip was in shock. But he had a job to do. He was an employee of Oxfam America, a disaster relief agency.

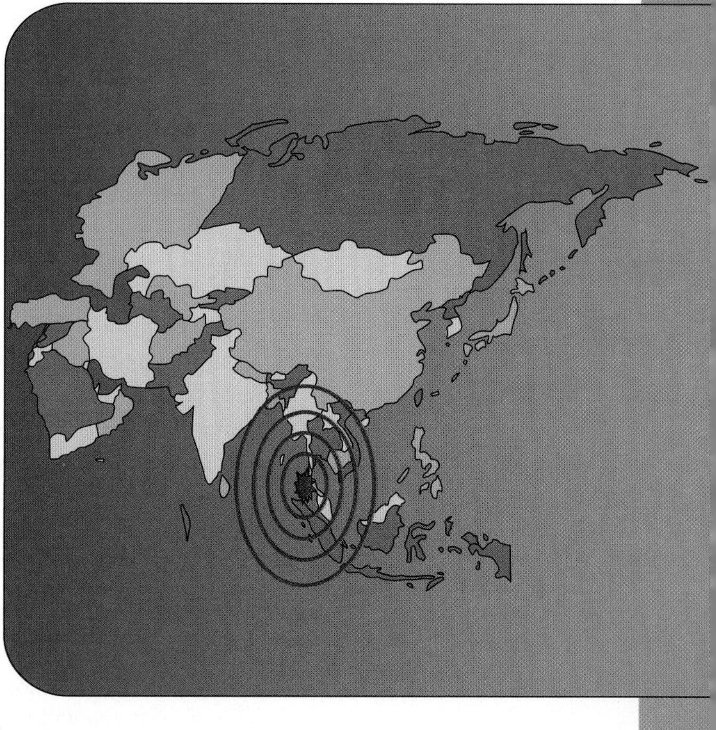

In another ocean village A.R. Mohamed Saifullah, also an aid worker employed by Oxfam America, faced a similar situation. Like fellow employees of Oxfam in other villages, Mohamed organized a group of volunteers for search and recovery. He coordinated his efforts with Oxfam managers in larger cities who were in contact with Oxfam's international headquarters in Boston, Massachusetts. Within hours of the disaster a cargo plane carrying tons of equipment and materials needed to build latrines and emergency water systems (one of Oxfam's specialties) was in flight to Sri Lanka from the United Kingdom. When materials arrived, Saifullah coordinated with other aid agencies and local officials to use the emergency resources. Looking for survivors, recovering the dead, and providing for sanitation and fresh water are just a few of the important disaster relief efforts needed in small ocean villages.

The scale of the tragedy was so enormous it is still difficult to comprehend. Over 200,000 people lost their lives, making this the third deadliest earthquake and the deadliest tsunami in recorded history. One-third of those killed were the most vulnerable—children. Those not killed or injured from the quake and tsunami faced other dangers in the weeks and months following including death from cholera, diphtheria, dysentery, and typhoid fever.

Over one million people were displaced, needing food, shelter, clean water, transportation, and many support services we take for granted in normal life. Hundreds of businesses were destroyed. The entire fishing industry in the Indian Ocean was disrupted, cutting off another important food supply to millions.

The planning and decision making needed for handling natural disasters is an illustration of systems thinking that we considered earlier in this book. For example, we naturally think about the horrid physical and social upheaval that a tidal wave can wreak. Local governments make decisions to issue land use permits and building permits. They enact zoning laws, housing subdivision regulations, and enforce building codes that either encourage or discourage people from populating low-lying areas near the ocean.

Planners also must study local geological formations known as tsunami inundation zones. This information guides planners for developing future communications, training, plans for how to deal with specific buildings that are at high risk, and even the possibility of

Source: © Tommy E Trenchard/Alamy.

Disaster relief workers can do their job best when their managers plan ahead.

population migrations. They must identify and label evacuation routes. Someone needs to manage the process of producing maps, signage, preparedness checklists, public communication, and citizen education. Planners must prepare for the allocation of personnel such as public safety, communication, response, and rescue workers.

Each disaster becomes a learning experience. Yet disasters are some of the most difficult things to plan for. Huge disasters are rare. A hazardous chemical spill from one truck in one community does not give disaster planners and decision makers the scale of operations they would face with a major earthquake. Those who respond to today's catastrophic earthquake are not necessarily the same people who learned from the last one. A generation or more may have passed. Because of this, many first responders will lack the hands-on experience at the scale needed for the truly monstrous catastrophe. And yet when they don't distribute food, water, and shelter to victims fast enough, they are easily criticized for not being ready.

Who Cares About Planning and Decision Making?

The response to natural disasters such as earthquakes and tsunamis requires planning and decision making on a grand scale, involving thousands of local managers like Philip Manuel and Mohamed Saifullah. But managers in other situations plan on a smaller scale every day.[4] As a manager, even in the more mundane dimensions of work, planning and decision making make up a lot of what you will do on a daily basis. The jobs of decision making and planning are two of the most important reasons why organizations hire managers. So important is planning that it has been called the primary management function.[5]

When you think about it, very little would ever be accomplished in this world if we did not have the capacity to think about what might happen in the future, consider our goals and options, make decisions, and then take action accordingly. Yet uncertainty about the future makes it very difficult to predict the effects of our decisions. Strangely enough, to help ourselves deal with this uncertainty, we plan and make decisions as if we did know the future, thinking creatively about its possibilities.

As individuals, we engage in the planning process on a daily basis and sometimes multiple times each day. Planning occurs so often and sometimes is done so informally that we may not recognize it as planning. It's just how we get things done in life. When we go to bed, it is natural to think about what needs to be done the next day. This is a form of planning. Think about all of the "to-do" lists that you make on a daily or weekly basis. This, too, is a form a planning. Whether they are kept on our cell phones, on our computers, on a piece of paper, or simply in our memory, our lists serve multiple purposes. They help us be responsible and stay on course. These lists are sometimes the place where we record our goals for the day or the week. Managers, likewise, rely on lists to record what has been accomplished and what priorities lie ahead for the next few days and weeks.

Source: Stylephotographs/Dreamstime.com.

A manager's "To Do" list is one of the more simple, yet effective, planning tools.

Only the simplest kinds of routine work activities don't require making plans every time we do them. But this does not mean that planning didn't occur. Managers and non-managers both participate in establishing or revising work routines. This is a legitimate form of planning. The result of their planning becomes what we call *standard operating procedures*.

More complicated activities, such as when an assembly plant moves to a new building, require extensive planning and decision making that consumes enormous amounts of time and money. Here the process is formal. A move of an assembly plant requires the careful sequencing of activities to minimize the time that production machines and workers are sitting idle. Managers in other departments will probably be involved either because their department has a stake in the move or just because extra people are needed for coordinating and moving materials and equipment.

The concepts of planning and decision making lead us to the heart of the Management Pyramid model.

Management Pyramid on Planning and Decision Making

As we have seen, management is largely mental work. The Management Pyramid in Exhibit 6-1 illustrates how integrated planning and decision making are with each other and with the pyramid's levels of being and becoming, thinking and feeling, and action. Action is never separated from decision making and planning; planning is never separated from awareness of purpose. But purpose

EXHIBIT 6-1

The Management Pyramid: Planning and Decision Making

Source: Courtesy of Michael E. Cafferky, © Michael E. Cafferky 2011.

Actions that move the organization toward its goals **Actions that result in employee development** **Communication about plans and decisions** **Decisions that lead to implementation of plans**	**Action**
Anticipating what will likely occur in the future and what this will mean for you and for others **Articulating expectations for what should be done** **Thinking about duties and consequences of actions** **Discussing action alternatives**	**Thinking & Feeling**
Beliefs about how others will act when decisions and plans are made **Awareness of the purpose for decisions and actions** **Intuition which informs thinking and action** **Personal and organizational values** **Assumptions regarding constraints on decisions and plans**	**Being & Becoming**

arises from our deepest values and beliefs. It is at this level of belief that the reason for having goals to act exists. We might even say that the moment of decision or when a manager conceives of a plan is an action taking place in the manager's mind. Of course the mental work of planning and decision making eventually leads to physical actions. As a manager, your planning and decision making will set in motion the mental activities of others around you, which in turn will result in coordinated action toward achieving the organization's goals. See Exhibit 6-1.

Faith Perspective on Planning and Decision Making

For the Christian, planning and decision making are important dimensions of fulfilling the role of being a good steward of organizational resources while considering the needs of people. We will explore both ideas starting with planning. We begin with the Christian perspective because it is an important part of the Christian's personal beliefs and values (the "being and becoming" part of the Management Pyramid model).

Planning in the Bible

One thing that we notice in the Bible is that God is a planner and a decision maker.[6] His planning encompasses the entire earth, the nations, and his plan of salvation. When Jesus came to fulfill his part in that plan, he had an operational plan.[7] Some scientists observe the order of nature and believe that God must have had a design in creation. Like anyone else, biblical prophets were planners. Their ministry reveals that God plans. And their messages sometimes carried the details of God's plans for the future. The divine prophecies they told were essentially plans for what would happen. Some prophecies came in the form of dreams. Some prophecies are contingent on the response of humans. God's plan for unbelievers is sometimes unfulfilled when they refuse his grace.[8]

Because decision making and planning are done in service to God, these are essentially spiritual activities in the context of a larger setting of the community and God's will. Planners and decision makers take responsibility on behalf of others. Because of this, trust and trustworthiness are at the heart of decision making. This means that before we make a decision, we will consider the needs of those with whom we have primary relationships as well as those who are part of the extended relationships throughout the community. This is a way to live a covenant relationship.

Biblical wisdom on planning alludes to both efficiency and effectiveness.[9] Plans are closely connected with decision making and establishing purpose. Plans communicate expectations. They build trust. They are an important part of organizing work. Plans are the foundation for building commitment for concerted effort. Much of how Christians have come to conceive of planning and decision making in the Bible was recorded in the wisdom sayings in the book of Proverbs.[10] Other writers give us a wider understanding of how God thinks about planning. Scores of Bible stories illustrate how making arrangements to achieve a goal is important.

The Biblical Story of Esther

Read the book of Esther in the Bible. Based on her experience, grasp the significance of the accomplishments that occurred under the leadership of Esther. Make a mental note of the leadership strengths and weaknesses of Esther in terms of her planning and decision making. What leadership principles can we gain from the experience of Esther that are applicable today?

The Bible's teaching on the immanence (nearness) of God[11] and the faith relationship of the believer leads some to believe that if they maintain a close relationship with God, ask for guidance, and wait for the Holy Spirit to direct them, then God will give them guidance.[12] But God also is transcendent—far away and unknowable in a complete sense.[13] The Bible writers all agree: God is sovereign and in control, but human knowledge of the future is imperfect. From a human perspective, the future details of life are uncertain.[14] Because of our limited knowledge of an uncertain future, humans are expected to make decisions and take actions in the short run to minimize the risk of unfavorable events from occurring. Unless individual believers expect frequent direct revelations from God to help them in decision making, they cannot escape dealing with uncertainty. Lacking direct revelation, decision makers need to process all the information relevant to the decision through their understanding of God's will. This means discerning God's will through the lens of a particular worldview, which is shaped by understanding Scripture.

In contrast to human limitation, God knows the end from the beginning.[15] If humans could partner with God for decision making, then we might be able to make better decisions and have assurance that we are following his will. The Bible describes some situations where such collaboration existed. A few individuals received instructions from God through special revelation. Others asked for and received signs or other unusual events that gave them guidance.[16] But if we look at the pattern where God gave supernatural guidance, we see that this was the exception rather than the rule. Prophets received direct guidance from God, which they delivered to the people. Guidance was sometimes revealed in critical situations when the whole faith community especially needed it.[17]

Practical Nature of Planning

Bible writers consider planning a normal, practical part of living a successful life. The Bible portrays planning as thinking wisely about what will happen in the future. For example, planning how to develop agricultural assets, compared with buildings, should account for the long lead time to harvest and the seasons. Jesus told a story about 10 virgins, 5 of whom failed to prepare for a wedding in the future and were caught without oil in their lamps.[18] Planning assumes that the human being has some capability of anticipating the future consequences of actions. Planning is primarily a mental activity. Such mental work is necessary before undertaking any project, large or small.[19]

One major issue with planning is that the human mind has limitations. Because of this, under some circumstances good planning cannot be a solo activity. Sometimes it is a group or community activity that involves consulting trusted persons in the community who are wise with experience.[20]

Planning must include considering God's will. It is God who directs the actions of a careful planner. The manager who wants to be faithful to God will stay close to his will. Herein we see an interesting paradox of Christian faith. On the one hand, the Bible clearly establishes God's sovereignty over the world. On the other hand, humans are expected to make plans and implement them.[21]

Not every human plan may be realized. But those who commit themselves, their plans, and their work to God, believing that, in reality, they work for him, will find that their plans are established. Though they should take careful thought about the future, people who trust in God do not need to be anxious about what is to come.[22]

Biblical Examples of Practical Planning

The Bible reports many situations in which planning is important.[23] Planning and economic activity are closely linked in the Bible. When careful, deliberate planning is added with diligent work and listening to wise counsel, it leads to economic success. The person who acts in haste without adequate planning can lose economically. The simple-minded person will believe that anything is possible. But the practical person will think about things before acting rashly or in anger. Likewise, the wise person who sees danger ahead will make a plan to avoid it whenever possible. Those who make capital investments are trustworthy when they show their wisdom by carefully considering the investment before the purchase.[24]

Planning that includes specific, measurable objectives is illustrated in the story of Nehemiah. When Nehemiah asks to be released from his duties to the Persian king, the king wisely wants to know specifically how long Nehemiah plans to be gone. Sensing how important his departure is to the king Nehemiah gives him a definite time when he plans on returning.[25] Such information is helpful to a top-level leader who needs to know whom he can rely on at any time when situations arise.

Before investing, count not only the economic cost but also the loss to social influence that will result if a project fails for lack of planning. This is illustrated in a story told by Jesus to illustrate the importance of counting the cost of discipleship:

> For which one of you, when he wants to build a tower, does not first sit down and calculate the cost to see if he has enough to complete it? Otherwise, when he has laid a foundation and is not able to finish, all who observe it begin to ridicule him saying, "This man began to build and was not able to finish."[26]

EXHIBIT 6-2
Planners and Plotters in the Bible[27]

Esther's plan to save the Jews	Moses plans to spy in the land of Canaan
Joseph prepares an empire for famine	Jesus plans the last supper with the disciples
Satan's plan to test Job's faith in God	David's plan vs. Abigail's plot
Noah manages the ark-building plan	Christians' plan vs. the Jews' plot for Paul
Spies hatch a plan to save a Jericho harlot	Jonah tries to thwart God's plan for his life
King Ahab plots to get Naboth's vineyard	Balak has a project to curse Israel
Daniel's diet plan	Church leaders plan to help the widows
The plan to fetch the ark of the covenant	Josiah's project to restore the temple

Planning and constructing a building involved a variety of considerations from fund raising, site preparation, gathering and transporting construction materials such as stones, beams, and wood to fire kilns, manufacturing lime plaster (which involved the use of wood-fired kilns that had to be built), purchasing or making tools, lifting, attaching materials, and finishing surfaces.[28]

The Bible contains numerous examples of a variety of plans, as shown in Exhibit 6-2.The Bible teaches that whenever someone's action will affect other people, that individual should plan ahead for the benefit of all.[29]

Well-known leaders such as Noah, Elijah, Daniel, Nehemiah, Paul the Apostle, and Jesus were planners.[30] But planning was a part of everyone's lives. Some plans are known to us only because of the actions that were taken. Other plans are revealed for our benefit before the actions are taken. Some plans are clearly linked with God's leading in life.[31] In all cases, the plans that were developed had a central purpose behind them as their reason for being. Without this underlying purpose, plans would mean nothing.

Some biblical examples illustrate how inadequate planning can lead to impulsive decisions and regrettable outcomes. Esau was willing to trade his inheritance for a bowl of soup.[32] Impulsive Peter once drew his sword and maimed someone in the presence of Jesus.[33] Herod's daughter was dancing for her father on his birthday. When he impulsively asked her what she wanted, she replied that she wanted the head of John the Baptist on a platter. Herod complied with her request.[34]

The Bible also shows us examples of the danger of basing plans on faulty assumptions. For example, the Philistines tried to make sport of Sampson assuming that he was still weak because he was blind. Sampson, whose hair and strength had grown back after being imprisoned, mustered a final burst of strength and destroyed the Philistines in their temple.[35] In another example, the Philistine giant Goliath had a good plan for challenging the army of Israel. The plan was working. The problem was his assumption regarding young, relatively inexperienced shepherds. He didn't anticipate what David might be able to do with a slingshot.[36]

Closely related to planning is decision making. Plans suggest that decisions already have been made or will soon be made.

Decision-Making Methods in Biblical Times

Ancient cultures accepted a variety of decision-making methods, some of which are unusual to us today. Examples include casting lots, casting an arrow, reading water in a vessel, consulting spiritualist mediums, studying the stars, and the pagan practice of divination.[37] The Bible strictly forbids consulting spiritualist mediums and witches or resorting to divination even though they were common practices then.[38] Casting lots (like rolling dice in our time) was used to decide how to fairly distribute land and duties, how to determine who had done wrong (often used along with additional evidence), the selection of soldiers for the draft, the selection of the goat used on the Day of Atonement, and how to mete out punishment. When the disciples desired to replace Judas Iscariot, they cast lots. The lot fell to Matthias, who became the twelfth apostle.[39] Apparently the reason why casting lots was acceptable but other practices were not was that casting of lots resulted in an immediate unambiguous result. The lot was transparent while other practices required more subjective interpretation that could be open to question.[40]

The Bible provides several interesting examples of biblical characters making decisions and the different approaches they used. For example, Abram received direct guidance from God to take his family from his father's land and journey toward Canaan. He simply acted on this guidance.[41] Moses also received a direct communication from God when he was called to lead Israel. God gave the whole encampment direction on which way to go by leading with the pillar of cloud and the pillar of fire. When difficult questions could not be answered by the counselors, the priest's prayerful use of the Urim and Thummim resulted in direction. But when Moses needed to reorganize the Israelis, he depended on the counsel of a trusted person with more experience.[42] The decision proved to be wise.

When Gideon received instruction from God, in his doubt he asked for a special sign to confirm.[43] Rehoboam, who succeeded his father King Solomon to the throne, also asked for counsel of the elders. He chose to act contrary to their counsel. The end result was insurrection.[44] At times, God spoke through the prophets to provide spiritual direction to change their behaviors. We see a few examples of dreams and visions given to particular individuals.[45]

When Saul was converted, God directed him to go to the Christian faith community for instruction on what he should do next.[46] When the early church faced a difficult decision related to faith and practice, they counseled together and decided what to do as a group. When they needed to communicate their decision regarding circumcision to the churches, they chose official spokesmen to represent them.[47] We don't know the particular method they used to select these ambassadors.

Participation in Decision Making

The biblical portrayal of leaders includes an understanding that they have the unquestioned authority to make decisions.[48] Many decisions were apparently made individually, and others were made as a group.[49] The book of Proverbs advises us to get counsel from others before making decisions or plans. It does not specify the extent to which participation by counselors should be allowed.[50] As shown in Exhibit 6-3, we see a range of participation by subordinates in decision making in the Bible. At one end of the spectrum, we see managers making decisions on behalf of a group and then simply announcing the decision. At the other end of the spectrum, we see managers asking their subordinates what they prefer and then the manager following their wishes. Giving workers an active role in making decisions that affect their work life gives them an opportunity to be responsible stewards of the resources in which they are entrusted.[51]

King Rehoboam asked for advice from the leaders serving under him. After they gave their advice, he ignored them and decided to do the opposite. When he announced his decision, he verbally abused them. This resulted in their anger and rebellion.[52] We might deduce from Rehoboam's experience that it might be better if you don't ask for subordinates' advice if you know you won't follow it in the first place. If the advice you get from subordinates is not what you want to hear, don't verbally abuse them. Instead show them respect in your response.

EXHIBIT 6-3

The Spectrum of Participation in Decision Making

Leader-Centered Decision Making[53]	Leader-Follower Decision Making[54] (The degree of participation is ambiguous.)	Follower-Centered Decision Making[55]
Josiah makes executive decisions to cleanse the temple and revive religious services.	David first consults with military leaders and then announces his decision to the people.	David first announces his decision but then retracts it after the people give him counsel. He follows what they want him to do.
Jesus decides how he will make his entrance into Jerusalem. He announces it.	Jehoshaphat counseled with the people before making a decision.	The counselors of Darius tell him that he must sign a decree. He complies but reaps unfavorable consequences as a result.
Jesus decides to send 70 disciples on a missionary tour. He announces it to them.	Nebuchadnezzar gets counsel from others.	The family consults with Rebekah regarding her desire to go with Abraham's servant. She decides to go.

The gospels portray Jesus as making the decisions related to his ministry. He understood the value of getting counsel from others. In his own experience, his counsel came from God, not from his disciples.[56] He "did not run a democratic organization. Not once did he call for a vote on the course that should be followed."[57]

Based on the entire biblical record on decision making, the key takeaway is that participation by subordinates in decision making can be an appropriate method as long as the ultimate decision-making authority remains with the top-level leaders of the organization.

Unwarranted Optimism in the Bible

A recurring theme in the Bible is the warning that excessive behaviors lead to pride and insolence, which lead a person to forsake God. In turn, this leads to injustices and eventual dishonor before God.[58] The Bible contains some examples of individuals who were more pessimistic than they should have been.[59] We also see several examples of individuals who exhibited unwarranted optimism with respect to decisions they made, described in Exhibit 6-4.

Human Inconsistencies in Decision Making

Knowing what we should do and knowing what we want to do is a challenge for humans. The Bible's perspective on this comes primarily from the writing of Paul the Apostle. Here the root cause of this problem is nothing other than sin. Paul says that the law of God resides in his mind or the "inner man" which instructs him regarding what he should do. This is at work through the functioning of a reasoning mind. That which he naturally and selfishly wants to do comes from the desires of his body. The only way out of this impossible situation is by living in a relationship with Jesus Christ and making the complete commitment to follow the law of the Spirit instead of selfish desires. It is only by making such a full commitment to God in faith to follow his Law that true liberty can be experienced. The Bible calls this process of learning over time to make such choices *sanctification*.[60]

How Should Christians Make Decisions?

Many Christians believe that God reveals his will to those who earnestly seek him.[61] But the question of how the Christian manager should discern God's will is not simple. Christians have a variety of opinions on this topic but a common belief is that discernment is a partnership between the decision maker and God.[62] Some say, just read the Bible and you will find the answers to your questions.[63] Others focus on submitting your will to God.[64] Others believe the key is obedience to the revealed standard of moral values: the Ten Commandments.[65] Some believe that God will give them a special, miraculous sign to reveal his will to them.[66] Others emphasize the importance of asking for God's guidance in a prayer of faith.[67] Some emphasize learning how to hear God's voice,[68] while others suggest that God reveals his will through the counsel of trusted leaders in the community.[69] Still others emphasize that the Holy Spirit mysteriously works in us to do God's will.[70]

The basis for each of these viewpoints can be found in the Bible. However, while each contains an important point of truth regarding discerning God's will, each also tends to reduce a complicated matter down to a relatively simple formula.

EXHIBIT 6-4
Unwarranted Optimism in the Bible[71]

Lucifer claims he would ascend to God's throne	Belshazzar's lax security
The people who built the tower of Babel	Haman's decision to destroy the Jews
Samson reveals the source of his strength	Balaam's decision
Pharaoh's response to Moses	Planning the attack on the town of Ai
Nebuchadnezzar's defiance	The prodigal son's wasting his inheritance
Cain's behavior leads to dishonor	Pharaoh's hubris against Abraham's wife
Potiphar's wife's outrageous solicitation	Korah's rebellion

If the particular management decision is covered by a direct command or clear guidance, then this must be obeyed. But for many decisions there is no biblical guidance. For these situations, what is the Christian manager to do?

Bible scholar Gary Meadors offers a model for decision making that can be adapted to managerial situations as illustrated in Exhibit 6-5.[72] The decision maker should begin with God's revealed will as contained in the Bible. In this way, the manager will become familiar with Scripture.

The ancient Hebrews seemed to be aware of the concept of probability. Pure chance, however, implies complete independence from God, a view that the Bible writers do not have.[73] At the same time, while the people in the Bible believed that it is God who orders nature and human life, ancient wisdom, such as that portrayed in the book of Ecclesiastes, takes for granted that humans are free to choose and are capable of making and executing plans at the right time or as circumstances permit.[74]

For the Christian manager, this raises another significant concern: relying on your own mental functions while also relying on God.[75] On the one hand, the follower of God will wait patiently for God's Providence in situations. On the other hand, the manager will be proactive rather than passively waiting for things to happen.[76]

Christians have been interested in Providence for centuries.[77] God's **Providence** is defined by one respected scholar as "that continued exercise of the divine energy whereby the Creator preserves all His creatures, is operative in all that comes to pass in the world, and directs all things to their appointed end."[78] God's Providence works through the physical world, the political affairs of nations, and individual human life experiences.[79] For many Christians, being in the right place at the right time is not a matter of chance but rather the confluence of God's Providence working to preserve and care for people.[80]

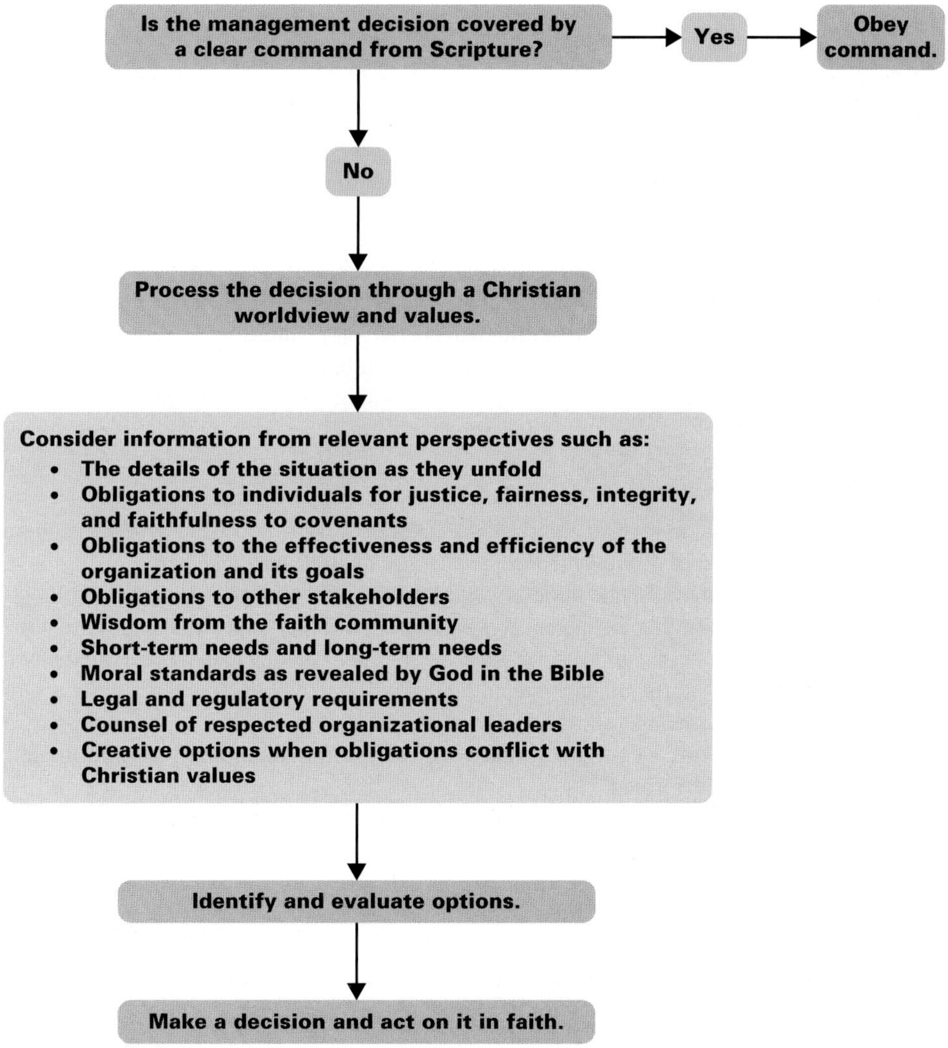

EXHIBIT 6-5

Biblical Decision-Making Process

Source: Adapted for managerial decisions from Meadors, G. T. (2003). *Decision making God's way: A new model for knowing God's will.* Grand Rapids, MI: Baker Books. p. 65. Used by permission of the author.

God's Hands *Off*; Human Hands On	God's Hands *Off* or Selectively *On*; Human Hands On	God's Hands *with* Human Hands	God's Hands Always *On*, Human Hands Off
God is no longer directly involved with the daily affairs of humans and nature on Earth. His involvement is through the unchanging laws that he created. God set in motion the natural physical and social laws but it is the actions of nature and individual humans that influence outcomes. Things can and do happen by chance. Randomness is one of God's created laws.	God is selective when he chooses to be directly involved in the daily affairs of humans and nature on Earth. Most of the time his involvement is through the natural laws he created and sustains. Some things happen by chance; some things happen because God is immediately at work. Sometimes God works directly without human involvement; other times God works with humans.	God is still actively involved with the affairs of humans and nature on Earth directly or indirectly. God uses the forces of nature and the actions of humans to carry out his will for the Earth. Events that may appear to be random are really events where God is at work. Humans are the hands of God participating with him in Providence.	God is directly, continually, and immediately involved with all affairs of Earth through specific, miraculous interventions in the lives of human beings. God does not use indirect means such as human actions to bring about his will. Nothing is random. There is no such thing as chance because God is in control.

EXHIBIT 6-6
Different Views of God's Providence

When comparing Christian beliefs on this subject we find a spectrum, which is summarized in Exhibit 6-6.

Ultimately all human decisions are processed through the Christian's understanding of what the Bible teaches. In addition, the Christian manager must consider relevant information as the situation unfolds such as obligations to individuals and to the organization, short-term and long-term implications, and legal requirements. Also, some situations require the counsel of experienced leaders. When obligations appear to conflict with the Christian worldview, the Christian manager will attempt to identify options that do not require value compromises.

Now that we have seen the Christian faith perspective on planning and decision making, we will explore these two interrelated concepts from the results of contemporary research and the practice of experienced managers.

Planning

Planning and decision making are so closely interrelated that it is impossible to separate them in practice.[81] However, we will give each concept separate, focused coverage here.

A **plan** is an expression of the actions you intend to take and the objective you hope to accomplish in the future. It can be expressed either verbally (informally) or in writing (formally). For example, if the aircraft manufacturer Boeing decides to acquire a company that supplies it with assembly parts, managers at all levels will make plans to integrate the acquired company for a closer working relationship with Boeing. Plans consider the resources and people available, the nature of the work that will be accomplished, and the environment in which the work will be performed.[82]

Planning helps us to bring order to complicated, chaotic situations. However, as we have seen, the basic reason why we plan is to anticipate the future, about which we are uncertain. If we don't know the future and if the future ends up being different from what we expect, then does this mean that planning is a waste of time? No.[83]

Planning is not just the manager's job; planning is something that all employees do. The more employees plan, the more responsibility they take for getting their work done.[84] This is good for two reasons. First, managers do not have time to plan every detail of work for every employee. Second, in some situations, employees are better able to plan the technical details of the work than their managers are because of the nature of the job.

EXHIBIT 6-7
Components of Effective Planning

Planning: A Way to Manage Goal Accomplishment

Planning in the context of organizational management begins with an awareness of three important elements: the purpose of the organization's existence, what the organization's members believe the organization can become in the future, and the beliefs that organizational members stand for. We often speak about these three elements as the organization's ***mission***, ***vision***, and ***values***, respectively.

These three broad guidelines are valuable but by themselves they are not enough to accomplish effective planning. Managers must also consider the strategic long-term commitments of the organization toward key resources such as property, equipment, and people that have particular types of talent and skills that will help the organization have a competitive advantage. In addition, planning requires determining specific objectives that need to be accomplished on a daily and weekly basis. Without a specific objective in mind, planning is useless. Exhibit 6-7 illustrates all of these components of effective planning.

Formal commitments to achieve measurable performance within a particular time frame are made by establishing objectives. To focus organizational members on their responsibilities, objectives should be specific, measurable, and achievable. See Exhibit 6-8.

One of the most popular approaches to planning based on objectives is the management by objectives (MBO) system made popular by management consultant Peter Drucker. Let's look at his approach.

Management by Objectives (MBO)

Peter Drucker[85] recommended a straightforward planning process based around objectives, actions, and self-control. Drucker's original model gradually transformed into a four-step process described here.

SETTING OBJECTIVES. Ideally the person responsible for the objectives is the one to set them. Drucker believed that objectives should not be imposed on employees from persons higher in authority. However, workers and their managers must agree on the objectives. In other words, the responsible person cannot set an objective that is in isolation from the thinking of others. Objectives are meant for self-control on the part of the responsible person; they are not meant to be the basis of one person dominating another.

Objective	Measure	Time Frame	Person Responsible
Describes what needs to be accomplished	Describes the tangible measure that gives evidence that the objective has been achieved	Specifies the time in which the objective needs to be accomplished	Identifies the person who is accountable for achieving the objective
Example: Achieve a sustained increase in production of Ultra Premium Geegaws by 10% no later than June 1 next year.			
Achieve a sustained increase in production of Ultra Premium Geegaws . . .	. . . by 10% . . .	. . . no later than June 1 next year.	Production Manager

EXHIBIT 6-8
Setting Objectives

DEVELOPING ACTION PLANS. **Action plans** are focused on specific tasks and projects that, when implemented, are designed to achieve measurable objectives. The person responsible for the accomplishment of the plan is the one who should take the lead in establishing the action plans. If the plan is simple and does not involve other people, usually the planner is the person who is responsible to carry out the plan. But if the plan affects other people and their work tasks, more than one person will be involved in developing the action plan. In Drucker's approach, supervisors collaborate with immediate subordinates to create the action plan details.

MONITORING RESULTS. Drucker recommended that the person responsible for the objectives also be the one who monitors the results. His assumption is that managers generally want to achieve their goals. This can be accomplished by generating a few simple reports that are shared with those involved in setting the objectives.

MAKING ADJUSTMENTS. Where results do not measure up to the performance standard, the one who set the objectives will want to make adjustments to improve the chances of achieving success. Sometimes this requires the supervisor to have a conversation with the subordinate. At other times, the subordinate uses his best judgment and makes adjustments which he reports to the supervisor.

The MBO approach to planning usually begins at the top-level management team. These leaders have the responsibility of aligning the MBO plans with the organizational mission and vision. For example, the Philippine Educational Theater Association might set its objectives as the production of an entire season of live performances, completion of an actor training program, the development of a team of understudy performers, and the securing of at least one alternative venue for performances.[86] Executives discuss their objectives with the CEO. These executives then have discussions with the division or department managers, who in turn set objectives and so on throughout the entire organization. When MBO is used extensively, eventually every employee gets involved in setting objectives, planning, and monitoring the results of their work.

Some managers who use Drucker's approach have taken it a step further than Drucker first envisioned by integrating the MBO process into annual employee performance reviews. At the beginning of the annual review cycle, the supervisor and employee set objectives and develop action plans. At the end of the cycle, the supervisor uses the MBO objectives, plans, and results to evaluate the employee.

Many variations on the basic MBO approach exist. Some of these have wandered from Drucker's strong emphasis on self-control toward an emphasis on top-down managerial control. This shift in emphasis, the fact that some MBO programs appear to be less effective than others, and the fact that a good proportion of managers are dissatisfied with how their MBO program works have generated a debate over the pros and cons of MBO.[87]

Most people agree in principle that setting objectives is important. Verifiable objectives naturally lead to action-oriented planning. Generally speaking, setting goals leads to higher performance. However, in practice, objectives are difficult to set in many situations. Many factors can influence whether measurable objectives can be achieved. When supervisors use the goal-setting process to control employees, some employees resist. Another problem is that the focus on a few measurable objectives can undermine the achievement of other objectives that may be just as important.

In practice, the MBO program looks simple, but it has been difficult to implement. Many managers are used to planning for work activities (the inputs) but not necessarily planning to achieve outcomes. If goals are arbitrarily set to appease a supervisor or if the supervisor arbitrarily sets objectives for a subordinate—something that Drucker counseled against—commitment is undermined. Using the supervisor–subordinate authority relationship to mandate objectives and monitor results contradicts the central principle of self-control on which Drucker developed the program. The debate over these and other issues with MBO has raised some moral questions about MBO. To these we turn next.

The Morality of MBO

One minor issue with goal setting is that not all employees desire the same degree of participation. Some prefer that their supervisor set the objectives for them. For this issue, the question is whether it is moral for supervisors to mandate that employees participate in setting objectives. A more difficult problem is that some supervisors say they want their subordinates to participate in setting objectives but then either subtly or overtly coerce the subordinate to accept the objectives that the supervisor wants to set. Another related problem is the pressure that some managers feel from their supervisors to set unrealistic measurable objectives. They achieve the objectives but then feel guilty about neglecting other important areas of work equally of value. If the setting of objectives is used by senior managers to simply ratchet up the performance from one time period to another, employees soon feel used, and the MBO becomes the whip from above rather than a self-imposed self-management system as Drucker originally designed. When the focus is solely on the performance of the organization, and the personal goals of the employees are not included in the MBO program, employees feel like they are a means to an end instead of in partnership with the firm.[88]

Making MBO part of the annual performance appraisal cycle, especially if wage increases are tied to performance, puts added pressure on employees to employ immoral actions to meet performance goals. An even larger issue is when the immoral use of an MBO program undermines the trust between supervisor and subordinate. Distrust grows like a cancer in the community of relationships in the organization, making effective leadership difficult.

The Christian Mind on Planning

"Planning is an effort not so much to control outcomes, but to increase options for action and to reduce unnecessary risks. We are God's moral agents, who are confronted constantly with choices between competing values and alternative uses of resources. We must make plans to help us sift through and select those options that assist us in matching our objectives to God's goals for his world." "Planning is deciding on a course of action. It should involve counsel and participation by those involved. Doing justice—doing what is right—requires good planning that involves everyone in the business and that is based on broad counsel and advice."[89]

Regardless of your opinions about the MBO program, one thing is for certain: setting objectives and creating plans to achieve those objectives focuses work on specific projects and work tasks. To this we turn next.

Project Planning and Management

Many organizations employ individuals to manage a succession of projects.[90] These *project managers* play a vital role when other managers are too busy with other tasks.

Managers plan because particular projects need to get done to achieve strategic goals. For example, the goal of improving the ability to move goods domestically in time of war led

U.S. President Eisenhower to establish the Interstate Highway system plan. Think about all the major innovations that have occurred in the scientific and commercial uses of familiar technology. They all relied on project planning to make the strategic goals become reality. For example, the Mercury, Gemini, and Apollo space programs each had scores of projects that needed to be completed to accomplish the goal of sending a human to the moon and returning safely to the earth.

Early in the 1970s, NASA engineers and managers proposed developing a reusable space transportation system that could be used for building a space station. The idea of the Space Shuttle was born. The Space Shuttle program became the organizing impetus for planning and completing scores of new projects. The idea behind a cellular telephone network was first developed by two engineers at Bell Labs in 1947. Project managers at Motorola and Bell Labs managing scores of projects over more than 25 years eventually put all the pieces together to publically demonstrate the system in 1973, but it would be another 5 years (and many more projects completed) before the systems were built for first commercial use.

These and all projects share a few common attributes familiar to project managers.[91] First, projects have a well-defined, specific, goal-oriented purpose that can be broken down into sets of specific work tasks. Second, projects are time-limited, meaning that once all the work tasks are complete and the goal is accomplished, the project is complete. We call this the **project life cycle**. This doesn't mean that managers work on just one project at a time. Busy managers will manage several related or unrelated projects and, in the process, manage the portfolio of projects, each of which is different in size, scope, and time.

Projects begin with the first phase, which involves developing the initial ideas of what needs to be done. For example, a plant manager decides it is a good idea to convert empty space into an area where workers can assemble a new product. This decision is instrumental in identifying the need. The manager will probably have discussions with supervisors who work in and around the space that is currently empty. Key people who are affected by the project need to be called for a meeting. Idle equipment and supplies stored in the empty space may have to be moved somewhere else. Electrical service may need to be added to the space so that assembly equipment and tools can be set up. This may require hiring a licensed electrical contractor to do the work. There will be a cost of purchasing equipment and tools and a cost for hiring new workers. All these considerations will be worked into a project budget.

During the second phase project managers create an overall plan, an implementation schedule, and a design for the assembly process. Building permits require approvals. Other types of projects may require managers to design and build prototypes or conduct studies of factors that drive costs and productivity.

Phase three involves obtaining the workers, materials, equipment, and support services to execute the plan according to schedule and budget. As unanticipated situations arise project managers must make adjustments. As new equipment is installed it is tested to make sure that it works according to the plan.

The final phase involves training personnel that work in the new assembly unit as well as those who support them. Managerial responsibility is delegated to appropriate supervisors. Ongoing resource allocations are established. Policies and procedures are put in place to promote routine functioning of the work unit.

Third, in most organizations, projects are part of a larger system of ongoing activities that help the organization as a whole achieve its objectives. This means that all projects, by nature, are interdependent with other projects or ongoing work. A fourth common attribute is that projects are unique, meaning that while there may be similarities in detail when comparing one project with another, every project has something that is slightly different from other projects. This means that the project manager must customize some or all of the project for a given situation.

A fifth attribute in common for projects is that because most projects occur in the context of other activities ongoing in an organization, projects must compete for time, money, and other needed resources. This competition for resources creates conflicts, which the project manager must manage. There are people inside and outside the project team that have an interest in particular projects because of the project requirements or because of the linkages that exist between them. This brings up a sixth common attribute: the reason why projects are used. Projects focus responsibility and authority for accomplishing tasks that are designed to achieve explicit goals. Without this focus, other things would get done but not the projects that lead to goal achievement.

Planning for and managing the completion of projects requires several important elements.[92] Managers in charge of projects must obtain adequate resources to get the job done. Most projects require personnel from more than one department or work team. These people often have other responsibilities. Project managers are motivated to get permission for the best performing employees to help on the project. This is good for the project manager, but it might pose a problem for the supervisor of the work team that depends on the high-performing employee on a day-to-day basis. This conflict requires a degree of political sensitivity and the ability to negotiate with other managers in the organization regarding project needs and how these fit into the larger picture of the organization.

With careful planning, managers can minimize but not entirely eliminate the effect of surprises. Early in the project life cycle, surprises often come in the form of barriers to access to key resources. Later in the life cycle, surprises can arise because it was impossible to anticipate what implementation would be like in every detail. Managers who have responsibilities for projects also may be required to make trade-offs among project goals, financial costs, time, and performance. For example, if the project involves remodeling the work space for an employee, the project manager might spend more money to get the remodeling done quickly. More desirable equipment initially might be more expensive but over time might offer the possibilities of saving money. If managerial responsibilities include multiple projects and ongoing operations, the manager may also have to make trade-offs between projects. For example, if remodeling a work space for an employee is high priority, then the manager may need to sacrifice improving the information system.

Project Planning Tools

Managers who plan and manage projects use a variety of practical tools. We will review some of these in this section.

SIMPLE WORK PLAN. One of the simplest tools available is the **work plan**, which simply lists the tasks, key resources needed, completion deadlines, and the persons responsible for task completion. See Exhibit 6-9.

SCHEDULING. Imagine what would happen if the manager of the customer service department didn't create a schedule for employees identifying which days and times during the week that each worker is expected to be at work. Productivity would alternate between having too many employees for the volume of activity or not having enough workers to support the customer service needs. Workers and customers would become frustrated. The department would find it extremely difficult to accomplish its purpose for the company. The manager will find it impossible to be responsible for the trust received from customers. To prevent this problem managers use schedules to time the application of people, resources, and activities important for carrying out the organization's goals. A **schedule** is simply a plan for performing work or specifying the expected sequence of activities. Such a plan is useful for specific projects as well as the ongoing operation of a department.

ACTION PLAN. Similar to a work plan, the action plan provides a little more detail that can be used in scheduling. See Exhibit 6-10 for an example.

WORK BREAKDOWN STRUCTURE. A larger project will have a more detailed work plan (sometimes called the work breakdown structure or WBS). Illustrating the breakdown of tasks in a WBS as they relate to the overall project goals is sometimes helpful. For example, a building project may have a WBS that looks like Exhibit 6-11.

Task	Person Responsible	Key Resources Needed	Completion Deadline
1.			
2.			
3.			

EXHIBIT 6-9
Sample Work Plan Template

EXHIBIT 6-10
Sample Action Plan

Tasks	Responsibility	Expected Duration	Precedence Step	Resources Needed
1. Develop new content for webpage			-	
1.a Decide on layout	Department Director	1 week	-	Team meeting
1.b Gather content	Office Manager	2 weeks	1.a	Team members' contributions
2. Create new webpage			-	
2.a Editing and Layout	Marketing Director	1 week	1.b	Webpage software
2.b Testing links	Office Manager	0.5 week	2.a	
2.c Upload live page	Marketing Director	0.5 week	2.b	Webpage software

EXHIBIT 6-11
Sample Work Breakdown Structure

1.0 Architecture and design
- 1.1 Establish goals and priorities
- 1.2 Define stakeholder needs
- 1.3 Establish size and scope
- 1.4 Decide on design and materials

2.0 Selection of contractor(s)
- 2.1 Bidding process
- 2.2 Selection of winning bid
- 2.3 Building permits obtained

3.0 Site preparation
- 3.1 Grading
- 3.2 Connections to city infrastructure

4.0 Construction
- 4.1 Foundations
- 4.2 Exterior
- 4.3 Interior
- 4.4 Finish work
- 4.5 Final inspections

5.0 Equipment installation and testing

6.0 Site clean-up

7.0 Landscaping
- 7.1 Design
- 7.2 Construction

8.0 Move in
- 8.1 Final walk through
- 8.2 List of final tasks
- 8.3 Inspection and approval to take occupancy
- 8.4 Move in

Moving to a new apartment	Week 1	Week 2	Week 3	Week 4	Week 5	Week 6
Select new apartment; sign contract	xxx	xxx				
Give notice to current landlord		xxx				
Pack and arrange for helpers to move			—	—	—	
Rent truck					—	
Move out of old apartment					—	
Move in and unpack						—
Return rental truck						—

Legend: (Showing some tasks complete and some incomplete)
— = Task planned
xxx =Task completed

EXHIBIT 6-12
Project Planning Bar Chart

Breaking down the work tasks like this provides an overall summary of the materials, personnel, and other organizations that make up the project. It shows many of the interrelationships among separate tasks. It also shows a rough idea of scheduling issues that need more details. The structure provides a natural way for project managers to give status reports to key stakeholders. When developing a WBS, it is natural to think about who has authority and responsibility for various decisions along the way. It also provides a structure for gathering information used in estimating costs and completion times.

PLANNING BAR CHART FOR SCHEDULING. Also known as a Gantt chart, the simple **bar chart** visually illustrates the sequential relationships between work tasks as well as the estimates for task completion times. Depending on the size and scope of the project being shown, the bar chart is divided into units of time (for example, days, weeks, or months). Task descriptions are used in the first column and then symbols are used to show the beginning and expected amount of time required for each task. Simple bar charts can be made using word processing or spreadsheet software. More detailed projects can be planned using project scheduling software. See Exhibit 6-12.

NETWORK TECHNIQUES. **Network techniques** take the basic information from the action plan and apply mathematical models to the data, which increases planning precision, important especially in complex projects. Complex projects require planning tools such as the Program Evaluation and Review Technique (PERT) and the Critical Path Method (CPM), which are more detailed than simple bar charts.[93] **PERT charts**, also called activity network diagrams or activity precedence diagrams, are commonly used in research and development situations while CPM activity network diagrams are used for construction projects. Exhibit 6-13 shows a

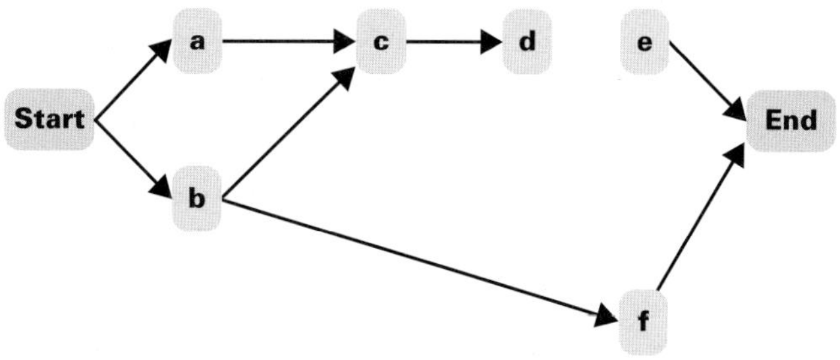

a = Purchase building materials
b = Hire workers
c = Dig foundation and pour concrete
d = Build the walls (frame and siding)
e = Put on the roof (frame and shingles)
f = Install landscaping (grass and trees)

EXHIBIT 6-13
Activity Precedence Diagram

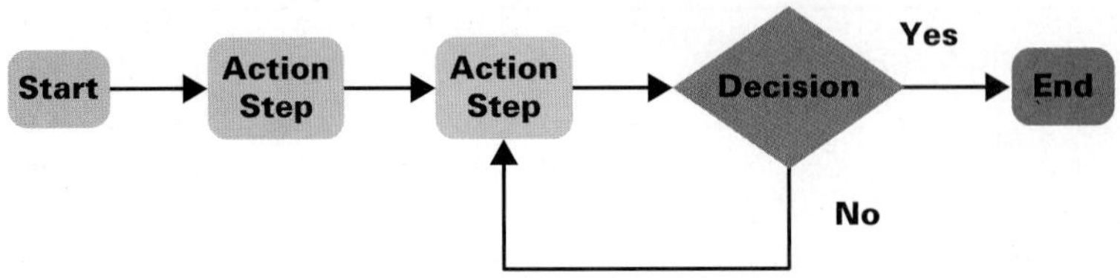

EXHIBIT 6-14
Process Flow Diagram

sample activity precedence diagram. The value of these systems is in lowering the risk of cost overruns. While simple versions of these charts can be created manually, several computer software applications are available to make the planning and management of complicated projects easier.

In the activity precedence diagram, each small box represents a work task. Arrows are connectors to the work tasks that show which tasks take precedence over (must be completed before) other tasks.

WORK (PROCESS) FLOW DIAGRAMS. Many projects involve the development of, or the ongoing management of, a process. **Process flow diagrams** are used to identify discrete steps in a process, as illustrated in Exhibit 6-14.

COMPUTER-AIDED PLANNING TOOLS.[94] The more complicated the project the more uncertain the project manager becomes regarding the completion times of various tasks. When hundreds or thousands of tasks are involved in a project, with each one depending on one or more other tasks being completed, the solution to managing this level of detail is to use sophisticated computer software. For example, planning software can mathematically determine the optimal solution to things like minimum waiting times, maximum completion times, linear programming problems to manage complicated processes, or the development of just-in-time inventory management systems.

BUDGETING. Without the resources, even the greatest of ideas will get nowhere. This is why every action plan carries with it one or more commitments for allocating resources. The wise manager will be interested in thinking about these allocations in advance and then monitoring the actual use of the resources as plans are implemented. The most common tool used for this managerial work is a budget. A **budget** is a quantitative description of the activities that are planned for the future. Budgets can be financial and long term in nature such as the **capital budget** where managers estimate the costs of selecting, purchasing, and installing new property, buildings, or major equipment that the company can use to pursue its purposes. In comparison, the **operating budget** describes the operating revenue and expenses expected to be incurred as the organization goes about its day-to-day activities. Budgets also can be measures of productivity where the amount of production, the number of worker hours spent, or other elements are tracked on a daily, weekly, monthly, quarterly, or annual basis.

When budgets are used as planning and monitoring tools, managers compare actual revenue and expenses to what is in the budget. A **budget variance** is any favorable or unfavorable difference between the expected, budgeted amount and the actual amount. Budget variances are often studied as a percentage of change from the budget amount and on a year-to-date basis. When budget variances occur, managers explore the reasons for variances to better understand the nature of the business and to improve their planning for the future.

MULTI-ATTRIBUTE UTILITY MODELS.[95] Many decisions that managers make involve the possibility of multiple consequences. There are many variables that can affect the outcomes of plans during implementation. An approach that managers use to address multiple consequences is called multi-attribute utility (MAU) models. A **multi-attribute utility model** is the attempt by decision makers to mathematically compare each decision alternative with known desirable attributes. It can also be used to conduct a "what if" analysis where decision makers make changes to the factors and check for the impact of such changes on the consequences. This is also known as sensitivity analysis.

MAU begins when someone identifies the problem and some of the alternatives available to solving the problem. Various factors that can affect outcomes are each given a mathematical weight (showing the relative importance or influence). Each factor is then scored based on its expected level of performance compared with other alternatives. For example, the production department in a small manufacturing firm wants to improve its production equipment. Each of the options requires a different mix of employees, inventory of materials, maintenance costs, and production cycle turnaround time (the time required to shut the machine off, change from one product to another, and then get the machine back up to full production again). Each of these and other factors will be given a mathematical weight and a performance score corresponding to the cost of production over a relevant range of time.

Such an approach requires managers to anticipate what work life will be like under each of the scenarios presented by the different machines. When a decision is made to purchase one machine, the planning has already begun for what needs to be done to prepare for using the machine when it is installed.

As this example shows, regardless of the type of planning tools used for projects or ongoing operations, they all involve managers making decisions. Let's explore this now.

Decision Making

Like planning, decision making is one of the most important functions of a manager. Decisions and their consequences naturally are both the beginning and the culmination of planning processes. Thus, the uncertainty in life that applies to planning also affects decision making.

At the moment you make an important complicated decision, you cannot know with 100 percent certainty whether the decision is good or bad. For example, when hiring a new employee, you cannot know for certain whether this person will perform as you hope. When you decide to purchase new equipment, you cannot know for certain whether the expected benefits will be realized. But as a manager you are expected to decide these and many other things regardless of this lack of certainty.

We might even say that the job of decision making is one of the most important reasons why owners of (or trustees of nonprofit) organizations hire managers. As long as organizations continue to exist, they will need decision makers to help focus and implement plans. This leads to one of the strange characteristics of organizations: the time spent on decision making is much less than the time spent living with and adjusting to the consequences of decisions.[96]

Managers will find many decisions at work to be relatively easy to make: whether to discuss with other employees the juicy details of why one employee was fired (no!), whether to reconcile the cash with the general ledger (yes!), or whether to obtain competitive bids on a price of new equipment that has been authorized (yes, if circumstances and policies allow it). These decisions often involve one-dimensional problems for which an efficient solution exists given the requirements and the constraints.

Other decisions are more difficult to make or have the potential to have a larger effect on the organization: whether to fire a particular employee, how to replace an employee who is let go, whether to purchase a new piece of equipment, what factors to address first that will likely have the most influence on improving cash flow and how to address them, and what strategic direction the organization should pursue. These decisions require judgment. Like it or not, for these judgment-based decisions there may be multiple right or wrong answers. You cannot approach these more difficult decisions using the same efficient technical solution approach. Here the manager's job is not to find the right solution to a technical problem. Instead, the bulk of the manager's work is focused on exploring the big questions that will guide a carefully thought-out choice.[97]

Decision Making: Rational and Nonrational

Like planning, decision making is a whole-brain cognitive activity. ***Whole brain*** refers to the complete collection of cognitive functions that involve all aspects of human awareness, information processing, perception, introspection, belief, volition, emotion, logical reasoning, language, imagery, memory, and judgment. How all these functions are combined in any given manager and for any particular decision depends on several factors including the following:

- the type of decision that is being made (routine or nonroutine, clear or ambiguous)
- the conditions of certainty or uncertainty
- the level of managerial responsibility in the organization
- the natural abilities and preferences of the decision maker (sometimes referred to as decision-making *style*)
- the time constraints
- human biases that affect our judgment
- widely shared cultural values that emphasize some decision-making styles over others

- moral values that define what is right and wrong
- emotional reaction to the problem and to the alternative solutions
- social influences such as our perception of what others will think of our decision
- organizational constraints such as policies, procedures, organizational structure, organizational systems, and processes.

The type of decision that is being made affects how we go about deciding. For the majority of routine task-oriented decisions in life, your brain allows you to make relatively effortless, automatic choices.[98] For example, you are at your desk when someone comes in to talk with you about a problem. To illustrate a point you want to make, you pull open the desk drawer and look for a pen. Glancing in the drawer you know instinctively which type of writing instrument to select based on what you are doing. You don't think much about it.

Some decisions appear on the surface to be only technical problems for which an efficient economic solution can be found. In reality, efficient, logical solutions cannot be achieved unless judgment, emotions, and values also are considered. For example, while we have several practical formulas to calculate the answers to financial questions, many financial decisions require judgment and values.[99]

For costly decisions, the decision maker typically needs time to work through a logical process, as shown in Exhibit 6-15: defining the problem, analyzing it, developing solutions, deciding on the best solution from among alternatives, and converting the decision into effective action.[100] But this logical, rational process assumes that the problem can be clearly defined, the best options can be known, information is available to evaluate alternatives, there are no time or cost constraints, and the outcomes from each of the alternatives can be measured. Such assumptions are often difficult to satisfy.

Humans are fully integrated whole beings and use all cognitive abilities. For example, our logical reasoning is combined with emotional responses. This doesn't mean that our emotional reaction is always consistent with our reasoning. Quite the opposite is sometimes the case. Humans often experience internal contradictions between what we want to do and what we believe we should do.[101] The point, however, is that we use our entire cognitive functioning when planning and making decisions. See Exhibit 6-16.

Decision-Making Styles

Our natural decision-making preferences, sometimes called *styles*, are another important factor.[102] People differ in their decision making along two dimensions: their way of thinking (logical–rational vs. intuitive–creative) and their tolerance for ambiguity or complexity (high or low). People also differ in terms of how many options they prefer to consider (one or many) and how much information they prefer to analyze (small amount vs. large amount). Likewise, some managers excel at the logical cognitive functions while others excel at introspection or imagery.[103]

EXHIBIT 6-15
Steps in the Rational Decision-Making Process

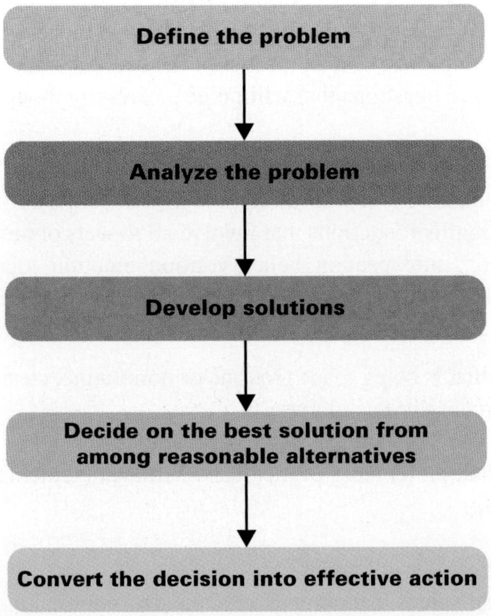

> Unless a person has a disease or injury that limits cognitive ability, generally speaking the human mind acts as a whole functioning unit. This means that no part of the brain lies dormant. The brain is a collection of interconnected neurological circuits. Multiple regions of the brain are used for all activities of life. The brain is capable of both serial and parallel information processing. It is capable of selective attention focusing on a few specialized details. Likewise, it is able to integrate all of the inputs available to it on a broad level.
>
> The mind does more than just process information. The mind develops meaning and judgment, which we use to adapt to our environment. A popular myth that has lasted for over a century is that humans use only about 10 percent of their brain's capacity every day. The reality is that we use our whole brain and its cognitive capacity every day.[104]

EXHIBIT 6-16

Assumptions Regarding Human Beings

Considering just the two variables of tolerance for ambiguity and preference for logic vs. intuition, we can see four different decision-making styles, as described in Exhibit 6-17.

These different profiles of decision-making styles are not meant to imply that if you have one dominant style then you don't have the others. Humans are amazingly adaptable. Even though we might prefer one style, we have the ability to use other styles depending on the circumstance we are in.

Each of these styles can come with trade-offs if the person is unwilling or unable to adjust his or her preferred style. For example, while **directive-style** decision makers are task-oriented, thorough, and objective, they can come across to others as being narrow-minded, controlling, overbearing, insensitive, or domineering. When working with someone with this style, be well organized and prepared. Be brief but be ready to answer questions with direct answers. Present your conclusions first.

EXHIBIT 6-17

Four Decision-Making Styles

	High Tolerance for Ambiguity	Low Tolerance for Ambiguity
Preference for Logical Reasoning (left-brain dominance)	**Analytical** • Desires more information because the best solution is valued. • Is unsatisfied by using just a few alternatives and a few key factors. • Careful in decision making. • Has the ability to adapt to new situations. • Enjoys problem solving through careful analysis.	**Directive** • Alternatives considered are limited in number. • Prefers less information over more. • The few key factors are identified and the decision is made quickly and efficiently. • Intuition may be used instead of logical reasoning. • The focus is on the short run. • Verbalizes the problems and solutions.
Preference for Intuition (right-brain dominance)	**Conceptual** • Has the ability to consider the big picture that has many alternatives. • Finds creative solutions to problems. • Achievement-oriented and future-oriented.	**Behavioral** • Focuses on how people will react to decisions. • Seeks to prevent or resolve conflict and disharmony. • Prefers face-to-face meetings. • Likes getting feedback from key stakeholders.

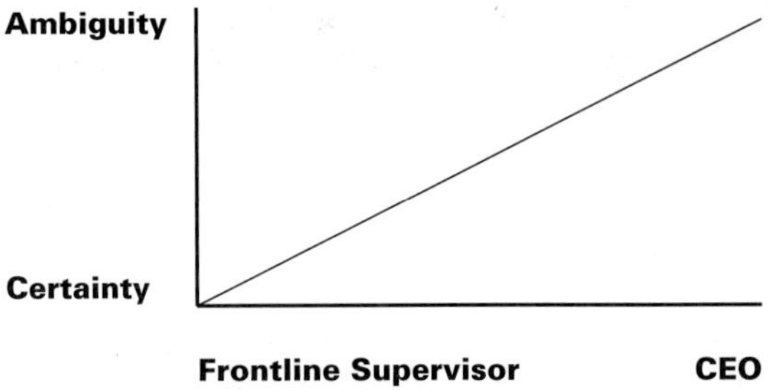

EXHIBIT 6-18
Decision-Making Conditions

Analytical-style decision makers are task-oriented, precise, and thorough in analysis before making a decision. They can come across to others as being stubborn, impractical, and indecisive. When working with an analytical-style person, be organized and prepared. Do thorough homework and provide documentation. This person may need time to think about what you are saying. Avoid making exaggerated claims or strong categorical statements.

Conceptual-style decision makers are oriented toward creative ideas that relate to the big picture. They are venturesome, enthusiastic, expressive, and future-oriented. But they can appear to others as being unrealistic, scattered, and impractical. The conceptual-thinking person may be more relational than the others. Help this person with big-picture thinking by positioning the issues in terms of the strategic issues the organization faces. Show how your ideas are creative. Expect that this type of thinker may expand the discussion beyond the main subject.

Behavioral-style decision makers are oriented toward people and relationships. They are empathetic and team-oriented. However, such a decision maker can be perceived as unbusinesslike, sentimental, and subjective. Help the behavioral-thinking person consider the effect of alternatives on people and relationships in the organization. When presenting your ideas, show that you have thought of how others will feel about it. If organizational harmony is at stake, show how implementation can maintain harmony.

Keep in mind that regardless of any differences in decision-making style, senior-level managers typically face decisions that are more ambiguous than those normally faced by middle managers. See Exhibit 6-18.

The Christian Mind on Decision Making

Daily life offers very few black and white decisions; oftentimes there is an unlimited amount of solutions. I have seen many managers hold the weight of the world on their shoulders, for some reason believing that workforce decisions do not require biblical review or prayer. As a manager, if you remember Proverbs 3:5–6, you will always have help with your decisions: "Trust in the Lord with all your heart; do not depend on your own understanding. Seek his will in all you do, and he will show you which path to take." The workforce will require faster and faster decision making to compete in a global market, and seeking his will could be your competitive advantage.

Dr. Jean Scheller-Sampson
Assistant Professor of Management
School of Business
McKendree University
Lebanon, IL

Intuition

When a problem is highly structured and well-known and the issues in the decision are clear, managers tend to use logical reasoning. Highly-structured problems are understood in terms of the current and the future state as well as the methods needed for a satisfactory solution. For example, you have to move an object from one room to another. The object is a heavy and bulky box. The solution is obvious based on the intuition of your experience: Moving the object will require the physical effort of two people to lift and carry it safely. But when the situation is complicated and stakeholders are likely to have a variety of opinions, managers tend to use insight and intuition. Others resort to acting quickly and then making decisions as their actions produce results.[105]

When uncertainty increases, time pressures mount, information is minimal, outcomes are unpredictable, and there is more than one right answer, managers resort to their instincts.[106] While logical reasoning is a conscious process, **intuition** is an automatic process of making holistic associations among all the details.

Intuition is fast. It is the ability to connect deep understanding of patterns and structures with emotional reactions to our judgments. Intuition is sometimes seen as a shortcut to making judgments about a complex situation. But using such a shortcut is not always advisable because speculation often leads to severe errors in judgment. Intuition works best in the following situations:[107]

- when problems that require judgment are complex
- when problems are less structured
- when a relatively short time is available to make the decision
- when the environment is rapidly changing
- when the decision maker has extensive experience in a particular relevant domain of knowledge (as much as 10 years of intense practice is often required to gain the level of expertise needed for intuition to be effective)

As a first-time supervisor, your brain has the same raw ability to intuitively process information as that of an experienced executive. However, the less experience you have in a particular business or industry, the more likely your intuition will be unreliable. Senior leaders have the advantage of years of experience guiding their intuitions in solving complex problems that affect the entire organization. This is not to say that inexperienced managers have nothing to contribute. Creative ideas can and do come from inexperienced managers who see problems in a new perspective.

Does this mean that as a middle manager you shouldn't contribute to discussions about the larger, more complicated problems of the organization? If you want to become more useful to an organization, then absolutely not! Three elements are needed to develop intuition: practice over a long time period, repetition, and specific feedback. Test your intuitions with more experienced managers and learn from their feedback to improve your ideas.

Social Influences on Decision Making

Decision making does not occur in a social vacuum. Like many other dimensions of management, it is communal by nature.[108] Not surprisingly, social influences are at work during the judgment, decision-making, and implementation processes.[109]

For example, research shows that judgment can be either enhanced or impaired when people believe they are being evaluated—regardless of whether the evaluators are present. Even when working alone, decision makers shape their behaviors in anticipation of how others will evaluate them. For complicated tasks, knowing that someone is looking over your shoulder can impair your decision making. For simple tasks, decision making is enhanced when you know others are evaluating your work.

Another example of the social influences on decision making is **social loafing**. As the size of a work group increases, responsibility for the outcomes of the group's decisions becomes diffused. This allows some members of the group to make decisions that decrease their commitment and the amount of work they perform.

Social influences can encourage or discourage employees to do what they know is right. Individuals and groups can pressure employees to compromise moral principles. Or they can provide support for standing true to your beliefs.

Other Problems and Challenges in Managerial Judgment

Many of the problems in managerial judgment occur in everyone regardless of their experience. For example, when attempting to predict the future, managers will tend to take shortcuts because they do not have perfect knowledge. This is called **heuristics**. We sometimes refer to this as using a "rule of thumb" or a simple guideline based on someone's experience. The problem is that an inexperienced person who attempts to take a shortcut to decision making will likely experience errors. For example, a manager might say to the workers, we need to produce about 10 cases per day. In actuality the rule of thumb for 10 cases per day may have been profitable 3 years ago but is not now. Business circumstances change such as when the cost of components increases or decreases or the fixed costs of the organization change. Let's review some of the other problems that bias judgment.

POSITIVE ILLUSIONS. When comparing themselves with others, people tend to perceive themselves as better than others on desirable attributes. This unrealistic **positive illusions** of self can bias them in their judgment. Such an optimistic bias leads people to believe that their future will be more positive than the experiences of others. For example, it is quite possible that some readers of this section are saying to themselves, "Other people will have problems in their decision making and judgment, but I tend to have fewer biases and illusions when making decisions." Another illusion is the belief that one can control a situation even though most, if not all, of the elements cannot be controlled.[110]

UNWARRANTED OPTIMISM. Related to positive illusions, **hubris** is excessive optimism when making decisions even though the evidence on which the decision is made doesn't warrant it.

SELF-SERVING BIASES. **Self-serving bias** is the tendency for people to accept a disproportionate amount of credit for success while taking too little responsibility for failures and, instead, blaming failure on external factors.

ESCALATION OF COMMITMENT.[111] Consider a manager who is authorized to purchase a $75,000 machine that holds promises of increasing efficiency. Eighteen months into the operation with the new machine, the increases of productivity have not been realized. The manager rationalizes this by saying that the software that came with the machine wasn't designed for the department's particular setup, but if time is allowed to get the software bugs corrected, the desired level of productivity will surely be achieved. **Escalation of commitment** is really a form of self-justification: Attitudes about the current situation are biased in a positive direction so that their previous actions are justified. Actions that support these attitudes usually result in allocation of additional resources such as money, personnel, or time in the hope of attaining a goal that heretofore was unattainable.

RISK-SEEKING VS. RISK-AVOIDANCE. Generally, managers tend to avoid risks. But whether the manager wants to avoid a loss or wants to achieve a gain can make the difference in how much the manager tends to avoid risk. Managers who want to avoid loss may take greater risks than when they want to achieve gains. For example, once a capital equipment investment decision has been made, the managers responsible for the performance of the capital may experience the tendency to hold onto underperforming capital equipment longer than they should, hoping that the performance will turn around.

EASE OF RECALL BIAS.[112] When an individual more easily recalls an event, it will seem to the person that this event occurs more frequently when, in fact, it might not. For example, a manager conducting the annual performance evaluation searches his memory for examples of specific behaviors. What he can recall from memory will appear to be more frequent behavior than other behaviors. Also, events that occurred recently, say in just the last few months, will be given more weight.

Benefits and Problems Peculiar to Group Decisions

Rarely will a manager plan or make decisions apart from the involvement of other employees. Including a group of employees in planning has the potential to generate more ideas. More than one perspective can be applied to solving problems.

The characteristics of the group can have a big influence on the planning processes and the outcomes of the decisions. For example, large groups bring more information from divergent points of view. This can slow down decision making. The size of the group can also make communication more difficult because one individual may interpret what is heard differently from other individuals. The cohesiveness of a group can affect group decisions. The more cohesive, the more likely the group will come to agreement. But cohesiveness can also minimize critical thinking. Diversity among group members means more points of view, which can increase creativity. But diversity can also be a barrier to communication.

GROUPTHINK.[113] A well-known example of the social pressures that affect decision making is *groupthink*. Recall from Chapter 5 that groupthink is the development of norms that push group members toward seeking agreement at the expense of realistic evaluation of alternatives. Such conformity impairs judgment and serves to stop group members from speaking up on important issues. The more cohesive a work group becomes, the more it is at risk for groupthink. Members of groups that develop such strong conformity come to share the illusion that the group is not vulnerable to being overly optimistic. Another illusion that develops is that because dissent is drummed out, silence is taken as a signal of support. This can lead the group to take unfavorable risks. Group members tend to discount or outright ignore warnings and apply direct pressure on others in the group who express concerns. Groupthink often leads to lowering moral standards to accommodate concurrence.

DECISION MAKING AS A CONTEST FOR SUPREMACY.[114] Two broad approaches are used in group decision making: inquiry and advocacy. Inquiry focuses on discovering the issues and assumptions that group members hold on a particular decision. Group members see their role as critical thinking inquirers looking for the best ideas. The focus is on discovery of a good workable solution through exploration. The goal is not to persuade the group to accept a particular point of view but rather to agree on the best course of action based on the issues. Inquiry encourages dissent and debate as long as such debate does not become personal. Inquiry assumes that the best solutions emerge from testing ideas. Group members come to own the solution that they have agreed on based on the best ideas, and their commitment to implementation is enhanced.

In contrast, the advocacy approach is a contest for personal supremacy. Group members see their role as advocates persuading others to agree with their position. Instead of debating ideas, assumptions, and issues, group members use persuasion and lobbying skills to influence each other. The advocacy approach assumes that the best solution comes from the test of strength of persuasion skills among competing positions. The debates usually degenerate into conflict that becomes personal. Group members lash out at other group members with personal criticisms to defend themselves or their positions. Advocacy usually ends with some people winning and others losing. Group members' commitment to implementation is then undermined.

The Biblical Story of David

Read the story of David found in 1 Samuel 8–31, 2 Samuel 5–24, and Psalm 51 in the Bible. Based on his experience, grasp the significance of the accomplishments that occurred under the leadership of David. Make a mental note of David's leadership strengths and weaknesses in terms of planning and decision making. What leadership principles can we gain from his experience that are applicable today?

Planning and Decision Making in Nonprofits

For-profit organizations and nonprofit organizations (NPOs) share many similarities in decision-making processes.[115] One area of similarity is that in both for-profits and nonprofits, top-level leaders spend very little time in actual decision making. Most of their time is spent in meetings trying to get information or facilitate discussion of issues.

Nonprofits do differ from for-profits, though, in some areas of decision-making processes. A large difference is that decision making can be particularly slow in nonprofits. One reason for this is that a nonprofit typically has more stakeholders whose interests it must consider. This means that decision making requires more consensus building, which usually requires more time. A second reason is that nonprofits tend to watch over and debate the significance of the historical and ideological roots that define their purpose. Third, nonprofits have multiple, and sometimes competing, goals they are trying to achieve. Fourth, some of their goals are ambiguous and can be interpreted in many ways, any one of which is just as valid as the other interpretations. Fifth, nonprofits rely on stakeholders to make significant commitments to share goals that

Suggestions that will help make your decision making more effective:

- Listen to the key stakeholders. If some of the key people are not talking about a proposed idea, ask them for their suggestions.
- Create transparency by facilitating conversations among those who have opposing points of view.
- Watch out for the interests of the historical values of the organization. Where historical values come into conflict, dialogue with organizational members is vital.
- Discuss the issues in terms of the organization's mission.
- Some members will get frustrated at the time spent in meetings. Reassure organizational members that time spent in discussion is important for the sake of the organization and its mission.

EXHIBIT 6-19
Decision Making in Nonprofit Organizations

stem from mission. But because mission can be interpreted in many ways in a nonprofit, it takes time to develop unified goal sharing. Sixth, because most nonprofits do not face the same economic pressures to build wealth for shareholders, they do not need to react as quickly to marketplace opportunities as for-profit organizations.

Consider also that the mission of the nonprofit is primarily not economic. This makes deciding how to measure success more difficult than in a for-profit. Some types of nonprofits (such as hospitals) are just as concerned about generating retained earnings as are for-profit firms. But most nonprofits are concerned with breaking even. While profit is not a measuring stick for success in nonprofits, prosperity is vital to the continued pursuit of their mission. And, because the bottom line is not as prominent, nonprofits tend to think that every activity they operate is good.

Motivating organizational members, many of whom may be volunteers, to support decisions is vital for success. One challenge in volunteer organizations is that volunteers have other things going on in their lives. The activities of the nonprofit organization represent just one small segment of their life. Contributions by many organizational members are on a part-time basis.

Goal conflicts and differing interpretations of the organization's mission make decision making more of a political process in nonprofits than we typically find in the for-profit world. See Exhibit 6-19.

Paradoxes of Planning and Decision Making

Many of the tensions highlighted in this book are, by nature, a part of the managerial function of planning and decision making. Many of the decisions and plans that a manager makes are attempts to deal with paradoxical tensions. In this chapter, we focus on just a few of the tensions that are central to your work in planning and decision making.

SPEED—THOROUGHNESS.[116] We are not the only ones in history who believe that the pace of managerial life is faster now than in the past.[117] Arguably, electronic communication has accelerated our life and managerial productivity. Managers are increasingly expected to be faster in their planning and decision making. Yet they also are expected to be thorough, which requires time. So full are some managers' schedules that they have less and less time for planning and decision making and must allocate part of their daily routine for important decisions. The demands of the present tend to crowd out the time needed to engage in short-term and the long-term thinking, which brings us to the next tension point.

LONG TERM—SHORT TERM.[118] Like no one else, organizational leaders must at the same time honor the difference between short-term needs and long-term needs and yet respect that both time frames are intertwined and inseparable. So fundamental is this tension point that Peter Drucker said this tension is "ever-present in every management problem, every decision, every action."[119] One danger is in solving an immediate management problem not realizing or not caring that the solution will likely sacrifice long-range success. The opposite danger is in focusing so much on the long-term, grandiose scheme that the decision about the present becomes irresponsible.

1. Left to themselves, the day-to-day operational concerns of an organization will drive out the strategic concerns. This is an example of what has been called Gresham's Law.
2. The present is vivid and understandable. The future is vague and ambiguous. People are prone to be more concerned about what is happening to them in the present because this is what they are experiencing.
3. The speed of change in the business world has increased the importance of the short term.
4. Investment managers are fascinated with quarterly earnings.
5. Some top-level leaders act in self-interest out of concern for their reputations.
6. Stocks are usually held for relatively short periods of time and then sold. Many stockholders attempt to gain by selling stock rather than by holding stock for their dividends.
7. Executive compensation packages emphasize short-term achievements. Executives typically have relatively short tenures. This further emphasizes what they can accomplish in the short term.
8. Many in business have an optimistic belief that if we take care of today, tomorrow will take care of itself.
9. Using accounting profits (instead of economic profits) to calculate incentive bonuses tends to emphasize the short-term performance.
10. Managers can be punished (demoted or fired) for mistakes made in the short term. Rarely, if ever, will they be punished for mistakes that cost the company in the long run.
11. Managers with a high need for achievement want quick feedback indicating that they are being effective.
12. Some managers have a weak ability to defer gratification.

EXHIBIT 6-20
Why the Short-Term Planning Horizon Dominates Decision Making[120]

Managers at all levels face this tension. More than anyone else, a top-level leader is responsible for directing the whole organization so that it can achieve tomorrow's results.

In American culture, the short-term focus dominates the experience of organizational leaders.[121] Exhibit 6-20 offers several factors that contribute to this focus.

Focus on an Organization

Christians in Commerce

Christians in Commerce is a cross-denominational organization that attempts to encourage Christians to live a Christ-like life in their workplaces. The mission of the organization is:

"We encourage and equip Christians to live the life of Christ by releasing the power of the Holy Spirit that is in them. We challenge them to be Christ to the people and circumstances in their workplaces by bringing his truth, healing, justice and excellence to the marketplace. We fulfill this mission by:

- Proclaiming with clarity the call to be filled with the Holy Spirit and live as Christ
- Partnering with churches, organizations and individuals committed to bringing about the kingdom of God
- Forming and supporting groups of businesspeople to transform their areas of influence."

More information about Christians in Commerce can be found at the organization's website: http://www.christiansincommerce.org/.

Chapter Summary

1. Because decision making and planning are done in service to God, these are essentially spiritual activities in the context of a larger setting of the community and God's will. Planners and decision makers take responsibility on behalf of others. Trust and trustworthiness are at the heart of decision making. Humans have limited knowledge of an uncertain future, yet managers are expected to make decisions and take actions in the short run to minimize the risk of unfavorable events from occurring. When careful, deliberate planning is added with diligent work and listening to wise counsel, it leads to economic success. When people act in haste without adequate planning, they can lose economically. We see a range of participation by subordinates in decision making in the Bible.
2. The Bible contains some examples of individuals who were more pessimistic than they should have been. We also see several examples of individuals who exhibited unwarranted optimism with respect to decisions they made.
3. Knowing what we should do and knowing what we want to do is a challenge for humans. Paul the Apostle said that which he naturally and selfishly wants to do comes from the desires of his body. The only way out of this impossible situation is by living in a relationship with Jesus Christ.
4. A plan is an expression of the actions you intend to take and the objective you hope to accomplish in the future. Planning helps us to bring order to complicated, chaotic situations. Planning helps focuses our energies to accomplish goals. The more employees plan, the more responsibility those employees take for getting their work done. Effective planning involves the consideration of several elements: mission, vision, values, strategic long-term goals, and specific short-term objectives.
5. Management by objectives (MBO) is an approach to planning that involves both supervisor and subordinate. MBO is a planning process that involves the following steps: setting objectives, developing action plans, monitoring results, and making adjustments. Some have criticized on ethical grounds how the MBO approach has been used.
6. Projects are part of a larger system of ongoing activities that help the organization as a whole achieve its objectives. A variety of project planning tools exist for managers including work plan, scheduling, action plan, work breakdown structure, planning bar chart, network techniques, activity precedence diagrams, work flow diagrams, computer-aided planning tools, budgets, and multi-attribute utility modeling.
7. The job of decision making is one of the most important reasons why owners of (or trustees of nonprofit) organizations hire managers. Decision making is a whole-brain cognitive activity which involves the complete collection of cognitive functions that involve all aspects of human awareness, information processing, perception, introspection, belief, volition, emotion, logical reasoning, language, imagery, memory, and judgment. How all these functions are combined in any given manager and for any particular decision depends on several factors.
8. Persons exhibit different decision-making styles based on their brain's natural preferences for logical reasoning and the person's tolerance for ambiguity: These styles are categorized as analytical, conceptual, directive, and behavioral.
9. Intuition is an automatic process of making holistic associations among all the details. Intuition is fast. It is the ability to connect deep understanding of patterns and structures with emotional reactions to our judgments. Intuition works better in some situations than in others.
10. Decision making does not occur in a social vacuum. Like many other dimensions of management, it is communal by nature. Social influences are at work during the judgment, decision-making, and implementation processes.
11. Decision making is not easy. It is associated with several problems including positive illusions, unwarranted optimism (hubris), ease of recall bias, escalation of commitment, self-serving bias, risk-seeking, and risk avoidance. When decisions are made in the context of groups additional problems can be encountered such as groupthink and decision making as a contest for supremacy.
12. Decision making in a nonprofit organization is typically different from that in the for-profit organization. Some of the differences for this include speed of decision making, consideration of the historical and ideological roots that define their purpose, multiple and sometimes competing goals, and ambiguous goals.
13. Many of the decisions and plans that a manager makes are attempts to deal with paradoxical tensions.

Key Terms

Discussion Questions

1. What important management perspective can we learn from the story in Luke 14:28–33?
2. Is it always a problem that organizational leaders focus on the short term?
3. What do you think is the remedy for this chronic short-term focus?
4. For the Christian, is the short-term focus encouraged or discouraged by the popular belief that ultimately God is in control and we should leave our worries with him? (See Matthew 6:25–31; Luke 12:24–27)
5. How do the three dimensions of planning a project—cost, time, and performance—interact?
6. You have been asked by your boss to manage the development of a new after-sale service for an automobile dealer. What are the various roles that need to be filled on your planning team?
7. Why is much of the planning that a manager completes focused on projects?
8. What types of questions can a project manager ask to determine the priority of an assigned project?
9. How can the Christian manager avoid decision-making hubris while at the same time be an encouragement to the stakeholders who must be relied on to vigorously support the decision?
10. If intuitive decision making is based on your history of decisions made with logical reasoning, in what way can it be said that intuition is *non*rational?
11. Can you think of a situation where awareness of your religious values would not be part of the cognitive functions used in decision making?
12. Is it possible that humans were created by God with the natural abilities of the mind wherein we must work through decisions about what we believe we should do when we feel like we want to do something else? In other words, is it an oversimplification to attribute cognitive-emotional inconsistencies to sin?
13. Because the behavioral-style decision maker considers the effect of decisions on people, is this style closer to a Biblical standard for decision making than the other styles?
14. If the Christian manager stays close to God's will as revealed in the Bible, will that manager be less susceptible to errors of bias in judgment?
15. What adaptive decision making activities might characterize the Christian manager?
16. Is hubris really just sinful pride called by another name, or is this part of the God-created phenomenon of human existence?
17. In terms of God's Providence in the world of business, how would you interpret the following verses of Scripture? 1 Samuel 6:9; 2 Samuel 1:6; Ecclesiastes 9:11; Luke 10:31.

STUDENT EXERCISES

1. Using an Internet search engine, survey the types and costs of project planning software that is available for different types of situations or industries.
2. Interview one of the leaders of the Student Association regarding the types of projects she is planning or managing. For example, find out what projects are underway, what new projects are being planned, who is involved in planning, and what planning tools, if any, are being used.
3. Interview the Director of Plant Services (Construction). Discuss the project planning tools and processes he uses.
4. Read the story of King Ahasuerus and his Queen Vashti in the book of Esther chapter 1. What were the options available to the king in response to the queen's refusal to attend his party? Did Vashti have the right to refuse the King because she was hosting her own party? How did the king's decision-making process help him? Is this a valid biblical example of how a leader should manage decision making when political risks are involved?
5. Find a current article in the *Wall Street Journal* that discusses major changes taking place in a corporation. From the details of the story:
   a. Make a list of the key decisions that need to be made
   b. Make a list of the projects that need to be assigned
6. Interview your campus chaplain to find out what new ministry programs are being planned. Who is involved with planning? What planning resources do they use?
7. Get involved with a student club or organization and take the responsibilities for managing at least one project from start to finish. Pay attention to the planning and decision-making activities during your work.

IN-CLASS EXERCISES

Issue Debates/Discussions

Divide the class into small groups of five to six people each. Hand out a sheet of paper containing the following quotations. Assign one half of the groups to develop a rationale why the first quotation is valid and the other half to develop a rationale for why the second quotation is valid. Give the groups 5 minutes to discuss. Then call for groups to give a summary of the rationale they developed. Discussion can follow.

Discussion Topic #1: How is the Christian to make decisions?

A. **Foundation of faith and a Christian worldview plus reason.** Proverbs 3:5–6 and Psalm 25:12 "are not to be read as pleas for, or promises of, additional revelatory guidance in the struggle of life. Rather, the writers bare their souls as wise teachers, dependent upon the character and instruction of God. Terms such as show, teach, guide, direct, seek, and instruct do not imply an immediate revelatory process of guidance. Rather, they are terms of exhortation within contexts that offer wisdom for life by moral and godly value development based on what God has already revealed."[122] Instead of waiting for special guidance that comes from personal revelation, believers should study the Bible because God's will is revealed there. Bible study will help the believer develop a Christian worldview based on biblical theology. This worldview will be the guide to values, which are vital when making decisions in which we do not have complete knowledge.

B. **Dependence on God for special guidance.** God's will is a private matter between God and us as individuals. If we have a close relationship with Jesus, and if we commit ourselves in faith to God, then the Holy Spirit will reveal his will for us to follow. The biblical record is clear: "Trust in the LORD with all your heart, And do not lean on your own understanding. In all your ways acknowledge Him, And He will make your paths straight." "Who is the man who fears the LORD? He will instruct him in the way he should choose."[123]

Discussion Topic #2: How important is short-term thinking?

A. **Short-term thinking is *overrated*.** Short-term thinking emphasizes short-term results that inevitably sacrifice the long-term effectiveness of the organization. Short-term thinking can divert decision makers from the overall goals of the firm. Excessive short-term thinking will undermine moral constraints. We should ask ourselves: What is the price we, as managers, are willing to pay by focusing so much on the short term that we do not give more influence to the long-range issues? It's the long term that needs more attention.

B. **Short-term thinking is *underrated*.** Managers have only a vague idea of what will come in the long-term future. Today's long-term vision of the firm will be different 6 or 9 months from now. Humans are limited in their ability to predict the future with any comfortable degree of confidence. Meanwhile managers have an organization to run—today. In reality, managers cannot completely ignore the long-range direction of their organization or of their industry. It is impossible for effective managers to make short-term decisions except in the context of their perception of the long-range issues and influences.

Discussion Topic #3: In terms of a Christian worldview, should so-called *positive illusions* be considered wrong and therefore be corrected?

A. **Positive illusions are negative and should be corrected.** Positive illusions are dangerous and can get you fired. Illusion simply postpones the inevitable task of dealing with the emotional effect of life's difficulties. What we need are people who are realistic. God's plan for humans is that they seek to find the truth about situations they are in. It is only in finding and dealing with the truth of a situation that the person can fully express the image of God. Living continually in a life of illusion is sinful because it focuses on the self at the expense of others and of reality. Illusions give short-term benefits but at the cost of long-term success.[124]

B. **Positive illusions are positive and should be left alone.**[125] The upside of positive illusions is that they tend to increase personal commitment for accomplishing tasks. Positive illusions contribute to psychological well-being. They help us persist when the going gets rough. They help leaders keep a hopeful vision in front of followers. When things are outside of our control, positive illusions help us cope. God created our minds with the ability to see the positive side of things.

Endnotes

1. Rogers Jr., F. (1997). Discernment. In Bass, D. C. (Ed.). *Practicing our faith: A way of life for a searching people.* San Francisco, CA: Jossey-Bass. p. 107.
2. Webber, R. A. (1972). *Time and management.* New York: Van Nostrand Reinhold Company. p. 126.
3. McCabe, C. (2005). Facing disaster: How we responded. *Oxfam Exchange.* Boston, MA: Oxfam America. Spring/Summer. pp. 6–10.
4. Cleland, D. I., & Ireland, L. R. (2007). *Project management: Strategic design and implementation.* (5th ed.). New York: McGraw-Hill. pp. 75–82.
5. Garvin, D. A., & Roberto, M. A. (2001). What you don't know about making decisions. *Harvard Business Review.* 79(8), 108–116; Kreitner, R. (2001). *Management.* (8th ed.). Boston, MA: Houghton Mifflin Company. p. 166; Brousseau, K. R., Driver, M. J., Hourihan, G., & Larsson, R.

(2006). The seasoned executive's decision-making style. *Harvard Business Review*. 84(2), 111. See also Drucker, P. F. (1954). *The practice of management*. New York: Harper & Row, Publishers. pp. 351–369.
6. For examples see Deuteronomy 7:6–7, 10:15, 12:5–26, 14:2, 16:2–16; Joshua 9:27; 1 Samuel 10:24, 16:8–10; 1 Kings 11:13–36; 1 Chronicles 28:4–10; John 13:18; Acts 1:2, 1:24, 9:15, 10:41; 1 Corinthians 1:28; Colossians 3:12; 2 Thessalonians 2:13; Titus 1:1; 1 Peter 2:9.
7. See Isaiah 50:7; Luke 9:51–53. See also comments on Jesus as a planner in Briner, B. (1996). *The management methods of Jesus: Ancient wisdom for modern business*. Nashville, TN: Thomas Nelson, Inc. pp. 1–4.
8. Chewning, R. C., Eby, J. W., & Roels, S. J. (1990). *Business through the eyes of faith*. San Francisco, CA: HarperSanFrancisco. p. 120. See also Genesis 41; Daniel 2; Jonah 3:10; Luke 7:30.
9. Dose, J. (2006). *Proverbs: Ancient wisdom for contemporary organizations*. Paper presented at the Christian Business Faculty Association annual conference. Dayton, OH. October.
10. In many languages there are two distinct terms that are used for planning depending on the purpose of the planning. If the plan is positive, one word is used. If the plan is to be harmful, another word is used. For example, in English the word *plan* is often used if the purpose is positive while the word *plot* is used when the purpose is negative. Also, a person *prepares* to accomplish a positive purpose but *schemes* to accomplish a harmful purpose.
11. Bible verses typically offered in support of the immanence of God include Genesis 26:3, 28:15, 39:2–3, 39:21; Exodus 3:2, 13:21–22, 19:4, 25:8, 33:9–10; Numbers 12:5, 14:14; Deuteronomy 4:5–7, 31:6, 31:15; Joshua 1:5, 3:7; 1 Kings 8:10–11; Psalm 27:14, 73:28, 119:151, 139:7–12; Isaiah 12:6, 40:28–31, 41:10, 43:5; Jeremiah 1:8; Ezekiel 43:7; Zephaniah 3:15–17; Haggai 1:13, 2:4; Zechariah 2:10; Matthew 28:20; Luke 17:20–21; John 1:14, 15:4; Acts 17:26–28; Romans 8:10; 1 Corinthians 2:1; 2 Corinthians 6:16, 13:5; Galatians 2:20; Ephesians 4:6; Colossians 1:17; Hebrews 1:3, 4:16, 10:22, 13:5; James 4:5, 4:8; Revelation 3:20, 21:3.
12. Psalm 145:18; Isaiah 30:18, 55:6–7; Matthew 7:7; Luke 11:9.
13. Bible verses typically offered in support of the transcendence of God include 1 Kings 8:27; 2 Chronicles 2:6; Job 11:7–9, 36:26, 37:23; Psalm 13:1, 42, 44:9, 90:2–4, 139:6, 145:3–5; Isaiah 40:13, 40:18, 57:15, 66:1; John 4:24; Acts 17:24; Romans 11:33; 1 Corinthians 2:6–16; 1 Timothy 6:16. On this theological paradox see also Barth, K. (1957). *Church dogmatics. Volume 2*. Edinburgh: T & T Clark, Ltd. pp. 313–314.
14. Job; Psalm 52:7; Proverbs 11:28, 23:5, 27:1, 27:23–26; Ecclesiastes 5:13–14, 6:12, 8:7, 9:11–12, 10:14, 11:1–6; Jeremiah 9:23–24, 17:8–9; Matthew 6:32–34, 24:42–50; Philippians 4:6–7; 1 Timothy 6:17; 1 Peter 5:7; James 4:13–16.
15. Meadors, G. T. (2003). *Decision making God's way: A new model for knowing God's will*. Grand Rapids, MI: Baker Books. pp. 32–33. Several Bible passages refer to the omniscience of God: Psalm 33:13, 139:1–4, 147:4–5; Proverbs 5:21; Isaiah 46:10; Matthew 10:29–30; John 21:17; Acts 15:18; 1 John 3:19–20; Hebrews 4:13.
16. Genesis 24:12–15, 37; Exodus 3, 28:30; Leviticus 16:8; Numbers 22:28–30, 26:55, 27:18–21; Joshua 13–21; Judges 6:15–22, 6:36–40, 7:13–15, 8:25–27; 1 Samuel 14:8; Proverbs 16:33, 18:18; Daniel 7; Acts 8:26–40, 9:3–4, 9:10–16, 10:5, 10:17–20, 12:7–8, 16:6–10, 18:9–10, 22:17–21, 21:10–11, 23:11.
17. Friesen, G., & Maxon, J. R. (1980). *Decision making & the will of God*. Portland, OR: Multnomah Press. pp. 90–92; Meadors, G. T. (2003). *Decision making God's way: A new model for knowing God's will*. Grand Rapids, MI: Baker Books. pp. 77–150. See examples: 1 Kings 3:28; Acts 6:2–4, 15:22–29, 15:36, 20:16; Romans 1:10–13; 1 Corinthians 6:1–6, 16:3–9; 2 Corinthians 1:15–2:4, 2:12–13; 1 Thessalonians 3:1–2; Philippians 2:25–26, 4:10, 4:14; Colossians 4:5.
18. Matthew 25:1–13.
19. Genesis 11:6; Proverbs 1:17, 14:8, 14:15, 16:3, 24:3–4, 24:27; Acts 27:42; Hebrews 4:12.
20. See for example 2 Kings 6:8; 1 Chronicles 13:1; 2 Chronicles 10:6, 20:21, 30:2, 32:3; Nehemiah 6:7; Proverbs 12:15, 13:10, 14:12, 15:22, 16:2, 16:25, 19:2, 21:2. See also Chewning, R. C., Eby, J. W., & Roels, S. J. (1990). *Business through the eyes of faith*. San Francisco, CA: HarperSanFrancisco. p. 123.
21. Chewning, R. C., Eby, J. W., & Roels, S. J. (1990). *Business through the eyes of faith*. San Francisco, CA: HarperSanFrancisco. p. 122. See also 1 Chronicles 29:18; Proverbs 16:9.
22. Proverbs 1:24–33; Romans 1:13. In the Bible the term plan and the term counsel are sometimes used interchangeably. Psalm 20:4; Proverbs 1:24–33, 16:3, 19:21; Isaiah 14:24; Matthew 6:25–34; Romans 8:28.
23. And in one passage the Bible suggests a time when planning is unimportant: Ecclesiastes 9:10. The implication of this passage is that humans should work with all their might and planning is an important part of achieving this. However, a person does not plan after he or she dies.
24. Proverbs 14:15–17, 21:5, 22:3, 31:11–16.
25. Nehemiah 2:6.
26. Luke 14:28–31.
27. Genesis 41–47; Numbers 13, 22; Joshua 2; 1 Samuel 4, 25; 1 Kings 1, 21; 2 Kings 21–23; Esther 4–8; Job 1; Daniel 1; Jonah; Matthew 26, 27; Acts 6, 9.
28. Clark, D. R. (2003). Bricks, sweat and tears: The human investment in constructing a "four-room" house. *Near Eastern Archaeology*. 66(1–2), 34–43.
29. Genesis 16, 30, 37:18–28; Exodus 18; Joshua 2; 5–8; 1 Samuel 20; Esther 2:22; Psalm 38:12; Matthew 12:14, 22:15, 26, 27:1; Mark 3:6; Luke 10; John 11:53, 12:10; Acts 9:24, 20:3, 23:21, 23:30, 27:42; 1 Timothy 4:13.
30. Genesis 6; Nehemiah 1–2; 1 Kings 18.
31. 1 Samuel 9.
32. Genesis 25:31–34.
33. Matthew 26:50–53.
34. Matthew 14:1–11.
35. Judges 16.
36. 1 Samuel 17.
37. Genesis 44:5; Leviticus 16:8, 19:31; Joshua 18:6–10; 1 Samuel 14:42, 28; 2 Kings 17:16–17, 23:4–5; 1 Chronicles 24:31, 25:8, 26:14; Nehemiah 10:34, 11:1; Psalm 22:18; Isaiah 8:19–20; Jeremiah 10:2–3; Ezekiel 21:21; Obadiah 1:11; Jonah 1:7; Nahum 3:10; Matthew 27:35; Mark 15:24; John 19:24; Acts 1:26.

38. Leviticus 19:26; Deuteronomy 18:9–13; 2 Kings 17:16–20.
39. Leviticus 6:3–10; Numbers 26:55; Joshua 7:16–18, 14:1–2, 18:10; Judges 20:9–10; 1 Samuel 14:40–42; 1 Chronicles 6:39 ff, 24:7–19, 31, 26:13; Nehemiah 10:34–37, 11:1; Proverbs 16:33, 18:18; Jonah 1:7; Acts 1:26.
40. An interesting discussion of the various forms of divination practices is presented in Walton, J. H. (2006). *Ancient Near Eastern thought and the Old Testament*. Grand Rapids, MI: Baker Academic. pp. 239–274.
41. Genesis 12:1–6.
42. Exodus 3, 13, 18, 28:13–30; Leviticus 8:8; Numbers 27:21; Deuteronomy 33:8–9; 1 Samuel 14:41, 28:3–6; Nehemiah 7:65.
43. Judges 6.
44. 1 Kings 12:6–19.
45. Genesis 15:1; Numbers 12:6; 2 Samuel 7:17; 2 Chronicles 26:5; Daniel 2:19, 8:1; Matthew 1:20, 2:12–22, 17:1–9; Luke 1:22, 24:23; Acts 9–10, 16:9–10, 18:9.
46. Acts 9.
47. Acts 15:22–27.
48. For examples, Sarah's servant is told to submit to her authority in Genesis 16:9; Joseph is granted broad decision-making authority in all of Egypt in Genesis 41; Kore the Levite and keeper of the eastern gate was given authority in 2 Chronicles 31:14–15; Haman had unquestioned authority in Esther 3; Daniel is given a great amount of authority in the empire in Daniel 5; the centurion in Matthew 8.
49. Genesis 13:11; Exodus 17:9; Numbers 11:16; Deuteronomy 1:13; 1 Samuel 13:2, 24:1–4; 1 Chronicles 12:19; 2 Chronicles 10:8, 22:5, 30:2, 30:23, 32:3; Ezra 5:17; Matthew 12:14–15, 27:1, 27:7, 28:12; Mark 3:6; Acts 6:5, 15:22, 15:40, 25:12, 27:12; 2 Corinthians 1:15–17, 1:23–2:1.
50. Proverbs 15:22, 20:18.
51. Tiemstra, J. P., Graham, W. F., Monsma, G. N., Sinke, C. J., Storkey, A., & Ebels, D. M. (1990). *Reforming economics: Calvinist studies on methods and institutions*. Lewiston, NY: The Edwin Mellen Press. p. 203.
52. 1 Kings 12.
53. 2 Kings 23:1–8; Matthew 21; Mark 11; Luke 10, 19; John 12:15.
54. 2 Kings 20:20–22; 1 Chronicles 13:1–4; Daniel 1.
55. Genesis 24; 2 Samuel 18:1–4; Daniel 6:6–9.
56. Briner, B. (1996). *The management methods of Jesus: Ancient wisdom for modern business*. Nashville, TN: Thomas Nelson, Inc. p. 15.
57. Briner, B. (1996). *The management methods of Jesus: Ancient wisdom for modern business*. Nashville, TN: Thomas Nelson, Inc. p. 15.
58. Leviticus 26:19; Deuteronomy 32:15.
59. For examples, Jonah and Job's friends.
60. Romans 6:17–23, 7:19–24, 8:1–4; 2 Corinthians 3:17; Galatians 5:13–24; Ephesians 5:9; Philippians 1:11; Colossians 1:10; 1 Peter 2:9–16.
61. Some of the Bible passages used in support of this include Psalm 25:14, 32:8–11; Ephesians 5:17.
62. Rogers Jr., F. (1997). Discernment. In Bass, D. C. (Ed.).*Practicing our faith: A way of life for a searching people*. San Francisco, CA: Jossey-Bass. p. 107.
63. Psalm 119:105; 2 Timothy 2:15, 3:16.
64. Job 35:12; Psalm 18:41, 37:4, 66:18; Proverbs 1:28, 21:13; Isaiah 1:15–16; Jeremiah 11:11–14; Micah 3:4; James 4:13–16.
65. Exodus 20:2–17; Deuteronomy 5:1–22, 10:12; Joshua 1:8; Psalm 19:8–11, 111:10, 112:1, 147:11; Proverbs 1:7; Ecclesiastes 12:13. Those who hold this view equate "the fear of the Lord" with keeping God's commandments.
66. Judges 6; 2 Chronicles 32:24.
67. James 1:5–7; 1 John 5:14.
68. Psalm 32:8.
69. Proverbs 1:5, 12:15, 13:10, 19:20, 20:18.
70. Philippians 2:13.
71. The passage in Isaiah 14:13–14 is believed by some scholars to refer to Lucifer. See other biblical examples: Genesis 4, 11:1–9, 12, 39; Exodus 5–15; Numbers 16, 22; Joshua 7; Judges 16; Daniel 5; Jeremiah 50–51; Luke 15. See also Muilenburg, J. (1965). Abraham and the nations: Blessing and world history. *Interpretation*. 19(4), 387–398; Anderson, B. W. (1978). Unity and diversity in God's creation: A study of the Babel story. *Currents in Theology and Mission*. 5(2), 69–81; See also commentary on this in Levine, D. B. (1993). Hubris in Josephus' Jewish antiquities 1–4. *Hebrew Union College Annual*. 64, 51–87; Stulman, L. J. (2008). Jeremiah as a messenger of hope in crisis. *Interpretation*. 62(1), 5–20.
72. Meadors, G. T. (2003). *Decision making God's way: A new model for knowing God's will*. Grand Rapids, MI: Baker Books. p. 65.
73. Rabinovitch, N. L. (1973). *Probability and statistical inference in ancient and medieval Jewish literature*. Toronto, Canada: University of Toronto Press. pp. 22–23. See Job 9:24, 21:17–18. See comments about these verses in Rabinovitch, pp. 25–26.
74. Whybray, R. N. (1989). Ecclesiastes. In Clements, R. E. (Ed.). *New century Bible commentary. Volume 21*. Grand Rapids, MI: William B. Eerdmans Publishing Company. p. 67.
75. Perkins, D., & Carter, D. L. (2000). *Human self-reliance vs. reliance on God: Understanding God's design for man's participation*. Paper presented to the Annual Conference of the Christian Business Faculty Association. Buffalo, NY. October.
76. Perkins, D., & Carter, D. L. (2000). *Human self-reliance vs. reliance on God: Understanding God's design for man's participation*. Paper presented to the Annual Conference of the Christian Business Faculty Association. Buffalo, NY. October. p. 4.
77. Many writers have addressed this topic (a topic too large to address in a textbook like this). Here are representative scholars from the Protestant tradition: Berkhof, L. (1941). Providence. In *Systematic theology*. Grand Rapids, MI: William B. Eerdmans Publishing Company. pp. 165–178; Grudem, W. (1994). God's providence. In *Systematic theology: An introduction to biblical doctrine*. Grand Rapids, MI: Zondervan Publishing House. pp. 315–354; Pieper, F. (1950). Divine providence, or the preservation and government of the world. In *Christian dogmatics, Volume 1*. St. Louis, MO: Concordia Publishing House. pp. 481–494.
78. Berkhof, L. (1941). *Systematic theology*. Grand Rapids, MI: William B. Eerdmans Publishing Company. p. 166.

79. Psalm 22:28, 66:7, 103:19, 104:14, 139:16; Proverbs 16:33; Daniel 5:35; Romans 8:28; Philippians 4:19.
80. Deuteronomy 33:12, 33:25–28; 1 Samuel 2:9; Nehemiah 9:6; Psalm 107:9, 127:1, 145:14–15; Matthew 10:29–30; Colossians 1:17; 1 Peter 3:12. Regarding Ecclesiastes 9:11: Some Christians believe that the Hebrews would have interpreted this verse to mean unexpected events (but not random). In 1 Kings 5:4 the English word "chance" can also be translated as an *evil event*. The Hebrew word *pega* means to encounter or misfortune. See Grudem, W. (1994). *Systematic theology: An introduction to biblical doctrine*. Grand Rapids, MI: Zondervan Publishing House. pp. 318–319.
81. Anthony, R. N. (1988). *The management control function*. Boston, MA: The Harvard Business School Press. pp. 3–23.
82. Fayol, H. (1949). *General and industrial management*. London: Sir Isaac Pitman and Sons, Ltd. p. 43.
83. Urwick, L. F. (1956). *The pattern of management*. Minneapolis, MN: University of Minnesota Press.
84. Drucker, P. F. (1954). *The practice of management*. New York: Harper & Brothers. p. 287.
85. Drucker, P. F. (1954). *The practice of management*. New York: Harper & Brothers. pp. 121–136; Drucker, P. F. (1973). *Management: Tasks, responsibilities, practices*. New York: Harper & Row Publishers, Inc. pp. 430–442.
86. See the article on MBO applied to a theater company at http://www.msuiit.edu.ph/ipag/studies/stagecraft/management.html.
87. Koontz, H. (1977). Making MBO effective. *California Management Review*. 20(1), 5–13; Ford, R. C., & McLaughlin, F. S. (1982). Avoiding disappointment in MBO programs. *Human Resource Management*. 21(2/3), 44–49.
88. Pringle, C. D., & Longenecker, J. G. (1982). The ethics of MBO. *Academy of Management Review*. 7(2), 305–312.
89. Chewning, R. C., Eby, J. W., & Roels, S. J. (1990). *Business through the eyes of faith*. San Francisco, CA: HarperSanFrancisco. pp. 122, 123.
90. Stewart, T. A. (1995). The corporate jungle spawns a new species: The project manager. *Fortune*. 132(1), 179–180.
91. Meredith, J. R., & Mantel Jr., S. J. (2003). *Project management: A managerial approach*. New York: John Wiley & Sons, Inc. pp. 8–10.
92. Meredith, J. R., & Mantel Jr., S. J. (2003). *Project management: A managerial approach*. New York: John Wiley & Sons, Inc. pp. 128–137.
93. Dean, B. V. (1985). *Project management: Methods and studies*. New York: Elsevier; Meredith, J. R., & Mantel Jr., S. J. (2008). *Project management: A managerial approach*. (7th ed.). New York: John Wiley & Sons, Inc. pp. 333–364; Heizer, J., & Render, B. (2001). *Operations management*. (6th ed.). Upper Saddle River, NJ: Prentice Hall. pp. 655–696.
94. Heizer, J., & Render, B. (2001). *Operations management*. (6th ed.). Upper Saddle River, NJ: Prentice Hall. pp. 739–862.
95. Edwards, W. (1982). *Multiattribute evaluation*. Beverly Hills, CA: Sage Publications. pp. 1–94
96. Pfeffer, J. (1992). Understanding power in organizations. *California Management Review*. 34(2), 37.
97. Drucker, P. F. (1954). *The practice of management*. New York: Harper & Row, Publishers. pp. 351–369.
98. For discussions of the dimensions and typical approaches to managerial decision making see Simon, H. A. (1997). *Administrative behavior: A study of decision-making processes in administrative organizations*. (4th ed.). New York: The Free Press. pp. 10–139; Mintzberg, H., & Westley, F. (2001). Decision making: It's not what you think. *MIT Sloan Management Review*. 42(3), 89–93; Stanovich, K. E., & West, R. F. (2000). Individual differences in reasoning: Implications for the rationality debate. *Behavioral and Brain Sciences*. 23, 645–665; Bazerman, M. H. (2006). *Judgment in managerial decision making*. (6th ed.). New York: John Wiley & Sons.
99. For examples, the Capital Asset Pricing Model (CAPM) requires an estimate of beta (β). Choosing a particular risk-free rate of return requires making a judgment. Using net present value (NPV) to make choices for investments, we contend here, cannot be done without also measuring the choices among alternatives through the filter of one's values, one's perception of how competitors will react, assumptions regarding future consumer behaviors, and moral and social responsibilities of the firm. Estimating the discount rate to apply to the NPV calculation requires an estimate based on judgment. As Peter Drucker said, " . . . managers who make effective decisions know that one does not start with facts. One starts with opinions." Drucker, P. F. (1974). *Management: Tasks, responsibilities, practices*. New York: Harper & Row, Publishers. p. 470.
100. More than one approach can be identified as the so-called "rational" decision making process. See Bazerman, M. H. (2006). *Judgment in managerial decision making*. (6th ed.). New York: John Wiley & Sons. pp. 4–5.
101. Bazerman, M. H. (2006). *Judgment in managerial decision making*. (6th ed.). New York: John Wiley & Sons. pp. 62–66.
102. Brousseau, K. R., Driver, M. J., Hourihan, G., & Larsson, R. (2006). The seasoned executive's decision-making style. *Harvard Business Review*. 84(2), 110–121; Rowe, A. J., & Boulgarides, J. D. (1992). *Managerial decision making*. New York: Macmillan Publishing Company; Rowe, A. J., & Mason, R. O. (1985). *Managing with style: A guide to understanding, assessing and improving decision making*. San Francisco, CA: Jossey-Bass; Leonard, N. H., Scholl, R. W., & Kowalski, K. B. (1999). Information processing style and decision making. *Journal of Organizational Behavior*. 29(3), 407–419. On the issue of tailoring your communication style to your supervisor's decision-making style see Williams, G. A., & Miller, R. B. (2002). Change the way you persuade. *Harvard Business Review*. 80(5), 65–73.
103. For a discussion on the concept of multiple intelligences see Gardner, H. (1993). *Multiple intelligences: The theory in practice*. New York: Basic Books. pp. 1–63; Gardner, H. (1999). *Intelligence reframed: Multiple intelligences for the 21st century*. New York: Basic Books. pp. 1–46.
104. Kellogg, R. T. (2007). *Fundamentals of cognitive psychology*. Los Angeles, CA: Sage Publications. pp. 1–30; Baars, B. J. (2007). Attention and consciousness. In Baars, M. G., & Gage, N. M. (Eds.). *Cognition, brain and consciousness: Introduction to cognitive neuroscience*. New York: Elsevier. pp. 225–254; Aamodt, S., & Wang, S. (2008). *Welcome to your brain: Why you lose*

your car keys but never forget how to drive and other puzzles of everyday life. New York: Bloomsbury. pp. 6–7.

105. Mintzberg, H., & Westley, F. (2001). Decision making: It's not what you think. *MIT Sloan Management Review*. 42(3), 89–93.
106. In modern times Chester Barnard raised our awareness to the role of intuition in his book: Barnard, C. I. (1938). *The functions of the executive*. Cambridge, MA: Harvard University Press. For helpful surveys of intuition and its role in managerial decision making see Dane, E., & Pratt, M. G. (2007). Exploring intuition and its role in managerial decision making. *Academy of Management Review*. 32(1), 33–54; Miller, C. C., & Ireland, R. D. (2005). Intuition in strategic decision making: Friend or foe in the fast-paced 21st century? *Academy of Management Executive*. 19(1), 19–30; Burke, L. A., & Miller, M. K. (1999). Taking the mystery out of intuitive decision making. *Academy of Management Executive*. 13(4), 91–99; Sadler-Smith, E., & Shefy, E. (2004). The intuitive executive: Understanding and applying "gut feel" in decision-making. *Academy of Management Executive*. 18(4), 76–91; Myers, D. G. (2002). The powers and perils of intuition. *Psychology Today*. 35(6), 42–52.
107. Dane, E., & Pratt, M. G. (2007). Exploring intuition and its role in managerial decision making. *Academy of Management Review*. 32(1), 33–54.
108. Garvin, D. A., & Roberto, M. A. (2001). What you don't know about making decisions. *Harvard Business Review*. 79(8), 108–116.
109. Plous, S. (1993). Social influences. In *The psychology of judgment and decision making*. Philadelphia, PA: Temple University Press. pp. 191–204.
110. Bazerman, M. H. (2006). *Judgment in managerial decision making*. (6th ed.). New York: John Wiley & Sons. pp. 68–76.
111. Staw, B. M. (1981). The escalation of commitment to a course of action. *Academy of Management Review*. 6(4), 577–587; Brockner, J. (1992). The escalation of commitment to a failing course of action: Toward theoretical progress. *Academy of Management Review*. 17(1), 39–61.
112. Bazerman, M. H. (2006). *Judgment in managerial decision making*. (6th ed.). New York: John Wiley & Sons. pp. 18–19.
113. Asch, S. (1956). Studies of independence and conformity. *Psychological Monographs*. 70(416); Janis, I. L. (1982). *Groupthink*. (2nd ed.). Boston, MA: Houghton Mifflin; Chapman, J. (2006). Anxiety and defective decision making: An elaboration of the groupthink model. *Management Decision*. 44(10), 1391–1404; Sims, R. R. (1992). Linking groupthink to unethical behavior in organizations. *Journal of Business Ethics*. 11(9), 651–662.
114. Garvin, D. A., & Roberto, M. A. (2001). What you don't know about making decisions. *Harvard Business Review*. 79(8), 108–116.
115. Drucker, P. F. (1992). *Managing the non-profit organization: Principles and practices*. New York: HarperBusiness; Euske, K. J. (2003). Public, private, not-for-profit: Everybody is unique? *Measuring Business Excellence*. 7(4), 5–11; Fottler, M. D. (1981). Is management really generic? *Academy of Management Review*. 6(1), 1–12; Hatten, M. L. (1982). Strategic management in not-for-profit organizations. *Strategic Management Journal*. 3(2), 89–104; James, E. (1983). How nonprofits grow: A model. *Journal of Policy Analysis and Management*. 2(3), 350–366; Knoke, D., & Prensky, D. (1984). What relevance do organization theories have for voluntary organizations? *Social Science Quarterly*. 65, 3–20; Newman, W. H., & Wallender III, H. W. (1978). Managing not-for-profit enterprises. *Academy of Management Journal*. 3(1), 24–31; Unterman, I., & Davis, R. H. (1982). The strategy gap in not-for-profits. *Harvard Business Review*. 60(3), 30–35; Bear, A. B., & Fitzgibbon, M. A. (2005). Leadership in a not-for-profit world: A mixed toolbox. In Sims, R. R., & Quatro, S. A. (Eds.). *Leadership: Succeeding in private, public and not-for-profit sectors*. Armonk, NY: M. E. Sharpe. pp. 87–104.
116. Dane, E., & Pratt, M. G. (2007). Exploring intuition and its role in managerial decision making. *Academy of Management Review*. 32(1), 33–54. This tension is alluded to in the discussion of "deciding too early" vs. "deciding too late" in Garvin, D. A., & Roberto, M. A. (2001). What you don't know about making decisions. *Harvard Business Review*. 79(8), 108–116.
117. Urwick, L. F. (1955). *The pattern of management*. Minneapolis, MN: University of Minnesota Press. pp. 5–6; Marshall, A. (1949). *Principles of economics*. (8th ed.). New York: The Macmillan Company, pp. 245–246.
118. Dodd, D., & Favaro, K. (2006). Managing the right tension. *Harvard Business Review*. 84(12), 62–74; Vancil, R. F. (1976). Strategy formulation in complex organizations. *Sloan Management Review*. 17(2), 1–18; Wacker, W., Taylor, J., & Means, H. (2000). *The visionary's handbook: Nine paradoxes that will shape the future of your business*. New York: HarperBusiness. pp. 77–96; Drucker, P. F. (1974). *Management: Tasks, responsibilities, practices*, New York: Harper & Row, Publishers, Inc. pp. 43–44; Andrews, K. R. (1971). *The concept of corporate strategy*, Homewood, IL: Dow Jones-Irwin, Inc. pp. 230–231; Maital, S. (1994). *Executive economics*. New York: The Free Press.
119. Drucker, P. F. (1974). *Management: Tasks, responsibilities, practices*, New York: Harper & Row, Publishers, Inc. p. 43.
120. Selznick, P. (1957). *Leadership in administration: A sociological interpretation*. Berkeley, CA: University of California Press. p. vi; Simon, H. A. (1993). Strategy and organizational evolution. *Strategic Management Journal*. 14, 131–142; Simon, H. A. (1997). *Administrative behavior*. (4th ed.). New York: The Free Press. p. 273; Andrews, K. R. (1971). *The concept of corporate strategy*, Homewood, IL: Dow Jones-Irwin, Inc.; Bazerman, M. H. (2006). *Judgment in managerial decision making*. (6th ed.). New York: John Wiley & Sons, Inc. p. 65; Rappaport, A. (2005). The economics of short-term performance obsession. *Financial Analysts Journal*. 61(3), 65–66; Cavanagh, G. F. (2006). *American business values: A global perspective*. Upper Saddle River, NJ: Pearson Prentice Hall. p. 28; De George, R. T. (2006). *Business ethics*. (6th ed.). Upper Saddle River, NJ: Pearson Prentice Hall. p. 10; Brealey, R. A., & Myers, S. C. (2000). *Principles of corporate finance*. (6th ed.). New York: Irwin McGraw-Hill. p. 325; Atkinson, S. K. (1956). Short and long-range considerations in cost analysis.

National Association of Cost Accountants NACA Bulletin. 38(3), 343–352.

121. Selznick, P. (1957). *Leadership in administration: A sociological interpretation*. Berkeley, CA: University of California Press. p. vi; Simon, H. A. (1993). Strategy and organizational evolution. *Strategic Management Journal*. 14, 131–142; Simon, H. A. (1997). *Administrative behavior*. (4th ed.). New York: The Free Press. p. 273; Andrews, K. R. (1971). *The concept of corporate strategy*, Homewood, IL: Dow Jones-Irwin, Inc. pp. 230–231; Bazerman, M. H. (2006). *Judgment in managerial decision making*. (6th ed.). New York: John Wiley & Sons, Inc. p. 65; Barnard, C. (1938). *The functions of the executive*. Cambridge, MA: Harvard University Press. p. 208; Rappaport, A. (2005) The economics of short-term performance obsession. *Financial Analysts Journal*. 61(3), 65–66; Cavanagh, G. F. (2006). *American business values: A global perspective*. Upper Saddle River, NJ: Pearson Prentice Hall. p. 28; De George, R. T. (2006). *Business ethics*. (6th ed.). Upper Saddle River, NJ: Pearson Prentice Hall. p. 10; Brealey, R. A., & Myers, S. C. (2000). *Principles of corporate finance*. (6th ed.). New York: Irwin McGraw-Hill. p. 325; Webber, R. A. (1972). *Time and management*. New York: Van Nostrand Reinhold Company; Atkinson, S. K. (1956). Short and long-range considerations in cost analysis. *National Association of Cost Accountants NACA Bulletin*. 38(3), 343–352.
122. Meadors, G. T. (2003). *Decision making God's way: A new model for knowing God's will*. Grand Rapids, MI: Baker Books. pp. 119–120.
123. Proverbs 3:5–6; Psalm 25:12. See also Jeremiah 33:3.
124. Cf. Bazerman, M. H. (2006). *Judgment in managerial decision making*. (6th ed.). New York: John Wiley & Sons, Inc. p. 74.
125. Cf. Bazerman, M. H. (2006). *Judgment in managerial decision making*. (6th ed.). New York: John Wiley & Sons, Inc. p. 73.

CHAPTER

7

Strategic Thinking

LEARNING OBJECTIVES

- Understand how personal values directly influence strategic decisions.
- Describe how a faith perspective can guide the strategic decision maker.
- Understand the strategic thinking process and content that are used to analyze a given situation to make strategic decisions.
- Describe the common patterns of strategic decision making across industries.
- Understand selected tension points that strategic managers face during the strategic thinking process.

"The critical difference between the traditional definition of strategic management and its Christian definition lies in the firm's need to demonstrate Christian values in its decisions and operations."[1]

"Most ethical issues that strategic management confronts arise from a potential conflict between the goals of the enterprise, or the goals of the individual managers and the fundamental rights of important stakeholders . . ."[2]

TOYOTA'S ASSUMPTIONS

During the third quarter of 2008, executives at Toyota released bad news to the investor community: The company would miss its annual sales projections. The story began several years earlier as Toyota strategists observed the growth in the highly profitable full-size pickup truck and SUV market. The big three U.S. automakers Ford, Chevy, and Dodge were doing well in this segment, so much so that Toyota leaders decided to begin head-to-head competition with them. Executives assumed that consumer demand for these gas-guzzling vehicles would continue in spite of the slow but steady increase in gas prices.[3]

As executives implemented their plan, Toyota "tooled up" for manufacture and assembly. Managers established a strategic alliance with parts suppliers. They cranked up their well-oiled marketing promotion efforts to stimulate demand in an attempt to leverage the company's strong reputation for quality. The result: Toyota created new products, such as the Tundra, that began selling successfully.

Source: Darren Brode/Shutterstock.

Then in 2008, gasoline prices increased dramatically to over $4 per gallon. The price of steel and other materials used in automobile manufacturing also increased, putting pressure on the profitability of Toyota's new products. In spite of its leading market share in the American auto market, sales of its new full-sized pickups and SUVs declined dramatically—a condition that led executives to revise their sales projections for the investor community and consider restructuring the company.

What happened? For one, the basis of Toyota executives' assumptions regarding demand and *price elasticity*—customer responsiveness to changes in price—was transformed within a few months. As a result, executives were forced to re-examine their assumptions. Toyota executives were not ignorant of other influences in the marketplace. Market preferences sometimes are paradoxical (contradictory). Some consumers demand larger, more powerful but less fuel-efficient work and sport vehicles such as the Tundra. Other consumers demand more fuel-efficient, environmentally friendly sedans such as the Prius.

Perhaps we should not be too quick to criticize strategy executives at Toyota. They did have accurate assumptions at the time. Based on their assumptions, the economic basis of their strategy was sound. However, eventually conditions changed as consumers began to change their preferences. The changes that took place outside the company required executives to rethink their plans and ideas and make new decisions.

We must assume that these decision makers were aware of other developments around the auto industry such as the vehicle designed by Aptera Motors that promised 300 miles per gallon of gasoline.[4]

Given Toyota's experience, several strategic questions give company executives reason to evaluate their strategic decisions:

- Should assumptions about the American market for full-size trucks and SUVs be revised?
- How much emphasis should incumbents (current automobile manufacturers) place on alternative fuel vehicles?
- How are microeconomic influences, such as price elasticity of demand, changing?
- With the proliferation of auto parts suppliers worldwide and the development of new technologies for environmentally clean engines, is the automobile market in the

United States beginning a major *microeconomic* restructuring? If so, what will the new market structure be like in the future and how will this change the basis of competition?

- What is keeping corporations such as General Electric from entering the automobile industry with an environmentally clean product?
- How can upstart automobile companies like Aptera Motors establish a successful foothold in this industry?
- Are these driving forces that are changing the auto industry likely to be temporary or permanent?
- If new segments of the automobile industry get established (H_2O-Hydrogen powered electric, battery electric, solar electric), are they likely to be profitable for investors?
- How can successful companies manage the fact that some of their assumptions about the market become obsolete quickly while other theories remain valid?

Toyota's experience is not unusual. Companies in many other industries have faced similar situations in which the marketplace changed while they were still operating on old assumptions. This leaves top-level managers with the challenge of thinking differently about the market as a whole and then deciding what the company should do, where to spend its money, what customer segments to target, how to finance operations, and how to organize workers. These and similar questions represent the strategic thinking of company leaders that we will consider in this chapter.

For the manager of faith who wishes to be true to fundamental principles, such as the stewardship of the environment, there are other questions. Because of the religious belief regarding stewardship of the environment, should Christian executives or entrepreneurs actively pursue the application of green technology in the transportation industries even if expected profits are lower than what can be gained by applying traditional fossil fuel technologies? Do Christian business executives have the privilege of expecting that God will bless their business with prosperity if they follow the principle of the stewardship of the environment faithfully?

Who Cares About Strategic Thinking?

Organizations hire managers to help them make strategic decisions and then implement their strategic plans. These managers are called to consider the broad strategic purposes for why the organization as a whole exists. Keeping broad purposes in focus, managers also shape the day-to-day activities for implementing strategic decisions and communicating with strategic decision makers about adjustments to strategy.

Some managers in every organization must take responsibility for the decisions that affect their entire company. For the small family business, the family leaders make these decisions. In the nonprofit organization, the administrator takes this role in collaboration with the board of trustees. In corporations, top-level executives and the governing board share these responsibilities. What is common in these examples is that the persons who are responsible for and who influence the overall viability of the organization are the ones who usually make the strategic decisions.[5] These are the persons whose work is not so much solving a problem as it is identifying the right questions that affect the entire organization.[6]

Even though most strategic decisions are made by the top-level leaders, mid-level managers get involved in strategic thinking, too.[7] Including mid-level leaders in strategic decisions increases their acceptance of the decisions after they are made. Mid-level managers may participate in strategic planning sessions by evaluating marketplace information or their own organization and then making recommendations. They have key information that top-level managers need but don't have to make good decisions. Without their coordinating efforts, implementation of grand ideas grinds to a halt. They interpret the big decisions for their employees so that subordinates can see the relevance of day-to-day work in support of what the company is trying to accomplish. And they communicate the results of implementation to top-level leaders, often making adjustments to the plans as unexpected issues arise. See Exhibit 7-1.

Frontline supervisors and team members receive instructions regarding the strategic decisions and then initiate actions. They are the key linkages between ideas and day-to-day ability to actually make things happen. As these individuals communicate with mid-level and senior managers, they play a key role in helping other managers revise their strategic ideas for what will work in practice.

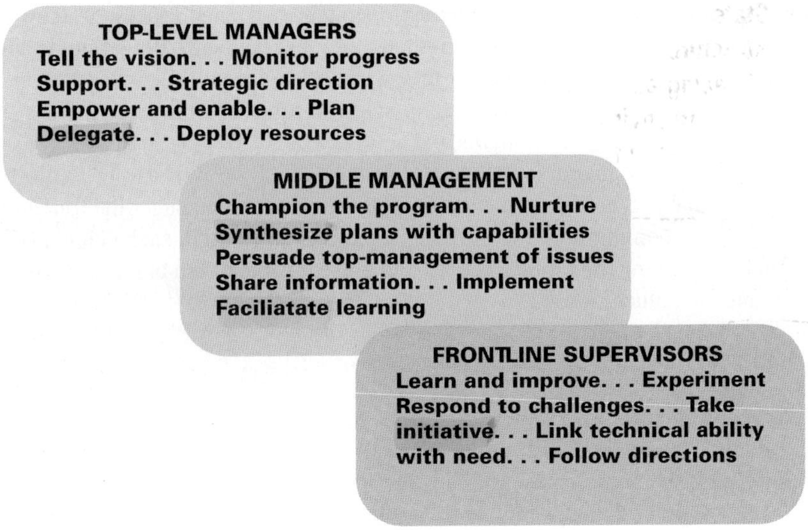

EXHIBIT 7-1

The Strategic Roles of Managers

Source: Based on Floyd, S. W., & Lane, P. J. (2000). Strategizing throughout the organization: Managing role conflict in strategic renewal. *Academy of Management Review*. 25(1), 159.

The Management Pyramid and Strategic Thinking

Making strategic decisions and then taking actions to implement strategy are the most visible dimensions of a manager's work. Chief among their actions are activities such as advocating their ideas to members of the governing board, hosting team meetings to discuss and clarify strategic decisions with employees, contacting leaders of other organizations that are needed to support company activities, allocating people to projects, and authorizing the purchase of equipment and other needed resources. But leaders can accomplish these and other strategic actions only as they spend a great amount of time thinking about the issues.

Here, as with managerial effort everywhere in the organization, the work of a manager is largely mental and emotional work. It would come as no surprise to learn that senior managers take their company's strategic issues and decisions home with them at night as they continue to think about the issues. But underneath the action and thinking on strategic issues lie the personal values and character of the manager, as illustrated in Exhibit 7-2. Strategy "begins in our minds, gets expressed in words, and then gets translated into action."[8]

There is no better illustration of the connection between being–thinking–action than strategic management. For example, when US Airways CEO Doug Parker faced the downturn in the economy, slumping demand for air travel, and rising costs of fuel and wages, the strategic decisions he and his team made emerged from their personal values. The leaders' values created perceptions of the environment and of the organization. These perceptions led to a cluster of issues to think about and then to decisions and actions such as in which cities they should maintain routes, whether to match competitors' prices, whether to downsize the organization by laying off some workers, and which types of aircraft to use.[9]

Analysis of the environment Discussions and debates Implementation of plans Organizing for implementation Establishing strategic alliances with other firms	Action
Thinking about the goals of the organization Thinking about the marketplace in which the organization operates Thinking about the competitive dynamics of the industry Thinking about the organization's resources	Thinking & Feeling
Awareness of the organization's purpose Commitment to organizational values Commitment to personal values Assumptions regarding how an organization should operate in its particular environment	Being & Becoming

EXHIBIT 7-2

The Management Pyramid: Strategic Thinking

Source: Courtesy of Michael E. Cafferky, © Michael E. Cafferky 2011.

Strategic managers bring their entire being to strategy tasks and processes. How aggressive they wish to compete in the market, the methods they use to "sell" the strategic ideas to the governing board and to employees, whether they wish to retaliate against rivals who successfully win customers away, and which individuals inside the organization receive their support all represent the values guiding their thoughts and actions.

In this chapter the Management Pyramid is the model we will use to explore strategic thinking, decision making, and implementation. For the Christian manager the foundation of this model is being and becoming in terms of biblical values. As we do in each chapter of this book, we will begin by reviewing the biblical record and present some of the big issues where strategic thinking is related to values.

Faith Perspective on StrategicThinking

It is in the creation account where we see the first suggestions related to strategic thinking. The original Strategic Thinker is God himself. God gives human beings the work of stewardship responsibilities over the entire earth. Humans are to keep the larger picture in mind when they engage in specific actions. Humans ultimately work for God and all work-related decisions should be made in the context of God and his will by fulfilling the commission given at creation.

The Bible highlights several persons as having the gift of strategic thinking to guide organizations.[10] These include notable strategic thinkers such as Abraham, Jacob, Moses, Joseph, David, Solomon, Daniel, Nehemiah, Jesus, and Paul. The features below and on the next page offer more details on two of these strategic managers: Jacob and Joseph. Joseph, for example, had the gift of dreams and interpretation of dreams but also had the ability to identify strategic issues, make reasonable recommendations for alternatives to consider, and then organize the efforts of many people to accomplish the implementation.[11] Joshua, the assistant to Moses, was yet another strategic thinker. In his relationship with God we see revealed the close working of God in strategic direction for the nation.[12] For example, Joshua followed God's leading in the decisions of what part of the land of Canaan Israel should approach—the unusual method of taking the city of Jericho. The story about the failed attack on the city of Ai reveals the centrality of values when making strategic decisions.

The Biblical Story of Jacob, the Strategic Manager

You may remember the story of how Laban, Jacob's father-in-law, used Jacob's love for Rachel as leverage to keep Jacob working for him for about 20 years. It is easy to see how Laban took advantage of Jacob and his knowledge of herding, as everything that Jacob touched seemed to become wealth.[13] But it is possible that Jacob had the last say in the matter.

The Bible[14] tells how when Jacob married both Leah and Rachel he wanted to leave Laban and move his family to his own home and country. But he waited until Rachel had borne a son, Joseph. It was then that Jacob asked for the freedom to leave. Laban asked Jacob what he wanted in wages. Instead of wages Jacob made a deal with Laban to select specific sheep from Laban's flocks as payment. Jacob used his technical knowledge of breeding sheep—knowledge that Laban evidently did not have—to carefully select strong sheep for his own flocks. Jacob ended up with the stronger, more valuable sheep while Laban ended up with the less valuable herds. Laban did not follow the ancient wisdom found in Proverbs to carefully watch over his herds.[15] In the process of careful selection, much of the wealth that had accrued to Laban through Jacob's 20 years of hard work essentially was transferred to Jacob. As you might guess, this result angered Laban and his family.

Evaluate the morality of Jacob's strategy in making the deal with Laban. Did Jacob do the right thing to drain much of Laban's wealth and take it before he returned to the land of Canaan? Regardless of what you think about Laban's fairness or unfairness with Jacob, was it fair for Jacob to use his specialized technical knowledge to gain a strategic advantage in the market when such an advantage hurts his competitor?

Members of the tribe of Issachar were known as having the ability to see the big picture.[16] David showed strategic thinking as a young man. This may be one reason why Samuel recognized in him the one who would become the successor to King Saul. When he needed to consolidate the national defensive force, David turned to the men of Issachar for strategic advice. Nehemiah's story is inspiring for it shows the value of focus and single-mindedness in implementation.[17] The Apostle Paul planned his missionary journeys to cities that were centers of influence such as Corinth, Ephesus, and Athens. Many of these cities also were commercial centers where he could pursue his tent-making trade. The strategy that Jesus used combined a ministry of healing and teaching to reach people where they were—many of them in the marketplace.

The Biblical Story of Joseph, the Strategic Manager

Most know the story of how Joseph was sold into slavery, how he was falsely accused of sexual misconduct, and after he was released from prison how he rose to power in the court of the Egyptian Pharaoh. At 30 years of age, Joseph became the prime minster of Egypt. Joseph's economic policies resulted in saving the Egyptians and the Hebrews (including his own family and all other surrounding nations) from starvation. But have you noticed the strategic macroeconomic policies that Joseph used? In the space of 14 years, the entire Egyptian economy was changed from essentially a free-market, decentralized political-economic system to a centrally planned and controlled political economy. Here is a summary:

- Joseph recommends to Pharaoh to set aside a proportion of the grain into long-term storage. For 7 years this was a 20 percent corn tax levied on all corn producers. The proceeds from the corn tax would be kept safe under a centrally controlled (but decentralized geographically) storage and distribution system all under Joseph's delegated Egyptian authority.[18]
- As the famine years came, Joseph sold the grain to whoever wanted to buy. The grain revenue went into the Egyptian treasury—so much so that not only did Joseph control all the grain, the Egyptian treasury owned all the money, too.[19]
- When the people were out of money, Joseph commanded that they must exchange real capital (livestock and work animals) for grain to survive. (The grain stores were able to support the livestock.) This resulted in Pharaoh coming to own all the money, all the residual grain, and all the important capital-producing animals.[20]
- With nothing but their own hands to work and the plots of land that they owned, the Egyptians offered to sell their labor and their lands in exchange for food. Joseph accepted their proposal and, as a result, Egypt came to own all property that could be used in production. The people became slaves for Pharaoh (with the exception of the land owned by priests).[21]
- Next Joseph commanded that the Egyptians were to take and use an allowance of seed grain, plant it, work, and harvest the fields. The 20 percent grain tax policy was continued indefinitely to replenish and keep fresh the strategic grain stores.[22]

Evaluate the strategic leadership of Joseph concerning the famine prevention program he initiated. How important did this famine prevention program become in terms of the promised Messiah? Why do you think Pharaoh selected Joseph, who was not Egyptian, to be second-in-command in the Egyptian Empire?

Environmental Analysis

An example of strategic analysis that leads to a strategic decision is recorded in Numbers 13 when Moses sends spies throughout the land to scan the environment.[23] It had been about 2 years since the children of Israel had come out of the land of Egypt. They had spent some time under the shadow of Mt. Horeb (Mt. Sinai) learning a new culture and new expectations. It is an 11-day journey from Mt. Horeb to Kadesh Barnea. At Kadesh, God sent an encouraging message. "You have come to the mountains of the Amorites, which the Lord our God is giving us. Look, the Lord your God has set the land before you; go up and possess it, as the Lord God of your fathers has spoken to you; do not fear or be discouraged."[24] It was at this point that the people requested that men be sent before the congregation to "search out the land for us, and bring back word to us of the way by which we should go up, and of the cities into which we shall come."[25] We might conclude that although the promise of possession and encouragement to accomplish this were given, there were questions about which was the best route to take and what the cities were like that they would be inhabiting. Moses' emphasis on evaluating the defensive positions and the strength of the people is counterbalanced by his instruction on evaluating the production potential and commercial value of the land.

Moses identifies several critical success factors that would influence what and how Israel would approach the problem of conquest in Canaan:

- Strength of the Canaanite peoples: strong or weak
- Number of people in the land: many or few
- Resources of the land: good or bad for supporting inhabitants and trade, rich or poor for growing crops, and whether plenty of trees were available
- Nature of Canaanite defenses: mobile camps or permanent fortresses

Ten of the spies falsely reported conditions in Canaan. They also failed to report items that could have been an encouragement to the people. The Israelite spies' self-contradictory, false reports and the resulting mutiny and arrogant revolt led to consequences: punishment of death and a 40-year delayed conquest. Their experience shows the enormous influence that honest and dishonest strategic reports can have on organizations.

The Wisdom literature of the Bible contains instructions for the top-level leader who carries the responsibility to make the decisions that affect the entire organization. Making decisions should not be entered into on a whim.[26] Yet knowing what to do for the future requires wisdom.[27] Wisdom is a gift that is given by God through those who have experience. In the Bible sometimes leaders listen to others for counsel,[28] and at other times we find them in prayer asking God for guidance.[29] Once a decision is made under God's guidance, the work of implementation requires the commitment of the person's whole being and work to God.[30] And while humans take actions that are designed to produce good results, there is an awareness on the part of Bible writers that in God's providence, it is God's will ultimately that is done in the end—not merely the will of humans.[31]

Issues from Religious Faith

Viewing strategic thinking from the perspective of religious faith[32] raises several issues for consideration. If we take the point of view that a faith-informed perspective will change some things but not everything in strategic thinking, then what are the aspects that it will change?[33] While there is more than one faith perspective, what follows is an example of how strategic thinking for a Christian might be different from that of other leaders. First, some Christians will see the idea of being a strategic leader in the context of the leader's relationship to God and in the context of a Christian worldview as noted in the following definition:

> "Christian strategic leadership refers to the top executives of an organization who are called and equipped by God to lead the entire organization and its resources from a Christian biblical worldview to the glory of God."[34]

This means that the vision for the future that the top-level leaders develop through their strategic thinking will be in alignment with what they believe God's mission to be.

This raises the question of how the Christian should relate to the whole idea of trying to achieve competitive advantage over other companies.[35] Exhibit 7-3 outlines four Christian viewpoints about competition. One view is that some persons of faith are troubled by the

		RELATIONAL: What kind of relationship should the Christian have with competition?	
		Engagement with Competition	**Estrangement from Competition**
REACTIONAL: What kind of reaction should the Christian have when he or she encounters competition?	Challenge Competition	Competition is an opportunity: Reform competition for the glory of God by changing the basis of competition and avoiding playing dirty tricks	Competition is bad: Resist and avoid competition because it will automatically lead you to compromise values
	Coexist with Competition	Competition is good: Accept and pursue a policy of competition: Be the best you can in a competitive market	Competition is neither bad nor good: Coexist with competition, but be wary of it because it can tempt you to compromise values

EXHIBIT 7-3

The Four Christian Views on Competition

prospect of attempting to gain extreme competitive advantage over competitors. They will promote business success as long as business actions avoid retaliation toward competitors or harm to other businesses to achieve an advantage. Instead, these Christian business leaders will promote cooperation and reconciliation as a way to fulfill Christ's principle of the Golden Rule while living out the principles of love and justice. Here competition is resisted. In a second view, Christians accept competition as a positive force as long as it does not result in pride or making business so important that it eclipses a relationship with God. These Christians view competition as a good that reduces prices for customers, creates jobs, and improves the standard of living for everyone in the marketplace. Here competition is embraced. A third group of Christians views competitive advantage as a necessary part of doing business that is neither inherently bad nor good. This viewpoint places the Christian in tension with, and wary of, competition while being willing to coexist with it. The fourth group of Christians views competitive advantage as a dimension of the marketplace that needs to be reformed. Here the Christian will participate in competitive business actions but in a way that changes the purpose of competition from a purely economic activity to an activity designed to promote the glory of God. Here competition is a dimension of business for reformation.

These four views raise fundamental questions for the Christian business leader to consider. If competition is bad, how can the Christian really avoid it? If competition is good, how can the Christian resist temptations to pride and idolatry? If competition is an opportunity to demonstrate God's glory, just how does the Christian do that? If the Christian is to live in tension coexisting with competition, how can the Christian be in the world of the marketplace but not embrace the negative dimensions of the market?

The second way that strategic thinking might differ for Christian leaders is that decisions regarding the *mission* (purpose) of the organization and the executive's vision for the organization's future depend to a large degree on the guiding moral values of decision makers. For some executives religious values will constrain the available strategic alternatives, making some off-limits. Short-run gains in profit will be compared with the long-run obligations to stakeholders such as employees, customers, suppliers, and the general public.[36] For example, some Christians may be unwilling to invest capital in certain industries that are viewed as producing "bad products." For others, the self-serving vision of what the company can become in the future might be limited by a covenantal commitment to maintain moral relationships over the long term.[37]

A third difference is the issue of forming long-term strategic alliances. Values are important in strategic thinking regardless of a person's religious beliefs. If a company forms a strategic alliance with an organization whose executives do not share particular Christian values, a long-term relationship with such an organization may be difficult for the Christian leader to manage while maintaining a life consistent with religious values.[38] One problem is that some Scripture passages imply that believers should be actively involved in their community[39] and their surrounding culture regardless of differing values. Another difficulty is that a potential strategic alliance partner may superficially profess to be a religious believer but may not actually follow religious values or not follow them to the same degree as the other party. The key to the alliance is a strategic partner who supports important values consistent with religious faith and not necessarily who shares a specific religion.

A fourth issue is that the setting in which the religious believer works may influence how prominently religious values affect strategic (and other) decisions.[40] An executive who works in a private firm owned by persons of faith will find this setting conducive to integrating faith into strategic decision making. In contrast, the executive who works in a public firm may not be able to express religious faith to the same degree.

A fifth difference is how the person of faith approaches the entire strategic management process through the eyes of faith. For example, when scanning the external environment for opportunities and threats, the Christian manager may evaluate them as opportunities both for business and for influencing others on behalf of God's kingdom. Likewise, the Christian manager may evaluate threats not merely from an economic perspective but also based on how likely a situation will make it more or less difficult to remain faithful to one's beliefs. When economic analysis of market and industry structure doesn't include constraints of values as a basis for developing strategic decisions, the risk may increase that strategic actions will be immoral.[41]

A sixth difference is that Christian leaders evaluate the success of the organization in achieving its strategic goals in terms of the organizational mission. The person of faith may likely, if given an opportunity, subordinate organizational goals to the religious values that influenced the formation of the company's mission. Success of the company in achieving above-average economic returns is a goal that the Christian can support. However necessary this may be, this will not be sufficient for all that the Christian leader is working to accomplish.[42]

Deciding how to integrate Christian faith in the work of business is a seventh strategic issue. There are several possibilities:[43]

- Business and Christian mission are kept as separate activities.
- Business exists for the financial support of Christian mission activities.
- Business exists as a platform for mission as work is a means to channel mission throughout the world.
- The business organization is a setting in which mission can be carried out on behalf of employees with the goal of leading them to a relationship with Jesus Christ.
- Business is mission where for-profit business activities minister to spiritual, social, and economic needs carried out in a cross-cultural setting, either domestic or international.

The last concept described is the broadest view encompassing all but the first possibility.

Finally, another implication for a faith-perspective is that some Christians may choose not to exploit low price elasticity of demand by raising prices or cutting back on quality. When consumers are in a dependent position, the Christian manager will want to provide care for consumers rather than use the firm's pricing power to capture as much economic value from the market as might be possible.

Some in the marketplace extol the virtues of aggressive competition in which the rules of the game involve downward pressures on morals to achieve upward pressure on profit. But in the process, some organizations get hurt.[44] In previous generations, highly regarded experts on executive behavior couched their observations regarding how to move the organization toward its goals in the context of acting responsibly.[45] And most university textbooks have revived the issue of ethical strategic decision making. Yet some practitioners seem to operate under a different set of guidelines in which business is like playing hardball—some win and some get hurt and lose.

The proponents of so-called hardball strategy describe the "hardball manifesto" as a complete concentration on competitive advantage in which the leaders of successful companies play to win even if it means being deceitful. Winners at the hardball become disciplined and toughened to deal with the hard realities of competitive marketplaces. They realize the power of a strong organization that is difficult for competitors to duplicate. If they are unable to succeed by attacking competitors directly with overwhelming force, hardball players deploy flanking maneuvers. Top-level leaders know that their employees want to win. They exploit this desire and help their employees become courageous and smart. Hardball players are aware of the ethical and legal limits of hardball tactics and they play as close to the edges of commonly accepted standards as possible when this is required to gain an advantage in the market. They are also careful not to step over the lines of what they believe society disagrees with. Hardball tactics include such actions as destroying a competitor's profit sanctuary, stealing business ideas, deceiving competitors, and luring competitors into situations in which they lose money.

We have considered here some of the fundamental values and issues that a Christian will face when participating in strategic management. Next we will review the fundamental ideas on strategy from contemporary business scholarship. In the next section notice how important values are for strategic thinking and action.

Strategic Thinking

For an organization to succeed in achieving its goals, a pattern of objectives across the whole organization must guide the thinking of managers at all levels as they coordinate their efforts together. This pattern is an integrated set of commitments and actions across the firm that help everyone stay focused. It leads the organization to do things that are different from other organizations, or to do the same things but in different ways.[46] Applied on a daily basis, the desired result is a competitive advantage and a full but efficient use of all the abilities and resources in the organization. In this section we will explore strategic thinking, its connection to values, its process, and its content.

Strategic thinking begins by attempting to make sense of the internal and external environment of the organization. From this sense-making process, one or more issues or problems emerge. Strategic thinkers make a cluster of interrelated plans that are designed to address these problems and achieve company goals. Employees implement the plans on an ongoing basis, making adjustments when necessary. This pattern of thinking and action is not a one-time process but rather is continuous. Strategic issues or problems can emerge at any time, and the need to adjust actions or a strategic decision can come up quickly. Exhibit 7-4 is depicted as a linear, sequential process. In reality any of the steps in the process can occur at any time the situation requires.

Strategic Thinking and Values

Strategic decisions, those that make a difference for the whole of a company, cannot be made in isolation from all the other decisions the company is making or in isolation from the decisions that others (such as suppliers, customers, competitors, etc.) make.[47] These decisions also cannot be made in isolation from the personal values of the decision makers. One could argue that it is at the level of personal values that strategic thinking begins. In this way strategic thinking is consistent with the intent of the Management Pyramid model presented in this book: Strategic thinking begins with who you are.

Personal values heavily influence what strategic decision makers want to do in spite of what the organization might do.[48] Values include making a judgment about what is good or bad, right or wrong. Values influence how top leaders perceive their market and their organization. They are like colored lenses through which the strategic decision makers view the key issues the company and its industry faces. Although we like to think of strategic decision making as purely a logical, rational process, values bias logic and judgment.

When top-level leaders value hard-driving market aggressiveness and rivalry, they foster a set of strategies that alternative values, centered on collaboration, fairness, trust, and preventing conflict, may not support. And, if leaders wish to flex the firm's pricing power in the market, short-term gains may be achieved but perhaps at the risk of undermining long-term support from

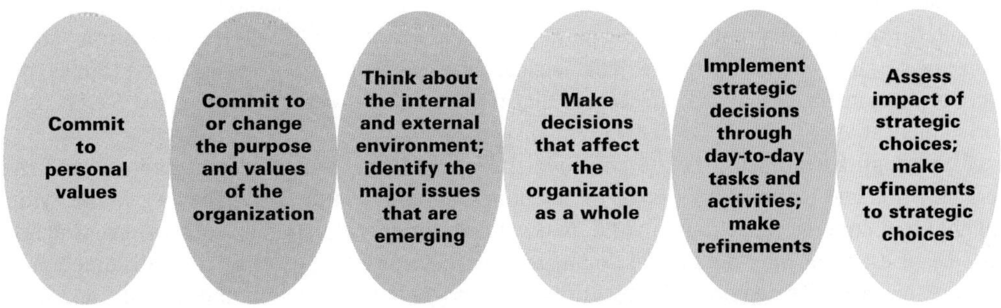

EXHIBIT 7-4
Strategic Thinking as Process

customers who will search for substitutes. Another leader may want to create confusion for customers to make it more difficult for customers to compare values and prices among rival firms.[49] The next executive may value openness and transparency and attempt to regain lost trust by clearing up price-value confusion created by a predecessor.

Members of an executive team likely will have differences of opinion regarding which information to analyze and the types of strategic actions to consider. One team member will think that the balance sheet is most crucial for understanding the company's situation. Another team member will place a higher value on data from outside the organization such as market research reports. A third team member may point to the microeconomic dimension. A fourth might focus on capital financing issues. An opinion of one vice president about what should be done will be tested through debate by other leaders with different perspectives. If one division of the company stands to gain or lose in budget allocations, then the top managers of these divisions will tend to take the strategy debates personally. At times these discussions can become "heated" as the decision makers attempt to help each other clarify their thinking.

Ironically, strategic planning discussions and debates rarely are directly about values that are at the root of the discussions. Even so, values always drive the discussions. During this process top leaders reveal personal opinions but also verbalize the values prized by other top managers and governing board members. Thus, to a large degree the strategic decision making work of a top leader such as a CEO is to manage the conversation about values among the top leaders and between these leaders and other stakeholders.[50]

With personal values as their guide, managers play a key strategic role by following a process of strategic thinking. To explore this we have divided the material into two sections: the process of strategic thinking and the content of strategic thinking. We will explore the process first.

Strategic Thinking Process

Strategic thinking is a constant process of thinking about the present and the future, the internal capabilities and the external situation, the specific products and the core competencies that are embedded in the ability to make and sell these products, specific issues that require decisions, and the organization as a whole. Decision makers must bring into their thinking awareness of competitors, customers, and the ability of their organization to coordinate internal efforts.[51] Successful strategic thinking requires putting yourself into the shoes of people outside your organization and thinking like customers, suppliers, and competitors.[52] It involves filtering everything through individual and organizational value systems. Ultimately, the thinking process involves either affirming previous decisions made by organizational leaders or making decisions that alter the future of the organization.

In some organizations strategic thinking is sequential and planned at times, such as when Volkswagen decided to build an assembly plant in North America. Top-level executives use formal data analysis and formal planning meetings. First, data is analyzed. Next decisions are made, and then implementation is carried out.

We might like to think of the strategic thinking process as sequential—we analyze first, decide second, implement third, and evaluate results last.[53] But the reality for many leaders is that in some organizations strategic thinking is emergent, less formal, and at times even chaotic.[54] Whenever the market changes significantly around an organization, new strategic issues can emerge quickly. For example, if cinema chain Carmike Cinemas purchases the new digital sound system offered by Iosono, it has the potential to transform the cinema experience for some moviegoers. Iosono, the creators of the MP3 digital compression, has developed a system that makes the sound dimension of the cinematic entertainment come alive through its computer control of 600 speakers around the cinema. If this new technology is accepted, such a change in the industry will require cinemas everywhere to rethink their assumptions about consumers. They will need to do the financial analysis to figure out how to pay for the $150,000 per screen investment. For retail operations that have 10 screens, for example, the $1,500,000 investment is huge.

Strategy formulation is the continual process of analyzing the marketplace and the organization and then making one or more decisions that affect the company as a whole. Most of the time strategic decisions involve making only minor adjustments to previous strategic choices. Less frequently do strategic managers make major changes to the overall direction of the organization. **Strategy implementation** is the process of carrying out the strategic decisions

Source: Jason Winslow/Splash News/Jason Winslow/Splash News/Newscom.

Organizations such as Carmikes Cinemas make strategic decisions that involve changing the technology resources which are used to deliver value to customers.

that are made. In practice, strategic formulation is sometimes difficult to distinguish from strategy implementation. See Exhibit 7-5.

For years the ideal strategic planning process included a review of the entire organization and its marketplace, analyzing market and industry structure looking for strengths, weaknesses, opportunities, and threats. The focus has been on writing carefully crafted strategic plans for presentation, discussion, and approval at the corporate office or the board of directors. This approach is still used. Strategic leaders find that planning for the organization as a whole once a year is not how strategic decisions actually are made in practice throughout the year.[55] The market does not wait for any company to complete its year-end strategic planning meetings. The market is dynamic, causing many issues for senior leaders to deal with on a weekly basis.

Strategic issues emerge from the implementation of strategic plans, from the actions of suppliers, lawmakers, and regulators, and from the actions of competitors trying to gain an advantage in the market. Thus, instead of conducting traditional planning sessions once every year or two, the leaders of some companies use a continuous process of developing and debating the strategic issues that emerge from normal marketplace activities and that need decisions. Senior leaders focus on gathering the data and debating the alternatives related to the few strategic issues. For example, should the company expand operations into India or China? Yum! Brands restaurants opened 88 new restaurants in mainland China in just 4 months.[56] Should some of the manufacturing or assembly be outsourced? Should the company launch a new

EXHIBIT 7-5

Strategy Formulation vs. Strategy Implementation: A Difference in Focus

Formulation	Implementation
Strategic thinking about the *whole* but not forgetting the parts	Strategic thinking about the *parts* but not forgetting the whole
In the context of *what can be done* during implementation	In the context of *what needs to be done* for strategy
Intent and purpose (not forgetting reality and limitations)	Reality and limitations (not forgetting intent and purpose)
Past, present, and future	Past, present, and future
Divergent thinking	Convergent thinking
Horizontal thinking	Vertical and horizontal thinking
Generic core competencies that can be applied in new markets or new products	Product-specific core competencies that need to be refined or improved day by day
The big picture	The details
Choice from among trade-offs	Choice from among trade-offs

Source: © Hupeng/Dreamstime.com.

Deciding whether to expand internationally is usually an important strategic decision.

product line? Should the firm acquire a supplier? Focusing on strategic issues takes advantage of the natural cycle of activities of the marketplace. As decisions are made with respect to strategic issues, budgets and implementation plans are adjusted accordingly.

Strategic planning processes differ from company to company and situation to situation. There is no single right way to manage the strategic planning process.[57] An effective strategic planning process is unique to its company. Every company has a top-level leader with a different approach to leadership. Every company faces a different marketplace situation. The skills and experiences of the senior leaders are different from company to company. The analytical techniques required for sound strategic thinking will be different depending on the particular approach that company takes to get products and services to market.

Regardless of where in the process it occurs, strategic thinking always leads to decisions. This involves wrestling with tensions and trade-offs. If the executives of a commercial bakery decide that their best alternative is to bake and package individual servings of tasty treats, which will be sold in grocery stores and convenience stores, then such a choice will require that the company purchase certain types of production and packaging equipment. Employee work teams will be organized for efficient implementation. Marketing promotion and distribution efforts will focus on the successful sale of this type of product. Companies that supply the ingredients and packaging materials will support the decision through purchase agreements and delivery schedules.

But deciding to focus on this particular type of product and market immediately limits other alternatives such as producing fresh-baked bread, pies, and cakes. The lesson here is that strategic decisions require making trade-offs. Companies cannot do it all and expect to have an advantage over competitors. Narrowing the choices down to a particular set of products and services or a particular approach to production to the exclusion of the alternatives means that over time the company potentially can become very good at what it does. This will strengthen the brand reputation and make it more difficult for competitors to copy what they do. It offers the hope that the company will achieve performance levels that are higher than average.[58] But strategic decision makers get nervous that their choices are too narrow. Narrowness of choice can be risky if consumer preferences change quickly.

This principle of making trade-offs affects nonprofit organizations just as much as it does for-profit companies.[59] When the nonprofit enjoys a period of prosperity, it might not seem like trade-offs are required. However, nonprofits often must deal with limited resources. There is never enough cash to do all the good things that the organization might do. There are not enough volunteers to engage in every program that might be offered to society. This requires strategic decision makers to place some limits on the mission of the organization.

Developing the ability to think like key players in the market who are outside your organization will result in a greater awareness of the value of your company's products and services as seen from their perspective. Thinking like they would think also gives you some sense of how they might react to strategic decisions made by your firm. Training yourself and other top-level leaders to think outside the walls of the firm educates your perceptions.[60] Including the perspective of others in your thinking requires practice at overcoming the natural bias that occurs because you know too much about your own organization.

Now that we have explored the thinking process, we will go a little deeper into what strategic decision makers think about as they formulate strategic plans. We address this in the next section.

Strategic Thinking Content

As we saw in the previous section, the traditional way to think about the big issues that an organization faces is to think in terms of two key influences:

- what is happening *outside* the organization in the marketplace and industry, and
- what is happening *inside* the organization in terms of its key personnel and resources needed to accomplish the organization's mission.

Using the insights gained from this analysis executives attempt to refine their thinking so that they can help their organization find the "sweet spot" where what the company does best and what the company can make money doing meets what the company's managers are passionate about.[61] This is sometimes called the *hedgehog concept*.[62] The sweet spot where the economic benefits, the passion, and the capabilities meet attracts company managers to improve the discipline of the day-to-day work. Strangely enough, the success that comes from this discipline creates opportunities for the company to grow outside the sweet spot. A company like eBay, the firm that for years simply provided a forum for individuals to sell their used articles, found that it had developed capabilities to sell overstocked and slightly used inventory worldwide.[63] Growing outside the sweet spot requires the company to move outside the zone where it developed its competencies but in a way that is related to what it already does. In other words, discipline on the sweet spot may create opportunities for exceptional companies to find additional sweet spots to pursue. However, this may actually create too many opportunities, requiring managers to make difficult choices to let some opportunities go for a time. See Exhibit 7-6.

People often confuse the two terms *strategy* and *tactics*.[64] **Strategy** is what orients the entire organization toward the pursuit of its mission or a big goal; strategy guides tactical day-to-day decision making and action. **Tactics** are the visible day-to-day activities, tasks, and maneuvers that need to get done to accomplish the mission or achieve the goal in a changing market. Sometimes tactical decisions reveal opportunities for changes to strategy. Most changes in strategy require corresponding changes in tactical maneuvers. See Exhibit 7-7.

In the natural world, strategy is the location above the river where the eagle chooses to soar in search of its prey. Tactics are the flight maneuvers that enable the eagle to successfully swoop down to catch a fish. For the undergraduate student strategy is the choice of which major to pursue in a bachelors degree. Tactics are the day-to-day tasks (attending class, submitting homework on time, and preparing for exams) that help a person succeed in courses.

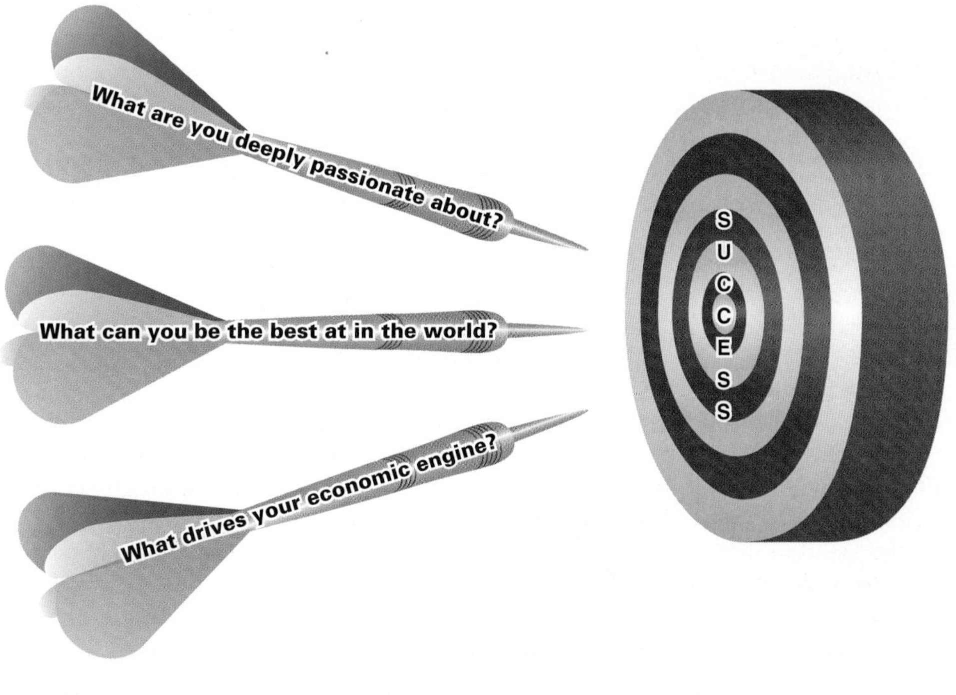

EXHIBIT 7-6
The Hedgehog Concept

Source: Based on Collins, J. (2001). *Good to great.* New York: HarperBusiness. pp. 90–119.

EXHIBIT 7-7
How to Determine if a Decision Is Strategic

While the distinction between strategic decisions and operational (tactical) decisions and goals can be fuzzy (especially in a nonprofit organization), the following are often used as indicators of *strategic* decisions.

- **Capital expense risk:** Puts at risk a major capital investment such as the purchase of property or major equipment.
- **Broad functional commitments:** Requires ongoing commitments of personnel, budget, time, and knowledge by most or all functional departments in the organization.
- **Response to external environment:** Is a response of the organization as a whole to a specific and significant external pressure, threat, opportunity, or emerging issue outside the organization.
- **Long-run impact on mission:** Has a long-run impact on the organization's purpose as a whole.
- **Focuses the whole on a clear objective:** Orients the whole organization toward a single clear objective; becomes a "big picture" guiding plan around which all departments programs organize themselves.
- **Difficult to implement:** Involves a high degree of operational coordination across many operating departments or divisions.
- **Difficult to reverse:** Requires changes and commitments of the organization that are difficult to "undo."
- **Competitive advantage:** Affects the overall advantage of the entire organization compared with its closest competitors or substitutes.

Strategy is the decision by executives at Volkswagen to establish a production facility in North America in 2010. The decision required millions of dollars of investment, a thorough site selection process, and 2 years of planning and construction to fully outfit the new assembly plant to make it ready for operations. Tactics are the week-to-week highly coordinated activities of engineers, human resource managers, lawyers, purchasing agents, construction workers, managers, marketing professionals, and finance specialists to successfully build, equip, and staff a fully functioning plant. Exhibit 7-8 gives additional examples of how these two ideas of strategy and tactics are different and yet interdependent.

EXHIBIT 7-8
Strategy vs. Tactics Examples

Strategy	Tactic
Pricing: Restructuring and maintaining the entire value chain both inside and outside the firm to support a low-cost leadership position for the long run.	**Pricing:** Offering products at a discount sale price for a short period of time to stimulate demand or win market share.
Product: Launching a new product line that is designed to meet the needs of new consumer groups. Achieve differentiation by remaking the entire process of product design, manufacturing, and assembly to achieve superior quality and performance over the long run.	**Product:** Improving one of the features of an existing model of an existing product this season.
Promotion: Divest all manufacturing, assembly, and distribution and become a marketing communication and sales organization to promote the sale of products.	**Promotion:** Spend $40,000,000 on a "pull" advertising campaign this quarter.
Distribution: Distribute products through a growing network of wholly owned retail stores; support these stores with regional distribution warehouses and a logistics information system.	**Distribution:** Open two new retail stores this month; add two long-haul trucks to the logistics management system.

We will now consider both the outside and the inside information that comprises the content of strategic thinking, starting with outside content: microeconomic market structure and dynamics, industry structure, and the forces that are driving change for the companies in the industry.

MARKET STRUCTURE AND DYNAMICS. In the for-profit sector the microeconomic structure of the market plays an influential role in the organization's ability to achieve strong economic performance.[65] Here we think of the traditional patterns of market structure such as monopoly, oligopoly, monopolistic competition, and perfect competition. **Monopoly** is a market in which a single company dominates the market or has dominant pricing power. In an **oligopoly** a few powerful companies dominate the market and interact in a fragile competitive relationship with each other, each reacting to the strategic and tactical moves of the others. Competition may be on price or on product features and benefits. In a market described as **monopolistic competition** many companies exist and each has a certain ability to differentiate its products from competitors. In **perfect competition** the market is flooded with companies that sell essentially the same commodity-like product.[66] See Exhibit 7-9 for more information about each of these market structures.

But markets change. A market dominated by a company with strong pricing power today can change toward an oligopoly as new companies enter the market offering customers new alternatives from which to choose. Likewise, an oligopoly today may actually be a marketplace

EXHIBIT 7-9
Microeconomic Market Structures[67]

Market Structure	Characteristics	Industry Examples
Perfect Competition	• Many similar firms compete in the market. • Each firm sells a small percentage of the total sold in the market. • Any one company has little to no influence on price. • Products offered in the market by competitors are essentially close substitutes or identical substitutes. • Consumer responsiveness to changes in price is very high.	• agricultural products • fish products • basic metals • stock markets • the foreign exchange market
Monopolistic Competition	• Many similar firms compete in the market. • Some firms have the ability to differentiate their products from competitors. • Companies have some, but not total, control over price because they can differentiate their products. • Customers are not as responsive to changes in price if they have accepted the product differences.	• retail trade • dresses • shoes
Oligopoly	• Relatively few companies dominate the market. • Competition can be on price or on differentiation of products. • Firms remain in a delicate, high rivalry where the actions of one firm affect all other firms.	• steel • aluminum • autos • farm implements • household appliances
Monopoly	• Fewer companies dominate the market. • Companies that dominate can set the price by controlling the quantity produced. • Customers have few viable substitutes available and because of this are less responsive to changes in price. • Competition can be based on promotion or on product differentiation.	• local utilities • "near monopolies" such as Intel, Wham-O Frisbees, De Beers diamonds

that is in transition toward monopolistic competition as more companies enter. And some markets that can be described as monopolistic competition also are in transition toward perfect competition as the products become more like commodities, such as agricultural products and raw materials that are mined out of the earth, and competition is based less on how different the products are and more on the selling price. Strategic decision makers think about not only the current structure of the market but also how it might be changing for the future. Likewise, price elasticity of demand may be low today if consumers have few substitutes available. But as the market structure changes, consumers' responsiveness also changes. The more substitutes available the more responsive customers are to changes in price.

INDUSTRY STRUCTURE AND INDUSTRY FORCES.[68] One of the chief concerns of investors is whether their investments will generate an acceptable return over the long run compared with other investments they might make. Some key drivers to such returns[69] lie outside the company, in the industry. Several forces affect the profitability of every industry and because of this the attractiveness of the industry for investors. For example, picture yourself as the CEO of a golf equipment company. An important influence on attractiveness of your industry is the intensity with which rival companies (your firm and your direct competitors) compete with each other. The higher the intensity of the rivalry, the lower profits will tend to become. **Bargaining power** is the degree of influence that a producer or consumer has in influencing what the selling price will be. The bargaining power of your suppliers (the firms that sell you materials used in making club handles and club heads) affects not only your profitability but the profitability of the industry as a whole (assuming that they sell to other golf club makers). The bargaining power of buyers (retail stores, golf course pro-shops, and mail-order customers) also affects industry profitability. The more pricing power that buyers have the lower profits tend to be as buyers compete with your firm for favorable pricing. New competitors entering the industry also tend to drive down economic profits for all firms. These are sometimes called **new entrants**. **Substitutes** are products that offer the same or similar values to customers. The presence of substitutes both inside and outside the industry also may have a downward pressure on profits and represents another type of threat. But substitutes can also bring opportunities. See Exhibit 7-10.

A force that can counteract the influence of substitutes and create opportunity is the presence of complementary products and services.[70] For some companies cooperation is just as important as competition, and strategic thinking must consider both.[71] This is called **co-opetition**. Firms that make complementary products can be firms inside or outside the industry. For example, automobiles need the complementary products of auto insurance, engine oil, tires, and gasoline. What **complements** have in common is that they provide something that customers need to get full value from the products they buy. For example, it makes no sense for a customer to purchase a set of golf clubs from your company if they cannot also purchase golf balls to use with the clubs or if they have no place to use the clubs such as a golf course. When deciding strategy for your golf club company, you must consider the actions of the golf ball manufacturing companies. Golf balls and golf courses are just two of

EXHIBIT 7-10
Industry Forces That Influence Strategic Thinking

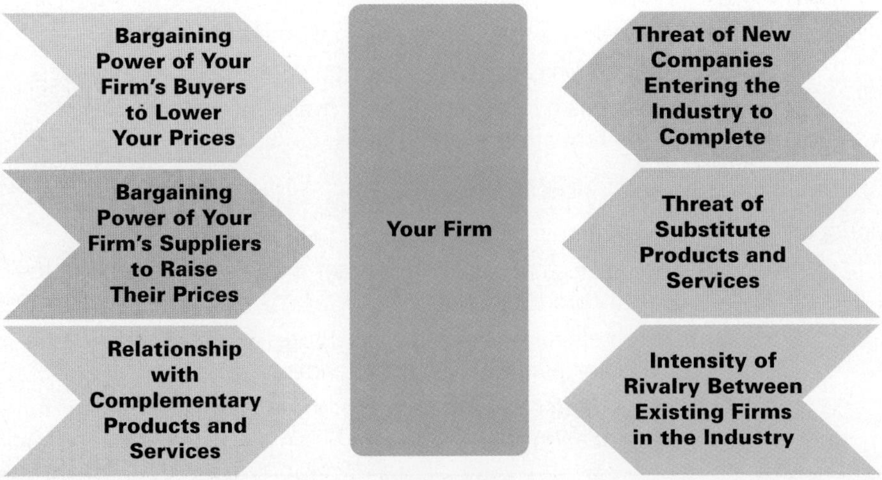

Source: DavidXu/Shutterstock.

Strategic choices that a gasoline retailer makes involves deciding what products can be sold that are complementary to the sale of fuel.

many complementary products that are needed by the customer to get the full value out of golf clubs. See Exhibit 7-11.

When a company works together with another company that makes complementary products to promote the success of the product, from the customer's perspective, demand grows and both companies succeed. This may require, in the short-run, that one or both of the companies take lower profits. These companies must also be on guard that their other-interest does not place them in a position of complete dependence on the companies that make stronger profits in the short run.

So while some firms are your competitors, some also can be complementary. Customers and suppliers can be both complementary and competition. The presence of complementary products makes the industry more attractive if their positive influence counteracts the downward pressure on profits from competitors. In most business situations organizations both compete and cooperate with each other. When suppliers work closely with companies and their customers,

EXHIBIT 7-11
Substitutes and Complements

Product	Substitutes	Complements
Sugar	Corn syrup, NutraSweet	Cereal, flour, other baking ingredients
Fiberglass insulation	Cellulose, rock wood, Styrofoam	Framing lumber, staples, nails
Business travel	Video conferencing	Briefcase, computer, luggage
Symphony concert	Radio, television, CDs, iPod	Formal wear, evening wear
Soft drinks	Fruit juice, bottled water	Snack food, ice cubes, drinking cups
Aspirin	Acetaminophen, ibuprofen	Water, juice
Beef	Chicken, ham, tofu	Steak knives, steak sauce, BBQ
FAX machine	Email, Express mail	Toner, paper, telephone line
Corn chips	Potato chips, fresh fruit	Beans, cheese sauce, salsa
Jif peanut butter	Skippy peanut butter	Jam, bread, bananas
Golf clubs	Tennis racket	Golf balls, golf shoes, bag
Shopping mall	Online shopping	Parking lots, restaurants
Universities	Private enterprise, libraries, community colleges	Computers, housing, hotels, local employers
Bachelors degree in business	Bachelors degree in history, on-the-job training	Textbooks, business scholars, business newspapers, stories

cooperation creates value for everyone. When customers try to use their bargaining power to get better quality or prices and when suppliers want to get better prices or reduce quality, competition can deplete value, making the value "pie" smaller.[72]

The Christian Mind on Environmental Analysis

Understanding the world around us requires us to be observant, so that we can see connections not always evident to others. While speaking to the people of Athens, at the meeting of the Areopagus, Paul remarks on the religious commitment of the people who even worship an "Unknown God." Paul uses this accepted altar as a point of connection to the Creator/Savior God (Acts 17:22–24). Likewise, managers will be able to draw parallels and connections with the world around them as they observe their environment. Seeing the Social, Technological, Economic, and Political (STEP analysis or PEST analysis) realities will help us make better decisions to navigate a course of action. Being in tune to the world around us will aid our ability to make better decisions, meet needs, and respond to the changing landscape. We are called to be wise and "understand our times" (I Chronicles 12:32 and Esther 1:13).

Dr. Ervin Starr
Associate Professor of Management & Entrepreneurship
Roberts Wesleyan College
Rochester, NY

DRIVING FORCES FOR CHANGE. Every industry is undergoing constant change. Executives make it their business to be aware of not only the changes but the things that are driving change. Some of the more common forces that drive strategic change include government regulations and legislation; invention of new technology that changes how products are manufactured, distributed, or used by customers; the development of specific technology standards for the whole industry; and changing consumer preferences that are shaped by culture.

We have been exploring the types of things that strategic decision makers think about that are *outside* the organization. But decision makers cannot forget what's going on *inside* the organization. Organization executives think about core competencies, organizational structure, assets, and the financial performance of the business model.

CORE COMPETENCIES. A **core competency** is the combination of resources and capabilities that allow a firm to grow in the future by making new products or selling its products to new customers.[73] A **resource** is something a business has, such as sophisticated equipment, a patent, access to raw materials, or a great location. A **capability** is what the organization does exceptionally well (compared with competitors) with its resources, such as the knowledge and skills to use resources. Thus, core competence is "a bundle of skills and technologies rather than a single discrete skill or technology."[74] The ability of the firm to find sizable cost benefits in production also is a core competence. To use an analogy from nature, core competencies are the roots of the tree that grows the fruit of future products and services and allows the company to enter new markets when its current market is saturated with products. See Exhibit 7-12.

The core competencies of Federal Express have grown its ability to manage a continual package routing and delivery system. Such a system depends on several things such as bar code

EXHIBIT 7-12
Core Competencies

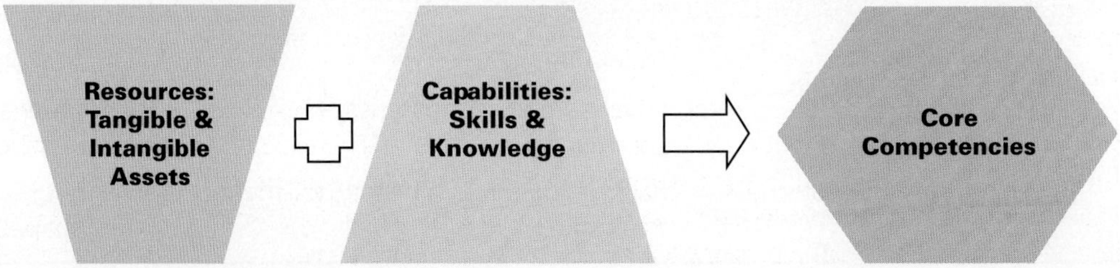

technology, computer controlled sorting, electronic communication, linear programming, staff and equipment scheduling, and skills required for managing a network.

Senior leaders are limited in the amount of time they can spend gathering information and thinking about everything. Because of this, it is natural that they are selective in what they pay attention to. Generally executives focus on the core competencies that lie at the center of the organization's ability to deliver value to its key customer groups over a long period of time.

But what reveals whether a competence is "core"? The identifying marks of a core competence are:[75]

- **Customer Value.** Compared with the influence of other internal factors, a core competence will make a disproportionate contribution to customer value.
- **Competitor Differentiation.** Core competencies of one firm set the company apart from competitors. However, there is a natural bias of company executives to overestimate their company's competencies compared with those of competitors. Executives also are biased in identifying what they believe are unique characteristics of their company when such characteristics may likely be found in competing firms as well.
- **New Products, New Markets.** A core competency can be extended beyond current products and services and applied to new products, new markets, and to solving new customer problems. This requires managers to think abstractly about particular product configurations in which the competence is embedded. SKF, a leading manufacturer of roller bearings, can define its core competence in a more fundamental way than simply making bearings. The firm's ability to make bearings is based on its knowledge of friction, antifriction, and precision engineering using hard metals and close tolerances, and on its ability to make spherical devices. A firm with the ability to manufacture electronic display systems such as a laptop display may have the core competencies to develop displays for a wide variety of products that are applied in a wide variety of industries and consumer use: calculators, automotive dashboards, devices for computer controlled manufacturing and robotics, etc.
- **Difficult to Imitate.** When a core competency involves the coordination of people, systems, skills, and technology, it becomes increasingly difficult for a competitor to copy it. "A rival might acquire some of the technologies that comprise the core competence, but it will find it more difficult to duplicate the more or less comprehensive pattern of internal coordination and learning."[76]

ORGANIZATIONAL STRUCTURE. Core competence is about understanding which skills and technology are central to the ability of the organization to deliver value and then harmonizing these effectively.[77] Harmonizing work effort requires structure to the organization, so organizational structure, and whether changes are needed to it, becomes an important consideration for executives when they are making strategic choices.

ASSETS. The current property, facilities, and equipment will play an important role in strategy implementation. It is only natural that top-level leaders consider these items when deciding what to do in the future. While the strategic decisions might involve the purchase of new assets, existing assets will either be sold or also used.

FINANCIAL PERFORMANCE OF THE BUSINESS MODEL. The ability of the organization as a whole to generate revenue and manage its costs contributes to its ability to accomplish its mission. We sometimes refer to the revenue stream and expense structure as the **business model.** The business model is comprised of two elements. The business model is first of all a story that describes how the enterprise as a whole works and the key assumptions that support the story. It describes the economic logic of why revenue is generated. The business model also contains financial estimates that describe the way the organization will add cash to investors as a result of the operations of the revenue stream and expense structure. The business model can be expressed in terms of any one of several typical financial statements and analyses such as the following: the income statement, the statement of cash flows, the balance sheet, and break-even (cost-volume-profit) analysis.[78] See Exhibit 7-13.

The revenue stream represents the value that customers are willing to exchange for what the organization offers in its products and services. "Hidden" in this revenue stream are a host of assumptions about how best to price, promote, and distribute the products downstream toward consumers. The revenue stream eventually becomes free cash flow for investors. The expense structure part of the model represents the supply chain relationships upstream and assumptions

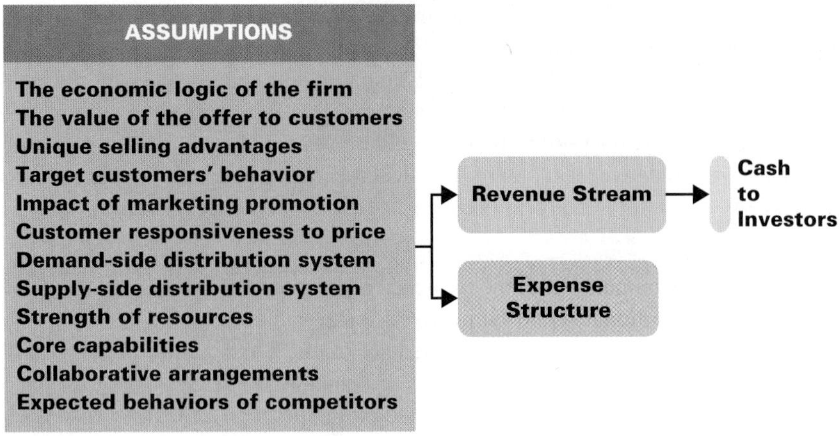

EXHIBIT 7-13
The Business Model

regarding the core competencies that are required to create and deliver value to customers on a consistent basis. The financial accounting report of profit and loss (income statement) is a common representation of the business model assumptions. Statements of cash flow and balance sheets also describe the business model from slightly different perspectives.

SWOT Analysis

As the executive team thinks about the situation outside and inside the organization, it is natural for leaders to make judgments about the state of affairs as they understand it. Major issues will have emerged that have the potential for impacting the entire organization. This thinking leads to summarizing the major issues in what is known as the **SWOT analysis**. SWOT stands for Strengths, Weaknesses, Opportunities, and Threats (See Exhibit 7-14). SWOT analysis refers to the process of evaluating whether what is found is favorable or unfavorable to the company.

An evaluation of the internal situation of the company will reveal favorable strengths and unfavorable weaknesses. Strengths and weaknesses can arise in terms of core competencies, organizational structure, assets, financial performance, and key personnel. These raise strategic issues inside affecting the organization as a whole that must be addressed. For example, strategic decision makers realize that compared with competitors the company has one of the best locations (a strength), but that because of the high population density in the area the size of their customer parking lot is inadequate (a weakness). This represents an ongoing strategic issue that strategic decision makers must address.

Similarly, an evaluation of the external marketplace will reveal favorable opportunities and unfavorable threats. Opportunities and threats result from changes in market structure or industry structure, the influence of driving forces, the actions of competitors (foreign and domestic), the actions of companies making complementary products, changes in consumer preferences, macroeconomic influences, and government regulations. See Exhibit 7-15.

The SWOT analysis is not something that strategic decision makers do only every 2 or 3 years during a strategic planning meeting. Instead, it is a continual process of thinking about internal and external issues that the organization must address in order to be successful. As new opportunities or threats arise company leaders evaluate them and use their judgment regarding how important they are and what to do about them. Likewise, as company leaders notice favorable and unfavorable changes taking place inside the organization, they make judgments regarding the importance of these changes for the future of the company. These judgments then lead to decisions.

EXHIBIT 7-14
Factors Considered in SWOT Analysis

	Internal	External
Favorable	Strengths	Opportunities
Unfavorable	Weaknesses	Threats

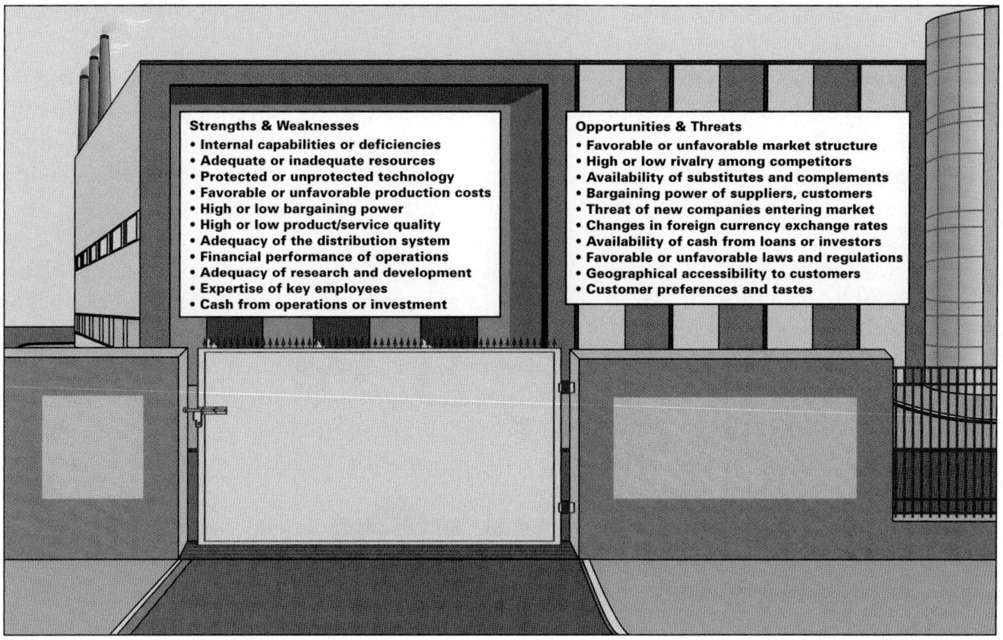

EXHIBIT 7-15
What to Look for in the SWOT Analysis

Strategic Decisions and Actions

While strategic thinking never stops for top-level managers, it leads to making decisions and taking actions that, when implemented, become the major commitments of resources, people, and activities needed to achieve organizational goals. To explore this, we will consider the concept of strategy formulation next.

Strategy Formulation

Strategic thinking leads either to reaffirming previous strategic choices or to making new choices that affect the future of the entire organization. From a broad perspective, the types of strategic choices that executives make fall into common patterns. We will review two of the models that strategy scholars have developed to identify these patterns.[79]

Igor Ansoff, who worked in the aircraft manufacturing industry as a strategic planner, identified four basic patterns of strategic growth opportunities open to a business.[80] Each of the patterns represents a different combination of emphasis on products and markets or product lines and the mission the company has with each of the major markets it serves. Ansoff called these choices the **product-market strategy choices**. When the company leaders choose to continue selling more of their existing products to the current market (doing more of the same), they are choosing the **market penetration strategy**. The company can accomplish this by increasing the volume of sales to current customers or attracting new customers from the same market to purchase its products. Of the four choices, this strategic choice usually represents the lowest risk. See Exhibit 7-16.

When a firm chooses to adapt its current products to a new mission (by making some modifications to its products), it is using a **market development strategy**. An example of this is when an aircraft company modifies its passenger jets and attempts to sell the same basic aircraft

		Markets (Missions)	
		Existing	**New**
Product Lines	Existing	Market Penetration	Market Development
	New	Product Development	Diversification

EXHIBIT 7-16
Ansoff's Product-Market Strategy Model[81]

to cargo transportation companies. These two patterns of strategy emphasize the growth of the company by leveraging its current products.

A company can also develop new products. A **product development strategy** is when the company creates new products and attempts to sell these to its current customers, thereby continuing to enhance its ability to achieve its current mission. With this strategy, the products developed will serve the current market. An aircraft company may decide to design and build a different size of aircraft that its current commercial airlines customers may want to help them pursue their goals.

When a firm chooses to sell new products in completely new markets, its strategic choice is **diversification**. The diversification approach to growth requires developing new skills and knowledge. New relationships with suppliers, customers, and regulators are required. Also, this choice usually leads to changes in the structure of the organization. A company can diversify by getting involved with products and customers that are related to its current products and mission (lower risk), or it can diversify into completely unrelated products and customer groups. Unrelated diversification carries the highest risk because the company is venturing into new territory for products and customer groups to serve.

Large businesses with plenty of financial capital available and with the management expertise will follow more than one strategy simultaneously. Smaller, family-owned businesses can, as they grow over time, follow these strategic choices, too.

An example of Ansoff's model is Green Mountain Coffee Roasters, a company that began as a house brand in a small café in Waitsfield, Vermont, in 1981.[82] At first the owners of this small business employed a *market penetration strategy* to grow demand for their coffee brand primarily through word of mouth. Visitors began asking for bags of coffee to take home with them. Then people from out of town began asking for coffee to be sent to them through mail order. This led the company toward the *market development strategy* of serving people in other geographical markets. Low price elasticity of demand allowed the company to charge a premium for its coffee. Mail-order sales increased when the company developed a catalog (both print and online). The success of the mail-order revenue stream gave the company new opportunities to grow by expanding its product line as they followed the *product development strategy*. They began selling coffee mugs, coffee machines, coffee bean roasters, pancake mixes, and many other products. In 1993, the company went public by selling stock on the New York Stock Exchange.

The simplicity of Ansoff's model makes it fairly easy to characterize a company's strategic choices. His model represents a balance of both the internal and external perspective required for strategic thinking. However, what Ansoff's model lacks is the perspective of market structure and industry structure. This perspective has been provided by Harvard professor Michael Porter's generic strategies model.[83]

Strategic choices cannot be reduced to a simple recipe that when followed will automatically bring success.[84] Every market and every industry is different. Markets and industries are constantly changing. However, when we look at the strategic choices that many companies in many industries have made over the years we see some interesting commonalities and patterns. It is the pattern of commonalities that Michael Porter's model offers when you consider the core issues at stake in both market and industry structure. What emerges is a pattern of choices that reveal how broad (or narrow) in scope a company's strategic efforts are pushed as well as the economic position the company attempts to establish and maintain in its market.

Some companies attempt to serve a broad marketplace and many customer segments with products designed for many segments. For example, a large, national public accounting firm such as Ernst & Young serves companies of all sizes and in most all industries. Other firms choose to serve a more narrow set of customers (geographic segments, demographic segment, business segment, etc.). As an example, Michael R. Bell and Company is a local public accounting firm in Spokane, Washington, offering public accounting services for hospitals, home health agencies, nursing homes, and health clinics in the northwest. There is nothing inherently better about one scope or another.

Another pattern emerges when we consider the economic position options available to companies. Some companies in a given industry attempt to produce at a lower cost per unit than their competitors. Often these companies charge a price that is lower than their rivals. We sometimes call this **low-cost leadership**. Tata Motors of India is an example of a company that is attempting to compete in the global automobile market with one of the lowest-cost vehicles available. Low-cost leadership can be a solid competitive position or a tenuous position depending on how easy it is for competitors to copy a company's low-cost expense structure. Also, if customers are relatively price sensitive and are unwilling to pay a price premium for a similar product that is different, then the low-cost leadership approach makes sense. The low-cost leadership strategy also makes sense when the product that is being sold is a *search good*—a product that is purchased after the consumer has searched and compared one company's product with other offerings.

If the market structure supports opportunities for *differentiation*, then other companies may decide to produce products that can command a premium price. A **differentiation strategy** is based on providing a product that offers distinctive features or benefits that are qualitatively different from other companies and that customers demand. This is sometimes called **benefit leadership**. For example, British Airways has become known for its ability to distinguish itself from other airlines based on excellent customer service.

The ability of any particular firm to successfully emphasize a position of differentiation depends on the price elasticity of demand as consumers evaluate the advantage that this firm's products offer compared with competitors. If there are many product attributes that the customer considers when making the purchase decision and if customers disagree about the attractiveness of one or more attributes, then the benefit leadership strategy is more likely to be successful. The benefit leadership strategy makes obvious sense when there are no foreseeable means to do better than the current low-cost leader firms in terms of restructuring costs without sacrificing the minimum level of quality that customers desire. It also makes sense when the product is an *experience good*, that is, a product in which the customer must purchase and use the product before they can fully understand its benefits.[85] For an illustration of Porter's generic strategies model see Exhibit 7-17.

If customers are not very responsive to changes in price, then cutting the price will not effectively attract new customers,[86] and price increases may not result in losses in market share. But if customers are more responsive to price changes, then developing the low-cost leader position can result in increases in market share.

Some companies attempt to get the benefits of a low-cost strategy mixed with the benefits of a differentiation strategy. This is sometimes called the *best-cost* strategy. The products the firm makes are at attractive prices (though perhaps not the lowest prices) and the products carry features and benefits that distinguish them from competitors' products. Toyota has developed a reputation for following this type of strategy.

Another approach is the **transaction strategy**, in which the firm attempts to improve the ability of the company and its customers to complete transactions with fewer resources. This can involve improving the convenience or the cost of transactions. For example, Staples office products retailer started an Internet marketing company that became very successful at selling office products online. But Staples realized that some customers need the flexibility of ordering online *and* visiting the retail stores. Customers who order online and visit the Staples store spend up to four times as much at Staples as the customer who shops only online. Staples now has integrated its in-store, online, catalog marketing, and its direct sales efforts to small businesses.[87]

The Broad Metropolitan Interstate Freeway

Low-cost products demanded by a broad market

Differentiated (higher priced) products demanded by a broad market

The Narrow Country Lane

Low-cost niche products

Differentiated (premium price) niche products

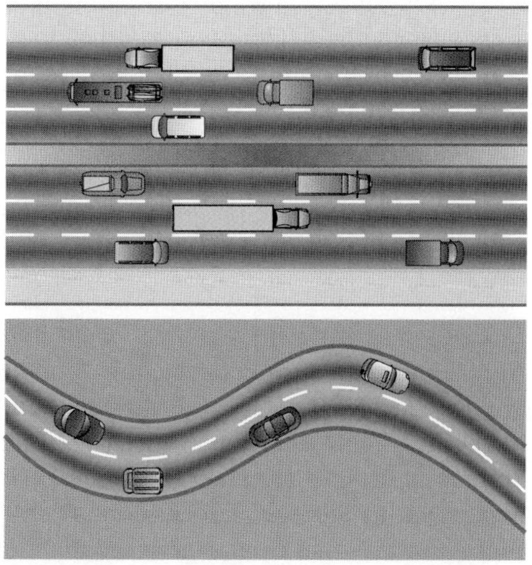

EXHIBIT 7-17

Porter's Generic Strategies Model: A Metaphor

Staples also enjoys a degree of synergy from its integrated operations. **Synergy**, whether achieved within a company or between different businesses owned by a larger corporation, occurs when the value of two or more revenue-producing units working together is greater than it would be if these units worked independent of each other.[88] While synergy is still the hope of many company leaders, in practice it is difficult to achieve.

The Christian Mind on Strategy Formulation

"The critical difference between the traditional definition of strategic management and its Christian definition lies in the firm's need to demonstrate Christian values in its decisions and operations . . . For the Christian, the ability for one human being to alter or influence the environment should be quite familiar. The Bible teaches that we are the salt of the earth and that we are to season/preserve our environment with good works. We are to let our lights shine before men to expose our good deeds and bring praise to the Father (see Matt. 5:13–16). Given the scriptural commands on witness through good works, it seems that organizational strategy can and should become an additional vehicle for Christians to influence their environment. A strategy providing purpose and direction for organizational activities is a natural tool for producing good works."[89]

Steven J. Musser, PhD
District Superintendent, Eastern District
Evangelical Free Church of America

Strategy and Nonprofit Organizations

The process of strategic decision making in a nonprofit organization can be different from that in the for-profit world because of some key differences between the two settings.[90] For nonprofits the value they create in the form of services is often intangible and difficult to measure. While for-profits must consider customers and their preferences, this type of knowledge may be less influential in the nonprofit organization where mission is more prominent.

Mission is the key force and the primary influence for integration in the nonprofit while economic incentives is a much stronger force for integration in the for-profit world. Strategic planning is often focused on the input of resources needed for organizational programs and service functions. This is in contrast to the output-orientation mentality of value-producing processes in for-profits. Indeed, strategic planning sessions may not even be called that. Instead such thinking and planning might be called "visioning for the future" or simply planning. Because nonprofit organizations include a wider range of stakeholders than the for-profit business, they have a wider range of perspectives to consider. This means that decision making for the long-term future might take longer than it would in the for-profit arena. The big decisions tend to be more political than in the for-profit world. Compared with the resources available in a for-profit organization, the resources of a nonprofit are fewer in volume and more varied in quality.

In the nonprofit the business model is continually strained. Pressures for operating revenue do not subside as the organization becomes prosperous. The reason is that as prosperity occurs, decision makers expand programs and services making the expense structure increase. This, in turn, places more pressure on the need to generate more operating revenue.

The Gap Between Formulation and Implementation

According to research conducted by Marakon Associates, a strategy consulting firm, on the average companies achieve roughly two-thirds of the financial performance that they hope to achieve by implementing their strategy.[91] As hard as top-level executives work to improve their assumptions about the marketplace, their ability to get it right 100 percent of the time and then to implement it effectively and consistently 100 percent of the time is limited. We can easily say from this study and from experience that doing the work of strategy is more difficult than it

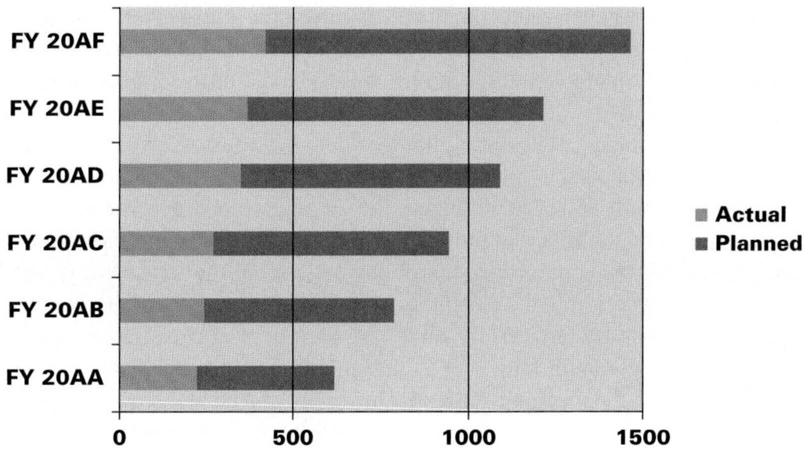

EXHIBIT 7-18
Actual Performance Implementing Strategy

Source: Based on Mankins, M. C., & Steele, R. (2005). Turning great strategy into great performance. *Harvard Business Review*. 83(7/8), 67.

appears on the surface when merely thinking about strategy work. This raises the question of why most companies fall short of their performance projections. Exhibit 7-18 shows how strategic decision makers expect that their strategy will generate results that are far superior to what can be obtained in practice.

Researchers have found that one of the reasons for this gap is that companies rarely track their actual performance against specific expectations outlined in their strategic plans. After the strategic planning debates and discussions, after the strategic plan is presented to the governing board, and after assignments are made and implementation tasks delegated, executives get busy solving the implementation problems. They spend a large amount of time selling the strategic decision internally so that mid-level managers and frontline supervisors understand and commit to supporting the plans. When executives do track their firm's performance against the projected performance, a pattern emerges that is called the venetian blind or hockey stick charts.

Some financial forecasts are unreliable. When executives are unable to tie the capital expense budget approval process to the strategic decision-making process, they are less likely to achieve their projected gains. And, when it comes time to allocate strategically relevant resources for implementation, if these actions are not coupled directly with the strategic thinking and goals, then performance will suffer. Day-to-day operational needs can be so important to care for that it becomes extremely difficult to have the strategic plan drive operational thinking.

Researchers also found that some business units that are failing to produce long-run wealth for investors receive capital expense allocations while other value-creating business units are starved for capital. Sometimes it is difficult to predict that a business unit that is struggling this year will actually fail in the future. Executives hope that providing such a unit with more capital will help it turn around. In other cases, the allocation of capital becomes so political that business units that have the most potential for creating long-term wealth suffer if their executive leaders are unable to win approval of funds.

Factors that can influence the gap between projections and actual performance include the following:

- Inadequate resources allocated or available
- Poorly communicated strategy
- Actions required to execute strategy not clearly defined
- Unclear accountabilities
- Organizational silos and organizational culture blocking execution
- Inadequate performance monitoring
- Inadequate consequences or rewards for failure or success
- Poor senior leadership
- Uncommitted leadership
- Unapproved strategy
- Other obstacles

Researchers propose several factors that can repair the gap between performance and projection.[92] First, keep the strategy simple. The best projections are concrete and measurable. Avoid long, drawn out, or complex descriptions of lofty goals. Instead, stick to clear language that people can understand to describe the course of action.

Second, debate the marketplace assumptions, but not the numbers in the forecasts. Strategic planning is often a negotiated settlement and highly political. To improve the chances that the truth about the market will be revealed during the strategic planning process, keep financial forecasting separate from where assumptions are hammered out—assign these to two separate teams. This ensures that the economic assumptions underlying the long-term goals reflect the real economics of the markets and the performance of the company relative to competitors.

Third, use a rigorous framework for analysis. Members of the strategic planning team should learn to speak a common language to minimize misunderstandings. Discuss resource deployments early during the planning process. This improves the realism of forecasts. Some of the deployment questions to ask include: How long will it take us to change customer purchase patterns? How fast can we deploy our new sales force? How quickly will competitors respond? Fourth, clearly identify priorities. Most strategic plans are highly detailed and managers can get lost in the details losing sight of the priorities.

The best strategies will always compete with other day-to-day activities going on in the firm. Therefore, continuously monitor actual results against projected results. Without this monitoring, strategic decision makers will not have the information they need to make adjustments when a gap develops. Finally, reward and develop managerial capabilities.

Successful implementation requires careful management of both top-down visioning and bottom-up communication of what really works. Executives have the responsibility of identifying where strategic priorities conflict with other priorities. Only by clarifying values and priorities can such executives give clear behavior-guiding signals to subordinates. The CEO may need to change some members of the senior leadership team. In other cases, senior leaders may need coaching on how they can become more effective. Successful implementation requires far more communication between subordinates and bosses than many realize. Likewise, horizontal coordination across the organization is far more important and more difficult to achieve than most managers expect.[93]

Paradoxes of Strategic Thinking

Just like many of the other management activities we are exploring in this book, strategic thinking comes with its own set of interesting tension points. The whole process of strategy can be thought of as the process of mentally embracing many tensions: intuition versus logical analysis, ambiguity versus precision, focusing on specifics versus being flexible, and the big picture versus the little details.[94] Here are the most common tensions.

FORMULATE STRATEGIC DECISIONS—IMPLEMENT DECISIONS.[95] This is perhaps the fundamental tension that all strategic managers face. Mentally they must continually be thinking about and refining their understanding of what the company must do and what the company is now doing.

RISK TAKING—CONSTANCY.[96] Many top-level leaders find that their company's situation calls for risk taking. At the same time, these leaders must maintain some level of constancy. Prematurely implementing a particular strategy can be just as damaging as maintaining constancy when it's time to change.

TOP-DOWN—BOTTOM-UP.[97] Senior leaders must assimilate all the information coming from all directions and then communicate top-down the strategic decisions that are made. Top-down visioning, however, works against the bottom-up communication by the frontline workers who know the day-to-day difficulties of implementing strategy. Yet emphasizing the bottom-up interests of frontline workers without senior leaders' assistance will make it difficult for frontline workers to focus their ideas into a cohesive vision for the future.

CONCENTRATE—DIVERSIFY.[98] If a company concentrates its resources on just a few products and services, it can become exceptional at producing. But this limits its ability to spread its risks. However, if a company attempts to diversify too broadly by producing and selling a wide variety of products, it will become more difficult to become very good at any particular product, and, as a result, its brand reputation might weaken.

Focus on an Organization

Christian Leadership Alliance

Christian organizations such as large churches, para-church ministries, and other religious nonprofit organizations have come to realize how important management and leadership is to be successful. The Christian Leadership Alliance (CLA) is an organization whose mission is to help develop Christian organizations and leaders. CLA was formed in April 2008 when the former Christian Management Association merged with the Christian Stewardship Association. This international organization is comprised of over 6,000 members working in over 2,500 organizations. Several metropolitan areas in the United States have a local CLA chapter where members can meet several times each year to learn from each other about how to improve their ability to manage.

CLA "seeks to build the body of Christ by building people—enhancing the effectiveness of Christian organizations and large churches."

The CLA, in collaboration with the Engstrom Institute, provides many educational resources to help develop the character and effectiveness of Christian leaders. The association conducts an annual conference.

Information about the CLA can be obtained from the association's website: http://www.christianleadershipalliance.com/.

Chapter Summary

1. There may be differences between Christians and others in terms of how religious faith influences strategic thinking. For example, Christians hold different views regarding competition. The religious values of a strategic leader may constrain the organization's mission or affect the selection of long-term alliances. The setting in which the religious believer works may influence how prominently religious values affect strategic decisions. How the external environment is scanned through the eyes of religious faith will shape how a person views opportunities and threats and the degree to which organizational goals are subordinated to biblical principles, to what degree business will be linked with the mission of evangelism, and to what degree taking advantage of temporary market opportunities will conflict with religious beliefs.
2. The Management Pyramid model is used in this chapter to explore strategic thinking and action. Values are the foundation of strategic thinking. Values always drive discussions and debates among strategic leaders.
3. Strategic thinking is a constant process of thinking about the present and the future, the internal capabilities and the external situation, the specific products and the core competencies that are embedded in the ability to make and sell these products, specific issues that require decisions, and the organization as a whole. In some organizations the strategic thinking process is more sequential, planned, and formal. In other circumstances and in some organizations strategic thinking is emergent, less formal, and at times even chaotic. Strategy formulation is the continual process of analyzing the marketplace and the organization and then making one or more decisions that affect the company as a whole. Strategy implementation is the process of carrying out the strategic decisions that are made. There is no single right way to manage the strategic planning process, but strategic decisions require making trade-offs.
4. The content of strategic thinking includes what is happening *outside* the organization in the marketplace and industry, and what is happening *inside* the organization in terms of its key personnel and resources needed to accomplish the organization's mission. The content of strategic thinking involves keeping in mind a distinction between strategic issues and tactical issues. Strategy is what orients the entire organization toward the pursuit of its mission or a big goal; strategy guides tactical day-to-day decision making and action. Tactics are the visible day-to-day activities, tasks, and maneuvers that need to get done to accomplish the mission or achieve the goal in a changing market. Strategic thinkers have an awareness of how the microeconomic structure of the market influences the organization's ability to achieve strong economic performance. Competitive and cooperative forces in the industry also influence the thinking of strategic

managers: bargaining power of buyers and sellers, the presence of substitutes, the threat of new entrants, the rivalry of existing companies, and the presence of complementary products. Strategic leaders also keep aware of the driving forces for change taking place in their marketplace. They think about their firm's core competencies and the ways the company is able to add value to products and services.

5. This thinking leads to summarizing the major ongoing issues in what is known as SWOT analysis. SWOT stands for internal Strengths and Weaknesses, and external Opportunities and Threats.
6. Strategic thinking leads either to reaffirming previous strategic choices or to making new choices that affect the future of the entire organization. Igor Ansoff identified four basic patterns of strategic growth opportunities open to a business. When the company leaders choose to continue selling more of their existing products to the current market (doing more of the same), they are choosing the market penetration strategy. The firm can choose a market development strategy by adapting its current products to a new mission (by making some modifications to its products). A product development strategy is the decision to create new products and attempt to sell these to current customers. Diversification, the most risky of the four patterns, is when the firm decides to make new products and offer them to new customers.
7. Michael Porter's model of strategic patterns reveals that some companies attempt to serve a broad marketplace and many customer segments with products designed for many segments while other companies attempt to serve a narrow part of the market. Likewise, some firms attempt to be low-cost leaders in their market while other firms attempt to offer products that are differentiated from competitors in terms of product features and benefits. In some markets firms attempt to offer their products at the best cost and best value. Synergy, whether achieved within a company or between different businesses owned by a larger corporation, occurs when the value of two or more revenue-producing units working together is greater than it would be if these units worked independently.
8. The process of strategic decision making in a nonprofit organization can be different from that in the for-profit world because of some key differences between the two settings.
9. Several factors appear to influence why a gap exists between strategic choices and actual performance.

Key Terms

Discussion Questions

1. Can a Christian be faithful to principles of Scripture and at the same time attempt to create a monopoly in which consumers are more vulnerable? Under what conditions would a Christian attempt to increase the company's pricing power over consumers, for example, moving toward a monopoly position in the market?
2. Are there some industries that a Christian business owner would choose not to invest in because of the nature of the products being sold or because of the commonly accepted practices that require the believer to compromise religious beliefs?
3. Is it ever wrong for a Christian executive to attempt to gain a competitive advantage over rival companies? If so, under what conditions?
4. How can Christian strategic managers manage the balance in their life (being present for family and for worship), particularly when complex strategic decisions must be made?
5. Describe how personal values influence strategic decisions.
6. How can the Christian strategic decision maker fully live the eternal principles of love, justice, and redemption while engaging fully in a competitive market where the struggle for economic success is never-ending?
7. To what degree can a Christian executive who works in a publically traded corporation implement a "business as mission" strategy? How will this type of strategic choice be different in a private company owned by a Christian?

8. What are the influences that cause a change in the core values on which company strategy is made?
9. How influential are the personal values of a company's founders 10 years after the company is established? 25 years later? 50 years later?
10. If a company founder dies or retires, how long will the core values that guided the company strategy continue to have a strong influence?
11. When a company goes public, does this increase the risk that core values will be changed? Why?
12. Will the Christian strategic decision maker place more or less emphasis on values than a non-Christian?
13. Should a Christian be willing to become unequally linked with individuals who don't support fundamental Christian values through a merger or acquisition?
14. How great are the risks that a company such as Tata Motors will reduce its costs so much that the product fails to meet minimum customer expectations for performance and safety?
15. If a merger requires downsizing of one or both of the firms, should the Christian manager engage in restraint because these actions have a direct negative economic effect on the lives of workers who are let go?

STUDENT EXERCISES

1. Identify one of the companies that you are most interested in. Using resources on the Internet try to identify whether this company is striving to achieve a low-cost leadership, differentiation, or best-cost strategy.
2. Identify a company that is currently going through a strategic decision-making process. To do this, find an article from a recent issue of the *Wall Street Journal*, *Forbes*, *Business Week*, or another business magazine or newspaper that discusses the strategic issues and decisions that the company faces. What are the biggest issues the company is facing? What type of strategy does the company seem to be following?
3. Identify a company whose assumptions are no longer completely valid. What seems to be incorrect about the company's assumptions now?
4. Find a company that seems to have as its guiding principle diversification into related products and services. How has this company been pursuing such a strategy: by merger, by acquisition, or by growing new companies on their own?

IN-CLASS EXERCISES

Memory-Repetition Feedback

Before beginning the lecture, divide the class into small teams of four to five members each. Each group should meet for a few minutes to discuss what they already know about the topic of the chapter. Groups record what they know on index cards. At the end of the class period ask groups to meet again, this time to record what elements of the lecture need repetition. These ideas also are recorded on the cards. Cards can be submitted to the professor for review. At the beginning of the next class period the professor can select some of the cards that address issues that need repeating.

Content Review Cards

Divide the class into small teams of four to five members each. Give each class member an index card. On one side of the card the team member writes a review question. Cards are handed to other members of the team who write a summary of the answer to the review question on the back of the card. Cards from one team are passed to another team who add to the answers that were written. Cards can be handed in. Content from these cards can be posted online such as in a blog for all students to review and add to.

Issue Debate/Discussion

Divide the class into small groups of five to six people each. Hand out a sheet of paper containing the following quotations. Assign half of the groups to defend the first perspective and the other half to defend the second quotation as valid. Give the groups 5 minutes to discuss. Then call for groups to give a summary of the rationale they developed. Discussion can follow.

Discussion Topic #1: The Christian and the low-cost leadership strategy. If a Christian pursues business activities that pursue religious values of justice and love, such actions might include raising wages of workers compared with what other firms pay. This, in turn, can raise the cost of doing business, making it more difficult for that business to achieve a cost-leadership strategy with respect to competitors. If this economic reasoning is accurate, does this mean that a low-cost leadership strategy is the best approach for the Christian business to pursue?

A. **Yes.** Pursuing a cost leadership strategy is a way of being a faithful steward of resources. Low-cost leaders can offer lower prices to low-income consumers. Being a low-cost leader requires creativity—a principle founded at creation that is consistent with the image of God.
B. **No.** Pursuing a cost leadership strategy in competition with secular companies will result in the secular company always winning that battle. Secular companies will pay their workers less and will be more willing to contract with foreign suppliers who pay their workers less. The more the Christian tries to surpass the secular company in terms of costs, the more pressure the Christian decision maker will be under to compromise principles of religious faith.

Discussion Topic #2: The Christian and the differentiation strategy. Companies pursue the differentiation strategy by trying to offer products and services that are meaningfully different from competitors' products and services. The costs of producing differentiated products are often higher as materials may be of higher quality and cost more, and employees may be paid more. This translates into higher costs of doing business. However, companies that offer differentiated products can sometimes charge higher prices to customers. If this economic reasoning is accurate, does this mean that a differentiation strategy is the best approach for the Christian business to pursue?

A. **Yes.** Offering a differentiated product allows the Christian business leader to be more just in paying employees and suppliers. Differentiation requires the business leaders to be creative. This is consistent with humans being created in the image of God.

B. **Not necessarily.** If Christian leaders in a company have a better opportunity to pursue a low-cost leader strategy, they should do so. Paying workers higher wages will help them, but the higher prices charged to consumers mean that the products and services are less accessible to them.

Discussion Topic #3: Mergers and acquisitions. Should a Christian consider a merger or acquisition simply because such an action represents an opportunity to extend the Christian's influence for the gospel to the newly acquired company employees?

A. **Yes.** The Christian will always consider first the opportunities for extending Christian values throughout the market. Because the principles of the gospel are consistent with good business, such an action will bring God glory and business success.

B. **No.** God does not want strategic leaders to be economically reckless and thereby bring him dishonor. The Christian must consider the economic implications of such actions. While Christian values guide the Christian leader in decision making, the Gospel Commission is not always the sole reason for taking a strategic action such as a merger or acquisition. Buying a failing company just for the purpose of helping the workers may very likely set the company up for failure in achieving both goals.

Endnotes

1. Musser, S. J. 1990. Biblical principles applied to strategic management. In Chewning, R. C. (Ed.). *Biblical principles & business: The practice*. Colorado Springs, CO: Navpress, p. 33.
2. Hill, C. W. L., & Jones, G. R. (2004). Strategic management theory: An integrated approach. Boston, MA: Houghton Mifflin Company. p. 3.
3. Murphy, J. (2008). International business: Toyota pulls back on sales goal; lowering '09 target is rare concession; a sign of the times. *Wall Street Journal* (Eastern Edition). August 29, p. B.2.
4. http://www.aptera.com/.
5. Finkelstein, S., & Hambrick, D. C. (1996). *Strategic leadership: Top executives and their effects on organizations.* Minneapolis/St. Paul: West Pub. Co. p. 2; Haskins, D. R., & Smith, Y. (2004). *Christians in strategic leadership: Towards an integration of faith and the top management team.* Paper presented to the Christian Business Faculty Association Annual Conference, San Antonio, TX. October 28–30. p. 7.
6. Drucker, P. F. (1954). *The practice of management.* New York: Harper & Brothers. p. 353.
7. Hall, R. H., & Tolbert, P. S. (2005). *Organizations: Structures, processes and outcomes.* (9th ed.). Upper Saddle River, NJ: Pearson Prentice Hall.
8. Kouzes, J. M., & Posner, B. Z. (2003). Character development: It's what leadership development is all about. *Executive Excellence*. 20(9), 3.
9. Andrews, K. R. (1971). *The concept of corporate strategy.* Homewood, IL: Dow Jones-Irwin, Inc. pp. 237–238; Kouzes, J. M., & Posner, B. Z. (2003). Character development: It's what leadership development is all about. *Executive Excellence*. 20(9), 3; Harvey, M. (2001). The hidden force: A critique of normative approaches to business leadership. *SAM Advanced Management Journal*. 66(4), 38. See the story about US Airways in Foust, D. (2009/October 5). Boxed in at US Airways. *Business Week*. 4149, 34.
10. 1 Corinthians 12:28. The Greek word (transliterated as) kubernesis. This word is from the root kubernao meaning *to steer*. From this word we have derived the English word *governing*.
11. Genesis 39–47.
12. Joshua 6–7.
13. Genesis 30:30.
14. Genesis 30:25–31:55.
15. Proverbs 27:23–24.
16. 1 Chronicles 12:32.
17. Nehemiah.
18. Genesis 41:33–35.
19. Genesis 41:53–57, 47:13–15.
20. Genesis 47:15–17.
21. Genesis 47:18–22.
22. Genesis 47:23–26.
23. Also, Numbers 14, Deuteronomy 1. See Keil, C. F., & Delitzch, F. (1949). *Biblical commentary on the Old Testament, Vol. 3 The Pentateuch*, Grand Rapids, MI: Wm. B. Eerdmans Publishing Company; Kuntz, J. K. (1974). *The people of ancient Israel: An introduction to Old Testament literature, history and thought.* New York: Harper & Row Publishers. pp. 123–149; Noth, M. (1968). *Numbers: A commentary*, Philadelphia, PA: The Westminster Press; Cafferky, M. E. (2005). *Teaching strategic environmental analysis using Numbers 13 & 14: The first 2 × 2 strategy matrix in Scripture?* Paper presented to the Christian Business Faculty Association Annual Conference. San Diego, CA. October.
24. Deuteronomy 1:20, 1:21.
25. Deuteronomy 1:22.
26. Proverbs 14:15, 21:5.

27. Proverbs 19:8.
28. Proverbs 11:14, 20:18.
29. Psalm 25:12, 32:8; 1 Kings 22:5.
30. Proverbs 16:3; Psalm 37:5.
31. Proverbs 16:9.
32. Martinez, R. (2003). Teaching strategic management from a Christian perspective. *Journal of Biblical Integration in Business*. Fall, 69–97; VanderVeen, S. (2004). A radical, reformed Christian rejoinder to Martinez's "Teaching strategic management from a Christian perspective." *Journal of Biblical Integration in Business*. Fall, 7–13; Musser, S. J. 1990. Biblical principles applied to strategic management. In Chewning, R. C. (Ed.). *Biblical principles & business: The practice*. Colorado Springs, CO: Navpress, pp. 31–42; Tiemstra, J. P., Graham, W. F., Monsma, G. N., Sinke, C. J., Storkey, A., & Ebels, D. M. (1990). *Reforming economics: Calvinist studies on methods and institutions*. Lewiston, NY: The Edwin Mellen Press. pp. 176–182.
33. This is adapted from Marsden, G. M. (2005). Faith-informed scholarship. In Henderson, J. W., & Pisciotta, J. (Eds.). *Faithful economics: the moral worlds of a neutral science*. Waco, TX: Baylor University Press. p. 21.
34. Haskins, D. R., & Smith, Y. (2004). *Christians in strategic leadership: Towards an integration of faith and the top management team*. Paper presented to the Christian Business Faculty Association Annual Conference, San Antonio, TX. October 28–30. p. 9.
35. Bretsen, S. N. (2006). *In competition with godless hoards: Are some strategic approaches more appropriate for a faithful business*. Paper presented to the Christian Business Faculty Association Annual Conference. Dayton, OH. October; Smith, Y., Johnson, S. G., & Hiller, E. M. (2003). *God of the games: Towards a theology of competition*. Paper presented to the Christian Business Faculty Association Annual Conference. San Antonio, TX. October; Johnson, S. G., & Smith, G. (2002). *Perspectives on competition—Christian and otherwise*. Paper presented to the Christian Business Faculty Association Annual Conference. Boise, ID. October.
36. Musser, S. J. (1990). Biblical principles applied to strategic management. In Chewning, R. C. (Ed.). *Biblical principles & business: The practice*. Colorado Springs, CO: Navpress, pp. 31–42.
37. Hoksbergen, R. (1994). Is there a Christian economics: Some thoughts in light of the rise of postmodernism. *Christian Scholar's Review* 24, 126–142. See also the discussion on "bluffing" in Porter, B. E. (2004). The compatibility of Christianity and business. *Journal of Biblical Integration in Business*. Fall, 5–21.
38. Some Christians may cite 2 Corinthians 6:14 as the basis of their concern. This passage is based on the Deuteronomic instruction not to join two different animals together under the same yoke. (Deuteronomy 7:2, 22:10). See also Galatians 1:6–10; 1 John 2:15–17.
39. Matthew 5:13–16; John 17:14; Mark 16:15; Hebrews 12:14; 1 Peter 2:9–12. For comments on this see Musser, S. J. (1990). Biblical principles applied to strategic management. In Chewning, R. C. (Ed.). *Biblical principles & business: The practice*. Colorado Springs, CO: Navpress, pp. 31–42.
40. Musser, S. J. (1990). Biblical principles applied to strategic management. In Chewning, R. C. (Ed.). *Biblical principles & business: The practice*. Colorado Springs, CO: Navpress, p. 34.
41. Miles, G. (1993). In search of ethical profits: Insights from strategic management. *Journal of Business Ethics*. 12(3), 219–225.
42. Haskins, D. R., & Smith, Y. (2004). *Christians in strategic leadership: Towards an integration of faith and the top management team*. Paper presented to the Christian Business Faculty Association Annual Conference, San Antonio, TX. October 28–30. p. 20.
43. Stevens, R. P. (2006). *Doing God's business: Meaning and motivation for the marketplace*. Grand Rapids, MI: William B. Eerdmans Publishing. p. 80; Johnson, C. N. (2009). *Business as mission: A comprehensive guide to theory and practice*. Downers Grove, IL: InterVarsity Press. pp. 25–57.
44. Stalk Jr., G., & Lachenauer, R. (2004). Hard ball: Five killer strategies for trouncing the competition. *Harvard Business Review*. 82(4), 62–71; Stalk Jr., G. (2006). Curveball strategies to fool the competition. *Harvard Business Review*. 84(9), 114–122; Barach, J. A. (1985). The ethics of hardball. *California Management Review*. 27(2), 132–139.
45. Barnard, C. I. (1938). *The functions of the executive*. Cambridge, MA: Harvard University Press. pp. 258–284; Andrews, K. R. (1971). *The concept of corporate strategy*. Homewood, IL: Dow Jones-Irwin, Inc.
46. Besanko, D., Dranove, D., Shanley, M., & Schaefer, S. (2007). *Economics of strategy*. (4th ed.). New York: John Wiley & Sons. pp. 223–247; Hitt, M. A., Ireland, R. D., & Hoskisson, R. E. (2009). *Strategic management: Concepts & cases*. (8th ed.). Mason, OH: South-Western Cengage Learning; Porter, M. E. (1996). What is strategy? *Harvard Business Review*. 74(6), 61–78.
47. Brandenburger, A. M., & Nalebuff, B. J. (1996). *Co-opetition*. New York: Doubleday. p. 7.
48. Andrews, K. R. (1971). *The concept of corporate strategy*. Homewood, IL: Dow Jones-Irwin, Inc. p. 104; Freeman, R. E., Gilbert Jr., D. R., & Hartman, E. (1988). Values and the foundation of strategic management, *Journal of Business Ethics*. 7(11), 821–834; Liedtka, J. (2000). In defense of strategy as design. *California Management Review*. 42(3), 8–30. See also the thought: "It is impossible to be totally rational about strategy. Hence, values creep in, and most agree that they should. An organization needs a set of values, but these also constrain strategic decision-making." Higgins, J. M., & McAllaster, C. (2004). If you want strategic change, don't forget to change your cultural artifacts. *Journal of Change Management*. 4(1), 63–73. (p. 67)
49. Andrews, K. R. (1971). *The concept of corporate strategy*. Homewood, IL: Dow Jones-Irwin, Inc. p. 51. See also Besanko, D., Dranove, D., Shanley, M., & Schaefer, S. (2007). *Economics of strategy*. (4th ed.). Hoboken, NJ: John Wiley & Sons. pp. 302–304; Brandenburger, A. M., & Nalebuff, B. J. (1996). *Co-opetition*. New York: Doubleday. pp. 223–224.
50. McDonald, M. L., & Westphal, J. D. (2003). Getting by with the advice of their friends: CEOs' advice networks and firms' strategic responses to poor performance. *Administrative Science Quarterly*, 48, 1–32; Boatright, J. R. (1988). Ethics and the role of the manager. *Journal of Business Ethics*. 7(4), 303–312.

51. Narver, J. C., & Slater, S. F. (1990). The effect of a market orientation on business profitability. *Journal of Marketing*. 54(4), 20–35; Kohli, A. K., & Jaworski, B. J. (1990). Market orientation: The construct, research propositions, and managerial implications. *Journal of Marketing*, 54(2), 1–18; Prahalad, C. K., & Hamel, G. (1990). The core competence of the corporation. *Harvard Business Review*, 68(3), 79–91; Best, R. J. (2009). *Market-based management: Strategies for growing customer value and profitability*. (5th ed.). Upper Saddle River, NJ: Prentice Hall.
52. Brandenburger, A. M., & Nalebuff, B. J. (1996). *Co-opetition*. New York: Doubleday. pp. 60–64.
53. Hitt, M. A., Ireland, R. D., & Hoskisson, R. E. (2009). *Strategic management: Concepts & cases*. (8th ed.). Mason, OH: South-Western. pp. 5–6.
54. Mintzberg, H., & Lampel, J. (1999). Reflecting on the strategy process. *Sloan Management Review*. 40(3), 21–30; Mintzberg, H. (1994). *The rise and fall of strategic planning: Reconceiving roles for planning, plans, planners*. New York: The Free Press. pp. 5–34.
55. Mankins, M. C., & Steele, R. (2006). Stop making plans start making decisions. *Harvard Business Review*. 84(1), 76–84.
56. Alberts, H. R. (2009). Yum! Brands grow in China. *Forbes.com*. http://www.forbes.com/2009/10/07/yum-brands-earnings-markets-equities-china.html.
57. Campbell, A. (1999). Tailored, not benchmarked: A fresh look at corporate planning. *Harvard Business Review*. 77(2), 41–50.
58. Phills, Jr., J. A. (2005). *Integrating mission and strategy for nonprofit organizations*. Oxford: Oxford University Press. p. 48.
59. Drucker, P. F. (1992). *Managing the non-profit organization: Principles and practices*. New York: HarperBusiness; Phills, Jr., J. A. (2005). *Integrating mission and strategy for nonprofit organizations*. Oxford: Oxford University Press.
60. Brandenburger, A. M., & Nalebuff, B. J. (1996). *Co-opetition*. New York: Doubleday. pp. 62–63.
61. Collins, J. (2001). *Good to great*. New York: HarperBusiness. pp. 90–119.
62. Collins, J. (2001). *Good to great*. New York: HarperBusiness. pp. 90–119.
63. Spors, K. (2009). EBay changing its strategy again. WSJ Blogs. http://blogs.wsj.com/independentstreet/2009/03/12/ebay-changing-its-strategy-again/.
64. Peter Drucker was one of the first management scholars to distinguish between strategy and tactics. See Drucker, P. F. (1954). *The practice of management*. New York: Harper & Brothers. pp. 352–353.
65. Pindyck, R. S., & Rubinfeld, D. L. (2001). *Microeconomics*. (5th ed.). Upper Saddle River, NJ: Prentice Hall. pp. 251–455; Hitt, M. A., Ireland, R. D., & Hoskisson, R. E. (2009). *Strategic management: Concepts & cases competitiveness and globalization*. (8th ed.). Mason, OH: South-Western. pp. 13–18.
66. Besanko, D., Dranove, D., Shanley, M., & Schaefer, S. (2007). *Economics of strategy*. (4th ed.). Hoboken, NJ: John Wiley & Sons. pp. 31–35, 199–202; Pindyck, R. S., & Rubinfeld, D. L. (2001). *Microeconomics*. (5th ed.). Upper Saddle River, NJ: Prentice Hall. pp. 252–253.
67. Pindyck, R. S., & Rubinfeld, D. L. (2001). *Microeconomics*. (5th ed.). Upper Saddle River, NJ: Prentice Hall. pp. 251–455.
68. Porter, M. E. (1980). *Competitive strategy: Techniques for analyzing industries and competitors*. New York: The Free Press. pp. 3–33; Porter, M. E. (2008). The five competitive forces that shape strategy. *Harvard Business Review*. 86(1), 78–93.
69. Here the difference between accounting profits and economic profits is important. Accounting profits are reported in the firm's financial statements. Economic profits take into consideration the accounting profits but also factor in the *opportunity cost of capital*.
70. Brandenburger, A. M., & Nalebuff, B. J. (1998). *Co-opetition*. New York: Doubleday. pp. 11–39.
71. Besanko, D., Dranove, D., Shanley, M., & Schaefer, S. (2007). *Economics of strategy*. (4th ed.). Hoboken, NJ: John Wiley & Sons. p. 313.
72. Brandenburger, A. M., & Nalebuff, B. J. (1998). *Co-opetition*. New York: Doubleday. p. 36.
73. Fuchs, P. H., Mifflin, K. E., Miller, D., & Whitney, J. O. (2000). Strategic integration: Competing in the age of capabilities. *California Management Review*. 42(3), 118–147; King, A. W., Fowler, S. W., & Zeithaml, C. P. (2001). Managing organizational competencies for competitive advantage: The middle-management edge. *The Academy of Management Executive*. 15(2), 95–106; Leonard-Barton, D. (1992). Core capabilities and core rigidities: A paradox in managing new product development. *Strategic Management Journal*. 13, 111–125; Mascarenhas, B., Beveja, A., & Jamil, M. (1998). Dynamics of core competencies in leading multinational companies. *California Management Review*. 40(4), 117–132; Prahalad, C. K., & Hamel, G. (1990). The core competence of the corporation. *Harvard Business Review*. 68(3), 79–91; Smith, R. (2008). Harnessing competencies, capabilities and resources. *Research Technology Management*. 51(5), 47–53.
74. Hamel, G., & Prahalad, C. K. (1994). *Competing for the future*. Boston, MA: Harvard Business School Press. p. 202.
75. Prahalad, C. K., & Hamel, G. (1990). The core competence of the corporation. *Harvard Business Review*. 68(3), 79–91; Hamel, G., & Prahalad, C. K. (1994). *Competing for the future*. Boston, MA: Harvard Business School Press.
76. Prahalad, C. K., & Hamel, G. (1990). The core competence of the corporation. *Harvard Business Review*. 68(3), 84.
77. Prahalad, C. K., & Hamel, G. (1990). The core competence of the corporation. *Harvard Business Review*. 68(3), 79–91.
78. Magretta, J. (2002). Why business models matter. *Harvard Business Review*. 85(5), 86–92; Schweizer, L. (2005). Concept and evolution of business models. *Journal of General Management*. 31(2), 37–56.
79. Other models include the following: Miles, R. E., & Snow, C. C. (1978). *Organizational strategy, structure and process*. New York: McGraw Hill; Kim, W. C., & Mauborgne, R. (2005). *Blue ocean strategy*. Boston, MA: Harvard Business School Press.
80. Ansoff, H. I. (1957). Strategies for diversification. *Harvard Business Review*. (Sept–Oct), 113–124.

81. Ansoff, H. I. (1957). Strategies for diversification. *Harvard Business Review*. (Sept–Oct), 114.
82. Lowy, A., & Hood, P. (2004). *The power of the 2 × 2 matrix*. San Francisco: Jossey-Bass. pp. 134–138; http://www.greenmountaincoffee.com/.
83. Porter, M. E. (1985). *Competitive advantage: Creating and sustaining superior performance*. New York: The Free Press. pp. 62–163.
84. Besanko, D., Dranove, D., Shanley, M., & Schaefer, S. (2007). *Economics of strategy*. (4th ed.). Hoboken, NJ: John Wiley & Sons. p. 363.
85. Besanko, D., Dranove, D., Shanley, M., & Schaefer, S. (2007). *Economics of strategy*. (4th ed.). Hoboken, NJ: John Wiley & Sons. pp. 370–373.
86. Besanko, D., Dranove, D., Shanley, M., & Schaefer, S. (2007). *Economics of strategy*. (4th ed.). Hoboken, NJ: John Wiley & Sons. p. 371.
87. Spulber, D. (2003). *Management strategy*. New York: McGraw-Hill/Irwin. p. 273.
88. Hitt, M. A., Ireland, R. D., & Hoskisson, R. E. (2009). *Strategic management: Competitiveness and globalization*. Mason, OH: South-Western Cengage Learning. p. 175; Porter, M. E. (1985). *Competitive advantage: Creating and sustaining superior performance*. New York: The Free Press. pp. 317–319.
89. Musser, S. J. (1990). Biblical principles applied to strategic management. In Chewning, R. C. (Ed.). *Biblical principles and business: The practice*. Colorado Springs, CO: NavPress. p. 33.
90. Newman, W. H., & Wallender III, H. W. (1978). Managing not-for-profit enterprises. *Academy of Management Journal*. 3(1), 24–31; Hatten, M. L. (1982). Strategic management in not-for-profit organizations. *Strategic Management Journal*. 3(2), 89–104; Unterman, I., & Davis, R. H. (1982). The strategy gap in not-for-profits. *Harvard Business Review*. 60(3), 30–35; Steinberg, R. (2006). Nonprofit organizations and the market. In Powell, W. W. (Ed.). *The nonprofit sector: A research handbook*. (2nd ed.) New Haven, CT: Yale University Press. pp. 117–139; Nutt, P. C., & Backoff, R. W. (1987). A strategic management process for public and third-sector organizations. *Journal of the American Planning Association*. 53(1), 44–57; Bryce, H. (1999). *Financial & strategic management for nonprofit organizations*. (3rd ed.). Upper Saddle River, NJ: Prentice Hall. p. 41; Drucker, P. F. (1992). *Managing the non-profit organization: Principles and practices*. New York: HarperBusiness; Simon, H. A. (1993). Strategy and organizational evolution. *Strategic Management Journal*. 14, 131–142; Oster, S. M. (1995). *Strategic management for nonprofit organizations: Theory and cases*. New York: Oxford University Press; Euske, K. J. (2003). Public, private, not-for-profit: Everybody is unique? *Measuring Business Excellence*. 7(4), 5–11; Rangan, V. K. (2004). Lofty missions, down-to-earth plans. *Harvard Business Review*. 82(3), 112–119; Phills Jr., J. A. (2005). *Integrating mission and strategy for nonprofit organizations*. Oxford: Oxford University Press.
91. Mankins, M. C., & Steele, R. (2005). Turning great strategy into great performance. *Harvard Business Review*. 83(7/8), 64–72.
92. Mankins, M. C., & Steele, R. (2005). Turning great strategy into great performance. *Harvard Business Review*. 83(7/8), 64–72.
93. Beer, M., & Eisenstat, R. A. (2000). The silent killers of strategy implementation and learning. *Sloan Management Review*. 41(4), 29–40; Bourgeois III, L. J. (1980). Performance and consensus. *Strategic Management Journal*. 1(3), 227–248.
94. Liedtka, J.. (2000). In defense of strategy as design. *California Management Review*. 42(3), 8–30.
95. Ginsberg, A., & Venkatraman, N. (1985). Contingency perspectives of organizational research: A critical review of the empirical research. *The Academy of Management Review*. 10(3), 421–434.
96. Parnell, J. A., & Lester, D. L. (2003). Towards a philosophy of strategy: Reassessing five critical dilemmas in strategy formulation and change. *Strategic Change*. 12(6), 291–303.
97. Abell, D. F. (1999). Competing today while preparing for tomorrow. *Sloan Management Review*, 49(3), 73–81; Parnell, J. A., & Lester, D. L. (2003). Towards a philosophy of strategy: Reassessing five critical dilemmas in strategy formulation and change. *Strategic Change*. 12(6), 291–303; Denison, D. R., Haaland, S., & Goelzer, P. (2004). Corporate culture and organizational effectiveness: Is Asia different from the rest of the world? *Organizational Dynamics*. 33(1), 98–109; Mulhare, E. M. (1999). Mindful of the future: Strategic planning ideology and the culture of nonprofit management. *Human Organization*. 58(3), 328–340.
98. Porter, M. E. (1997). Creating tomorrow's advantages. In Gibson, R. (Ed.). *Rethinking the future*, London: Nicholas Brealey Publishing; Porter, M. E. (2001). Strategy and the Internet. *Harvard Business Review*. 79(3), 63–78; Drucker, P. F. (1992). *Managing the non-profit organization: Principles and practices*. New York: HarperBusiness.

CHAPTER

8 Organization

LEARNING OBJECTIVES

- Be aware of why organizing is such an important role for managers to play.
- Understand the principles of organizing found in the Bible and how they apply to today's managers.
- Understand the key elements of organizing such as division of labor, coordination, span of control, and decision-making authority.
- Know the basic differences in organizational design options.
- Value trust as an organizing principle and be aware of how organization influences moral decision making.
- Evaluate the impact that large organizations have on individual workers and understand the reasons for and results of downsizing an organization.
- Identify selected tension points that managers face as they fulfill their role as organizers.

"Significance is partly about work itself, but even more about how the work is understood. . . . The gift of significance helps people sustain their faith rather than burn out and retire on the job."[1]

"When we think that we have solved a problem, well, by the very process of solving, new elements or forces come into the situation and you have a new problem on your hands to be solved."[2]

JOE GIBBS RACING

When Joe Gibbs, a committed Christian, Pro Football Hall of Famer, and three-time Super Bowl Champion head coach of the Washington Redskins professional football team, wanted to expand his well-known auto racing organization, he had a few organizational choices to make. For years Joe Gibbs Racing, based in Huntersville, North Carolina, had operated three race teams in the NASCAR Nextel Series (now known as the Sprint Cup series) and two teams in the Busch Series (now known as the Nationwide Series). Gibbs' racing teams had also competed in the Funny Car, Top Fuel, and Pro Stock drag racing events of the National Hot Rod Association (NHRA). Gibbs decided to expand his company by fielding teams to compete in off-road motorcycling competitions.[3]

Over the years Joe Gibbs Racing has focused on working with the best people it can find. Over 450 people are employed by the company. To Joe Gibbs, integrating faith is as important as winning races. The company's facilities include personal weight training, a banquet hall, a theater-style auditorium, and a lunchroom where employees can enjoy weekly Bible studies. The company's philosophy is that you win with people, not with machines. While this is an important foundation, even champions find it difficult to perform at their highest level unless they are in a well-organized environment.

Source: Iakov Filimonov/Shutterstock.

Organizing is not new to Joe Gibbs. When you have auto racing teams that use hundreds of motors each year—each engine used for just one race—you need to be organized. The Huntersville facility is highly organized down to every car having its own set of parts bins that move with the car if it changes location inside the building. Cars are grouped by which tracks they race on.

In expanding his business to include motocross racing, Gibbs faced several organizing decisions: How many drivers should he hire to launch this new effort? Should the motocross team members be located in one place? Should they work out of the Huntersville, North Carolina, facilities where the three Sprint Cup NASCAR teams are based? If so, should the drivers, mechanics, and other support staff report to one of the NASCAR team managers? Locating the motocross team near the NASCAR teams might allow team members to share creative ideas with the other teams. For example, engineering experts who have been working in NASCAR for years might be able to serve as coaches and mentors to the engineers working for the motocross team. Or, to achieve more efficiency, engineers might be assigned the task of working for both NASCAR teams and the motocross teams.

Another question was should the motocross team have its own identity, budget, manager, and facility? With its own identity, it may have more influence over resource allocation decisions. It might also be able to respond to changes taking place in the motorcycle racing environment more quickly than if leaders steeped in the NASCAR environment had to make the decisions for them. What are the key tasks that need to be accomplished and who should be assigned to these tasks? These are just a few of the organizing decisions that Gibbs needed to make.

In the end Joe Gibbs appointed his youngest son, Coy Gibbs, to run the new motocross racing division of Joe Gibbs Racing Motocross (JGRMX). Jeremy Albrecht, an experienced motocross racer and championship mechanic, was appointed team manager of JGRMX. Gibbs decided to field two teams to compete in each of the World Supercross GP races and the AMA Supercross Series. The two motocross teams are based in Huntersville and have an organization similar to the auto racing teams. Unlike some other motocross competitors that might have components of a team in more than one geographic location but come together on race days, JGRMX decided to locate all the components together: mechanics shop, test track, trainers, engineers, transportation team, other support staff, and, of course, the riders. The benefit of operating in one location is that the team can learn to work together every day of the week, not just on race day. To take a video tour of the Joe Gibbs Racing facilities in Huntersville, North Carolina, visit: http://www.jgrmx.com/cgr/community/home.htm.

Who Cares About Organizing?

Think about the last time you were given an assignment to work with a small team of people. It could have been a group assignment in a course or a project at work. One of the first things that you needed to do was to get organized. You needed to consider the task as a whole, as well as specific job assignments.

The success of any company depends on two fundamental requirements: strategy and organization. Strategy can often be copied. Organization of core competencies is far more difficult to copy and is one of the few remaining sustainable sources of competitive advantage.[4] For example, at Anderson Landscape Construction company, a firm that specializes in installing expensive landscaping for upscale homes, company managers have learned how to work closely with homeowners in ways that many of their competitors have not. The company has established a customer–field worker communication program that shortens the time between when a customer wants to discuss a concern and when the construction worker onsite communicates with the company owner. Another competitive advantage is how Anderson works as the mediator between customer and landscape architect as the installation occurs. Someone must take responsibility to make sure that the big picture ideas from the architect actually fit precisely with the existing terrain and buildings on site. How Anderson organizes these processes is difficult for many companies to copy.

When inexperienced managers organize their workers and then problems arise, they can easily blame the individuals for the problems. Or they might question the way they have been treating their employees: If they were just a little nicer, or a little more respectful, then the workers would not exhibit problems. Another common thought is that one or more of the workers may be mismatched with the job. Workers are sometimes selected for jobs in which it is difficult for them to perform at their best. These thoughts may be valid depending on the circumstance. But looking at organization from a structural point of view helps the responsible manager move past the oversimplified solution of blaming individuals for organizational problems.[5]

In both for-profit and nonprofit organizations, managers must have a wider market awareness of how their organizational choices affect customers, clients, and the general public. This market orientation, in part, depends on managers' abilities to coordinate their efforts with each other throughout the company. This is a job not just for the marketing director but for everyone. Coordination does not occur simply because someone announces in a manager's meeting that it will be a new priority.[6] It takes work.

To properly understand the importance of structural elements in organizations, we need to go back to the beginning.

Management Pyramid: The Organization

Peter Drucker realized that an enterprise is a community of human beings founded on common beliefs.[7] The values and beliefs shared by the organization (or society) drive shared thinking and feeling patterns (both operational and strategic), which in turn influence patterns of action. Just as with individual behavior, the long-term results of *organizational* action affect how the members of the organization think and what the organization as a whole becomes. See Exhibit 8-1.

Concerted action is vital to an organization's ability to carry out its mission and strategy. But concerted action depends on shared thinking and feeling about how to solve the organization's problems. Shared thinking stems from a shared cluster of values and assumptions that guide

It is the complexity of the work itself and the complexity of the business environment outside the organization that requires division of labor. For example, construction crews might be divided based on the primary skills of workers. People skilled in framing might specialize in that while masons specialize in laying cement blocks and bricks. Another example is that the increase in federal government regulations for environmental safety has influenced some companies like colleges and universities to hire a specialist to train employees and monitor the disposal of hazardous waste.

Division of labor makes the organization more complex and establishes interdependencies between the workers and between the organization and its environment. When a worker in a bicycle assembly plant becomes a specialist in assembling tires on rims, there is an immediate need for this person to coordinate with the worker who specializes in installing the brakes. The more tasks are divided the more likely efficiency will be improved. At the same time, without attention to coordination, effectiveness might be jeopardized. Thus, managers or workers must coordinate work efforts to deal with the *organizational complexity* created by division of labor.[41] **Organizational complexity** is the number of different types of workers and the various levels of decision-making authority in the organization. It also includes the various approaches the organization takes to coordinate the efforts of workers. **Environmental complexity** is the number of different entities and people that the organization must maintain active relationships with. It also includes how complicated and how rapidly the environment around an organization is changing. **Task complexity** is the number of different types of work action that must be performed to accomplish a task. See Exhibit 8-5.

EXHIBIT 8-5
Fundamental Organizing Problems and Solutions

Problems	Solution
Environmental complexity: For example, a variety of government regulations, the variety of types of resources that organizations need, the variety of suppliers companies need to work with, and changing customer tastes create environmental complexity. **Task complexity:** For example, assembling an automobile requires hundreds of different parts made by scores of companies put together in a carefully orchestrated sequence. **Lack of efficiency:** For example, making one entire refrigerator from start to finish would take days to complete, but by dividing the work into a series of specific tasks, a refrigerator can be assembled in just a few minutes.	**Division of labor:** To solve these types of problems, organizations divide the tasks and train workers to become very good at their tasks.
Interdependencies: For example, manufacturing is interdependent on research and development and sales when planning production. **Organizational complexity:** For example, in organizations of all sizes, the more work is divided up to improve efficiency the more workers need to coordinate with each other to get all the work done.	**Coordination and integration of labor:** To solve these types of problems, organizations can coordinate scheduling of inventory, the placement of workers, and the sequencing of activities for all workers in the assembly, packing, and shipping processes. Organizations must also coordinate sales with marketing, accounting, and production, and quality control with production and purchasing.

(continued)

Lack of effectiveness:
For example, when the work of assembling a refrigerator is divided into many small tasks, workers must carefully sequence their activities to keep the assembly process moving.

Key Management Issue: It is at the point(s) of division of labor where coordination and integration problems will occur regardless of the level where the division is made.

EXHIBIT 8-5
Continued

THE BENEFITS. Managers divide up the work for several reasons.[42] They give orders to subordinates so that all the work is accounted for. (See Exhibit 8-6.) Organization reduces uncertainty for both managers and non-managers. By dividing up the work, managers can save time and lower costs. As they divide up the work, managers can take into consideration the natural differences in human ability among workers. The economic return increases for each unit of work accomplished. When managers divide the tasks, they can more easily analyze the job that needs to be done and find ways to improve efficiency and effectiveness. For example, when possible, managers at an assembly plant such as Honda will ask engineers to devise mechanical or robotic systems to assist workers or to accomplish the tasks that workers formerly performed.

Productivity is important especially in the work areas that are devoted to fulfilling the primary purpose of the company. Because of this, we sometimes observe a higher degree of specialization of tasks among workers at the core of the organization where the products and services are made. **Specialization** is the dividing of the total work into specific, well-defined

EXHIBIT 8-6
Mary Parker Follett on "Giving Orders"[43]

During the 1920s and 1930s, Mary Parker Follett became one of the forward-thinking students of management and a pioneer in organizational theory and behavior. She made insightful observations from her study of political organizations, social service organizations, and businesses. In her day, managers were expected to give the commands and subordinates were expected to carry out the commands without questioning. Even managers who held strong religious beliefs tended to "lord over" their subordinates, continually reminding them who was in charge and who had the authority. She noticed that successful managers were more sophisticated than using a simplistic approach that emphasized their power and authority.

In Follett's opinion giving a subordinate an order should not be about the manager exercising authority over the subordinate. Instead, it should be about the work situation, what the task is, and why it is needed to move the goals of the organization forward. This allows the employee to see meaning in the delegated task.

When a manager issues arbitrary commands, the manager will lose valuable contributions from subordinates. Employees will clam up and let the manager figure things out alone. Arbitrary demands on workers cause unnecessary social friction. Arbitrariness destroys the sense of pride that workers have in their work. Worst of all, it destroys the sense of personal responsibility that workers would normally have otherwise.

Follett's instructions are to:

- Depersonalize the delegated task (it's not about you).
- Identify the basic issues that emerge from the work itself (let the "work" give the commands).
- If the reasons are not self-evident, then give subordinates the reasons for the task.
- As much as possible, replace "giving orders" with teaching.

Benefits of Division of Labor	Costs of Division of Labor
Improves accountability	The greater the division of labor the higher the risk that the overall mission of the organization might get lost without coordination.
Reduces uncertainty	Differences between workers increase in terms of their mental orientations and goals.
Saves time and costs	Pieces of important processes can get scattered among several work units.
Takes into consideration the natural skills and abilities of each worker	Coordination becomes more costly.

EXHIBIT 8-7
The Costs and Benefits of Division of Labor

steps. Higher degree of specialization means that any given employee has just one or very few different specific tasks to perform. Low specialization means that employees have several or many different specific tasks to perform.

THE COSTS. Division of labor also comes with a downside. The more work is divided, the higher the risk that the mission of the whole organization will get lost. With specialization comes differences in work styles and mental orientations of workers. If not coordinated, differences in goals can threaten the overall effectiveness of the organization. For example, the time frame of the production department can be different from the time frame of the purchasing department. The ways in which the top-level administrative leaders interact with each other can be quite different from how the staff of support departments work with each other. Differences in mental orientations can result in employees focusing on specific activities in their own jobs rather than the organizational goals. Employees in large bureaucratic organizations can develop a "that's not my job" response to things that need to get done. We sometimes call these *silos* or *stove pipes* because the subcultural differences that develop tend to isolate one group of workers from other groups.

As an organization becomes more divided up, pieces of the important business processes become scattered across many specialized departments. In very large organizations these lines of division come with geographical separation that ranges from yards to city blocks to hundreds or thousands of miles. As a result, coordination of effort becomes more difficult and more costly. Even under the best of circumstances the risk increases that details will fall through the cracks. Filling customer orders, purchasing materials and supplies, obtaining feedback from customers, and improving product quality are examples of crucial activities that can be difficult to coordinate the more specialized the tasks become.[44]

See Exhibit 8-7 for a summary of the costs and benefits of division of labor.

The Christian Mind on Division of Labor

The Bible demonstrates that organizing is part of the social fabric of how humans relate with each other. Ancient biblical society included a clear specialization of social roles: prophet, priest, king, merchants, tradesmen, agricultural specialists, and other specialized occupations. Inside organizations labor was divided among specialists.

From a faith perspective, work relationships should be based on the principle of covenant. Just as individuals in a covenant work hard to support the covenant relationship, so the organizational choices that managers make should support the relationship by serving the needs of individuals, as well as the needs of the company as a whole. Division of labor is not an end in itself. Work should be divided in such a way that promotes harmony of effort and well-being for all those affected at the same time as fostering efficient production.

EXHIBIT 8-8
Integration and Coordination

Influences that promote *integration* of effort:[45]	**Activities that promote coordination:**[46]
Desire for economic gain	Authority of supervisors
Organizational goals	Schedules, plans, policies, procedures
Organizational mission	Direct contact between employees
Shared mental and emotional responses toward common problems	Interdepartmental liaisons
Moral principles and personal values	Task forces, committees, teams, coordinating departments

Coordination and Integration

Division of work and integration of effort are the opposite (inverse) of each other and yet must go hand-in-hand.[47] Division separates; integration unites. **Integration** and **coordination** are the combining of separate parts of an organization so that they work together in concert. A symphony orchestra is an excellent analogy of coordinated effort among highly trained experts performing specialized tasks.[48] The conductor and the musical score act as control systems with the musicians who willingly submit to the conductor's authority and the composer's will. This is one way that the players become unified in their effort. The other path to unification of effort is through the integration that comes from having shared norms and values. In an orchestra, this is displayed in terms of a shared understanding of the style of music being performed as well as an awareness of the intent of the composer. Shared values regarding precision of entrances and cut-offs, tone quality, and the rules of musical score interpretation all contribute to the integration of effort.[49] See Exhibit 8-8.

Several important points to keep in mind: First, implementing more complicated, costly coordinating mechanisms (such as teams and task forces) does not replace the simpler, less costly approaches (such as direct contact and schedules). Second, even if coordinating mechanisms are used, this does not diminish the need for the integrating influences from shared values and goal alignment. Third, as an organization grows in size, diversity increases and it becomes increasingly difficult to achieve unity with shared values alone. Fourth, organizations need to use systems of control to manage the diversity of perspectives and values that result when tasks are divided up among many workers.[50] See Exhibit 8-9.

EXHIBIT 8-9
Mary Parker Follett on Coordination[51]

Most management scholars now agree that Mary Parker Follett was way ahead of her time. In her mind, the universal goal of organizing is the integration of individual effort into a synergistic whole of the organization. Her mantra was "control through unity." She found that the best organizations are ones where coordination is so complete that it fuses the various components of the whole organization into a whole organism. But to be effective, coordination requires the application of a universal principle: a pattern of reciprocal or circular feedback between management and workers. There is no one best way to accomplish this. As Follett observed many different kinds of organizations she found four characteristics that set successful leaders apart:

1. Whenever possible, coordinate using direct contact between those who are responsible (the managers) and those doing the work.
2. Coordination during the early stages of a project or a work assignment is vital.
3. Coordination must involve the reciprocal relationships of all key people and their resources.
4. The work of coordination is never finished. In successful organizations, it is a continual process.

Delegating tasks to others means that as the manager you keep the responsibility for the task but you give the authority to someone else to do the work. "When it comes to delegating, most inexperienced supervisors make two big mistakes: (1) They fail to delegate enough. (2) They fail to do it skillfully. The primary reason for both mistakes is that it's easy to agree to the idea of delegation, but difficult to put into actual practice."[52]

There are four reasons why supervisors fail to delegate as much as they should:

- Some managers do not have faith in their subordinates' ability to perform the work well.
- Managers are keenly aware of their responsibility. Delegation means giving up some control and increasing the risk that they will not please their own boss.
- Some managers desire to get personal credit for accomplishing certain tasks. This is selfish and short-sighted, but it is a reality for some weak managers.
- Some managers misjudge the value of time. Spending an hour today delegating a task can save many hours later that can be used to accomplish other tasks.

EXHIBIT 8-10
Why Managers Fail to Delegate

Delegation

Dividing up the work and coordinating the work usually means that managers must ask others to help them get the work done. We think of this in terms of delegating responsibilities. **Delegation** is when someone in a position of higher authority asks someone else to perform a work task that needs to be done.

Generally, managers who delegate responsibilities to subordinates try to make clear the delegated expectations. (See Exhibit 8-10.) This prevents confusion and promotes efficiency. The more permanent the organizational structure and the more stable the external environment, the more likely roles will become specific and clear. But clear expectations also narrow the perspective of subordinates as they add to the separation between workers. The more specific the delegated role, the more likely the subordinates will become rigid in their performance considering other tasks not their job.

When delegated tasks are not clearly defined, a situation called **role fuzziness** emerges. Role fuzziness encourages integration and responsiveness as workers must communicate with each other. One downside is that overlaps (redundancies) and gaps can occur. This approach to delegation can lower efficiency and create frustration. But it also can promote flexibility. Sometimes role fuzziness may be necessary, such as when a new department is being formed to perform new tasks or when two departments are being joined together for the first time and adjustments must be made as the work progresses. When an organizational structure is less permanent or the external environment is unstable, we expect to see more role fuzziness and flexibility so that cooperation and mutual adjustments are made between people. Stability and permanence tend to encourage role clarity.

Span of Control

Span of control is the number of subordinates that report to one supervisor.[53] A manager who supervises just five subordinates has a relatively narrow span of control. In contrast, a manager who supervises 25 subordinates has a wide span of control. All things being equal, the narrower the span of control, the better the integration. But this comes at a cost because narrower spans of control require the organization to hire more managers.

So what is the optimal span of control? Several factors influence the best span of control for any given situation. One influence is the ability of the manager to coordinate and control and the ability of the subordinates to perform their work with minimal direct supervision. If tasks are routine and interrelated, employees will need less supervision and managers can use a wider span of control. If workers are in close geographical proximity to each other, managers can use wider spans of control. If the amount of interaction between subordinate and supervisor is large or if the type of interaction is complex, managers would likely need to use a narrower span of control.[54]

Decision-Making Authority

Work is normally divided among workers based on the particular work tasks that each is expected to perform. But another way to divide work is between those who perform the work and those who make decisions and supervise the work. This is a way of dividing up decision-making authority.[55]

In **centralized authority**, top-level managers have the authority to make the decisions that affect the entire organization. Decentralized authority shares the decisions affecting the entire organization with mid-level and lower-level managers. **Decentralized authority** means that individual work groups (or individuals) have the freedom to act decisively and spontaneously without obtaining permission from those in higher positions of authority. As more people participate in decision making on more issues, power becomes more decentralized.[56] Two categories of decisions are important in this discussion.[57] One is the authority to allocate resources. The other is the authority to monitor the implementation of work after resource allocation decisions have been made. In a centralized organization, employees at lower levels of the organization are limited in both categories.

Small organizations often are quite centralized. As organizations increase in size, or as government regulation of the industry increases, top-level leaders feel a dual pressure to be involved in decision making, but at the same time to delegate some decisions to lower-level managers as their workloads increase.[58] This increase in size usually makes the organization more decentralized for some decisions.

Centralized organizations tend to allow minimal participation by mid-level managers. In these organizations, leaders perceive the environment to be either relatively stable or changing so fast that they must make the key decisions. The assumption is that lower-level workers do not have the inclination, time, knowledge, or judgment to make certain decisions. These organizations are often driven by goals of efficiency where strict managerial oversight follows the detailed production procedures. For example, in a manufacturing plant that makes millions of cans used in the food processing industry, managers and workers have established the best ways to be efficient. The company develops standard operating procedures that reduce the decision-making authority of the frontline supervisor and workers but maintain a high level of efficiency.

Centralization offers several advantages.[59] Top-down communication is efficient. Accountability is clear. Using the legitimate authority of supervisors, coordination is accomplished, as long as such coordination promotes the maintenance of standard work routines.

The bad news is that highly centralized organizations can experience more decision-making bottlenecks, which can slow decision making. More complicated decisions require that more detailed information be accessible to the decision makers. But top-level leaders can become isolated from the details making it more difficult for them. Yet in these organizations mid-level managers are given few opportunities to develop their decision-making abilities. What is worse, highly centralized organizations can unintentionally discourage lower-level managers and frontline workers from taking initiative.

The Christian Mind on Decision-Making Authority

The Christian worldview includes both centralized and distributed models of decision-making authority. The pattern revealed in the Bible reveals a tendency for humans to consolidate decision-making authority rather than distribute it. Moses adjusted his centralized leadership behavior by distributing decision-making authority among many.[60] The desire for a king for Israel in whom authority might be consolidated challenged the distributed model wherein the people looked directly to God as their Ruler.[61]

Counsel should, when possible, be sought widely before decisions are made.[62] This model applied by the New Testament reveals a radical distribution of authority among the believers of the early church; each member bore the responsibility for their spiritual gift for ministry and that of decision making within the body of Christ.[63]

Stanley Patterson, PhD
Associate Professor of Christian Ministry
Andrews University
Berrien Springs, MI

Companies have been moving away from the design of highly centralized organizations.[64] The external environment for many industries has become increasingly complicated and uncertain, making it more difficult for top-level leaders to make all the key decisions fast enough. Advances in managerial control technologies help top-level managers ensure that lower-level decisions are in alignment with organizational objectives. Those who are closest to the place where the decision will have the most impact are more familiar with the situation. When these individuals have the opportunity to practice wise decision making, they develop good judgment. In this environment, frontline supervisors and their employees are trained to become organization-wide leaders. Employees learn that taking initiative is rewarded, and they tend to be more creative in problem solving.

Are decentralized organizations the panacea for the organizational problems of the future? Not always. Decentralized organizations have some important trade-offs.[65] Until managers (at any level) develop good judgment, they can make costly mistakes. Decentralization can unintentionally encourage individual departments to begin acting more autonomously, which can divert the organization from the overall goals to particular goals of specific departments. Decentralization requires increased trust between individuals at different levels of authority. It can increase conflict among departments. When decisions are made by groups of mid-level managers, accountability is more difficult to define.

In decentralized organizations, top-level leaders face an important dilemma: how much autonomy to give to lower-level managers. Too much autonomy can destroy the organization's effectiveness and efficiency. Too little autonomy can stunt the organization's growth and its ability to respond to a changing environment.

Managerial decision makers need good information, and their decisions need to be in close alignment with the organization's objectives.[66] The farther away from the chief executive you get in the organization, the better the information and the lower the cost of getting good information. However, the farther away from the chief executive, the more likely decisions will be made that are not in alignment with the organization's objectives. Mid-level managers will more likely attempt to accomplish objectives that benefit their own work units, which may be out of alignment with the overall organizational objectives.

Formality

Organizing fosters efficiency and effectiveness. Another structural element that does this is the creation of formal policies, procedures, and other guidelines.[67] The more formal an organization becomes, the more routines and controls are embedded into the organization's culture. Examples of formal guidelines include the following:

- Employee manuals
- Standard operating procedures (SOP)
- Written job descriptions
- Organization charts
- Facility physical space allocation plans
- Project work plans
- Printed work schedules, staffing schedules
- Job classification–wage scale systems
- Computerized inventory management systems, purchasing systems, payroll systems, accounts receivable and accounts payable systems
- Time and attendance record-keeping systems

Formal guidelines for how work gets done reduce the amount of discretion that employees have in performing certain tasks. This is an advantage when the environment is stable. It increases the predictability, making it easier to create and monitor budgets. When carefully planned and orchestrated, formal policies and procedures act as important coordinating devices, without which all the good work that is being done could not mesh together easily. These guidelines reinforce the organization's shared values, helping employees to share the same work values. As organizations get busier, formal ways of getting the work done minimize confusion and preserve order.

If you have ever worked in an organization that is chaotic, then you know how much of a relief even a little formalization can bring to reduce the chaos. But too much formalization comes

Source: Phase4Photography/Shutterstock.

Even a little formality such as drawing an organizational chart can help reduce confusion.

with some important trade-offs.[68] Formal guidelines can reduce the amount of discretion that employees have. The more formal an organization becomes the more difficulty it has creating innovations. The organization becomes less flexible. Personal initiative can decrease. For those who believe that their way of doing things is better than the organization's way, formal guidelines start to feel like "red tape" as rules come to be more important than the organizational goals they were designed to promote.

Small organizations can operate successfully with less formality than larger businesses. But the larger the business, the more formal it needs to be. This is one reason why very large organizations become less flexible in responding to changes in the environment.

Formalization, in part, is why large bureaucracies can be unpleasant for some workers. Managers and scholars have grown concerned about this nature of large organizations.[69] We will return to this issue later in this chapter in the section "Are Big Organizations Unhealthy?"

Organizational Management Styles

We have been looking at some of the most important individual structural elements in organizations. But combine some of these elements into clusters, and you can begin to look at the organization from a little broader perspective. When we do this, taking into consideration the environment in which the organization operates, how employees coordinate their efforts, how authority is divided up, and how formal or informal the organization is, we find some interesting patterns. Let's look at two common patterns.[70]

Organizations operating in relatively stable environments tend to divide and subdivide the work into ever-smaller, highly specialized tasks. If, in addition, decision-making authority is kept centralized and coordination is mainly through the subordinate–boss relationship with formal rules and procedures, then we have a **mechanistic style of organizational management**. The emphasis here is on the hierarchy of authority, vertical communication, predictability, accountability, and highly specialized roles.[71] Examples of organizations that tend to be mechanistic include the U.S. Postal Service, factories, government organizations, and libraries.

In contrast to the mechanistic style, in the *organic approach* the organization is more likely to operate in a changing environment, and, because of this, it needs to be flexible, adaptable, and innovative. To accomplish this, in the **organic style of organizational management** decision-making authority is more decentralized and coordination occurs through horizontal and vertical relationships. Workers tend to do more than one specific task rather than specialize in their work. Horizontal communication and higher reliance on mutual adjustment between coworkers is needed as the organization responds to changes in the outside environment. Hospitals, research and development laboratories, and construction companies tend to be organic organizations.

Let's look now at organizations from an even broader perspective: the organization's overall design.

Organizational Designs

Organizational designs range from simple to complicated. Consider, for example, Underwood's Exxon gas station, a typical small, family-owned and operated business. Overall, this business has a simple structure. The physical building in which the employees work is small, and employees are located close together. Decision making is centralized with Mr. Underwood and his son. This is an example of unity of command: There is one person who is the boss. Everyone reports directly to Mr. Underwood, or if he is gone they report to his son. This suits a family business very well up to a point. If Mr. Underwood wants the business to grow (either in terms of the types of products and services offered or in the geography covered), then he will likely need to change the structure. The larger an organization becomes, the more likely it will need to replace a simple design with more complicated approaches in order to continue to grow.

One tool that helps us visualize an organization's design as well as its reporting relationships is the organizational chart. See Exhibit 8-11.

An **organizational chart**, or *org chart*, shows the reporting relationships by depicting the individuals and work units of an organization as small boxes joined with connecting lines. You can usually look at a chart and know quickly who you should contact in the organization if you need help making a decision. Organizational charts identify the managers by their position title. Top-level managers with more decision-making authority are usually at the top of the chart. In large, formal organizations, organizational charts can be found in department policy manuals or posted on bulletin boards. They are sometimes used in new employee orientation programs.

Organizational charts are limited in their usefulness.[72] They do not describe the extent to which decision-making authority is centralized or decentralized. Also, they do not show all the coordinating integrating mechanisms in place, which are hidden in the white space of the chart. Similarly, organizational charts are not adequate pictures of the interdependencies that need to be managed.

THE TRADITIONAL FUNCTIONAL DESIGN. While many organizations face rapid change in their external environments, the default design is what we traditionally have called the **functional** or **hierarchical design**. It is called functional because the work is divided according to the functions (tasks) that people perform. In addition, individuals who perform similar or closely related tasks are often grouped into the same department reporting to the same manager. So, in a company like Flowserve Corporation that uses a functional design to make pumps, valves, seals, actuators, and other products, we expect to see Human Resources, Accounting, Marketing, Manufacturing, Research & Development, and Purchasing as functional departments. In manufacturing companies that have a wide product line, we expect to see

EXHIBIT 8-11
The Organization Chart

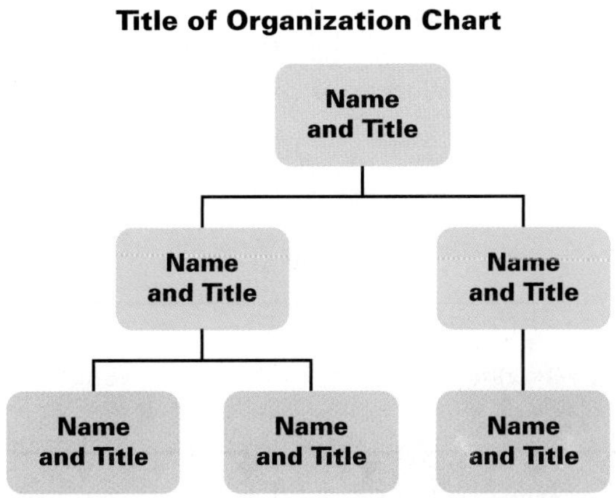

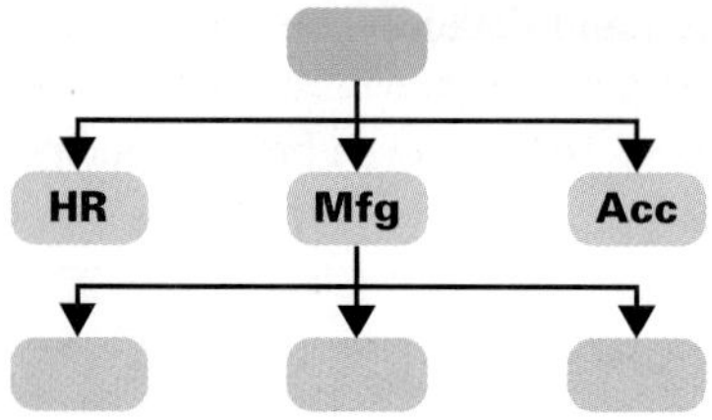

EXHIBIT 8-12
The Functional Design

multiple manufacturing or production departments, each one focused on a particular product line. See Exhibit 8-12.

Companies with a functional design are typically stable and efficient. The division of labor is clear. With practice at the specific tasks assigned to them, individuals can become very skilled in their work. Coordination within departments is easy to accomplish with the department manager and department members working closely together.[73]

In spite of its benefits, the traditional functional design has some problems. It is the functional design that is most closely related to the often-maligned term "bureaucracy." Individual workers or managers can become so focused on their specialized tasks that they can lose sight of the overall purpose of the organization. This contributes to rigidity, making it difficult for the organization to change. The mental orientation of the department can breed conflict with other departments, each of which has its own but often quite different mental orientation and goals peculiar to its own needs and interests. Coordination of effort can be difficult to achieve across departments. The larger the organization becomes the less efficient it becomes. Individual behaviors can come to mirror the parochial mental orientations of the department. Individuals start to protect their own turf, act insensitively toward other individuals, and think of themselves as more important than they truly are.

MULTI-DIVISIONAL DESIGN. As functional organizations grow in size they come to a point when it is difficult to grow larger unless they adjust their structure. Around 1920, General Motors discovered this and learned that to continue growing, it needed to adjust its traditional hierarchical design. Out of this, the *multi-divisional design* (also known as the *M-form* design) was born.[74] See Exhibit 8-13.

The **multi-divisional design** divides a large organization into several semiautonomous business units, each of which can be of any design, though frequently each is a functional designed unit. The top executives in each business unit are allowed a considerable amount of decision-making authority to operate the organization in a way that makes it successful in its market. This allows the corporation as a whole more flexibility and keeps the company close to the market. Each operating unit is responsible for profit and loss.

Dividing the work of the company into semiautonomous units can be accomplished along the lines of products, customer groups, or geography. Deciding which of these to select is driven primarily by where the organizational control needs to be kept.[75] For example, if the key issue the company faces is the customization of products to meet the needs of customers located in different geographic areas, then geographic divisions is the likely choice.

Besides General Motors, some well-known corporations that have used this design effectively include Procter & Gamble, which is divided along product groups, Ford Motor Company, and Heinz foods. Very large corporations like General Electric may have scores of semi-autonomous divisions operating in dozens of countries worldwide, employing hundreds of thousands of employees.

EXHIBIT 8-13
The Multi-Divisional Design

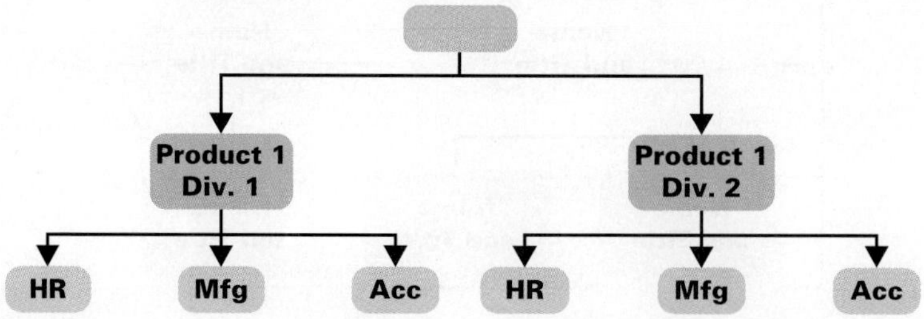

One of the challenges in managing this design is in the relationship between the corporate office and each of the divisions in terms of how much authority to give them. Give each division too much authority and the needs of the whole organization will be more difficult to meet. Give divisions too little authority and their ability to be effective in their market will diminish. Another issue is that because each division is focused on the needs of its market, communication and coordinating across divisions becomes difficult. Because each division is a semiautonomous operating unit, each unit must have its own human resources, accounting, purchasing, production, and marketing functions (to name a few). This means that there is duplication of functions across the business units.

THE HORIZONTAL DESIGN. In the **horizontal design**, the key work processes, rather than functional tasks, are the basic building blocks of the organization.[76] For example, a horizontally designed company will structure around key business processes or work flows that link employees to customers. A company that assembles a variety of appliances might be organized by assembly lines. The traditional departments of sales, customer service, and order fulfillment might be organized around the customer management process with a process manager appointed in charge. The emphasis is on teams of individuals such as the teams that manage customer order fulfillment, customer billing (sometimes known as the *revenue cycle process*), new product development, product manufacturing, and product installation. See Exhibit 8-14.

Focusing on interlinked and often cross-functional work processes that are linked with customers and their needs promotes flexibility. Individual workers' mental orientation is on the production and delivery of value. Individuals are assigned tasks in a particular process. They learn to work together with others who have the same assignment as they take responsibility, achieving better coordination across the entire set of activities. This can make work in progress run smoothly because the key workers in the process coordinate their efforts. IBM, Owens-Corning, and Texas Instruments are examples of companies that have organized around processes.[77]

In some organizations, the pure horizontal process design is difficult to achieve. One reason is that functional specialists are still needed to do some of the work necessary to keep the company in operation. Some functions do not easily lend themselves to being assigned to a particular process. For example, a support department like landscaping and building maintenance in Pfister, which manufactures faucets, has a set of tasks that is not directly related to that of workers who are assembling and packaging bathroom faucets. There is no need to assign these departments to the assembly process. Another reason is that processes tend to be divided from each other, making coordination across processes a challenge. Process team leadership can be a shared leadership, leaving the role of the process manager ambiguous. Because of these drawbacks, some organizations are unwilling to make the commitment to a complete horizontal structure. Those organizations may use a hybrid approach instead, in which part of the organization is functionally organized and the core of the business that creates the value offered to customers is organized around processes.

THE MATRIX DESIGN. Organizations that use the **matrix design**, also known as the *dual authority* or *lattice* structure (because of how the organizational chart looks), attempt to maintain a dual

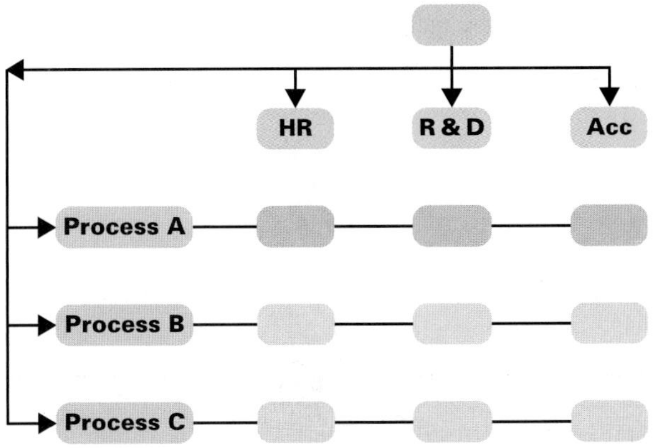

EXHIBIT 8-14
The Horizontal Design

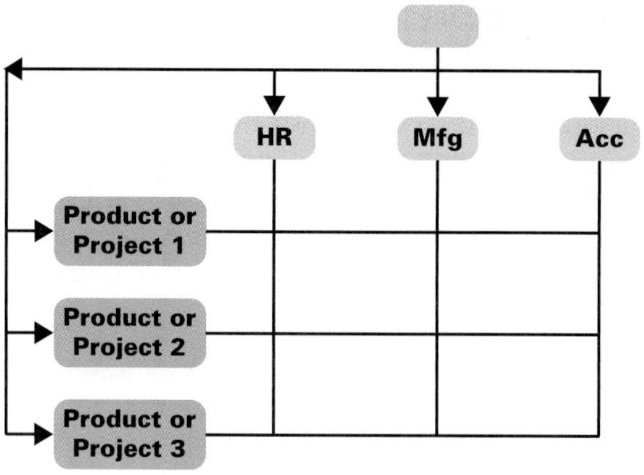

EXHIBIT 8-15
The Matrix Design

focus both on functional tasks and on either projects, product lines, or customer groups.[78] Some employees have dual (and even triple or more) reporting relationships. For example, engineers might report not only to their manager but also to one or more project leaders or product group leaders. NASA, TRW, Unilever, Xerox, and Caterpillar have implemented the matrix design. Most hospitals have traditionally employed a form of matrix design where the medical (physicians) authority is overlaid onto the technical and support staff functional organization (nurses and other non-physician health care professionals). See Exhibit 8-15 for an example of the matrix design.

Organizations use the matrix design because it promises several advantages. It attempts to achieve efficiency. It focuses employees on multiple (though sometimes conflicting) business goals such as lowering cost and improving quality. By requiring the participation of many functional experts, it also fosters cooperation and innovation while it improves a companywide focus instead of a department or work unit focus. Perhaps its most important advantage over other designs is that it allows for flexibility and adaptability in a changing environment.

But the matrix design also comes with some significant trade-offs. Dual reporting relationships can create power struggles, overlap in responsibilities, and confusion and conflict between managers in positions of authority, leaving those who report to multiple managers caught in the middle. Unity of command is more difficult to achieve when two bosses are involved in decision making. If resources are scarce, there is heightened conflict. As much as the matrix is designed for improved responsiveness and flexibility in a changing environment, it can have a slow reaction time because of the complexity of getting decisions made. Vertical top-down communications are less efficient. Matrix organizations find that compared with the traditional vertical functional organization there are many more meetings for managers and project groups. The overall cost of coordination is much higher compared with other designs. The higher degree of psychic energy that managers must invest in their work can be taxing. It takes a special breed of manager to work in such an environment where company politics are more intense than in other organizations.

Some organizations are not truly matrix in design but simulate a matrix by overlaying cross-functional teams and ad hoc project groups to the existing functional or process structure. In these environments, functional managers or process managers learn "matrix management" as they collaborate more with each other.

THE NETWORK DESIGN. Of all the design options considered thus far, the network design is the most flexible for responding to rapid changes in the marketplace.[79] In a **network design**, the company forms a central coordinating team whose job is to establish and maintain relationships with other organizations who perform either functions or processes under contract with the company. A key driver in the selection of the network design is the variety of materials and processes that are needed to create the product. One reason that networked organizations can operate effectively is the use of electronic information and communication systems. See Exhibit 8-16 for an example of the network design.

Networked organizations have been successful in apparel (Liz Claiborne™, Reebok™, Nike™) and computer-related products (Dell, Sun Microsystems), and in automobile

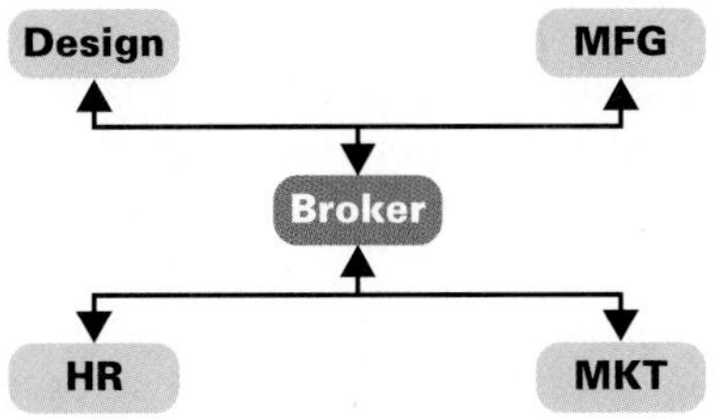

EXHIBIT 8-16
The Network Design

manufacturing, assembly, and distribution (Toyota, Chrysler). Networked organizations have the ability to increase their global competitiveness, as strategic alliance partners can be located in many different places around the world to take advantage of location-specific qualities. They can narrow their internal focus and develop deeper expertise in a few areas while they depend on other firms for expertise in other areas. Network partner firms can reduce production costs. Growth and variety can occur simply by adding more strategic alliance partners to the network.

Just like other design options, the network design has drawbacks. Contract firms can learn from the networked firm and eventually become competitors. Because the key point of division is between the company and its partners, coordination and control problems can exist *across* the networked partners. The networked company sacrifices hands-on control and must trust that the strategic alliance partners will maintain appropriate monitoring and control on its behalf.

Another problem that networked organizations face is that because they have less control over the contracted firm, they need a much higher degree of trust than would be required in other design structures to conduct successful business. Contract vendors that are at an arms length have more opportunity to take advantage of the network relationship, skimp on quality, or engage in practices that do not match the moral standards of the networked firm. A moral lapse of any vendor can have a negative effect on the reputation of the networked organization that uses the products and services of the vendor.

CELLULAR DESIGN. A **cellular design** is a network of small quasi-independent or autonomous units integrated, or held together, by a common goal, philosophy, ideology, or shared mission.[80] A manufacturing company may appoint teams of workers to accomplish production goals. Cells are allowed to form their own internal structure of authority for decision making, within limits. A liaison connects one cell as needed to the rest of the organization. An example of the cellular design is the cell church growth movement, where small congregations form within a larger congregation but are still connected through a common belief system. Leaders of cells are still accountable to the central authority of the congregation. Another example is Technical and Computer Graphics of Sydney, Australia, which is comprised of 13 small, relatively independently operating firms in the organization. Each cell can operate independently of other cells in the organization by seeking and serving its own set of customers. But each cell also can collaborate with one or more other cells on specific projects. See Exhibit 8-17 for an example of the cellular design.

Cellular design offers the ultimate in flexibility. Cells can be highly mobile. Depending on the organization, the operational work of one cell may not need to coordinate with that of other cells. Coordination within each cell is easily managed. Cell members can take on multiple tasks

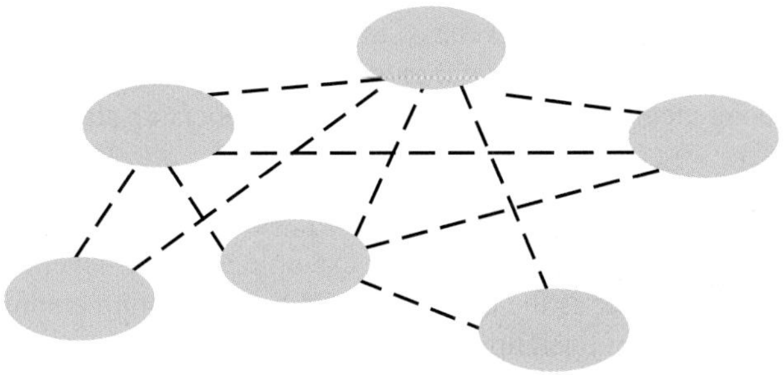

EXHIBIT 8-17
The Cellular Design

as the need demands. Leadership is appointed from within the cell. Decision-making authority may be decentralized for operational activities but centralized for activities related to the organization's mission. In political and religious organizations cell design also offers a platform for continued growth. Each new cell that is formed can take advantage of local conditions and resources to help it fulfill a mission.

Cells also have some disadvantages. Leaders must work hard to integrate individual members into the organization's mission. This requires an exceptionally strong surrounding subculture, clearly established values, and a high degree of trust. Communication between cells can be fragmented and coordination of access to centralized resources is a challenge.

No single approach to organizing is the best. Each design choice has trade-offs. According to Peter Drucker, "The simplest organization structure that will do the job is the best one."[81] In spite of their shortcomings, functional organizations appear to remain the default design even if other designs are used. Many organizations must make changes to the design when they experience control problems. As you move from the functional design toward the cellular design, it becomes more and more difficult to monitor the behavior of functional teams, enforce agreements, maintain high moral standards among the stakeholders, and ensure that trust is the glue to hold the relationships together.[82]

Working with Groups and Teams

In order for organizations to achieve their goals they often need employees to work together in groups and teams. A **group** is two or more interacting and interdependent persons who work toward a common goal.[83] For example, going to the mall as a group means that the group members share a common goal: shopping. It might mean riding together in the same car, but not necessarily. Going as a group requires little in the way of mutual accountability for how much the group as a whole spends on products and services. When one member of the group makes a purchase, the other group members are not necessarily needed.

Some groups in organizations are permanent and others are temporary. Formal work groups are part of the organizational structure, each with its designated set of work tasks. Informal groups also are part of organizational life, but these groups do not show up on the organizational chart since they form primarily to achieve social relationship goals.

A group becomes a **team** when group members work toward a specific goal in ways that require mutual accountability and collective effort by everyone on the team.[84] All teams are groups but not all groups are teams. Teams share some of the characteristics of groups but they go beyond groups in terms of the extent to which and how team members must work together to achieve specific goals. For example, going to the mall as a team means that team members develop a clear understanding of how team members will help each other during shopping to purchase one or more products that the team as a whole want to have. One person may have the role of checking prices online and relaying this information to other team members. Another person may have the task of finding alternative retailers who sell similar products and then communicating this to the team. Other team members may have the task of evaluating the features and benefits of specific products and discussing the advantages and disadvantages of purchasing one over another before coming to a decision that the team as a whole can live with given its objectives.

In some work situations a group is all that is required to get tasks done. In other situations teamwork is required. Understanding the difference is important to become a successful manager.

Group Structural Characteristics

Groups and teams display characteristics that distinguish one group or team from another and that account for differences in effectiveness. Structural characteristics include the roles that members fulfill, the norms that guide member behaviors, shared values, relative size, the degree of cohesiveness among members, a means to establish membership status, and the methods used to make decisions.[85]

ROLES. For most formal groups and teams each person will have an assigned set of behaviors that other members expect. We call these **roles**. For example, in a top-level executive team group roles will include a person who is the chair of the strategic planning committee. This might be the chief executive or the chief operational officer. This person will have a certain set of tasks to prepare the agenda for meetings, keep the meetings on track, and help the committee to make decisions. Other roles might require the use of expertise to gather, analyze, and report on strategically relevant information such as marketing, accounting or financial information. Another person will be tasked with the job of reflecting to the committee the expected impact that strategic choices will have on employees or the organization as a whole. Formal roles are often focused on the tasks that the group or team has been assigned; however, some informal roles are fulfilled to help the group or team function effectively.

NORMS. In order for groups and teams to work effectively and efficiently members expect of each other certain minimal standards of behavior.[86] We call these group **norms**. For example, in some teams members are expected to show up to work on time, complete all homework assignments before the next team meeting, speak in team meetings showing respect and courtesy to others present, and be actively involved in team discussions. Group norms can either enhance or hinder the ability of the group to accomplish its goals. Norms that expect high performance of individuals and of the team as a whole usually result in higher productivity compared with teams with weaker performance norms. This is especially true of teams that are cohesive and share weaker performance norms.

SHARED VALUES. Each group and team will develop shared values peculiar to its forming a subculture, an idea we considered in Chapter 3. For example, a new product development team will develop mental orientations related to the importance of experimentation and innovation. Team members are expected to be creative. Members of some innovation teams may develop comparatively less interest in keeping a lid on the costs of innovation.

RELATIVE SIZE. Another structural characteristic of groups and teams is that of size, that is, the number of persons who are part of the group. While there is no particular group size for optimal effectiveness, groups comprised of 5 to 7 members generally perform better than much larger groups (more than 12 people). Larger groups usually mean that a greater diversity of ideas will be represented; however, the larger the group, the more likely members will become dissatisfied or take less responsibility for completing their share of the tasks. Large groups may perform better at complex problem solving compared with smaller groups.[87]

COHESIVENESS. **Cohesiveness** is the strength of group members' desire to be an active part of the team and its work. When individual goals and team goals are in close alignment, this tends to increase cohesiveness. Generally, we think of cohesive teams as being more effective than teams that are weak in cohesion; however, if the team develops goals that are in conflict with the organization's goals and cohesiveness is strong, the overall impact of the team may be less than desired. Cohesiveness also is a function of group size. Smaller groups tend to be more cohesive. Improving group or team cohesiveness is a typical manager's task. Several ideas can be used when these are appropriate. Reducing the size of the group is one way. Encouraging agreement with group goals is another. Encouraging group members to spend more time together usually will increase cohesion. Increasing the importance of the group's work and the status of the group also will tend to have a positive impact on cohesion.

STATUS. Most groups develop ways in which group members demonstrate social respect for differences among group members and their contributions to the group. **Status** is the hierarchical rank or prestige conferred by group members to each other.

GOALS. Each group has certain task-oriented goals and some relationship goals. Most of the time groups spend their effort on attaining task goals; however, some time must be spent on achieving and maintaining goals of positive relationships among group members. When goals are clear, groups tend to perform better.[88]

Stages of Group Development

Putting people together in the same room to solve a problem doesn't mean that they have truly formed a group. Groups develop over time through a process.[89] During the first phase of the process group members are developing self identities related to participation in the group. They are getting to know the tasks and roles, learning of each other's skills and expectations, and testing each other's commitment. We call this phase **forming**. A second stage in the process is involves storming. **Storming** is characterized by members setting unrealistic goals, questioning the purpose of the group, competing for control over influence, debating the real issues at stake, and complaining about the organizational barriers to their tasks.

As group members strengthen their ability to work together, they reach the norming stage. **Norming** is the stage when the group comes to agreement on what is expected of each other. Group members begin accepting each other's ideas. The group is better able to define the parameters of the problem it is attempting to solve. Group members give and receive constructive feedback. The group begins to value individual differences. The norming stage positions the group to be effective in accomplishing its goals through high performance.

During the **performing** stage of group development, the group makes progress towards its goal. Team members help each other diagnose and overcome obstacles. The group begins to improve its ability to work together. Group members actively seek feedback in order to make more improvements. During this stage the group sees the results of its work in terms of decisions being made and accepted by others, solutions to problems implemented, and the actual performance of the organization improved.

When the work of problem-solving groups is complete, the group can be disbanded and the employees can go back to their normal routines. During the **adjourning** stage of group development, the group prepares for disbanding. The group may prepare a final report that it presents to other groups or teams inside or outside the organization. Team members celebrate the accomplishments of the team.

Maintaining Team Effectiveness

Making a group into an effective team is not always easy, yet this is one of the more important roles that managers fulfill in organizations. Taking a systems view of a team requires the manager to see the team in the context of the larger environment of the organization or society. Team effectiveness can depend on this context. For example, if resources that the team needs are difficult to obtain, team effectiveness will be lower than desired. If the team lacks leadership, is poorly structured in terms of team member assignments, or has weak mechanisms for coordination, effectiveness will suffer.

Managers can improve their team's effectiveness by paying attention to the following dimensions:[90]

- Purpose. Help the group know why it exists.
- Goals and tasks. Establish clear measurable goals and tasks to help group members focus their efforts. As a result they will be more effective.
- Competence. A team can have laudable goals, but if team members lack competencies in skills relevant to the goals, effectiveness will suffer.
- Communication. Good communication helps team members by providing clear understanding of expectations as well as key information that the team needs to carry out its work.
- Loyalty. As team members make commitments to the team's goals by contributing their fair share of effort and even giving extra effort when needed, loyalty and team effectiveness is built.
- Conflict management. By nature teams that are made up of interdependent persons will have conflict over what work should be done and how work should be done. When teams learn how to manage this conflict, their effectiveness increases. Effective teams tend to be teams that have one or more persons on the team who are skilled in negotiation that help the team resolve differences.
- Leadership. Team effectiveness improves when persons who lead participate as members of the team. Leaders watch out for team goals, communication, loyalty, trust, and many other elements that positively affect team effectiveness.
- Trust. Managers can improve team effectiveness by ensuring an atmosphere the supports mutual trust.

Self-Managed Teams

Some organizations are turning to self-managed teams to work on projects. Teams are given a measure of autonomy to decide how to organize members and how to go about performing work. Managing workers who are divided into self-managed teams requires some thought. For example, group autonomy will have a positive impact on cohesiveness and effectiveness; however, individual autonomy among members of the self-managed team can conflict with group cohesion and group effectiveness.[91] Thus, even for a self-managed team, managers still have a role to play to monitor to what degree the team has developed team norms and set clear goals and tasks.

Trust as an Organizing Principle

As organizations expect their middle managers to participate more in decision making and as these managers include their subordinates more in decisions that affect them, the psychology of managing is changing.[92] Managers at all levels are more closely involved with their subordinates, focusing on maintaining commitment. This means that the more participative an organization is, the more its managers will need to understand the personalities of their workers when trying to motivate them.

As organizations face increasingly ambiguous marketplaces, trust between managers and subordinates is even more important than in the past.[93] Managers and subordinates will not have all the answers. Certainly individual behaviors are important to build trust. But can trust be a principle on which the company is organized? Some scholars think so.[94]

Trust is a willingness to be vulnerable based on the expectation that the behaviors of another person are well-intentioned. It is required in all organizations. **Trustworthiness** means being deserving of trust based on actual behavior in the past. Trust and trustworthiness are interdependent and co-evolve. When individuals trust others who have shown themselves to be trustworthy, trust can become an organizing principle.[95] Trust develops as the people in power who have access to the important, relevant information share what they know with others who need this information. Keeping secrets, when they are not necessary, undermines trust.

Organizing is a way to manage interdependencies and deal with uncertainty. But one of the persistent problems in organizations is that some individuals and work groups in the company are in a position of security while others are in positions of vulnerability. Vulnerability increases the risk that some in the organization will be opportunistic and take advantage of the vulnerable individuals. For example, lower-level, unskilled workers are relatively more vulnerable than are top-level managers. Trust is acceptance of the vulnerability based on the assumption that those in positions of security will serve the interests of those who are vulnerable. If workers in a more vulnerable position expect that those with more security intend to be fair, they are more willing to cooperate. Opportunism, while apparently serving the short-term needs of the dominant person or group, will, in the long run, undermine trust.

Trust influences organizing in two ways. First, when people trust each other, they do not need immediate positive payback for good things they do for each other. They trust that someone else who has a different role will be willing to work together with them to get the job done. Second, trust mobilizes people to take action when tasks are delegated. Employees who trust superiors and each other are more likely to cooperate as they work together to solve problems. If difficulties arise, those who trust are willing to suspend judgment on other people who have the opportunity to abuse the relationship. If trust is broken, workers begin spending more time and energy monitoring each other's behaviors as a safeguard.

This means that trust is a vital influence when supervisors oversee subordinates. But trust works both ways. Supervisors must trust that subordinates are trustworthy and vice versa. The more trust that is alive in the organization, the more autonomy can be allowed and, as a result, the organization operates more efficiently. Trust by itself does not guarantee trustworthy behavior.

Reinforcing Moral Values Through Organization

Many people believe that the only way to have permanent change toward higher moral standards in business is for businesses to change from the inside rather than have changes imposed from the outside. Appointing ethics officers, revising corporate codes of ethics, and ethics training can help. But if the structure of the organization encourages immoral behavior, these types of internal changes become no more than window dressing.[96] For example, if the top-level executives who have a great amount of decision-making authority are the ones who have low moral standards, then an ethics officer and code of ethics will do little to prevent moral problems.

Enron Corporation, once one of the world's largest buyers and sellers of natural gas and electricity, had a "code of ethics" that was lauded as a model for other organizations to follow. However, its 64-page manual on ethics was insufficient to prevent the kinds of moral lapses that eventually ruined the company.

In hierarchical bureaucratic organizations, decision-making authority is typically at the top of the organization, centralized with the top executives. When decision-making authority is centralized and when an opportunity exists for top-level executives to promote their personal interests, the organizational structure is a weak support for high moral standards. Opportunistic situations are more prevalent when decision making is centralized with a small group of individuals. When lower-level employees feel compelled by senior leaders to act immorally or if they believe they lack the authority to choose a moral alternative, they are more likely to act immorally.

Responsibility is shared more widely in decentralized organizations as managers are expected to consult with others and bear the burden of responsibility for their decisions. Here the more decisions are decentralized and shared among many managers, the fewer the opportunities for one manager to act in self interest, regardless of the level of authority any one manager has.[97]

The danger here is that when key decisions are made by committees, the moral responsibility for decisions can become so diffused that any given individual can easily say, "that wasn't my decision." We can conclude from this that organizations that tend to share decision-making authority widely and that have in place firm monitoring systems to ensure that individuals take responsibility are more likely to promote moral decision making.[98]

Other structural elements influence moral decision making, too.[99] Financial incentives and other nonfinancial rewards can, if poorly designed, entice employees to make immoral decisions. Performance evaluation systems that are poorly designed will fail to detect immoral conduct and can even encourage this behavior by creating the perception that unethical behavior will be tolerated or even expected. When the chain of command is unclear and when decision-making responsibility is ambiguous, employees are more likely to engage in immoral behavior.

We have seen the importance of organizing in managerial work. In some organizations managers supervise individuals who are spread out geographically around the globe. This presents a special challenge for organizing. To this we turn next.

Are Big Organizations Unhealthy?

According to Peter Drucker, for efficient functioning and survival, society in developed countries depends "on the effectiveness of large-scale organizations, on their performance and results, on their values, standards, and self-demands."[100] Compared to the environment of a hundred years ago, the demand for products is much larger today. To meet this demand, organizations have become "special-purpose institutions. They are effective because they concentrate on one task."[101] This means that managers must learn how to build high-performance organizations. Large organizations do a lot of good for society by providing employment and creating and distributing goods and services to millions of people globally.

But large organizations are not without their problems. One problem is that the larger the organization the more likely the work that is accomplished is far away from the contribution of any individual worker. Large, complex organizations have multiple books of rules (departmental and organizational policies) that dictate behavior, constrain individuality, and inhibit creativity. These pressures, coupled with the impersonal nature of organizational objectives, can cause workers to feel alienated from the larger purpose of the organization. Top-level leaders and mid-level managers in these large hierarchical organizations wield their hierarchical authority that negates autonomy, freedom, and spontaneity. Some consider this to be one of the worst characteristics of big organizations.[102] The constant focus on the organization's goals becomes coercive to individual employees. Employees become merely a means to an economic end and cease to be important as beings created in the Image of God. See Exhibit 8-18.

Some people believe that humans need more freedom and that increased freedom will result in higher performance, improved market responsiveness, and higher levels of satisfaction from work. However, more individual freedom undermines the ability of the organization as a whole to achieve its goals. Without controls placed on individual behaviors, organizations would disintegrate and self-destruct.

The larger the organization the more likely mid-level managers, frontline supervisors, and rank-and-file employees will perceive organizational constraints as coercive. Effective managers will

Large Organizations Are *Good*	Large Organizations Are *Bad*
Organizations exist for the purpose of achieving commonly shared goals of providing employment as well as goods and services of value to society. In this, organizations are succeeding.	The organization exists for the purpose of generating wealth. In this it is succeeding, but at the expense of individual relational needs of workers and other stakeholders.
Organizations exist for the sake of the results that are produced for those outside the organization in the market. This provides a means for employees to lead satisfying, meaningful lives by contributing to something larger than themselves.	Organizations are impersonal settings; division of labor and the management methods needed for coordination dehumanize individuals.
Large organizations are an efficient means of providing a high volume of products and services to a complex society.	Large organizations are inefficient and filled with red tape, inertia, and bureaucratic waste.
Hierarchical authority prevents confusion over tasks and minimizes conflict over authority and access to resources as it ensures accountability and coordinates work effort.	Hierarchical authority seduces, coerces, and demeans because the primary focus is on the organization's goals and efficiency.
Hierarchical authority prevents the demoralization of employees by creating predictability and reducing chaos and ambiguity.	Organizations dictate behavior, constrain individuality, enable dependencies, and foster passivity while they inhibit creativity and self-actualization. This results in workers feeling alienated.
Managers in large organizations provide a means for allocating (budgeting) resources when a variety of perspectives in the whole organization must be considered. They provide an avenue for appeal when employees have disputes over allocation of resources.	Managers in large hierarchical organizations wield dictatorial authority that negates autonomy, freedom, and spontaneity and dignity of subordinates while feathering their own nests. The resource allocation process is biased against new ideas.

EXHIBIT 8-18
The Two Faces of Large Organizations

counteract this tendency. They will ensure that working relationships are healthy and humane. Also, they will help employees keep a clear vision of the organizational goals, why they are important, and the particular contribution the employee is making toward these greater goals.

Managers can counteract the negative influences of large organizations by maintaining ongoing communication. This may require periodic town-hall meetings or employee focus groups. Reporting to employees on their progress can help them to know whether they are making a difference. However, reporting progress when true progress has not been made will result in cynicism and distrust. Chaotic environments can be repaired with attention to how the work is organized.

Downsizing and Its Consequences

Downsizing, also called "restructuring," has always been one of the risks inherent in a free-market economy. Since the late 1980s, downsizing has become a standard practice in many companies, large and small. Anyone who expects to take a job in management needs to be aware of the possibility that the employer might choose to downsize. **Downsizing** is the action that organizational leaders take to eliminate jobs or positions (including managers). This reduces the cost structure of the organization.

Downsizing can be precipitated by any number of things.[103] An economic recession, which reduces demand for products and services, may spark companies to reduce expenses. Overhead as a proportion of total sales may be higher than that of competitors. The ability of the company to service its debt may be challenged. Supply and materials costs can increase. New technologies can emerge. A company may acquire or merge with another organization. Deregulation can spark competition. Years of mismanagement can culminate in cost restructuring. Or, a company may decide to outsource some of the work formerly done by employees so that the company can focus on its core competencies.

When an organization's leaders decide to downsize, they attempt to reduce the red tape of bureaucracy, promote faster decision making, improve organizational communications and coordination, and encourage a spirit of innovation and change among the workforce. In general, the leaders try to make the organization more efficient (perform the same work with fewer resources), more effective (changing the kind of work performed, reducing the assets, or refocusing the range of activities performed by the organization), or both.[104]

Like many important decisions that leaders make, downsizing comes with a mixed bag of results. Because the decision is made at the top level, middle managers and frontline supervisors may fail to understand or endorse the reasons for downsizing. Part of the social cost of downsizing is that managers and other workers experience a wide range of emotions that are difficult to deal with. While some managers will feel hopeful and confident that the changes are necessary, others will end up feeling alienated. Managers can feel anger and resentment toward the top-level leaders and, in particular, the chief executive. If they believe that full information is not disclosed, they can feel anxious and cynical.

If downsizing is not carefully planned, the firm can end up rehiring some of the laid-off workers as independent contractors. Without adequate planning, downsizing can actually cause more coordination problems rather than less. Surviving managers, the very people who are needed for effective coordination and communication, have more work to do and as a result are unable to devote as much time as needed for coordination. Some firms end up hiring workers as independent contractors but at a much higher cost than the wages they previously paid. Or, the corporate office may hire consultants to replace support staff. The cost of quality can increase.

Firms who successfully downsize concentrate on refocusing the firm and improving effectiveness. Some of these firms must make short-term, across-the-board reductions. But they also find ways to make systemic improvements to the organizational culture. Firms who merely cut jobs in an attempt to be more efficient without focusing on the *strategic* use of assets or improving the corporate culture have a more difficult time achieving positive gains.

What seems to make the difference is when managers focus on several important dimensions.

- Expect that downsizing actions will be accomplished quickly. Dragging out the process destroys morale.
- Expect to engage in extensive conversations. Managers may need to quickly help make the plans for how to pick up the pieces after downsizing. In some cases, this time period can be as short as a few hours to a few days.
- Conduct a town-hall type meeting with employees to minimize the chances of rumors undermining the work that needs to be done to restructure and move toward a positive future.
- Apply fairness when making the decision to lay off workers.
- Allow laid-off workers to leave with dignity.
- Help those displaced to find a new job.
- Communicate with surviving employees about the goals of the company, the nature of the downsizing, the expectations for the future, the need for restructuring work tasks, and the positive gains that are achieved. This will promote loyalty and trust.
- Always be polite and courteous even in the face of anger and cynicism. Acknowledge and be respectful of the positive achievements of the past.
- Avoid bad-mouthing senior leaders as this will only add fuel to the fire of anger, resentment, and low morale.
- When possible, allow frontline supervisors and rank-and-file employees the opportunity to participate in recommending changes to operations of the organization.
- Monitor the total net effect from downsizing and provide honest, straightforward feedback to top-level leaders.

The social cost of life in organizations has an important spiritual dimension not lost to the manager of faith. Managers who work from a religious faith perspective will find downsizing and other organizational changes as opportunities to provide a level of care normally not thought of in many so-called secular organizations.

The Christian Mind on Downsizing

All organizations, whether Christian-based or managed by a Christian, may face the economic reality that would require the release of employees. Economic downturns require more careful attention and management of an organization's resources. Of all the resources utilized by a manager only one, according to the Creation accounts in Genesis, is created in the image of God, and that is man or woman. Resources (people) created in the image of God are not simply those we "turn off" and quit using. This God-like stamp carried by people in our organizations has implications for how a downsizing decision should be approached. It necessitates clear and forthright communication of information. It would suggest the appropriateness of respect from the manager and the firm for the individuals impacted and for a proper exit strategy, which may include career development and/or employment assistance.

Doyle J. Lucas, Ph.D.
Professor of Management
Falls School of Business
Anderson University
Anderson, IN

Paradoxes of Organizing

As with other dimensions of managerial work, organizing brings its own particular set of paradoxical tensions. Here are some of the interrelated organization tensions that managers face.

DEPENDENCE—INDEPENDENCE.[105] Organizational leaders sometimes work to eliminate red-tape bureaucracy and foster more independence among the organization's work groups. This promotes the ability to respond to changes in the marketplace. Paradoxically, becoming more independent actually involves the development of interdependencies. For example, the employees involved with purchasing materials and other resources needed by the company to make and sell its products cannot be fully independent of the production departments. They can come to function independently but only when they have a close working relationship with the production managers. An organization can function only if the individual work groups are able to depend on each other. Emphasizing independence too strongly will undermine group synergy and cohesiveness, while ensuring connectedness with the group will foster excessive conformity and loss of individual initiative.

LOOSE—TIGHT.[106] Organizations that live by this tension point are tightly controlled (at least on financial matters) and at the same time insist on autonomy to foster innovation and an entrepreneurial approach. Managers monitor revenue and expenses closely. But they also allow workers an appropriate amount of freedom for making decisions for how the work will be done.

RULES—THE DOUBLE-EDGED SWORD OF BUREAUCRACY.[107] The larger an organization becomes, the more the need for rules increases. Those of us who work in large organizations come to both love and hate the rules. Rules, also known as policies, in an organization represent the collective memory of the organizational leaders regarding the most efficient way to get work done or at least what is believed to be the most workable solution to difficult dilemmas that arise when competing interests are at stake. Rules both foster cooperation and, at times, block cooperation. Rules help to channel effort as well as stifle it. They reinforce stability but at the same time create inflexibility to change.

Focus on an Organization

Fellowship of Companies for Christ International (FCCI)

In 1977, Robert "Bobby" Mitchell, an Atlanta businessman, joined with a handful of other Christian business leaders to consider the question, "What would Jesus do if he ran my business?" The outcome of that discussion, among other things, was the formation of a Business Leader Group to share ideas and to encourage one another to find ways to integrate their faith with their work.

The organization grew and brought clarity to its mission: "In pursuit of Christ's eternal objectives, we equip and encourage business leaders to operate their businesses and conduct their personal lives in accordance with biblical principles. As we do, we thrive personally, professionally, and in serving others. Our influence grows, our lives become an example for others to follow and Christ is honored in the workplace."

Business Leader Groups (operating under the name Christ@Work) are comprised of 6 to 12 members in a particular geographical area who meet on a regular basis to share counsel and support for each other. Group members pray for each other and worship. In Canada, they are called Council of Business Advisors.

Fellowship of Companies for Christ International manages a website (http://www.fcci.org/) where information is provided regarding the organization's publication, membership, and meetings.

Chapter Summary

1. The creation story in Genesis gives insight into the nature of organized society. The acts of creation bring order out of chaos. More than this, God's character and actions at creation provide us with a window of understanding the fundamental *organizing* principles found in every level of society. The Bible supports the use of division of labor to increase efficiency. More than once Scripture emphasizes the importance of respecting legitimate authority. Managers have the opportunity to make improvements to the structure of their organizations and thereby improve the efficiency and effectiveness of the company while also improving the ethical decision making that takes place.
2. Several elements are the foundation of effective organizing:
   a. Division of labor makes the organization more complex and establishes interdependencies between the workers and between the organization and its environment. Managers or workers must coordinate work efforts to deal with the *organizational complexity* created by division of labor.
   b. Integration and coordination are the combining of separate parts of an organization so that they work together in concert. A symphony orchestra is an excellent analogy of coordinated effort among highly trained experts performing specialized tasks.
   c. Delegation is when someone in a position of higher authority asks someone else to perform a work task that needs to be done.
   d. Managing the span of control is important to prevent managers from becoming overloaded and subordinates becoming frustrated.
   e. Under centralized authority top-level decision makers make most of the important decisions. Decentralized authority shares the decisions affecting the entire organization with mid-level and lower-level managers.
   f. The more formal an organization becomes, the more routines and controls are embedded into the organization's culture.
3. The mechanistic management style emphasizes hierarchy of authority, vertical communication, predictability, accountability, and highly specialized roles. The organic style of organizational management decision-making authority is more decentralized and coordination occurs through horizontal and vertical relationships.
4. An organizational chart, or *org chart*, shows the reporting relationships by depicting the organization as small boxes with connecting lines.
5. Several designs are used to organize workers. The traditional functional design divides work according to the functions (tasks) that people perform. The multi-divisional design builds on the functional design but separates each business unit into separate divisions. The horizontal design divides work into identifiable processes. The matrix design establishes dual-authority relationships involving both functional leaders and product leaders. The network design uses

a central coordinating team, whose job is to establish and maintain relationships with other organizations that perform either functions or processes under contract with the company. A cellular design is a network of small quasi-independent or autonomous units integrated, or held together, by a common goal, philosophy, ideology, or shared mission.

6. A key distinction must be made between a group and a team. Groups and teams display characteristics that distinguish one group or team from another and that account for differences in effectiveness. Structural characteristics include the roles that members fulfill, the norms that guide member behaviors, shared values, relative size, the degree of cohesiveness among members, a means to establish membership status, and the methods used to make decisions. As task groups develop they typically go through five phases or stages: forming, storming, norming, performing, and adjourning. Managers of teams can increase the effectiveness of the team by helping them establish a clear purpose, goals and tasks, competence in team members, communication, loyalty and commitment, conflict management, leadership, and trust.
7. Trust can be an important organizing principle. Trust is a willingness to be vulnerable based on the expectation that the behaviors of another person are well-intentioned. It is required in all organizations. Trustworthiness means being deserving of trust based on actual behavior in the past. Trust and trustworthiness are interdependent and co-evolve.
8. Organizations that tend to share decision-making authority widely and that have in place firm monitoring systems to ensure that individuals take responsibility are more likely to promote moral decision making.
9. Whether large organizations promote well-being for humans is debated among scholars and practitioners. Some believe that large organizations provide many positive benefits to workers and for society. Others believe that large organizations are harmful to humans.
10. Downsizing is the action that organizational leaders take to eliminate jobs or positions (including managers). Like many important decisions that leaders make, downsizing comes with a mixed bag of results.

Key Terms

Adjourning stage 266
Cellular design 263
Centralized authority 256
Cohesiveness 265
Coordination 254
Decentralized authority 256
Delegation 255
Division of labor 250
Downsizing 269
Environmental complexity 251
Forming stage 265
Functional design 259
Group 264
Hierarchical design 259
Horizontal design 261
Integration 254
Matrix design 261
Mechanistic style of organizational management 258
Multi-divisional design 260
Network design 262
Norming stage 266
Norms 265
Organic style of organizational management 258
Organizational chart 259
Organizational complexity 251
Performing stage 266
Role fuzziness 255
Roles 264
Span of control 255
Specialization 252
Status 265
Storming stage 265
Task complexity 251
Team 264
Trust 267
Trustworthiness 267
Unity of command 249

Discussion Questions

1. Has the traditional hierarchical bureaucracy completely outlived its usefulness to businesses?
2. How can the leaders in a large bureaucracy humanize the work environment without destroying the structural elements that contribute to efficiency?
3. What can an individual mid-level manager do to humanize the work environment for subordinates? For other managers?
4. How can college student organizations improve how they are managed by using structural changes?
5. When working with volunteers such as in a nonprofit organization, how differently might this type of organization be structured compared with a for-profit organization? How will individual structural elements be used differently?
6. In what ways might changing an organization's structure allow it to reach the next higher level of growth in market share?
7. What might be some of the structural barriers preventing small businesses and start-up entrepreneurial ventures from growing?

8. Should a manager emphasize the human side of work or the organizational side of work?
9. Are modern horizontally designed organizations and matrix organizations unbiblical?
10. In the traditional hierarchical organization where decision-making authority is centralized, who really has the power—those at the top or those at the bottom?
11. What are the assumptions and beliefs behind the desire to organize groups for accomplishing work? Which of these assumptions, if any, might conflict with biblical principles?
12. Given the definition of management used in this book, how is a manager able to fulfill this in practice when working in a large, complex organization?
13. Why is it that a structural change to solve one problem is very likely to create a new problem that also needs to be solved?

STUDENT EXERCISES

1. Select an organization that does not have a formal organizational chart. Your task is to draw an organizational chart for the organization showing reporting relationships. Boxes in the chart contain titles but not names. Solid lines show direct reporting relationships between superiors and subordinates. Dotted lines show liaison (or other coordinating) relationships between individuals or departments. You can draw the charts by hand or use software such as Microsoft Word, Excel, or PowerPoint.
2. Divide the class into teams of four to five individuals. Choose a class objective such as raising money for a special project such as a mission, organizing volunteer work teams to help a family that is in need in the community, and so on. Assign the teams the task of organizing their efforts over a 2-week period. Allocate time in class for teams to report on their activities. Focus discussion in class on the organizing dimension of your work.
3. Using the Internet, conduct a study of Enron Corporation, focusing in particular on the organizational structure of the company. What conclusions can you draw regarding how the organizational structure contributed to the moral lapses which eventually led to the destruction of the organization as a whole?
4. Evaluate a club or ministry organization at a college or university in terms of how it is structured. How centralized is the organization? How is work divided? How is coordination accomplished?
5. Select a small organization and offer to draw a chart of the organization. Use each box to represent the key titles or positions. Connect the boxes using solid lines indicating a direct reporting relationship. Interview selected employees and managers to gather the information needed to draw the chart. Bring the organizational chart to class and discuss the merits of alternative arrangements that might be considered for that organization.
6. Think of an organization you work or live in. What is the one rule or policy that is the most difficult for individuals to stomach? Why is it so offensive? What past events might have occurred that sparked the interest in making this rule? What underlying reason does the rule exist? In what way is it excessive in fostering the underlying principle? What would happen in the organization if the rule was completely abolished? How would you change the rule so that it is less offensive? What impact on the whole organization would your idea for change have if it was adopted?
7. Review Exhibit 8-18, "The Two Faces of Large Organizations." Have you ever worked for a large organization that seemed "unhealthy"? What did you do to manage your experience? What can a manager do to help employees who feel like they are an in an unhealthy environment? Are large organizations inherently contradictory to God's intentions for human beings?

IN-CLASS EXERCISES

The Bible and Organizing

Organize the class into four or five teams of students. Give each team a short list of Bible verses that describe or illustrate something related to organizing. Ask each team to develop a skit, improvisation, or class game (Taboo or Pictionary, for example) that illustrates the story or situation in the Bible verse. Class members have the job of guessing what the Bible situation or story is.

Divide the class into small groups. Assign each small group one of the following Bible passages. Each group has the task of reading the passage and then discussing what the passage teaches about management.

a. Exodus 18
b. Luke 7:1–10
c. Acts 6:1–7
d. Acts 15:1–35
e. Luke 16

Syllabus Decisions: Centralized or Decentralized

Engage the class in a discussion of "What would happen if . . ." course syllabi were created with the students participating in some of the decisions. Ask for specific suggestions regarding which portions of the course syllabus students would prefer to participate. Such a discussion usually fairly quickly shows students the impact of diversity of opinion on decentralized decision making! It also may result in new ideas that both students and professors can use in the future. Note to instructors: Some instructors will not see inherent value in having students

Dovid

participate in developing a course syllabus. Doing so takes valuable time. However, engaging students in discussion of the syllabus and its elements has the potential for creating an environment for all to learn from each other.

Issue Debate/Discussion

Divide the class into small groups of five to six people each. Choose a set of "Discussion Topic" statements from the list that follows. Hand out a sheet of paper containing the two "Discussion Topic" statements. Assign half of the groups to defend the first statement (A) as valid and the other half to defend the second statement (B) as valid. For this exercise, students do not necessarily need to agree with the perspective they are asked to defend. In fact, defending a point of view that a student disagrees with can be an amazing teaching-learning experience for undergraduates by helping them to intellectually go outside their usual thinking patterns and develop critical thinking skills. Give the groups 5 minutes to discuss. Then call for groups to give a summary of the rationale they developed. Discussion can follow.

Discussion Topic #1: Is downsizing an inevitable positive consequence of God-given ability to innovate or the negative result of a free-market economy run amuck? Which of the following statements best explains the fundamental reason for downsizing?

A. **An inevitable positive consequence of God-given ability to innovate.** As technological developments continue to advance in ways that increase productivity through the use of computer-controlled devices at work, it is inevitable that organizations will reduce their workforces by laying off some workers who are replaced by machines.

B. **A negative result of a free-market run amuck.** In the free-market capitalist tradition, the workforce is merely an impersonal *labor* production factor inevitably to be replaced by even more impersonal *capital* equipment as senior managers dictate. The reason for this is the constant push for building shareholder wealth at the expense of seeing human beings as valuable in themselves.

Discussion Topic #2: What should be the Christian manager's primary goal in terms of work: employee enjoyment of work or high performance at work?

A. **Enjoyment of work.** Christian managers have a responsibility to redeem work that has been negatively affected by unhealthy work structures or unhealthy work relationships. Organizational structure and bureaucracy get in the way of employee enjoyment. These should be changed so that workers become happier. When work becomes enjoyable and workers are happier, this is evidence that work and the organization are being redeemed from the ravages of sin. Happy workers are spiritually healthier than unhappy workers. Further, happy workers, not organizational structure, will produce high performance.

B. **Performance at work.** Humans were created for work. Christian managers have a responsibility to help people become high-performing workers. In addition, high performance creates a by-product of happiness some of the time. But some kinds of work by nature are not as enjoyable as others. In these situations, happiness may not be a by-product. In settings where the work by nature is not enjoyable, the Christian manager's first priority should be in encouraging in subordinates a stronger sense of responsibility rather than making unenjoyable work more enjoyable. Higher performance can many times be achieved by being more organized. It is through high performance that humans come closest to revealing the Image of God in them. Healthy spirituality recognizes the enjoyable *and* unenjoyable dimensions of life's experiences.

Discussion Topic #3: How should the Christian manager deal with "upward delegation?" Upward delegation (also called "reverse delegation") occurs when a subordinate brings back to the supervisor an uncompleted task that had been delegated to the subordinate but that the subordinate finds too difficult to complete. The subordinate hopes that the supervisor will take back the task assignment, relieving him or her of the responsibility for its completion.

A. **The manager's job is to effectively serve the subordinate's needs.** If employees have difficulty accomplishing a delegated task, they should bring these back to their manager for help. The manager should offer to help the employee with the difficult parts of the task since this is the biblical thing to do. Managers who refuse to take back assignments that are too difficult for subordinates are acting selfishly. Subordinates do not exist to serve the managers; managers exist to serve the subordinates.

B. **The manager's job is to effectively delegate tasks to subordinates.**[108] Upward delegation is mismanagement and a poor expression of biblical stewardship. The more the manager allows subordinates to upward delegate, the less responsibility the subordinate needs to take for task completion and the less discretionary time available for the manager to deal with organizational issues. Upward delegation causes a bottleneck of decision making at the manager's desk. Upward delegation is nothing short of enabling "work avoidance" on the part of the subordinate. It kills initiative on the part of subordinates. It is inefficient since the subordinate must wait for the manager's action before the subordinate can continue working. If the manager allows this, the manager is not doing his or her job as a manager.

Discussion Topic #4: Downsizing: Is it a symptom of wise management or of mismanagement?

A. **Downsizing is a sign of wise management.** When economic environment (such as a decline in demand for a company's products) threatens a company's profitability, wise managers cut expenses in the short run. When these managers add new employees to boost production to meet increased demand, they cannot always predict when demand will decline. These managers are wise to increase the number of employees to meet growing demand. When demand declines, these same managers are also wise in laying off workers. Owners of stock appreciate managers who respond to changes in the market to keep the company profitably healthy during economic downturns. Layoffs signal that the company will reorganize for a more efficient future. This bolster's investor confidence in the company's stock. Investors will buy stock.

B. **Downsizing is a symptom of *mis*management.** When the economic situation gets tough, companies that downsize consistently underperform compared with companies that do not downsize.[109] Investors consider layoffs a sign that managers allowed the organization to get too "fat" with too many employees or were not paying close attention to changes in customer demand in order to make adjustments more quickly. Declining confidence leads investors to sell their stock.

Discussion Topic #5: The Christian manager and downsizing. Having to lay off workers for any reason is one of the most unpleasant tasks as a manager. A layoff can cause economic chaos for the person and his or her family. For the sake of discussion, place yourself into the "shoes" of a Christian manager who must decide whether to carry out a layoff because the company will be unable to continue earning a profit if it does not cut its expenses. How should the Christian manager act in this situation? What assumptions must be made to carry out each of the following actions?

A. **Instead of laying off workers, gradually downsize by not replacing people who retire or who voluntarily terminate employment.** This is the humane way to handle the problem. It may take more time, but workers who choose to stay will not lose their jobs. Having such a policy in place will lead a manager to make wiser decisions and thus prevent the need to lay off workers when times get tough.

B. **Instead of laying off workers, change the other things in the organization.** A lot of alternatives exist: Costs can often be cut in other areas instead of laying off people. Improve the quality of the products. Offer early retirement with generous severance packages to older workers. Reducing everyone's workweek by a half day will share the burden of cost reduction. Change suppliers so that the company pays less for its materials and supplies. Change the company's strategy to be more competitive. Improve marketing and sales to stimulate demand for products. Increase prices to correct a profitability problem.

C. **Get the layoff over with quickly and then move on.** This is the humane way to handle it. If you don't lay off some workers, the entire company could be jeopardized and you may have to lay off everyone. A Christian manager must watch out for the interests of the workers and their families as well as the needs of the organization. While the worker is part of the organization the manager will watch out for the worker's needs. However, if the company needs to continue without a particular worker, the Christian manager should wish the person well and send them on their way quickly.

D. **Lay off workers, but do it with compassion, helping those who are laid off to find other work and giving them severance pay.** This is the humane way to handle the situation. The manager can take care of the company's needs and some, but not necessarily all, of the workers' needs at the same time.

E. **Other:** Think of another alternative action.

Discussion Topic #6: In God's economy is the hierarchy of authority for work recognized?

A. **No.** Other than the difference in authority between the Creator and creation, "God's economy displays no hierarchy of work."[110]

B. **Yes.** The Bible clearly recognizes that some humans have more decision-making authority than others. The Bible writers do not criticize this.[111]

Endnotes

1. Bolman, L. G., & Deal, T. E. (2003). *Reframing organizations: Artistry, choice and leadership.* (3rd ed.). San Francisco, CA: Jossey-Bass, pp. 405–406.
2. Follett, M. P. (1937). The process of control. In Gulick, L., & Urwick, L. (Eds.). *Papers on the science of administration.* New York: Institute of Public Administration. p. 166.
3. Joe Gibbs Racing (2007). Joe Gibbs racing forms motocross and supercross team. News Release. August 31. From http://www.joegibbsracing.com/season_2007/news_misc/070831_jgrmx.php, accessed June 9, 2008.
4. Child, J. (2005). *Organization: Contemporary principles and practice*. Malden, MA: Blackwell Publishing. p. 23; Prahalad, C .K., & Hamel, G. (1990). The core competence of the corporation, *Harvard Business Review*. 68(3), 79–91.
5. Bolman, L. G., & Deal, T. E. (2003). *Reframing organizations: Artistry, choice and leadership.* (3rd ed.). San Francisco, CA: Jossey-Bass. pp. 25–44.
6. Best, R. J. (2000). *Market-based management: Strategies for growing customer value and profitability*. (2nd ed.). Upper Saddle River, NJ: Prentice Hall. pp. 6–21; Day, G. S. (1994). The capabilities of market-driven organizations. *Journal of Marketing*. 58(4), 37-52; Day, G. S. (2007). *The market driven organization*. New York: The Free Press. pp. 3–26, 186–208. Kotler, P. (1972). A generic concept of marketing. *Journal of Marketing*. 36(2), 46–54; Kohli, A. J., & Jaworski, B. J. (1990). Market orientation: The construct, research propositions, and managerial implications. *Journal of Marketing*. 54(2), 1–18; Narver, J. C., & Slater, S. F. (1990). The effect of a market orientation on business profitability. *Journal of Marketing*. 54(4), 20–35; Katz, R. L. (1974).

Skills of an effective administrator. *Harvard Business Review*. 52(5), 90–102.
7. Drucker, P. F. (1954). *The practice of management*. New York: Harper & Row. p. 64.
8. Narver, J. C., & Slater, S. F. (1990). The effect of a market orientation on business profitability. *Journal of Marketing*. 54(4), 20–35.
9. 1 Corinthians 14:33–40; Titus 1:5.
10. Genesis 1:27–28, 2:7, 2:18–25.
11. Genesis 2:18, 2:20.
12. This governing principle is found implicitly in Scripture in many places. More explicit references to this are in passages such as the following: Genesis 13:8; Leviticus 19:18; Deuteronomy 5:14, 5:15; Matthew 7:12; Luke 6:31; Romans 13:9; Galatians 5:14; Philippians 2:3–4; Romans 12:10, 15:1–3; 1 Corinthians 10:24, 12:27, 13:4–5; James 2:8.
13. For an interesting discussion of how the Christian can work to bring redemption at the organizational level see the following: Hardy, L. (1990). *The fabric of this world: Inquiries into calling, career choice, and the design of human work*. Grand Rapids, MI: William B. Eerdmans Publishing Company. pp. 124–185.
14. Genesis 4:2, 4:17–22, 9:20, 11:1–9, 13:1–12. See also Gordon, B. J. (1989). *The economic problem in biblical and patristic thought*. New York: E. J. Brill. p. 5.
15. Exodus 17:5, 18; Numbers 11:14–17; Deuteronomy 1:13–18, 16:18–20. Robert Greenleaf asserts that Moses accepted "bad advice from Jethro [Moses' father-in-law] on how to structure the leadership of the people so that his own natural power striving would be diminished and his serving enhanced. Missing was the necessary guardianship of strong trustees and an astute chairman." Greenleaf, R. K. (1977). *Servant leadership*. New York: Paulist Press. p. 84.
16. Mead, J. K. (2007). *Biblical theology: Issues, methods and themes*. Philadelphia, PA: Westminster John Knox Press. p. 237.
17. Exodus 18:19–22.
18. Genesis 1:26–28; Exodus 32:15–24; Numbers 12:1–16, 16:1–35, 17:1–10, 25:1–5; Nehemiah 3, 7:2; Proverbs 19:10; Isaiah 14:13–15; Matthew 22:21; Luke 7:1–10; Romans 13:1–7; Revelation 12:7–9.
19. Exodus 31:1–6, 31:36–38.
20. Genesis 39:1–6, 41:39–57.
21. 2 Samuel 8.
22. Daniel 1:20, 2:27, 3:1–3, 5:11.
23. Matthew 10:1, 11:1, 14:14–21, 15:32–38, 21:1–7, 26:18–19; Luke 10:1–20, 22:8–14.
24. Matthew 5:20, 6:24, 8:5–13, 16:1–6; John 11:46–57.
25. Acts 6:1–7, 15:1–16:5; 1 Timothy 3:1–7.
26. 1 Corinthians 12:27–31.
27. See for examples Genesis 6:13–22 (here the detailed building plans were used to coordinate the building of the ark); Genesis 11:1–9 (here removing the coordinating function of a common language resulted in the failure to complete the tower); Genesis 50:16; Exodus 3–13 (several coordinating activities are recorded during the process of preparing for the Exodus out of Egypt); Exodus 2–31 (detailed plans for the construction and organization of the wilderness sanctuary are given to Moses); Exodus 32 (Aaron gives instructions to the people to prepare for making a golden idol while Moses delays).
28. Matthew 6:24; Luke 16:13.
29. Genesis 24.
30. 2 Samuel 11.
31. Esther 4–5.
32. Matthew 2.
33. John 2.
34. Matthew 26.
35. John 3:5–8, 7:39, 14:26, 15:26, 16:13, 17:23, 20:22; Acts 1:2–8; Ephesians 4:3, 4:13.
36. McCann, D. P. (2002). Business corporations and the principle of subsidiarity. In Cortright, S. A., & Naughton, M. J. (Eds.). *Rethinking the purpose of business: Interdisciplinary essays from the Catholic social tradition*. Notre Dame, IN: University of Notre Dame Press. pp.169–189; Alford, H. J., & Naughton, M. J. (2001). *Managing as if faith mattered: Christian social principles in the modern organization*. Notre Dame, IN: University of Notre Dame Press. pp. 77–78.
37. Hardy, L. (1990). *The fabric of this world: Inquiries into calling, career choice, and the design of human work*. Grand Rapids, MI: William B. Eerdmans Publishing Company. pp. 124–185.
38. Marshall, A. (1890). *Principles of economics*. London: Macmillan and Company, Ltd.; von Mises, L. (1966). *Human action: A treatise on economics*. Chicago, IL: Contemporary Books, Inc. pp. 143–164.
39. George Jr., C. S. (1972). *The history of management thought*. Englewood Cliffs, NJ: Prentice-Hall, Inc.
40. Mintzberg, H. (1979). *The structuring of organizations: A synthesis of the research*. Englewood Cliffs, NJ: Prentice-Hall, Inc. pp. 69–72.
41. Adapted from Blau, P. M., Heydebrand, W. V., & Stauffer, R. E. (1966). The structure of small bureaucracies. *American Sociological Review*. 31(2), 179–192.
42. Mill, J. S. (1862). *Principles of political economy*. London: Parker, Son and Bourn. pp. 134–148; McConnell, C. R., & Brue, S. L. (2002). *Microeconomics: Principles, problems and policies*. Boston, MA: McGraw-Hill Irwin. p. 62; Mintzberg, H. (1979). *The structuring of organizations: A synthesis of research*. Englewood Cliffs, NJ: Prentice-Hall, Inc. pp. 69–72.
43. Follett, M. P. (2001). The giving of orders. In Shafritz, J. M., & Ott, J. S. (Eds.). *Classics of organization theory*. (5th ed.). Belmont, CA: Wadsworth Thomson Learning. pp. 150–158.
44. Lawrence, P. R., & Lorsch, J. W. (1969). *Organization and environment: Managing differentiation and integration*. Homewood, IL: Richard D. Irwin, Inc. pp. 23–53.
45. Child, J. (2005). *Organization: Contemporary principles and practice*. Malden, MA: Blackwell Publishing. pp. 79–110; Schendel, D. E. & Hofer, C. W. (1979). *Strategic Management: A new view of business policy and planning*. Boston, MA: Little, Brown and Company. pp. 258–259.
46. Schendel, D. E., & Hofer, C. W. (1979). *Strategic management: A new view of business policy and planning*. Boston, MA: Little, Brown and Company. pp. 258–259; Hall, R. H. & Tolbert, P. S. (2005). *Organizations: Structures, processes and outcomes*. (9th ed). Upper Saddle River, NJ: Pearson Prentice Hall. pp. 34–44.

47. Things that are inverse are things that undo the effect of the other or that are opposites. Addition is the inverse of subtraction. Division is the inverse of multiplication. In management both opposites need to be present in order for work to get accomplished. See Church, A. H. (1914). *The science and practice of management*. New York: The Engineering Magazine Company. pp. 101–102; Gulick, L. (1937). Science, values and public administration. In Gulick, L., & Urwick, L. (Eds.). *Papers on the science of administration*. New York: Institute of Public Administration. p. 198.
48. Drucker, P. F. (1993). *Post-capitalist society*. New York: HarperBusiness. p. 54.
49. Katz, D., & Kahn, R. L. (1978). *The social psychology of organizations*. (2nd ed.). New York: John Wiley & Sons. pp. 104–118.
50. Katz, D., & Kahn, R. L. (1978). *The social psychology of organizations*. (2nd ed.). New York: John Wiley & Sons.
51. Fox, E. M. (1968, Nov/Dec). Mary Parker Follett: The enduring contribution. *Public Administration Review*. 28, 250–260; Parker, L. D. (1984). Control in organizational life: The contribution of Mary Parker Follett. *Academy of Management Review*. 9(4), 734–745; Graham, P. (Ed.). (1995). *Mary Parker Follett—Prophet of management: A celebration of writings from the 1920s*. Boston, MA: Harvard Business School Press; Sethi, N. K. (1962, December). Mary Parker Follett: Pioneer in management theory. *Academy of Management Journal*. 5, 214–221.
52. Urbaniak, A. J. (2005). Giving others authority. *SuperVision*. 66(4), 3.
53. Hatch, M. J., & Cunliffe, A. L. (2006). *Organization theory: Modern, symbolic, and postmodern perspectives*. New York: Oxford University Press. p. 34; Jones, G. R. (2007). *Organizational theory, design and change*. (5th ed.). Upper Saddle River, NJ: Pearson Prentice Hall. pp. 124–126; Child, J. (2005). *Organization: Contemporary principles and practice*. Malden, MA: Blackwell Publishing. p. 69; Hodge, B. J., Anthony, W. P., & Gales, L. M. (2003). *Organization theory: A strategic approach*. (6th ed.). Upper Saddle River, NJ: Prentice Hall. pp. 40–41.
54. Hodge, B. J., Anthony, W. P., & Gales, L. M. (2003). *Organization theory: A strategic approach*. (6th ed.). Upper Saddle River, NJ: Prentice Hall. p. 41.
55. Simon, H. (1997). *Administrative behavior* (4th ed.). New York: The Free Press; Jones, G. R. (2007). *Organizational theory, design and change*. (5th ed.). Upper Saddle River, NJ: Pearson Prentice Hall.
56. Hall, R. H., & Tolbert, P. S. (2005). *Organizations: Structures, processes and outcomes*. (9th ed.). Upper Saddle River, NJ: Pearson Prentice Hall.
57. Jensen, M. C. (1998). *Foundations of organizational strategy*. Cambridge, MA: Harvard University Press. pp. 117–118.
58. Hall, R. H., & Tolbert, P. S. (2005). *Organizations: Structures, processes and outcomes*. (9th ed.). Upper Saddle River, NJ: Pearson Prentice Hall.
59. Hall, R. H., & Tolbert, P. S. (2005). *Organizations: Structures, processes and outcomes*. (9th ed.). Upper Saddle River, NJ: Pearson Prentice Hall. pp. 54–62; Hatch, M. J., & Cunliffe, A. L. (2006). *Organization theory: Modern, symbolic, and postmodern perspectives*. New York: Oxford University Press. pp. 101–140; Chamberlain, N. W. (1962). *The firm: Microeconomic planning and action*. New York: McGraw-Hill. pp. 384–405.
60. Exodus 18:13–26.
61. Judges 8:22–23 and 1 Samuel 8:4–5.
62. Proverbs 11:14.
63. Matthew 16:19, 18:18.
64. Hall, R. H., & Tolbert, P. S. (2005). *Organizations: Structures, processes and outcomes*. (9th ed.). Upper Saddle River, NJ: Pearson Prentice Hall. pp. 54–62; Hatch, M. J., & Cunliffe, A. L. (2006). *Organization theory: Modern, symbolic, and postmodern perspectives*. New York: Oxford University Press. pp. 101–140; Thompson, A. A., Gamble, J. E., & Strickland, A. J., (2006). *Strategy: Winning in the marketplace, core concepts, analytical tools, cases*. (2nd ed.). New York: McGraw-Hill Irwin.
65. Hall, R. H., & Tolbert, P. S. (2005). *Organizations: Structures, processes and outcomes*. (9th ed.). Upper Saddle River, NJ: Pearson Prentice Hall. pp. 54–62; Hatch, M. J., & Cunliffe, A. L. (2006). *Organization theory: Modern, symbolic, and postmodern perspectives*. New York: Oxford University Press. pp. 101–140.
66. Jensen, M. C. (1998). *Foundations of organizational strategy*. Cambridge, MA: Harvard University Press. pp. 114–123.
67. Hodge, B. J., Anthony, W. P., & Gales, L. M. (2003). *Organization theory: A strategic approach*. (6th ed.). Upper Saddle River, NJ: Prentice Hall. p. 38.
68. Hall, R. H., & Tolbert, P. S. (2005). *Organizations: Structures, processes and outcomes*. (9th ed.). Upper Saddle River, NJ: Pearson Prentice Hall, pp. 44–54.
69. Leavitt, H. J. (2007). Big organizations are unhealthy environments for human beings. *Academy of Management Learning & Education*. 62(2), 253–263.
70. These patterns were made popular by the research conducted by Burns and Stalker. See Burns, T., & Stalker, G. M. (1961). *The management of innovation*. London: Tavistock Publications.
71. Hatch, M. J., & Cunliffe, A. L. (2006). *Organization theory: Modern, symbolic, and postmodern perspectives*. (2nd ed.). New York: Oxford University Press. pp. 101–140; Child, J. (2005). *Organization: Contemporary principles and practice*. Malden, MA: Blackwell Publishing.
72. See Perrow, C. (1986). *Complex organizations: A critical essay*. (3rd ed.). New York: McGraw-Hill, Inc. p. 35; Oxman, J. A., & Smith, B. D. (2003). The limits of structural change. *MIT Sloan Management Review*. 45(1), 77–82.
73. Drucker, P. F. (1973). *Management: Tasks, responsibilities, practices*. New York: HarperCollins. pp. 558–563; Jaques, E. (1990). In praise of hierarchy. *Harvard Business Review*. 68(1), 127–133; Weston Jr., F. C. (1991). Functional goals are often in conflict with each other. *Industrial Engineering*. 23(11), 25–29.

74. Chandler, A. D. (1962). *Strategy and structure: Chapters in the history of the industrial enterprise*. Cambridge, MA: The MIT Press. pp. 42–51; Sloan, A. P. (1963). *My years with General Motors*. Garden City, NY: Doubleday & Company; Sheldrake, J. (2003). *Management theory*. (2nd ed.). London: Thomson Learning. pp. 128–132; Jones G. R. (2007). *Organizational theory, design and change*. (6th ed.). Upper Saddle River, NJ: Prentice Hall. pp. 153–167; Drucker, P. F. (1973). *Management: Tasks, responsibilities, practices*. New York: HarperCollins. pp. 572–589.
75. Jones, G. R. (2007). *Organizational theory, design and change*. (5th ed.). Upper Saddle River, NJ: Pearson Prentice Hall. p. 164.
76. Ostroff, F., & Smith, D. (1992). The horizontal organization. *The McKinsey Quarterly*. 1, 148–168; Stalk, G., & Black, J. (1994). The myth of the horizontal organization. *Canadian Business Review*. 21(4), 26; Garvin, D. A. (1995). Leveraging processes for strategic advantage. *Harvard Business Review*. 73(5), 77–90.
77. Hammer, M., & Stanton, S. (1999). How process enterprises really work. *Harvard Business Review*. 77(6), 108–118.
78. Sy, T., & D'Annunzio, L. S. (2005). Challenges and strategies of matrix organizations: Top-level and mid-level managers' perspectives. *Human Resource Planning*. 28(1), 39–48; Atkinson, P. (2003). Managing chaos in a matrix world. *Management Services*. 47(11): 8–11; Bartlett, C. A., & Ghoshal, S. (1990). Matrix management: Not a structure, a frame of mind. *Harvard Business Review*. 68(4), 138–145; Larson, E. W., & Gobeli, D. H. (1987). Matrix management: Contradictions and insights. *California Management Review*. 29(4), 126–138.
79. Dess, G. G., Rasheed, A. M. A., McLaughlin, K. J., & Priem, R. L. (1995). The new corporate architecture. *The Academy of Management Executive*. 9(3), 7–20; Schilling, M. A., & Steensma, H. K. (2001). The use of modular organizational forms: An industry-level analysis. *Academy of Management Journal*. 44(6), 1149–1168; Daboub, A. J. (2002). Strategic alliances, network organizations, and ethical responsibility. *SAM Advanced Management Journal*. 67(4), 40–48; Powell, W. W. (1990). Neither market nor hierarchy: Network forms of organization. *Research in Organizational Behavior*. 12, 295–336.
80. Cellular design is seldom used in business. However, religious and political organizations have used cellular design effectively. For example, see: Stockstill, L. (1998). *The cell church*. Ventura, CA: Regal Publishing; Comiskey, J. (2007). *The church that multiplies: Growing a healthy cell church in North America*. Moreno Valley, CA: CCS Publishing; Assadi, D., & Lorunser, B. (2007). Strategic management analysis of al Qaeda: The role of worldwide organization for a worldwide strategy. *Problems and Perspectives in Management*. 5(4), 57–71; Mayntz, R. (2006). Control of a terrorist network: Lessons from the 9/11 Commission report. *International Public Management Journal*. 9(3), 295–311.
81. Drucker, P. F. (1973). *Management: Tasks, responsibilities, practices*. New York: HarperCollins. p. 601.
82. Daboub, A. J. (2002). Strategic alliances, network organizations, and ethical responsibility. *SAM Advanced Management Journal*. 67(4), 40–48.
83. Robbins, S. P., & Coulter, M. (2009). *Management*. (10th ed.). Upper Saddle River, NJ: Prentice Hall. p. 233. For discussions of groups and teams see Coghlan, D. (1994). Managing organizational change through teams and groups. *Leadership & Organizational Development Journal*. 15(2), 18–23.
84. Katzenbach, J. R., & Smith, D. K. (1992). Why teams matter. *McKinsey Quarterly*. 3, 3–27; Katzenbach, J. R., & Smith, D. K. (1993). The discipline of teams. *Harvard Business Review*. 71(2), 111–120; Katzenbach, J. R., & Smith, D. K. (1993). *The wisdom of teams*. Cambridge, MA: Harvard University Press.
85. This section based on Robbins, S. P., & Judge, T. A. (2010). *Essentials of organizational behavior*. (10th ed.). Upper Saddle River, NJ: Prentice Hall. pp. 112–142.
86. Feldman, D. C. (1984). The development and enforcement of group norms. *Academy of Management Review*. 9(1), 47–53.
87. Manners Jr., G. E. (1975). Another look at group size, group problem solving, and member consensus. *Academy of Management Journal*. 18(4), 715–724; Maier, N. R. F. (1967). Assets and liabilities in group decision making. *Psychological Review*. 74(4), 239–249; Holloman, C. R., & Hendrick, H. W. (1971). Problem solving in different sized groups. *Personnel Psychology*. 24(3), 489–500.
88. O'Leary-Kelly, A. M., Martocchio, J. J., & Frink, D. D. (1994). A review of the influence of group goals on group performance. *Academy of Management Journal*. 37(5), 1285–1301.
89. Tuckman, B. W., & Jensen, M. C. (1977). Stages of small group development revisited. *Group & Organization Studies*. 2(4), 419–427.
90. Hellriegel, D., & Slocum, J. W. (2010). *Organizational behavior*. (13th ed.). Mason, OH: South-Western College Publishing; Robbins, S. P., & Judge, T. A. (2010). *Organizational behavior*. (14th ed.). Upper Saddle River, NJ: Prentice Hall; Mathieu, J., Maynard, M. T., Rapp, T., & Gilson, L. (2008). Team effectiveness 1997–2007: A review of recent advancements and a glimpse into the future. *Journal of Management*. 34(3), 410–476; Phillips, J. M., Douthitt, E. A., & Hyland, M. A. M. (2003). The role of justice in team member satisfaction with the leader and the attachment to the team. *Journal of Applied Psychology*. 86(2), 316–325; Langfred, C., & Shanley, M. (1997). The importance of organizational context, I: A conceptual model of cohesiveness and ineffectiveness in work groups. *Public Administration Quarterly*. 21(3), 349–369; Shanley, M., & Langfred, C. (1998). The importance of organizational context, II: An empirical test of work group cohesiveness and effectiveness in two governmental bureaucracies. *Public Administration Quarterly*. 21(4), 465–48; Shea, G. P., & Guzzo, R. A. (1987). Group effectiveness: What really matters? *Sloan Management Review*. 28(3), 25–31.
91. Langfred, C. W. (2000). The paradox of self-management: Individual and group autonomy in work groups. *Journal of Organizational Behavior*. 21(5), 563–585;

Langfred, C. W. (2004). Too much of a good thing? Negative effects of high trust and individual autonomy in self-managing teams. *Academy of Management Journal*. 47(3), 385–399.

92. Levinson, H. (1988). You won't recognize me: Predictions about changes in top-management characteristics. *The Academy of Management Executive*. 11(2), 119–125.
93. Young, S. (2003). *Moral capitalism: Reconciling private interest with the public good*. San Francisco, CA: Berrett-Koehler Publishers, Inc. p. 50.
94. McEvily, B., Perrone, V., & Zaheer, A. (2003). Trust as an organizing principle. *Organization Science*. 14(1), 91–106.
95. McEvily, B., Perrone, V., & Zaheer, A. (2003). Trust as an organizing principle. *Organization Science*. 14(1), 91–106.
96. Stanford, J. H. (2004). Curing the ethical malaise in corporate America: Organizational structure as the antidote. *SAM Advanced Management Journal*. 69(3), 14–21; James Jr., H. S. (2000). Reinforcing ethical decision making through organizational structure. *Journal of Business Ethics*. 28(1), 43–58.
97. Stanford, J. H. (2004). Curing the ethical malaise in corporate America: Organizational structure as the antidote. *SAM Advanced Management Journal*. 69(3), 14–21; Collins, D. (1997). The ethical superiority and inevitability of participatory management as an organizational system. *Organizational Science*. 8(5), 489–507; James Jr., H. S. (2000). Reinforcing ethical decision making through organizational structure. *Journal of Business Ethics*. 28(1), 43–58.
98. James Jr., H. S. (2000). Reinforcing ethical decision making through organizational structure. *Journal of Business Ethics*. 28(1), 43–58.
99. James Jr., H. S. (2000). Reinforcing ethical decision making through organizational structure. *Journal of Business Ethics*. 28(1), 43–58; Allison, R. E. (1998). Ethical values as part of the definition of business enterprise and part of the internal structure of the business organization. *Journal of Business Ethics*. 17(9/10), 1015–1028.
100. Drucker, P. F. (1967). *The effective executive*. New York: Harper & Row, Publishers. p. 171.
101. Drucker, P. F. (1993). *Post-capitalist society*. New York: HarperBusiness. p. 53.
102. There may be other influences at work in the broader culture as society as a whole becomes more complex. Thus, to claim that organizations per se are the cause of alienation may be an oversimplification. See the discussion of cultural complexity related to the growth of individualism in Triandis, H. C., Bontempo, R., Villareal, M. J., Asai, M., & Lucca, N. (1988). Individualism and collectivism: Cross-cultural perspectives on self-ingroup relationships. *Journal of Personality and Social Psychology*. 54(2), 323–338. Regarding the negative influences of large, bureaucratic organizations see Argyris, C. (1957). *Personality and organization: The conflict between system and the individual*. New York: Harper & Row, Publishers. pp. 175–208; Volf, M. (1991). *Work in the spirit: Toward a theology of work*. Eugene, OR: Wipf and Stock Publishers. pp. 157–201. See also Raelin, J. (2006). Finding meaning in the organization. *MIT Sloan Management Review*. 47(3), 64–68; Forrester, T. (1989). *High-tech society: The story of the information technology revolution*. Cambridge, MA: MIT Press; Kyle, D. T. (1993). *Human robots and holy mechanics: Reclaiming our souls in a machine world*. Columbus, NC: Swan Raven & Company; Bakke, D. W. (2005). *Joy at work*. Seattle, WA: PVG. pp. 41–84; Lebow, R., & Spitzer, R. (2002). *Accountability: Freedom and responsibility without control*. San Francisco, CA: Berrett-Koehler. pp. 25–40; Houston, J. (1992). *The heart's desire*. Oxford: Lion Publishing. p. 13; Mitroff, I. I., & Denton, E. A. (1999). A study of spirituality in the workplace. *MIT Sloan Management Review*. 40(4), 88; Martinez, R. J., & Franz, R. (2006). *Order out of chaos—Toward a Christian theology of organizing*. Paper presented at the Christian Business Faculty Association Annual Conference. October. Dayton, OH; Higginson, R. (1993). *Called to account—Adding value in God's world: Integrating Christianity and business effectively*. Guildford, Surrey: Eagle. p. 103.
103. Cascio, W. F. (1993). Downsizing: What do we know? What have we learned? *Academy of Management Executive*. 7(1), 95–104; Mabert, V. A., & Schmenner, R. W. (1997). Assessing the roller coaster of downsizing. *Business Horizons*. 40(4), 45–53; DeWitt, R. (1993). The structural consequences of downsizing. *Organization Science*. 4(1), 30–40; O'Neill, H. M., & Lenn, D. J. (1995). Voices of survivors: Words that downsizing CEOs should hear. *Academy of Management Executive*. 9(4), 23–33; Imberman, W. (1989). Managers and downsizing. *Business Horizons*. 32(5), 28–33.
104. Bruton, G. D., Keels, J. K., & Shook, C. L. (1996). Downsizing the firm: Answering the strategic questions. *Academy of Management Executive*. 10(2), 38–45; Cameron, K. S., Freeman, S. J., & Mishra, A. K. (1991). Best practices in white-collar downsizing: Managing contradictions. *The Executive*. 5(3), 57–73.
105. Smith, K. K., and Berg, D. N. (1997). *Paradoxes of group life: Understanding conflict, paralysis and movement in group dynamics*. San Francisco: The New Lexington Press. pp. 133, 141; Bennis, W., & Powell, S. (2000). Great groups and leaders. *Career Development International*. 5(2), 112; Lewis, M. W., & Dehler, G. E. (2000). Learning through paradox: A pedagogical strategy for exploring contradictions and complexity. *Journal of Management Education*. 24(6), 708–725.
106. Peters, T. J., & Waterman, R. H. (1982). *In Search of Excellence*. New York: HarperCollins Publishers, Inc. pp. 105–106; Perrow, C. (1986). *Complex organizations: A critical essay*. (3rd ed.). New York: McGraw-Hill, Inc. p. 148.
107. Perrow, C. (1986). *Complex organizations: A critical essay*. (3rd ed.). New York: McGraw-Hill, Inc. p. 26.
108. For discussions on the dangers of upward delegation see Oncken Jr., W., & Wass, D. L. (1999). Who's got the monkey. *Harvard Business Review*. 77(6), 178–186;

Oncken, W. (1999). Discretionary time. *Executive Excellence*. 16(10), 16; Brandt, J. R. (2005). Deflection by delegation. *Industry Week*. 254(9), 23; Stone, F. (2004). Smart management: Are you labeled high potential? *Executive Excellence*. 21(4), 8; Ensman, R. (2001). The games people play. *Incentive*. 175(9), 74; Sondak, A. (1991). Upward delegation—It's alive and well. *Supervisory Management*. 36(12), 7; Sondak, A. (1991). Delegation: Getting to the heart, or gut, of the matter. *Supervisory Management*. 36(3), 5; McConkay, D. D. (1987). Whose job are you working on? *Business Quarterly*. 51(4), 39–42; Allen, L. A. (1973). How to stop upward delegation. *Nation's Business*. 61(7), 67–69.

109. Rigby, D. (2002). Look before you lay off. *Harvard Business Review*. 80(4), 20–21.
110. Jensen, D. H. (2006). *Responsive labor: A theology of work*. Louisville, KY: Westminster John Knox Press. p. 56.
111. Genesis 39, 41; 2 Samuel 8; Acts 6, 15; 1 Timothy 3:1–7.

CHAPTER 9

Human Resource Management

LEARNING OBJECTIVES

- Gain an increased awareness of the importance of human resource management.
- Describe the principles of human resource management from a faith perspective.
- Explain the major steps in the human resource management process.
- Understand the legal constraints on human resource management.
- Explain the issues related to religious discrimination in the workplace in the United States.
- Describe selected tension points that managers face in human resource management.

"The human resource—the whole man—is, of all resources entrusted to man, the most productive, the most versatile, the most resourceful."[1]

"The work exists for the person as much as the person exists for the work. Put another way, the business exists as much to provide meaningful work to the person as it exists to provide a product or service to the customer."[2]

MERYL BARCLAY

7:30 a.m. Human resources specialist Meryl Barclay arrives at work. Her first task is to check her to-do list. New employee orientation dominates the day. Meryl checks the education and training room to make sure all is ready for the 8:15 start time. She reviews the names of new employees and the positions for which they were hired. At 9:30, during the orientation, the vice president of marketing will speak to the new employees, and Meryl must remember to meet with the company president for 20 minutes to discuss the recruitment of a new manager. Later in the day at 1:00 p.m., when the new employees are finished with the first of the 2-day orientation program, they will go to their assigned work units and spend the rest of the afternoon with their respective supervisors for the first of their department orientations. This is when Meryl's day in her office really begins.

8:05 a.m. Jeremy Horne, the first of 10 new employees, arrives at the human resource management department looking for the meeting room. Meryl greets Jeremy and the others as they come in. She remembers most of them from the pre-employment screening interviews she conducted.

Source: Stephen Coburn/Shutterstock.

8:15 a.m. The new employee orientation begins with a welcome by the company president. He talks about his vision of the company's future. After a 30-minute video on the history of the company, Meryl introduces in turn the chief financial officer, the vice president of operations, and the vice president of marketing. Each will talk with the new employees regarding parts of the organization for which they are responsible.

12:15 p.m. Meryl escorts the new employees to the lunchroom where they enjoy relaxed conversation around good food together. Meryl finds it difficult to relax. She knows that in a few minutes she will need to switch gears and move fast to complete everything else on her schedule.

1:40 p.m. The meeting with the health insurance representative runs late but the issues brought up in the conversation couldn't wait. Meryl puts a note on her to-do list that she must meet with the chief financial officer and the president as soon as possible to give them a report on the proposed changes to the healthcare insurance program. Before Meryl can get to the telephone messages that have come in from people looking for work, her phone rings. It is the manager of the storage and shipping department calling. He tells Meryl that he is fed up with one of his employees and that he plans to fire him today, and asks for Meryl's help. Meryl gets more details from the manager. It seems that the employee has been late for work a few days in a row and one day skipped work without calling to inform him. Meryl glances at her to-do list again. Most of the items will need to be delayed to help the manager. With the manager on the phone, Meryl checks the storage and shipping department employee's official file folder. She does not find any written document warning the employee regarding any performance problem. After a short conversation with the manager, Meryl determines that the manager has not talked with the employee regarding his performance problem. She provides counsel to the manager on how to proceed, explaining the discipline process and exploring what to do next. Above all, the manager is not to fire the employee today unless the employee takes an action that is on the short list of "these things will get you fired immediately," such as physically assaulting the manager or brandishing a weapon.

2:45 p.m. The supervisor in the assembly department walks in to inform Meryl that one of the assembly employees injured her hand while trying to retrieve something she dropped into the machinery. It looks like it could be a bad injury and the paramedics have taken the employee to the hospital. Meryl reviews with the supervisor the paperwork that must be completed and the steps in the workers compensation program that must be followed. She gives the supervisor forms to complete and sign. She also calls the worker's home to inform her family.

5:15 p.m. In between returning calls to job applicants, calling the local newspaper to place an advertisement for hiring a new director of quality improvement, checking with the warehouse and shipping manager to see how his conversation with the employee went, reading and signing three performance review forms that have come in to be filed, and checking on the injured employee at the hospital, Meryl wonders how the hours of her day could have flown by so fast.

Companies hire workers to get work done, but in and around all the work, the company and the employee have a relationship to maintain. This requires paying attention to many aspects of work life in addition to the work itself. We call this *human resources management*.

Who Cares About Human Resource Management?

Organizations hire managers to help them manage the relationships with employees. Collaborating with human resources specialists, managers carry the responsibility of making informed choices regarding the types of people that will match well with the shared values of the organization. As an advocate on behalf of employees and their needs, managers listen to employees and fairly represent their interests when considering the needs of the organization.

When you are applying for a job at a particular company and you don't know whom you should contact, you can always ask for personnel or human resources. The support staff members in such a department are often the first contact that prospective employees have with the company. If you are a job applicant or if you are the manager trying to hire a new employee, how the human resources support staff conduct their work is vital to representing the company and the jobs that are available.

Human resources specialists at organizations like Chiquita Brands International, American Express, and the State of Virginia provide support for recruiting, selecting, hiring, and training employees. In large corporations and government organizations human resource departments are large and well organized. The Virginia Department of Human Resource Management, for example, employs 79 persons to assist the thousands of state employees with their personnel needs.[3] Beyond this, most managers, whether they realize it or not, depend on human resources personnel to help build or repair trust among employees.[4] As few as 40 percent of employees say they trust senior-level leaders.[5] When employees feel like they are not being heard by senior-level managers, they sometimes trust the personnel department to listen. Trust cannot be engineered with superficiality. Human resources (HR) often becomes an advocate for employees who have concerns about how they are treated by the organization, workplace safety, and balancing the responsibilities of work and family.

An important dimension of HR work is communication. When senior-level managers find themselves too busy to communicate effectively, HR staff members get involved in the communication process. HR personnel who are loyal to the organization but who also are watching out for the interests of employees will create opportunities for senior-level leaders to communicate with employees face-to-face. When bad news needs to be given to employees, HR staff can help senior-level leaders interpret the news so that employees understand the reasons behind the news.

Focus on an Organization

The Society for Human Resource Management

Managers who enjoy helping organizations build relationships with employees sometimes choose human resource management as a career. The Society for Human Resource Management offers professional development through networking and continuing education for career HRM specialists. See the website at http://www.shrm.org/Pages/default.aspx.

Hiring, promoting, evaluating, terminating **Negotiating** **Communicating with employees and prospective employees** **Training and developing employees** **Handling grievances and complaints**	**Action**
Strategic thinking about the organization's needs of employees **Operational thinking about the employees' needs of the organization and the organization's needs of employees**	**Thinking & Feeling**
Assumptions regarding employees and their needs **Beliefs regarding fairness** **Moral values** **Shared organizational values** **Assumptions regarding specific legal constraints**	**Being & Becoming**

EXHIBIT 9-1

The Management Pyramid and HRM

Source: Courtesy of Michael E. Cafferky, © Michael E. Cafferky 2011.

Another important dimension is helping the organization go through change such as restructuring, downsizing, or merging with another organization. During change, employees can feel anxious about being left out of the loop on the major decisions. Effective human resources managers will stay involved in the communication process.

Management Pyramid on Human Resource Management

All human resource management (HRM) activities that we consider in this chapter begin with a set of beliefs and assumptions about employees and their needs. Moral values define fairness. This foundation guides the manager in how to think strategically about the organization's needs of employees. Operational thinking leads to managing the HRM process, which we will outline below. Finally, beliefs and thought patterns influence the actions that comprise the HRM process. See Exhibit 9-1.

For the Christian involved with human resources work this close connection between being, thinking, and action ultimately comes from biblical principles. We explore these in the section that follows. Before we consider contemporary ideas on human resource management, we first look at the Christian faith perspective because it is an important part of the Christian's personal beliefs and values (the "being and becoming" part of the Management Pyramid model).

Faith Perspective on Human Resource Management

Did you ever think that when you work productively you are engaging in a holy activity? Many Christians consider work to be a sacred activity. The biblical worldview sees work as a fulfillment of God's creative purpose for our lives. We work, in part, to fulfill being created in the Image of God. We work to contribute to the needs of those around us in the larger community and thereby to serve God. Work gives us a sense of purpose. It binds us to each other, contributing to our feeling that we belong. Through this, our work brings glory to God. This goes for all lawful occupations whether they are highly acclaimed in society, garner large economic payoffs, or are the so-called menial, low-paying jobs. Every job contributes to the well-being of ourselves and the larger community around us. This offers line managers and human resources managers a perspective that can guide them through the human resources relationships and activities of the organization.

The Employment Relationship

Like many other business topics, the Bible provides guidance on fundamental values, ways of thinking, and ways of doing things that honor God in the area of human resource management.[6] In this section we will explore the biblical guidance.

In biblical times, in addition to family members and in-laws working for the family business, sometimes more workers were needed to get the job done.[7] The Bible recognizes that both work itself and the employment relationship are legitimate.[8] Jesus spoke of employers and

EXHIBIT 9-2
Examples of Hired Workers in the Bible

King Josiah hires workers to restore the temple[9]	Abimelech hired people thought to be worthless[10]
Prodigal son becomes a laborer and then asks to become his father's hired hand[11]	Moses hires Bezalel to be the lead craftsman for the tabernacle and its furnishings[12]
Obadiah is the manager of King Ahab and Jezebel's household[13]	Haman was hired, promoted, and then "fired" as the king's chief prince[14]
Pharaoh hires Joseph to be Prime Minister[15]	Kings Belshazzar and then Cyrus hire Daniel[16]

employees in his parables. In these he gave no suggestion that working for pay is wrong.[17] Humans were created for work. Even when poor people were unemployed, they were expected to work.[18] It is through work that humans can bring glory to God.[19] See Exhibit 9-2 for examples of hired workers in the Bible.

The employer–employee relationship that involves working for pay and paying for workers to work is one way that humans created in God's image can glorify God. Employers and employees alike can glorify God by modeling God's character traits in the employment relationship: honesty, fairness, trustworthiness, kindness, wisdom and skill, faithfulness in keeping covenant relationships, the careful use of power, and the proper response to authority.[20]

The employment relationship carries the risk that both employee and employer will misuse the relationship. The employer may act harshly and unfairly. The employee may be tempted to be dishonest, to steal, or to be careless.[21] By proportion, the Bible probably puts slightly more emphasis on the responsibilities of the employer than on the obligations of the employee. This may be because employers generally have an economic advantage over the employees.

The employment relationship, by nature, is personal. Even in large corporations employees have personal face-to-face conversations with at least one manager who represents the interest of the employer. But there is also an impersonal dimension in the relationship. A biblical example where both dimensions seem to be present is the story of the business owner who hired workers at various times of the day. He had a personal relationship with each employee. However, his relatively impersonal employment policy was to pay everyone the same regardless of how many hours they worked.[22]

Community-Covenant Nature of the Employment Relationship

Employment, like most other business relationships, is embedded in the larger community of which businesses are a part. The workplace also is an important community of relationships inside the company. And the businesses employees work for are important elements in the broader community.[23]

The employment relationship is among persons in a community inside the company who work for the greater good of the larger community outside the company.

Source: © Deanm1974 / Dreamstime.com.

Human communities of all kinds are networks of human interdependence. This applies to the inside of a company, between the company and other organizations, and to the geographic community in which the organization is located. It also applies at a much larger scale to national and international communities of industries and nations. Successful communities involve patterns of cooperation in which individuals share similar values and goals that are designed to support the common good of all who are in the community. This fundamental biblical principle is called **solidarity**.[24]

It also means that both the employer and the employee are vulnerable to each other, though an individual employee is in a weaker position because the company holds economic power to hire and fire the employee. However, the company is vulnerable to the employees if, as a group, they are in a stronger position to start and stop work. Thus, the covenant employer–employee relationship is built on mutual trust and the desire for mutual goodwill.

Employee Selection and Hiring

The examples of Jesus and others in the Bible show us how important employee selection can be. Jesus hand-picked the 12 people who were destined to be his closest associates. Yet, after his ascension to heaven, Jesus made a special call to Saul of Tarsus to be the evangelist who surpassed all but a few of the original 12 apostles.[25] When Jesus recruited disciples, he gave them an honest and realistic picture of what to expect. He taught that the cost of discipleship is high.[26]

Employers should select their employees with care for several reasons. Like any other managerial task, employee selection should be done to bring glory to God. Given that the employer and new employee will be forming a covenant relationship, select wisely so that the relationship has the best opportunity for long-term success.

The idea of matching the employee to the tasks is not new to contemporary management thought. It was first taught in the Bible. See Exhibit 9-3.

The effects of the hiring decision will be felt by everyone inside and outside the organization. Choose new employees carefully because you are responsible for the choices you make. The book of Proverbs describes this in graphic terms: "Like an archer who wounds everyone, so is he who hires a fool . . ."[27]

Human Development and Training

The principle of training and developing employees for more effective and efficient service is consistent with biblical thinking. For example, when Moses was called by God to become the leader of Israel, God promised that he would teach Moses "just-in-time" what he was to do in his negotiations with the Egyptian leader.[28] God chose Bezalel to lead the artisans and construction workers who built the tabernacle, and also gave him the role of teaching others how to perform the skillful work.[29] The work of Jesus is one of the best examples of training and human development. Jesus gave his disciples training in several dimensions. Over just a few years he gave them a sense of mission. He told them what they should do and grounded them in the reasons for the tasks. He gave them practical, hands-on experience.[30]

By the time that Jehoshaphat became king, the role of teacher had become firmly established in the culture.[31] The ancient teacher's role developed from the belief that the spiritual life of the nation could be enhanced through training. The giving of the law was accompanied by teachers, using Spirit-filled reason to show how the law was to be applied in everyday life.[32] Individuals could hear the law read to them if they could not read. The topics for teaching run the spectrum of information relevant to life in the community from spiritual life, technical training, and health and safety training. So powerful is teaching's influence on people that leaders must make careful choices regarding what things should be taught.[33] So highly prized is teaching and learning that the Bible sternly warns us not to be so self-centered that we are unwilling to learn from others. Unwillingness to be taught is foolish.[34]

EXHIBIT 9-3
Examples of Worker Selection Criteria Used in the Bible[35]

Selection of leaders to assist Moses	Selection of spies
Selection of Bezalel and his assistants	Selection of Moses
Selection of Church elders and bishops	Selection of deacons
Selection of Joshua as leader	Gideon's selection of soldiers

EXHIBIT 9-4

The Management Pyramid Applied to Training and Development

Instruction in the *what* of actions; training in skills, procedures, techniques, and practices relevant to the expectations from God's will as revealed in his Law.	**Action**
Instruction in the *how* of thinking about the issues facing the individual, his or her family, and the whole community.	**Thinking & Feeling**
Instruction in the *why* of thinking and behaving; teaching the shared values, beliefs, and assumptions that guide the community as a whole in following God's will.	**Being & Becoming**

Source: Courtesy of Michael E. Cafferky, © Michael E. Cafferky 2011.

The principles of teaching and learning carried on through the centuries following Israel's first experiences in training. In the New Testament we find that teaching was a major part of the ministry of Jesus and the apostles.[36] See Exhibit 9-4.

Performance Evaluation and Discipline

Selecting and hiring a new employee begins a covenantal relationship with that person. So in the same way, disciplining and firing the employee should be taken seriously in the context of the covenantal relationship. If the employment relationship is seen as a covenantal relationship, then when a person needs to be let go, the employer will consider the future of the employee and will want to sever the employment in a way that preserves the relationship.

When God created, he did very good work. Humans are to follow his example. At the root of this, human relationships in the Bible either are patterned after or find their fundamental principles in the relationship with God. Humans who live for the glory of God never forget for whom they live and work. Ultimately it is God who determines whether humans' relationships with him measure up to his standard.[37] It is precisely because humans, on their own, cannot measure up to God's high standard of righteousness that they need God's help.

In the human realm, the Bible assumes that it is proper to evaluate employee performance. This occurs not because the supervisor alone is interested in controlling the worker but because the group of workers is held accountable to the goals of the organization. But it is not proper to evaluate the performance of someone else's employee.

The biblical expectation to judge work performance is not in contradiction to the commands of the Bible not to judge one another. Ultimately, all humans work for God, and it is not proper for one human to judge another human in terms of the other person's walk with God.[38]

When an employer evaluates the performance of an employee and the performance is less than expected, the employer is expected to discipline the employee. The Bible teaches that keeping an employee in the organization that is slack in his or her work is destructive.[39]

The Bible talks about discipline in terms of reproof and admonition, meaning gentle criticism. It is better to bring reproof than not because this promotes integrity for both the employee and the manager. The challenge for the manager is to bring discipline in a way that treats the person with dignity and respect. The wise manager will offer discipline mixed with mercy, understanding, and humility. Reserve conversations designed to help an employee improve performance or eliminate disruptive behaviors for settings where the employee will not be embarrassed or subject to peer ridicule.[40]

The Bible recognizes that some people do not respond to discipline. For these individuals, the manager is better off not continuing to reprove with the hope that they will change.[41] In such a case, it is better for the organization and the individual to terminate the employment relationship. Termination can thus be seen as a redemptive action for both the employee and the organization. Redemption comes to the employee by giving him or her a chance to find a better-matched employment in another organization. Redemption comes to the organization by freeing it of someone whose performance is blocking the organization from achieving its goals.

Retaliation and Conflict Management

One important dimension that the follower of God will use as a guide is the principle of not retaliating when an employee does something that brings anger. The biblical principle related to this problem is clear: Do not repay evil for evil. Such retaliation only stirs up more conflict and brings more problems to the one retaliating. Instead, treat others with respect and respond with gentleness. For example, if you must let someone go because of insubordination, let them go with dignity, without strife, and in a spirit of forgiveness.[42] This applies as much to subordinates as it does to managers.[43] These principles apply equally to the problem of managing conflict at work. The Bible holds up before us how much happier we are when we seek peace.[44] We cannot control how others behave toward us, but we can choose to behave peaceably toward others. Our responsibility is to make a good-faith effort to resolve conflict quickly so that the covenant relationship is redeemed and nourished.[45]

Fairness in the Employer–Employee Relationship

In a biblical covenant relationship all parties look out for the interests of the others because each has equal status with God. A manager who desires to follow biblical principles will work to keep covenants that the organization makes with employees. This is a weighty responsibility to be taken seriously.

Covenant requires that the employer treat employees with fairness whether deciding wages, promotion, recognition, or anything else.[46] Some employees will come from a national culture or subculture in which certain behaviors are at best incomprehensible and at worst offensive. Some personality traits of employees may grate on the manager's nerves. But the manager's job is to be fair regardless of these and other differences.

Covenant also requires the employee to be honest and fair with the employer. Stealing money, supplies, material, inventory, or equipment from the employer is wrong for three reasons. First, it is an offense against God who gives so much in abundance to humans. This is a way of making profane God's name.[47] Second, stealing is a sin against the community because it undermines trust, which is fundamental to a smoothly functioning society created by God. Third, stealing is a sin against the owners of the business and other employees who work hard to acquire that which was stolen. Stealing from the employer's reputation by telling lies such as to gain an advantage during a performance evaluation prevents the employer from helping you and the company to achieve desired performance.

Because both employers and employees fall short of these ideals, Christian managers will see their role, in part, to participate with God by redeeming broken employer–employee relationships. This can happen consistently only when managers see their role in the context of a covenant with both the employer and the employee. In this way, managers become ministers of the relationship to heal and care for it.

Perhaps the first, most direct statements in the Bible about dealing fairly with others are the Commandments: "Thou shalt not steal" and "Thou shalt not lie."[48] These are stated in negative terms. The positive side of these might be stated as "Be fair; be truthful," or act with integrity. The application of the principle goes far beyond financial dealings embracing how we treat each other in terms of sharing influence, mediating conflict between employees, offering due process during disputes, and in any other situation in which there is opportunity for personal benefit.[49]

The manager who walks with integrity walks securely. But if the manager spoils integrity, more than likely that manager will be discovered.[50] In terms of human resource management, the Christian's prayer is like that of Paul the Apostle: that we serve others in the world of work not in mere wisdom of the world but in the grace of God and in a manner worthy of God.[51]

Fairness extends beyond compensation. The Bible promotes the virtue of hard work; however, employers would not work an animal beyond its capacity. The employer should be sensitive to the limitations of human capacity for accomplishing tasks.[52] We find in the book of Exodus that the upper limit of human capacity was tested by oppressive work supervisors. This oppression of workers was long-remembered and often used as an illustration of how humans can take advantage of one another and, in so doing, dishonor God.

The Bible provides important guidance for managers in terms of dealing with employees. In addition to following these fundamental principles it is important for a manager to understand the human resource management process. One of the reasons for this is that human resource activities make up an important portion of managerial work.

The Biblical Story of Deborah

Read the story of Deborah in Judges 4 in the Bible. Based on her experience, grasp the significance of the accomplishments that occurred under the leadership of Deborah. Make a mental note of the leadership strengths and weaknesses of Deborah. What leadership principles can we gain from the experience of Deborah that are applicable today?

Human Resource Management Process

An organization's personnel dimension boils down to managing the process of the organization forming and maintaining relationships with individual employees. Specifically this usually involves planning for personnel needs, fairly and legally recruiting and selecting new employees, developing employees' potential for high performance, evaluating performance, providing safe working conditions, advocating on behalf of employees, and managing compensation and benefits so that employees are dealt with fairly. Unfortunately, sometimes it means disciplining employees and, when training and disciplinary action fails, terminating the employment relationship fairly and with dignity.

Human resource management considers a wide range of issues that affect the entire relationship between employer and each employee. For this reason alone, human resource management is an integral part of every manager's work. It also has become a specialized management support function in organizations of all sizes.

With the increased population and the need to transport commodities and other products long distances to meet the needs of humans around the globe, the exchanges in the market have become impersonal.[53] In spite of this, the employment relationship remains primarily personal because in most organizations it is difficult to become an employee without having someone to whom you personally report.

If you work as a manager in an organization you will get involved in most of the human resource management activities even if your company is large enough to have a personnel department. For example, suppose you are one of three team supervisors of an accounting department. As a supervisor, you are involved in recruiting, interviewing, selecting, and training new employees. The manager of your department participates in deciding the pay scales for your workers. Also, you and your fellow supervisors are likely the primary individuals who conduct performance evaluations and, when necessary, make the decision to terminate an employee. Through all of this, the personnel department members may act as internal consultants to you, your fellow supervisors, and your manager.

The personnel department at organizations like Lockheed Martin and Dow Chemical Company has support staff authority to provide advice, help with communication with potential employees, keep up-to-date records, maintain an awareness of current best practices, and assist in the recruitment process. If the organization is large enough to support additional personnel support staff, there may be employees who specialize in recruitment or who are experts in training. Others might specialize in helping managers keep job descriptions current (job analysts) or manage the employee benefits program by making sure employees have the latest information about health insurance and are using the benefits appropriately, and by collaborating with outside providers of benefit services.

HRM Strategic Planning

If organizing workers is one of the last sources of strategic, sustainable competitive advantage, then an organization's group of employees is the other.[54] Strategic issues usually focus on the organization's ability to match its internal resources with the marketplace's opportunities and threats. This cannot be accomplished except by individual workers performing their work in close alignment with the company's strategic direction. But this, in turn, requires that the organization have the right people in the organization who are a good fit for and who are committed to pursuing its strategic direction with the highest performance possible. For example, when Service Master decides to grow its business through mergers and acquisitions, its managers need to make sure that the newly acquired organization has just the right number of employees with the right skills and training resources to help them perform. HRM also helps accomplish the organizational culture fit between Service Master and the acquired company.

In organizations in which strategy-critical categories of workers are in short supply, human resources works with top leaders and frontline employees to forecast the availability of future employees. In some industries the annual turnover rate can be between 10 and 20 percent. In other industries it can be much higher. For example, Covenant Transport, like all other national trucking firms, constantly faces the need for qualified drivers. Annual turnover in the industry is high, sometimes exceeding 100 percent. But without drivers, Covenant Transport cannot operate its business much less carry out its strategy.

Worker shortage is one problem, but the opposite situation is also a problem that HR managers help with. If the organization must downsize to respond to changes in the market, then human resources will play a key role in planning and implementing the downsizing process.

The Christian Mind on Strategic Human Resource Management

As Christian managers we celebrate employees as image-bearers, inherently worthy of dignity as the stewards of God's world. But we also must also see them as wise investments. Thus, we should celebrate the rise in prominence of HR as a strategic business function. Only 25 years ago the HR function was viewed as a cost center with the mandate of constraining the costs associated with the personnel of the firm. Today the HR function is viewed as a strategic investment center, and personnel are viewed as critical human resources and sources of human capital.

In fact, the empirical and theological reality is that there is no resource more precious to business than human beings. And the belief that financial capital is more important than human capital is false, as conveyed by the parable of the talents in Matthew 25. Consistent with this parable, emerging HR management research demonstrates that human capability is the ultimate source of wealth generation. One seminal study found that publicly-traded firms that adopt a strategic/investment-orientation toward the HR function have a higher market value—as much as $100,000 *per employee*—than do organizations that have maintained a cost-orientation toward the HR function.[55]

As Christian managers, we have an exciting opportunity to contribute to God's creative activity in business by heavily investing in employees and the HR function. The emerging research suggests that the result is a healthier bottom line. And sound theology suggests that the result is a healthier creation. Not a bad combination.

Dr. Scott Quatro
Associate Professor of Management
Covenant College
Lookout Mountain, GA

Recruitment and Selection

Recruitment and selection of employees are two important parts of the HRM process shown in Exhibit 9-5. **Recruitment** is a set of activities in which HR specialists and operational managers engage in tactical maneuvers to identify and attract suitable employees that will help the organization achieve high levels of performance.[56] **Selection** is the process of deciding which of the job candidates to offer the job. Because having quality employees is closely linked with the ability of the organization to carry out its strategic activities, most HR managers and top-level executives believe that employee recruitment and selection are two of the most important strategic and operational activities that managers do. The recruitment and selection process can be broken down into several steps including starting with a plan and rationale, conducting a job analysis, writing a job description, recruiting applicants, and making the selection.

PLAN, RATIONALE, AND BUDGET. Hiring always means that organizational costs are affected. Thus, making a commitment to hire a person should not be made until the budget has been

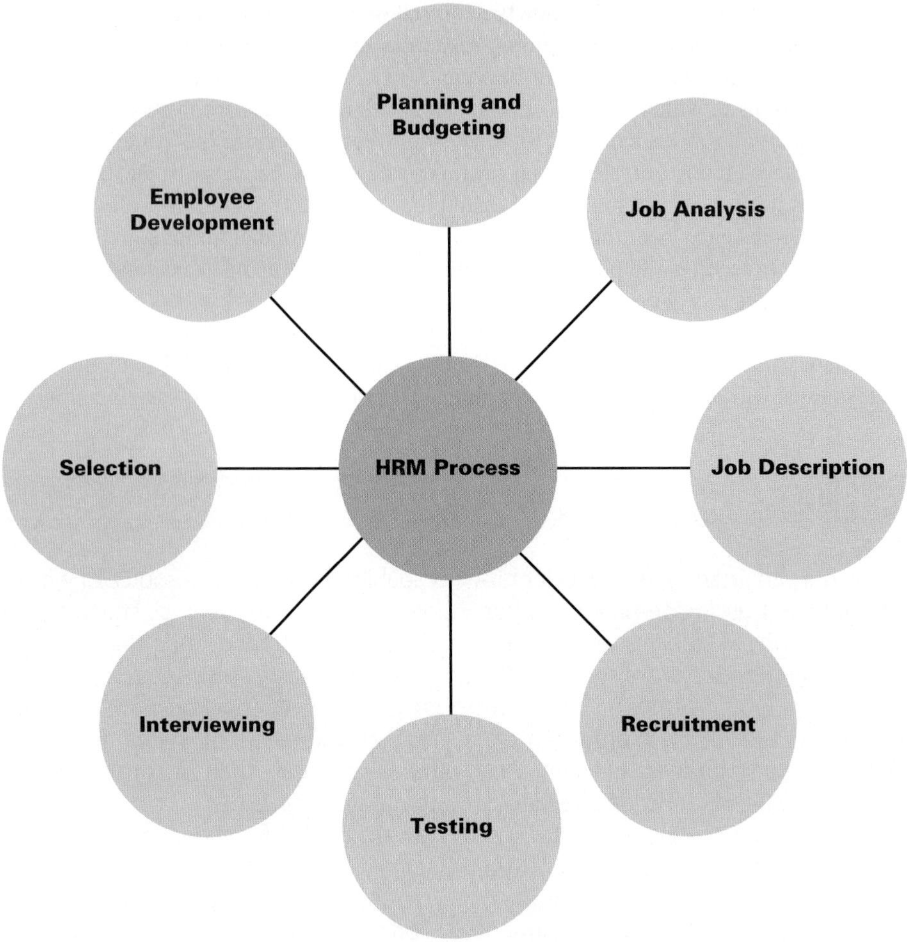

EXHIBIT 9-5
The HRM Process

approved. In some cases approval will be automatic if the company is hiring to replace someone who has terminated employment. In other cases, approval is not automatic, such as when the organizational leaders are looking for ways to cut costs or to reorganize.

When an existing employee terminates employment, decision makers should take the opportunity to review the organization's need for that particular job. Someone in the organization should be charged with the responsibility of challenging the status quo by asking the hard questions such as: Why do we need to replace this employee? Can this person's termination be the catalyst for making an organizational change? Do the current and expected future demands of the environment continue to support performing this particular job? Has the job changed significantly since the previous person was hired? If the person is not replaced, how will this affect the workload and morale of other employees? If not replaced, can these changes be incorporated into tasks assigned to other people?

JOB ANALYSIS. Determining whether to fill an existing job with a new employee begins by studying the job that needs to be completed and the traits and experience required to do the work well. This is called **job analysis**. To complete the job analysis, the HR specialist will interview the manager of the department that needs the new employee. This interview will reveal information regarding the work activities, working conditions, work schedules, and special qualifications needed. For example, the HR specialists in companies like Bank One and GlaxoSmithKline pharmaceuticals will ask supervisors questions such as: What is the job and what does it involve? What knowledge is required to do the work? What skills and abilities are needed to excel in this type of work? What environmental conditions are present when this job is performed? What are the minimum educational, training, or experience qualifications needed by an applicant? The HR specialist also might use a questionnaire or conduct face-to-face observation of the actual work being performed.

The information generated in the job analysis can be used in several places such as writing a job description, creating performance review guidelines, making adjustments to the organization, deciding whether to hire a temporary worker, advertising, screening and interviewing applicants, reviewing and adjusting the pay scale, and developing and enhancing training programs. Documentation of the requirements of the job is important for showing compliance to Equal Employment Opportunity regulations.

WRITING OR REVISING A JOB DESCRIPTION. A **job description** is a written document that contains information regarding what work is performed, the responsibilities of the job, and the working conditions most likely to be encountered by the worker. Information contained in the job description can be used in new employee orientations, annual performance reviews, organizational restructuring, and employee discipline. See Exhibit 9-6.

Some very small companies do not use written job descriptions if the owner also is the manager, works closely with all employees every day, and can direct employees' work on a daily basis. For example, a building contractor that specializes in laying tile in residential properties may have a crew of two people helping him every day. Expectations are communicated on a daily basis as needed and adjustments are made from job to job depending on the work that needs to be done. Larger companies find that job descriptions minimize misunderstandings between supervisor and subordinate. They can encourage continuity when managers are changed. When there is a change in personnel, the job description can be the basis for revising the job and recruiting a replacement employee. Exhibit 9-7 provides a sample job description.

RECRUITMENT OF APPLICANTS. Generating a pool of qualified applicants is the next goal in the process. This means promoting the availability of the open position among people who might be interested in applying for the job. Having a ready list of individuals who are interested in working for your organization is ideal. But there are thousands of organizations, and only a select few stand out. Thus, in reality most organizations must engage in some form of promotion to signal to prospective employees that a job opportunity exists. We know from research that the image that prospective applicants have of the organization is related to the likelihood of people applying for work.[57] In some organizations, reputation may be the dominant force in the organization's ability to find qualified applicants.

Recruitment can involve a number of promotional activities. For example, one company recruiting a Dietary Manager may advertise in a regional newsletter that experienced dietary supervisors read. Or it might mean posting a notice on the national Internet site of the Dietary

EXHIBIT 9-6
Elements of a Job Description

- **Job title.** Job titles help distinguish one job from another. For example, one job title might be *Accounting Clerk I* for a junior accountant whose job is to make journal entries.
- **Job summary.** This provides in one to three sentences an overall description of the job and its responsibilities.
- **Reporting relationships.** This identifies which manager (described by job title, not by name) is the immediate supervisor for this job. If the job involves supervision of other employees, these supervisory relationships are described using job titles.
- **Qualifications.** This section identifies minimum education level, work experience, or other credentials required. If certifications are required these should be listed. For example, if the dietary manager needs to be someone who is a certified dietary manager through the Dietary Managers Association, a diet technician registered with the American Dietetic Association, or an executive chef certified by the American Culinary Federation, this should be stated.
- **Responsibilities.** This section describes the regular, ongoing job duties that are assigned to the person who performs this job. It should describe the essential functions of the job that the employee must be able to perform.
- **Working conditions.** This section describes the general working conditions that the employee should expect to encounter. Special working conditions should be identified such as exposure to hazardous substances, heat or cold, and noise. These allow job applicants to make an informed decision as to whether they are fit for the job.
- **Physical requirements.** This section identifies the physical demands on the employee. For example, one job may be primarily sedentary (sitting), while other jobs require the employee to stand, lift, climb, carry, and perform other strenuous physical activities.

Job Description: Assistant Manager of Logistics

- **Job title.** Assistant Manager of Logistics
- **Job summary.** Provide assistance to the Logistics Department Director in carrying out the responsibilities of the department as it satisfies the needs of customers.
- **Reporting relationships.** The Assistant Manager reports directly to the Logistics Department Director. Reporting to the Assistant Manager are the members of the Order Preparation Team and the Outbound Order Fulfillment Team.
- **Qualifications.** The Assistant Manager must:
  - be a holder of a college or university undergraduate degree in operations management, supply chain management, or comparable degree.
  - have a minimum of 5 years experience working in outbound logistics.
  - be competent in using standard word processing, spreadsheet, and database software applications.
  - have demonstrated a positive track record in relating with fellow employees and working as an active member of a work team.
- **Responsibilities.** The Assistant Manager is responsible for:
  - overseeing the order preparation and order fulfillment work processes.
  - using the company's information system effectively to monitor the efficiency of outbound logistics.
  - coordinating and controlling the work of the order preparation and order fulfillment teams.
  - analyzing logistical problems and, in collaboration with others, introducing improvements in outbound logistics performance of the organization.
  - analyzing operational and financial data related to outbound logistics.
  - coordinating with internal and external freight carriers.
  - monitoring the flow of goods and materials.
  - planning to handle routine and special needs of customers.
  - planning and implementation of work team staffing schedules responding to the changing needs of customers.
  - conducting or arranging for team member training events.
  - following company health and safety policies and procedures.
  - participating in companywide performance improvement efforts as requested.
  - performing other duties and complete projects as assigned by the Logistics Department Director.
- **Working conditions.** General working conditions include working in offices, warehouses, and inside and outside as needed for the effective discharge of duties. All employees of the company are at risk of exposure to hazardous substances, heat or cold, and noise. Proper safety equipment must be worn and used at all times as dictated by the situation.
- **Physical requirements.** The Assistant Manager of Logistics will experience a mix of various physical demands including sedentary office work, standing, lifting, climbing, carrying, and performing other strenuous physical activities as required to support team members' abilities to perform their work efficiently and effectively.

EXHIBIT 9-7
Sample Job Description

Managers Association. General job Internet sites also are available for posting open positions. Depending on the type of job that is open, a classified advertisement in the local newspaper may be the best way to communicate the opening.

Word of mouth is often one of the most effective ways to get the word out. There may be employees working in the company who are looking for a change. Fellow employees play a key role in these individuals finding out about job opportunities that have opened up. In addition to word of mouth, some companies post job opportunities on bulletin boards or the company's internal website (intranet) accessible to employees.

Other means of finding qualified candidates also exist. For example, attending career fairs is one way to recruit new employees for jobs requiring a college or undergraduate professional education. Contracting for a fee with an employment agency or an executive recruitment firm can be helpful in finding highly specialized workers. The local office of the State Employment Agency also has contact with individuals looking for work.

USE OF AN APPLICATION FORM. Job applicants come from a variety of backgrounds and experiences. If each applicant gave the employer different kinds of information, it would make the decision-making process difficult to manage. Employers have found that having a standard set of questions set in the same format from applicant to applicant helps them compare one applicant with another more efficiently. It can improve the thoroughness with which decision makers review individual backgrounds.

Most application forms require the applicant to tell the employer specific, verifiable information including full legal name, educational background, employment history, personal contact information, interests and achievements, military service, Social Security number, and whether the applicant has been convicted of a felony. They may ask for additional information such as language skills, computer software skills, or skills in operating particular types of equipment relevant to the company. Some forms also have a space for the applicant to provide information regarding **references**—people that the employer can contact to obtain additional information regarding the applicant's work experience, work habits, or character traits.

Even though many companies have turned to online application forms submitted over the Internet, some employers expect the application form to be completed in the job applicant's original handwriting or to be typewritten. Other employers require that job applicants complete the form while being observed by someone.

TESTING. No manager wants to intentionally set up a new employee to fail right from the start when, for example, the job requires a minimum level of pre-employment proficiency in using a particular piece of equipment and the applicant has not used that type of equipment before. Employers may use **pre-employment testing** to determine whether there is a good match with the job. Some jobs require specific skills at minimum proficiency levels. For example, an applicant's keyboard typing ability may be important for a data entry job at Motorola or Texas Instruments. An applicant seeking a job in customer service will be given a personality test or sales aptitude assessment.

Such tests are administered as a way to screen for applicants that might be inappropriate for the job. But pre-employment tests have become controversial. One issue is the effectiveness of tests to screen out inappropriate applicants. Another issue is that some tests ask questions that can reveal underlying mental health conditions, which violates provisions in the Americans with Disabilities Act. Another problem is that with the increased use of the online application process, the use of online pre-employment testing encourages some applicants to cheat on the test to obtain a more favorable score. Still another problem, some argue, is that pre-employment aptitude tests give an unfair advantage to people of some ethnic backgrounds while creating a disadvantage to others. In spite of these and other debatable issues, pre-employment testing is still used in many organizations.[58]

SCREENING INTERVIEWS. Managers at most businesses want to surround themselves with the people who are best suited for the jobs that need to be accomplished.[59] In some ways, each step in the employee recruitment and selection process is designed to achieve this objective. Information provided in the job application will be used to determine whether the applicant should be invited to participate in a screening interview.

A **screening interview** is an interview designed to narrow the pool of applicants down to the individuals who are potentially good matches for the organization. At the same time, a screening interview also keeps qualified applicants in the pool of applicants until the selection decision is made and the job offer is accepted. It is a time to get acquainted with the applicants, evaluate their ability to communicate, determine their level of confidence, clarify information provided on or omitted from the application form, and gauge their enthusiasm and knowledge of the job for which they are applying. During the screening interview, the person representing the organization can provide information about the company to the applicant. To save time, screening interviews can be conducted over the telephone.

During screening interviews, applicants are also gathering information that helps them decide whether to continue as an applicant. Traits and behaviors of the interviewer provide important signals to job applicants regarding the organization and what it is like to work there. Interaction

During the job interview the employer and the applicant gather information that help them decide whether the job and the organization are a good match for each other.

Source: Adam Gregor/Shutterstock.

with the interviewer also is interpreted by applicants in terms of the likelihood of receiving a job offer. For example, some research has shown that the warmth of the interviewer is important to job applicants.[60] Interviewers who are warm seem to signal to applicants that the organization is a good place to work. It also raises applicants' expectancies that they will receive a job offer.

A decision that must be made during the interview phase of the process is how much information to give to applicants and how realistic this information should be. Being realistic about the job with the applicant is generally thought to have a positive influence on job satisfaction, commitment, and performance. The reason is pretty straightforward: Applicants going into a job with realistic expectations are more likely to have their expectations met than not. Research results indicate that the more intelligent, committed, and experienced applicants are, the more they will be positively influenced by an employer being realistic about the job with them.[61]

Researchers say that when selecting a new employee who is well-suited to the job, the best managers select for talent.[62] A job applicant can lack the experience compared with others, not be as smart as others, or may even exhibit apparent lower determination, but they can be wildly successful in the job if they have the talents that are needed for success in that job.

Talent is not the same as skill and knowledge. **Skills** are capabilities in fulfilling your role. You can train people to acquire new skills. For example, you can train a person in accounting skills. **Knowledge** is factual and experiential information that you are aware of. This, too, can be improved as a result of training and experience. **Talents** are the recurring and quite spontaneous patterns of thoughts, feelings, or behaviors that naturally emerge in social situations. These are transferrable from one work situation to another. Most habits are talents. See Exhibit 9-8.

Talents come in three dimensions:

- *Striving* talents are the reasons why a person attempts to do good work, works diligently to achieve good results, and why one employee is motivated more by social interaction while another employee is motivated by developing excellent technical competence. The degree of and the type of drive a person has is an important dimension of striving talent.

EXHIBIT 9-8
Knowledge and Skills Are Not Talents

- *Thinking* talents explain the basic ways people naturally think and how they make decisions. Some people are quantitative thinkers, converting the information they receive into terms that are as measurable as possible. Others have talent for thinking of the economic forces at work in a situation. Others have talent for thinking of the human relations dynamics that are present.
- *Relating* talents explain whom the job applicant forms relationships with, whom he or she confronts (or doesn't), and whom he or she ignores.

SELECTION INTERVIEWS. The purpose of **selection interviews** is to narrow the applicant pool to the individual who is the best fit for the organization. This round of interviews is conducted with applicants who have passed the screening interview step. This interview digs a little deeper into the applicant's past behavior patterns, accomplishments, and past experiences.[63] It also is designed to reveal more about the applicant's traits and values. While there is no way of knowing for sure how a job applicant will do before being hired, the reasoning behind the interview is that knowing more about the applicant's past behaviors and current traits is the best predictor of future behaviors.

Many experts believe that the selection interview is best accomplished in a conversational approach rather than simply asking a list of questions on a page. A conversational approach helps the applicant relax. See Exhibit 9-9 for a list of the dos and don'ts of interviewing.

CHECKING AND VERIFYING. Many companies conduct criminal background checks (through the state police), pre-employment drug screening, and reference checks on the short list of applicants that make it to the final stage. Verifying the truthfulness of information provided on the job application form and the resume is vital. Obtaining feedback from references can provide valuable information regarding past behaviors. This step cannot be bypassed even if you are very busy.

EXHIBIT 9-9
Dos and Don'ts of Interviewing[64]

- Do set the right tone from the beginning. First impressions last. Alert the front desk that Mr. or Ms. So-and-so will be coming (giving that person the name) for an interview.
- Don't use closed-ended, yes-no questions too much. For example, asking an applicant "Are you good with people?" requires a yes or no answer. Who in their right mind would ever answer "No" to such a question? Naturally, exceptions to this rule include when the interviewer needs to know whether the applicant is interested in accepting the job if it is offered and whether the applicant can start on a particular day of the week to begin employment.
- Do use open-ended questions that require the applicant to speak about past experiences that are related to the job being applied for.
- Don't play mind games with the applicant by asking absurd loaded questions requiring the applicant to choose which of two bad behaviors is the lesser evil. This is simply a power game and communicates to the applicant that power may be abused in the organization.
- Do pose situations in which the applicant is encouraged to tell stories that reveal past behaviors. For example, say to the applicant: "Suppose you were in the following situation . . . What would you do?"
- Don't settle for one-word or one-phrase answers. Ask the applicant to give an example.
- Do take the applicant to the work area to let them see the tasks being performed. The exception to this is when proprietary technology is used and confidentiality needs to be preserved.
- Don't ask more than one question at a time. This can needlessly confuse the applicant.
- Do use a structured interview with a prepared interview guide, but conduct the interview in a conversational tone. Use information from the application form and the resume as a basis for discussion rather than complete information.
- Don't allow the applicant to control the conversation. You want the applicant to do most of the talking but not to stray too far from the topic of conversation.

(continued)

- Do use a behavioral simulation, situations, and scenarios to help the applicant demonstrate behavior patterns. For example, suppose you are interviewing an applicant for a managerial job. You give the person a short stack (prepared ahead of time) of envelopes, telephone message slips, reports, and emails. This is called *The In-box Exercise*. These documents ask for advice and require decisions, memos, phone calls, or letters in response, and planning or organizing. Give the applicant 5 minutes to scan the documents and then discuss with the interviewer what he or she would do with each of the items. Use a simulation that is directly relevant to the tasks required in the job. For example, an applicant for a customer-service representative job can be asked to role-play a confrontation with an angry customer.
- Don't ask questions that could lead you into allegations of discrimination. For example, do not ask questions about national origin, religious beliefs and affiliations, race, marital status, physical or mental disabilities, physical health or illness, age, or military history.
- Do plan for and manage the use of time during the interview. Allow for some flexibility in your schedule in case the interview runs over time. This way, the schedules of others who are depending on you are not disrupted.
- Don't make exaggerated claims about the job, the company, the working relationship with the supervisor, or a promise of the job (unless the selection decision has already been made).
- Do use an interview form on which to record impressions and ratings for how the applicant rates on key issues, traits, and behaviors.
- Don't make snap judgments regarding applicants. First impressions are important, but there is more to a person than what is revealed in just the first few minutes.
- Do allow one or more other individuals in your department to interview the applicant. Training these persons ahead of time regarding the kinds of questions that can and cannot be asked is vital. Give each of these interviewers a copy of the interview form on which to record their impressions.

EXHIBIT 9-9
Continued

SELECTION. If a team decision is the approach used in your organization, conduct a team meeting in which together you review all the applicants in one session if possible. Make a short presentation regarding each of the finalist applicants, followed by discussion. If the team cannot reach a clear consensus during this discussion, an additional discussion might be needed or the decision may be left up to the manager.

Once the selection has been made, the organization makes a formal offer of employment to the final candidate. A telephone call is usually followed up with a letter offering the job. The letter should state the job title, the beginning compensation, and benefits that are offered. Other finalist job applicants usually are not informed that they were not selected until the job has been accepted.

Each of these recruitment and selection tools is limited in its ability to provide useful information in new employee decision making. Questionnaires can be faked. Resumes can be falsified. Applicants can conceal vital information they believe will lower their chances of being selected. References may hold back information. Interviews rely on subjective interpretation, which will be biased. Job applicants may shine during an interview while their job performance is dull. Nevertheless, when used together, these tools will minimize the risk of making a decision that the manager or new employee may later regret. Good decision making reduces the risk of turnover. Combined, these tools help the manager maintain fairness, minimize the risk of discrimination, and improve the overall chances that the new employee will be productive on the job.

Employee Development

Successful organizations have found that the job of human resource management is not completed when the employee has been hired. What comes next is just as important: orienting and training new and existing employees. We can think of this as **employee development**. Orientation and training meet short-term needs and long-run goals. We will address each of these briefly, giving relatively more emphasis to orientation than training.

Source: Digital Vision/Thinkstock.

Developing the skills and talents of employees after they are hired is just as important as selecting the best people to be employees.

ORIENTATION.[65] The process of recruiting, acquiring, and retaining employees is expensive. This is one of the reasons why employee turnover is so costly, in addition to the lost productivity when a worker leaves a job. Curiously, many organizations find that they are so busy or have so much backlog of work that needs to be done by the new employee that they allow the employee to dive right into work without going through an orientation program. These companies fail to realize that orientation can help reduce costs and improve retention by quickly aligning the employee's expectations with those of the organization, socializing the employee into the mix of shared values, and, at the same time, getting the new employee quickly into a productive work cycle.

World-class organizations known for their commitment to orienting new employees include Walt Disney and Citicorp. Such organizations usually provide new employees with 2 or more full days in general orientation to the company. These training programs cover important topics such as the mission and values of the organization, the function of the organization in its market, safety, applicable policies and procedures, employee benefits, work schedules and work rules, the physical layout of the facilities, and general skills such as how to give superior customer service that all employees need to know regardless of where they work.

Supervisors play just as important a role in completing the orientation process by providing specific orientation to the new employee's work unit, the specific skills required, the responsibilities, the performance expectations, and the relationships. This involves providing the new employee a formal introduction to the primary and secondary work groups, the assignment of a mentor or coach, locating specific areas for rest and lunch breaks, location of time clocks, materials, and other resources that the employee will use. Orienting the new employee to the work team and the job itself are two of the most important parts of the process. Clearly state department policies and procedures and give the new employee a chance to ask clarification questions. If employee handbooks and procedure manuals are used, show the new employee where these are located and how to use them.

Experts recommend that the new employee's primary supervisor conduct the very first, specific orientation. During the few days that follow, the employee should attend the first available organization-wide orientation program. Most large organizations have new employee orientation programs weekly, every 2 weeks, or once a month depending on the number of new employees being brought into the organization on a daily basis.

The very first day a new employee is on the job is not a good time for that employee's supervisor to take a much-needed vacation. Don't leave orientation up to fellow workers. Orientation is not just showing the new employee where the bathroom is, where the work resources are, and where the lunchroom and the time clock are. The more complicated the work and the working relationships, the more time it can take for orientation to be complete. Because of this, depending on the job, orientation can take several days, weeks, or even months.

TRAINING.[66] The goal of training is to develop the knowledge, skills, and abilities of new or existing employees so that they can perform their work at the highest level possible. Like the process of employee recruitment and selection, training must start with analysis, planning, and budgeting. Training occurs not only at the beginning of an employment relationship but continues as long as the employee stays with the company. In most organizations, the needs for training are greater than the resources available to carry out the training. Analysis will uncover the most important training needs that are at the core of why the organization exists. Training needs usually are connected with obvious employee performance deficiencies, the prevalence of accidents, or quality deficiencies. For example, at Ames Rubber in New Jersey, training programs include technical training as well as English as a Second Language training. Analysis also can reveal ideas for the instructional methods that are most important. Planning for training should include a measurable dimension so that outcomes can be tracked to determine the degree to which the training had an effect on the underlying need for training. Budgeting involves making a specific commitment for training time and resources to be spent conducting the training events. The training budget should include not only the cost of the trainer and training materials used but also the employee's time spent in training.

Training can take many forms. For example, a new employee can work with a mentor in on-the-job training until the new employee's skill is up to standard. An existing worker whose performance is lower than expected can be paired for a few hours or days with a high-performing worker to learn work techniques and processes that lead to higher performance. A small group of workers might watch a video on how to safely handle hazardous materials. Simulations, computer-based training, case studies, video teleconferencing, and Internet training through "learning portals" all are used depending on the situation and the training needs.

Performance Appraisals

Performance appraisal, also known as performance evaluation or performance review, is the process of maintaining satisfactory levels of performance that are needed to meet organizational needs.[67] It would be difficult to think of an organization whose members do not engage in some form of performance appraisal, either formal or informal. Normally the performance review is completed after the first 90 days of beginning employment and then once every year or more often if the employee's performance does not meet expectations.

Ideally, the performance review begins with the supervisor and subordinate's mutual understanding regarding the goals and expected performance standards. Some of the expectations are recorded as performance standards in the job description. Other expectations may be in terms of productivity goals and adherence to procedures and rules. In many organizations a common approach is to complete the performance review using a written criteria-based performance appraisal form. Such a form can incorporate a rating scale for various behavioral traits and performance indicators. Some forms place the performance indicators and rating scales on a grid. The supervisor completes the grid allocating a rating for each item. This rating can then be used as the basis of discussion and goal setting for the future time period. See Exhibit 9-10.

EXHIBIT 9-10
Sample Criteria-Based Performance Appraisal Form

Employee Name:
Employee Number:
Department: Maintenance
Job Title: Grounds Keeper Level I
Hire Date:

Review Reason:
___ Introductory/Probationary period completed
___ Annual Review
___ Special Review

Rating Scale:
1 = Does not meet standard
2 = Meets standard
3 = Exceeds standard
4 = Exceptional
5 = Does not apply

Critical Performance Area 1: Knowledge, Quality, Quantity of Completed Tasks	**1**	**2**	**3**	**4**	**5**
Mows lawns					
Knows how to operate power lawn mower					
Dumps outside trash cans					
Knows how to safely apply lawn chemicals					
Trims grass along sidewalks and curbs					
Maintains sprinkler system					
Replaces flowers, shrubs, and trees					
Replaces outside light bulbs					
Able to work independently					
Maintains sidewalks during inclement weather					
Critical Performance Area 2: Initiative					
Performs and completes duties in an independent and timely manner					
Recognizes and performs other necessary duties					
Recognizes and anticipates problems and takes preventive action					
Informs supervisor of suggestions and recommendations					
Works to identify solutions within his/her control					
Critical Performance Area 3: Attendance and Reliability					
Uses personal time off appropriately in accordance with company policy					
Provides proper notification for absence, tardiness, or leaving early					
Adjusts personal schedule to complete workload when requested					
Begins work at the start of assigned shift					
Complies with company policy regarding rest breaks and lunch breaks					
Critical Performance Area 4: Other Behavioral Factors					
Observes company dress code and wears identification name badge					
Operates equipment in a safe manner					
Understands emergency procedures as outlined in the emergency plan					
Assists in orientation of new staff members as needed					
Maintains a clean and safe work environment					
Reports any unusual or extraordinary incidents to supervisor					
Attends required in-service education and training programs					
Works in a cooperative manner with other company personnel					

Other observations and notes:

Goals:

Employee Comments/Response:

Employee Signature:

Supervisor Signature:

Administrative Signature:

EXHIBIT 9-10
Continued

The supervisor should monitor performance on a routine basis providing feedback, coaching, and correction as needed. By the time a performance review meeting occurs, there should be no surprises. It is unfair to the employee and to the organization not to provide feedback during the year and then hit the employee with a negative report of poor performance at the time of the annual performance review.

Information gathered and reviewed should be specific and, whenever possible, measureable. For example, weekly productivity data can be kept and charted for each employee in a service department showing the number of customer-service events that were completed and the average number of minutes per service event. If the chart is kept up to date, the chart can be reviewed at the performance review meeting. For employees who continually meet or exceed productivity standards, the performance review meeting is a validation or reinforcement for a job well done. For employees who have struggled meeting performance standards, the review meeting provides an opportunity to review the goals and what is needed to help the employee achieve higher performance.

Some organizations such as Deloitte and Touche use what is called a **360-degree review** in which the supervisor, peers, the employee, and other key employees evaluate the employee's performance. Each of the individuals is asked to complete the performance review form. The supervisor gathers the results for discussion. The advantage of using a 360-degree feedback is that each employee gains the benefit of seeing how people other than the supervisor view his or her work. The downside is that political tensions in the organization increase, more bureaucratic paperwork is required, such a program can undermine trust, and it takes more time. Also, this approach complicates relationships at work where peers become judges.[68] See Exhibit 9-11.

Successfully employing this method requires that managers be willing participants themselves and active role models. Managers should encourage peers to provide qualitative feedback as well as supportive coaching to help them improve performance.

Successful organizations take both a short-run and a long-run view of performance appraisals. Performance appraisals measure current and past performance against standards and objectives. This is a valuable short-term perspective. Managing employee potential, which is more difficult than measuring performance, involves looking to the future and predicting an employee's capabilities in the future. This requires a long-run perspective.[69]

Progressive Discipline

One of the unpleasant but necessary tasks of the manager is to provide **progressive discipline**, also known as corrective action, for employees who stray from the expectations given them when they are hired or whose performance falls below what is required.[70]

Discipline is a serious business matter and should never be personal. Employees are hired for business reasons to help the organization achieve its goals. Likewise, the reasons why a manager needs to discipline an employee are related to the goals of the organization. If an employee's performance is below standard, then there is a business reason why the employee needs to take corrective action. Insubordination is directly linked with a business reason for discipline—if the employee refuses to follow orders, work cannot get accomplished. Business reasons for discipline include not following policies and procedures such as safety rules or

EXHIBIT 9-11
Tensions with 360-Degree Feedback

- Peers are the people who may know best the performance of an employee. But they are likely to give conservative, positively biased feedback so that the relationships are not strained.
- The 360-degree feedback doesn't reveal how a work group behaves as a group. This approach can undermine group performance. Some employees will resist participating.
- Using a quantitative rating system oversimplifies the results and overlooks the qualitative feedback that can help an employee know how to improve.
- The focus tends to be on the rewards that result from the feedback rather than on the feedback that can be used to improve performance. When peers know that compensation will be influenced by what they say about a peer, they hesitate to provide negative feedback.

exhibiting behaviors that have a negative effect on the performance of other workers. Absenteeism and tardiness also are directly linked to obvious business reasons for discipline.

Poor performance may not go away by itself. Some managers avoid progressive discipline. Managers who want to be liked by all their workers do not like to confront poor performance. The employee with the performance problem may have previously displayed agitation or anger that the manager does not want to experience. If the manager will have a difficult time filling the job because qualified workers are in short supply, the manager may hesitate disciplining an employee.

Progressive discipline programs might vary slightly from company to company, but the basic ideas of the process are similar across most organizations. The first step to follow when the supervisor notices an employee's performance is unacceptable is to have a private discussion with the employee. Once you have observable facts, don't wait. The longer you wait the more difficult it is to convince the employee that it is poor performance that needs to be changed. Keep your cool even if the behavior you observed is upsetting to you. Focus on the specific, observable behaviors and the business reasons for why these are unacceptable. Start with a simple statement that does not judge. For example, the supervisor may simply say to the employee, "Let's talk about what happened today on the shop floor. . . . Help me see it from your point of view. . . . Here's why it is important to the company that we not see this behavior again. . . . This affects all of us. . . . Do you see why this is important for the team as a whole? . . . I need your commitment to not exhibit this behavior again."

One of the outcomes of this meeting is to have an agreed-upon plan with specific commitments of who will do what and why it is important. Check for understanding by asking the employee to summarize the situation and the agreement regarding the expectation for the future. See Exhibit 9-12 for what to avoid during a progressive discipline session.

If the employee exhibits unacceptable performance behaviors a second time, the supervisor must have a second meeting with the employee as soon as possible. Even if the specific behavior is different from what was discussed during the first session, this is the second time the supervisor

EXHIBIT 9-12
What to Avoid During a Progressive Discipline Session

- Ask yourself: Could the problem be caused by lack of ability, or is there an unwillingness to act in appropriate ways?
- What social factors might be active? The behaviors of others may have aggravated the situation and you haven't heard that part of the story yet.
- What organizational structure issues might be present?
  - Are there financial incentives influencing one person while different goals are affecting the other person?
  - What's in it for the employee you are talking to?
- Avoid generalities and vague feelings: Stick to the observable facts and actions that were unambiguous without feeling the need to put a spin on them:
  - Instead of saying "You are often back late from lunch," say "You have been more than 30 minutes late back from lunch seven times in the last 2 weeks."
  - Instead of saying "I don't like your attitude," say "This morning you engaged in insubordinate conduct when you responded to my request to complete the Jones' file by the close of the business day. You stated loudly in front of other members of the staff, 'If you want that file completed by the end of the day, do it yourself! I need to be left alone!' Such comments are unacceptable because they are disrespectful and violate company standards of performance and conduct."
- Focus on performance-relevant actions over which the employee has control, not on people. If you personalize it, you will get resistance. You will undermine the other person's confidence and enthusiasm. If you stray too far from job performance, you undermine your credibility.
- After you ask a question, listen. Don't interrupt the person even if you feel the urge to correct an inaccurate statement or to try to get your point across.
- Motivate by exploring natural consequences. Describe for the employee those who are affected that are not present.

has had to spend time correcting the employee. As before, focus on specific, observable behaviors and the business reasons why these behaviors are unacceptable. The difference is that with this session the employee is given something in writing that documents the situation and what change is expected. This written document should contain a strong statement that if the employee fails to correct the behavior, or if the employee exhibits additional unacceptable behaviors in the future, the employee could be terminated.

A third session may be needed if the employee fails to correct behavior in the agreed upon time frame or if additional unacceptable behaviors are observed. Take the same approach to introduce the conversation: Focus on the observable behaviors and on the business reasons why these behaviors are unacceptable. In addition, now focus on the relationship between the company and the employee. Some organizations use this third meeting to inform the employee that they are being suspended with or without pay to think about the commitment needed for the future. A written document is given to the employee (and a copy placed in the personnel file) stating that this is the final warning. Additional performance problems will result in termination.

The Christian Mind on Progressive Discipline

Anyone in a management position will have to deal with employees who are not performing at an acceptable level. Most organizations have policies as to how progressive discipline is to be handled (verbal, written, and termination are standard in many companies). Those who approach this with the mind of Christ will have a servant's attitude when dealing with employees. First, ask God to help you with the words you say and write. Second, put yourself in the employee's position and determine how you would feel hearing/reading the words. Third, remember that God's Word tells us we should care enough to confront. Simply allowing an unacceptable work trait to continue does *not* show a genuine concern for the employee. Our attitude should be one of assisting individuals to perform at the highest level. I highly recommend "Caring Enough to Confront" by David Augsberger.

Dr. Harriet Rojas
Indiana Wesleyan University
Marion, IN

Advocacy

Assisting other managers with counsel on how to manage a fair progressive discipline process is one way that the HR specialist fulfills an advocacy role on behalf of employees. There are other ways the advocacy role can be fulfilled by helping other managers. For example, the HR specialist will desire to speak on behalf of employees during the strategic planning process. Such a person can counsel managers how to improve communication with employees, how to create a work environment where work teams are motivated to superior performance, and how to develop the abilities of employees. A line manager can often benefit from discussing with the HR specialist the most effective ways to set department goals, track performance, and provide feedback to employees. If a department must make major changes, this can be stressful for some employees. The HR specialist can help the manager create a plan for change that takes into consideration the needs of employees.

HR specialists can also be advocates by being available to employees. Employees who are unhappy, under stress at work, or who are experiencing conflict with other employees may feel more comfortable talking with someone other than their immediate supervisor. The HR specialist can help the employee express the reasons for unhappiness and provide counsel on how to handle conflict. Interviewing an employee can reveal ways in which the company can help develop the employee's skills. Finding the best match between an employee's talents and company needs is an advocacy role in which the HR specialist can help both the employee and the company.

Compensation and Benefits Management

Paying workers fairly and offering benefits for their work comprise the total **compensation** that workers receive. In many organizations, the personnel department staff manage the wage and salary scale and are in charge of making sure that employees receive the promised benefits, such as health insurance and time off for vacations. In small organizations, the personnel department works closely with employees who process the payroll checks each pay period so that records are accurate.

Organizations must consider several legal constraints when setting wage rates. In the United States federal law mandates the minimum wage before taxes that an employee must be paid and the pay rate for hourly workers who work overtime, which is usually one and a half times the usual pay for any hours worked over 40 in a workweek. Federal law mandates that women must be paid the same as men if they do equivalent work. The law also requires that employers not discriminate against a worker in wages and benefits because of the person's race, color, national origin, religion, or sex. State laws may have minimum wage laws that mandate higher minimum wages than required by federal law. Another legal constraint involves organized labor. Companies that have signed agreements with labor unions have legal guidelines they must follow to honor the labor agreement in terms of pay and benefits.

The cost of paying employees is often the single-largest expense of many companies. Managers fulfill their stewardship responsibilities when they are careful in managing this expense while they also do their best to be fair to employees. Company policy (authorized in formal decisions made by top-level leaders of the organization) may have established a formal wage and salary scale or grid that lists each job title and the range of pay for individuals that hold each of the jobs. The levels on the scale are sometimes called pay grades. Wage scales create openness, consistency, and equity. They also minimize the risk that individual department managers begin setting compensation too high to meet their individual department goals.[71]

In addition to the compensation the company provides an employee, many companies also offer certain additional benefits such as health insurance, employee assistance programs, educational opportunities, ongoing training and a variety of other resources to help employees. The human resources department typically is involved with the oversight of the medical and dental insurance programs that are offered to employees. The health insurance benefit plan requires someone to coordinate the benefits offered by the company with benefits that the employee may receive from other health insurance policies. The employees need someone they can talk with to answer their questions about the details of health insurance coverage in an accurate and timely manner. The HR department may be in charge of managing the use of paid time off for holidays, vacation days, and sick days. If the company offers a retirement program, the HR staff members ensure that any matching funds that are promised the employee are applied correctly. If an employee assistance program is offered, employees need information about how to access the services.

Compensation and benefits management is one area of the employment relationship where legal issues are prominent. Equal employment opportunity is another legal issue.

Legal Issues in Human Resource Management

The United States Constitution, federal laws, federal regulations, and state laws establish the legal environment in which the employer–employee relationship is managed. In general, these legal constraints work to provide equal employment opportunities for all legal employees. The federal **Equal Employment Opportunity Commission (EEOC)**[72] has the task of enforcing specific federal laws related to equal employment and for providing oversight and coordination for all federal employment regulations, practices, and policies. State-level Fair Employment Practices Agencies (FEPAs) serve in a similar capacity over their respective jurisdictions.

While there are many federal and state laws that constrain employers, the major laws affecting employment and preventing discrimination are the following:[73]

- The Equal Pay Act of 1963 mandates that men and women who perform substantially equal work in the same organization must be paid the same.
- Title VII of the Civil Rights Act of 1964 is a broad legal statute that prohibits employment discrimination based on race, color, religion, sex, or national origin.
- The Age Discrimination in Employment Act (ADEA) of 1967 protects individuals who are 40 years of age or older from discrimination in the workplace.

Managers who learn about the legal requirements relating to employer-employee relationship can prevent difficulties for both the employee and for the organization.

- The Occupational Safety and Health Act of 1970, enforced by the Occupational Safety and Health Agency (OSHA), regulates the work safety practices of employers protecting workers from accidents and other hazardous working conditions.
- The Employee Retirement Income Security Act (ERISA) of 1974 regulates employee benefits and retirement plans.
- Title I and Title V of the Americans with Disabilities Act (ADA) of 1990 prohibits employment discrimination against qualified persons with disabilities.
- The Civil Rights Act of 1990 provides for the payment of monetary damages to individuals who have intentionally been discriminated against.
- The Family Medical Leave Act (FMLA) of 1993, enforced by the U.S. Department of Labor, allows eligible employees to take up to 12 workweeks of leave during any 12-month period to care for a newborn or a spouse, child, or parent with a serious health condition without fear that they will lose their job or health insurance benefits during the 12-week period.

All companies employing 15 workers or more (20 workers or more for the ADEA law) must comply with these laws. This includes U.S.-based companies that employ U.S. citizens outside the United States or its territories. The federal government also is included under the provisions of this law. Virtually all employers are subject to the Equal Pay Act of 1963 and the Fair Labor Standards Act, which covers the federal wage and hour law.

Federal law prohibits discrimination based on several factors: age, race, color, religion, sex, or national origin. To illustrate how the law applies we will use religious discrimination as an example.

Religious Discrimination

Every year thousands of persons contact the Equal Employment Opportunity Commission (EEOC), charging that their employer has discriminated against them. For example, in 2009, over 93,000 claims of discrimination were submitted to the EEOC. Of these claims, 36 percent involved charges of discrimination based on race compared to 30 percent for discrimination based on sex, 24 percent for age, 23 percent for disability, 3.6 percent for religion, and 1 percent for equal pay. An interesting observation is that as a proportion of total claims of discrimination, charges of racial discrimination are 10 times the charges of religious discrimination. Racial discrimination has remained at the top of the list between 1992 and 2009 ranging from 33.8 to 40.9 percent of the total. Exhibit 9-13 compares the trends in claims of discrimination for various types between 1992 and 2009.

Though a small proportion of the total, claims of religious discrimination received by the EEOC have been on the increase. As shown in Exhibit 9-14, between 1992 and 2009, religion-based claims of discrimination grew from 1,388 to 3,386—an increase of 144 percent. During this period, the annual total monetary awards paid increased over 400 percent from $1.4 million to $7.6 million. This does not include monetary benefits gained from litigation through the courts.

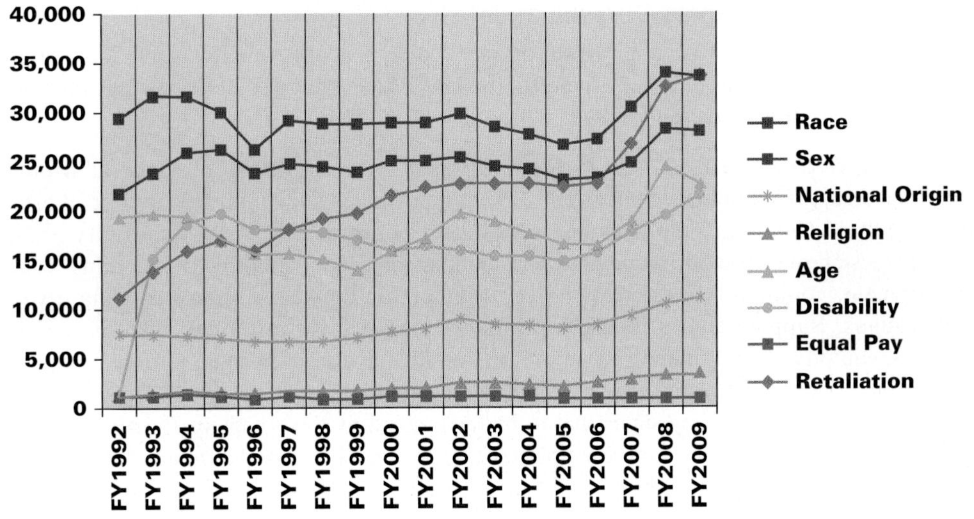

EXHIBIT 9-13

Claims of Discrimination Submitted to the EEOC by Type

Source: http://www.eeoc.gov/eeoc/statistics/enforcement/religion.cfm, accessed January 9, 2011.

During the time period of 1992–2009, between 44 and 65 percent of the religious-based discrimination claims resolved were found to have no reasonable cause based on the evidence obtained during EEOC investigations. Between 11 and 32 percent of resolved claims were found to have reasonable cause or merit for resolving the claim in favor of the claimant. Some claims are closed for administrative reasons and are not fully investigated by the EEOC.[74]

Reasonable Accommodation

When an employer's company policies interfere with an employee's religious practices, the employee can ask for a reasonable accommodation. For example, a person of the Muslim faith is required to attend prayer services at a mosque on Friday afternoons. This can conflict with scheduled work time. A **reasonable accommodation** is a change to the workplace policies that allow the employee to engage in religious practices as long as such a change is not too costly or too difficult for the employer to provide. Reasonable accommodations apply to other protections such as for workers with disabilities. The issue of cost or difficulty in making a change is sometimes called the *undue hardship* rule. Of course the employee might have a different opinion from the employer regarding what constitutes an undue hardship on the employer. Undue hardship must be based on an individualized assessment of a particular situation that shows that a specific accommodation would cause a significant difficulty or expense.[75]

The EEOC can provide more detailed information for specific situations. But if the employer refuses to make an accommodation for the employee's religious practices, or if the employer retaliates with what is known as an *adverse action* toward the employee, the employee has the right to contact the EEOC to file a claim of religious-based discrimination.[76]

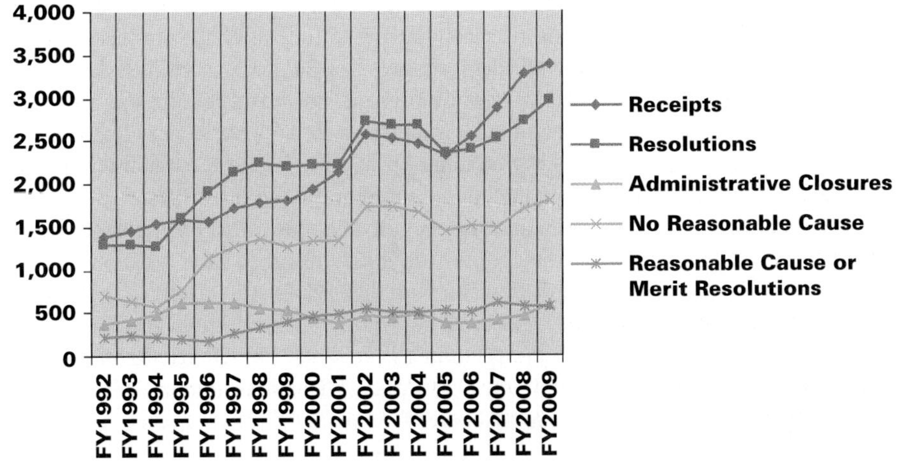

EXHIBIT 9-14

Religion-Based Claims of Discrimination under Title VII of the 1964 Civil Rights Act 1992–2009

Source: http://www.eeoc.gov/eeoc/statistics/enforcement/religion.cfm, accessed January 9, 2011.

Case Examples of Religious Discrimination

Whether the issue is discrimination based on race, color, sex, age, religion, or national origin, court cases are influential in how to interpret the law. Three examples of court cases involving alleged religious discrimination follow.[77]

***MORANSKI* v. *GENERAL MOTORS*.**[78] John Moranski, an employee of General Motors, submitted an application in December 2002 to company management for the purpose of establishing a "GM Christian Employee Network" affinity group. GM supports affinity groups because these groups provide employees with opportunities for mentoring, networking, career development, community outreach, and communication between employees from diverse backgrounds. Support comes in the form of offering certain resources such as meeting facilities, equipment, and funding to support the group's goals. To form an affinity group, one or more employees must register their intent with the company and adhere to the policy related to affinity groups. The policy states that to be recognized by the company, the affinity group must be open to all current, active employees who share the group's goals. Also, affinity groups cannot be formed for the purpose of promoting or advocating a particular religious position.

GM officials denied Moranski's application based on the policy forbidding groups to promote particular religious positions. Believing that he had been discriminated against, Moranski filed a claim with the EEOC in June 2003. The EEOC reviewed his situation and issued him a letter in January of 2004 indicating that he had a basis to bring a suit against GM under the provisions of Title VII of the Civil Rights Act of 1964. GM filed a motion with the district court asking that the suit be dismissed on the grounds that its denial was based on the affinity group being religious in nature, not because it was to be a Christian group. GM stated that it would have done the same for any proposed affinity group based on any other religion. GM believed that a group based on religion has the potential for causing divisiveness and harassment in the workplace. GM also stated that each company has the right to determine its own policies regarding the formation of affinity groups, and while some other companies might allow groups to form based on religion, GM does not. When the court agreed with GM, Moranski appealed, but the appellate court upheld GM's motion to dismiss the suit.

***EEOC* v. *CONOCOPHILLIPS*.** Clarence Taylor, a pipe-fitter working for the ConocoPhillips oil refinery in New Jersey, asked for accommodation for his religious beliefs when he was asked to work on Sundays for 2 months. Taylor was a deacon and lay leader in his congregation. ConocoPhillips' managers did not offer an accommodation. Instead, managers told Taylor he could use his vacation time.[79] Taylor contacted the EEOC, which reviewed his case. The EEOC filed a religious discrimination lawsuit against ConocoPhillips on behalf of Taylor. The two parties settled out of court, and Taylor was awarded $7,500 and 5 extra vacation days. Taylor designated that a local food bank should receive the other $12,500 awarded in the case. ConocoPhillips also was required to revise its antidiscrimination policies and provide training regarding discrimination at the refinery. A spokesperson for ConocoPhillips stated that the company disagrees with the EEOC's charges and admits no wrongdoing but that it settled out of court for business reasons.

***GOLDMEIER* v. *ALLSTATE INSURANCE CO*.** A husband and wife who were working as insurance agents for Allstate Insurance Company resigned their positions after the company announced plans to have its offices remain open on Friday evenings and Saturday mornings. An open office did not explicitly require that the Goldmeiers be present, but it did require the presence of a licensed insurance agent at all times, and the Goldmeiers were the only licensed agents working for the office. Because the couple were practicing Orthodox Jews, the company policy would conflict with their religious beliefs. For the couple to comply with the Allstate policy and their religious beliefs they would need to hire another agent to keep the office open.[80] Fifty-eight days before the policy was to take effect, the couple voluntarily resigned their positions. After they resigned, they filed a religious discrimination suit with the U.S. District Court in Ohio. The court found no evidence that Allstate had deliberately created an intolerable or hostile working environment with the intent to force the Goldmeiers to quit. The District Court also found that the couple had not been constructively discharged but had voluntarily terminated their employment. Their claim against Allstate Insurance Company failed.

Who is covered under the EEOC rules with respect to discrimination? A person who:

- files a claim of discrimination with the EEOC;
- participates in a discrimination proceeding such as an investigation by the EEOC or a lawsuit;
- has a close personal association with another person who is protected under EEOC rules. For example, terminating an employee because the employee's spouse participated in a discrimination claim or investigation is forbidden; or
- requests an accommodation related to employment discrimination.

EXHIBIT 9-15
Covered Individuals and Their Protected Activities

Retaliation

Some managers get frustrated when an employee claims to the EEOC that the company is discriminating against them. Some managers retaliate. Cases of retaliation submitted to the EEOC have increased over 110 percent between 1992 and 2009. In 2009, the EEOC received over 33,500 claims of retaliation discrimination.[81] This is roughly 10 times as many claims as for religious discrimination. The EEOC actively pursues the resolution of these claims. In 2008, almost 26,000 claims were resolved through the EEOC investigation processes and more than $111 million in monetary benefits were paid to claimants and other aggrieved persons. These funds do not include monetary awards that were obtained from cases brought to court.

Retaliation is an action that an employer takes in revenge for the employee filing or participating in a claim of discrimination or participating in an investigation by the EEOC or with a court. Three basic concepts are important when considering the issue of retaliation.[82] First, an employer, labor union, or employment agency is forbidden from taking an **adverse action** against an employee who engages in a protected activity defined by the EEOC with respect to discrimination. Adverse actions include firing, demoting, harassing, threatening, assaulting, writing an unjustified negative performance evaluation, or increasing surveillance of the employee without justification. Second, individuals covered under the EEOC rules are people who take action with respect to discrimination or who participate in a discrimination proceeding such as an investigation by the EEOC. Third, certain activities related to discrimination are protected. See Exhibit 9-15.

Paradoxes

The work of human resources is so fully interconnected with all other managerial work that many of the tension points highlighted in other chapters throughout this book apply to human resource management. But here we select three paradoxes that seem to relate to the current emphases in HRM.

UNIVERSAL—PARTICULAR.[83] It would be nice if organizational managers could tailor-make policies and procedures that consider the full range of differences between individuals at work. Considering the particular needs of employees might increase the level of personal satisfaction at work. However, to do this would potentially undermine the interests of the organization and justice. This is one reason why policies and procedures tend to be more universal in application. This is particularly relevant to HRM professionals who must implement organizational compensation systems and benefit allocations on an impartial basis. But while policies must apply across the entire organization, they also must consider particular circumstances. This tension, recognized as one of the classical tensions in all of society, is intertwined with the next one.

HEAD—HEART.[84] HR managers (and managers that conduct work that is related to human resources) must at the same time be coolly analytic and subjective. This requires making decisions that support unambiguous, quantitative, bottom-line results and yet also promote soft-hearted values that are based on the higher ideals. If cool headedness prevails at the expense of the higher ideals (and some scholars have pointed out that this is the tendency in business), then human relationships will be minimized. However, if subjectivity—using opinions and feelings—dominates, then deadlines will tend to be missed, standards will become lower, and quotas will become mediocre.

PRODUCTIVITY—EQUITY.[85] One of the roles that HRM professionals fill is that of advocacy. HR specialists often find themselves in the middle, advocating on behalf of both the employee and the organization. On the one hand, HR managers will support the organization's need to reduce its costs and improve productivity as the company faces downward pressure on prices and profits. On the other hand, they will advocate on behalf of the organizational commitments made to employees.

Focus on an Organization

Christianity 9 to 5

Christianity 9 to 5 is a website devoted to providing resources that equip Christians to do their jobs as Jesus would. The website contains a library of articles, case studies, and self-assessment tools designed to encourage the application of Christian principles of faith at work. Access the website at http://www.epiphanyresources.com/9to5/index.htm.

Chapter Summary

1. The biblical perspective sees work and work relationships as an important means by which humans glorify God. The Bible provides guidance on fundamental values, ways of thinking, and ways of doing things that honor God in the area of human resource management. Employers and employees alike can glorify God by modeling God's character traits in the employment relationship: honesty, fairness, trustworthiness, kindness, wisdom and skill, faithfulness in keeping covenant relationships, the careful use of power, and the proper response to authority. The Bible offers guidance for employee selection, training, discipline, fairness, and avoiding retaliation.
2. An organization's personnel dimension boils down to managing the process of the organization forming and maintaining relationships with individual employees. Specifically this usually involves planning for personnel needs, fairly and legally recruiting and selecting new employees, developing employees' potential for high performance, evaluating performance, providing safe working conditions, advocating on behalf of employees, and managing compensation and benefits so that employees are dealt with fairly.
3. The HRM process includes planning and budgeting, job analysis, developing and revising job descriptions, recruitment, testing, interviewing, selection, and employee development. Job analysis involves studying the job that needs to be completed and the traits and experience required to do the work well. Recruitment is a set of activities in which HR specialists and operational managers engage in tactical maneuvers to identify and attract suitable employees that will help the organization achieve high levels of performance. Selection is the process of deciding which of the job candidates to offer the job.
4. Employee development involves the process of orienting, training, and evaluating the performance of employees.
5. HR specialists play an important role advocating on behalf of employees by working with line managers to improve their approaches in working with employees, voicing the needs of employees during strategic planning, and by working with employees who need counsel.
6. Managing the compensation and benefits function of the organization is another important role that HR specialists often play.
7. Many federal and state laws constrain the relationship between employers and employees. These include the Equal Pay Act of 1963, Title VII of the Civil Rights Act of 1964, the Age Discrimination in Employment Act (ADEA) of 1967, the Occupational Safety and Health Act of 1970, the Employee Retirement Income Security Act (ERISA) of 1974, Title I and Title V of the Americans with Disabilities Act (ADA) of 1990, the Civil Rights Act of 1990, and the Family Medical Leave Act (FMLA) of 1993. All companies employing 15 workers or more (20 workers or more for the ADEA law) must comply with these laws.
8. Several types of employment discrimination are forbidden in the United States, including discrimination based on race, age, sex, national origin, religion, and disability. Racial discrimination is the most common claim submitted to the EEOC. Although religious discrimination is small in proportion to the other types of discrimination, it is on the increase. A reasonable accommodation is a change to the workplace policies that allow an employee to engage in religious practices as long as such a change is not too costly or too difficult for the employer to provide. Court cases illustrate how the law has been applied to specific situations involving claims of religious discrimination. Retaliation toward an employee who participates in a claim of discrimination is forbidden.

Key Terms

360-degree review 302
Adverse action 309
Compensation 305
Employee development 298
Equal Employment Opportunity Commission (EEOC) 305
Job analysis 292
Job description 293
Knowledge 296
Performance appraisal 300
Pre-employment testing 295
Progressive discipline 302
Reasonable accommodation 307
Recruitment 291
References 295
Retaliation 309
Screening interviews 295
Selection 291
Selection interviews 297
Skills 296
Solidarity 287
Talents 296

Discussion Questions

1. What important management perspectives can we learn from Matthew 20:1–16 (Parable of the workers in the vineyard)?
2. When is discrimination in employment decisions unlawful? How might evidence of discrimination be determined?
3. From Exhibit 9-9 discuss topics that employers should avoid in application forms, interviews, or other parts of the selection process.
4. When managers expect workers to perform their jobs with the lowest possible expense in terms of capital equipment, materials, and work time, shouldn't workers rightly expect that managers perform their work with the lowest possible expense in terms of equipment, materials, work time, and perks?
5. When civil law requires that a Christian HR professional take an action that goes against God's will, what is the HR professional to do?
6. What contributes to the fact that are there roughly 10 times as many claims to the EEOC for alleged retaliation as there are claims for religious discrimination?
7. Are talents the same as spiritual gifts? Why? Why not?
8. How might differences in culture hide a person's true talents during a job interview?
9. What are the fundamental talents needed to be successful as a manager? For example, what talents lead to success for the following types of managers?
   a. Assembly-line supervisor in an automobile factory
   b. Building construction supervisor
   c. Nurse manager
   d. Retail store owner-manager
   e. Sales manager
   f. Supervisor in an accounting department
   g. Chief executive of an injection molding factory
   h. Chairperson of the board of trustees for a nonprofit museum
10. In a covenantal employment relationship, is the first responsibility toward the individual worker or toward the community of workers (the organization) and the greater community of which the organization is a part?

STUDENT EXERCISES

1. **Internet Resources—Job Descriptions.** Go online and find two websites that offer job descriptions or job description templates for businesses. From a site that offers free sample job descriptions download a job description for a job you think you might like to have someday. Evaluate the details of the job description in terms of the kind of experience you need to obtain before you are qualified to take such a job.
2. **Job Analysis Practice.** Contact an employee and manager at an organization and ask for permission to practice interviewing the employee and the manager for the purpose of writing a job analysis. Offer to present the job analysis to the employee and manager or to an HR specialist for discussion. Ask for their suggestions on how you can improve your job analysis skills.
3. **Job Application Forms.** Obtain a job application form for a job that is currently open in a company near you. Your task with this document is to analyze the types of information being requested on the form. Write a short "white paper" with your analysis of why each type of information is being requested. In other words, what use will the company make of the information when the job applicant provides it?
4. **Job Classified Advertisements.** Find two classified advertisements for jobs that sound interesting to you or that you are curious about. (These can be two different jobs.) These can be found on the Internet, in the local newspaper, in a business magazine, or in another publication. One of the advertisements should be short (approximately 50 words or less) and the other one long (approximately 100 words or more). Write a half-page paper evaluating the effectiveness of each advertisement in terms of what it provides the prospective job applicant. Make a recommendation for how the advertisement might be improved.
5. **Classified Advertisement Contest.** This contest is to see who can find the shortest (measured by the number

of words) and the longest classified advertisement for jobs. Your professor may choose to limit your search to just local newspapers, certain Internet websites, or other publications. Evaluate why classified advertisements for some jobs are long and detailed while others are very short. Are short advertisements inherently less effective than long advertisements?

6. **Resume Practice.** Recruiting employees is the flip side of job hunting. Learning about the recruitment process can help you improve your own job-hunting skills. For example, in addition to completing the job application form some prospective employees are asked to provide a typed resume of their experience. Using a template that you find on the Internet (for example, you can find resume templates that have been created for Microsoft Word®), write your own resume and ask a practicing manager or HR specialist to evaluate it and give you feedback. Their feedback can be given in the margins right on your resume that you submit to the instructor. Based on their feedback be prepared to discuss with the class how you would improve your resume.
7. **Talent Search**. Your instructor will give you a job title and written job description for a particular job that is available in your community. Based on this information, talk with people who do that kind of work to identify at least one example of each of the three dimensions of talent (striving, thinking, relating) considered in this chapter. Organize your findings into the three dimensions of talent and type your findings on one page. Be prepared to discuss your findings in class.

IN-CLASS EXERCISES

Mock Applicant Selection Interview

Using information contained in a job description or a classified advertisement for an open position provided by your instructor, write 10 interview questions that you would use to evaluate a job applicant's suitability for the job. Show your list to a practicing manager who supervises this type of worker or an HR specialist and get their feedback (written on the page) on the questions you recommend. Bring this document to class for discussion.

Reflection on Scripture: Read 1 Corinthians 13:1–12. What parts of this passage relate directly to the work of a manager? How?

1 Corinthians 13:1–12 If I speak with the tongues of
men and of angels, but do not have love, I have become a
noisy gong or a clanging cymbal. 2 And if I have *the gift*
of prophecy, and know all mysteries and all knowledge;
and if I have all faith, so as to remove mountains, but do
not have love, I am nothing. 3 And if I give all my posses-
sions to feed *the poor*, and if I deliver my body to be
burned, but do not have love, it profits me nothing. 4 Love
is patient, love is kind, *and* is not jealous; love does not
brag *and* is not arrogant, 5 does not act unbecomingly; it
does not seek its own, is not provoked, does not take into
account a wrong *suffered*, 6 does not rejoice in unright-
eousness, but rejoices with the truth; 7 bears all things,
believes all things, hopes all things, endures all things. 8
Love never fails; but if *there are gifts of* prophecy, they
will be done away; if *there are* tongues, they will cease; if
there is knowledge, it will be done away. 9 For we know
in part, and we prophesy in part; 10 but when the perfect
comes, the partial will be done away. 11 When I was a
child, I used to speak as a child, think as a child, reason as
a child; when I became a man, I did away with childish
things. 12 For now we see in a mirror dimly, but then face
to face; now I know in part, but then I shall know fully
just as I also have been fully known. (New American
Standard version)

Issue Debate/Discussion

Divide the class into small groups of five to six people each. Choose a set of "Discussion Topic" statements from the list that follows. Hand out a sheet of paper containing the two "Discussion Topic" statements. Assign half of the groups to defend the first statement (A) as valid and the other half to defend the second statement (B) as valid. For this exercise, students do not necessarily need to agree with the perspective they are asked to defend. In fact, defending a point of view that a student disagrees with can be an amazing teaching-learning experience for undergraduates by helping them to intellectually go outside their usual thinking patterns and develop critical thinking skills. Give the groups 5 minutes to discuss. Then call for groups to give a summary of the rationale they developed. Discussion can follow.

Discussion Topic #1: Applying the "Golden Rule." What is the Christian's response to the fact that people at work are all different and because of this, may need to be treated differently?

A. **"Do unto others as you would have them do to you."**[86] There can be no clearer or more fundamental statement of the Christian's responsibility in life than what is stated in the Golden Rule. One basis for this is that as we treat others, God will treat us. Even if there are differences among people, the need to treat people fairly always trumps the need to consider individual differences. If managers don't treat people all the same, they create worker dissatisfaction. All managerial decisions and actions at work are moral or have an implicit moral basis. The Golden Rule is a moral basis for all managerial action. In addition, what workers might want their manager to do to them may not be in the workers' best interest in the long run. The Christian manager must do what is best for the employee based on moral principles.
B. **Do unto others as they would want you to do to them.** "The best managers break the Golden Rule every day. They would say *don't* treat people as you would like to be

treated. This presupposes that everyone breathes the same psychological oxygen as you. . . . The thinking [of the Golden Rule] is well intended but overly simplistic. . . . So the best managers . . . say, treat each person as he would like to be treated, bearing in mind who he is. Of course, each employee must adhere to certain standards of behavior, certain rules. But within those rules, treat each one differently, each according to his needs."[87] Who knows better how a worker should be treated than the worker himself? Doing unto others as you would have them do to you assumes that everyone is just like you. This is not true. How can a manager truly know what is best for the worker without understanding what the worker wants? Because every worker is different, it is not fair to them treat all workers the same. Treating all people the same breeds mediocrity. If you try to treat all people the same (assuming that this is even possible), you create worker dissatisfaction. In short, the Golden Rule is talking about moral decisions and actions. It should not be applied to other actions at work where differences between workers must be an important consideration.

Discussion Topic #2: Is there an essential difference between a secular approach and using religious principles for treating employees fairly?[88]

A. **They are the same.** Fairness is fairness regardless of whether a person looks at it from the perspective of religious values or humanism. Fairness is essentially impartiality on which both religious beliefs and secular philosophies can agree. Whether you start with a religious understanding of the world or not, you still must end up at the same place as someone working from a secular perspective: dealing with specific actions for specific employees. Ultimately, fairness is about taking action. At the point of action it doesn't really matter whether you have theological motives or secular motives for the actions.

B. **They are different.** The basic ideas may be the same but the starting point for understanding fairness is essentially different. Religious principles ground fairness in beliefs regarding God, humans, and God's relationship with human beings. Humans have dignity and should be treated fairly because of the God-given dignity. This goes deeper than merely saying that specific actions for one employee should be the same for another employee to be fair. Fairness is further based on a deeper awareness of the importance of community. Thus, fairness from religious principles is based on a completely different understanding of the basis of the relationship and, because of this, will lead the manager beyond just the outward actions of fairness to a covenant-like relationship with the employee.

Discussion Topic #3: Should the employment relationship be more personal or more impersonal?

A. **More personal than impersonal.** The Bible emphasizes the personal nature of human relationships. Indeed, while the impersonal nature of organizations may be important for achieving organizational goals, it also is one of the factors that can create spiritual crisis at work. Employees are not just agents fulfilling an impersonal role. They are living, breathing, thinking, and feeling persons who interact in the community collectively to create meaningful contributions of value to society by serving higher spiritual goals. Creating distance and impersonality in the relationship also creates the opportunity for both managers and subordinates to engage in self-interest behaviors at the expense of the other. Ultimately values must be personal to the people who prize them. Further, there is a danger in viewing work as impersonal in that this viewpoint tends to promote materialism seeing work as no more than a force needed for production of goods that can be sold. A corporation is an impersonal entity and while we may with validity talk about a corporate culture as exhibiting certain values, this can only be so if the personal values of leadership are present with strength. Human beings work in organizations. By nature human beings are personal, emotional beings. True, humans at work must place boundaries around their emotions so that the organizational goals can be accomplished. But, the manager–subordinate relationship is, by nature, personal. An impersonal relationship would create distance that undermines employee responsiveness and loyalty to the organization's goals. Trust, a vital element in achieving organizational goals, is personal. Ultimately, to become truly impersonal is not possible because we are talking about human relationships. Without the personal element, workplaces could never be a place where community could be built. And community is vital to achieving organizational goals.[89]

B. **More impersonal than personal.** The Bible allows for impersonality in organizational relationships. Business organizations exist for the sake of the results that are produced for those *outside* the organization in the market. "This also requires that an organization appraise and judge itself and its performance against clear, known, impersonal objectives and goals."[90] The market that organizations serve is impersonal and the organization must posture itself to meet the impersonal demands of the market. Organizations by their very nature tend to produce a set of values focused on the legal, impersonal, impartial, and disinterested. The reason for this is the relentless drive to achieve the organization's goals. Without impersonality, individual workers would be allowed to pursue self-interests at the expense of the organization. But the organization and its goals are bigger than any one individual who performs tasks for the company. Bureaucratic organizations emphasize management on an impersonal, rational basis through such elements as clearly defined authority and responsibility, formal record keeping, separation of management and ownership, and policies and procedures. Impersonality supports trust because employees are dealt with fairly. Rewards and punishments in organizations must not become personal. Time, a commodity that everyone in business worldwide must follow to effectively serve each other, is impersonal.[91] To be fair, managerial decisions must be made from an impartial point of view. This, too, requires a degree of impersonality.

Discussion Topic #4: Based on your experience are managers too quick to discipline employees?

A. **Managers are too quick to discipline employees.** Managers who are too quick to discipline employees don't give the employees a chance to make corrections on their own. The Christian approach to HR management suggests that managers should be patient and gentle with employees whose performance is less than desirable. Employees who are disciplined are embarrassed even if discipline is carried out in private conversation. This undermines human dignity. The decision of whether to subject employees to such embarrassment is a wonderful opportunity to show redemptive, Christian love. Instead, the manager should spend more time educating the employees and building a close relationship with the them so that the employees will want to change out of loyalty to their manager.

B. **Managers are too slow to discipline employees.** The Christian loving thing to do with employees whose performance is lacking is to help them make a change in their performance or help them get on with their lives by letting them go and letting them work in another organization where they can be more productive. Discipline can be carried out in a way that is respectful and focused on the needs of the employees as well as the needs of the organization. But delaying discipline does not show respect; in the long run it shows disrespect. Managers who delay discipline are not showing love; they are being disrespectful to someone created in God's image. Coddling employees usually will do no practical good anyway. It's not the way to a redemptive relationship with employees. It is a sign of weakness and merely gives low-performing employees license to continue low performance. Potentially it sets up the organization for a nasty legal fight later if and when discipline is finally used; later employees can claim that the manager didn't tell them that they were supposed to change their behavior.

Endnotes

1. Drucker, P. F. (1954). *The practice of management.* New York: Harper & Brothers. pp. 262–263.
2. Greenleaf, R. K. (1977). *Servant leadership: A journey into the nature of legitimate power & greatness.* Mahwah, NJ: Paulist Press. pp. 154–155.
3. http://www1.dhrm.virginia.gov/Directory/StaffDirectory.aspx.
4. Caudron, S. (2002). Rebuilding employee trust. *Workforce.* 81(10), 28–34.
5. According to a survey of employees on four continents, 75 percent of employees said they trust their immediate supervisor while just 60 percent trust the senior-level leaders. In the USA, Canada, and Mexico only about 50 percent trust the senior-level leaders. In other surveys the proportion who trust senior leaders is less than 40 percent. See Executive Briefing. (2008). Employees trust managers more than top brass. *HRMagazine.* 53(10), 10; Aparna, N. (2008). Trust issues. *Training & Development.* 62(8), 14; Krell, E. (2006). Do they trust you? *HRMagazine.* 51(6), 58–65; Hatch, N. (2005). Let it rip. *HRMagazine.* 50(9), 64–68; Anonymous. (2002). Declining employee trust poses threat. *Financial Executive.* 18(7), 10.
6. Hoover, D. J. (1990). Biblical principles applied to human resources. In Chewning, R. C. (Ed.). *Biblical principles and business: The practice.* Colorado Springs, CO: NavPress. pp. 145–159. The only full-length treatment of the topic from a biblical point of view is: Nyambegera, S. M. (2005). *Human resource management: A biblical perspective.* Nairobi, Kenya: Uzima Publishing House.
7. Genesis 29 (Jacob); Exodus 3:1 (Moses).
8. Leviticus 25:6, 25:40, 25:50, 25:53; Deuteronomy 15:18; Job 7:1–2, 14:6; Isaiah 16:14, 21:16; Matthew 20. See comments on this point in Grudem, W. (2003). *Business for the glory of God: The Bible's teaching on the moral goodness of business.* Wheaton, IL: Crossway Books. pp. 31–34.
9. 2 Chronicles 24:12–13.
10. Judges 9:4; 2 Samuel 10:6.
11. Luke 15:15–19.
12. Exodus 31.
13. 1 Kings 18.
14. Esther 3: 6–7.
15. Genesis 41.
16. Daniel 5–6.
17. Grudem, W. (2003). Employment. In *Business for the glory of God: The Bible's teaching on the moral goodness of business.* Wheaton, IL: Crossway Books. pp. 31–34.
18. Leviticus 19:9–10; Deuteronomy 24:19–22; Ruth 2. See the comments on this by Wilkinson, B. W. (1991). Biblical principles and unemployment. In Chewning, R. C. (Ed.). *Biblical principles and public policy: The practice.* Colorado Springs, CO: NavPress. pp. 57–74.
19. Genesis 1:26–28; Exodus 20:8–12, 23:12; Deuteronomy 14:29, 15:10; Psalm 1–4:23; Proverbs 12:24, 14:23; Ecclesiastes 2:24, 3:13; Ephesians 4:28; 1 Timothy 5:8.
20. Grudem, W. (2003). Employment. In *Business for the glory of God: The Bible's teaching on the moral goodness of business.* Wheaton, IL: Crossway Books. pp. 31–34; Wilkinson, B. W. (1991). Biblical principles and unemployment. In Chewning, R. C. (Ed.). *Biblical principles and public policy: The practice.* Colorado Springs, CO: NavPress. pp. 57–74. Some of the Bible admonitions with respect to the employment relationship are given in the context of slaves and masters. However, Christians believe that the fundamental principles are as

applicable to the employer–employee relationship as to the master–slave relationship. See Ephesians 6:5–8; Colossians 3:22–25, 4:1; 1 Timothy 6:1–2; Titus 2:9; 1 Peter 2:18–20.

21. Grudem, W. (2003). Employment. In *Business for the glory of God: The Bible's teaching on the moral goodness of business*. Wheaton, IL: Crossway Books. p. 34. See also the following Bible verses to which Grudem refers: Leviticus 19:13; Deuteronomy 24:14; James 5:4; Proverbs 18:19; Titus 2:9–10.
22. Matthew 20.
23. Pembroke, N. (2008). Partnership in the workplace: Covenant and management-labor relations. *International Journal of Practical Theology*. 12(2), 242–255; Herman, S. (1995). The potential of building covenants in business corporations. In Stackhouse, M., & McCann, D. (Eds.). *On moral business: Classical and contemporary sources for ethics in economic life*. Grand Rapids, MI: William B. Eerdmans Publishing. pp. 514–520.
24. Alford, H. J., & Naughton, M. J. (2001). *Managing as if faith mattered: Christian social principles in the modern organization*. Notre Dame, IN: University of Notre Dame Press. p. 78.
25. Matthew 10:1–5; Mark 3:16–19; Acts 9. See comments on the selection and eventual preeminence of Paul in Briner, B. (1996). *The management methods of Jesus: Ancient wisdom for modern business*. Nashville, TN: Thomas Nelson, Inc. pp. 9–10.
26. Matthew 10:24–25, 13:52, 16:24; Luke 14:26–33.
27. Proverbs 26:10.
28. Genesis 4:12–15.
29. Exodus 35:30–34.
30. Matthew 10:1–11:1; Mark 6:7–13; Luke 10.
31. 2 Chronicles 17:5–7.
32. Exodus 18:20; Deuteronomy 4:10.
33. Deuteronomy 4:14, 5:31, 6:1, 6:7, 11:19, 20:18, 24:8; Psalm 25:4–5, 32:8, 78:5, 90:12, 143:10; Proverbs 9:9.
34. 2 Chronicles 36:16; Proverbs 1:7, 1:25–30, 5:12, 6:23, 12:1; Isaiah 5:21.
35. Exodus 4:1–12, 18:21, 31:1–6; Numbers 13:1–3, 27:16–18; Deuteronomy 1:10–18; Acts 6:3, 15:37–39; 1 Timothy 3:107; Titus 1:7.
36. Matthew 5:2, 11:1; Mark 1:21, 4:1, 6:2; John 8:2; Acts 1:1, 5:21; 1 Corinthians 4:17; 1 Timothy 1:3, 4:11, 6:2; 2 Timothy 2:2, 2:24.
37. 1 Samuel 15:27–28; 2 Kings 10:30; Jeremiah 27:5; Matthew 21:43, 24:45–46.
38. Matthew 7:1; Luke 6:37; Romans 2:1–2, 14:3–4, 14:10–13; James 4:11–12. God evaluated the performance of Moses (Numbers 12:7; Hebrews 3:5). The entire Christian faith community evaluated the work of Jesus Christ (Hebrews 3:6). Jesus employed the principle of performance evaluation in his parables (Matthew 25:21; Luke 12:41–48).
39. Proverbs 18:9.
40. Proverbs 6:23, 12:1, 3:18–20, 15:31–32, 25:12, 27:5, 28:23; Matthew 18:15; Luke 6:36; Galatians 6:1; 1 Thessalonians 5:14; Hebrews 12:11.
41. Proverbs 9:8–9.
42. Exodus 23:4–5; Leviticus 19:18; Deuteronomy 32:35; Proverbs 10:12, 11:3, 15:1, 15:18, 16:7, 17:13–14, 20:22, 24:17, 24:29, 25:15, 25:21–22, 26:21, 29:22, 30:33; Obadiah 1:12; Matthew 5:38, 5:43; Romans 12:17–19; Galatians 5:15, 6:7–10; Colossians 3:13; 1 Thessalonians 5:13–15; 2 Timothy 2:24; 1 Peter 3:8–11.
43. Ecclesiastes 10:4.
44. Psalm 34:14; Proverbs 12:20; Matthew 5:9, 23; Romans 12:18, 14:19; 2 Corinthians 13:11; Philippians 2:3–4; Hebrews 12:14; James 3:17. The Old Testament concept of the "cities of refuge" are consistent with this. In the ancient cultures individuals were expected to act on personal revenge in an eye-for-an-eye fashion. The cities of refuge allowed for community justice system which was a marked improvement on the old code of personal revenge.
45. Matthew 5:9, 5:25. See the comments on this passage in Briner, B. (1996). *The management methods of Jesus: Ancient wisdom for modern business*. Nashville, TN: Thomas Nelson, Inc. pp. 91–92.
46. For a discussion on the Christian view of fair wages see Alford, H. J., & Naughton, M. J. (2001). *Managing as if faith mattered: Christian social principles in the modern organization*. Notre Dame, IN: University of Notre Dame Press. pp. 125–151; Chewning, R. C., Eby, J. W., & Roels, S. J. (1990). *Business through the eyes of faith*. San Francisco, CA: HarperSanFrancisco. pp. 27–29.
47. Proverbs 30:9.
48. Exodus 20:15–16; Leviticus 19:11–13; Deuteronomy 5:19, 25:13–16, 24:14; Proverbs 11:1; Malachi 3:5; Matthew 15:19, 19:18; Luke 10:7, 18:20; Romans 4:4, 13:8–10; 1 Corinthians 6:10, 9:9; Colossians 3:8–9; 1 Thessalonians 4:6; 1 Timothy 2:6, 5:18; 1 Peter 2:1; James 5:4.
49. Exodus 23:2; Leviticus 19:15; Deuteronomy 16:19, 24:17, 27:19; 1 Samuel 8:3; Psalm 82:3; Proverbs 11:3, 14:5, 16:13, 19:5, 21:3, 24:23–28, 25:18; Isaiah 1:17–23, 33:15, 56:1, 61:8; Amos 5:24; Micah 6:8; Mark 12:33; Colossians 4:1.
50. Proverbs 10:9.
51. 2 Corinthians 1:12; Colossians 1:10.
52. Genesis 33:13–14; Exodus 5:6–19; Proverbs 12:10.
53. Hill, P. J., & Lunn, J. (2007). Markets and morality: Things ethicists should consider when evaluating market exchange. *Journal of Religious Ethics*. 35(4), 627–653.
54. Dessler, G. (2004). *A framework for human resource management*. (3rd ed.). Upper Saddle River, NJ: Pearson Prentice Hall. pp. 9–15; Mathis, R. L., & Jackson, J. H. (2008). *Human resource management* (12th ed.). Mason, OH: Thomson South-Western. pp. 35–64.
55. Becker, B. E., Huselid, M. A., Pickus, P. S., & Spratt, M. F. (1997). HR as a source of shareholder value: Research and recommendations. *Human Resource Management*, 36(1), 39–47.
56. Barber, A. E. (1998). *Recruiting employees: Individual and organizational perspectives*. Thousand Oaks, CA: Sage Publications. p. 124.
57. Barber, A. E. (1998). *Recruiting employees: Individual and organizational perspectives*. Thousand Oaks, CA: Sage Publications. p. 50.
58. O'Connell, V. (2009). Test for dwindling retail jobs spawns a culture of cheating. *Wall Street Journal* (Eastern Edition). New York. January 7. p. A.1; Prager, J. H. (2000). Nasty or nice: 56-question quiz. *Wall Street Journal* (Eastern Edition). New York. February 22. p. 4; Smith, A. (2008). Experts: Tests, job steering raise flags. *HRMagazine*. 53(6), 36.

59. Collins, J. (2001). *Good to great*. New York: HarperBusiness. pp. 41–64; Buckingham, M., & Coffman, C. (1999). *First break all the rules: What the world's greatest managers do differently*. New York: Simon & Schuster.
60. Barber, A. E. (1998). *Recruiting employees: Individual and organizational perspectives*. Thousand Oaks, CA: Sage Publications. p. 56.
61. Barber, A. E. (1998). *Recruiting employees: Individual and organizational perspectives*. Thousand Oaks, CA: Sage Publications. pp. 85–92.
62. Buckingham, M., & Coffman, C. (1999). *First break all the rules: What the world's greatest managers do differently*. New York: Simon & Schuster. pp. 71–108.
63. Byham, W. C. (1994). Recruitment, screening, and selection. In Tracey, W. R. (Ed.). *Human resources management & development handbook*. (2nd ed.). New York: AMACOM. pp. 190–203.
64. Yate, M. (1990). *Hiring the best: Hot to staff your department right the first time*. Holbrook MA: Bob Adams, Inc. Publishers; Byham, W. C. (1994). Recruitment, screening, and selection. In Tracey, W. R. (Ed.). *Human resources management & development handbook*. (2nd ed.). New York: AMACOM. pp. 190–203; Dessler, G. (2004). *A framework for human resource management*. (3rd ed.). Upper Saddle River, NJ: Pearson Prentice Hall. p 129.
65. Davis, V. D., & Kleiner, B. H. (2001). How to orient employees into new positions successfully. *Management Research News*. 24(1/2), 43–49; Shea, G. F. (1994). Induction and orientation. In Tracey, W. R. (Ed.). *Human resources management & development handbook*. (2nd ed.). New York: AMACOM. pp. 986–1000.
66. Dessler, G. (2004). *A framework for human resource management*. (3rd ed.). Upper Saddle River, NJ: Pearson Prentice Hall. pp. 157–181.
67. Jette, R. D., & Wertheim, E. G. (1994). Performance appraisal. In Tracey, W. R. (Ed.). *Human resources management & development handbook*. (2nd ed.). New York: AMACOM. pp. 274–302; Dessler, G. (2004). *A framework for human resource management*. (3rd ed.). Upper Saddle River, NJ: Pearson Prentice Hall. pp. 191–216.
68. Peiperl, M. A. (2001). Getting 360° feedback right. *Harvard Business Review*. 79(1), 142–147.
69. Mucha, R. T. (2004). The art and science of talent management. *Organization Development Journal*. 22(4), 96–100. (quote from p. 99)
70. Liberman, V. (2009). The perfect punishment. *Conference Board Review*. 46(1), 32–39; Mathis, R. L., & Jackson, J. H. (2008). *Human resource management*. (12th ed.). Mason, OH: Thomson South-Western. pp. 511–513; Patterson, K., Grenny, J., McMillan, R., & Swizler, A. (2005). *Crucial confrontations*. New York: McGraw Hill; Sandler, L. (1989). How managers create monsters. *Personnel Journal*. 68(1), 24–30; Brown, W. S. (1992). The case of the incompetent employee. *Supervisory Management*. 37(11), 1–2; Falcone, P. (2001). When employees have a 'tude. *HRMagazine*. 456(6), 189–193; Sujansky, J. G. (2007). The poor performer confrontation handbook: Eight rules for dealing with employees who are bringing your company down. *Cost Engineering*. 49(8), 14–15; Gallagher, D. G., & Veglahn, P. A. (1994). Employee discipline. In Tracey, W. R. (Ed.). *Human resources management & development handbook*. (2nd ed.). New York: AMACOM. pp. 653–667; Campbell, D. N., Fleming, R. L., & Grote, R. C. (1985). Discipline without punishment—at last. *Harvard Business Review*. 63(4), 162–169; Cottringer, W. (2003) The abc's of employee discipline. *Supervision*. 64(4), 5–7; Bielous, G. A. (1993). How to discipline effectively. *Supervision*. 54(4), 17–19; Harvey, E. L. (1987). Discipline vs. punishment. *Management Review*. 76(3), 25–29.
71. Gibbons, T. P. (1994). Employee compensation. In Tracey, W. R. (Ed.). *Human resources management & development handbook*. (2nd ed.). New York: AMACOM. pp. 531–546.
72. Information about the EEOC can be obtained at the Commission's website: http://www.eeoc.gov/.
73. Information from the EEOC website: http://www.eeoc.gov/abouteeo/overview_laws.html. See also Tracey, W. R. (1994). HRM in perspective. In Tracey, W. R. (Ed.). *Human resources management & development handbook*. (2nd ed.). New York: AMACOM. pp. 3–18.
74. These reasons include some claimants withdraw their claim, litigation of a legal claim generates a result that would make an EEOC investigation futile, some claimants do not respond to the EEOC communications, and after filing the claim some claimants cannot be located by EEOC investigators.
75. http://www.eeoc.gov/policy/docs/accommodation.html#undue.
76. This information is from the Equal Employment Opportunity Commission website: http://www.eeoc.gov/facts/backlash-employee.html. See also Wolf, M., Friedman, B., & Sutherland, D. (1989). *Religion in the workplace: A comprehensive guide to legal rights and responsibilities*. Chicago, IL: American Bar Association Publishing. pp. 42–47.
77. Examples of cases can be found many places including http://www.eeonews.com/news/religious/index.html.
78. http://cases.justia.com/us-court-of-appeals/F3/433/537/546180/.
79. http://www.employment-lawyer-blog.com/2009/06/religious-discrimination-workp.html.
80. *Goldmeier* v. *Allstate Ins. Co.*, 157 L. Ed. 2d 891, 2004.
81. http://www.eeoc.gov/eeoc/statistics/enforcement/charges.cfm, accessed January 9, 2011. These claims of retaliation are related to discrimination of all types, based on race, color, sex, religion, national origin, age, and disability, as well as wage differences between men and women performing substantially equal work.
82. http://www.eeoc.gov/types/retaliation.html, accessed May 14, 2009.
83. Parsons, T., & Shils, E. A. (1962). *Toward a general theory of action: Theoretical foundations for the social sciences*. New York: Harper & Row. pp. 77–99.
84. Lowy, A., & Hood, P. (2004). *The power of the 2 × 2 matrix: Using 2 × 2 thinking to solve business problems and make better decisions*. San Francisco, CA: Jossey-Bass. pp. 37–57; Pascale, R. T. (1990). *Managing on the edge: How the smartest companies use conflict to stay ahead*. New York: Simon and Schuster; Vancil, R. F. (1976). Strategy formulation in complex organizations. *Sloan Management Review*. 17(2), 1–18.

85. Nutt, P. C., Backoff, R. W., & Hogan, M. F. (2000). Managing the paradoxes of strategic change. *Journal of Applied Management Studies*. 9(1), 5–31.
86. Leviticus 19:18; Deuteronomy 5:14, 6:4–9; Matthew 7:12, 22:36–40; Luke 6:27–38, 10:25–37; Romans 2:1–5, 13:9–10; 1 Corinthians 13:4–10; Galatians 5:14; 6:2.
87. Buckingham, M., & Coffman, C. (1999). *First break all the rules: What the world's greatest managers do differently*. New York: Simon & Schuster. pp. 151–152. [Emphasis in original]
88. Some authors have sought to make a distinction between these. See Koys, D. J. (2001). Integrating religious principles and human resource management activities. *Teaching Business Ethics*. 5(2), 121–139.
89. On this point of the importance of community see Martin, J., Knopoff, K., & Beckman, C. (1998). An alternative to bureaucratic impersonality and emotional labor: Bounded emotionality at the Body Shop. *Administrative Science Quarterly*. 43(2), 429–469.
90. Drucker, P. F. (1993). *Post-capitalist society*. New York: HarperBusiness. p. 55.
91. Webber, R. A. (1972). *Time and management*. New York: Van Nostrand Reinhold Company. p. 4.

CHAPTER 10

Communication

LEARNING OBJECTIVES

- Understand the importance of communication for managerial success.
- Describe the Christian worldview on managerial communication.
- Explain the process, purpose, and barriers of business communication.
- Understand how to manage confrontations with employees.
- Understand the principles of managing the informal communication network in organizations.
- Be aware of the influence of nonverbal communication.
- Describe the benefits and problems associated with electronic communication.

"Leaders who do not know the language of their staff cannot communicate with them effectively, and without effective communication they cannot motivate them."[1]

"No step in the administrative process is more generally ignored, or more poorly performed, than the task of communicating decisions."[2]

KROY, INC.

Managers at Kroy, Inc., a sign manufacturer located in Scottsdale, Arizona, faced an interesting communication problem. The company couldn't pay its bills and it was fast heading toward bankruptcy.[3]

Founded in 1982, Kroy Sign Systems, LLC, a subsidiary of Kroy, LLC, operates sign manufacturing, production, assembly, and distribution. The company makes and distributes ADA-compliant interior and exterior signs for government, healthcare, and corporate customers.

Times were good in the early 1980s. Kroy's managers succeeded in growing annual revenues to $75 million in 1984. Then the success began to unravel. Employees stopped listening to customer needs. They developed an attitude that they knew better than their customers what was needed. Products were no longer state-of-the-art in quality. In 1986, Kroy, Inc., went through a leveraged buyout, which resulted in accumulating a huge amount of debt—too much as it turned out. In 1989, revenues were less than $40 million. The company had $5 million to meet its $6 million in annual interest charges on the debt. Top-level management shut itself off from employees. As might be expected, employee morale was at an all-time low.

Source: Alamy Images Royalty Free

Kroy's owners contracted with Howard Klemmer, a financial turnaround expert, to become chief executive officer in August 1989. As part of the turnaround plan, Klemmer helped the company prepare for the difficult task of going through a Chapter 11 bankruptcy court in August 1990. Eighty-eight days after the court proceedings began, the company was out of bankruptcy.

Because the greatest challenge was to keep the company operating as usual during the difficult time, Klemmer divided his time working on the financial reorganization plan and focusing on relationships with dealers and employees. He found out that employees did not know very much about what was going on. Under a cloud of secrecy, rumors ran rampant about what might happen. He decided to take drastic action. On the first day when changes were announced, he physically removed the top managers' office doors from their hinges. "No more closed door meetings and no more secrets" was both the symbolic and actual message he gave employees. Employees could come in at any time and ask any top-level manager anything they wished, including the scariest rumors, and they could expect an honest answer.

Klemmer instituted other communication changes, too. He conducted monthly employee surveys. He also began conducting monthly open-forum style employee meetings to give employees up-to-date information and to answer questions. He created a team of five trusted employees who were given responsibility to communicate with other employees regarding what the details of the bankruptcy plan would mean to them. Klemmer walked among employees on a daily basis, stopping to answer questions. The communication program kept employees aware of when layoffs were to occur and other cost-cutting tactics that were needed. Managers prepared booklets with answers to frequently asked questions such as "What is Chapter 11 bankruptcy?" "Will I get my paycheck as usual?" and "Will the plant be closed?" These booklets were made available to employees, customers, suppliers, and distributors.

Management also produced and sent a video to all dealers explaining why the changes were needed. A toll-free hotline staffed by senior-level executives was established.

Interestingly enough, only a handful of calls came into this hotline. Key managers were assigned to make personal telephone contact with companies they dealt with. These managers were required to visit with dealers or suppliers to talk about what was happening.

Employee confidence in top managers' ability to help the company weather the crisis increased. Morale scores on a 10-point scale went up from 4 to 8. In the end, not one distributor—the key link with end-user customers—abandoned the company.

It is not every day that such a drastic approach to communication is required in a company. But Kroy's story illustrates how important open, truthful communication is to companies regardless of how successful the company is. Klemmer had a key role to play in communication, but he could not do it alone. He had to get others involved, too. It makes you wonder: Just how important is communication for managers? Is it perhaps more important than we at first think?

Who Cares About Business Communication?

Organizations hire managers to take responsibility to communicate information in and around the organization. Managers promote truthfulness and trustworthiness by how and what they communicate.

In each chapter of this book, we have been covering the various managerial functions and activities as reasons why organizations need managers. But of all these many functions and activities, which one is the most important?[4] Which one is central to the ability of the manager to be effective and efficient? Which one is at the core of what it means to express one's faith at work?

Many practicing managers and management thinkers claim that communication is at the heart of what it means to be a manager.[5] Based on sheer volume of activity alone, one might argue that managers spend more time on communication than on any other activity. As much as 80 percent of the manager's time is spent communicating.[6] One reason for this is that managers play a key role in coordinating the work that gets done. This requires communication. For example, managers at Beauty 4 Ashes®, maker of all-natural hair and skin care products, spend a great amount of time communicating with people inside and outside the organization. Leaders at Beauty 4 Ashes consider customer service a Christian ministry. From this perspective alone communication is important. Communication with customers is at the core of the company's relationship with them. Because products are made fresh to order, communication inside the company among employees is vital to fulfilling orders promptly and correctly.

We care about communication when we want to persuade our boss to approve our request for an increase in our expense budget or when we want our subordinates to understand the rationale for why we follow a new procedure. We care about communication when we send a memo to other managers asking them for pertinent information that we need to accomplish a project. We care about communication on special occasions such as at the moment when we stand up in a manager's meeting and give a presentation for which we are not prepared or when our boss returns a written report asking us to rewrite it.

But, you might be saying, these situations involve formal communication and everyone knows that formal communication is important. Informal communication is just as important. For example, a camp counselor at Cedarbrook Camp in Southern California has a casual conversation with the camp director at the copy machine. This conversation may be as important as official announcements that the camp director makes at a staff meeting. Informal communication networks in organizations make up the bulk of communication. Some estimate that as much as 70 percent of the communication in an organization occurs through informal channels. If this is true, then we might say that managers spend more than half of their time communicating using informal communication networks in their organization.

Individuals who have never been a manager can mistakenly think to themselves: *When I become a manager, I'll not have to write. I'll just telephone or text message. If something absolutely must be put in writing, then my secretary can do that.* Consider this a myth. The reality: Managers are expected to write far more than they expect.

As Bonnie Wurzbacher, a manager at the Coca-Cola Company, advanced in her responsibilities to the level of senior vice president, communication became increasingly important. What she writes and says often creates legal or moral obligations that must be fulfilled. With increased responsibility comes a greater need to communicate effectively to minimize misunderstandings, explain the rationale for decisions, and persuade others for particular ways of thinking and action. She believes that developing the social world around us is, in part, a fulfillment of God's original purpose for us at creation to be fruitful and multiply.[7] This includes all cultural forms such as business organizations, technological inventions, agriculture, and the arts. Communication is one important way in which humans participate with God's work of creation.

But let's get closer to home. When you are looking for your dream job (or any job), verbal and written communication becomes top priority. Depending on the job and the qualities that other applicants bring, your ability to communicate effectively can be what sets you apart from other job applicants.

To see how managerial work is an integrated whole that includes who you are, how you think, and what you do, let's review the Management Pyramid in terms of communication.

Management Pyramid

Each level of the Management Pyramid plays an important role in managerial communication. At the heart of communication in organizations, the goal is to create shared understanding and beliefs, shared thinking, and collaborative action. Communicating through speech or in writing is the visible, action part of the pyramid. Underneath the action of communication lies the thinking and feeling dimension. It is at this level where trust occurs. Below this level lie the beliefs, values, and assumptions that communicators and their audiences have. See Exhibit 10-1.

Differences exist in values, beliefs, and assumptions. This makes communication even more important. Communication contributes to the common sharing of basic organizational values. Without employees agreeing on the organizational values and goals, achieving the goals becomes more difficult. For example, in a company like office products retailer Staples, one of the top "green" companies in America, top-level leaders create an opportunity through their communication for strategic thinking to be shared among store managers. Through this process many people come to think alike regarding what the organization might do. Frontline workers who communicate their operational concerns to store managers create an opportunity for shared thinking about what the organization can do.

The faith perspective on communication is an important part of each level of the Management Pyramid, including the being and becoming part of the model. In the section that follows we will explore the Bible record on communication as it relates to the work of a manager.

Faith Perspective on Communication

Few things mentioned in the Bible are as versatile and powerful as a simple word or gesture. When God speaks, his words are powerful to create new realities.[8] Communication was the beginning action that moves toward attaining his goal. Because humans are created in God's Image,

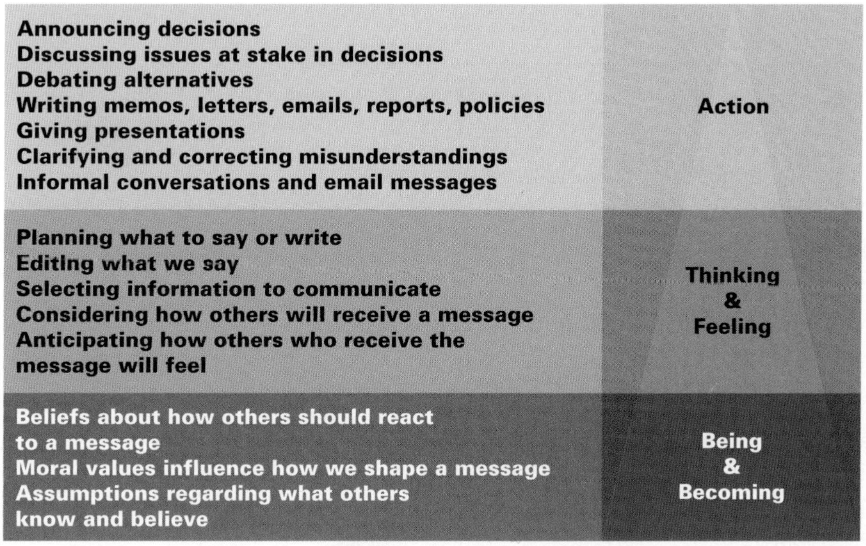

EXHIBIT 10-1

The Management Pyramid: Communication

Source: Courtesy of Michael E. Cafferky, © Michael E. Cafferky 2011.

in the human sphere communication has power for humans to get things accomplished not in a supernatural sense but in our sphere of responsibility.[9]

In the Bible when parties to an agreement speak to each other, they do so in a way that establishes an obligation for follow-through. Unless one party to an agreement becomes unfaithful, the word of a person is as good as the action because all parties trust the actions to automatically follow. So important is trust in the Bible that being unfaithful to a spoken or written commitment was a serious offense.

Writing details of business and legal agreements was a way for details of the agreement to be placed on record for the future. God's law written down had significance, placing on permanent record the obligations under covenant living.[10] The idea of writing a record was used as a metaphor of spirituality. If writing the law on tablets of stone created a permanent record of the law of God for the people to read and hear again, then writing the law on a person's heart meant placing the law permanently into the very center of a person's life—for out of the heart comes all speech and action.[11]

Communication Is for a Flourishing Community

The Bible writers begin with the assumption that people in the community communicate with each other for the purpose of carrying out the work of the community. This means that when we communicate, we are aware that what we say or write affects not only individual relationships but also group relationships. Communication is communal by nature for four reasons. First, few things said or written can be kept a secret in a community. Eventually everyone will find out because people talk to each other. Second, commitments to each other are made in the context of a community whose job, in part, is to monitor faithfulness to commitments, integrity of reports, and the permanence of relationships. In essence this is a covenantal protection role that the community shares in. Third, communication is the relational food that keeps social relationships in the community vibrant and healthy. Fourth, community relationships are based on trust. Without trust the community would disintegrate. But communication is a two-edged sword: It can help trust or hurt it. See Exhibit 10-2 for positive results of communication in the Bible.

You probably have heard that listening is "the cornerstone of good communication."[12] In the Christian faith perspective listening requires us to practice humility. Communal living is not easy. It is perhaps the most complicated system in all of human experience. Listening means that we respect the insights that others in the community offer us. For example, when a worker brings us an idea, as a manager, we must respect the idea and the person bringing it. The fact that a worker has the courage to speak to a manager indicates trust. It is by listening that we learn what others' needs are. In this way, we can become more effective servants and stewards for each other.[13]

Because spoken or written words are so powerful in affecting relationships, several problems can occur in our communication.[14] See Exhibit 10-3, which lists negative results of communication in the Bible. One problem with communication is that when one person in the community does something to irritate us, we sometimes talk with other people about it initially instead of communicating directly with that person first. Talking with other people first instead of the one who has offended us undermines the fabric of community relationships.[15]

EXHIBIT 10-2
The Blessing of the Tongue

The Bible describes the good things that communication can do for ourselves and the community:

- Words bring healing, blessing, saving life, and preservation to the community.[16]
- Telling the truth promotes trust.[17]
- Reasoning and persuading with each other and with God moves toward action.[18]
- Advocating on behalf of justice and mercy promotes redemption.[19]
- What you say brings the fruit of good things to enjoy.[20]
- With gentleness and love correct others.[21]
- To promote fairness, confirm the testimony of witnesses in a dispute.[22]
- When we listen more than we speak, we support vibrant community relationships.[23]
- Soundness of speech can prevent condemnation from others.[24]

The Bible also tells the bad things that communication can do for ourselves and others in the community:

- Arrogance and boasting undermines relationships.[25]
- Deceit and lying destroys relationships.[26]
- Flattery destroys trust.[27]
- Our words can bring destruction.[28]
- If we do not follow God's will, our words become a channel for injustice.[29]
- Our words can come back to harm ourselves.[30]
- Being two-faced (double-hearted) destroys community because it undermines trust.[31]
- We harm the whole community when we slander, gossip, and backbite.[32]
- Left to itself, our tongue will naturally tend toward harming others. Our words need vigilance, restraint, and guarding.[33]
- Not speaking up when we should also brings evil, just as speaking too hastily can cause harm.[34]

EXHIBIT 10-3
The Curse of the Tongue

Another problem occurs in communication when we do not tell the truth. This doesn't mean that we must be blunt when speaking the truth. While speaking the truth, we always need to be aware of the effect that our words have on others and on the relationship. We must speak the truth in a way that demonstrates love and does not hurt others.[35]

Defensiveness gets in the way of effective communication and true dialogue by making it difficult for the listener to concentrate on the message. An example of this in the Bible is the reports of the spies when they returned from their journey through Canaan. Ten of the spies created a sense of threat among the listeners. They attempted to control and manipulate the listeners. They implied their own superiority and spoke with categorical certainty.[36] Some of the most violent reactions to communicators in the Bible come when communicators fake genuine interest when they have no interest.[37]

Communication Supports Covenants

Speaking and writing have significance for covenant relationships and are not to be done lightly. Living for God means that we will communicate with others in a way that supports relationships based on covenant principles. This means that when we talk with even just one person, we keep in mind that there are others who may hear us talking, read what we write, or hear what we say through word of mouth. See Exhibit 10-4, Covenant and Communication.

Making a statement about a future action requires that we monitor our speech so that we do not make thoughtless or shallow promises.[38] Written communication also is covenantal by nature, calling all readers or hearers of the word for all time in the future to take note of and be faithful to commitments that are made.[39]

Communicating in a way that supports a long-term covenant relationship means we must always consider the listener or reader who receives our words.[40] This covenant is based on Paul's

Communication is at the foundation of covenantal relationships:

- All parties in a covenant relationship attempt to build trust and loyalty.
- Covenant relationships are long term. Long-term relationships are impossible without open, honest communication.
- Covenant emphasizes the relationships built on faithfulness and loving kindness. These qualities cannot be sustained without communication.
- Covenant relationships honor the interdependencies that exist among the parties. These cannot be sustained without communication.
- Communication strengthens commitment and provides opportunities to resolve conflicts and to express value toward other parties.

EXHIBIT 10-4
Covenant and Communication

principle of looking to the interests of others just as God looked out for our interest when he sent Jesus Christ.[41] This idea will be explored in the next section.

God's Model for Communication Is Incarnational

Incarnational means being modeled after God's actions when Jesus became a human being in order to reveal to us what God is like.[42] Before Jesus came, God gave the Ten Commandments through Moses. He guided the people through the work of Isaiah, Jeremiah, Ezekiel, and many other prophets. But through the Incarnation, God revealed himself to humans in a new way.[43]

In terms of communication, the Incarnation means that God chose to communicate with humans in terms they could understand—by entering into a specific, local, and historical community, living and working among them as they lived and worked. Watching Jesus Christ in action, contemplating his teachings, and observing his life and work as the fulfillments of prophecy gave the first-century citizens of Palestine a much clearer picture of God.

People who want to model their communication after the Incarnation will likewise take responsibility to overcome obstacles in communication and not wait for the listeners to do this for themselves. They will attempt to adapt their communication to the needs of the recipients. This is not only modeled after God's character, it is also a wise thing to do.

Nonverbal Communication in the Bible

We give others in the community a picture of our thoughts and feelings toward them when we communicate nonverbally. **Nonverbal communication** is the information we give to others, either consciously or unconsciously, through tone of voice, eye movement, facial expressions, gestures, body posture, and actions other than the actual words we say. Because our nonverbal communication behaviors can be highly symbolic, they can be as powerful for communication as words. See Exhibit 10-5.

Communication Methods in the Bible

The Bible is filled with communication. The Bible itself is communication. In terms of verbal communication in the Bible we find examples of improvisational drama,[44] teaching and preaching,[45] reports,[46] and debate.[47] Just like today, managers in biblical times had face-to-face meetings with subordinates in which information was given and received. Leaders gave inspirational speeches to groups or engaged in dialog with individuals.[48]

Written communications include letters containing instruction, answers to questions and concerns, encouragement, and requests. Managers took full advantage of communication technologies available to them. They wrote official notices on papyrus scrolls, clay tablets, or stones. Sometimes simple but powerful symbols were used.[49] Leaders erected guideposts and other markers that communicated boundaries and directions.[50] Bible writers used a variety

EXHIBIT 10-5
Nonverbal Communication in the Bible

Many examples of nonverbal communication are given in the Bible:

- Wagging the head, looking at a person with wide open mouth, taking a sandal off the foot, spitting in someone's face, making a hissing sound, covering the ears, or sticking out the tongue all show disrespect.[51]
- Putting your hand over your mouth signifies humility or guilt.[52]
- Facial expressions show shame, sadness, anger, sternness, arrogance, false humility, or being troubled.[53]
- Bowing the face to the ground shows respect or humility.[54]
- Lifting up hands in blessing, folding hands, spreading out hands, washing hands, clapping hands together in anger or in joy, laying on of hands.[55]
- Embracing, kissing, or throwing a kiss.[56]
- Raising the eyelids indicates arrogance.[57]
- Turning away from a person.[58]
- Waving your hand in contempt.[59]
- Speaking in a loud, troubled, or joyful voice, crying out, groaning, or screaming.[60]
- Mimicking the sound of someone else's footsteps to deceive someone.[61]

of methods including repetition and parallelism,[62] parables,[63] stories, proverbs,[64] allegories,[65] paradox,[66] satire,[67] personification,[68] irony,[69] metaphors and similes,[70] and hyperbole (exaggeration).[71]

Word of Mouth in the Bible

One day the friends of a man who was deaf and could not speak brought him to Jesus.[72] Taking him aside from the multitude privately, Jesus put his fingers into the man's ears and then touched his tongue. At Jesus' prayer, the man was healed. Jesus ordered them to tell no one. And we find out what happens next:

Mark's Gospel account is laden with irony on this story point. Jesus, the Creator of the Universe, introduces to them the Kingdom through a dramatic healing of a deaf-mute. He then charges those who witnessed the healing to remain mute. Clearly, Jesus has just demonstrated his power to heal. Yet, surprisingly, the astonished crowd suddenly has more power than he has. Their zeal to proclaim increased proportionately.

On more than one occasion Jesus tried to discourage word of mouth.[73] On other occasions he allowed it and even encouraged the healed person to go home and show his friends.[74]

We have seen evidence of the power of word of mouth in the Gospels. But in the Old Testament we see word of mouth wielding a different kind of power—power that affected an entire nation. For example, word-of-mouth referral is observed in the experiences of Joseph and Daniel.[75] In both cases a person refers an interpreter of dreams to a perplexed king who needs assistance during a crisis. In the case of Joseph, we find that after he performed a valuable service to one of his jail mates, he asked for and eventually received a referral that affected his release from prison. We find Daniel in Babylon under the rule of the evil king Belshazzar when mysterious handwriting appears on the wall. The queen remembers the interpretation of a dream that Daniel had provided to Belshazzar's father Nebuchadnezzar. She refers Belshazzar to Daniel for help. Daniel's interpretation of the handwriting results in his promotion to a position of power in the empire.

Word of mouth is two-sided: Negative word of mouth can be a kiss of death to someone's reputation.[76] In contrast, positive word of mouth can be a tremendous force for good for someone's reputation.

In the Bible, your name spoken and interpreted by others carries the essence of your reputation for (or against) you when you are not present.[77] Name and fame are constantly paired in the Bible. Bible translators seemed to understand this inseparable connection between word of mouth and reputation.[78] "A good name is to be chosen rather than great riches, and favor is better than silver or gold."[79] If you are fortunate to have been blessed with a good name (reputation), the Bible says you should be thankful.[80] But Scripture counsels us to avoid grasping for and boasting about our reputation.[81] Selfish grasping for human acclaim derails us from our relationship with God and with each other.[82] When the desire for favor with others rises above the desire for favor with God, it is cause for scorn.[83]

In the long run, reputation is held in trust by, and ultimately belongs to, the community that grants it. When the conditions on which the reputation is granted are breached, you risk breaking that community trust at the same time as offending the vulgar sensibilities of those around.

Source: Peter Elvidge/Shutterstock.

Word of mouth is two-sided: it can be the kiss of death to someone's reputation or it can be a tremendous force for good for someone's reputation.

Self-aggrandizement was seen in ancient times as a foul odor coming out of a boastful mouth and into the nostrils of those who have to put up with the egotist. In contrast, the ointment of a good reputation coming out of the mouth of the community smells sweet both to those who give it and to the person who receives it.[84]

The Expansion of the Church

A good example of a word-of-mouth recommendation is in the experience of Saul after his Damascus Road experience. Before Saul was converted, negative word of mouth about his deeds preceded him among the believers.[85] When Saul arrived in Jerusalem wanting to join the community of leading disciples, many were skeptical, but a report of his Damascus experience somehow got through to at least one person. Saul benefited by the word-of-mouth recommendation of Barnabas, who stood up in the group of disciples and said, "Allow me to tell you a story about this man." Indeed, Barnabas had a lot to lose by taking the risk of making a recommendation that could turn out to be harmful to the church community. The courage of Barnabas opened the door for Saul to meet with the disciples and confess Christ.

When Paul selected Timothy as an assistant, word of mouth played a part in his selection.[86] When Paul later gave directions to Timothy for the selection of elders, one of the important selection criteria was that the elder must have a good reputation with the non-Christian public.[87] If an elder does not have the positive reputation, then it is easy for prejudice to be stirred up against him and the cause of the Gospel. But a good reputation will silence critics that otherwise may lay in wait to destroy the Church.[88]

Paul's word selection is important. Just as confessing Christ (what we say) and giving one's own life (what we do) are forms of witness, so also is a Christian's reputation (what others say about us) a form of witness.[89]

Communication Principles

The biblical worldview on communication leads us to a few principles that we can apply in business communication:[90]

1. Communicate in a way that will glorify God and respect those in the community.
2. Communicate by telling the truth. Do not deceive as this undermines community trust necessary for business.
3. Communicate in a way that others are blessed and helped rather than hurt. Provide encouragement whenever possible. Always look out for the interests of others who are directly or indirectly affected by your communication.
4. If you need to correct someone, do so in a way that is respectful and loving.
5. Share wisdom and knowledge with the community in a way that is acceptable to them. This requires being aware of what your listeners or readers know. Relate your message to what people already know or have experienced. "A message that is hooked to some cue—something we will think about or experience again—is more likely to come to mind in the future. When the cue pops up, it may call to mind the message associated with it."[91]
6. Use concrete examples. Illustrations and stories offer the power to sway judgment and attitudes. Being specific, definite, and concrete holds the attention of others.
7. Use repetition and other communication methods such as figures of speech to capture attention and communicate the core ideas efficiently.
8. Foster active listening.
9. Actions shape attitudes, and beliefs and can be as powerful as your words.

Having considered the biblical principles of communication, next we will look at the fundamental ideas and principles of business communication in contemporary practice.

The Biblical Story of John the Baptist

Read the story of John the Baptist in Matthew 3–14 and Luke 7–9 in the Bible. Based on his experience, grasp the significance of the accomplishments that occurred under his leadership. Make a mental note of the leadership strengths and weaknesses of John the Baptist. What leadership principles can we gain from the experience of John the Baptist that are applicable today?

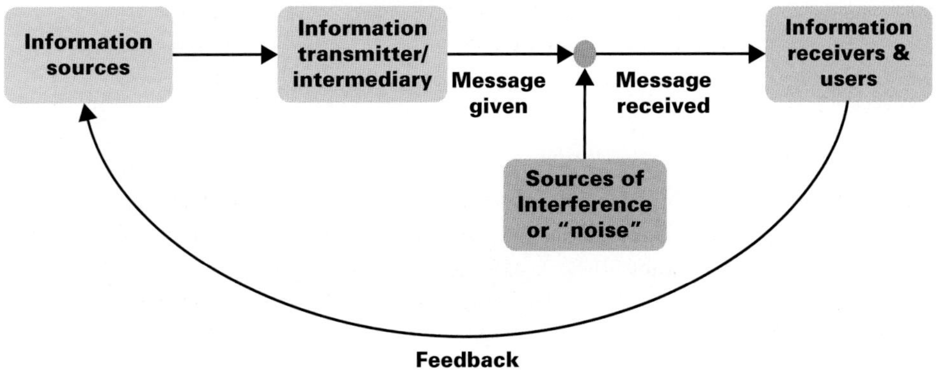

EXHIBIT 10-6
The Traditional Model of the Communication Process

Business Communication

In this section, we will consider communication as a process and explore its purposes, which provide important guides for managers. We will also look at the barriers to interpersonal communication and how to overcome them.

The Communication Process

The traditional model of the communication process focuses on senders of information encoding their ideas into symbols, putting out information to other people, using communication channels efficiently, and getting past barriers in the communication channel. It also focuses on recipients interpreting the symbols and giving a response or feedback from information they receive.[92] The process assumes that telling and receiving are the primary purpose; feedback or dialogue is secondary. The traditional model also emphasizes the technical elements of the process of using language. See Exhibit 10-6.

The traditional model helps us diagnose communication problems at each stage in the process. It helps us to be aware of our language. The sender may not know clearly what needs to be transmitted and may choose communication symbols (words, pictures, metaphors, tone of voice, gestures) that are ineffective in delivering a clear message. Barriers to communication may get in the way of sending or receiving the information. The term **noise** is simply any disruption that interferes in the communication process. Traditionally with this model noise is seen as coming from outside the message sender or the receiver. However, the perceptions and biases of sender and receiver also may interfere with the intended message. See Exhibit 10-7.

In reality, both the sender and the receiver are quite capable of generating enough noise on their own such that the message does not get through or the wrong message is sent or received.

Considering the traditional model of communication raises an important question regarding the purpose of communication. It is important to understand this if we are to be effective managers. We discuss the purpose of communication next.

The Christian Mind on the Communication Process

As a representative of Christ in the workplace, it is our responsibility to honor God in our communications. As Paul simply stated "*Let no unwholesome word proceed from your mouth, but only such a word as is good for edification according to the need of the moment, so that it will give grace to those who hear*" (Ephesians 4:29, NAS). Character is revealed in the communication with others. While character is developed internally, it is revealed externally. Being wise and prudent in how we communicate with other people requires that our "*conversations be always full of grace, seasoned with salt, so that you may know how to answer everyone*" (Colossians 4:6 NIV). The way in which we communicate reveals our heart to others.

Karen Jacobs
Assistant Dean, School of Business
LeTourneau University
Longview, TX

	Problems	Solutions
The sender	• Sender does not know what to communicate. • Sender chooses words and symbols that are ineffective. • Sender is not thinking of the needs of the receiver. • The sender's verbal and nonverbal messages are contradictory. • Sender does not account for barriers to communication.	• Gather information; make a decision about what to communicate. • Select symbols and codes to match the message. • Shape the message to the needs of the receiver. • Be aware of nonverbal messages. • Pay attention to communication barriers and make provisions to overcome these.
The receiver	• Receiver is not listening, not paying attention, or tries to interpret the message before all the information is received. • Receiver misunderstands the information from the codes and symbols. • Receiver does not give feedback. • Receiver has incorrect assumptions regarding the intent of the message. • Receiver has perceptions or biases that change the message from its original intent.	• Focus on listening. • Ask the sender to clarify the information. • Provide the sender with feedback in order to clarify the correct interpretation of the message; the sender asks for feedback.

EXHIBIT 10-7
Problems with the Sender and Receiver

The Purpose of Communication

We naturally think that the purpose of communication is for one person, using language correctly, to give information to another person or to a group.[93] While this is true it is only part of the story. At a deeper level, communication is a people process, not a language transmission process.[94]

Communication is for more than just transmitting information. In **vertical communication** up and down the chain of command, leaders communicate with followers and followers with leaders in attempts to change each other's behavior or coordinate activities. Subordinates communicate with supervisors and supervisors with subordinates, in part, to fulfill their obligations to keep them informed. They give each other reports on the status of operations or the exceptions to expected routines. Managers communicate with subordinates to reinforce standards of behavior. Believing that most workers come to work motivated to do their best, managers will communicate to prevent workers from becoming unmotivated. Subordinates communicate with managers to help them make decisions. When necessary, frontline workers ask managers and top-level leaders to create policies that apply across more than one department. To create policies, managers communicate with people at many levels of the organization. Managers disseminate carefully written policy documents to those who are affected by them for their review and feedback.

In **horizontal communication**, workers communicate with each other to solve problems, create procedures for recurring problems, or establish ways to handle routine situations. In organizations where frontline workers are empowered to make adjustments without managers needing to be involved, an employee of one department will communicate with an employee of another department to modify procedures when unusual situations arise. For example, employees transporting partially finished goods from one room to another may need to adjust the stacking of boxes because of their unusual size or shape. Employees who come to that room to remove these materials for further work may want to know that their usual expectations need to be changed for particular materials. These conversations are usually quickly accomplished without difficulty. At other times, however, when one work team needs to make more complicated adjustments to how it carries out its work, such changes can make more difficulties for other work teams.

Source: Polka Dot Images/Thinkstock.

Communication is a two-way street where people from different perspectives come together in their understanding and move forward together in their actions.

The conversations that take place for more complicated situations take more time and might involve managers if the workers cannot find a solution that works for both teams.

Top-level managers want to know what frontline workers are thinking and feeling about their work. To find out, they may institute a grievance system, implement an employee suggestion program, conduct exit interviews of employees who voluntarily terminate, or conduct employee attitude surveys. They may ask the human resources department to help conduct such a survey.

Individuals at the outside boundaries of the organization communicate with others inside and outside the company in an attempt to understand the changes taking place. For example, purchasing department workers communicate with suppliers for routine orders. The purchasing department manager and other managers communicate with suppliers when unusual situations arise such as when one material is being replaced by a completely new material.

Communication is a two-way street where people from different perspectives come together in their understanding and move forward together in their actions. Effective communication helps managers maintain an environment in which employees are engaged even under difficult circumstances.[95] Communication helps employees understand how their particular work contributes to the overall goals of the organization. Communication sets the context for people to understand what is happening inside and outside the company. Communicating the vision answers the question "Why do we need to do this?" It is the context that connects employees with the organization as a whole. This connectedness with the larger purpose is vital for employees to understand the meaning of their work. Effective communication is dialogue that permits employees to participate in decision making about the things that matter to their work. Communication also provides a way for employees to be recognized for their contributions. This strengthens the sense of belonging to the organization and the community it serves.

These deeper purposes of communication are sometimes not achieved because of communication barriers that we face. Understanding the barriers to communication will help you become a more effective communicator.

Barriers to Interpersonal Communication

Communication is a process that involves people. Because of this, individuals or the organizational structures they create can get in the way of communication. We already introduced the idea of noise getting in the way. Here we review some of the barriers to communication that make the job of a manager challenging, starting with one of the most serious barriers, defensiveness.

Defensiveness is an emotional reaction to interpersonal communication in which the receiver of a message perceives a personal threat or a threat to the community he represents such as his work group or his department. A receiver's natural reaction is to defend a wrong that he perceives has been done. When people communicate in ways that judge the listeners, attempt to control them, attempt to manipulate them, fail to show concern, suggest superiority, and couch their words in categorical certainty, defensiveness is more likely to result.[96]

With adjustments, communication can become supportive. Instead of attempting to control or manipulate listeners, the effective communicator can minimize defensiveness by focusing on the issues and simply describing the facts without judgment. Transparency on the part of the communicator will build trust that a hidden agenda is not lurking around the corner. Instead of ignoring the concerns of the listener, the effective communicator will show empathy. Instead of communicating an attitude of superiority, the communicator can respect equality. Instead of being dogmatic about a particular opinion, the effective communicator will suggest that ideas are open for improvement, reducing defensiveness and promoting open dialogue.

Another barrier to communication can be organizational hierarchy. Dividing up the decision-making authority usually makes for a smooth-running organization. Without a clear chain of authority chaos would reign. The trend in many organizations has been to push decision-making authority down to the lowest possible level, giving persons who are closest to the action more authority. Add to this the trend that organizations have become flatter with fewer levels of managers in the middle. This leaves more work for both lower-level and upper-level managers, reducing the amount of time available for communication but, in some cases, increasing the need for communication. This puts managers at all levels more at risk of being overloaded with information.

Also, people with more discretionary decision-making authority generally have a higher social status than people with less authority. People who have the same status in an organization tend to communicate with each other more often than they communicate with people at lower levels of status.[97] The effect of this is that communication between the various levels of authority becomes restrained.

There also is a tendency for workers of a lower status to direct their emotional and social communication upward to people in higher-status positions. Individuals in the highest status positions also tend to direct their communication upward more than toward people of lower status. This is natural given that everyone is responsible to someone at a higher status level. The effect of this is that those with the lowest status receive the least amount of this type of communication.

Communication provides an important way for us to correct each other in organizations. For example, a manager reports what she believes to be a fact ("We produced at 92 percent capacity last week," or "This machine needs to be serviced today."). Someone else hearing the capacity report has the opportunity to make a correction. A person receiving the direction to service the machine may be aware that the machine was recently serviced and that it is not due for service for another month. Those aware of the service-record facts can correct the person giving the order. In this way truth is uncovered, allowing everyone to share the same understanding. This is an important part of maintaining integrity in an organization. For many kinds of communication the error-correcting function works pretty well. However, research shows that workers at a lower level of authority fear the consequences of giving bad news to their boss, and because of this they edit what they say.[98] We sometimes call this **filtering**.

Communication provides an important way for us to correct each other.

Source: Andresr/Shutterstock.

All people have perceptual biases that affect their ability to communicate. A **bias** is a strong inclination of thinking toward or a preconceived opinion about something or someone. Another way to think about bias is in terms of using a preformed judgment about what someone is telling us rather than taking the message at face value. For example, some people develop the opinion that accountants are concerned only about the money. When an accountant gives a message about the organization, a person with such a bias toward accountants will more easily write off the validity of the message simply because it is an accountant who is stating it. Biases will lead a person to distort the meaning and intention of another person's message.

Perception is a mental process that helps us interpret the information we receive and experiences we have in our environment. Perception is an important part of making sense out of our world. Our personality, temperament, and our experiences shape our perceptions about people. Perception of what we think others tell us cannot be avoided. But the wise manager will be open to adjust perceptions of other people. When communicating the manager will check to see what message was perceived by those who received it and then provide corrections when necessary.

The emotional reaction of a group of workers to the behaviors of managers can be another barrier to communication. When organizations go through drastic changes in response to changes taking place in their market, they may have to make important adjustments to operational decisions. Such changes can leave frontline workers skeptical when they do not share the same perspective as the top-level leaders. Skepticism also can result when the sheer volume of information is greater than workers can assimilate in the time available.[99]

These barriers to communication illustrate two different types of communication in organizations: goal-based and need-based communication.[100] **Goal-based communication** focuses on talking about the work that needs to be done, the tasks that must be accomplished, and the strategic goals of the organization. Here the focus is on repairing problems and making decisions based on verifiable facts using appropriate channels of behavior. Boundaries are maintained between people. Minimal controls are employed to promote accountability. When problems arise, the focus is on the work processes and systems rather than on blaming people. In contrast, **need-based communication** focuses on meeting the emotional needs of members of the organization. For example, employees who have an exceptionally difficult task to complete may experience discouragement. In this situation the manager can show empathy with the employees by reflecting on the difficulty of the work and by showing appreciation. Individual employees who appear to be discouraged may benefit from personal words of encouragement. When need-based relationships become dysfunctional, they raise communication barriers. Dysfunctional need-based relationships sometimes involve inappropriately crossing boundaries, betraying trust, unnecessarily needing to control, controlling through emotional manipulation, promoting a conspiracy of silence, focusing on personalities, and blaming people.

Conversation is a social process. From early childhood we are socialized to communicate in particular patterns.[101] Factors such as cultural background, region of the country, and gender influence our communication patterns. People growing up in one area of the country develop different linguistic styles compared with people in other parts of the country. There is evidence that even though there are individual differences, men and women tend to exhibit different patterns of communication. Even among people who are part of the same cultural subgroup, gender differences exist. As a manager, you should not assume that when you hear people speak that they mean the same thing you would mean if you used the same words. See Exhibit 10-8 for examples of communication differences between men and women.

Finally, as organizations become more diverse, cross-cultural communication increases in importance. Barriers can emerge when information is lost in translation from one language to another or when the message comes across with an unintended connotation when translated.

Given all of the barriers that we have considered, communication is clearly a critical reason why organizations need managers. Managers share with others the responsibility of preventing and overcoming these communication barriers. To this we turn next.

Preventing and Overcoming Communication Barriers

For good communication to occur between two people, both need to be good listeners and both need to be good at conveying their thoughts to the other. We often think of good listening as something that the person receiving a message does while someone else is talking.

Issue	Men	Women
Ritual behaviors learned in childhood	Boys learn to put others down and take a dominant position in conversations.	Girls learn to take a less dominant position but assume that the other person will recognize the ritual and will pull them back up.
Recognizing status differences and building rapport	Focus on status; sensitive to power dynamics, positioning themselves in a superior power position	Focus on rapport; speak in ways that help others save face
Taking credit	Tend to put themselves forward to get credit	Tend to be more reluctant to put themselves forward to get credit
Doubt and certainty; humility and confidence	More likely to minimize their doubts; tend to exhibit confidence	More likely to downplay their certainty; tend to exhibit humility
Asking for directions	Less willing to ask directions; tend to avoid losing face for not knowing the answer	More willing to ask directions; less concerned regarding losing face
Apologizing	More likely to avoid apologizing because it puts them in a lower power or status position	More likely to apologize to show concern for the other person
Ritual vs. Literal	Apologizing, mitigating criticism with praise, and exchanging compliments are taken literally; opposition (debates/verbal fighting) is ritual	Apologizing, mitigating criticism with praise, and exchanging compliments are taken as ritual; opposition (debates/verbal fighting) is taken as literal
Talking about accomplishments	Tend to talk up accomplishments	Tend to downplay accomplishments
Giving criticism as a supervisor	Tend to show less concern about the other person's feelings	Tend to show more concern about the other person's feelings
Giving criticism as a subordinate	Tend to show more concern about the other person's feelings	Tend to show less concern about the other person's feelings
Direct vs. Indirect	Tend to be indirect when admitting fault or weakness	Tend to be indirect when telling others what to do

EXHIBIT 10-8
Communication Differences between Men and Women[102]

Factors such as cultural background, region of the country, and gender influence our communication patterns.

Source: bikeriderlondon/Shutterstock.

(See Exhibit 10-9.) But it is also something that the person who is talking does after he or she has given a message.

It might seem counterintuitive to say that managers who need to communicate with others must be good listeners before they initiate communication. This is true but in a way that you might not expect. Effective communication occurs when managers first consider the people who will receive the information—an incarnational approach. Managers can accomplish this in several ways.[103]

When thinking about the message that they need to give, managers can listen by considering how others will react to the message as a whole and to the messenger. The manager probably believes the message is important, but do the recipients? Boil the message down to its kernel and

EXHIBIT 10-9

How to Be a Good Listener

In conversations "we hear half of what is said, listen to half of what we hear, understand half of it, believe half of that, and remember only half of that."[104] Do the math:

What the other person says	100%	For every 8 hours of conversation
What we hear	50%	4 Hours
What we listen to	25%	2 Hours
What we understand	12.5%	1 Hour
What we believe	6.25%	30 Minutes
What we remember	3.12%	15 Minutes

Good listening is a skill that we can learn with practice. The following are suggestions for how to improve this ability:[105]

- Be aware of your feelings toward the person talking with you. Negative feelings can influence you to prejudge what you think she is going to say. Attempt to listen objectively. You can always learn something of value in a conversation even from someone you don't like.
- Before you react with preconceived notions about what you know is needed, stop for a moment. What might the person be telling you that will help you get to the truth of a situation? Which of your preconceived notions may be weak or lack hard evidence to support it?
- The urge to react by way of defense, correction, or teaching can raise a barrier in the communication. Manage your emotional reaction to what someone tells you. Your emotional reaction is a sign that you have made up your mind about what the person has told you (or is about to tell you) and what it means to you personally. This doesn't mean that you must stop being human and not have emotional reactions. It means that to improve your ability to listen, you must manage your emotional reaction.
- The urge to think about what you will say in response may blind you to the essential message that you are receiving. If you find that while listening to the other person you are spending more time planning your reply and not understanding what you are hearing, then you are increasing the risk that you will miss something important and unexpected.
- Curb your daydreaming. Yes, we all have many things to accomplish that are waiting for our attention as soon as the conversation ends. And yes, the human mind can work five times faster than humans normally speak using conversational speech. It is natural to allow your mind the luxury of going to topics other than the one the speaker is on. Fidgeting or letting your eyes wander around the room or toward the exit communicates that you are impatient and do not want to listen.
- Take notes and ask clarifying questions. This will help ensure that you are getting the information you need to understand its significance.
- For especially sensitive situations, restate in your own words what you heard the other person saying and ask him to correct or confirm what you heard.

ask the following questions: What is being said and is this important to others? If not, what is important to them? How can the importance of the message be communicated ethically so that others grasp its importance? How will the fact that the message is from a particular individual affect how others react to it?

Another dimension is to consider what the recipients already know and how much new information recipients need. Because it is impossible to get into the minds of your audience, this is a place where it is easy to make a mistake. Unless the topic is familiar to the audience, they may need much more information than you expect. Remember that the recipients may be focused on other things in their work. They don't necessarily think about this topic as much as you do. They may have forgotten some of the details of information received in the past, even though you may remember it clearly. Or they may need to be reminded of the context or the rationale for the information.

Listening before communicating also involves anticipating the barriers that exist. When you know that recipients will automatically disagree or be opposed to something in your message, consider this disagreement when shaping your message. If you know that certain words or phrases are "red flags" of concern, are controversial, or will tend to raise an emotional reaction in your audience that will get in the way of your message, make an effort to choose other words. You may need to address the opposition in your message, though it is usually best to begin where you know there is agreement.

Many management decisions come with trade-offs. The benefits you hope to gain from a course of action can come at a price. Do not sugarcoat a message by telling only the expected positive benefits or by exaggerating the positive outcomes hoped for. Most listeners will see right through this. Here is where integrity will build trust. If you acknowledge the downside but also emphasize the positive benefits, then you will increase your credibility. When you acknowledge the downside to choices but also present options for managing the downside, this gives encouragement to fellow workers.

Select a tone and create an atmosphere that is appropriate to the situation. For example, if you are presenting a new project to your employees for the first time, it would be inappropriate to say something like, "This project is pretty silly, but we need to get it done anyway." It would be much better to say, "This project is important because it will help us make improvements in how we serve customers." Another example is if you are giving the employee of the year award at your company's annual meeting, you will probably take a personal but more formal approach than you might if you were talking to the employee in the hallway after lunch and thanking that person for a job well done.

If your communication is written, consider what the recipients expect from you. If you are writing the report of a feasibility study for senior-level leaders to read, be aware that they may not have time to read the entire report immediately. Including an *executive summary* on the first page gives readers a digest of what the report contains. It provides clues about what to look for in the details. As you craft your message, consider what the readers will need, such as graphs, tables, or other visual illustrations, to understand your message. Anticipating these needs is an important form of listening before you communicate.

Recruiting a new employee is an important time for communication. How you manage the communication process during job interviews can make the difference between setting up a new employee for failure or for success. As a manager, you want to get as much information as possible about the job applicant. Likewise, the job applicant wants to get accurate information about what it is like to work in your organization. For example, during a job interview you might be tempted to exaggerate the positive dimensions of your organization. You might be tempted to say something like, "We value employee suggestions and regularly give recognition to employees who tell managers their ideas" when you know that this seldom occurs. In so saying you might think you are influencing the person to accept a job offer. However, you could be influencing this person's expectations, setting him or her up for disappointment or even termination when expectations are not met.[106]

If the message is particularly important or you know that there are elements of the situation that are controversial, it can pay to get counsel from someone with more experience before you give the message. If you plan to put your message in writing, have a trusted coworker read and react to it. If you plan to deliver the information verbally, describe to a trusted coworker the points you plan to make using some of the words and phrases that you plan to use. With a coworker's help, you can check your understanding of recipients and their probable reactions. For additional ideas see Exhibit 10-10.

Listening for feedback after you provide a message, deliver a speech, or write a memo is important, too. It shows that you respect those with whom you communicate. Feedback will give

Managers frequently communicate decisions as part of their job. Here are some tips to improve this dimension of managerial work.

- **What is the central message that needs to be shared?** Make an outline of the points you want to address. If other managers need to share the same message with others in the organization, develop a common list of *talking points*.
- **How is the decision related to company mission, vision, goals, and strategy?** Most operational decisions can be linked to strategic goals and the overall purpose of the organization. But managers should not assume that others in the organization see this relationship.
- **What is the purpose of the decision?** Curiosity is a natural part of the human experience especially when other people make decisions that affect us. The purpose of the decision is clear to the decision makers, but it might not be evident to other people.
- **Who will carry the message?** Some decisions should be conveyed by specific individuals. For example, announcing a merger should be made by the highest ranking leader in the organization. Hiring a new employee for the department calls for the department director to make the announcement. If more than one person needs to be communicating the decision, be sure that each person understands the what and why of the decision.
- **What is the best communication method to use?** Some decisions need to be put in writing such as in a memo, policy, procedure, or other document. Other decisions can be delivered with a phone call.
- **What is the deadline when the communication needs to be accomplished?** Most decisions are time-sensitive and involve future actions. If the decision carries with it expectations for specific people to do specific activities, then timing of the communication is important. Timing also is important when communicating sensitive or controversial decisions.

EXHIBIT 10-10

Suggestions for Improving the Communication of Decisions

you a chance to clarify misunderstandings. Feedback also gives you insight into what is important to listeners and readers. As a manager, you will have opportunities to ask people for their reactions to the message. A simple question of "Did you have a chance to look at my memo?" can open the door for feedback.

Busy managers sometimes forget that other employees also are busy with their work. It is easy to forget what managers told them. In addition, individuals naturally learn and remember things in different ways. One way to overcome this is to repeat key points in a message in more than one way. For example, when announcing changes to the company benefit plan, a manager might describe the changes in terms of what employees can see (for the visual learners). Then the same information might be repeated in terms of what employees can do (for kinesthetic learners). Wrapping up for a summary of the central message the manager can describe the new situation in terms of how employees feel (emotive learners), or what they are hearing (auditory learners).

Managing Confrontations with Employees

In Chapter 13 we will explore some of the communication principles when managing conflict. In this chapter we will address the thorny issue of confronting a subordinate employee whose performance lags or is inappropriate. Communicating during a confrontation can be one of the most difficult of all situations for a manager.[107]

Confrontation should occur when you respect the feelings and dignity of the employee who needs the conversation. Without respect, it will be difficult for you as a manager to obtain the employee's commitment to change. The subordinate's behavior may irritate you or make you downright angry. For example, an employee might begin to show tardiness or begin missing important deadlines. Here are some suggestions to help you be effective during these difficult conversations:

1. Keep your cool. Showing your anger will get in the way of change. Calm, self-control that also is assertive in focusing on solving the problems of the organization will keep the focus where it should be: on overall performance.

2. If the other person shows anger, remain calm but verbalize that you understand he is upset and that the situation is important to him.
3. As soon as you notice a pattern, have the conversation with the employee. Waiting will only complicate the matter.
4. Talk with the employee in private. Embarrassing an employee in front of peers will show disrespect and make you the enemy.
5. Consider the individual's needs. Everyone deals with confrontation and correction differently. Some people are sensitive and need only a gentle reminder of your expectations. Others need more emphasis to get their attention.
6. State the purpose of your conversation. For example, say, "The reason I want to talk with you is that I have noticed that you have been late three out of the last five days."
7. Be specific as to the observed behaviors. Avoid talking about the employee's attitude because attitude is subjective and the employee can easily disagree with your interpretation.
8. Focus on the things over which the employee has control. Bringing up other issues will only provide an opportunity for the employee to deflect the conversation away from the behavior.
9. When you ask questions, avoid the use of the word "why." Instead of saying, "Why isn't that project done on time?" say, "Help me understand the reason for the delay in getting the project done."
10. Discuss only the issue that needs attention. Wandering to other issues or unrelated problems will communicate to the employee that you have been saving up things you have wanted to say for a while and now you are unloading all at once.
11. Ask for the employee's opinion. You may learn more about organizational systems, policies, or procedures that are influencing employee behavior.
12. Agree on what needs to be done.

While these conversations are not easy, they are opportunities for true redemptive action on the part of both you and the employee. Successfully talking with a difficult employee can send you home with a deep sense of accomplishment as a manager.

Talking About Work

What you say about your work and your organization has an impact on those you supervise as well as your superiors.[108] Complaints made about your job to subordinates or other employees raise questions about your loyalty. Subordinates can get the idea that they can complain, too. This will spread discontent. Motivation for high performance may decrease. Complain about your supervisor and you can assume that this complaint will be passed along by word of mouth to your boss. Comments about your supervisor, even if said in a joking manner, usually will have a negative impact on others. Comparisons you make by using metaphors that have negative connotations will also have a negative impact.

If you have a disagreement with company policy, or your boss's personality or values, take the matter up directly with the boss instead of with other employees in the organization. If you are unable to resolve your differences with your boss or with company policy, it might be time to consider whether you should continue as an employee.

Managing the Company Grapevine

Experts suggest that the majority of communications within an organization is through its **grapevine**, the informal network of communication that is a natural part of the organization's complete communication system.[109] The informal network of communication may be much faster than traditional formal channels. It reaches in all organizational directions.

Much of the time, the grapevine carries accurate information. But sometimes the information people receive through this medium is not accurate. Inaccuracies can occur when someone receives only part of the information. Pressed for time, a person walking past you in the hallway may say, "Did you hear about . . . ?" But without adequate time to explain all the details, your well-meaning coworker hurries along, leaving you to wonder about the details not said. Under these circumstances it is easy to make assumptions about what else might be true. When passed by word of mouth, message details can get filtered or reinterpreted as one person takes in the information and recasts it when passing it along to the next person. This creates a barrier to managerial communication. While organizational grapevines are here to stay and can be efficient in carrying a message around an organization, they create another problem because of the amount of time people spend talking with one another. If such conversations divert attention from work tasks, this can become a drain on productivity.

If you are thinking that because of the problems with informal communication managers should not pay attention to the grapevine, think again. Managers who are out of the informal networks either by their own choice or because of others' choices are not getting enough information.

Another problem with informal communication networks is rumor.[110] **Rumors** are conversations that workers have with each other regarding information that cannot be verified by authority or clear evidence as to its truthfulness. Rumors are an attempt by people to manage the fact that something unusual has occurred and they do not have all the information necessary to make sense of the situation. Humans naturally want to reduce uncertainty. When there is uncertainty regarding things that are important to us such as our work situation (which is tied directly to our ability to earn a living), we want to get to the truth of the matter. When we lack the details necessary to establish the truth, we develop plausible explanations and then discuss these with other workers. See Exhibit 10-11.

There are three ways that managers typically deal with rumors. First, managers will do their best to communicate with employees in ways that minimize the chance that harmful rumors get started. Prevention can be achieved if managers anticipate what might be ambiguous and then provide as much of an explanation as possible. For example, announcing that one of the workers has resigned will naturally raise questions among the other workers such as, "Who will we hire to replace this person? When will the company replace this person? How will my work be affected until a replacement is hired?" Skipping these natural curiosities will create an opportunity for rumors to get started. Anticipating when a rumor might start because of a rapidly changing situation or because of an anxiety-producing event is a skill that you can develop as you gain experience. If you can anticipate the potential rumor you can communicate to employees ahead of time, minimizing their anxiety.

Practicing open communication builds trust. This creates an atmosphere in which an employee who has a question or who has heard a rumor can come directly to you and just ask whether it is true. For example, conducting a team meeting periodically in which you give team members a chance to ask questions sets the stage for them to distrust rumors that are weak or are implausible. Vibrant trust is rumor prevention in itself because employees who trust you and who hear a rumor are less likely to believe it because it did not originate with you.

A final way to encourage prevention is by having a good early detection system. As the organization enters a change or encounters an anxiety-producing event, listen more to employees. Ask a trusted employee or two to be your eyes and ears to help you detect rumors. Explain why rumor detection is so important. Explain that they do not need to be a tattletale by naming persons who are passing rumors or indicating where in the organization they heard the rumor.

Second, some rumors will die relatively quickly on their own as members of the organization come to realize that the rumor is not true. If we accept the premise that a rumor is a search

EXHIBIT 10-11
How Rumors Work[111]

1. Rumors do not begin with the truth. Instead, rumors are an attempt by members of a social group to find the truth about a situation they believe is important.
2. How fast and how far a rumor spreads is related to the importance of the issues and the ambiguity of the information.
3. Rumors spread because they are socially accepted, not because they are true.
4. Rumors spread less from objective facts than from the beliefs about facts.
5. Rumors have worth to people because they contain information that is not available from official sources.
6. The more current the information contained in a rumor, the more valuable the rumor becomes. Therefore the social group must make use of the rumor as quickly as possible to get the most value out of the information.
7. A rumor's power grows when the information that it contains agrees with people's intuition or when it conveys a community hope or fear.
8. It is the social group that is in control of a rumor. Once a rumor is identified as a rumor by those who use it, the rumor usually stops spreading.

for the truth, then allowing a rumor to die without taking the time to refute it makes sense. This will work if the rumor is not very important or has an obvious weakness or flaw.

But some rumors do not die. As the issues related to a rumor increase in importance, and if the details are ambiguous and too difficult for the social group to verify the truth, then members of the group will persist in their search for truth. Rumors that have strong emotions tied to them, such as anxiety over impending layoffs, should not be ignored. Employees will hear a rumor like this and attempt to interpret new information in light of the rumor. For example, if it is rumored that top management plans to lay off workers, the fact that a top-level leader is seen talking with the human resources manager or with the workers' supervisor will be added to the rumor mill. Some who hear about this will interpret the personal conversation as evidence that the rumor might be true.

If you are asked whether a rumor is true, avoid saying "No comment." To many people this is equivalent to saying "Yes, I just can't tell you that it's true." Your response gives added credence to the rumor without giving the complete story. This fuels the rumor to be spread more. Instead of saying "no comment," provide a comment. If there are details that must be kept confidential, explain that you cannot talk about all the details. If the rumor is false, just say so, dismissing it as absurd. If you have not heard the rumor before and you do not know whether it is true, you can always tell the person that you will investigate to find the answer.

Third, if a rumor persists, begins to spread widely, and its content is important to the stability of the organization, then managers will help employees by publicly refuting or confirming the rumor. This is done by addressing the specific rumor and providing credible evidence of how the rumor is or is not true because of other factual information. If the rumor is false, say so and then tell the truth so that employees can understand quickly how it became rumor. Make your explanation easy to understand. If it is complicated, take the time to walk through the details.

Many rumors begin because they contain an element of the truth. Confirming the true details of a rumor and providing a context for employees to understand how the details were distorted through the rumor mill can take care of many rumors. If the rumor concerns employees' anxiety about layoffs, then the person with the closest access to the factual information should be selected to respond. This might be the human resources manager or another top-level leader in charge of operations. The more credible the source, the more likely workers will believe the facts and the more likely that the rumor will come to an end.

Just as managing the informal grapevine is vital to managerial effectiveness so too is the task of managing the nonverbal messages that we give to others in conversations. In the next section we will explore this important topic.

The Christian Mind on the Informal Communication Network

Informal communication networks (ICNs) are commonplace and inevitable in most organizations today. Whether it is called "the rumor mill" or "the gossip train" these ICNs can be a very valuable tool. Not only can an ICN provide a faster means to move information across the organization, but it can also provide a means by which people can build stronger social ties that bind them together to be more effective. As Christian leaders we must be careful how to use ICNs. Paul warns us in his Epistle to the Romans that gossip is a serious sin right along with sexual immorality and murder (Romans 1:28–32). Jesus encourages us in Matthew 18 to always look to spread positive information and not evil gossip that may damage a relationship. When we gossip (or allow gossip to happen) we destroy God's intention for us to have relationships with each other, and hence destroy the social ties within the organization. Therefore, misuse of an ICN can lead to a separation from God's love and will. By being obedient to God, we can experience the benefits of ICNs to help us meet organizational strategic goals, while at the same time, glorifying God and avoiding the potential dangers of ICNs.

Dr. Monty Bohrer
Assistant Professor of Marketing
East Texas Baptist University
Marshall, TX

Nonverbal Communication

Some researchers have claimed that humans transmit less than 10 percent of what they say through words. The rest we transmit through our tone of voice and body motions such as hand and arm gestures, facial expressions, eye movements, and posture.[112] This type of communication is called body language or *nonverbal communication*. From infancy we learn how to use tone of voice and body language from our cultural surroundings.

Because nonverbal communication comprises the bulk of how we communicate in conversations and presentations, effective managers will pay attention to their own body language and that of others. For example, when making presentations the manager will develop nonverbal skills that exude confidence, empathy with the audience, and credibility. When interviewing a job applicant, effective managers will observe the nonverbal messages given as the person speaks. When conducting annual performance evaluations with subordinates, managers will tune into the nonverbal messages given. When meeting with top-level managers, mid-level managers will observe their body language at the same time as monitoring their own. All this occurs in the split seconds in and around all the words that we say and hear.

Experts say that nonverbal communication occurs through five zones of our body: face, arms, hands, legs/feet, and the lean of our torso.

Smiling and frowning, two of the basic social skills we learn as infants, also are basic nonverbal communication tools in management. The power of a genuine smile cannot be underestimated in work situations. A smile communicates receptiveness and respect. It helps others relax during tense situations. It says to others in the room that you appreciate being there with them. As long as it is not given with an air of superiority or is not fake, a genuine smile usually involves the entire face. Such behavior can disarm opponents during a heated debate. A fake smile usually involves the lips only while the eyes and skin tautness communicate the rest of how the person is feeling. Faking a smile is usually interpreted as a sign of disrespect and disdain.

The face has the ability to communicate scores of emotions such as anger, gladness, sadness, or shame. With a simple facial expression, a person can show interest or disinterest, delight or disgust, and boredom or belligerence. Facial skin color can, under different situations, reveal embarrassment, anger, or fright. Taut facial skin around the jaw and neck indicates anger, tension, or stress. How your eyes move communicates your degree of interest. For example, when someone is talking to you, do your eyes roam around the room looking for other people? Furtive eyes can indicate lack of interest, nervousness, or deception. See Exhibit 10-12 for information on a computer system that analyzes nonverbal behavior.

Gesturing with your hands open and relaxed with palms facing up indicates openness and receptiveness to other people. Hands that reach to touch parts of the face or clothing indicate

Because nonverbal communication comprises the bulk of how we communicate in conversations and presentations, effective managers will pay attention to their own body language and that of others.

Source: Jason Stitt/Shutterstock.

Source: Benjamin Loo/Shutterstock.

Source: elwynn/Shutterstock.

EXHIBIT 10-12

New Computer System Detects Deception

Researchers at Manchester Metropolitan University in the United Kingdom have created a noninvasive computer program that analyzes nonverbal behavior.[113] It is called Silent Talker. Using artificial neural networks, Silent Talker is able to detect different nonverbal behavior patterns that indicate whether a person is telling a lie or telling the truth. Based on the assumption that nonverbal behavior is, in part, involuntary and unintended, the software receives images of a person's body captured by a video camera. Hundreds of measurements of bodily movements, such as the head, eyes, eyebrows, lips, and nose, are statistically compared with expected movements. The software has been shown to be accurate in identifying deception three out of four times. Statistically this accuracy is significantly above what we might expect by chance ($p < 0.05$). Software such as this might be used in pre-employment screening.

tension. For example, experts say that people who repeatedly place their hand up to or over their mouth while speaking are uncomfortable about the information they are giving. It can indicate that the person is telling a lie or they are concerned about how the listener will react to what they say. Tightly clasped hands or fists indicate anger or rejection. Rubbing palms together usually means that you expect something positive to happen. Hands held together with the fingertips touching in the shape of a steeple can indicate confidence.

Arm and leg positions also indicate a subtle message. Experts say that crossed limbs form a social barrier to others. This usually indicates that the person is defensive or nervous about what they are hearing. Crossed arms with clenched fists indicate defensiveness and anger. Be careful though: Crossed arms might simply indicate that a person is cold. Or the person might be thinking about something else.

Upper body posture also communicates. Leaning your upper body slightly toward the speaker indicates interest. Leaning away communicates disinterest or suspicion.

Single body movements or gestures may not mean anything by themselves. But experts say that a pattern or series of body gestures during a conversation convey a message.

We may not think of verbal and nonverbal communication as being technologically sophisticated. However, these standard communication "tools" may be more complex than we believe them to be on the surface. Compared with verbal communication, nonverbal communication may be more difficult to master, but like other communication skills, it can be improved with practice.

Mechanical or electrical communication devices have been used for many years as technological means for improving communication. In recent times, the emergence of electronic communication tools has changed the way managers do their work. Managers who wish to be responsible for the trust placed in them to help their work community achieve its goals will learn to use these resources effectively.

Electronic Communication

Electronic communication devices are everywhere people do business. These devices make communication quick and efficient. Unfiltered news about what is happening in the company can be rapidly shared with everyone in an instant. The proliferation of electronic devices among employees creates opportunities for feedback and participation in decision making. One problem is that brief summaries of reactions to events widely disseminated can contribute to employees being less educated about company issues than managers want them to be. Another problem, especially with texting and emailing, is with the brevity of the information. For some situations such as confirming that you received a message, a short reply such as "I got your message. Thank you." is all that may be necessary. However, the same situation can pose a risk in communication with brief words and phrases, especially if the parties communicating have different assumptions regarding where they are to meet. Here, more information is better than less. See Exhibit 10-13.

Email is widely used in many organizations. Each organization develops a set of written or unwritten norms regarding electronic communication. When you join an organization, observe the patterns of email behavior before you jump in with your own messages. For example, some organizations do not want employees sending out messages to all other employees that are personal, such as "I have free puppies to give away" or "Car For Sale." Keep in mind the following guidelines as you get used to your organization's rules:[114]

1. Do not express anger using email. Conflict with other workers should be worked out face to face.
2. Typing words in all CAPITAL letters is considered the same as shouting. In some organizations writing a message in all caps is considered to be rude.
3. Send only the messages that people need. Avoid sending messages to your boss unless he or she has asked for them.
4. Email can be forwarded without your knowledge or your consent, so be careful what you send. Email messages can be printed and given to anyone. Be prudent in what you send.
5. All the principles of good writing apply equally to emails as they do for any other medium. Use a spell-checker. Before hitting the "Send" button read your message, checking for proper grammar and syntax.

Texting and instant messaging is becoming common throughout society. In some business environments, text messengers may encounter constraints that they are not used to living with during leisure time activities. Here are some suggestions for effective texting at work:

1. Learn your company's culture. In most organizations text messaging is not the primary form of communication. In other organizations text messaging is so widespread it is considered commonplace. In some organizations the use of text messages during a committee meeting is considered rude. In other organizations this is expected as managers are expected to multitask.
2. Know when it is proper to silence the ringer on your phone.
3. Texting when someone else (such as a customer or your superior) is talking with you at work may be considered rude.
4. While on the job, limit the amount of personal text messages you respond to. Remember that when you are at work, you are on company time, and your employer is paying you for that time. When you are having fun texting, you are not completely focused on the tasks of your work. Some people consider overuse of personal email and texting as theft of company time—time you should be spending working toward organizational goals. This is all the more important if your company pays the cost of your cell phone.
5. Keep text messages short. In-depth messages should be given and received using the telephone or face-to-face communication.
6. Sending chain texts can be as annoying as forwarding emails without the permission of recipients.

EXHIBIT 10-13
Effective Email and Texting

There are so many options available for communicating that it can be confusing to the first-time manager as to which medium is best under which circumstance. For example, how do you know when to call a face-to-face team meeting versus sending an email to team members? First-time managers may find the guidelines in Exhibit 10-14 helpful (not a comprehensive list).

Media Options	Managerial Situations
Face-to-face group meeting	• Introducing a new project • Explaining how the project contributes to the overall objectives of the organization • When a project is complex or is changing rapidly and team members need to clarify changing expectations
Face-to-face meeting with an individual	• Discussing the person's performance • Discussing disciplinary action • Discussing something that has the potential for a strong emotional response
Telephone call	• Making appointments to meet • Getting counsel when it is inconvenient to meet face-to-face • Gathering facts that require a conversation to clarify expectations and meaning • Coordinating arrivals and departures
Email	• Confirming an expectation • Acknowledging receipt of information • Giving facts that others may need • Documenting a decision • Asking for advice
Text message	• Sending a quick alert that a more detailed conversation is needed • Sending confirmations of receipt, arrival, departure • Sending a question or answer related to a fact or detail
Printed memorandum	• When an official, printed copy of a decision or announcement is needed for later reference
Written policy and procedure	• When current and future employees need to be reminded of how and why certain actions are required
Employee newsletter	• Announcing actions and decisions that affect the entire organization • Providing a forum for recognizing employee accomplishments • Providing a forum for top-level leaders to communicate strategic initiatives, organizational mission, vision, and values
Social media (Facebook®, Twitter®, etc.)	• Informally connecting organizational members and others • Sharing information about personal activities and interests with others • Building community based on characteristics of organizational members that go beyond work roles and tasks • Promoting

EXHIBIT 10-14
Selecting Communication Media

Focus on an Organization—Legatus

Protestants are not the only Christians who see a vision of managers being ministers in the marketplace. Legatus is an organization founded in 1987 by Thomas Monaghan to provide networking, peer support, and spiritual growth for Roman Catholic top-ranking business executives and their spouses. Monaghan is the former owner of Domino's Pizza and the Detroit Tigers professional baseball franchise. He says, "As corporate executives, most of us know what we have to do, and economic conditions may leave us no choices. The question then becomes how to do it in the best way, and the moral guidance Legatus offers helps make the tough calls a little easier."

Since its founding, the organization has grown to over 60 chapters internationally. The purpose of Legatus is threefold:

1. Study: Provide ongoing education in which members who have a thirst for knowledge are provided materials for continuing education based on the Roman Catholic tradition.
2. Live: Help members learn how to translate the teachings of Christ and the social teachings of the church into practical applications in the market.
3. Spread: Encourage members to become ambassadors by living (rather than proclaiming) their faith through good example, good deeds, and high ethical standards.

For more information about Legatus, see the organization's website: http://www.legatus.org/public/index.asp.

Paradoxes and Dilemmas

Communication presents its own set of tension points for the manager. The communication process itself is inherently paradoxical.[115]

HORIZONTAL COMMUNICATION TRADE-OFFS.[116] When employees in different departments are allowed to communicate directly with each other without being required to first go up the hierarchical chain of command, they can more easily solve day-to-day problems. This saves time. The downside of this, however, is that managers higher up in the organizational hierarchy can become isolated from changes that are taking place at the front lines.

COMMUNICATION AND CHANGE. Times when more communication is needed, such as when the organization is going through major changes or is in a crisis, are the very times when those who need to be communicating with others seem to have the least amount of time for communication. During these periods of transition, communication becomes a priority that rivals the demands of caring for the other elements of the changing situation.

Chapter Summary

1. The biblical worldview of communication provides a religious-based model for Christian managers to follow. Communication is an important part of maintaining a flourishing community. Communication supports covenantal relationships. Biblical communication is incarnational following the model of Jesus Christ. The biblical record shows that a variety of communication methods should be considered. Word-of-mouth communication is one of the most powerful methods of communicating. Biblical principles of communication include the following:
   a. Communicate in a way that will glorify God and respect those in the community.
   b. Communicate by telling the truth.
   c. Communicate in a way that others are blessed and helped rather than hurt. Provide encouragement whenever possible. Always look out for the interests of others who are directly or indirectly affected by your communication.
   d. If you need to correct someone, do it in a way that is respectful and loving.
   e. Share wisdom and knowledge with the community in a way that is acceptable to them.
   f. Use concrete examples.
   g. Use repetition and other communication methods such as figures of speech to capture attention and communicate the core ideas efficiently.

h. Foster active listening.
i. Actions shape attitudes and beliefs and can be as powerful as your words.

2. The traditional model of the communication process focuses on senders of information encoding their ideas into symbols, putting out information to other people, using communication channels efficiently, and getting past barriers in the communication channel. At a deep level communication is a people process not merely a language transmission process. Communication of meaning, values, interests, needs, and the results of actions occurs both horizontally and vertically in organizations.
3. Several barriers exist that make effective communication more difficult. These include defensiveness, organizational hierarchy, social status, filtering, biases, perceptions, dysfunctional need-based communication, gender differences, and language barriers.
4. Preventing and overcoming communication barriers is an important role of an effective manager. Effectively communicating begins with active listening. It involves preparing for communicating by understanding the listeners and their needs.
5. Managing confrontations with employees is another managerial opportunity to serve the common good. Several principles are useful when managing confrontations with subordinates.
6. Experts suggest that the majority of communications within an organization is through its grapevine, the informal network of communication that is a natural part of the organization's complete communication system. A manager can manage rumors in the grapevine.
7. Some researchers have claimed that humans transmit less than 10 percent of what they say through words. The rest we transmit through our tone of voice and body motions such as hand and arm gestures, facial expressions, eye movements, and posture. Because nonverbal communication comprises the bulk of how we communicate in conversations and presentations, effective managers will pay attention to their own body language and that of others.
8. Electronic communication is an important part of managerial work. Just like traditional methods of communication, electronic communication technologies provide benefits and challenges to managers.

Key Terms

Discussion Questions

1. Why is it sometimes better to listen than to speak even if the person you are listening to seems to have incorrect information?
2. How do a person's communication patterns reflect the personal values of the communicator?
3. What important management perspectives can we learn from Matthew 13:10–17 (The Purpose of Parables) and Genesis 11:1–9 (The Tower of Babel)?
4. Give examples of problems that can occur within each stage of the communication process.
5. Discuss the types of communication media and when each would be appropriate and inappropriate. What other media can managers use to communicate with members of the organization? What are the appropriate circumstances for these other media to be used?
6. Think about an organization that you are a member of. What suggestions do you have for improving communication inside the organization? What is your rationale for these suggestions?
7. Comparing top-down communication with bottom-up communication, which of these two is the more difficult to control? Why?
8. Consider the following communication situations for managers:
   a. Exit interview with an employee who is voluntarily terminating employment
   b. Informal conversation with an employee at employee's workstation
   c. Formal team meeting to discuss changes in staffing schedule
   d. Employee suggestion system
   e. Writing a weekly manager's blog to keep employees informed about things happening in the organization
   f. Sending an email informing other managers about a decision that has been made that might affect them

   What are the possible shortcomings of each of these? How can a manager overcome the shortcomings?
9. What role does a manager have to facilitate or impede the use of the informal grapevine?
10. Think about the most common conversations you have with friends. What are the reasons you have difficulty actively listening to them?
11. Under what circumstances might a manager communicate with others too much?
12. Consider the software tool called "Silent Talker" described in this chapter. Is this something that effective managers will want to use? Would using this software at work with employees be an invasion of privacy?

STUDENT EXERCISES

1. Write a memo introducing yourself. In a memo written to your instructor, introduce yourself telling about your background, your interests, why you are in the course, and what you hope to accomplish as a result of this course. Use the following memo format and any other instructions provided by your instructor:

   Date:

   To:

   From:

   Subject:

   Body:

2. Conduct an experiment and record it on digital video.[117] In this experiment you will record the same script acted by an actor showing two different sets of nonverbal signals. The video can then be used to test viewers' perceptions of the likelihood of the actor being believed. To start this, write a short script in which the actor attempts to persuade someone else regarding a certain course of action such as to purchase a certain book or enroll in a particular course. Ask someone to play the role of actor. In the first scene, the actor delivers the script using body-language behaviors that show enthusiasm such as arm gestures, leaning forward, and speaking quickly. In the second scene, the same actor delivers the script using nonverbal behaviors that show caution such as leaning back and slowing down, using gestures that indicate pushing away. Ask a series of individuals to watch both scenes and react by saying how likely they would be persuaded by the person in each scene.
3. Conduct an experiment regarding the power of smiling and frowning. On a given day practice walking up to small groups of individuals at work or other settings with a frown. Note the reactions you get such as the types of nonverbal messages they give off when you arrive or the types of things they say to you. On another day walk up to small groups of individuals with a natural smile. Note the reactions you get. What differences can you detect in how others respond to you?
4. Write a resume that effectively communicates your career objective and your work experience. Share it with an experienced manager who works in the same or similar type of work and ask this person to write comments in the margin. Based on the feedback you receive, how will you revise your resume so it is more effective?

IN-CLASS EXERCISES

Issue Debates/Discussions

Divide the class into small groups of five to six people each. Choose a set of "Discussion Topic" statements from the list that follows. Hand out a sheet of paper containing the two "Discussion Topic" statements. Assign half of the groups to defend the first statement (A) as valid and the other half to defend the second statement (B) as valid. For this exercise, students do not necessarily need to agree with the perspective they are asked to defend. In fact, defending a point of view that a student disagrees with can be an amazing teaching-learning experience for undergraduates by helping them to intellectually go outside their usual thinking patterns and develop critical thinking skills. Give the groups 5 minutes to discuss. Then call for groups to give a summary of the rationale they developed. Discussion can follow.

Discussion Topic #1: What effect do high-technology communication systems have on the human community?

A. **Loss.** High technology-based communication systems reduce direct interpersonal communication. This impoverishes the natural communication patterns in human communities. As a result, the community is more fragmented. Separation makes it more difficult to experience meaningful community life.

B. **Gain.** High technology-based communication systems enhance interpersonal communication. In addition to improving efficiency, these technologies increase the amount of communication between humans. They are important for effective coordination. They provide new forms of and forums for community.

Discussion Topic #2: Is it moral for a manager to "plant" information into the informal communication grapevine rather than use the formal information channels such as staff meetings, memos, announcements, and employee newsletters?

A. **Yes.** There is nothing wrong with sharing information that you know will be passed along the grapevine. The grapevine is a natural part of social organizations. People expect to get true information through the grapevine. In a practical sense, the grapevine is efficient.

B. **No.** "Planting" information into the grapevine is a form of manipulation. Also, if you share something that is important for everyone to hear, but you single out just a few people to hear the message, then others will come to think that you are playing favorites. This will undermine trust.

Discussion Topic #3: If an organization fully implemented biblical principles of communication, would there be a need for the informal grapevine?

A. **Yes.** Whether the organization is Christian or not does not eliminate the fact that it is still a social organization. Social organizations require information communication among the members. Information communication builds trust and loyalty among the members. Furthermore, the presence of an informal communication network does not indicate that an organization is non-Christian.

B. **No.** Biblical communication means that everyone is completely open with each other. Under such a system, managers would be proactive with information. They would become experts at anticipating when anxiety might arise under changing or unusual circumstances, and they would discuss this with employees before changes take place.

Discussion Topic #4: Are rumors inherently good or bad?

A. **Rumors are bad.** They are disruptive. They may carry a kernel of the truth, but they often also carry errors. They prey on people's anxieties and stir up emotions unnecessarily. They may be the reason that some employees take an action (such as resigning their position) when such actions are not necessary. Rumors undermine trust. They provide opportunities for individuals who have less-than-honorable intentions to undermine management's authority and cause chaos. Rumors are an indication that managers have failed in their duties to communicate with employees.

B. **Rumors are good.** Rumors are a natural part of human beings seeking to find the truth. The presence of rumors indicates that employees are interested in what is going on in the organization. Rumors are workers' way of saying to managers, we want to know what is happening! Yes, humans fail in their abilities to make sense of a situation in which credible details are lacking. In their attempt to understand an ambiguous situation, some humans will distort the interpretation. Rumors do not, by themselves, indicate that managers have failed in their job to communicate. Managers have limitations on their time and resources. Some situations change rapidly for everyone including managers. We should not expect managers to be superhero communicators to anticipate and prevent every possible rumor. Rumor management is a responsibility of everyone in an organization, not just the manager's.

Discussion Topic #5: Refer to Exhibit 10-8. Who has the more difficult time living their Christian faith through their communication styles?

A. **Men**
B. **Women**

Discussion Topic #6: Consider the proposition that organizations develop communication styles that are modeled by the top-level leaders. Assume that there are verifiable differences in communication style as described in this chapter. If an organization's leaders are predominantly men, are women at a disadvantage because of the differences between men and women in communication style?

A. **No.** Women can and do learn to adjust so that they can thrive and be fully contributing members of the organization. To suggest that women are at a disadvantage is to suggest that they are weak. This places them inappropriately in the position of being victim.
B. **Yes.** Women are at a disadvantage because they are caught in a communication style that goes against the dominant male-oriented communication style.
C. **Yes.** Women are at a disadvantage because men have not made adjustments from their communication style to accommodate the communication style of women.

Notebook Exercise

Divide the class into teams of 8 to 10 people each. Team members should sit in a row. Give the first team member a spiral notebook. The following rules must be observed: (a) No talking is allowed; (b) Only the notebook can be used for communicating; (c) Those who use only words to communicate in the notebook will alternate with those who use only drawings; each person has just 60 seconds to complete the assigned task. The first page contains a word or phrase identifying a building, object, or familiar location. The first person's task is to draw a simple picture of this item on the next page. After completing the drawing, this person passes the book to the next person on the team. The next person turns to the next blank page and writes a word or phrase identifying the item that was drawn on the previous page. Team members pass the book down the line so that each one can communicate in the notebook using their communication gift (but no other). When the last person has written (or drawn), the activity is complete. Team members should gather in a circle and beginning with the first page flip through the pages and see how the team communicated with each other. Discussion can focus on the difficulties of communicating under a constrained situation. What can be learned regarding managerial communication?

Endnotes

1. Corrigan, P. (1999). *Shakespeare on management.* London: Kogan Page. p. 155.
2. Simon, H. (1997). *Administrative behavior: A study of decision-making processes in administrative organizations.* (4th ed.). New York: The Free Press. p. 116.
3. McMillan, S. (1991). Squelching the rumor mill. *Personnel Journal.* 70(10), 95–99; DiFonzo, N., Bordia, P., & Rosnow, R.L. (1994). Reining in rumors. *Organizational Dynamics.* 23, 47–62; Mason, J. C. (1991). On the road to recovery. *Management Review.* 80(4), 23–26; Hansen, C. D., & Salerno, T. J. (1991). Making the best of bankruptcy. *Bankers Monthly.* 108(4), 21–23; Faser, J. A. (1991). Bankruptcy: Speeding up chapter 11. *Inc.* 13(6). 139–140. Additional information about Kroy Sign Systems products and services can be found at the company's website: http://www.kroysignsystems.com/.
4. Limiting the answer to just one managerial idea may reveal a built-in flaw to the question. Managerial success may be derived from the cluster of functions, skills, and abilities rather than focusing on just one or another.
5. Hall, R. H., & Tolbert, P. S. (2005). *Organizations: Structures, processes, and outcomes.* (9th ed.). Upper Saddle River, NJ: Prentice Hall. pp. 137–153.
6. Klauss, R., & Bass, B. M. (1982). *Interpersonal communication in organizations.* New York: Academic Press. See also Mintzberg, H. (1973). *The nature of managerial work.* New York: Harper & Row; Mintzberg, H. (1975).

The manager's job: Folklore and fact. *Harvard Business Review, 53*(4), 49–61.
7. From an article by Bonnie Wurzbacher published on the Internet: http://arenewingthought.org/christianbusiness worldview.
8. Genesis 1; Psalm 33:6–9; Isaiah 11:4, 34:16, 40:5, 45:23, 48:3, 55:11, 58:14, 59:21; Hebrews 11:3; 2 Peter 3:5.
9. Pawluk, S. (2009). Personal conversation with the author. Southern Adventist University. Collegedale, TN. October 8.
10. Exodus 24:12; Deuteronomy 24:1–3; 2 Kings 23:21; Luke 16:6–7.
11. Deuteronomy 11:18–20, 30:14; Psalm 12:2; Proverbs 3:3, 6:21, 7:3, 16:23, 24:2, 26:23–24; Jeremiah 17:1, 31:33; Matthew 12:34–35, 15:11, 15:18; Luke 6:45; Romans 10:10; 2 Corinthians 3:3; Hebrews 10:16.
12. Chewning, R. C., Eby, J. W., & Roels, S. J. (1990). *Business through the eyes of faith.* San Francisco, CA: HarperSanFrancisco. p. 181. See also Ecclesiastes 3:7; James 1:19.
13. Chewning, R. C., Eby, J. W., & Roels, S. J. (1990). *Business through the eyes of faith.* San Francisco, CA: HarperSanFrancisco. pp. 181–185.
14. Proverbs 18:21.
15. Chewning, R. C., Eby, J. W., & Roels, S. J. (1990). *Business through the eyes of faith.* San Francisco, CA: HarperSanFrancisco. p. 185. See also Matthew 18:15–17.
16. Job 16:5; Proverbs 10:21, 12:18, 13:17, 14:3, 14:25, 15:4, 15:23, 16:24, 18:20–21, 22:17–18, 25:11–12, 31:26; Ecclesiastes 10:12; Ephesians 4:29; Colossians 4:5–6; James 3:8–10.
17. Proverbs 12:22; Ephesians 4:15.
18. Job 23:4; Proverbs 16:21, 16:23, 25:15.
19. Proverbs 31:8–9.
20. Proverbs 13:2, 18:20.
21. Proverbs 9:8, 15:4, 15:12, 28:23.
22. Matthew 18:16.
23. Proverbs 11:12, 15:28, 17:28, 18:13; Ecclesiastes 3:7; James 1:19.
24. Titus 2:7–8.
25. Deuteronomy 29:29; Judges 7:2; 1 Samuel 2:3; 2 Kings 19:28; Psalm 5:5, 10:3, 12:3–4, 17:10, 31:18, 49:6, 52:1, 59:12, 73:9, 75:4; Proverbs 20:14, 27:1, 30:32; Isaiah 16:6, 37:29; Jeremiah 9:23–24; Hosea 7:16; Romans 1:30, 2:23; 1 Corinthians 1:28–29, 3:21, 5:6; James 3:5, 4:16; Jude 1:16.
26. Job 20:12, 27:4; Psalm 10:7, 36:3, 50:19, 52:2–4, 59:12, 78:36, 120:2; Proverbs 4:24, 6:16–19, 10:8–11, 12:17, 12:19–20, 12:22, 19:5, 19:9, 21:6, 26:28; Micah 6:12; Zephaniah 3:13.
27. Psalm 5:9, 12:3, 26:28, 28:23; Romans 16:18; 1 Thessalonians 2:5; Jude 1:16.
28. Psalm 10:7, 52:2, 57:4, 59:7, 64:3, 140:3; Proverbs 10:8–11, 10:14, 12:6, 12:18, 17:4, 18:6, 18:20–21, 19:28, 26:28; Jeremiah 9:8; Hosea 7:16; Ephesians 4:29; 2 Timothy 2:17; James 3:8.
29. Job 6:30, 27:4; Psalm 10:7.
30. 2 Samuel 1:16; Job 15:6; Psalm 64:8; Proverbs 6:2, 12:13, 14:3, 18:7; Ecclesiastes 10:12; James 3:5–6.
31. Psalm 12:2; 62:4; Jeremiah 9:8; Matthew 15:8.
32. Psalm 15:3; 41:6–7; Proverbs 10:18, 11:9, 20:19, 25:23, 26:20; Colossians 3:8.
33. Psalm 39:1, 141:3; Proverbs 4:23, 10:19, 13:3, 17:27, 21:23; Ecclesiastes 5:3; Micah 7:5; James 1:26; 1 Peter 3:10.
34. Proverbs 16:30; James 1:19.
35. Chewning, R. C., Eby, J. W., & Roels, S. J. (1990). *Business through the eyes of faith.* San Francisco, CA: HarperSanFrancisco. pp. 188–189. See also Psalm 10:7, 36:3, 50:19; Proverbs 12:22; Matthew 5:37; Ephesians 4:15.
36. Numbers 13.
37. 1 Kings 12.
38. Leviticus 5:4; Numbers 30:2; Deuteronomy 23:23; Psalm 50:16, 89:34.
39. Deuteronomy 32:3–4; 2 Samuel 7:15; 1 Corinthians 1:8–9, 10:13; 1 Thessalonians 5:23–24; Habakkuk 2:4.
40. Chewning, R. C., Eby, J. W., & Roels, S. J. (1990). *Business through the eyes of faith.* San Francisco, CA: HarperSanFrancisco. p. 181.
41. 1 Thessalonians 2:3–8; 2 Corinthians 2:17, 4:2, 7:2; Philippians 2:1–11.
42. The Incarnation is described directly or alluded to in several passages: Matthew 3:17, 17:5; John 1, 6:38, 8:42, 10:36, 13:3; Romans 8:32; 1 Corinthians 2:8; Galatians 4:4; Philippians 2; Colossians 1:16–17; Hebrews 1:1–2; 2:11–14; 1 Timothy 3:16; 1 John 4:9–10, 14. In the Old Testament the mobile Tabernacle along with the pillar of cloud by day and the pillar of fire by night was the center of God revealing himself to the people by dwelling among them. Later Solomon's Temple was seen as the place where God came to dwell with his people. See Exodus 13, 14, 25:8, 29:45–46; Leviticus 26:12; Numbers 5:3; 35:34; 1 Kings 6:13; Isaiah 12:6. The Messiah was prophesied in terms of God coming to dwell with his people. See Ezekiel 37:27, 43:7; Zechariah 1:10, 8:3. In John's revelation this same image of God dwelling with his people is used to describe the joys of living in heaven. See Revelation 21:3. The study regarding the precise divine-human nature of Jesus Christ is known as Christology. The details of this concept have been a source of debate among Christians for centuries.
43. Hebrews 1:1–2.
44. Jeremiah 13; 19.
45. Jeremiah 7–10; Jonah; Matthew 3:1, 4:23, 7:28–29, 9:35, 12:41, 13:54; Mark 1:14, 1:22; Acts 2:42, 4:2, 5:25–28, 8:4; Romans 10:14; 1 Timothy 2:7, 4:13, 5:17; 2 Timothy 3:16.
46. Genesis 32:7; Exodus 23:1; Numbers 13:32, 14:36–37; Deuteronomy 1:25; 1 Samuel 2:24; 2 Samuel 13:30–33; 1 Kings 10:6–7; 2 Chronicles 9:5–6; Ruth 2:11; Isaiah 21:6; Jeremiah 36:16; Matthew 2:8, 8:33, 11:4, 14:12, 18:31, 28:11; Mark 5:14, 6:30, 16:10–13; Luke 7:18, 8:20, 8:34–36, 9:36, 14:21, 16:1; Acts 5:22.
47. Genesis 31; Acts 17.
48. Genesis 32:3–6, 50:16; Numbers 20:14, 21:21, 22:5, 24:12; Deuteronomy 2:26; Joshua 6:17, 6:25; 1 Samuel 23:27; 2 Samuel 11:19–25, 15:3; 1 Kings 19:2, 22:13; 2 Kings 5:10, 6:32–33, 9:18, 10:8; 2 Chronicles 19:12; Job 1:14; Proverbs 13:17, 17:11, 25:13; Ecclesiastes 5:6; Isaiah 41:27, 42:19; Jeremiah 51:31; Malachi 2:7, 3:1; Philippians 2:25.
49. Exodus 12:7, 21:6.
50. Jeremiah 31:21; Ezekiel 21:19, 39:15.
51. Deuteronomy 25:9; Job 16:10, 27:23; Psalm 22:7, 22:13, 109:25; Isaiah 57:4; Matthew 26:67; Acts 7:5.

52. Job 29:9, 40:4; Proverbs 30:32.
53. Genesis 4:5–7, 40:7; 1 Samuel 1:8, 18; Nehemiah 2:1–3; Job 9:27; Psalm 10:4; Proverbs 21:29, 25:23; Ecclesiastes 7:3, 8:1; Ezekiel 27:35; Matthew 6:16.
54. 1Samuel 25:41, 28:14; 2 Samuel 24:20; 1 Kings 1:31; 2 Chronicles 20:18.
55. Genesis 48:14; Leviticus 19:22, 24:14; Numbers 8:10–12, 24:10, 27:23; Deuteronomy 21:6, 34:9; 1 Samuel 21:13; 2 Chronicles 6:12–13; Ezra 9:5; Nehemiah 8:6; Job 27:23, 34:37; Psalm 47:1; Ecclesiastes 4:5; Matthew 27:24; Mark 6:5; Luke 13:13; Acts 8:17, 9:17, 13:3; 1 Timothy 4:14.
56. Genesis 29:13, 33:4, 49:10; Exodus 18:7; Ruth 1:14; 2 Samuel 19:39; Job 31:27; Matthew 26:49; Luke 15:20; Acts 20:37.
57. Proverbs 30:13.
58. 1 Kings 21:4; 2 Chronicles 30:9; Isaiah 53:3.
59. Zephaniah 2:15.
60. Genesis 21:16, 27:27, 29:11, 37:35, 39:15, 39:18; Numbers 11:4; Deuteronomy 1:45, 34:8; Judges 2:4; 1 Samuel 28:12; 2 Samuel 15:23; 19:4; 1 Kings 18:27–29; 2 Kings 18:28, 19:22; 2 Chronicles 29:18, 32:18; Ezra 3:12, 10:12; Nehemiah 9:4; Psalm 38:8; Proverbs 29:2; Isaiah 42:14; Jeremiah 22:23, 25:10, 51:52; Lamentations 1:21; Ezekiel 9:4, 21:6; Daniel 6:20; Mark 1:26, 5:7, 15:34; Luke 1:42, 8:28, 11:27, 17:15, 18:39, 19:37, 23:46; John 11:35, 11:43, 20:11; Acts 7:57, 7:60, 8:7.
61. 1 Kings 14:6.
62. Genesis 9:8–17; Psalm 14:2, 37:21, 24:7–9, 119:105; Proverbs 3:1, 10:1, 11:19–20, 12; Isaiah 6:10; 44:22; Amos 9:14; Matthew 3:3, 3:12, 7:7–8, 11:29–30, 12:18–20, 13:15, 19:30; Mark 12:11; Luke 1:46–55, 1:68–79, 4:18–19, 6:21, 6:25, 7:32; Romans 2:7–10, 3:10–18; Ephesians 5:14; 1 Timothy 1:8–11; Revelation 4:2–8.
63. 2 Samuel 12:1–7; Psalm 78:2; Jeremiah 18; Ezekiel 17:2, 20:49, 24:3; Hosea 12:10; Matthew 13:3, 13:10, 13:34–35, 21:45, 22:1; Mark 4:11.
64. Proverbs; Galatians 6:7.
65. John 3:14; Galatians 4:21–29.
66. Psalm 8:2; Proverbs 11:24–25, 13:7; Ecclesiastes 2:18–24; Isaiah 7:14; Matthew 10:16, 10:39, 16:25, 19:30; Luke 12:33, 18:22; Romans 8:3; 1 Corinthians 1:27; 2 Corinthians 12:9; Ephesians 3:19; Philippians 2:5, 3:7, 3:19; 1 Timothy 5:6; 2 Timothy 3:12; Hebrews 11:1.
67. 1 Samuel 2:1–10; Matthew 23:2–33; Mark 12:13–40; Luke 11:39–54.
68. Genesis 4:10; Psalm 73:9; 114:3–4; Proverbs 1, 2:1–9, 8, 9; Matthew 6:34, 23:37.
69. 2 Samuel 6:20; 1 Kings 18:27, 22:15; Job 12:2; Isaiah 2:10; Ezekiel 28:3–5; Amos 4:4; Matthew 22:16; Mark 2:17; Luke 6:42; John 19:14; 1 Corinthians 4:8.
70. Genesis 49:27; 2 Chronicles 1:15; Job 19:20; Psalm 18:42, 23:1, 42:1; Proverbs 26:11; Ecclesiastes 10:1; Isaiah 7:2, 40:15; Ezekiel 26:14; Matthew 19:23–26; John 15:5; Ephesians 5:28; Hebrews 4:12; 2 Peter 2:2; Revelation 1:14–15.
71. Exodus 8:17; Deuteronomy 1:28; 2 Kings 18:5, 23:25; Psalm 91:7; Proverbs 4:16; Song of Solomon 4:7; Isaiah 13:20; Ezekiel 5:9; Matthew 3:5, 5:29, 23:24, 24:21; Luke 10:4,14:26; John 12:19; Galatians 1:8.
72. Mark 7:31–37.
73. Matthew 8:4, 9:27–31; Mark 1:25, 1:34, 1:44, 3:12; Luke 5:14–15; 8.
74. Mark 5:19–20: Luke 8:38–39.
75. Genesis 41:1–14; Daniel 5:11, 12.
76. Ezekiel 36:3; Deuteronomy 28:36–37; Jeremiah 24:9; 2 Chronicles 7:19–20; Psalm 44:13,14.
77. See for example Genesis 25:26, 27:36 and 1 Samuel 25:25.
78. Acts 10:22, 22:12.
79. Proverbs 22:1; see also Ecclesiastes 7:1.
80. See Proverbs 22:1.
81. Proverbs 27:2.
82. See 2 Corinthians 10:18; 1 Thessalonians 2:6.
83. John 12:42, 43.
84. Ecclesiastes 7:1.
85. Acts 9:13.
86. Acts 16:1–2.
87. 1 Timothy 3:7.
88. See also 1 Peter 2:12.
89. 1 Timothy 3:7. The key English word "witness" is from the Greek root word for martyr.
90. Some of these points are observed in Myers, D. G., & Jeeves, M. A. (2003). *Psychology through the eyes of faith.* San Francisco, CA: HarperSanFrancisco. pp. 79–83.
91. Myers, D. G., & Jeeves, M. A. (2003). *Psychology through the eyes of faith.* San Francisco, CA: HarperSanFrancisco. p. 81.
92. Shannon, C. E. A. (July, 1948). Mathematical theory of communication. *Bell System Technical Journal.* 27, 379–423; Shannon, C. E. A. (October, 1948). Mathematical theory of communication. *Bell System Technical Journal.* 27, 623–656; Weiner, N. (1948). *Cybernetics: Or control and communication in the animal and the machine.* New York: John Wiley & Sons. pp. 16–115.
93. For example, see Hall, R. H., & Tolbert, P. S. (2005). *Organizations: Structures, processes, and outcomes.* (9th ed.). Upper Saddle River, NJ: Prentice Hall. p. 139.
94. Gibb, J. R. (1961). Defensive communication. *The Journal of Communication.* 11(3), 141–148.
95. Shaffer, J. (2009). Playing to win. *Communication World.* 26(2), 16–21.
96. Gibb, J. R. (1961). Defense level and influence potential in small groups. In Petrullo, L., & Bass, B. M. (Eds.). *Leadership and interpersonal behavior.* New York: Holt, Rinehart and Winston. pp. 66–81; Gibb, J. R. (1961). Defensive communication. *The Journal of Communication.* 11(3), 141–148; Baker, W. H. (1980). Defensiveness in communication: Its causes, effects and cures. *Journal of Business Communication.* 17(3), 33–43.
97. Hall, R. H., & Tolbert, P. S. (2005). *Organizations: Structures, processes, and outcomes.* (9th ed.). Upper Saddle River, NJ: Prentice Hall. p. 144.
98. Hall, R. H., & Tolbert, P. S. (2005). *Organizations: Structures, processes, and outcomes.* (9th ed.). Upper Saddle River, NJ: Prentice Hall. p. 145. See also Blau, P. M., & Scott, W. R. (1962). *Formal organizations: A comparative approach.* San Francisco, CA: Chandler Publishing. pp. 121–124.
99. D'Aprix, R. (2009). *The credible company: Communicating with today's skeptical workforce.* San Francisco: Jossey-Bass. pp. 17–134.
100. Baker, J. S., & Jones, M. A. (1996). The poison grapevine: How destructive are gossip and rumor in the

workplace. *Human Resource Development Quarterly*. 7(1), 75–86.

101. Tannen, D. (1995). The power of talk: Who gets heard and why. *Harvard Business Review*. 73(5), 138–148.
102. Tannen, D. (1995). The power of talk: Who gets heard and why. *Harvard Business Review*. 73(5), 138–148.
103. Locker, K. O. (2003). *Business and administrative communication*. (6th ed.). New York: McGraw-Hill Irwin. pp. 66–69.
104. Hathaway, P. (2001). Building rapport. *Executive Excellence*, 18(7), 13.
105. Adapted from Swindle, R. E., & Swindle, E. M. (1989). *The business communicator*. (3rd ed.). Englewood Cliffs, NJ: Prentice Hall.
106. Sandler, L. (1989). How managers create monsters. *Personnel Journal* 68(11), 24–30.
107. Brown S. (1992). The case of the incompetent employee. *Supervisory Management*. 37(11), 1–2; Carter, J. H. (1991). How to cope with angry employees or colleagues. *Supervisory Management*. 36(4), 6–7; Falcone, P. (2001). When employees have a 'tude. *HRMagazine*. 46(6), 189–193; Grassell, M. (1989). How to supervise difficult employees. *SuperVision*. 50(7), 3–4, 23; Sujansky, J. G. (2007). The poor performer confrontation handbook: Eight rules for dealing with employees who are bringing your company down. *Cost Engineering*. 49(8), 14–15.
108. Ramsey, R. D. (2002). Watch how you talk about your job. *SuperVision*. 63(10), 17–19.
109. Crampton, S. M., Hodge, J. W., & Mishra, J. M. (1998). The informal communication network: Factors influencing grapevine activity. *Public Personnel Management*. 27(4), 569–584; Mishra, J. (1990). Managing the grapevine. *Public Personnel Management*. 19(2), 213–228.
110. Akanda, A., & Odewale, F. (1994). One more time: How do you stop company rumors? *Leadership Organization Development Journal*. 15(4), 27–30; Kapferer, J. N. (1990). *Rumors: Uses, interpretations and images*. New Runswick, NJ: Transaction Publishers; Rosnow, R. L., & Fine, G.A. (1976). *Rumor and gossip: The social psychology of hearsay*. New York: Elsevier; Zaremba, A. (1988). Working with the organizational grapevine. *Personnel Journal*. 67(7), 38–42; Festinger, L., Cartwright, D., Barber, K., Fleischl, J., Gottsdanker, J., Keysen, A., & Leavitt, G. (1948). A study of a rumor: its origin and spread. *Human Relations*. 1(4), 464–486; DiFonzo, N., Bordia, P., & Rosnow, R. L. (1994). Reining in rumors. *Organizational Dynamics*. 23, 47–62.
111. Adapted from Kapferer, J. N. (1990). *Rumors: Uses, interpretations and images*. New Runswick, NJ: Transaction Publishers.
112. Raghavan, A. (2009). Watch your body language. *Forbes*. 183(5), 92–93; Gorman, C. K. (2008). Watch your language. *T&D*. 62(8), 94–95; Shepherd, L. C. (2007). Reading body language can offer insights to HR pros. *Employee Benefit News*. 21(6), 22; Underwood, A. (2006). How to read a face. *Newsweek*, 10/23/2006, 148(17), 65; Larson, J., & Kleiner, B. H. (2004). How to read nonverbal communication in organisations. *Management Research News*. 27(4/5), 17–22; Hathaway, P. (2001). Building rapport. *Executive Excellence*, 18(7), 13; Morgan, N. (2001). The kinesthetic speaker: Putting action into words. *Harvard Business Review*. 79(4), 112–120; Latiolais-Hargrave, J. (2001). *Strictly business body language: Using nonverbal communication for power and success*. Dubuque, IA: Kendall/Hunt Publishing Company; Mehrabian, A. (1971). *Silent messages*. Belmont, CA: Wadsworth Publishing; Drucker, P. F. (1967). *The effective executive*. New York: Harper & Row, Publishers. p. 61; Hall, E. T. (1959). *The silent language*. New York: Doubleday & Company.
113. Rothwell, J., Bandar, Z., O'Shea, J., & McLean, D. (2006). Silent talker: A new computer-based system for the analysis of facial cues to deception. *Applied Cognitive Psychology*. 20, 757–777.
114. Locker, K. O. (2003). *Business and administrative communication*. (6th ed.). New York: McGraw-Hill Irwin. pp. 20–21.
115. Hall, R. H., & Tolbert, P. S. (2005). *Organizations: Structures, processes, and outcomes*. (9th ed.). Upper Saddle River, NJ: Prentice Hall. p. 139. Hall & Tolbert cite the following sources: Brunsson, N. (1989). *The organization of hypocrisy: Talk, decisions, and actions in organizations*. New York: John Wiley; Manning, P. (1992). *Organizational communication*. New York: Aldine de Gruyter.
116. Hall, R. H., & Tolbert, P. S. (2005). *Organizations: Structures, processes, and outcomes*. (9th ed.). Upper Saddle River, NJ: Prentice Hall. p. 147.
117. Adapted from Hutson, M. (2008). Know your audience. *Psychology Today*. 41(4), 27.

CHAPTER 11

Motivation

LEARNING OBJECTIVES

- Be aware of how important motivation of employees is for managers.
- Understand motivation from a Christian worldview perspective.
- Recognize the many factors that influence motivation and performance.
- Examine the assumptions about human nature and how these assumptions affect managerial work.
- Explain how physiological, psychological, and social needs shape work behavior.
- Understand the variety of perspectives that have come to shape our understanding of motivation at work.
- Identify tension points in managing worker motivation.

"The heart of man is his worst part before it is regenerated, and the best afterward; it is the seat of principles and the fountain of actions. The eye of God is, and the eye of the Christian ought to be, principally fixed upon it."[1]

"Only the relationship to his Creator and that to his family antedate man's relationship to his work; only they are more fundamental. And together with them the relationship to his work underlies all of man's life . . . "[2]

MOTIVATION THE RITZ-CARLTON WAY

Organizations with many employees sometimes find it difficult to keep employees motivated for high performance every day. Managers at the Ritz-Carlton Hotels believe they have found a solution to this problem: stories![3]

Hotels of all types desire to create such a good experience for their guests that these customers choose their hotel first. Luxury hotels are no different, and the Ritz-Carlton has developed a worldwide reputation for treating its guests like kings and queens. Every employee is expected to provide high-performance warmth, friendliness, graciousness, eagerness to serve, and courtesy to 100 percent of the guests that come to a Ritz-Carlton hotel.

The Ritz-Carlton trains every manager and every employee in what it calls *12 service values*. These service values are a condensed and revised version of the Ritz-Carlton's original *20 rules*. The 12 values are a mix of about one-third functional values and two-thirds emotional engagement values. For example, the first service value focuses on the role that each employee plays in building a long-term relationship with guests. Other values focus on being responsive, employee involvement in planning work, protecting privacy and security for hotel guests, and creating memorable hotel experiences.

Source: © Holger Burmeister/Alamy.

Each employee carries a laminated card that contains these values. Every day employees from each department have a short staff meeting to discuss the guest experiences of the day. They resolve issues with current guests and brainstorm ways to improve service. During daily staff meetings managers do not focus on what employees have done wrong. They do this in private conversations as needed. Instead, during the staff meeting managers help employees talk about how to improve their work tasks.

The 12 service values are kept as the focus of stories and employee discussions. The same stories are provided to managers at all Ritz-Carlton facilities worldwide so that at the daily employee meeting employees around the globe hear and react to the same value-laden story. A bellhop in San Francisco hears the same story as the housekeeper in Berlin and the restaurant server in Kuala Lumpur. Each story represents the experience of an employee in the Ritz-Carlton organization who went above and beyond what was expected and delivered exceptional service to a guest. These stories recognize specific contributions of specific employees in front of peers. They give managers a chance to show the passion they feel for "wowing" guests. This passion is caught and relived in the work lives of employees throughout that day. Stories also reinforce at least one service value, helping employees and managers make the connection between the abstract value and real-world actions.

Each daily staff meeting is just 15 minutes long. That doesn't seem like much of a commitment for keeping employees energized to high performance as well as training them in how to give high performance. But every day is a new opportunity to serve customers exceptionally. And, do the math. Over the course of 365 days, 15 minutes each day adds up to over 90 hours of training delivered to 35,000 Ritz-Carlton employees worldwide. What other company do you know that spends over 2 weeks of time every year wowing its employees?

The Ritz-Carlton way of motivating employees to high performance combines many of the ideas we consider in this chapter. It integrates what the employee is all about with what the guest is all about. It gets at the heart of what most managers at most contemporary organizations desire to see: employees who are engaged and passionate about what they do by serving others.

Who Cares About Motivation?

One reason organizations hire managers is to ensure that the organization can achieve sustained high performance. Managers are called to develop themselves and others around them to give their very best efforts to serve each other and the needs of the organization.

Ask many people how you motivate workers to sustain exceptional performance and you might hear many of them say, "Just pay workers more." Because motivation is so common to our own experience, all of us have some knowledge about some of the things that motivate us to action. For this reason, it is not uncommon for some studying the subject for the first time to assume that (a) motivation is pretty straightforward and a relatively simple matter of offering rewards or (b) the problem of motivation can easily be solved with practical insights from popular self-help books.[4]

Motivation is not very far away from you if you look closely. The issues are everywhere. Just ask someone to help you with an unpleasant task. How do you persuade that person to help you? Take a look at your own daily schedule. Which activities do you find yourself easily doing? Which activities do you delay doing? Now search your heart to find clues regarding why these patterns exist. What motivates you to go to the library to study: the hunger for learning, the threat of punishment, the expectation of getting "paid" with a grade on an assignment, the desire to hang out with friends, or something else? Or is it a combination of motives at work? Are there some activities you like doing simply because of the enjoyment they bring without any tangible reward? Would you read an article or a book just because it is interesting, or would you read it only because you know your grade will depend on it? Have you ever wanted to do something only to find out that there were obstacles in your way that discouraged you from following through on your desire?

Religious beliefs are a powerful force motivating people to engage in some behaviors while avoiding other activities. Christianity is not bashful about prescribing the virtues of humility, gratitude, loyalty, and love as guides for behavior. For many activities, this makes the problem of choosing what to do much clearer. The religious perspective emphasizes relationships and sees motivation as part of relational living.

Management Pyramid on Motivation

When you hire a new employee to perform a specific set of tasks, you cannot hire just the task-specific abilities. The whole person comes along with these abilities. For example, at PRO-TEC Coating Company, producer of coated sheet steel products in northwest Ohio, motivation of workers begins in the hiring process when managers select new workers who are deemed capable of exhibiting three important qualities: ownership, responsibility, and accountability in their work.[5] Managers also look for evidence that the new employee is open to diverse thinking. Does the person listen to others? Is the new employee respectful of others? Does the person work for the good of the team? Wholeness of an individual means that actions are inseparable from the thoughts and feelings that are forever connected with the individual's underlying motives. But wholeness requires that the person also be forever connected with social groups around them. Thus, from a social perspective, motives, to some degree, result from social interaction.[6]

The concept of motivation naturally leads us to seek and understand the reasons for human action or lack of action. Motives have their foundation in who we are and who we are becoming. See Exhibit 11-1.

Motives are sometimes hidden, but they bear fruit in terms of the thoughts and feelings of the manager. For example, an excessive interest in protecting one's ego from the reactions of subordinates and coworkers will play out in how managers interpret the behavior of those around them. These interpretations will result in emotions, which feed the dominant motives lying deeper in the soul. In turn, the thoughts and emotions fuel managerial action.

Then the reciprocal process occurs. With experience, managers who survive the early years eventually learn to allow both their subordinates and their superiors to influence how they behave. These managers change their behaviors to model successful managers around them.

Changing the work environment or the job itself **Implementing reward and recognition systems** **Reinforcing a culture of excellence** **Using the chain of command**	**Action**
Thinking about what encourages employees to enliven their passion to high performance **Planning employee training, development, rewards, and a work environment conducive to high performance**	**Thinking & Feeling**
Assumptions regarding employees and what motivates them to high performance **Motives of workers and managers** **Beliefs regarding the value of intrinsic vs. extrinsic rewards** **Beliefs regarding human nature**	**Being & Becoming**

EXHIBIT 11-1

The Management Pyramid on Motivation

Source: Courtesy of Michael E. Cafferky, © Michael E. Cafferky 2011.

The changes in behaviors spawn new ways of thinking and feeling about what they do and how others view them. Over time, these new ways of thinking and feeling gradually influence a change in the motivation in both the managers and those around them.

This chapter puts the spotlight on issues and ideas related to motivation. We start with the Christian faith perspective because it is an important part of the Christian's personal beliefs and values (the "being and becoming" part of the Management Pyramid model).

Faith Perspective on Motivation

Motivation in the context of the work environment has received much attention from management experts over the last hundred years.[7] Some ideas we have today regarding motivation follow a long history of awareness starting in the narratives and teachings of the Bible. Let's review the Bible record on motivation to work, starting with the heart.

Keeping the Heart

In the Bible motivation is primarily a matter of the heart. The Bible sometimes refers to the heart as the *inner man*. The heart is the most important human body term in the Old Testament. It has the power to control the rest of the body. It is multidimensional, yet mysterious.[8] In the Old Testament mental functions were attributed to the heart.[9] The book of Proverbs illustrates the many uses of the word, as shown in Exhibit 11-2.

EXHIBIT 11-2

The Versatility of the Human Heart in the Book of Proverbs

Function of the Heart	The Book of Proverbs
Thinks and contemplates	24:12
Experiences emotions	12:25, 14:10, 14:30, 15:15
The seat of wisdom	14:33
Discerns (makes judgments and decisions) and prompts action	2:10, 10:13, 15:14. Compare these with Exodus 14:5, 35:21; Numbers 32:9; 1 Kings 12:27, 18:37.
Makes plans	6:14, 6:18, 16:9
Serves as the center of internal spiritual activity	3:5, 14:33, 17:20, 20:9, 26:23–25
Serves as the center of ethical activity	23:17
Acts as a barrier to or receptor of correction	5:12, 28:14. Compare with Isaiah 6:10; Matthew 13:5.
Controls the eyes, ears (the two gateways to the heart), tongue, and all other body parts	2:2, 4:21–27, 6:18, 15:13, 15:28

From the Bible we see that while some motivations can come from outside a person, they ultimately go through the thoughts and emotions before they come to fruition in a person's actions. The Bible does not analyze motivation in a scientific way per se. Nor does it address questions of motivation from the point of view of contemporary motivation theories. But the Bible's stories provide the context for many situations from which we can infer and understand the motives behind human actions.[10]

The Bible instructs us to watch over our hearts. In his Beatitudes Jesus pronounced a special blessing on those whose heart is pure.[11] Bringing God's Law into the heart is the way to keep motives pure. However, because humans are prone to selfishness or having altruistic and self-interested motives, as much as we might fix our eye on our heart, it can easily deceive us.[12] Above all things it is the heart that is in need of renewal—a process that only God can accomplish.[13]

Three Powerful Motivators

Three motives stand out as being the most powerful: faith, hope, and love—the three theological virtues.[14] Faith and hope are closely related as motivating forces.[15] Faith is the support for what we expect (hope) for the future. Faith and hope are tied to our expectations of the future but grounded in our memory of what God has done for us in the past. God is both the source and object of hope and faith because of his acts of loving kindness rooted in his character. The very message of this good news brings a positive expectation of the future.[16] See Exhibit 11-3.

So powerful are faith and hope that human beings seemingly at the point of utter despair can be revived at even the faintest reason to hope. A beautiful metaphor of hope is given in the story of Job in which the person is described as a tree stump, which would normally have no reason to expect a positive future as a tree. But the mere scent of water causes the stump to flourish because of the expectation of what is to come. Another biblical metaphor for hope is that of a helmet, which provides security or safety.[17] Jesus used the parable of a tiny mustard plant seed and the parable of the grain farmer to illustrate the power of faith.[18]

Compared with faith and hope, love is the greatest motive: love to God and love to each other. Love is defined by the moral law contained in the Ten Commandments. Love is the fulfillment of this law. It is the most powerful force in guiding human behavior.[19] The link between love and motivation to serve can be summed up in the concept of gratitude. Gratitude is the foundation for Christian service.[20] This, in turn, is replicated in others who after experiencing our service of love also desire to serve.[21]

Ideally, it is this desire to serve God and others that is a fundamental motive to work. We might even think of work as the result of this desire to serve. From this perspective, work takes on a great significance. Difficult work that on the surface appears to be drudgery ultimately is work that is performed in service to others. Thus, the desire to serve for the common good of the organization and of society is an expression of this love.

Other Motives

Besides faith, hope, and love, the Bible alludes to a variety of motivational forces including human dignity, compassion, imitating God, fear of punishment, and promises of well-being.[22] Legitimate motives related to physical survival are assumed in Scripture. Anger at injustice,

EXHIBIT 11-3
Three Powerful Motivators

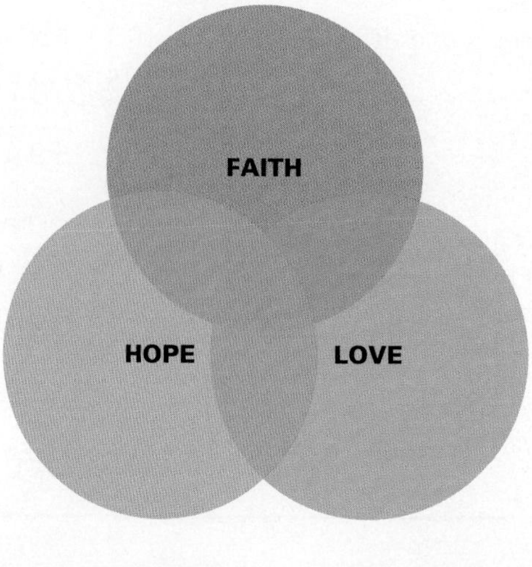

Israelites were motivated to donate goods for the building of the Tabernacle
Jonah was motivated to resist going to Ninevah
Lot did not want to leave Sodom
Friends of a paralyzed man were motivated to lower him down through a roof to be healed

EXHIBIT 11-4
Examples of Motivation in the Bible[23]

illustrated in the lives of Moses and Jesus, is another motive.[24] Five of the Ten Commandments reference motivation. A fundamental theme in these references is the human reaction to God's acts of creation and, after the fall, deliverance (redemption).[25]

The motive of hunger, the desire to avoid harm and death, and the desire for honor are all present in the wisdom of Proverbs.[26] In Proverbs we see portrayed the individual who is an integral part of a community and who must choose her behavior. Yes, there are social influences around the individual that influence behavior, but the individual still has the power to choose based on values rooted in character that is built on a relationship with God. Things don't just happen to a person by forces outside the control of the person. Rather, we all can affect what happens to us based on the choices that we make.[27] In Proverbs we also can see a connection between emotions and motivation.[28] For example, the righteous person acts with the hope of finding gladness as a consequence.

Loyalty toward one's family and community was considered central to life in biblical times. When Jacob and his family ran out of food in Canaan, they asked to be allowed to move to Egypt to obtain food. Jairus made the choice to look for Jesus so that his daughter could be healed. Concern for her people motivated Queen Esther to choose to become their advocate. Zaccheus the tax collector went through a spiritual conversion experience. As a result, he was instantly motivated to give back that which he had taken by fraud.[29]

The Bible shows us many other examples of motivated people (see Exhibit 11-4). Some of these people were motivated by God-created physiological needs of food and safety.[30] Others appear to have been motivated by cognitive or spiritual needs. Some were motivated by selfish desires for money, revenge, influence, or other reasons. In many of the stories we see multiple motives at work.

Cause and Effect in Work Situations

Cause and effect in social relationships is clearly understood in the Bible. The foundation for this is our relationship with God.[31] Closely linked with this is the cause and consequences in the human sphere.[32] A common metaphor is from the world of agriculture: The diligent work of a farmer pays off with the reward of fruit. Apparently the farmer is motivated to work diligently by his desire for fruit. Similarly, the reward for a person's work (such as wages) is discussed using the metaphor of fruit.[33]

This leads us to the concept of incentives. Scripture describes and implies a variety of incentives to action.[34] For example, to the person who killed the giant Goliath, the king promised great wealth, his daughter for marriage, and freedom for his family from certain obligations.[35] Exhibit 11-5 lists incentives in the book of Genesis and the book of Proverbs.

EXHIBIT 11-5
Incentives in the Book of Genesis and the Book of Proverbs

Book of Genesis	Book of Proverbs
Peer pressure: 3:12–13, 3:17	Desire for a good reputation: 22:1
Fear: 3:10, 3:24, 4:15, 9:5–6, 12:12–13	Desire for honor: 22:4
Jealousy: 4:8, 13:7, 16:5, 20:10	Desire for a positive reaction of parents: 10:1
Resentment: 4:23, 9:25	Fear of poverty: 22:16
Fame: 11:4, 12:2	Fear of being an abomination: 21:27
Family loyalty: 14:14, 20:11	Fear of shame: 10:5
Integrity: 14:22–24	
Faith: 15:6	
Hospitality, generosity: 18:3–8, 19:2	
Physical necessity: 2:17, 3:3, 6:13–14, 13:6	

Intrinsic vs. Extrinsic Rewards and Punishments

Scripture portrays two broad categories of incentives: rewards and punishments.[36] Some rewards and punishments are extrinsic and material while others are intrinsic and spiritual, as shown in Exhibit 11-6. Both are legitimate in Scripture.[37] Some rewards in the Bible could be both intrinsic and extrinsic.[38] Standing above all other kinds of rewards is the promise of a close relationship with God.[39]

Extrinsic rewards can induce people to perform beyond the bare minimum. They are effective because people are self-interested. God appeals to our self-interest to motivate us to follow his will. But when self-interest seeks self-gain at the expense of others, the Bible forbids it. Human motivation is complex. Self-interest is only one of many motivations.

Jesus' interest in intrinsic motivation does not come from its inherent moral superiority but rather from his desire to encourage the disciples to focus on their mission and not on themselves.[40] When King David led his armies to capture the stronghold of Zion, his opponents told him that the city was so strongly fortified that only blind and lame guards were necessary to keep intruders out. David offered an incentive that whoever would successfully lead the charge would be commander of the army. Joab responded and received the promotion.[41]

One of the problems with extrinsic rewards is that these appeal to our selfish natures. Extrinsic motivation eventually undermines effective discipleship by leading the person toward a deep-seated self-focus and self-absorption. Intrinsic interests in motivated activities wane. It undermines the nurturing of the desire for loving service. Even religion becomes weakened by extrinsic thinking. How is a person to reclaim the power of intrinsic motivation that has been undermined by the use of extrinsic rewards? Some Christians believe that this can occur only through repentance and developing a thriving faith relationship with God that leads the person to love God for God's and other people's sake. Another problem with extrinsic rewards is that they originate with someone other than the person who takes the action. This suggests that behavior might change because of a reward but the attitudes that underlie the behavior might not necessarily change.[42]

The distinction between intrinsic and extrinsic rewards should not be taken to the extreme, because they are not always mutually exclusive. The reward of hard work in the fields brings not only satisfaction from good food but also gladness.[43] Wisdom carries an inherent reward for living a sensible and prudent life, yet it also influences the capability to build wealth, which is tangible, and social power, which may be tangible or intangible.

Goal Setting

We know from modern research on motivation that goal setting is positively correlated with increased motivation and work performance. While the Bible writers do not attempt to analyze the goal-motivation-performance linkage, they show the connection between goals and action with the motivation implied or stated.

One of the chief goals that a sovereign God has for humans is that they respond to his love and have a repentant, saving relationship with him.[44] Likewise, from the perspective of human beings the highest human goal in the Bible is to enjoy the full relationship with God in heaven. Such a goal enlivened the Apostle Paul toward the action of spreading the

EXHIBIT 11-6
Intrinsic and Extrinsic Rewards in Scripture

Intrinsic, Spiritual Rewards	Extrinsic, Material Rewards
Keeping the law carries its own spiritual reward.[45]	Wealth and successful families will result from obedience.[46]
A close relationship with God is the highest reward.[47]	People offer tangible rewards of gifts and honor for doing favors, for providing service, and for honest labor.[48]
Wisdom and knowledge are rewards.[49]	Adults reward children.[50]
Work brings its own reward of pleasure.[51]	Inheritance is a reward.[52]

God gave Noah a goal: build an ark for safety.[53]
When humans organize, their goals will be realized.[54]
Joseph set goals for accumulating food during years of plenty.[55]
Uzziah prepares armaments of war to lay siege.[56]
The goal of the Messiah: destroy the works of the devil.[57]

EXHIBIT 11-7
Goal Setting in the Bible

Good News of the Kingdom.[58] In Paul's letter to Timothy he explains the goal of his instruction: love from a pure heart and a good conscience. Paul explains his goal in writing to the church at Corinth: to test them. The goal of his prayer for the churches is that God will fulfill his plan for their good.[59] Exhibit 11-7 describes several more examples of goal setting in the Bible.

Fairness

The gospel of Matthew gives an illustration of how the principle of fairness of rewards was part of the consciousness of people in the first century A.D.[60] Jesus tells the story of the land owner who hired day laborers to work in his fields. When those who were hired early in the morning saw that they received the same wages as those who were hired at the end of the day, they complained. This gave Jesus the opportunity to discuss how God's grace works in a way that doesn't seem fair when using human concepts. But the story also illustrates what we now know as *equity theory*. As humans, it is natural for us to compare with others the amount of work we produce along with the rewards we receive for that level of production. When there is an unfavorable discrepancy between what we think we should get and what we believe others are getting, we are displeased. This principle of fairness, to a large degree, depends on perception. The workers in the story Jesus told had tangible evidence of the differences among workers in terms of inputs (the number of hours worked) and outputs (the amount of pay).

The Community Setting of Motivation

The story of paying workers the same also illustrates that motivation seldom, if ever, can be isolated from our social relationships. Though we might think of motives as occurring in the heart and mind of an individual, we can also say that motivation is rooted in community. The reasons for action involve other people. The actions themselves either involve other people or directly affect them.[61]

The Bible writers recognize the social influences on motives. For example, the book of Proverbs contains many guidelines that represent the influence we have on each other. The ministry of Jesus Christ gives many examples of how he taught by modeling behaviors. On the one hand, Christians are instructed to use their influence with those around them. On the other hand, as humans, we are especially vulnerable to the influence of others around us. Because of this we should be wary of the social relationships we maintain because these can influence the shape and direction of our motives.[62]

Although motives are often hidden from view, they are an important dimension of our life as they are the spark for either action or resistance to action.

The Biblical Story of Peter

Read the story of Peter in the Gospels and Acts in the Bible. Based on his experience, grasp the significance of the accomplishments that occurred under the leadership of Peter. Make a mental note of Peter's leadership strengths and weaknesses. What leadership principles can we gain from the experience of Peter that are applicable today?

Motivation and Performance

Having considered the Bible's perspective on motivation, we will now look at motivation in practice in business. We will begin by offering a definition of motivation. We will also explore many of the factors that influence a person's motivation to work.

While work motivation can be defined in many ways, we offer the following definition: "Work **motivation** is a set of energetic forces that originate both within as well as beyond an individual's being to initiate work-related behavior and to determine its form, direction, intensity and duration."[63]

Notice that this definition allows for multiple forces to be at work influencing work behavior. Notice also that this definition allows that some forces are outside the individual worker.

The relationship between motivation and performance at work is the focus of this chapter. **Performance** is the actual carrying into action or execution of plans and objectives. It means the degree of accomplishment or achievement in action that is attained. A number of factors influence work motivation and performance.[64] You may have heard people say things like, "All these workers need are a good kick in the pants," or "If workers would just take initiative once in a while, this department could outperform all the others." Such statements oversimplify reality. In many instances only some of the factors that influence performance are within the control of the individual employee or the manager.[65] For example, an employee's supervisor might knowingly or unknowingly limit an employee's productivity by requiring that the work be accomplished in one particular way or using particular resources when other ways or resources might just as well be used. Organizational policies adhered to rigidly can tie employees' hands—sometimes unnecessarily. This doesn't mean that we should do away with company policies. It means that managers need to be watchful for the times when policy needlessly constrains performance.

There are many more examples of factors that are beyond an individual's control and yet still affect performance: The tools needed for the tasks may be lacking, damaged, substandard, or inappropriate. The physical layout of the work space might be a barrier. The sporadic availability of key resources can limit productivity. Competing goals and objectives may require an employee to compete with his own behavior. The organizational structure might be getting in the way of high productivity. For example, employees at the core of the organization's purpose normally are closely dependent on each other and on the support services of the organization. Employee motivation at the core of the organization might be high, but the challenges that other departments face may be outside the control of these core employees.

An otherwise highly motivated employee may lack the skills necessary to perform at a high level. For example, a junior financial analyst working in a mergers and acquisition department of a large corporation may be highly motivated to perform. But this person may lack the depth of understanding of the industries that the department is exploring. Or the person might lack either the quantitative skills or the qualitative human relations skills to be effective. These are just some of the influencing factors. See Exhibit 11-8.

Just as some factors limit a highly motivated employee from achieving high performance, other factors can have a destructive effect on motivation itself. Because of this, productivity might suffer. For example, few things are as destructive to employee motivation as when an

Performance on the job can be influenced by may factors.

Source: Pryzmat/Dreamstime.com.

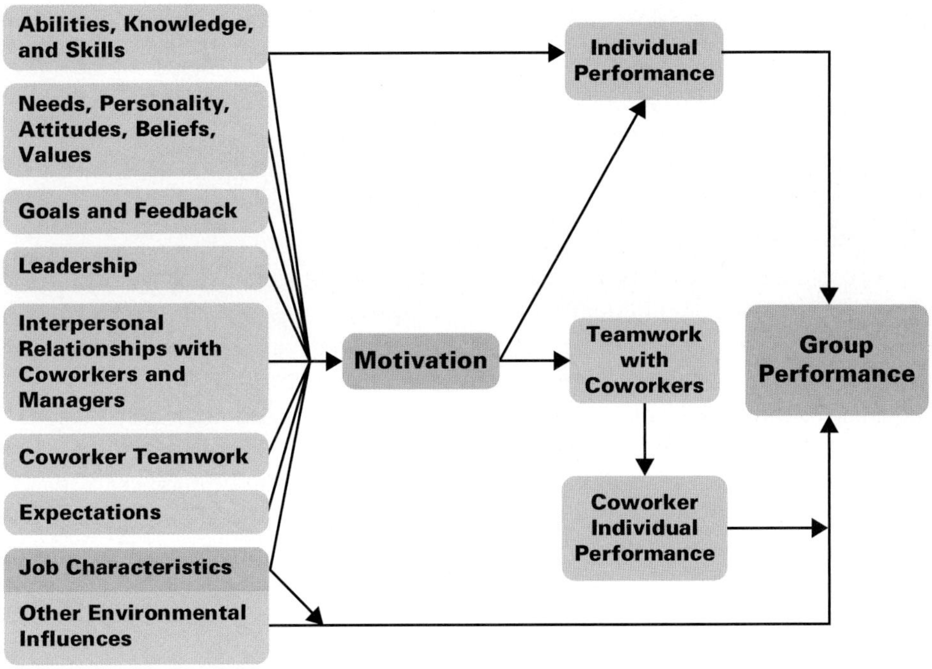

EXHIBIT 11-8
Influences on Motivation and Performance

employee must wait for a manager to figure out what to do next. But if you allow the employees to participate in developing the vision for what needs to be done next, then you may find that motivation for work increases. When a manager hoards unnecessary employees to use when unusual situations occur, the manager must make work for these employees. Other employees who see this happening may become demoralized, believing that the work is an unnecessary waste of company resources. Such situations may reveal lack of sufficient planning or the manager's desire to control. They undermine employees' respect for managers.[66]

This tendency to think that performance problems are caused by something inside and under the control of the employee rather than by factors outside the employee's control is an example of the **fundamental attribution error**. Managers are just as susceptible to making this error as anyone else in the organization. This tendency illustrates how a manager's belief about employees plays an important role in shaping managerial behavior toward employees. To this we turn next.

Assumptions About Human Nature

When we study motivation, it is natural to think about what we believe to be true regarding human beings. We might even say that business as a whole depends on our assumptions regarding humans and what we expect they will do.[67] Exhibit 11-9 describes some of the assumptions that we make as we begin this study of human motivation in the workplace.

If you lined up 10 workers in a room, how many of them would you predict to be ambitious, eager to work, altruistic, and interested in assuming responsibility? How might your prediction affect how you manage?

Consider three contrasting sets of assumptions about human nature and how these can affect three traditional approaches to increasing worker motivation. First, if managers assume that workers who are satisfied will show higher performance, then managers will attempt to provide good working conditions, fair wages, and job security. Managers will treat workers with respect and show concern for their problems. Some scholars call this *paternalism*. Second, if managers assume that workers are motivated to high performance based on the rewards and punishments they receive, then managers will carefully control the working environment, offer wage incentives, and threaten punishments for unacceptable performance. This approach was used extensively under *scientific management*. Third, if managers assume that workers do better when they have a say in how the work is done, then managers will attempt to improve motivation by avoiding autocratic decisions whenever possible and encouraging workers to *participate* in decision making. Exhibit 11-10 outlines the contrasts among these three traditional approaches to motivation.

- Humans are conscious beings. Consciousness is at the root of all values, thoughts, and feelings.
- Humans are social beings. They desire to work in association with others or are willing to engage in social interaction to accomplish their goals.
- Human thought processes, perceptions, emotions, physical sensations, and personality traits form an integrated whole that cannot be separated from an individual's experience with the social environment.
- Humans have physical, psychological, and social needs. Human behavior choices at work are made, in part, in response to these needs.
- Each human has a variety of skills or talents that can be applied to work situations. Generally, humans prefer to use some or all of this variety.
- Human values, beliefs, perceptions, and personality traits contribute to a person's desire to work toward a high level of performance.
- Humans exhibit individual differences in terms of personality, preferences, values, and needs.
- Humans have strong drives to behave in moral ways. However, humans also fail in living up to their moral standards. They behave immorally.
- Humans have and use the ability to anticipate the future. They use this to set goals, plan, and order their actions accordingly.
- Human beings strive for equity in their work relationships.
- Humans who are rewarded will shape their behavior so as to maximize the promised rewards. We sometimes refer to this tendency as "gaming the system."
- Humans usually exhibit consistency between their values and their behaviors. However, they can also exhibit inconsistency.
- Humans exhibit contradictory behaviors. At times they seem to have a strong interest in work and high performance. At other times they seem to dislike work and want to avoid it. At times they demonstrate a wonderful capacity for altruism. Without being asked they will help each other. At other times they are destructively selfish.

EXHIBIT 11-9

Assumptions Regarding Human Nature and Work

EXHIBIT 11-10

Three Traditional Approaches to Motivation Contrasted[68]

Approach	Paternalism	Scientific Management	Worker Participation
Assumption	**Satisfaction causes good performance:** Workers will respond with gratitude, loyalty, and hard work if they are satisfied at work.	**Rewards and punishments cause good performance:** Workers will respond to rewards and will try to avoid punishments.	**Increased power causes good performance:** Workers will respond better if they participate in deciding the things that affect their work.
Principle	Treat all workers equally.	Base rewards on individual performance.	Equalize decision-making power in the organization.
What Managers Do	Treat all workers with the same degree of respect, show equal concern for their needs, provide good working conditions for all, and offer fair wages to all.	Offer extrinsic incentives based on performance: status symbols and supervisor verbal approval. Threaten punishment for low performance.	Avoid autocratic decisions. Allow workers opportunities to participate in the decisions that affect their work such as how work is performed, the design of their jobs, goal setting, and feedback.
Weaknesses	It has the least support from research and fails to deal with individual differences. Higher performers may become dissatisfied and exit, leaving mediocre performers behind.	It fails to explain how jobs can intrinsically motivate and ignores individual and situational differences. (Some people do not value extrinsic rewards as highly as other people.)	It fails to account for why extrinsic rewards influence motivation and for why not everyone responds in the same way to the opportunity to participate in decision-making.

Personality Traits, Attitudes, Beliefs, and Values

Of all the influences on motivation and performance what influence does a person's personality have? Are there some personality traits that lead to higher levels of motivation at work? **Personality traits** are the clusters of habitual patterns of thinking, behavior, and attitudes. Some scholars believe that some personality traits do influence what job characteristics a person prefers, what behaviors a person chooses, what types of people a person tends to interact with at work, how much effort the person gives for job activities, and how persistent the person is in such actions.[69]

For example, if a work situation offers an opportunity for employees to express their personality traits that are valued by coworkers and managers, then those employees are likely to be motivated to work toward high performance. Also, the more a job allows employees to be autonomous in their work, the more likely a person's personality will predict effective performance.

An example of a cluster of personality traits that has been studied in terms of job performance is what is known as the **Big Five personality dimensions.**[70] These five dimensions have become good predictors of job performance. They are:

1. *extroversion* (sociable, outgoing, talkative, active, ambitious)
2. *emotional stability–instability* (anxious, depressed, embarrassed, insecure)
3. *agreeableness* (likeable, good-natured, cooperative, forgiving, tolerant)
4. *conscientiousness* (careful, thorough, dependable, organized, hard-working, achievement-oriented, persevering)
5. *openness to experience* (imaginative, cultured, curious, broad-minded, intelligent)

The personality traits of conscientiousness and emotional stability may be good predictors of behavior across more than one job situation. Extroversion is a valid predictor of strong performance for managers and sales personnel.

Attitudes and the beliefs on which they are founded are long-lasting positive or negative thoughts and feelings a person has toward something such as a work task.[71] Although attitudes are relatively stable, they are influenced by the social situation, which might change as circumstances change.

Beliefs are the mental acceptance of the truthfulness of certain propositions about work. Beliefs involve estimating the probability that a work task or situation will be consistent with the perception of one or more attributes of the work. For example, beliefs regarding the task of taking out the garbage, depending on the situation, may involve a perception that the smell of garbage is distasteful. Thinking about taking out the garbage will likely involve making a judgment of how smelly the garbage will likely be on this trip to the dumpster.

For many work situations there are probably many types of beliefs that, when combined, form attitudes about the work. Beliefs can come from personal experience at the particular tasks, from merely thinking logically about the work based on general knowledge and experience, or from trusted outside information sources.

Values are the standards that a person holds that satisfy underlying needs and that guide behaviors and serve as the basis for making choices.[72] The assumption regarding values is that humans will make choices to pursue things, activities, and situations through work-related behaviors that are believed to result in the outcomes they value. Some values, called **terminal values,** are the ultimate, end result that is prized. Other values represent the means of achieving a goal or end result—these are called *extrinsic* or **instrumental values.**[73] Exhibit 11-11 provides examples of terminal and instrumental values.

EXHIBIT 11-11
Terminal and Instrumental Values

Terminal Values	Instrumental Values
A comfortable life	Capability
Sense of accomplishment	Persistence
Social acceptance	Love
Inner peace	Honesty
Financial security	Ambition

The connection among values, beliefs, attitudes, and motivation is that values act as the compass guiding the decisions to pursue outcomes through particular actions. Beliefs form the basis for thoughts and feelings toward an action or situation. Attitudes influence our intention to act. They also influence how we believe we should fulfill the action. For example, a so-called negative attitude toward a work task such as preparing a monthly expense reports may reduce the intention to fulfill that task as well as the effort put forward when completing it. One person completing such a disfavored task might take longer than they otherwise might if they favored it. Another person might attempt to complete the task in the shortest amount of time and, in the process, be willing to sacrifice quality of performance in order to be done with it quickly. Still another person might feel the same aversion toward preparing the report but hold an attitude of no matter how difficult or distasteful the action, it should be performed as well as possible.

Attitudes are comprised of three dimensions or components. The *cognitive* component is the thought process that a person has regarding an object or an action. The cognitive component can involve comparing observed reality against your expectation. The *affective* component is the emotional reaction the person has when thinking about an object or action. The *behavioral* component is either the intention to act or the actions that come from the cognitive processes and the emotional reaction to these. You may be able to see elements of the Management Pyramid model used in this book in these three components. Exhibit 11-12 describes the three components of attitudes.

Theories of Motivation

In addition to the influences that personality, values, and attitudes have on motivation and performance, there are other influences, too. Some managers and scholars who realize that motivation is not just a matter of common sense have developed different explanations for how motivation works. We call these simply *motivation theories*. Each theory has offered an intriguing perspective on motivation that has captured the attention of both practicing managers and motivation researchers alike. We begin with something called "Theory X, Theory Y," which is really an explanation about managers rather than their employees.

Theory X, Theory Y

Many managers consider workers, by nature, to be uninterested in taking responsibility, selfish, not too eager to work, and lacking in ambition. To deal with such workers, these managers have resorted to rewards and punishments to prod them into working when they would otherwise not work. Using observational research, Douglas McGregor, an industrial psychologist, professor of psychology, and management consultant, observed this type of manager. These managers were aloof, arrogant, and intolerant of subordinates. They closely monitored workers' performance. They displayed short tempers. They shouted at workers. They didn't ask; they demanded. If workers did not respond as the manager desired, then they withheld rewards. These managers

EXHIBIT 11-12
Three Components of Attitudes

	Attitude Component		
	Cognitive	**Affective**	**Behavioral**
Example 1	"That report is incomplete."	"I get frustrated when reading incomplete reports."	"Before I read the next report from that employee, I'm going to give it back if it is incomplete."
Example 2	"The boss is 15 minutes late for my appointment again."	"I feel disrespected when the boss is late and doesn't bother to let me know."	"Next time I go to the boss's office for my appointment, I'll call ahead to make sure he is on schedule."
Example 3	"The employee took initiative to solve the problem."	"I feel relieved and happy when employees take initiative."	"I give verbal recognition to employees who take initiative."

acted as if the employees would do nothing significant unless the manager demanded it. This becomes a self-fulfilling prophecy as in return workers resist, resent, and retreat from responsibility. The vicious cycle continues. McGregor believed that over the centuries workers had become like this not because they were lazy by nature but because of how they had been treated by managers.

McGregor, more than most other scholars, raised awareness that what managers assume about human nature shapes their behavior toward workers. From his observations he identified two general patterns of assumptions, which he called Theory X and Theory Y. **Theory X** is the traditional, more common way of viewing employees as, by nature, lacking ambition, the eagerness to work, and the desire for responsibility, as described in the preceding paragraph. **Theory Y** is the pattern in which managers believe that employees are ambitious, eager to work, and interested in assuming responsibility. McGregor observed that managers who held to this belief treated their employees with respect. They allowed employees to participate in decisions that affected their work. They acted as if employees accepted responsibility and wanted to perform at a high level.

McGregor believed that if managers would change their assumptions to align with Theory Y, then they would start treating workers differently. This change would bring about a new positive self-fulfilling prophecy and virtuous cycle. The different way of managing would result in employees exhibiting self-control and initiative. They would welcome responsibility. They would be eager to achieve the goals of the organization.

Many who have followed McGregor agree with his conclusion that Theory Y should be used more often than Theory X. For example, management guru Peter Drucker commented that when a manager employs Theory X assumptions he or she corrupts employees.[74] Others have said that sometimes the manager has no choice but to act in ways that are based on Theory X assumptions. Others believe that if managers are able to more closely align the organization's interests with the individual employee's interest, then they can depend on Theory Y assumptions more frequently.[75]

McGregor offered little data to back up his recommendation. In his model, Theory X and Theory Y seem to be mutually exclusive. However, in practice it may be more difficult to generate positive results with Theory Y behavior than with Theory X. Practicing managers have come to understand that *participative management*, in which workers participate in decision making, is more complex than McGregor realized. Also, we have come to understand that the reality of work situations cannot be placed into just two categories. The human experience may be a mixture of both Theory X and Theory Y. See The Christian Mind on Theory X, Theory Y.

The Christian Mind on Theory X, Theory Y

The Christian meta-narrative of Creation→Fall→Redemption→Consummation provides an insightful framework relative to McGregor's theory.

Creation . . . God created all things good. God's original design is for all employees to be completely Theory Y in their behavior. As Christian managers, we must affirm this original design.

Fall . . . all things have fallen from their original goodness. God's original design has been attacked by sin. In our fallen world, all employees are partly Theory X in their behavior. As Christian managers, we must acknowledge this reality.

Redemption . . . God has redeemed all things through Jesus Christ. God's original design for employees to be completely Theory Y in their behavior has been reaffirmed. Yet sin and Theory X employee behavior still abound as God's work of making all things new continues. In short, God's world is already redeemed, but doesn't yet fully reflect that ultimate reality. As Christian managers and God's agents of renewal, we must foster Theory Y employee behavior as God's original and reaffirmed design while contending with ongoing employee sin.

Consummation . . . Jesus Christ will return and establish the fully consummated kingdom wherein all employees will be completely Theory Y in their behavior. As Christian managers, we will delight and prosper in this reality forever.

Dr. Scott Quatro
Associate Professor of Management
Covenant College
Lookout Mountain, GA

For example, consider Premier, Inc., a healthcare alliance owned by 200 nonprofit hospitals and health system organizations.[76] The alliance offers group purchasing and supply chain management services and insurance and risk management services to its owners. Premier's managers use a four-step employee performance management system. It begins by leaders communicating expectations to employees. These expectations are based on the assumptions that employees will respond with high performance. Managers also provide employees with ongoing feedback, coaching, and, when necessary, redirection to encourage continued performance. Here a clear assumption is that sometimes workers need direction. During annual performance reviews managers complete formal evaluations and discuss with employees both their strengths and opportunities for improvement. Premier uses an incentive pay system to attempt to keep employee goals aligned with the company goals.

In spite of the weaknesses in McGregor's model, practicing managers and scholars saw truth in McGregor's teaching about assumptions. Even today there is an implicit belief by many that what managers assume to be true about workers will influence their beliefs about motivation as well as their managerial behaviors.

Another belief that became popular in the 1950s and 1960s and has continued since then is the notion that human beings have needs. Our work behaviors are, in part, an attempt to satisfy those needs. McGregor developed his ideas, in part, based on this idea of needs. To this we turn next.

Physiological, Psychological, and Social Needs

You may have heard the saying, "Some people work to live and other people live to work." This statement reflects the fundamental influence that needs have on work behavior as well as some of the differences in people's needs. Some are focused on working to get their paycheck so they can pay the rent and buy food and clothing. The need to generate economic value from our work doesn't go away. Once we are able to satisfy our economic needs, other needs become important, such as the need to enjoy the inherent value from work itself. The point of this section is that when we talk about motivation to work, we must include the role that satisfaction of human needs plays.[77]

Managers should be aware of several interesting things regarding human needs. Some needs pull us favorably toward some behaviors while other needs lead us to avoid other behaviors. Needs may be conscious or unconscious. Needs guide our perceptions. For example, the hunger need increases the attentiveness toward the clock and toward proximity to food. If we are hungry, we may likely delay a business meeting with someone until after we eat lunch, or we may organize our daily routine to have lunch with the person. Either way the need for food has an organizing influence on our behavior.

Some needs are more intense than others. We experience some needs as momentary forces on our behavior while other needs influence us over a longer time. Emotions are important indicators of need. Managers who become skilled at understanding human emotion may be more adept at understanding their employees' needs. Another interesting thing about needs is that they cannot be observed directly. We can only infer what needs are present when we observe human behaviors. We often take experiences of our own needs to draw conclusions about the needs that people around us must be experiencing. The problem is that humans are all different. Personal experience may not be a valid basis for predicting the behaviors or motivations of those around you.[78]

More than most others in the field of management, American psychologist Abraham Maslow has raised awareness of the importance of needs in work motivation.[79] Maslow, who studied psychology at the University of Wisconsin, claimed that his model was not perfect and that others would build on his observations.[80]

From his observations of individuals who were struggling to cope with the Great Depression of the 1930s, Maslow detected five categories of human needs. He believed that these needs were some (but not all) of the forces that determine human behavior: physiological needs, safety needs, social needs, esteem needs, and self-actualization needs. We will explore each in turn.

Physiological needs are the most basic human needs, such as food and sleep. When these needs are deprived they become more intense. But when these needs are satisfied other higher needs emerge that influence behavior. In Maslow's model need gratification is as important as need deprivation because it sets the person free from the domination of the need. Satisfaction of need permits the emergence of other needs that are social in nature. When the physiological needs are continuously gratified, they cease to be active determinants of behavior. However, the potential that these needs will emerge again is always present. See Exhibit 11-13.

Safety needs, the need for protection, shelter, warmth, security from assault, and psychological safety such as freedom from fear, emerge when the physiological needs are met. Maslow included the need to organize our perceptions of the universe into a coherent and meaningful

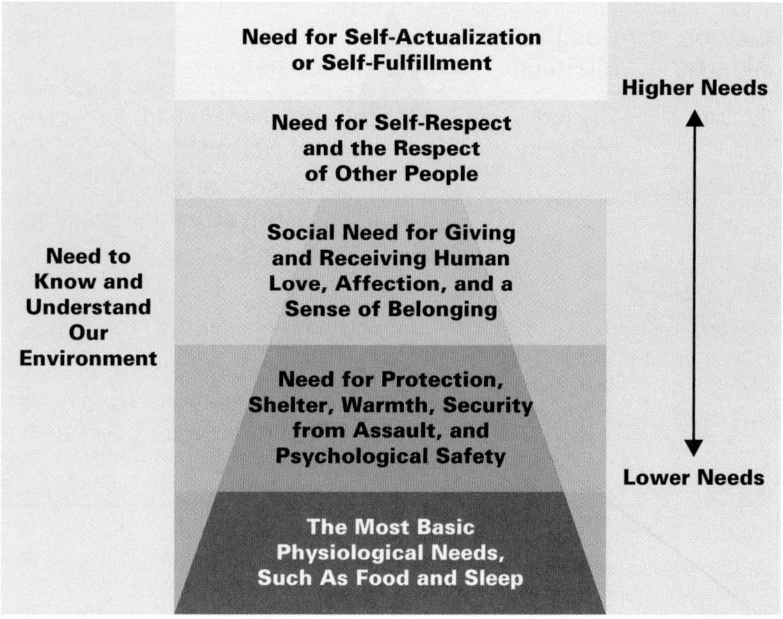

EXHIBIT 11-13

Maslow's Scheme of Higher and Lower Needs

Note: This scheme is typically called "Maslow's Hierarchy of Needs." Typical illustrations of Maslow's scheme include only five categories of needs arranged in the form of a triangle; however, originally he proposed six categories as shown in this exhibit but he did not provide a drawing.

Source: Maslow, Abraham H.; Frager, Robert D. (Editor); Fadiman, James (Editor), *Motivation and Personality, 3rd,* © 1987. Printed and electronically reproduced by permission of Pearson Education, Inc., Upper Saddle River, NJ.

whole as an expression of one of the safety needs. Participating in organized religion is one way humans satisfy this need. When safety needs are continually satisfied they, too, cease to be strong determinants of behavior.

In addition to the two categories of lower-level physiological and security needs, Maslow saw three categories of higher-level social needs. The **social need** for giving and receiving human love, affection, and a sense of belonging will emerge as both the physiological and safety needs are well satisfied. Maslow believed that deprivation of love is the fundamental reason why humans experience problems of maladjustment and mental illness.

Everyone has **esteem needs** for self-respect and the respect of other people. This category of needs includes the needs for achievement, social respect from others, social reputation, the need for confidence to face the world, and the need for independence and freedom. Satisfying these needs leads to self-confidence, self-worth, and strength while deprivation of these needs leads to the feeling of inferiority, weakness, and a sense of helplessness.

The need for **self-actualization** or self-fulfillment is a universal human need. We all want to live up to our personal potential in society. In Maslow's model this is the highest level of social need that humans experience.

In addition to these five sets of needs, Maslow also saw another category of needs related to the desire to know and understand our environment. From this need flows the motivations of curiosity, learning, scientific research, and the development of philosophical explanations for what and how we know. Human beings have a tendency toward gathering information, organizing it, analyzing it, and then looking for relationships and meaning in the information.

While some have incorrectly interpreted Maslow's model of needs as a fixed or rigid hierarchy, Maslow warned against this. It may be true that the physiological needs must be met before the social needs emerge as dominant. However, we should not conclude that the love need must be met before esteem needs emerge. For example, for some people the need for esteem is more dominant than the need for love.

Following Maslow's work, Clayton Alderfer, also an American psychologist, grouped human needs into three broad categories.[81] Alderfer's three categories, known as ERG, are needs for existence, social relatedness, and growth in the ability to master one's environment. This last category includes the idea of self-actualization but also the other needs that Maslow observed such as the need to know and understand. Maslow taught that the higher-level needs of esteem and self-actualization are present but are less dominant while a person is attempting to satisfy the lower-level needs. Unlike Maslow's model, Alderfer's model does require that lower-level needs be satisfied before the higher-level needs emerge.

As popular as the hierarchy of needs has been over the years, many scholars have criticized it. Maslow himself saw the limitations of his own theory. One problem is that Maslow's model has been misunderstood and often oversimplified. Another criticism is that it is difficult to use

	Abraham Maslow	Clayton Alderfer	Douglas McGregor	Frederick Herzberg
	Self-actualization and reaching full potential	Growth	The focus of Theory Y	The **Abraham** View: Humans were created in the Image of God and have innate potential.
Knowing and understanding	Esteem and social respect	Relatedness		Factors that meet social needs related to our work are **Motivators** that promote job satisfaction.
	Love and belonging			
	Safety and security			The **Adam** View: Because of sin, humans must work hard to avoid suffering.
	Physiological	Existence	The focus of Theory X	Factors that meet needs related to basic survival are **Hygiene Factors**, which prevent job dissatisfaction.

EXHIBIT 11-14
Needs Models Compared

Maslow's model to accurately predict human behavior. We need behaviors as evidence of needs, but the behaviors are the only things we can measure. This makes the job of research on needs difficult to accomplish. Maslow used his own perceptions to identify subjects who were at the self-actualization stage.[82] In addition to these criticisms, the whole idea of categories of need that drive work behaviors has been criticized.[83] Another concern is that attempts to validate Maslow's hierarchy with empirical research have proved inconclusive.[84]

Some Christian scholars consider Maslow's model invalid because in their mind his model proposes that self-actualization can be achieved without a relationship with God. To them, his theory would make more sense if it were explained in the context of the creation–fall–redemption–consummation story of the Gospel.[85]

Herzberg's Two-Factor Theory

Frederick Herzberg, another influential American psychologist, and his colleagues developed another approach to explain motivation to work that is also based on the idea of human needs.[86] Herzberg, trained in clinical psychology, viewed his theory from his assumption that all humans have two sets of needs: needs for human survival and social needs related to our work. Herzberg linked needs for survival to his belief in the human situation that results from sin, which he called *the Adam view*. Because of sin, humans must work hard to avoid the suffering that results from basic survival. Herzberg linked social needs to the innate human potential that results from being created in the image of God, which he called *the Abraham view*.[87] According to Herzberg, one of the responsibilities of the organization is to provide for the two sets of needs of humans. Exhibit 11-14 compares the needs models of Maslow, Alderfer, McGregor, and Herzberg.

Herzberg's theory is sometimes called the motivation-hygiene theory or the **two-factor theory**. Whether these two sets of needs are met or not met can result in satisfaction or dissatisfaction in the work environment. Herzberg believed that a fundamental difference exists between the things that cause positive job attitudes, which he labeled *job satisfaction*, and the factors that cause negative attitudes toward work, which he labeled *job dissatisfaction*. In other words, to Herzberg job satisfaction is not the opposite of job dissatisfaction as different factors influence each. Another way to see his distinction is that the opposite of dissatisfaction is not satisfaction but rather simply the lack of dissatisfaction. Also, an employee might be satisfied about some elements related to work and yet at the same time dissatisfied about other elements related to work. See Exhibit 11-15.

The researchers interviewed hundreds of engineers and accountants asking them to think of times during their work when they felt "exceptionally good" and "exceptionally bad" about their jobs. Data from the interviews were broken down into 500 separate ideas. The researchers then categorized these items into 16 groups that Herzberg called factors. They looked to see which factors were linked with good memories of their jobs and which were linked with bad memories of their jobs. They found that factors related to memories of positive job satisfaction include the work itself, verbal recognition, achievement, more responsibility, and a promotion. They labeled these factors

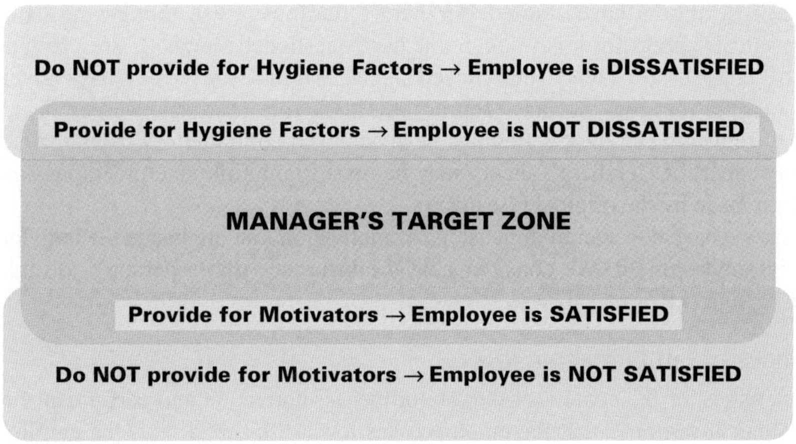

EXHIBIT 11-15
The Two-Factor Theory

Source: Based on Herzberg, F., Mausner, B., & Snyderman, B. B. (2008). *The motivation to work.* Piscataway, NJ: Transaction Publishers; Lawler III, E. E. (1994). *Motivation in work organizations.* San Francisco, CA: Jossey-Bass. p. 90.

satisfaction **motivators**. When these factors are present, employees experience positive feelings toward their jobs and improved performance. Some of these factors, such as verbal recognition and achievement, have a short-term effect on employees and need to be repeated to reproduce the effect.

Researchers found that factors related to memories of job dissatisfaction include company policies, the quality of supervisory skill, a worker's interpersonal relationship with the supervisor, the physical working conditions, job security, and wages and benefits. They labeled these factors **hygiene factors** because they are needed to create a minimum level of satisfaction and job performance. When hygiene factors are lacking or inadequate, workers tend to become dissatisfied. When these factors are present, dissatisfaction is removed and performance improves but only up to a point. However, these factors cannot be relied on to create job satisfaction. Only motivators can do that. See Exhibit 11-16.

In the study, some factors believed to be motivating, such as recognition and opportunities for advancement, actually increased frustration in workers who expressed job dissatisfaction. When recognition is not given to the degree that some employees believe it should be given, it can add to dissatisfaction. Also, when opportunities for career advancement through promotion do not come up very often, it can add to dissatisfaction.

In a follow-up to this initial study, Herzberg and his fellow researchers found that compensation is primarily a hygiene factor. However, money can become a symbol for social recognition or social status, and because of this, it can also be a motivator.

Herzberg recommended that to achieve a basic level of performance, managers should provide for hygiene factors. To achieve higher levels of performance, managers should use motivators. One of the best ways a manager can do this is by enriching workers' jobs where possible by introducing motivators—especially the intrinsic rewards that come from the work itself. Managers should see that the work itself provides direct feedback to employees regarding their performance and their improvement. Linking the employee closer to the customer will give the employee a higher level of purpose. Allowing employees to choose the manner in which they perform their work and increasing their responsibility also promotes higher motivation for higher performance.

	When Motivating Factors Are Present:	**When Motivating Factors Are Missing:**
When **Hygiene Factors** Are Present:	The **best** situation: The employee is not unhappy (hygiene factors are present) but also is happy (motivators are present).	Managers need to provide job enrichment: The employee is not unhappy (hygiene factors are present) but also not very happy (motivators are missing).
When **Hygiene Factors** Are Missing:	Managers need to provide for basic needs: The employee is unhappy (hygiene factors are missing) and happy (motivators are present).	The **worst** situation: The employee is both unhappy (hygiene factors are missing) and lacking happiness (motivators are missing).

EXHIBIT 11-16
Motivating and Hygiene Factors[88]

Several researchers have studied Herzberg's findings. Even though the theory is still popular, practical support for it is weak. Some have questioned Herzberg's research methods as being highly subjective. Those interviewed in the original study may have given socially desirable answers that may not have represented their true attitudes. Researchers who have attempted to replicate Herzberg's findings have achieved contradictory results. Also, the data gathered in support of Herzberg's theory may be open to multiple interpretations—not just the interpretation made by the original researchers.

Thus far we have considered dimensions of motivation that are inside the individual person or the social environment. We consider next the influence that a person's job itself has on motivation to high performance.

The Influence of Job Characteristics

Job characteristics, or the content of the job, influence motivation and performance because of the psychological response that the employee has toward the work.[89] If the employee feels a sense of responsibility for the results of the work, if the employee believes that the work matters, and if the employee knows that he or she is being effective in performing the work, then motivation and performance will increase. These three factors have come to be known as the **Job Characteristics Model (JCM)**. The basic ideas of this model are consistent with the recommendations of Frederick Herzberg, which we reviewed earlier.

Jobs that allow for increased worker autonomy in terms of learning, improvement, performance, and satisfaction, without compromising the need for interaction with other employees, will result in higher performance. **Autonomy** is the degree to which the job provides freedom, independence, or discretion. Generally, humans do not appreciate being micromanaged, that is, being told every detail of what do to, how to do their work, when to do it, and where to do it. Increased autonomy enhances the worker's sense of responsibility for results. In turn, this improves job satisfaction. Exhibit 11-17.

Meaning from work derives from the variety of skills required at work, known as **task variety**. More variety leads to increased sense of meaning. Meaning also derives from **task identity**, which is the degree to which the job requires completion of a process from beginning to end. If the worker is responsible for only a small portion of the entire job, this decreases motivation and performance. It also may result in a sense of alienation. Human beings prefer to work at jobs in which they can understand the whole of the work and how their particular part contributes to the whole. Finally, meaning derives from **task significance**, which is the perception of the employee that what the employee is doing makes a difference for other human beings.

When the worker gets immediate *feedback* from the work process regarding the results, this can have a positive effect on motivation and performance. **Feedback** is information about work performance that comes to the worker. The feedback that helps workers know the results of their work might be in the form of information observed from indicators on machines, or it might be immediate feedback from a supervisor or other workers. For example, a worker at a chemical processing plant will observe temperature, volume, or pressure gauges, as well as other devices that indicate whether the process is operating within the desired parameters. Feedback provides cues that workers use to judge the likelihood that desired performance is achievable. It also helps

EXHIBIT 11-17
Job Characteristics that Influence Motivation

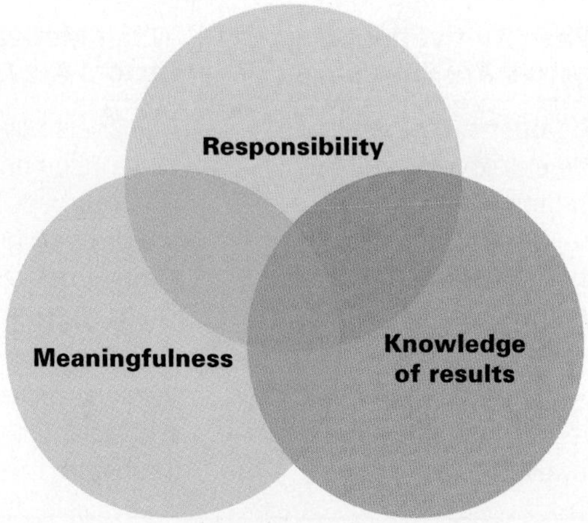

workers improve for the future. Workers attempt to perform at a level that is consistent with their beliefs regarding their abilities. If workers are assigned a job for which they believe they have strong capabilities, then they will strive for high performance.

If job characteristics have an influence on motivation and performance, then it is natural to think about the manager's role in making adjustments to the job so that employees have a higher motivation and performance. This is known as **job enrichment** or *job design*.[90]

Job enrichment is based on the assumption that jobs should be complex, challenging, and interesting. For example, if an employee's job can be made more interesting by creating increased task variety, then workers will respond with higher performance. This is easier said than done, however. If the increase in task variety is not relevant to the set of skills of the employee, then such a change might decrease performance. It is difficult to predict in advance whether a particular employee will find the adjustment interesting or not. Another approach is to have employees change jobs temporarily. Experts believe that a change in job can provide employees with a richer understanding of the significance of their work. As employees experience other important tasks, they will better understand how their job contributes to the organization as a whole.

Job enrichment can be difficult to implement. What is enrichment to the manager may not be enrichment to the subordinate. Further, some employees will perceive job enrichment as simply a means to get employees to do more work without corresponding compensation.

Participation

Organizations have a long history of preserving the hierarchical authority structure between supervisors and subordinates. This differentiation in decision-making authority emphasizes more participation in decisions by supervisors and proportionately less by subordinates. Because of this, the discussion on participation usually focuses on how decision-making authority is shared. Depending on the situation and whether the person is a supervisor or nonsupervisor, participation can take many forms. Exhibit 11-18 describes some of the forms of participation by subordinates.

Some Christian scholars so clearly believe in the importance of sharing participation with subordinates that they call this a commonsense truth.[91] Others believe that organizations are gradually becoming more democratic, and in this process participation by subordinates will be required more in the future than was done in the past.[92] As a practicing manager, you will understand what this means. But is this common sense confirmed by research? Do projections about the future have any basis from the research conducted in the past?

Consider the following results of decades of study. First, when workers believe that they can achieve their work goals, they are motivated toward high performance. By participating in decision making on the details related to job tasks, workers develop expectations regarding how achievable the goals are. Participation also increases their commitment to the goals.[93] Second,

EXHIBIT 11-18
The Many Faces of Participation by Subordinates

Making suggestions to supervisors	Making decisions regarding job design that improve the meaningfulness of tasks and increase the autonomy of workers
Participation in quality improvement teams	Giving feedback to upper management through opinion surveys
Being a member of a committee that affects the organization-wide decisions	Obtaining information about the organization from supervisors
Sharing knowledge with each other and with supervisors	Involvement in employee forums
Analyzing a work situation and giving recommendations to the supervisor	Making decisions regarding work processes and systems
Clarifying initial thinking by senior-level leaders regarding products and markets	Communicating the vision and strategy of the organization to other employees
Testing the viability of senior-level leaders' ideas	Helping frontline employees to relate their jobs to the overall strategic direction of the firm

EXHIBIT 11-19
Inputs and Outcomes[94]

Inputs	Outcomes
Education	Pay
Experience	Social status
Skills	Intrinsic rewards of work
Work effort	Working conditions
Collegiality	Job "perks"

some researchers have concluded that productivity increases when workers participate in decision making. Other researchers see less of a direct effect on performance but a significant effect on employee satisfaction. The reason for the differences in research outcomes may be due to other factors in the work situation such as an employee's desire for autonomy, the manager's attitudes toward subordinate participation, and differences in national culture.[95] Third, workers who participate develop a sense of accomplishment and healthy pride in completing important tasks.[96] Fourth, the quality of planning improves when the people who are going to do the work participate in the planning. One reason for this is that participating workers are less resistant to change.[97] Fifth, workers will develop increased motivation to take responsibility if they and managers share the same vision for the organization. Participation helps them develop this vision.[98]

Equity and Fairness

In many nations, the idea of fairness is fundamental to society. When one person is treated unfairly compared to how others are treated, it can result in a social problem. This same principle of justice is at work in organizations, too. "Few things kill an individual's motivation faster than the feeling that someone else is getting a better deal."[99] In other words, when there is perceived inequity, an employee's motivation will likely decrease.

Workers evaluate what they put into or bring to their jobs (inputs) with what they receive from their job (outcomes).[100] See Exhibit 11-19.

Workers must perceive the attributes of inputs that they bring to a job situation as relevant to that situation. Likewise, workers must believe that the outcomes are relevant for the type of work done or the type of position they are in. We can illustrate the relationship between outcomes (O) and inputs (I) using the math ratio of O ÷ I. This is sometimes called *the equity ratio*. See Exhibit 11-20.

For example, according to this theory, a secretary may really enjoy the work she does for the company. It is natural that eventually she will compare her own experience with what she believes that other secretaries experience in her organization. She may compare her situation with the situation for a secretary in another company.

As long as the secretary believes that what she is getting is fair for what she is putting into her job, she will continue to be motivated toward positive performance. If she begins to believe that she is getting more for her inputs than others might be getting, she is unlikely to complain. But when the employee senses that there is unfairness, she will begin to feel uncomfortable. At this point she will have several options available. Some inputs, such as education and experience, cannot be immediately changed. She can take classes or seminars, which will add to her skills or help her obtain certifications for new skills, but this takes time. In the meantime she might choose to lower some inputs such as work effort or the quality of her work.

This person can attempt to change outcomes such as her pay by asking for a raise. She also might be able to change how she thinks about the differences between her own experience and that of others. But assuming that relevant inputs, outcomes, and reference points are used, this might be difficult to accomplish.

EXHIBIT 11-20
Equity Theory

The Equity Question:

Do workers' perception of their $\text{experience}_{(1)}$ = their perception of the experience of someone $\text{else}_{(2)}$? In other words, does:

$$O_1 \div I_1 = O_2 \div I_2?$$

If not, then a perceived inequity exits.

Another option is to change the reference point by comparing herself with someone else. For example, instead of comparing her experience with that of a secretary in a much larger company, she might choose to compare it with a secretary in a similar sized or similar type of organization. Failing to rectify a situation that she perceives to be unfair, her last resort is to terminate her employment and seek an employment situation where equity is restored.

Fairness is in the eye of the beholder. Workers compare their own experience with their perception of what other relevant people achieve for their inputs. Workers might not view their situation in the same way that their supervisor views it. And, when two people view each other's situation, each might believe that an inequity exists. Managers can unwittingly cause feelings of inequity by how they provide outcomes for employees. They will be liked by some employees and disliked by other employees.[101]

PRO-TEC Coating Company, mentioned earlier in the chapter, provides an example of how a company can manage fairness. PRO-TEC was a 2007 winner of the prestigious Malcolm Baldrige National Quality Award Program. PRO-TEC's managers intentionally engage the organizational culture to teach the three qualities of ownership, responsibility, and accountability for all employees. To support high performance among the workers, each worker has goals specific to their position. High performers receive opportunities for ongoing development and improvement. Employees' needs and desires for learning are assessed. Managers develop a specific training plan for each associate. Associates are offered task-specific training to help them improve their job performance. They also have access to one-on-one mentoring from more experienced employees. A salary progression system rewards performance that meets above-average expectations. High-performing associates also receive verbal recognition. Low-performing employees receive a corrective performance development plan. With this person-specific plan, managers can handle perceptions of inequality by focusing on the goals, performance, and the resources that have been committed by both the employee and the organization.

The Christian Mind on Equity Theory

It seems natural for workers to compare themselves with others. When that occurs in the workplace, it often boils down to pay. God's Word in I Timothy 5:18 speaks to fair and equitable wages for work productivity and skill set, so this issue has been a concern since biblical times. When one takes into account the words of Christ in Luke 6:31, it is important to note that he admonished everyone to treat others as they want to be treated. Those with a Christian worldview understand that equity doesn't need to be legislated, because the Bible instructs one to be fair and honest in all dealings. We should be striving to create a workplace where all employees feel appreciated for the work they do and are paid sufficient wages for that labor. When that environment exists, employees need not be concerned about inequity.

Dr. Harriet Rojas
Indiana Wesleyan University
Marion, IN

Expectancy Theory

We have seen how motivation is directly linked with the way people think about themselves and their work situation. This cognitive activity has been the focus of much research on motivation. One part of cognitive activity that has been studied is the influence that expectations about a job and its outcomes have on the worker. The motivation theory that Victor Vroom, a professor of organization and management at Yale University, developed (and others later refined) around this idea is called **expectancy theory**.[102]

Expectancy theory begins with an assumption that humans at work freely make choices from among possible outcomes they can obtain from their work. Some outcomes are desired and others are not. This theory also assumes that there are multiple possible outcomes. Workers have expectations regarding how likely their effort will lead to intended job performance. They also have expectations regarding how likely certain outcomes will be realized from their job

EXHIBIT 11-21

Effort, Expected Job Performance, and Expected Outcomes

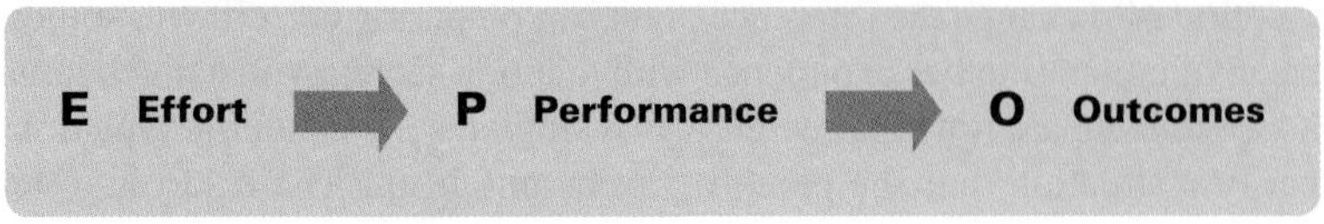

performance. The theory describes how workers will make choices for certain work-related actions over others based on their expectations and their preferences. The desirability of the expected outcomes and the strength of the expectation regarding the link between job performance and outcomes influence which outcomes the worker attempts to achieve. See Exhibit 11-21.

Several influences determine the expectations regarding the link between effort and job performance. Self-perception either increases or decreases the ability to see the link between effort and performance. Low self-esteem workers have more difficulty than high self-esteem workers in estimating their own abilities. But over time, all workers learn from experience how well they are performing and what outcomes are directly linked with job performance. They get information from other workers. The actual work situation itself also provides clues about their performance.

Similar influences determine workers' expectations regarding the link between job performance and desired outcomes. Workers learn by experience. They learn from other workers with credible experience. The actual situation may make the linkage explicit. The attractiveness of the outcomes also plays a part. A worker's personality also has an influence. For example, the employee who believes she can influence what happens, known as *internal control*, is more likely to be motivated to give effort because she sees the connection between her own effort, performance, and expected outcomes. In contrast, the employee who believes that he cannot influence what happens, known as *external control*, is less likely to be motivated to work hard for desired outcomes. Other influences are the organization policies and management practices.

An organization's reward system can influence worker expectations regarding the link between effort, performance, and desired outcomes.[103] Organizations use four general types of reward systems sometimes known as *merit-raise systems.* **Individual incentive plans** such as piece-rate pay systems pay workers based on the amount of output. Each worker receives a bonus based on performance. Individual incentives tend to encourage competition. Offering individual incentives for performance generally results in better performance.[104] **Group incentive plans** encourage cooperation as they pay workers based on the performance of the group. Group incentives such as bonuses tend to produce lower performance as the group size increases. The larger the group the more distant any individual's contribution becomes from the performance of the group. Compared with individual incentive plans, group incentives are likely to produce less motivation. **Organization-wide incentive plans** usually offer every member of the organization payment based on the overall performance of the organization. For example, one measurement of the overall performance is profitability. The larger the company, the more distant each individual's contribution is from the performance of the organization. A **combination incentive plan** seeks to gain some of the advantages of an individual incentive plan and the advantages of a group or organization-wide plan. One example of this is known as the Lincoln Electric Plan in which bonuses are paid based on the overall performance of the organization, but the amount the individual receives is based on the evaluation of that individual's performance either quantitatively or qualitatively estimated.

Incentive systems are not perfect. Each individual worker may value the incentive plan differently from other workers. Even within an individual worker there may be differences in how the person values certain incentives from situation to situation. In addition, several unintended consequences have been observed in organizations that use incentive systems. One problem with merit-raise systems is the subjectivity of measurement and political influences that can come to bear on the evaluation process. Sometimes it is difficult to measure the contribution of individual members. Sometimes the data used to calculate bonuses is not a valid measure of the type of performance desired for the organization. Another problem with individual incentive plans is that they can spark competition among members. In a sales organization this can work well, but in some other work settings this can become dysfunctional. Incentives tied to specific performance measures may result in other important performance measures becoming neglected.

Interpersonal influence is another area that can affect effort, performance, and outcomes. A worker's supervisor plays an important role in terms of interpersonal influence. It is the supervisor who has authority to implement incentive systems (an extrinsic reward) or redesign a worker's job (an intrinsic reward). Some workers are more influenced by the social relationships they have at work. They have a stronger need for autonomy than do other workers. Thus, when a supervisor focuses both on the needs of workers and on the needs of getting the job done, these workers have higher motivation from the social rewards they receive from their effort. When a democratic-styled supervisor allows such workers to participate in decision making, their performance tends to increase. In contrast, other workers may be influenced more by the tangible, extrinsic rewards from work. These workers will likely experience higher motivation under a relationship with a more authoritarian-styled supervisor who lays out a clear system of rewards based on measurable performance.

Coworkers also influence effort, performance, and outcomes. Coworkers provide feedback on worker performance. They provide some of the extrinsic and intrinsic rewards. For example, coworkers can praise each other for work well done. Their presence on the job and how pleasant it is to work with them is a form of intrinsic reward. Coworkers also affect how much autonomy a worker enjoys. Autonomy-seeking workers employed in a setting in which coworkers limit autonomy may experience decreased motivation.

Coworkers as a group have the ability to influence motivation through the group norms that develop at work because the group has some control over the outcomes that most people value. Coworkers reward certain behaviors with verbal praise. They also can punish workers who do not conform to group norms. The more cohesive a work group, the more influence it tends to have on motivation and performance. This does not mean that cohesiveness automatically creates higher performance. But when cohesiveness is coupled with a strong organizational goal orientation, higher performance is usually the result.

Job enrichment also has the potential for influencing the effort, performance, and outcome expectations. Job enrichment through cross-training can provide employees with a better understanding of the importance of their role as well as give them added skills with which to serve the organization. It also will likely improve efficiency in the organization by minimizing the need to hire temporary or full-time workers for certain tasks. For some employees jobs that offer a level of complexity that is challenging and jobs that are interesting have a positive influence on effort and outcomes. As discussed previously in this chapter, what is enrichment for one person may not be for another.

Goal Setting

Goals and goal setting are an important part of everyday life in both positive and negative ways. No other set of principles of motivation in organizations has been studied more or found to be more useful than goals. Check the last time a group you were a part of failed to achieve what it wanted: Were specific, measurable goals used?

Goals affect the information that a person pays attention to and acts on. Goals regulate behaviors. People use goals to monitor their current progress. Goals provide purpose. They shape the direction of a person's activities toward a goal. They affect whether a person works hard or slacks off to just get by. Goals encourage people to develop strategies that will help them complete tasks. Goals also affect whether a person stays with a task or stops when the going gets difficult.[105] When individual goals and group goals are well-matched, group performance is improved. The opposite also is true. If an individual worker's goals are too far out of alignment with the goals of the work team or the goals of the organization, then group performance is usually weakened.

Some goals represent personal preferences and desires. Other goals are set because the person believes certain actions are required. When a person is blocked by other persons from achieving a goal, conflict arises. "When two ore more people believe that their goals are competitively rather than cooperatively related, they are likely to be tempted to pursue their self-interest single-mindedly."[106]

Goal setting and intention to act on goals affect a person's motivation and performance at work. Goals that are too broadly defined, too vague, or too far removed from present activities have less of an influence on motivation and performance. Goals are effective when they are specific, closer in proximity to everyday work activities but directly related to longer-term goals, and set in a context of work that is constantly changing or uncertain.

Establishing challenging, yet attainable, goals has a positive effect on motivation and performance. Of course this assumes that the worker possesses the ability to perform the tasks. If the goal is too easy, able workers will slack off and perform at a lower level than they would if the goal was difficult to achieve. If the goal is too difficult and perceived as impossible to attain, then motivation and performance will decrease. For example, leaders at Cargill Corn Milling North America, based in Minneapolis, Minnesota, understand the importance of goal setting.[107] Cargill manufactures corn and sugar-based products for food, feed, and fermentation market segments. The annual business planning process deploys production plans to each product line and each work team. These plans are the basis for individual employee goals that Cargill managers call "Key Result Areas."

Employees are given the authority to create their own performance goals and development plans with guidance from their immediate supervisor. The supervisor's involvement in goal setting is vital so that the individual goals remain in alignment with the organization's goals. In addition, supervisors give each employee specific feedback on the Key Result Areas and how well these results align with the organization-wide leadership values of learning capacity, execution capacity, knowledge, and behaviors that reflect integrity, conviction, and courage. Performance feedback from supervisors is coupled with a well-developed compensation, recognition, reward, and incentive system to reinforce high performance. In addition, high-performing employees receive opportunities for additional skill-based cross training to enhance their ability to serve the organization in more than one job.

Feedback is an important element in the effectiveness of goals. If a goal is set but inadequate feedback is available to workers, they will find it difficult to judge to what degree they have progressed toward goal attainment. Feedback provides workers with a sense of achievement. Feedback of positive results brings recognition. Feedback of less-than-desired results indicates that the worker needs to step up effort or increase efficiency or effectiveness of current efforts. The more specific the feedback, the more likely the worker will attempt to adjust effort focused on achieving the desired level of performance. But this is not always the case. Task-focused workers will use feedback to channel their mental activity toward tasks. Ego-focused workers will use feedback to channel their mental activity toward themselves. Exhibit 11-22 provides a summary of the characteristics of effective goals.

Moral issues are present with respect to goal setting in the workplace.[108] When people sense that others will feel exploited as a result of attaining their goals, they are tempted to be deceptive. If goals are believed to be mutually beneficial, however, this reduces the risk that one person will attempt to exploit the other. Managers who are rewarded with bonuses or pay increases may be

EXHIBIT 11-22
How to Set Effective Goals

Using goals in the workplace can have a positive effect on performance. But to be effective, goals need to be:

- Specific and, where possible, measurable. Workers need to understand how the goal will be measured. However, goals that are too specific can blind some workers to other important interests.
- Challenging (assuming that workers have the ability to attain the goals).
- Time-related. Goals should have a short-term time horizon but also be linked with long-term objectives of the organization.
- Ranked, if there are multiple goals involved. This gives workers clarity in terms of the expected priorities. Without clear priorities, too many measurable goals can create conflicts among goals, trapping workers in difficult dilemmas. If priorities are clear, then workers will be able to pursue multiple goals effectively.
- Related to the work tasks at hand but directly related to the larger objectives of the work unit or organization.
- Clearly communicated with employees and supported by the immediate supervisor.
- Coupled with specific measurable feedback that emerges from the work tasks and that can be easily understood by employees. Feedback in the visual form of tables, charts, and graphs plotted over time are effective.
- Coupled with specific provisions for coordination of effort. In most organizations, goal achievement requires coordination of effort from more than one person or work unit. Goals cannot ignore these important integrating mechanisms.
- When possible, open to allowing workers to participate in setting work goals as long as the goals truly are challenging. But be aware that participation in setting goals may not have the same effect in all work settings or conditions. Participation may reduce the likelihood that conflicts will arise among competing goals.
- Modified only if workers lack ability or knowledge needed to achieve the goals.
- Balanced by attention to other duties such as living by high moral standards. Without moral standards, goal setting can easily degenerate into a mentality of "anything goes" to achieve the goals.

tempted to deceive their supervisors regarding how difficult it is to attain their goals. This form of cheating can be found in organizations that use extrinsic incentives. Also, some workers may be tempted to focus only on the specific goals that are measured and rewarded, ignoring other important dimensions of work tasks. Or they may be tempted to use shortcuts that reduce quality or deceive their supervisor, or engage in other immoral behavior when trying to attain difficult goals.

How to prevent or remedy cheating needs more study.[109] One way to minimize the tendency toward immoral behavior resulting from using specific, challenging goals may be for the supervisor to specify the moral expectations related to the goals and work behaviors. This will raise workers' awareness of the importance of morality. It also gives a clear signal regarding the expectations of the legitimate authority. And it will reduce the likelihood that workers will attempt to *compartmentalize* their morals. Compartmentalization means to have one set of moral values to use under certain circumstances and another, different set of values to follow under different circumstances. For example, under some circumstances an employee might believe that other people will not find out if he engages in unethical conduct. In other circumstances, the employee might believe that there is a risk that others will find out if he does something immoral. Another way to minimize the risks of immoral behavior may be to give employees a chance to participate in goal setting. Employees who participate may be more likely to think about the behaviors that will be needed to attain the goals. Supervisors and employees can exchange frank discussions of the expected behaviors.

Paradoxes of Worker Motivation

A few tension points exist for the manager who is interested in worker motivation.

COOPERATION AND COMPETITION. Cooperation and competition appear to be opposites.[110] Yet in experiments, researchers have found that both cooperation among workers and competition among workers improve performance. In some situations competition can stimulate higher performance and new ideas, but it can also breed actions that are destructive of the work that others contribute. Because both cooperation and competition require social interaction depending on the particular work situation, both can improve performance over that found with individuals working in isolation.

COLLABORATION PARADOX.[111] Managers sometimes approach the task of motivating employees in a logical, reasoned manner assuming that the worker is motivated by the same economic interests that managers view as important. But some of these approaches do not work out as well as they are intended. The reason is that the schemes that managers create to promote collaboration may actually get in the way of collaboration. The reason these managerial attempts fail is that the managers who devise the methods do not see the situation through the eyes of the workers. For example, the manager may decide to offer subordinates a free pizza dinner after work on Friday if the group meets the very high performance goal. Ordinarily free food along with the verbal recognition that is served up with the food will encourage workers. However, if this is the Friday just before a holiday weekend such as Memorial Day weekend, workers may prefer to just get home so that they can get out of town with their families. Looking at the situation from the worker's point of view, the astute manager will delay the pizza dinner until the following week.

Focus on an Organization

Women of Influence Ministries[112]

Women of Influence Ministries exists to provide Bible-based leadership training for women who work in a variety of settings including the world of commerce and the world of church organizations. Women live with the stresses that come from managing work, family, and church relationships. These stresses may be contributing to a decline in church attendance and volunteerism among women. Women of Influence Ministries offers three dimensions in its program: practical training in leadership, coaching designed for women, and Bible exploration. What sets this organization apart from others is that trainers and coaches take into account the particular needs of women.

Additional information can be obtained from the website: http://www.woiministries.com/index.html.

Chapter Summary

1. In the Bible motivation is primarily a matter of the heart. Different motivational forces can be observed in the Bible, including human dignity, compassion, imitating God, fear of punishment, loyalty, and promises of well-being. Three powerful motivators dominate: faith, hope, and love. The Bible describes the relationship between cause and effect. Intrinsic and extrinsic rewards can be distinguished. Motivation has a community dimension to human experience; the Bible writers recognize the social influences on motives.
2. A number of factors influence work motivation and performance. The tendency to think that performance problems are caused by something inside and under the control of the employee rather than by factors outside the employee's control is an example of the fundamental attribution error.
3. Assumptions about human nature are important influences in what managers believe are the best ways to motivate workers.
4. Some scholars believe that some personality traits do influence what job characteristics a person prefers, what behaviors a person chooses, what types of people a person tends to interact with at work, how much effort the person gives for job activities, and how persistent the person is in such actions. An example of a cluster of personality traits that has been studied in terms of job performance is the Big Five personality dimensions. Other factors that influence motivation include attitudes, beliefs, and values.
5. Over the years several theories of motivation have been offered. The following are reviewed in this chapter:
   a. Theory X, Theory Y. When managers hold certain assumptions about workers, these assumptions influence the behavior of managers which, in turn, has an effect on workers.
   b. Needs: Physiological, psychological, and social. Unmet needs influence behaviors designed to satisfy these needs.
   c. Two-factor theory. Job satisfaction is not the opposite of job dissatisfaction as different factors influence each.
   d. Job characteristics, or the content of the job, influence motivation and performance because of the psychological response that the employee has toward the work.
   e. Allowing workers to participate in decisions that affect their work will increase their motivation to high performance.
   f. When workers perceive that an inequity exists between what they do and the rewards they get compared with other workers, this can have a negative impact on motivation.
   g. When workers expect that their effort will result in expected performance and when the performance will result in desirable outcomes, they will increase their performance efforts.
   h. Goal setting and intention to act on goals affect a person's motivation and performance at work. Goals are effective when they are specific, closer in proximity to everyday work activities but directly related to longer-term goals, and set in a context of work that is constantly changing or uncertain.

Key Terms

Discussion Questions

1. Review the chapter opener regarding the Ritz-Carlton Hotel. What motivation principles seem to be at work in the company's approach?
2. Is it a valid belief that there is a cause-and-effect relationship between our assumptions about human nature and our actions as managers?
3. Which of the Ten Commandments refer to motivation? What motives are at stake in these?
4. In what way might the beliefs of Douglas McGregor predisposed him to see more of Theory X assumptions and behaviors than Theory Y?
5. Some people believe that the Theory X, Theory Y model portrays two extreme viewpoints and that reality lies somewhere in the middle with a mixture of beliefs about human nature. If this is true, how would you describe a model of human nature that includes some of both Theory X and Theory Y? How would such a model influence managerial behavior?
6. How should managers' belief that humans are made in the image of God affect what they do to improve performance of their workers?
7. Think of an experience you have had or have heard about regarding a company and its managers. What managerial behaviors seem to illustrate the belief that workers are created in the image of God? Now think of a contrasting example of an organization whose managers seem to emphasize the belief that humans are sinful. What managerial behaviors appear to illustrate that belief?
8. If a manager needs to discipline an employee, how can this be accomplished taking into consideration that humans are both created in the image of God *and* are sinful? What elements of employee discipline respect the belief in the image of God and what elements of employee discipline respect the belief in the sinfulness of humans?
9. Which of Maslow's five categories of needs become important in the workplace? How can managers help satisfy these needs?
10. If Maslow's model is correct that the need for safety is met, in part, by participating in religious behaviors, then is it possible that the need for God is one of the fundamental human needs that must be met before the social needs become dominant? But, because participating in a religious organization is a social experience, too, is it possible that this facet of Maslow's safety need is a combination of social and spiritual needs?
11. Herzberg believed that humans have a dual nature, that is, they are sinful and they have great positive potential. Assuming that motivation is essentially something that takes place in the heart and mind of a worker, what should a Christian manager do to encourage motivation?
12. Imagine that you are a manager. One of your employees comes to you and complains that he is not getting paid what he is worth. Considering the implications of equity theory, how would you respond to this employee?
13. Acting in a fair and just manner toward all employees is highly valued in the Christian faith community. But if it is true that fairness is in the eye of the beholder, then how is the Christian manager able to achieve fairness for all employees? If fairness is not in the eye of the beholder, then who is to determine what fairness is in any given situation? On what basis does this person determine what is fair?
14. What elements in human nature account for the observations that specific task-related goal setting increases performance *and* can increase the chances that workers will cheat?
15. The results of practical research on participation's effect on performance are mixed. What does the Christian worldview offer to this question?
16. Should the Christian manager encourage employee participation when employees do not want to share decision-making power such as when employees have a low desire for autonomy?

STUDENT EXERCISES

1. Visit a company and watch and listen to the actions of managers toward employees. Try to replicate the observational research that Douglas McGregor did in the 1950s. What pattern do you see? Do Theory X and Theory Y assumptions appear to be present with managers? What evidence would you put forward from your observations in support of your conclusions?
2. Research the difference between motivation and manipulation. Under what conditions is manipulation wrong for the Christian manager?
3. Assign small groups of students to complete one or both of the following assignments:
   - **Truth statements.** Meet as a group and create a half-page document containing at least seven things that the group members know must be true regarding motivating workers.
   - **Evaluating assumptions.** Meet as a group to examine the list of assumptions presented in this chapter. Identify the assumptions that seem to have a weaker basis. Identify the assumptions that might have a stronger basis. Discuss what criteria should be used to determine a strong or weak basis for assumptions.
4. After considering the issues in this chapter, write a one- or two-page reaction paper addressing the following questions: What elements of motivation theory and practice do you question the most? What ideas are new to you? What ideas have you seen in practice? What ideas really hit home? What facets of motivation are you the most curious about? What elements of Christian faith are consistent with (or inconsistent with) the principles of motivation addressed here?

IN-CLASS EXERCISES

Visualization

The concepts in this chapter are abstract, yet they have practical value for practicing managers. One way to process abstract ideas is to visualize them. Assign small groups the task to illustrate visually on a poster a key concept of their choice from the chapter. Allow some class time to start the pictures. If groups need additional time after class, they can be allowed to bring their poster back to class in the following class period. When the posters are completed, ask each group to present and explain their poster to the rest of the class.

Issue Debates/Discussions

Divide the class into small groups of five to six people each. Choose a set of "Discussion Topic" statements from the list that follows. Hand out a sheet of paper containing the two "Discussion Topic" statements. Assign half of the groups to defend the first statement (A) as valid and the other half to defend the second statement (B) as valid. For this exercise, students do not necessarily need to agree with the perspective they are asked to defend. In fact, defending a point of view that a student disagrees with can be an amazing teaching-learning experience for undergraduates by helping them to intellectually go outside their usual thinking patterns and develop critical thinking skills. Give the groups 5 minutes to discuss. Then call for groups to give a summary of the rationale they developed. Discussion can follow.

Discussion Topic #1: Is Maslow's hierarchy valid from the Christian perspective?

A. **No.** "... Maslow believed that people had created their gods in their own image. Christians maintain that God is the original, and that he created us in his image ... Maslow discovered the image of God in humans, but, being an atheist, he has confused the original with the copy."[113]

B. **Yes.** "... God has created us with normal human needs and limitations, and we function best when these are attended to. Both experience and Scripture attest to the truth of this claim. Maslow's hierarchy reminds us of areas of human experience to which we can usefully direct our attention as we attempt to communicate God's truth in a way that strikes a responsive chord."[114]

Discussion Topic #2: Which of the three traditional management approaches is most appropriate from your understanding of the Christian worldview? Why?

A. **Philosophy of fear: Force workers to be docile; use rewards and punishments.** "Operating from the point of view that their job was to get the organization's purpose achieved through manipulating the ingredients, some managements simply said, 'Well, if people won't be docile, we'll make them.' The philosophy behind the tactics of such a management was, essentially, 'Be strong, be tough, break down resistance and antagonism, and get the job done that way.' The trick is to make people afraid through fear of unemployment."[115]

B. **Philosophy of paternalism: Keep them docile but happy by being good to workers.** "Some managements made an altogether different attack on this problem. They said in effect, 'Be good. If you're good, people out of loyalty and gratitude will do what you want them to do.' Notice that the notion of docility is still there. The idea is that management has a job to do: to accomplish the organization's purpose through people. It can only accomplish that purpose if people do what they are told—if they are docile and accept orders."[116]

C. **Philosophy of participation and cooperation: Encourage workers to work because they want to.** "We do not regard people as a commodity now; we do not ask them to be docile. We say that management's task is to get people's cooperation, to create the conditions under which people will willingly and voluntarily work toward organizational objectives."[117]

Discussion Topic #3: Can human beings achieve self-actualization and attain their true potential without a relationship with God?

A. **A gift from God in creation.** The drive toward and the ability to achieve self-actualization is a God-created gift for all humans, known as *common grace*. Self-actualization is a social, community experience that is a part of what it means to be human. Whether a person espouses faith in God, such a person can be as successful in achieving self-actualization as a believer in God. Furthermore, all humans are sinful. Thus, all share the same limitations imposed by sin in achieving self-actualization. Christians who believe that only they can achieve self-actualization through faith are arrogant and self-centered, not recognizing that there are many people in society who have developed the ability to live up to their God-given potential.

B. **A gift from God in salvation.** The ability to live up to one's true potential can only truly be accomplished when the spiritual dimension of life is included in the discussion. Here the concepts of "self-actualization" and "true potential" must include our relationship with God. We were created to live in a faith relationship with God, and such a relationship is necessary if we expect human relationships to be experienced to their fullest. To claim that humans can attain true self-actualization and reach their true potential without God is to make a mockery of the plan of salvation.

Discussion Topic #4: How can a relationship with God be the source of motivation to work? When thinking about the answer to this question, consider the following passage of the Bible from Psalm 40:1–10:

Psalm 40:1–10[1] I waited patiently for the LORD; And He inclined to me, and heard my cry.[2] He brought me up out of the pit of destruction, out of the miry clay; And He set my feet upon a rock making my footsteps firm.[3] And

He put a new song in my mouth, a song of praise to our God; Many will see and fear, And will trust in the LORD.[4] How blessed is the man who has made the LORD his trust, And has not turned to the proud, nor to those who lapse into falsehood.[5] Many, O LORD my God, are the wonders which Thou hast done, And Thy thoughts toward us; There is none to compare with Thee; If I would declare and speak of them, They would be too numerous to count.[6] Sacrifice and meal offering Thou hast not desired; My ears Thou hast opened; Burnt offering and sin offering Thou hast not required.[7] Then I said, "Behold, I come; In the scroll of the book it is written of me;[8] I delight to do Thy will, O my God; Thy Law is within my heart."[9] I have proclaimed glad tidings of righteousness in the great congregation; Behold, I will not restrain my lips, O LORD, Thou knowest.[10] I have not hidden Thy righteousness within my heart; I have spoken of Thy faithfulness and Thy salvation; I have not concealed Thy loving kindness and Thy truth from the great congregation. (New American Standard version)

Discussion Topic #5: What does the greatest motivator (love) actually mean in the practice of a manager?

A. **Showing care and concern for the situation workers are in** (tender love). People come to work and face many challenges. Their home lives may be in chaos. There may be things that happen to them that are outside of their control. The resources they need to get their jobs done efficiently are not as great as they wish. Differences between workers' personalities, temperaments, and attitudes make it difficult for some workers to get along. One of the great needs that workers have is for a supervisor who cares about them as people, one who shows flexibility, mercy, patience, and kindness. Loving kindness is one of the greatest motivators.

B. **Expecting workers to live up to their responsibilities** (tough love). When people come to work, they choose to give up some of their personal interests to help an organization achieve its goals of serving society. Personal problems, when brought into the company, will divert the organization from its goals. Employees should develop contingency plans so that they can still fulfill their obligations at work when things happen to them that are outside of their control. Workers must be encouraged to deal with scarce resources at work just as they do at home. They must get past the individual differences in personalities, temperaments, and attitudes that make it difficult to get along. One of the greatest needs that workers have is for a supervisor to show workers that they have responsibilities to fulfill to each other, to the company, and to society by getting their work done. As workers we cannot truly serve each other unless we get work done.

Endnotes

1. Flavel, J. (1972). *Keeping the heart*. Wilmington, DE: Sovereign Grace Publishers. p. 5. http://www.the-highway.com/heart_TOC.html.
2. Drucker, P. F. (1954). *The practice of management*. New York: Harper & Brothers. p. 262.
3. Gallo, C. (2007). How Ritz-Carlton maintains its mystique. BusinessWeek.com. http://www.businessweek.com/smallbiz/content/feb2007/sb20070213_171606.htm. February 13; Gallo, C. (2008). Employee motivation the Ritz-Carlton way. BusinessWeek.com. http://www.businessweek.com/smallbiz/content/feb2008/sb20080229_347490.htm. February 29; Hotels Magazine (2006). Values evolve at the Ritz-Carlton. http://www.hotelsmag.com/article/362998-Values_Evolve_at_the_Ritz_Carlton.php. August 31.
4. Pinder, C. C. (2008). *Work motivation in organizational behavior*. (2nd ed.). New York: Psychology Press. p. 9.
5. Information from the 2007 PRO-TEC Malcolm Baldrige Application Summary submitted to the Malcolm Baldrige National Quality Award Program.
6. Pinder, C. C. (2008). *Work motivation in organizational behavior*. (2nd ed.). New York: Psychology Press. p. 47.
7. Surveys of the topic include the following works: Latham, G. P. (2007). *Work motivation: History, theory, research and practice*. Thousand Oaks, CA: Sage Publications. pp. 1–121; Lawler III, E. E. (1994). *Motivation in work organizations*. San Francisco, CA: Jossey-Bass. pp. 1–13; Pinder, C. C. (2008). *Work motivation in organizational behavior*. (2nd ed.). New York: Psychology Press. pp. 25–60.
8. Goldingay, J. (2006). *Old Testament theology. Vol. 1: Israel's faith*. Downers Grove, IL: IVP Academic. pp. 548–560.
9. This table was constructed based on Waltke, B. K. (2004). *The book of Proverbs Chapters 1–15*. The New International Commentary on the Old Testament. Grand Rapids, MI: William B. Eerdmans Publishing Company.
10. Chewning, R. C., Eby, J. W., & Roels, S. J. (1990). *Business through the eyes of faith*. San Francisco, CA: HarperSanFrancisco. p. 169. See Proverbs 27:19; 1 Corinthians 4:5.
11. Matthew 5:8; Proverbs 3:1, 4:4. See the comments on this in Chewning, R. C., Eby, J. W., & Roels, S. J. (1990). *Business through the eyes of faith*. San Francisco, CA: HarperSanFrancisco. pp. 136–137.
12. Genesis 6:5, 8:21; Proverbs 6:14, 6:18, 11:20, 12:8, 12:20, 18:2, 26:5; Jeremiah 17:9; James 4:3.
13. Genesis 6:5, 8:21; Exodus 35:21–26; 1 Chronicles 28:9, 29:18; Psalm 7:9, 19:14, 51:10, 51:17; Proverbs 4:23, 6:14, 6:18, 12:20; Jeremiah 17:9, 22:17; 1 Corinthians 4:5; Philippians 1:17; James 4:3.
14. 1 Corinthians 13:13; Galatians 5:5–6.
15. Psalm 22:9, 40:4, 65:5, 71:5; Proverbs 1:33, 14:26, 22:19; Hebrews 11:1.
16. Job 8:13, 27:8; Psalm 42:11, 43:5, 62:5, 71:5, 130:7, 146:5; Lamentations 3:21–26; Zechariah 9:12; 1 Corinthians 9:10; Ephesians 2:12; Colossians 1:23–27; 1 Thessalonians 1:3; 2 Thessalonians 2:16; 1 Timothy 1:1, 4:10, 5:5, 6:17; Titus 2:13; Hebrews 6:11; 1 Peter 1:3–9, 1:21; 1 John 3:3.

17. Job 14:6–9, 19:10–26; 1 Thessalonians 5:8. The dimension of security or safety that hope provides is illustrated by the Septuagint (Greek) translation of the Hebrew Bible in certain passages: Judges 18:7–10; Psalm 4:8, 14:6, 16:9, 61:2, 62:7, 73:28, 78:53; 91:9, 94:22, 142:5.
18. Matthew 13:31, 17:20, 21:21; Mark 4:31; Luke 8:13–15, 13:19, 17:6, 18:42. See also the stories of individuals whose faith moved them to action (Matthew 8:5–10, 9, 15:28).
19. Chewning, R. C., Eby, J. W., & Roels, S. J. (1990). *Business through the eyes of faith*. San Francisco, CA: HarperSanFrancisco. p. 43. See also 2 Corinthians 5:14.
20. 1 John 4:19. See comments on this principle in Porter, B., & VanderVeen, S. (2002). Motivation from a Christian Perspective. Paper presented to the Christian Business Faculty Association Annual Conference. Boise, ID. October.
21. Beisner, E. C. (1990). Biblical incentives and an individual's economic choices. In Chewning, R. C. (Ed.). *Biblical principles and economics: The foundations*. Colorado Springs, CO: NavPress. p. 196. See also Matthew 22:37–39; Romans 13:8–10; 2 Corinthians 8:8, 9:6–15.
22. Hildebrandt, T. (1992). Motivation and antithetic parallelism in Proverbs 10–15. *Journal of the Evangelical Theological Society*. 35(4), 433–444. In his article Hildebrandt cites several Scripture passages in support of these: Deuteronomy 25:3; Exodus 20:11–12, 22:26; Leviticus 19:3, 19:20, 21:9. See also the promises that faithful believers will experience the flourishing that comes from shalom: 1 Kings 2:33; Psalm 29:11, 72:7, 89:15–18, 92:12–13, 119:165; Proverbs 3:13–17, 11:28, 14:11; Isaiah 60:17.
23. Genesis 19:15–22; Exodus 36:3–6; Jonah 1:1–3, 4:1–9; Mark 2:1–12; Luke 5:17–26.
24. Exodus 2:11–15; John 2:13–17.
25. Chirichigno, G. (1981). A theological investigation of motivation in Old Testament law. *Journal of the Evangelical Theological Society*. 24(4), 303–313.
26. Hildebrandt, T. (1992). Motivation and antithetic parallelism in Proverbs 10–15. *Journal of the Evangelical Theological Society*. 35(4), 433–444. He points out that Maslow's hierarchy of needs and motivation and the wisdom of Proverbs intersect. See as examples Proverbs 10:3, 10:7, 10:15, 10:21, 13:25, 15:15.
27. Hildebrandt, T. (1992). Motivation and antithetic parallelism in Proverbs 10–15. *Journal of the Evangelical Theological Society*. 35(4), 433–444. He comments on the concept of "internal local of control" portrayed in Proverbs.
28. Proverbs 10:1, 10:28, 11:10, 12:20, 15:23, 15:30.
29. Genesis 37:17–38, 47:1–27; 2 Samuel 13–15; Esther; Mark 5:22–43; Luke 19:1–8.
30. On the point that fundamental human needs were created by God see Porter, B., & VanderVeen, S. (2002). *Motivation from a Christian perspective*. Paper presented at the Annual Conference of the Christian Business Faculty Association. Boise, ID. Fall. p. 10.
31. Genesis 22:18, 26:5; Exodus 20:6; Leviticus 25:18–19, 26:3–7; Deuteronomy 4:40, 6:3, 6:18, 11:13–21; 1 Samuel 26:23; Psalm 58:11; Ecclesiastes 12:14; Isaiah 1:16–20, 40:10–11; Jeremiah 22:3–4; Matthew 10:32, 16:24–27; Mark 10:21, 13:13; Luke 6:22–23; Hebrews 10:34–36, 11:25–26; 1 Peter 1:10–11.
32. Exodus 20:12; 1 Samuel 30:24; 2 Samuel 4:10, 12:6, 12:10, 18:22, 19:36–37; 1 Kings 13:7; 2 Chronicles 15:7; Proverbs 10:12, 10:14, 11:15, 11:18, 12:13–14, 22:29; Isaiah 3:11; Matthew 5:46–47; Luke 6:38; Romans 2:10; 1 Corinthians 3:8; Ephesians 6:1–3. See also House, H. W., & Durham, K. M. (1997). *Living wisely in a foolish world*. Grand Rapids, MI: Kregel Publications. pp. 200–203.
33. Genesis 15:1; 2 Chronicles 15:7; Psalm 58:11; 127:3; Proverbs 11:18, 13:2, 18:20, 18:21, 27:18, 31:16, 31:31; Isaiah 3:10, 40:10, 62:11.
34. Beisner, E. C. (1990). Biblical incentives and economic systems. In Chewning, R. C. (Ed.). *Biblical principles and economics: The foundations*. Colorado Springs, CO: NavPress. pp. 168–186, 302.
35. 1 Samuel 17:25–27.
36. Beisner, E. C. (1990). Biblical incentives and economic systems. In Chewning, R. C. (Ed.). *Biblical principles and economics: The foundations*. Colorado Springs, CO: NavPress. pp. 168–186.
37. Beisner, E. C. (1990). Biblical incentives and economic systems. In Chewning, R. C. (Ed.). *Biblical principles and economics: The foundations*. Colorado Springs, CO: NavPress. p. 174; Hildebrandt, T. (1992). Motivation and antithetic parallelism in Proverbs 10–15. *Journal of the Evangelical Theological Society*. 35(4), 433–444.
38. Genesis 15:1; Ruth 2:12; 1 Samuel 24:19; 2 Chronicles 15; Proverbs 11:18, 25:21–22; Ecclesiastes 9:5; Matthew 6:1–5; 10:41.
39. Beisner, E. C. (1990). Biblical incentives and economic systems. In Chewning, R. C. (Ed.). *Biblical principles and economics: The foundations*. Colorado Springs, CO: NavPress. p. 173; Alford, H. J., & Naughton, M. J. (2001). *Managing as if faith mattered: Christian social principles in the modern organization*. Notre Dame, IN: University of Notre Dame Press. pp. 63–64. See also Psalm 16:5–11, 17:15, 37:4, 42:2, 43:4, 63:3, 73:25, 89:6, 104:34, 143:6–8; Isaiah 26:8–9; Habakkuk 3:17–18; Matthew 5:8; Philippians 3:8; Revelation 21:3.
40. Olson, D. L., & Henning, L. H. (1987). The dynamics of faithfulness. *Currents in Theology and Mission*. 14(5), 339; Faw, H. W. (1995). *Psychology in Christian perspective: An analysis of key issues*. Grand Rapids, MI: Baker Books. p. 76; Beisner, E. C. (1990). Biblical incentives and economic systems. In Chewning, R. C. (Ed.). *Biblical principles and economics: The foundations*. Colorado Springs, CO: NavPress. pp. 176–177. See also James 5:1–6.
41. 2 Samuel 5:6–8; 1 Chronicles 11:6.
42. Smith, V. O., & Smith, Y. S. (2003). *An analysis of power in Christian leadership*. Paper presented to the annual conference of the Christian Business Faculty Association. Virginia Beach, VA. October 16–18. p. 7.
43. Acts 14:17.
44. Exodus 34:6; Numbers 14:18; Psalm 78:38, 86:15; Isaiah 30:18, 46:13, 63:7–10; Luke 18:7–8; Romans 2:4; 1 Timothy 2:4; 2 Peter 3:9; Revelation 3:20.
45. Psalm 19:11.
46. Leviticus 26:3–4; Deuteronomy 7:12–15.

47. Psalm 17:15, 65:4, 73:25; Proverbs 19:23; Jeremiah 31:14; Matthew 5:6.
48. 2 Samuel 18:22; 1 Kings 13:7; Daniel 2:6; Luke 10:7.
49. Proverbs 5:1–2.
50. Psalm 17:14, 127:3.
51. Ecclesiastes 2:10, 3:22, 5:18–19, 9:9.
52. Genesis 31:14; Proverbs 17:2.
53. Genesis 6.
54. Genesis 11:6; Judges 6–7; Acts 6.
55. Genesis 41:29–49.
56. 2 Chronicles 26:14–15.
57. 1 John 3:5–8. See also Genesis 3:15; Isaiah 27:1; Mark 1:24; John 12:31; Colossians 2:15; Hebrews 2:14.
58. Philippians 3:14. See similar thoughts expressed in Matthew 10:22, 24:13; Mark 13:13; John 3:16; Romans 2:7; 2 Corinthians 4:17–18, 5:1; Hebrews 3:6, 14; 2 Timothy 4:7–8; 1 Peter 3:9; James 1:12; Revelation 2:10, 3:21.
59. 2 Corinthians 2:9; 1 Thessalonians 2:13; 2 Thessalonians 1:11; Philippians 1:9–11; Colossians 1:9–13; 1 Timothy 1:5; Philemon 1:21.
60. Matthew 20:1–16. See also Matthew 9:37–38, 10:10; Luke 10:2.
61. Maehr, M. L. (2005). The meaning that religion offers and the motivation that may result. In Miller, W. R., & Delaney, H. D. (Eds.). *Judeo-Christian perspectives on psychology: Human nature, motivation and change.* Washington, DC: American Psychological Association. p. 140.
62. Matthew 5:13–16. See the comment on this in Faw, H. W. (1995). *Psychology in Christian perspective: An analysis of key issues.* Grand Rapids, MI: Baker Books. pp. 76, 176. See also Numbers 33:55–56; Deuteronomy 20:8; Proverbs 1, 13:20, 14:7, 22:24, 24:1; Matthew 16:5–12; 1 Corinthians 5:9–11, 15:33; 2 Thessalonians 3:6–7.
63. Pinder, C. C. (2008). *Work motivation in organizational behavior.* (2nd ed.). New York: Psychology Press. p. 10.
64. Because of space limitations in this chapter we limited the discussion of motivation theories. Theories not reviewed here include classical conditioning, operant conditioning, and social cognitive theory.
65. Lawler III, E. E. (1994). *Motivation in work organizations.* San Francisco, CA: Jossey-Bass. pp. 143–252; Pinder, C. C. (2008). *Work motivation in organizational behavior.* (2nd ed.). New York: Psychology Press. pp. 16–22.
66. Drucker, P. F. (1954). *The practice of management.* New York: Harper & Brothers. p. 305.
67. Chewning, R. C., Eby, J. W., & Roels, S. J. (1990). *Business through the eyes of faith.* San Francisco, CA: HarperSanFrancisco. p. 39.
68. Summarized from the discussion in Lawler III, E. E. (1994). *Motivation in work organizations.* San Francisco, CA: Jossey-Bass Publishers. pp. 253–257.
69. Tett, R. P., & Burnett, D. D. (2003). A personality trait-based interactionist model of job performance. *Journal of Applied Psychology.* 88, 500–517. See also Stewart, G. L., & Barrick, M. R. (2004). Four lessons learned from the person-situation debate: A review and research agenda. In Schneider, B., & Smith, D. B. (Eds.). *Personality and organization.* Mahwah, NJ: Lawrence Erlbaum. pp. 61–86.
70. Barrick, M. R., & Mount, M. K. (1991). The big five personality dimensions and job performance: A meta-analysis. *Personnel Psychology.* 44, 1–26; Barrick, M. R., & Mount, M. K. (1993). Autonomy as a moderator of the relationships between the big five personality dimensions and job performance. *Journal of Applied Psychology.* 78(1), 111–118; Tett, R. P., & Burnett, D. D. (2003). A personality trait-based interactionist model of job performance. *Journal of Applied Psychology.* 88(3), 500–517; Block, J. (2010). The five-factor framing of personality and beyond: Some ruminations. *Psychological Inquiry.* 21, 2–25; Goldberg, L. R. (1993). The structure of phenotypic personality traits. *American Psychologist,* 48(1), 26–34.
71. Ajzen, I. (2005). *Attitudes, personality and behavior.* (2nd ed). Buckingham: Open University Press. pp. 1–24.
72. Pinder, C. C. (2008). *Work motivation in organizational behavior.* (2nd ed.). New York: Psychology Press. p. 92.
73. Rokeach, M. (2000). *Understanding human values.* New York: Free Press. pp. 47–70.
74. Drucker, P. F. (1973). *Management: Tasks, responsibilities, practices.* New York: Harper & Row Publishers, Inc. p. 441.
75. Bolman, L. G., & Deal, T. E. (2003). *Reframing organizations: Artistry, choice and leadership.* San Francisco, CA: Jossey-Bass. pp. 118–119.
76. From the 2006 Premier, Inc. Malcolm Baldrige National Quality Award Application. Available at http://www.baldrige.nist.gov/PDF_files/Premier_Application_Summary.pdf.
77. Lawler III, E. E. (1994). *Motivation in work organizations.* San Francisco, CA: Jossey-Bass. pp. 13–51; Latham, G. P. (2007). *Work motivation: History, theory, research, and practice.* Thousand Oaks, CA: Sage Publications. pp. 30–33.
78. Pinder, C. C. (2008). *Work motivation in organizational behavior.* (2nd ed.). New York: Psychology Press. pp. 68–70.
79. Maslow, A. H. (1943). A theory of human motivation. *Psychological Review,* 50, 370–396; Maslow, A. H. (1954). *Motivation and personality.* New York: Harper & Row.
80. This proved to be the case. For examples, see McGregor, D. (1960). *The human side of enterprise.* New York: McGraw Hill Book Company; Alderfer, C. P. (1969). An empirical test of a new theory of human needs. *Organizational Behavior and Human Performance.* 4, 143–175; Alderfer, C. P. (1972). *Existence, relatedness, and growth.* New York: Free Press; McClelland, D. C. (1961). *The achieving society.* Princeton, NJ: Van Nostrand Reinhold; McClelland, D. C. (1965). Achievement motivation can be developed. *Harvard Business Review.* 43(6), 6–24, 178; Ryan, R. M., Connell, J. P., & Deci, E. L. (1985). A motivational analysis of self-determination and self-regulation in mediation. In Ames, C., &

Ames, R. E. (Eds.). *Research on motivation and education: The classroom milieu.* New York: Academic Press. pp. 13–51; Ryan, R. M., & Deci, E. L. (2000). Self-determination theory and the facilitation of intrinsic motivation, social development, and well-being. *American Psychologist*, 55(1), 68–78.

81. Alderfer, C. P. (1969). An empirical test of a new theory of human needs. *Organizational Behavior and Human Performance*. 4, 143–175; Alderfer, C. P. (1972). *Existence, relatedness, and growth.* New York: Free Press.
82. Heylighen, F. (1992). A cognitive-systemic reconstruction of Maslow's theory of self-actualization. *Behavioral Science,* 37(1), 39–59; Pinder, C. C. (2008). *Work motivation in organizational behavior*. (2nd ed.). New York: Psychology Press. pp. 74–75.
83. Salancik, G. R., & Pfeffer, J. (1977). An examination of need-satisfaction models of job attitudes. *Administrative Science Quarterly*. 22, 427–456.
84. Lawler III, E. E., & Shuttle, J. L. (1973). A causal correlation test of the need hierarchy concept. *Organizational Behavior and Human Performance*. 7, 265–287; Schneider, B., & Alderfer, C. (1973). Three studies of measures of need satisfaction in organizations. *Administrative Science Quarterly*. 18, 498–505.
85. Porter, B., & VanderVeen, S. (2002). Motivation from a Christian perspective. Paper presented to the Christian Business Faculty Association Annual Conference. Boise, ID. October. pp. 22–23.
86. We address it briefly here since it is still popular among many managers. See Herzberg, F., Mausner, B., Peterson, R. O., & Capwell, D. F. (1957). *Job attitudes: Review of research and opinion*. Pittsburgh, PA: Psychological Service of Pittsburgh; Herzberg, F., Mausner, B., & Snyderman, B. B. (1959). *The motivation to work*. New York: John Wiley & Sons; Herzberg, F. (1968). One more time: How do you motivate employees? *Harvard Business Review*. 46(1), 53–62. For a short description of the controversial nature of Herzberg's theory and references to scholars who have reviewed Herzberg's work see Pinder, C. C. (2008). *Work motivation in organizational behavior*. (2nd ed.). New York: Psychology Press. pp. 32–39.
87. Herzberg, F. (1966). *Work and the nature of man*. Cleveland, OH: World Publishing. p. 56.
88. Adapted from Herzberg, F. (1968). One more time: How do you motivate employees? *Harvard Business Review*. 46(1), 53–62; Miner, J. B. (2005). *Organizational Behavior 1: Essential theories of motivation and leadership*. Armonk, NY: M. E. Sharpe. pp. 61–74.
89. Research related to the Job Characteristics Model (JCM) has been described by several scholars. Conceptually these scholars built on the ideas put forward by Frederick Herzberg. See Hackman, J. R., & Oldham, G. R. (1976). Motivation through the design of work: Test of a theory. *Organizational Behavior and Human Performance*. 16, 250–279; Hackman, J. R., & Oldham, G. R. (1980). *Work redesign*. Reading, MA: Addison-Wesley. pp. 71–98; Vroom, V. H. (1995). *Work and motivation*. San Francisco, CA: Jossey-Bass. pp. 276–294; Latham, G. P. (2007). *Work motivation: History, theory, research, and practice*. Thousand Oaks, CA: Sage Publications. pp. 36–42, 157–161; Pinder, C. C. (2008). *Work motivation in organizational behavior*. (2nd ed.). New York: Psychology Press. pp. 209–213.
90. Frederick Herzberg is sometimes lauded as being the "father" of job enrichment. He and others have contributed to the research in this area. See Herzberg, F., Mausner, B., & Snyderman, B. B. (1959). *The motivation to work*. New York: John Wiley & Sons; McGregor, D. M. (1960). *The human side of enterprise*. New York: McGraw Hill; Staw, B. M. (1976). *Intrinsic and extrinsic motivation*. Morriston, NJ: General Learning Press. See also the review of job enrichment in Pinder, C. C. (2008). *Work motivation in organizational behavior*. (2nd ed.). New York: Psychology Press. pp. 205–236.
91. Alford, H. J., & Naughton, M. J. (2001). *Managing as if faith mattered: Christian social principles in the modern organization*. Notre Dame, IN: University of Notre Dame Press. p. 77.
92. Hamel, G. (2007). *The future of management*. Boston, MA: Harvard Business School Press. pp. 165–169; Cardy, R. L., & Selvarajan, T. T. (2001). Management interventions. In Anderson, N., Ones, D. S., Sinangil, H. K., & Viswesvaran, C. (Eds.). *Handbook of industrial, work and organizational psychology*. (Vol. 2). Thousand Oaks, CA: Sage Publications. pp. 346–376.
93. Pinder, C. C. (2008). Work motivation in organizational behavior. (2nd ed.). Psychology Press. pp. 394–397.
94. Roethlisberger, F. J., & Dickson, W. J. (1939). *Management and the worker*. Cambridge, MA: Harvard University Press; Coch, L., & French, J. R. P. (1948). Overcoming resistance to change. *Human Relations*. 1, 512–532; Argyris, C. (1957). *Personality and organization: The conflict between system and the individual*. New York: Harper & Row, Publishers. pp. 145–153; McGregor, D. (2005). *The human side of enterprise annotated edition*. New York: McGraw Hill Book Company. pp. 165–178; Herzberg, F., Mausner, B., & Snyderman, B. B. (1959). *The motivation to work*. New York: John Wiley & Sons. pp. 127–128, 136–137; Vroom, V. (1964). *Work and motivation*. New York: John Wiley & Sons. pp. 133–138, 257–268; McGregor, D. (1966). *Leadership and motivation*. Cambridge, MA: The M.I.T. Press; Emery, F. E., & Trist, E. L. (1969). Sociotechnical systems. In Emery, F. E. (Ed.). *Systems thinking*. London: Penguin. pp. 53–62; Lawler III, E. E. (1994). *Motivation in work organizations*. San Francisco, CA: Jossey-Bass. pp. 262–263; Miller, K. L., & Monge, P. R. (1986). Participation, satisfaction and productivity: A meta analytic review. *Academy of Management Journal*. 29, 727–753; Wagner, J. A. (1987). Shared influence and organizational behavior: A meta analysis of situational variables expected to moderate participation-outcome relationship. *Academy of Management Journal*. 30, 524–541; Cotton, J. L., Wollrath, D. A., Lengnick-Hall, M. L., & Jennings, K. R. (1988). Employee participation: Diverse forms and different outcomes. *Academy of Management Review*. 13, 8–22; Wagner, J. A. (1994). Participation's effects on performance and satisfaction: A reconsideration of the research evidence. *Academy of Management Review*. 19, 300–312; Cardy, R. L., & Selvarajan, T. T. (2001). Management interventions. In Anderson, N., Ones, D.S., Sinangil, H. K., & Viswesvaran, C. (Eds.)

Handbook of industrial, work and organizational psychology. (Vol. 2). Thousand Oaks, CA: Sage Publications. pp. 346–376.

95. Drucker, P. F. (1954). *The practice of management*. New York: Harper & Brothers. p. 308.
96. Drucker, P. F. (1954). *The practice of management*. New York: Harper & Brothers. p. 309. See also Coch, L., & French, J. R. P. (1948). Overcoming resistance to change. *Human Relations*. 1, 512–532.
97. Drucker, P. F. (1954). *The practice of management*. New York: Harper & Brothers. p. 307.
98. Latham, G. P. (2007). *Work motivation: History, theory, research, and practice*. Thousand Oaks, CA: Sage Publications. p. 95. For a survey of the history of the concept and research regarding participative management see Cardy, R. L., & Selvarajan, T. T. (2001). Management interventions. In Anderson, N., Ones, D. S., Sinangil, H. K., & Viswesvaran, C. (Eds.) *Handbook of industrial, work and organizational psychology*. (Vol. 2). Thousand Oaks, CA: Sage Publications. pp. 346–376.
99. Adams, J. S. (1963). Toward an understanding of inequity. *Journal of Abnormal and Social Psychology*. 67, 422–436; Adams, J. S. (1963). Wage inequities, productivity, and work quality. *Industrial Relations*. 3, 9–16.
100. Adapted from Miner, J. B. (2005). *Organizational behavior 1: Essential theories of motivation and leadership*. Armonk, NY: M. E. Sharpe. p. 136.
101. Pinder, C. C. (2008). *Work motivation in organizational behavior*. (2nd Ed.). New York: Psychology Press. pp. 318–319.
102. Vroom, V. H. (1964). *Work and motivation*. New York: John Wiley & Sons. pp. 20–31; Porter, L. W., & Lawler III, E. E. (1968). *Managerial attitudes and performance*. Homewood, IL: Dorsey. pp. 10–13; Lawler III, E. E. (1994). *Motivation in work organizations*. San Francisco, CA: Jossey-Bass. pp. 57–74.
103. Lawler III, E. E. (1994). *Motivation in work organizations*. San Francisco, CA: Jossey-Bass. pp. 143–187.
104. Lawler III, E. E. (1994). *Motivation in work organizations*. San Francisco, CA: Jossey-Bass. p. 151.
105. Good reviews of the current literature on goal-setting theory and motivation can be found in Pinder, C. C. (2008). *Work motivation in organizational behavior*. (2nd ed.). New York: Psychology Press. pp. 392–406; Latham, G. P. (2007). *Work motivation: History, theory, research, and practice*. Thousand Oaks, CA: Sage Publications. pp. 175–206; Latham, G. P. (2004). The motivational benefits of goal-setting. *Academy of Management Executive*. 18(4), 126–129; Miner, J. B. (2005). *Organizational behavior 1: Essential theories of motivation and leadership*. pp. 159–183; Latham, G. P., & Locke, E. A. (2006). Enhancing the benefits and overcoming the pitfalls of goal setting. *Organizational Dynamics*. 35(4), 332–340; See also Lock, E. A., Shaw, K. N., Saari, L. M., & Latham, G. P. (1981). Goal setting and task performance. *Psychological Bulletin*. 90, 125–152.
106. Latham, G. P. (2007). *Work motivation: History, theory, research, and practice*. Thousand Oaks, CA: Sage Publications. p. 180.
107. From the Cargill Corn Milling North America 2008 Malcolm Baldrige National Quality Award Application. Available at http://www.baldrige.nist.gov/PDF_files/2008_Cargill_Corn_Milling_%20Application_Summary.pdf.
108. Locke, E. A., & Latham, G. P. (2009). Has goal setting gone wild, or have its attackers abandoned good scholarship? *Academy of Management Perspectives*. 23(1), 17–23; Latham, G. P. (2007). *Work motivation: History, theory, research, and practice*. Thousand Oaks, CA: Sage Publications. pp. 180–188; Barsky, A. (2008). Understanding the ethical cost of organizational goal-setting: A review and theory development. *Journal of Business Ethics*. 81, 63–81; Schweitzer, M. E., Ordonez, L., & Douma, B. (2004). Goal setting as a motivator of unethical behavior. *Academy of Management Journal*. 47(3), 422–432.
109. Locke, E. A., & Latham, G. P. (2009). Has goal setting gone wild, or have its attackers abandoned good scholarship? *Academy of Management Perspectives*. 23(1), 17–23.
110. Blau, P. M., & Scott, W. R. (1962). *Formal organizations: A comparative approach*. San Francisco, CA: Chandler Publishing. p. 120.
111. Roethlisberger, F. J. (1941). *Management and morale*. Cambridge, MA: Harvard University Press. p. 38.
112. Information gleaned from the organization's website http://www.woiministries.com/.
113. Koteskey, R. L. (1991). *Psychology from a Christian perspective*. (2nd ed.). Lanham, MD: University Press of America. p. 63.
114. Faw, H. W. (1995). *Psychology in Christian perspective: An analysis of key issues*. Grand Rapids, MI: Baker Books. p. 108.
115. McGregor, D. (1966). *Leadership and motivation*. Cambridge, MA: The M.I.T. Press. p. 35.
116. McGregor, D. (1966). *Leadership and motivation*. Cambridge, MA: The M.I.T. Press. pp. 36–37.
117. McGregor, D. (1966). *Leadership and motivation*. Cambridge, MA: The M.I.T. Press. p. 39.

CHAPTER 12

Leadership

LEARNING OBJECTIVES

- Understand the community nature of leadership.
- Describe the biblical perspective of leadership.
- Evaluate the various perspectives on leadership: leadership as a process, traits, behaviors, and relationships.
- Distinguish between the role of a leader and the role of a manager.
- Consider some of the paradoxes of leadership.

"Successful corporate leaders of the twenty-first century will be spiritual leaders. They will be comfortable with their own spirituality, and they will know how to nurture spiritual development in others."[1]

"Leadership is a reciprocal process between those who aspire to lead and those who choose to follow."[2]

NEHEMIAH

Sometimes even the best leaders can't hide their emotions.[3] Such was the case with Nehemiah after he heard the report from someone who had just returned from Jerusalem to Persia with bad news.[4] Nehemiah was devastated. Jerusalem's walls were crumbling; the city gates had been destroyed by fire.

Nehemiah slipped into a state of sorrow as deep as if he had received news that a close family member had just passed away.[5] His empathy with the plight of his fellow countrymen got to him. For several days his every waking moment was filled with thoughts and prayers about the Jews in Jerusalem. Someone had to take drastic action.[6]

One of the most trusted servants in the royal court, Nehemiah was cupbearer to Artaxerxes, king of Persia. As cupbearer to the king, it was Nehemiah's job to make sure that no unscrupulous characters had slipped him poison. This could be a risky job.

Source: Noel Powell, Schaumburg/Shutterstock.

When the king asked the reason for Nehemiah's sadness, Nehemiah told him the whole story, whereupon the king asked what Nehemiah wanted. Nehemiah asked for permission to return to Jerusalem and rebuild the city walls using Persian building materials from the king's stores.[7] The rest is a story that reveals characteristics and behavior of a leader that today we might do well to emulate.[8]

Nehemiah's first action after hearing the news was to think, meditate, and pray about the situation. When the opportunity for a solution presented itself in the invitation of the king, he unashamedly used his relationship with the person of influence to obtain permission to serve those in need. A 3-day survey of the conditions at Jerusalem gave Nehemiah the detailed knowledge he needed to discuss the situation with local leaders. Nehemiah had received the highest authority to perform the work. But he also respected local leaders. He used persuasion by communicating the vision of what could be done if he could obtain their commitment to the project.[9]

Rebuilding the walls meant that unfriendly tribal leaders from two neighboring villages would no longer be able to go in and out of Jerusalem at will. These leaders set about to thwart Nehemiah's work. At first they hurled ridicules at Nehemiah.[10] When these had no effect, they attempted to set a trap to harm him.[11] Suspecting foul play, Nehemiah did not acquiesce to their request for a "summit meeting." Instead, he instructed workers to arm themselves and post guards at strategic locations to protect the city until the wall was completed. When the opposition turned to political backstabbing, telling lies about Nehemiah's intentions, Nehemiah wasted no time in refuting them.[12] Next these enemies tried to entice him into committing a sacrilegious act by suggesting that he take refuge in the temple. Again Nehemiah saw through their wiles and refused. Meanwhile, the work continued.

Nehemiah kept his singleness of purpose in constant focus. He organized the work so that workers could work on portions of the wall near their own families. Nehemiah kept the workers informed. He encouraged them during the psychological attacks by the enemy. Just 52 days after the work began, the Jerusalem wall was once again secure.

But Nehemiah's work was not done. Leadership sometimes spans situations greater than the immediate project that needs immediate attention. He remembered the spiritual reasons why the nation had been taken into captivity. He set about to improve economic conditions. He worked to stop exploitation of the poor, restored Jewish national identity, and reformed religious practices.[13] In so doing, he brought shalom-like wholeness to the community.

Based on the ancient records available as far as we know, leadership as an activity may not have been studied in ancient times like it is today. Now the subject of leadership is one of the most popular fields of research and writing. Best-selling books are produced every year on this topic.

In this chapter we will consider the current dimensions of leadership that are so important for organizations and why managers need to think about their leadership as well as management skills.

Who Cares About Leadership?

Organizations hire managers in hopes that leaders will emerge who can help the organization achieve its objectives. Companies ask employees of all types to exercise leadership by understanding what needs to be done, communicating the vision and purpose of the organization, and helping the organization move forward together.

Have you ever taken a leadership role in a club or organization? If so, you are already aware of how important leadership can be. Student groups at the university level are notorious for being difficult to lead. Members are usually volunteers who have multiple competing interests like homework, recreation activities, work, and volunteer service that vie for attention. Leaders of these groups can command only a small slice of commitment from such volunteers.

You might be thinking, "I do not aspire to be a top-level executive. Why should I read about leadership?" The answer is that even if you are not an official leader (someone with a job title that sounds like it entails leadership), it is very likely that you will have opportunities somewhere in your life to lead regardless of your job. You can exercise leadership at home, at work, during recreation, and at church—even without carrying the title of "leader."

There are other reasons why leaders are needed in organizations. First, organizations are never perfect. In an ideal world, once all the organizational problems are solved and policies and plans are written to maintain these solutions, the continuing need for leaders should diminish. But reality is far more complex and variable than company policies can account for. Second, occasionally individual members of an organization attempt to achieve their own self-interests at the expense of the organization. Some even attempt to sabotage the organization's plans and policies to gain something. Leaders must step forward to watch out for the interests of the organization. Third, every organization has inseparable connections and interrelationships with others in the larger society. Changes in the environment will leave the organization behind if leaders are not active in helping the organization adapt. Fourth, most organizations work in the global environment where most of the factors for success can be purchased somewhere in the global market. The world is changing in ways that will make access to success factors less important. Leadership is becoming more difficult to purchase as it becomes a more important source of competitive advantage.[14]

The Management Pyramid Applied to Leadership

Earlier in the book we introduced the connections between being, thinking, and action. This set of interrelationships also applies to leadership, as shown in Exhibit 12-1.

Leadership is an **inside-out process**, meaning it is a process of transformation that begins with the inner core of both followers and leaders and flows out through the whole group. Leaders cannot escape the values that drive their judgment and decisions. Leaders' values grip them; they embrace their values and use them as important guideposts. Personal values are probably the most essential, most enduring factor in leadership success.[15]

To become a credible leader, values must come first. If you expect followers to embrace your values, then you must understand them, clarify them, and embrace them yourself. This is why leading self-responsibly is the essential first focus of a leader.

Character traits are developed in the crucible of leaders and followers interacting, disagreeing, persuading, coming to mutual purposes, and spiritually experiencing attempts to make real changes, failing, and trying again. In other words, leadership development is not just about developing skills and practices, though these are helpful in forging productive relationships.

Implementing change **Taking action with an awareness that leading is a constant relationship** **Repeatedly communicating the organizational vision** **Inspiring trust in others** **Empowering others to lead** **Empowering others to make the vision a reality**	**Action**
Sharing leadership **Developing a vision for the organization** **Developing innovative ideas** **Considering the community and the relationships** **Asking "What?" and "Why?"**	**Thinking & Feeling**
The leader's character and values **Transformation during the leadership process** **Beliefs regarding the nature of the relationships** **Beliefs regarding human nature** **Willingness to let others lead** **Willingness to follow**	**Being & Becoming**

EXHIBIT 12-1
The Management Pyramid: Leadership

Source: Courtesy of Michael E. Cafferky, © Michael E. Cafferky 2011.

It is about developing people whose shared values guide them as individuals and guide the relationships in the whole group.[16]

Leaders and followers alike must think about the common purposes at work within the whole community. Leaders will encourage followers to think about the central issues from the perspective of the external environment. Followers will encourage leaders to think about the issues from the perspective of the followers closest to the frontline action of the organization.

To be authentic, a virtuous person with character and solid values will not sit idly by just thinking when action is needed. Leaders will work to create a voice that represents the common interests. They will take action. Leadership involves "getting your hands dirty" in the work of implementing changes and then working with fellow leaders and followers to make corrections when things don't work out just as expected.

This chapter focuses on issues and ideas related to effective leadership. We start with the Christian faith perspective because it is an important part of the Christian's personal beliefs and values (the "being and becoming" part of the Management Pyramid model).

Faith Perspective on Leadership

The biblical teaching on leadership begins with the understanding that humans who follow the call of God ultimately serve God in all that they do. Central to this idea is that we should be imitators of God who first served us. God's call to serve is inherent in the first great commandment to love God with all our heart, soul, and mind. Service to God can be in the form of human hands and hearts caring for some of the least of humanity as a responsible citizen or in the context of one's career.[17]

Biblical Principles of Leadership

The Bible presents several principles that apply to leaders who view their work in terms of service to God. See Exhibit 12-2.

We also can learn a lot about leadership by considering the examples of leaders mentioned in the Bible.

Biblical Examples

Scripture narrative offers contrasting examples of leaders. The experiences of Abraham, Moses, Joshua, Gideon, Saul, Daniel, David, Samson, Solomon, Esther, Rahab, and Joseph are well known.[18] But the experiences of less prominent leaders are described, too, such as Barak, Deborah, and Jephthah.[19] For many of them, like those who were official leaders chosen to help Moses, we have no names.

Sometimes a leader's ego can have drastic consequences if the leader is unwilling to change. King Herod's sister-in-law Herodias, the wife of his brother Philip, complained about John the Baptist. Herod had John imprisoned at her request.[20] On Herod's birthday the daughter of

EXHIBIT 12-2
Biblical Leadership Principles

- The fundamental requirement for leaders is that they be found trustworthy.[21]
- Leaders are people of integrity.[22]
- Leaders need to have wisdom and good judgment.[23]
- The person who is faithful in lesser tasks will be faithful in greater tasks.[24] The focus here is not on the opportunities for promotion that faithful leaders gain but rather on the character of the leader regardless of the task. The corollary to this is that to whom much is given, much is required.[25]
- The mere action of claiming to be a Christian can increase the expectations of others. Thus the Christian leader has a responsibility to be a model of moral behavior.[26]
- Followers of Christ will not "lord it over" by imposing or abusing their power and authority on subordinates. Rather, they will serve with compassion and humility.[27] At the same time, the Bible writers respect the leader's need at times to give orders to others so that things can be accomplished.[28]
- Leaders serve on behalf of others not merely for self-interests or for an occasion to put aside moral principles.[29]
- Whoever desires to be great among others will become a servant to them.[30]
- It is when the leader serves others that God is glorified.[31]
- Leaders do to others as they would have others do to them.[32]
- Leaders develop the same mind that was in Jesus Christ when he came to earth. The ministry of leadership should be a process of becoming a humble servant both to God and to others. This is a model of leadership not based on position but on relationship.[33]
- Leaders who serve God are the type of people who treat others with love, respect, and dignity.[34]
- Subordinates come to share the values that leaders prize.[35]
- Leaders who serve God have a responsibility to serve those in need, to correct injustices, and to serve with integrity.[36]
- Leaders who submit to the life-changing influence of God will develop character traits patterned after the fruit of the Spirit.[37]
- Leaders will engage in self-examination being wary of the tendency to have an inflated sense of self.[38]

Herodias danced for Herod. So pleased was he that he made an oath that whatever she asked for would be hers. When she asked for the head of John the Baptist, he was caught in a self-made dilemma. Perhaps to save face he complied with her request.

At other times when the leader is willing to change from what is expected, the whole community gains by it. An illustration of this is when David ascended to the throne succeeding Saul. It was customary in ancient times that a new king ascending the throne would destroy everyone in the household of the former king to prevent any revengeful uprising in the future. But because of David's oath to King Saul's son Jonathan, David refused to kill the sole remaining heir of Saul, Mephibosheth. In this touching story of redemption and loyalty, King David went against custom and saved Mephibosheth.[39]

A Biblical Story of Moses

In his article "The Leadership Qualities of Moses," Rabbi Ari Zivotofsky[40] explores three biblical vignettes from Exodus 2 that may reveal why Moses was selected as the leader for Israel. These stories expose the changes in Moses that prepared him to lead. In the passages from Exodus, "Moses is consistently portrayed as not only caring and concerned for others, but also as willing and ready to act upon those feelings."[41] Here is a summary of Moses' experiences that qualified him for selection as leader of the nation of Israel:

1. Exodus 2:11–12: Moses sees an Egyptian abusing one of the Hebrews. Seeing the injustice and incited to anger, Moses becomes a man of action.
2. Exodus 2:13–14: Moses again goes out among his people and attempts to intercede, not physically but verbally, on behalf of one Hebrew who was being abused by another. His chief leadership attribute emerges: his readiness to act against injustice.
3. Exodus 2:15–19: The third vignette reinforces this leadership attribute but advances the portrait of Moses further. When Moses observes Jethro's daughters being harassed by the Midianite shepherds, he intercedes in a nonviolent manner between two groups of non-Israelites. In addition, Moses moves past peacemaking and becomes a servant, providing water for Jethro's daughters and their herds.

"In each succeeding story there was seemingly less reason for him to get involved and yet, in all of these three archetypal cases, he intervened and attempted to save the victim(s) from the aggressor(s)."[42]

Moses was powerful in words and actions.[43] Moses, however, was not perfect as a leader. He had his faults. Besides his anger management problem, Moses was not a skilled delegator. He sometimes preferred to work alone instead of consulting with other leaders. Moses was sometimes not easy to work with, especially when he could not handle well people who had differences of opinion with him. These weaknesses may be what kept Moses humble.[44]

Several styles of leadership exist in Scripture.[45] In one story about King Nebuchadnezzar we see two contrasting styles of leadership.[46] King Nebuchadnezzar, like many kings in ancient times, ruled by fear and coercion as a dictator. Daniel, who eventually was elevated to a high official position of leadership, began as a slave. He showed that even slaves can lead by suggesting a plan whereby he and his fellow slaves could be tested and thereby avoid the king's wrath but still remain faithful to their moral principles.[47] In the experience of Jesus we see contrasting styles. At times he is as gentle and caring as a loving parent.[48] At other times his actions appear harsh. The effective leader bears the pain that followers experience as they confront the prospects of changing.[49]

A Biblical Story of Joshua[50]

Joshua grew up in a family that had been oppressed by slavery. He certainly knew hardship. But Joshua's influence lasted for a generation following his death. (Judges 2:7) And, at the end of his life, Joshua was called the servant of God. (Numbers 27:18–19) When Joshua was appointed the official leader of the Children of Israel, it was at a time of one of the greatest logistical challenges the nation had faced since leaving Egypt. The manna had stopped and the nation needed a way to obtain food. (Exodus 16:14, 16:31; Joshua 5:12)

Joshua was one of the few who, at the end of the day, was found faithful in obedience to his convictions. By this he was in the company of people such as Noah, Lot, Esther, Micaiah, and Job. (Genesis 6:8, 19:15; Esther 2:10; 1 Kings 22:8) He was a good follower and assistant. Joshua spent 40 years in the wilderness with the people who had disobeyed God. (Numbers 14:28–35)

One of the elements of Joshua's calling as a leader involved intercessory prayer on behalf of his people. (Joshua 7:6–15, 10:12–14) Faith was one of his gifts, which he used to encourage others to have faith, too. (Numbers 14:7–10) But Joshua had his weaknesses. Although otherwise his obedience to God was stellar, he slipped on one occasion. When God prohibited Israel from making any treaties with the Gibeonites, Joshua weakened under the influence of the Gibeonite emissaries. (Joshua 9:1–27) But Joshua learned from his mistakes and never repeated the same mistake again.

EXHIBIT 12-3
Individual–Group Leadership

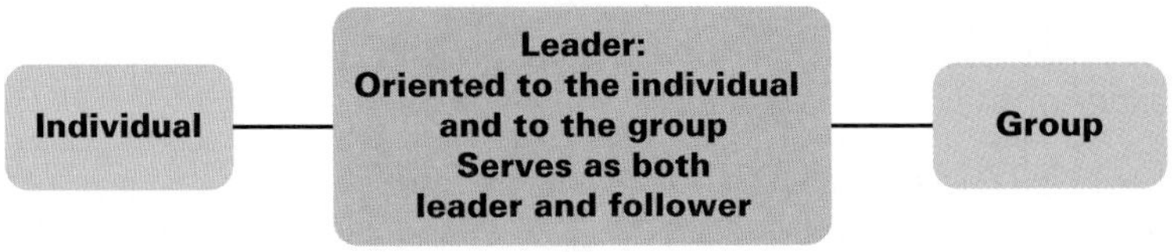

When King Rehoboam was put in office, he appeared to be interested in the opinions of his advisors on how to govern the people. His advisors were quick to point out the value of being a servant to the people.[51] Unfortunately Rehoboam rejected their advice and the result was rebellion.

A Beautiful Tension

Every leader is at the same time one person with ideas and interests that are separate from the group; however, the leader is forever connected with the group. It is at creation that we first see this inseparable connection. Human beings are whole creatures as persons interacting in a community.[52] From the creation account we conclude that God's plan was not that certain humans would dominate others but that self-interest would be tempered by interest for others. Likewise, humans were not created to be isolated from each other. Humans are interdependent, and because of this, serving one another is not optional. We were created free, autonomous beings that are responsible to and forever connected with our community, to the environment, and to God. See Exhibit 12-3.

Wholeness means caring for the needs of one person while also respecting true wholeness by caring for the needs of the group. There is a stunning beauty in this understanding of wholeness even if the aesthetic value is more abstract than the natural beauty that exists in physical creation. God gives leaders the privilege of continually standing in front of this great work of social-structure art as they carry out their work.[53]

The creation account also states the commission given humans—stewardship. Stewardship begins with the belief that it is God who is the owner of all the earth's assets. God has given humans the privilege of serving as stewards. And because of the stewardship relationship, humans are accountable for their actions to God and to the larger community. Stewardship applies equally to the relationships among humans and between humans and the environment. Because humans are stewards, they should be careful how they manage their resources. On the one hand, they are stewards of the relationship with each other. On the other hand, stewards have the responsibility of watching out for the interests of the organizations they serve.[54] See Exhibit 12-4.

EXHIBIT 12-4
Individual–Group Tension

Individual–Group Tension at All Levels of Organizational Leadership*

Needs of the Smaller Unit		Needs of the Next Larger Unit
Person	↔	Work group
Work group	↔	Department
Department	↔	Organization
Organization	↔	Corporation, industry, market
Corporation, industry, market	↔	Regional and national commercial groups
National commercial groups	↔	Global commerce
Nation	↔	World of nations

*** This tension exists for all levels of civic relationships: individual, family, neighborhood, township, county, state, nation, and international.**

Other Biblical Models for Leadership

Another interesting perspective with which to view leadership is the idea of covenant, which some believe is the template for all relationships including organizational relationships.[55] Scripture states that covenantal loving kindness and faithfulness will be the guiding principle.[56] Under a covenant relationship, leading is more than just doing things and expecting followers to take action in return. A covenant requires that the parties live a way that fosters the relationship for the long term. When an official leader is granted a disproportionate degree of power with respect to followers, an asymmetrical relationship is established. A relationship based on covenant principles prevents a leader from abusing power.

The biblical covenants encompassed both individuals and groups. When using covenant as a model for leadership, it matters whether you view the covenant as first being between God and community or first being between God and individuals.[57] If the covenant is viewed as primarily between God and the community, then the Christian leader will likely manage the individual–group tension in favor of the organization and its goals. But, if the focus of the covenant is seen as individual, then the leader may likely manage the tension in favor of individual interests. Strangely, in Western society, which tends to favor individualism, the organizations in which we work and serve tend to emphasize the protection of organizational interests.

Another biblical model of leadership is the New Testament concept of the body.[58] Paul describes the church in terms of the body. Jesus is the head of the church and each church member, because of the spiritual gifts members enjoy, can be a leader for the faith community. Human anatomy and physiology demonstrates the interdependence of the various body parts. The head needs the heart. The heart needs the lungs. The internal organs need the bones. Bones need muscles and connective tissue. For the human being to be whole, all the various parts and systems need to be present and fully functioning. So it is with the faith community of the church. We need each other for the experience as a believer to be fully enjoyed. Spiritual wholeness means that we are connected with Jesus Christ, the head of the church, and with each other.

One of the popular Bible passages that describes the incarnation of Christ offers another model for leadership. Just as Christ was fully God and fully human, so leaders will be fully oriented toward persons in the community while fully committed to foster the community's interests. Such leaders will not need to grasp for power but will be willing to serve by sharing power with others, in humility, realizing that others have been given gifts that the broader community needs. Every leader has legitimate self-interests. This cannot be avoided. But leaders who wish to model their lives after the ministry of Jesus are willing to also consider the interests of others. When needed, they are even willing to put aside their own self-interests for the good of the whole. The natural tendency under these circumstances is to shore up your own leadership power, thinking that you are on the verge of losing something important to leadership.[59]

From these biblical models—creation, covenant, body, and incarnation—we find support that covenantal leadership means caring for the needs of individuals and caring for the needs of the group as a whole.[60] This contributes to leadership being a group process, not just a matter of

Source: James Steidl/Shutterstock.

The biblical concept of covenant is one of several biblical models for leadership.

individual action. Sometimes leadership is letting frontline employee followers take the lead. You become the follower. This does not require that the official leader abdicates responsibility. But for some, it means that at times they must relax their need to promote their own ideas.[61] It means sharing leadership with followers. At the end of the day, it is not the leader's position or legitimate authority that makes the difference; it is through sharing both the leadership and followership process with others in the organization that leaders find the most effective means to manage the needs of individuals and the needs of the group.

The call to full-time leadership is like no other calling. Not everyone can live creatively and confidently in the midst of the tensions we've described. These tension-filled opportunities for service are like mini-Sabbath experiences, holy times and places where leaders walk with God.

Kingship and Leadership

The biblical ideal of kingship offers interesting food for thought by contemporary leaders who want to be covenantal in their leadership. Some scholars see planted in Genesis the seed that later developed into the idea of kingship. When God created humans, he created us in his own image and in royal fashion gave both men and women the royal status of having dominion over the whole earth representing God.[62] Just as God created the world to serve his creation, so all human beings rule over the earth in a way that creates harmony, peace, and well-being for all of creation. Humans serve each other not to oppress or diminish each other but to treat everyone with royal dignity.

Biblical kings were at the same time merely one human from among the community which they served. They were expected to be loyal followers of Yahweh, making Yahweh's kingship over the earth a pattern for their own work and watching out for and guarding the interests of the covenant across the entire community (nation).[63]

Moses gave directions that established elements of the ideal conduct of the king in his relationship to God and to the nation.[64] Not just anyone could become king: The king was to be chosen by God. The king was to make a personal copy of the Law in his possession. This gave him immediate accessibility for personal reference to God's Law on a daily basis. He was to copy the Law in the presence of the priests. This would assure the larger community of the nation that the king had not changed the Law to suit his own desires. This also established the balance of power with the priesthood.

The king was to read the Law every day to learn piety, as someone who faces perplexing problems and complicated political issues needs daily devotions. He was to be a model to others by observing the Law: The standard of behavior among the community will rise no higher than that of the king. This would promote humility reminding him that he is one from among many in the community. In response, God would bless the king with a long life and power to accomplish much good on the earth.

The people expected the king to come before them annually and renew his commitment to follow the covenant relationship with God. In this service of humility, which took place at the New Year Festival, the king expressed his sincere desire to promote justice and peace by his personal conduct throughout the land.[65]

The Christian Mind on Humility: The Danger of Making Comparisons with Others

Humility is a lost art in today's society. Filled with many good things that demand our attention, the ability to truly focus on those around us can be difficult at times. An individual that possesses true humility has a genuine desire to discover what other people can offer. Humility is freedom from pride and arrogance . . . freedom to discover the true worth of individuals that surround us on a daily basis.

Following in the footsteps of Christ *"who, being in very nature God, did not consider equality with God something to be grasped"* (Philippians 2:6, New Living Translation), true humility provides self-confidence that allows us to go about our tasks in the strength that God provides. Rooted in our character, true humility allows us to *"shine like stars in the universe"* (Philippians 2:15, NIV) and reflect the character of God to the world.

Karen Jacobs
Assistant Dean, School of Business
LeTourneau University
Longview, TX

The king's power had to be limited to prevent him from abusing his power. He was not authorized to develop such a large standing army that he could then rule as a tyrant over the nation. He was not to take into marriage too many daughters of foreign kings because doing so would create too many complicated entanglements for the nation. He also was limited in terms of the personal wealth he could develop. Such a limitation would prevent him from taking extraordinary control over the economic system so that he could gain power above his fellow countrymen.

In these limitations we see tensions. First, the king was to adequately defend the nation against foreign intrusion but at the same time not have such a powerful military that he could use it to abuse his power. Second, the king was to extend his influence into other nations but at the same time not become entangled in international politics through marriages. Third, the king was an important force for economic prosperity but at the same time was not to build his personal wealth above his fellow citizens.[66]

Just before popular King David died he added to the counsel of Moses, proclaiming God's intent for national leaders to fear God, rule over the nation with righteousness, and do good for the nation.[67] So loved was he that ever after David became the benchmark when considering the ideal king. The people came to define the ideal king as a person whose heart is transformed by the Holy Spirit, signified by the anointing with oil at the coronation ceremony. He is God's Anointed One, holy to serve God, the ruler of the whole earth, and the people in a way similar to the priests being anointed for their spiritual service.[68] He is a mediator between God and the nation. His close relationship with God gives him the power to bring peace, well-being, justice, and harmony to the land. With the covenant as his guide, the king is the protector and restorer of the people not only from foreign powers but also from moral lapses. Under his reign good fortune would result for everyone.[69] These ideas became so powerful in the minds of the people that they began to see the future hope of the Messiah as a David-like king.[70] See Exhibit 12-5.

Unfortunately not every king measured up to this high standard. Some kings let their status and power corrupt their relationships. Instead of working for the good of the people, they worked for their self-interests.

EXHIBIT 12-5
Ideal King—Ideal Leader

Ideal King	Ideal Leader
Meditates daily on covenant	Bases leadership on God's revealed will
Has a heart transformed by the Holy Spirit	Has a heart and mind transformed by the Holy Spirit
Becomes anointed for spiritual service to God, who is the ultimate King of the whole earth	Has a clear sense of spiritual calling; fulfills work that is essentially spiritual in nature
Has limited military, foreign relations, and economic power to avoid being a tyrant	Limits power with respect to the community, outside organizations, and personal wealth to avoid abusing power
Works to bring peace, justice, well-being, and harmony for the good of all people who are created in God's image	Focuses on the needs of the community instead of only self-interests; treats others with respect and dignity that royalty deserves
Protects and restores moral authority	Has the courage to ground decisions on solid moral basis; willing to make corrections for previous moral mistakes

Relationships with Followers

The Bible narratives describe leadership as based primarily on relationships. When the group of followers is relatively small, the leader can maintain a relationship with each person. In larger groups, the leader maintains a close relationship with a small group of followers. For example, Jesus chose just 12 disciples with whom to develop a closer relationship than with most of the other people who followed him. He also had a relationship with a group of 70 disciples, but the Gospel writers lead us to believe that he spent proportionately more time with the 12. Among the 12 disciples, he seems to have had still a closer relationship with Peter, James, and John. Although Jesus treated everyone fairly, he spent extra time with his disciples teaching them. This doesn't mean that he valued them more and others less. He explained more about the vision of the Kingdom of God in private to his disciples than he told the large group of followers. Jesus engaged his disciples in many two-way dialogues. He gave them opportunities to ask clarifying questions and voice their feelings. He delegated special assignments to them. He empowered them to do specialized work. He worked through his disciples to pursue the commonly shared vision.[71]

Leadership

Now that we have seen leadership portrayed in the Bible, what can we learn from contemporary research that will help us become more effective leaders? Let's begin by considering several definitions of leadership.

Definitions of Leadership

Over time, scholars and practitioners have offered a variety of definitions of leadership.[72] Some define it in terms of being a process: "Leadership is a process used by an individual to influence group members toward the achievement of group goals in which the group members view the influence as legitimate."[73] Others have defined it primarily in relational terms: "Leadership is a relationship between those who aspire to lead and those who choose to follow."[74]

But leadership can also be defined as an influence relationship *among* followers and leaders.[75] This definition offers several key ideas: First, leadership is a relationship in a community based on influence, but this influence is not one-directional from the leader to the follower—instead, it is multi-directional. Followers are not relegated to a passive role of "followership" in which they simply receive the influence of the leader. Leaders can become followers for a while; followers can become leaders for a while. The more complicated the organization, for example, a company such as General Electric, the more followers also need to take on leadership roles. Second, influence is noncoercive. Coercive relationships are about power and authority. In leadership relationships freedom is essential. Without freedom, followers could never influence leaders and vice versa. When a follower is influencing another leader, such a person may have unequal influence at that time. So the influence patterns experienced in the leadership relationship fluctuate. Third, the focus of the influence is change. Not all changes can be accomplished to the degree that everyone desires. Leadership is about attempting to make real changes together. Fourth, mutuality is what binds leaders and followers together. If the purposes are shared, then the actions that the community takes to make change will not represent only what the leaders want but rather what the community wants. This does not require that the purpose that one group of followers (or leaders) holds must be identical with the purpose of all others in the community.

Leadership as a Group Process

To understand leadership as a group process, let's consider the following example. Ellen, the nurse manager in the long-term care unit of a small hospital, stood in the doorway to the vice president's office, question marks sprouting from her eyes. She had just reported to the vice president what some of her employees had proposed to her and she was unsure whether their idea was a good one.

In a long-term care unit, a good share of the physical labor is done by nurse aides. It is largely a thankless job. The turnover rate and the number of employee no-shows can be high. One of the nurse aides had come to Ellen with a simple proposal: Let the nurse aides as a team do the scheduling. They would take full responsibility for scheduling as well as making last-minute adjustments when employees call in sick.

Source: Jupiterimages/Thinkstock.com.

The proposal that Ellen's employees brought to her was not typical. They wanted to share in leadership.

Ellen and her vice president discussed the proposal and after his encouragement she decided to give it a try. Ellen gave the team time to hammer out the details in a team meeting every week or two. Shifts and days were negotiated and assigned as a team. The team made the effort to accommodate individual scheduling needs of employees who had personal challenges to contend with. One of the informal leaders took on the task of encouraging her fellow employees who called in sick. The encouragement quickly took on the form of, "You made a commitment to us for this shift. If you are really sick, then stay home and get well. But if you are just taking the day off, that is not acceptable. We are all in this together." It wasn't long before employees who whiffed on a scheduled shift got the message from the team: Don't leave us in a lurch! We will support you, but you support us.

What happened next was remarkable. Turnover dropped and the number of "no shows" declined. Morale improved. Quality of care improved. The quality of Ellen's work life improved. The facility spent less on overtime pay and employee recruitment.

Ellen's experience illustrates the power that comes from sharing with others the job of managing the fundamental problem that exists in every organization and at every level of society around the globe: meeting the needs of the individual employee at the same time as meeting the needs of the group.

She also experienced through this process that the essence of leadership is not leadership from the official manager to the frontline employees but leadership with frontline employees who wanted to make real changes. Leadership requires an intentional movement away from the command and control structures of a managed context in favor of leveraging the trust and competency of the group.[76]

Many people think of leadership as something that can be found only in a few persons at the very top of just a few organizations in society. The reality is that leaders are found everywhere in society.[77] Others think about leadership in terms of competent, charismatic individuals doing things that result in other people (usually subordinates) making commitments to do what these leaders want done. Such a viewpoint focuses on the individual leader's thoughts and actions. People with this idea of leadership emphasize the importance of training individuals to be more competent in being an active leader of other individuals who are passive followers. The problem with this approach is that in reality leaders do not function in isolation from followers.[78] If you have ever been a leader, then you know after trying your best and making all the right decisions or doing all the right things and still not accomplishing all that you intended that it's not all about you.

There must be more to it. Leadership is a collective, group process more than merely the behavior of one person. It emerges from the inseparable, interdependent relationship rooted in and shared by many in the community. This idea is called *shared leadership*. **Shared leadership** is leadership that is distributed to the members of the entire group rather than being the job of just one person. Whether the leader has an official job title that sounds like "leadership" is irrelevant in many situations. Leadership is a shared activity, and learning to lead is about learning to share in both leadership and followership.[79]

As a manager who values shared leadership, you will understand the limitations of your own knowledge. You will want your workers to give suggestions for solving the problems that you share in common. You will value followers who speak up and attempt to persuade the group to consider an alternative to what you have suggested. You will seek advice from other leaders including the person to whom you report. When the situation requires, you will assert your own ideas for the good of the organization. And when followers cannot agree on the best course of action, you will listen to their ideas and, when necessary, make the decision. When this happens, you will respect their intelligence and thoughtful participation by explaining the rationale for your decision.

Top-level leaders cannot merely bring their authoritative expertise or simply announce solutions. Some solutions for adaptive challenges must shift to the people who perform the day-to-day work. Every worker has specialized knowledge or information that comes from his or her work. Thus, the work of a leader is about fostering a community of helping each other understand the core problems we face and to find solutions rather than imposing the solutions.[80]

It is not just the top-level leaders who face adaptive challenges. Leadership is needed at all levels and in all functions in the organization. Department managers who need quick solutions to technical problems depend on frontline workers. When the frontline employee notices a difference between the organization's goal and the task, that worker has the opportunity to lead from below.[81]

The idea that effective leadership is a shared activity is not new.[82] However, the traditional views on leadership have been so strong that empirical research (based on experience) of shared leadership is relatively recent.[83] From the focused study of this dimension of leadership we have learned several things, as outlined in Exhibit 12-6. First, leadership is embedded in the social interactions that occur among members of a group. Leadership occurs when all members of the team "are fully engaged in the leadership of the team and are not hesitant to influence and guide their fellow team members in an effort to maximize the potential of the team as a whole."[84] Second, shared leadership may be more complex and time-consuming than the traditional approach, which focuses on the work of an individual leader.

Third, the more workers are interdependent with each other the greater the need for shared leadership. Fourth, tasks requiring high levels of creativity benefit from shared leadership. Fifth, if leadership is a shared activity, then team members have authority to participate in charting the direction for the group.[85] Sixth, shared leadership does not necessarily do away with the need to designate someone to take responsibility. The official leader may still be needed to *manage the team's boundaries*, meaning to manage the relationships between the group and those outside the group, to provide intervention to encourage participation in shared leadership, to mediate between the team and the overall goals of the organization, and to encourage team members influencing supervisors.

EXHIBIT 12-6
Shared Leadership

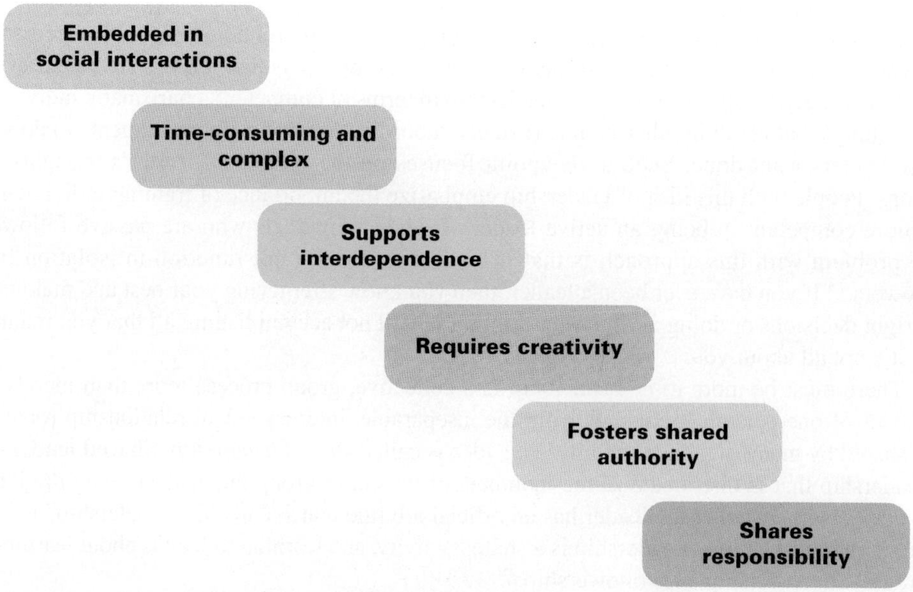

This notion of shared leadership is a way of integrating other perspectives such as traits, behaviors, and contingencies. For example, just because leadership is shared does not mean that individual traits and characteristics of persons who become leaders are unimportant. Likewise, individual behaviors are important in the shared leadership concept if leaders expect to influence the future direction of the group. To these other perspectives we turn next.

Leadership as Personal Traits

Before leadership became a topic of focused study, management scholars concentrated on the individual characteristics of persons who became successful leaders of large organizations, such as religious leaders, military officers, politicians, corporate executives, and famous scientists. Successful leaders were studied in terms of their personality, character traits such as confidence and courage, and even physical appearance. If leadership is an inside-out process, then this makes sense.

This individual perspective assumes that leadership is primarily an individual activity in which one person attempts to get others to do things that the individual wants to get done. This perspective has sometimes been called the **Great Man Theory**.[86]

As scholars realized that leadership is more than individual characteristics, eventually personal traits fell out of favor as a theory to explain why some leaders are more successful than others. Even so, scholars have recognized that traits are a necessary, but not sufficient, precondition that leads to success.[87] Traits that are believed to be associated with successful leadership include:

- Drive: A high degree of achievement motivation, effort, tenacity, and initiative
- Motivation to be a leader: Thinking about leading others, desiring to influence others, and the need for power
- Self-confidence and emotional stability
- The ability to inspire others
- Competence in getting things done
- Cognitive ability: The ability to process quickly large amounts of information, make judgments about which information is the most significant, and then bring conceptual order to the data for decision making
- Knowledge of the business environment in which the person works
- Other traits: charisma (though not necessary), creativity, originality, and flexibility
- Credibility, integrity, and trust

The traits credibility, integrity, and trust are important for all leadership situations. We will explore these next.

Credibility-Integrity-Trust Connection

Most leadership experts agree that credibility, integrity, and trust are fundamental elements required for effective leadership. As Exhibit 12-7 illustrates, these three elements are interrelated.

The logic of credibility is straightforward. When followers believe that the leader is trustworthy, competent, forward-looking, and inspiring, they attribute credibility to the leader.[88]

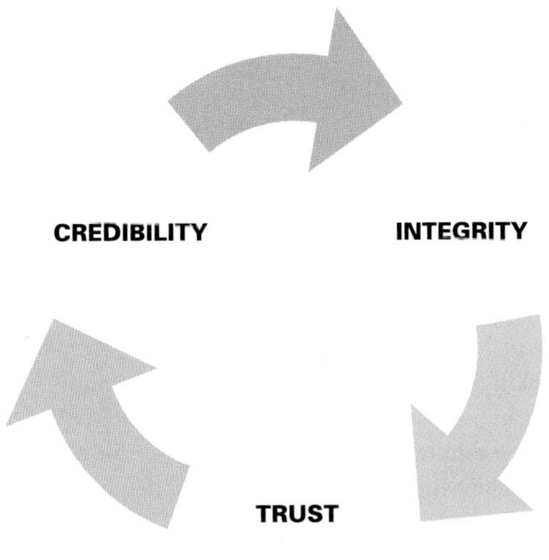

EXHIBIT 12-7
Credibility-Integrity-Trust Connection

Credibility is not easily earned but can be easily lost. In the aftermath of the 2008–2009 collapse of the mortgage finance industry in the United States, the credibility of leaders of companies such as Citigroup, Lehman Brothers, Goldman Sachs, Merrill Lynch, Morgan Stanley, and AIG fell when the public heard about the huge salaries, bonuses, and perks executives were receiving.[89] Upon hearing reports that some Tylenol products smelled bad, managers at the product's company, Johnson and Johnson, did not react immediately. When they did finally respond, the Food and Drug Administration heavily criticized the company for its slow response.[90]

You might be asked to assume the role of leader because of your technical knowledge and experience with the work processes of a company. This expertise provides you with a certain amount of credibility. Workers know that they can come to you for advice on how to solve problems because you have seen these problems before and know what it takes to solve them. You are trustworthy and competent.

Over time, however, your leadership will depend more and more on your expertise in dealing with people as well as the work processes. Once you are removed from the minute-to-minute working of a work process or once the current technology is changed for newer, computer-controlled technology, your technical expertise may decline. Now your credibility will depend almost entirely on your trustworthiness with people, your competence with people, and your ability to be forward-looking in terms of the people and the whole organization.

Being open and honest creates trust. One of the things that kills both candor and trust is when a leader hoards information. Information is the lifeblood of leaders and followers who are engaged in the organizational processes. Some information is highly sensitive and such details are shared only on a need-to-know basis with subordinates left out. But the need-to-know information arises under unusual circumstances and should be a very tiny fraction of the total information that is shared between leaders and followers.

Strangely enough the very people who need to be sharing the information widely across the organization are the very ones who tend not to share it. Sometimes this occurs because the leader is simply busy or absent-minded regarding others' need for information. Other times, getting and keeping information is a way that the leader can selfishly maintain control. If the leader develops a habit of keeping others in the dark, then workers will tend to become increasingly dissatisfied with their working conditions. Their morale will drop. Productivity will decline.

Trust is an essential element of leadership regardless of the perspective you take. The contributors to trust include competence, constancy, caring, fairness, candor, and authenticity.[91] The logic of trust is straightforward: If others do not trust you, then they will not believe you. If they don't believe you, then they will lack motivation to collaborate with each other in working vigorously toward the vision you present. If they are not motivated, then they will not act to help achieve the reality of that vision.[92]

In summary, without integrity, credibility is not established. Without integrity and creditability, followers will not loan their trust. And without trust, followers will be hesitant to give their commitment and collaborative effort.

Leadership as Individual Behavior

Wouldn't it be great if we simply knew the particular behaviors that effective leaders exhibit? If we knew the best leadership behaviors that get results, then we could simply train people to practice such behaviors. Unfortunately, leadership is more complicated than that.

Even so, scholars think that they have identified some important elements. Take, for example, two sets of leader behaviors. On the one hand, leaders can exhibit behaviors that show friendly concern for employees' emotional well-being, considering personal interests of and building personal relationships with employees. These leaders listen to their concerns and ideas. They ask employees for their ideas. On the other hand, leaders can behave in ways that support the job that needs to get done by assigning tasks, monitoring performance, and focusing on the job. These leaders give feedback to employees when the quality of their work is low or their performance is less than expected. They emphasize meeting deadlines and following standards. Which of these behavior patterns will be most effective? To be successful, should leaders let employees participate in decision making on issues that affect the organization and its ability to accomplish its goals?

The first researchers to tackle these questions began their work in the late 1940s at the University of Michigan.[93] They found that leaders generally were effective when they concentrated on **task-oriented** behaviors such as planning and coordination of work, clear delegation of

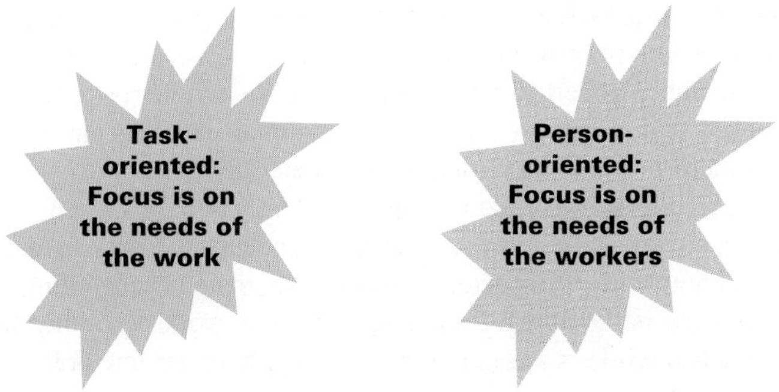

EXHIBIT 12-8
Two Major Categories of Leadership Behavior

tasks, setting performance goals, and monitoring performance. Researchers also found that leaders were effective when they were **person-oriented**: friendly and considerate, listening sincerely to employee concerns and problems, watching out for the development of employees, keeping employees informed, and showing appreciation for employees' contributions and accomplishments. When they were both task-oriented and person-oriented, performance was even better. Researchers also found that leaders who employed group supervision were more effective than those who employed one-on-one supervision. Group supervision uses group meetings, group decision making, and conflict resolution. See Exhibit 12-8.

Around this same time, researchers at The Ohio State University began studying similar ideas.[94] They labeled the person-oriented behaviors "consideration" and the task-oriented behaviors "initiating structure" behaviors. Analyzing information gathered from questionnaires that leaders completed, the researchers found that these two sets of behaviors are relatively independent of each other.

Some leaders can rate low on one set of behaviors and high on the other set, low on both, or high on both. Intuition might suggest that leaders who are more person-oriented get better results. They found that followers are more satisfied when their leader behaves in more person-oriented ways, but this doesn't mean that workers always showed better performance.

These findings led other scholars to develop a two-dimensional managerial grid.[95] According to this view, effective leaders do not flip-flop back and forth between the two types of behavior but rather simultaneously emphasize both person-oriented behaviors and task-oriented behaviors.

Some unresolved problems remain with the two factors of task-oriented and person-oriented behavior.[96] For example, in some work situations the demands of the job might require the leader to ask employees to make personal sacrifices or suffer hardships that a strictly person-oriented leader may not ask of employees. Also, an excessive emphasis on either person-oriented or task-oriented behaviors increases the risk of undermining effectiveness. If, for example, the leader becomes too personal with employees, it will undermine the ability of the work group to focus on getting the job done. But if the leader overemphasizes the tasks, the leader will progressively become more controlling of the details of the work. This, too, will undermine performance.

As scholars came to realize that leadership effectiveness is more complex than just two types of behaviors, they began to study other elements including the influence of situational factors.

Effective Leadership Depends on the Situation

The idea that, depending on the situation, effective leaders will adjust the pattern of their leadership behavior was first studied in the 1960s.[97] Building on the results of the research at the University of Michigan and The Ohio State University, other researchers studied two different patterns of leader behaviors under different conditions.[98] They found that person-oriented leaders seek to maintain good interpersonal relationships with followers. But here the leaders' certainty about their influence is important. Under conditions of uncertainty, leaders may likely spend time with subordinates to solicit their support by being considerate of their needs and preferences.

Task-oriented leaders will naturally gravitate toward behaviors focused on getting the job done, especially if they are uncertain about their influence. But as the structure of the tasks increases, the relationship with workers improves, and the leader's power becomes secure, the situation becomes highly favorable for the leader. In such a situation, the leader will be willing to relax with subordinates and show more interest in the relationship. Task-oriented leaders also do well under extremely unfavorable situations. Person-oriented leaders do best when conditions are moderately favorable. We might conclude that task-oriented leaders are better at achieving short-run improvements in organizational performance while person-oriented leaders might be better for achieving long-run improvements in performance.

Management researcher Robert House studied the effect of other factors on leadership effectiveness.[99] He believed that at least two types of situational variables can influence leadership effectiveness: differences between individual workers and differences in the tasks of the work. He called this the *path-goal theory* of leadership.

House and his associates studied four types of leadership behavior patterns. **Directive leaders** let followers know what is expected of them, participate in scheduling of work, and give specific guidance to workers. Directive leadership behaviors work best when tasks are ambiguous and complex or when workers are inexperienced and there are few policies and procedures available. But when work is routine and well-known by workers, workers will react unfavorably to directive leadership behaviors.

Supportive leaders show concern for the needs of workers by showing personal interest in their welfare and being friendly toward them. Supportive leadership behaviors are effective when the work is stressful, dangerous, or in other ways unsatisfying.

Participative leaders consult with followers and consider their suggestions before making a decision. This leadership behavior style works best when the task is unstructured and employee participation can bring clarity to what needs to be done.

Achievement-oriented leaders present challenging goals to their workers and communicate the expectation that followers will succeed. This increases employees' expectancy that their efforts will result in higher performance.

The Christian Mind on Leadership

The Bible writers distinguish between two types of leaders which we might call "masters" and "lords."[100] This is illustrated by the following table. Masters are seen as cruel. Lords, not to be confused with those who "lord it over others," serve.

Masters	**Lords**
Unjust (1 Kings 12:11, 21; Jeremiah 22:13)	Have a royal passion for justice (Psalm 82)
Oppressive (1 Samuel 8:11–17)	Judge the wicked (Psalm 72)
Pretentious: came to think of themselves as gods (Exodus 20:3)	Follow a mandate of social action: Frees people from the oppression of the wicked
Follow a lust for power (Judges 9:8–15)	Intolerant of social inequity
	A blessing to the nations
	Promote the covenant
Take	Give

Do the most effective leaders allow followers to participate while the ineffective leaders make the decisions for followers? The answer is that it may depend on the situation.[101] Several dimensions of a situation influence how much decision-making influence leaders will allow their followers and, in turn, their leadership effectiveness. For example, when acceptance of and commitment to a decision is vital to the outcome, effective leaders will more likely involve followers in the decision making. If there is enough time to include others in the decision making, the leader will more likely do so. Also, if the leader lacks key information but followers have the missing pieces, then the leader will likely include followers when making the decision. In other situations the leader may be more likely to make decisions alone, such as when the leader has adequate information to make the decision, when the problem being solved is highly structured, and when the leader is reasonably certain that followers will accept the decision made without their participation.

Leader-centered decision making

- **Leader makes and announces decision to followers**
- **Leader sells decision to followers**
- **Leader presents ideas and invites questions from followers**
- **Leader presents a tentative decision and gets followers' reactions**
- **Leader presents problem and invites suggestions from followers**
- **Leader defines limits for followers to decide; followers decide and report their decision to leader.**
- **Followers function within the same limits as leader; followers report their decision to the leader.**

Follower-centered decision making

EXHIBIT 12-9
Leader-Centered vs. Follower-Centered Decision Making

Thus, the leader has several options available. The leader can behave in a *leader-centered* (autocratic) style in which the leader makes the decisions and then announces these to followers. The leader might consult employees individually, getting their opinions on the issues to be decided, and then make the decision. The leader might bring the issue before a group of employees and entertain a group discussion after which the leader makes the decision. Another alternative, which gives more decision-making influence to followers, is that the leader brings a decision to the group and facilitates a discussion in which the group makes the decision. Or, at the other extreme, the leader can behave in a *follower-centered* (participative) style in which the leader asks followers to make the decision. See Exhibit 12-9.

Which leader behavior to apply depends on three sets of factors. *Managerial* factors include the value system of the leader, the degree of trust and confidence that the leader has with followers, the primary inclination of the leader toward being directive or participative, and the leader's perceived security of his or her influence. *Follower-related* factors include the followers' need for independence, whether followers are ready to assume decision-making responsibility, how well followers tolerate ambiguous situations, and how important the decision is to the followers. Last, *situational* factors such as the type of organization, the complexity of the organization, the nature of the problem, and whether a time pressure exists for making a decision also influence which behavior pattern the leader will select.

A similar approach to leadership style based on the two sets of leader behaviors (task-oriented and person-oriented) is that developed by leadership experts Hersey and Blanchard.[102] They were interested in the differences among followers in terms of their readiness to perform the needed work. They defined readiness in terms of two different variables: the ability and the willingness of the employee to perform the task.

If employees are unwilling and unable, the appropriate leadership style requires that the leader simply *tell* employees what needs to be done. The focus of this style is task-oriented or *directive*. Little emphasis is placed on people-orientation or *supportive* behavior. If, at the other extreme, employees are both willing and able, the leader can be successful by focusing minimally on both people-orientation and task-orientation. In this situation, the leader simply *delegates* the tasks, and the employees will likely perform well in accomplishing it. In the middle we have a situation in which the employees lack the ability but are willing to work. Here the leader must *sell* the task to the employees using a high degree of both people-orientation and task-orientation. The last scenario involves employees who have the ability but are unwilling. To be effective, the leader will focus on people-orientation to gain employees' commitment to *participate*.

In spite of scholars' emphasis on the two types of behaviors (person-oriented and task-oriented), two factors alone are insufficient to capture the complexity of leadership, followers, and the many situational variables that come into play. A two-factor theory does not explain why in some situations high performance is not achieved even when the leader engages in so-called "correct" behaviors. Most leadership scholars today, while recognizing the enduring importance of leader behavior, believe that simple models based on a few categories of behaviors are inadequate. While the influences of the situation and the followers are considered, the main focus of the behavioral approach to leadership is still on the individual behaviors of the official leader and does not account for the dynamic relationship that exists between leaders and followers. Behaviors are important especially when we consider that leadership is an experience shared among members of a group and not just the action of a single individual.[103]

The next perspective we'll explore attempts to go beyond mere leader behaviors to encompass the relationship that exists between leaders and followers.

Servant Leadership

The popular term **servant leadership** was coined by Robert Greenleaf in 1970 when he described what work life would be like if leaders saw themselves as servants first.[104] Greenleaf, a mathematician, became a manager at AT&T working in this quasi-public utility until 1964.[105] Greenleaf understood economics, but in spite of this, he encouraged leaders to go against the usual economic pressures if doing so meant that they became better servants.

In Greenleaf's view, leaders should be servants, focusing first on serving the needs of employees.[106] This inverts the traditional view that followers are expected to serve the leaders and employees generally are expected to serve the needs of the organization. The purpose of an organization is to provide meaningful employment. With this purpose in mind, the primary aim of leaders is the personal growth of the employees because it is the employees who serve the customers. The highest priority of the leader is to make sure that other people's needs are being met.

Servant-first leaders are opposites of leader-first leaders. They start with what Greenleaf thought was a natural feeling that they want to serve. The aspiration to lead comes second as a conscious choice. Servant leaders make it their business to make other people's priorities more important than their own interests.

At the heart of the servant leadership concept is trust, appreciation for others, and empowerment.[107] Becoming a servant leader can take time because it requires an entire transformation of the person, a whole new way of being.[108]

Servant leaders know how to listen to others. They empathize with the concerns of people. Service to others is an opportunity to bring healing and wholeness to those who have been broken. Servant leaders are self-aware. They use noncoercive persuasion rather than imposing the legitimate power of their position. These leaders practice conceptual thinking about the larger implications of specific activities. This ability corresponds with the abilities to think about the future consequences of decisions and act as an accountable steward. All of these areas of emphasis are directed at the growth of people. As organizations have grown larger, individuals have become fragmented from their communities. Servant leaders attempt to rebuild the sense of community from this fragmentation.[109]

Greenleaf proposed three tests to determine the effectiveness of servant leadership:

1. Do those who are served grow as persons?
2. Do they, while being served, become healthier, wiser, freer, more autonomous, and more likely to become servants themselves?
3. What is the effect of leadership on the least privileged in society? Will they benefit or be further deprived?

Greenleaf extended his concept of servant leadership to encompass the entire organization in its role of servant to workers and to the rest of society. Simply put, organizations are to be servants, too.

Servant leadership can be threatening to some who are focused on wielding their power and authority within a traditionally hierarchical structure. It is an affront to the human's need for power. Servant leadership offers a perspective that is quite different from what might be found in many high-energy, aggressive for-profit organizations that compete in dynamic industries. Its focus is not on the power and authority of the leader but rather on the needs of the followers. Serving others as the number one priority and the emphasis on human dignity are consistent with the principle of selfless love. Work life in large organizations is sometimes in need of redemption. Servant leadership offers hope that meaningful work life can be regained through a more humane culture that fosters a community of caring. Servant leadership promotes self-awareness and maintenance of mature, responsible relationships.[110]

Some have criticized servant leadership. For example, the idea that employees and their needs come ahead of stockholders and their needs conflicts with the obligation that managers must fulfill the needs of the owners and the organization. This can be potentially destructive to the organization. Although the idea of service is appealing, servant leadership does not adequately address the fact that there is more than one legitimate stakeholder group who needs to be served and that different stakeholder groups will at times have competing interests.[111] Another criticism is that the concept emerged from a setting in which the cold reality of the marketplace was not fully experienced by Greenleaf in his organization. Some question whether servant leadership is realistic in some situations such as dynamic for-profit environments.[112] Also, an extreme emphasis on workers and their goals may encourage passivity of leaders or, even worse, set up some servant leaders for manipulation by their less naïve followers.[113]

Christian scholars have differing opinions regarding servant leadership.[114] Some consider servant leadership to be not distinctly biblical. They point out that servant leadership can just as easily be supported by an atheist as by a Christian. They say the fact that believers and non-believers agree on an idea should immediately raise serious concerns about the biblical truthfulness of the idea. The biblical passages typically used in support of servant leadership may not have originally been intended to talk about the nature of leadership but rather the selfish motives that come from ambition.[115] The central biblical idea needed for understanding leadership is that the leader serves primarily God and from the relationship with God comes the motivation to serve others. Another perspective[116] is that the core ideas of servant leadership can be shared by Christians and non-Christians alike. While service to God is the foundation for leadership, service to others is a legitimate way of serving God.[117]

Transforming Leadership

Many people assume that if the leader does his work, then followers will follow. As a leader, you offer a reward to followers to line up with your vision. If they do, then you give them a reward. James MacGregor Burns[118] called this view **transactional leadership**.

But Burns also recognized a contrasting view called *transforming leadership*. **Transforming leadership** (also known as **transformational leadership**) is focused not merely on transactional exchanges that encourage compliance by followers[119] but on helping followers to trust the leader and to develop a loyalty toward the common vision. Leaders demonstrate transforming leadership when they help others accept the purpose of the group. They intellectually stimulate others in the organization to become thinkers of what the organization is all about. They encourage others to look beyond self-interests to the interests of the group. They pay attention to the emotional needs of others and consider individual differences. They also help others become better and develop as people.[120]

It is easy to see that transforming leadership is more than just followers getting rewards in exchange for getting a job done. Transformational leaders are genuinely interested in followers as persons in a community. They avoid authoritarian, command, and control behaviors.

The Christian Mind on Transformational Leadership

The essence of Christian leadership is the drawing of people to Jesus and leading their transformation into his likeness—all other tasks within the framework of Christianity and its mission serve this essential purpose. It follows that leaders within the Christian context will contribute to this transformational focus of discipleship. A test that may be applied is whether or not those led are better off when we leave them than they were when we found them. Are they more capable of contributing to the leadership process of the church than before? Are they more capable leaders themselves? Are they more like Jesus? This process of changing people in character and competency is the groundwork of the Gospel Commission.

Stanley Patterson, PhD
Associate Professor of Christian Ministry
Andrews University
Berrien Springs, MI

Leader-Member Exchange

Leadership researchers noticed that in many organizations leaders had relatively close relationships with some persons but did not have the same degree of closeness with others.[121] They also noticed that leaders do not show the same behaviors toward all followers. These observations led researchers to think about leadership in terms of the collection of individual relationships, called *dyads*, between the leader and each follower. The study of leader-follower relationships became known as **Leader-Member Exchange (LMX)**.

Two general types of relationships emerged based on the types of exchanges between leader and follower. With some followers, leaders developed closer, informal relationships and gave followers some influence. Roles and responsibilities were negotiated between follower and leader. Researchers called the followers with this type of relationship members of the *in-group*. With other followers, leaders tended to have a more formal, though fair, employment contract kind of relationship in which roles and responsibilities were not negotiated. Researchers called this group of followers the *out-group*. Individual personality differences and how well followers and leaders work together seemed to influence whether a follower became a member of an in-group or an out-group. Followers who were willing to expand their usual job responsibilities, taking on new tasks or projects, tended to become members of the in-group.

Further research on the relationship between leaders and members revealed that the higher the quality of the relationship, the higher the performance in terms of lowering turnover, increasing organizational commitment, improving attitudes toward the job, and higher performance with work tasks.

Experts in leader-member exchanges suggest that leaders who over time are able to develop a positive partner-type relationship with each subordinate that reports directly to them will bring benefits to themselves and to their organizations.

At first, the relationship may be distant as the follower tends to be self-interested. The exchanges between follower and leader start out at low quality. The influence is one-way, from leader to follower. The leader defines the subordinate's role. As the relationship develops, the exchanges are higher quality. The follower's interest shifts from self-interest to group interests. Influence becomes reciprocal. The follower's role becomes more negotiated with the leader.

Some have criticized Leader-Member Exchange theory on the basis that it seems to be contradictory to fundamental ideas of fairness and justice.[122] But there are practical issues that should be considered. For example, the leader has limited time available to spend developing a close relationship with each subordinate. If subordinates are allowed the freedom to act on their desires to expand their role by taking on more tasks or projects, then it is natural that their leader will develop a closer relationship with them. Because of their giftedness, some followers will more likely be able to contribute proportionately more to the good of the organization than other followers. Leaders will naturally have closer relationships with these persons.

While we have considered some of the dimensions of leadership, we need to distinguish between management and leadership to fully understand it.

The Distinction between Leaders and Managers

Many scholars have pointed out that *leader* and *manager* are related but not identical terms.[123] Yet it is difficult to precisely distinguish between the two concepts because both leaders and managers lead. Even so, the following distinctions help us better understand the two terms.

Many leadership experts think that the essence of leadership is the relationship between leaders and followers.

Source: Dean Mitchell/Shutterstock.

Managers must focus on the day-to-day operational challenges of the organization using reason, cost-benefit analysis, and decision-making skills to overcome the barriers to success. They analyze, structure, and order the work tasks and operational systems so that the organizational goals can be accomplished. Managers administer the work by focusing on how the work will get done, when, by whom, and with what resources. Their focus is on today's efficiency, keeping the current systems operating through planning, budgeting, controlling, and problem solving.

Leaders, while not ignoring day-to-day operational issues, bring to the organization the broad perspective of the outside world blended with the passion to attempt greatness in the future. Leaders focus on relationships between people. They innovate by focusing on the what and why. Their focus is on tomorrow's effectiveness and, if need be, calling for change when effectiveness suffers.

Understanding this distinction is important. One observation we can easily make is that all managers need to demonstrate leadership and all leaders need the ability to manage. Sometimes, such as in the experience of successful entrepreneurs, we can observe tremendous leadership ability and great managerial skill in the same person. At other times, individuals will excel at either leading or managing with some complementary abilities in the other area. Another observation is that a manager who chooses leadership behaviors does not relinquish management or control authority but rather chooses not to rely on it as a primary approach. Exhibit 12-10 shows the traditional characteristics of both managers and leaders.

While a distinction between the two terms is important, one unintended consequence has been that the two callings have come to be valued differently when viewed superficially.[124] Leaders, it is sometimes thought, make more of a difference to an organization than do managers. Leaders are at the top of the echelons in positions of authority over managers. They are paid more. Leaders inspire their underlings to greatness. With this approach, leaders are considered the thinkers who use their imaginations creatively to solve the future problems of the organization. In contrast, managers are stuck in the ruts of their policies and procedures. Managers are sometimes characterized as plodding along just doing what leaders tell them to do, controlling and being controlled. However, this is not necessarily the case because most managers need to exercise leadership. Thus, considering managers separate from leadership and leaders separate from management is incomplete.

Such a superficial view creates an unnecessary adversarial relationship between the two roles, which in practice are often inseparable. In this conflict, managers stifle leaders and leaders ignore managers. When this becomes ensconced in the organizational culture, it becomes

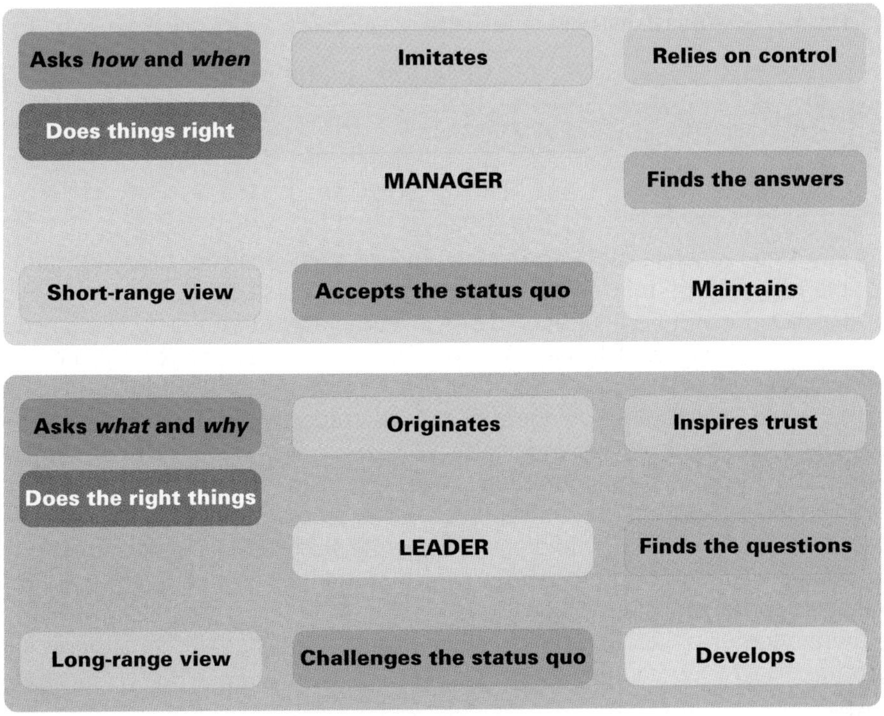

EXHIBIT 12-10
Managers vs. Leaders

Source: Based on Bennis, W. (1989). *On becoming a leader*. Reading MA: Addison-Wesley, pp. 44–46.

destructive. In reality leaders could never accomplish great things unless managers partnered with them to achieve success.

Paradoxes of Leadership

Because organizations are such complex organisms, organizational leadership is filled with its own set of paradoxical tension points. When providing direction, leaders will at times define the problems and the solutions and at other times identify the key questions and issues and ask others to define the problems and solutions. Because they are looking out for the interests of the entire organization, leaders must shield the organization from external threats but at the same time let the organization's members feel external pressures to a degree that they can handle them.[125]

As part of their visioning work, leaders provide orientation to members of the organization by clarifying roles and responsibilities. At the same time, leaders have the job of challenging current roles and, at times, resisting pressure to define new roles too quickly. When conflict arises, leaders must restore order. But sometimes they must allow conflict to emerge so that the organization can change. One of the core elements of a leader's work is in managing the norms that guide individual behaviors. Leaders work hard to maintain the positive norms that contribute to organizational effectiveness. At the same time, these same leaders have the responsibility to challenge unproductive norms when these get in the way of effectiveness.

Many other tension points exist for leaders. The following is a representative sample of these.

PATIENCE—URGENCY. Leaders have a sense of urgency about pursuing the vision so that no opportunity goes unused. This focuses their minds on the top priorities. At the same time, leaders need a degree of patience with the process and the people they are leading. It takes time for change processes to unfold and reveal opportunities. It takes time for people to integrate the vision into their day-to-day priorities. It takes time for people to transform.

LEADERSHIP WEAKNESSES.[126] Leadership expert Warren Bennis said, "It is one of the paradoxes of life that good leaders rise to the top in spite of their weaknesses while bad leaders rise because of their weaknesses."

CLEARNESS OF VISION—FLEXIBILITY.[127] You often hear about the importance of leaders communicating the vision of the organization. Leaders who are clear in their expression of the vision will garner support for the vision. However, clearness of vision creates rigidity and may be impractical for implementation. Leaders who listen to organizational stakeholders may be more flexible. Leaders must include sound judgment from the community when implementing the vision. However, some stakeholders may see such flexibility as a vision that is ambiguous and lacking direction.

Focus on an Organization

Leadership Edge Inc.

Many organizations exist to encourage practicing managers to share their faith in the marketplace, but few specialize in encouraging students. Leadership Edge Inc. is a nonprofit organization based in Durham, North Carolina, that encourages students who want to be leaders at Duke University and the University of North Carolina.

The mission of Leadership Edge is to provide leadership development based on scriptural principles to college and university students. The intent is that participants prepare for future leadership positions in their families, careers, and communities based on three fundamental concepts: character, competence, and commitment. Since its beginning in 1993, hundreds of university students have participated in the organization's mentoring program in which students are linked with practicing managers and business professionals.

More information about Leadership Edge can be obtained at the organization's website: http://www.lead-edge.com.

Chapter Summary

1. The biblical record on leadership presents many examples of successful and unsuccessful leaders. From these biblical models—creation, covenant, body, and incarnation—we find support that leadership means caring for the needs of individuals and caring for the needs of the group as a whole. The biblical ideal of kingship offers interesting food for thought by contemporary leaders who want to be covenantal in their leadership. The Bible narratives describe leadership as based primarily on relationships.
2. Leadership can be defined as an influence relationship *among* followers and leaders. Leadership is a shared group process. Shared leadership is leadership that is distributed to the members of the entire group rather than being the job of just one person.
3. Scholars believe that some personal traits explain why some leaders are more effective than others. These traits include drive, the motivation to be a leader, self-confidence and emotional stability, the ability to inspire others, competence in getting things done, cognitive ability, knowledge of the business environment in which the person works, charisma, creativity, originality, flexibility, credibility, integrity, and trust.
4. When followers believe that the leader is trustworthy, competent, forward-looking, and inspiring, they attribute credibility to the leader.[128] Credibility is not easily earned but can be easily lost.
5. Two sets of individual leader behavior have been studied. Some leaders concentrate on task-oriented behaviors such as planning and coordination of work, clear delegation of tasks, setting performance goals, and monitoring performance. Other leaders are person-oriented: friendly and considerate, listening sincerely to employee concerns and problems, watching out for the development of employees, keeping employees informed, and showing appreciation for employees' contributions and accomplishments.
6. As scholars came to realize that leadership effectiveness is more complex than just two types of leader behaviors, they began to study other elements including the influence of situational factors. For example, the path-goal theory of leadership describes particular situational variables which influence leadership effectiveness: differences between individual workers and differences in the tasks of the work.
7. At the heart of the servant leadership concept is trust, appreciation for others, and empowerment. Servant leaders know how to listen to others. They empathize with the concerns of people. Service to others is an opportunity to bring healing and wholeness to those who have been broken. Servant leaders are self-aware. They use noncoercive persuasion rather than imposing the legitimate power of their position.
8. Transforming leadership is focused not merely on transactional exchanges that encourage compliance by followers but on helping followers to trust the leader and to develop a loyalty toward the common vision. Leaders demonstrate transforming leadership when they help others accept the purpose of the group. They intellectually stimulate others in the organization to become thinkers of what the organization is all about. They encourage others to look beyond self-interests to the interests of the group. They pay attention to the emotional needs of others and consider individual differences. They also help others become better and develop as people.
9. Leadership can also be seen in terms of the collection of individual relationships, called dyads, between the leader and each follower. This approach to leader-follower relationships became known as Leader-Member Exchange (LMX).
10. Understanding the distinction between leading and managing is important. Managers must focus on the day-to-day operational challenges of the organization using reason, cost-benefit analysis, and decision-making skills to overcome the barriers to success. Leaders, while not ignoring day-to-day operational issues, bring to the organization the broad perspective of the outside world blended with the passion to attempt greatness in the future.

Key Terms

Discussion Questions

1. Select one of the Bible characters mentioned in this chapter and describe his experience as a leader.
2. Based on your experience as an employee, how would you define "effective leadership"? How would you define "ineffective leadership"?
3. Is Adolf Hitler an example of "good leadership"? Why or why not?
4. Reflect on a personal experience you have had as a leader (either official or unofficial). Which dimensions of this experience were rewarding? Which were unpleasant?

5. Is there an essential difference between individuals who are official leaders and others who become informal leaders unofficially?
6. Can you think of a specific situation in which your own characteristics as a follower affected your response to a leader?
7. In what way do so-called secular leadership theories agree or disagree with what is taught in the Bible?
8. Based on the many elements that are part of leadership experience, draw a map of the key concepts that you think are the most important for effective leadership.
9. What are the trade-offs that can be experienced with each of the various leader behavior patterns?
10. Of the two leadership styles (supportive, person-oriented and directive, task-oriented), which have you seen most often in your work? Which was most effective and why? In what way did the situation influence the effectiveness of the leader?
11. How can a person be person-oriented *and* still be task-oriented at the same time?
12. Do you think a person who values religious faith will tend to be more of a person-oriented leader or more of a task-oriented leader? Why?
13. Which behavioral styles of leadership, if any, seem to contradict the teachings of the Bible? Why?
14. Scenario: You are promoted from employee to manager. What should you do to build credibility and trust as a leader?
15. This chapter says that the foundation of effective leadership is being and becoming. On what basis do you agree or disagree?
16. Given all that is said in this chapter regarding leadership, would you say that leadership is something that can be learned? Why or why not?
17. If a leader is truly living the principles of Christ-like leadership, shouldn't the leader be willing to continue working with an underperforming employee indefinitely? Under what circumstances would a Christian leader discipline or fire an employee?
18. What important management perspectives can we learn from Philippians 2:1–11 (Imitating Christ's Humility) and John 4:1–42 (The Woman at the Well)?
19. Discuss the circumstances when task-oriented leaders are most successful and when person-oriented leaders are most successful.
20. Discuss the components of transformational leadership.
21. Discuss servant leadership and what types of activities and attitudes would characterize a servant leader.

STUDENT EXERCISES

1. Read one of the "Royal Psalms" and write a summary of the code of conduct for a king described in the Psalm you chose.[129] The "Royal Psalms" are the following: Psalm 2, 18, 20, 21, 45, 72, 89, 101, 132, 144; 2 Samuel 23.
2. Your assignment is to take a leadership role in an organization to manage a team of people or a one-time project. Write a personal journal of your experiences. Each journal entry should include the following:
   a. **The Situation and My Emotional Reaction to It:** Write a narrative describing an event, activity, or a conversation that you have as part of your leadership experience. Also describe your emotional reaction to the situation. This may require more than one paragraph. If you have difficulty identifying your emotional reaction to the situation, try completing the following sentence: "When ______________ happened, I felt ___________ because I ___________."
   b. **Learning about Leadership:** Describe what you learned about leadership from the situation, activity, or conversation. This can be one or more paragraphs. You should state something specific about leadership rather than just a generic statement such as "It takes good leadership to get things done." Yes, but what dimension(s) of leadership did you learn from the specific situation you experienced?
   c. **Learning about Myself:** Describe what you learned about yourself as a result of the situation, activity, or conversation. This can be one or more paragraphs. If you have difficulty verbalizing what you learned about yourself consider completing one or more of the following sentences:
      i. "I learned that I . . ."
      ii. "I am . . . " (referring to a character trait or personality trait)
      iii. "I learned that I need . . ." (referring to a personality trait)
      iv. "I can . . ." (referring to skills or abilities that you have)
      v. "I feel . . . when . . . happens." (referring to emotions that you experience)
      vi. "I prefer . . ." (referring to the types of people or situations at work)
3. Your assignment is to read the entire book of Proverbs in the Bible. Submit a one-page typed outline of specific passages from Proverbs and one sentence for each passage explaining in your own words what you think it offers as instruction to leaders.

Wisdom Literature on Leadership

Bible Passage	Comment

4. Your assignment is to read one of the four Gospels (Matthew, Mark, Luke, or John) in the Bible. Submit a one-page typed table of specific passages from that Gospel and one sentence for each passage explaining in your own words what you think it offers as instruction to leaders today. A minimum of five passages is required.

Leadership from the Gospel of ________

Bible Passage	**Comment**

5. **The Mirror.** Write a one-page, typed description of yourself as a leader *based on your past experiences* as a leader. Include at a minimum the following items:
   a. Strengths: Personality trait(s) and/or temperament(s)
   b. Weaknesses: Personality trait(s) and/or temperament(s)
   c. One leadership success you have enjoyed and what you learned as a result
   d. One leadership failure you have experienced and what you learned as a result
6. **Shadowing a Leader.** Make arrangements to "shadow" a leader for a day attending meetings, sitting in on conversations, discussing leadership situations. Write a two- to three-page typed discussion of what you observed and what you learned about leadership as a result.
7. **Prayer for a Leader.** Write a one-paragraph typed prayer for a leader in a specific situation that you or another leader is facing. This can come from something you observed, heard about, or read about this semester. Be prepared to share your prayer in class with students. Think about it: How do the words of this prayer reflect your own personality trait(s) and/or temperament(s)?

IN-CLASS EXERCISES

Issue Debates/Discussions

Divide the class into small groups of five to six people each. Choose a set of "Discussion Topic" statements from the list that follows. Hand out a sheet of paper containing the "Discussion Topic" statements. Assign some of the groups to defend one statement as valid and other groups to defend the other statement(s) as valid. For this exercise, students do not necessarily need to agree with the perspective they are asked to defend. In fact, defending a point of view that a student disagrees with can be an amazing teaching-learning experience for undergraduates by helping them to intellectually go outside their usual thinking patterns and develop critical thinking skills. Give the groups 5 minutes to discuss. Then call for groups to give a summary of the rationale they developed. Discussion can follow.

Discussion Topic #1: Which of the following definitions/descriptions of a leader's humility best describes the Christian perspective?

A. **Humility is not self-contempt.** "To paraphrase C. S. Lewis, humility does not exist in handsome people trying to believe they are ugly and clever people trying to believe they are fools. Tiger Woods can acknowledge his greatness at golf without violating the spirit of humility. False modesty regarding one's gifts can actually lead to pride—pride in one's better-than-average humility." "Humility is more like self-forgetfulness. It is flowing with life with minimal self-consciousness, as when we become totally absorbed in a challenging task, an exciting game, or even a life mission."[130]

B. **Humility is the quality of not being proud because you are aware of your bad qualities.** Humility is the quality of being humble or having a lowly opinion of oneself; meekness, lowliness, humbleness: the opposite of *pride* or *haughtiness*.[131]

Discussion Topic #2: You are a shift manager at a retail store. One of your employees (a professed Christian) appears to be involved in stealing from the store. This employee has not been caught in the act but you have strong suspicions (and some evidence) to suggest that merchandise items are leaving the store with this employee without the employee paying for them. Based on the following approaches to leadership, what would you do? As a Christian, what biblical support do you have for your leadership response? (Assign each of these perspectives to a different group):

A. **Theory X** (from Chapter 11, Motivation)
B. **Theory Y** (from Chapter 11, Motivation)
C. **Servant Leadership**
D. **Shared Leadership**

Discussion Topic #3: How do the Beatitudes apply to leadership? The *Oxford English Dictionary* defines "beatitude" as "a declaration or ascription of special blessedness." Consider the Bible passage from Matthew 5:1–12. Identify elements in this passage that apply to leaders and their work.[132]

> **Matthew 5:1–12**[1] And when He saw the multitudes, He
> went up on the mountain; and after He sat down, His
> disciples came to Him.[2] And opening His mouth He
> *began* to teach them, saying,[3] Blessed are the poor in
> spirit, for theirs is the kingdom of heaven.[4] Blessed are
> those who mourn, for they shall be comforted.[5]
> Blessed are the gentle, for they shall inherit the earth.[6]
> Blessed are those who hunger and thirst for righteous-
> ness, for they shall be satisfied.[7] Blessed are the
> merciful, for they shall receive mercy.[8] Blessed are
> the pure in heart, for they shall see God.[9] Blessed
> are the peacemakers, for they shall be called sons of
> God.[10] Blessed are those who have been persecuted
> for the sake of righteousness, for theirs is the kingdom
> of heaven.[11] Blessed are you when *men* cast insults at
> you, and persecute you, and say all kinds of evil against
> you falsely, on account of Me.[12] Rejoice, and be
> glad, for your reward in heaven is great, for so they
> persecuted the prophets who were before you. (New
> American Standard version)

In what ways are leaders specially blessed?

Discussion Topic #4: To be effective, leaders who are managers must learn how to be servants.

A. **Managers must *learn* how to be servants of subordinates.** Servant leadership for the manager means more than just doing the managerial job. Because they face the pressures of monitoring, organizational structure, and control, managers do not automatically tend toward service of their subordinates. They tend to think of subordinates as servants who need structure and control. Servant leadership, therefore, is not natural. It must be learned.

B. **Managers are *automatically* servants of subordinates.** By its nature, the work of a leader who also is a manager means serving others. Managers today have less discretionary time than managers of the early 1900s. Today's managers are expected to engage in community activities to have an active presence in the community. Thus, community activity is not something that managers can perform exclusively on their own time. Because of the extreme time pressures at work, many managers work at home doing paperwork or reading to keep up with things at work. They are expected to entertain others in the business world. Work could not get accomplished if managers were not serving their subordinates. Managers typically spend over 40 percent of their time responding to and involved in communications that others have initiated. Communication from subordinates and peers consumes most of this communication.[133] To say that to be a *true* servant leaders must add to this the responsibility of attempting to make their subordinates better people (meaning, help them become servant leaders) underrepresents and undervalues the service-nature of a leader's work. Such an expectation that results in feeling guilty (for not doing more to help people change themselves) is manipulation.

Discussion Topic #5: Review the Hersey-Blanchard Model presented in this chapter that presented four leadership styles. With the strong Christian emphasis on serving others and on fostering covenantal relationships with employees, is it appropriate for a Christian leader to engage in supportive person-oriented behaviors just enough to get the job done?

A. **Yes.** All leaders, whether they are Christians or not, have a limited amount of time to spend on task-oriented behaviors and person-oriented behaviors. If the Christian leader maintains a high degree of person orientation on a constant basis, employees will take advantage of the leader and tasks will not be accomplished efficiently. This does not mean that the leader must be disrespectful and mean to employees. Focusing on the tasks does not mean that the Christian is breaking a covenant. Part of covenantal relationships is helping others get tasks done that are valued by the community.

B. **No.** The Christian leader will constantly focus on people and on the relationships. This is the essence of covenantal thinking. It is the people who get the job done. Without them, a task orientation is meaningless. The Christian cannot engage in too much supportive person-oriented behaviors. Also, focusing on the workers and their needs does not need to compete with focusing on the work and its needs. These two can be integrated.

Discussion Topic #6: Organizational leaders have the job of influencing members of the organization to achieve organizational objectives. To accomplish this to what degree should leaders attempt to change the underlying values and beliefs of individual organizational members?[134]

A. **To a great degree.** Leaders have a responsibility to see that organizational goals are achieved. If changes are necessary on a large scale, they must encourage the values and beliefs of organizational members to change accordingly. The changes in values and beliefs eventually become integrated into the organizational culture, which supports the changes on a long-term basis. Without changes in values and beliefs, change will not be permanent. Further, leading change of values and beliefs is an opportunity for the Christian leader to infuse Christian values and beliefs into the changes that take place.

B. **To a limited degree.** Even if the organizational goals and outcomes are worthy and expected to benefit members of the organization or those they serve, attempting to change underlying values and beliefs is not moral. Leaders do not always know what is best for the organizational members. However, some leaders will abuse their influence over weak and insecure members, coercing them to believe in ways that support the leader's power. Even if a Christian leader has laudable goals, coercing organizational members to accept Christian values and beliefs is contrary to Christian principles of freedom of choice. Requiring organizational members to believe as Christians believe is essentially using one's leadership power to evangelize non-Christians. This is not appropriate in the work setting.

Endnotes

1. Hendricks, G., & Ludeman, K. (1996). *The corporate mystic: A guidebook for visionaries with their feet on the ground.* New York: Bantam Books. p. xviii.
2. Kouzes, J. M., & Posner, B. Z. (2002). *The leadership challenge.* (3rd ed.). San Francisco, CA: Jossey-Bass. p. 23.
3. Moses, David, Saul, Solomon, Peter, and Jesus all are examples of leaders who, at times, displayed emotions.
4. Nehemiah 1:1–3. Nehemiah lived during the 5th century B.C. See Brueggemann, W. (2003). *An introduction to the Old Testament: The canon and Christian imagination.* Louisville, KY: Westminster John Knox Press. pp. 363–374.
5. Nehemiah 1:4–11.
6. Brueggemann, W. (2003). *An introduction to the Old Testament: The canon and Christian imagination.* Louisville, KY: Westminster John Knox Press. p. 369.

7. The king's only stated concern was how long Nehemiah would be gone to manage the rebuilding of the walls and gates.
8. Maciariello, J. (2003). Lessons in leadership and management from Nehemiah. *Theology Today*. 60(3), 397–407.
9. Nehemiah 2:17–18.
10. Nehemiah 4:1–5.
11. Nehemiah 4:7–15.
12. Nehemiah 6:1–8.
13. West, J. K. (1981). *Introduction to the Old Testament*. (2nd ed.). New York: Macmillan Publishing Company, Inc. pp. 406–414.
14. Kotter, J. P. (1988). The leadership factor. *McKinsey Quarterly*. 2, 78.
15. Burns, J. M. (2003). *Transforming leadership: A new pursuit of happiness*. New York: Atlantic Monthly Press. pp. 211–213; Lattore, P. (2005). Leadership. In Stevens, R. P., & Banks, R. (Eds.). *The workplace ministry handbook*. Vancouver, BC: Regent College Publishing. pp. 131–136.
16. The metaphor of head, hand, and heart was used to explain the concept of whole-person shepherd leadership by McCormick, B., & Davenport, D. (2004). Leader as shepherd. *Executive Excellence*. 21(2), 6. See also Griffin, T. J., & Gustafson, J. (2007). Balancing the leadership paradox. *T + D*. 61(5), 50–54; Chewning, R. C., Eby, J. W., & Roels, S. J. (1990). *Business through the eyes of faith*. San Francisco, CA: HarperSanFrancisco. p. 133; De Pree, M. (1989). *Leadership is an art*. New York: Doubleday. p. 136; Kouzes, J., & Posner, B. (2003). Character development: It's what leadership development is all about. *Executive Excellence*. 20(9), 3–4; Senge, P. (1996). *Synchronicity: The inner path of leadership*. San Francisco, CA: Berrett-Hoehler. p. 1; Drucker, P. F. (1954). *The practice of management*. New York: Harper & Row. p. 157; Byler J. (2006). *The heart of Christian leadership*. Lancaster, PA: Global Disciples. p. 8; Ramsey, R. D. (2004). Understanding the culture of your workplace. *Supervision*. 65(8), 4. Also see 1 Samuel 16:7.
17. This assumes that the human is aligning personal behavior with biblical principles. Several Bible passages are usually referred to in support of this: Genesis 1:28; Leviticus 19:18; Deuteronomy 28; Ecclesiastes 12:13–14; Proverbs 3:9; Matthew 25:40; Luke 10:27; Romans 13:9–10; 1 Corinthians 1:9, 10:31; 2 Corinthians 5:18–20; Galatians 5:13–14; Ephesians 3:14–19, 5:1; Colossians 3:17, 3:23–25; 2 Timothy 2:20–21; 1 Peter 4:11. One example of a leader serving God whose story is recorded in the Bible is that of Moses. Following his death Moses repeatedly is called the "servant of the Lord" (e.g., Joshua 1:1, 1:13, 8:31). An example of the pervasiveness of this idea in Christian thought comes from the *Westminster Shorter Catechism*: "*Q. 1. What is the chief end [purpose]of man? A. Man's chief end is to glorify God.*" Scripture passages offered in support of this are Psalm 86; Isaiah 60:21; Romans 11:36; 1 Corinthians 6:20, 6:31; Revelation 4:11. *The Heidelberg Catechism* expresses a similar thought in its opening question: *"Question 1. What is the only comfort in life and death? Answer: That I with body and soul both in life and death, (a) am not my own, (b) but belong unto my faithful Savior Jesus Christ . . . who . . . makes me sincerely willing and ready, henceforth, to live unto him."* Scriptures offered in support of this include Romans 14:7–8; 1 Corinthians 3:23, 6:19. See also Stevens, R. P. (2006). *Doing God's business: Meaning and motivation for the marketplace*. Grand Rapids, MI: William B. Eerdmans Publishing Company. pp. 22–24.
18. Some of these are mentioned in Hebrews 11:32–38.
19. Judges 4:6–22, 11–12.
20. Matthew 14.
21. 1 Corinthians 4:2. Several writers have contributed to our understanding of biblical principles of leadership, including Higginson, R. (1996). *Transforming leadership: A Christian approach to management*. London: SPCK. pp. 29–34.
22. Leviticus 19:15; Deuteronomy 1:16–17, 16:18–20, 17:14–20, 19:18–19, 25:13–15, 27:19; 1 Samuel 12:1–4; 2 Samuel 18:11–12; 2 Chronicles 19:6–7; Nehemiah 5:14–18; Proverbs 10:9, 17:7, 20:28, 24:23–26, 25:2, 29:4, 29:14, 31:4–9; Ecclesiastes 10:16–17; Isaiah 16:5, 60:17; Zechariah 8:16; Acts 20:32–37; Romans 12:8; Luke 19:1–8. For an interesting review of biblical principles of leadership see Woolfe, L. (2002). *The Bible on leadership: From Moses to Matthew—Management lessons for contemporary leaders*. New York: AMACOM. pp. 2–23.
23. Genesis 41:33; Deuteronomy 1:13; Proverbs 16:10, 16:12.
24. Luke 16:10.
25. Luke 12:48.
26. Chewning, R. C., Eby, J. W., & Roels, S. J. (1990). *Business through the eyes of faith*. San Francisco, CA: HarperSanFrancisco. p. 137.
27. Numbers 12:13; Judges 18:7; 1 Kings 12:7, 21:29; 2 Samuel 9:7; 2 Chronicles 12:6–7; 1 Kings 12:7; Proverbs 28:16; Isaiah 2:12; Ezekiel 28:3; Matthew 18:4, 20:25–28; Mark 10: 42–45; Luke 3:15, 22:25–27; John 3:28; Colossians 3:12–17; Ephesians 4:32; 1 Peter 5:2–3, 10:4–11; Luke 10:34–34. This trait of serving for the greater good of the community rather than for the self-interest of the leader is parallel to ideas in the writings of some Greek and Roman philosophers such as Plato, Dio Chrysostom, and Epictetus before and during the 1st century A.D. See Seeley, D. (1993). Rulership and service in Mark 10:41–45. *Novum Testamentum*. 35(3), 234–250.
28. See Matthew 8:9; 2 Thessalonians 3:4. Also, note these New Testament passages where the Greek word (*kel-yoo' o*) for "to command" is used: Matthew 8:18, 14:9, 14:19, 14:28, 18:25, 27:58, 27:64; Luke 18:40; Acts 4:15, 5:34, 8:38, 12:19, 16:22, 21:33–34, 22:24, 22:30, 23:3, 23:10, 23:35, 24:8, 25:6, 25:17, 25:21, 25:23, 27:43. The Old Testament also uses the word (*tsaw-vaw*) many times. Here are a few examples of the 474 uses of the Hebrew word: Genesis 2:16, 6:22, 12:20, 28:6, 32:4, 32:19, 42:25, 49:29, 49:33; Exodus 1:22, 31:6, 34:32, 36:6; Ruth 2:15, 3:6; 1 Samuel 17:20, 18:22; Esther 4:10, 4:17. See the discussion of the tension between directing and serving in Chewning, R. C., Eby, J. W., & Roels, S. J. (1990). *Business through the eyes of faith*. San Francisco, CA: HarperSanFrancisco. pp. 143, 151.
29. Deuteronomy 17:14–20; Ezekiel 34:1–16; 1 Corinthians 8–9. This trait of serving for the greater good of the community has a parallel ideas in the writings of some Greek and Roman philosophers before and after the 1st century A.D. See Seeley, D. (1993).

Rulership and service in Mark 10:41–45. *Novum Testamentum*. 35(3), 234–250.
30. Proverbs 15:33, 16:19, 22:4, 29:23; Matthew 23:11; Mark 9:35–37; Luke 9:46–48, 22:24–27. See also Chewning, R. C., Eby, J. W., & Roels, S. J. (1990). *Business through the eyes of faith*. San Francisco, CA: HarperSanFrancisco. p. 91.
31. 1 Peter 4:8–11.
32. Matthew 7:12; Matthew 22:39.
33. John 15:15; Philippians 2:3–11.
34. Proverbs 3:27; Matthew 7:1–4; Romans 12:9–21, 15:1–2; 1 Corinthians 13:4–7; Colossians 3:12; Ephesians 4:31–32.
35. Proverbs 29:12.
36. Deuteronomy 24:14; 2 Chronicles 19:4–11; 2 Samuel 8:15; Psalm 72:1–17; Zechariah 7:10; Matthew 8:1–3 21:12–13, 23:13–29; Mark 2:15–17; Luke 11:42–52; James 2:1–4.
37. Joshua 1:7–8; Ezra 7:25; Galatians 5:22–23; Philippians 4:8; Colossians 3:12–15; 1 Timothy 2:1–2; Titus 1:5–9. Some scholars suggest that the Beatitudes of Matthew 5 are good characteristics of the Christian leader. See Chewning, R. C., Eby, J. W., & Roels, S. J. (1990). *Business through the eyes of faith*. San Francisco, CA: HarperSanFrancisco. pp. 133–137.
38. Proverbs 16:18–19, 25:27, 26:12; Romans 12:3; 1 Corinthians 12:7–11; Galatians 6:3; Philippians 2:3–8.
39. 2 Samuel 9; 21.
40. Zivotofsky, A. Z. (1994). The leadership qualities of Moses. *Judaism*. 43(3), 258–269.
41. Zivotofsky, A. Z. (1994). The leadership qualities of Moses. *Judaism*. 43(3), 259.
42. Zivotofsky, A. Z. (1994). The leadership qualities of Moses. *Judaism*. 43(3), 263.
43. Acts 7:22.
44. Numbers 12:3.
45. Rush, M. (1983). *Management: A biblical approach*. Wheaton, IL: Victor Books. pp. 209–224.
46. Daniel 2:1–13.
47. Higginson, R. (1996). *Transforming leadership: A Christian approach to management*. London: SPCK. pp. 134–139.
48. Matthew 19:14.
49. John 2:13–16. On this see the book Friedman, E. H. (2007). *A failure of nerve: Leadership in the age of the quick fix*. New York: Seabury Books.
50. Based on the book by Blackaby, H., & Blackaby, R. (2004). *Called to be God's leader: How God prepares his servants for spiritual leadership*. Nashville, TN: Thomas Nelson Publishers.
51. 1 Kings 12:7–13. See comments on this in Rush, M. (1983). *Management: A biblical approach*. Wheaton, IL: Victor Books.
52. Hoeksema, H. (1966). *Reformed dogmatics*. Grand Rapids, MI: Reformed Free Publishing Association. p. 199; Berkof, L. (1941). *Systematic theology*. Grand Rapids, MI: William B. Eerdmans Publishing Company. p. 192; Berkouwer, G. C. (1962). *Man: The image of God*. Grand Rapids, MI: William B. Eerdmans Publishing Company. p. 203. Creation theology has been cited by scholars (Roman Catholic and Protestant) as one of the pivotal foundations for understanding the believer's place in business. See for example Grudem, W. (2003). *Business for the glory of God: The Bible's teaching on the moral goodness of business*. Wheaton, IL: Crossway Books. pp. 11–17; Griffiths, B. (1984). *The creation of wealth: A Christian's case for capitalism*. Downers Grove, IL: InterVarsity Press. pp. 49–53; Stevens, R. P. (2006). *Doing God's business: Meaning and motivation for the marketplace*. Grand Rapids, MI: William B. Eerdmans Publishing Company. pp. 19–39, 164–183; MacKenzie, A., & Kirkland, W. (2003). *Where's God on Monday? Integrating faith and work every day of the week*. Colorado Springs, CO: NavPress. pp. 17–20; Novak, M. (1996). *Business as a calling: Work and the examined life*. New York: The Free Press. p. 127; Beed, C. (1990). *God's economic strategy: A biblical study*. Monograph published by the author. Melbourne, Australia. p. 22; Rossouw, G. J. (1994). Business ethics: Where have all the Christians gone? *Journal of Business Ethics*. 13(7), 557–570.
53. Romans 1:20; Ephesians 2:10. The Christian worldview "declares from the outset that each of us is unique and in the image of God, but that the God in whose image we are made is communal." Sire, J. W. (1990). *Discipleship of the mind: Learning to love God in the ways we think*. Downers Grove, IL: InterVarsity Press. p. 64.
54. Many Christian scholars have highlighted the concept of stewardship. The following are representative: Grudem, W. (2003). *Business for the glory of God: The Bible's teaching on the moral goodness of business*. Wheaton, IL: Crossway Books. pp. 47–60; Hill, P. J. (1991). Biblical principles applied to a natural resources/environment policy. In Chewning, R. C. (Ed.). *Biblical principles and public policy: The practice*. Colorado Springs, CO: NavPress. pp. 169–182; Acton Institute. (2007). *Environmental stewardship in the Judeo-Christian tradition*. Grand Rapids, MI: Acton Institute. pp. 1–119. See also the following Scriptures that are often used in support of this idea: Genesis 1:26–28; Exodus 19:5–6; Psalm 24:1, 50:10–12; Leviticus 25:23; Proverbs 3:9; Luke 16:12; 1 Corinthians 4:7.
55. McCann, D. P. (1997). On moral business: A theological perspective. *Review of Business*. 19(1), 12.
56. Proverbs 20:28; Micah 6:8.
57. Novak, D. (2000). *Covenantal rights: A study in Jewish political theory*. Princeton, NJ: Princeton University Press. p. 78. For a discussion on the community and individual nature of biblical covenants also see Robertson, O. P. (1980). *The Christ of the covenants*. Grand Rapids, MI: Baker Book House. pp. 280–300.
58. 1 Corinthians 12.
59. Galatians 5:22–26; Philippians 2:2–8; 1 Peter 4:8–11.
60. The doctrine of the Trinity also can be seen as a biblical model of the individual–community interdependence inherent in leadership relationships. On this see Griffiths, B. (1984). *The creation of wealth: A Christian's case for capitalism*. Downers Grove, IL: InterVarsity Press. pp. 53–55. For a discussion regarding the dangers of emphasizing either one to the extreme see Triandis, H. C. (1995). *Individualism and collectivism*. Boulder, CO: Westview Press.
61. See Ephesians 4:1–6.
62. This section based on: Cafferky, M. E. (2010). *Biblical kingship: Lessons for contemporary top-echelon leaders*. Paper presented at the Christian Business Faculty

Association Annual Conference. Lakeland, FL. October 21–23. See also Genesis 1:26–28; Psalm 8; Von Rad, G. (1972). *Genesis*. John Marks (Trans.). Philadelphia, PA: Westminster; Schneider, J. R. (2002). *The good of affluence: Seeking God in a culture of wealth*. Grand Rapids, MI: William B. Eerdmans Publishing Company. pp. 41–49. The idea that humans are royal is picked up in various places in the Bible. See Daniel 7:18, 7:27; Matthew 19:28, 25:34; Luke 22:30; 1 Corinthians 6:2–3; 2 Timothy 2:12; Revelation 1:6, 2:26–27, 3:21, 5:10, 20:6, 22:1–5.

63. Kenik, H. A. (1976). Code of conduct for a king: Psalm 101. *Journal of Biblical Literature*. 95(3), 391–403.
64. Deuteronomy 17:14–20. See on this Block, D. I. (2005). The burden of leadership: The Mosaic paradigm of kingship (Deut. 17:14–20). *Bibliotheca Sacra*. 162 (647), 259–278; Dutcher-Walls, P. (2002). The circumscription of the king: Deuteronomy 17:16–17 in its ancient social context. *Journal of Biblical Literature*. 121(4), 601–616.
65. The "Royal Psalms" record the speeches and hymns that kings presented at this annual event. See for example Psalm 2, 18, 20, 21, 45, 72, 89, 101, 132, 144; 2 Samuel 23. See also on this Kenik, H. A. (1976). Code of conduct for a king: Psalm 101. *Journal of Biblical Literature*. 95(3), 391–403.
66. Launderville, D. (2003). *Piety and politics: The dynamics of royal authority in Homeric Greece, biblical Israel, and old Babylonian Mesopotamia*. Grand Rapids, MI: William B. Eerdmans Publishing Company. pp. 289–340; Dutcher-Walls, P. (2002). The circumscription of the king: Deuteronomy 17:16–17 in its ancient social context. *Journal of Biblical Literature*. 121(4), 601–616.
67. 2 Samuel 23:1–4.
68. Several anointing ceremonies and references to the Anointed One are in the Bible, including one reference to anointing used in a parable. For example, see Judges 9:8; 1 Samuel 9:16, 15:1, 16:3, 16:13; 2 Samuel 2:4–7, 5:3, 5:17, 19:10; 1 Kings 1:34, 1:39, 19:15; 2 Kings 9:1–6, 11:1–12, 23:30; 1 Chronicles 11:3, 14:8, 29:22.
69. Isaiah 4:2, 4:5, 9:1, 16:5, 32:2; Jeremiah 17:25, 23:4–6, 33:15; Ezekiel 17:23, 34:23ff; Micah 5:3; Zechariah 9:9.
70. Launderville, D. (2003). *Piety and politics: The dynamics of royal authority in Homeric Greece, biblical Israel, and old Babylonian Mesopotamia*. Grand Rapids, MI: William B. Eerdmans Publishing Company. pp. 289–340; Mowinckel, W. (2005/1956). *He that cometh: The messiah concept in the Old Testament and later Judaism*. Grand Rapids, MI: William B. Eerdmans Publishing Company. pp. 155–180. See also Isaiah 9:6, 11:1, 11:10, 16:5, 55:3ff; Micah 5:1; Jeremiah 17:25, 23:5, 33:17, 30:9; Ezekiel 34:23ff, 37:24ff; Amos 9:11.
71. Dose, J. J. (2005). *Leader-member exchange in Scripture: Insights from Jesus, Noah, and Abraham*. Paper presented to the Annual Conference of the Christian Business Faculty Association. San Diego, CA. October 13–15. See also Matthew 11:1, 13:11, 16:20, 17:1–2, 17:19, 26:37; Mark 4:34, 9:2–3, 10:23, 14:32–34; Luke 9:21, 9:28–29, 22:7.
72. For one of the best comprehensive reviews of the various definitions see Rost, J. C. (1993). *Leadership for the twenty-first century*. Westport, CT: Praeger Publishers. pp. 37–96.
73. Howell, J. P., & Costley, D. L. (2006). *Understanding behaviors for effective leadership*. (2nd ed.). Upper Saddle River, NJ: Pearson Prentice Hall. p. 4.
74. Kouzes, J. M., & Posner, B. Z. (2002). *The leadership challenge*. (3rd ed.). San Francisco, CA: Jossey-Bass. p. 20.
75. Rost, J. C. (1993). *Leadership for the twenty-first century*. Westport, CT: Praeger Publishers. p. 102.
76. Kouzes, J. M., & Posner, B. Z. (2002). *The leadership challenge*. (3rd ed.). San Francisco, CA: Jossey-Bass. p. 29.
77. Kouzes, J. M., & Posner, B. Z. (2002). *The leadership challenge*. (3rd ed.). San Francisco, CA: Jossey-Bass. p. 20.
78. This was recognized decades ago by scholars such as Mary Parker Follett, Robert Tannenbaum, and Fred Massarik. For examples see Sethi, N. K. (1962, December). Mary Parker Follett: Pioneer in management theory. *Academy of Management Journal, 5*, 214–221; Tannenbaum, R., & Massarik, F. (1957). Leadership: A frame of reference. *Management Science*. 4(1), 1–19.
79. Raelin, J. (2006). Finding meaning in the organization. *MIT Sloan Management Review*. 47(3), 64–68; Pearce, C. L., & Conger, J. A. (Eds.). (2003). *Shared leadership: Reframing the hows and whys of leadership*. Thousand Oaks, CA: Sage Publications; Gibb, C. A. (1954). Leadership. In Lindzey, G. (Ed.). *Handbook of social psychology*. (Vol. 2). Reading, MA: Addison-Wesley. p. 884.
80. Heifetz, R. A., & Laurie, D. L. (1997). The work of leadership. *Harvard Business Review*. 75(1), p. 129.
81. Heifetz, R. A., & Laurie, D. L. (1997). The work of leadership. *Harvard Business Review*. 75(1), p. 134.
82. Gibb, C. A. (1954). Leadership. In Lindzey, G. (Ed.). *Handbook of social psychology*. (Vol. 2). Reading, MA: Addison-Wesley. pp. 877–917; Katz, D., & Kahn, R. L. (1978). *The social psychology of organizations*. (2nd ed.). New York: John Wiley & Sons. p. 332; Pearce, C. L., & Conger, J. A. (Eds.). (2003). *Shared leadership: Reframing the hows and whys of leadership*. Thousand Oaks, CA: Sage Publications. pp. 1–18.
83. This concept of shared leadership is not to be confused with the concept of "co-leadership" where two or more individual official leaders guide the organization. Rost, J. C. (1993). *Leadership for the twenty-first century*. Westport, CT: Praeger Publishers; Carson, J. B., Tesluk, P. E., & Marrone, J. A. (2007). Shared leadership in teams: An investigation of antecedent conditions and performance. *Academy of Management Journal*. 50(5), 1217–1234; Pearce, C. L. (2004). The future of leadership: Combining vertical and shared leadership to transform knowledge work. *Academy of Management Executive*. 18(1), 47–57; Louis, D. J., Lamothe, L., & Langley, A. (2001). The dynamics of collective leadership and strategic change in pluralistic organizations. *Academy of Management Journal*. 44(4), 809–837. For an insightful article on co-leadership see O'Toole, J., Galbraith, J., & Lawler III, E. E. (2002). When two (or more) heads are better than one: The promise and pitfalls of shared leadership. *California Management Review*. 44(4), 65–83.
84. Pearce, C. L. (2004). The future of leadership: Combining vertical and shared leadership to transform

knowledge work. *Academy of Management Executive*. 18(1), 47–57.

85. Cox, J. F., Pearce, C. L., & Perry, M. L. (2003). Toward a model of shared leadership and distributed influence in the innovation process. In Pearce, C. L., & Conger, J. A. (Eds.). (2003). *Shared leadership: Reframing the hows and whys of leadership*. Thousand Oaks, CA: Sage Publications. pp. 48–76.
86. This term "Great Man" reveals the fact that this theory developed in the West during a time when a strong gender bias was imposed on the concept of leadership. Most leaders were expected to be male.
87. Tannenbaum, R., & Massarik, F. (1957). Leadership: A frame of reference. *Management Science*. 4(1), 1–19; Kirkpatrick, S. A., & Locke, E. A. (1991). Leadership: Do traits matter? *Academy of Management Executive*. 5(2), 48–60; Northouse, P. G. (2007). *Leadership: Theory and practice*. (4th ed.). Thousand Oaks, CA: Sage Publications. pp. 15–26; Yukl, G. (2010). *Leadership in organizations*. (7th ed.). Upper Saddle River, NJ: Prentice Hall. pp. 190–220; Kouzes, J. M., & Posner, B. Z. (2002). *The leadership challenge*. (3rd ed.). San Francisco, CA: Jossey-Bass. pp. 24–32.
88. Kouzes, J. M., & Posner, B. Z. (1990). The credibility factor: What followers expect from their leaders. *Management Review*. 79(1), 29–33; Kouzes, J. M., & Posner, B. Z. (2008). *The leadership challenge*. (4th ed.). San Francisco, CA: Jossey-Bass. pp. 27–44.
89. Reports of executive compensation were published in several national newspapers. For one example see http://www.usatoday.com/money/companies/management/2008-09-28-executive-pay-ceo_N.htm.
90. http://money.cnn.com/2010/01/15/news/companies/over_the_counter_medicine_recall/.
91. Bennis, W. (1999). The end of leadership: Exemplary leadership is impossible without full inclusion, initiatives, and cooperation of followers. *Organizational Dynamics*. 28(1), 78.
92. Corrigan, P. (1999). *Shakespeare on management*. Dover, NH: Kogan Page Publishing. p. 102; Russell, R. F. (2001). The role of values in servant leadership. *Leadership & Organizational Development Journal*. 22(2), 76ff.
93. Bass, B. M. (1960). *Leadership, psychology, and organizational behavior.* New York: Harper & Brothers. pp. 96–102; Katz, D., & Kahn, R. L. (1952). Some recent findings in human relations research in industry. In Swanson, E., Newcommb, T., & Hartley, E. (Eds.). *Readings in social psychology*. New York: Holt. pp. 650–665. See a summary of the findings in Likert, R. (1961). *New patterns of management*. New York: McGraw Hill. pp. 5–25; Likert, R. (1967). *The human organization: Its management and value*. New York: McGraw Hill.
94. Fleishman, E. A. (1953). The description of supervisory behavior. *Personnel Psychology*. 37, 1–6; Stogdill, R. M. & Coons, A. E. (1957). *Leader behavior: Its description and measurement*. Columbus, OH: Bureau of Business Research, Ohio State University.
95. Blake, R. R., & Mouton, J. S. (1964). *The managerial grid*. Houston, TX: Gulf Publishing.
96. Yukl, G. (2002). *Leadership in organizations*. (5th ed.). Upper Saddle River, NJ: Prentice Hall. p. 60.
97. Fiedler, F. E. (1967). *A theory of leadership effectiveness*. New York: McGraw-Hill; Vroom, V. H., & Jago, A. G. (1974). Decision making as a social process. *Decision Sciences*. 5, 743–755; Hersey, P., Blanchard, K. H., & Natemeyer, W. E. (1979). Situational leadership and power. *Group and Organizational Studies*. 4(4), 418–428.
98. Fiedler, F. E. (1964). A contingency model of leadership effectiveness. In Berkowitz, L. (Ed.). *Advances in experimental social psychology*. New York: Academic Press. pp. 149–190; Fiedler, F. E. (1967). *A theory of leadership effectiveness*. New York: McGraw-Hill.
99. House, R. J. (1971). A path-goal theory of leader effectiveness. *Administrative Science Quarterly*. 16, 321–339; House, R. J., & Mitchell, T. R. (1974). Path-goal theory of leadership. *Contemporary Business*. 3, 81–98.
100. Klein, R. W. (1982). Liberated leadership: Masters and "lords" in biblical perspective. *Currents in Theology and Mission*. 9(5), 282–290.
101. Vroom, V. H., & Yetton, P. W. (1973). *Leadership and decision making*. Pittsburgh, PA: University of Pittsburgh Press; Vroom, V. H., & Jago, A. G. (1988). *The new leadership: Managing participation in organizations*. Englewood Cliffs, NJ: Prentice Hall.
102. Hersey, P., Blanchard, K. H. & Johnson, D. E. (2007). *The management of organizational behavior*. (9th ed.). Upper Saddle River, NJ: Prentice Hall. pp. 107–126, 171–203.
103. Houghton, J. D., Neck, C. P., & Manz, C. C. (2003). Self-leadership and superleadership. In Pearce, C. L., & Conger, J. A. (Eds.). (2003). *Shared leadership: Reframing the hows and whys of leadership*. Thousand Oaks, CA: Sage Publications. pp. 123–140.
104. Greenleaf, R. K. (1977). *Servant leadership: A journey into the nature of legitimate power and greatness*. New York: Paulist Press; Greenleaf, R. K. (1996). *On becoming a servant leader*. San Francisco, CA: Jossey-Bass Publishers.
105. Harvey, M. (2001). The hidden force: A critique of normative approaches to business leadership. *SAM Advanced Management Journal*. 66(4), 36–47.
106. Greenleaf, R. K. (1977). *Servant leadership: A journey into the nature of legitimate power and greatness*. New York: Paulist Press. pp. 21–61.
107. Russell, R. F. (2001). The role of values in servant leadership. *Leadership & Organizational Development Journal*. 22(2), 76; Spears, L. C. (2004). Practicing servant-leadership. *Leader to Leader*. 34, 7–11.
108. Spears, L. C. (2004). Practicing servant-leadership. *Leader to Leader*. 34, 7.
109. See also Russell, R. F., & Stone, A. G. (2002). A review of servant leadership attributes: Developing a practical model. *Leadership & Organizational Development Journal*. 23(3/4), 145–157. The Greenleaf Center for Servant Leadership maintains a website that contains more information: http://www.greenleaf.org/.
110. Johnson, C. (2001). *Meeting the ethical challenges of leadership*. Thousand Oaks, CA: Sage Publications. p. 136.
111. Beadles II, N. A. (2000). Stewardship-leadership: A biblical refinement of servant-leadership. *Journal of Biblical Integration in Business*. Fall, 25–37.
112. Johnson, C. (2001). *Meeting the ethical challenges of leadership*. Thousand Oaks, CA: Sage Publications. p. 136.
113. Bowie, N. (2000). Business ethics, philosophy and the next 25 years. *Business Ethics Quarterly*. 19(1), 7–20.

114. Rush, M. D. (1990). Biblical principles applied to management. In Chewning, R. C. (Ed.). *Biblical principles and business: The practice*. Colorado Springs, CO: NavPress. pp. 49–60; Beadles II, N. A. (2000). Stewardship-leadership: A biblical refinement of servant-leadership. *Journal of Biblical Integration in Business*. Fall, 25–37; Porter, B. (2000). A response to "Stewardship-leadership: A biblical refinement of servant-leadership." *Journal of Biblical Integration in Business*. Fall, 38–42; Smith, V. (2000). Response to "Stewardship-leadership: A biblical refinement of servant-leadership." *Journal of Biblical Integration in Business*. Fall, 43–47.
115. For example, Matthew 20:25–28; Mark 10: 42–45. See also Tucker, B. A., Stone, A. G., Russell, R. F., & Franz, G. P. (2000). The importance of leader visibility in servant-leadership. *Journal of Biblical Integration in Business*. Fall, 9–24.
116. Porter, B. (2000). A response to "Stewardship-leadership: A biblical refinement of servant-leadership." *Journal of Biblical Integration in Business*. Fall, 38–42.
117. See Matthew 25:40; John 13:12–17.
118. Burns, J. M. (1978). *Leadership*. New York: Harper & Row. pp. 257–397; Burns, J. M. (2003). *Transforming leadership: A new pursuit of happiness*. New York: Atlantic Monthly Press. The term "transforming leadership" was taken by Bass and revised for the corporate environment. Bass refers to it as "transformational leadership." See Bass, B. M. (1985). *Leadership and performance beyond expectations*. New York: Free Press.
119. For an interesting discussion of the historical roots of transformational leadership see Humphreys, J. H. (2003). Nothing new under the sun: Transformational leadership from a historical perspective. *Management Decision*. 41(1/2), 85–95. Also see Burns, J. M. (1978). *Leadership*. New York: Harper & Row, Publishers, pp. 141–254.
120. Bass, B. M. (1990). From *transactional to transformational leadership: Learning to share the vision. Organizational Dynamics*. 18(3), 21.
121. Graen, G. B., & Uhl-Bien, M. (1995). Relationship-based approach to leadership: Development of leader-member exchange (LMX) theory of leadership over 25 years: Applying a multi-level, multi-domain perspective. *Leadership Quarterly*. 6(2), 219–247; Dansereau, F., Graen, G. B., & Haga, W. (1975). A vertical dyad linkage approach to leadership in formal organizations. *Organizational Behavior and Human Performance*. 13, 46–78.
122. Harter, N., & Evanecky, D. (2002). Fairness in leader-member exchange theory: Do we all belong on the inside? *Leadership Review*. 2(2), 1–7; Scandura, T. A. (1999). Rethinking leader-member exchange: An organizational justice perspective. *Leadership Quarterly*. 10(1), 25–40; Dose, J. J. (2005). *Leader-member exchange in Scripture: Insights from Jesus, Noah, and Abraham*. Paper presented to the Annual Conference of the Christian Business Faculty Association. San Diego, CA. October 13–15.
123. Bennis, W. (1989). *On becoming a leader*. Reading, MA: Addison-Wesley Publishing Company. pp. 39–51; Hickman, C. R. (1990). *Mind of a manager soul of a leader*. New York: John Wiley & Sons; Kotter, J. P. (1990). What leaders really do. *Harvard Business Review*. 68(3), 103–111; Kotter, J. P. (1999). *John P. Kotter on what leaders really do*. Cambridge, MA: Harvard College; Kent, T. W. (2005). Leading and managing: It takes two to tango. *Management Decision*. 43(7/8), 1010–1017; Zaleznik, A. (1990). The leadership gap. *The Executive*. 4(1), 7–22; Griffin, T. J., & Gustafson, J. (2007). Balancing the leadership paradox. *T + D*. 61(5), 50–54; Zaleznik, A. (1977). Managers and leaders: Are they different. *Harvard Business Review*. 55(3), 67–84; Rost, J. C. (1993). *Leadership for the twenty-first century*. Westport, CT: Praeger Publishers. pp. 129–152; Kotterman, J. (2006). Leadership versus management: What's the difference? *Journal for Quality & Participation*. 29(2), 13–17; Covery, S. R. (1990). *Principle-centered leadership*. New York: Simon & Schuster. pp. 244–249; Howell, J. P., & Costley, D. L. *Understanding behaviors for effective leadership*. (2nd ed.). Upper Saddle River, NJ: Pearson Prentice Hall. p. 8; Higginson, R. (1996). *Transforming leadership: A Christian approach to management*. London: SPCK. pp. 25–26, 31–44.
124. Hickman, C. R. (1990). *Mind of a manager soul of a leader*. New York: John Wiley & Sons; Klay, R., Lunn, J., and TenHaken, V. (2004). Middle management as a calling. *Journal of Biblical Integration in Business*. Fall, 118–137.
125. Heifetz, R. A., & Laurie, D. L. (1997). The work of leadership. *Harvard Business Review*. 75(1), 124–134.
126. Bennis, W. (1989). *On becoming a leader*. Reading, MA: Addison Wesley. p. 47.
127. Johnson, B. (1996). *Polarity management: Identifying and managing unsolvable problems*. Amherst, MA: HRD Press. pp. 29–38.
128. Kouzes, J. M., & Posner, B. Z. (1990). The credibility factor: What followers expect from their leaders. *Management Review*. 79(1), 29–33; Kouzes, J. M., & Posner, B. Z. (2002). *The leadership challenge*. San Francisco, CA: Jossey-Bass.
129. Kenik, H. A. (1976). Code of conduct for a king: Psalm 101. *Journal of Biblical Literature*. 95(3), 391–403.
130. Myers, D. G., & Jeeves, M. A. (2003). *Psychology through the eyes of faith*. San Francisco, CA: HarperSanFrancisco. p. 173.
131. Definitions can be found in the *Cambridge Dictionary* online at http://dictionary.cambridge.org/ and the *Oxford English Dictionary* online at http://www.oed.com/.
132. For a discussion of this see Chewning, R. C., Eby, J. W., & Roels, S. J. (1990). *Business through the eyes of faith*. San Francisco, CA: HarperSanFrancisco. pp. 133–137.
133. Webber, R. A. (1972). *Time and management*. New York: Van Nostrand Reinhold Company. pp. 23–24.
134. Adapted from Yukl, G. (2010). *Leadership in organizations*. (7th ed.). Upper Saddle River, NJ: Prentice Hall. pp. 411–412.

CHAPTER 13

Change, Power, and Conflict

LEARNING OBJECTIVES

- Understand why managing change, power, and conflict is important to being a successful manager.
- Explain the Bible's perspective on change, power, and conflict.
- Understand how to successfully lead an organization that is changing.
- Describe the dynamics and proper use of power.
- Understand the two different types of conflict and the tactics that managers can use to manage conflict.
- Consider some of the paradoxes of leading change, using power, and managing conflict.

"Not understanding the degree to which the situation is politicized may cause a person either to use power and influence when it is unnecessary, and thereby violate behavioral norms as well as waste resources, or to underestimate the extent to which power needs to be employed, and fail in the task of implementation."[1]

"Some power-driven leaders (and organizations) can succeed in the short term, but experience suggests that power-driven individuals invariably 'contain the seeds of their own destruction' based on an apparently infinite need to prove themselves."[2]

JOHN'S EXPERIENCE WITH POLITICS AND CONFLICT

For the first half of his career, John Iverson[3] worked in staff support departments of various organizations in a dynamic service industry. Early in his career he worked in employee training. When the company he worked for downsized his department, he had an opportunity to transfer to the marketing department and become a market analyst. The only complaint he received from his new boss was that he worked slowly. John picked up the pace. He enrolled in marketing courses at the local university and over the next 3 years gradually developed his understanding of marketing. When the opportunity came to become a marketing director for another organization, he jumped at the chance to advance his career.

His first few senior-level discussions occurred at budget time. Reflecting on this later John remarked, "This was an eye-opener for me! I hadn't realized before this how important angling and pushing for budget allocations was for these leaders. When my opinion was asked on several budget issues, I felt completely unprepared to deal with the political dimensions to the questions." Another eye-opener was the difference in mentality he experienced in the new job. "Many staff support people in our industry are soft-hearted folks. Senior-level managers over profit centers are much more tough-minded." In spite of the challenges of learning company politics, John survived. Gradually he became more comfortable with the company politics.

Source: Jupiterimages/Thinkstock.com.

After 7 years as marketing director, John started feeling the itch for a new, larger career challenge. After about a year of job hunting, John landed a job in a small but successful organization. In his new job he had the opportunity to use his marketing skills to grow a newly acquired division. John was not a part of the acquisition and deal making. He was hired after labor contracts and supplier contracts were signed by the new owners. Looking back at his career path, John realized that it was in this new job that he learned the most about company politics and managing conflict.

John's marketing skills did prove to be helpful for growing the volume of business served by the division. However, the new division was not as profitable as top leaders wanted. The primary reason was the expense structure—a major portion of which was the salaries and benefits of several professional service providers. John felt that his hands were tied. He had discussions with the service providers and their support staff regarding other ways to reduce expenses. Gradually he and his management team reduced other operating expenses by 20 percent, but not without conflict in the process.

Next, John started discussions with the service providers regarding their employment agreements. He quickly realized that if he attempted to renegotiate the employment agreements, many of the professionals would bolt because they had other alternatives available to them. But John came under increasing pressure to achieve a better bottom line.

One afternoon 3 years into his work, John was summoned to the president's office where he received the news that he was being asked to resign. Given the increased pressure he had been under for the previous year, this was not a complete shock.

The president suggested that John might better succeed in his career if he took a job as a consultant, remarking, "You had trouble working with the senior-level management team and the service providers in your division."

Over the next 18 months, as John looked for his next career position, he reflected on the feedback from his boss. He had to admit that there was some truth to what the president had said. It was painful to see himself in the mirror that the president had held up to him. He also knew that the reason for being let go was not entirely his fault because the expense structure was, to a large degree, out of his control.

John Iverson's experience is not uncommon. Making the shift from non-managerial to managerial work requires more out of you in terms of managing change, company politics, and conflict than your previous job. Making the shift from mid-level managerial work to higher level leadership requires greater political skills. Moving from a staff support function to profit-center management requires quite a different mental approach to managing change, company politics, and conflict.

Who Cares About Change, Power, and Conflict?

One reason organizations hire managers is to help the organization integrate many different points of view on issues that arise. Managers are called to responsibly use their influence to get things done. This often involves helping organizational members navigate the difficult journey through conflict.

Like many managerial concepts we are exploring, change, politics, and conflict are found all around you. Roommates disagree on how their apartment should be organized. You and your spouse try to decide where to go for year-end holidays: Should you visit her family or his family? Conflict can erupt between parents and a young adult child if there is a disagreement regarding which college to attend or which career path to follow. One political party attempts to gain dominance over the other through the democratic process. This contest for power involves framing and reframing points of view. Candidates contrast their visions for the future. Party loyalists jockey for positions in leadership. In business, for example, a manager in one department at Archer-Daniels-Midland thinks that all managers should park their cars farther away from their office buildings to give employees parking spaces closer to the building. Other managers think just the opposite. They want closer parking spaces because they need quick access to their vehicles during the day. Even a change such as installing new carpet at church can involve power and conflict. Redecorating the church can represent a change in ministry focus that may be unsettling for some who desire to preserve traditional values as symbolized by present architecture and décor. For others, a change will represent an opportunity to connect the church with contemporary people in terms that they understand. Personal preferences over the aesthetic dimension of worship will clash as members attempt to use their influence during the decision-making process. Add to this mix the potential that such a change will involve major allocation of funds, and you have a recipe for more intensity in the political processes.

Change, power, and conflict management are integral to the managerial experience but especially so the higher up the chain of command your career takes you. Just recognizing when a situation is becoming, or already has become, political is important. Middle managers are sometimes unaware of the battles for supremacy that can be waged around conference room tables at the higher levels of leadership. Capital budget allocations are at stake. The ability of the departments and work units to achieve their separate goals is at stake. If bonuses are tied to operating performance and if operating performance is tied to the capital resources available to work units, then change, power, and conflict will be part of any strategic planning. Some argue that your ability to learn all you can about managing change, power, and conflict is what prepares you to serve an organization in a broader capacity. Your success in an organization can depend not on how smart you are or how hard working you are, but rather on your ability to negotiate and persuade others to support your ideas.[4]

One of the assumptions in this book is that dealing with change, company politics, and conflict is unavoidable if you expect to serve in management. These three interrelated dimensions of your work are so important that we must devote a portion of this text to this topic.

Persuading others to agree with you **Changing specific behaviors that lead to new ways of thinking and feeling** **Negotiating with someone to achieve a compromise** **Debating alternatives and assumptions** **Forming a coalition of support** **Correcting misunderstandings**	**Action**
Thinking of persuasive ways to frame the issues **Changing thoughts and feelings that lead to shared values** **Anticipating how others will react to change** **Considering how others will receive a message** **Evaluating the reasons for or against change** **Evaluating the external forces that drive change** **Feeling secure or insecure**	**Thinking & Feeling**
Beliefs about the significance of certain issues **Moral values influence which issues are top priority and which battles to fight** **Assumptions regarding what others know and believe** **Personality patterns in response to threats**	**Being & Becoming**

EXHIBIT 13-1

The Management Pyramid: Change, Power, and Conflict

Source: Courtesy of Michael E. Cafferky, © Michael E. Cafferky 2011.

Management Pyramid on Change, Power, and Conflict

It should be evident by now that the interconnections between who you are, how you think and feel, and what you do apply to just about every managerial setting and situation. The same is true when we consider the issues surrounding change, power, and conflict management as outlined in Exhibit 13-1.

Who you are includes a collection of beliefs, motives, values, and assumptions that you carry with you when you deal with change, company politics, and conflict. For example, your personality factors may lead you either to want more dominance or to be content with the influence you now have.[5] Also, your values become one of the most important influences with respect to your work when it comes to leading change, exercising power, and managing conflict. From thousands of years of human experience we have learned that the opportunity to exercise power unchecked by spiritual values will lead to the abuse of power.[6]

How you think and feel also affects how you manage change, power, and conflict. Your ability to anticipate how others will react to your vision for change can help you communicate the need for change in terms that are relevant to their concerns. Your abilities to manage your own emotions during change, to use influence, and to manage conflict play a role in your success as a leader. Change, power, and conflict all bring increased risk that as a leader you will be criticized (with or without justification) for what others believe are your motives, your point of view, or your actions. If you don't already have thick skin, then you will develop this as you learn how to survive and thrive in the midst of organizational politics and change.

Your actions in managing change, power, and conflict have consequences for your work.[7] Spending time getting to know who in your organization has power is vital if you want to use your influence to promote or resist change. For example, at Caterpillar, Inc., how managers manage their relationships with their subordinates will have a positive or negative effect on their influence in the organization. Developing expertise in some skill or knowledge that is valuable to your organization can increase your power. Perhaps the single most valuable way to increase your influence, lead change, and manage conflict is to develop your own competencies for positive relationships with people.

This chapter focuses on managing change, power, and conflict. We begin with the Christian faith perspective because it is an important part of the Christian's personal beliefs and values (the "being and becoming" part of the Management Pyramid model).

Faith Perspective on Change, Power, and Conflict

The dynamics of change, organizational power, and conflict all are represented in Scripture. Like other dimensions of life, it is impossible to completely separate these three dimensions in our experience. We will briefly look at each one separately.

Leading Change

We can glean the principles of change management in the Bible by reading the experiences of several leaders such as Joseph, Moses, Joshua, David, Solomon, Josiah, Nehemiah, Peter, and Paul. For example, Joseph was just 30 years of age when Pharaoh asked him to be Egypt's prime minister.[8] The environment for Egypt and the surrounding nations was changing rapidly. In one of the most unusual passages of Scripture we find Joseph making changes to national economic policies. In the space of just 15 years Egypt became more centralized in the control of all the key resources needed for survival. Tax laws were changed. The people eventually sold all their wealth-building assets to the government in exchange for food.

King Josiah is also evidence that age is not an important factor for leading change.[9] When he became king at the age of eight, the nation had fallen away from faith in God. A succession of unfaithful kings had led the nation to a state of disbelief. Prophets began foretelling the fall of Jerusalem. For example, it had been many years since the nation had celebrated the Passover. Josiah's first action to reform the government involved asserting fundamental religious values and changing the religious cultural symbols. He repaired Solomon's temple that had not been kept up under his father's leadership.

When workmen found the book of the covenant, they brought it to Josiah. The king immediately recognized that this book contained the statements of core values that were needed to bring true change not only in the government but also among the people. After studying it, Josiah called the government leaders, the temple leaders and the prophets, and the citizens of Jerusalem to meet with him for a renewal of the covenant with God. Josiah made a public declaration of his intention to follow the principles of God's covenant. The leaders and the citizens joined in the consecration service. Next, Josiah cleansed the temple of the idols and other materials that had been used for worshiping false gods. He proclaimed that the Passover would be celebrated again. In spite of the changes that Josiah brought to the government, so corrupt had the relationships with other nations become that his reforms alone were not enough to change the course of events that followed. The Israelite nation suffered under the hand of first the Egyptian and then the Babylonian empires. Under the Babylonian dominance, the nation's leaders were taken captive to Babylon where they remained for decades.

An experience of the early church illustrates how leaders went about the process of change. Some men from Judea were teaching Antioch Christians that salvation for the Gentiles could not be complete unless the Gentile men were circumcised. Paul and Barnabas vehemently disagreed with these teachers, arguing that Christ's death on the cross was sufficient alone for salvation. Paul and Barnabas were unable to convince the Judean teachers on the strength of their arguments. And the believers, most of them Jews, were confused. As a result, the church in Antioch selected Paul and Barnabas to be delegates from Antioch to bring the question to the church leaders in Jerusalem.[10]

The Jerusalem church leaders gathered to debate the situation. Open debate followed after which Peter stood up and gave his opinion on the matter: Requiring circumcision would place an unnecessary burden on Gentile believers. Further, salvation is based on the grace of Christ alone. Paul and Barnabas were asked to give their perspective, which they did by recounting the stories of how gentiles were converting to the Christian faith. Another Jerusalem leader, James, stated that he agreed with Peter. He suggested that Gentiles not be required to become circumcised but that instead they should be admonished to abstain from idol worship and from unchastity. Also, they should be encouraged to eat kosher meat.

These examples of leading change illustrate several important principles. First, change comes about when someone (or a small group of people) sees the need for change. They begin communicating the need to others. Sometimes the need for change involves dialogue and even debate. Second, solid values become central to the reason for change. Third, we find change leaders using existing reporting relationships to affect change. Fourth, commitments of time, energy, and resources are made as individuals submit to each other and to their belief in God's will. Fifth, leaders listen to others. Sixth, leaders are themselves willing to be changed.

Managing Power

The idea of power in Scripture stems from three root ideas. First, God is omnipotent as evidenced by his sovereign ability to create and to redeem.[11] Unrestrained, the power of God would be destructive to sinful humans. Balancing his own power to destroy is God's omnipotent love.

Bases of Power	Biblical Examples	Internal vs. External
Reward	Deuteronomy 5:16; Psalm 81:13–16; Proverbs 3:27, 18:21, 22:1, 27:2; Ecclesiastes 7:1	External
Punishment (compulsion)	Exodus 5:9–11, 20:2–6; Leviticus 25:43–53; Deuteronomy 15:6; Judges 8:22; 1 Samuel 9:17; Ephesians 6:9	External
Legitimate power of position	Genesis 1:26–28; Exodus 20:12; 1 Kings 9:19; Psalm 8:6; Proverbs 1:8–9, 23:22-25; Romans 13:1–8; Ephesians 6:1–3; Colossians 3:20; 1 Timothy 5:17; 1 Peter 5:3	Internal, External
Expertise, knowledge, wisdom, information	Genesis 41–47; Leviticus 19:32; Proverbs 12:24, 24:5; Ecclesiastes 7:19; Acts 7:22	Internal
Identification (referent): feeling closely associated with the person in power; desiring to model the leader's behavior	Genesis 24:12–14, 39:21, 40:14, 47:29; Joshua 2:12–14; 2 Kings 22-23; 1 Chronicles 12:33; Ruth 3:11; Mark 1:7, 6:22–23, 10:35; John 6:68–69, 21:15–19; Acts 9:26–30; 1 Corinthians 1:12; Philippians 3:10; 2 Timothy 1:7–9	External
Ecological power (the power to restructure jobs, work environment, organization, culture)	Exodus 5 (Pharaoh's control over work environment), 18 (Moses restructures leadership); Jesus adjusts the shared values of his followers (many verses)	External
Physical or military strength	Deuteronomy 4:38; Judges 6:2, 15–16; 1 Samuel 9:1–2; 2 Chronicles 26:13	Internal
Wealth	Deuteronomy 15:6; Proverbs 12:24,18:23, 22:7	Internal, External
Inheritance	Genesis 31:14; Judges 8:22–23; Colossians 3:24	External
God	1 Samuel 2:7–8; 1 Chronicles 29:11; 2 Chronicles 20:6, 25:8; Psalm 33:6, 62:11, 68:35; Philippians 3:21; Colossians 1:16–17; Hebrews 3:4	External

EXHIBIT 13-2
Sources of Power in the Bible[12]

Second, God created humans with the ability to use their power to serve each other.[13] Humans exercise their power of choice.[14] Some choose to use their power in responsible ways; others abuse their power. Third, the Bible writers recognize that in society there are differences in the distribution of power when comparing humans with each other and with the rest of creation. This is not arbitrary, capricious power but rather power that has a moral foundation of right doing and justice. Exhibit 13-2 outlines the sources of power in the Bible. The third column in the exhibit describes whether the source of power comes from outside or inside a person. For example, rewards come to a person from the outside, such as from the person's boss or coworkers. The power that comes from knowledge or expertise is an internal source of power because it comes from within the person. Later in this chapter we will cover the sources of power in more detail.

Power, Covenant, and Community

Because of the disparity in power distributed throughout the community, the biblical pattern is that those with the most power such as the king must have limits placed on their power to protect the community. These restrictions put kingship in the context of covenant and community.[15] This relationship is significant. It is only within community relationships that power can be exercised. And it is the community who stands to gain or benefit from the use of power. For the king to fulfill his God-given responsibility and the community its responsibility, both must exercise their full allegiance to God in all decisions.

Power in the biblical community is based on the covenant concepts of right doing (*sedeq*) and justice (*mispat*).[16] In a community, certain individuals or groups are invested with the power to act on behalf of the rest of the community to carry out justice. These individuals are usually recognized community leaders. When a community leader takes an action that is in support of what the community believes to be right, the community accepts the leader's power. But members of the community will resist the leader's actions if the action is against what the community believes to be right. Thus a community leader's power is derived, at least in part, from the moral convictions of members of the community. If a contradiction exists, then the leader's power is weakened. Power is therefore a matter of right doing and carrying out justice in a community setting. Leaders have power because people consent to obey. But the consent to obey is conditioned on the leader sharing with the community a common understanding of what is right. This congruence between what is right doing and what is justice ultimately comes from God, whose throne is described as being founded on both concepts.

One of the ideal types of power described in the Hebrew Bible is that of the power of loving kindness.[17] God gives this loving kindness as an example to humans. In return, humans express loyalty through obedience to God's will. In social relations when one person treats another with loving kindness, this creates a bond of loyalty that leads the other person to fulfill the requests of the loving-kindness person.[18] Another interesting observation from the Bible is that the term for loving kindness is sometimes paired with the term for truthfulness.[19] Those who are loyal to the person who shows loving kindness will be truthful. This nourishes a deep-seated trusting covenant relationship.

The New Testament's focus on the concept of authority deals with both the church and civil government contexts. The premise is that God has established an order for communal life that involves leaders having a recognized official office. It is the office to which authority is given, not just to the person holding the office. In the church, believers willingly subordinate to church leaders and cooperate with them.[20] All leaders who receive power exist only in the larger context of the community of people who voluntarily subordinate self-interests to the interests of the community.

Scripture often refers to power using the imagery of over and under.[21] If a person or nation is in a dominant position with respect to another, they would be referred to as having power over. Power in the mind of the Bible writers is to be found in a person's hand.[22] To put your hand on or over another means that you have the dominant influence and could direct the other person to act as you desired.

Distribution of Power

When one person or group dominates another, the other is dependent and vulnerable. For example, strangers are dependent and vulnerable. With their disadvantages that come from not knowing the language and their unfamiliarity with how to obtain life's necessities in a new place, others can take advantage of them.[23]

Scripture acknowledges the legitimate place of power in social settings as the following examples show: Parents have power over their children. In biblical times, a master would have power over the slave but should never use this power harshly.[24] The servant in a family would be subject even to the children. However, when children are foolish, they become subject to the servant. An employer has power over the employee but is expected not to use this power harshly. Judges have power over those who are judged. Kings and princes have power over their subjects, but these subjects ultimately are God's people. Normally, older siblings have power over younger siblings, and when this arrangement is threatened, older siblings act to reclaim the power. The poor are vulnerable and should not be oppressed. The borrower is servant to the lender. Some tribes are more powerful than others. Some armies are more powerful than other armies. Some nations are more powerful than other nations. Humans rule over the environment. Power is not just a one-way street with those in power in control all of the time. The way society is structured, we share power with one another. As a safeguard against corruption, we should use our power in humble and not arrogant ways.[25] The employer has power over the employee but also depends on the employee for production. Even oppressed people will wield the power that they have when they have suffered long enough. Each person's reputation is subject to the power of speech among those in the community. One person may have political power over others and still be dependent on those with specialized knowledge to provide counsel and guidance. Indeed, knowledge is power.[26]

Power Used for Good	Power Used for Evil
Pharaoh is fair to Abraham.[27]	Sarah oppresses Haggar.[28]
Joseph establishes fair policies.[29]	Samuel's sons take bribes.[30]
Pharaoh treats Jacob's family with respect.[31]	Ahab confiscates Naboth's vineyard.[32]
Josiah uses his power to implement reforms.[33]	Rehoboam oppresses the people.[34]

EXHIBIT 13-3
Power for Good and Evil

Although this may not have been the original intent at creation, there now are differences in power distributed throughout society. This suggests that power relationships will be or should be subject to redemption, just like any other dynamic in life.

Scripture offers several examples of individuals who used their power for good. Just as many, if not more, examples show what happens when individuals use their power to pursue self-interests at the expense of others. See Exhibit 13-3.

An interesting example of abuse of power occurred in the household of King David.[35] David became the most powerful of Israel's kings. He unified the nation and built it into a world power among the community of nations. He unified the government under a common set of religious values.

These accomplishments are all the more significant when you consider that David was a shepherd boy at the time he was swept into a position of influence. But David's rise to power was not without its difficulties. David's son Absalom used his position to undermine his father's legitimate authority. Absalom deceived companions, manipulated those around him, faked religious piety, and spread false reports.[36] Absalom took over the throne and David fled to safety.

A Biblical Story of King David: A Complex but Powerful Leader of Change[37]

David, one of the most popular and powerful of Israel's kings, is highly revered even to this day. More is written in the Bible about David than about any other king. David was a complex individual who displayed a variety of character traits. On the one hand, he was a caring individual. On the other hand, he displayed the ability to use violence to consolidate his power. He showed the ability to form strong friendships. He exhibited extraordinary oratory skills and astute political skills. Yet he succumbed to the temptation to lie.

David was not content to sit back and discuss the moral virtues of a situation, though he did plenty of contemplation as illustrated in the many Psalms he wrote. He was a man of action when leading change.

One of the great turning points in David's life was his adultery with Bathsheba, the wife of Uriah whom he sent into battle to be killed. This act of treachery, coercion, and disloyalty had a major effect on the nation. Violence and disloyalty plagued David the rest of his reign even though he experienced a complete spiritual transformation through accepting responsibility for his actions and repenting. This violence began in his own household and spread throughout the kingdom, becoming the chief reason why David was unable to complete his dream of building a temple.

Not every corrupt, power-abusing leader meets the same end as Absalom, who was killed by one of David's soldiers. But a concern in Scripture is that some use their disproportionate amount of power to harm others. Liberty from such abuses of power is highly prized. Leaders who follow God are expected not to "lord it over" their subordinates as do the unrighteous.[38]

An interesting tension point appears to exist in the Biblical record on power. Selfishly seeking power has no place in God's Kingdom.[39] However, we should use our power to serve. "Power is from God and if we reject it, we reject His will."[40]

Scripture looks forward to the day when God will right all wrongs and at the judgment day remove all earthly dominions and powers. Until that time, Christians have a responsibility to use power wisely and morally.

Managing Conflict

The central message of the Bible is a story about God's character and great works. God is a God of peace and not chaos.[41] Whenever self-interest is at odds with the interest of the community, conflict will surely result. God is sovereign and could have chosen immediately to simply wipe evil out of existence. Instead, for a time, he allows evil to exist with good. This conflict sets in motion the great plan of redemption.[42] Foreshadowed in the covenants and the prophets, the Messiah is all about redemption, without which conflict would be terribly destructive.

The ideal in life is that we live at peace with one another. But reality is usually far from the ideal. Whether because of pride, envy or greed, unwise talking, anger, scarcity of resources, ideology, or simply differences in perspective, conflict is an unavoidable part of life.[43] See Exhibit 13-4.

In the experience of Jesus and the early church leaders, we find a curious mix of conflict avoidance and resolution. But other times these individuals appear to stir up controversy.[44] Sometimes Jesus is outspoken in his judgment of the religious leaders of his day. At other times, his soft-spoken manner turns away their wrath.[45]

There is value in preventing unnecessary conflict.[46] But where conflict arises, conflict resolution is a community process rather than merely an individual matter. Because conflict is embedded in the social experiences of life, the resolution of conflict also is a social process.

If there is conflict, the Bible's direction is to first attempt resolution by speaking to the other party in private.[47] This allows both parties to save face in the community and resolve the conflict efficiently. Quick resolution is as important as other spiritual activities such as community worship. The one who is seeking resolution of conflict should remember that there is a built-in bias that each person has: It is easier to see another person's faults than it is to see our own faults. For some situations the wise leader will get counsel from someone with more experience before working to resolve the conflict.[48]

How you approach conflict resolution is important. The Bible's guidance is to always begin from the posture of doing good and, in humility, consider the other as better than yourself.[49] Think about what is needed to be fair.[50] Being patient in the midst of conflict is not easy, but patience promotes goodwill. Do not approach conflict resolution with the spirit of revenge.[51] This is likely

EXHIBIT 13-4
Examples of Conflict in the Bible

Parties	Issues	Outcome
Abraham and Sarah[52]	What to do with Ishmael	Ishmael is sent away and becomes a great nation; the descendents of Ishmael are in continual conflict with the descendents of Isaac.
Abraham and Lot[53]	Fighting over scarce resources	They separate and the conflict ends.
Cain and Able[54]	Proper worship, self-interest	Cain kills Able; Cain is exiled.
Paul and Barnabas[55]	Whether to take Mark on missionary trip	Paul and Barnabas separate.
Early church leaders[56]	Whether to require gentiles to be circumcised	They conduct a conference and debate in Jerusalem.
James and John and the other disciples[57]	Who would have power next to Jesus in his Kingdom	Jesus teaches regarding servant leadership.

to only make matters worse. Instead, approach the other party in a spirit of forgiveness. Your integrity is on the line during these sacred moments of reconciliation.[58] Remember that as a leader you are accountable not only to yourself and to the community you serve, but also to the other person and ultimately to God.

If a private conversation does not resolve the conflict, try taking one or two others from the community with you to attempt a resolution. A mediator that is trusted by both parties can go a long way to find a resolution. Taking two persons with you offers the advantage that words spoken will less likely be misrepresented later. Finally, if the dispute continues even after two good-faith attempts, then include the wider community in the process. If contention is caused by an intractable individual, the harshest of solutions is to separate the person from the community.[59]

Conflict can be constructive, but it also can be destructive. The Bible considers it honorable when a person resolves conflict with others.[60] Applying this to the leader's work we see that the leader is to participate with God in redemption by working for reconciliation in the settings in which the leader serves. The leader reconciles by helping both parties of the conflict to be transformed. Ultimately resolution of conflict comes from spiritual transformation of the heart.[61] Through this process, the peace of God is brought into the community.

In spite of our best efforts, sometimes conflicts do not get resolved. We are left with chronic tension in the relationship. Our natural inclination is to find a way to retaliate toward the other party. In such situations the follower of God has a responsibility to show honor and respect to the other party. The Bible's counsel is clear: Do not take vengeance into your own hands. Harboring animosity or holding a grudge is destructive. Speaking to or about others in a way that is disrespectful is dangerous and should be avoided. This can be one of the most difficult things to do. Pray for grace to put away bitterness and for forgiveness when you are not able to do what you know to be right.[62]

The Biblical Story of Solomon

Read the story of Solomon contained in 1 Kings 3–11 in the Bible. Based on Solomon's experience, grasp the significance of the accomplishments that occurred under his leadership. Make a mental note of the leadership strengths and weaknesses of Solomon. What leadership principles can we gain from the experience of Solomon that are applicable today?

Ken Sande, of Peacemaker Ministries, proposes several principles for Christian conflict management.[63] First, believers who want to resolve personal conflict with fellow Christians must begin with a heart's desire to glorify God.[64] Wanting to get your own way at any cost will only make the conflict worse. Second, instead of attacking another person's faults, take care of your own faults.[65] Criticizing the faults of others will only invite counterattacks that escalate the conflict. In contrast, by overlooking the minor flaws in other people while openly acknowledging our own failings decreases tension and opens the way for sincere dialogue. Third, gently help the opposing parties see how they have contributed to the conflict.[66] If the opposing parties refuse to acknowledge their contribution to the conflict, involve respected friends or church leaders who have an objective perspective. Fourth, make the commitment to restore the damaged relationship while negotiating an agreement that promotes justice.[67]

Leading Change

Now that we have seen what the Bible says about these three interrelated concepts, let's consider what is honorable not only in the sight of God but also in the sight of those around us.[68] For this we turn to information gleaned from the work of researchers and scholars.

From a systems view of organizations, it is relatively easy to understand why organizations constantly change. Adaptations that organizations make to their changing environment trigger changes that individual workers and work teams need to make as well.

Some changes are as simple as using new materials for a routine process or rearranging the objects and equipment in a work space at a company like Abbott Laboratories. Other changes might mean working with a new subcontractor or implementing the results of a performance improvement team's effort. It could mean making changes to standard operating procedures. Adding a new product line will require changes. Acquiring or merging with another company requires changes by almost everyone in both organizations. Some change comes in the form of new organizational structures such as new reporting relationships, adding to or removing assigned tasks, adding a new manager, and dividing up or combining work groups.

Change inside an organization happens for a reason. Usually it is because there is something new that has occurred in the external environment that requires an adaptation of some kind. But voices calling for change can come from just about anywhere inside or outside the organization. Working through the process of change is an important job for leaders and followers.

In this section we will explore some of the barriers to change that make a leader's job challenging. We will also explore models of change leadership that help us understand this complex process a little better.

Barriers to Change

Changes outside the organization stimulate the need for change on the inside. This does not mean that change will automatically come to the organization. But it raises the question, "If change occurs for all organizations and if change is necessary for survival, then why is change so often resisted?"

Several barriers make change difficult to accomplish.[69] Internal barriers to change are inevitable. To be effective, leaders must understand these barriers to be able to communicate with those who are affected. Let's explore these barriers.

BENEFITS OF STABILITY. It is sometimes easier to do nothing about a situation than to do something. People in organizations like routine, predictable activities. Change threatens to upset these. Change always brings an element of the unknown into the equation. Managers often prefer the familiarity of their current or past experiences over the unfamiliarity of what is unknown or uncertain in a future of change. If the ways of doing business have been successful in the past, then there will always be some who believe that change is unnecessary.

CALCULATED OPPOSITION. When change is introduced or suggested, individuals will attempt to block the change by using their influence. These individuals want to protect the status quo and they may have good reasons. They might want to prevent or delay the costs of changing. The economic costs of change may be the first to be argued in opposition to change. Change can mean the threat of loss of or disruption to work relationships. Change signals potential loss of influence or resources in the organization. For others, it might mean the potential loss of their job. The emotional reaction of anxiety about change might be enough for some to block change. Or it might come from a lack of trust in those who are promoting change. Individuals who work in areas where there are well-oiled routines can consider change interference. Some individuals simply want more, not less, autonomy. Calculated opposition to change can take the form of active speaking about the dangers of change, as shown in Exhibit 13-5.

Opposition can also be subtle, such as when a manager apparently supports the change but is passive-aggressive in undermining change through actions. Similarly, individuals who hear about a potential change in the organization may continue to act silently in support of the former organizational values—values that are now in opposition to the proposed changes. This opposition is both difficult to detect and difficult to speak against.

MENTAL BLINDERS. Mental blinders are the patterns of thinking that make it difficult for us to understand the full value that can be gained by change. They can come from several places. Managers in organizations generally work hard to ensure that the organizational shared values permeate throughout. This can have an unwanted side effect of causing rigidity toward change. Organizational values are often used when recruiting and selecting new employees whose personal values are in close alignment. Employees who do not share the organizational values are weeded out, meaning that they are either marginalized by being placed in positions that have little influence or are encouraged to leave the organization. Excessive focus on costs can become a mental blinder to change. Another mental blinder can be the organizational structure, which is a strong influence on how employees think. When an organization is experiencing difficulties with

- It's not part of our job.
- It sounds good on paper, but . . .
- We tried that before and it didn't work.
- That might work someplace else, but not here!
- We don't have enough employees to do that.
- Our budget won't allow for that.
- We have too many projects to work on right now.
- Let's appoint a committee to study this.
- That will conflict with our compliance with regulations.
- Whose idea is this?
- We will need board approval to do that.
- Did the people who dreamed that up bother to see what is happening over *here*?
- With everything else we have, that is too big of a project.

EXHIBIT 13-5
Common Phrases That Can Kill Change

the organizational structure, such as coordination problems, these structural problems can become obstacles to change. Another mental blinder is that for some organizations the day-to-day activities needed to solve the problems of work dominate the mental space of managers and non-managers. As a result, they have little time or energy to put toward making changes that might make work easier in the long run. As one senior manager said to his middle managers when describing their organization, "It is hard to drain the swamp when you are busy killing alligators."

SYSTEMIC OBSTACLES. Most organizations involve many interdependent relationships between workers and between the organization and other entities in the environment. They each need each other to achieve their goals. These interdependent relationships come with a host of ongoing expectations and commitments that can easily compete with the need to change. Some of these interdependent relationships are based on formal agreements such as a strategic alliance partnership between an assembly plant and parts suppliers. For example, Blue Planet Foods is a subsidiary of the McKee Foods Corporation supplying McKee with cereals used in baking the many treats and snack foods that McKee is known for. The arrangements increase predictability and stability. But they also are obstacles to change. Government laws and regulations have the same effect. Organizational policies can become obstacles to change even though they offer benefits.

Active resistance to change indicates that core values are being tested and perhaps threatened. Emotional reactions to this indicate that a great amount of energy is potentially available in support of change once those who oppose change are given a chance to view the situation differently.[70]

No one is immune to the barriers to change. This doesn't mean that resisting change is never beneficial. As a manager, you will likely resist change more than once during your own career. When barriers to change occur, how is the manager to work through these barriers? To help answer this question, let's explore some of the models of the change process.

Kurt Lewin on Change Management

The observations in 1941 of Kurt Lewin, a social psychologist, regarding change in society have guided the thinking of many in more recent years as they try to understand change in organizations.[71] Lewin observed a cluster of forces at work on three levels: on individuals (from the groups to which they belong), on groups (from the society of which they are a part), and ultimately on societies (from forces at work on them from other societies). Some forces are pushing toward change. Other forces are pushing against change. When added together, these forces are a part of a whole field of forces that are constantly at work. Lewin called this a **force field**. See Exhibit 13-6.

According to Lewin, when change is needed, leaders should make changes to the force field whenever possible. These forces normally affect groups of workers rather than just individuals. Lewin believed that, all other things being equal, it is easier to change a group of persons than to change just an individual within that group. The reason is that group values are a powerful force in the life of the individuals who make up the group. As long as the group values are unchanged, individuals will continue to resist change. But if you can change the group values, then individual resistance will diminish. For example, in the United States the typical workday begins at around 8:00 a.m.

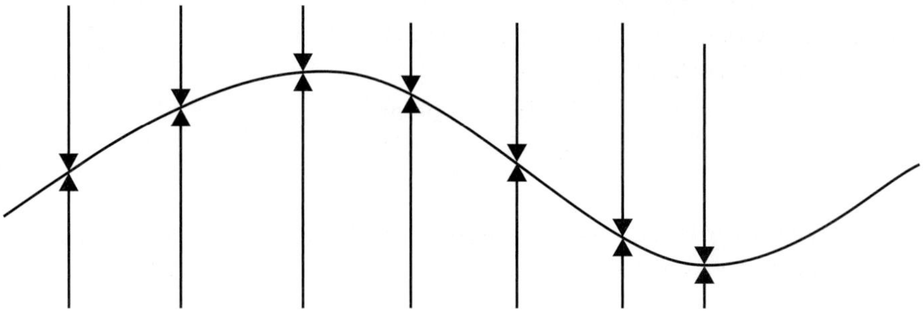

EXHIBIT 13-6
The Force Field: Forces For and Against Change

Coincidently, the school day begins around the same time. For decades now workers and their families have arranged their personal schedules around this start time. Of course there are exceptions, such as banks that often open later in the morning, for example, at 9:00 a.m.

What do you think would happen if one day the president of a bank announced to the workers that work will now begin at 6:30 a.m. instead of 9:00 a.m.? The president's proclamation would be a force for change. There would be resistance to changing the start time if for no other reason than many individuals are not prepared to quickly adjust their family and personal schedules. This would be a force against change.

Of course the conundrum is: How do you change the group values without changing individuals? The answer is that you must first engage the forces that affect the group from the outside such as a new legal requirement, actions of a competitor that require a response, new technology, or changes in customer preferences. Returning to our example, the bank president would need to provide a convincing argument for the real need for such a change. But argument alone probably would not be enough to change the group values on this particular issue. There would need to be something bigger from the outside that is pushing the company to change in order for it to survive. In other words, something might need to be big enough to threaten the very existence of the company before workers are likely to accept such a drastic change in their family routines. If the argument is simply to please the whim of the bank president, forget implementing such a change. But if something drastic were to take place with the bank customers such that they needed to do their banking very early in the morning and if the bank could not respond to such a need in any other way, then the bank would be in great danger of losing its customers. In such a drastic situation, the bank president needs to paint the picture of what would happen if a change is not made.

The type of change envisioned in this model can be described in terms of three stages: *unfreezing* the current balance of forces in the force field, moving toward change, and after change is made, embedding the change into the group's value system. Lewin called this last step *refreezing*.

Helping an organization move away from old ways of doing business, embedding these changes into organizational values and then making the changes last is important work for a leader.

Source: Stockbyte/Thinkstock.

Destabilizing or **unfreezing** the status quo is equivalent to changing the equilibrium among the current field of forces affecting a group. This needs to be done before permanent change can be established. It involves a deep psychological change.[72] Such change is possible only in the presence of data that disconfirms that the organization can remain unchanged. But that is not enough on its own. Disconfirming data must be important enough that it causes anxiety or anticipated guilt if no change is made. And there must be psychological safety available in a proposed solution so that individual and group identity or integrity is not destroyed in the process. But destabilizing is not the goal.

Moving toward change requires developing a practical solution to the need for change. This may require repeated trials and errors to adjustments in work routines, technology, materials, and human resources. During this phase of the process, individuals make adjustments to their expectations and behaviors. Gradually the group develops commonly shared values that have been adjusted. Moving toward change may require employee training or redesigning roles and responsibilities.

Refreezing attempts to embed the new work routines and processes within the group so that stability is restored to the group. Work processes are changed to support the new direction. Policies, procedures, and job descriptions are revised. The organizational structure might need to be adjusted. New symbolic and ceremonial activities may need to be implemented to reinforce the newly emphasized values. All these new behaviors must be consistent with the group's identity. They also must be congruent with the shared values. Unless the group values can be adjusted, individual behaviors won't stick.

Lewin's three-stage model of change has been the source of debate among scholars.[73] Some think his model is oversimplified. Nevertheless, the basic ideas have been a solid foundation on which to better understand leading change. One of those who built on Lewin's work is John Kotter, a researcher and organizational consultant. To his model we now turn.

John Kotter on Change Management

Kotter, like other experts on leading change, assumes that the external environment changes regardless of whether managers in a particular organization recognize it. Unless organizations adapt to these changes, they risk failing to accomplish the reason for their existence. For example, managers at Colgate-Palmolive constantly face a changing environment for their personal care products as consumer tastes change. Successful organizations will remain open to their environment without sacrificing the core values on which the organization has been built. But leading change is not easy. Some leaders fail in the change process.

Kotter identifies eight reasons why change efforts fail. He presents these reasons in the carefully planned sequence of what is needed for successful change leadership, revealing his eight-step model. The first four steps in any effective change leadership process involve defrosting the hardened status quo. The next three steps introduce new practices that have the potential to bring success. The last step is critical because it is here that the change becomes embedded into the organizational culture.[74] Let's look at the eight reasons for failure and their corresponding solutions for successful change leadership.

COMPLACENCY. According to Kotter, the biggest mistake that leaders make is not establishing a strong sense of urgency for change among those needed to support it. Without a sense of urgency, employees will continue on their path of focusing on their day-to-day activities to accomplish the goals the organization has established. The solution: Establish and repeat the sense of urgency. This can be accomplished by helping organizational members examine the realities outside the organization. Multiple discussions will usually be necessary to help managers and non-managers understand the magnitude of the crisis or potential crisis present in the environment.

LACK OF A COALITION OF SUPPORTERS. The problem: Most leaders underestimate the need for building a coalition of supporters for change. Tradition, self-interest, and ongoing expectations compete for the commitment of key people who need to support change. In all but only small organizations an individual manager alone will lack the necessary resources to overcome such organizational inertia. The solution: Successful change leaders are those who vigorously work to build a coalition of active support among employees. Managers who believe they have accomplished the necessary support with just a handful of people will likely fail in leading change. Coalitions of support may need to comprise as much as 20 percent or more of the members of the organization. Effective coalitions will be comprised of people that have some influence in the organization. They will be people who are recognized for their expertise or experience. Effective coalition members will be credible leaders whom others are willing to follow.

LACK OF A COMPELLING AND CLEAR VISION. When the need for change is not carried on the back of a compelling and clearly articulated vision, the details will be subject to endless debates. Disagreements will emerge over the smallest details and the change process will grind to a halt. A simple test that indicates that your vision is not clear and compelling is if you cannot describe the vision for a change initiative in 5 minutes or less and get a reaction that signals both understanding and interest. Successful leaders work hard to craft a compelling and understandable vision of what is needed. Such a vision will describe a clear picture of an appealing future but one that is feasible and focused.

INSUFFICIENT COMMUNICATION. Many change leaders incorrectly assume that after publishing the vision for change in the company newsletter and making an announcement about it in a manager's meeting, all the key people who need to support the change will begin their active support. Reality is often quite different from this. Successful change efforts must be communicated through every available communication channel possible. Repetition and two-way dialogue are vital. Communication is accomplished by words and actions. But leadership actions speak louder than words and signal to everyone your priorities. If leader behavior is inconsistent with the words about change, then the behavior will drown out the verbal messages. Thus, guiding a coalition requires that role models step forward to exhibit the expected behaviors.

PERMITTING OBSTACLES THAT BLOCK CHANGE EFFORTS. Three types of obstacles get in the way of change. First, the organizational structure formalizes the system of reporting relationships, rewards, and discretionary authority. Traditional hierarchical, functional structures fragment the resources needed to successfully change. These organizational barriers can make it difficult for employees to act on the vision. Information systems also can get in the way of following the vision. Subordinates whose manager bad-mouths the vision or in other ways discourages action become barriers themselves. Mental orientations that develop in task-specific managers and work teams create silos of separation between them and other parts of the organization. Second, psychological blocks can make it difficult for workers to see the positive possibilities that might come from change. Third, one well-placed blocker with influence can stop an entire change effort. On the positive side, successful change leaders will act to empower broad-based action. Those in charge of leading change may sometimes make the difficult decisions to change systems and the structure. Unnecessary interdependencies may need to be eliminated. Also, after spending time and effort helping the individual blockers understand the necessity for change, leaders may decide to remove those individuals who continue to block change. This is more easily done in a for-profit organization than in a nonprofit organization.

NOT PLANNING FOR AND GETTING SHORT-TERM SUCCESS. Without short-term (within 6 to 18 months) successes, employees may give up hope. Or they might join active opposition to change because the change efforts are going nowhere and are costing them time and resources.

Source: © Cultura Creative/Alamy.

Leading change often requires multiple conversations with employees reinforcing the urgency for change, describing the vision of what needs to be done and listening to responses from employees.

This is why successful change leaders plan for success and then work to create the success. Early success enables leaders to show the connection between new behaviors and the desired outcomes. Short-term wins need to be highly visible so that large numbers of employees can see that the success is real and not just "leadership hype." These successes need to be unambiguous in terms of the direct relationship between the behaviors and the outcomes.

DECLARING VICTORY TOO SOON. The problem: Early successes should be celebrated, but any suggestion that these early successes mean that the job of change has been accomplished will undermine future success. Long-term success in leading change can take years to accomplish in large, complex organizations. New activities associated with change are fragile. Premature celebration of victory will actually stop the momentum that is needed until the change has become anchored in the corporate culture. The solution: On the positive side, successful change leaders will work vigorously to use early success to reinforce the need for continued changes. They will begin changing policies and procedures to support the new direction. They will hire and promote individuals who can implement the changes. Early victories may need to be followed by a renewed emphasis on change under a new (but closely related) theme or project.

NOT ANCHORING CHANGE IN CORPORATE CULTURE. Many change efforts stop before the shared values of the organization have become changed. Change must begin at the level of very specific behaviors and from there gradually work its way into the shared thinking and feeling patterns of organizational members to become permanently rooted in shared values. In other words, behavior is the first to change. Organizational culture is the last to change. But unless organizational values also change, the change leadership efforts will not be effective. This may require changing some of the organizational cultural artifacts that we discussed in Chapter 3 such as stories, rituals, and physical objects.

Leaders must not assume that workers automatically see the connection between new behaviors and improved performance. Helping employees by showing these important connections contributes to building new shared values. This may require assisting employees in getting the reactions of customers. Or it might involve developing a graphical representation of performance-related behaviors that support positive outcomes. When new employees are hired, leaders will encourage the new generation of managers to personify the values underlying the change.

According to Kotter, all eight steps in the model must be followed. Leaders will fail if they attempt to speed up change by skipping one or more steps. In addition, when earlier steps have been accomplished, such as a general awareness that there is an urgent need for change, these steps may need to be revisited later. Do not assume that successful awareness of urgency will remain. And do not assume that a coalition of supporters will remain intact over the course of a long-term change process. Coalitions are constantly in change themselves. The successful leader of change will monitor the coalition of support and, where needed, work to maintain cohesion of support when it begins to weaken.

Most change initiatives are made up of many smaller change-oriented projects, each of which might go through all eight steps. This has the potential for creating a complex matrix of change leadership activities in which all eight problems are addressed simultaneously for different projects related to the vision for change. It also reveals that the change process is sometimes messy and even chaotic.

Given this change process that is rooted in actions, thoughts and feelings, and deeper values (the three elements of the Management Pyramid), we can conceive of the leader's job as creating or facilitating the conditions for transforming the organization from the outside. This is paradoxical because actions spring from thoughts and feelings, which depend on values. Change is unlikely to succeed unless it is put into the concrete terms of a specific problem that needs a solution. Indeed, it may be impossible at first to see how some changes will require adjustments in the organizational culture. It is only when specific goals are identified that leaders can identify which shared values will support or detract from the change.[75]

Adaptive vs. Technical Change

Leadership expert Ronald Heifetz claims that an important distinction must be made between technical challenges and adaptive challenges.[76] **Technical challenges** are problems with solutions that can be found if enough technical knowledge is used. Leadership with technical challenges requires expert answers, decisiveness, and promoting a specific vision for the future and then aligning followers with this vision. In contrast, **adaptive challenges** are problems for which there are no clear solutions even when plenty of technical knowledge is available. Adaptive challenges require people in the organization to learn new ways. These challenges require experimentation. Heifetz says that adaptive work is difficult "because it requires that we relinquish some of our deeply held beliefs and learn new skills where old ones are insufficient."[77]

Most leaders, he says, fall into a common error of treating change as if it is primarily a technical problem. People expect such leaders to know more than most people about the problems that need solving. With this expert knowledge such leaders, it is assumed, can then describe a vision of what needs to be done to change.

To overcome this error Heifetz proposes five principles. First, leaders and followers must identify the adaptive challenges that the organization faces. Second, members of organizations can learn only so much fast. They must be given time to absorb what they learn and what the new ways of working mean for them. Third, leaders must help their organizations stay focused on the issues they face. This is especially important as changes normally result in a multitude of points of view that organizational members have to the changes in their work. If focus on the key issues is not maintained, the organization will fragment. Fourth, people at all levels need to have the authority to adapt to unforeseen circumstances. Last, organizational members at lower levels of authority need to be protected when they speak. Squelching the voice of those at the front lines of strategy implementation will close the organization off from learning to adapt.

Moral Implications of Change Leadership

The change leadership process generates some interesting moral questions. For example, to shake members of an organization out of their complacency, organizational leaders need to describe the dire circumstances the organization will be in unless change happens. Raising the level of urgency can be accomplished by any number of ways, as described in Exhibit 13-7. But are all these ways moral? Is it moral for organizational leaders to actually create a crisis by allowing financial loss? Some workers might lose their jobs under such a circumstance. Is it moral for managers to allow problems to mushroom and get out of control (instead of being corrected) to create crisis which is then used to initiate change?[78]

Managing the change process that is begun can bring up other moral issues.[79] For example, the change leader normally will act in a way that watches out for the good of the organization. After all is said and done, needed change is often for the good of the organization. With this in mind, should individual employees be overtly coerced or covertly manipulated into participating in projects that are designed to bring about organizational change? How much freedom should top-level leaders give managers to opt out of change programs if such programs conflict with their deeply held personal values? Is it moral to disguise the ultimate intention of change when seeking the support of organizational members? How much information should leaders give to organizational members who might be directly affected by changes? For example, if a leader knows that certain people will likely lose their jobs as a result of making changes, should the leader disclose this to them?

Both initiating change and managing the change process require the leader to exercise power to get things done in a moral manner. To this important topic we turn next.

EXHIBIT 13-7
Raising the Urgency Level

Create a crisis by allowing financial loss, exposing managers to major weaknesses vis-à-vis competitors, or allowing errors to blow up instead of being corrected at the last minute.

Eliminate obvious examples of excess (for example, company-owned country club facilities, company-owned jets, gourmet executive dining room).

Set revenue, income, and productivity targets so high that these cannot be reached by conducting business as usual.

Start holding managers accountable for the broader organizational measures of business performance.

Insist that managers talk regularly with unsatisfied customers, unhappy suppliers, and disgruntled shareholders.

Bring in a consultant who has current, relevant data.

When major decisions are made such as decisions:

- at the upper echelons of leadership in the organization
- that involve reorganizing
- regarding budget allocations

Situations in which performance is difficult to measure such as for support staff rather than line production.

Other work situations when:

- there is likely to be uncertainty and disagreement
- individuals or work units are interdependent
- there is a diversity of opinion or perspective
- resources are scarce
- objectives are unclear

EXHIBIT 13-8
When Power Is Important[80]

Power

Power may be the most pervasive social phenomenon.[81] Any time change occurs in an organization, leaders and followers will attempt to use their power to influence change.

Organizations are social environments. Whenever decisions are made that affect people, individuals are likely to attempt to influence the decision. See Exhibit 13-8.

Power Defined and Described

Power can be seen in no other way but in the context of social relationships.[82] In a word, power is communal. We should distinguish between power as a need and power as a goal. As a need, power is a variable influencing motivation at work. As a goal, power is the means of achieving influence and getting things accomplished. In its simplest forms, power can be described in terms of influence, dependence, and goal achievement. We will look at each of these ideas.

INFLUENCE. Entity A has power over entity B if A can get B to do something that B ordinarily would not do.[83] In this view, entities can be individuals, groups, organizations, or societies. The core idea with this definition is influence or force over the behavior of others. This definition of power is based on the assumption that differences exist in the distribution of influence; we might say that power is unequally distributed. Notice that this definition does not specify that only those at the higher levels of authority have power. Power of influence can reside in any person or work group depending on the situation. In addition, such balance of power is subject to being shifted depending on the situation.

Although the terms power and influence are often used interchangeably, there is a distinction.[84] The concept of **power** really refers to just the potential to influence other people's behavior. **Influence** refers to the specific tactics employed to realize the desired behaviors.

DEPENDENCE. When one entity is dependent on another for something important, a power relationship exists.[85] Dependence might exist because one person has information or tangible resources that others need. When the boss's secretary controls access to the boss's schedule, that secretary can wield a lot of power as time with the boss is a highly valued resource among managers. The more a resource is vital to the organization's ability to achieve its objectives, the more likely that resource will be depended on by more than one person or group. Also, the more uncertainties the organization faces or the more unexpected situations come up at work, the more influence those individuals with credible expertise related to these uncertainties will have. In most situations dependence is not a one-way relationship. Because of the complexities, our society is usually characterized by interdependence in which individuals (or work units) depend on each other.

GOAL ACHIEVEMENT. Power is about initiating and sustaining action so that ideas become reality.[86] When there are conflicting goals in an organization, power is the ability of persons or groups to achieve their goals when others prefer the achievement of different goals. This definition assumes scarcity of resources. This goal-oriented definition suggests that power is a zero-sum game, namely that if you get what you want, then others will be unable to get what they want.

The Christian Mind on Power

The saying "power corrupts and absolute power corrupts absolutely" describes nicely some of the seductive dangers involved in the exercise of power. *Power over* another person is a trap managers might all too readily fall into as they attempt to influence the behaviors of colleagues and friends. So how can a manager who chooses to integrate beliefs with practice begin to navigate the issues associated with power? One idea that seems at first a paradox is found in Christ's teaching to the Apostles, that "a man can have no greater power than to lay down his life for his friends" (John 15:13). The context is Christ talking to his Apostles, trying to help them see that power need not be *over*. Rather, it can come from a place of vulnerability. Our lives, Christ reminds them, are the core of our vulnerability.

An example of this approach would be that, when faced with ambiguity in a management situation that requires a decision, we open ourselves to the truth about our confusion and fear rather than pretend to an heroic style of leadership. We talk about the fullness of the shared situation, which becomes a situation that belongs to the group or community. When we are honest and accept power as part of our service to others, when we involve community, power *over* can shift to power *with*, which greatly changes the dynamic of power and reduces its dangers. This approach is close to servant leadership.

Jeanne M. McNett, PhD
Professor of Management
Assumption College
Worcester, MA

Kathleen M. Fisher, PhD
Associate Professor of Theology
Assumption College
Worcester, MA

Abuse of Power—Apathy Toward Power

Using one's power in an organization is important to get things done that otherwise might not get done to achieve rewards. When managers exercise their power, they are exercising their hierarchical authority. Because subordinates are in a position of dependence on their manager, the opportunity for managers to abuse their power exists. Whenever individuals are highly committed to achieving goals along with a belief that they can achieve them, they will use their power to achieve their goals.[87]

Power can be used to either increase or decrease other people's feelings of dignity.[88] For example, disrespect for dignity can be expressed in many forms such as asking a subordinate to perform an illegal action, verbally harassing a worker, requiring a subordinate to perform a personal service, gossiping about an employee to others, or by making insincere promises.

Performance can also diminish when subordinates do the work but the manager secretly attempts to gain the credit for their work, when the manager arbitrarily withholds key information from an employee who needs it to perform the job, or when the manager unfairly or capriciously gives rewards to some employees but not to others who deserve the rewards.

Power that is focused on self-interest and power over others will almost inevitably become corrupted and, because of this, abusive.[89] The alternative is responsibility-driven and other-focused power. Self-interested power is about gathering and hoarding. Responsibility-focused leadership is about sharing. The following examples can help us further understand abusive power.[90]

FIGHTING TURF WARS. Managers who are responsible for productivity based on the allocation of particular assets and workers will be tempted to protect their control over these resources that they believe might be threatened. When managers use their influence to maintain control or increase the scope of control over key resources, we call this fighting a **turf war**. A manager must protect key resources and not be run over by others. But using managerial influence to engage in internal political behavior that is disruptive or deceptive can be abusive. For some, political behavior that is focused on protecting one's power can become a goal in itself.

INGRATIATION. We sometimes refer to this as "kissing up" or "sucking up" to a person whom you want to think more highly of you. When a person deliberately tries to misrepresent himself in an attempt to gain an advantage at work, the person is abusing power—this is called **ingratiation**. For example, a person may make it seem that the issue she is discussing is her only concern, when in reality the goal is to enhance the other person's perception of her.

BULLYING. Repeatedly treating subordinates using intimidation, ridicule, sarcasm, humiliation, or loud vulgar language are examples of a form of abuse of power called **bullying**. Also abusive is the practice of setting work goals or deadlines that are impossible to achieve. Using tyranny to rule workers with an iron fist may yield temporary compliance for getting work done. In the long run, however, it usually creates more problems because employees subjected to bullying will lower their commitment to the organization. They may begin modeling the bullying behavior toward coworkers, causing disruption, unnecessary conflict, and lower productivity.

RETALIATION. When a subordinate irritates the manager, the manager will feel the urge to retaliate. In government organizations, retaliation usually is forbidden. But retaliation is difficult to prove. **Retaliation** can affect job performance and the ability of workers to achieve desired rewards. It can take many forms, as described in Exhibit 13-9.

SEXUAL HARASSMENT. Power abuse is often one of the root causes of sexual harassment at work. For example, a supervisor may use his legitimate power to attempt to engage in sexual behavior toward a coworker who does not want such a relationship. But power need not stem from a supervisor–subordinate relationship. One individual may attempt to use other forms of power to sexually harass a coworker.

CORRUPTION. Another type of power abuse is using your power in an organization to obtain personal favors (economic or otherwise) in exchange for using your influence on another person's behalf.

Just as serious an issue as abuse of power is its opposite: not using power to do things that need to get done. This is an especially difficult problem in highly centralized organizations in which even seemingly small decisions are made at the highest levels. In such environments, mid-level managers and frontline supervisors learn not to exercise their influence. Instead, they wait until senior managers decide. Sidestepping issues of power or ignoring power won't make it go away. Managerial apathy toward power may be as destructive as the abuse of power.[91] Implementation of managerial decisions suffers if we fail to use legitimate power. What's more, when moral issues are at stake, avoiding the use of power to avoid immoral actions can make the manager complicit in the immoral behavior.

Using your power responsibly and humbly means recognizing that in almost every organization there are varying interests. People have different ideas of what should be done and why. The wise manager will spend time attempting to understand the "political landscape" of the organization to know what the key "interests" are and who is in support of each. Using power also means figuring

EXHIBIT 13-9
Forms of Retaliation = Abuse of Power

Denying adequate support staff or other critical resources needed to perform required tasks	Refusing to assign meaningful work when such work is available and the employee is qualified
Transferring the employee involuntarily to another work team	Removing the employee from a decision-making committee or team
Removing tasks from the employee's job description	Demoting the employee
Writing an unsubstantiated letter of reprimand	Completing an unsatisfactory performance review without cause
Piling on work so that it is difficult for the employee to accomplish all required tasks	Publicly embarrassing the employee
Not inviting the employee to an important meeting but expecting the employee to know the information that is given	Subjecting the employee to a hostile working environment
Openly showing vindictive anger to the employee	Bad-mouthing the employee to a prospective employer

out why these interest groups have the particular perspective they have and what their perspectives mean for the issues important to you. Managing with power means fully accepting the idea that to get things done you need power. As we will discuss in the next section, you will need to know where power comes from in your organization and how these sources of power can be developed. Using power also means understanding the ethical tactics for using power in organizations. These include the use of timing, the use of organizational structure, how people use their influence to help or undermine your agenda, and how to get people to make commitments to your perspective.

Where Does Power Come From?

Many people think of power as if it flows from one place to another. For example, a machine on the factory floor breaks down. No work can be accomplished on that machine until the mechanic is summoned to complete the repairs. In this situation, power flows immediately to the mechanic. In another situation a worker is underperforming and his manager initiates the progressive discipline process. Both manager and subordinate can exercise power. Some power will flow to the employee if he responds by improving performance. If, however, the subordinate does not improve performance even after being given the opportunity to improve, then he loses power. Power that has flowed to the manager from her appointment as a legitimate authority (agent) may be used by the manager to dismiss the employee.

One way to view power is flowing from the top down: power flows from those in higher positions of authority to those in lower positions of authority. In this view, power is dominance that is achieved and exercised by official leaders over followers who are duty-bound to obey. In the Western world, this top-down view may have been heavily influenced by the influence of a religious organization—the church.

The opposite way to view power is to see it flowing from the bottom up in an organization.[92] Think about it: If your subordinates and others in the organization refuse to consent to your influence, then you don't have influence. Delegating responsibilities to subordinates gives them an opportunity to support you. In the process, your influence is reinforced. The thinking of this perspective is that ultimately power is given by the consent of members of an organization. Subordinates are the ones who decide whether what their superiors ask of them should be followed. Without this consent, there is no power to give orders and expect that they will be followed.

These two viewpoints on the flow of power are both correct. Without subordinates exercising their power of consent, top-down power is stymied. However, individuals in positions of decision-making authority have *legitimate power* that comes downward from the company's owners.

Notice that it would be impossible to talk about managers who have power in a meaningful way without including others in the organization who are the ones being influenced by those with power. The idea that power flows captures another important dimension of power: Power is dynamic, not static. Also, power is not generalized. In other words, the power that one manager has is context-specific, meaning that this power can be effectively applied in some situations and for some issues but not for every situation or issue. Another important aspect is the sources or bases of power in organizations.[93] Consider the bases of power shown in Exhibit 13-10 and discussed next.

Receiving an appointment for work in an organization always comes with a certain amount of discretionary authority for decision making known as **legitimate power**. The amount or scope of this authority is determined by those in positions of authority above the person. Sometimes the requirements of the job being performed or professional licenses also influence the scope of authority. Authority that is given because of one's position is formal. It is embedded in the legal and financial relationship between owners and the workers they hire. Often it is described in one or more written documents such as job descriptions and organizational policies. When new members are brought into an organization, they usually agree to comply with the directions they receive from individuals who are in a higher authority. Continued compliance is an important part of power relationships. When workers accept the authority of those above them, they perceive these leaders and managers as being *legitimate* in their positions. Exhibit 13-11 offers several guidelines for using legitimate authority.

EXHIBIT 13-10
The Bases of Power

EXHIBIT 13-11

Guidelines for Using Legitimate Authority

Make polite, clear requests.
Explain the reasons for the request.
Don't exceed your scope of authority.
Verify authority if necessary.
Follow proper channels of authority.
Follow up to verify compliance.
Insist on compliance if appropriate.

Source: Yukl, Gary A., *Leadership in* Organizations, 7e. © 2010. Printed and electronically reproduced by permission of Pearson Education, Inc., Upper Saddle River, NJ.

All other things being equal, workers will normally be willing to comply with direction, requests, instructions, and orders they receive "from above." (See Exhibit 13-12.) If workers begin to view the manager as abusing authority or otherwise as illegitimate in authority, then they will withdraw their support. Under such difficult circumstances compliance will either be grudgingly provided (if the tasks require it) or may even be withdrawn if workers desire to assert their power to veto the manager's authority.

In most organizations, outright insubordination to legitimate authority is not tolerated and is grounds for dismissal. However, when leaders have undermined their authority by abusing or hoarding it to the detriment of subordinates, a general breakdown in consent by subordinates and peers may occur. Such a situation sometimes is resolved by removing the manager who is in crisis. With legitimate authority comes the power to give rewards or to coerce through threat of punishment. To these we turn next.

If it is within a manager's scope of authority to give an employee a raise in pay for a job well done or a promotion in responsibilities, then the manager has *reward power*. **Reward power** is the authority to control the distribution of tangible and intangible rewards to subordinates. In many organizations, such reward power is limited by policy or by the discretionary authority of those higher in the organizational hierarchy. Managers can exercise reward power if they have control over necessary resources that subordinates need. For example, a manager with budget authority can approve (or deny) requests to purchase a newer model of a desired piece of small equipment. Or it might mean allocating a larger portion of the expense account for the workers being rewarded. If the manager does not hold power to authorize the purchase of bigger ticket (capital equipment) items, this manager still may have the power to exert some influence in the capital budgeting process by representing the needs of the workers. Another type of reward is the reward that comes from recognition among one's peers. Thoughtful managers will be quick to give credit where credit is due both in telling that manager's superiors as well as telling the story to the rest of the organization.

EXHIBIT 13-12

Follett on Giving Orders[94]

Leadership expert Mary Parker Follett understood orders and commands as arising out of the work itself rather than being vested in the person of the leader. Because of this, she recommended that orders should not be seen as personal, arbitrary commands but rather as an exploration of the nature of the work and of the situation at hand.

She saw *four disadvantages of arbitrary commands:*

1. Arbitrary commands diminish the contributions from those directed.
2. They are likely to cause unnecessary conflict between workers and managers.
3. They destroy pride in work.
4. They decrease the sense of personal responsibility.

Instead of commanding workers, the wise manager will follow *four simple rules*:

1. Depersonalize the order.
2. Find the law of the work situation that requires the order.
3. As far as possible, replace orders with teaching.
4. Give reasons with the order.

When one person has the legitimate authority to discipline an employee or withhold key resources this is called **coercive power**. A century or two ago coercion was used more frequently than it is used today. For thousands of years coercion even included the use of physical force such as flogging to induce desired employee behaviors. In most Western nations the use of physical force is prohibited by law. We also now recognize that compelling workers may induce desired behavior, but at the same time, it will undermine their commitment. Coercion is likely to result in resentment, which turns into either active or passive retaliation. In modern organizations the power to compel workers with threat of punishment is rarely used, however, it always is available as part of legitimate authority. The best way to use coercive power is to follow the progressive discipline process without favoritism. Of the power bases associated with legitimate power, the power to reward and the power to punish carry the most risk of abuse.[95] Because of this, the wise manager will be vigilant not to abuse legitimate power.

Every organization needs people who are experts in their work or who have knowledge that is important for the organization to solve its problems. This is called **expert power**. For example, an Internet marketing company like QualitySmith, Inc., would have a difficult time adapting to the changing needs of its customers if it didn't have ready access to expert software developers who could quickly make changes to the company's web pages. The more the organization depends on such individuals, the more power the software developers have. From a power perspective, this is a positive thing for the software developers. However, the trade-off is that their expertise becomes a magnet for requests from many places in the organization to make improvements in the web pages. As the number of requests increases, time pressures on the software developers also increase, making it more and more difficult for the software developers to respond equally to all requests. Having specialized knowledge or expertise is necessary, but alone it is not sufficient. Others in the organization must value this knowledge and expertise and see it as credible and directly relevant to the needs of the organization.

Power can also come from control of an important resource. Besides the knowledge or expertise of individual workers, individuals in the organization depend on each other for key resources to get their work done. One key resource is specialized information. For example, because of their connections with information sources outside the organization, some managers are in a position of power to control what information is shared with workers and what interpretation is given to the information. Control over information raises an important moral issue. Managers with access to information should use this information to influence others. However, they must be careful not to distort the information, selfishly bias their interpretation, or present false information. In addition, control of specialized information can present a temptation to the manager to use this access to cover up mistakes.

Other key resources include the inventory of materials used in work processes or equipment that is shared by more than one worker or work team. The manager in charge of inventory or equipment is in a position of power because of the dependence that others have for the resource. Those who depend on these resources will watch that access is offered fairly according to organization policies.

Power can also come through social connections with influential people inside and outside the organization. Managers may not have all the sources of power directly available to them. However, important social connections create access to resources, knowledge, expertise, and legitimate authority that a manager might lack. Most managers will tell you that developing a network of others to whom you can turn for advice, resources, and influence is one of the most important intangible assets.

When subordinates and peers feel a sense of loyalty and admiration toward a manager, they are more willing to do the things that the manager asks of them. We call this **referent power**. Such power is developed through paying personal attention to the needs of others and treating others with respect and trust. When a manager is loyal to subordinates and attends to their needs, this builds a reciprocal loyalty to the manager. The power of loyalty that comes from loving kindness is the both the basis of and result of a covenantal relationship. Perhaps the reason is that power to build loyalty and identification is the relational power to engender faith and trust. *Identification* is a subordinate's desire to model personal behavior after a person in power. It also means that the subordinate has a growing feeling of close association with the person in power. This is the extreme opposite of the power to compel with force. It is more subtle than other bases of power. Trust may be the strongest source of power and the strongest motivation for high performance. However, once it is established, it will not maintain itself indefinitely. The one with the power from loyalty must continually demonstrate trustworthiness.[96]

EXHIBIT 13-13
Mary Parker Follett on Power[97]

> Power is simply the ability to make things happen, to be causal agent, to initiate change. Power is not a measure of strength, for both the weak and the strong have power in organizations. True power is *power-with,* not *power-over,* others.

From this short discussion of the bases of power, a few observations are clear. First, from its many possible sources, power is available to everyone in the organization. As a manager you will see this as a good thing, especially when you want your subordinates to use their power to get things done. Second, if this is true, then power is a community experience in which everyone participates. When organizational members voluntarily consent for others to have influence, they are acting on behalf of the community of people in the organization. Giving voluntary consent should not be equated with inferiority or subservience. Truly, those who give consent to leaders to have power are acting with a power at least equal to those to whom consent is given. In this frame of reference, subordination itself is a powerful force to be respected by all, especially by managers and leaders. Third, in most organizational situations you will find people using more than one form of power. Fourth, some forms of power are more dangerous than others. Fifth, some forms of power will be preferred over others. For example, the power that comes from identification and loyalty to the manager is one of the most preferred forms of power to develop.[98] Sixth, the manager or leader has a dual task with respect to managing power. The first task is to win consent from others that breeds voluntary cooperation by them. The second task is to manage the balance of power to maintain these voluntary commitments.[99] See Exhibit 13-13.

Managing Conflict

Leading change and using influence in and around the organization are two important elements of a manager's work, but they often result in conflicts. **Conflict** is the mental and emotional struggle that occurs between persons who have differences of opinion about how things should be at work or who have opposing needs and desires. When one person or group opposes another person or group and there is no apparent way to resolve the differences conflict will arise.

Conflict in organizations is a natural part of working together to achieve organizational goals. Conflict can be disruptive to getting work done. Emotions tend to run high. What's at stake often is important. When conflict occurs, communicating appropriately is important for managerial success.

Similar to the two types of communication (goal-based and need-based) reviewed in Chapter 10, two types of conflict are typical in work groups.[100] One type of conflict is over the work that needs to be done and the methods or work processes. This is sometimes called **task conflict** or **functional conflict** since it involves differences of opinion regarding the best ideas that should be pursued to achieve the goals. The focus is on the work, the goals, and the processes. Functional conflict can slow down decision making, but vigorous debate that occurs during functional conflict can result in improved performance. The other type of conflict is relational conflict. **Relational conflict** or **dysfunctional conflict** tends to be personal, meaning one individual attacks another person. It involves blaming others, undermining another person's relationships, or making interpersonal attacks on another person. Relational conflict is often associated with employee dissatisfaction. It demoralizes workers. When a worker attacks the motives, character, intelligence, or personality of another person, this incites either a fight or flight, violent (verbally or in rare instances physically), or silent reaction. See Exhibit 13-14 for a listing of reasons for conflict.

EXHIBIT 13-14
Reasons for Conflict

- When people are interdependent
- When parties interfere with one another's goal attainment
- When people show disrespect to others
- When there are scarce organizational resources such as power and esteem
- When the organization is changing
- When there are differences in values: personal, organizational, cultural
- When there are competing goals: personal, organizational, policy
- When there are misunderstandings regarding expectations, roles, responsibilities, and authority

As a manager you will find yourself either as a participant or a mediator in conflict situations. Managers sometimes need to spark functional conflict to spur workers toward innovation and problem solving, or to counteract the effects of groupthink. Managers should always be aware of functional conflict occurring and provide leadership to prevent functional conflict from escalating into dysfunctional conflict. Managers are expected to refrain from personal attacks and stay out of dirty fights that involve themselves. They are expected to quickly resolve dysfunctional conflict.

When conflict becomes dysfunctional, what can a manager do to resolve it? Let's consider an example: Mikki and Laura, two employees in an accounting department, were irritating each other. First Mikki went to her manager and complained about Laura. Then Laura went to her manager to complain about Mikki. Other employees were starting to take sides with one or the other. Realizing that this conflict was dysfunctional, the manager separately asked both Mikki and Laura to have a private meeting to discuss and resolve their differences before they left work that day. The next day the manager realized that this had not happened. He asked both Mikki and Laura to meet him in the conference room later that morning. When the three of them had assembled, he simply stated that the conflict they were having was interfering with getting work done and he expected that they would be able to resolve their differences through a civil conversation. He said, "Don't come out of this room until you have resolved this issue." Thirty minutes later Mikki and Laura had aired their feelings and apologized to each other, making a commitment to cooperate instead of combat each other. With the conflict resolved, the performance of the whole department increased.

Some approaches to conflict actually make conflict worse or transform task conflict into relational conflict. For example, a person who demeans or devalues fellow workers or uses sarcastic language when referring to a fellow worker or what the worker has said tends to make the conflict personal rather than task oriented. Also, avoiding conflict or simply giving in to the opposing person strengthens the relational conflict and weakens the task conflict.

The wise manager will use constructive methods instead of destructive methods:

- **Take time to cool down.** When faced with a conflict, the wise manager will take some time to cool down the emotions. This might mean suggesting that the people take a short break or that the issues can be brought up at a later meeting.
- **Establish ground rules.** If conflict is intense and persons involved have transitioned from task conflict into relational conflict, the manager may need to call a temporary break from the conversation in order to agree on a few communication "ground rules." **Ground rules** are rules of conduct that all persons agree to follow before continuing the conversation. For example, ground rules might include agreeing:
  - to show common courtesy when speaking
  - not to use obscenities when speaking
  - not to interrupt others while they are speaking
  - to keep conversation focused on the problems related to tasks and organizational goals
  - to show respect and dignity to others even when disagreeing with them.
- **Be just as concerned about how you speak as what you say.** Tone of voice, innuendo, the use of comparisons, and the use of words that are heavily "loaded" with negative connotations will undo even the best of intentions.
- **Understand the other person's point of view.** When you are able to show the other person that you understand their point of view and that you respect their position or have empathy toward their values, this disarms them of the need to be personal about it.
- **Emphasize a superordinate goal. Superordinate goals** are common objectives held by conflicting parties that are more important than their conflicting individual goals. They are bigger than individual goals and usually encompass the entire department or the whole organization. Superordinate goals establish a common frame of reference. Increased commitment to superordinate goals will reduce conflict. For example, two work teams may be in conflict because the members of one team perceive the other team as not fulfilling their fair share of the responsibilities in taking care of the machine. Without proper cleaning and maintenance, the machine will eventually break down, preventing both teams from using this key resource. Here the superordinate goal, the goal that both groups have an interest in, is maintaining continual access to a reliable machine. Supervisors for both groups will keep this the focus of conversation with group members when allocating

maintenance responsibilities, following up on commitments, and talking with members of the other group.

- **Reduce differences of viewpoint.** Some conflict arises because employees from one team see the issues only from their perspective. Helping each team experience the point of view of other teams can reduce these differences. The manager can reduce differences by having a departmental convention in which other departments are invited to a show and tell, demonstrations, poster board sessions, and presentations that describe what the department accomplishes and why.
- **Increase the amount of communication that focuses on understanding.** Understanding breeds wisdom and unselfishness. Managers can support conflict resolution by engaging in direct communication involving the key stakeholders. Talking behind someone's back will undermine success. Some issues may require more than one conversation to resolve the conflict. Some managers use socializing after work such as playing softball or engaging in team-building activities.
- **Reduce task interdependence.** Much conflict arises simply because of task interdependence. While it is usually impossible and not advisable to completely eliminate task interdependence, in some cases interdependence may be too high and managers may need to create boundaries between two teams that are in conflict. For example, managers may need to divide a key resource over which there has been conflict so each party has exclusive use of part of it. Or the work processes may need to be changed such as combining sequential jobs so they form a pool of interdependence on the same team. For example, one employee may be serving customers who have questions and another employee operating the cash register. The manager may decide to combine both tasks in the same job and ask both employees to do both tasks. In another situation, the manager may need to assign two interdependent workers or work teams to report to the same manager.
- **Clarify rules and procedures.** Some conflicts arise from ambiguous rules regarding allocation of resources or allocation of responsibilities. If this is the source of conflict, managers can establish clearer rules and procedures that all agree on. For example, managers may need to establish a schedule for when certain machines can be used by whom or under what circumstances supplies can be accessed. Managers can also help workers by clearly identifying who is in charge and by clarifying job responsibilities of team members. Even in fast-changing situations responsibilities may need better clarification. As changes occur and responsibilities shift, managers can engage workers to minimize the chances that functional conflict turns dysfunctional.

Rarely will one work team have so much autonomy that what it does has no effect on other workers. Conflict management may require the manager to collaborate with other managers and higher-level managers to develop solutions that work for everyone.

Managing Innovation

Managers in many organizations are often called upon to create new ways of doing work, develop new products and services, and find ways to do work better. In some fast-changing industries, innovation is an expected part of the daily routines of work. **Innovation** is both a process and a result of introducing new products, services, new categories of products, and new work procedures. **Creativity** is "the generation or production of ideas that are both novel and useful."[101]

Creativity is a fascinating concept that deserves more attention by managers. Creativity offers intrinsic rewards; the marketplace offers extrinsic rewards for creating products that customers value. The process of creating new and useful ideas can be both conscious and unconscious. Also, the process of innovating can involve the use of structured, formal innovation teams as well as less structured or informal groups whose members collaborate.

Several implications for managers exist. First, managers may need to build in some flexibility of work time to allow employees opportunities for creating innovations. On the surface this seems to be inefficient; however, creativity sometimes needs time for new ideas to incubate before coming to the surface for testing. Second, not all persons in an organization appreciate innovations. Some subordinates view innovation as a threat to efficient work procedures while others see the normal routines of work as stifling the innovations that are needed to help the organization improve its competitiveness in the market. Third, the organizational culture that supports innovation must be present for successful management of innovation. For example, if creativity is essential to the future of the organization, subordinates must feel safe in offering creative ideas for consideration. If creativity is expected of employees, the cues for this must be unambiguous. Job descriptions should mention this expectation. Team and staff meetings must include time spent on reporting and reviewing innovations that are under development. Leaders and managers must act in ways that are clearly supportive of innovation. Fourth, managers will provide for important social linkages to other departments in the organization or to outside organizations that can provide important elements used in creativity. Isolating an innovation team from its outside environment will likely stifle the very thing that the manager wishes to be accomplished.

Wise managers will consider the ethical dimension of managing creativity, too.[102] For example, some approaches to innovation allow or even encourage breaking the rules in order to get past the barriers to creativity. It can be ambiguous which rules can be broken and which ones must be supported. If a creative person breaks a rule, does this require compromising ethical standards? The manager's job is to maintain clear support for ethical standards, but it may not always be clear whether allowing employees to "bend" a rule also implicitly encourages employees to consider that rules are optional, especially when innovation is imperative for success.

Another example is when creativity is encouraged at the cost of intra-group competition which, in turn, encourages destructive competition. How far should a manager go to encourage the creative thinking that comes from intra-organizational conflict? Here the manager's influence during the innovation process will either reinforce ethical norms or lower them for the sake of innovation.

Innovations sometimes require employees and their managers to take risks they normally would not take. This may require tolerating greater ambiguity about which risks are right and which ones are wrong. Here the manager has the job to monitor the risk-taking behaviors and protect the ethical constraints of the organization while encouraging innovation.

Paradoxes in Leading Change, Using Power, and Managing Conflict

The cognitive tensions that complicate managerial work are no less present when it comes to leading change, developing and using power, and managing conflict in organizations. Here are some examples of the complexity in this arena.

STABILITY—CHANGE.[103] The role of the leader is to be the mediator between two contradictory forces constantly at work in and around organizations: the influences of the external environment pulling the organization inevitably toward change and the forces within the organization that maintain stability so that the maximum can be obtained from existing operating systems. The push for stability pays off in continuity, loyalty, and relational security. It appears to lower risks. But the downside is that stability creates stagnation. A risk-averse organization may have difficulty adapting to changing circumstances. Pushing for change can bring new energy and new perspectives to an organization. Change almost always brings not only new challenges but also new knowledge and expertise. The downside of change is that some routines are turned into chaos. Insecurity mounts. Loyalty is jeopardized. The constant adjustments from change stress working relationships.

MANAGERIAL SYSTEMS—PROXIMITY TO CHANGE PARADOX. Have you ever tried to give someone driving directions without a map and at the same time listen to the sound of the car engine and diagnose why it is sounding "funny?" Difficult to do, isn't it? We can multitask at some things, but the more complex the tasks become the more difficult it is to accomplish both at the same time. This principle holds true for leaders who are leading change. A leader must be close (emotionally, intellectually) to a particular situation to understand it and interact with the people who are dealing with it. At the same time, the effective leader will remain at enough of an intellectual and emotional distance from the particular details to see what else is going on in and around the system and how the situation affects and is affected by other elements in the organization and external environment. Another way of thinking about this is in terms of the ability to remain, to a certain extent, aloof but also present. If the leader is not fully engaged in the key relationships, effectiveness will suffer. But being fully engaged can blind the leader to the overall effect the situation is having—like "missing the forest for the trees." If while engaged in the details of a situation managers are unable to observe the effect of their leadership, their influence will suffer. The challenge is to enjoy both the forest and a particular tree but not become fully engulfed by either one alone.

CONSENT—DISSENT.[104] Power creates the conditions for resistance to power while at the same time limiting that resistance. Those who resist power draw on the very power that they want to reject! Leadership power limits resistance because followers expect disciplinary action in response to open resistance. Those who want to resist do so in subtle, disguised ways. They may appear on the surface to consent to leadership control while concealing their dissent or resistance. Such consent is often destructive though not openly insubordinate. But if the leader would allow constructive dissent without fear of retaliation, new and better ideas would surface that could help the entire organization.

Focus on an Organization

Christians in Commerce

Working to bring change to a workplace is a challenge as old as organizations. Managing change is not easy, especially when the values of the change makers are different from the values of other stakeholders.

Some Christians believe that only through a close personal relationship with God can you be effective in bringing change to an organization. Christians in Commerce has dedicated itself to helping Christian managers bring change to their organizations.

Christians in Commerce has dozens of local chapters around the United States and is also expanding internationally. Each local chapter hosts a weekly meeting of small "Challenge Groups" to consider how Scripture applies to their personal life. Challenge Group members seek ways to change their own relationship with God and seek guidance from God in their daily work. When a Challenge Group grows to be eight members, it is encouraged to divide into two groups. Small groups of four to five members are preferred because this group size allows for everyone to participate.

More information about Christians in Commerce can be obtained at the organization's website: http://www.christiansincommerce.org/about.html.

Chapter Summary

1. The Bible contains examples of leaders that illustrate several important principles of leading change. Change comes about when someone (or a small group of people) sees the need for change. Solid values become central to the reason for change. Change leaders use existing reporting relationships. Commitments of time, energy, and resources are made as individuals submit to each other and to their belief in God's will. Leaders listen to others. They are themselves willing to be changed. Because of the disparity in power distributed throughout the community, the biblical pattern is that those with the most power such as the king must have limits placed on their power to protect the community. It is only within community relationships that power can be exercised. And it is the community who stands to gain or benefit from the use of power. One of the ideal types of power described in the Hebrew Bible is that of the power of loving kindness. Scripture acknowledges the legitimate place of power in social settings. Power relationships should be subject to redemption like any other dynamic in life. Selfishly seeking power has no place in God's Kingdom. However, we should use our power to serve. The Bible offers instructions for how believers can manage conflict with each other.
2. When leaders want to change their organization, they often encounter many barriers to change including the desire to enjoy the benefits of stability, calculated opposition from persons with different points of view, mental blinders, and systemic obstacles.
3. The observations of Kurt Lewin regarding change in society have guided the thinking of many in more recent years as they try to understand change in organizations. Lewin's model included three phases of change management: unfreezing the organization from its current values, making changes to routines

embedding revised values into daily work life, and then refreezing the organization with its revised values.

4. John Kotter identifies eight reasons why change efforts fail. He presents these reasons in the carefully planned sequence of what is needed for successful change leadership, revealing his eight-step model. The first four steps in any effective change leadership process involve defrosting the hardened status quo. The next three steps introduce new practices that have the potential to bring success. The last step is critical because it is here that the change becomes embedded into the organizational culture.
5. Some leaders and their followers make a common mistake by missing the distinction between technical challenges and adaptive challenges. Technical challenges have knowable solutions. Adaptive challenges are problems where no specific technical solutions exist but the members of the organization must learn to do their work in new ways.
6. Managing change raises several moral issues that leaders should consider.
7. In its simplest forms, power can be described in terms of influence, dependence, and goal achievement. Using one's power in an organization is important to get things done that otherwise might not get done to achieve rewards. Power that is focused on self-interest and power over others will almost inevitably become corrupted and, because of this, abusive. One way to view power is flowing from the top down: power flows from those in higher positions of authority to those in lower positions of authority. In this view, power is dominance that is achieved and exercised by official leaders over followers who are duty-bound to obey. The opposite way to view power is to see it flowing from the bottom up in an organization.
8. There are several bases of power in organizations including legitimate power, reward power, coercive power, expert power, and referent power. From its many possible sources, power is available to everyone in the organization.
9. We generally think about conflict in terms of two broad types: functional and dysfunctional. Functional conflict is conflict that arises in a group when the members have a diversity of values and opinions regarding what and how work should be performed. Dysfunctional conflict tends to be personal, meaning one individual attacks another person. Conflict management approaches that are constructive involve the following: Take time to cool down, establish ground rules, be concerned about how you speak, understand the other person's point of view, emphasize a superordinate goal, reduce differences of viewpoint, increase the amount of communication, reduce task interdependence, and clarify rules and procedures.
10. Managers are often called upon to help their employees to create new and useful products, services, and new work procedures. Several factors are important when managers take this responsibility. Managers must create the appropriate context in which innovations can be created but within ethical standards.

Key Terms

Adaptive challenges 431
Bullying 435
Coercive power 438
Conflict 439
Creativity 441
Dysfunctional conflict 439
Expert power 438
Force field 427
Functional conflict 439
Ground rules 440
Influence 433
Ingratiation 435
Innovation 441
Legitimate power 436
Power 433
Referent power 438
Refreezing 429
Relational conflict 439
Retaliation 435
Reward power 437
Superordinate goals 440
Task conflict 439
Technical challenges 431
Turf war 434
Unfreezing 429

Discussion Questions

1. After considering the issues presented in this chapter, do some soul searching. What level of management are you qualified to fulfill now given your current skills in leading change and managing politics and conflict? If you aspire to become a company president or vice president, what are you doing now to develop your political skills?
2. Is the quest for power inherently sinful or is it simply a mix of personality factors and situational/environmental factors?
3. Ken Sande's biblical model for resolving conflict is designed primarily for Christians in conflict with other Christians. How might the model work for Christians who are in conflict with non-Christians?
4. Consider Kurt Lewin's force field model. Think of a situation you have been in where certain "forces" were preventing the organization from changing when it really needed to change. What forces were at work pushing the organization toward the change?
5. John Kotter presents eight steps in leading change. In your experience which of the eight steps has been the most difficult for leaders to follow? Why do you think this happens?

6. Based on your experience, which barriers to change are the most important?
7. Of the barriers to change described in this chapter, which one might be the most difficult for a manager to overcome?
8. How should a manager respond when his or her supervisor attempts to implement a change that the manager disagrees with?
9. Which is worse: abuse of power or avoiding the use of power? Why?
10. In the organizations of which you have been a member, which was the most common problem: abuse of power or avoiding the use of power?
11. How can a manager de-escalate dysfunctional conflict?
12. Will the need to use power ever conflict with the need to show love? Under what circumstances might this occur?
13. What Bible example best illustrates how to manage conflict successfully? Why?
14. Compare the experiences of King Solomon and his son Rehoboam in the Bible. In terms of managing change, power, and conflict, what accounts for their differences in leadership success?
15. Which of the bases of power do you think are most commonly used by frontline supervisors in a factory? What bases of power do you think are most commonly used by the top-level executive managers of the factory?

STUDENT EXERCISES

1. Assign students to perform an in-class skit demonstrating a conflict situation. Students choose one of the methods and create an approach to manage the conflict. Students then choose a second approach to manage the conflict. Evaluate which is the best approach for that situation.
2. Assign students one of the following passages of the Bible. Students are to study the passage and write a description of how conflict was managed.
   a. 2 Samuel 14:1–15:37
   b. 2 Samuel 13
   c. Acts 6
   d. Acts 15
   e. John 8
3. Find a Bible story that illustrates one of the following:
   a. An approach to conflict resolution
   b. Managing power
   c. Managing change
4. Use one of the following Bible stories in which conflict existed. Create an alternative conflict resolution approach.
   a. 2 Samuel 14:1–15:37
   b. 2 Samuel 13
   c. Acts 6
   d. Acts 15
   e. John 8
5. During the next week, observe other people around you. Write a description of what conflicts you observe. Describe how you would resolve the conflicts.
6. Attempt to persuade a small group of friends to do an activity. Alternative: If you are an officer of a club or organization, attempt to persuade club members or other officers to do an activity. Write a personal journal of the attempts to use influence and the outcomes.
7. Attend a meeting of a club, church group, or employee group. Watch the leaders in action and evaluate the bases of power they are using. Write a short description.

IN-CLASS EXERCISES

Visualization

The concepts in this chapter are abstract, yet they have practical value for practicing managers. One way to process the abstract ideas is to visualize them. Assign small groups the task to illustrate visually on a piece of poster paper one of the key concepts of their choice from the chapter. Allow some class time to start the pictures. If groups need additional time after class, they can be allowed to bring their poster back to class in the following class period. When the posters are completed, ask each group to present/explain their poster to the rest of the class.

Role-Playing

Choose a small group to role-play the scenario that follows. Divide the rest of the class into small groups to discuss how to manage the conflict. Alternative: Assign each group to a particular approach and have each group demonstrate or explain how its approach would be used in this situation. Scenario: You are an account manager for a professional software development organization. You have several clients assigned to you. This week, you have been planning to discuss current issues related to billing and future projects for one particular client. One of your lead project managers told the customer that one of the key project deadlines would be missed, but he didn't tell you. When you show up for the meeting with the client, the client is angry about the deadline problem, and this is the first you have heard of the issue.

Issue Debates/Discussions

Divide the class into small groups of five to six people each. Hand out a sheet of paper containing the following statements. Assign half of the groups to develop a rationale why the first quotation is valid and the other half of the groups to develop a rationale for why the second quotation is valid. Give the groups 5 minutes to discuss. Then call for groups to give a summary of the rationale they developed. Discussion can follow.

Discussion Topic #1: You are a manager and your boss describes a change that she wants you to support. You disagree with the change. Is it right for you to build a coalition of supporters that agree with you rather than support your boss?

A. **Yes.** Without a coalition of supporters to back you, your influence will be much less than it otherwise might be. Some bosses are stubborn and won't take action unless they realize that there are several people who are organized in their concerns. When there are conflicting interests and many different kinds of people with different perspectives, getting organized may be the only way for you to have your voice heard.

B. **No.** Managers are expected to be loyal and supportive of their superiors. There are good reasons why the boss wants to make a change. Whether you agree is immaterial. Your job is to support and carry out the change as best you can.

Discussion Topic #2: How quickly should a leader fire a subordinate who resists change?

A. **Quickly.** Waiting will only embolden others who want to resist, and it will delay the inevitable.

B. **Slowly.** If you fire the person too quickly, then others will have fear and will be silent about their concerns—concerns that need to be aired to move beyond resistance.

Discussion Topic #3: You are the CEO of a company. For several months you have been asking employees to cut costs wherever possible. A few months later you are conducting a managers' meeting and one of the employees says, "You have been asking us to cut costs and we have been giving more than a lukewarm response to you doing our best. It is a little difficult for us to dig even deeper to cut costs when we find out that you are building a second office. We heard that the furniture alone will cost $150,000." As the CEO, how do you respond?

A. **Cut the discussion short and move on to other agenda items.** If you let the employee talk, you lose "face," meaning you will be embarrassed by the employee in front of your subordinates. Encouraging more feedback on that issue will encourage unrest among the very managers whom you, as the CEO, need for cost cutting.

B. **Encourage honest feedback and allow more discussion on that question.** If you let the employee talk, you allow truth to be considered. Cutting the discussion short will make you a hypocrite.

Endnotes

1. Pfeffer, J. (1992). *Managing with power: Politics and influence in organizations.* Boston, MA: Harvard Business School Press. p. 33.
2. Lloyd, B. (1996). The paradox of power. *The Futurist.* 39(3), 60.
3. The name has been changed. The story of this situation was provided in a personal interview with the author.
4. Pfeffer, J. (1992). *Managing with power: Politics and influence in organizations.* Boston, MA: Harvard Business School Press. p. 47.
5. See for example Murray, H. A. (1955). Types of human needs. In McClelland, D. C. (Ed.). *Studies in motivation.* New York: Appleton-Century-Croft. pp. 63–66; Edwards, A. L. (1959). *Edwards personal preference schedule.* New York: The Psychological Corporation; Cattell, R. B. (1962). *Handbook for the sixteen personality factor questionnaire.* Institute for Personality and Ability Testing; Wolman, B. (Ed.). (1973). *Handbook of general psychology.* Englewood Cliffs, NJ: Prentice Hall, Inc. pp. 793–816.
6. Vredenburgh, D., & Brender, Y. (1998). The hierarchical abuse of power in work organizations. *Journal of Business Ethics.* 17(12), 1337–1347; Chewning, R. C., Eby, J. W., & Roels, S. J. (1990). *Business through the eyes of faith.* San Francisco, CA: HarperSanFrancisco. pp. 146–154.
7. For an example of the kinds of tactical abilities to develop see Keys, B., & Case, T. (1990). How to become an influential manager. *The Executive.* 4(4), 38–51.
8. Genesis 41–47.
9. 2 Kings 21–23; 2 Chronicles 34–35.
10. Acts 15.
11. Genesis 1:1; 1 Chronicles 29:11–12; Psalm 33:6, 66:7, 102:25; Isaiah 45:12, 45:18; Jeremiah 16:21; John 1:3, 1:10; Romans 11:36; Ephesians 3:9; Philippians 3:21; Colossians 1:16–17; Hebrews 1:2–12; Hebrews 3:4; Revelation 4:11.
12. Adapted from Smith, V. O., & Smith, Y. S. (2003). *An analysis of power in Christian leadership.* Paper presented to the Annual Conference of the Christian Business Faculty Association. Virginia Beach, VA. October 16–18. pp. 5–7. See also French Jr., J. R. P. (1956). A formal theory of social power. *Psychological Review.* 63, 181–194; French Jr., J. R. P., & Raven, B. H. (1959). The bases of social power. In Cartwright, D. (Ed.). *Studies in social power.* Ann Arbor, MI: University of Michigan Press. pp. 150–167; Raven, B. H. (1965). Social influence and power. In Steiner, I. D., & Fishbein, M. (Eds.). *Current studies in social psychology.* New York, NY: Holt Publishing. pp. 371–382; Yukl, G. (2010). *Leadership in organizations.* (7th ed.). Upper Saddle River, NJ: Prentice Hall. pp. 154–164; Chewning, R. C., Eby, J. W., & Roels, S. J. (1990). *Business through the eyes of faith.* San Francisco, CA: HarperSanFrancisco. pp. 148–150; Yukl, G. (2010). Leadership in organizations. (7th ed.). Upper Saddle River, NJ: Prentice Hall. pp. 154–164.
13. Colossians 1:16. See the comment on this in Smith, V. O., & Smith, Y. S. (2003). *An analysis of power in Christian leadership.* Paper presented to the Annual Conference of the Christian Business Faculty Association. Virginia Beach, VA. October 16–18. p. 418. See also 1 Samuel 2:7–8; 1 Chronicles 29:12; 2 Chronicles 25:8, 32:27–29; Proverbs 8:14–16, 22:2;

Ecclesiastes 5:19, 6:2; Daniel 2:21; Luke 1:52; Acts 13:22.

14. Deuteronomy 30:15–19; Joshua 24:15; 1 Kings 18:21; Psalm 25:12; Proverbs 3:31, 10:4; Ezekiel 28:4–7.
15. Dutcher-Walls, P. (2002). The circumscription of the king: Deuteronomy 17:16–17 in its ancient social context. *Journal of Biblical Literature*. 121(4), 601–616. Quoted comment is from p. 604.
16. Walsh, J. P. M. (1987). *The mighty from their thrones: Power in the biblical tradition*. Minneapolis, MN: Augsburg Press. pp. 5–7, 179; Johnson, B. (2003). Sadaq; sedeq; sdaqa; saddiq. In Botterweck, G. J., Ringren, H., & Fabry, H. J. (Eds.). *Theological dictionary of the Old Testament*. (Vol. 12). Grand Rapids, MI: William B. Eerdmans Publishing Company. pp. 239–264; Johnson, B. (1998). Mispat. In Botterweck, G. J., Ringren, H., & Fabry, H. J. (Eds.). *Theological dictionary of the Old Testament*. (Vol. 9). Grand Rapids, MI: William B. Eerdmans Publishing Company. pp. 86–98. See also Psalm 89:14, 97:2, 119:121; Proverbs 1:3, 2:9.
17. For a discussion of the theology of *chesed* (loving kindness) in the Old Testament see Harris, R. L., Archer Jr., G. L., & Waltke, B. K. (Eds.). (1980). *Theological word book of the Old Testament*. Chicago, IL: Moody Press.
18. See as examples Genesis 24:12–14, 39:21, 40:14, 47:29; Exodus 15:13, 20:6; Joshua 2:12–14; Ruth 3:11.
19. See as examples Genesis 24:49, 32:10, 47:29; Exodus 34:6; Joshua 2:12–14; Psalm 25:10, 26:3, 40:10–11, 57:3; Proverbs 3:3, 14:22, 16:6, 20:28.
20. Kleinig, J. W. (2005). Ordered community: Order and subordination in the New Testament. *Lutheran Theological Journal*. 39(2/3), 197.
21. Genesis 41:40–45, 42:6; Genesis 39:3, 39:5, 41:33, 41:40–41, 41:43, 41:45, 42:6; Exodus 1:8, 1:11, 2:14, 5:14, 18:21, 18:25; Numbers 10:15, 27:16; Deuteronomy 1:15, 17:14–15, 28:36; Judges 9:14–15, 9:18, 11:11; 1 Samuel 8:7, 8:9, 8:11, 8:19, 9:16, 10:1, 10:19, 11:12, 12:1, 12:12–14, 13:1, 13:14, 14:47, 15:1, 15:17, 15:26, 15:35, 18:5, 19:20, 22:2, 23:17, 25:30; 2 Samuel 2:4, 2:7, 2:9–11, 3:10, 5:2–3, 5:5, 5:12, 5:17, 7:8, 7:11, 8:15, 12:7, 19:22, 20:23; 1 Kings 1:34–35, 2:11, 2:35, 4:1, 4:4–7, 5:7, 5:14, 5:16, 8:16, 9:5, 9:23, 11:37; 2 Kings 11:18; 2 Chronicles 1:11; Esther 8:2; Matthew 10:1, 11:27, 20:25, 28:18; Mark 10:42; Luke 1:33, 9:1, 10:19, 12:14, 19:14–19, 19:27, 22:25; John 3:35, 5:22–27; Acts 2:24, 2:32, 7:10, 7:18; 1 Peter 3:22; Revelation 9:11.
22. Genesis 21:36–39; Exodus 15:6, 32:11; Deuteronomy 8:17–18; Judges 8:22; 1 Samuel 10:18; 1 Chronicles 29:12; 2 Chronicles 20:6, 21:8; Ezra 8:22; Nehemiah 1:10; Job 1:12; Psalm 8:6; Proverbs 3:27, 12:24; Isaiah 10:13, 19:4, 50:2; Jeremiah 38:19, 46:26; Lamentations 5:8; Daniel 2:38, 6:27.
23. Exodus 22:21.
24. Genesis 1:26–28, 37:8; Leviticus 25:43–53; Deuteronomy 15:6; Joshua 17:17; Judges 6:2, 8:22; 1 Samuel 9:17; 1 Kings 9:19; 2 Chronicles 1:11–12, 26:13; Psalm 8:6; Proverbs 17:12, 18:23, 19:10, 22:7.
25. Smith, V. O., & Smith, Y. S. (2003). *An analysis of power in Christian leadership*. Paper presented to the Annual Conference of the Christian Business Faculty Association. Virginia Beach, VA. October 16–18. p. 4.
26. 1 Kings 12:8–20; Proverbs 18:21, 22:1, 24:5, 27:2, 27:21; Ecclesiastes 7:1.
27. Genesis 12:15–20.
28. Genesis 16:6.
29. Genesis 41–47.
30. 1 Samuel 8:1–5.
31. Genesis 47–50.
32. 1 Samuel 8:10–18; 1 Kings 21:1–16; 2 Kings 9:26.
33. 2 Kings 22–23.
34. 1 Kings 12:8–10.
35. 2 Samuel 13, 15. An interesting discussion of Absalom's corruption can be found in Wood, B. M. (2006). *Business the Bible way: Christlike communication within corporate culture*. Greenville, SC: BJU Press. pp. 53–61. For a discussion of King David's rise to power see McConkie, M. L., & Boss, R. W. (2001). David's rise to power—and the struggle to keep it: An examination of the change process. *Public Administration Quarterly*. 25(2), 190–228.
36. 2 Samuel 15:1–10.
37. Based on the discussion in McConkie, M. L., & Boss, R. W. (2001). David's rise to power—and the struggle to keep it: An examination of the change process. *Public Administration Quarterly*. 25(2), 190–228.
38. Matthew 20:25–26; Mark 10:42–43; Luke 22:25–26; 1 Peter 5:3.
39. Matthew 20:20–28; Mark 10:35–41.
40. Smith, V. O., & Smith, Y. S. (2003). *An analysis of power in Christian leadership*. Paper presented to the Annual Conference of the Christian Business Faculty Association. Virginia Beach, VA. October 16–18. p. 5. For additional commentary on the Christian view of power see Marshall, P. (2005). Power. In Stevens, R. P., & Banks, R. (Eds.). *The workplace ministry handbook*. Vancouver, BC: Regent College Publishing. pp. 193–195; Gill, D. W. (2005). Power, workplace. In Stevens, R. P., & Banks, R. (Eds.). *The workplace ministry handbook*. Vancouver, BC: Regent College Publishing. pp. 196–199.
41. 1 Corinthians 14:33; 2 Corinthians 13:11; 2 Thessalonians 3:16.
42. Genesis 3:14–15.
43. Psalm 133:1; Romans 12:18, 13:13–14, 14:17–19; Ephesians 4:1–3; Philippians 2:3–4, 2:13–16; 1 Thessalonians 5:13; Hebrews 12:9–14; 1 Peter 3:11.
44. Matthew 15:12–14, 16:6–12, 17:24–27, 21:12–13, 22:15–21; Mark 2:16–19, 3:1–6; Luke 5:30–32, 11:38–47.
45. John 8:4–9. See also Proverbs 15:1, 25:15.
46. Proverbs 17:14, 30:10; Matthew 17:24–27; 1 Corinthians 6:12, 10:23; 1 Timothy 6:5–6; 2 Timothy 2:22–26.
47. Proverbs 25: 9–11; Matthew 18:15–20.
48. Proverbs 13:20; Matthew 5:23–26, 7:3; Ephesians 4:26–27.
49. Psalm 37:3–4; Proverbs 11:24–25, 12:18, 14:29, 16:32, 29:23; Matthew 7:12; Luke 14:11; 1 Corinthians 10:24; Galatians 5:25–6:5, 6:9–10; Philippians 2:3–4; 1 Peter 2:17.
50. Psalm 119:33–36; Matthew 22:39; James 2:9.
51. Leviticus 19:18; 1 Kings 8:46–50; Psalm 141:3–4; Proverbs 17:9, 17:13, 20:22, 24:29; Matthew 5:43–44, 6:12–15, 18:27; Mark 11:25; Luke 17:3–4; Ephesians 4:32; Colossians 3:13.

52. Genesis 21:5–18.
53. Genesis 13.
54. Genesis 4:1–18.
55. Acts 15:35–39.
56. Acts 15.
57. Mark 10:35–44.
58. Deuteronomy 23:23; Proverbs 3:1–4, 3:27–28, 3:32, 4:24, 10:9, 11:3, 12:22, 22:1, 25:28; Matthew 5:16, 25:40; Colossians 3:17.
59. Proverbs 22:10, 26:17–25.
60. Proverbs 20:3; Matthew 5:9, 12:25; Acts 15; Galatians 5:15; James 3:13–18.
61. Deuteronomy 17:8–9, 19:14–20, 25:1–3; Exodus 18:13–26, 22:9; 1 Kings 3:16–28; 2 Chronicles 19:8–11; Ezekiel 44:15, 44:23–24; Mark 9:33–35; Galatians 5:19–23; James 3:13–18.
62. Exodus 23:4–5; Leviticus 19:18; Proverbs 24:17–19; Ecclesiastes 7:9; Matthew 5:43–44; Romans 12:14–19; Ephesians 4:31; Colossians 3:8; 1 Peter 2:1; James 4:11, 5:9.
63. See the book: Sande, K. (2004). *The peace maker: A biblical guide to resolving personal conflict*. (3rd ed.). Grand Rapids, MI: BakerBooks.
64. 1 Corinthians 10:31; Colossians 3:23; 1 Peter 4:11.
65. Matthew 7:5.
66. Matthew 18:15–17; Galatians 6:1.
67. Matthew 5:24.
68. 2 Corinthians 8:21.
69. See the book: Kaufman, H. (1971). *The limits of organizational change*. Tuscaloosa, AL: University of Alabama Press; Connor, D. R. (1995). *Managing at the speed of change: How resilient managers succeed and prosper where others fail*. New York: Villard Books; Kotter, J. P. (1996). *Leading change*. Boston, MA: Harvard Business School Press. pp. 33–158; Connor, P. E., Lake, L. K., & Stackman, R. W. (2003). *Managing organizational change*. (3rd ed.). Westport, CT: Praeger. pp. 151–163; Hannan, M. T., Pólos, L., & Carroll, G. R. (2003). The fog of change: Opacity and asperity in organizations. *Administrative Science Quarterly*. 48(3), 399–432.
70. Yukl, G. (2010). *Leadership in organizations*. (7th ed.). Upper Saddle River, NJ: Prentice Hall. pp. 299–301.
71. Lewin, K. (1951). *Field theory in social science*. New York: Harper & Brothers. For two influential examples see Schein, E. H. (2004). *Organizational culture and leadership*. (3rd ed.). San Francisco, CA: Jossey-Bass. pp. 319–337; Kotter, J. P. (1996). *Leading change*. Boston, MA: Harvard Business School Press.
72. Schein, E. H. (2004). *Organizational culture and leadership*. (3rd ed.). San Francisco, CA: Jossey-Bass. pp. 319–325.
73. Burnes, B. (2006). Kurt Lewin and the planned approach to change: A reappraisal. In Gallos, J. V. (Ed.). *Organization development*. San Francisco, CA: Jossey Bass. pp. 133–157.
74. Kotter's eight steps are outlined in his book: Kotter, J. P. (1996). *Leading change*. Boston, MA: Harvard Business School Press.
75. Schein, E. H. (2004). *Organizational culture and leadership*. (3rd ed.). San Francisco, CA: Jossey-Bass. p. 334.
76. Heifetz, R. A., & Linsky, M. (2002). A survival guide for leaders. *Harvard Business Review*. 80(6), 65–72; Heifetz, R. A., & Laurie, D. L. (2001). The work of leadership. *Harvard Business Review*. 75(1), 124–134; Heifetz, R., Grashow, A., & Linsky, M. (2009). Leadership in a (permanent) crisis. *Harvard Business Review*. 87(7/8), 62–69; Heifetz, R. A., & Laurie, D. L. (2003). Learning to lead: Real leaders say, "I don't have the answer." *Ivey Business Journal*. 67(3), 1–9; Heifetz, R. A. (1998). *Leadership without easy answers*. Boston, MA: Harvard University Press.
77. Heifetz, R. A., & Laurie, D. L. (2003). Learning to lead: Real leaders say, "I don't have the answer." *Ivey Business Journal*. 67(3), 1.
78. These are two examples offered by John Kotter in his book. See Kotter, J. P. (1996). *Leading change*. Boston, MA: Harvard Business School Press. p. 44.
79. For example, see Connor, P. E., Lake, L. K., & Stackman, R. W. (2003). *Managing organizational change*. (3rd ed.). Westport, CT: Praeger. pp. 221–236; White, L. P., & Wooten, K. C. (1983). Ethical dilemmas in various stages of organizational development. *Academy of Management Review*. 8(4), 690–697; Connner, D. R. (1993). *Managing at the speed of change: How resilient managers succeed and prosper where others fail*. New York: Villard Books. pp. 266–277.
80. Pfeffer, J. (1992). *Managing with power: Politics and influence in organizations*. Boston, MA: Harvard Business School Press. pp. 37–41.
81. Grimes, A. J. (1978). Authority, power, influence, and social control: A theoretical synthesis. *The Academy of Management Review*. 3(4), p. 724.
82. For this discussion of power see Pinder, C. C. (2008). *Work motivation in organizational behavior*. (2nd ed.). New York: Psychology Press. pp. 145–161.
83. Dahl, R. (1957). The concept of power. *Behavioral Science*. 2, 201–215; Pfeffer, J. (1992). *Managing with power: Politics and influence in organizations*. Boston, MA: Harvard Business School Press. pp. 14, 30; Etzioni, A. (1975). *A comparative analysis of complex organizations on power, involvement, and their correlates*. New York: The Free Press. p. 4; Kanter, R. M. (1979). Power failure in management circuits. *Harvard Business Review*. 57(4), 65–75.
84. Koslowsky, M., & Stashevsky, S. (2005). Organizational values and social power. *International Journal of Manpower*. 26(1), 23–112; Collinson, D. (2005). Dialectics of leadership. *Human Relations*. 58(11), 1419–1442.
85. Emerson, R. M. (1962). Power-dependence relations. *American Sociological Review*. 27, 31–40. See also Jacobs, D. (1974). Dependency and vulnerability: An exchange approach to the control of organizations. *Administrative Science Quarterly*. 19(1), 45–59; Salancik, G. R., & Pfeffer, J. (1977). Who gets power and how they hold on to it: A strategic-contingency model of power. *Organizational Dynamics*. 5(3), 2.
86. Perrow, C. (1986). *Complex organizations: A critical essay*. (3rd ed.). New York: McGraw-Hill, Inc. p. 259; Bennis, W., & Nanus, B. (2003). *Leaders: strategies for taking charge*. New York: HarperBusiness. p. 14.
87. Vredenburgh, D., & Brender, Y. (1998). The hierarchical abuse of power in work organizations. *Journal of Business Ethics*. 17(12), 1338.

88. Vredenburgh, D., & Brender, Y. (1998). The hierarchical abuse of power in work organizations. *Journal of Business Ethics*. 17(12), 1337–1347.
89. Lloyd, B. (1996). The paradox of power. *The Futurist*. 39(3), 60.
90. See the discussion on abuse of power in Pinder, C. C. (2008). *Work motivation in organizational behavior*. (2nd Ed.). New York: Psychology Press. pp. 151–161.
91. Pfeffer, J. (1992). Understanding power in organizations. *California Management Review*. 34(2), 29–50.
92. Barnard, C. (1938). *The functions of the executive*. Cambridge, MA: Harvard University Press; Gazell, J. A. (1970). Authority-flow theory and the impact of Chester Barnard. *California Management Review*. 13(1), 68–74; Raadschelder, J. C. N., & Stillman II, R. J. (2007). Towards a new conceptual framework for studying administrative authority. *Administrative Theory & Praxis*. 29(1), 4–40.
93. Over the years several different types or bases of power have been reported and debated in the literature. What we present here is a summary of the most commonly described bases. See as examples French Jr., J. R. P. (1956). A formal theory of social power. *Psychological Review*. 63, 181–194; French Jr., J. R. P., & Raven, B. H. (1959). The bases of social power. In Cartwright, D. (Ed.). *Studies in social power.* Ann Arbor, MI: University of Michigan Press. pp. 150–167; Raven, B. H. (1965). Social influence and power. In Steiner, I. D., & Fishbein, M. (Eds.). *Current studies in social psychology*. New York, NY: Holt Publishing. pp. 371–382; Mintzberg, H. (1983). *Power in and around organizations*. Englewood Cliffs, NJ: Prentice Hall, Inc. p. 24; Pfeffer, J. (1992). *Managing with power: Politics and influence in organizations*. Boston, MA: Harvard Business School Press. pp. 69–186; Stupak, R. J., & Leitner, P. M. (2001). Managers and leaders: An active strategy for understanding and using power. *Journal of Power and Ethics: An Interdisciplinary Review*. 2(2), 130–143; Bolman, L. G., & Deal, T. E. (2003). *Reframing organizations: Artistry, choice and leadership*. San Francisco, CA: Jossey-Bass. pp. 194–196; Koslowsky, M., & Stashevesky, S. (2005). Organizational values and social power. *International Journal of Manpower*. 26(1), 23–34; Yukl, G. (2010). *Leadership in organizations*. (7th ed.). Upper Saddle River, NJ: Prentice Hall. pp. 154–164; Fairholm, G. W. (2009). *Organizational power politics: Tactics in organizational leadership*. (2nd ed.). Santa Barbara, CA: ABC-CLIO, LLC. pp. 22–30.
94. Graham, P. (Ed.). (1995). *Mary Parker Follett—Prophet of management: A celebration of writings from the 1920s.* Boston, MA: Harvard Business School Press.
95. Smith, V. O., & Smith, Y. S. (2003). *An analysis of power in Christian leadership*. Paper presented to the Annual Conference of the Christian Business Faculty Association. Virginia Beach, VA. October 16–18. p. 6.
96. Smith, V. O., & Smith, Y. S. (2003). *An analysis of power in Christian leadership*. Paper presented to the Annual Conference of the Christian Business Faculty Association. Virginia Beach, VA. October 16–18. p. 69. Here Smith and Smith refer to Riker, W. H. (1974). The nature of trust. In Tedeschi, J. T. (Ed.) *Perspectives on social power*. Chicago, IL: Aldine Publishing Co. pp. 63–81.
97. Graham, P. (Ed.). (1995). *Mary Parker Follett—Prophet of management: A celebration of writings from the 1920s*. Boston, MA: Harvard Business School Press; Sethi, N. K. (1962, December). Mary Parker Follett: Pioneer in management theory. *Academy of Management Journal,* 5, 214–221.
98. Smith, V. O., & Smith, Y. S. (2003). *An analysis of power in Christian leadership*. Paper presented to the Annual Conference of the Christian Business Faculty Association. Virginia Beach, VA. October 16–18. p. 5.
99. Selznick, P. (1957). *Leadership in administration: A sociological interpretation*. Berkley, CA: University of California Press. pp. 63–64.
100. De Dreu, C., & Weingart, L. (2003). Task versus relationship conflict, team performance and team member satisfaction. *Journal of Applied Psychology*. 88(4), 741–749; Flanagan, T., & Runde, C. (2009). How teams can capitalize on conflict. *Strategy & Leadership*. 37(1), 20–22; Garvin, D. A., & Roberto, M. A. (2001). What you don't know about making decisions. *Harvard Business Review*. 79(8), 108–116.
101. George, J. M. (2007). Creativity in organizations. *Academy of Management Annals*. 1, 439. See also Perry-Smith, J. E. (2006). Social yet creative: The role of social relationships in facilitating individual creativity. *Academy of Management Journal*. 49(1), 85–101.
102. Baucus, M., Norton, W., Baucus, D., & Human, S. (2008). Fostering creativity and innovation without encouraging unethical behavior. *Journal of Business Ethics*. 81(1), 97–115.
103. Mintzberg, H. (1978). Patterns in strategy formation. *Management Science*. 24(9), 934–948; Kanter, R. M. (1989). *When giants learn to dance*. New York: Simon and Schuster. p. 279; Pascale, R. T. (1990). *Managing on the edge: How the smartest companies use conflict to stay ahead*. New York: Simon and Schuster. pp. 15–115; Abell, D. F. (1999). Competing today while preparing for tomorrow. *Sloan Management Review*, 49(3), 73–81; Johnson, B. (1996). *Polarity management: Identifying and managing unsolvable problems*. Amherst, MA: HRD Press. pp. 142–159.
104. Collinson, D. (2005). Dialectics of leadership. *Human Relations*. 58(11), 1419–1442.

CHAPTER 14

Managerial Control and Accountability

LEARNING OBJECTIVES

- Explain the biblical teaching on accountability and agency.
- Understand the importance and purpose of managerial controls.
- Describe the steps in the managerial control process.
- Discuss the different levels and approaches to managerial control.
- Understand the moral implications of managerial control.
- Explain the various approaches to and the fundamental elements of performance improvement.
- Understand the challenges that managers of NPOs face when promoting accountability and implementing controls.
- Describe the paradoxes and dilemmas of managerial controls and performance improvement.

"Living with the tension of responsibility without control is the essence of a good manager. To achieve this managers have to know that they can manage their own experience of that tension. They take responsibility in the knowledge that they cannot control everything."[1]

". . . the existence of responsibility is a fact of our spiritual nature, of our general experience of existing as a human being in the world. We are accountable to the world as it exists, whether we like it or not."[2]

EDSEL PAYNE'S JOURNEY TO AFRICA

Some managers go to great lengths to perform the fairly straightforward tasks of managerial control. Consider Edsel Payne, a manager of a multimillion dollar corporation.[3] The management project that took him to Africa was not due to his work. Instead, it involved volunteering his time and energy along with several other people to raise money needed to dig a freshwater well in Homa Bay, Kenya. Raising the funds, it turned out, was the relatively easy part. The difficult part was spending the money so that the needed well could become fully operational.

Homa Bay, Kenya, with a population of approximately 85,000 people, is located on the edge of Lake Victoria in western Kenya. The nearest large city is Kisumu, 100 kilometers northeast. Over 60 percent of the population lives in poverty. Various estimates of the prevalence of HIV/AIDS range from 15 to 30 percent. At one time, 16,000 orphans were living in Homa Bay. Housing is substandard. Most of the water used in Homa Bay comes from Lake Victoria, the single largest source of freshwater in the region—if you can call it fresh. The problem: Lake Victoria also is the dumping ground for untreated and incompletely treated sewage. There are some freshwater wells that provide clean water but not nearly enough to serve everyone.

Source: Design Pics/Newscom.

Edsel Payne's group is not the only one doing humanitarian work in and around Homa Bay. UN-Habitat, CARE, ADRA, and several other nongovernment organizations (NGOs) operate programs. Some of these organizations operate clinics and other social service organizations in the area. By comparison, Edsel Payne's group had a more modest goal: Dig one well and put it into operation.

After the funds were sent to Homa Bay, no well was completed. Weeks and months passed. Still no well was in operation. Seasoned manager that he is, Edsel Payne became frustrated at not seeing the group's goal achieved. As he puts it bluntly, "We give money for a well; I want to see clean water coming out of a pipe."

Payne decided to go to Kenya and see for himself why it was so difficult to put a well into operation. In one of the airports en route, Payne met a young lady who inquired about the purpose of his trip. "I'm performing the fourth management function," he said.

She looked puzzled.

Payne told her about the well project and why he was traveling to Homa Bay. "Our team already did the planning, organizing, and leading. Now I'm doing the fourth managerial function: controlling. If we don't exercise managerial control, our dream of providing fresh water for the people of Homa Bay will be worthless." She nodded in understanding.

When Payne arrived in Homa Bay, he went straight to the mayor's office.

"What can I do for you?" the mayor asked.

Payne smiled. "Put that well into service that we paid for!"

Not too many days later clean water was coming out of a new well pipe in Homa Bay, Kenya. Had it not been for one person taking responsibility to see that the money raised actually brought about the desired result, who knows how long the people of Homa Bay would have had to wait for more clean water.

Who Cares About Managerial Controls?

One reason organizations need managers is that organizational goals are difficult to accomplish without individuals helping other organizational members remain accountable to each other, to the organization, and to the greater good of society.

Edsel Payne's team used a few simple operational controls to monitor progress during its fundraising campaign. The team monitored the amount of money coming in to the fund each week. It checked the cumulative total funds received against the goal. It communicated with those who had donated to inform them of the progress. But until Payne flew to Africa, no one on the team could properly manage strategic control to see that the overall goal was achieved.

Unless you work as a manager in international business, you will seldom need to travel as far as Edsel Payne to exercise managerial control. However, over the course of even one week, you will likely make many phone calls; read, write, and respond to official reports; send and receive dozens of emails and text messages; and have several face-to-face conversations—all contributing to managerial control. Depending on what and where you manage, you may need to travel from one office to another, across town or across the country, or from your office to a customer's location, and take any number of other trips just to confirm that what you expect to be getting done is actually getting done.

University students exercise managerial control all the time. For example, they check the financial balance on their account at the school and check their monthly bank statement against their checkbook. Students also are generally in charge of making the choices for their academic career. For example, students must look at all the degree requirements and then check to see which requirements have been completed as they plan for the next school year. They must balance these requirements with other obligations or commitments to work, family, and church.

We all are subject to control processes in our lives. The highway patrol officer using radar to monitor the speed of drivers is a necessary control device to enforce the legal speed limits. Paying your credit card bill late usually triggers an automatic control mechanism at the bank: The computer does a simple calculation and slaps a penalty on your account for late payment. We break an apartment rental agreement by leaving the apartment dirty when we move out. The result: The manager of the apartment building completes an evaluation of the extent of the cleaning and damage and deducts this from our rental deposit.

A common thread throughout these and all other managerial control activities is individuals taking responsibility to determine where they or their team stands in terms of their goals. Without this fundamental activity, it would be difficult if not impossible to accomplish what we want in life. The same thread runs through managerial control at work.

Management Pyramid and Managerial Control

Managerial control, like all other managerial activities, begins with the values, assumptions, and perceptions you have regarding a specific situation. An important value at the root of managerial control is the desire to be accountable to yourself, your team, and your organization. For the Christian, it also means desiring to be accountable to God. This belief is founded on the biblical principle of working at your best in every thing because it is not merely humans we work for.[4] Control also requires the manager to evaluate specific work processes, such as on an assembly line at a factory, to better understand how the work is being done efficiently. A key part of accountability is the desire to know the truth about a situation. This usually leads to someone gathering measurable facts about work processes rather than relying on someone's subjective opinion. See Exhibit 14-1, The Management Pyramid: Control.

Managerial control is designed to influence the behavior of humans and the performance of machines on which the organization depends to achieve its objectives. Because of this focus, the assumptions we have about human behavior naturally influence how we design and manage control systems. For example, consider the following assumptions regarding human behavior as it pertains to managerial control:[5]

- **Rationality.** Humans are rational creatures. They have the ability to plan actions, anticipate the consequences of actions, and make adjustments to behavior accordingly. However, humans also take action on grounds other than pure rationality. Personal values, beliefs, and emotions influence decision making as well. A manager's assumption regarding the

Gathering data that reveals the truth about work processes and their efficiency **Calculating productivity ratios** **Conducting a team meeting to discuss performance data** **Discussing performance reports with individual employees** **Choosing a performance-improvement project** **Selecting a performance-improvement team leader** **Implementing performance-improvement changes** **Reporting the results of a performance-improvement project**	**Action**
Following the control process **Thinking about constraints that affect work processes** **Analyzing process flow diagrams** **Clarifying the underlying problem for a performance improvement** **Developing innovative ideas** **Asking "What?" and "Why?"**	**Thinking & Feeling**
The desire to be accountable to yourself, to your organization, to society, and to God **Assumptions and values regarding managerial controls** **Expectations of how hard employees will work to make improvements to organizational performance**	**Being & Becoming**

EXHIBIT 14-1

The Management Pyramid: Control

Source: Courtesy of Michael E. Cafferky, © Michael E. Cafferky 2011.

rationality of workers and superiors will influence how the manager describes to others the importance of gathering and analyzing data regarding work processes. For example, the manager may promote data gathering because in the long run it will help workers justify their perceived needs for additional resources such as more efficient equipment. The data will also provide a basis for fair performance evaluations.

- **Creativity.** Humans are by nature creative. When faced with a problem, humans will attempt to create a solution. If a manager assumes that the work team members are creative and desire to solve efficiency problems, then he or she is more likely to involve workers in analyzing the data gathered on their performance and in brainstorming ways to make improvements.
- **Mastery.** Humans are "wired" for performance. They have a basic desire to achieve a level of performance that masters any given task. Once such a level of performance is achieved, humans desire to maintain it. The manager who assumes this will work with employees to set performance goals.
- **Barriers to High Performance.** Barriers exist that prevent some humans from performing at optimal levels all the time. Barriers to mastery include organizational structural variables and individual behavior variables. Where barriers exist, managerial control systems contribute to achieving high performance in spite of the barriers. The manager who assumes this to be true will work to remove barriers that prevent workers from achieving high performance. For example, the manager may make a structural change so that work assignments are closely aligned with each employee's talents and temperament. When an employee lacks training, the manager will provide training with the resources available or will lobby senior-level leaders on the need to allocate additional resources (time and money) for training.

Managerial control is not only your managerial perception, values, and how you think about a situation. It also is what you do to monitor and track progress toward achieving goals. The *managerial control process* is a series of steps in which you compare what you want to achieve with the truth of the actual situation. With this information, you and your work team will be better equipped to formulate positive changes that result in improvements. Before we explore managerial controls, we begin by exploring the Christian perspective on accountability because it is an important part of the Christian's personal beliefs and values (the "being and becoming" part of the Managerial Pyramid model).

Faith Perspective on Accountability

The Bible gives a few examples of managerial control at work but its main focus is on the fundamental principle of responsibility. The idea of taking responsibility for the actual state of affairs compared with what is desired is addressed in Scripture in the form of two similar ideas—using modern terminology we are talking about *accountability* and *agency*. We will explore each.

Accountability and Control

When the Bible addresses accountability, it is primarily from the perspective of accountability to God with respect to moral issues. God is a God of truth. His law is the standard of truth against which human behavior is judged. It is in this truth that we should walk.[6]

In God's economy all are accountable.[7] God is the Supreme example of what it means to be faithful over all that he owns. God holds himself accountable to his promises in the covenant. Humans are accountable to each other and to God. Humans will be judged compared with God's standard of truth, his perfect law. God's ability to uncover truth is perfect. It is not just observable behavior that God judges. He also tests the thoughts and intentions of a person's heart.[8] If the person desires to escape the judgment of God, then the only recourse is to acknowledge sin, ask forgiveness, and turn away from sin. Spiritual leaders and fellow believers also have a role to play to correct one another with gentleness. Because of this role, fellow believers are accountable to themselves, to each other, and ultimately to God.

Accountability is fundamental to positive, trust-filled relationships. It is based on the assumption that a standard exists outside of any one person in the community. It also assumes that humans can anticipate the consequences of their actions. We can make decisions, in part, based on what we anticipate. The community has a collective awareness of what is good and bad behavior. Each person lives in a responsibility relationship with other persons. With this knowledge the community holds members of the community accountable in all dimensions of life including economics. The connection with community is central to why the organization as a whole exists—to serve the greater good of society. We might even say that organizations are merely the structures that hold together many relationships that are built on a foundation of accountability. As a collection of relationships, the organization is itself accountable for the greater good of society.[9]

Accountability also plays a role in God's system of order and authority. Organizations run more smoothly when persons are in charge and are held accountable to each other for the common good.[10] Subordinates are held accountable by their superiors; superiors are held accountable by everyone in the organization as well as some outside the organization.

Accountability is an aspect of biblical love: the commitment to seek what is best for others in the community by restraining our own behavior. It is the only way that we can experience true freedom.[11]

Humans have failed in their accountability to God and to each other. Humans can find the truth about most human affairs such as business transactions, but humans are flawed in their consistency in telling the truth. Here the biblical role of the witness is the community's way of ensuring accountability to the truth.[12] In an interesting twist on the concept of accountability, God is the one who has taken the accountability for humans and placed on Jesus Christ this burden that humans are unable to bear on their own.[13]

The biblical concept of truth is a concept of action.[14] When the king, emulating God's character, builds his throne on truth, he builds it on actions of faithfulness. In essence, advancing truth means advancing the cause of faithfulness to commitments both to individuals and to the community. Because of this truth is directly related to the concept of shalom. It is reliability, stability, and faithfulness that accompany complete well-being and prosperity.

Examples of Accountability in Scripture

The Bible refers to accountability in the context of organizations a few times. For example, Joseph tested the truthfulness of his brothers' words. Nehemiah's experience illustrates the principles of managerial control. He set goals and standards, made corrections, and established work procedures designed for improvement.[15]

When Josiah rebuilt the temple, he asked that funds be allocated to the carpenters, stone masons, and craftsmen. So complete was Josiah's trust in the honesty of these workmen, he stated that no accounting of the use of funds would be required from them.[16] Trust and trustworthiness are rooted in a person's relationship with God; it grows out of shalom.[17] The spiritual reforms that Josiah implemented had a deep influence on the trustworthiness of temple employees.[18]

The idea of monitoring the results of work is accepted implicitly in the teaching and work of Jesus. Jesus monitored the conversations of his disciples (a qualitative measure). When necessary, he corrected them. He tells a story about the shepherd who counts his sheep (a quantitative measure) and, finding that one is missing, immediately takes corrective action by going out to find it. In parables we find managers monitoring servants, requiring them to give an account of their work.[19] In Paul's ministry, he and Barnabas reported to the elders in Jerusalem regarding the controversy over the religious practices of non-Jews.[20]

In ancient times most work was accomplished by hand labor. Few machines controlled production. Exceptions were grinding grain using a millstone turned by animal power or the use of pack animals to transport goods, for example. Naturally the biblical record on accountability for work is focused on the production and accountability of individual workers rather than on the control of complex work processes.

What can we conclude from this review of the biblical record? Accountability is communal and relational in nature.[21] Accountability looks to past performance; responsibility looks to the future.[22] When trust is high and self-control reigns, the need for control mechanisms decreases. Those in positions of authority should monitor and correct in patience, gentleness, love, humility, and wisdom but not with harshness. The purpose of monitoring behavior should be to build up and encourage rather than to destroy. Honesty and the search for the truth is one key to accountability. Those in positions of authority legitimately review the work of those who have been entrusted to them. Accountability requires openness or transparency so that the truth can be revealed. This requires trust. Another is the willingness to submit to be corrected by legitimate authority. It is this idea of submitting to authority to which we turn next.

Agency

The first Great Commission given in the Bible is the commission regarding management work delegated to humans at creation.[23] Humans were given a broad set of tasks to perform in relation to the physical creation. Implicit is the awareness that humans perform such work for God and his glory.[24] The Commission is founded in a relationship between the Creator and humans. God is the owner of all the earth; humans are God's commissioned responsible agents.[25]

In addition to this Commission that applies to all humans, at times specific individuals received a special assignment to perform a work on behalf of God and others. For example, God commissioned Noah to build the ark. God asked Moses and Aaron to serve as agents of liberation by leading the children of Israel out of Egyptian bondage. The prophets acted as agents of God to correct wayward people. Jesus was appointed to be the Messiah to fulfill God's promises.[26]

The idea that some humans can act on behalf or as representatives of each other also is reported many times in Scripture.[27] Today we label this the *agent relationship*. Individuals performing the role of agent are described using various terms such as servants, stewards, messengers, ambassadors, rulers, elders, and bishops. Abraham sent his oldest servant, Eliezer, on a mission to find a wife for his son Isaac. Jacob sent agents to contact his brother Esau. Pharaoh appointed Joseph as his agent complete with his signet ring, fine linen garments, and authority over all people to establish and enforce national economic policy and laws. When a potential conflict of interest came up when Joseph's family wanted to move to Egypt, Joseph informed Pharaoh and asked permission. Aaron became an unfaithful agent of Moses while Moses was on Mount Horeb. The 12 spies sent into Canaan were agents working on behalf of the entire nation. Messengers were sent to Balaam. Judges Gideon and Jephthah, and Kings Saul, David, and Josiah, all used agents to carry out their interests. The story of King Darius offers an interesting commentary regarding the need for agents. The ancient kingdom of Babylon spanned a large territory over what is now Iran and parts of Iraq. King Darius appointed agents over his kingdom so that he would suffer no loss.[28]

When Jesus sent out his disciples he illustrated the relationship between agent and someone in higher authority such as the owner. His disciples were official representatives of Jesus everywhere they went. If the people rejected them, the people were rejecting Jesus.[29] The parable of the pounds shows that in an agency relationship either implicit or explicit expectations exist that the agent will faithfully pursue positive outcomes on behalf of the one who gave him a task to perform.[30]

The root idea in being a servant or steward of someone else is being responsible for a resource committed for protection or for a task to accomplish on behalf of another. Two things are implied in committed resources: (1) the legitimacy of resource ownership or task accomplishment, namely that the one who asks for a steward to care for a resource is the legitimate owner of the resource, and (2) the authority of the one who is asking another to serve on his or her behalf.

Characteristics of the Ideal Agent

Agency is a concern of a *community,* not just of an individual: Both owner and hired agent are responsible for the property and interests upon which they and others are dependent.[31] Members of the community are to care for the interests of each other if key assets are threatened. For example, Moses taught that if you see a stray farm animal, it is your responsibility to return it to its legitimate owner.[32] Jesus showed his implicit awareness of this principle when he directed his disciples to go into Jerusalem and get an animal to use. He knew that people in the neighborhood would take responsibility for the animal. This principle of taking responsibility for someone else's assets extended even to a person's enemy—a radical way of implementing the principle of "love your enemies."[33] Above all else an agent is expected to be as faithful in carrying out responsibilities as the owner of the property would be.[34] Faithfulness extends to the responsibility to honestly report to the owner.[35] Unfaithful stewards should expect to be relieved of their responsibilities.

Faithfulness is one way we bring glory to God and fulfill the image of God in us.[36] Three biblical examples of such faithful *agents* are David, the shepherd chosen as king; Timothy, of whom Paul spoke in glowing terms as he compared Timothy with others; and Hananiah, who was put in charge of Jerusalem when it was being rebuilt.[37]

In Deuteronomy we see an example of when individuals are allowed to personally benefit from other people's assets.[38] The people are allowed to eat the produce of a field during harvest season. However, they may not gather extra produce to take out of the field. In this way, the employer provides for some, but not all, of the needs of workers while the worker respects the assets of the employer and does not take advantage of the employer.

A good illustration of this in Scripture is the relationship between the owner of sheep and the hired shepherd. Raising animals such as sheep and asses was one way that people in ancient times could build their wealth.[39] But Scripture advised that because the future is uncertain, owners of flocks should pay attention to the condition of their animals.[40] Rachel, Laban's daughter, served as her father's agent by caring for his sheep.[41] Because she was a family member, we can only assume that she paid close attention to her father's sheep and goats. Later, after making a deal with Laban to care for the spotted, speckled, and black sheep and goats, Jacob, the hired servant and son-in-law, started a selective breeding program. Yes, he cared for Laban's sheep and goats, but he also started taking care of his own self-interests. In the end, Laban's assets devalued and Jacob's assets grew in value so much that he became exceedingly prosperous.[42] Another example is the steward-shepherd David who remained faithful to his father's sheep when wild animals attacked his sheep. Later he remained faithful to his shepherd duties while he served the king. The biblical imagery of shepherd and sheep is powerful. It carries through the entire Bible, conveying a message about the relationship between God and his people. Exhibit 14-2 provides some examples of people as God's wealth-building asset—His sheep.

Human Limitations

In spite of the expectation of commitment and faithfulness, the Bible recognizes that human agents falter in their faithfulness when they pursue their self-interests at the expense of the interests of those to whom they have given their commitment.[43] Caring for someone else's assets can be downright unpleasant.[44] Yet the agent still has a responsibility.

Humans are naturally selfish.[45] In this sense, the biblical teaching on human nature is consistent with contemporary agency theory that starts from the premise that humans naturally seek their own good.

Shepherding Sheep: An Agent at Work

The Hebrew teaching regarding animal sacrifices states that sacrifices should involve only unblemished animals.[46] Traditionally Christians take this as a symbol foretelling the Messiah to come who would be without sin. But we often forget the economic significance of using the very best of the herd for sacrifice rather than for building wealth. The first-born sheep, goat, or oxen was considered holy and could not be consecrated for or by the owners.[47] In ancient times people were taught to think that the ultimate questions of life were not to be answered in terms of one's return on assets but rather in one's relationship with God.

Occasion/Situation	References
Jacob is the first to use the metaphor of Shepherd to refer to God.	Genesis 48:15; 49:24
Moses realizes that the congregation needs a Shepherd leader to care for them; Joshua is chosen.	Numbers 27:17
Moses predicts the scattering of Israel if the people are unfaithful to the Covenant.	Leviticus 26:33; Deuteronomy 4:27; 28:64; 30:3
David, prefiguring the Messiah, is chosen as shepherd of the people.	2 Samuel 5:2; 7:7–8; 1 Chronicles 11:2; 17:6–7
Micaiah the prophet speaks to the King of Israel.	1 Kings 22:17; 2 Chronicles 18:16
David uses the metaphor of people as sheep and God as Shepherd.	Psalm 23; 28:9; 44:11–12, 22–23; 49:14; 74:1; 78:52, 71–72; 79:13; 80:1; 95:7; 100:3; 106:27; 119:176
The prophets evaluate the people in terms of the sheep metaphor, false shepherds, scattering of God's people (sheep) in fulfillment of Moses' prophecy, God as the Lion which threatens the sheep, and God as the true Shepherd who gathers his scattered sheep.	Isaiah 11:11–12; 13:14; 40:11; 53:6–7; Jeremiah 9:15–16; 12:3; 13:24; 17:16; 18:17; 23:1–6; 30:11; 31:10; 32:37; 50:6, 17; 56:9–12; Lamentations 4:16; Ezekiel 6:8; 11:16–17; 12:15; 20:23, 34–41; 28:25; 22:15; 34:4–12; 36:19; 37:24–26; Hosea 5:14; 6:1; 13:7; Joel 3:2; Amos 3:12; Micah 2:12; 3:1–4; 5:2–4; Nahum 3:18; Zephaniah 1:1, 8; 3:3–4; Zechariah 1:19–21; 7:14; 10:2; 11:16; 13:7
Nehemiah prays that God will fulfill His promise to gather His scattered people; he refers to Moses' prophecy.	Nehemiah 1:1–11
The Messiah is viewed as the fulfillment of God's promise to gather the scattered sheep and predicts the future of the church in terms of sheep.	Matthew 2:6; 9:36; 10:6; 15:24; 18:12–14; 25:31; 26:31; Mark 6:34; 14:27; Luke 15:4–6; John 10:1–27; 11:52. (Cf. Zechariah 11:16; Micah 5:2–4; Acts 5:37)
Jesus asks Peter to become a shepherd of spiritual Israel—the Church.	John 21:16–17 (See also Acts 20:28)
Jesus is considered the great Shepherd of the Sheep.	Hebrews 13:20
Peter evaluates the church in terms of sheep.	1 Peter 2:25; 5:2–4
John offers his prophecy that the Lamb (Jesus) is also the Shepherd.	Revelation 7:17

EXHIBIT 14-2
People as God's Wealth-Building Asset—His Sheep

The Hebrews were consecrating not only a sheep symbolic of God's grace for the sacrifice—they were consecrating their wealth-building capabilities to God. We can think of this as a spiritual tithing program in which all of the assets of the family were consecrated to God, the ultimate owner of all the sheep. The first fruits of the labor of the shepherd further were designated for the benefit of the Levites who served in the tabernacle.[48]

Care of assets was also intermingled with the concept of community service. Whenever someone in the community observed a stray sheep, it was that person's community responsibility to make sure that the asset was returned to the proper owner.[49]

So familiar were people with the commitment needed to care for flocks that more than one prophet used this illustration to warn the spiritual leaders of Israel who were unfaithful shepherds of God's people. Later, Jesus used the parable of the lost sheep to show the faithfulness of God in reaching out with salvation to his unfaithful people. Jesus also highlighted a common expectation that shepherds who are not the owners of sheep sometimes limit their commitment to the sheep as they pursue their own interests when doing so is more convenient. When a wild animal comes, the hireling shepherd runs away to protect his own life, leaving the sheep vulnerable to attack. This is something the owner of the sheep would not do. The hired servant is more interested in his wages than in faithfully pursuing the interests of the owner of the sheep.[50] Further, the metaphor of the Shepherd caring for the sheep was not lost to the Gospel writers. For example, in Mark's gospel we find Jesus feeding the 5,000 in a pastoral setting much like a shepherd would feed his flocks. Mark's comment is that he began to teach (care for) them as if a shepherd would care for sheep that had been without a shepherd. This feeding culminated in the actual feeding of the people.[51]

The story of the gospel can be told in terms of the shepherd-asset metaphor. Humans are like sheep harassed and scattered having no shepherd. But Jesus is the faithful Shepherd, the Chief Shepherd who comes to save his vulnerable sheep from destruction.[52]

One of the special challenges that a Christian manager faces is when the duty to loyalty conflicts with the duty to be true to one's religious beliefs, such as when the owner asks the believer to do something that the believer considers immoral.[53] A biblical example of this is Obadiah, who was the manager in charge of King Ahab and Jezebel's household.[54] Queen Jezebel had killed the prophets. Obadiah risked his life to hide 100 prophets in caves and provide them with food and water. Another example is that of Daniel, who negotiated a creative solution in which he took on risk.[55] When the Hebrew Daniel and his friends arrived in Babylonian captivity, they received orders to enter the king's palace and learn the language of the Chaldeans. The purpose was to prepare them to enter the service of the King. As part of the arrangement they were to receive the choicest food from the king. However, there was one problem. The food that the king served conflicted with the dietary habits of the Hebrews. To openly defy the king by refusing his food carried a high risk. Daniel negotiated the opportunity to follow the Hebrew diet for a period of 10 days.

The biblical imagery of the shepherd is an illustration of the principle of agency. The agency problem: hired shepherds are not always willing to risk their own lives for the safety of sheep owned by someone else.

Source: © Didenko/Dreamstime.com.

One extreme position, being completely submissive to one's superior, reduces the conflict but undermines faith. At the other extreme, the agent challenges the authority of the owner, choosing instead to obey his or her beliefs in God and not humans. The owner may perceive such an agent who pursues loyalty to God in a legalistic manner as less useful, and, because of this, might let him or her go. However, the believer can attempt to accommodate the wishes of the owner, confronting only the requests that are intolerable or resigning from employment when the situation becomes intolerable.

The Bible's record on accountability and agency is primarily theological. But the fundamental principles found in the Bible are consistent with the modern-day concept of managerial controls. To this we turn next.

Managerial Controls

In 1954, the famous management scholar Peter Drucker wrote that managers give life to organizations in which they work.[56] This is still true today. One reason for this is the burden that each manager carries to watch out for the interests of the organization and the interests of the employees. Nowhere is this more clearly seen than in managerial control.

The Purpose of Managerial Control Systems

Managerial control is "the process by which managers influence other members of the organization to implement the organization's strategies."[57] At times the members of the organization allow their behavior to become out of alignment with the needs of the organization when their own needs become more important. When the needs of the employees and the needs of the organization are in close alignment, the requirements for a managerial control system are minimal. Generally employees tend to do what is required to help the organization achieve its goals because doing so meets their own needs, too. At other times, employees allow their self-interests to divert them from the goals of the organization. In most work processes humans are working against natural conditions such as gravity, temperature, pressure, wind, rain, ice, molecular bonds, and friction. Humans also must create useful products in the presence of impurities, mold, pests, bacteria, viruses, and other things harmful to humans. Certain raw materials decay rapidly, break easily, or escape when not properly contained. These and thousands of other factors make achieving productivity difficult. It is because of these challenges that all workers, including managers, need controls.

Managerial control involves two types of managerial activity. **Strategic control** is when managers work with other managers to ensure that together they carry out organizational strategies as a whole.[58] **Task control** is focused on the efficient and effective execution of specific tasks of individuals and work teams. Here the interaction is primarily between managers and non-managers, in which both work to ensure that the work procedures are followed. The interaction can also be between humans and machines, in which the human attempts to control

Source: wrangler/Shutterstock.

Managerial control involves two types of managerial activity: strategic control and task control. Both focus on the results of work activity.

the output of the machine according to predetermined specifications. Control can work the opposite way, too. When human labor is dependent on the machine, the machine acts as a control on employee behaviors. For example, managers set the controls on the speed of a moving assembly line. The speed of the line acts as a control on the line workers who must keep up their pace.

Managerial controls focus on results of work activity.[59] Regardless of how quantitative they are, by nature managerial controls are not truly objective and morally neutral. Controls represent the values of managers who have discretionary authority to use them in the organization.

The Control Process

Managers do not have the luxury of exercising control once in a while or only when someone is asking them to give a report. Control is an ongoing process. Exhibit 14-3 illustrates the steps in this control process.

The first step in an effective control process is for managers to set achievable performance or productivity goals. In addition to being achievable, the goals must be closely related to the key success factors for the organization.[60] See Exhibit 14-4, Sources of Key Success Factors.

EXHIBIT 14-3

Steps in the Control Process

Source: Based on Maciariello, J. A., & Kirby, C. J. (1994). *Management control systems: Using adaptive systems to attain control*. Upper Saddle River, NJ: Prentice Hall. pp. 41–45.

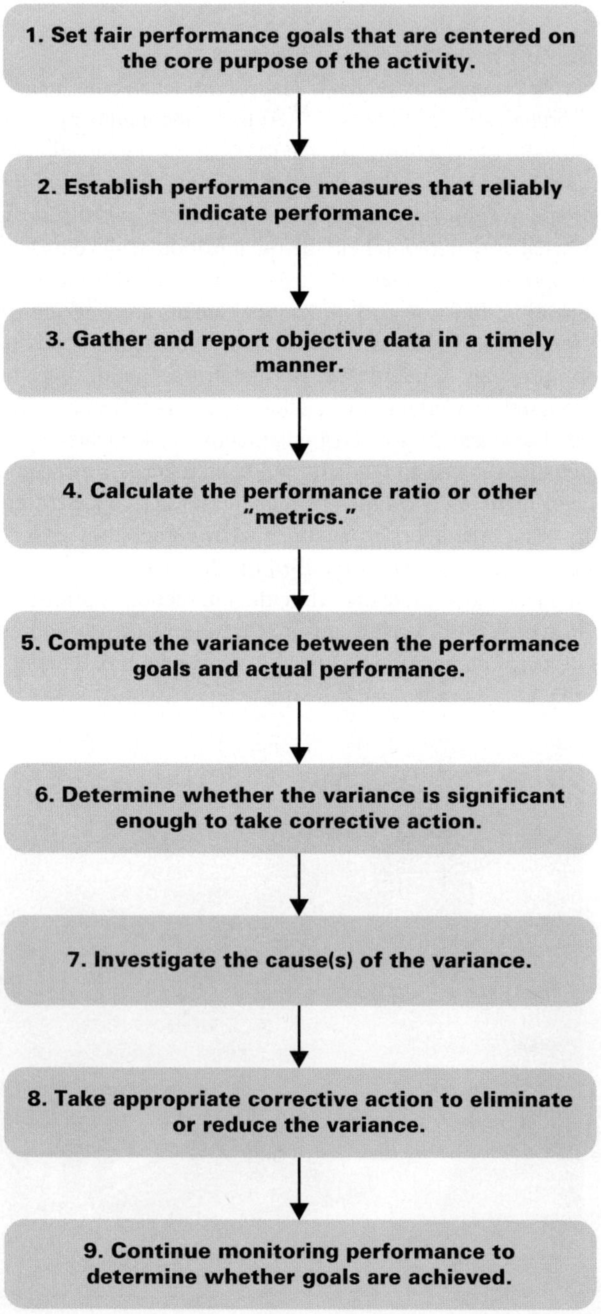

- ***Industry characteristics.*** Every industry is different. For example, in manufacturing, lowering costs is a key success factor. For magazine publishers, identifying and attracting specific socioeconomic customer groups is vital. In hospitals, aligning with physicians is a key success factor.
- ***Competitive strategy.*** For example, recall from Chapter 7 that a business that selects a differentiation strategy for a focused segment of the market must monitor its ability to generate demand from this segment by creating significantly different products. A company that chooses to be the low-cost producer must focus its monitoring and control efforts on lowering costs.
- ***Environmental forces.*** Forces in the general economic and political environment affect businesses differently. For example, a magazine publisher is affected by changes in postal rates. Hospitals are affected by changes in reimbursement rates.
- ***Significant problems.*** Every industry has its own set of problems when dealing with suppliers, customers, employees, creditors, and other entities. Monitoring how well these problems are managed can be crucial for success.
- ***Functional issues.*** Each functional manager (managers in charge of specific tasks or work processes) focuses on a number of key variables that contribute to the success of the particular tasks that are performed. Sales managers are concerned with the efficiency of sales staff. Production managers are concerned with the output-to-input ratio of production and the quality of goods. Managers attempt to establish controls before work is performed, monitor work while it is being performed, and track success after work is performed.

EXHIBIT 14-4
Sources of Key Success Factors[61]

For example, fast-food restaurants such as Jack in the Box, In-n-Out Burger, McDonald's, Taco Bell, and others must pay close attention to several key factors to be successful in their industry.[62] Managers must track overall profitability and profitability per transaction. They must have carefully planned work procedures, without which it is easy to waste money in the fast-food business. Owners must set goals and closely monitor portion size and waste that comes from incorrectly filled orders and damaged food products. The manager's ability to schedule workers efficiently around periods of low and high demand is crucial for profitability. Understaffing during peak demand will result in lost revenue when customers go away. Overstaffing raises expenses and threatens profitability. Owners must closely monitor how efficiently times of peak and low demand are matched with appropriate staffing.

Source: Steve Mason/ThinkStock.com.

A fast-food restaurant manager must monitor several measurements of performance on a daily, weekly, and monthly basis.

The second step in the control process is to establish performance measures that reliably indicate performance. Quantitative performance goals are often stated in the form of a mathematical ratio of output to input. Qualitative performance measures also can be used if no suitable quantitative measure is available. In such a case, managerial judgment must be used to interpret information from a management situation.

Managers must establish practical, objective measures that are valid voices of the work process being managed. Being a valid voice means that the data is drawn directly from the work process itself (whenever possible) instead of being filtered through a human's perception and biases. These measures need to be reliable indicators of the degree to which goals are being achieved. They should be timely and allow opportunity for corrective actions.

Selecting a performance measure that is economically feasible to use with the data that is available is crucial. The manager at a small bicycle shop might decide to gather data on 100 percent of the bikes assembled. In another organization in which millions of units are produced, this would be impractical because it disrupts work too much or is too expensive. In such situations, statistical sampling is more feasible.

With performance measures set, managers then create mechanisms for gathering objective data, the third step, which reveals the truth about the organization's operations. Gathering data might mean simply counting the number of completed projects or products. Or, it might mean counting the number of errors made. Whenever possible, use data that is generated directly from the use of technology while the technology is being used. Mechanical or electronic counters are attractive options to managers. In the fourth step, managers calculate the performance ratio. More than one type of ratio can be used with quantitative data. One approach is to compare the amount of output produced for a given amount of input or resources. The opposite approach is to calculate the ratio of input used for each unit of output produced. A third approach is to compare the units of actual output with the expected amount of output. See Exhibit 14-5, Generic Control Ratios.

Some problems can be unintentionally created at this point. For example, if only financial measures and short-term operational measures are used, then the control system can become imbalanced.[63] Workers may attempt to "game the system" to achieve their goals and in so doing shortchange the organization's ability to achieve other goals. Another factor that can cause an imbalance is when only one measure of performance is used. Ideally the data is generated as the work is done with minimal if any interruption to the work. Where possible, computer-controlled machines automatically capture and report data. If this is not possible, then managers need to create a manual data-tracking system and assign someone to gather and report the information.

During the fifth step in the control process managers compare the gathered data for actual performance with performance goals to determine whether a favorable or unfavorable variance has occurred. In more sophisticated control systems, acceptable variances are established in advance using statistical techniques.

The sixth, seventh, and eighth steps in the control process are closely tied in dealing with variances. If managers deem a variance unfavorable, then they call for those responsible to investigate the causes of the variance to isolate and remove them. This may require either formal or informal performance improvement efforts that lead to corrective actions. The objective at this point becomes a focus on eliminating or, where this is not possible, reducing the variance into tolerable limits.

EXHIBIT 14-5
Generic Control Ratios

Productivity = Input ÷ Output, or*
Productivity = Output ÷ Input, or*
Productivity = Actual Output ÷ Expected Output
Short-Term Financial Performance of a work unit = Percent variance from expected (or budgeted) performance; for example, profitability, return on capital
Financial Performance of the organization = Market Value (the present value of future income)

*Which type of ratio to use will depend on the conventional approach used in the particular business or industry.

In the final step, successful performance improvement efforts must be followed by continued monitoring of performance to determine whether the corrections work as expected. Performance goals are reviewed either formally or informally. And with this step, the control process starts again.

Agency

Consider the following example: Imagine that you are one of the officers of the Student Association planning a spring music and arts festival for campus. Your and your team's job is to decorate the venue. As part of the preparation you send a team of students downtown to purchase supplies not available on campus. But you don't have time to go along with them.

When their return is delayed by three or four hours, you call the driver to find out what is happening. The conversation that ensues goes something like this: "Hello. Where are you guys? I expected you to be back here by now."

"Ah, well, we ah, ur, we stopped at a restaurant for some food on the way and then one of the girls wanted to stop in the mall to talk with one of her friends who works there—so we had to wait for that. We're just starting back now. Isn't that right guys?" You hear laughter in the background.

Your phone call is a simple managerial control action. What you have just experienced is an example of what is known as the *agency problem*. You had to spend your time checking up on people who got sidetracked doing their own thing.

If you had to do all the work yourself, you probably wouldn't get everything done. When you ask someone to act on your behalf, delegating to them authority to perform work or incur expenses on behalf of the organization, as long as the action you ask the individual to perform is legal, you are appointing that person as an agent.

The concept of agency involves a financial relationship between an owner—the **principal**—and the owner's hired manager—the **agent**.[64] In a nonprofit organization, the agent might be a volunteer or an employee who willingly takes on a task requested by the administrator or the board of trustees. The principal has certain responsibilities toward the agent. The agent and all employees who are subordinate to the agent have responsibilities toward the principal.

In a relationship between principal and agent, the agent is expected to act in the best interest of the principal and must do so without a conflict of interest. Assuming both parties want to get the most out of the relationship, their interests may sometimes conflict. The agent will at times act out of self-interest. Principals monitor their agents by using managerial control systems.

When managers set goals for work teams and for the organization as a whole, they usually assign responsibility to an individual. For example, a department manager is the logical person to assign responsibility for the production goals of the entire department. But in some situations, assigning accountability to achieve a specific goal is more difficult. For example, inventory levels at a company such as Premium Connections, Inc., which makes and imports gifts, gadgets, and incentive premiums, are affected by purchasing, production, and sales.[65] The people in charge of each of these tasks look at inventory from the point of view peculiar to the task and will work to achieve performance of their own area of responsibility. No single department manager (excluding perhaps the general manager) can take responsibility for keeping inventory at a financially optimal level. In such a situation, the goals of sales, production, and purchasing must be reviewed carefully. Managers must set department goals so that they do not unintentionally compete with each other and create unfavorable inventory levels.

One consequence of the managerial control process is that tasks needing to be done to achieve organizational effectiveness must be subordinated to the organizational purpose. For example, at a company like Parc Center Industries, which provides full-service maintenance including metal fabrication and welding, a staff welder must stay focused on completing projects assigned to him. He can't use company time and resources to weld himself a backyard barbeque. Managerial controls can require individual employees to make changes in their level of performance. The staff welder may prefer to take more time to weld a project than is allotted, fearing that working faster will sacrifice too much quality in order to meet the production quota. Such focus may be unpleasant for employees who wish to have more freedom than that allowed by a control system that they perceive as being too tight. But when employees choose not to fully support a control system they think is oppressive, managers may view them as obstructing organizational progress. In such organizations some workers may develop strong

The Christian Mind on Being a Responsible Agent

Agents owe a duty to their principal. The principal pays the agent. The principal is legally bound by contracts entered into by the agent. He is liable for any harm the agent causes in the course of the agency. The purpose of agency is to allow the principal to act through the agent, and in order to make that relationship possible the agent must agree to perform in the principal's best interests. The Bible recognizes this duty of agents to their principals. It describes it in terms of "stewardship" and "faithfulness." The Bible, however, also acknowledges a higher kind of agency. By virtue of the *imago Dei* all humankind is in an agency relationship with God. We are responsible to act upon the earth according to His wishes. As Christians we are further called to live for Christ, to do His work, and to represent Him to a lost world. In business, when a Christian is asked to act in a manner that would violate the express will of God, it creates a conflict between one level of agency and another. Scripture is clear that while we are responsible to obey our earthly masters, we are not thereby absolved from responsibility to God. Sometimes, with candid disclosure, "We must obey God rather than man." (See Acts 5:29.)

Larry G. Locke, JD, MBA, MATh.
Assistant Professor of Management, Entrepreneurship & Marketing
University of Mary Hardin-Baylor
Belton, TX

concerns about the priorities of the organization that are placed before what they perceive as the needs of the workers. Control systems, it seems then, are not immune from the moral questions that emerge in organizations.

Morality and Managerial Controls

Moral behavior influences managerial controls in three ways. First, the controls used to align behavior are themselves based on the deep-seated moral values of those who establish the control standards. For example, one manager may believe that employees are able to increase their speed at work without sacrificing quality. That manager will employ a control system to make changes in the employees' work activities to meet the control standards. Successively ratcheting up the production goals may, at some point, reach a maximum limit of employee ability and create a situation in which employees are caught between needing to produce more and maintaining high quality.

Second, the structure of a control system, when combined with an incentive pay system, can result in employees who "game the system" and act immorally to achieve larger pay. Temptations to achieve goals can be very strong.[66] Add to this a situation in which some organizational goals compete with each other. Here the manager is in a difficult spot where apparently the only way out is to compromise on one goal so that the other can be met. For example, a production manager notices that the assembly department is behind schedule in assembling a certain model of product. Pressure to meet the delivery schedule promised to the customer may push the manager to cut corners in the quality of assembly. This may increase the probability that defective products are shipped to the customer.

Third, ironically, the principles of the control process can be applied to monitor, prevent, and, when necessary, correct immoral behavior.[67] Managers must establish moral performance goals. Then they must train subordinates regarding what constitutes immoral behavior. Managers then monitor employee behavior. When managers detect immoral behavior, they must take corrective action. After changes are made, managers must continue to monitor the behavior of employees to ensure that the changes had the desired effects.

Three Levels of Control

Controls can be applied at the individual level, operational task level, and the strategic level.

INDIVIDUAL-LEVEL SELF-CONTROL. Although control measures can be imposed on both managers and subordinates from those higher in authority, much of what gets done in an organization happens because everyone exercises self-control. Self-control is vital to an organization's success because it would be impossible for managers to devise and implement formal control measures for all types of actions for everyone. All workers have final authority over the specific tasks for which they are responsible. Authority resides in the job itself, not in the top executive who must share a portion of it with subordinates. Thus, each person doing a particular part of the work commands full authority over that phase of the operation.[68]

Employees in the organization interpret the goals and purposes of the organization and then make judgments and decisions about what actions to take. They monitor their own behavior. They watch the behavior of those with whom they work closely. They have discussions when they think the organization is getting off course.

OPERATIONAL TASK CONTROL. Most information generated in an organization comes from the accomplishment of tasks. This operational task level is the concern of frontline supervisors, mid-level managers, and their superiors.[69]

To accomplish managerial control at this level, organizations gather information to compare with expectations or other standards. This can occur frequently, every minute or every hour of the workday for some types of tasks, or less frequently for other types of tasks. For example, a manufacturing company might compare information about the number of units produced in a shift with the number of hours worked that shift. It might monitor the production hours lost due to equipment downtime on a weekly or monthly basis. It might track employee turnover on a quarterly or annual basis. A service organization might compare customer waiting time with the resources available in the customer service department. A consulting business might track the number of employee hours spent per client. A law firm would analyze the ratio of actual billable hours to expected billable hours.

Within any given company, each department can have its own productivity measurement. For example, the marketing department might monitor market share or the percentage of customers who are very happy with the product. The research and development department might track the ratio of the expected time to create a new prototype to the actual time. The engineering department can control for the number of hours spent per project. The sales team will track sales revenue per salesperson or the percentage of repeat orders. The order fulfillment team might track the percent of order fulfillment accuracy or the time it takes from receiving the order to when the order is received by the customer. Production might track the percent of capacity used or the percentage of jobs expedited by bumping other jobs from the schedule. The warehouse could track the number of pallets shipped per person per hour. The billing department can monitor the number of days in accounts receivable or the percentage of invoices disputed. Exhibit 14-6 provides more sample performance measures.

Several other control devices are available for managers. Managers use financial reports to track operational performance. For example, a monthly operating budget for the machining department helps the manager track actual labor costs compared with expected costs.

EXHIBIT 14-6
Sample Performance Measures

Divisional productivity = Return on capital invested in the division (ROI)
Business unit productivity = (Sales revenue – Input costs)/(Labor + Capital inputs)
Overall marketing productivity = Total marketing expenses/Total sales
Production department productivity = Number of units produced per unit of time or labor
Primary market research efficiency = Cost per completed market research survey
Physician's office = Number of service units produced per day or per month
Service organization = Total productive hours ÷ Total units of workload
Inbound logistics = Percent of shipments received on time
Outbound logistics = Number of actual shipments delivered on time compared with the goal

EXHIBIT 14-7
Examples of Three Categories of Control Devices

Prospective (feed-forward)	Real Time (concurrent)	Retrospective (feedback)
Planning sessions	Face-to-face discussions with subordinates during work	Analysis of sales per employee
Training for workers/suppliers regarding standards	Monitoring of indicators during production	Final quality inspection
Settings for moving assembly-line speed	Collection of customer feedback during service	Output ÷ Input for last week's production
Inspection and testing of raw materials before they are used in manufacturing	Cash-register-management software to monitor cashiers' activities	Benchmarking performance compared with best practices or industry standards
Safety policies and procedures	A manager's "To Do" list	Financial statement analysis
Cash control procedures	Video monitoring of an assembly line	Quality improvement projects
Selection of new employees for a good fit with desired organizational values	Locked access to expensive materials with only certain employees allowed a key	Annual individual employee performance evaluation meeting

Organizational policies and procedures are control devices that align a variety of behaviors with organizational goals. For example, in large organizations written policies guide a manager in how to obtain permission to hire a new worker or purchase new equipment. In a professional service organization such as a dentist's office, the schedule acts as a control device to keep workers moving efficiently. The speed of a moving assembly line system in a factory acts as a control device to keep workers working efficiently.

We can see from this discussion of control mechanisms three broad categories of managerial control devices:

- **Prospective**, or feed-forward: Control devices that are established before work is done
- **Real time**, or concurrent: Control devices that are used as work is performed
- **Retrospective**, or feedback: Control devices that are used after work is completed

Most managers will use a combination of all three types. Exhibit 14-7 provides examples for each of the three categories of control devices.

The Christian Mind on Productivity

A developed Christian theology of work emphasizes the inherent importance of and connection between worship and work. As Christians, to worship God is to imitate Him. The Bible clearly teaches us that Jesus was an intense and diligent worker. A Christian interpretation of *productivity* is based on the understanding that work has deep spiritual significance and is rooted in the desire to imitate the example of Jesus as an act of worship.

Dr. Franco Gandolfi
Professor of Management
Regent University Virginia Beach, VA

Corné J. Bekker, D. Litt. et Phil.
Associate Professor
School of Global Leadership & Entrepreneurship
Regent University

Strategic Controls	Operational Controls
Less precise	More precise
Subjective	Objective
Political	Rational
Focused on the whole organization	Focused on specific tasks or work units
Criteria is both efficiency and effectiveness	Criteria is efficiency
Medium- to long-range time horizon	Immediate to short-term time horizon
Summaries	Details
Domain of managers	Domain of individual workers or machines
More emphasis on planning	Less emphasis on planning
Responsible person: the manager who is responsible for both plans and results	Responsible person: the manager responsible for results

EXHIBIT 14-8

Comparing Strategic Controls and Operational Controls[70]

STRATEGIC-LEVEL CONTROL. Controls should be applied to strategic goals as well as to operational goals. This is the territory of senior-level managers and the board of directors. In reality, however, few organizations identify and use many explicit strategic control measures.[71] One important reason for this is that strategic controls are more difficult to identify and use. Because of this, the relatively simple financial ratios of return on investment, return on assets, or other similar devices are sometimes used to track performance toward strategic goals.

There are many differences between strategic and operational controls, as outlined in Exhibit 14-8. In contrast to operational controls, which emphasize short-term task-related activities, strategic control measures focus on the long term for the whole organization. But they are less precise. Because they are more subjective, they tend to be more hotly debated among managers and top-echelon leaders and are subject to organizational political influences. But strategic controls by nature ignore the day-to-day operations. Because of this, they leave out calculations of operational efficiency. For example, one strategic control measure for a new electric automobile company might be answering the question, "Are we stimulating enough demand to break even?" or "Do we have a large enough dealer support network for customers?" Another example is when a company acquires another company, a strategic control question might be, "Are we sharing core competencies across these two businesses as we had hoped?"

Dilemmas of the Ideal Managerial Control System

When considering the entire organization as a whole, the ideal control system will balance the short term and long term, and the operational and strategic. The ideal control system should be economical to use, congruent with organizational goals, and relatively simple to use on a day-to-day basis. Finally, it must be meaningful to those who are benefiting from its use.[72]

If too many goals are used for managerial control, the risk increases that some goals will conflict with other goals. If too few goals are used, they tend to encompass too much of the organization to be truly effective in monitoring performance.

Managerial control measures are often tied to managerial bonuses. If managers are rewarded based on operational performance, they will more likely trade strategic choices for short-term performance. This will undermine long-term effectiveness.

Under some circumstances formal managerial control mechanisms might actually undermine an important ingredient in organizational leadership: trust.[73] When employees believe that their manager is looking over their shoulder and scrutinizing the details of their work, they will resent the manager's work and begin to mistrust. Another negative influence on trust can be how intrusive the monitoring system is to the normal routines of work. The more the control system disrupts work routines, the more trust is damaged. A third negative influence on trust is the actual or perceived loss of autonomy that results from control mechanisms being imposed on workers. What does this mean for you as a manager? Employees may perceive personal surveillance by a manager as the greatest threat to autonomy. Measuring the outcomes of work processes requires less scrutiny and intrusion and has much less effect on autonomy because the work has already been performed

Managers must exercise control over the work but this creates a dilemma. Ideally, the manager will work in a collaborative relationship with subordinates outlining the goals and the limits within which they must work. In some work settings the manager will be able to give employees freedom to complete the work as effectively as they can (even though it might be done differently from the way the manager prefers). In other settings employees will receive less freedom because of the nature of the product being created.

Other Approaches to Control

The dilemmas just covered reveal some of the weaknesses of a managerial control system that is based on hierarchical authority. Another term for this approach to control is **bureaucratic control**. Implicit in this approach is the centrality of a superior–subordinate relationship. It turns out that this is not the only perspective on accountability.[74] Other models of control exist as well.

If an employee's boss can act as a control influence, then can fellow workers be an influence on control? Under some situations the answer is yes. Known as **clan control**, this approach taps into the power of peer pressures and the informal social structures at work to influence behaviors. Clan control can be effective when it is difficult to measure the performance of every individual, for example, when the tasks are ambiguous, are highly interdependent, or require constant close teamwork. With clan control, managers are careful to select supervisors who have integrated the organization's values and objectives into their thinking and behavior. Managers use extensive socialization processes to shape the values of all new members to the work group. On a day-to-day basis, supervisors emphasize coordination more than measuring outcomes and defects. When either one member of the work group messes up or the team as a whole experiences performance difficulties, group members help each other solve problems. They also confront each other to reinforce the boundaries of individual freedom and accountability.

Without the close social relationships of a team, peer influence and support will be limited. Clan control also requires a high degree of trust among the team members. Another requirement is that some individuals in the group must have strong interpersonal skills to deal with conflicts concerning performance issues. Clan control is effective, for example, in industries such as health-care services and airline transportation services because of the high degree of interdependence that exists among the various work groups. The more work teams need each other, the more likely they will experience conflict and the more they must work together to manage performance.

Other types of work are not as compatible with clan control. In some situations employees need a great degree of autonomy to perform their work. Putting them into a team may have limited usefulness. For example, in a large organization, purchasing agents need the guidelines and boundaries within which they should work to negotiate prices, but they need flexibility during the negotiations. What might work better in this type of situation is the use of incentives to encourage individual purchasing agents to get good deals for the company. Rewarding employees for meeting or exceeding individual goals becomes the mechanism to encourage alignment with organizational objectives. For this reason, this model of control is sometimes called a **market mechanism** or *market control*.

Many organizations use a combination of various approaches. For example, a sales department might use market controls and bureaucratic controls. A hospital will use clan controls and bureaucratic controls. The fact that combinations of various approaches to control are needed suggests that any single approach, by itself, has limited usefulness.

When considering the various dimensions of managerial control, keep in mind that the purpose of control is based on the following values:

- Accountability
- Trust
- Integrity and truth seeking
- Commitment to the organization and to following the truth about systems and processes
- Freedom of choice

Managers play a key role, regardless of the managerial control systems they use, in encouraging the formation of these values at work. These common-thread values are in close alignment with the fundamental Christian values.

Sharing Control Responsibilities

When managerial control devices are imposed on employees, all things being equal, employees are likely to resist the imposition. The more coercive the control system, the more likely employees will perceive it as negative. The exception is that employees tend to accept the use of controls when the tasks they perform are highly technical and require skill.[75] If, however, employees are included in the process of developing control mechanisms, they will more likely support the system and perceive it as less alienating.

If the organization can use generally accepted norms to align behavior, the need for coercive control systems diminishes. This is easier to accomplish in some organizations than in others. A church or a university will find it easier to use commonly shared values as control devices. A factory will need to depend on practical productivity measuring devices. A high-risk environment such as a dangerous coal mine will likely need to impose coercive control devices.

Whenever possible, include employees in the development and monitoring of performance. If employees understand the thinking behind a productivity ratio such as how this particular ratio is the best indicator of work process success, then they will trust it to represent their own work. If they understand how data is gathered, then they will trust the interpretation of the data.

Approaches to Performance Improvement

The need to make improvements in an organization's work processes can come from any of several sources. Routine monitoring of operational work processes, whether by managers or non-managers, will reveal opportunities to make improvements. For example, the manager of a production department notices that it is taking much longer than usual to get the paint room set up and usable for each new color being used. This delay has caused a corresponding delay for production workers who must wait for the paint department to get ready. Looking into the situation further, the manager finds that a problem in the paint department has been going on for some time. The worker who usually solved the recurring problem without anyone knowing resigned from his job last week.

Other sources are prevalent, too. Customer requirements for improved quality can spark the need to make improvements. Actions of competitors to improve quality or lower cost can influence the need for managers to spend time managing improvements. In most organizations, the opportunities for making improvements outnumber the amount of time and resources available to make improvements. This requires managers to make choices regarding which improvement efforts to focus on and which ones to delay. See Exhibit 14-9, How to Identify a Performance Improvement Project.

If managers and their subordinates simply monitor the status of the organization but never do anything substantial to make improvements, we must ask: Of what value is the managerial control system?

EXHIBIT 14-9

How to Identify a Performance Improvement Project

One that integrates well with the strategic plan	A process that experiences repeated problems
One that builds customer loyalty	Where a safety problem exists
Where the cost of poor quality is too high	Where frontline employees can participate
Where expected net cost savings are significant	One that has high visibility in the organization
When capacity needs to be increased	Something within the work team's control
One that can be accomplished in a reasonable amount of time	A process that is at the core of the company's purpose
One that is related to a high volume of customer complaints	Where the most waste is generated
Where sales personnel continually must make price or service concessions to make the sale	Where the organization is consistently having difficulty meeting its promises

Most of the commonly used approaches to performance improvement share several basic characteristics:

- Focused on specific improvements. Employees who work on improvement efforts focus on specific work tasks or processes.
- Reality-based. Employees engage in a continual search for the truth of a situation.
- Data-driven. Employees depend on observable facts that can be analyzed. Results must be measurable.
- Objective. Employees are willing to suspend judgment and personal bias until the facts are revealed.
- Aware of systems view. Managers and non-managers develop the awareness that one work task or process is inseparable from other work tasks and processes. If improvements (changes) are made in one, then changes will likely be required elsewhere in the organization.

Several approaches to performance improvement are widely used in organizations. We will introduce each one here.

INFORMAL APPROACHES. In many organizations and work teams in large organizations, this may be the most commonly used approach. When problems come up in the normal expected routines of work, those closest to where the action is make adjustments as needed if they have the power to do so. Some problems in complex organizations exceed the ability of any given work team to create solutions. The reason is that the work of the work team is interdependent and interconnected with many other units of the organization. Solutions to complex problems can sometimes require a more formal approach that considers the needs of the other units.

TIME AND MOTION STUDIES. This approach, which became the backbone of the Scientific Management movement discussed in Chapter 2, can be used wherever physical tasks are performed. This approach focuses on the elemental movements of humans and machines attempting to create the most efficient set of actions for definable physical tasks. The Scientific Management movement developed formal approaches using measurement technologies such as timing devices and distance measurements. In some organizations, time and motion analysis is less formal where a manager or a work team uses trial and error methods to make improvements. The more flexibility that the organization needs to maintain its work processes, the less likely it will use formal approaches to time and motion analysis.

FOCUS-PDCA MODEL.[76] Based on the work of Edwards Deming and Joseph Juran, two of the best-known proponents of quality improvement, the FOCUS-PDCA model is based on a management philosophy that guides a constant striving to improve optimization of work processes. It assumes that most of the difficult problems that affect financial performance and quality are so complex that they need an organization-wide management system to find solutions. Because of this, these approaches are embedded in a whole way of thinking about the organization. As an example of such a philosophy see Exhibit 14-10, Deming's 14 Points of Management.

The **FOCUS-PDCA** approach, like some other approaches, is interested in identifying and eliminating the sources of variation in a work process. The assumption is that variation increases costs and decreases quality. By isolating the sources of variation that are due to chance, which cannot be controlled, from those that are due to changes in the process, which are controllable, the team will first change what can be controlled. For example, slight variations in temperature,

EXHIBIT 14-10
Deming's 14 Points of Management

Source: Deming, W. Edwards, *Out of the Crisis* pp. 23–24, © 2000. Massachusetts Institute of Technology, by permission of the MIT Press.

W. Edwards Deming, one of the notable proponents of quality management, identified 14 points of an integrated management system devoted to continual performance improvement:

1. **Create constancy of purpose for product and purpose.** Management needs to determine a set of its core values and mission that does not change over time.
2. **Adopt the new philosophy.** We are in a new economic age. Western management must awaken to the challenge, learn its responsibilities, and take on leadership for change.

(continued)

3. **Cease dependence on mass inspection.** Eliminate the need for inspection on a mass basis by building quality into the product in the first place.
4. **End the practice of awarding business on the basis of price tag alone.** Instead, minimize total cost. Move toward a single supplier for any one item, on a long-term relationship of loyalty and trust.
5. **Improve constantly and forever the system of production and service.** Improve quality and productivity, and thus constantly decrease costs.
6. **Institute training.** Employees contribute to overall success through their continuous learning.
7. **Institute leadership.** The aim of supervision should be to help people, machines, and gadgets to do a better job. Supervision of management is in need of overhaul, as well as supervision of production workers. Leadership is the engine that drives systems toward optimization.
8. **Drive out fear.** Deming felt that supervision is often fear-based and mistake-driven, impairs contribution, and promotes safeguarding techniques such as padding the numbers or being a "yes" person to the boss.
9. **Break down barriers between staff areas.** Optimization of systems is impossible unless all components recognize their systemic function and have some feedback concerning the way their activities are affecting the system performance.
10. **Eliminate slogans, exhortations, and targets for the workplace.** Such exhortations focused at the workers only create adversarial relationships, because the bulk of the causes of low quality and low productivity belong to the system and thus lie beyond the power of the workforce. Management must learn that the responsibility of improving the business system is theirs, not the workers.
11. **Eliminate numerical quotas for the workforce and numerical goals for management.** Deming felt that numerical quotas were a barrier to quality improvements, as quotas cannot improve quality. Deming claimed that numerical goals are set when management does not know the capabilities of the system they are managing.
12. **Remove goals that rob people of workmanship.** This means abolish the annual or merit rating and management by objective. Give all the workers the tools and training they need to do a job they can take personal pride in.
13. **Encourage education and self-improvement for everyone.** Systems will improve because of applied knowledge, which is linked to education.
14. **Take action to accomplish this transformation.** Put everybody in the company to work to accomplish the transformation. The transformation is everybody's job.

EXHIBIT 14-10
Continued

vibration, electrical voltage, humidity, and atmospheric pressure can have a small but difficult-to-measure effect on some work tasks. Depending on the work environment and technology available, some of these can be controlled but some cannot. These are causes that are natural to or inherent in the process. If they cannot be controlled, they become random or common-cause sources of variation. Exhibit 14-11 explains the FOCUS-PDCA model and the meaning of its name.

Other sources of variation have specific, measurable effects on the process. These sources are due to irregular or unnatural causes that are not inherent in the process. For example, a worker adjusts the dials on a machine control device and forgets to change them back to the default settings. This will likely create a variance in the process output that is assignable to that error. There are sometimes other unusual events that occur such as equipment failure or a significant change in the quality of the raw materials that are used. These, too, can often be classed as unusual events that cause variation.

SIX SIGMA.[77] Started by the Motorola company, the **Six Sigma** program is based on a few rudimentary principles: (a) all work occurs in the context of an interconnected system of work

FOCUS:
Find a process to improve
Organize a team to improve the process
Clarify current knowledge about the process
Understand the sources of variation
Select the part of the process to improve

PDCA:
Plan the improvement and the data collection needed
Do the improvement and collect data for analysis
Check the results of implementation by interpreting data
Act to hold and continue improvements until more improvements are needed

EXHIBIT 14-11
FOCUS-PDCA Model

processes, (b) variation occurs in all work processes, and (c) understanding and correcting sources of variation is the key to success. Six Sigma is widely known for its emphasis on eliminating nearly all defects and making improvements to a process that can be directly linked to improved profitability. One of the most popular starting points in the Six Sigma approach is the needs of the customer. This is chosen because of the assumption that ultimately customer needs and preferences guide customer behaviors and are the key connecting link between the value that the organization creates and the price the customer is willing to pay.[78]

LEAN PRODUCTION SYSTEMS.[79] An area of emphasis common to many approaches to performance improvement is a continual attempt to drive out all activities and resources that do not contribute to the creation of value for the customer. This minimization and simplification of resources is why this approach is called **lean production**. Popularized by such companies as Toyota and United Parcel Service (UPS), lean production is a management philosophy centered around minimizing waste and on continual learning. Lean production often involves *just-in-time* inventory management (minimizing the space and time costs of inventory waiting to be used), eliminating defects, developing close relationships with suppliers, encouraging employees at the front lines to take more responsibility, and encouraging employees to participate in decision making that removes unnecessary resources from the system.

CONSTRAINT MANAGEMENT.[80] Every process is subject to limitations that restrict the maximum performance of the process. **Constraint management** is a management philosophy that focuses relentlessly on the interconnections between work processes and the larger systems of which they are a part. Managerial work is centered on identifying and correcting the places in the work processes that limit optimal performance. We sometimes refer to these places as the *bottlenecks* in the process.

The practical work of constraint management begins with a process that is already in place and that is central to the purpose of the organization's existence. See Exhibit 14-12, Identifying the Core Processes That Create Value. This could be a product assembly process, a material fabrication process, or a service process.

Once you have selected a process for improvement, perform the following five steps in constraint management:

1. Study the process to find where the process is constrained. Potentially every step in the process can constrain the optimal performance of the entire process (known as *throughput*). The step in the process that causes the most constraint is the one to find first.
2. Adjust work routines, materials, staffing, and equipment to optimize the point(s) at which constraint occurs. The objective is to optimize the constraint.
3. Subordinate all non-constraint steps to the needs of the step where the constraint occurs. This means that the work activities surrounding the bottleneck take priority.
4. Make adjustments to the point of constraint to increase capacity (reduce the constraint) of the process. While you should expect to achieve improved performance, be aware that other issues will likely surface during this push to optimize the performance of the overall process and the systems to which it is connected.

Define the purpose (mission) of the organization:

- **What set of values are created by this organization?**
- **What is the essence of what this organization does?**

→

Identify the work processes that are closest to the organization's purpose:

- **Where (what processes, departments, work units, individuals, or locations) is the bulk of the value created for customers/clients? Another way to look at this: If you removed these processes, would the organization still exist to fulfill its mission?**
- **To begin constraint management, select the process that is at the "center of gravity" for the organization's purpose.**

→

Identify the key linkages between these core processes, all supporting work units, individuals, processes, and outside organizations.

EXHIBIT 14-12
Identifying the Core Processes That Create Value

5. Start over and identify new constraints that have surfaced. This improvement process can be repeated as many times as necessary until managers believe that they have reached optimality.

Comparing the various approaches to performance improvement yields some interesting findings. Although there are slight differences in emphasis, the values needed for successful performance improvement are similar. They are also similar to those that form the basis of managerial controls: accountability, trust, integrity and truth seeking, and commitment to follow wherever truth leads to optimal performance.

The Biblical Story of Josiah

Read the story of Josiah recorded in the book of 2 Kings 22–23. Grasp the significance of the accomplishments that occurred under Josiah's leadership after he became king. What leadership principles can we gain from the experience of Josiah that are applicable today? What contributed to the state of affairs that Josiah faced so that he did not need to require workmen to give an account to him?

Accountability and Controls in NPOS

Many nonprofit organizations (NPOs) face new environments in which they are in competition for donors, volunteers, and public recognition.[81] These competitive pressures make it increasingly difficult for nonprofit leaders to manage the tension between the pull of their mission and passion for service and the need to view their work in business terms. This can be difficult for some nonprofit organizations that are so heavily mission-driven that they minimize some traditional business activities. Let's explore some challenges that NPOs face when attempting to ensure accountability and implement managerial controls.

Strategic controls in service firms and NPOs are more difficult to create and monitor than in for-profit organizations.[82] They are more subjective. The presence of human interactions makes the work processes and outcomes less certain. Operational controls are used in these organizations, too. In nonprofit organizations, financial reports are important but less so than in for-profits because they do not directly measure the nonfinancial goals of the nonprofit. Other information from operational tasks may be similar to for-profit service organizations. But NPOs may find such measures more difficult to use consistently.

In an NPO, productivity measures can be seen as a threat to some stakeholders whose services may be operating at less than optimal efficiency. Strident differences of opinion can undermine unity around the organization's purpose. Thus, organizational top-level leaders who limit conflict in the organization may choose to forego the use of some measurement devices to preserve harmony. In place of productivity measures, leaders resort to restatement of the organization's mission and vision as a way to encourage stakeholders to stay focused on their work.

One challenge inherent in the nonprofit's work is the dominant focus on service rather than on measuring organizational performance. NPO leaders must lead with their hearts and keep the mission of service paramount in the minds of employees and volunteers. Focusing on efficient performance detracts from this service emphasis.

A second challenge is embedded in an oversight paradox: Nonprofit leaders must partner with their board of trustees at the same time the board of trustees must exert oversight to ensure accountability. When board members begin emphasizing the operational details by getting involved in the day-to-day management of various departments or projects in order to improve them, they not only get in the way of the organization's employees and volunteers but the lines between governance and management blur. This can compromise the board's oversight responsibility while emasculating managers. It will lead to emotional tensions between the board and the managers. Board members usually mean well by getting involved in the minutia such as visiting managers and recommending that they purchase certain pieces of equipment or change the work flow or work processes. Some board members own or operate their own for-profit business and have authority to make these decisions in their work. In one small hospital, a board member visited the dietary department one day and told the dietary manager to purchase a new toaster that could produce toast much faster, meaning that the toast would be warmer for more people. Both the manager and the head accountant felt pressured by the board member. They purchased a $2,500 high-volume toaster at this board member's insistence. The toaster was used for one month and then put on a shelf in a storage building never to be used again. The reason: The counter space devoted to the toaster was needed for food preparation more frequently than the toaster was needed, and because the kitchen was so small, there was no room to put a movable cart to hold the toaster.

Another challenge in ensuring accountability is that compared with for-profit firms, nonprofits find it more difficult to effectively measure success in a meaningful manner. Defining success is difficult because most of what the nonprofit does is considered worthy. Getting comparable benchmark data from similar organizations is difficult. The organization's mission is the dominant focus in the organization. Yet operating the organization efficiently can be crucial to the organization's ability to continue serving its constituents in the future. When the organization is prosperous, the focus tends to shift more to mission. But when the organization runs into financial difficulties, it places more emphasis on the business dimensions.

Another issue is that in nonprofits (especially religious NPOs) that emphasize the redemption of society, managers find it more difficult to hold the line with employees who misuse their relationship with the organization. For example, if an employee is lax in productivity such as chronically wasting organizational resources, coming in late, or using work time to socialize, managers who discipline this employee may be perceived as attacking the employee's "style of ministry." Add to this the tendency to be patient with the employee in hopes that the person will change, and you have a recipe for enabling inefficiency and ineffectiveness.[83]

Paradoxes of Managerial Control

Several tension points emerge from the discussion of managerial controls, some of which we have already briefly mentioned. Let's consider some examples.

BUSINESS RESULTS—PEOPLE RESULTS.[84] This is a recurring tension point across a wide spectrum of managerial work. In dynamic organizations, leaders push for business results as measured by maximum economic output. This serves the needs of the organization. But without the effectiveness of the organization in terms of its people results, true success is not achieved. The development of people is more difficult to measure yet no less important. Here the key questions are whether employees develop and whether the organizational culture improves. Managerial control systems exist for the purpose of helping the organization to learn from its mistakes and improve or otherwise to stay on a course that will lead to accomplishing its purpose. So on the one hand, managers are expected to use effective managerial control systems to keep work tasks subordinated to organizational goals. Thereby the manager helps the organization contribute to something of greater good for society. On the other hand, managers also are expected to watch out for the interests of employees, especially when managerial control systems become too tight or oppressive to workers.

FLEXIBILITY—CONTROL.[85] Managers have the job of maintaining an organization that is stable and, because of this, to a certain extent predictable. Clarifying goals and direction and centralizing decisions that affect many people in the organization creates predictability and stability. However, managers also must innovate and adapt. They encourage commitment and the development of meaning in work. These require flexibility that comes from decentralizing decisions that affect smaller groups or individuals. If controls are followed too rigidly, then control destroys flexibility. If the drive for flexibility is followed too diligently, then controls are undermined and rendered useless.

THE CORE LEARNING DILEMMA.[86] Managing effective control systems is based, in part, on an interest in constantly learning the truth about the work that is performed. The dilemma is that while we want to learn from our experience, we rarely experience directly the consequences of many of our most important decisions.

Focus on an Organization

Christians in Action International Network (CIAIN)

As we have demonstrated in prior chapters, some Christian organizations exist for the purpose of helping business professionals learn how to integrate their faith with their work. While this is one of the objectives of Christians in Action International Network (CIAIN), its primary objective is to provide a forum for Christian networking that fosters an ethical approach to economic growth and development of Christian businesses.

The organization hosts an annual Christians in Action Trade Show. It also offers training in how to network to promote your business.

Membership dues range from $165 to $850 per year to participate.

Additional information about CIAIN can be found at the organization's website: http://www.christiansinactionnetwork.com/index.php.

Chapter Summary

1. When the Bible addresses accountability, it is primarily from the perspective of accountability to God. God is the Supreme example of what it means to be faithful over all that he owns. Accountability is fundamental to positive, trust-filled relationships. The idea of monitoring the results of work is accepted implicitly in the teaching and work of Jesus. It is communal and relational in nature. Accountability looks to past performance; responsibility looks to the future.
2. The idea that some humans can act on behalf or as representatives of each other also is reported many times in Scripture. The root idea in being an agent is being responsible for a resource committed for protection or for a task to accomplish on behalf of the other. Above all else an agent is expected to be as faithful in carrying out responsibilities as the owner of the property would be. A good illustration of this in Scripture is the relationship between the owner of sheep and the hired shepherd. In spite of the expectation of commitment and faithfulness, the Bible recognizes that human agents falter in their faithfulness when they pursue their self-interests at the expense of the interests of those to whom they have given their commitment. One of the special challenges that a Christian manager faces is when the duty to loyalty conflicts with the duty to be true to one's religious beliefs such as when the owner asks the believer to do something that the believer considers immoral.
3. Managerial controls focus on results of work activity. Managerial control involves two types of managerial activity. Strategic control is when managers work with other managers to ensure that together they carry out organizational strategies as a whole. Task control is focused on the efficient and effective execution of specific tasks of individuals and work teams. The control process involves several steps, including setting performance goals, establishing performance measures, gathering data, calculating performance metrics, computing the variance between goals and actual performance, determining the significance of variance, investigating the causes of variance, taking corrective action, and continuing to monitor performance.
4. The concept of agency involves a financial relationship between an owner—the principal—and the owner's hired manager—the agent. In a relationship between

principal and agent, the agent is expected to act in the best interest of the principal and must do so without a conflict of interest. Moral behavior influences managerial controls in three ways. First, the controls used to align behavior are themselves based on deep-seated moral values of those who establish the control standards. Second, the structure of a control system, when combined with an incentive pay system, can result in employees who "game the system" and act immorally to achieve larger pay. Third, the principles of the control process can be applied to monitor, prevent, and, when necessary, correct immoral behavior.

5. Controls can be applied at the individual level, operational task level, and the strategic level. Much of what gets done in an organization happens because everyone exercises self-control. Operational task control addresses the productivity in accomplishing tasks. Controls should be applied to strategic goals as well as to operational goals. When considering the entire organization as a whole, the ideal control system will balance the short term and long term, and the operational and strategic. The ideal control system should be economical to use, congruent with organizational goals, and relatively simple to use on a day-to-day basis. Finally, it must be meaningful to those who are benefiting from its use.
6. Bureaucratic control is based on hierarchical authority. Implicit in this approach is the centrality of a superior–subordinate relationship. Clan control taps into the power of peer pressures and the informal social structures at work to influence behaviors. Rewarding employees for meeting or exceeding individual goals becomes the mechanism to encourage alignment with organizational objectives and is sometimes called a market mechanism or market control.
7. When managerial control devices are imposed on employees, all things being equal, employees are likely to resist the imposition. The more coercive the control system, the more likely employees will perceive it as negative. Whenever possible, include employees in the development and monitoring of performance. If employees understand the thinking behind a productivity ratio such as how this particular ratio is the best indicator of work process success, then they will trust it to represent their own work.
8. Most of the commonly used approaches to performance improvement share several basic characteristics: Focused on specific improvements, reality-based, data-driven, objective, take a systems view. Approaches to performance improvement include informal methods, time and motion studies, the FOCUS-PDCA model, Six Sigma, lean production methods, and constraint management techniques.
9. Applying managerial controls in nonprofit organizations can be more difficult than in for-profit firms.

Key Terms

Agent 463
Bureaucratic control 468
Clan control 468
Constraint management 472
FOCUS-PDCA 470
Lean production 472
Managerial control 459
Market mechanism 468
Principal 463
Prospective 466
Real-time 466
Retrospective 466
Six Sigma 471
Strategic control 459
Task control 459

Discussion Questions

1. How does the Biblical perspective on accountability and agency guide us regarding the challenge of balancing the needs of the organization and the needs of individual workers?
2. Should Christian managers be expected to achieve the highest quality products produced by the highest performing systems?
3. Which of the following assumptions about human nature is correct most of the time?
   a. Humans perform better with assistance to stay focused on achieving organizational goals.
   b. Humans perform better without assistance to stay focused on achieving organizational goals.
4. Is the drive toward greater autonomy at work a God-created, healthy drive, or is it a sinful desire?
5. Think about a place where you work now or have worked in the past. What would have to be changed in order for managerial controls to be discontinued?
6. In the illustration based on the officer in the Student Association, what could have been done before the telephone call? What should be done when the students do return? What do you think the student leader will do?
7. Given the social nature of work in most organizations, is it possible to completely eliminate the process of control? Explain.
8. Bureaucratic control mechanisms can be diagrammed as a process. How useful would such a diagram be to describe the concepts of *clan control* and *market control*?
9. If managers gave proportionately more emphasis to shared norms and values, how would this change the need for the imposition of managerial controls?
10. Describe a situation you have experienced or that you anticipate might happen at work in which the values of performance improvement clash with the values for human development of the workers.

11. If workers who participate actively in performance improvement efforts also grow and develop, can we say that there ever would be a time when the need for organizational performance improvement will clash with religious values? If so, under what circumstances?
12. How do you think human development efforts might be blended with organizational performance improvement efforts so that no clash exists between caring for the needs of the organization and caring for the needs of individuals?
13. Some critics say that endless performance improvement or quality improvement is a battle that can never truly be won, so why put so much energy and cost into it? Do you agree or disagree? Explain.
14. Of the paradoxes and dilemmas described in this chapter, which one do you think might be the most challenging for a manager? Explain.
15. When Obadiah hid God's prophets in caves and deceived Ahab (1 Kings 18) was he being moral or immoral?
16. Evaluate the morality of Jacob's strategy in making the deal with Laban (Genesis 30–31): Did Jacob do the right thing to drain much of Laban's wealth and take it before he returned to the land of Canaan? Regardless of what you think about Laban's fairness or unfairness with Jacob, was it fair for Jacob to use his specialized technical knowledge to gain a strategic advantage? Did Jacob's specialized knowledge actually hurt Laban's family?

STUDENT EXERCISES

1. Discuss with your friends the various processes at your college/university. From a student's perspective, which processes have the greatest needs for improvement and are at the core of why the institution exists? Why? Is it possible to identify one person in charge of that process, or are several people responsible for it? Discuss your ideas with some of the managers or non-managers involved in that process. As a result of these conversations, write a one- to two-page explanation of why this process has not or cannot easily be improved.
2. Read the nursery rhyme "Little Boy Blue:"

   Little Boy Blue, come blow your horn,
   The sheep's in the meadow, the cow's in the corn.
   Where is the boy who looks after the sheep?
   He's under a haycock, fast asleep.
   Will you wake him? No, not I,
   For if I do, he's sure to cry.

   Why do people not feel comfortable about confronting others who are not fulfilling their duties as an agent? Write your own nursery rhyme about a situation you have observed in which the individual was not fulfilling his or her role as a responsible agent.
3. The class will be divided into small teams of no more than five (5) members per team. Each team will select a business, department, nonprofit organization, or government organization to observe some aspect related to the *efficiency* or *productivity* of the organization. Limit your observations to efficiency or productivity. It is the team's responsibility to initiate contact with the entity and arrange all appointments associated with completing the assignment. Select a process that is at the core of the reason why the organization exists. Break down the process into steps and try to draw a flow diagram of the process. Ask yourself the questions: Where are the most problems experienced in this process? Where can this process be improved? What data can be used to inform us about the efficiency of the process? For this project teams should see their role as an *outside consulting team* gathering information on which to make an informed judgment of what can be done to improve the process. Teams should counsel with the instructor regarding problems encountered, guidance in structuring the project, and writing the report. Consider all information you gather as confidential. The written report you create must contain six elements/sections used in grading the project:

   - Executive Summary of the project
   - Description of the process observed
   - Description of the observation methods used
   - Description of the findings and observations
   - Description of what might be done to improve efficiency or productivity of this process
   - Statement regarding the implications for personal faith and business integration

   The length of the written report will be a minimum of 5 and a maximum of 10 pages, typewritten, double-spaced.

IN-CLASS EXERCISES

Memory-Repetition Feedback

Before beginning the lecture, divide the class into small teams of four to five members each. Each group should meet for a few minutes to discuss what they already know about the topic of the chapter. Groups record what they know on sheets of paper or 5″ × 7″ cards. At the end of the class period, ask groups to meet again, this time to record what elements of the lecture need repetition. These ideas also are recorded on the cards. Cards can be submitted to the professor for review. At the beginning of the next class period, the professor can select some of the cards that address issues that need repeating.

Content Review Cards

Divide the class into small teams of four to five members each. Give each class member a 3″ × 5″ card. On one side of the card the team member writes a review question. Cards are handed to other members of the team who write a summary of the answer to the review question on the back of the card. Cards from one team are passed to another team who add to the answers that were written. Cards can be handed in. Content from these cards can be posted online such as in a blog for all students to review and add to.

Visualization

Some of the concepts in this chapter are abstract, yet they have practical value for practicing managers. One way to process the abstract ideas is to visualize them. Assign small groups the task to illustrate visually on one sheet of poster paper a key concept of their choice from the chapter. Allow some class time to start the assignment. If groups need additional time after class, they can be allowed to bring their poster back to class in the following class period. When the posters are completed, ask each group to present/explain its poster to the rest of the class.

Process Improvement

Ask another department (marketing, public relations, fundraising, etc.) if it has any envelopes that need stuffing. If not, bring 100 No. 10 envelopes and 100 copies of a flier (such as from the school of business, the dormitory dean, or other department) that need to be folded and stuffed into envelopes. Ask for volunteers to form two teams of five persons at the front of the class. Explain the goal of the activity: Fold 50 fliers and stuff these into 50 envelopes in as short amount of time as possible. Each team will be given the same amount of supplies. Ask each team to take 3 minutes to plan in private the process they will use. Allow the teams 2 minutes to "set up" their workers and materials. All other class members are "consultants" who are to observe the processes in action and prepare a verbal report regarding how the process can be improved. Assign some class members to observe one team and the other class members to observe the other team. At the command "Go!" start a timer. Both teams begin to use their process to accomplish the task. At the conclusion listen to both the "consultants" and the team members regarding what could be done to improve the process. What can each team learn from the other team?

Issue Debate/Discussion

Divide the class into small groups of five to six people each. Hand out a sheet of paper containing the following discussion topics. Assign half of the groups to defend the first quotation and the other half to defend the second quotation. Give the groups 5 minutes to discuss. Then call for groups to give a summary of the rationale they developed. Discussion can follow.

Discussion Topic #1: With the tremendous pressures that white-collar workers (such as managers) are now facing to achieve ever-higher levels of performance in their organizations, are white-collar workers the ones now working in a new kind of sweatshop?

A. **White-collar workers never had it so bad.** "Overwork is epidemic, for men and women whose job demands keep increasing, not because of career advances, but because of corporate environment that had depended upon squeezing more work out of fewer people with fewer resources." With the plethora of electronic communication technologies that white-collar workers are expected to use, they find it impossible to completely leave work at the office when they go home. Even when they go on vacation they are expected to check in with the office periodically to make sure everything is okay. White-collar workers may be spending as much or more time on the job now as they did a century ago.[87]

B. **White-collar workers never had it so good.** A century ago white-collar workers were mainly the mid-level managers, supervisors, and technical experts such as engineers. These individuals worked under tremendous pressure from top-level leaders (most of whom were the owners of the business). These mid-level supervisors were required to be dictatorial. They were expected to mistreat workers to cow them into submission to achieve higher levels of productivity. The push for productivity is no different now from then. But managers today have many more tools available to them, including the use of technology and employee teams to bear some of the responsibility for productivity. Also, managers now are expected to find ways to integrate their work with the rest of their life so they can find balance in both. White-collar workers use electronic communication technologies in their personal life as much as at work. They have choices regarding whether to turn these devices off when they go home or when they go on vacation. Class discussion can follow regarding the definition of the term "sweatshop" and whether, in the push for higher productivity, today's managers find themselves in similar (though post-modern form of) sweatshops. How should managers deal with this?

Discussion Topic #2: If a manager does not pay attention to subordinates and their behaviors, is this a way of trusting them to work for the interests of the company or is the manager encouraging workers to slack off or steal from the company?

A. **Trust is the highest form of motivation for performance.** Workers dislike managers "looking over their shoulders." Constantly monitoring behaviors shows that the manager distrusts his or her workers. This results in *lower* performance. Employees become resentful and will find subtle ways to get back at the company such as by stealing. Managers should explain what needs to be done and why and then get out of the way to let subordinates perform. Like Josiah did when rebuilding the temple, instead of closely monitoring workers, managers should spend their time inspiring workers to do their best work. Trust feeds faithfulness and this brings blessings to both the worker and the company.[88]

B. **Ignoring subordinates encourages them to slack off or to steal.** If managers do not monitor performance and behaviors of subordinates, they should not be surprised when workers decrease their performance or, worse yet, steal materials from the company. Human nature naturally leads people to selfish, immoral behaviors. Managers should not be enablers of immorality. In other words, manages should not *tempt* selfish humans by letting them work unmonitored. This is equivalent to placing a stumbling block in front of a blind person.[89]

Endnotes

1. Corrigan, P. (1999). *Shakespeare on management.* London: Kogan Page. p. 27.
2. Koestenbaum, P., & Block, P. (2001). *Freedom and accountability at work: Applying philosophical insight to the real world.* San Francisco, CA: Jossey-Bass/Pfeiffer. p. 41.
3. The account of the story was provided the author by Edsel Payne, February 2009.
4. Colossians 3:23–24.
5. See Maciariello, J. A., & Kirby, C. J. (1994). *Management control systems: Using adaptive systems to attain control.* Upper Saddle River, NJ: Prentice Hall. p. 7.
6. Psalm 25:10, 26:3, 86:11, 117:2, 119:43, 142, 151; Proverbs 20:28; 1 Kings 2:4, 3:6; 2 Kings 20:3; Isaiah 8:3; John 17:17; Galatians 2:14; 2 John 4; 3 John 3–4.
7. Harrison Jr., W. T. (1990). Biblical principles applied to accounting. In Chewning, R. C. (Ed.). *Biblical principles & business: The practice.* Colorado Springs, CO: NavPress. pp. 110–111.
8. Psalm 26:2, 139:23; Proverbs 17:3; Jeremiah 1:20, 12:3; Zechariah 13:9; 1 Thessalonians 2:4.
9. Proffitt, D. (2000). *Agency theory as a basis of business ethics.* Paper presented to the Annual Conference of the Christian Business Faculty Association. Buffalo, NY. October. On the relationship between organizations and society see Jensen, M. C., & Meckling, W. H. (1976). Theory of the firm: Managerial behavior, agency costs and ownership structure. *Journal of Financial Economics.* 3, 305–360; Drucker, P. F. (1954). *The practice of management.* New York: Harper & Row Publishers, Inc. pp. 34–48, 381–392.
10. Harrison Jr., W. T. (1990). Biblical principles applied to accounting. In Chewning, R. C. (Ed.). *Biblical principles & business: The practice.* Colorado Springs, CO: NavPress. p. 112.
11. Chewning, R. C. (1990). Editor's perspective. In Chewning, R. C. (Ed.). *Biblical principles & business: The practice.* Colorado Springs, CO: NavPress. pp. 121–124.
12. "As recorded in Genesis 23:10–18; Ruth 4:1–9; and Jeremiah 32:10, land was purchased in the presence of witnesses. John 8:17 reiterates the Old Testament law that the testimony of two men is needed to prove the validity (truth) of a proposition." Harrison Jr., W. T. (1990). Biblical principles applied to accounting. In Chewning, R. C. (Ed.). *Biblical principles & business: The practice.* Colorado Springs, CO: NavPress. p. 119.
13. Numbers 32:23; Deuteronomy 32:4; Psalm 31:5, 58:11, 90:3, Proverbs 28:13; Ecclesiastes 4:9–10; Isaiah 3:11–14, 42:3, 53:6; Jeremiah 23:24; Ezekiel 3:18–19, 16:43, 18:20; Zephaniah 2:3; Matthew 12:36–37, 25:14–20; Luke 16:2, 19:12–27; Romans 2:2, 3:19, 14:12; 1 Corinthians 4:5, 11:28; 2 Corinthians 3:5, 5:10; Galatians 6:1–2; Colossians 3:16; 1 Thessalonians 5:11–12; Hebrews 4:12–13, 10:19–26; 2 Timothy 4:2; Titus 2:15; 1 Peter 4:4–5; James 5:16–20; 1 John 1:8–9; Revelation 22:12.
14. Berkovitz, E. (1969). *Emeth*, the concept of truth. In *Man and God: Studies in biblical theology.* Detroit, MI: Wayne State University Press. pp. 253–291.
15. Johnson, S. (1988). *Values-driven people: A Christian approach to management.* Dallas, TX: Probe Books. p. 39.
16. 2 Kings 12:15, 22:7.
17. Smith, V. O. (1999). Organizational control through trust: A biblical system? *Journal of Biblical Integration in Business.* Fall, 77–102.
18. See the comments of the prophet Isaiah regarding the impact that spiritual renewal would have in terms of oversight: Isaiah 60:17.
19. Genesis 42:16; 2 Kings 5:20–27, 22:3–7; Matthew 18:12, 23, 25; Mark 9:33; Luke 12:47, 48; Luke 16:1–8, 19:15; Acts 5:1–10.
20. Acts 15:1–12. See Hammond, P. (2005). Accountability, relational. In Stevens, R. P., & Banks, R. (Eds.). *The workplace ministry handbook.* Vancouver, BC: Regent College Publishing. pp. 13–14.
21. 1 Corinthians 12; Ephesians 4:15; Colossians 3:9, 16; 1 Timothy 4:2; Hebrews 10:24; James 5:16; 1 Peter 5:2–3. See the comment on the community basis of accountability in Chewning, R. C., Eby, J. W., & Roels, S. J. (1990). *Business through the eyes of faith.* San Francisco, CA: Harper San Francisco. pp. 156–157.
22. Hammond, P. (2005). Accountability, relational. In Stevens R. P., & Banks, R. (Eds.). *The workplace ministry handbook.* Vancouver, BC: Regent College Publishing. pp. 13–14.
23. Genesis 1:28, 2:5, 19–20.
24. See also 1 Corinthians 10:31; Ephesians 2:10; Colossians 3:23; 1 Peter 4:11.
25. Genesis 1–2; Leviticus 25:23; Psalm 50:10–11; Proverbs 3:5, 9–10.
26. Genesis 6; Exodus 3–4; Jonah; Isaiah; Jeremiah; Ezekiel; Philippians 2.
27. For an exploration of the biblical concept of agency see Cohn, G., & Friedman, H. H. (2002). Improving employer-employee relationships: A biblical and Talmudic perspective on human resource management. *Management Decision: Focus on Management History.* 40(10), 955–961; Hill, A. D. (1991). The loyal Christian agent. In Trunfio, E. J. (Ed.). *Christianity and business: A collection of essays on pedagogy and practice.* Christian Business Faculty Association.
28. Genesis 15:2, 24, 32:3–6, 41:37–45, 43:19, 44:4, 45–47; Exodus 4:28, 32; Numbers 13, 22:5; Judges 7:24, 11:12–19; 1 Samuel 16:19, 19:11–21; 1 Chronicles 28; 2 Chronicles 35:21; Psalm 105:17–22; Daniel 6:1–2; Matthew 20:8; 1 Corinthians 4:1–2; Titus 1:7.
29. Luke 10:16. See comments on this in Barlow, D., & Usrey, K. (2000). *Contracts and agency principles in the Bible.* Paper presented at the Annual Conference of the Christian Business Faculty Association. Buffalo, NY. October.
30. Luke 19:11–27.
31. 1 Peter 5:1–7.
32. Exodus 22:14; Deuteronomy 22:1.
33. Exodus 23:4–5; Matthew 5:44; Luke 6:27; 1 Peter 3:9. See also Proverbs 25:21; Romans 12:20.
34. Genesis 31:6, 38–41; Colossians 3:22–4:1; Ephesians 6:5–9.
35. Harrison Jr., W. T. (1990). Biblical principles applied to accounting. In Chewning, R. C. (Ed.). *Biblical principles & business: The practice.* Colorado Springs, CO: NavPress. p. 113.

36. Numbers 12:7; Deuteronomy 7:9; 1 Samuel 22:14; Psalm 40:10, 89; Proverbs 25:13, 28:20; Matthew 25:14–29; Luke 12:42–48, 16:2–4, 12, 19:13–26; 1 Corinthians 4:1–2.
37. Philippians 2:19–23; Nehemiah 7:2.
38. Deuteronomy 23:24–25. In Hebrew tradition this applied as much to the employer–employee relationship as it does to neighbor relationships. See Cohn, G., & Friedman, H. H. (2002). Improving employer-employee relationships: A biblical and Talmudic perspective on human resource management. *Management Decision: Focus on Management History.* 40(10), 955–961.
39. Sasson, A. (2010). *Animal husbandry in ancient Israel: A zooarchaeological perspective on livestock exploitation, herd management and economic strategies*. London: Equinox Publishing; Finklestein, J. J. (1968). An old Babylonian herding contract and Genesis 31: 38f. *Journal of the American Oriental Society* 88, 30–36; Golding, T. A. (2006). The imagery of shepherding in the Bible, Part 1. *Bibliotheca Sacra.* 163, 18–28; Golding, T. A. (2006). The imagery of shepherding in the Bible, Part 2. *Bibliotheca Sacra.* 163, 158–175; Gordon, C. H. (1940). Biblical customs and the Nuzu tablets. *The Biblical Archeologist.* 3(1), 1–12; Mabee, C. (1980). Jacob and Laban: The structural judicial proceedings (Genesis 31:25–42). *Vetus Testamentum.* 30(2), 192–207; Mein, A. (2007). Profitable and unprofitable shepherds: Economic and theological perspectives on Ezekiel 34. *Journal for the Study of the Old Testament.* 31(4), 493–504; Morrison, M. A. (1983). The Jacob and Laban narrative in light of Near Eastern sources. *Biblical Archeologist.* 46(3), 155–164.
40. Proverbs 27:23–27. For an interesting story regarding the owner of asses going to great lengths to find his lost animals see 1 Samuel 9–10.
41. Genesis 29:6–10.
42. Genesis 30:28–43.
43. For an example of the agency problem see: Numbers 20:2–12; Matthew 24:45–51; Luke 16:1–3.
44. Luke 15:15–18.
45. Cf. Romans 3:10–23. This point is well made by Proffitt, D. (2000). *Agency theory as a basis of business ethics.* Paper presented to the Annual Conference of the Christian Business Faculty Association. Buffalo, NY. October.
46. Exodus 12:5; Leviticus 1:10, 22:19; Deuteronomy 17:1.
47. Leviticus 27:26; Numbers 18:17.
48. Deuteronomy 18:3–4.
49. Deuteronomy 22:1.
50. Genesis 30:32–43; 1 Samuel 17:34–37; 2 Samuel 12:2; 1 Samuel 17; Ezekiel 34:1–16; Luke 15:4–6; John 10:12–13; Job 7:1–2.
51. Mark 6:34. See also the comments on this in Johnson, S. E. (1968). The Davidic-royal motif in the gospels. *Journal of Biblical Literature.* 87(2), 136–150.
52. Psalm 100:1–5; Matthew 9:36, 10:6; John 10:2–27; Hebrews 13:20; 1 Peter 5:4.
53. Hill, A. D. (1991). The loyal Christian agent. In E. J. Trunfio (Ed.). *Christianity and business: A collection of essays on pedagogy and practice*. Christian Business Faculty Association. pp. 109–124.
54. 1 Kings 18.
55. Daniel 1.
56. Drucker, Peter F. (1954). *The practice of management.* New York: Harper & Row. p. 3.
57. Anthony, R. N. (1988). *The management control function.* Boston, MA: The Harvard Business School Press. p. 10.
58. Anthony, R. N. (1988). *The management control function*. Boston, MA: The Harvard Business School Press. p. 7.
59. Drucker, P. F. (1973). *Management: Tasks, responsibilities, practices*. New York: HarperBusiness. pp. 496–498.
60. Maciariello, J. A., & Kirby, C. J. (1994). *Management control systems: Using adaptive systems to attain control.* (2nd Ed.). Upper Saddle River, NJ: Prentice Hall. pp. 77–79.
61. Maciariello, J. A., & Kirby, C. J. (1994). *Management control systems: Using adaptive systems to attain control.* (2nd Ed.). Upper Saddle River, NJ: Prentice Hall. p. 79.
62. This is just a sample. Other key success factors include selecting good locations, maintaining a clear market position, and the ability to franchise operations for continued growth. Some factors affect the corporate success for franchised organizations. Other factors affect the success at the retail level. Based on an *IbisWorld* Industry Report for Fast Food Restaurants in the US NAICS Code No. 72221. Updated January 2009. http://www.ibisworld.com.
63. More than one scholar has contributed to the discussion regarding the inherent flaws of overusing short-term measures of performance. One interesting discussion of this is found in Neal, A., & Hesketh, B. (2001). Productivity in organizations. In Anderson, N., Ones, D. S., Sinangil, H. K., & Viswesvaran, C. (Eds). *Handbook of industrial, work and organizational psychology. Volume 2. Organizational Psychology*. Thousand Oaks, CA: Sage Publications. pp. 7–24.
64. Young, S. (2003). *Moral capitalism: Reconciling private interest with the public good.* San Francisco, CA: Berrett-Koehler Publishers, Inc.; Scott, W. R. (2003). *Financial accounting theory*. (3rd Ed.). Toronto: Prentice Hall. pp. 305–323; Keown, A. J., Martin, J. D., Petty, J. W., & Scott Jr., D. F. (2005). *Financial management: Principles and applications*. Upper Saddle River, NJ: Pearson Prentice Hall. pp. 17–18; Eisenhardt, K. M. (1989). Agency theory: An assessment and review. *The Academy of Management Review*. 14(1), 57–73; Jensen, M. C. (1998). *Foundations of organizational strategy*, Cambridge, MA: Harvard University Press.
65. This illustration was first given in Newman, W. H., & Summer Jr., C. E. (1961). *The process of management: concepts, behavior and practice*. Englewood Cliffs, NJ: Prentice-Hall, Inc. p. 565.
66. Maciariello, J. A., & Kirby, C. J. (1994). *Management control systems: Using adaptive systems to attain control.* Upper Saddle River, NJ: Prentice Hall. p. 649.
67. Maciariello, J. A. & Kirby, C. J. (1994). *Management control systems: Using adaptive systems to attain control.* Upper Saddle River, NJ: Prentice Hall. pp. 648–654.
68. Sethi, N. K. (1962, December). Mary Parker Follett: Pioneer in management theory. *Academy of Management Journal,* 5, 214–221; Parker, L. D. (1984). Control in organizational life: The contribution of Mary Parker Follett. *Academy of Management Review,* 9, 734–745.
69. For a discussion on the operational and strategic levels of control see Child, J. (2005). *Organization: contemporary principles and practice*. Malden, MA: Blackwell Publishing. pp. 113–115.

70. Based on comparisons made by Anthony, R. N. (1988). *The management control function*. Boston, MA: The Harvard Business School Press. pp. 40–59.
71. Goold, M., & Quinn, J. J. (1990). The paradox of strategic controls. *Strategic Management Journal*. 11(1), 43–57.
72. Drucker, P. F. (1973). *Management: Tasks, responsibilities, practices*. New York: HarperBusiness. pp. 498–504.
73. Christ, M. H., Sedatole, K. L., Towry, K. L., & Thomas, M. A. (2008). When formal controls undermine trust and cooperation. *Strategic Finance*. 89(7), 39–44.
74. For an early discussion of this see Blau, P. M., & Scott, W. R. (1962). *Formal organizations: A comparative approach*. San Francisco, CA: Chandler Publishing Company. Other discussions of the topic offer various "models" or "strategies" of control: Ouchi, W. G. (1979). A conceptual framework for the design of organizational control mechanisms. *Management Science*. 25(9), 833–847; Ouchi, W. G. (1980). Markets, bureaucracies, and clans. *Administrative Science Quarterly*. 25, 129–141; Ouchi, W. G. (1978). The transmission of control through organizational hierarchy. *Academy of Management Journal*. 21(2), 173–192; Heinsman, H., de Hoogh, A. H. B., Koopman, P. L., & van Muijen, J. J. (2006). Competency management: Balancing between commitment and control. *Management Revue*. 17(3), 292–306; Gittell, J. H. (2000). Paradox of coordination and control. *California Management Review*. 42(3), 101–117; Walton, R. E. (1985). From control to commitment in the workplace. *Harvard Business Review*. 63(2), 77–84; Long, C. P., Bendersky, C., & Morrill, C. (2006). Fair control: Complementarities between types of managerial control and employees' fairness evaluations. *Academy of Management Proceedings*, F1–F6; Child, J. (2005). *Organization: Contemporary principles and practice*. Malden, MA: Blackwell Publishing. pp. 118–134.
75. Etzioni, A. (1975). *A comparative analysis of complex organizations*. (Rev. Ed.). New York: The Free Press; Etzioni, A. (1964). *Modern organizations*. Englewood Cliffs, NJ: Prentice-Hall, Inc.
76. Deming, W. E. (1982). *Quality, productivity and competitive position*. Cambridge, MA: Massachusetts Institute of Technology Center for Advanced Engineering Study; Deming, W. E. (1986). *Out of the crisis*. Cambridge, MA: Massachusetts Institute of Technology Center for Advanced Engineering Study; Juran, J. M. (1992). *Juran on quality by design: The new steps for planning quality into goods and services*. New York: McGraw Hill; Juran, J. M. (1995). *Managerial breakthrough: The classic book on improving management performance*. New York: McGraw Hill; Juran, J. M. (1989). *Juran on leadership for quality: An executive handbook*. New York: Free Press.
77. Antony, F. (2004). Some pros and cons of Six Sigma: An academic perspective. *The TQM Magazine*. 16(4), 303–306; Lakhavani, S. T. (2003). Six Sigma implementation: Trials, tribulations and lessons learned. *Proceedings of the ASQ Annual Quality Congress*. 57, 643–647; Eckes, G. (2003). *Six Sigma team dynamics: The elusive key to project success*. New York: John Wiley; Larson, A. (2003). *Demystifying Six Sigma: A company-wide approach to continuous improvement*. New York: AMACOM; Pande, P. S. (2000). *The Six Sigma way: How GE, Motorola and other top companies are honing their performance*. New York: McGraw-Hill.
78. A good exposition of this connection can be found in Maital, S. (1994). *Executive economics: Ten essential tools for managers*. New York: Free Press.
79. Pascal, D. (2002). *Lean production simplified: A plan language guide to the world's most powerful production system*. New York: Productivity Press; Carreira, B. (2005). *Lean manufacturing that works: Powerful tools for dramatically reducing waste and maximizing profits*. New York: AMACOM; Alukal, G. (2006). All about lean. *Quality Progress*. 39(2), 74–75; Snee, R. D. (2005). When worlds collide: Lean and Six Sigma. *Quality Progress*. 38(9), 63–65.
80. Goldratt, E. M. (1986). *The goal: A process of ongoing improvement*. (2nd Ed.). Great Barrington, MA: North River Press, Inc.; Hsu, P. F. & Sun, M. H. Using the theory of constraints to improve the identification and solution of managerial problems. *International Journal of Management*. 22(3), 415–425; Mabin, V. J., & Baldersone, S. J. (2003). The performance of the theory of constraints methodology: Analysis and discussion of successful TOC applications. *International Journal of Operations & Production Management*. 23(5/6), 568–595.
81. Bear, A. B., & Fitzgibbon, M. A. (2005). Leadership in a not-for-profit world: A mixed toolbox. In Sims, R. R., & Quatro, S. A. (Eds.). *Leadership: Succeeding in private, public and not-for-profit sectors*. Armonk, NY: M. E. Sharpe. pp. 87–104; Phills Jr., J. A. (2005). *Integrating mission and strategy for nonprofit organizations*. Oxford: Oxford University Press; Drucker, P. F. (1992). *Managing the non-profit organization: Principles and practices*. New York: HarperBusiness; Letts, C., Ryan, W. P., & Grossman, A. (1999). *High performance nonprofit organizations: Managing upstream for greater impact*. New York: John Wiley & Sons, Inc.
82. Coff, R. W. (1999). How control in human-asset-intensive firms differs from physical-asset-intensive firms: A multi-level approach. *Journal of Managerial Issues*. 11(4), 389–405; Anthony, R. N. (1988). *The management control function*. Boston, MA: The Harvard Business School Press.
83. Osten, C. (2005). The challenges of interpersonal relationships, employee discipline, and leadership effectiveness in religious nonprofit organizations. In Sims, R. R., & Quatro, S. A. (Eds.). *Leadership: Succeeding in private, public and not-for-profit sectors*. Armonk, NY: M. E. Sharpe. pp. 105–116.
84. Griffin, T. J., & Gustafson, J. (2007). Balancing the leadership paradox. *T + D*. 61(5), 50–54; Quinn, R. E., Faerman, S. R., Thompson, M. P., & McGrath, M. R. (1996). *Becoming a master manager: A competency framework*. (2nd Ed.). New York: John Wiley & Sons, Inc. pp. 1–28.
85. Quinn, R. E., Faerman, S. R., Thompson, M. P., & McGrath, M. R. (1996). *Becoming a master manager: A competency framework*. (2nd Ed.). New York: John Wiley & Sons, Inc. pp. 1–28.
86. Senge, P. M. (1990). *The fifth discipline: The art & practice of the learning organization*. New York: Doubleday. p. 23.
87. Fraser, J. (2001). *White-collar sweatshop*. New York: W. W. Norton & Company. p. 146; Schor, J. (1993). *The overworked Americans*. New York: Basic Books.
88. 2 Kings 12:15, 22:7; Proverbs 28:20.
89. Leviticus 19:14; Deuteronomy 27:18; Matthew 13:41, 18:7; Luke 17:1; Romans 14:13; James 1:13.

CHAPTER 15

Spirituality, Faith, and Management

LEARNING OBJECTIVES

- Describe the concepts of spirituality and calling and understand their importance in management.
- Understand the faith perspective on spirituality and the distinction between spirituality and religion.
- Understand the linkages between spirituality and management.
- Contrast the two broad approaches to Christian spirituality.
- Understand the connection between work and worship, and the ongoing work of God.
- Understand the models of faith integration for the Christian.

"Spirituality is the essence of management."[1]

"To call on Christians to divorce faith from work is to urge the church, as a body, toward scandal, and to foist on its individual members the absurd notion that they have a kind of public moral or political duty to shirk their religious duty."[2]

MICHAEL VALLESKEY

At lunchtime Michael Valleskey, a real-estate research analyst for Sears Holding Corporation, leaves his office and walks to one of several Bible study and prayer group gatherings in his office complex located in Hoffman Estates, Illinois. The office complex where Valleskey has worked for 13 years is headquarters for Sears, but it also accommodates offices of other companies. This multi-company, multi-faith cluster of small groups also serves as an informal support network for Valleskey and other workers whose companies are going through changes such as downsizing, reorganizing, and scrambling to keep up with changing consumer behaviors. Valleskey also participates in the Sears Associate Gospel Choir, which rehearses at lunchtime.

Commenting about his experience with these small affinity groups that he helped to establish, Valleskey says, "I don't know what I would have done without my coworkers of similar faith. They have been there to support me, encourage me, make me a better worker. They are family. It's basically church. I have a church in the workplace."[3]

Source: Design Pics/Design Pics CEF/Thinkstock.com.

People of all faiths are looking for ways they can appropriately express their religious values in the workplace. They are looking for fellowship experiences at work. They are looking for opportunities to worship God at work. Participating in a Bible study group, a prayer group, or a Gospel choir are just three of the many ways that individuals express their religious beliefs. When you consider the actions that leaders of some organizations take to bring the organization into a posture of religious faith expression, the variety only increases.

Is spirituality so private that it cannot or should not be included when considering the work of a manager? What is spirituality? How is it connected to management? Why people and organizations do what they do when expressing religious faith at work is a curious question that scholars are increasingly considering. This chapter will encourage you to explore these and similar questions.

Who Cares About Spirituality and Management?

Managers develop the spiritual dimension of their work so that they and other workers bring meaning *to* their work as much as they all find meaning *from* their work.[4] Christian managers will be open to experiencing God and his call in the context of work as well as apart from work. Christian managers will seek to match their gifts with opportunities for service to others. Through the years, theologians and church leaders have called for Christians everywhere to live their life of faith regardless of their occupation. Many Christian managers have responded to this call, desiring to intentionally integrate their faith in the context of their work. They want to learn how they can do this more effectively and appropriately. But at times and in some settings this is not easy.

Just as there is a variety of denominations, there is also a variety of approaches to integrating faith at work. This chapter will explore some of this variety. It will also explore some of the underlying contributing factors that influence the choices that Christians make as they integrate faith at work.

Perhaps it is the mystery of spirituality that influences us to keep our own spiritual experiences a closely guarded secret. In terms of the work of a manager, this raises several questions.

For example, if you were completely open about your spiritual struggles at work, what would happen? Would coworkers judge you in a negative light? Would your supervisor immediately rush to support you in your ambivalence? Or would your supervisor encourage you to focus on your work? When was the last time you openly talked with coworkers about your most private spiritual thoughts and feelings? Some thoughts and feelings are best left private matters.[5] As a manager, would it ever be appropriate to discuss spirituality with employees? If so, in what terms will your employees be comfortable talking about it? With what will they be uncomfortable?

Just what is the connection between spirituality and management? Although not all agree, many scholars think that the concept of spirituality has a natural place at work. Based on their observations, spirituality and management researchers Mitroff and Denton believe that organizations benefit when they develop a strong sense of spirituality.[6] Based on their research, they found that compared with organizations without a strong sense of spirituality, employees in these organizations:

- are less fearful,
- are less likely to compromise beliefs and values,
- perceive their organizations as more profitable, and
- are able to bring more of their complete selves to work.

While spirituality brings these benefits to organizations, it also adds complexity and is far from being a magic formula to resolve all managerial problems.[7]

Of all the factors that influence managerial behavior, spirituality may be one of the most influential. If we start with an assumption that human beings want to engage in activities that are meaningful, then we must allow that spirituality might be at the core of managerial work for three reasons. First, all workers will experience this drive toward meaning. This is true for workers who feel they must put aside spiritual values to be successful in their work. But it also is true of workers who already find meaning in their work when what they do closely aligns with a sense of accomplishment of serving others and at the same time supports their deep beliefs. Second, managers will want to create job characteristics and work environments conducive to sensing the meaning in work. Third, managers themselves share this drive toward meaning. They want to know that what they do makes a difference.[8]

Management Pyramid

It is easy to think of spirituality as something occurring in the soul of a person, something that is mainly mental/emotional in nature and hidden from view. But spirituality is more than just a private mental experience. It involves the same three dimensions of the Management Pyramid model that we've been discussing throughout this text: who you are, how you think and feel, and what you do.[9]

Because the concept of spirituality is difficult to define, we often resort to describing it rather than precisely defining it. The term *spirituality* sometimes makes people think of inner mystical mental and emotional experiences or altered states of consciousness.[10] While these are experienced by individuals, spirituality is a much broader concept encompassing all of life.[11] For many Christians, spirituality is rooted in the fundamental experience of Christian belief and practice. Although spirituality may be defined in various ways it still remains a mystery.[12]

While historically in Western nations spirituality has been inseparably linked with religious experience, some scholars now believe that spirituality can be religious or nonreligious.[13] Christian or **religious spirituality** is rooted in an experience shared with other people who are members of an organized religion.[14] Christian spirituality is founded on several key beliefs such as the existence of God, the origin of sin, God's plan of salvation to take care of the sin problem, the believer's religious experience of faith, and living a life that is aligned with God's revealed will. Defined free of religious beliefs, **nonreligious spirituality** is the ability to see the sacredness in every dimension of life.[15] It emphasizes a person's values (religious or otherwise). Nonreligious spirituality is rooted in human experience that is common to all persons whether or not they are members of an organized religion. One assumption of nonreligious spirituality is that a person does not need to be a member of a religious organization to develop spirituality. Even so, it is hard to deny that many of the concepts of nonreligious spirituality are closely aligned with Christian teachings.[16] Looking across the variety of Christian denominations we find several common elements that describe spiritual experience, as outlined in Exhibit 15-1.

Christian Traditions[17]	Nonreligious Spirituality[18]
Spirituality is concerned with the physical, material, and mundane as well as the nonphysical, and with hunger and yearning for a relationship with God.	Spirituality is concerned with hunger or yearning for meaning and purpose in life and work and with transformation of consciousness.
Spirituality is individual (personal) and corporate or communal (organizational).	Spirituality includes a sense of connectedness with community and relationships.
Spirituality is private and public, inward and outward.	Spirituality involves contemplation, service, and moral action in society.
Spirituality is churchly and worldly (sacred and secular).	Spirituality is seeing the sacred in everyday life.
Spirituality is concerned with relationship with God and with human relationships.	Spirituality is concerned with interdependence and balance or interconnectedness with everything in the universe—self, others, nature, and with divine power.

EXHIBIT 15-1

Commonly Accepted Dimensions of Spirituality

Spirituality as a dimension of business has become a popular subject of study apart from religious teachings.[19] Some believe that bringing spirituality to work enhances a person's ability to live a more integrated life as a whole.[20] But not everyone accepts the religious foundation for spirituality in the business world, and not all Christians accept a concept of spirituality separate from religion. Exhibit 15-2 provides some examples of Christian criticisms of corporate spirituality.

Some teachings of nonreligious spirituality that are promoted in the marketplace may be in opposition to commonly accepted Christian teachings. These include the following:

- *The belief that all humans are intrinsically good.*[21] Here an important distinction must be made. Most Christians claim that while the image of God in humans is not totally destroyed by sin, humans are by nature sinful beings and are in need of the righteousness that comes only through the person and work of Jesus Christ. This doesn't mean that sinful humans cannot exhibit behaviors that are considered good or beneficial to others. Humans are capable of both good and bad behavior.
- *The belief that all humans possess divine power.*[22] While most Christians believe that God's power can be experienced in a person's life through faith, they believe that human beings are not divine beings.
- *Pantheism.*[23] It is one thing to view all of creation as sacred. It is quite another thing to believe that God is everything and everything is God—*pantheism*—a belief that Christians reject. Christians believe that God exists independent from the environment.
- *The belief that there are no moral absolutes.*[24] Christians believe that God has established moral absolutes in the form of the two great commands (supreme love to God and unselfish love to others) and the Ten Commandments.[25]

- The spirituality at work movement tends to marginalize the church as a social structure of importance.
- Corporate spirituality forces the church into marketplace goals and values.
- Corporate spirituality maintains a distance from historic Christianity while using traditional Christian concepts, values, and symbols.
- Spirituality at work encourages people to measure the value of spirituality in terms of what it does for them, such as their happiness, self-esteem, work motivation, or career success. This diverts attention from Jesus Christ and absorbs the church by commerce while robbing the church of its prophetic and eschatological emphasis.
- Corporate spirituality cheapens true spirituality and a person's relationship with Jesus Christ.

EXHIBIT 15-2

Some Christian Criticisms of Corporate Spirituality[26]

EXHIBIT 15-3

The Public and Private Dimensions of Spirituality

Source: Based on that presented in Mitroff, I. I., & Denton, E. A. (1999). *A spiritual audit of corporate America: A hard look at spirituality, religion and values in the workplace*. San Francisco, CA: Jossey-Bass. pp. 26–27; based on Wilber, K. (1996). *A brief history of everything*. Boston, MA: Shambhala. See also Steingard, D. S., & Fitzgibbons, D. E. (2007). Toward a spiritual integrated theory of management. In Biberman, J., & Whitty, M. D. *At work: Spirituality matters*. Scranton, PA: University of Scranton Press. pp. 47–46. Pyramid courtesy of Michael E. Cafferky, © Michael E. Cafferky 2011.

		Community	Individual
Outward	Action	What the community does as a group that affects everyone	What we do that affects others
Inward	Thinking & Feeling	Thoughts and feelings that are expressed to or shared by others	A personal inner experience
	Being & Becoming	Beliefs, assumptions, and desires shared by the community	Who we are; personal beliefs and assumptions

Through the lens of the Management Pyramid, spirituality is first who you are. Think about your character, spiritual values, beliefs about God, your desire to live a life that aligns with particular religious beliefs, and your assumptions about human existence. For example, you may have opinions about performing the work of the organization in a manner that expresses concern for organizational interests as well as considers the needs of others. Spirituality does not remain bottled up inside. Eventually it is expressed in behaviors that affect other people.

Spirituality also has both individual and community (public) dimensions,[27] as shown in Exhibit 15-3. One assumption in this text is that generally it is difficult to separate your actions from your thinking and feeling. There may be inconsistencies between your beliefs and your actions, but, one way or another, what goes on inside your mind and heart will be revealed on the outside through your actions even if some of these actions are not observable by others.[28]

This chapter focuses on integrating spirituality and faith in the work of a manager. As we have done with other chapters, we begin with the Christian perspective because it is an important part of the Christian's personal beliefs and values (the "being and becoming" part of the Management Pyramid model).

Faith Perspective on Spirituality

Two broad traditions of spirituality have been practiced among Christians around the world: (1) Spirituality lived through actions in life including work, which is called **kataphatic spirituality**; and (2) reflective, prayerful, contemplative spirituality experienced through temporary separation from the world, which is called **apophatic spirituality**.[29] Another way of describing this is in terms of attachment and detachment. **Attachment** is the attempt to be fully engaged with people and the world around us. It means connecting with the world through service and stewardship. Attachment emphasizes the importance of finding God in the context of human relationships. **Detachment** is the temporary separation for a period of time from some relationships for the purpose of contemplation and spiritual renewal. The emphasis here is on solitude, silence, and self-sacrifice to get close to God through meditation, prayer, Scripture reading, journaling, or contemplation.[30]

Apophatic spirituality is based on the belief that a wide chasm exists between God and humans. Because of this great distance, God is best known through negation or removal of common, worldly thoughts, symbols, and images. In this perspective, little in our worldly life can connect us with God. Those who follow this tradition will emphasize separation from the cares of this world.[31] If this is your thinking on spirituality, then you probably prefer taking time away from work and family life to be alone with God, to meditate in a setting that is free of worldly distractions. Or it might simply mean attending church services on a weekly basis.

In contrast is the opposite belief that God is close to us while we are in the midst of the common experiences of life including work. Those who follow kataphatic spirituality emphasize spiritual development that takes place in the context of their day-to-day life. If this is your thinking of spirituality, then you probably prefer growing spirituality in the midst of life's cares

Source: Stockbyte/Thinkstock.

Detachment is the temporary separation for a period of time from some relationships for the purpose of contemplation and spiritual renewal.

and responsibilities. Thoughts, symbols, and images of everyday life are not distractions to spirituality. Rather, they enhance spiritual awareness.

For some Christian managers, spirituality means finding opportunities for meditation, reflection, and prayer within managerial work itself. Reflection in the midst of managerial work creates an openness to find Divine influence.[32] The reality is that because of the heavy demands of the mental work of management, it is difficult to engage in reflection about work. For other managers whose work requires constant attention, managing the rhythm of withdrawal and engagement means creating a few quiet times during the day, for example, simply closing your office door for a few minutes.[33] For still others who have high intensity work, this means attending to the material, detailed issues of work and family, with quiet time of personal prayer, Scripture reading, or meditation daily before or after work. Managers who find it difficult to mentally leave their work at the office at the end of the day may find the weekend the time when they can get away from it all for spiritual renewal. See Exhibit 15-4.

Which approach is best? It might be argued that both approaches are appropriate as long as neither approach is allowed to dominate to the exclusion of the other. To see how these two perspectives are relevant to the world of work, we will explore the concept of Christian worship.

Attachment is the attempt to be fully engaged with people and the world around us. It means connecting with the world through service and stewardship.

Source: © Pastoor/Dreamstime.com.

***Within* Managerial Work**	***Between* Managerial Work**
Practicing the presence of God by meditation and contemplation as you perform management tasks; maintaining an openness to learn, to change	**Finding time for contemplation throughout the workday; using break time for meditation and prayer; maintaining an openness to learn and to change**
Keeping focused on spiritual values and foundational principles while engaged in the work of management; prayer at work; gradually transforming the work and, through this, changing the organization	**Finding quiet time alone at the beginning or end of a workday for journaling, meditation, Scripture reading, or prayer**
Looking with expectancy for evidence that God is at work in the mundane, the details, and the lives of others in the marketplace; being aware that work is part of a larger scheme of existence than what is present in a specific situation	**Taking time for reflection and meditation at the end of the workweek; participating in religious services with other people in a faith community (church)**
Sensing that all of life is sacred; that spirituality means fully participating in life and is not merely a spectator activity, that God is present in every management and leadership situation, that management is full-time ministry and full-time worship, and that ultimately the manager's work, though imperfect, is accomplished for God and his glory	**Planning time for retreat at the conclusion of major projects or periodically every few weeks or months**

EXHIBIT 15-4
The Rhythms of Spirituality

Dimensions of Worship

Worship is a state of spiritual being in which the person and the faith community experience a transformed responsiveness to God.[34] We normally think of worship, which in some faith communities is called liturgy, as something that occurs inside a church building or, at the very least, something that occurs when a religious congregation gathers for organized spiritual meetings. Worship has many dimensions that are not exclusively the domain of congregational events conducted in church buildings. The dimensions of biblical worship include:[35]

- **Thoughts and actions:** Worship is a subjective experience of both the heart and mind (being and thinking). It also is an objective social activity (action).[36] Worship is the hidden work of the soul as it is moved by God. But worship also is the visible work of the soul as the person expresses glory to God.
- **Individual** (by yourself) **and corporate** (with the congregation) **settings:** Individual worship occurs in solitude or apart from the gathering of believers in a group, while corporate worship occurs in the setting of a group.[37]
- **Spontaneity and order:** Worship involves freedom and "unexpectedness of the Spirit as well as the ordered life of spiritual rigor and discipline."[38]

- **Expressions of joy and sorrow:** Joyous celebration is a valid dimension of worship just as is the cry of emotional pain during a time of grief or despair.[39]

These dimensions of worship are usually applied when discussing worship in the context of religious services at church. To these dimensions we can add a fifth:

- **Temporary withdrawal from and then engagement with day-to-day activities in service to others:** Worship is firmly rooted in the time-place-history of God's redemptive activities of the past. It also is expressed within the context of present life and engagement with the contemporary world as followers of God participate with God in his ongoing activities. This includes activities at the workplace.[40] "There is a deep organic connection between the life of the liturgy and the life of society."[41]

The following section builds on the explanation for this last dimension.

Managerial Work: An Extension of Worship

Most scholarship on the concept of worship among the Christian faith traditions is focused on the religious services and events that occur at church. The activities most often discussed in terms of biblical worship are liturgies, rituals, rites, ceremonies, artistic expression through the arts, reading and preaching of God's word, and prayer. While these are the dominant ideas in worship, nowhere in Scripture is it taught that to worship, a person must be limited to a particular time, place, and form such as in a church building, at a program organized by a religious congregation, or only one day of the week such as a designated day of worship.[42]

Worship "means a stepping aside from normal life in order to perceive it in a deeper and more significant way."[43] From this perspective, worship is a temporary withdrawal from the world of work and leisure time. But it is more. It is a means of "encountering the world on a deeper level than that of our normal consciousness."[44]

With a broader understanding of worship, it is understandable how worship can be seen as imbedded in the concept of work. Indeed, the Christian concept of work is rooted in several worship-related ideas such as fulfilling God's intention for humans, being God's instruments of sustenance, and following Christ's example of service. These ideas are becoming common to many Christians. See Exhibit 15-5.

Temporary withdrawal from the world is not the same as completely escaping from the world.[45] To be authentic, worship must be firmly linked to or rooted in the realities of real time

EXHIBIT 15-5
Christian Views on Work[46]

Since the 19th century, the Protestant and Roman Catholic theological views of work have converged on several key concepts, which follow. The traditional Protestant views have been shaped by Martin Luther, John Calvin, and other Bible students. The modern Roman Catholic views have been shaped by Pope Leo XIII's encyclical *Rerum Novarum*, Pope John Paul II's *Laborum Exercens*, Pope Benedict XVI's *Caritas in Veritate*, and other papal encyclicals (papal letters delivered to bishops).

1. Work is at the center of God's intention for humans since the Creation.
2. Work is an expression of the Image of God in humans.
3. Through the work of human hands, God provides for the sustenance of his creatures.
4. Human social systems are part of a larger economy that encompasses the sphere in which God exists. As such, humans are interdependent with each other; each person contributes to the whole using particular gifts.
5. Work is one way in which the believer follows Christ in his example of redemptive suffering on behalf of others.
6. There is no conflict between loving God and loving one's neighbor. To serve one's neighbor is to serve God.
7. Individuals and society as a whole are corrupted by sin. Believers have an obligation to reform where sin abounds. Among other things, work is one of those settings that have been corrupted by sin. Believers should work to redeem work from sin's destructive influences.

Source: niderlander/Shutterstock.

Source: © Udra11/Dreamstime.com.

Worship involves the whole of one's life—words and actions inside and outside of religious programs. This means that the work of a Christian manager is worship.

and space existence. Because of this, many believe that we do not meet God by attempting to *escape* this present world. Rather we meet God within this world "by coming to a deeper understanding of the nature of the world itself and what God is doing in it."[47]

The Greek word *latreia* used in the Bible is often translated as service or worship. "The concept of service, then, is fundamental in understanding worship."[48] Even the idea of **liturgy** (leitourgia) is that of a work performed by God's people.[49] But liturgy and worship are broader concepts that encompass our whole life of service at work, at home, or wherever we are. Worship may begin in the church building, but it extends out to everywhere the believer goes. Worship involves the whole of one's life—words and actions inside and outside of religious programs.[50]

Applying these ideas to the work of a manager we see that mission is "to do whatever you do in a way that will reflect God's heart to those around you. Your mission is to worship . . . with everything you say and all you do."[51] This doesn't mean that managers should impose religious worship practices on employees. Managers should realize that if their words and actions represent the character of God to others, then they will desire to live a life that is consistent with what they believe God's character to be.

Calling in the Old Testament

Calling is described in the Old Testament in terms of God sending his Spirit upon those who were called for unusual duties relevant to serving the needs of the larger community. When Bezalel was appointed to be in charge of the craftsmen making components for the Tabernacle, he was filled with the Spirit of God in wisdom, understanding, knowledge, and craftsmanship.[52] Bezalel's calling was not just as the most expert craftsman but also as a manager of the craftsmen and women. Bezalel needed the spiritual gifts of wisdom and understanding for working with the other craftsmen and with his boss Moses just as much as the technical craftwork skills.

Moses selected 70 elders to assist him in managing the Children of Israel.[53] The elders' calling is described in terms of taking a portion of the Spirit that had rested on Moses and sharing it with the 70 so that they could share in the leadership burden that Moses was bearing on behalf of the nation. When Joshua was appointed to succeed Moses, when judges were called to lead the people, when Saul was called to become King, and David after him, God sent his Spirit upon them.[54] In the king's coronation, calling was symbolized by the anointing with oil, a ceremony conducted by the prophet signifying that the calling to be a leader originated with God. David was aware that God had filled him with the Spirit. After his sin of adultery with Bathsheba and murder of her husband, David worried that God might remove the Spirit from him (and thereby end his reign as king), just as God did with Saul.[55] The calling of a prophet was usually attended by the falling of the Spirit of God on the person giving them words to utter on behalf of the larger work of the nation. The calling of the Messiah is described in similar terms.[56]

A person's calling can follow from personal experiences they have with someone else who has a particular calling. This seemed to be true for Elisha, who shared the same calling as Elijah.[57]

Calling in the New Testament

In the New Testament *calling* is rooted in God's call to a saving relationship with him through Jesus Christ.[58] Spiritual gifts are closely associated with calling in the New Testament. They are the foundation for how the individual is expected to answer calling in the context of an occupation or other service. These gifts are considered permanent, and a person should not try to change God's gifts.[59] Spiritual giftedness comes with a belief that some social behaviors are expected for specific calling.[60] For example, those who are called to be leaders in the church are expected to behave in certain ways. Church leaders should be above reproach, live a monogamous lifestyle, and be temperate, prudent, respectable, hospitable, and able to teach. They also should not be addicted to wine or be pugnacious, but instead gentle, uncontentious, and free from the love of money.[61] Teachers are expected to live to a higher standard than are their students.[62]

God's calling is noble. And while a person's calling is not based on good works performed, followers of God should work vigorously to demonstrate the validity of their calling.[63]

Calling and the Manager

You have probably heard admonishments that "life is more than what you own."[64] But you may find it difficult to think of your career in any other way than working successfully, earning a good salary, advancing in your career, and eventually having an income that gives you the opportunity to buy whatever you want.

In truth there is more to life than earning enough to have things. That more to life is your *calling*. Calling forms a bridge between religious beliefs and your work as a manager. This bridge is like a daily conversation embracing the current community you serve, yourself, and your sense of God's purpose for your life.[65] It is "the place where your deep gladness and the world's deep hunger meet."[66] Exhibit 15-6 highlights some perspectives on calling shared by the Roman Catholic and Protestant traditions.

EXHIBIT 15-6
Calling in the Roman Catholic and Protestant Traditions[67]

In the Roman Catholic tradition, calling has several similarities to the Protestant view. Calling embraces the following elements and themes:

- Work is at the center of God's original plan for human beings.
- Work is an important way we respond to God and express his image.
- Through work, we participate in God's providence.
- By serving our neighbor (everyone is our neighbor), we are serving God.
- The purpose of calling is to work for the common good of the community. Community includes both the organization for which one is employed and the larger society. Thus, all work involves a calling to be fully a person who works industriously for others. In this way, work is vital to caring for the interdependence between human beings in which we serve each other.
- Work is a way to follow Jesus Christ by engaging in "redemptive suffering" on behalf of others whom we serve.
- Work is accomplished in a social setting and is not merely utilitarian or economically instrumental in nature.
- Calling is both earthly and transcendent, involving a higher purpose.
- Calling involves a commitment to solidarity with the larger community including the global community. As such, workers are intentionally aware of the effect of their participation in the organization as well as on the world around them. In fulfilling their Christian calling, workers will work toward bringing human dignity and freedom.
- Work is the means by which human beings improve the social structures of work including organizations and institutions in which work is performed.

EXHIBIT 15-7
The Relationship Between Job and Calling

Who you are and who you are becoming equals the means to accomplish your calling. Calling equals your higher purpose (the end or the why) in who you are and who you are becoming. From the perspective of employment, this reduces to: Your Job = The Means to accomplish your calling. Your Calling = The higher purpose (the End) of your life and your work.

People often confuse calling with occupation, profession, or a job. But calling does not require paid employment. An unemployed person also has a calling. "Daily work we do is an expression of our calling, but it is not itself that calling."[68] As Exhibit 15-7 shows, a succinct way of thinking about calling is to think of your job as the means to accomplish your calling and your calling as the end or purpose of your job. Calling may be the answer to the question: What is the spiritual opportunity in what I am doing?[69]

To better understand what calling means, let's consider 12 characteristics of a calling:

- **Calling is a call to follow God.**[70] More than being focused on an occupation, calling has meaning in your relationship with God.
- **Calling is a call to a certain identity.** This is a call to who you are[71] and who you are becoming rather than just to what you do. The entire person is called, not just the person's work skills.[72] "The people we become attached to, as well as the roles we choose and commit ourselves to in work, contribute to a coherent sense of self-identity. This firm sense of who we are, which we gain through commitments and emotional self-integration, helps promote our capacity to be faithful."[73]
- **Calling is a call to serve others.**[74] "Organizational leaders must . . . remember that the nature and meaning of that calling materializes only in relationship with the people whom God places on their paths."[75] It is the community through which God's providence works that creates opportunities for you to explore your options in vocation. It is the community that supports you when you need guidance or emotional support. In addition, the community context for the call is broader than the faith community.
- **Calling is a call to the ministry of reconciliation.**[76] God's great work is one of reconciliation. And God gives humans the privilege of participating in this work. Managers have an unbelievable opportunity to work for reconciliation at several levels:
  - Personal reconciliation between people
  - Organizational reconciliation between groups or between individuals and the organization
  - Conceptual reconciliation between the goals springing from religious beliefs and the goals springing from the material, practical demands of organizational goals
  - Ethical reconciliation of finding the moral path between two seemingly opposing but equally justifiable ways of behaving in the marketplace
- **Calling is a call to be a coworker with God.**[77] As a manager, being a coworker with God involves participating in God's work of creating, sustaining, redeeming, and consummating. We will explore this characteristic in more detail later in this chapter.
- **Calling is a call to live with uncertainty.** "When we invest ourselves in work and construe work as vocation, we do so with no firm or concrete evidence that our investment will yield the hoped-for return. We must jump in without certainty of where we will land, or of what shape we'll be in when we do."[78]
- **Calling is unique to the individual.** "Each of us is as unique in our calling as we are in being made in the image of God . . . Each person reflects only a small—but beautiful—part of the whole."[79] Consider your unique cluster of temperaments, personality traits, passions, spiritual experience, and historical experiences. All of these and more contribute to defining your calling.
- **Calling is the call to serve using your current set of talents.** Talents are the necessary preconditions for a calling.[80] For our calling to be right, it must fit our spiritual gifts.

- **Calling is the call to love.** Every calling can come with tasks that most people would rather not do. This is true regarding a managerial calling. But unless these, too, are welcomed, "the claim to be called has a hollow ring."[81]
- **One indicator that calling is expressed in the context of work is the experience of joy or deep satisfaction that comes from the work itself.** Calling is bigger than a person's occupation, yet calling can be expressed through one's work. When calling is expressed through managerial work, the manager will experience joy through the work itself. But this does not mean that every particular task of a manager or every management situation is enjoyable. Sometimes managers must accomplish very difficult work such as helping an organization get through a financial turnaround situation. In such a situation the manager may experience suffering that comes from critical, unhappy people.
- **For some, calling is not easy to discover.** Sometimes people will want to be able to fulfill one purpose in work when they have talents for something entirely different. Some try and fail. They take another job hoping that their original idea for their career will work out in the new situation. They find that they learn something else about themselves. And they may try again.[82]
- **For a manager, calling is a call to live in the midst of complexity.** Some people have technical jobs but they are called to manage. Some managers do the work of a manager but have a calling that pulls them into technical work. Not everyone is cut out to be at the vortex of organizational complexity like a manager. This calling requires an ability to constantly learn about yourself and other people.

In exploring what calling is, it is also helpful to consider what calling is not. Let's look at some of the misunderstandings that people have regarding calling.

Misconceptions of Calling

In her book *Career and Calling*,[83] youth ministry expert Ginny Ward Holderness discusses five common misconceptions of calling:

- **God's call refers only to church professions.** The term *call* is sometimes limited to church-related professions such as pastors, Bible teachers, missionaries, and evangelists. The truth is that "God's call is for everyone, in all walks of life, in all professions, in all circumstances."[84]
- **There is only one call of God for each person.** People who hold this misconception believe that their task is to find that one calling. Regardless of what job you have at any one time, God has a calling for you in that particular job. A calling can be fulfilled by any number of occupations or by nonpaid volunteer work.
- **God calls other people, but not me.** Calling is not just for people who are highly religious. Instead, you might even see that God's call for you is, in part, for the purpose of changing you as much as it is for the purpose of you serving others.
- **Certain vocations are more pleasing to God than others.** This view is based on the assumption that occupation is identical with vocation and calling. Some people have a hierarchical view of occupations, namely that some occupations are inherently more valuable to God than others.
- **One's relationship with God is a private matter, to be lived out at church and at home but rarely at work.** Many people now question this traditional view. Faith is personal, but it is not private. Faith requires not only the community of faith but also the larger culture for its full expression. As Holderness says: "To compartmentalize life and live for God only on Sundays or only in private lives at home is to miss out on the wonderful way God intended it to be."[85]

The biblical understanding of calling for the manager is inseparable from the belief that God is a Being who works. This we explore next.

Management and the Ongoing Work of God

The Bible teaches that human beings are made in God's image.[86] According to theologian R. Paul Stevens, one of the implications of this is that humans have the privilege of participating in the four major types of ongoing work that God does: creating, sustaining, redeeming, and consummating.[87] In this view managers are needed in a variety of organizations that serve God

	Creating	Sustaining	Redeeming	Consummating
The manager has a purpose related to God's ongoing work through the organization	Creating new products, services, and experiences for others: for example, information technology, financial services, arts, politics, engineering, science, architecture, construction, design, and marketing	Service organizations that keep the infrastructure of communities functioning: for example, transportation, distribution, logistics, healthcare, accounting, maintenance, consulting, and cleaning	Service organizations that repair, mend, and transform: for example, auto and truck repair, appliance repair, counseling, healthcare, social services, accounting, environmental protection, law, religious organizations, and consulting	Work that points to the meaning of life; work that helps bring people to new levels of maturing: for example, writing, publishing, education, politics, pastoral work, healthcare, counseling, consulting, parenting, public relations, marketing, and media
The manager has a purpose related to God's ongoing work with persons inside the organization	Creating new policies, procedures, processes and systems to get work done; testing new ideas; hiring new workers; negotiating; planning; strategic thinking; creating new relationships with workers, suppliers, and customers	Monitoring and maintaining the systems and processes on which workers, customers, and suppliers depend in any organization; organizing and coordinating; preserving organizational culture; maintaining equipment and relationships	Leading in quality improvement efforts, reorganizing work during transitions, employee discipline, improving policies and procedures, controlling, resolving conflict, challenging assumptions, encouraging and supporting relationships	Communicating the vision of the organization; helping workers see the connection between their work, the mission of the organization, and God's work; leading; changing organizational culture; helping others see the value of the relationships

EXHIBIT 15-8
Management and the Ongoing Work of God

by co-working with him in his ongoing work through and with the organization as it serves society. But managers are also needed because God has ongoing work with persons inside the organization. Exhibit 15-8 outlines the role of managers in the ongoing work of God.

CREATING. The **creating** role of a manager involves working in an organization that creates new products, services, and experiences for others is a way of participating in creation. Creative work can occur in any type of organization. Anytime managers are asked to begin something new for the benefit of workers, customers, or suppliers, their work participates in the ongoing creative work of God. This may require openness and flexibility to experience new ways of getting the work done.

SUSTAINING. Some organizations have as their primary purpose helping to sustain the life of humans, communities, and all living things. The manager's **sustaining** role is crucial to pursuing the mission of sustaining life, such as through making decisions and following policies and procedures that run the business efficiently. To be successful in the sustaining work of a manager, a person needs to be dependable, honest, trustworthy, fair, and respectful.

REDEEMING. The **redeeming** work of a manager includes but goes beyond spiritual redemption. Redemption is an ongoing activity that encompasses all relationships including humans' relationship with the earth, with ourselves, with each other, and with God. The Bible teaches that work is one of the things most affected by sin. It should be no surprise then that work itself is in need of redemption.[88] While all workers can participate in the redemption of work, managers have a special role in helping workers move past working purely for self-interest to working for the common good. Working together, managers and workers can restore work by helping workers find meaning in work, minimize the sorrow of work, eliminate discrimination, and where possible heal the drudgery of work. Organizations that work for peace; provide spiritual guidance; communicate the gospel; provide healthcare and social services; and repair broken equipment, systems, and relationships all are examples of what it means to be coworkers with God. Managers who are successful in redemptive work will approach others with understanding, care, faithfulness to covenants, unselfishness, and honesty.

CONSUMMATING. Other organizations participate in God's work of consummation when they bring people and relationships to new levels of maturity. The idea of **consummating** comes out of the larger story of the Bible which portrays God as bringing his solution to the sin problem to a final and complete conclusion where sin will be no more.[89] Some of these organizations help customers and suppliers to better understand the meaning of life. Managers who lead by communicating the vision of the organization and the work group help others mature. The type of person the manager is (for example, reflective, perceptive, self-aware, objective, willing to change self) will have an influence on how well the work of consummation is fulfilled.

Finding Your Calling

Every person engaged in the marketplace has the opportunity to identify his or her calling. This applies to individuals who hold paid positions as well as to those who volunteer. This is no different for managers. Theologian R. Paul Stevens[90] suggests four factors that contribute to finding your calling. First, coming to know what motivates you and what you feel passionate about is foundational. A second factor is your particular cluster of talents, gifts, and personality traits. Third, providential circumstances provide (or block) opportunities for you to learn from managerial and leadership experiences. When others see managerial potential in you, they give you an opportunity to try. Last, some individuals have an intense religious experience with God that includes receiving what they believe to be direct instruction from God to engage in managerial work.

The Biblical Story of Gideon

Read the story of Gideon recorded in Judges 6–8 in the Bible. Grasp the significance of the accomplishments that occurred under the leadership of Gideon. What strengths and weaknesses did Gideon exhibit in his leadership? What leadership principles can we gain from the experience of Gideon that are applicable today?

Expressing Faith at Work

Expressing personal faith occurs at various levels including the individual, organizational, industry and professional association, and economic system. What is appropriate at each level may vary according to the context. We will briefly introduce each level.

Four Levels of Expression

INDIVIDUAL. At the individual level, who you are may be one of the most attractive features of your Christian witness. It may also be the most powerful. A work life consistent with what you believe to be right can counteract the suspicions of many that Christians talk a good game but don't walk the walk.

Organizations expect managers to act in moral ways through honesty, integrity, justice, and honoring commitments. But some Christians desire to express their faith beyond these minimum expectations. Keeping aware of the legal and cultural expectations regarding talking about religion at work, they wonder how they should share their faith through actions and words. They wonder what priority they should place on the economic dimension of life when their religious faith encourages them to promote the Gospel. See Exhibit 15-9 for examples of the four levels of expression.

Individual	• Including a Bible text in the automatic signature line in email messages that you send out • Asking someone (coworker, client, or supplier) if you can pray with them when they are in your office • Sending a text message to someone sharing a Bible verse, a meditation thought, or a prayer • Engaging in small acts of humility on behalf of another without an expectation for a returned favor • Wearing a crucifix or other religious symbol as a clothing accessory • Playing religious music at your workstation • Saying phrases such as "Praise the Lord" when you hear someone share good news • Asking someone if they are interested in studying the Bible outside of work time
Organization	• Allocate space for an informal employee group to engage in religious practices at break time or lunchtime • Retain employees on the payroll during a transition period such as temporary work stoppage, loss of a key customer, or shortages of materials and supplies • Sponsor employees to attend a 2-day conference on the topic of workplace spirituality • Refuse to sign a contract with a supplier or a customer if the contract provisions will increase the risk that religious values will need to be compromised • Allow workers of all faith traditions to adjust their work schedules for the purpose of participating in religious practices
Industry/Profession	• Working on an industry ethics committee through a national professional association • Presenting papers and participating in formal panel discussions at the regional or national level and, through these venues, representing fundamental biblical principles • Writing letters to the editor or articles for trade publications advocating for industry-wide actions • Speaking to others regarding the fairness of existing or proposed relationships with other industries or professions
Economic System	• Participating in political party meetings when party platforms are discussed • Lobbying lawmakers to improve laws or regulations that encourage injustice • Writing letters to state or federal lawmakers encouraging a particular policy point of view consistent with religious beliefs

EXHIBIT 15-9
Four Levels of Expression

ORGANIZATIONAL. As a manager, most of your actions will affect the organization for which you work, for example by influencing policies, procedures, and organizational structure. At the organizational level, the Christian manager works hard to achieve the organization's mission while constantly watching out for the interests of employees, suppliers, and customers. It is at this level that the question becomes how should the Christian manager show and tell religious faith through actions that affect the organization as a whole? Perhaps more important, you play a major role in shaping the collective sense of identity and shared purpose in the organization which, in turn, shapes the actions of employees. The principles you stand for will speak loudly of your faith.

INDUSTRY/PROFESSION. At the industry and professional association level, a Christian manager's actions may have a broader influence than the organization. Here we are concerned with the beliefs and values that may influence the actions of regional or national organizations. It is at this level that the Christian enters public or civic debates about the morality of actions of an entire industry or professional association.[91]

ECONOMIC SYSTEM. It is at the economic system level that the manager can influence the larger society, for example in decisions that affect the structure of government. Shaping public policies will affect how scarce resources are distributed in society and in what ways regulations will limit the activities of commercial and nonprofit organizations.

Influencing Factors

Thinking about one's faith provides important ground rules for participating in public life.[92] Belief is never separated from actions.[93] In particular, how Christians think about the purpose of the faith community influences what they do in the marketplace. For example, if you believe that the purpose of the church is to heal social injustice, then this will guide your decisions regarding how you should live out your faith at the workplace. Under this concept you might work to ensure fairness among workers, using company resources to help individuals who are discriminated against and providing employment to the marginal members of the community. But if you see the purpose of church as being primarily proclamation, then your expression of faith at work might be characterized more by talking about your relationship with God or encouraging others to consider the claims of your faith tradition.

Another assumption is that participating in church means a 7-days-per-week practice of faith. It is easy to think of "going to church" as merely meaning attending the weekly worship service. However, nowhere in Scripture is the concept of church limited in this way.[94]

A third assumption is that a person's inclination toward a particular style of integrating faith at work may be a result of many factors,[95] grouped as religious belief factors and contextual factors. We will briefly explore each.

RELIGIOUS BELIEF FACTORS. **Religious belief factors** are the elements of Bible doctrine that shape Christians' shared understandings regarding the believer's role in society. These elements include beliefs regarding the purpose of the church, the biblical definition of outreach, and beliefs regarding the relationship between the faith community and the larger culture.

One way to think about the purpose of a business is to ask, "Why does this organization exist?" Similar questions can be asked of the Church: "Why does the Church exist?" "What do you hope the Church will accomplish?" The Scriptures portray two broad task-oriented dimensions of what it means to be a part of the faith community.[96] One dimension is more internally focused on serving the needs of church members while the other dimension is externally focused on serving the needs of persons who are not members. See Exhibit 15-10.

Internally focused faith integration may involve awareness that to be effective in your role in the faith community you must invite others to come into the church and its settings. This might take the form of inviting others to attend worship services and special programs hosted by your congregation. Externally focused faith integration at work may be a keen awareness that outreach is more than just inviting people to come to church. The circumstances you deal with during the workweek are valid settings for expressing faith in appropriate ways in the moment. These two dimensions of purpose in the faith community are not mutually exclusive. In practice, there is no perfect way to distinguish between what is only internal work for members and what is only external work for others. Some of the activities in the faith community can be both simultaneously. The discussions among leaders of a church can sometimes get hung up on the debate over which purpose leaders should emphasize. Both dimensions are legitimate. Neither should take the place of the other.[97]

A person's religious beliefs regarding the proper definition of outreach also has an influence on faith integration at work. Two views of what **outreach** is exist. With one view, the task of verbal proclamation dominates outreach activities. Such mission activities are characterized by talking to others about God, sin, and salvation. One justification for this is the belief in the need for reconciliation with God as the ultimate concern in life. In this view, works of service are helpful but only as they lead to opportunities for telling the Gospel message. With this perspective, the faith community sees itself as the bearer of a message of salvation to a lost and dying world.[98]

EXHIBIT 15-10
Two Broad Dimensions of Purpose for the Church

The other view considers outreach to the world primarily as God's mechanism for social service and social change.[99] Here the goals of mission are humanization, reconciliation, and peace. Four justifications can be offered for this perspective. First, individuals who suffer under oppression, inhumanity, and injustice need temporal, or material, needs met before they are ready to hear proclamation of the Gospel. Second, a life of unselfish service is necessary for spiritual development on the part of the one serving and the one being served. Another justification is that social action that reconciles the oppressed is not only a means to prepare for evangelism but is in itself a true manifestation of evangelism. Fourth, given the skepticism of some people toward things religious, a life of service may be the most effective way to witness in a secular society.[100]

In terms of integrating faith at work, there are situations in which it will be more appropriate to engage in outreach simply through actions without proclamation, just as there may be an appropriate time and place for proclamation.

Another influence on faith integration is the set of religious beliefs regarding the relationship of the faith community with the larger culture.[101] Some Christians view the surrounding culture as something so entirely evil that it must be avoided. Because worldly culture is completely opposite religious values, these members withdraw into their religious subculture and talk about the evil of the surrounding culture. Others see no essential difference between the demands of culture and the demands of being a Christian. They have harmonized life in the world with life in the faith community. Still others believe that the larger culture has some authority, but the authority of Christian teaching supersedes cultural authority. Whenever the larger culture is not in conflict with Christian values, it is embraced and integrated into life. Whenever the demands of culture are in conflict with Christian teaching, Christian values have more authority, and the cultural expectations are to be avoided. Some see the evil side of culture at the same time as seeing its value. They attempt to resolve the tension by honoring each. Other members of the faith community seek to change the larger culture so that it represents or is in closer alignment with their understanding of Christian values.

Another way of looking at the relationship between the church and the larger culture is in terms of a Christian identity.[102] Christians who hold to an **exclusive identity** attempt to live a distinctive life defined in the faith community. Those who hold to an **inclusive identity** desire to live a life that is relevant to those in the larger culture. Inherent in this discussion is a central, never-ending point of tension: "The gospel must be neither captive to the local culture nor alienated from it."[103]

CONTEXTUAL FACTORS. **Contextual factors** include organizational culture, personality and temperament, spiritual gifts, legal constraints, and current issues in society. A person's approach to expressing faith at work may be heavily influenced by the work context in which the person chooses to be in.[104] Like the various religious belief factors, the connection between contextual factors and faith expressions at work needs more research. National culture, organizational culture, personality and temperament, spiritual gifts, competency, organizational level, legal constraints, and current issues faced by customers and suppliers all may affect an individual's choice of faith expression.

ORGANIZATIONAL CULTURE. As we explored in Chapter 3, organizational culture is the collection of shared values and beliefs that the company learned as together the employees solved company problems. If the company you work for prizes openly discussing spiritual values, then its environment may be more conducive to verbal expressions of religious faith. In a different company, the expectation may be that spiritual values are not expressed openly. The company that is more closed to verbal expressions of spiritual issues may exert social pressure on individuals who desire to openly express religious faith.

PERSONALITY AND TEMPERAMENT. Personality is comprised of many facets, some of which may influence an individual's approach to expressing faith at work. Take, for example, the dynamic of introversion and extroversion. Extroverts gain energy and stimulus from interacting with others while introverts gain energy and stimulus from reflection. Religious experience for extroverts may be more social than the experience of introverts who prefer solitary times of meditation. When we view the narrative of the New Testament, we can see the variety of personalities. Peter is impetuous, assertive, and confrontational. Andrew prefers to refer people to others. Paul, the tent maker and intellectual debater-evangelist, raises and answers objections he finds in the culture. The blind man healed by Jesus is nonconfrontational even if he is focused on his experience. Dorcas is content to serve the physical needs of others. Yet Scripture does not attempt to explain all the reasons for these differences. Persons strong in dominance[105] or social boldness may be more forceful or aggressive in expressing religious beliefs than those who are not. Likewise, they may be less sensitive to the possibility that others are offended when they share their faith.

SPIRITUAL GIFTS. One person is gifted with the ability to persuade. Another is gifted to analyze. A person's giftedness is another potential influence on faith expression.[106] A person gifted with the courage to speak out prophetically will more likely confront the culture of business that is not in alignment with religious values. Such a person may find support or criticism of the prophetic nature of her talk. A person gifted in evangelism may be more likely to witness directly regarding faith in God, sin, and salvation.

LEGAL CONSTRAINTS. In Chapter 9 we considered some of the legal issues related to sharing one's faith at work. Legal constraints attempt to provide for a fair management of freedoms while preventing one person's free expression from becoming a hostile working environment. The opportunities for abuse of power in this area exist, even if used for laudable religious goals. For this reason, legal constraints are one of the strongest influencing contextual factors.

CURRENT ISSUES IN SOCIETY. The current issues present in society or in the industry represent opportunities to discuss religious values. Just listen to the talk the next time a business magazine or newspaper reports alleged white-collar crime or breaches of moral trust in a boardroom. Morality, ethics, values, and other spiritual issues will surface in discussions, creating opportunity to share personal beliefs.

Models of Faith Integration

So what are the patterns of behavior among Christians who wish to integrate their faith with their work? The models of faith integration range from simple to complex depending on your perspective.

SIMPLE MODEL. Perhaps the simplest way to understand the different approaches in practice is by thinking of sharing one's faith in terms of the following formula:[107]

What we do[108]
+ What we say[109]
+ What others say about us[110]
= Sharing faith (witnessing)

Direct witnessing (what we say) is the attempt to represent one's religious faith to others in various ways. This may be the most controversial approach because it has the most potential for offending people. A major concern about overt witnessing is the potential for a manager to unfairly use managerial power to coerce or influence employees' religious choices.[111] **Indirect witnessing** (what we do) is living a moral life rather than talking about faith and God. It emphasizes the lifestyle choices of the manager, which set up opportunities to talk with others about personal faith. An example of indirect witnessing is disguising faith "in the rational language of business problem solving."[112] For instance, instead of a manager saying to subordinates, "God wants us to be as responsive as possible to employees and their needs," the manager would use the language of business that explains the rationale for being responsive to employees. The concern about disguising faith in rational language is that the distinctive feature of religious faith might lose its effect.

Theologian R. Paul Stevens sees witness as being comprised of four dimensions.[113] First is the ministry of responsible service by meeting legitimate needs and wants. Second is the ministry of competent service. Third is the ministry of working with Christian love, honesty, and justice. Last is the ministry of words.

MILLER'S FIVE-PART MODEL. After his survey of the history of the faith at work movement in the United States, theologian David Miller developed a five-part model to represent the variety of experiences in how various Christians approach integrating their faith at work. The five dimensions are as follows:[114]

- **Ethics Type** people and groups integrate their faith through personal virtues, business ethics, and devoting their energies toward addressing social and economic justice. They emphasize discerning right actions and following biblical instructions. Making the ethical decision can at times require a trade-off of short-term corporate profits and one's personal career. The challenge that the Ethics Type people face is that many of the dilemmas in business are gray areas where there are no clear biblical teachings that provide an immediate, simple solution.

- **Evangelism Type** people express personal faith primarily through evangelization. They focus on introducing others to Jesus Christ as Lord and Savior. Evangelization activity can range from the gentle to the aggressive. Individuals who emphasize evangelism at work may find that it impedes them from doing their jobs well or that it disrupts the basic functions and responsibilities of their job. The risk for Evangelism Type people is that they may neglect the ethical and social justice issues, which also are important to being a Christian.
- **Experience Type** people focus on their vocation or calling. Their faith integration is in terms of the central meaning or purpose of their work. The work itself can be of central theological value. But it also can be instrumental in bringing value to others. Regardless, it always has a greater purpose than what appears on the surface of the job tasks. One risk for Experience Types is that overemphasis on calling and purpose can result in a form of elitism in which only the most stimulating work is considered a calling.
- **Enrichment Type** people focus primarily on the inner religious experiences that occur during spiritual disciplines such as prayer and meditation. Personal transformation or healing through more generic, nonreligious spirituality can become the focus for Enrichment Types. But when this becomes the exclusive focus, it can lead to narcissism, stressing self-improvement over the needs of others.
- **Everywhere Type** people desire to exhibit behaviors characteristic of more than one of the four types.

COPING STRATEGIES MODEL. The coping strategies model was developed by Laura Nash and Scotty McLennan, researchers who interviewed business executives, as well as clergy, regarding their Christian faith integration behaviors.[115] Their belief is that Christians face several tensions when desiring to integrate their faith in the marketplace. For example, the Christian is faced with the responsibility to one's faith at the same time as making a profit. At times, these dual responsibilities can come into conflict with each other. To cope with these tensions Christians choose different coping strategies. Nash and McLennan grouped their findings into seven profiles of coping strategies, which they then organized along a continuum representing the degree to which faith is integrated at work.

- **Secularists** are individuals who may not profess a religious faith and have no reason to attempt to integrate their faith in their work. Secularists may prize spiritual values such as human dignity and social responsibility to society. Secularists who are Christians believe in radical separation of business from their faith.
- **Cynics** are resigned in their belief that no integration of their religious faith in the world of business is possible. They believe that the influences of the market are just too strong. Their coping strategy separates their business expectations from their religious values.
- **Atomists**, like other Christians, have strong religious faith but attempt to cope with the tensions of integrating faith at work by keeping business separate from religion. They try to preserve their faith and fit it into business culture by compartmentalization.
- **Percolators** believe that their faith influences their work in the business world. For them, faith "percolates up," unconsciously guiding them. They are sensitive to the fact that those around them may be offended at open expressions of religious faith. Because they value tolerance and freedom from discrimination, they choose not to push their religious beliefs. In short, they attempt to remain relevant but disguised.
- **Generalists** believe that their personal religious faith must operate all the time throughout all of their life. They are optimistic about their religious faith and about capitalism, and they believe strongly in both. But they sidestep the difficult questions that come up when these two are in potential conflict with each other.
- **Justifiers** believe that total integration of faith and work is possible. They see no distinction between sacred and secular. Their key question when faced with a dilemma in the market is, "What would Jesus do?" Justifiers view the positive elements of their work as evidence that being faithful to God is the key to business success.
- **Resacralizers** have an expectation that there is no distinction between sacred and secular, that everything a believer does in the market is guided by God. They work toward the day when economic life is governed by religious beliefs. Resacralizers cope with the tension by attempting to reform the economic system.

Spirituality in the Workplace

Since the 1990s, a growing interest in spirituality at work has emerged and can be understood in relation to the larger societal trends taking place. Layoffs and downsizing have had a demoralizing effect on workers.[116] The disparity in wages between top executives and frontline workers has added to this low morale. For some workers, their place of employment is their primary community, the place where they feel the most connected. Others, dissatisfied with the spirituality offered by churches, have turned to eastern religions, some of which encourage meditation and emphasize highly desired values and virtues.

One result of these and other factors is that people are "less willing [than in the past] to put their spiritual strivings on hold while at work"[117] But they do not always know *how* to include their spiritual desires in their work without offending others. Also, there seems to be a fundamental dilemma regarding spirituality at work, as described in Exhibit 15-11.

Spirituality at work is about expressing yourself, to discover who you really are as a person in the middle of a big universe, to transcend the difficulties of life, and to find the essential purpose for your life. We look for meaning in all of life including our life at work. Often it is a crisis that precipitates people to embark on a focused spiritual journey in which they attempt to live their values more fully.[118]

To see an example of spirituality at work in practice, let's consider Jensen DJ Construction, owned and operated by Don Jensen. When you walk into the company's offices, you are met by an octagonal feng shui mirror hanging by the door. Inside, the walls are decorated with multiple colors and traditional images related to spirituality. Butterfly kites are on the ceiling. Lush green plants add to the atmosphere. Spiritual-themed posters, religious icons, and a religious altar also contribute to the ambience.

But for Don Jensen spirituality in business goes deeper than decorating. Jensen established company policies that support spirituality. While state law requires that employees receive a few minutes paid break from work every few hours, Jensen takes this further and offers employees the option of using a 20- to 30-minute paid meditation break each day over and above the state-mandated work breaks. Employees are not required to participate.

Given the added expense of meditation breaks, why would a business owner do this? Jensen wanted to have his work environment aligned with his personal life. He wanted to have an effect on other people's lives. Has it worked? While he can't show a direct connection with company profits, Jensen believes that he has happier, more productive workers. In his mind, his company has matured as a result.[119]

Not all Christians will consider feng shui to be as valid as other ways of expressing spirituality such as talking about religious subjects, praying, or placing religious symbols at work. Exhibit 15-12 presents five models of spiritual development in the workplace.

Regardless of how you define proper expressions of spirituality, there are companies whose leaders promote spirituality but whose workers still run afoul of commonly accepted values. For example, ServiceMaster has a reputation for its emphasis on Christian spirituality rooted in the Bible. Its founder and its leaders are known for talking openly about God. But not all of the 75,000 employees in ServiceMaster share these values. ServiceMaster's

EXHIBIT 15-11
A Spiritual Dilemma

Researchers Mitroff and Denton[120] believe that a deep ambivalence exists within corporate America. Employees, managers, and executives feel they are caught in a dilemma:

- On the one hand, they wish they could express themselves more fully in the workplace.
- On the other hand, they fear that expressing their own spirituality could result in criticism.
- But if they don't express more of their whole selves, then the development of their spirituality will be seriously stifled, "possibly even halted."

Many people experience a similar dilemma when they desire to express their spirituality more fully at work but fear that doing so will offend coworkers.[121]

Researchers Mitroff and Denton conducted in-depth interviews with over 90 high-level managers and executives in American companies. As a result of their research, they describe five models of how organizations have attempted to develop spirituality in the workplace:

1. The *religion-based* organization intends to actively bring religion into the workplace. These managers attempt to place all decisions under the authority of Scripture. God is the key stakeholder who makes everything possible in business. These managers make a conscious choice to limit economic growth and manage greed. This is the most controversial of the five models.
2. The *evolutionary* organization starts out from one spiritual perspective and evolves over time. A crisis might spur the organization to change. Managers in this type of organization maintain a deep spiritual openness to change. They tolerate deeply felt emotions. The key stakeholder is the next generation of workers and their families.
3. The *recovering* organization behaves somewhat like Alcoholics Anonymous, a program based on the foundational principles of clear constraints that help manage addiction, which in this case means addiction to greed and power. Managers must give over their entire being and the organization to a higher power. Managers will intentionally limit the size of organizational units to prevent the development of excessive power. The organization emphasizes results that indicate improvements are being made toward moving the organization completely away from greedy behavior.
4. The *socially responsible* organization works on the basis of the social contract. Business is necessary to solve social problems, but the organization must constrain its own behaviors so that the greater good of society can be promoted. Good consequences result from the practice of good values. Power comes from day-to-day living of socially responsible values. Managers focus on living publicly espoused values to create a spiritually uplifting work environment.
5. In the *values-based* organization managers believe that personal spiritual values produce an ethical organization. Trust is the cornerstone of all values. The Golden Rule is universal. Managers focus on treating people as whole persons. Achieving profit is important, but other values are more important. In this type of organization spirituality is meaningless unless it is described in terms of values.

EXHIBIT 15-12
Models for Spiritual Development in the Workplace[122]

Terminix pest-control business unit admitted taking advantage of customers and polluting groundwater.[123]

It is clear from the experience of large and small companies, some of which have stellar reputations for integrating their religious faith-based spirituality in their work, that spirituality does not prevent all moral and legal lapses. But in spite of the examples of moral problems that surface, company leaders and managers in many industries are promoting spirituality.[124]

The Linkage Between Management and Spirituality

How are management and spirituality connected? We will explore six aspects of the connection between management and spirituality, as outlined in Exhibit 15-13. First, just as spirituality is part of humans being connected with a community, so management exists for the purpose of serving a community (an organizational community and the good of the broader societal community). It is performed in the context of fostering trust and responsibility for self and for helping others achieve their goals.

Second, spirituality cannot be separated from physical, social, material, psychological, and historical dimensions of life.[125] But, like management, spirituality also is inseparable from the contradictions, the "uncomfortable commitments and murky trade-offs" inherent in working in the business world.[126]

Third, spirituality and management are both an inner experience of the mind and an outer expression through action. Fourth, a common element in spirituality and management is the

Spirituality	Management
Spirituality is an individual and community experience of trust, responsibility, and service.	Management exists to build trust, encourage responsibility, and to serve a community.
Spirituality is inseparable from the inherent tensions of life.	Management is provided in the midst of tensions.
Spirituality is both an *inner* experience and an *outer* expression through action.	Management is about *who you are*, how you *think and feel*, and *action*.
Spirituality is the striving for a sense of purpose, identity, transcendence, and meaning in life.	Clarity of purpose and self-identity strengthen management effectiveness.
Spirituality is dynamic. Spiritual growth occurs when we are willing to be transformed from the inside out.	Management is dynamic.
Spirituality provides a focus of awareness to all of life.	Management focuses on creating value and meaning in the products and services for the broader societal community.

EXHIBIT 15-13

The Linkages Between Spirituality and Management

striving for a sense of purpose and meaning in life.[127] Researchers have found that the more congruent an employee's values and spiritual aspirations are with the organization, the more likely that employee is to find meaning at work.[128] Similarly, self-awareness is another fundamental dimension of both spirituality and successful management.

Fifth, spirituality is dynamic. Spiritual experience changes throughout life and from one situation to another and from one level of maturity to another. Individuals will experience spirituality differently from others. Spiritual maturity means being open to change. Spirituality involves the common goal of being transformed from the inside out at three levels: individual, organizational, and societal.[129] Management also is dynamic. Managerial effectiveness is rooted in the willingness of the manager to change while serving a community that is changing.

Sixth, spirituality provides a particular focus of awareness to managerial work,[130] creating value from hopes and fears, joys and sorrows, and successes and failures. Another way of understanding this is to think of spirituality as a grid that is used to filter managerial experiences in a way that is consistent with your worldview. As such, spirituality is an essential part of who you are.

Supported by these connections, we argue that spirituality is inseparable from the work of management. Some even believe that "spirituality is an integral part, if not the very essence, of management."[131] Striving to be an effective manager runs parallel with seeking to mature spiritually. Thus, management is more than a job. It is an opportunity for spiritual growth.

Organizational Spirituality

Some scholars suggest that spirituality operates at both the individual level and the organizational level.[132] Describing individual behaviors that promote spirituality is one thing. Describing spirituality in terms of organizational actions is more difficult.[133]

One example of many organizations whose leaders want spirituality to pervade organizational activities is WAI Wetherill Associates, Inc., a privately owned worldwide distributor of starters, alternators, and other auto parts. One policy of the firm is that field representatives give and discuss with customers a document titled *Quality Assurance Manual*, which outlines the products the firm offers as well as the spiritual and ethical basis for the firm's existence.[134] After spending years teaching others about spirituality-based management principles through speeches and publications, Richard W. Wetherill founded WAI in 1978. One of his central beliefs was that work should be a place where people can be happy. To this end, Wetherill established a basic operating philosophy of the "principle of right action." The corporate policy of Wetherill Associates, Inc. states:[135]

> "It is a company policy to avoid all the nasty personality situations which tend to make people's working lives miserable. We find that it really can be done. We want everybody's cooperation in that effort. We trust that each and every person will do everything

EXHIBIT 15-14
Indicators of Organizational Spirituality

Atmosphere in which employees feel comfortable to share their ideas
Openness to discuss personal and organizational values
Encouragement of balance between work and family
Dedicated space for use in contemplation
Encouragement of employees to volunteer and even payment for some hours of volunteer service
Company leaders who openly reflect on the meaning of the contributions of specific employees
A corporate culture that rewards honesty with self
Open acknowledgement of commitments to stakeholders
Selection of employees who are a good match with corporate spiritual values
Open, transparent communication with all stakeholders both inside and outside the organization
Encouragement of individual employees to find their match with the best job for them
Socialization of new employees who share the espoused spiritual values widely shared
Organizational climate that emphasizes integrity and customer value rather than simply building shareholder wealth

possible to make this policy keep on succeeding. Let this be a really happy place to work."

Richard W. Wetherill
Chairman

Organizations by their very nature tend to produce a set of values focused on the legal, impersonal, impartial, and disinterested. The reason for this is the relentless drive to achieve the organization's goals and the impersonal nature of most markets. The organization is bigger than any one individual who performs tasks for the company. While the impersonal nature of organizations may be important for achieving organizational goals, it also is one of the factors that can create spiritual crisis at work. Employees are not just agents fulfilling an impersonal role. They are living, breathing, thinking, and feeling persons who interact in a community collectively to create meaningful contributions of value to society by serving higher spiritual goals.

If you were thinking of applying for a job at an organization, how would you know whether the organization is spiritual? Exhibit 15-14 provides some of the characteristics that scholars have identified as indicators of spirituality at an organizational level.[136]

One element of spirituality in the context of organizational life is the task of balancing legitimate self-interests while looking out for the interests of others (altruism) and the organization as a whole. This is fundamental to being an effective leader but not always easy to live consistently. It is also an illustration of how spirituality is expressed at the level of the individual person and the level of the organization.

The Christian Mind on Altruism vs. Self-Interest

The Bible encourages altruism: acting out of concern for the welfare of other persons even if it means giving up something for yourself. The Bible also supports fulfillment of legitimate self-interests (physical, social, spiritual, economic).[137] The tension between altruism and self-interest is not always easy to manage. The following table illustrates how both altruism and self-interest is shown at the individual and organizational level.

		Spiritual Values	
		Altruism	**Self-Interest**
Level	Individual	Acting out of concern for the welfare of other individuals	Seeking fulfillment of legitimate personal needs (physical, social, spiritual, economic)
	Organizational	Pursuing actions in the market that promote the good of the community outside the firm	Seeking fulfillment of legitimate organizational goals (physical, social, spiritual, economic)

Spirituality vs. Religion

Spirituality and its historical root religion are closely related and compatible but not necessarily identical.[138] One might think of religion as organized, formal, and communal[139] spirituality, meaning a group of people in a community who agree around a particular common set of beliefs. The group shares common symbols, practices, ceremonies, and rites as they practice their religion. Christianity requires commitment of behavior patterns valued by the group.[140] Also, religion has as its primary focus salvation. Religion tends to be defined by boundaries of things like, "we believe this (and we are correct) and you believe that (and you are wrong)."

One problem that can be experienced is when institutional religion is used in place of spiritual experience rather than being used to enhance spiritual development.[141] When this occurs, religion becomes coercive, attempting to prevent individual members of the faith community from thinking outside the confines of the boundaries of the religious system.

An opposite problem is when people attempt to separate spirituality from religion, something that "deprives the soul of valuable symbolic and reflective experience."[142] Without incorporating the sacred into all of life, "religion can become so far removed from the human situation as to be irrelevant. People can be extremely religious in a formal way and yet profess values in everyday life that are thoroughly secular."[143]

Both religion and spirituality can be found in the workplace but both are not equally embraced at work. In a survey of executives regarding religion and spirituality at the workplace researchers Mitroff and Denton found that 60 percent of respondents had positive views of spirituality and negative views of religion.[144] Only 30 percent viewed spirituality and religion positively. For this group spirituality and religion are synonymous and inseparable. Executives see both as sources of basic beliefs and universal values. In their view spirituality is developed only through religion. A small number (8 percent) of those surveyed reported a negative orientation toward both spirituality and religion. For these executives universal values can be defined and attained independently of religion and spirituality.[145] Researchers have identified the same negative attitudes.

Religion gives depth to spirituality but, in part because of this, it can be divisive. For this reason some business leaders emphasize the generic expression of fundamental values, virtues, and character traits that all religions support.[146] Fundamental virtues offer the benefit of being a test for the appropriateness or inappropriateness of spirituality for the workplace.[147]

In spite of the differences people have regarding expressing religious values at work, religion plays a key role in guiding moral behavior. Religion holds before the adherent's eyes an ideal of universal principles in which the needs of the individual and the needs of the community are harmonized. Because religion occurs in the context of a community, it acts as a force for binding together the individuals.[148] Many believe that without religion, it is more difficult to develop spirituality to a satisfying depth.[149]

Sacred-Secular: An Outdated Distinction?

Since the Renaissance and perfected in modern times, people in western European cultures came to believe that spiritual is something you do in church and secular is something you do elsewhere. Such an understanding artificially splits reality into two fundamentally distinct categories: holy and profane, and sacred and secular.[150] This distinction when applied broadly to life in general, many now believe, violates reality, which is an integrated whole.

These distinctions are giving way for a renewed understanding that all of life is integrated; all of life is sacred. Yes, we have special religious places that we treat with reverence and awe such as a church sanctuary or cathedral and other religious objects. But sacred and secular of life as a whole should be viewed not as independent and mutually exclusive but rather as similar and interpenetrated in a fundamental way. God is the God of all of life, not just religious things. Writers who have been seeking to understand management in terms of spirituality are coming to believe that the hours that precede and follow the workday are not disconnected from work.[151] Likewise, the hours that precede and follow a day of worship are not disconnected from worship. People live a whole life.

Paradoxes of Spirituality

Like the rest of life as a manager, spirituality itself is filled with paradoxes that over time we learn to hold in dynamic tension. Let's consider a few of them.

INWARD FOCUS THAT IS OUTWARD DIRECTED.[152] This is the first of two fundamental spiritual paradoxes. Spirituality is intensely internal, sometimes overwhelming our thoughts and feelings. But if it is not also outward directed, then spirituality becomes no more than being self-absorbed which, paradoxically, can be destructive to spirituality. On the positive side, spiritual fulfillment increases when we give to others, being willing to step away from our own selfish interests and get genuinely involved with the interests of someone else. It is making a difference in another's life that brings meaning to our own life.

THE ETERNAL AND THE HERE-AND-NOW.[153] This is the second fundamental spiritual paradox. The former monk and author Thomas Moore observed that a person is interested in eternal issues but at the same time cannot completely avoid being embedded in the mundane particulars of everyday life. It is in being linked to both the inspiring and the pragmatic that we avoid the dual traps of getting lost in inspiration and not being able to fulfill our purpose.

PERSONAL TRANSCENDENCE IN AN INSTITUTIONAL SETTING.[154] Spirituality, at least in part, is a personal search for transcendence in the midst of our work. But as managers we cannot separate ourselves from our work. Further, we cannot separate ourselves from the shared values of the organization we work for. This means that the very thing we may want to achieve transcendence from is that which can prevent us from achieving this.

WORKING TO LIVE OR LIVING TO WORK.[155] Work is one of the chief integrators of our life. Apart from the obvious economic benefits that we derive from work, generally people view work as a good thing. Few of us prefer to be unemployed. Yet we are ambivalent in our feelings toward work. Every job has its drudgery elements. At various times even the most appealing work can be very unappealing when the people we work with or the boss we work for create an atmosphere that detracts from the pleasant dimensions of work. Thus most of us have two opposing attitudes toward work that oscillate in our hearts and minds: At the same time as we live to work by fulfilling a greater good to the community, we sometimes find that we must simply work to live when work appears to shortchange us on the meaning it offers.

THE PARADOX OF FAITH. The paradox of faith is that for faith to be true faith, it must be faith in the context of being uncertain. Faith "is always planted in the soil of wonder and questioning."[156] But how can what we know be the object of faith if it is something we already know? In other words, one cannot believe unless one doubts. For faith is never built on certainty but on the foundation of simply not knowing.[157]

Focus on an Organization

LifeChasers

Founded by Verla Gillmor Wallace, the mission of LifeChasers is to encourage, inspire, and model how to live out a winsome, genuine faith and how to be an effective and strategic influence in our culture, believing we are invited by God to be both salt and light. The LifeChasers network publishes encouraging stories, interviews, and profiles of Christians "from the trenches" who embody the LifeChasers marketplace ministry philosophy. Verla Gillmor Wallace is the author of an inspirational book for Christians interested in pursuing God with purpose, passion, and commitment: *Reality Check: A Survival Manual for Christians in the Workplace.*[158]

Chapter Summary

1. Two broad traditions of spirituality have been practiced among Christians around the world: (1) spirituality lived through actions in life including work, which is called kataphatic spirituality; and (2) reflective, prayerful, contemplative spirituality experienced through temporary separation from the world, which is called apophatic spirituality. The dimensions of biblical worship include thoughts and actions, individual (by yourself) and corporate (with the congregation) settings, spontaneity and order, expressions of joy and sorrow, and the temporary withdrawal from and then engagement with day-to-day activities in service to others. With a broader understanding of worship, it is understandable how worship can be seen as imbedded in the concept of work.
2. Calling forms a bridge between religious beliefs and your work as a manager. This bridge is like a daily conversation embracing the current community you serve, yourself, and your sense of God's purpose for your life. Calling does not require paid employment. Twelve characteristics of calling show how it is distinguished from an occupation, profession, or a job. People have misconceptions of calling. Calling involves participating in the creating, sustaining, redeeming, and consummating of God.
3. Expressing personal faith occurs at various levels including the individual, organizational, industry and professional association, and economic system. Several influencing factors may affect how people express their faith at work, including religious beliefs and the context in which a person works. What is appropriate at each level may vary according to the context.
4. Various models of expressing religious faith at work have been offered. Direct witnessing (what we say) is the attempt to represent one's religious faith to others in various ways. Indirect witnessing (what we do) is living a moral life rather than talking about faith and God. David Miller's five-part model represents the variety of experiences in how various Christians approach integrating their faith at work. The Nash-McClennan Coping Strategies Model is based on the belief that Christians face several tensions when desiring to integrate their faith in the marketplace. To cope with these tensions Christians choose different coping strategies.
5. Since the 1990s, a growing interest in spirituality at work has emerged and can be understood in relation to the larger societal trends taking place. The chapter presents five approaches to spiritual development at the workplace. The religion-based organization intends to actively bring religion into the workplace. The evolutionary organization starts out from one spiritual perspective and evolves over time. The recovering organization behaves somewhat like Alcoholics Anonymous, a program based on the foundational principles of clear constraints that help manage addiction, which in this case means addiction to greed and power. Managers must give over their entire being and the organization to a higher power. The socially responsible organization works on the basis of the social contract. In the values-based organization managers believe that personal spiritual values produce an ethical organization.
6. The chapter explores six aspects of the connection between management and spirituality. Some scholars suggest that spirituality operates at both the individual level and the organizational level.
7. Spirituality and its historical root religion are closely related and compatible but not necessarily identical. Religion is organized, formal, and communal spirituality, meaning a group of people in a community who agree around a particular common set of beliefs. Also, religion has as its primary focus salvation. Religion tends to be defined by boundaries.
8. Since the Renaissance the traditional understanding of life artificially splits reality into two fundamentally distinct categories: holy and profane, and sacred and secular. This distinction when applied broadly to life in general, many now believe, violates reality, which is an integrated whole.

Key Terms

Apophatic spirituality 486
Atomists 500
Attachment 486
Calling 490
Consummating 495
Contextual factors 498
Creating 494
Cynics 500
Detachment 486
Direct witnessing 499
Enrichment Type 500
Ethics Type 499
Evangelism Type 500
Everywhere Type 500
Exclusive identity 498
Experience Type 500
Generalists 500
Inclusive identity 498
Indirect witnessing 499
Justifiers 500
Kataphatic spirituality 486
Liturgy 490
Nonreligious spirituality 484
Outreach 497
Percolators 500
Redeeming 494
Religious belief factors 497
Religious spirituality 484
Resacralizers 500
Secularists 500
Sustaining 494
Worship 488

Discussion Questions

1. Considering the possibility that as a manager you might be called on to also be a minister is a provocative idea. Consciously inserting yourself into a situation containing spiritual challenges or crises, though laudable for serving the needs of the person, can jeopardize the other legitimate managerial roles and responsibilities to the firm. In addition, because most managers are untrained in counseling psychology, they are not equipped for professional ministry of caring for the soul. How should a manager decide when to get involved and when to focus solely on the needs of the organization?
2. Which of the ministry activities do you feel least comfortable in providing to a subordinate who seems to be going through a difficult time spiritually? Which activities do you feel least comfortable in offering to a supervisor?
3. What personal characteristics of a manager might be important for participating with God in each of the following types of God's ongoing work?
   a. Creating
   b. Sustaining
   c. Redeeming
   d. Consummating
4. Considering that creation in many settings involves the institutions of commerce, where in creation can the person of faith see God at work?
5. Where are the places that tension exists between the ultimate spiritual realities and the pressing needs of today's work most apparent in the life of a manager?
6. How can a manager come to increased clarity about reality through contemplation?
7. Think about some of the more difficult jobs that a manager is called on to perform. How can the performance of these tasks be a channel for redemption?
8. In your own faith tradition, is work seen as worship? If so, in what way?
9. Do you have an idea of what your calling might be?
10. Can anyone ever be completely certain regarding the definition of their calling? Why or why not?
11. How would you distinguish between religion and spirituality? Where have you seen what might be called religion without spirituality?
12. If management work is worship, as this chapter asserts, then how is firing someone for low performance an act of worship?
13. If meaning in life is closely tied to calling, what happens to a person's spirituality when that person's job is lost?
14. Can you think of a legitimate occupation that by its very nature is meaningless?
15. Why do persons who are unemployed feel a vacuum, an unfulfilled void within?
16. Of the five spiritual models identified in Exhibit 15-12, which type of organization would you most want to work for? Why?
17. Comparing spirituality through *attachment* with spirituality through *detachment*, which of the two do you find yourself attracted to? What might be the reasons for this?
18. Is it possible to engage in contemporary business without embracing some of the culture of business?
19. What is more important: the message or the way in which it is delivered?
20. Should the Christian make works of service so visible that the connection between the work and Christian faith cannot be missed ("let your light shine before men that they may see your good works and glorify God . . . " – Matt 5:16)?

STUDENT EXERCISES

1. Following is a list of four management activities. How might each activity be considered in a spiritual light?
   - Hire new employee
   - Prepare operating budget
   - Prepare monthly operating report for the boss
   - Celebrate with employees the successful completion of a project

2. Following is a list of management activities. Select an activity and write a short prayer that a manager might pray before or after the activity.
   - Review monthly budget report
   - Discipline employee for poor performance
   - Tell employees that you have been asked to downsize the department
   - Conduct a planning meeting for a special project
3. Interview a manager from a different religion from your own. Come to class with a report based on your conversation. Ask this person:
   - How do you define spirituality?
   - What spiritual actions of employees, customers, or suppliers have you observed at work?
   - What dimensions of spirituality are your employees the most uncomfortable with? Why?
4. Write a three- to five-page typewritten paper describing your personal calling. This paper should include a discussion about your early life experiences, choices you have made regarding your career path up to the present, feedback from family and friends regarding personal gifts, how your calling serves the greater good of society, what dimensions of your calling you are able to fulfill inside the context of your current (or a recent) job, and what dimensions of your calling you are able to fulfill outside the context of paid employment.
5. Identify and gather information about one company in which the leader(s) has attempted to integrate faith at work. The instructor may give you the opportunity to present your mini-case with the class. A one-page outline must be written and submitted. Information to share includes the following minimum elements:
   - Name of company (Who is it?)
   - Location (Where are they?)
   - Type of business (What do they do?)
   - Type of industry and key success factors of the industry
   - How is faith integrated at this company?

   Where did you get the information? (published sources, personal interviews, etc.)
6. Interview a practicing manager who is a Christian. Ask this person questions regarding his or her style of faith integration. Try to identify a model from this chapter that seems to describe the manager's style.
7. Get permission to walk through a company taking photographs that you will use to create a digital photo journal. The photographs should be of interactions that are related to expressing religious faith at work. For each photo, provide a written explanation that addresses the issues present in the interaction.
8. Write a parable or short story (fictional or true) about integrating faith and business. Be sure that the story contains the following elements:
   - An existing situation in which a protagonist has a goal to accomplish and an obstacle or incident blocks the protagonist from achieving the goal.
   - An antagonist that takes a series of actions or a series of obstacles that arise which block the protagonist.
   - How the protagonist deals with each new situation.
   - How the story is resolved: Did the protagonist achieve the goal or not?
9. Start a faith-oriented affinity group at your place of employment. Write a personal journal of your experience of getting it established.

IN-CLASS EXERCISES

1. Review the list of faith integration activities described earlier in the chapter. Have a small group discussion on the following questions: Which ones are strong approaches to faith integration? Which ones are weak approaches? What makes a particular approach strong or weak?
2. Review the legal issues of expressing faith at work that we covered in Chapter 9, Human Resource Management. Have a small group discussion evaluating the list of faith integration activities in terms of legal risks.
3. Using the models presented in this chapter, share with the rest of the class where your style lines up best. Explain the rationale for your approach based on religious belief factors and contextual factors.
4. **Work v. Meditation.** The purpose of this exercise is to consider how work and spiritual meditation are interrelated. Divide the class into teams of five or six students per team. Each team will have two tasks: (a) complete a work task such as stuffing envelopes, folding brochures, etc.; (b) meditate on a Scripture verse or the text of a prayer. After the second exercise, discuss with students the differences between the two sets of activities.
   - What does the experience of each activity tell you about spirituality?
   - Why might it be difficult to meditate under some work situations?
   - Why might focusing on a secular task block thinking about God?
   - How might work and prayer nourish each other?
   - How can a manager stay focused on the work of managing and at the same time be focused on the spiritual dimension of life?

Issue Debates/Discussions

Divide the class into small groups of five to six people each. Hand out a sheet of paper containing the Bible verse and the question that follows. Assign the groups to develop a list of ways that the work of a manager is represented in the Lord's Prayer. Give the groups 5 minutes to discuss. Then call for groups to give a summary of the rationale they developed. Discussion can follow.

Discussion Topic #1: The Lord's Prayer is one of the most famous passages in the Bible: Matthew 6:9–13 [9]Pray, then, in this way: Our Father who art in heaven, Hallowed be Thy name. [10]Thy kingdom come. Thy will be done, on earth as it is in heaven. [11]Give us this day our daily bread. [12]And forgive us our debts, as we also have forgiven our debtors. [13]And do not lead us into temptation, but deliver us from evil. For Thine is the kingdom, and the power, and the glory, forever. Amen. (See also Luke 11:1–10)

A. In what elements of the Lord's Prayer do you see a reflection of a manager's work?
B. Imagine a work situation that is familiar to you. You are just arriving at that work situation on Monday morning. Share with the group what you might be praying about.

Discussion Topic #2: Promoting spirituality in the workplace is a controversial topic to some Christians. How do you view the issue?

A. Spirituality is a dimension of all of life including a person's relationship to the church, leisure time, and work.
B. True spirituality involves a call of the Gospel and a personal response to that call. Anything else diverts attention from a person's relationship with Jesus Christ.
C. Spirituality is one of the strongest motivational forces for improving performance at work, improving our home life, and improving all social relationships.
D. Spirituality stripped of historical Christian beliefs becomes a counterfeit of true faith. The counterfeit nature suggests that it is of Satan rather than of God.
E. We must recognize that people of other religious faiths are in the workplace. Christians should not be so arrogant as to say that only their particular way of spirituality is a valid expression of this dimension of life.
F. Other: ________________________________.

Discussion Topic #3: Are Christians the only persons capable of living exemplary, altruistic lives?

A. **Yes.** True spirituality comes from a person's relationship with Jesus Christ. Ultimately all altruistic actions come from God through believers. A non-Christian may be able to exhibit altruistic behaviors on an occasional basis but such behaviors probably result from selfish motives. The Christian will engage in altruistic behavior on a consistent basis and not from selfish motives.
B. **No.** We can find many examples of individuals who are not Christian but who live an altruistic life of giving to others. Also, if Christians were the only ones capable of true altruism, then why do not more Christians exhibit such behavior? Is it because they are Christians in name only but not truly Christian? All altruistic actions may ultimately come from God, but people other than believers can be channels for God to work through just as God works through believers.

Discussion Topic #4: Read the following Bible verses. How can you explain the paradox of being salt and light in the context of the workplace?

A. **Matthew 5:13–16** You are the salt of the earth; but if the salt has become tasteless, how will it be made salty *again*? It is good for nothing anymore, except to be thrown out and trampled under foot by men. You are the light of the world. A city set on a hill cannot be hidden. Nor do *men* light a lamp, and put it under the peck-measure, but on the lampstand; and it gives light to all who are in the house. Let your light shine before men in such a way that they may see your good works, and glorify your Father who is in heaven.
B. **Matthew 6:1–3** Beware of practicing your righteousness before men to be noticed by them; otherwise you have no reward with your Father who is in heaven. When therefore you give alms, do not sound a trumpet before you, as the hypocrites do in the synagogues and in the streets, that they may be honored by men. Truly I say to you, they have their reward in full. But when you give alms, do not let your left hand know what your right hand is doing.

Endnotes

1. Mitroff, I. I. (1998). On the fundamental importance of ethical management: Why management is the most important of all human activities. *Journal of Management Inquiry*. 7(1), 77.
2. Alford, H. J., & Naughton, M. (2001). *Managing as if faith mattered: Christian social principles in the modern organization.* Notre Dame, IN: University of Notre Dame Press. p. 12.
3. Sweeney, K. (2007). The merger of faith and work. *The Strategist*. Spring, 6.
4. Mitroff, I. I. (1998). On the fundamental importance of ethical management: Why management is the most important of all human activities. *Journal of Management Inquiry*. 7(1), 68–79; Mitroff, I. I., & Denton, E. A. (1999). A study of spirituality in the workplace. *MIT Sloan Management Review*. 40(4), 83–92; Boatright, J. R. (1988). Ethics and the role of the manager. *Journal of Business Ethics*. 7(4), 303–312.
5. Mitroff, I. I., & Denton, E. A. (1999). A study of spirituality in the workplace. *MIT Sloan Management Review*. 40(4), 86.
6. Mitroff, I. I., & Denton, Elizabeth A. (1999). *A spiritual audit of corporate America: A hard look at spirituality, religion and values in the workplace*. San Francisco, CA: Jossey-Bass. p. xiv.
7. Franz, R. S., & Wong, K. L. (2005). Spirituality and management: A wider lens—a comment on D. Steingard's "Spiritually-informed Management." *Journal of Management Inquiry*. 14(3), 250. See also comments on the complexity faced by Christian managers in Johnson, S. (1988). *Values-driven people: A Christian approach to management*. Dallas, TX: Probe Books. p. 3.

8. Pauchant, T. C. (2002). Introduction: Ethical and spiritual management addresses the need for meaning in the workplace. In Pauchant, T. C. (Ed.). *Ethics and spirituality at work: Hopes and pitfalls of the search for meaning in organizations.* Westport, CT: Quorum Books. pp. 1–28.
9. Stiver, D. R., & Aleshire, D. O. (1990). Mapping the spiritual journey. In Leonard, B. J. (Ed.). *Becoming Christian: Dimensions of spiritual formation.* Louisville, KY: Westminster John Knox Press. p. 26. See also Luke 17:21.
10. Krishnakumar, S., & Neck, C. P. (2002). The "what," "why" and "how" of spirituality in the workplace. *Journal of Managerial Psychology.* 17(3), 153–154.
11. "Those who write about spirituality in the workplace do not always agree on what the term means." Garcia-Zamor, J. C. (2003). Workplace spirituality and organizational performance. *Public Administration Review.* 63(3), 355. See also the discussion on definitions of spirituality in Ottaway, R. N. (2003). Defining spirituality of work. *International Journal of Value-based Management.* 16(1), 23–35; Krishnakumar, S., & Neck, C. P. (2002). The "what," "why" and "how" of spirituality in the workplace. *Journal of Managerial Psychology.* 17(3), 153–164. While recognizing that nonreligious definitions of the term *spirituality* are used by some, the use of the term in this book will be primarily from the Judeo-Christian religious perspective.
12. Stiver, D. R., & Aleshire, D. O. (1990). Mapping the spiritual journey. In Leonard, B. J. (Ed.). *Becoming Christian: Dimensions of spiritual formation.* Louisville, KY: Westminster John Knox Press. p. 20.
13. Cavanagh, G. F., & Bandsuch, M. R. (2002). Virtue as a benchmark for spirituality in business. *Journal of Business Ethics.* 38(1/2), 109.
14. Stevens, R. P. (2006). *Doing God's business: Meaning and motivation for the marketplace.* Grand Rapids, MI: William B. Eerdmans Publishing Company. p. 127.
15. Nash, L., & McLennan, S. (2001). *Church on Sunday, work on Monday.* San Francisco, CA: Jossey-Bass. p. 16. For an extended discussion of nonreligious spirituality see Brussat, F., & Brussat, M. A. (1996). *Spiritual literacy: Reading the sacred in everyday life.* New York: Scribner; Solomon, R. C. (2002). *Spirituality for the skeptic: The thoughtful love of life.* New York: Oxford University Press.
16. Stevens, R. P. (2006). *Doing God's business: Meaning and motivation for the marketplace.* Grand Rapids, MI: William B. Eerdmans Publishing Company. p. 133; Ashmos, D. P., & Duchon, D. (2000). Spirituality at work: A conceptualization and measure. *Journal of Management Inquiry.* 9(2), 134; Howard, S. (2002). A spiritual perspective on learning in the workplace. *Journal of Managerial Psychology.* 17(3), 231; Cavanagh, G. F., & Bandsuch, M. R. (2002). Virtue as a benchmark for spirituality in business. *Journal of Business Ethics.* 38(1/2), 109; Mitroff, I. I., & Denton, E. A. (1999). *A spiritual audit of corporate America: A hard look at spirituality, religion and values in the workplace.* San Francisco, CA: Jossey-Bass. pp. 15–30; Turner, J. (1999). Spirituality in the workplace. *CA Magazine.* 132(10), 41; Cacioppe, R. (2000). Creating spirit at work: Re-visioning organization development and leadership—Part I. *Leadership & Organization Development Journal.* 21(1/2), 49; Nash, L., & McLennan, S. (2001). *Church on Sunday, work on Monday.* San Francisco, CA: Jossey-Bass; Brussat, F., & Brussat, M. A. (1996). *Spiritual literacy: Reading the sacred in everyday life.* New York: Scribner; Cavanagh, G. F. (1999). Spirituality for managers: Context and critique. *Journal of Organizational Change Management.* 12(3), 186–199; Day, N. E. (2007). Religion in the workplace: Correlates and consequences of individual behavior. In Biberman, J., & Whitty, M. D. *At work: Spirituality matters.* Scranton, PA: University of Scranton Press. pp. 115–145; Cavanagh, G. F. (2007). Spirituality for managers: Context and critique. In Biberman, J., & Whitty, M. D. *At work: Spirituality matters.* Scranton, PA: University of Scranton Press. pp. 147–165.
17. Stevens, R. P. (2006). *Doing God's business: Meaning and motivation for the marketplace.* Grand Rapids, MI: William B. Eerdmans Publishing.
18. Mitroff, I. I., & Denton, E. A. (1999). A study of spirituality in the workplace. *MIT Sloan Management Review.* 40(4), 83; Higgens, J. J. (1975). *Thomas Merton on prayer.* New York: Doubleday. p. 9.
19. Many authors have contributed to this perspective including the following: Bolman, L., & Deal, T. (1995). *Leading with soul: An uncommon journey of spirit.* San Francisco, CA: Jossey-Bass; Renesch, J. (Ed.). (1992). *New traditions in business: Spirit and leadership in the twenty-first century.* San Francisco, CA: Berrett-Koehler Publishers; Wilber, K. (2000). *A theory of everything: An integrated vision for business, politics, science, and spirituality.* Boston: Shambhala; Biberman, J. & Tischler, L. (2008). *Spirituality in business: Theory, practice and future directions.* New York: Palgrave Macmillan; Giacalone, R. A. (2010). *Handbook of workplace spirituality and organizational performance.* Armonk, NY: M.E. Sharpe.
20. Cavanagh, G. F. (1999). Spirituality for managers: Context and critique. *Journal of Organizational Change Management.* 23(3), 186–199.
21. Stevens, R. P. (2006). *Doing God's business: Meaning and motivation for the marketplace.* Grand Rapids, MI: William B. Eerdmans Publishing Company. pp. 125–142.
22. Ashmos, D. P., & Duchon, D. (2000). Spirituality at work: A conceptualization and measure. *Journal of Management Inquiry.* 9(2), 135–136; Myers, D. G., & Jeeves, M. A. (2003). *Psychology through the eyes of faith.* San Francisco, CA: HarperSanFrancisco. p. 104.
23. Cavanagh, G. F. (1999). Spirituality for managers: Context and critique. *Journal of Organizational Change Management.* 12(3), 186–199; Daniels, D., Franz, R. S., & Wong, K. (2000). A classroom with a worldview: Making spiritual assumptions explicit in management education. *Journal of Management Education.* 24(5), 540–561.
24. Nash, L., & McLennan, S.. (2001). *Church on Sunday, work on Monday.* San Francisco, CA: Jossey-Bass. p. 84.
25. See Exodus 20; Leviticus 19:18; Luke 10:27; Romans 13:9–10; Galatians 5:13–14; Ephesians 3:14–19.
26. Strong criticisms of spirituality in the workplace have come from Budde, M. L., & Brimlow, R. W. (2002).

Christianity incorporated: How big business is buying the church. Grand Rapids, MI: Brazos Press. pp. 47–54.

27. Simmons, P. D., & McSwain, L. L. (1990). Ethical maturity and spiritual formation. In Leonard, B. J. (Ed.). *Becoming Christian: Dimensions of spiritual formation*. Louisville, KY: Westminster John Knox Press. pp. 59–61.
28. See Jeavons, T. H. (1994). *When the bottom line is faithfulness: Management of Christian service organizations*. Bloomington, IN: Indiana University Press. p. 48.
29. Egan, H. D. (1978). Christian apophatic and kataphatic mysticisms. *Theological Studies*. 39(S), 399–426; Kelsey, M. T. (1995). *Companions on the inner way: The art of spiritual guidance*. (2nd ed.). New York: Crossroad Publishing Company. The distinction between contemplative (inner) and lived (outward) spirituality is described in Cavanagh, G. F., & Bandsuch, M. R. (2002). Virtue as a benchmark for spirituality in business. *Journal of Business Ethics*. 38(1/2), 116; Garcia-Zamor, J. C. (2003). Workplace spirituality and organizational performance. *Public Administration Review*. 63(3), 356; Larive, A. (2004). *After Sunday: A theology of work*. New York: Continuum. pp. 45–49.
30. See the discussion on the twin foci of fleeing and seeking, detachment and attachment in Kelsey, M. T. (1996). *Companions on the inner way: The art of spiritual guidance*. (2nd ed.). New York: Crossroad Publishing Company. pp. 24–25; Hardy, L. (1990). *The fabric of this world: Inquiries into calling, career choice, and the design of human work*. Grand Rapids, MI: William B. Eerdmans Publishing Company. pp. 119–121; Robinson, J. A. T. (2002). Worldly holiness. In *Honest to God*. (40th Anniversary Edition). Louisville, KY: Westminster John Knox Press. pp. 84–104; Jones, C., Wainwright, G., & Yarnold S. J. E. (1986). *The study of spirituality*. New York: Oxford University Press. pp. 1–44.
31. Ashmos, D. P., & Duchon, D. (2000). Spirituality at work: A conceptualization and measure. *Journal of Management Inquiry*. 9(2), 135.
32. See the comments on the belief that "God makes himself known in our everyday life . . . " Stevens, R. P. (2006). *Doing God's business: Meaning and motivation for the marketplace*. Grand Rapids, MI: William B. Eerdmans Publishing Company. pp. 186–194.
33. Mitroff, I. I., & Denton, E. A. (1999). A study of spirituality in the workplace. *MIT Sloan Management Review*. 40(4), 87.
34. McElrath, H. T., & Leonard B. J. (1990). Spirituality and worship. In Leonard, B. J. (Ed.). *Becoming Christian: Dimensions of spiritual formation*. Louisville, KY: Westminster John Knox Press. pp. 46–58.
35. Some of these dimensions were put forward by McElrath, H. T., & Leonard, B. J. (1990). Spirituality and worship. In Leonard, B. J. (Ed.). *Becoming Christian: Dimensions of spiritual formation*. Louisville, KY: Westminster John Knox Press. pp. 46–58.
36. Wiersbe, W. W. (1986). *Real worship: It will transform your life*. Nashville, TN: Oliver Nelson Books. pp. 21, 24.
37. Many writers emphasize the individual and corporate nature of worship. For example, White, J. F. (1967). *The worldliness of worship*. New York: Oxford University Press. p. 23; Gibbs, E., & Bolger, R. K. (2005). *Emerging churches: Creating Christian community in postmodern cultures*. Grand Rapids, MI: Baker Academic. p. 230.
38. McElrath, H. T., & Leonard, B. J. (1990). Spirituality and worship. In Leonard, B. J. (Ed.). *Becoming Christian: Dimensions of spiritual formation*. Louisville, KY: Westminster John Knox Press. p. 49.
39. Ibid. See also White, J. F. (1967). *The worldliness of worship*. New York: Oxford University Press. p. 25.
40. As an example of the integration of worship and work see Brother Lawrence. (1982). *The practice of the presence of God*. New Kensington, PA: Whitaker House.
41. Alford, H. J., & Naughton, M. J. (2001). *Managing as if faith mattered: Christian social principles in the modern organization*. Notre Dame, IN: University of Notre Dame Press. p. 238.
42. John 4:21, 4:23–24; John 15:26; Colossians 3:17.
43. White, J. F. (1967). *The worldliness of worship*. New York: Oxford University Press. p. 20.
44. White, J. F. (1967). The worldliness of worship. New York: Oxford University Press. pp. 59, 75, 86.
45. Wiersbe, W. W. (1986). *Real worship: It will transform your life*. Nashville, TN: Oliver Nelson Books. p. 23.
46. Hardy, L. (1990). *The fabric of this world: Inquiries into calling, career choice, and the design of human work*. Grand Rapids, MI: William B. Eerdmans Publishing Company. pp. 44–76; Brady, B. V. (2008). *Essential Catholic social thought*. Maryknoll, NY: Orbis Books. pp. 184–211; Thompson, J. M. (2010). *Introducing Catholic social thought*. Maryknoll, NY: Orbis Books. pp. 78–102.
47. White, J. F. (1967). *The worldliness of worship*. New York: Oxford University Press. p. 81.
48. White, J. F. (1980). *Introduction to Christian worship*. Nashville, TN: Abingdon. p. 23.
49. The connection between work and worship has been seen in both Protestant and Roman Catholic traditions. See the discussion of the connection between work and liturgy in Alford, H. J., & Naughton, M. J. (2001). *Managing as if faith mattered: Christian social principles in the modern organization*. Notre Dame, IN: University of Notre Dame Press. pp. 229–241.
50. White, J. F. (1980). *Introduction to Christian worship*. Nashville, TN: Abingdon. pp. 67, 89, 119. See also the comments on this in Smith, Y. S. (2002). *Three myths of good hard work*. Paper presented to the Annual Conference of the Christian Business Faculty Association. Boise, ID. Fall; Larive, A. (2004). *After Sunday: A theology of work*. New York: Continuum. pp. 142–146; Jensen, D. H. (2006). *Responsive labor: A theology of work*. Louisville, KY: Westminster John Knox Press. pp. 67–96; Volf, M. (1991). *Work in the Spirit: Toward a theology of work*. Eugene, OR: Wipf and Stock Publishers. pp. 136–141; Kaiser, E. G. (1966). Work and worship. In *Theology of work*. Westminster, MD: The Newman Press. pp. 457–469.
51. Adapted from Giglio, L. (2006). Everyday worship. *Ignite Your Faith*. 65:(2), 9.
52. Exodus 31:1, 35:30.
53. Numbers 11:17–29.
54. Deuteronomy 34:9; Judges 3:9, 6:34, 11:29; 1 Samuel 10:10, 11:6, 16:13–14, 19:20.
55. Psalm 51:11.

56. 2 Chronicles 12:18, 15:1, 20:14, 24:20; Isaiah 11:1–2, 42:1, 61:1; Ezekiel 3:24, 11:5; Matthew 3:16, 12:18; Mark 1:10; Luke 3:22; John 1:32; Acts 1:8, 4:31, 13:52.
57. 2 Kings 2:15.
58. Romans 1:6, 8:28–30, 9:24; Ephesians 1:18, 4:4; 2 Thessalonians 2:13–14; Hebrews 3:1; 1 Peter 5:10.
59. Romans 11:29; 1 Corinthians 7:20.
60. Ephesians 4:1.
61. 1 Timothy 3:1–7.
62. James 3:1.
63. Philippians 3:14; 2 Thessalonians 1:11; 2 Timothy 1:9; 2 Peter 1:10.
64. See Luke 12:15.
65. Banks, R. (2000). Moving from faith to faithfulness. In Banks, R., & Powell, K. (Eds.). (2000). *Faith in leadership: How leaders live out their faith in their work—and why it matters*. San Francisco, CA: Jossey-Bass. pp. 3–18; Roels, S. J. (2000). Dealing with vulnerability. In Banks, R., & Powell, K. (Eds.). (2000). *Faith in leadership: How leaders live out their faith in their work—and why it matters*. San Francisco, CA: Jossey-Bass. pp. 123–139.
66. Buechner, F. (1992). *Listening to your life: Daily meditations with Frederick Buechner*. New York: HarperOne. p. 186.
67. Hardy, L. (1990). *The fabric of this world: Inquiries into calling, career choice, and the design of human work*. Grand Rapids, MI: William B. Eerdmans Publishing Company. pp. 67–76; Chamberlain, G. L. (2004). The evolution of business as a Christian calling. *Review of Business*. 25(1), 27–36.
68. MacKenzie, A., & Kirkland, W. (2003). *Where's God on Monday?* Colorado Springs, CO: NavPress. p. 70; Bursk, E. D. (1959). *Business and religion: A new depth dimension in management*. New York: Harper & Brothers Publishers. pp. 160–163; Richardson, A. (1952). *The biblical doctrine of work*. London: Student Christian Movement Press, Ltd.
69. Nash, L., & McLennan, S. (2001). *Church on Sunday, work on Monday*. San Francisco, CA: Jossey-Bass. p. 248.
70. See 1 Corinthians 1:9; Mark 3:14. The Puritan theologians distinguished between the "general calling" and the "particular calling." The dimension identified here aligns with the general calling. See Hardy, L. (1990). *The fabric of this world: Inquiries into calling, career choice, and the design of human work*. Grand Rapids, MI: William B. Eerdmans Publishing Company. pp. 80–81; McCann, D. P. (1997). On moral business: A theological perspective. *Review of Business*. 19(1), 9–14; Roels, S. J. (2000). Dealing with vulnerability. In Banks, R., & Powell, K. (Eds.). (2000). *Faith in leadership: How leaders live out their faith in their work—and why it matters*. San Francisco, CA: Jossey-Bass. p. 135. See also Holderness, G. W., & Palmer Jr., F. C. (2001). *Career and calling*. Louisville, KY: Geneva Press. p. 16; Nash, L., & McLennan, S. (2001). *Church on Sunday, work on Monday*. San Francisco, CA: Jossey-Bass. pp. 240, 248; Chamberlain, G. L. (2004). The evolution of business as a Christian calling. *Review of Business*. 25(1), 27–36; Klay, R., Lunn, J., & TenHaken, V. (2004). Middle management as a calling. *Journal of Biblical Integration in Business*. Fall, 118–137.
71. Holderness, G. W. (2001). *Career and calling*. Louisville, KY: Geneva Press. p. 19.
72. Klay, R., Lunn, J., & TenHaken, V. (2001). Middle management as a calling. *Journal of Biblical Integration in Business*. Fall, 118–137.
73. Gooden, W. E. (2000). Confidence under pressure: How faith supports risk taking. In Banks, R., & Powell, K. (Eds.). (2000). *Faith in leadership: How leaders live out their faith in their work—and why it matters*. San Francisco, CA: Jossey-Bass. p. 49.
74. See 1 Corinthians 1:2; Colossians 3:12. See also Nash, L., & McLennan, S. (2001). *Church on Sunday, work on Monday*. San Francisco, CA: Jossey-Bass. p. 208; Chamberlain, G. L. (2004). The evolution of business as a Christian calling. *Review of Business*. 25(1), 27–36; Klay, R., Lunn, J., & TenHaken, V. (2004). Middle management as a calling. *Journal of Biblical Integration in Business*. Fall, 118–137.
75. Roels, S. J. (2000). Dealing with vulnerability. In Banks, R., & Powell, K. (Eds.). (2000). *Faith in leadership: How leaders live out their faith in their work—and why it matters*. San Francisco, CA: Jossey-Bass. p. 137.
76. See 2 Corinthians 5:18–19.
77. Stevens, R. P. (2006). *Doing God's business: Meaning and motivation for the marketplace*. Grand Rapids, MI: William B. Eerdmans Publishing Company. p. 36.
78. Gooden, W. E. (2000). Confidence under pressure: How faith supports risk taking. In Banks, R., & Powell, K. (Eds.). (2000). *Faith in leadership: How leaders live out their faith in their work—and why it matters*. San Francisco, CA: Jossey-Bass. p. 49.
79. Novak, M. (1996). *Business as a calling: Work and the examined life*. New York: The Free Press. p. 34.
80. Novak, M. (1996). *Business as a calling: Work and the examined life*. New York: The Free Press. p. 34.
81. Novak, M. (1996). *Business as a calling: Work and the examined life*. New York: The Free Press. p. 35.
82. Novak, M. (1996). *Business as a calling: Work and the examined life*. New York: The Free Press. p. 35.
83. Holderness, G. W., & Palmer Jr., F. C. (2001). *Career and calling*. Louisville, KY: Geneva Press. pp. 14–16.
84. Holderness, G. W., & Palmer Jr., F. C. (2001). *Career and calling*. Louisville, KY: Geneva Press. p. 14.
85. Holderness, G. W., & Palmer Jr., F. C. (2001). *Career and calling*. Louisville, KY: Geneva Press. p. 15.
86. Genesis 1:26–28.
87. Stevens, R. P. (2006). *Doing God's business: Meaning and motivation for the marketplace*. Grand Rapids, MI: William B. Eerdmans Publishing Company. Many other authors emphasize the co-creation privilege of humans. Not all scholars will agree with Stevens' inclusiveness. For example, "Peddling insurance policies and manufacturing car parts might seem unworthy of consecration, as too mundane and crass to warrant reverence." Ashforth, B. E., & Vaidyanath, D. (2002). Work organizations as secular religions. *Journal of Management Inquiry*. 11(4), 360.
88. See Romans 8:18–23; Ephesians 1:9–12; Colossians 1:20. Several scholars view the human side of the work of redemption as extending into economic life of business. See for example Stevens, R. P. (2006). *Doing God's business: Meaning and motivation for the marketplace*. Grand Rapids, MI: William B. Eerdmans Publishing Company p. 125–142; Mackenzie, A., & Kirkland, W. (2003). *Where's God on Monday? Integrating faith and work every day of the week*.

Colorado Springs, CO: NavPress. pp. 27–36; Diddams, M., & Daniels, D. (2008). Good work with toil: A paradigm for redeemed work. *Christian Scholar's Review*. 38(1), 61–82.

89. The book of Revelation portrays this in eschatological terms. Other books of the Bible also discuss God's ultimate plan of salvation for the entire earth.
90. Stevens, R. P. (2006). *Doing God's business: Meaning and motivation for the marketplace*. Grand Rapids, MI: William B. Eerdmans Publishing Company. pp. 204–209.
91. For discussions regarding Christians entering public dialog regarding political and economic issues see the following books and articles: Land, R. D., & Moore, L. A. (1994). *Citizen Christians: The rights and responsibilities of dual citizenship*. Nashville, TN: Broadman & Holman Publishers; Thiemann, R. F. (1991). *Constructing a public theology: The church in a pluralistic culture*. Louisville, KY: Westminster John Knox Press; Budzieszewski, J. (2006). *Evangelicals in the public square: Four formative voices on political thought and action*. Grand Rapids, MI: BakerAcademic; Boersema, J. (1999). *Political-economic activity to the honour of God*. Winnipeg, MB: Premier Publishing. Stackhouse, M. I. (2004). Civil religion, political theology and public theology: What's the difference? *Political Theology*. 5(3), 275-293; Cavanaugh, W. T. (2001). Is public theology really public? Some problems with civil society. *Annual of the Society of Christian Ethics*. 21, 105–123; Breitenberg Jr., E. H. (2003). To tell the truth: Will the real public theology please stand up? *Journal of the Society of Christian Ethics*. 23(2), 55–96.
92. Toulouse, M. G. (2006). *God in public: Four ways American Christianity and public life relate*. Louisville, KY: Westminster John Knox Press. p. 108.
93. Jeavons, T. H. (1994). *When the bottom line is faithfulness: Management of Christian service organizations*. Bloomington, IN: Indiana University Press. p. 48. Here Thomas Jeavons cites James 2:14–18 as an illustration.
94. See the comments about this in Hamon, B. (2002). *The day of the saints*. Shippensburg, PA: Destiny Image Publishers. pp. 252–253.
95. Miller, D. W. (2007). *God at work: The history and promise of the faith at work movement*. Oxford: Oxford University Press. p. 128.
96. Three dimensions are identified (worship, nurture, witness) by Clowney, E. P. (1995). *The church: Sacraments, worship, ministry, mission*. Downers Grove, IL: IVP Academic. pp. 137–186. Clowney, like most scholars, acknowledges the two broad categories of being *called* (inward focus) and being *sent* (outward focus). An early proponent of these two views was De Deitrich, S. (1958). *The witnessing community*. Philadelphia, PA: Westminster Press.
97. Bosch, D. J. (1991). *Transforming mission: Paradigm shifts in theology of mission*. Maryknoll, NY: Orbis Books, pp. 385–386. See also the comments regarding the emerging churches who first experimented with focusing almost solely on sending: "We have found that it's too simplistic and ultimately unhelpful for people's spiritual formation to say that church has nothing to do with gathering." Gibbs, E., & Bolger, R. K. (2005). *Emerging churches: Creating Christian community in postmodern cultures*. Grand Rapids, MI: Baker Academic. p. 106.
98. Here the term "outreach" is used. The preferred term among theologians is "mission." However, using this term may be confusing to management students who apply the term in its secular context to refer to organizational *purpose*. For a discussion on the two views of the church's mission see Stott, J. R. W. (1975). *Christian mission in the modern world*. Downers Grove, IL: InterVarsity Press. pp. 25–31; Bosch, D. J. (1991). *Transforming mission: Paradigm shifts in theology of mission*. Maryknoll, NY: Orbis Books. p. 381.
99. Another way of seeing this dichotomy is the difference between *life* and *word*. See Clowney, E. P. (1995). *The church*. Downers Grove, IL: InterVarsity Press. p. 184; Bosch, D. J. (1991). *Transforming mission: Paradigm shifts in theology of mission*. Maryknoll, NY: Orbis Books, p. 381. See also Matthew 20:26–27, 25:31–46; Galatians 5:13; Philippians 2:5–18; James 1:22, 2:8–18; 1 John 3:16–18.
100. Jeavons, T. H. (1994). *When the bottom line is faithfulness: Management of Christian service organizations*. Bloomington, IN: Indiana University Press. pp. 54–55.
101. Some of the relevant Scripture verses considered in discussions on this issue include the following: Matthew 5:13–16; Mark 16:15; John 17:14; Romans 12:1–2; 1 Corinthians 5:9–13, 9:20–21; 2 Corinthians 6:14–15; Galatians 1:6–10; 1 John 2:15–16. See also van Wensveen, S. L. (1989). Christ and business: A typology for Christian business ethics. *Journal of Business Ethics*. 8(11), 883–888; Niebuhr, H. R. (1951). *Christ and culture*. New York: Harper & Row. pp. 1–44; Kraft, C. (1984). *Christianity in culture*. Maryknoll, NY: Orbis Books; Hollinger, D. P. (2002). *Choosing the good: Christian ethics in a complex world*. Grand Rapids, MI: Baker Academic. pp. 189–215; Webber, R. (1986). *The church in the world: Opposition, tension or transformation*. Grand Rapids, MI: Zondervan. pp. 81–144; Stassen, G., Yeager, D., & Yoder, J. H. (1996). *Authentic transformation: A new vision of Christ and culture*. Nashville, TN: Abingdon Press; Wuthnow, R. (1996). *Poor Richard's principle: Recovering the American dream through the moral dimension of work, business, and money*. Princeton, NJ: Princeton University Press. pp. 292–328.
102. Suess, P. (1999). Evangelization and inculturation: Concepts, options and perspectives. In Scherer, J. A., & Bevans, S. B. (Eds.). (1999). *New directions in mission and evangelization 3: Faith and culture*. Maryknoll, NY: Orbis Books. p. 166.
103. Scherer, J. A., & Bevans, S. B. (Eds.). (1999). *New directions in mission and evangelization 3: Faith and culture*. Maryknoll, NY: Orbis Books. p. 12.
104. Reference to these influences has been made by Nash, L. (1994). *Believers in business*. Nashville, TN: Thomas Nelson Publishers; Miller, D. W. (2007). *God at work: The history and promise of the faith at work movement*. New York: Oxford University Press.
105. Here selected items from the *16 Personality Factors* introduced by Raymond Cattell PhD in the 1940s is used. See Conn, S. R., & Reike, M. L. (1994). *The 16PF technical manual*. (5th ed.). Champagne, IL: Institute for Personality and Ability Testing, Inc. Other approaches to

describing elements of the personality may be useful. See also Hirsh, S. K., & Kise, J. A. G. (2006). *Soul types: Matching your personality and spiritual path.* (2nd ed.). Minneapolis, MN: Augsburg Fortress. pp. 1–240; Page, E. C. (1981). *Finding your spiritual path/Following your spiritual path.* [Training handout]. Gainesville, FL: Center for Applications of Psychological Type; Richardson, P. T. (1996). *Four spiritualities: Expressions of self, expressions of spirit: A psychology of contemporary spiritual choice.* Palo Alto, CA: Davies-Black Publishing.

106. See the spiritual gifts discussed in Romans 12; 1 Corinthians 12; Ephesians 4.
107. This model is similar to that put forward by Nash, L. L. (1994). *Believers in business.* Nashville, TN: Thomas Nelson Publishers. pp. 247–265; Solomon, L. (2004). *Evangelical Christian executives: A new model for business corporations.* New Brunswick: Transaction Publishers.
108. Matthew 10:42, 25:34–40; Hebrews 6:10.
109. See the comments on witnessing as both doing and saying by Deihl, W. E. (2000). Sharing personal faith at work. In Banks, R., & Powell, K. (Eds.). (2000). *Faith in leadership: How leaders live out their faith in their work—and why it matters.* San Francisco, CA: Jossey-Bass. p. 140. See also Scripture passages such as 2 Timothy 4:2; 1 Peter 3:15.
110. See 1 Timothy 3:7 where Paul gives instructions regarding how to select church elders. One of the selection criteria is that the elder must have a good reputation in the community. This implies that Paul understood the power of word of mouth in sharing one's faith. The Greek word used here for reputation is based on the same root word often translated as martyr or witness. Regarding the influence of nonbelievers also see 1 Peter 2:12. Nonbelievers may be overly simplistic in evaluating the life of the Christian. Nevertheless, what they say has an effect on others. See the comments on this in Nash, L. L. (1994). *Believers in business.* Nashville, TN: Thomas Nelson Publishers.
111. See the discussion on use of power in Diehl, W. E. (2000). Sharing personal faith at work. In Banks, R., & Powell, K. (Eds.). (2000). *Faith in leadership: How leaders live out their faith in their work—and why it matters.* San Francisco, CA: Jossey-Bass. pp. 140–156.
112. Nash, L. L. (1994). *Believers in business.* Nashville, TN: Thomas Nelson Publishers. p. 262.
113. Stevens, R. P. (2006). *Doing God's business: Meaning and motivation for the marketplace.* Grand Rapids, MI: William B. Eerdmans Publishing Company. p. 55. Here he summarizes the work of Dan Jessen from an unpublished paper.
114. Miller, D. W. (2007). *God at work: The history and promise of the faith at work movement.* Oxford: Oxford University Press. pp. 125–142.
115. Nash, L., & McLennan, S. (2001). *Church on Sunday, work on Monday.* San Francisco, CA: Jossey-Bass.
116. Spirituality and work have a long history of connection and because of this it is difficult to identify specific historical turning points. The 1990s is selected here based on the comments by Garcia-Zamor, J. C. (2003). Workplace spirituality and organizational performance. *Public Administration Review.* 63(3), 355. See also in support of this Cacioppe, R. (2000). Creating spirit at work: Re-visioning organization development and leadership—Part I. *Leadership & Organizational Development Journal.* 21(1/2), 49; Harrington, W. J., Preziosi, R. C., & Gooden, D. J. (2001). Perceptions of workplace spirituality among professionals and executives. *Employee Responsibilities and Rights Journal.* 13(3), 155; Ashmos, D. P., and Duchon, D. (2000). Spirituality at work: A conceptualization and measure. *Journal of Management Inquiry.* 9(2), 134–135; Mitroff, I. I., Denton, E. A., & Alpaslan, C. M. (2009). A spiritual audit of corporate America: Ten years later. *Journal of Management, Spirituality and Religion.* 6(1), 27–41; Barrett, R. (2009). What's right and wrong with spirituality in the workplace. *Journal of Management, Spirituality & Religion.* 6(3), 261–268; Oswick, C. (2009). Burgeoning workplace spirituality? A textual analysis of momentum and directions. *Journal of Management, Spirituality & Religion.* 6(1), 15–25.
117. Ashforth, B. E., & Vaidyanath, D. (2002). Work organizations as secular religions. *Journal of Management Inquiry.* 11(4), 363.
118. Ashmos, D. P., & Duchon, D. (2000). Spirituality at work: A conceptualization and measure. *Journal of Management Inquiry.* 9(2), 134–135; Garcia-Zamor, J. C. (2003). Workplace spirituality and organizational performance. *Public Administration Review.* 63(3), 360; Mitroff, I. I., & Denton, E. A. (1999). A study of spirituality in the workplace. *MIT Sloan Management Review.* 40(4), 88.
119. Finlayson, C. (2001). Belief in your business: Jensen DJ Construction incorporates spirituality into workplace. *Oregon Business.* August 1.
120. Mitroff, I. I., & Denton, E. A. (1999). *A spiritual audit of corporate America: A hard look at spirituality, religion and values in the workplace.* San Francisco, CA: Jossey-Bass. pp. 6–7.
121. Mitroff, I. I., & Denton, E. A. (1999). *A spiritual audit of corporate America: A hard look at spirituality, religion and values in the workplace.* San Francisco, CA: Jossey-Bass. p. 44.
122. Mitroff, I. I., & Denton, E. A. (1999). *A spiritual audit of corporate America: A hard look at spirituality, religion and values in the workplace.* San Francisco, CA: Jossey-Bass. pp. 57–186.
123. Gunther, M. (2001). God and business. *Fortune.* July 9. 144(1), 58ff.
124. Examples of literature that supports the assertion that spirituality is popular in many organizations include Brandt, E. (1996). Corporate pioneers explore spirituality. *HRMagazine.* 41(4), 82–87; Pandey, A., Gupta, R. K., & Arora, A. P. (2009). Spiritual climate of business organizations and its impact on customers' experience. *Journal of Business Ethics.* 88, 313–332; Lee, C., & Zemke, R. (1993). The search for spirit in the workplace. *Training.* 30(6), 21–28; Miller, D. W. (2007). *God at work: The history and promise of the faith at work movement.* New York: Oxford University Press; Hicks, D. A. (2003). *Religion and the workplace: Pluralism, spirituality, leadership.* Cambridge: Cambridge University Press; Mitroff, I. I., & Denton, E. A. (1999). A study of spirituality in the workplace. *MIT Sloan Management Review.* 40(4), 83–92.
125. Franz, R. S., & Wong, K. L. (2005). Spirituality and management: A wider lens—A comment on D. Steingard's "Spiritually-informed management." *Journal of*

Management Inquiry. 14(3), 248. On the community nature of spirituality see also Jeavons, T. H. (1994). *When the bottom line is faithfulness: Management of Christian service organizations*. Bloomington, IN: Indiana University Press. p. 53. Note that from a Christian point of view "Our humanity, in the image of God, is essentially a cohumanity. We are social-cultural beings, called by God to work together in developing and cultivating the creation." Walsh, B. J., & Middleton, J. R. (1984). *The transforming vision: Shaping a Christian world view*. Downers Grove, IL: InterVarsity Press. p. 55.

126. Nash, L., & McLennan, S. (2001). *Church on Sunday, work on Monday*. San Francisco, CA: Jossey-Bass. p. 30. Nash and McLennan use a variety of terms to refer to these tensions including the following: uncomfortable details (53), inherent conflict (59), complex social or financial factors (62), mixed motives (63), sharp tensions (95), messy details (109), the pragmatics of capitalist economic activity (114), ambiguous questions (139), ambivalence (157), religious tension (165), soul-wracking problems (173), and the crucible of pragmatism. While Nash and McLennan state that Christians can do more to integrate their faith with their work, these tension points never go away entirely. Hence, Christians must do their best in using "coping strategies."
127. Ashmos, D. P., & Duchon, D. (2000). Spirituality at work: A conceptualization and measure. *Journal of Management Inquiry*. 9(2), 135.
128. Harrington, W. J., Preziosi, R. C., & Gooden, D. J. (2001). Perceptions of workplace spirituality among professionals and executives. *Employee Responsibilities and Rights Journal*. 13(3), 162.
129. Howard, S. (2002). A spiritual perspective on learning in the workplace. *Journal of Managerial Psychology*. 17(3), 233. Differences between men and women in terms of spiritual experience have been described by Garcia-Zamor, J. C. (2003). Workplace spirituality and organizational performance. *Public Administration Review*. 63(3), 357. See also Brewer, E. D. C. (1979). Life stages and spiritual well-being. In Moberg, D. O. (Ed.). *Spiritual well-being: Sociological perspectives*. Washington, DC: University Press of America. pp. 99–112. The quote by Thomas Moore is interesting: "Growing old is one of the ways the soul nudges itself into attention to the spiritual aspect of life. The body's changes teach us about fate, time, nature, mortality, and character. Aging forces us to decide what is important in life." Moore, T. (1992). *Care of the soul: A guide for cultivating depth and sacredness in everyday life*. New York: Harper Perennial. p. 216. See also Steingard, D. S. (2005). Spiritually-informed management theory: Toward profound possibilities for inquiry and transformation. *Journal of Management Inquiry*. 14(3), 234; Larkin, E. E. (1967). Christian spirituality. In *New Catholic encyclopedia*. (Vol. 13). New York: McGraw-Hill. p. 602; Howard, S. (2002). A spiritual perspective on learning in the workplace. *Journal of Managerial Psychology*. 17(3), 235; Turner, J. (1999). Spirituality in the workplace. *CA Magazine*. 132(10), 41.
130. Howard, S. (2002). A spiritual perspective on learning in the workplace. *Journal of Managerial Psychology*. 17(3), 235.
131. Mitroff, I. I. (1998). On the fundamental importance of ethical management: Why management is the most important of all human activities. *Journal of Management Inquiry*. 7(1), 77. See also the comments on this in Steingard, D. S. (2005). Spiritually-informed management theory: Toward profound possibilities for inquiry and transformation. *Journal of Management Inquiry*. 14(3), 237.
132. Garcia-Zamor, J. C. (2003). Workplace spirituality and organizational performance. *Public Administration Review*. 63(3), 360. Research by Mitroff and Denton identified different ways in which spirituality was expressed organizationally. Mitroff, I. I., & Denton, E. A. (1999). A study of spirituality in the workplace. *MIT Sloan Management Review*. 40(4), 90; Cacioppe, R. (2000). Creating spirit at work: Re-visioning organization development and leadership—Part I. *Leadership & Organization Development Journal*. 21(1/2), 51; Krishnakumar, S., & Neck, C. P. (2002). The "what," "why" and "how" of spirituality in the workplace. *Journal of Managerial Psychology*. 17(3), 153–164; Barrett, R. (2009). What's right and wrong with spirituality in the workplace. *Journal of Management, Spirituality & Religion*. 6(3), 261–268.
133. Konz, G. N. P., & Ryan, F. X. (1999). Maintaining an organizational spirituality: No easy task. *Journal of Organizational Change Management*. 12(3), 200–210.
134. Wagner-Marsh, F., & Conley, J. (1999). The fourth wave: The spiritually-based firm. *Journal of Organizational Change Management*. 12(4), 292ff.
135. From the Wetherill Associates, Inc., corporate website: http://www.wai-wetherill.com/contacts/in_memoriam.cfm, accessed August 27, 2007.
136. Turner, J. (1999). Spirituality in the workplace. *CA Magazine*. 132(10), 42; Wagner-Marsh, F., & Conley, J. (1999). The fourth wave: The spiritually-based firm. *Journal of Organizational Change Management*. 12(4), 292ff; Marcic, D. (2000). God, faith and management education. *Journal of Management Education*. 24(5), 632–634; Konz, G. N. P., & Ryan, F. X. (1999). Maintaining an organizational spirituality: No easy task. *Journal of Organizational Change Management*. 12(3), 200–210; Barrett, R. (2009). What's right and wrong with spirituality in the workplace. *Journal of Management, Spirituality & Religion*. 6(3), 261–268.
137. Matthew 19:19, 22:39; Mark 12:31; Romans 15:1; 1 Corinthians 10:24, 12:25, 13:3–5; Galatians 5:13, 6:2; Ephesians 5:29; Philippians 2:3; James 2:8.
138. Garcia-Zamor, J. C. (2003). Workplace spirituality and organizational performance. *Public Administration Review*. 63(3), 358; Thompson, W. D. (2000). Can you train people to be spiritual? *Training & Development*. 54(12), 18; Mitroff, I. I., & Denton, E. A. (1999). A study of spirituality in the workplace. *MIT Sloan Management Review*. 40(4), 86; Turner, J. (1999). Spirituality in the workplace. *CA Magazine*. 132(10), 41; Harrington, W. J., Preziosi, R. C., & Gooden, D. J. (2001). Perceptions of workplace spirituality among professionals and executives. *Employee Responsibilities and Rights Journal*. 13(3), 156; Pauchant, T. C. (2002). *Ethics and spirituality at work: Hopes and pitfalls of the search for meaning in organizations*. Westport, CT: Quorum Books. pp. 192–193.
139. Mitroff, I. I., & Denton, E. A. (1999). A study of spirituality in the workplace. *MIT Sloan Management Review*. 40(4), 88. See also a similar distinction made in

Miller, W. R., & Delaney, H. D. (2005). *Judeo-Christian perspectives on psychology: Human nature, motivation and change*. Washington, DC: American Psychological Association. pp. 12–14; Howard, S. (2002). A spiritual perspective on learning in the workplace. *Journal of Managerial Psychology*. 17(3), 232; Steingard, D. S. (2005). Spiritually-informed management theory: Toward profound possibilities for inquiry and transformation. *Journal of Management Inquiry*. 14(3), 228. The first to discuss the distinction between personal and institutional spirituality was James, W. (1902). *The varieties of religious experience*. New York: Modern Library. pp. 26–46.

140. Nash, L., & McLennan, S. (2001). *Church on Sunday, work on Monday*. San Francisco, CA: Jossey-Bass. p. 36.
141. McBride, J. L. (1998). *Spiritual crisis: Surviving trauma to the soul*. New York: The Haworth Pastoral Press. pp. 126–129.
142. Moore, T. (1992). *Care of the soul: A guide for cultivating depth and sacredness in everyday life*. New York: Harper Perennial. pp. 211–212.
143. Moore, T. (1992). *Care of the soul: A guide for cultivating depth and sacredness in everyday life*. New York: Harper Perennial. p. 215. Not everyone agrees with Moore on this point. See for example Solomon R. C. (2002). *Spirituality for the skeptic: The thoughtful love of life*. New York: Oxford University Press.
144. Mitroff, I. I., & Denton, E. A. (1999). A study of spirituality in the workplace. *MIT Sloan Management Review*. 40(4), 83–92.
145. Mitroff, I. I., & Denton, E. A. (1999). A study of spirituality in the workplace. *MIT Sloan Management Review*. 40(4), 83–92.
146. Cavanagh, G. F., & Bandsuch, M. R. (2002). Virtue as a benchmark for spirituality in business. *Journal of Business Ethics*. 38(1/2), 112.
147. Cavanagh, G. F., & Bandsuch, M. R. (2002). Virtue as a benchmark for spirituality in business. *Journal of Business Ethics*. 38(1/2), 112. This is much like the "fruit of the spirit" described in Galatians 5:22–23.
148. Sauser Jr., W. I. (2005). Ethics in business: Answering the call. *Journal of Business Ethics*. 58, 345–357.
149. Cavanagh, G. F. (1999). Spirituality for managers: Context and critique. *Journal of Organizational Change Management*. 12(3), 186–199.
150. Walsh, B. J., & Middleton, J. R. (1984). *The transforming vision: Shaping a Christian world view*. Downers Grove, IL: InterVarsity Press. pp. 95–97; Diddams, M., & Daniels, D. (2008). Good work with toil: A paradigm for redeemed work. *Christian Scholar's Review*. 38(1), 61–82. For a discussion regarding three popular views see Wuthnow, R. (1996). *Poor Richard's principle: Recovering the American dream through the moral dimension of work, business, and money*. Princeton, NJ: Princeton University Press. pp. 301–305; Nash, L. L. (1994). *Believers in business*. Nashville, TN: Thomas Nelson Publishers.
151. Brandt, J. R. (1995). Spirituality-business: An enduring link. *Industry Week*. 244(9), 6.
152. McDonald, T. (1997). Getting in the spirit. *Successful Meetings*. 46(6), 22; Peppers, C., & Briskin, A. (2000). *Bringing your soul to work: An everyday practice*. San Francisco, CA: Berrett-Koehler Publishers, Inc. p. 194.
153. Moore, T. (1992). *Care of the soul: A guide for cultivating depth and sacredness in everyday life*. New York: Harper Perennial. p. 223; Peppers, C., & Briskin, A. (2000). *Bringing your soul to work: An everyday practice*. San Francisco, CA: Berrett-Koehler Publishers, Inc. pp. 129–130.
154. Ashforth, B. E., & Vaidyanath, D. (2002). Work organizations as secular religions. *Journal of Management Inquiry*. 11(4), 359–371.
155. Hardy, L. (1990). *The fabric of this world: Inquiries into calling, career choice, and the design of human work*. Grand Rapids, MI: William B. Eerdmans Publishing Company. p. 6. See also Ecclesiastes 1:3–14, 3:13–22.
156. Moore, T. (1992). *Care of the soul: A guide for cultivating depth and sacredness in everyday life*. New York: Harper Perennial. p. 253.
157. See Hebrews 11:1. Restating a quote from the theologian Paul Tillich. In Smith, K. K., & Berg, D. N. (1997). *Paradoxes of group life: Understanding conflict, paralysis and movement in group dynamics*. San Francisco: The New Lexington Press. p. 148.
158. Gillmor, V. (2001). *Reality check: A survival manual for Christians in the workplace*. Camp Hill, PA: Horizon Books.

Chapter Appendix

Assumptions in the Field of Management

LEARNING OBJECTIVES

- Understand the importance of managerial assumptions.
- Understand the faith perspective on selected assumptions and some of the fundamental tensions that Christians experience working in the marketplace.
- Describe prominent modern managerial assumptions.
- Describe managerial assumptions that are becoming obsolete and those that are emerging for future managerial success.
- Explain selected paradoxes of managerial assumptions.
- Understand some of the opportunities for further research concerning faith integration and managerial practice.

"A Christian approach to business is not a cookbook of simplistic recipes for resolving complex business problems."[1]

"It's the commonly held assumptions that require the greatest scrutiny. Since these beliefs seem noncontentious, they seldom get examined."[2]

THE SECRECY TRAP

Most top-level leaders assume that when they need to make a major change, they must keep this secret until the right time. In some organizations, people receive information on a need-to-know basis and top leaders assume that initially most other people don't need to know about impending changes. After all, when a big change is coming to an organization, even the top-level leaders may not have all the details that information-hungry employees desire. But a policy of secrecy often fails. Here's an example.

In 2003 the ultra-secret United States National Security Agency wanted to install a computer in the San Francisco offices of AT&T at its Folsom Street building,[3] apparently to secretly monitor telephone traffic for terrorist activities. In retrospect, knowing human nature, is it any surprise that when AT&T employees saw a stranger working in their building they got more than a little curious? By the time the computer was installed in a secret location, AT&T employees with detailed information about the project were scheduled to appear on the television program *Frontline* to talk about it to the world.[4] So much for the assumption that keeping secrets would actually work.

Not all organizational secrets will backfire like that one. But managers usually find it difficult to keep secrets in organizations, at least for very long. In spite of this, they keep trying. True, managers cannot talk about just anything and everything to all employees such as when a manager fires an employee or when a human resources employee receives private health information about an employee. But for most of the things that managers can talk about, some still try to keep secrets. Most of the time, it is impossible to keep a secret about something as big as a merger, an acquisition, a downsizing, or another major event.

Source: © Brooks Kraft/Corbis.

Secrecy-prone managers might assume that employees will not be able to handle the truth in a mature way, that some really good employees will find a job elsewhere, or that other employees will jump to conclusions and misinterpret data, causing problems ahead of time. They might assume that by carefully controlling key information, they will be able to control the reaction to the situation when it is time to announce it. They might also assume that if they control when they release the information, then they can control how the information is framed so that the receivers accept it in the terms that the managers want them to interpret it.

Maybe the opposite assumptions can safely be made most of the time. Maybe employees are smart enough to figure out that something is about to happen, even if they don't know all the details. Maybe employees are mature enough to handle bad news. Maybe employees prefer bad news instead of no news. Maybe, just maybe, employees will trust managers more when managers keep fewer secrets.

Assumptions that managers make regarding the situation they are in and how employees will react to their decisions are at the basis of much managerial success and disappointment. Assumptions that are generally accepted as valid form the foundation of all managerial action. For the Christian, managerial assumptions potentially can conflict with Christian beliefs, creating tension.

Who Cares About Assumptions?

You get up one morning and instead of cooking breakfast you decide to go to a restaurant. To accomplish this small task you depend on several assumptions. You assume that your chosen mode of transportation is available. Unless you have been having car trouble, your bicycle tire

Source: Dmitriy Yakovlev/Shutterstock.

We make assumptions every day regarding things as common as having breakfast.

has been low on air, or you have heard on the news that the public transportation system is running late, you don't give the issue of reliable transportation much, if any, thought. It is not something you are likely to discuss with anyone unless something different from your assumption occurs. You also assume that your chosen restaurant is open for business, that it will have your preferred selection of food, that you will be served in a timely and courteous manner, that the food will taste as good as it usually does, and that you will have enough time to eat and get to work on time.

These assumptions are analogies for the hundreds of assumptions that managers must make after they get to work every day. Indeed, managers and the organizations they lead would get very little done if they did not work based on assumptions.

Management is not just a collection of techniques and activities but also perceptions and beliefs about the behavior of human beings.[5] It is the collection of assumptions that we use in management. An **assumption,** also called a presumption or presupposition, is something that you accept as true, or probably true, without question or scientific proof. Assumptions form the basis of all reasoning, analysis, learning, decisions, and actions. An assumption is an unstated, implicit belief that supports more explicit reasoning.[6]

Assumptions matter for three reasons. First, assumptions contribute to the definition of a situation. For example, you have an employee who comes to you with a complaint about wages. What you assume regarding this employee's motivation, the degree of fairness of the current wage scale, and the effect on the organization if this employee decides to voluntarily terminate are just a few of the things that will drive your thinking and actions. Second, assumptions establish what we care about and what we want to achieve. Third, they influence what we believe to be our choices. We consider some options to be more important than others, and we eliminate some options altogether just because of our assumptions.[7] So important are our assumptions that we could argue that compared with everything else in management practice, assumptions matter the most.

We rarely bring our assumptions up for discussion unless something occurs that is contrary to what we believe to be true. Assumptions help us greatly to simplify our complicated lives. They allow us to live a relatively routine, stable life focusing our attention on other things.

Not all assumptions about the marketplace, the organization, or our managerial activities are actually true even if we believe them to be true. Managers sometimes experience problems when they depend on faulty assumptions or assumptions that were once true but are no longer because something important has changed. Regardless of whether they are true or false, assumptions help guide our thinking, decision making, and actions. Managers play a key role in shaping the shared assumptions in and around the organization. Managers take the lead in allowing their assumptions to be tested by others who have different points of view.

Applying a Christian worldview, we will explore and evaluate several core managerial assumptions that have been generally accepted over the years.

Management Pyramid and Assumptions

Assumptions are part of who we are and who we are becoming. They comprise what we hold quietly in the back of our minds that we believe to be true. See Exhibit A-1 for how assumptions play a role in thinking and action. Identifying our assumptions about a business situation is sometimes difficult simply because we seldom talk about assumptions. They are elusive! Somewhat like a balance sheet, assumptions about life in an organization or about the organization's situation in the marketplace are good only at a point in time or for short ranges of time. Our assumptions last year or last quarter may not be valid next year or next quarter. This is because (we assume!) things in dynamic marketplaces change.

At times our assumptions become a part of our conscious thinking. When our actions do not produce the desired results, we explore what we assumed would happen and we make more assumptions about why the results turned out differently. We experience an emotional response.

Assumptions are sometimes the subject matter of our decisions and actions. For example, as we get new information regarding a situation, we either refine or completely transform our assumptions for the future. During discussions with others, we may find that they have different assumptions from ours. This may become a point of debate as we test the validity of each other's assumptions.

Faith Perspective on Assumptions

Consider an assumption in business strategy that top-level leaders make strategic decisions based on economic reasoning. For example, executives at one company might assume that customers value the unusual features and benefits of their product so highly that they will be willing to pay a premium price to obtain them. If you follow this or any other assumption backward to the most fundamental assumptions of all, you arrive at one of two beliefs about the origin of the universe:

a) Humans were created by God who gave them the ability to reason. This is one of the ways that humans are different from other life forms. This is based on a central cluster of assumptions that God exists and that we exist.

b) Humans evolved from lower life forms that spontaneously occurred by chance over a long period of time and developed the ability to reason in order to survive. This is based on the assumption that God does not need to exist for evolution to "work" as the origin of life.

Notice that regardless of which premise you hold, your starting point for reasoning is based on faith. In the second premise, accepting the theory of evolution as the explanation of the origin of life requires faith that life-generating and life-sustaining conditions on Earth occurred by chance.[8]

The theological assumptions regarding human origins and human nature are an important foundation for exploring assumptions. For the Christian, theological assumptions shape the worldview through which all else is understood.[9] These form the context or backdrop for all of life including our most fundamental managerial assumptions.

Selecting information to use to test or validate assumptions and beliefs **Talking about assumptions with other people when important decisions must be made** **Choosing to reject a previously held assumption** **Revising actions when assumptions must be changed**	**Action**
Mentally exploring or testing assumptions when new information comes that is contradictory **Reacting emotionally when assumptions are proven true or false**	**Thinking & Feeling**
The things you accept as true without question **Unstated expectations of what other people and organizations will do under certain circumstances** **Unstated, implicit beliefs that support reasoning** **Christian worldview assumptions about the nature of reality**	**Being & Becoming**

EXHIBIT A-1
The Management Pyramid: Assumptions

Source: Courtesy of Michael E. Cafferky, © Michael E. Cafferky 2011.

THE AUTHORITY OF THE BIBLE. Perhaps the most significant assumption is that regarding the nature of Bible authority. This single belief is the basis from which all other Christian beliefs issues stem. Most Christians believe the Bible to be the ultimate authority on faith and practice. Christians believe it is the result of God's inspired self-revelation to mankind. It contains universal norms that are applicable across all world cultures; however, knowing how to apply biblical principles in another culture is not always easy. Once Bible authority is accepted, the next question is how a believer should go about the process of interpreting the Bible.[10]

REALITY OF GOD. Christians believe that an unseen, empirically untestable spiritual realm exists outside the human experience. Some call this the realm of the spirit. In the great monotheistic religions this spirit is God. Christians believe that God is ever present through his Holy Spirit, guiding humans toward God's will for their lives and encouraging them to do what they know to be right.[11]

THE PERSON AND WORK OF JESUS CHRIST. Jesus Christ is central to Christian belief. Christians believe that Jesus was born as a human, served in ministry, died on the cross, was raised from the dead, and is ascended to heaven. Jesus Christ is one with God. He is both our Savior and our Judge. Only through a faith relationship with Jesus Christ is it possible for humans to obtain salvation. Christians attempt to emulate Jesus in every dimension of their lives.[12]

HUMANS ARE NOT DIVINE BEINGS. On their own, humans do not establish the ultimate standards of right and wrong behavior. An absolute standard of right and wrong exists, independent of how humans think about it. Although humans are not divine, they were created in the image of God and reflect, in part, God's nature.[13]

RELATIONAL BEINGS. Humans are relational creatures. They make choices in the context of social relationships. They are meaning makers and their behavior is motivated by moral standards. The relational nature of human life is inseparable from moral standards of right and wrong.[14]

SIN. Humans have the potential for both good and evil, altruism and self-centeredness, virtue and vice. But they do not measure up to the absolute standard of right and wrong. Humans are aware of the opportunities to be altruistic, but this is in constant tension with our awareness that we want to place own needs above those of other people.[15]

HUMAN RESPONSIBILITY. Humans are held accountable by society (and by God) for the choices that they make. Human responsibility is not only toward other individuals but to the entire community. The concept that best depicts the depth of this community relationship is shalom (peace). Living in community with others means that we should take responsibility for each other. Ultimately, we are responsible to God the Creator.

HOPE. Even though humans are unable of their own power to live up to the absolute standard of right and wrong, the existence of God means that humans are not alone. God has provided a way through faith in Jesus Christ.[16]

TRANSFORMATION. Humans can have hope that through God's power of his Spirit, transformation is possible.[17]

Depending on the denominational perspective you take on these and other theological assumptions, other things can be added here that are central to Christian faith. Let's look at some examples from the Bible of persons who made correct or incorrect assumptions about people around them.

Examples of Assumptions in the Bible

The Hebrew Old Testament contains several examples of how people make incorrect assumptions. When Abraham encountered Abimalec, King of Gerar, he assumed that because the people of Gerar did not believe in his God, they would kill him and take Sarah. Jacob had second thoughts just before he went in to deceive his father for the birthright blessing. He assumed that his father would recognize his smooth skin and know that it was not Esau, who was a hairy man. Sometimes our assumptions set us up for strong emotional reactions. For example, when Naaman, a captain in the army of the King of Aram, went to meet the prophet Elisha for healing, he expected that Elisha would come out of the house, wave his hand ceremoniously, and heal him of his leprosy. Instead, when Elisha instructed Naaman to dip into the Jordan River seven times, he was furious.[18]

The New Testament contains examples as well. On more than one occasion Jesus had to address the incorrect assumptions that people had regarding him and his mission. They assumed that if he was the Messiah, then he would install his kingdom immediately. He also addressed faulty assumptions that people had regarding pious behaviors. For example, he told the people that they should not assume that meaningless, repetitious prayers would improve their chances that God would listen to them. One day the disciples of Jesus saw him walking on the Sea of Galilee, but they assumed it was a ghost and were fearful.[19] One night a man named Nicodemus came to Jesus inquiring about salvation. He assumed that Jesus was sent from God because, as he stated, "no one can do these signs that you do unless God is with him."[20]

While incorrect assumptions lead to problems, correct assumptions become a blessing. We can assume that the usual daily and monthly cycles involving the sun and moon will continue. We can safely assume that in loving kindness God is faithful to his promises. We can assume that if we ask for wisdom, peace, or other qualities, God will answer our prayer. We can assume that if we confess our sins to God, God is faithful to forgive us.[21]

Using a Christian worldview, we will explore some managerial assumptions that have become generally accepted as being reliable.

Managerial Assumptions and the Christian Worldview

We need to distinguish between two types of assumptions. One type includes the beliefs that a manager holds regarding the marketplace such as customers, competitors, and other entities. We call these **market assumptions**. Managers must maintain their ability to continually reexamine their underlying assumptions about the market. Otherwise managers stop thinking and stop questioning. When managers do not test their market assumptions, they cannot continue to do the right things when the assumptions on which they have built the organization no longer match with reality.[22] In contrast, **managerial assumptions** are the unquestioned beliefs about managerial work. This is the category of assumptions we will focus on in this appendix. We have introduced some of these in previous chapters and will revisit them here. Both market and managerial assumptions can be either *descriptive* or *prescriptive*. **Descriptive assumptions** are implicit beliefs regarding reality. **Prescriptive assumptions** are beliefs regarding how reality should be. Descriptive market assumptions describe what managers believe is real in the marketplace. Prescriptive managerial assumptions are value-based assumptions portraying the actions managers believe they should take or the goals they believe they should pursue. Exhibit A-2 provides some examples of the different types of assumptions.

As we discussed in Chapter 1, the Bible reader must make a judgment whether information presented in the Bible that is connected to management and leadership is consistent with the rest of the Bible as an expression of God's will. The Bible reader also must consider the broader themes of the Bible such as creation and covenant.

When evaluating modern managerial assumptions from a Christian worldview, we should look for the following categories: (1) modern managerial assumptions that are in full agreement with the Bible, (2) those that are in partial agreement, (3) those that are not in disagreement with the Bible, and (4) those that are contradicted by the Bible. Recall from Chapter 1 that the Christian worldview is not monolithic. There will be differences of opinions among faithful believers regarding which category any given assumption should be placed in. Let this thought guide your personal consideration of your own beliefs as you review the assumptions presented here.

EXHIBIT A-2
Examples of Assumptions

	Market Assumption	Managerial Assumption[23]
Descriptive	Customers are changing their tastes from large, heavy vehicles to smaller, fuel-efficient vehicles.	Top-level leaders assume that by keeping impending change a secret, the outcome will be more favorable.
Prescriptive	The company will capture market share if it makes and sells small hybrid fuel vehicles.	It is generally better to be open with information than to keep secrets.

Modern assumptions about managerial work encompass a broad spectrum of ideas.[24] We present here selected assumptions about individuals, organizations, and the economic environment in which management takes place. This list is not intended to be comprehensive. Scholars will differ regarding which assumptions are the most important. An appropriate starting place for considering managerial assumptions is with an economic perspective.

MANAGERS WORK TO BUILD SHAREHOLDER WEALTH. While wealth is not the primary purpose of most organizations, without positive economic profits, organizations cannot continue to pursue their mission. This assumption drives much managerial thought and behavior. For example, managers who take this assumption seriously will be concerned about the economic implications of their decisions and will seek ways to increase revenue, reduce expenses, or both. In nonprofit organizations the related assumption is that managers work to build prosperity for the organization.[25]

Microeconomics is at the basis of much managerial action: Maximize economic profit.[26] From a slightly different perspective, the goal of the organization is to minimize the costs of exchanging resources in the environment and the costs of managing exchanges inside the organization.[27] More wealth is better than the same or less. Growing wealth decreases resource dependence, increases cash flow, and increases influence in distribution channels and supply chains. More wealth improves operating stability and adds to the organization's reputation. While producing economic profits is not the purpose of business, it is the most commonly used measurement to evaluate performance. Given this, is it any surprise that managers are expected to put economic performance first and the social effect of business second?

The upside of this assumption is self-evident: increase in efficiency and shareholder wealth. But the raw push for efficiency and wealth offers nothing substantial regarding how managers should act to obtain these goals.[28] The downside is that organizations can put the drive toward efficiency before moral standards and the needs of people, namely workers, customers, suppliers, and the general public.[29] This ripens the business situation for conflicts between moral standards and efficiency.[30] For example, pushing for economic efficiency places the manager smack in the middle of moral dilemmas regarding use of workers, what is a fair wage, or how much work should be expected of subordinates. Seemingly stripped of moral boundaries, almost anything might be allowed in terms of managerial behavior as long as that behavior does not violate the basic moral foundations of economics in a free market.

An important question, therefore, is whether or to what degree personal faith tradition supports this assumption. Aligning business reality with Christian teaching is not easy. It may be difficult during hard economic times when company managers feel the downward pressure on prices and the upward pressure on costs.[31] In the Christian tradition this has long been a point of tension. Some Christians see this assumption in contradiction with the Bible—pursuit of wealth is synonymous with love of money and greed. Others see this assumption as not disagreeing with

In the Christian tradition beliefs regarding wealth have long been a point of tension.

Source: Keith Brofsky/Thinkstock.com.

the Bible. Because this assumption is central to understanding managerial work in a for-profit context and because this text has not reviewed this assumption in previous chapters, comparatively more space will devoted here to reviewing the biblical record on the issues.

The Bible contains many passages that address questions about the morality of generating wealth. It is remarkable how collectively the Bible writers demonstrate an inherent tension between the use of material and wealth-producing resources and spiritual values. In particular, two sets of tensions appear to be present in Scripture: "diligence versus contentment, and acquiring wealth versus charitable giving." We will explore each side to this tension.

We were created for work.[32] It is no surprise that humans should find pleasure in being diligent in their work. Diligent work, in part, demonstrates the Image of God in human beings. Diligent, honest work produces honest gain, though such gain is not automatic. Some who are diligent also lack economic plenty. In the Bible, both economic gain and economic loss are seen as gifts from God.[33] "Because God both created and redeemed the world, the laws of nature and biblical wisdom are complementary. God's laws are not arbitrary. They really do reflect what is best for people."[34]

Unless circumstances outside the control of the worker come up, diligent workers should lack nothing, as a result of diligence in following biblical principles of wisdom, and such persons will be able to help others.[35] Diligence that yields progress represents the character of God to others. Diligence is positively commanded while sloth is forbidden.[36] More than anything else, our diligence and service to others should be seen as a response to God's gifts placed as a divine loan during the limited days of our life and not as a means of obtaining God's favor.

In tension with diligence is the concept of contentment, also found in Scripture. The truly wealthy person is the one who is content with his or her wealth, be it small or great. Three dimensions of contentment are present in the Bible. First, as much as diligence is held in high regard in the Bible, economically unproductive time and activity is allowed.[37] Ecclesiastes says that one handful of rest is better than two handfuls of work.[38] Second, in work itself we can find pleasure and contentment.[39] Third, while diligence produces quantitative economic gain, contentment with that which is produced also produces a qualitative gain from work.[40] We might deduce from this that in some ways, diligence itself produces contentment.

The Apostle Paul wrote from prison to the church of Philippi and said: "I have learned in whatever state I am to be content. I know how to be abased and I know how to abound, I have learned the secret of facing plenty and hunger, abundance and want. I can do all things in him who strengthens me."[41] Did Paul learn this from his entrepreneurial experiences where he may have seen wide swings in cash flow? In Paul's teaching, abundance is implicitly valued. Paul does not seem to instruct the believers to shun prosperity but rather to find, through Christ, the secret of being content with one's level of economic attainment no matter what that level is.

However much we might value wealth and assets that produce wealth, some things have still higher value.[42] By itself wealth will not produce contentment. The other qualitative dimensions of life listed here will bring contentment. For example, love is more valuable than money. A good name is more valuable than riches. Peace, integrity, wisdom, harmony, righteousness, and our relationship with God trump all the wealth-building assets of the earth.[43] For wealth to be a positive influence we must use our wealth responsibly and we must not equate the level of our wealth, be it great or small, with our true worth in God's sight. Our worth is defined by our relationship with God who gives each of us the task of being a faithful steward over our wealth and wealth-producing assets as long as we live.[44]

Without contentment, diligence can easily be taken to an extreme where selfish economic gain becomes more important than relationships with self, with others, with God, and with the environment. However, without diligence, contentment degenerates into a selfish slothfulness where the lazy person depends on the diligence of others for support.

Even though the central theme of Scripture is human beings' relationship with God, the economic side of life has a respectable place in the Bible. In Scripture the material dimension of life cannot be separated from spirituality. The material world is a result of God's creation. This world was pronounced "very good." A relationship with God that guides our economic affairs is founded on the belief that God is the owner of all wealth-producing assets. God's divine sovereignty is the basis of human existence. Everything that humans produce is to represent this fundamental belief.[45] God has made all the primary physical materials, which humans transform creatively into the products that we exchange with each other.[46]

EXHIBIT A-3
How God Gives Power to Obtain Wealth

1. God created all the wealth-building assets in the earth in abundant supply.
2. He created human beings with the capacities for exchange, creativity, judgment, learning, courage, communication, negotiation, persistence, ingenuity, initiative, goal-setting, monitoring of our results, and adjustments to our behavior. With these capacities humans have gradually learned how to subdue the earth and have dominance over it. This dominance has resulted in the development of new materials and technologies that are derived from nature and its God-created laws. These new materials and technologies provide solutions to the plethora of human needs.
3. God created humans as social creatures to serve each other's needs. This social setting is the God-created context in which wealth is built and for which it is designed.
4. Through their own efforts, humans participate in God's Providential working for society by finding opportunities to serve and build wealth. This sometimes occurs through circumstances and being in the right place at the right time.
5. God created human beings to learn cumulatively from mistakes. This learning, known as wisdom, can be transferred from one person to another in the community.
6. God has gifted some individuals with entrepreneurial ability to take risks on behalf of the other members of society while they add to the wealth they are building.

Giving the power to build wealth is described in covenantal terms. "But you shall remember the LORD your God, for it is He who is giving you power to make wealth, that He may confirm His covenant which He swore to your fathers."[47] The covenant was not just a promise of economic prosperity (though it included prosperity in its scope). Rather, it was a promise of a full covenantal relationship with God, with family, with the community, and with all nations based on spiritual abundance. Under God's covenant with Abraham, the whole world would be blessed in every dimension of shalom including prosperity. God gives the power to obtain wealth in several ways. See Exhibit A-3.

The assets by which a person could build wealth in biblical times included land, precious metals, jewels, animals, equipment, and the harvest that was dependent on the sun and the rain.[48] The Israelites were concerned with the productive capability of the land when they entered Canaan after their long wilderness journey. The land owner was expected to act responsibly with the harvest.[49] Productive land was also a concern in the New Testament.[50] Trade was expected and even encouraged. Employment of workers was expected to increase production.[51] But the one hiring workers was expected to be just.[52] Also, spending of money, by itself, is not criticized per se, though wasting money is criticized.[53] Surveying the entire scope of scriptural teaching on wealth, we can conclude that for the believer wealth is not self-centered but rather God-centered.

Through diligence and creativity wealth is designed to bring honor to God.[54] Wealth also brings honor to humans. Abraham, Jacob, Job, David, Jehoshaphat, and Hezekiah are examples of wealthy persons who are honored in the Bible. Compared with the others, Solomon is considered to have achieved the greatest wealth.[55]

Not all humans intend to bring God honor from their wealth-building activities. Some acquire wealth with integrity, others with dishonesty. But both the righteous and the unrighteous should expect to obtain wealth.[56] God does not reserve the benefits of wealth-producing wisdom and hard work just for the person of faith. In his love to all creatures he offers these to everyone.

The cliché "You can't take it with you" represents the understanding that wealth and wealth-producing assets are on loan during a person's life span. As beneficial as wealth is during a human's life, it is of no use to our relationship with God.[57] In the Bible wealth has several purposes (see Exhibit A-4). These purposes require that we develop a simple faith in God that as we are diligent in our work he will supply for all our needs.[58] Such faith may be the single most important influence that prevents us from needing to steal or commit fraud to acquire more wealth.

As stewards of that which ultimately belongs to God, individuals should do their best to manage what has been entrusted to them.[59] The Bible represents wealth as temporary. Sometimes wealth is acquired by chance.[60] This is an additional rationale for paying attention to

1. Wealth when efficiently and justly used will provide for one's own needs and the needs of one's family.[61]
2. The connection between the individual and the larger community cannot be forgotten. Those who have been blessed with accumulating great wealth should not hoard it but rather contribute to the greater good of the larger community by creating wealth-producing organizations that offer employment opportunities for others.
3. The purpose of wealth is to provide a way for those with means to help those who are facing difficult financial circumstances.[62] While the Bible consistently calls us to share with the poor, poverty is not highly valued and the question of what proportion or how much to give is not answered in the Bible.[63]
4. The purpose of wealth is to provide a means of support for expanding the kingdom of God on Earth through the ministry of the gospel.[64] So, acquiring wealth is to serve both individual needs and the needs of the greater community through charitable giving.[65]
5. Regardless of the amount, wealth encompasses the previous four purposes: it is a way to love God and bring him glory.[66]

EXHIBIT A-4
The Purpose of Wealth in the Bible

that which holds the power to build wealth. We should expect good economic times and times of economic difficulty.[67]

The double-edged principle of acquiring wealth and sharing charitably also comes with a caution: Beware of letting money have too much influence in your life. Jesus warned about the dangers of loving wealth. While money is good and can do much good when used wisely, the love of money is the root of evil.[68] Current assets are important when operating an organization. It is the relationship between current assets and current liabilities that define the working capital necessary for operating the business. But when the steward begins to love generating current assets, this is the root of evil. Greed is sin.[69] When the person pursuing wealth, whether that person be wealthy or poor, believes that God has no effect on our ability to obtain wealth, that person is denying God's existence.[70] Wealth creation, while legitimate, is not autonomous.[71]

Jesus criticized the rich, money-loving Pharisees for their greed and unethical practices that made them wealthy, but not for their wealth. Yet he accepted dinner invitations from the rich and accepted resources provided by others.[72] He warned others to be on guard against all kinds of greed.[73] He counseled a wealthy manager to sell all that he possessed and to give to the poor, but he did not make this a general principle that everyone should follow.[74] For example, when Zacchaeus, the wealthy chief tax collector, accepted Jesus, he sold a portion of his goods. Jesus did not command him to sell the rest.[75] Jesus was aware of his father Joseph's experience as a carpenter. Jesus helped his disciples in their trade.[76] He never questioned the right to own

Source: Brand X Pictures/Thinkstock.com.

Just as the Bible honors the ability to gain wealth, it also places a strong emphasis on giving to those in need.

Managers succeed by promoting efficiency.
The business environment in which an organization operates is an open system.
Business takes place in one or more communities.
Effective managerial action depends on the situation.
Administrative authority improves efficiency.
Managers have the right to define organizations and their work.
Managers can be a force for moral good in the organizations they serve.
Human nature is complex.
Motives expressed in business are complex.
Managers and subordinates attempt to influence each other's behavior.
Managers and their subordinates are inescapably present with each other as long as the employment relationship lasts.
Cooperation imposes costs on both managers and their subordinates.
Managers are limited in terms of rational decision making.
Managers exercise influence to achieve better results.
Managers organize through specialization and coordination to improve efficiency.
Organizations work best when rationality prevails over personal preferences.
Organizational culture is the set of values that drives organizational performance.
Top managers are the most influential members of the organization's culture.

EXHIBIT A-5
Selected Managerial Assumptions

property. And many of his healing miracles resulted in helping the sick and disabled to become well not only in body and spirit but also in their ability to provide for themselves economically.[77]

An important tension exists here. Prosperity is born through diligence and the wisdom[78] that comes from God through our own experience and the experience of trusted, God-fearing members of the community to which we should listen.[79] The problem is that when prosperity is obtained, people can easily begin to trust in the wealth and ungratefully take themselves away from God who has provided the ability and resources to build that wealth.[80]

This and several other generally accepted managerial assumptions can be reviewed from a biblical perspective. See Exhibit A-5 for these assumptions, which we discuss next.

MANAGERS SUCCEED BY PROMOTING EFFICIENCY. Recall from Chapter 1 that efficiency and effectiveness are two major points of emphasis in managerial work.

What is the Bible's record on efficiency? Combing the Bible we find that Scripture assumes that humans will attempt to be as productive as possible.[81] Theologian Wayne Grudem says that human desire to be productive represents a God-given desire to exercise dominion and stewardship over the earth.[82] Diligence that yields progress represents the character of God to others. Humans are expected to be useful, and when they are not, they are considered to be destructive.[83] For example, people do not work hard to plant and tend their fields without expecting that they will get something good in return.[84] When they know that harvest season has come, they will persist in attempting to gather the produce that belongs to them.[85]

Specific biblical instruction regarding care for the wealth-building asset of sheep appears in Proverbs 27:23–27. Here the writer commands the sheep owner to know the faces of his flocks well. Paying attention to assets is not merely a rational mental activity but also the activity of the "inner man"—the heart of the shepherd.[86]

God made the earth with the capability to flourish and be productive. Flourishing of the land is an important element of the concept of shalom. It is God's desire that there be shalom on the earth. People should seek and pursue shalom.[87] Unusual circumstances occur that limit productivity, but generally we can rely on the earth to yield a good harvest from what is sown.[88] Fruitfulness, God's original plan for the earth and for society, is contrasted with barrenness and waste, which result from sin. So powerful is this contrast that the fruitfulness of the land and the wasted land ideas were used as metaphors for how God will bless or destroy.[89]

Practical usefulness and sensibleness are closely related to diligence. The Bible writers hold in high regard things and people who are useful for practical purposes.[90] The Scripture assumes

Source: © Getty Images.

The Bible encourages us to be productive.

that humans will attempt to be as productive as possible. It is unwise to use technology that is inefficient or useless. Wasting time and energy on debates over minor details is useless. We are encouraged to make the most of every opportunity.[91] Other implicit encouragement to be efficient is found in Ecclesiastes. Here Solomon explains the trade-off that comes from not using a sharp axe. Either sharpen the axe or become stronger.[92] The implication is that it is foolish to toil with a dull axe. The Bible suggests the importance of establishing the proper sequence of work tasks in order to have the most desirable outcome.[93] Here the farmer understands that there is a right time for each activity. A first cousin of practical usefulness might be self-control.[94]

People in Bible times understood the impact of useful technology on costs and dynamic efficiency. Hundreds of different types of technology are referred to in the Bible.[95] Setting a bird snare in the presence of a bird was considered foolish since such a snare would be useless.[96] When Solomon was building his house the stones used were cut with saws "according to measure." These were the costly stones.[97] Solomon hired Hiram, a bronze worker from Tyre, to make fancy decorative art. One of the notable features of Hiram's work was his use of one mold and form for the 10 basin stands that he made.[98] This suggests the understanding of how a single mold used repeatedly can improve efficiency as well as reducing variation in the art work.

We find in Scripture several examples of diligence and efficiency including Nehemiah, Hezekiah, Gideon, Ruth and Naomi, Solomon, and the apostles. Joseph's national policy of sacrificing during years of abundance, setting aside resources for future lean years, is highly regarded.[99] Isaac and Jacob are admired for their efficiency in breeding animals. We see in the experience of Jesus how diligent he was in pursuing his mission.[100]

The Bible speaks of unproductive resources in disapproving tones.[101] When a resource became unproductive, it was expected that the owner of the resource would correct the problem or simply get rid of the unproductive resource, replacing it with something else that produces. The principle of destroying unproductive assets and replacing them with productive assets may be the rationale behind Solomon's wisdom that there is a time to plant and a time to uproot that which is planted when the asset cannot be salvaged and becomes irreversibly unproductive.[102] Solomon was an experienced vineyard and orchard owner. One might argue that Solomon had experience in managing productivity and likely knew well what needed to be done with unproductive vines and trees.[103]

A key ingredient in this is economic efficiency. Pruning fruit-bearing plants results in higher production.[104] In grain farming, certain factors increase yield.[105] The implication is that higher yield is to be more highly valued than lower yield. It is unwise to use technology that is inefficient or useless. Using technology must be done in a wise manner so that the full purpose of the technology can be achieved.[106] These practical examples highlight the spiritual principle that it is God who owns the land; humans are coworkers with God in helping the land produce. The land, and by extension all that it contains including technology that is used in commerce, is holy.[107]

The spiritual experience of the people is represented in how they care for the land and its resources. Under the ancient Hebrew economy, every 7 years the land was allowed to return to its natural abilities without human effort applied to production. Because of this, those engaged in agricultural businesses could not earn a profit from the land during the sabbatical year. By observing the sabbatical year, the people were acknowledging God's ownership while they also showed their trust in his sustenance.[108]

This principle of asset utility maximization was used in the Bible to illustrate important spiritual truths.[109] This suggests that for the Bible writers the fundamental principle of maximizing utility was viewed as a good thing. For example, God's word is described as being useful to transform people. Individuals who have faith in God will be like trees firmly rooted near permanent sources of water—they will flourish. The Bible describes God as being interested in the utility of his power to change lives. Christians are encouraged to make the most of every opportunity for the sake of the Kingdom.[110]

At the same time as encouraging utility and productivity, the Bible condemns achieving utility by immoral actions. Stealing, which in some instances is the most efficient way to obtain goods, is condemned. For example, stealing Naboth's vineyard is wrong.[111]

THE BUSINESS ENVIRONMENT IN WHICH AN ORGANIZATION OPERATES IS AN OPEN SYSTEM. When managers plan, decide, and act they have no choice but to include in their frame of reference elements outside their organization, such as consumers, technology, competitors, social forces, government regulations, and laws.[112] An important task of management, according to Peter Drucker, is managing the social responsibilities of the organization. His view is shared by many: A business does not exist by itself or as an end to itself. Every business ultimately exists for the sake of society. From the larger perspective of the economic system in which business operates in Western nations, the free-enterprise system cannot be justified on the basis that it is good for business. The only valid justification for free-enterprise is that it is good for society.[113] The Christian tradition takes open systems to a scope larger than that considered in the physical or social sciences. We operate in an open universe with "principalities and powers" much larger than what we can observe using empirical research.[114]

BUSINESS TAKES PLACE IN ONE OR MORE COMMUNITIES.[115] Moral decision making is a communal process often requiring dialogue with key stakeholders and other members of the community. Other processes such as planning, decision making, communication, leadership, motivation, and the process of deciding what is right and wrong all involve community in one way or another. The entire employment relationship is both a form of community and a part of the larger community in which people live and work. Human resources development is communal. Accountability and agency both have community dimensions. Spirituality has a community dimension that cannot be completely avoided.

A related assumption is that organizations are formed to fulfill social purposes in the marketplace. Business is inherently a social activity. It is an organized way humans go about the process of exchanging things of value to meet their needs and wants.

This text has offered for consideration a Christian worldview that is consistent with this assumption.[116] From the Creation story forward the Bible describes humans as living together in community of interdependent persons. Motivation, leadership, managerial controls, planning and decision making, communication, and many other facets of managerial work are rooted in community.

EFFECTIVE MANAGERIAL ACTION DEPENDS ON THE SITUATION. This assumption must account for two levels of experience.[117] First, before making decisions managers must consider the micro-level factors such as the characteristics and tasks of individual members of the organization. Differences between workers and their mental orientations affect the degree to which the individual fits the job and the organization. Second, managers must consider the macro-level characteristics of the organization as a whole as well as its external environment. This contingency theory, as it is now called, has been studied in terms of leadership, human resources issues, organizational behavior, organization theory and design, and strategy.

In the Christian tradition, many believe that if Christians trust in God, they will be shown the way—not just any way, but God's plan for the one best way. Belief in an omniscient, all-powerful Supreme Being who also personally interacts and intervenes in the affairs of humans sometimes carries a corresponding belief among some Christians that God's will must be a singular direction or command for every situation. In one version of this belief, there is only one true contingency: God's all-powerful, unerring will. It is the Christian's responsibility to be open to determine God's will and then to follow it.

This belief causes inner tension for Christian managers who see the complexity of a situation as they evaluate several alternative actions and believe that there is more than one way to do business.

ADMINISTRATIVE AUTHORITY IMPROVES EFFICIENCY. Hierarchy of decision-making authority is essential for coordination of effort. Supervisors fulfill this responsibility by being a vertical channel of communication. Establishing a manager's authority over workers and processes is central in most organizations. Managers use this legitimate source of power to pursue the economic objectives through such actions as giving direction and commands, monitoring performance of both the company and individuals, structuring rewards and punishments, assigning decision-making rights and responsibilities, and trusting yet verifying.[118] This assumption has remained ingrained in the minds of practitioners and academics for decades. It has been only recently that some have questioned the traditional concept of authority.

Authority means having bounded discretionary power to make decisions and hold subordinates accountable for their actions. Subordination of individual interests to the interests of the organization as a whole is vital for organizational success. Ultimately this is a choice made by each person in the organization. However, managers have a legitimate role to play to ensure subordination of personal interests. Even in so-called self-managed teams, the issue of authority and reporting to superiors never goes away entirely.

Scripture depicts authority as something that should be respected and supported. When Aaron's authority was questioned, God confirmed Aaron's authority and then punished the people for their insubordination. David represented a firmly held belief that one should not "put forth his hand" against the Lord's anointed. In the writings of the early Christians, submission to appointed authority is a clear behavioral expectation. We could say that there is a covenant between employer and employee including the fact that one party is in a position of authority and the other is in a subordinate position. Faithfulness to such a covenant is in concert with the foundation of the Law of God. In addition, while the Ten Commandments are not specific in addressing this assumption, the fifth commandment to honor thy father and mother suggests an underlying principle of respect for and preservation of authority.[119] While loyalty to legitimate authority is valued in the Bible, the Bible also recognizes that sometimes loyalty can get in the way of ethical behavior when it is followed at all costs. Also, with the position of authority comes the increased risk of abuse of hierarchical power.

MANAGERS HAVE THE RIGHT TO DEFINE ORGANIZATIONS AND THEIR WORK. Managers hold legitimate authority to establish organizational values, mission, goals, work processes, productivity measures, and a host of other things. They are charged with the responsibility to foster accountability to the organization and its mission. They define the terms of the employer–employee relationship. They control access to key resources such as budget allocation, information, and influence. Managers use their legitimate authority to delegate tasks, monitor compliance, and provide corrective guidance to employees when necessary.

After reviewing the biblical record on management issues and topics, we conclude that, in general, the Bible supports the assumption of managerial authority; however, when managers abuse their legitimate authority by oppressing their workers, they are breaking other important principles of the Scripture.[120]

MANAGERS CAN BE A FORCE FOR MORAL GOOD IN THE ORGANIZATIONS THEY SERVE. Whether or not they engage other workers in ethical debates, managers model through their own actions what they believe is right and wrong behavior. Managers have the responsibility to manage the organization's moral values in all the decisions they make. Managers are in a position to challenge values that are contrary to moral standards. The Bible clearly supports this assumption.

HUMAN NATURE IS COMPLEX. Recall from Chapter 11 that Douglas McGregor and other researchers grappled with the implications of a manager's beliefs about reality in terms of extrinsic and intrinsic employee motivation. He showed that belief about the nature of human beings is an important influence in managerial behavior. Humans have the capability to show their desire to be productive. They want more responsibility and get satisfaction from accomplishing meaningful work. But humans also show lack of desire to work. Certainly the Bible supports this assumption as it presents the many facets of human experience.

MOTIVES EXPRESSED IN BUSINESS ARE COMPLEX. Human motives can simultaneously include both ultimate, transcendent concerns and immediate temporal concerns. We sometimes refer to this as having mixed motives. What motivates one worker may have much less influence to motivate another worker. We have seen in Chapter 12 how complex motivations are from the biblical perspective.

MANAGERS AND SUBORDINATES ATTEMPT TO INFLUENCE EACH OTHER'S BEHAVIOR. To accomplish this, several types of power are available. Influence can come from one's position such as legitimate power, coercive power, reward power, or the power that comes from control of access to information. It also can come from personal sources such as from expert power or referent power.[121]

Influencing another person's behavior is legitimate in the eyes of the Bible writers as long as such influence is aligned with the principles of right and wrong behavior. As we saw in Chapter 13, the Bible presents several bases of power that are recognized by contemporary scholars. With power comes responsibility to use power in just ways.

MANAGERS AND THEIR SUBORDINATES ARE INESCAPABLY PRESENT WITH EACH OTHER AS LONG AS THE EMPLOYMENT RELATIONSHIP LASTS. The employment relationship is interdependent. Managers and employees are vulnerable to each other. Because of this, the employment relationship is characterized by both cooperation and conflict. The complex, ongoing nature of the manager–employee relationship requires that the relationship be based on a covenant. While the Bible does not comment on this assumption directly, we conclude that the whole of the biblical record is in support of this assumption.

COOPERATION IMPOSES COSTS ON BOTH MANAGERS AND THEIR SUBORDINATES. Cooperation requires managers and employees to give up a measure of their external coercive power in favor of encouraging the other toward self-imposed restraint. Cooperation requires attention and effort. It does not eliminate the need for each party to attempt to shape the wills of the other. The biblical record supports the importance of self-restraint for the good of others.[122]

MANAGERS ARE LIMITED IN TERMS OF RATIONAL DECISION MAKING. It is incorrect to say that managerial decision making is non-rational, a term that would imply irrationality. It is better to state that the rational processes for decision making are limited. A corollary to this assumption is that in addition to purely rational processes, decision making is made with the aid of intuition, which itself may be a result of learning from previous rational decisions, and emotion, which may be a result of an unconscious or conscious logical evaluation of decision alternatives.

The Scripture supports the assumption that managers are limited in their ability to predict and control future events. Managerial knowledge is limited. The future is uncertain.[123] The Christian manager makes decisions in the context of both faith and reason. Scripture calls for humans to in all our ways acknowledge God and he will direct our paths.[124] However, created with the power to think, create, and reason, we are expected to use these God-created gifts, too.

MANAGERS EXERCISE INFLUENCE TO ACHIEVE BETTER RESULTS. Achieving results is implicit in managerial work in the for-profit sector. This assumption is clearly supported in the Bible.[125] Israel was instructed to prune fruit-bearing plants as a means to prepare for the sabbatical year. Pruning results in higher production.[126] When searching out the land of Canaan the Israelite spies were instructed to evaluate the productivity of the land.[127] The implication is that higher production is better than lower production. Careful breeding of sheep will result in a wealthier flock.[128] While managers are expected to use their power to achieve results, organizational power requires responsible use.

Four factors provide opportunity for abuse: hierarchical authority, control of resources, centrality, and a high degree of autonomy in the exercise of power. Abuse of power includes actions that decrease the subordinate's feelings of dignity and self-respect (such as gossiping harmfully, publicly embarrassing the subordinate) and that diminish the subordinate's job performance or rewards (such as making arbitrary personnel selection decisions, assuming credit for subordinates' work, and depriving subordinates of resources).[129]

MANAGERS ORGANIZE THROUGH SPECIALIZATION AND COORDINATION TO IMPROVE EFFICIENCY. Two fundamental purposes of management in terms of coordinating can be seen in this assumption. First, coordination is integral to hierarchy and allocation of authority. Second, organizing is an important tool for achieving efficiency. Given this assumption, it is not surprising that managers also believe that problems and performance gaps arise from structural deficiencies.

The Bible clearly supports the assumption regarding organizing workers through specialization and coordination. If the tasks that need to be accomplished are too great or too complex for individual workers effectively to perform by themselves, the manager should organize workers, dividing up and then coordinating the work.

The issue of freedom of choice that stems from personal faith tradition also arises in the context of organizing workers. All organizations are founded on a paradox. Organizing is, in effect, an effort to exert power and control over individuals and the work groups they are in. On the one hand, the organization needs people who are capable of behaving autonomously, meaning they can think for themselves, but on the other hand, it wants these autonomous people to give up a measure of that autonomy to serve the broader interests of the firm.

In some Christian faith traditions organization is a form of order. The Bible exhorts Christians to do everything in the church decently and in order. Exactly how order is defined depends on who is in charge and the perceived degree to which the order conforms to the biblical models and examples. Christians often turn to the experience of the early church as the model of organization. The New Testament model is based on top-down hierarchy and a functional design. Unfortunately the New Testament does not discuss the complexity of the task environment or of technology that modern organizations experience. Applying the functional design to every situation can result in lower performance, increased conflicts, and even ethical dilemmas. Christian managers want, on the one hand, to follow biblical examples. But on the other hand, they are faced with situations in which organizing must vary from the biblical model.

ORGANIZATIONS WORK BEST WHEN RATIONALITY PREVAILS OVER PERSONAL PREFERENCES. The assumption of rationality derives from the economic assumptions mentioned earlier. If managers work hard to build shareholder wealth, and if they seek the most efficient ways to conduct business operations, then the best approach is a rational approach that weighs the costs and benefits of each decision.

The Bible recognizes that managerial decisions involve the use of rational thought processes; however, many decisions have an ethical dimension that must be considered. For some Christians a purely rational approach is overly utilitarian and places a lower value on the human dimension of business activities. For them, rationality is insufficient to meet the economic needs of the organization as well as the needs of Christian values.

Although the assumption of rationality has prevailed for years, there is a growing awareness that organizational politics and other influences produce less than purely rational decisions.

ORGANIZATIONAL CULTURE IS THE SET OF VALUES THAT DRIVES ORGANIZATIONAL PERFORMANCE. Corporate cultures that are strong are believed to reduce performance variability and improve reliability. A strong corporate culture is present when norms and values are shared widely throughout the firm and intensely held. These shared values define order, align the goals, and act as a social control mechanism that shapes employee behaviors, frames the interpretations of events, energizes employees, and increases the consistency of stakeholder behavior. All this, it is believed, leads to increased firm performance.[130]

Successful organizations strive to obtain rock-solid acceptance of all pivotal norms and values while fostering creativity along the lines of other non-pivotal norms and values as this will promote creative problem-solving in fast-paced environments. But this is difficult to achieve. One unwanted side effect of the socialization process is that some individuals become over-conformed to corporate norms. This undermines creativity. Another dilemma is that while organizations perform better when there is unity among employees, diversity is needed to respond to rapid changes in the environment.

In many evangelical denominations, freedom of choice is embedded in the theological pillars of the belief systems. Anything that appears to be manipulation or coercion is flatly rejected. This sets up a difficult dilemma in terms of socialization of new organizational members. Organizational leaders want to achieve conformity to pivotal organizational norms but they also want to reject manipulation.

TOP MANAGERS ARE THE MOST INFLUENTIAL MEMBERS OF THE ORGANIZATION'S CULTURE. Organizational culture is influenced to one degree or another by every stakeholder in the organization. But founders and senior-level leaders have extraordinary influence in the corporate culture.[131] Culture flows downhill from top-level managers to frontline employees. However, top-level leaders are limited in the influence they have on others. Not all beliefs and values prized by top-level leaders will become accepted by the rank-and-file employee.[132]

We conclude that the Bible supports this assumption. Top-level leaders have a responsibility to maintain the key values around which the organization pursues its goals.

Assumptions in Transition

History teaches us that the more we learn about the complexities of managing and organizations, the more we should be prepared to let go of outdated assumptions. In this section we will first consider the underlying assumptions about managing organizations from the past century that have become obsolete.[133] Then we will explore some of the assumptions that have been put forward as important for the future of management. See Exhibit A-6 list the assumptions we will discuss next.

THERE IS ONLY ONE RIGHT WAY TO ORGANIZE WORKERS. We now know that every business is in a slightly different situation, and one organizational design won't work equally well everywhere. We also have learned that there are multiple ways to organize workers. Each approach comes with trade-offs.

WOMEN CANNOT HOLD LEADERSHIP POSITIONS. For years men controlled access to leadership positions. Leadership was a fraternity. It has taken a few decades to unravel this assumption. In some organizations, notably the largest global organizations, men still dominate the ranks of chief executives.

MANAGEMENT PRINCIPLES APPLY ONLY TO FOR-PROFIT BUSINESS ORGANIZATIONS. The reality is that for-profit, nonprofit, and governmental organizations need managers. Many of the issues that managers in for-profit businesses experience are also present in nonprofit and governmental organizations.

EXHIBIT A-6
Assumptions in Transition

There is only one right way to organize workers.
Women cannot hold leadership positions.
Management principles apply only to for-profit business organizations.
There is "one best way" to manage people.
Top-down command and control-style hierarchy is the most effective management style.
Technologies, markets, and end users are fixed and rarely overlap.
The scope of management applies only to running an organization, managing its assets and its employees.
Employees provide purely an instrumental economic value to the company.
Management's job is to concentrate on running the business rather than on what is happening outside the business.
Management is internally focused on the organization and its workers.
National boundaries define the environment of business.
People are best persuaded by reason and logic.
Religion and business don't mix.

THERE IS "ONE BEST WAY" TO MANAGE PEOPLE. On this fundamental assumption rests all the other assumptions we make about people in organizations. We now know that there are dozens of ways to manage people. The workforce is changing. The skill sets of workers are changing. Organizations are changing.

TOP-DOWN COMMAND AND CONTROL-STYLE HIERARCHY IS THE MOST EFFECTIVE MANAGEMENT STYLE. During the last century the human race has experienced the effects of heavy-handed, authoritarian leaders at all levels of society. This traditional assumption has given way to an interesting ambivalence. Humans want the comfort that hierarchy provides, but we do not want people to control us. We want more influence over what affects our life.

TECHNOLOGIES, MARKETS, AND END USERS ARE FIXED AND RARELY OVERLAP. During the 19th century and early 20th century, this assumption might have been true. But today, technologies apply in multiple industries, not only in the industry in which they were first developed. Organizations routinely look outside their own industry for new technologies. Computers were once viewed as word and number processors; now they are integral to communication networks.

THE SCOPE OF MANAGEMENT APPLIES ONLY TO RUNNING AN ORGANIZATION, MANAGING ITS ASSETS AND ITS EMPLOYEES. True, organizations expect managers to manage assets and employees. But they also expect them to act as entrepreneurs looking for new opportunities outside the organization that will help the organization succeed.

EMPLOYEES PROVIDE PURELY AN INSTRUMENTAL ECONOMIC VALUE TO THE COMPANY. With this assumption, managers will treat workers as if they are merely a raw material that needs to be exploited to obtain a profit. A more modern, enlightened view of employees contends that workers offer important knowledge, influence, and commitments that need to be worked with, not worked over.

MANAGEMENT'S JOB IS TO CONCENTRATE ON RUNNING THE BUSINESS RATHER THAN ON WHAT IS HAPPENING OUTSIDE THE BUSINESS. We now know that almost every manager has a boundary-spanning role of gathering marketplace information, interpreting it, assimilating it, and communicating it inside the organization. The manager's job is to organize company resources to create results *outside* the organization. The customers and the primary mission of most organizations are outside of the organization.

MANAGEMENT IS INTERNALLY FOCUSED ON THE ORGANIZATION AND ITS WORKERS. While the internal focus is still present, as we introduced in Chapter 3 we now realize that to be successful managers must consider the dynamics of both the internal and the external environments of an organization.

NATIONAL BOUNDARIES DEFINE THE ENVIRONMENT OF BUSINESS. This used to be generally true but is no longer true. Now many businesses serve in a multinational environment. This has changed the nature of doing business.

PEOPLE ARE BEST PERSUADED BY REASON AND LOGIC. Reason and logic are important, but by themselves they are insufficient. Persuasion involves capturing the imagination and the passion of people. These are not contradictory to reason, but without them, reason alone won't be very effective in persuading people.

RELIGION AND BUSINESS DON'T MIX. From one point of view, this is still true. Open discussions about religion in the workplace can offend some workers who may perceive them as a hostile working environment or harassment. But from another point of view, humans have found that it is difficult to leave their religious beliefs at the door when they go to work even if they do not speak openly of these beliefs. As we have shown throughout this book, religious beliefs influence many of our thoughts and actions.

OTHER ASSUMPTIONS THAT ARE PARTIALLY TRUE. Some people, though perhaps not the majority, see other assumptions as being only partially true or true under some but not all circumstances.[134] Some business professionals believe it is a half-truth that self-interest is the sole perspective excluding an interest in society. Pure self-interest creates distrust. From a purely pragmatic viewpoint, it doesn't work to be only self-interested. Another half-truth is that corporations exist to maximize shareholder value. Shareholders need to obtain a fair return on their investment. But maximizing shareholder value at the expense of other stakeholders doesn't work in the long run. Imagine what would happen in an organization if only the shareholders were considered in managerial decisions. Such an organization would alienate its customers. The belief that companies need to be lean and mean is another half-truth. Top-level managers highly prize leanness, in terms of efficiency and productivity. Promoting meanness, however, will yield some unsavory results such as burned out managers, angry workers, and poor-quality products and services. Yet another half-truth is that a rising tide (of the economy) lifts all boats. The free market is the most successful approach to global economic development known. However, the gap between the rich and the poor is great and growing. Another assumption that has not completely changed but has been found to be true only under certain circumstances is the belief that organizations work best when there is predictable order. This is true for what is known, but when a situation changes rapidly or temporarily becomes complicated, a certain amount of disorder must be allowed to deal with the unpredictability of the situation.

To this list we add a few maxims that are only partially true. **Maxims** are propositions that express generally accepted principles or rules. Maxims are like assumptions in that most people implicitly consider them to be valid descriptions of managerial life. Consider the following two maxims that are partly true.

YOU CAN DELEGATE AUTHORITY BUT NOT RESPONSIBILITY. While it is true that a superior cannot delegate ultimate responsibility to a subordinate, delegation becomes meaningless unless the superior delegates the responsibility to complete the task along with the task itself.

THE PETER PRINCIPLE. The **Peter Principle**, named after Lawrence J. Peter, co-author of the popular book by that title, states that employees tend to be promoted to the level of their incompetence.[135] In other words, employees grow and develop to an upper maximum level of competence beyond which they do not grow. They then are promoted to a position of higher authority but bring with them a level of competence that they do not improve on. This is true from the perspective of the technical abilities required for work to be done. An opposing perspective is that employees are promoted to higher levels of authority because they have developed other abilities to manage and lead. What the Peter Principle ignores is that if only employees who had fully developed all the skills needed to be successful in all dimensions of management and leadership were promoted, then we would have few managers and leaders available. Management and leadership are learned with experience. Many managers are promoted and then grow into their new roles with experience. They may be deficient in some skills but have other well-developed valuable skills.

Business author and strategy consultant Gary Hamel has put forward a cluster of assumptions that he believes are important for the future of management.[136] These deserve consideration. See Exhibit A-7 for the assumptions for the future of management that we discuss next.

EXPERIMENTATION IS BETTER THAN PLANNING. Management of the future will look for ways to continually introduce diversity of opinions and information. The capability to experiment with new ideas may become a source of competitive advantage.

MARKETS REQUIRE FLEXIBILITY. Managers of the future will be better at listening to the wisdom that is in the marketplace—wisdom that comes from distributors, suppliers, and customers—than today's managers. Listening to the market will require flexibility to quickly change how resources are allocated. While this is a value now, few companies have actually organized themselves for flexible reallocation of resources based on information they receive from the market in real time.

DEMOCRACY IMPROVES MANAGERIAL DECISION MAKING. In the past most organizations were not run as democracies. Hamel claims that this must change. Successful leaders will

EXHIBIT A-7
Assumptions for the Future of Management

Experimentation is better than planning.
Markets require flexibility.
Democracy improves managerial decision making.
The mission matters.
Managers succeed when they organize for serendipity.

encourage the company to hear dissenting voices. Employees will be encouraged to share in leadership. Doing so will make the organization more responsive to the needs of the workers who are at the front lines of creating value for customers. It will improve the wisdom of decision making and reduce the dependence on a single manager or a small group of managers.

THE MISSION MATTERS. Managers will be more successful if they help workers commit to the bigger purposes of the organization. It is through integration of the higher-order goals into the personal goals of the worker that success is achieved.

MANAGERS SUCCEED WHEN THEY ORGANIZE FOR SERENDIPITY. This means creating organizational structures, organizational values, and promoting more interactions among employees of all types. Serendipity results from creating an organizational culture that values the eccentric employee with creative ideas as much as the employee who lacks eccentricity.

The Christian Mind on the Importance of Managerial Assumptions

Successful managers are people of ACTION (they know what to do), ARTICULATION (they know what to say), and ASSESSMENT (they know what to measure). They are also people who carefully consider the ASSUMPTIONS that underwrite actions, articulation, and assessment. An assumption is not merely a speculation or guess—it is a belief about what is fundamentally true and fundamentally of value. While assumptions are less concrete than "facts" or "data" their role has a very concrete impact—they tie together the facts and data they see into patterns (like cause-and-effect, primary-and-secondary), and these patterns provide the basis for strategic and operational decisions. The Christian faith provides the "plumb line" that allows managers to determine how their assumptions align with God's design and will. Because assumptions can either accurately inform or erroneously mislead, the Christian faith allows assumptions based on the ultimate truth and value contours of God's character and wisdom.

Dr. Sharon G. Johnson
Charleston Southern University
Charleston, SC

"Every business operates with assumptions about human nature. . . . A familiar Christian belief is that we are all created in the image of God. . . . This is a foundational truth that should permeate our thinking, for it is at the core of what it means to be a human." "We were created to know God and have God's view of reality; in knowing God we can come to know and do what is right in his sight; and in knowing God and doing right we can separate ourselves from evil and be holy." "The fact that Adam and Eve and every one of us since then has chosen to sin dramatically shapes the way we do business. Sin is not only personal; it has become rooted in our organizations and ways of thinking. Much of what we do is oriented toward recovering from and controlling its effects."[137]

Richard Chewning, John Eby, & Shirley Roels
Business Through the Eyes of Faith

Assumptions in Tension for the Christian

Scholars and Christian business practitioners have identified a few common points of tension between Christian belief and business assumptions—tensions that believers must continually manage in the marketplace.[138] Consider these tensions:

- Love for God vs. the pursuit of profit
- Love vs. the competitive drive

- People needs vs. profit obligations
- Humility vs. the ego of success
- Commitment to family vs. commitment to work
- Charity vs. wealth
- Faithful witness vs. living in the secular culture
- The desire to witness for the Gospel vs. the desire to avoid invasion and hostility at work

Each of these tension points offers both a threat and an opportunity. These tensions represent threats in that some believers may find that they begin compromising their Christian faith to survive in a dynamic marketplace. A pattern of compromise can create pressure from acting in one way while believing in another that is difficult to manage. These tensions also represent opportunities for believers to explore on an ongoing basis the richness of their faith and the complexity of the markets in which they serve.

Achieving balance in these tension points may be an elusive though worthy goal. Pursuing economic success may drive out time and energy available to spend in developing a relationship with God. Managers are notorious for working long hours and allowing the demands of work to encroach on family time. This challenge of balance leaves the Christian with the responsibility to intentionally decide to lay aside work, turn the cell phone off, and ignore email to give family undivided attention. It may require the Christian to forego some profit if doing so means expressing love to God in ways that are respectful of God's creation.

Final Thoughts on Paradox

Paradox describes contradictory, mutually exclusive elements that exist simultaneously for which no permanent resolution apparently exists. Humans often emphasize one side of the paradox at the expense of the other.[139] In this section we review a few paradoxes relevant to managerial assumptions.

CLARITY—PERPLEXITY. At a fundamental level our assumptions can bring both clarity and perplexity to managerial thinking. Assumptions, whether true or untrue, bring clarity to our thinking. Such clarity helps us organize our thoughts about what to do. These help us prioritize our values and goals. At the same time, assumptions can perplex us as we discover evidence that appears to be contrary to what we believe.

SAFETY—DANGER. Assumptions provide us with a measure of safety. Faced with a host of unknowns and options regarding what to do and how to think in particular situations, managers press forward in faith that what they know and what they assume will ultimately lead to success. The safety of our managerial assumptions comes with a degree of bounded certitude. If we hold too firmly to certain assumptions, we will selectively find evidence in support of our assumptions, which will tend to reinforce what we believe. This can leave us in jeopardy if good evidence for an alternative point of view surfaces later. Assumptions about the marketplace that are untested are dangerous. If our assumptions turn out to be false with respect to reality, then we will make some important decisions that could waste a lot of money or put in jeopardy the company's ability to compete effectively. People lose their jobs because faulty assumptions went untested or unchallenged. Assumptions must constantly be tested. The metaphoric highway of business history is littered with examples of companies that used untested assumptions that resulted in the failure of new or existing products. For example, the manufacturers of powerful steam locomotives assumed incorrectly that the invention of the diesel engine would have no effect on railroad transportation.

ACCEPTANCE—REJECTION.[140] As Christians interact in a global economy, God calls them to face the ongoing tension between living in this world but not to live of the world. We must interact with the economic systems, industries, and companies in which we work. To conduct business, Christians must accept some economic rules of the game where these rules do not openly conflict with Christian belief and practice. At the same time, Christians must reject some generally accepted practices that are in conflict with belief and practice. Acceptance and rejection also applies at the level of managerial assumptions. On the one hand, we must accept certain assumptions as being valid in order to make any progress in managerial work. On the other hand, we must be open to challenge and even reject some of our assumptions as we gain more experience in managing.

For Further Research

The discipline of management offers many opportunities for research too numerous to mention here. In terms of integrating Christian faith and managerial work, the opportunities for further research are plentiful while the resources are few.

THEORY AND CONCEPTUAL FRAMEWORK DEVELOPMENT. Serious scholarship in the field of the Christian worldview of management is in its infancy. Few conceptual frameworks have been put forward for consideration. To date, no true theories have been offered for empirical testing. Most business scholars lack formal training in such disciplines as biblical studies, biblical languages, and theology. Conversely, most scholars with advanced training in the study of the Bible generally lack interest or advanced training in the business disciplines. Most Christian business scholars are busy teaching at institutions where they have heavy teaching loads. This makes it difficult to devote much time to scholarly research and development.[141] In-depth evaluation of various management theories from a Christian worldview perspective is waiting for additional study.

PRIMARY RESEARCH ON FAITH INTEGRATION BEHAVIORS. Work has begun on conducting primary descriptive research regarding faith integration behaviors. Much more can be done in this area. For example, research is needed to identify which religious belief factors and which contextual factors are the most influential determinants of faith integration behaviors in the workplace. Other research needs to study the intensity of conflict between various managerial assumptions and elements of Christian faith. Hundreds of organizations and thousands of practicing managers offer relatively untapped sources of in-depth interviews and case studies. Case studies focusing on managers who work in so-called secular publicly traded firms are needed.

PRIMARY RESEARCH ON SPIRITUALITY AND MANAGEMENT. A solid stream of dialogue about spirituality has come out of the *Academy of Management* and its publications. This stream of research holds promise for further work in this area in the future.

PRIMARY AND SECONDARY RESEARCH ON THE BIBLICAL STUDIES AND SYSTEMATIC THEOLOGY. The footnotes containing Bible references in this book are evidence that a significant portion of the biblical record touches on management-related concepts. In many ways the ideas presented here touch just the surface of what might be done in the future through word studies, concept studies, and careful exegesis of specific Bible passages. If business scholars would collaborate with theologians, then more advances in the integration of faith and business could be made in scholarship. The journals published by the *Christian Business Faculty Association* and other publications contain examples of the kinds of scholarship that has been accomplished in the past. The contributions of these scholars are waiting for us to build on in the future.

Appendix Summary

1. Regardless of what premises you hold regarding the origin of the universe, your starting point for reasoning is based on faith. All assumptions in life can be logically traced back to such fundamental assumptions. Fundamental Christian theological assumptions guide thinking and practice. These include the authority of the Bible, the reality of God, the person and work of Jesus Christ, the nature of humans beings, sin, human responsibility, hope, and transformation.
2. We can distinguish between two types of assumptions. One type includes the beliefs that a manager holds regarding the marketplace such as customers, competitors, and other entities. We call these market assumptions. In contrast, managerial assumptions are the unquestioned beliefs about managerial work. Both market and managerial assumptions can be either *descriptive* or *prescriptive*. Descriptive assumptions are implicit beliefs regarding reality. Prescriptive assumptions are beliefs regarding how reality should be.
3. Selected assumptions regarding managerial work are reviewed in terms of the biblical record, including:
   - Managers succeed by promoting efficiency.
   - The business environment in which an organization operates is an open system.
   - Business takes place in one or more communities.
   - Effective managerial action depends on the situation.
   - Administrative authority improves efficiency.
   - Managers have the right to define organizations and their work.
   - Managers can be a force for moral good in the organizations they serve.
   - Human nature is complex.
   - Motives expressed in business are complex.

- Managers and subordinates attempt to influence each other's behavior.
- Managers and their subordinates are inescapably present with each other as long as the employment relationship lasts.
- Cooperation imposes costs on both managers and their subordinates.
- Managers are limited in terms of rational decision making.
- Managers exercise influence to achieve better results.
- Managers organize through specialization and coordination to improve efficiency.
- Organizations work best when rationality prevails over personal preferences.
- Organizational culture is the set of values that drives organizational performance.
- Top managers are the most influential members of the organization's culture.

4. Several traditional assumptions about management are now being questioned in terms of their validity:
   - There is only one right way to organize workers.
   - Women cannot hold leadership positions.
   - Management principles apply only to for-profit business organizations.
   - There is "one best way" to manage people.
   - Top-down command and control-style hierarchy is the most effective management style.
   - Technologies, markets, and end users are fixed and rarely overlap.
   - The scope of management applies only to running an organization, managing its assets and its employees.
   - Employees provide purely an instrumental economic value to the company.
   - Management's job is to concentrate on running the business rather than on what is happening outside the business.
   - Management is internally focused on the organization and its workers.
   - National boundaries define the environment of business.
   - People are best persuaded by reason and logic.
   - Religion and business don't mix.
5. In thinking about the future of management Gary Hamel presents several assumptions that should be considered:
   - Experimentation is better than planning.
   - Markets require flexibility.
   - Democracy improves managerial decision making.
   - The mission matters.
   - Managers succeed when they organize for serendipity.
6. This book assumes that several points of tension exist for the Christian manager including the following:
   - Love for God vs. the pursuit of profit
   - Love vs. the competitive drive
   - People needs vs. profit obligations
   - Humility vs. the ego of success
   - Commitment to family vs. commitment to work
   - Charity vs. wealth
   - Faithful witness vs. living in the secular culture
   - The desire to witness for the Gospel vs. the desire to avoid invasion and hostility at work

Key Terms

Assumption 520
Descriptive assumptions 523
Managerial assumptions 523
Market assumptions 523
Maxims 536
Peter Principle 536
Prescriptive assumptions 523

Discussion Questions

1. Evaluate the assumption about secrecy described in the opening scenario. When is a policy of secrecy appropriate? What are the risks of openness regarding major changes that are expected?
2. Which fundamental Christian beliefs are most visibly in conflict with generally accepted assumptions about business and management?
3. What transformations must Christians make in the way they do business so that their religious faith is compatible with the world of business?
4. In addition to the assumptions discussed in the chapter that have changed over the last hundred years, what other assumptions about management do you think should be questioned? Explain.
5. Review Gary Hamel's list of assumptions that are needed for future managerial success. What are the inherent risks of each of his assumptions?
6. Which of the ongoing tensions are the most difficult for managers to deal with? Explain.

STUDENT EXERCISES

1. Complete the following chart to illustrate what you believe to be the Christian worldview on managerial assumptions. Place a check mark in the column that best represents your viewpoint. Make written notes in support of your point of view.

SELECTED MANAGERIAL ASSUMPTIONS	In full agreement with Christian belief	In partial agreement with Christian belief	Not in disagreement with Christian belief	Contradicted by Christian belief
Managers work to build shareholder wealth.				
Managers succeed by promoting efficiency.				
The business environment is an open system.				
Business takes place in one or more communities.				
Effective managerial action depends on the situation.				
Administrative authority improves efficiency.				
Managers have the right to define organizations and their work.				
Managers can be a force for moral good in the organizations they serve.				
Human nature is complex.				
Motives expressed in business are complex.				
Both managers and employees attempt to influence each other's behavior.				
Managers and their employees are inescapably present with each other as long as the employment relationship lasts.				
Cooperation imposes costs on both managers and their employees.				
Managers are limited in terms of rational decision making.				
Managers exercise influence to achieve better results.				
Managers organize through specialization and coordination to improve efficiency.				
Organizations work best when rationality prevails over personal preferences.				
Organizational culture is the set of values that drive organizational performance.				
Top managers are the most influential members of the organization's culture.				

2. During the next week, carry a notepad with you, and every time you notice someone depending on an assumption in a conversation, record it. When possible, discuss these assumptions with the person. Evaluate the validity of the assumptions you identify.

IN-CLASS EXERCISES

Issue Debates/Discussions

Divide the class into small groups of five to six people each. Hand out a sheet of paper containing the following statements. Assign half of the groups to develop a rationale why the first quotation is valid and the other half of the groups to develop a rationale for why the second quotation is valid. Give the groups 5 minutes to discuss. Then call for groups to give a summary of the rationale they developed. Discussion can follow.

Discussion Topic #1: Can a person in business often please God?

A. **No.**

- **a.** "Business is in itself an evil for it turns men from seeking true rest, which is God."[142]
- **b.** "A merchant can seldom if ever please God."[143]
- **c.** "Commerce is satanic, because it is the basest and vilest form of egoism. The spirit of every businessman is completely depraved. Commerce is natural, therefore shameful."[144]
- **d.** "But those who want to get rich fall into temptation and a snare and many foolish and harmful desires which plunge men into ruin and destruction. For the love of money is a root of all sorts of evil, and some by longing for it have wandered away from the faith, and pierced themselves with many a pang."[145]
- **e.** "And again I say to you, it is easier for a camel to go through the eye of a needle, than for a rich man to enter the kingdom of God."[146]

B. **Yes.**

- **a.** "With persons as his 'hand' or 'coworkers,' writes Gustaf Wingren in his study of Luther's concept of vocation, 'God gives his gifts through the earthly vocations, towards man's life on Earth (food through farmers, fishermen and hunters; external peace through princes, judges, and orderly powers; knowledge and education through teachers and parents . . . ' As we pray each morning for our daily bread, people are already busy at work in the bakeries."[147]
- **b.** " . . . business has a special role to play in bringing hope—and not only hope, but actual economic progress—to the billion or so truly indigent people on this planet. Business is, bar none, the best real hope of the poor. And that is one of the noblest callings inherent in business activities: to raise up the poor."[148]
  "Truly I say to you, to the extent that you did it to one of these brothers of Mine, *even* the least *of them*, you did it to Me."[149]
- **c.** "As each one has received a *special* gift, employ it in serving one another, as good stewards of the manifold grace of God. . . . whoever serves, *let him do so* as by the strength which God supplies; so that in all things God may be glorified through Jesus Christ."[150]
- **d.** "Honor the LORD from your wealth, And from the first of all your produce."[151]
- **e.** "And whatever you do in word or deed, *do* all in the name of the Lord Jesus, giving thanks through Him to God the Father."[152]

Discussion Topic #2: How should the faithful Christian view the following statement by Peter Drucker?

"What we generally call profits, the money left to service equity, is usually not profit at all. Until a business returns a profit that is greater than its cost of capital, it operates at a loss. Never mind that it pays taxes as if it had a genuine profit. The enterprise still returns less to the economy than it devours in resources. It does not cover its full costs unless the reported profit exceeds the cost of capital. Until then, it does not create wealth; it destroys it."[153]

A. **Drucker has it all wrong.** Christians may need to be marginally less interested in generating the type of profit that Drucker discusses when doing so allows the Christian to pursue other goals such as doing the right thing; treating employees, suppliers, or customers fairly; and caring for the company's environmental effect. Under such circumstances a certain amount of economic wealth might end up being "destroyed" as Drucker puts it, but other, higher spiritual values will be achieved.

B. **Drucker is right on target.** Christian managers must be creative to learn ways that they can care for others (such as employees, suppliers, customers) and for the environment and at the same time avoid destroying wealth. One of Drucker's often overlooked points is that if a company devours more economic resources than it generates, then this has potentially harmful effects on the economy as a whole. Christians who do not pay attention to this are at risk of undermining the economic needs of not only their company but the whole economy.

Endnotes

1. Chewning, R. C., Eby, J. W., & Roels, S. J. (1990). *Business through the eyes of faith*. San Francisco, CA: HarperSanFrancisco. p. 5.
2. Hamel, G. (2007). *The future of management*. Boston, MA: Harvard Business School Press. p. 131.
3. Larkin, T. J., & Larkin, S. (2008). The secrecy trap. *Communication World*. 25(6), 21–23.
4. For more information about this watch the episode of *Frontline* titled "Spying on the Home Front" at www.pbs.org/wgbh/pages/frontline.
5. Simon, H. A. (1997). *Administrative behavior*. (4th Ed.). New York: The Free Press. pp. 1–28; Drucker, P. F. (1999). *Management challenges for the 21st century*. New York: HarperBusiness. pp. 1–40; Lozano, J. M. (1996). Ethics and management: A controversial issue. *Journal of Business Ethics*. 15(2), 227–236.
6. Browne, M. N., & Keeley, S. M. (2007). *Asking the right questions: A guide to critical thinking*. (8th ed.). Upper Saddle River, NJ: Pearson Prentice Hall. pp. 53–69; Schein, E. H. (2010). *Organizational culture and*

leadership. (4th ed.). San Francisco: John Wiley & Sons. pp. 7–23; Werhane, P. (1999). *Moral imagination and management decision-making*. Oxford: Oxford University Press. pp. 47–68. Business author Gary Hamel has described managerial assumptions as managerial DNA—the fundamental principles of management that are rarely questioned. See Hamel, G. (2007). *The future of management*. Boston, MA: Harvard Business School Press. pp. 150–151.

7. Neustadt, R. E., & May, E. R. (1986). *Thinking in time: The uses of history for decision-makers*. New York: The Free Press. p. 136; Lozano, J. M. (1996). Ethics and management: A controversial issue. *Journal of Business Ethics*. 15(2), 227–236.
8. See for example the discussion in Pun, P. (2007). Integration and confrontation of contemporary world-view: Evolution and intelligent design. *Perspectives on Science and Christian Faith*. 59(2), 102–109.
9. Adapted from Miller, W. R., & Delaney, H. D. (Eds.). (2005). *Judeo-Christian perspectives on psychology: Human nature, motivation and change*. Washington, DC: American Psychological Association. pp. 3–29.
10. Proverbs 6:23; Psalm 119:105; 1 Corinthians 10:11; 2 Timothy 3:16; 2 Peter 1:20–21; Hebrews 4:12.
11. Genesis 1–2; Exodus 20:3, 24:9–11, 33:18–23; Deuteronomy 10:17; Joshua 22:22; Psalm 19:1–2, 82:1, 89:6, 95:3, 102:25–27; Daniel 7:9; 1 Corinthians 8:5–6; Revelation 1:10–17.
12. Matthew 11:27, 24:30; John 1:1–2, 5:28–29, 8:58, 10:30, 14:9, 17:21; 2 Timothy 4:1–3; Titus 2:13.
13. Psalm 8:4–8.
14. Leviticus 19:18; Matthew 19:19, 22:39.
15. Ecclesiastes 7:20; Romans 3:9, 3:19, 3:23, 5:12–16; James 3:2; 1 John 1:8–10.
16. Matthew 12:21; Romans 5:2–5, 7:15, 8:20–25, 12:12, 15:12–13; 2 Corinthians 1:10; Galatians 5:5; Ephesians 1:12–13; Colossians 1:27; 1 Timothy 1:1, 4:10; Titus 1:2.
17. Romans 6:19–20; 2 Corinthians 7:1; 1 Thessalonians 4:3–4, 4:7, 5:23; Hebrews 12:10, 12:14; 1 Peter 1:15–16; Revelation 22:11.
18. Genesis 20:11, 27:11; 1 Samuel 1:13, 18:11; 2 Kings 5:1–15.
19. Matthew 3:9, 6:7; Mark 6:49; Luke 19:11.
20. John 3:2.
21. Deuteronomy 7:9; Psalm 89:37; 1 Corinthians 1:9, 10:13; 1 Thessalonians 5:24; 2 Thessalonians 3:3; 2 Timothy 2:13; Hebrews 2:17, 10:23; 1 John 1:9.
22. Drucker, P. F. (1994). The theory of business. *Harvard Business Review*. 72(5), 95–104.
23. Like other assumptions, these may be open to debate.
24. McGregor, D. (1967). *The professional manager*. New York: McGraw-Hill Book Company; Cavanagh, G. F., Moberg, D. J., & Velasquez, M. (1981). The ethics of organizational politics. *The Academy of Management Review*. 6(3), 363–374; Anderson, C. R., & Paine, F. T. (1975). Managerial perceptions and strategic behavior. *Academy of Management Journal*. 18(4), 811–823; Drucker, P. F. (1999). *Management challenges for the 21st century*. New York: HarperBusiness; Bolman, L. G., & Deal, T. E. (2008). *Reframing organizations: Artistry, choice and leadership*. (4th ed.). San Francisco: Jossey-Bass. pp. 23–44; Hatch, M. J., & Cunliff, A. (2006). *Organization theory: Modern symbolic and postmodern perspectives*. (2nd ed.). Oxford: Oxford University Press. pp. 3–24; Herman, S. W. (1997). *Durable goods: A covenantal ethic for management and employees*. Notre Dame, IN: University of Notre Dame Press; Schein, E. H. (2010). *Organizational culture and leadership*. (4th ed.). San Francisco, CA: John Wiley & Sons; Pattison, S. (1997). *The faith of the managers: When management becomes religion*. London: Cassell. pp. 10–58.
25. Phills Jr., J. A. (2005). *Integrating mission and strategy for nonprofit organizations*. Oxford: Oxford University Press. pp. 48–70.
26. Pindyck, R. S., & Rubinfeld, D. L. (2008). *Microeconomics*. (7th ed.). Upper Saddle River, NJ: Prentice Hall. pp. 251–286; Drucker, P. F. (1954). *The practice of management*. New York: Harper & Row. p. 11.
27. Jones, G. R. (2004). *Organizational theory, design and change*. Upper Saddle River, NJ: Pearson Prentice Hall.
28. Boatright, J. R. (1988). Ethics and the role of the manager. *Journal of Business Ethics*. 7(4), 303–312.
29. Crainer, S. (2000). *The management century: A critical review of 20th century thought and practice*. San Francisco: Jossey-Bass Publishers. pp. 14–18.
30. Tiemstra, J. P., Graham, W. F., Monsma, G. N., Sinke, C. J., Storkey, A., & Ebels, D. M. (1990). *Reforming economics: Calvinist studies on methods and institutions*. Lewiston, NY: The Edwin Mellen Press. p. 189.
31. Rossouw, G. J. (1994). Business ethics: Where have all the Christians gone? *Journal of Business Ethics*. 13(7), 557–570.
32. Genesis 1–2; Exodus 20:9; Deuteronomy 5:13; Ecclesiastes 3:9–13, 5:18–20.
33. Deuteronomy 8:18; 1 Samuel 2:7; 1 Chronicles 29:12; Proverbs 22:2.
34. Chewning, R. C., Eby, J. W., & Roels, S. J. (1990). *Business through the eyes of faith*. San Francisco, CA: HarperSanFrancisco. p. 13.
35. Psalm 37:7, 128:1–2; 1 Thessalonians 2:9, 4:11–12; 2 Thessalonians 3:11–12; Titus 3:14; Romans 12:11; Hebrews 6:10–12; Ephesians 4:28.
36. Proverbs 6:6–11, 10:4–5, 10:16, 10:26, 12:9, 12:24, 12:27, 13:4, 13:11, 14:23, 15:19, 18:9, 19:15, 19:24, 20:4, 20:13, 21:5, 21:25, 22:29, 23:4, 24:30–34, 26:14–16, 27:23, 28:19, 31:13–17, 31:26–27; Ecclesiastes 5:15, 9:10, 10:18, 11:4–6; Matthew 20:6–7; Romans 12:11; 2 Thessalonians 3:10–12; 1 Timothy 5:8–13.
37. Exodus 20:8–11, 23:10–12; Leviticus 23:3–5, 23:4–44; Deuteronomy 5:12, 15:7–11; 2 Chronicles 36:20–21; Mark 6:31. For comments on the need to balance work and rest to experience contentment see Smith, G., & Wheeler, B. G. (1999). The nature and purpose of work and productivity. *Journal of Biblical Integration in Business*. Fall, 127–141.
38. Ecclesiastes 4:5–6.
39. Ecclesiastes 2:24–26, 3:4, 3:10–15, 5:18–20, 7:14.
40. Judges 19:6; 2 Kings 6:3; Psalm 37:16, 112:1–5, 128:1–2; Proverbs 15:16, 16:8, 22:2, 23:4–5, 30:8; Haggai 1:6–9; Luke 3:14; Philippians 4:11; 1 Timothy 6:6; Hebrews 13:5–6.
41. Philippians 4:10–13.
42. See the comments on this in Wilkinson, B. W. (1991). Biblical principles and unemployment. In Chewning, R. C. (Ed.). *Biblical principles and public policy: The practice*. Colorado Springs, CO: NavPress. p. 69.

43. Job 28:16; Proverbs 3:13–15, 8:11, 11:4, 11:28, 15:17, 16:8, 17:1, 19:1, 19:22, 22:1, 28:6, 28:20; Matthew 6:33, 19:21.
44. Job 34:16–22; Proverbs 22:2.
45. Genesis 14:19; Leviticus 25:23; Deuteronomy 10:14; 1 Chronicles 29:11–14; Psalm 24:1, 50:10–12, 104:24; Proverbs 3:5, 3:9–10; Haggai 2:8.
46. Beed, C. (1990). *God's economic strategy: A biblical study*. Monograph published by the author. Melbourne, Australia. p. 13.
47. Deuteronomy 8:18. See also Genesis 12:2–3, 22:18, 24:1, 26:4; Leviticus 26:9; Deuteronomy 28:4–11, 30:9, 30:15; Psalm 25:13, 37:11.
48. Genesis 13:2, 24:35, 26:12–13; Job 1:1–10.
49. Numbers 13:17–20, 32; Deuteronomy 24:21; Proverbs 3:13–18, 11:26, 27:23–24; Ruth 2:1–19.
50. Matthew 3:10, 7:19, 13, 21:19; Mark 4:28; Luke 8, 13:7–9; John 15:1–2.
51. Deuteronomy 24:14–15; Mark 1:20; Matthew 20:14–15.
52. Matthew 10:10; James 5:1–6.
53. Luke 7:37, 15:11–32; Matthew 26:7; Mark 14:3.
54. Deuteronomy 26:2; Proverbs 3:9. See also Colossians 1:16 where Paul states that all things were created by God and *for* Him.
55. Genesis 13:2, 30:43; Job; 1 Kings 10:23; 1 Chronicles 29:28, 32:27–29; 2 Chronicles 9:20–22, 17:5.
56. Psalm 17:4, 37:16, 49:5–6, 52:7, 73:3, 73:12, 92:7, 109:8, 123:4; Matthew 5:44–45.
57. Isaiah 2:17–20; Psalm 39:6, 49:10; Proverbs 11:4, 13:8, 13:22; Revelation 6:15.
58. Philippians 4:11–19.
59. Psalm 104:24. Griffiths, B. (1984). *The creation of wealth: A Christian's case for capitalism*. Downers Grove, IL: InterVarsity Press. p. 47.
60. Ecclesiastes 9:11.
61. Genesis 30:30; Psalm 17:14; Proverbs 13:22; 31:26–27; 1 Timothy 5:8–13; Titus 3:14.
62. See Chewning, R. C., Eby, J. W., & Roels, S. J. (1990). *Business through the eyes of faith*. San Francisco, CA: HarperSanFrancisco. pp. 222–226.
63. Leviticus 25:25–39; Deuteronomy 15:4–11, 24:12–15; Proverbs 14:21, 14:31, 17:5, 19:17, 22:9, 22:16, 22:22, 28:27, 29:7; Matthew 6:3–4, 19:21; Luke 3:11, 14:13–21, 19:8; Romans 12:8, 12:13, 15:26–27; 1 Corinthians 16:1–2; 2 Corinthians 9:11; Galatians 2:10; Ephesians 4:28; James 2:2–6, 2:15–16; 1 John 3:17.
64. Matthew 6:1–4; 2 Corinthians 9:13; Philippians 4:14–19; James 2.
65. For a discussion on the communal nature of money in the New Testament see Piper, O. A. (1959). That strange thing money. *Theology Today*. 16(2), 215–231.
66. Deuteronomy 6:5, 10:12; Matthew 22:37; Mark 12:30–33; Luke 10:27.
67. Proverbs 23:5, 27:23–27; Ecclesiastes 11:6.
68. Psalm 62:10; Proverbs 6:1–2, 11:15, 11:28, 15:27, 17:18, 22:7, 23:4, 28:22; Ecclesiastes 5:10; Jeremiah 9:23; Malachi 3:8–9; Matthew 6:19–20, 13:22, 19:24; Mark 4:18–19, 10:24; Luke 3:13, 6:24, 12:15, 12:20–21, 12:33–34, 16:14–15, 18:24; John 6:25–27, 6:51; 1 Timothy 6:9–10.
69. Exodus 20:17; Deuteronomy 5:21; Isaiah 57:17; Mark 7:22; Romans 1:29; Ephesians 5:3; 1 Thessalonians 2:5; 2 Peter 2:14.
70. Deuteronomy 6:10–12, 8:10–14, 31:20; Job 31:24–28; Proverbs 30:7–9.
71. Griffiths, B. (1984). *The creation of wealth: A Christian's case for capitalism*. Downers Grove, IL: InterVarsity Press. p. 61.
72. Griffiths, B. (1984). *The creation of wealth: A Christian's case for capitalism*. Downers Grove, IL: InterVarsity Press. p. 61. See also Hollis, C. (1961). *Christianity and economics*. New York: Hawthorn Books. p. 8; Matthew 23:25; Luke 11:39; 16:14.
73. Luke 12:13–15.
74. Luke 18:18–30.
75. Hollis, C. (1961). *Christianity and economics*. New York: Hawthorn Books. p. 9. See also Luke 19:1–10.
76. John 21:6–11.
77. Gordon, B. (1989). *The economic problem in biblical and patristic thought*. Leiden: E. J. Brill. p. 44.
78. Deuteronomy 8:10–20; 1 Chronicles 29:12; 2 Chronicles 1:11–12; Proverbs 3:13–20.
79. Exodus 31:3; Deuteronomy 8:17–18; Nehemiah 8:3; Job 12:11, 28:18, 32:8; Psalm 1, 119:125, 119:144; Proverbs 2:7, 3:21, 4:5–8, 8:11, 9:9, 10:17, 12:1, 12:15, 13:10, 15:31–32, 16:16, 18:15, 19:8, 20:18, 23:4, 23:12, 29:26; Ecclesiastes 7:5, 7:12, 9:10; Isaiah 50:5; Jeremiah 6:10; Ezekiel 28:4. On the issue of the ears being the seat of intelligence see Doukhan, J. B. (1993). *Hebrew for theologians: A textbook for the study of biblical Hebrew in relation to Hebrew thinking*. Lanham, MD: University Press of America. p. 194.
80. Proverbs 11:28.
81. Matthew 5:13–16; 2 Timothy 2:21, 4:11; Philemon 1:11.
82. Grudem, W. (2003). *Business for the glory of God: The Bible's teaching on the moral goodness of business*. Wheaton, IL: Crossway Books. p. 28.
83. Proverbs 18:9; Titus 3:14.
84. Deuteronomy 20:6; Proverbs 27:18; 1 Corinthians 9:7.
85. Matthew 21:33–41; Mark 12:1–9; Luke 20:9–15.
86. See on this passage commentary by Golding, T. A. (2006). The imagery of shepherding in the Bible, Part 2. *Bibliotheca Sacra*. 163, 161.
87. Psalm 34:14, 72:7, 122:6–7; Romans 14:19; 2 Timothy 2:22; Hebrews 12:14; 1 Peter 3:11.
88. Genesis 1:11–12, 1:29. Sowing and reaping are mentioned several times in Scripture. The implication is that agrarian workers sowed seed with the expectation that the harvest (yield) would exceed the amount sown. Sometimes these terms refer to actual agrarian activities. Other times the concepts are used metaphorically to refer to spiritual dynamics. On sowing and reaping see Leviticus 25:11; 2 Kings 19:29; Ecclesiastes 11:4; Isaiah 37:30; Hosea 8:7, 10:12; Micah 6:15.
89. Genesis 1:22, 1:28, 8:17, 9:1, 9:7, 17:6, 17:20, 26:22, 28:3, 35:11, 41:52, 47:27, 48:4; Exodus 1:7, 23:30; Leviticus 26:9; Psalm 105:24, 107:33–40; Isaiah 5:5–6, 24:1–3, 45:18.
90. Proverbs 18:9; Matthew 5:13–16; 2 Timothy 2:21, 4:11; Titus 3:14; Philemon 1:11.
91. 1 Samuel 12:21; Job 22:2; Proverbs 1:17, 14:15, 26:7; Ecclesiastes 10:10; Isaiah 59:6; Jeremiah 13:7–10; Ezekiel 15:3–5; Luke 14:35; Ephesians 4:28, 5:16; Colossians 4:5; 1 Thessalonians 3:5; 2 Timothy 2:14, 2:21, 3:16, 4:11; Titus 1:8, 2:2–6, 3:9; Philemon 1:11; Hebrews 6:7.

92. Ecclesiastes 10:10.
93. Isaiah 28:23–29.
94. Proverbs 25:28; Acts 24:25; 1 Corinthians 7:5, 9:24–27; Galatians 5:16–17, 5:23; Romans 7:15–25; 2 Timothy 3:3; 2 Peter 1:6.
95. See Appendix D: Technology in the Bible.
96. Proverbs 1:17.
97. 1 Kings 7:9–11.
98. 1 Kings 7:37.
99. Genesis 47–51.
100. Genesis 26:12–25; 2 Chronicles 31:21; Ruth; Nehemiah; Judges 6; 1 Corinthians 4:12; Matthew 20, 25; Luke 15; Acts 5:42, 20:33–35; 2 Corinthians 8:22.
101. Deuteronomy 29:23; 2 Kings 2:19; Proverbs 26:7; Ezekiel 15:3–5; Luke 13:6–7, 14:35; Hebrews 6:8.
102. Ecclesiastes 3:2. See also Matthew 3:10; Luke 3:9, 13:6–7.
103. Whybray, R. N. (1989). Ecclesiastes. In Clements, R. E. (Ed.). *New century Bible commentary*. (Vol. 21). Grand Rapids, MI: William B. Eerdmans Publishing Company. pp. 53–54. See also Ecclesiastes 2:4–6; Song of Solomon 6:11, 7:12, 8:11–12. Though these passages may be symbolic of Solomon's romantic relationship, they reveal practices of tending vineyards.
104. Leviticus 25:3–4; John 15:1–2.
105. Genesis 26:12; Matthew 13:8, 13:23; Mark 4:8, 4:20; 2 Corinthians 9:6.
106. Proverbs 1:17, 24:27; Ecclesiastes 10:9–10.
107. Proverbs 16:11.
108. Kiuchi, N. (2007). Leviticus. In Baker, D. W., & Wenham, G. J. (Eds.). *Apollos Old Testament commentary*. (Vol. 3). Downers Grove, IL: Intervarsity *Press*.
109. Deuteronomy 32:2; Psalm 1:3, 92:12–14; Isaiah 55:10–11; Matthew 3:10, 7:18–19; Luke 3:9, 13:6–9, 14:34–35; John 15:1–2; Hebrews 6:7–8; Jude 1:12.
110. Ephesians 5:16; Colossians 4:5.
111. Exodus 20:15; Leviticus 19:11; Deuteronomy 5:19; 1 Kings 21; Matthew 19:18; Mark 10:19; Luke 18:20; Romans 13:9; Ephesians 4:28.
112. Kast, R. E., & Rosenzweig, J. E. (1972). General systems theory: Applications for organization and management. *Academy of Management Journal*. 15(4), 447–465; Katz, D., & Kahn, R. L. (1978). *The social psychology of organizations*. (2nd ed.). New York: John Wiley. pp. 1–34; Scott, W. R. (1987). *Organizations: Rational, natural and open systems*. Englewood Cliffs, NJ: Prentice Hall; Koontz, H. (1980). The management theory jungle revisited. *The Academy of Management Review*. 5(2), 175–187.
113. Drucker, P. F. (2001). *The essential Drucker*. New York: HarperBusiness.
114. Romans 8:38–39; Ephesians 3:10, 6:12; Colossians 1:16, 2:15; 1 Peter 3:22.
115. Bretsen, S. N. (2008). The creation, the Kingdom of God, and a theory of the faithful corporation. *Christian Scholar's Review*. 38(1), 140; Herman, S. W. (1997). *Durable goods: A covenantal ethic for management and employees*. Notre Dame, IN: University of Notre Dame Press; Byron, W. J. (1988). Twin towers: A philosophy and theology of business. *Journal of Business Ethics*. 7(7), 525–530; Rossouw, G. J. (1994). Business ethics: Where have all the Christians gone? *Journal of Business Ethics*. 13(7), 557–570; Rodger SJC, (1998). A summary of Christian social teaching. In Oslington, P. (Ed.). *Economics and religion. Volume I*. Northampton, MA: Edward Elgar Publishing. pp. 446–492; Alford, H. J., & Naughton, M. J. (2001). *Managing as if faith mattered: Christian social principles in the modern organization*. Notre Dame, IN: University of Notre Dame Press. pp. 1–98; Williams CSC, O. F. (Ed.). (2003). *Business, religion, and spirituality: A new synthesis*. Notre Dame, IN: University of Notre Dame Press. pp. 31–52. Compare with the assertions of Peter Drucker who advocated that we view business as integral with society. See Drucker, P. F. (2001). *The essential Drucker*. New York: HarperBusiness. pp. 3–68.
116. See for example Romans 12:4–5; 1 Peter 4:8–11; Higginson, R. (1993). *Called to account—Adding value in God's world: Integrating Christianity and business effectively*. Guildford, Surrey: Eagle. pp. 49–51; Goldingay, J. (2006). *Old Testament theology. vol. 1: Israel's faith*. Downers Grove, IL: IVP Academic. pp. 527–537, 564–567; Tiemstra, J. P., Graham, W. F., Monsma, G. N., Sinke, C. J., Storkey, A., & Ebels, D. M. (1990). *Reforming economics: Calvinist studies on methods and institutions*. Lewiston, NY: The Edwin Mellen Press. p. 167.
117. Thompson, J. D. (1967). *Organizations in action*. New York: McGraw-Hill; Lawrence, P. R., & Lorsch, J. W. (1967). *Organization and environment*. Homewood, IL: Richard D. Irwin; Duncan, R. (1972). Characteristics of organizational environment and perceived environmental uncertainty. *Administrative Science Quarterly*. 17, 313–327; Shepard, J. M., & Hougland Jr., J. G. (1978). Contingency theory: "Complex man" or "complex organization"? *The Academy of Management Review*. 3(3), 413–427; Mealiea, L. W., & Lee, D. (1979). An alternative to macro-micro contingency theories: An integrative model. *The Academy of Management Review*. 4(3), 333–345; Simon, H. A. (1997). *Administrative behavior*. (4th ed.). New York: The Free Press. pp. 29–54; Mintzberg, H., & Westley, F. (2001). Decision making: It's not what you think. *MIT Sloan Management Review*. 42(3), 89–93; Drejer, A. (2004). Back to basics and beyond: Strategic management—an area where practice and theory are poorly related. *Management Decision*. 42(3/4), 508–520.
118. Housman, D. M., & McPherson, M. S. (1993). Taking ethics seriously: Economics and contemporary moral philosophy. *Journal of Economic Literature*. 32(2), 671–731; Barnard, C. I. (1938). *The functions of the executive*. Cambridge, MA: Harvard University Press. pp. 82–113; Schein, E. H. (1989). Reassessing the "divine rights" of managers. *Sloan Management Review*. 30(2), 63–68.
119. Exodus 20:12; Numbers 16:1–35, 17:1–10, 25:1–5; 1 Samuel 24:1–7, 26:9; 2 Samuel 19:21; Romans 13:1–5; Titus 3:1; Hebrews 13:17; 1 Peter 5:4–5.
120. Deuteronomy 1:17; 2 Samuel 23:4ff; Proverbs 3:27, 10:9–10, 11:1, 11:17, 11:26, 12:17, 16:11–13, 17:23, 21:3, 23:24–25, 24:28, 25:13, 28:16, 29:4; Ecclesiastes 7:7, 8:9.
121. Fairholm, G. W. (2009). *Organizational power politics*. (2nd ed.). Santa Barbara, CA: Praeger. pp. 23–30.
122. Leviticus 19:18; Mark 12:33; Luke 10:27; 1 Corinthians 9:25; Galatians 5:22–23; Titus 1:8.

123. Job; Psalm 52:7; Proverbs 11:28, 23:5, 27:1, 27:23–26; Ecclesiastes 5:13–14, 6:12, 8:7, 9:11–12, 10:14, 11:1–6; Jeremiah 9:23–24, 17:8–9; Matthew 6:32–34, 24:42–50; Philippians 4:6–7; 1 Timothy 6:17; 1 Peter 5:7; James 4:13–16.
124. Proverbs 3:6.
125. Matthew 25:14–30; Luke 16:1–12.
126. Leviticus 25:3–4; John 15:1–2.
127. Numbers 13:19–20. Cf. Joshua 5:12.
128. Genesis 30–31, 30:43; Proverbs 27:23–24.
129. Vredenburgh, D., & Brender, Y. (1998). The hierarchical abuse of power in work organizations. *Journal of Business Ethics*. 17(12), 1337–1347.
130. Sorensen, J. B. (2002). The strength of corporate culture and the reliability of firm performance. *Administrative Science Quarterly*. 47, 70–91; Chatman, J. A., & Cha, S. E. (2003). Leading by leveraging culture. *California Management Review*. 45(4), 20–34.
131. Hambrick, D. C., & Mason, P. A. (1984). Upper echelons: The organization as a reflection of its top managers. *The Academy of Management Review*. 9(2), 193–206.
132. Hatch, M. J., & Cunliff, A. (2006). *Organization theory: Modern symbolic and postmodern perspectives*. (2nd ed.). Oxford: Oxford University Press. p. 207.
133. Drucker, P. F. (1998). Management's new paradigms. *Forbes*. 162(7), 152–169; Drucker, P. F. (1999). *Management challenges for the 21st century*. New York: HarperBusiness. pp. 1–40; Stamps, D. (1997). A conversation with doctor paradox. *Training*. 34(5), 42–48; Gorman, C. K. (2008). Watch your language. *T&D*. 62(8), 94–95; Locke, R. R. (1996). *The collapse of the American management mystique*. Oxford: Oxford University Press. pp. 158–208.
134. Simons, R., Mintzberg, H., & Basu, K. (2002). Five half-truths of business. *Fast Company*. 59, 117–121; Kurtz, C. F., & Snowden, D. J. (2003). The new dynamics of strategy: Sense-making in a complex world. *IBM Systems Journal*. 42(3), 462–483.
135. Peter, L. J., & Hull, R. (1969). *The Peter principle: Why things always go wrong*. New York: William Morrow.
136. Hamel, G., & Breen, B. (2007). *The future of management*. Boston, MA: Harvard Business School. pp. 154–183.
137. Chewning, R. C., Eby, J. W., & Roels, S. J. (1990). *Business through the eyes of faith*. San Francisco, CA: HarperSanFrancisco. pp. 39–42. See also the discussion of the tension between humans as sinners and humans as bearing the image of God in Carson, K. (2001). *Tensions facing Christians in business: A proposed framework for guiding students*. Paper presented to the Annual Conference of the Christian Business Faculty Association. Bourbonnais, IL. Fall.
138. As examples see Nash, L. L. (1994). *Believers in business*. Nashville, TN: Thomas Nelson Publishers. pp. 56–266; Nash, L., & McLennan, S. (2001). *Church on Sunday, work on Monday*. San Francisco, CA: Jossey-Bass. pp. 3–69; Carson, K. (2001). Tensions facing Christians in business: A proposed framework for guiding students. Paper presented to the Christian Business Faculty Association Annual Conference. Bourbonnais, IL. October; Hoyce, G. (1981). The dilemmas of Christians in business. *The Christian Century*. 98(25), 802–804; Chewning, R. C., Eby, J. W., & Roels, S. J. (1990). *Business through the eyes of faith. San Francisco*, CA: HarperSanFrancisco. pp. 73–83; Johnson, S. (1988). *Values-driven people: A Christian approach to management*. Dallas, TX: Probe Books. pp. 16–22; Hicks, D. A. (2003). *Religion and the workplace: Pluralism, spirituality, leadership*. Cambridge: Cambridge University Press. pp. 63–88.
139. Cameron, K. S., & Quinn, R. E. (1988). Organizational paradox and transformation. In Quinn, R. E., & Cameron, K. S. (Eds.). *Paradox and transformation: Toward a theory of change in organization and management*. Cambridge, MA: Ballinger. pp. 1–18; Lewis, M. W., & Dehler, G. E. (2000). Learning through paradox: A pedagogical strategy for exploring contradictions and complexity. *Journal of Management Education*. 24(6), 708–725.
140. Blank, R. M. (2005). Market behavior and Christian behavior. In Henderson, J. W., & Pisciotta, J. (Eds.). *Faithful economics: The moral worlds of a neutral science*. Waco, TX: Baylor University Press. p. 49.
141. Martinez, R. J. (2004). Defining and developing a space for business scholarship in the Christian academy. *Christian Scholar's Review*. 34(1), 55–74.
142. Attributed to St. Augustine of Hippo.
143. Attributed to St. Jerome, quoted in Chewning, R. C., Eby, J. W., & Roels, S. J. (1990). *Business through the eyes of faith*. San Francisco, CA: HarperSanFrancisco, p. ix.
144. Baudelaire, C. P. (1957). *The intimate journals*. Isherwood, C. (Trans.). Boston, MA: Beacon Press. p. 51. [Baudelaire was a French poet and art critic.]
145. 1 Timothy 6:9–10.
146. Matthew 19:24.
147. Hardy, L. (1990). *The fabric of this world: Inquiries into calling, career choice, and the design of human work*. Grand Rapids, MI: William B. Eerdmans Publishing Company. p. 48.
148. Novak, M. (1996). *Business as a calling: Work and the examined life*. New York: The Free Press. p. 37.
149. Matthew 25:40.
150. 1 Peter 4:10–11.
151. Proverbs 3:9.
152. Colossians 3:17.
153. Drucker, P. F. (1995). The information executives truly need. *Harvard Business Review*. 73(1), 59.

Appendix A
Selected Hebrew and Greek Words Relevant to Managers

The following selected Hebrew and Greek words found in the Bible are relevant to the study of management from the Christian perspective. They are provided for students who wish to engage the Bible on the topic of management at a deeper level. Hebrew and Greek words have been transliterated into English. For each Hebrew and Greek word one or more Bible passages are given where that particular word is used. This is not intended to be a comprehensive listing of all management concepts for which the Bible offers instruction. Also, it is not intended to be a comprehensive list of all Hebrew and Greek words related to management or all passages where these words are found. For some words that are commonly used in the Bible representative passages are provided. Hebrew and Greek words are organized into groups according to contemporary management concepts. These groups are listed alphabetically.

The groups presented here are as follows:

Accountability
Agent
Authority
Command
Communication
Conflict
Covenant
Decision making
Managers, leaders
Motivation
Organize
Peace (Shalom)
Planning
Power
Quality
Safety
Utility maximization
Wages
Wealth
Work

Accountability

Key English words: test, judge, judgment, conceal, truth, account, examine, prove, proving, tried, try.

Old Testament Hebrew

Bachan (test) Job 7:18, 12:11; Psalm 11:4, 17:3, 26:2, 66:10, 95:9, 139:23; Jeremiah 12:3, 17:10, 20:12; Zechariah 13:9; Malachi 3:10, 3:15.

Chaphas (to search) Lamentations 3:40.

Emeth (faithfulness, firmness, truth) Exodus 18:21, 34:6; Judges 9:16, 9:19; 1 Samuel 12:24; 2 Samuel 2:6, 7:28, 15:20; 1 Kings 2:4, 3:6, 17:24, 22:16; 2 Kings 20:3, 20:19; 2 Chronicles 18:15; Esther 9:30; Psalm 15:2, 25:5, 25:10, 26:3, 31:5, 43:3, 85:10–11, 86:11, 86:15, 89:14, 108:4, 111:7–8, 115:1, 117:2, 119:43, 119:142, 119:160, 145:18; Proverbs 3:3, 8:7, 14:22, 16:6, 20:28, 23:23, 29:14.

Emunah (firmness, steadfastness, fidelity) Proverbs 12:17.

Omnam (verily, truly) Job 9:2.

Nakar (to regard, recognize) Genesis 37:32, 38:25.

Nasah (test, try) Exodus 16:4, 20:20; Numbers 14:22; Deuteronomy 6:16, 8:16, 33:8; Judges 2:22, 3:1, 6:39; 1 Kings 10:1; 2 Chronicles 9:1, 32:31; Psalm 26:2, 78:18; Ecclesiastes 2:1; Isaiah 7:12; Daniel 1:12.

Paqad (attend to, visit, muster) Job 7:18.

Qadash (to be set apart, consecrated) Ezekiel 20:41, 36:23.

Tsaraph (smelt, refine, test) Judges 7:4; Psalm 18:30, 26:2.

Yakach (to decide, adjudge, prove) Job 6:25, 19:5.

New Testament Greek

Adokimos (not standing the test, rejected) 2 Corinthians 13:5–6.

Aletheia (truth) Mark 5:33, 12:14; Luke 4:25; John 1:14, 1:17, 3:21, 4:23–24, 8:32, 8:44–46, 14:17, 15:26, 16:13, 17:17, 17:19, 18:38; Romans 1:18, 1:25, 2:8, 2:20; 1 Corinthians 13:6; 2 Corinthians 4:2, 6:7, 7:14, 13:8; Ephesians 4:21, 4:24; 1 John 5:7.

Aletheuo (speak the truth) Ephesians 4:15, 4:25, 5:9, 6:14.

Anakrino (to examine, investigate) 1 Corinthians 4:3, 9:3, 14:24.

Anetazo (to examine judicially) Acts 22:29.

Apodeiknumi (to bring out, show forth, declare) Acts 25:7.

Asphaleia (certainty, security) Luke 1:4.

Diegeomai (to relate fully) Luke 9:10.

Dokimazo (test, to approve) Luke 14:19; 1 Corinthians 3:13, 11:28; 2 Corinthians 8:8, 13:5; 1 John 4:1; Romans 12:2; Galatians 6:4; 1 Thessalonians 5:21.

Dokime (process of trial, proving, approval) 2 Corinthians 2:9.

Ekpeirazo (test thoroughly, tempt) Matthew 4:7; Luke 4:12, 10:25; 1 Corinthians 10:9.

Episcope (a visiting, overseeing) Luke 19:44; Acts 1:20; 1 Timothy 3:1; 1 Peter 2:12.

Ginomai (to become, come into being) John 15:8; Acts 26:19; Romans 15:31; 1 Corinthians 15:10; Philippians 2:15; James 1:22; 1 Peter 3:13, 5:3.

Krino (to judge) Acts 23:3, 25:10.

Logos (word, speech) Matthew 12:36; Luke 16:2; Romans 14:12; Philippians 4:17; Hebrews 13:17; 1 Peter 3:15, 4:5.

Logizomai (to reckon, to consider) Romans 4:8; 1 Corinthians 13:5.

Paristemi (to place beside, to present, appear) Acts 24:13.

Peirazo (make proof of, test, tempt) Mark 8:11; Luke 11:16; John 6:6; Acts 5:9, 15:10; 2 Corinthians 13:5; Hebrews 3:9; Revelation 2:2, 3:10.

Sunistemi (to commend, establish, stand near) Galatians 2:18.

Agent

Key English words: steward, messenger, servant.

Old Testament Hebrew

Asher (steward) Genesis 43:16, 44:1, 44:4.

Basar (to bear tidings) Isaiah 41:27.

Malak (messenger) 1 Samuel 23:27; 2 Samuel 11:19, 11:22–23, 11:25, 15:13; 1 Kings 19:2, 22:3; 2 Kings 5:10, 6:32–33, 9:18, 10:8; 2 Chronicles 18:12; Job 1:14; Proverbs 13:17, 17:11; Ecclesiastes 5:6; Isaiah 42:19; Ezekiel 23:40; Haggai 1:13; Malachi 2:7, 3:1.

Nagad (to be conspicuous) Jeremiah 51:31.

Sakan (to be of service) Isaiah 22:15.

Teem (taste, judgment, command) Daniel 6:2.

Tsir (envoy) Proverbs 25:13.

New Testament Greek

Aggelos (messenger, angel) Matthew 11:10; Mark 1:2; Luke 7:27; 2 Corinthians 12:7.

Apostello (to be sent) Mark 3:14.

Apostolos (one sent on a mission, messenger, an apostle) Matthew 10:12; Mark 6:30; Luke 6:13, 9:10, 11:49, 17:5, 22:14, 24:10; John 13:16; Acts 1:2, 1:26, 2:37, 2:42–43, 4:33, 4:35–37, 5:2, 5:12, 5:18, 5:29, 5:40 [and many other times in Acts]; Romans 1:1, 11:13, 16:7; 1 Corinthians 1:1, 4:9, 9:1–2, 9:5; Philippians 2:25; 1 Thessalonians 2:6–7.

Epitropos (administrator, one having authority) Luke 8:3.

Oikonomos (manager of household) Luke 12:42, 16:1–3, 16:8; Titus 1:7.

Presbeuo (to be the elder, take precedence) 2 Corinthians 5:20.

Authority

Key English words: authority, over.

Old Testament Words

Al (upon, above, over) Genesis 39:3, 39:5, 41:33, 41:40–41, 41:43, 41:45, 42:6; Exodus 1:8, 1:11, 2:14, 5:14, 18:21, 18:25; Numbers 10:15, 27:16; Deuteronomy 1:15, 17:14–15, 28:36; Judges 9:14–15, 9:18, 11:11; 1 Samuel 8:7, 8:9, 8:11, 8:19, 9:16, 10:1, 10:19, 11:12, 12:1, 12:12–14, 13:1, 13:14, 14:47, 15:1, 15:17, 15:26, 15:35, 18:5, 19:20, 22:2, 23:17, 25:30; 2 Samuel 2:4, 2:7, 2:9–11, 3:10, 5:2–3, 5:5, 5:12, 5:17, 7:8, 7:11, 8:15, 12:7, 19:22, 20:23; 1 Kings 1:34–35, 2:11, 2:35, 4:1, 4:4–7, 5:7, 5:14, 5:16, 8:16, 9:5, 9:23, 11:37; 2 Kings 11:18; Esther 8:2.

El (to, into, towards) 1 Samuel 22:14; 2 Samuel 2:9, 23:23.

Hod (splendor, majesty, vigor) Numbers 27:20; Isaiah 30:30.

Kisse or *kisseh* (seat of honor, throne) Esther 3:1.

Mashal (rule, dominion) Exodus 21:8; Judges 14:4, 15:11; Psalm 8:6; Proverbs 22:7.

Memshalah (rule, dominion, realm) Isaiah 22:21.

Mimshal (dominion, ruler) Daniel 11:3.

Moshel (dominion) Daniel 11:4.

Radah or *radaph* (to have dominion, rule, dominate) Leviticus 25:43, 25:46, 25:53, 26:17.

Seeth (exaltation, dignity, swelling, uprising) Habakkuk 1:7.

Shallat (to domineer, be master of) Ecclesiastes 8:9.

Shallit (having mastery, domineering) Ecclesiastes 8:8; Daniel 5:29.

Shelet (to have power, rule) Daniel 5:7, 5:16.

Tachath (underneath, below, instead of) Numbers 5:19–20, 5:29.

Toqeph (power, strength, energy) Esther 9:29, 10:2.

Tsaphan (to hide, treasure up) Job 34:13.

Yad (hand) Genesis 16:9, 41:35; Judges 9:29; 2 Chronicles 23:18, 31:13, 31:15; Jeremiah 5:31, 38:10–11.

New Testament Words

Authenteo (to govern, exercise authority) 1 Timothy 2:12.

Baros (weight) 1 Thessalonians 2:6.

Epi (upon) Luke 1:33, 9:1, 10:19, 12:14, 19:14, 19:27; Acts 7:10, 7:18, 7:27; Revelation 9:11, 11:6, 13:7, 16:9.

Epitage (a command) Titus 2:15.

Exousia (power to act, authority) Matthew 7:29, 8:9, 9:6, 9:8, 10:1, 21:23–24, 21:27, 28:18; Mark 1:22, 1:27, 2:10, 3:15, 6:7, 11:28–29, 11:33; Luke 4:32, 4:36, 5:24, 7:8, 9:1, 10:19, 12:5, 19:17, 20:2, 20:8, 20:20; John 5:27, 10:18, 17:2, 19:10–11; Acts 1:7, 8:19, 9:14, 26:10, 26:12; Romans 13:1–3; 1 Corinthians 7:37, 11:10, 15:24; 2 Corinthians 10:8, 13:10; Ephesians 1:21; Colossians 2:10; Jude 1:25; Revelation 2:26, 6:8, 12:10, 13:2, 13:4–5, 13:7, 13:12, 17:12, 17:13, 18:1.

Exousiazo (to exercise authority over) Luke 22:25; 1 Corinthians 7:4.

Huperecho (to hold above, to rise above, to be superior) 1 Peter 2:13.

Huperoche (a projection, eminence) 1 Timothy 2:2.

Katexousiazo (to exercise authority over) Matthew 20:25; Mark 10:42.

Kuriotes (lordship) 2 Peter 2:10; Jude 1:8.

Command

Key English words: command, commanded, commanding, charge.

Old Testament Hebrew

Amar (to utter, say) Esther 1:10, 1:17, 9:25.

Dabar (speak) Exodus 1:17.

Mitsvah (commandment) Leviticus 4:2.

Tsavah (to lay charge, to give charge, command, order) Genesis 2:16, 3:11, 3:17, 6:22, 7:5, 7:9, 7:16, 12:20, 21:4; Exodus 1:22, 7:6, 19:7, 31:6, 36:5, 38:22; Deuteronomy 28:45; Joshua 1:7, 1:10, 4:17, 6:10, 7:11, 8:4; Judges 2:20, 21:10, 21:20; Ruth 2:9, 2:15, 3:6; 1 Samuel 17:20, 18:22, 20:29; 2 Samuel 4:12, 7:7, 7:11, 13:28–29, 14:19, 21:14; 1 Kings 2:46, 22:31; 2 Kings 11:9, 16:15, 17:35, 22:12; Esther 2:20, 3:2.

New Testament Greek

Appaggello or *paraggello* (to announce what must be done; to order) Matthew 10:5, 15:35; Mark 6:8, 8:6, 16:8; Luke 5:14, 8:29, 8:56, 9:21; Acts 1:4, 4:18, 5:28, 5:40, 10:42, 15:5, 16:18, 16:23, 17:30, 23:22, 23:30; 1 Corinthians 7:10, 11:17; 1 Thessalonians 4:11; 2 Thessalonians 3:4, 3:6, 3:10, 3:12; 1 Timothy 1:3, 4:11, 5:7, 6:13, 6:17.

Entellomai (to give definite orders, implying authority or official sanction) Matthew 4:6, 17:9, 19:7, 29:30; Mark 10:3, 13:34; Luke 4:10; John 8:5, 14:31, 15:14, 15:17; Acts 1:2, 13:47; Hebrews 9:20, 11:22.

Epitimao (to command with the implication of a negative consequence that might follow if the command is not obeyed) Matthew 8:26, 12:16, 16:22, 17:18, 19:13, 20:31; Mark 1:25, 3:12, 4:39, 8:30, 8:32, 8:33, 9:25, 10:13, 10:48; Luke 4:35, 4:39, 4:41, 8:24, 9:21, 9:42, 9:55, 17:3, 18:15, 18:39, 19:39, 23:40; 2 Timothy 4:2; Jude 1:9.

Keleuo (order, command, to state with force or authority what others must do) Matthew 8:18, 14:9, 14:19, 14:28, 18:25, 27:58, 27:64; Mark 7:36; Luke 18:40; Acts 4:15, 5:34, 8:38, 12:19, 16:22, 21:33–34, 22:24, 22:30, 23:3, 23:10, 23:35, 25:6, 25:17, 25:21, 25:23, 27:43; 1 Thessalonians 4:16.

Communication

Key English words: mouth, tongue, speech, speak, speaks, speaking, spoke, spoken, lips, throat, slander, babbling, integrity, answer, gossip, boast, boasting, boasted, boastful, talk, mock, scoff, scoffed, scoffer, scoffers, mocked, mock, voice, voices, write, written, reply, report, reports, reported, reporting, teaching, preaching, letter, letters, keep silent, keeps silent, kept silent, messenger, messengers, message.

Old Testament Hebrew

Amar (to speak, to utter, to say) Genesis 12:12–13, 12:19, 32:4, 45:17; Exodus 3:13, 3:15–16, 20:22; Numbers 5:12.

Barak (to kneel, bless) Deuteronomy 29:19.

Dabar (to speak, word) Genesis 18:27; Exodus 4:15; Leviticus 1:2; Deuteronomy 3:26; Joshua 4:10; Judges 9:2; 1 Samuel 2:3, 15:16; 2 Samuel 3:19; Proverbs 23:33.

Dibbah (whispering, defamation, evil report) Genesis 37:2; Numbers 13:32; Psalm 31:13; Proverbs 10:18.

Emer (speech, word) Isaiah 32:7.

Hagah (to moan, growl, utter, speak, muse) Psalm 71:24; Proverbs 8:7.

Halal (to be boastful, to praise) 1 Kings 20:11; Psalm 34:2, 52:1, 75:4; Proverbs 27:1; Jeremiah 9:23.

Lashon, lashan, lashonah (tongue) Exodus 4:10; Job 27:4; Psalm 12:3, 52:2; Proverbs 6:17, 10:31, 12:18–19, 15:2, 17:4, 30:10.

Millah (a word, thing) Daniel 5:15, 5:26.

Naba (to flow, spring, bubble up) Psalm 78:2, 119:171, 145:7.

Nathan (to give, put, set) Psalm 50:20.

Pathah (to be spacious, wide, or open) Proverbs 20:19.

Peh (mouth) Numbers 30:2; Deuteronomy 8:3, 18:18, 30:14, 32:1; Joshua 1:8, 6:10; 1 Samuel 1:12, 2:1, 2:3.

Ragal (to go about on foot) Psalm 15:3.

Saphah (lips) Leviticus 5:4; Psalm 12:2, 12:4.

Shemuah or *shema* (a report) Exodus 23:1; Isaiah 28:9, 53:1; Jeremiah 49:14.

New Testament Greek

Aggelia (message, report) 1 John 1:5, 3:11.

Akoe (hearing) 1 Thessalonians 2:13.

Apologeomai (to give an account of oneself, to defend oneself) Luke 12:11.

Apophtheggomai (to speak forth) Acts 26:25.

Blasphemeo or *blasphemia* (to slander, to speak lightly or profanely of sacred things) Mark 3:28, 7:22; Ephesians 4:31; Colossians 3:8.

Didomi (to give) 1 Corinthians 14:9.

Ereugomai (to spit, to speak aloud) Matthew 13:35.

Glossa (tongue) James 1:26, 3:5–6; 1 Peter 3:10.

Kakologeo (to speak ill of) Mark 9:39.

Katalalia or *katalaleo* (evil speaking) 1 Peter 2:1, 2:12.

Kauchaomai or *kauchema* (to boast) Romans 2:17, 2:23, 4:2; 1 Corinthians 1:29, 1:31, 3:21, 4:7, 9:15–16; Galatians 6:13–14; Ephesians 2:9; Hebrews 3:6; James 4:16.

Laleo (to talk) Matthew 10:19–20, 12:34, 12:36, 12:46–47; Ephesians 4:25.

Lego (to say) Matthew 10:27, 11:7,12:32; Luke 12:10.

Logos (word, statement, speech) Luke 4:32, 4:36; Acts 4:4, 10:44, 15:32, 20:7; 1 Corinthians 2:4; Ephesians 1:13; 2 Thessalonians 2:2.

Psithurismos (a whispering, gossip) 2 Corinthians 12:20.

Rhema (word) Acts 5:20, 10:22.

Stoma (mouth) Matthew 5:2, 12:34–35; Ephesians 4:29; Colossians 3:8.

Conflict

Key English words: adversary, controversy, strife, contention, controversies, dispute, disputes, disputation, disputations, peace, shalom, accuse, conflict, quarrel, complain.

Old Testament Hebrew

Anah (answer, respond) Deuteronomy 19:16; 2 Kings 5:7.

Anan (complain, murmur) Numbers 11:1.

Dabar (speech, word) Exodus 18:16, 8:19, 8:22, 8:26.

Din (judgment) Proverbs 22:10; Ecclesiastes 6:10.

Galah (expose, lay bare) Proverbs 20:3.

Garah (stir up strife) Jeremiah 50:24.

Madon (strife, contention) Psalm 80:6; Proverbs 6:14, 15:18, 16:28, 22:10, 26:20, 28:25; Jeremiah 15:10; Habakkuk 1:3.

Matstsah (strife, contention) Proverbs 13:10, 17:19; Isaiah 58:4.

Matstsuth (strife, contention) Isaiah 41:12.

Medan or *medon* (strife) Proverbs 6:19, 10:12, 29:22.

Meribah (strife) Genesis 13:8; Numbers 27:14.

Ragaz (agitated, excited, perturbed) Genesis 45:24.

Rib (strife, dispute) Genesis 13:7, 26:22; Exodus 17:2, 17:7, 21:18, 23:2–3, 23:6; Deuteronomy 1:12, 17:8, 19:17, 21:5, 25:1; Judges 12:2, 21:2; 2 Chronicles 19:8, 19:10; Job 9:3, 33:13; Psalm 31:20, 55:9; Proverbs 15:18, 17:1, 17:14, 18:6, 20:3, 26:17, 26:21, 30:33; Isaiah 58:4; Jeremiah 15:10, 25:31; Ezekiel 44:24; Hosea 12:2; Habakkuk 1:3.

Satan (act as an adversary) Zechariah 3:1.

Shaphat (to judge) Proverbs 29:9.

Siach (to muse, complain, talk of) Job 7:11; Psalm 55:17.

Tsaba (army, warfare) Daniel 10:1.

Yakach (to decide; adjudge, prove) Micah 6:2.

Zaaq (to cry out, to call) 2 Samuel 19:28.

New Testament Greek

Agon (gathering, contest, struggle) Philippians 1:30.

Antilogia (gainsaying, contradiction) Hebrews 6:16, 7:7.

Athlesis (contest) Hebrews 10:32.

Eris (strife) Romans 1:29, 13:3; 1 Corinthians 3:3; 2 Corinthians 12:20; Galatians 5:20; Philippians 1:15; 1 Timothy 6:4; Titus 3:9.

Eritheia (ambitious rivalry) 2 Corinthians 12:20; Galatians 5:20.

Erizo (to wrangle, strive) Matthew 12:19.

Kategoreo (make accusation) Matthew 12:10; Mark 3:2, 15:3; Luke 6:7, 23:2; John 5:45; Acts 24:2, 24:8, 24:13, 25:11.

Logomachia (strife of words) 1 Timothy 6:4.

Mache (fight) Titus 3:9.

Philoneikia (love of strife) Luke 22:24.

Polemeo (make war) James 4:2.

Stenazo (to groan within oneself) James 5:9.

Sukophanteo (to accuse falsely) Luke 3:14.

Suzetesis (disputation) Acts 28:29.

Zetesis (a search, questioning) Titus 3:9.

Covenant

Key English words: oath, covenant, swear, swore, pledge, vow.

Old Testament

Abot (a pledge, article pledged) Deuteronomy 24:10.

Alah (to swear) 1 Samuel 14:24; Proverbs 29:24.

Berith (covenant) Genesis 6:18, 9:9, 9:11, 15:18, 17:2, 17:4, 21:27, 26:28, 31:44; Exodus 2:24, 6:4, 19:5, 34:28; Deuteronomy 4:13, 29:1; 2 Samuel 5:3; 1 Kings 5:12; 1 Chronicles 16:15; Ezekiel 34:25.

Chabal (to bind, pledge) Exodus 22:26; Deuteronomy 24:6.

Erabon (a pledge) Genesis 38:17–18, 20; Job 17:3.

Neder, *nadar*, or *nedar* (vow) Genesis 28:20, 31:13; Leviticus 22:21, 22:23; Numbers 6:2, 6:5; Deuteronomy 12:11, 23:21; Ecclesiastes 5:5.

Oth (a sign) Joshua 2:12.

Shaba or *shebuah* (to swear) Genesis 21:31, 24:8, 50:24; Exodus 22:11; Leviticus 5:4; Numbers 5:19; Deuteronomy 7:8; 1 Samuel 14:26, 20:17; Nehemiah 5:12; Psalm 105:9; Ecclesiastes 8:2.

New Testament

Anathematizo (to declare anathema, devote to destruction) Acts 23:12, 23:14.

Arrabon (an earnest payment—in advance) 2 Corinthians 1:22, 5:5; Ephesians 1:14.

Diatheke (testament, will, covenant) Matthew 26:28; Mark 14:24; Luke 1:72, 22:20; Acts 3:25, 7:8; Romans 11:27; 1 Corinthians 11:25; 2 Corinthians 3:6, 3:14; Galatians 3:15, 3:17; Hebrews 7:22, 8:6, 8:8, 13:20.

Epaggelia or *epaggello* (a summons, a promise) Luke 24:49; Acts 2:33, 2:39, 7:17, 13:23; Romans 4:13–14, 4:16, 4:20, 9:8–9; Galatians 3:14, 3:17–19; Ephesians 2:12, 3:6; Hebrews 6:13, 6:15, 6:17.

Euche (prayer) Acts 18:18, 21:23.

Omnuo (to swear) Matthew 5:34, 5:36.

Hikanos (sufficient, fit) Acts 17:9.

Horkomosia (affirmation on oath) Hebrews 7:20–21, 7:28.

Horkos (an oath) Matthew 14:7, 26:72; Luke 1:73; Acts 2:30; Hebrews 6:16–17; James 5:12.

Decision Making

Key English words: lots, certain, uncertainty, chose, choose, decide, decided, decision, change, conferred, counsel, counsels, consult, consulted, consultation, divination, instruct, judge, judged, know, knowledge, guidance, medium, mediums, mind, reveal, revealed, sorcerer, sorcerers, spiritist, spiritists, understanding, will, wills, wisdom, "do not know."

Old Testament Hebrew

Bachar (choose) Genesis 6:2, 13:11; Exodus 17:9, 18:25; Numbers 16:5, 17:5; Deuteronomy 4:37, 7:7, 10:15, 12:5, 12:11, 12:18, 23:16, 30:19; Joshua 8:3, 9:27, 24:15; 1 Samuel 2:28, 13:2, 17:40; 2 Samuel 6:21, 17:1, 24:12; 1 Kings 8:16, 11:34, 18:23, 18:25; 1 Chronicles 15:2, 21:10, 28:4; 2 Chronicles 6:5; Nehemiah 9:7; Job 7:15, 9:14, 29:25; Psalm 25:12, 65:4, 78:67–68, 78:70; Proverbs 1:29, 3:31; Isaiah 7:16, 56:4, 58:5–6, 65:12, 66:4; Jeremiah 33:24; Ezekiel 20:5; Zechariah 1:17, 2:12.

Barah (to eat) 1 Samuel 17:8.

Goral (lot) Ezekiel 24:6.

Yahab (to give) Deuteronomy 1:13.

New Testament Greek

Eklego (to choose) Mark 13:20; Luke 6:13; John 6:70, 15:16, 15:19; Acts 6:5, 12:22, 13:17, 15:7; Ephesians 1:4; James 2:5.

Eklektos (select, favorite) Romans 16:13; 1 Peter 2:4, 2:6.

Ekloge (divine selection) Romans 9:11, 11:5, 11:28; 1 Thessalonians 1:4.

Epilego (to call or name, to choose) Acts 15:40.

Haireomai (to take, choose) Philippians 1:22.

Managers, Leaders

Key English words: dominion, rule, ruler, appoint, oversee, overseer, captain, governor, inspector, chief, command, prefect, prince, manager, administer, director, preeminent, leader, delegate, taskmaster, taskmasters.

Old Testament Hebrew

Addir (majestic) Jeremiah 30:21.

Alluph (to be a leader or governor) Zechariah 9:7, 12:5–6.

Attud (male goat) Isaiah 14:9.

Ayil (a leader, chief) Exodus 15:15.

Baal (owner, lord) Judges 9:2, 9:3, 9:39, 9:46–47, 9:51.

Mashal (to rule over or have dominion over—just as one nation rules over another and just as God rules over all creation) Judges 8:22–23, 9:2; Genesis 45:26; 2 Chronicles 23:20; Psalm 22:28; Isaiah 3:12; Jeremiah 30:21.

Mismereth (having responsibility for or being in charge of) Numbers 1:53; 1 Chronicles 26:12; 2 Chronicles 23:6, 31:16, 35:2.

Nagas (to press, drive, oppress, exact) [taskmaster] Exodus 3:7, 5:6, 5:10, 5:13–14; Deuteronomy 15:2–3; 1 Samuel 13:6, 14:24; Job 3:18, 39:7; Isaiah 3:5, 3:12, 9:4, 14:2, 53:7, 58:3, 60:17; Zechariah 10:4.

Nagid (leader, ruler, prince) 1 Kings 14:7, 16:2; 2 Kings 20:5; 1 Chronicles 5:2, 12:27, 13:1, 17:7, 28:4; 2 Chronicles 6:5, 11:22; Nehemiah 11:11; Proverbs 28:16; Isaiah 55:4; Ezekiel 28:2.

Nahag (leading, to drive, conduct) 2 Samuel 6:3.

Nasi (one lifted up, chief prince) Exodus 16:22; Leviticus 4:22; Numbers 1:16, 1:44, 2:3, 2:5, 2:7, 2:10, 2:12, 2:14, 3:24, 3:30, 3:32; 1 Kings 8:1; 1 Chronicles 2:10, 4:38, 5:6; 2 Chronicles 1:2.

Nathan (to set upon, to appoint or to delegate) Genesis 41:43; Exodus 18:25.

Natsach (preeminent or enduring) (choir director) Psalm 4:1, 5:1, 6:1, 8:1, 9:1.

Paqad (to appoint, to care for, oversee, to punish) Genesis 39:4, 40:4, 41:34; Leviticus 26:16; 1 Samuel 29:4; 2 Kings 7:17.

Paqid (overseer, inspector, chief governor) Nehemiah 12:42; Jeremiah 20:1.

Pechah (governor, captain, viceroy) 1 Kings 10:15; 2 Chronicles 9:14; Ezra 8:36; Nehemiah 2:7, 2:9, 3:7, 5:14–15, 5:18; Haggai 1:1, 1:14; Malachi 1:8; Ezra 5:3, 5:6, 5:14, 6:6–7, 6:13.

Pera (leader) Judges 5:2.

Qatsiyn (to be a chief ruler or commander) Joshua 10:24; Judges 11:6, 11:11; Proverbs 6:7, 25:15; Isaiah 3:6–7.

Radah (to rule over or tread down) Genesis 1:26, 1:28; 2 Kings 11:15, 11:18, 12:11; Isaiah 14:2.

Razan (to be weighty, judicious, or commanding) Judges 5:3; Psalm 2:2; Proverbs 8:15, 31:4; Isaiah 40:23; Habakkuk 1:10.

Rosh (head) Ezra 7:28; Nehemiah 9:17, 11:17; Hosea 1:11; Micah 3:11.

Sagan (to be a subordinate ruler) Ezra 9:2; Nehemiah 4:14, 4:19; Jeremiah 51:57; Ezekiel 23:12.

Sar (chieftain, chief, ruler, official, captain, prince) Exodus 18:21, 18:25; Judges 7:25, 8:3, 8:6; Judges 10:18; 1 Kings 11:24; 1 Chronicles 15:27; Jeremiah 32:32; Ezekiel 11:1.

Sarar (to rule over or have power over) Numbers 16:13; Esther 1:22; Proverbs 8:16; Isaiah 32:1.

Shalat (to dominate or lord it over others) Nehemiah 5:15; Esther 9:1; Psalm 119:133; Ecclesiastes 2:19, 5:19, 8:9.

Shallit (ruler, governor) Genesis 42:6.

Shoter (official, officer) Exodus 5:10.

Shawmar (to keep, to protect, to preserve, to have charge of) Genesis 4:9, 28:15, 30:31; Proverbs 4:6, 21:23; Ecclesiastes 5:1; Nehemiah 2:8, 3:29; 1 Kings 20:39; 2 Kings 11:5, 22:4, 22:14; 1 Chronicles 23:32; Esther 2:3, 2:8, 2:14–15.

Sigenin (prefect, governor) Daniel 2:48, 3:2–3, 3:27, 6:7.

Ul (leading man, noble) 2 Kings 24:15.

New Testament Greek

Archisunagagos (ruler of a synagogue) Acts 18:8, 18:17.

Architriklinos (chief of a triklinium, i.e., superintendent of a banquet). John 2:8–9.

Archon (ruler, chief) Luke 14:1.

Epitropay (commission, permission, authority to carry out an assignment, full power, full authority) Acts 26:12.

Epitropo (to give permission, to permit, to let, to allow; order, instruct, to allow someone to do something) Acts 26:1.

Epitropos (foreman, manager, guardian, to instruct, steward, leader, guardian, person who guides, directs, shows concern for; someone to whom something is committed) Matthew 20:8; Luke 8:3; Acts 12:20.

Ethnarkas (governor, ruler of the people) 2 Corinthians 11:32.

Hêgemon (leader, governor, guide, one going before) Matthew 10:18, 27:2, 27:11, 27:14–15, 27:21, 27:23, 27:27; Matthew 28:14; Luke 20:20; Acts 23:24, 23:26, 23:33–34; Acts 24:1, 24:10; Acts 26:30; 1 Peter 2:14.

Hêgeomai (to lead, guide, go before) Luke 2:2, 3:1.

Kathegetes (teacher) Matthew 23:10.

Oikonomeo (to manage a household, to be a steward, manage, to administrate achievement of a project, regulate, administer a plan) Luke 16:2.

Oikonomia (management, administration, to put into effect, plan, trust, responsibility to manage, the work of an estate manager, administration for apostles; arrangement, order, plan, state of being arranged; program of instruction, training) Luke 16:2–4.

Oikonomos (given a trust, manager, administrator, trustee, director, manager of a household or estate, public treasurer, treasurer, one who is entrusted with management in connection with transcendent matters, administer) Luke 12:42, 16:1, 16:3, 16:8; 1 Corinthians 4:1–2; Titus 1:7; 1 Peter 4:10; Romans 16:23.

Protos (first, chief) Mark 6:21; Luke 19:47; Acts 13:50, 16:12, 17:4, 25:2, 28:7, 28:17.

Motivation

Key English words: motives, intent, intend, intended, intention, intending, reward, recompense, desire, punish, punished, punishment, correction, chasten, rod.

Old Testament Hebrew

Amar (to utter, say) Exodus 2:14; 2 Samuel 21:16.

Avon (iniquity, guilt, punishment for iniquity) Genesis 4:13, 19:5; Leviticus 5:17, 18:25; 1 Samuel 28:10; 2 Kings 7:9; Job 19:29.

Besorah (tidings) 2 Samuel 4:10, 18:22.

Bittachon (trust, hope) Ecclesiastes 9:4.

Chashab (to think) Job 6:26; Jeremiah 23:27.

Cheleq (portion, tract) Genesis 31:14; Leviticus 6:10, 6:17; Numbers 18:20; Deuteronomy 10:9, 12:12, 14:27, 14:29, 32:9; 1 Samuel 30:24; Proverbs 17:2; Ecclesiastes 2:10, 3:22, 5:18–19, 9:9.

Eqeb (consequences, heel) [This word may refer to the fact that consequences follow at the heel, i.e., close behind us, because of our actions.] Genesis 22:18, 26:5; Deuteronomy 7:12, 8:20; 2 Samuel 12:6, 12:10; Psalm 19:12; Proverbs 22:4.

Gamul (recompense) Judges 9:16, 16:28; 2 Samuel 19:37.

Gemulah (a dealing, recompense) 2 Samuel 19:36–37.

Leb (inner man, mind, heart, will) Genesis 6:5, 8:21, 24:45, 27:41; Exodus 35:5, 35:21–22, 35:25–26; 1 Kings 3:9, 3:12, 4:29, 8:23; Psalm 7:9, 51:10, 51:17; Proverbs 2:2, 2:10, 3:3, 4:23, 6:14, 6:18, 7:3, 8:5, 10:21, 11:12, 11:20, 12:8, 12:11, 12:20, 14:33, 15:14, 15:21; Jeremiah 17:9, 22:17.

Lebab (heart, inner man, mind, will) 1 Chronicles 22:7, 28:2; Daniel 11:27; Isaiah 44:18.

Mabbat (expectation) Isaiah 20:5–6.

Mattath (gift) 1 Kings 13:7.

Mezimmah (purpose, discretion, device) Job 21:27; Psalm 10:2, 10:4, 21:11; Jeremiah 30:24.

Miqveh (a hope) 1 Chronicles 29:15; Ezra 10:2; Jeremiah 14:8, 17:13, 50:7.

Musar (discipline, chastening, correction) Proverbs 13:24, 22:15; Isaiah 26:16, 53:5; Jeremiah 2:30, 5:3, 7:28, 17:23.

Naqam (to avenge, to take vengeance) Exodus 21:20.

Natah (to stretch out, spread out, extend, incline) Psalm 21:11.

Nebizbah (a reward) Daniel 2:6.

Paqad (visit, attend to, muster, appoint) Exodus 32:34; Leviticus 26:18, 26:28; Judges 20:10; Psalm 59:5; Isaiah 10:12, 13:11, 24:21–22.

Peri (fruit) Psalm 58:11; Proverbs 13:2, 18:20–21, 27:18, 31:16, 31:31; Isaiah 3:10.

Peullah (work recompense) Psalm 109:20; Isaiah 49:4, 62:11.

Qavah (to wait for) Isaiah 59:9, 59:11; Jeremiah 14:22.

Ruach (breath, wind, spirit) Proverbs 16:2.

Sabar (hope) Psalm 119:166; Isaiah 38:18.

Sabea or *saba* (to be sated, satisfied or surfeited) Genesis 25:8; Leviticus 26:26.

Sakal or *sakar* or *seker* (hire, wages) Genesis 15:1; 2 Chronicles 15:7; Psalm 127:3; Proverbs 11:18; Isaiah 40:10, 62:11.

Sebar (think, intend) Daniel 7:25.

Seber (hope) Psalm 119:116, 146:5.

Shalem (complete) Ruth 2:12; Proverbs 25:22.

Shaqad (watching, wake) Isaiah 29:20.

Shebet (rod, staff, club, scepter, tribe) Psalm 2:9, 23:4, 89:32; Proverbs 10:13, 13:24, 14:3, 22:15, 23:13–14, 26:3, 29:15.

Shochad (present, bribe) Isaiah 45:13.

Taavah (a desire) Proverbs 13:12.

Temurah (recompense, exchange) Leviticus 27:10, 27:33; Ruth 4:7; Job 15:31, 20:18.

Tiqvah (a hope, expectation) Ruth 1:12; Job 4:6, 5:16, 6:8, 7:6, 8:3, 11:18–20, 14:7, 14:19, 17:15, 19:10, 27:8; Psalm 9:18, 62:5, 71:5; Proverbs 10:28, 11:7, 19:18, 23:18, 24:14, 26:12, 29:20; Jeremiah 29:11, 31:17; Lamentations 3:29; Ezekiel 19:5, 37:11; Hosea 2:15; Zechariah 9:12.

Tocheleth (hope) Psalm 39:7; Proverbs 10:28, 11:7; Lamentations 3:18.

Yachal (to hope, expect, wait) Job 13:15; Psalm 31:24, 33:18, 38:15, 42:5, 42:11, 43:5, 71:13–14, 119:49, 130:5, 130:7, 131:3; Lamentations 3:21, 3:24; Ezekiel 13:6.

Yasar (discipline, chasten, admonish) Deuteronomy 21:18, 22:18; Psalm 6:1, 38:1, 39:11, 94:12; Jeremiah 30:11; Hosea 7:12, 10:10.

Yetser (form, framing, purpose) Genesis 6:5; Deuteronomy 31:21; 1 Chronicles 28:9.

Zamam (to consider, purpose, devise) Deuteronomy 19:19.

Zimmah (plan, device, wickedness) Proverbs 21:27.

New Testament Greek

Antapodosis (recompense) Colossians 3:24.

Boule (counsel) 1 Corinthians 4:5.

Boulema (design) Acts 27:43.

Boulomai (to will) Acts 5:28, 5:33, 12:4; Philippians 1:12; 1 Timothy 2:8, 5:14, 6:9; Titus 3:8; Philemon 1:13; Hebrews 6:17; James 1:18, 3:4, 4:4; 2 Peter 3:9; 3 John 1:10; Jude 1:5.

Dialogismos (reasoning) James 2:4.

Ekdikeo (to vindicate, to avenge) 2 Corinthians 10:6.

Ekdikesis (vengeance, vindication) 1 Peter 2:14.

Elpis (expectation, hope) Acts 2:26, 16:19, 23:6, 24:15, 26:6, 27:20, 28:20; Romans 4:18, 5:2–5, 8:20–24; Romans 12:12, 15:4; 1 Corinthians 9:10, 13:13; 2 Corinthians 1:7, 3:12, 10:15; Galatians 5:5; Ephesians 1:18, 2:12, 4:4; Philippians 1:20; Colossians 1:5, 1:23, 1:27; 1 Thessalonians 1:3, 2:19, 4:13, 5:8; 2 Thessalonians 2:16; 1 Timothy 1:1; Titus 1:2, 2:13, 3:7; Philemon 1:22; Hebrews 3:6, 6:11, 6:18, 7:19, 10:23; 1 Peter 1:3, 1:21, 3:15; 1 John 3:3.

Elpizo (to expect, to hope) Matthew 12:21; Acts 26:7; Romans 8:25, 15:24; 1 Corinthians 16:7; 2 Corinthians 1:10, 1:13, 5:11; Philippians 2:19, 2:23; 1 Timothy 4:10, 5:5, 6:17; 1 Peter 1:13; 2 John 1:12; 3 John 1:14.

Ennoia (thinking, thoughtfulness, moral understanding) Hebrews 4:12.

Epanorthosis (correction) 2 Timothy 3:16.

Epinoia (thought, design) Acts 8:22.

Epitimia (punishment) 2 Corinthians 2:6.

Eukodia (good pleasure) Ephesians 1:5, 1:9.

Hagnos (pure motives) Philippians 1:17.

Kata (down, against, according to) 1 Corinthians 15:32.

Kolasis (correction) Matthew 25:46; 1 John 4:18.

Kolazo (to chastise) 2 Peter 2:9.

Mello (to be about) John 6:15, 7:35, 12:4; Acts 20:7.

Misthapodosia (payment of wages) Hebrews 10:35, 11:26.

Misthos (hire, wages) Matthew 5:12, 5:46, 6:1, 6:5, 6:16, 10:41–42; Mark 9:41; Luke 6:23, 6:35; 1 Corinthians 3:8, 3:14, 9:17–18; 2 John 1:8; Revelation 11:18.

Noutheteo (to admonish, exhort) Acts 20:31; Romans 15:14; 1 Corinthians 4:14; 1 Thessalonians 5:14; 2 Thessalonians 3:15.

Paideuo (to chasten, to train children, to correct) 2 Corinthians 6:9.

Paraineo (to exhort, advise) Acts 27:9.

Phroneo (to have understanding, to think) Matthew 16:23; Romans 12:3, 12:16, 14:6, 15:5; 2 Corinthians 13:11; Galatians 5:10; Philippians 1:7, 2:2, 2:5, 3:15, 3:19, 4:2.

Proelpizo (hope before) Ephesians 1:12.

Rhabdos (a staff, rod) 1 Corinthians 4:21; Revelation 2:27, 12:5, 19:15.

Thelo (to will, wish) Mark 6:48; Acts 19:33.

Timoreo (to help, avenge) Acts 22:5, 26:11; Hebrews 10:29.

Organize

Key English words: appoint, appointed, arrange, array, arrayed, order, ordered, separated.

Old Testament Hebrew

Amad (to take one's stand, stand) 1 Chronicles 6:31, 15:16–17; 2 Chronicles 8:14, 11:22, 19:5, 19:8, 20:21, 31:2; Ezra 3:8; Nehemiah 6:7, 7:3, 12:31, 13:30; Esther 4:5.

Araq (to arrange, to set in order—often a military term) Genesis 14:8, 40:23; Joshua 2:6; Judges 20:20, 20:22, 20:30, 20:33; 1 Samuel 4:2, 17:21; 2 Samuel 10:9, 23:5; 1 Chronicles 12:33; Joel 2:5.

Asah (to make) 1 Samuel 12:6; 2 Kings 17:32; 2 Chronicles 2:18.

Atsar (to lay up, store) Nehemiah 13:13.

Badal (to be divided, separate) Leviticus 20:24; Numbers 16:9; Nehemiah 9:2, 10:28.

Chalaq (to divide, share) 2 Samuel 19:29.

Chatsah (to divide) Numbers 31:42.

Gebulah (border, boundary) Deuteronomy 32:8.

Kun (to be firm) Joshua 4:4.

Malak (to become king or queen, to reign) 1 Samuel 8:22, 12:1.

Manah (to count, number, reckon) Daniel 1:11; Jonah 1:17, 4:6–8.

Menah (to number, to reckon) Ezra 7:25; Daniel 2:24, 2:49, 3:12.

Nathan (to set, put, give) Exodus 31:6; Numbers 14:4; Deuteronomy 16:18; 1 Kings 2:35; 2 Kings 8:6; 1 Chronicles 6:48, 16:4; 2 Chronicles 25:16, 32:6; Nehemiah 9:17, 13:4; Isaiah 42:6; Jeremiah 1:5, 1:10; Ezekiel 3:17, 33:7, 44:14.

Parad (to divide) Genesis 10:5, 10:32, 13:11, 13:14; Deuteronomy 32:8.

Paqad (appoint, attend to, muster, visit) Genesis 41:34; Numbers 1:50, 27:16; Deuteronomy 20:9; 1 Kings 11:28; 2 Kings 7:17, 11:15, 25:22–23; 2 Chronicles 23:14, 36:23; Ezra 1:2; Nehemiah 7:1, 12:44; Esther 2:3; Psalm 109:6; Isaiah 62:6; Jeremiah 40:5, 40:7, 40:11, 41:2, 49:19, 50:44, 51:27.

Pequddah (oversight, mustering, visitation) Numbers 3:36.

Qum (to arise, to set) Ezra 6:18; Daniel 5:11, 6:1, 6:3.

Sum or *sim* (to put, place, set) Deuteronomy 1:13; 1 Samuel 8:1, 8:5, 8:12, 18:13; 2 Samuel 15:4, 23:23; 2 Kings 11:18; 1 Chronicles 11:25; Ezra 5:14; Isaiah 7:3; Hosea 1:11; Habakkuk 1:12.

Tsavah (to lay charge upon, to give charge to, command) 1 Samuel 13:14, 25:30; 2 Samuel 6:21; 1 Kings 1:35; Nehemiah 5:14.

Yakach (to decide, to prove) Genesis 24:44.

Yasad (to establish, found, fix) 1 Chronicles 9:22.

New Testament Greek

Anadeiknumi (to lift up and show, show forth) Luke 10:1.

Apochorizo (to separate, part asunder) Acts 15:39.

Cheirotoneo (to vote by stretching out the hand, to appoint) Acts 14:23; 2 Corinthians 8:19.

Diatasso (to arrange thoroughly, to charge) 1 Corinthians 11:34.

Epidiorthoo (to correct, to set right) Titus 1:5.

Horizo (to mark off by boundaries, to determine) Acts 10:42.

Poieo (to make, do) Mark 3:14, 3:16.

Procheirizo (to put into the hand, to take into one's hand, hence to determine) Acts 26:16.

Prokatartizo (to make ready before hand) 2 Corinthians 9:5.

Kathistemi (to set in order, appoint) Titus 1:5.

Kathizo (to make to sit down) 1 Corinthians 6:4.

Kosmeo (order, arrange) Matthew 12:44.

Taxis (an arranging, an order) Luke 1:8; 1 Corinthians 14:40; Hebrews 6:20.

Tithemi (to place, to lay, to set) John 15:16; 1 Corinthians 12:28; 1 Timothy 2:7; 2 Timothy 1:11.

Peace (Shalom)

Key English words: peace, peaceful, peace offerings, flourish, prosper, prospers, prospered, prospering, prosperity, prosperous, successful, succeed, welfare.

Old Testament Hebrew

Dashen (to be fat, grow fat) Deuteronomy 31:20; Judges 9:9; Psalm 22:19, 23:5 (anointed), 36:9, 63:5, 65:11; Proverbs 11:25, 13:4, 15:30, 28:5; Isaiah 30:23, 55:2; Jeremiah 31:14.

Kosharah (prosperity) Psalm 68:6.

Parats (to break through) [prosperous, increased, broken through] Genesis 30:30, 30:43; Exodus 19:22, 19:24; 2 Samuel 6:8; Nehemiah 1:3; Proverbs 3:10.

Sakal or *sekel* (to be prudent) [prosperous, succeed, successful, instruct, discernment, discretion, insight, understand] Genesis 3:6; Deuteronomy 29:9; Joshua 1:7–8; 1 Samuel 18:5, 18:14–15, 18:30; 1 Kings 2:3; 2 Kings 18:7; 1 Chronicles 22:12, 28:19; 2 Chronicles 2:12, 30:22; Ezra 8:18; Psalm 2:10, 14:2, 32:8, 36:4; Proverbs 1:3, 3:4; Jeremiah 10:21.

Shalam (covenant of peace) [complete, safety, friendly] Genesis 15:16, 33:18, 34:21; 1 Kings 22:44.

Shalem (a sacrifice or alliance of friendship, peace offering) Exodus 20:24; Leviticus 3:1.

Shalev (ease, quiet) [carefree] 1 Chronicles 4:40; Job 16:12, 20:20, 21:23; Psalm 30:6, 73:12; Jeremiah 49:31; Ezekiel 23:42; Zechariah 7:7.

Shalom (completeness, soundness, welfare, peace) Genesis 15:15, 26:29, 37:14, 43:27; Exodus 4:18, 18:7, 18:23;

Judges 18:15, 19:20; 1 Samuel 17:18; 2 Samuel 11:7; 1 Kings 2:33, 4:24; 1 Chronicles 22:9; Esther 10:3; Psalm 29:11, 35:27, 37:11, 55:18, 72:3, 72:7, 85:10; Proverbs 3:17; Ecclesiastes 3:8; Isaiah 9:7, 26:3, 32:17, 38:17, 39:8, 54:10; Jeremiah 8:15, 14:13, 15:5, 29:7, 29:11; Ezekiel 34:25, 37:26.

Shalvah (quietness, ease) [complacency] Psalm 122:7; Proverbs 1:32, 17:1; Jeremiah 22:21; Ezekiel 16:49.

Tobah or *tob* or *tub* (welfare, benefit, good things, good) Deuteronomy 23:6, 28:11, 30:15; 1 Kings 10:7; Ezra 9:12; Nehemiah 2:10; Psalm 25:13, 106:5, 128:5; Proverbs 13:21; Ecclesiastes 7:14; Jeremiah 14:11, 17:6; Zechariah 1:17.

Tsaleach or *tselach* or *tsalach* (to advance, prosper) Genesis 24:21, 24:40, 24:42, 24:56, 39:2; Joshua 1:8; Judges 18:5; 1 Chronicles 22:11; Ezra 6:14; Nehemiah 1:11; Psalm 118:25; Isaiah 48:15.

New Testament Greek

Eirene or *eireneou* (peace) Matthew 10:13, 10:34; Mark 5:34, 10:50; Luke 1:79, 2:14, 7:50, 8:48, 10:5–6, 12:51, 14:32; John 14:27, 16:33, 20:19, 20:21, 20:26; Acts 10:36, 15:33; Romans 1:7, 2:10, 5:1, 8:6, 12:18, 14:17, 14:19, 15:13; 1 Corinthians 7:15, 14:33; Galatians 5:22; Ephesians 2:14–15, 2:17, 6:15; Philippians 4:7; Colossians 3:15; 1 Thessalonians 5:13; 2 Thessalonians 3:16; 2 Timothy 2:22; Hebrews 12:14; James 3:18; 1 Peter 3:11; 2 Peter 1:2.

Eirenopoieo (to make peace) Colossians 1:20.

Euporia (prosperity, plenty) Acts 19:25.

Perisseuo (to be over and above, abound) Philippians 4:12.

Planning

Key English words: advice, advise, counsel, devise, make ready, plan, plans, planning, prepare.

Old Testament Hebrew

Arak (to arrange, to set in order) Psalm 23:5; Isaiah 30:33.

Asar (to tie, to bind) Genesis 40:3; Exodus 14:6; Numbers 30:2–3; Judges 15:10; 1 Samuel 6:7; 1 Kings 18:44; 2 Kings 9:21.

Athod (to be ready) Proverbs 24:27.

Chaphas (to search) Psalm 64:6.

Charash (to cut in, engrave, plow, devise) Proverbs 3:29, 12:20, 14:22.

Chashab (to think, account) 2 Samuel 14:14; Nehemiah 6:2, 6; Psalm 35:4, 35:20, 36:4, 41:7, 140:2; Proverbs 16:9, 16:30, 24:8; Ecclesiastes 9:10; Isaiah 10:7; Jeremiah 18:18, 26:3, 36:3; Ezekiel 11:2, 38:10; Daniel 11:24; Hosea 7:15; Micah 2:3; Nahum 1:9; Zechariah 7:10, 8:17.

Dabar (speech, word) Judges 20:7; 2 Samuel 17:4, 17:6, 19:43; Esther 5:14.

Damah (to be like, resemble) Numbers 33:56.

Etsah (counsel, advice) 2 Samuel 16:20, 16:23, 17:7; 1 Kings 12:13–14; 2 Chronicles 10:14; Nehemiah 4:15; Job 5:13; Proverbs 20:5; Isaiah 8:10, 14:26, 16:3, 19:11, 25:1, 29:15, 30:1; Jeremiah 49:20, 49:30, 50:45; Ezekiel 11:12.

Hagah (to moan, growl, utter, speak, muse) Psalm 38:12; Proverbs 24:2.

Kun (to be firm) Genesis 43:16; Exodus 16:5; Deuteronomy 19:3; Joshua 1:11; 2 Chronicles 2:9; Psalm 7:12, 11:2, 78:8; Proverbs 20:18; Isaiah 14:21; Ezekiel 7:14.

Maarak (arrangement) Proverbs 16:1.

Machashabah (thought, device) Psalm 33:10–11; Proverbs 6:18, 15:22, 15:26, 16:3, 19:21, 20:18, 21:5; Jeremiah 6:19, 18:11–12, 18:18, 29:11; Ezekiel 38:10.

Mahar (hasten) Genesis 18:6.

Melek (counsel, advice) Daniel 4:27.

Mezimmah (purpose, discretion, device) Job 21:27.

Mishpat (judgment) Exodus 26:30; 1 Kings 6:38.

Panah (to turn) Isaiah 57:14.

Sod (council, counsel) Psalm 83:3.

Tabnith (construction, pattern, figure) 1 Chronicles 28:11–12.

Toknith (measurement, proportion) Ezekiel 43:10.

Uts (counsel, plan) Isaiah 8:10.

Yaats (advice, counsel) Isaiah 32:8; Jeremiah 38:15.

Zamam (a plan, device) Psalm 140:8.

Zimmah (a plan, device, wickedness) Job 17:11.

New Testament Greek

Boule (counsel) Luke 23:51; Acts 2:23, 5:38, 27:42.

Entaphiazo (to prepare for burial) Matthew 26:12.

Hetoimazo or *hetoimos* (to prepare) Matthew 3:3, 25:10, 26:17; Mark 1:3, 14:12, 14:15; Luke 1:17, 1:76, 3:4, 17:8, 22:8–9, 22:12; John 14:2–3; 1 Peter 3:15; Philemon 1:22; Revelation 19:7; 21:2.

Kataskeuazo (to prepare) Matthew 11:10; Mark 1:2; Luke 7:27.

Meletao (to care for, practice, study) Acts 4:25.

Paraskeuazo (to prepare, make ready) 1 Corinthians 14:8.

Peitharcheo (to obey authority) Acts 27:21.

Peitho (to persuade, to have confidence) Acts 5:40.

Promeletao (to premeditate) Luke 21:14.

Power

Key English words: power, mighty, might, rule over.

Old Testament Hebrew

Addir (majestic) Ezekiel 32:18.

Atsom (vast, numerous) Psalm 69:4; Daniel 11:23.

Az (strong, mighty) Genesis 49:3.

Chayil (strength, efficiency) Psalm 59:11, 110:3.

Chazaq (strong) Exodus 13:9.

Chesen (royal power) Daniel 2:37, 4:30.

Chozeq (strength) Exodus 13:3; Haggai 2:22.

Ezuz (strength, might) Psalm 145:6.

Geburah (strength, might) 1 Chronicles 29:11, 29:30; Psalm 21:13, 54:1, 71:18, 80:2, 145:11; Proverbs 8:14; Daniel 2:20.

Kaph (flat of the hand) 1 Samuel 4:3.

Koach (strength, power) Genesis 9:16; Exodus 15:6, 32:11; Numbers 14:17; Joshua 17:17; 2 Chronicles 22:9;

Proverbs 24:5; Ecclesiastes 4:1; Isaiah 10:13, 50:2; Jeremiah 10:12, 51:15; Daniel 11:6.

On (vigor, strength) Job 40:16.

Otsmah (might) Isaiah 40:29, 47:9.

Oz (strength, might) Psalm 62:11, 63:2, 66:3, 90:11; Ezekiel 24:21, 30:6, 30:18, 33:28.

Pala (surpassing) Job 10:16.

Qavqav (might) Isaiah 18:2, 18:7.

Rab (many, great) 2 Chronicles 14:11.

Taatsuma (might) Psalm 68:35.

Toqeph (power, strength) Daniel 11:17.

Yad (hand) Genesis 16:6, 31:29; Exodus 3:8, 4:21, 14:31; Numbers 11:23; Deuteronomy 34:12; Judges 1:35, 6:2, 7:2; 1 Samuel 10:18; Job 2:6; Psalm 63:10; Proverbs 3:27, 18:21; Isaiah 8:11, 47:14, 64:7; Jeremiah 46:24; Ezekiel 35:5.

Zeroa (arm, shoulder, strength) Psalm 77:15, 79:11; Ezekiel 22:6; Daniel 11:6.

New Testament Greek

Dunamis (power) Luke 10:19.

Dunatos (strong, mighty, powerful) Acts 7:22; Romans 9:22; 2 Corinthians 10:4.

Exousia (power to act, authority) Luke 22:53; Ephesians 2:2; Revelation 9:3, 9:10, 9:19, 11:6, 14:18.

Ischus (strength, might) 2 Thessalonians 1:9.

Kratos (strength, might) Hebrews 2:14.

Quality & Excellence

Key English words: choice, desire, delight, excellence, excellent, fresh, good, new, perfect, pleasant, pure, purify, repairs, restore, restored, very good.

Old Testament Hebrew

Anog (soft, delicate, dainty) Job 22:26, 27:10; Psalm 37:4, 37:11; Isaiah 55:2, 58:14.

Arab (to be sweet or pleasing) Jeremiah 31:26.

Athiq (eminent, surpassing, choice) Isaiah 23:18.

Bachar or *bachur* (to choose) Deuteronomy 12:11; Judges 20:15–16, 20:34; 1 Samuel 9:2; 2 Samuel 10:9; 1 Chronicles 19:10; 2 Chronicles 25:5; Psalm 78:31; Proverbs 10:20; Song of Solomon 5:15, 7:13.

Barar (to purify, select) 1 Chronicles 7:40; Nehemiah 5:18.

Beriah (a creation, a thing created) Numbers 16:30.

Chadash (new, renew, repair) Exodus 1:8; Leviticus 23:16, 26:10; Numbers 28:26; Deuteronomy 20:5, 22:8, 24:5, 32:17; Joshua 9:13; Judges 5:8, 15:13, 16:11–12; 1 Samuel 6:7, 11:14; 2 Samuel 6:3, 21:16; 1 Kings 11:29–30; 2 Kings 2:20; 1 Chronicles 13:7; Job 10:17, 29:20, 32:19; Psalm 33:3, 40:3, 51:10, 96:1, 98:1, 103:5, 104:30, 144:9, 149:1; Ecclesiastes 1:9–10; Song of Solomon 7:13; Isaiah 41:15, 42:9–10, 43:19, 48:6, 62:2, 65:17, 66:22; Jeremiah 26:10, 31:22, 31:31, 36:10; Lamentations 3:23, 5:21; Ezekiel 11:19, 18:31, 36:26.

Chay (alive, living) Isaiah 57:10.

Chayil (strength, efficiency, wealth, army) Ruth 3:11; Proverbs 12:4, 31:10.

Chelqah (smooth part, smoothness, flattery) Isaiah 30:10.

Chemdah (desire, delight) Jeremiah 3:19, 12:10, 25:34; Psalm 106:24; Ezekiel 26:12; Zechariah 7:14.

Chemed (desire, delight) or *chamad* (to desire, take pleasure in) Isaiah 32:12; Amos 5:11; Proverbs 1:22; Song of Solomon 2:3.

Chephets or *chaphets* (delight, pleasure) 1 Samuel 15:22; 2 Samuel 15:26, 24:3; Nehemiah 1:11; Psalm 1:2, 16:3, 40:8, 40:14, 51:16, 51:19, 109:17, 111:2, 119:35, 147:10; Proverbs 18:2, 31:13; Ecclesiastes 5:4, 8:6, 12:1; Isaiah 58:2, 62:4, 65:12, 66:4; Jeremiah 6:10, 9:24; Hosea 6:6; Malachi 3:1.

Gaon (exaltation) Exodus 15:7.

Gemar (complete) Ezra 7:12.

Geuth (majesty) Isaiah 12:5.

Kalil (entire, whole) Ezekiel 16:14, 27:3, 28:12.

Maadan or *maadannah* (a dainty [food], delight) Proverbs 29:17.

Machmad (desire, desirable thing) Lamentations 2:4.

Maklul (a thing made perfect, a gorgeous garment) Ezekiel 27:24.

Masos (exultation, rejoicing) Isaiah 32:14.

Mathoq or *mathuq* (sweet, sweetness) Ecclesiastes 5:12, 11:7.

Meged (excellence) Deuteronomy 33:13–16; Song of Solomon 4:13, 4:16.

Mibchor (choice) or *mibchar* (choicest, best) 2 Kings 3:19, 19:23; Isaiah 37:24; Ezekiel 17:21, 24:4.

Migdanah (a choice or excellent thing) 2 Chronicles 32:23.

Naem or *naim* (to be pleasant, delightful, or lovely) Genesis 49:15; 2 Samuel 1:23, 1:26; Psalm 16:6, 133:1, 141:6, 147:1; Proverbs 2:10, 9:17, 22:18, 24:4, 24:25; Song of Solomon 1:16.

Noam (delightfulness, pleasantness) Proverbs 3:17, 15:26, 16:24.

Oneg (daintiness, exquisite delight) Isaiah 58:13.

Path-bag (portion, delicacies) Daniel 1:5, 1:8, 1:13, 1:15, 1:16, 11:26.

Raah (to see) Esther 2:9.

Ratsah (to be pleased with, accept favorably) 1 Chronicles 29:3; Psalm 62:4, 68:30, 70:2; Proverbs 23:26; Hosea 8:13; Micah 6:7.

Ratson (goodwill, favor, acceptance, will) Proverbs 11:1, 11:20, 12:22, 15:8, 16:13.

Reshith (beginning, chief) Exodus 23:19; Ezekiel 48:14.

Rob (multitude, abundance, greatness) Psalm 150:2.

Sameach (glad, joyful, merry) Proverbs 2:14.

Shaa (to sport, take delight in, delight) Psalm 94:19, 119:16, 119:47, 119:70.

Shaashuim (a delight) Psalm 119:24, 119:77, 119:92, 119:143, 119:174; Proverbs 8:30–31.

Shemen (fat, oil) Isaiah 25:6.

Simchah (joy, gladness, mirth) Jeremiah 15:16.

Soreqah or *soreq* (choice vine) Genesis 49:11; Jeremiah 2:21.

Sus or *sis* (rejoice, delight) Deuteronomy 28:63.

Taanug (daintiness, luxury, exquisite delight) Micah 1:16, 2:9.

Taavah (desire) Genesis 3:6.

Tam (complete) Song of Solomon 5:2, 6:9.

Tamam (to be complete or finished) Job 22:3.

Tamim (complete, sound) Leviticus 22:21; Deuteronomy 32:4; 1 Samuel 14:41; Job 36:4, 37:16; Psalm 19:7.

Tirosh (fresh or new wine) Genesis 27:28, 27:37; Deuteronomy 7:13, 11:14, 12:17, 14:23, 18:4, 28:51, 33:28; Judges 9:13; 2 Kings 18:32; Nehemiah 5:11, 10:37, 10:39; Psalm 4:7; Proverbs 3:10; Isaiah 24:7, 36:17, 62:8; Jeremiah 31:12; Hosea 2:8–9, 2:22, 4:11, 7:14, 9:2; Joel 1:10, 2:19.

Toaphah (eminence) Job 22:25.

Tob (pleasant, agreeable, good) Genesis 18:7, 29:7; 1 Samuel 9:2; 2 Kings 2:19; Jeremiah 42:6; Hosea 4:13.

Yatab (to be good, well, glad, or pleasing) Ecclesiastes 11:9.

Yether (remainder, excess, preeminence) Proverbs 17:7.

Zaqaq (refine, purify) Isaiah 25:6.

New Testament Greek

Anakainizo or *anakainoo* (renew) 2 Corinthians 4:16; Colossians 3:10; Hebrews 6:6.

Ananeoo (renew) Ephesians 4:23.

Arete (moral goodness) Philippians 4:8; 2 Peter 1:3, 1:5.

Diaphero (to carry through, carry about, to differ, to make a difference, to surpass) Philippians 1:10.

Diaphoros (verying, excellent) Hebrews 1:4, 8:6.

Epiteleo (to complete, accomplish) Philippians 1:6.

Hapas (all, the whole) 1 Timothy 1:16.

Holokleria (completeness, soundness) Acts 3:16.

Huperbole (a throwing beyond, excess, superiority) 1 Corinthians 12:31.

Kainos (new, fresh) Matthew 13:52, 26:29, 27:60; Mark 1:27, 2:21, 14:25, 16:17; Luke 5:36, 22:20; John 13:34, 19:41; Acts 17:19, 17:21; 1 Corinthians 5:7, 11:25; 2 Corinthians 3:6, 5:17; Galatians 6:15; Ephesians 2:15, 4:24; Hebrews 8:8, 8:13, 9:15; 2 Peter 3:13; 1 John 2:7–8; 2 John 1:5; Revelation 2:17, 3:12, 5:9, 14:3, 21:1–2, 21:5.

Kalos (beautiful, good) 1 Peter 2:12.

Katartizo (to complete, prepare) 1 Peter 5:10.

Kratistos (strongest, noblest) Luke 1:3; Acts 23:26, 24:3, 26:25.

Neos (young, new) Matthew 9:17; Mark 2:22; Luke 5:37–39; Colossians 3:10; Hebrews 12:24.

Neophutos (newly planted) 1 Timothy 3:6.

Prosphatos (freshly slain, generally new) Hebrews 10:20.

Teleioo (to bring to an end, to complete, perfect) Philippians 3:12; Hebrews 2:10, 5:9, 7:19, 7:28, 9:9, 10:1, 11:40, 12:23.

Teleios (complete, perfect) Matthew 5:48; Romans 12:2; 1 Corinthians 13:10; Philippians 3:15; Colossians 4:12; Hebrews 9:11; James 1:4, 1:17, 1:25; 3:2; 1 John 4:18.

Teleiotes (completeness, perfection) Colossians 3:14.

Safety

Key English words: safe, safety, safely, injury, harm, harmed, harmful, hurt.

Old Testament Hebrew

Betach (security) 1 Kings 4:25; Psalm 4:8; Jeremiah 32:37, 33:16; Ezekiel 39:6; Hosea 2:18.

Maoz (a place or means of safety, protection) Isaiah 30:2–3.

Shalom (completeness, soundness, welfare, peace) Genesis 28:21; 1 Samuel 20:13, 20:21, 20:42; 2 Chronicles 19:1; Isaiah 41:3.

Yesha (deliverance, welfare, rescue, salvation, safety) Job 5:4, 5:11; Psalm 12:5.

Uz (to take or seek refuge) Exodus 9:19; Jeremiah 6:1.

New Testament Greek

Asphaleia (safety) 1 Thessalonians 5:3.

Asphales (certain, secure) Philippians 3:1.

Utility Maximization

Key English words: useless, useful, produce, produces, produced, waste, barren, worthless, fruit, fruitful, unfruitful, yield, yielded, bear fruit, reap, reaped, reaping, reaper, reapers, harvest.

Old Testament Hebrew

Al (worthless) Job 24:25.

Asah (to make) Genesis 1:11–12; Isaiah 5:10, 37:31; Jeremiah 17:8; Ezekiel 17:6, 17:8, 17:23; Hosea 8:7, 9:6.

Bakar (to bear new fruit, to constitute as first-born) Ezekiel 47:12.

Beliyyaal (worthlessness) Deuteronomy 3:13; Judges 19:22, 20:13; 1 Samuel 1:16, 2:12, 10:27, 25:17, 25:25, 30:22; 2 Samuel 16:7, 20:1, 23:6; 1 Kings 21:10, 21:13; Job 34:18; Psalm 101:3; Proverbs 6:12, 16:27.

Beushim (stinking or worthless things, wild grapes) Isaiah 5:2, 5:4.

Chinnam (out of favor) Proverbs 1:17; Malachi 1:10.

Elil (insurficiency, worthlessness) Job 13:4; Zechariah 11:17.

Ephes (ceasing) Isaiah 41:29.

Hebel (vapor, breath) Jeremiah 10:15, 51:18; Lamentations 4:17.

Masas (dissolve, melt) [worthless] 1 Samuel 15:9.

Masseh (work) Habakkuk 3:17.

Nasa, nasah (to lift, carry, take) Ezekiel 17:8, 36:8.

Nathan (to give, put or set) Genesis 4:12, 49:20; Leviticus 25:19, 26:4, 26:20; Numbers 20:8; Deuteronomy 11:17; Psalm 85:12; Ezekiel 34:27; Joel 2:22; Zechariah 8:12.

Nub (to bear fruit) Psalm 92:14.

Parah (to bear fruit, be fruitful) Isaiah 11:1; 45:8.

Qatsar (to reap, harvest) Leviticus 19:9, 23:10, 23:22; 25:5, 25:11; Ruth 2:9; 1 Samuel 8:12; 2 Kings 19:29; Job 4:8, 24:6; Psalm 126:5; Proverbs 22:8; Ecclesiastes 11:4; Isaiah 37:30; Jeremiah 12:13; Hosea 8:7, 10:12; Micah 6:15.

Raa (to break) Jeremiah 11:16.

Req (empty, vain) Judges 9:4, 11:3; 2 Chronicles 13:7.

Riq (emptiness, vanity) Leviticus 26:16, 26:20; Psalm 4:2.

Sakan (to be of use or service) Job 22:2.

Shakol, shakal (to be bereaved) 2 Kings 2:19.

Shav (emptiness, vanity) Isaiah 1:13; Jeremiah 18:15; Hosea 10:4, 12:11.

Sheker (deception, disappointment, falsehood) Psalm 119:118.

Tebuah (product, revenue) Exodus 23:10; Leviticus 19:25; Deuteronomy 33:14; Joshua 5:12; Proverbs 8:19; Isaiah 30:23.

Tsaleach or *tsalach* (to advance, prosper) Ezekiel 15:4.

Yebul (produce) Deuteronomy 32:22.

Zalal (to be light or worthless, to make light of) Jeremiah 15:19.

Zara (to sow, scatter seed) Genesis 1:11–12, 1:29.

New Testament Greek

Achreios (usless) Matthew 25:30.

Achreoo (to make useless) Romans 3:12.

Adokimos (not standing the test, rejected) Titus 1:16; Hebrews 6:8.

Akarpos (unfruitful) Matthew 13:22; Mark 4:19; 1 Corinthians 14:14; Ephesians 5:11; Titus 3:14; 2 Peter 1:8.

Argos (inactive, idle) James 2:20; 2 Peter 1:8.

Didomi (to give—either literally or figuratively) Matthew 13:8; Mark 4:7–8.

Euchrestos (useful) 2 Timothy 2:21, 4:11; Philemon 1:11.

Euthetos (well placed) Hebrews 6:7.

Karpophoreo (to bear fruit) Mark 4:20; Luke 8:15; Romans 7:4.

Mataios (vain, useless) 1 Corinthians 3:20, 15:17; Titus 3:9; James 1:26.

Phero (to bear, carry, bring forth) John 15:2, 15:4, 15:8, 15:16.

Poieo (to make, do) Matthew 3:10, 7:19; Luke 3:9.

Poneros (toilsome, bad) Luke 19:22.

Ptochos (one who crouches or cowers) [worthless] Galatians 4:9.

Therizo (to reap) Matthew 6:26, 25:26; Luke 12:24; John 4:38; 1 Corinthians 9:11; 2 Corinthians 9:6; Galatians 6:7–9; Revelation 14:15.

Wages

Key English words: hire, wages, pay.

Old Testament Hebrew

Ethnan (wages of a harlot) Isaiah 23:17.

Maskoreth (wages) Genesis 29:15, 31:7.

Mechir (price, hire) Deuteronomy 23:18.

Nathan (to give, put, set) 2 Kings 2:15.

Peullah (a work, recompense) Proverbs 10:16.

Sakar or *seker* (hire, wages) Genesis 30:18; Exodus 22:15; Deuteronomy 15:18; 1 Samuel 2:5; 1 Kings 5:6; Malachi 3:5.

Yegia (toil, product) Isaiah 55:21.

New Testament Greek

Apodidomai (to give up, give back, return, restore) Matthew 20:8, 21:41.

Dapanao (to spend freely) Acts 21:24.

Misthoo (hire) Matthew 20:1.

Misthos (wages, hire) Matthew 20:8; Luke 10:7; John 4:36; 1 Timothy 5:18; 2 Peter 2:13; James 5:4.

Opsonion (provisions, wages) Luke 3:14; Romans 6:23; 2 Corinthians 11:8.

Wealth

Key English words: profit, successful, prosper, gain, belong, abundance, wealth, riches.

Old Testament Words

Ashar (to be or become rich) Proverbs 23:4.

Athereth (abundance) Jeremiah 33:6.

Chayil (strength, efficiency, wealth, army) Genesis 34:29; Deuteronomy 8:17–18; Ruth 2:1, 4:11; 2 Kings 15:20; Job 5:5, 15:29, 31:25; Psalm 49:6, 49:10, 73:12; Proverbs 13:22; Isaiah 8:4, 60:5, 60:11, 61:6; Jeremiah 15:3, 17:3; Obadiah 1:11, 1:13; Micah 4:13; Zephaniah 1:13; Zechariah 9:4, 14:14.

Chemdah (desire, delight) Haggai 2:7.

Chosen (wealth, treasure) Proverbs 15:6; Isaiah 33:6; Jeremiah 20:5.

Deshen (fatness, ashes of fat) Psalm 36:8; Isaiah 55:2; Jeremiah 31:14.

Hamon (sound, murmur, roar, crowd, abundance) 1 Chronicles 29:16; Psalm 37:16; Ecclesiastes 5:10; Isaiah 60:5; Ezekiel 28:19, 30:4.

Hem (moaning, wailing, wealth) Ezekiel 7:11.

Hon (wealth, sufficiency) Psalm 112:3; Proverbs 1:13, 3:9, 8:18, 10:15, 13:7, 13:11, 18:11, 19:4, 19:14, 28:8, 28:22, 29:3; Ezekiel 27:12, 27:18, 27:27, 27:33.

Kabar (to be much or many) Job 36:31.

Kabod (abundance, honor, glory) Genesis 31:1; Isaiah 10:3; Nehemiah 2:9.

Koach (strength, power) Job 6:22.

Male (full) Psalm 73:10.

Matmon (hidden treasure, treasure) Isaiah 45:3.

Meod (muchness, force, abundance) Genesis 41:49.

Nekes (riches, treasures) 2 Chronicles 1:11–12; Ecclesiastes 5:19, 6:2.

On (vigor, wealth) Job 20:10; Hosea 12:8.

Osher (riches) Genesis 31:16; 2 Chronicles 1:12; Ecclesiastes 9:11.

Pissah (abundance, plenty) Psalm 72:16.

Rab (much, many, great) Psalm 18:14.

Rabah (to be or become much, many, or great) 2 Chronicles 31:5; Nehemiah 5:18; Ecclesiastes 1:16; Jeremiah 40:12.

Rekush (property, goods) 2 Chronicles 32:29.

Revahah (saturation) Psalm 66:12.

Rob (multitude, abundance, greatness) Genesis 27:28; Deuteronomy 28:47; 1 Samuel 13:5; 2 Samuel 17:11; 1 Kings 1:19, 1:25, 4:20, 10:10; 1 Chronicles 29:2, 29:21; 2 Chronicles 2:9, 11:23, 32:29; Nehemiah 9:25; Psalm 49:6, 52:7, 72:7; Proverbs 11:14, 20:15, 24:6; Isaiah 7:22; Ezekiel 27:12, 27:16, 27:18, 27:33, 28:16; Zechariah 14:14.

Saba (plenty, satiety) Genesis 41:29–31; Psalm 37:19.

Shepha (abundance) Deuteronomy 33:19.

Shiphah (abundance, quantity) Job 22:11, 38:34.

Soba (satiety, abundance) Psalm 78:25.

Tobah or *tob* or *tub* (welfare, benefit, good things, good) Deuteronomy 23:6, 28:11, 30:15; 1 Kings 10:7; Ezra 9:12;

Nehemiah 2:10; Psalm 25:13, 106:5, 128:5; Proverbs 13:21; Ecclesiastes 7:14; Jeremiah 14:11, 17:6; Zechariah 1:17.

Tsaleach or *tsalach* (to prosper, to be successful) Genesis 24:21, 24:40, 24:52, 24:56, 39:2–3, 39:23; Numbers 14:41; Deuteronomy 28:29; Joshua 1:8; Judges 14:6, 14:19, 15:14, 18:5; 1 Samuel 10:6, 10:10, 11:6, 16:13, 18:10; 1 Kings 22:12, 22:15; 1 Chronicles 22:11, 22:13, 29:23; 2 Chronicles 7:11, 14:7, 18:11, 8:14, 26:5, 31:21, 31:30; Nehemiah 1:11, 2:20; Psalm 1:3, 37:7, 118:25; Proverbs 28:13; Isaiah 48:15, 53:10, 55:11; Jeremiah 2:37, 5:28, 12:1, 22:30; Ezekiel 17:10; Daniel 8:12, 8:24–25.

Yesh (being, substance, existence, is) Proverbs 8:21.

Yether (remainder, excess, preeminence) Job 22:20; Psalm 17:14.

Yithrah (abundance, riches) Isaiah 15:7; Jeremiah 48:36.

New Testament Words

Bios (life, living) Luke 15:12, 15:30.

Dunamis (power, might, strength) Revelation 18:3.

Perisseia (superfluity) Romans 5:17; 2 Corinthians 8:2.

Perisseuma (superfluity) 2 Corinthians 8:14.

Perisseuo (to be over and above, to abound) Matthew 13:12, 25:29; Luke 12:15; 2 Corinthians 1:5, 9:8; Philippians 4:12, 4:18.

Ploutos (wealth) 2 Corinthians 8:2; Colossians 2:2; Revelation 18:17.

Timiotes (preciousness, worth) Revelation 18:19.

Work

Key English words: deeds, fellow worker, labor, laborer, serve, service, toil, task, work, workers.

Old Testament Hebrew

Abad (to work, serve) Genesis 15:14, 25:23, 27:40; Exodus 4:23, 5:18, 7:16, 8:1, 20:5; Leviticus 25:40; Deuteronomy 28:14, 28:47; 2 Samuel 22:44; 1 Kings 12:4; Ezekiel 48:18–19.

Abodah (labor, service) Genesis 29:27, 30:26; Exodus 27:19; Leviticus 23:7 (laborious); Numbers 3:7; 1 Kings 12:4; 1 Chronicles 6:48, 9:19; Isaiah 14:3.

Amal (trouble, labor, toil) Deuteronomy 26:7; Ecclesiastes 1:3, 9:9, 10:15.

Asah (do, make) Exodus 5:9, 31:5; 2 Chronicles 2:7; Ruth 2:19; Psalm 101:3.

Atseb or *atstsab* (toiler) Isaiah 58:3.

Charash (engraver, artificer) 2 Chronicles 24:12.

Itstabon (a pain, toil) Genesis 3:17, 5:29.

Maaseh (a deed, work) Genesis 5:29; Exodus 5:4, 5:13, 18:20, 23:12, 26:1, 26:31, 26:36, 28:6, 28:15; Judges 2:7; Psalm 8:3, 90:17; Ecclesiastes 2:17.

Melakah (occupation, work) Genesis 2:2–3; Genesis 39:11; Exodus 12:16, 20:9–10, 31:14; Leviticus 16:29, 23:7; 1 Kings 5:16; 2 Kings 12:11; 1 Chronicles 9:13, 9:19, 27:26, 29:6; Nehemiah 2:16.

Paal or *poal* (do, make) Numbers 23:23; Ruth 2:12; Job 34:8, 34:22; Psalm 14:4, 44:1, 53:4; Proverbs 10:29, 21:15; Isaiah 31:2.

Siblah (a burden) Exodus 1:11.

Teleah (weariness, hardship) Exodus 18:8; Numbers 20:14; Nehemiah 9:32; Lamentations 3:5.

Teun (toil) Ezekiel 24:12.

Yad (hand) 1 Chronicles 6:31.

Yaga or *yagea* (to toil, grow or be weary) Joshua 7:3; Job 9:29; Jeremiah 51:58; Habakkuk 2:13.

Yegia (toil, product) Genesis 31:42.

New Testament Greek

Diakonia or *diakoneo* (service) Matthew 20:28; Mark 10:45; Acts 6:2; Romans 12:7, 15:31; Ephesians 4:12; 1 Timothy 1:12; 2 Timothy 4:11; Hebrews 1:14; Revelation 2:19.

Douleuo (to be a slave, to serve) Matthew 6:24; Luke 16:13; Romans 7:6, 9:12; Galatians 5:13; Ephesians 6:7; 1 Timothy 6:2.

Energo (to be at work, to work, to do) Matthew 14:2; Mark 6:14.

Ergates (worker) Matthew 9:37–38; 2 Corinthians 11:13; Philippians 3:2.

Ergazomai (to work, labor) Matthew 21:28; Luke 13:14; John 6:27; Romans 4:5; 1 Thessalonians 4:11.

Ergon (work) John 4:34, 10:33, 17:4; Acts 13:2, 13:41, 14:26, 15:38; Romans 2:15; 1 Corinthians 3:14; Ephesians 4:12; 2 Timothy 4:5.

Kopiao (to grow weary, toil) Matthew 6:28; Luke 12:27; 1 Corinthians 4:12; Philippians 2:16.

Kopos (laborious, toil) Matthew 26:10 (trouble); Mark 14:6; Luke 11:7; John 4:38; 1 Corinthians 3:8, 15:58; 2 Corinthians 6:5, 10:15, 11:23, 11:27; Galatians 6:17; 1 Thessalonians 1:3, 2:9, 3:5; 2 Thessalonians 3:8; Revelation 2:2, 14:13.

Latreuo (to serve) Matthew 4:10; Luke 4:8.

Leitourgia (a service, a ministry) 2 Corinthians 9:12; Philippians 2:17, 2:30.

Mochthos (toil, hardship) 2 Corinthians 11:27; 1 Thessalonians 2:9; 2 Thessalonians 3:8.

Oikourgos (working at home) Titus 2:5.

Paratithemi (to place beside, to set before) Mark 8:6.

Strateuo (to make war, to serve as a soldier) 2 Timothy 2:4.

Sunergos (fellow worker) Romans 16:3; 1 Corinthians 3:9; 2 Corinthians 1:24; Philippians 4:3; Colossians 4:11; Philemon 1:24; 3 John 1:8.

Appendix B
Occupations Mentioned in the Bible[1]

"Then Pharaoh said to his [Joseph's] brothers, 'What is your occupation?'" Genesis 47:3 (See also Jonah 1:8)

"Moreover, there are many workmen with you, stonecutters and masons of stone and carpenters, and all men who are skillful in every kind of work." 1 Chronicles 22:15

The following list is comprised of more than 180 occupations. Some of the terms are generic and could apply in more than one occupational context. Some are social and/or organizational roles. A few occupations listed are inferred from the Bible text. Based on what we know of the work of contemporary managers and leaders, approximately one-third of the occupations (marked in **bold**) may have involved managerial or leadership work.[2]

Occupation	Bible Reference
Administrator	Isaiah 60:17
Ambassador	Isaiah 30:4; 2 Corinthians 5:20
Archer	Genesis 49:23
Armor bearer	Judges 9:54; 2 Samuel 23:37
Artist	Song of Solomon 7:1
Astrologer	Isaiah 47:13
Author	Ecclesiastes 12:12; Judges 5:14
Baggage keeper	1 Samuel 17:22
Baker	Genesis 40:1–5; Hosea 7:4
Banquet superintendent	John 2:8–9
Barber	Judges 16:19
Binder of sheaves	Psalm 129:7
Blacksmith	1 Samuel 13:19; Isaiah 44:12
Bondwoman	Galatians 4:22–31
Bowman	Jeremiah 4:29
Brick maker	Genesis 11:3
Bronze worker	1 Kings 7:14
Builder	1 Corinthians 3:10; Luke 14:28
Burden bearer	2 Chronicles 34:13
Captain of a ship	Acts 27:11
Captain of the guard	Genesis 37:36; Acts 5:24
Carpenter	Ezra 3:7; Mark 6:3
Centurion	Matthew 8:5; Acts 10:1
Chariot driver	1 Kings 22:34
Chief baker	Genesis 40:2
Chief deputy	1 Kings 5:16
Chief gatekeeper	1 Chronicles 9:26
Chief jailor	Genesis 39:22
Chief Levite	1 Chronicles 15:22
Chief magician	Daniel 4:9
Chief magistrate	Acts 16:20–38
Chief minister	2 Samuel 8:18
Chief officer (supervisor)	1 Kings 9:23
Chief prefect	Daniel 2:48
Chief priest	2 Kings 25:18; Ezra 7:5
Chief prince	Daniel 10:13
Chief tax collector	Luke 19:2
Choir director	Psalm 4:1, 5:1
Commander	Ezra 4:8
Commissioner	Daniel 6:3
Concubine	Genesis 22:24; Judges 20:4
Conjurer	Daniel 1:20, 2:10
Cook	1 Samuel 9:23–24
Coppersmith	2 Timothy 4:14
Counselor	Daniel 3:3
Court official	Jeremiah 29:2
Craftsman	2 Kings 24:14
Cupbearer	Genesis 40:1
Dancer	Judges 21:3
Deacon	Philippians 1:1; 1 Timothy 3:8
Designer	Exodus 35:35
Diviner	Daniel 5:11
Domestic worker	Genesis 16:1
Door keeper	Ezra 7:24
Elder of the church	1 Timothy 5:17; Titus 1:5
Elder of the Jews	Ezra 6:7; Acts 25:15
Embalmer	Genesis 50:2

(Continued)

Occupation	Bible Reference
Embroiderer	Exodus 35:35
Engineer	Isaiah 22:9; 2 Kings 20:20
Engraver	Exodus 35:35
Eunuch	Esther 7:9
Evangelist	Acts 21:8
Executioner	1 Kings 2:25
Farmer	Joel 1:11; 2 Timothy 2:6
Fig grower	Amos 7:14; Luke 13:6
Fisherman	Isaiah 19:8; Matthew 4:18
Foreman (construction)	2 Chronicles 34:2
Fortune teller	Acts 16:16–19
Fowler (bird catcher)	Proverbs 6:5
Gardener	John 20:15
Garment worker	Proverbs 31:24
Gatekeeper	2 Kings 7:10
Gleaner	Leviticus 19:9–10
Goldsmith	Isaiah 40:19; Jeremiah 10:9
Governor of a city	1 Kings 22:26
Governor of a province	Ezra 8:36
Governor of the Jews	Ezra 6:7
Grape gatherer	Jeremiah 49:9
Grinder	Judges 16:21; Ecclesiastes 12:3
Guard	1 Kings 14:27
Harvest worker	Matthew 9:38; Luke 10:2
Herdsman	Amos 7:14
High priest	Numbers 35:28
Horseman	Jeremiah 4:29
Household manager	2 Kings 18:18
Hunter	Genesis 25:27
Idol maker	Habakkuk 2:18; Acts 19:24
Iron worker	2 Chronicles 24:12
Jailer	Acts 16:23–27
Judge	Exodus 18:3; 1 Chronicles 23:4
Keeper of the King's forest	Nehemiah 2:8
Keeper of the wardrobe	2 Kings 22:14
Keepers of the thresholds	1 Chronicles 9:19
King	2 Samuel 5:2
King's representative	Nehemiah 11:24
Lawyer	Matthew 22:35; Titus 3:13
Leader	Numbers 14:4; Luke 22:26
Leader of singers	Nehemiah 12:42, 12:46; Psalm 4:1
Leader of the congregation	Exodus 16:22
Leader of the synagogue	Acts 18:8
Levite	1 Chronicles 23:24
Linen worker	1 Chronicles 4:21
Magician	Genesis 41:8; Daniel 1:20
Magistrate	Daniel 3:3
Maid	Genesis 16:1; Ruth 3:9
Manager	Galatians 4:2
Mason	Ezra 3:7
Master	Matthew 6:24; Luke 16:13
Master builder	1 Corinthians 3:10
Mercenary soldier	Jeremiah 46:21
Merchant	Nehemiah 13:20
Messenger	1 Samuel 23:27
Midwife	Genesis 35:17
Mill worker	Lamentations 5:13
Miner	Deuteronomy 8:9
Minister	Acts 26:16; Colossians 1:23
Musician (instrumental)	2 Chronicles 34:12
Noble	Nehemiah 2:16; Daniel 4:36
Nurse	Genesis 24:59
Oarsman	Ezekiel 27:26–29
Olive grower	1 Samuel 8:14
Olive oil producer	Job 24:11
Overseer	Genesis 39:4; 1 Timothy 3:1
Pastor	Ephesians 4:11
Perfumer	Exodus 30:25; Nehemiah 3:8
Pharisee	Luke 7:39
Philosopher	Acts 17:18
Physician	Matthew 9:12
Pilot of a ship	Acts 27:11; James 3:4
Plowman	2 Kings 29:12
Potter	Isaiah 29:16; Jeremiah 18:4–6
Preacher	Romans 10:14
Prefect	Daniel 2:48
Priest	Genesis 14:18
Prince	Proverbs 17:7
Prophet	Genesis 20:7
Prophetess	Exodus 15:20
Queen	1 Kings 10:1
Rabbi	Mark 9:5
Reaper	Isaiah 17:5; Jeremiah 9:22
Refiner	Proverbs 25:4
Ruler of a province	Daniel 3:2–3
Sadducee	Matthew 3:7
Sailor	Revelation 18:17
Satrap	Ezra 8:36
Scribe	2 Kings 12:10; Matthew 8:19

Occupation	Bible Reference	Occupation	Bible Reference
Servant	Genesis 24:17	Tabernacle care taker	Numbers 4
Servant–girl	Matthew 26:69; Acts 12:13	Tax collector	Matthew 10:3
Shepherd	Genesis 46:34; John 10:11–16	Tanner	Acts 9:43, 10:16
Shepherdess	Genesis 29:9	**Teacher**	Ezra 8:16; Matthew 10:24–25
Ship builder	Genesis 6		
Silversmith	Judges 17:4; Acts 19:24	Temple servant	Ezra 7:7
Singer	1 Chronicles 9:33; Ezra 7:7	Tent maker	Acts 18:3
Slave dealer	Exodus 21:2–6	Thresher	1 Corinthians 9:10
Smelter	Isaiah 41:7	**Town clerk**	Acts 19:35
Soldier	John 19:23	Trader	Genesis 37:28; Ezekiel 17:4
Soothsayer	Isaiah 2:6	Trapper	Psalm 91:3, 124:7
Sorcerer	Jeremiah 27:9	**Treasurer**	Ezra 1:8; Daniel 3:2
Sower (of seed)	Isaiah 55:10; Matthew 13:3	Unskilled worker	Nehemiah 4:17
Spinner (making threads)	Exodus 35:25–26	Vine grower	Matthew 21:33
		Vinedresser	2 Kings 29:12
Steward	Genesis 43:16–19; Luke 12:42	Vineyard worker	Matthew 20:1–8
Stone mason	2 Samuel 5:11	Watchman	2 Samuel 13:34
Stonecutter	2 Kings 12:12	Weaver	Exodus 26:36, 36:37, 38:18
Supervisor	2 Chronicles 2:18	Woodcarver	Exodus 31:5
Seller of purple	Acts 16:14	Woodcutter	Jeremiah 10:3, 46:22

Illegitimate or questionable "occupations" and roles include:

Occupation or Role	Bible Reference
Bandit	Hosea 7:1
Drunkard	Joel 1:5; Matthew 24:49
Prostitute	Genesis 38:15; Hebrews 11:31
Robber	Proverbs 23:28
Sitting idle in the market	Matthew 20:3
Sluggard	Proverbs 19:24, 20:4, 24:30
Thief	Exodus 22:2; Matthew 6:19

Endnotes

1. Based on the New American Standard version.
2. See also Barnes, W. G. (2005). *Business in the Bible*. New York: Cosimo Classics.

Appendix C
Technology in the Bible

"The man shapes iron into a cutting tool, and does his work over the coals, fashioning it with hammers, and working it with his strong arm . . ." Isaiah 44:12

The following list contains over 160 items. Many types of technology are mentioned explicitly in the Bible.[1] Other types of technology used in the Ancient Near East during Bible times have been physically identified or inferred from the results of archeological research.[2] We can assume that many of these and other technologies were important to the work of workers, managers, and leaders in Bible times.

The word "technology" in contemporary management applies to more than just hardware and objects. It also includes the work processes of those who perform the work of transforming raw materials into finished goods and services as well as the work processes of those who manage the work. Even though the following list is comprised primarily of physical objects and equipment, the list will quickly grow if we add the various processes used by workers and their managers.

Technology	Scripture	Technology	Scripture
Anchors	Acts 27:13	Brazier	Jeremiah 36:23
Anvils	Isaiah 41:7	Breastplates	Isaiah 59:17
Aprons	Acts 19:12	Brick kiln	2 Samuel 12:31
Armor	Judges 9:54	Brick molds	Nahum 3:14
Arrows	1 Samuel 20:36	Bricks	Genesis 11:3
Awls	Exodus 21:6	Bridles	2 Kings 19:28
Awnings	Ezekiel 27:7	Bronze chains	Judges 16:21
Axes	Judges 9:48	Buckets	Numbers 24:7
Bags	Deuteronomy 25:13	Buckler	Psalm 35:2
Balances	Leviticus 19:36	Bugle	1 Corinthians 14:8
Bandages	1 Kings 20:38	Bulwark	Psalm 91:4
Banner	Psalm 60:4	Buttress	2 Chronicles 26:9
Bars	Exodus 36:33	Carts	Isaiah 28:28
Battering rams	Ezekiel 26:9	Chariots	Nahum 3:2
Battle axes	Psalm 35:3	Cistern	Leviticus 11:36
Beads	Song of Solomon 1:10	Clamps	1 Chronicles 22:3
Bellows	Jeremiah 6:29	Clasps	Exodus 26:6
Belts	1 Samuel 18:4	Club	Isaiah 28:27
Birthstool	Exodus 1:16	Conduit	2 Kings 18:17
Blindfold	Mark 14:65	Copper smelter	Job 28:2
Blocks	Jeremiah 6:21	Darts	Job 41:26
Boards	Exodus 26:15	Emery	Ezekiel 3:9
Bolts	Nehemiah 7:3	Engines (of war)	2 Chronicles 26:15
Books	Ezra 4:15	Facial paint (make up)	Jeremiah 4:30
Bottles	Judges 4:19	Fences	Psalm 62:3
Bows	1 Samuel 18:4	Fetters	2 Samuel 3:34
Bowls	Ecclesiastes 12:6	Fire pan	Exodus 27:3
Branding irons	1 Timothy 4:2	Fish nets	Matthew 4:18

Technology	Scripture	Technology	Scripture
Fishhooks	Job 41:1	Plow	Deuteronomy 22:10
Flint	Exodus 4:25	Plowshare	1 Samuel 13:20
Flint knives	Joshua 5:2	Plumb line	Isaiah 34:1
Floodgates	Genesis 7:11	Potsherd	Job 2:8
Forks	1 Samuel 13:21	Pruning hooks	Joel 3:10
Graving tool	Exodus 32:4	Pruning knives	Isaiah 18:5
Grinding mill	Ecclesiastes 12:4	Razor	Numbers 6:5
Guideposts	Jeremiah 31:21	Rims	1 Kings 7:33
Hammer	1 Kings 6:7	Road marks	Jeremiah 31:21
Handkerchiefs	Acts 19:12	Rods	Psalm 23:4
Hatchet	Psalm 74:6	Ropes	Judges 15:13, 16:11
Helmet	Isaiah 59:17	Sacks	Genesis 42:35
Hinges	Proverbs 26:14	Sails	Acts 27:40
Hoes	1 Samuel 13:20	Saws	2 Samuel 12:31
Hooks	Exodus 38:3	Scales	Micah 6:11
Hubs	1 Kings 7:33	Sharp instruments	1 Chronicles 20:3
Ink	2 John 1:12	Shields	1 Kings 10:17
Iron axes	2 Samuel 12:31	Ship rudders	James 3:4
Iron cutting tools	Isaiah 44:12	Ships	Proverbs 30:19
Iron tools	Deuteronomy 27:5	Shoes	Isaiah 20:2
Javelin	Job 41:26	Shovels	Exodus 27:3
Jugs	1 Samuel 1:24	Sickles	Deuteronomy 23:25
Keys	Matthew 16:19	Siegeworks	Ecclesiastes 9:14
Ladder	Genesis 28:12	Signposts	Ezekiel 21:19
Mattock	1 Samuel 13:20	Sling	1 Samuel 17:40
Measures	Proverbs 20:10	Snares	Job 18:9
Mill	Matthew 24:41	Snuffers	Exodus 25:38
Millstones	Numbers 11:8	Sockets	Exodus 26:19
Mortar	Numbers 11:8	Soldering	Isaiah 41:7
Muzzle	1 Corinthians 9:9	Spades	Deuteronomy 23:13
Nails	Isaiah 41:7	Spears	Job 41:26
Needles	Matthew 19:24	Spindle	Proverbs 31:19
Oars	Ezekiel 27:29	Spokes	1 Kings 7:33
Oven	Genesis 15:17	Sponge	Matthew 27:48
Pails	Exodus 38:3	Spoons	2 Kings 25:14
Paper (papyrus)	2 John 1:12	Staff	Psalm 23:4
Parchment	2 Timothy 4:13	Storehouses	Genesis 41:56
Pestle	Proverbs 27:22	Stove	Leviticus 11:36
Pitchers	Ecclesiastes 12:6	Swords	Micah 4:3
Planks	1 Kings 6:9	Tables	Matthew 21:12
Plaster	Leviticus 14:41–42	Tablets	Deuteronomy 4:13
Plating	Numbers 16:38–39	Tackle	Acts 27:19

(*Continued*)

Technology	Scripture	Technology	Scripture
Threshing floor	Numbers 18:27	Water distribution systems	Isaiah 22:9; 2 Kings 20:20
Threshing stages	2 Samuel 24:22	Water pots	John 2:6
Threshing wheel	Proverbs 20:26	Weaver's shuttle	Job 7:6
Torch	Genesis 15:17	Weights	Leviticus 19:36
Torches	Judges 7:16	Wheels	1 Kings 7:33
Utensils	Exodus 25:39	Whips	Nahum 3:2
Vats	Joel 2:24	Window frames	1 Kings 7:4
Vessels	Exodus 7:19	Wine cellars	1 Chronicles 27:27
Vials	Mark 14:3	Wine press	2 Kings 6:27
Wagons	Amos 2:13	Wine vats	Numbers 18:27
Wash bowls	Psalm 60:8	Yokes	Hosea 10:11

Endnotes

1. The English words used here are those used in the New American Standard version.
2. Beebe, H. K. (1975). Domestic architecture and the New Testament. *Biblical Archaeologist*. 38(3–4), 89–104; Clark, D. R. (2003). Bricks, sweat and tears: The human investment in constructing a "four-room" house. *Near Eastern Archaeology*. 66(1–2), 34–43; Ebeling, J. R., & Rowan, Y. M. (2004). The archaeology of the daily grind: Ground stone tools and food production in the Southern Levant. *Near Eastern Archaeology*. 67(2), 108–117; Fitzgerald, A. (1989). The technology of Isaiah 40:19–20 + 41:6–7. *Catholic Biblical Quarterly*. 51(3), 426–446. Frick, F. S. (1999). Oil from flinty rock (Deuteronomy 32:13): Olive cultivation and olive oil processing in the Hebrew Bible—a socio-materialist perspective. *Semeia*. 86, 3–17; Hiebert, T. (1998). Altars of stone and bronze: Two biblical views on technology. *Mission Studies*. 15(2), 75–84; Johnston, R. H. (1974). Biblical potter. *Biblical Archaeologist*. 37(4), 86–106; McNutt, P. M. (1990). *Forging of Israel: Iron technology, symbolism and tradition in ancient society*. Sheffield, UK: Sheffield Academic Press; Muir, J. C. (1938/2004). *Business men of the Bible: A study of the advance agents of trade and commerce*. Whitefish, MT: Kessinger Publishing; Neufeld, E. (1971). Hygiene conditions in ancient Israel. *Biblical Archaeologist*. 34(2), 42–66; Scott, R. B. Y. (1959). Weights and measures of the Bible. *Biblical Archaeologist*. 22(2), 22–40; Smith, R. H. (1964). Household lamps of Palestine in Old Testament times. *Biblical Archaeologist*. 27(1), 2–31; Wright, G. E. (1955). Israelite daily life. *Biblical Archaeologist*. 18(3), 50–79; Shortland, A. (2001). *The social context of technological change in Egypt and the Near East, 1650–1550 BC*. Oxford, UK: Oxbow Books.

Appendix D
The Christian as Manager and Leader: A Small-Group Study Guide

The purpose of this Small-Group Study Guide is to provide practicing managers, supervisors, top-level executives, and entrepreneurs a structured means to discuss with other Christian managers how to integrate their Christian faith with their work. The Study Guide is designed to be used with this book. The book provides coverage of both the biblical record and contemporary management thought and practice. The Study Guide provides relevant Scripture passages and questions to consider.

Organization of This Study Guide

This Study Guide is designed for Bible study, contemplation, and discussion in a small-group setting. The Study Guide is organized into 13 structured modules plus 2 bonus modules. Small groups who choose to meet weekly will be able to complete the series in one quarter of a year. Some groups may wish to meet twice each week or once every other week. Each module is subdivided into seven sections for the convenience of group members who wish to study and meditate on a portion of the material each day of the week. Each section contains suggested Bible readings and/or suggested discussion questions. These questions are merely to start discussion. Discussion leaders and group members will bring additional questions about issues that are important to them.

Organizing a Small Group

To get a small group of Christian managers together requires someone to take the lead in recruiting and organizing the group. This doesn't mean that the organizer must be the subject expert to whom everyone else turns for advice. This Study Guide assumes that managers at all levels will be able to contribute relevant information, ideas, and questions regardless of their reputation for being an expert.

A group size of 8 to 12 people is optimal. If more people are interested, then consider dividing into two groups. If the group is too large, then individual participation will decline for some group members while a few will dominate the discussions.

Look around you at work, at church, or any other organization to which you belong. How many Christians do you know who are in a supervisory or leadership position? How many might be interested in participating in a small group? Start organizing your group by talking with the people whom you know the best: your pastor, your neighbor, your friend who manages in a company across town, or a coworker. Consider asking permission to present or publish an announcement in church regarding your interest in forming a group. Provide your contact information.

If you live in a town that has a college or university, consider recruiting a few business students to join your group. Just about any business major can benefit from participating in such a group even if they believe that they will never be a manager during their career. They can benefit from hearing the perspective of practicing managers. Their idealism and creativity can be an inspiration to practicing managers. There may already be a Christian student group on campus that you can contact first. If no such formal student group exists, then canvass area churches for information regarding college students who might like to participate. Another option is for a student to lead a group of practicing managers in the 13-week series or a practicing manager to lead a group of business students through the series.

Consider kicking off your idea by collaborating with others to sponsor a prayer breakfast, panel discussion at church, or a church seminar on integrating faith at work.

Decide as a group where and when to meet. Many options are available limited only by the busy schedules of group members. Small groups may be able to meet in someone's home, at a church building, a health club, a restaurant, a community room, or at work. An alternative is to set up an online study group. The benefit of this venue is that you can recruit group members from just about anywhere in the world who have access to the Internet.

Regardless of which location you choose, go through the proper channels for permission. If you think that meeting at a workplace is ideal, you may need to seek permission to start an authorized affinity group. Check with your human resources management department or the executive in charge of operations of your organization. Be prepared to explain the purpose of the group such as Bible study, fellowship, prayer, and discussions of how the Christian faith guides managers to improve their work.

Picking a day of the week and time of day that works for everyone can be tricky. Managers are busy. You may find that meeting after church, in the early morning, or on Sunday evenings works best. Online discussion groups may try real-time instant messaging discussions, blogs, or asynchronous discussion boards.

As the group begins to form with the first two or three people giving tentative commitments, use the telephone, a personal meeting, or email to introduce group members to each other. Once you have enough people to start the group, such as four or five, obtain specific formal commitments for the number of weeks the group will meet and the length of each meeting. Limiting the commitment to just 13 weeks gives group members a chance to evaluate whether they want to continue. Discuss special needs of individual group members such as other commitments they have already made and adjust the schedule if necessary. Agree together on the expectations of group participation such as whether group members will be expected to have read and thought about the material ahead of time. Come to agreement regarding what resources group members should plan on bringing to each meeting (such as a Bible, an example from their own work life of one of the issues related to the module, etc.). Agree together on a policy regarding letting others join the group after it gets going. Smaller groups may want to build their membership. Larger, fully populated groups may want to encourage others to form a separate group. Come to agreement regarding what things need to be held confidential. When managers get together to talk, it can be natural for people to tell "war stories." Agree to be confidential when telling personal or organizational stories.

Leading a Small Group

Every group is different, but one common success feature is that the group designates at least one person as leader. One or two people may serve as the group discussion leaders, or the leadership role can be rotated among group members each week.

Structuring the group meeting can be accomplished in a variety of ways. Discuss the options among group members. As a starting idea, consider the following "agenda" outline:

1. Introduction of the theme for the meeting
2. Singing, sharing, and prayer
3. Highlights of the main issues in the Bible verses and study questions
4. Sharing of experiences and illustrations
5. Discussion of tension points for the Christian related to the meeting's theme
6. Exploration of how the Christian can appropriately share one's faith in the marketplace
7. Closing prayer and fellowship

Drawing group members into discussion is vital if you want to have a successful study group experience. Those who are predisposed to quickly giving their opinions will need to reign themselves in and take a leadership role by encouraging others to talk. If just one or two people dominate the discussion every week, expect that some group members will stop coming. Consider spending 1 or 2 minutes at the end of each group session for the group to give feedback to each other regarding the degree of participation that was observed at that meeting.

Monitor the level of interaction and enjoyment that group members seem to exhibit during the 13 weeks. Do group members genuinely enjoy each other's company and comments? Do group members encourage critical thinking? Do group members encourage each other? Does the group handle disagreements in a healthy, Christian way? Do the nonverbal messages that group members give each other indicate positive regard for each other and for the discussion process? Are all group members participating? Does the discussion stay on track or wander off topic?

As you near the completion of the 13-week series, consider planning a special spiritual dedication event in which group members and their families participate together.

Module 1	Theme: Work	Topics and Bible Verses to Read	Discussion Questions
	Day 1	Creation: God's work and ours Genesis 1:26–31 Psalm 8 Psalm 102:25 Ecclesiastes 8:17 Ephesians 2:4–11 Philippians 2:13	What do these passages teach us about why we work? How might it be possible for a person to experience both vanity and delight in work at the same management job?
	Day 2	For whom do we work Proverbs 3:9, 16:3, 16:11 Ecclesiastes 3:10–11 Acts 1:7–9 Romans 12:11 1 Corinthians 10:31 Ephesians 6:7 Colossians 3:17, 23 2 Timothy 2:12 1 Peter 4:11	In theory, Christians know that they ultimately work for God's glory. In practice, must Christians always maintain this constant awareness in the midst of a hectic work schedule? If you came to work tomorrow and Jesus met you at the door introducing himself as your supervisor, how would your work change?
	Day 3	Work is service to community Galatians 6:10 Ephesians 4:28 1 Peter 4:8–11 Titus 2:14 Hebrews 13:16	In what way is your management job service to the larger community? If coworkers have lost a sense of the bigger picture of their job, what can you do to help them regain an awareness of purpose in their work?
	Day 4	Fulfillment and vanity Psalm 90:17 Proverbs 22:29 Ecclesiastes 2, 3:1–13, 5:18–19, 9:7–9	When have you felt that work was mere vanity? What contributed to feeling like that? When have you felt that work was fulfilling a worthy purpose? What contributed to feeling like that? How can a manager minister to employees who have tasks that are inherently less fulfilling than other tasks?
	Day 5	Work, peace, and contentment Deuteronomy 15:10 Psalm 34:14 Proverbs 15:16 Matthew 6:32–33 Luke 3:14 Philippians 4:11–13 1 Timothy 6:6–8 Hebrews 13:5–6	Is ambition inherently sinful? On what basis does God want us to excel? How can a Christian transform the value of ambition by how work life is lived?
	Day 6	Rest Exodus 20:8–11, 23:12, 34:21 Deuteronomy 5:12–15 Psalm 23 Ecclesiastes 4:6 Hebrews 4:1–11	Review the Management Pyramid portrayed in the chapters of this book. How does the Management Pyramid apply to rest from work? What does it mean to truly rest from labor? Is rest a cessation of labor or something deeper? Consider the concept of the Sabbath. How can Christians bring the concept of Sabbath into their life of work? How long does it take you to unwind or decompress at the end of a hectic workweek? How does the busy executive "turn off" the mental dimension of work on the day of worship?

Module 1	Theme: Work	Topics and Bible Verses to Read	Discussion Questions
	Day 7	Use a Bible concordance to find and read Bible passages that mention the word diligence or diligent. How is it possible to keep diligent without becoming so absorbed in your work that your life gets out of balance? Do you feel fulfilled in the work that you do? If not, where outside of work do you find fulfillment? What might you do to change your work situation so that work is more fulfilling? How can you truly find rest for your soul? What can you do in your family and in your community to help others glorify God in and through their work? What are you doing in your family and in your community to help others gain fulfillment from their work? Are you working for God even when you are not doing the work of an evangelist at the workplace? How and why? If your job title was changed to "Minister" or "Pastor" how would that change your understanding of your role in working for God? Is it appropriate to think of your role at work as a spiritual ministry? Explain. As a group, write a prayer about work and working that encompasses some of the deepest heart desires of group members. Include each group member's thoughts. Save this written prayer for review and discussion at the end of the series.	
	For further reading	See: Chapters 1, 2, 15, and 16 of this book. Chewning, R. C., Eby, J. W., & Roels, S. J. (1990). *Business through the eyes of faith*. San Francisco, CA: HarperSanFrancisco. Hardy, L. (1990). *The fabric of this world: Inquiries into calling, career choice, and the design of human work*. Grand Rapids, MI: William B. Eerdmans Publishing Company. Stevens, R. P. (2006). *Doing God's business: Meaning and motivation for the marketplace*. Grand Rapids, MI: William B. Eerdmans Publishing Company. Volf, M. (1991). *Work in the Spirit: Toward a theology of work*. Eugene, OR: Wipf and Stock Publishers.	

Module 2	Theme: Accountability	Topics and Bible Verses to Read	Discussion Questions
	Day 1	God and truth Psalm 25:10, 26:3, 86:11, 117:2, 119:43 Proverbs 20:28 1 Kings 2:4, 3:6 2 Kings 20:3 Isaiah 8:3 John 17:17 Galatians 2:14 3 John 3–4	Why do you think truthfulness of God is highly revered by Bible writers? Why is finding the truth so important to managers? How can a manager seek the truth without coming across as trying to be God at work?
	Day 2	Accountability and community Genesis 23:10–18 Proverbs 13:17, 25:13 Ecclesiastes 4:9–10 Jeremiah 32:10 Luke 12:42 John 8:17 Galatians 6:1–2 Colossians 3:9, 3:16	Why was land to be purchased in the presence of witnesses in biblical times? How can the Christian community remain faithful in accountability to each other but not judge each other?

(*Continued*)

Module 2	Theme: Accountability	Topics and Bible Verses to Read	Discussion Questions
	Day 3	Accountability is scalable Matthew 25:15 Luke 12:48, 16:10–12 James 3:1	Can accountability be taught? How do you feel about being more accountable than your subordinates? Is it fair that managers have more responsibility than their subordinates? Why?
	Day 4	Accountable to God Numbers 32:23 Psalm 58:11, 96:13 Matthew 12:36–37 Romans 2:2, 3:19, 14:12	How should a Christian express accountability to God in terms of sharing faith at work? How does accountability to the organization demonstrate accountability to God?
	Day 5	The problem with unfaithfulness Numbers 13–14 Ezekiel 34	How should a Christian manager deal with subordinates when they are unfaithful at work? How should a Christian manager or employee respond when the business owner is unfaithful?
	Day 6	Accountability and peace Genesis 1:28, 2:5, 2:19–20 Ephesians 2:14	In what way do managers fulfill a covenant of peace with others through their work? How does accountability contribute to peace in a community?
	Day 7	How should a Christian manager ensure accountability while treating others with dignity and respect? In what ways should a Christian promote accountability at work? How do you know when you are promoting accountability to the organization at the expense of accountability to employees? What can you do differently to exercise managerial control at work in a way that brings glory to God? As a group, write a prayer about managerial control that encompasses some of the deepest heart desires of group members. Include each group member's thoughts. Save this written prayer for review and discussion at the end of the series. As a group, write a prayer about accountability that encompasses some of the deepest heart desires of group members. Include each group member's thoughts. Save this written prayer for review and discussion at the end of the series.	
	For further reading	See: Chapter 14 of this book.	

Module 3	Theme: Decision Making	Topics and Bible Verses to Read	Discussion Questions
	Day 1	God is the source of wisdom Deuteronomy 7:6–7 1 Samuel 10:24 Colossians 3:12 2 Thessalonians 2:13 James 1:5	Think of a time in your work that God gave you wisdom for a difficult decision. Did this wisdom come through other people or through your own thinking? How do you know when wisdom for a decision is from God?
	Day 2	Uncertainty Job Psalm 52:7 Proverbs 11:28, 23:5, 27:1, 27:23–26 1 Peter 5:7 James 4:13–16	What role should human reason play in making management decisions? When you face uncertainty, how do you turn this over to God for help? How does a Christian face uncertainty differently from a non-Christian?

Module 3	Theme: Decision Making	Topics and Bible Verses to Read	Discussion Questions
	Day 3	Human limitations in decision making Proverbs 27:1 Ecclesiastes 7:14, 11:6 Isaiah 55:8–9 Mark 4:26–29 2 Corinthians 9:6	What are the human limitations with respect to decision making? What role has your faith played in making a decision when you lacked information? What are the characteristics of a wise manager? How does a manager develop wisdom?
	Day 4	Human inconsistencies in decision making and the solution Romans 6:17–23, 7:19–8:4 Galatians 5:16–24 1 Peter 2:9–12	How does the human inability to be consistent in decision making complicate life? See the verse in 1 Peter 2. Can you think of a time when an action you took as a manager was at first criticized and later praised?
	Day 5	Discerning God's will Joshua 1:8 Psalm 18:41, 22:28, 25:14, 32:8, 66:7, 119:105 Proverbs 1:28, 12:15, 16:33, 19:20 Romans 8:28 Philippians 2:13, 4:19 2 Timothy 2:15 James 1:5–7	How should a Christian discern God's will in business and management situations? How does a leader gain the courage to go in a different direction than the other leaders want to go? How do you know that the opinion of others in the organization isn't God's will? What is your view of God's providence? (See the four models presented in Exhibit 6-6 of Chapter 6 of this book.) How does a Christian know when a situation is God's providential leading? Are all events in life God's providence?
	Day 6	Participation in decision making Genesis 24 2 Samuel 18:1–4 1 Kings 12 2 Kings 20:20–22, 23:1–8 1 Chronicles 13:1–4 Matthew 21 Luke 10 John 12:15	Read the accompanying Bible passages. What seem to be the differences in terms of subordinates participating in decision making? What happens when leaders make it appear that they are interested in subordinates participating but then ignore their advice? What would happen to the decision-making processes at work if Jesus were part of the committee?
	Day 7	Given what you know regarding what the Bible says on decision making, how is a Christian to make decisions under conditions of uncertainty? How should a Christian integrate faith and decision making at work? What can you do differently in your decision making at work in a way that brings glory to God? As a group, write a prayer about decision making that encompasses some of the deepest heart desires of group members. Include each group member's thoughts. Save this written prayer for review and discussion at the end of the series.	
	For further reading	See: Chapter 6 of this book. Meadors, G. T. (2003). *Decision making God's way: A new model for knowing God's will*. Grand Rapids, MI: Baker Books. Friesen, G., & Maxon, J. R. (2004). *Decision making & the will of God*. Portland, OR: Multnomah Press.	

Module 4	Theme: Quality and Excellence	Topics and Bible Verses to Read	Discussion Questions
	Day 1	Creation quality and God's excellence Genesis 1–2 Exodus 15:7 Deuteronomy 32:4 Psalm 150:2 Isaiah 12:5 Philippians 1:10 1 Timothy 4:4	What can we learn for our work today from the quality of God's work at Creation? How can I make my work reflect God's excellence? If Christians try to emulate God in everything, does this mean that nothing we do will be mediocre, or are there times when mediocrity is acceptable or necessary?
	Day 2	Placing high value on the best Exodus 23:19 Deuteronomy 20:25, 33:14, 33:16 1 Kings 11:29–30 Psalm 33:3, 96:1 Proverbs 27:25 Jeremiah 31:31 Mark 1:27 John 13:34 Acts 17:19 Revelation 2:17	What conclusions regarding quality can we draw from the Bible record on things that are new, choicest, and freshest? How can I affect the quality of work in my organization? Should a Christian manager always be at the forefront of leading quality improvement efforts in the organization? How does a Christian decide to limit resources allocated to quality improvement?
	Day 3	Repairing, renewing, and restoring Leviticus 14:42 Deuteronomy 30:3 2 Kings 12:5–12, 22:5–6 2 Chronicles 24:4–13 Psalm 51:10–12, 80:3–7 Lamentations 5:21 Galatians 6:1	Notice how important repairing, renewing, and restoring are in the Bible. What lesson can we learn for work in commerce? How do we know when it is better to cut losses and not repair? In what way is an emphasis on quality improvement an offering to God?
	Day 4	An experiment in quality improvement Daniel 1	What can Daniel's experience tell us about the importance of making careful choices to change outcomes in processes?
	Day 5	Jesus' example Mark 7:35–37	Should the Christian expect that following Christ's example of excellence will result in people talking about the quality of the work? If Jesus were on your quality improvement committee, how would your work be different from what it is now?
	Day 6	Our life of excellence Proverbs 17:7 Ecclesiastes 9:10 Romans 12:10–11 2 Corinthians 8:20–21 Galatians 5:22–24 Philippians 1:9–10, 4:8 1 Peter 2:12 2 Peter 1:5–6	What is excellent behavior among nonbelievers? How does a Christian live a life of excellence when it is so difficult being consistent? (cf. Romans 7:19–20) How open are you to receiving feedback regarding how you can improve as a manager?

Module 4	Theme: Quality and Excellence	Topics and Bible Verses to Read	Discussion Questions
	Day 7		In what ways can a Christian integrate faith and quality improvement efforts? In what way is a commitment to excellence and quality an inside-out process for a manager? When is it appropriate for transformation to come from the outside in? What work processes are in need of the most attention in terms of quality improvement? If quality improvement efforts were applied to every area of our life, would this resolve the tension a Christian experiences when trying to pursue profit and honor God? What can you do differently to improve excellence at work in a way that brings glory to God? Can you think of an example of someone who was or is excellent at "preaching" the Gospel only through his or her behavior? How can a person's actions be such a powerful force for God? As a group, write a prayer about excellence and quality that encompasses some of the deepest heart desires of group members. Include each group member's thoughts. Save this written prayer for review and discussion at the end of the series.
	For further reading	See: Chapter 14 of this book.	

Module 5	Theme: Communication	Topics and Bible Verses to Read	Discussion Questions
	Day 1	Communal nature of communication Job 16:5 Proverbs 10:21, 12:18, 13:17, 14:3, 14:25,15:4, 15:23, 16:24, 18:20–21, 22:17–18, 25:11–12, 31:26 Ecclesiastes 10:12 Ephesians 4:29 Colossians 4:5–6 James 3:8–10	Why is speaking evil of other people the same as cursing God? What does it mean to season your speech with salt? Contrast a situation in which a manager's response to an employee is thoughtless versus thoughtful. In what ways would we be more effective if we took time to help each other improve our communication?
	Day 2	Truth telling and community trust Proverbs 12:22 Psalm 12:2; 62:4; Jeremiah 9:8 Matthew 15:8 Ephesians 4:15	Why is the success of a community, company, or organization founded on truth-telling? How do you tell employees in an honest and loving way that their performance needs to improve? If Jesus attended your employee staff meeting in which you are in charge, how would you communicate differently from what you do now?
	Day 3	Communication is relevant and effective Psalm 49:3 Proverbs 15:2, 15:7, 18:4, 31:26	Why must a manager take responsibility to make sure that communication is appropriate to the situation?
	Day 4	Listen more than we speak vs. keeping silent when we should speak Proverbs 11:12, 15:28, 16:30, 17:28, 18:13 Ecclesiastes 3:7 James 1:19	How does a manager know when it is a time to be silent versus a time to speak? Give an example of a situation when you should have kept silent but didn't. How might the situation have turned out differently if you had remained silent? In what situations does keeping silent make a problem worse?

(Continued)

Module 5	Theme: Communication	Topics and Bible Verses to Read	Discussion Questions
	Day 5	Communication can be destructive Job 20:12, 27:4 Psalm 10:7, 36:3, 50:19, 52:2–4, 59:12, 78:36, 120:2 Proverbs 4:24, 6:16–19, 10:8–11, 12:17, 18:21, 18:19–20, 18:22, 19:5, 9:9, 21:6, 26:28	When is it appropriate for Christians to apologize for things that they say? How should Christians make amends after being destructive in their speech?
	Day 6	The power of word of mouth to do good or ill Deuteronomy 28:36–37 2 Chronicles 7:19–20 Psalm 15:3, 41:6–7, 44:13–14 Proverbs 10:18, 11:9, 11:13, 16:28, 20:19, 25:23, 26:20 Jeremiah 24:9 Ezekiel 36:3 Colossians 3:8	Is there a place for gossip in the Christian workplace? What are some ways that a Christian can manage gossip and rumor in the organization? When an employee brings you a juicy piece of gossip, as a Christian, how do you respond?
	Day 7	See Leviticus 5:4; Numbers 30:2; Deuteronomy 23:23; Psalm 50:16, 89:34. How does speech signify a covenant commitment and a heart that is intent on taking action? Review the story of the 12 spies in Numbers 13–14. What effect did their communication have on the nation? What are the best ways that a Christian can integrate faith and business communication? What can you do differently in your communication at work in a way that brings glory to God? As a group, write a prayer about communication that encompasses some of the deepest heart desires of group members. Include each group member's thoughts. Save this written prayer for review and discussion at the end of the series.	
	For further reading	See: Chapters 4 and 10 of this book. Muehlhoff, T., & Lewis, T. V. (2010). *Authentic communication: Christian speech engaging culture*. Downers Grove, IL: InterVarsity Press.	

Module 6	Theme: Planning	Topics and Bible Verses to Read	Discussion Questions
	Day 1	Planning is a community experience 2 Kings 6:8 1 Chronicles 13:1 2 Chronicles 10:6, 20:21, 30:2, 32:3 Nehemiah 6:7 Proverbs 12:15, 13:10, 14:22, 15:22	Why is it important for a manager to include others in planning for the future? If Jesus were physically present on your planning team, how would the planning process be different from what it is now?
	Day 2	Planning and God's sovereignty Job 42:2 Proverbs 16:3, 16:9, 19:21 Isaiah 14:27 Acts 5:38 James 4:13–16	If God directs our steps, then what is the point of planning? If God is in complete control, then why does he expect us to plan?
	Day 3	Committing our plans to God Proverbs 3:5 Matthew 6:25–34 Romans 8:28	What does it mean to commit your plans to God? What does it mean to not lean on our own understanding? Shouldn't a Christian use reason and judgment when planning for the future?

Module 6	Theme: Planning	Topics and Bible Verses to Read	Discussion Questions
	Day 4	The benefits of planning ahead Nehemiah 2:6 Proverbs 14:8, 14:15–17, 21:5 Luke 14:28–31	Will a Christian manager tend to be more cautious in planning than a non-Christian manager? Why?
	Day 5	Inadequate planning Genesis 25:31–34 Judges 16 1 Samuel 17 Matthew 7:26–27, 14–15, 26:50–53	Consider these examples of inadequate planning. How might the situations have turned out differently if the key people had planned for contingencies? How do a manager's assumptions reduce the need for planning? How can Christian managers test their assumptions about the future?
	Day 6	Examples of planners in the Bible Genesis 41 Esther 4–8 Matthew 26:18–19 Acts 6; 9	What can we learn about planning from Joseph, Esther, Jesus, and the early church leaders?
	Day 7	In what ways can a Christian integrate faith and the work of planning? What can you do differently in your planning at work in a way that brings glory to God? As a group, write a prayer about planning that encompasses some of the deepest heart desires of group members. Include each group member's thoughts. Save this written prayer for review and discussion at the end of the series.	
	For further reading	See: Chapters 6 and 7 in this book.	

Module 7	Theme: Leading	Topics and Bible Verses to Read	Discussion Questions
	Day 1	Trustworthiness Exodus 18:19–22 Proverbs 13:17 Luke 12:48, 16:10 1 Corinthians 4:2 1 Timothy 3:1–13	Consider the selection criteria that Moses used to choose leaders. Which of these criteria apply today? Review the selection criteria for church leaders. Which of these criteria apply today?
	Day 2	Integrity 1 Kings 9:4, 21:7–15 Job 2:3 Psalm 78:70–72 Proverbs 4:23–25, 19:1 Amos 5:10	What is the difference between honesty and integrity? Why is integrity so important for effective leadership? Where have you seen an example of a leader seizing a "vineyard"?
	Day 3	Humility and servant leadership 1 Kings 12:7 Proverbs 15:33, 16:19, 18:12, 22:4, 25:6–7, 29:23 Matthew 23:11 Mark 9:35–37 Luke 9:46–48, 22:24–27 Philippians 2:3–11 1 Peter 4:8–11, 5:5	What is humility? Why is this trait so important for effective leadership? Is it realistic that a humble leader in today's society can be effective? How or why? What does servant leadership look like where you work? If Jesus worked in your organization, how would he be serving as a leader?

(Continued)

Module 7	Theme: Leading	Topics and Bible Verses to Read	Discussion Questions
	Day 4	Working for justice Deuteronomy 24:14 2 Chronicles 19:4–11 2 Samuel 8:15 Psalm 72:1–17 Zechariah 7:10 Matthew 8:1–3, 21:12–13, 23:13–29 Mark 2:15–17 Luke 11:42–52 James 2:1–4	How does a Christian balance the need for justice with the need to care for the interests of the organization? How does a Christian decide how much to do when caring for the least advantaged employees? The least advantaged citizens in the community?
	Day 5	Leading change starts with transforming the leader Joshua 1:7–8 Ezra 7:25 Galatians 5:22–23 Philippians 4:8 Colossians 3:12–15 1 Timothy 2:1–2 Titus 1:5–9	Why does effectiveness in leading change begin with the leader being transformed? If Jesus were at your workplace tomorrow morning, what would he say regarding how you need to change yourself to be more effective as a leader?
	Day 6	Developing a realistic awareness of self Proverbs 16:18–19, 25:27, 26:12 Romans 12:3 1 Corinthians 12:7–11 Galatians 6:3 Philippians 2:3–8	How can Christians develop a realistic awareness of themselves? In what ways can a Christian help other leaders improve their self-understanding?
	Day 7	In what ways can a Christian integrate faith and leadership? What can you do differently to lead at work in a way that brings glory to God? As a group, write a prayer about leadership that encompasses some of the deepest heart desires of group members. Include each group member's thoughts. Save this written prayer for review and discussion at the end of the series.	
	For further reading	See: Chapters 1, 2, 3, and 12 of this book. Woolfe, L. (2002). *The Bible on leadership: From Moses to Matthew; management lessons for contemporary leaders*. New York: American Management Association. Borek, J., Lovett, D., & Towns, E. (2005). *The good book on leadership: Case studies from the Bible*. B&H Academic. Porter, J. (2005). *Leading lessons: Insights on leadership from women in the Bible*. Augsburg Books. Alford, H. J., & Naughton, M. J. (2001). *Managing as if faith mattered: Christian social principles in the modern organization*. Notre Dame, IN: University of Notre Dame Press.	

Module 8	Theme: Organizing	Topics and Bible Verses to Read	Discussion Questions
	Day 1	Chain of command Matthew 6:4 Luke 16:13	What is the fundamental principle that Jesus refers to? Does this passage absolutely forbid having dual reporting relationships in an organization?
	Day 2	Organizing: Division of labor (specialization) and coordination Genesis 1:26–28, 2:7, 2:18–25, 4:2, 4:17–22, 9:20, 11:1–9; 13:1–12, 39–41 Exodus 3–13, 25–32 2 Samuel 8 Daniel 1–5	Notice the variety of specialized jobs described in the Bible. Is there anything inherently wrong with specialization? In what way, if any, does the Great Commission to subdue the earth apply to understanding all we can about how organizations work?

Module 8	Theme: Organizing	Topics and Bible Verses to Read	Discussion Questions
	Day 3	Jesus and organizing Matthew 10:1, 11:1, 14:14–21, 15:32–38, 21:1–7, 26:18–19 Luke 10:1–20, 22:8–14	If you asked Jesus to recommend improvements to your organization, what do you think he would say? Why? How can Christian managers prevent becoming so focused on the organization that they lose sight of the people in the organization?
	Day 4	Decision-making authority Genesis 1:26–28 Exodus 32:15–24 Numbers 12:1–16, 16:1–35, 17:1–10, 25:1–5 Nehemiah 3, 7:2 Proverbs 19:10 Isaiah 14:13–15 Matthew 22:21 Luke 7:1–10 Romans 13:1–7	What is the proper place of authority in an organization? Is it ever appropriate for a person in higher decision-making authority to take over the responsibility that has been delegated to someone in lower authority?
	Day 5	Authority of the Holy Spirit Isaiah 60:17 John 3:5–8, 7:39, 14:26, 15:26, 16:13, 17:23, 20:22 Acts 1:2–8 Ephesians 4:3, 4:13	To what degree must transformation of the heart be accomplished before the need for human oversight goes away?
	Day 6	Redeeming the organization Exodus 18	What does it mean to redeem an organization? Why do organizations need to be redeemed? Where does the organization in which you work need to be redeemed?
	Day 7	See Acts 6:1–7, 6:15; 1 Corinthians 12:27–31; 1 Timothy 3:1–7. How would you describe the structure of the early church? Is it possible to employ other organizational designs and still do things "decently and in order"? In what ways can a Christian integrate faith and organizing? What can you do differently to organize at work in a way that brings glory to God? As a group, write a prayer about organizing that encompasses some of the deepest heart desires of group members. Include each group member's thoughts. Save this written prayer for review and discussion at the end of the series.	
	For further reading	See: Chapter 8 and Appendix C of this book. Hardy, L. (1990). *The fabric of this world: Inquiries into calling, career choice, and the design of human work*. Grand Rapids, MI: William B. Eerdmans Publishing Company.	

Module 9	Theme: Human Resources	Topics and Bible Verses to Read	Discussion Questions
	Day 1	Employment: A covenant relationship Ephesians 6:5–8 Colossians 3:22–25, 4:1 1 Timothy 6:1–2 Titus 2:9 1 Peter 2:18–20	How is the employment relationship a covenant? What principles discussed in terms of masters and slaves from biblical times apply to employers and employees? How far should the concept of covenant be applied to the employer–employee relationship?
	Day 2	Employee recruitment and selection Proverbs 26:10 Matthew 10:1–5, 10:24–25, 13:52, 16:24 Mark 3:16–19 Luke 14:26–33 Acts 9	If Jesus were in charge of selecting new employees in your organization, how would the process be different from what it is now? Would Jesus select new employees that are the best match for the organization or the best candidates that need character development?

(*Continued*)

Module 9	Theme: Human Resources	Topics and Bible Verses to Read	Discussion Questions
	Day 3	Employee development Exodus 4:12–15, 35:30–34 2 Chronicles 36:16 Proverbs 1:7, 1:25–30, 5:12, 6:23, 12:1 Isaiah 5:21 Matthew 10:1–11:1 Mark 6:7–13 Luke 10	How much should a manager expect employees to do for themselves to develop skills and expertise at work? How does a Christian manager decide when it is appropriate for the organization to spend resources to develop employee skills and expertise?
	Day 4	Employee performance evaluations and discipline Deuteronomy 1:17 Proverbs 3:18–20, 6:3, 9:8–9, 12:1 Matthew 7:1, 18:15 Luke 6:36–37 Romans 2:1–2, 14:3–4, 14:10–13 1 Corinthians 4:2 Galatians 6:1 Colossians 3:13 1 Thessalonians 5:14	If Jesus conducted the performance evaluations at your organization, in what ways would the process be different from what it is now? Using the concept of the covenant relationship, describe how you would carry out employee discipline as a Christian manager?
	Day 5	Fairness Exodus 23:2 Leviticus 19:15 Deuteronomy 16:19, 24:17, 27:19 Psalm 82:3 Proverbs 21:3 Isaiah 1:17–23, 33:15, 56:1, 61:8 Amos 5:24 Micah 6:8 Mark 12:33 Colossians 4:1	How is an act of justice at work better in God's sight than participating in a religious ceremony?
	Day 6	Retaliation Exodus 23:4–5 Leviticus 19:18 Proverbs 10:12, 11:3, 15:1, 15:18, 16:7, 17:13–14, 20:22, 24:17, 24:29, 25:15, 25:21–22, 26:21 Obadiah 1:12 Romans 12:17–19; Galatians 5:15 1 Peter 3:8–11	How should a Christian deal with the urge to retaliate against people who take advantage of us, undermine our influence, or attack us?
	Day 7	What can you do differently with respect to human resources management at work in a way that brings glory to God? As a group, write a prayer about human resources management that encompasses some of the deepest heart desires of group members. Include each group member's thoughts. Save this written prayer for review and discussion at the end of the series.	
	For further reading	See: Chapters 5 and 9 of this book. Grudem, W. (2003). *Business for the glory of God: The Bible's teaching on the moral goodness of business*. Wheaton, IL: Crossway Books. Herman, S. W. (1997). *Durable goods: A covenantal ethic for management and employees.* Notre Dame, IN: University of Notre Dame Press.	

Module 10	**Theme: Motivation**	**Topics and Bible Verses to Read**	**Discussion Questions**
	Day 1	Three greatest motivators: Faith Matthew 13:31, 17:20, 21:21 Mark 4:31, 9:23, 11:23 Luke 17:6 1 Corinthians 13:2, 13:13 Galatians 5:5–6	What is faith? What makes faith such a great motivator?
	Day 2	Three greatest motivators: Hope Job 14:6–9 Psalm 22:9, 40:4, 65:5, 71:5 Proverbs 1:33, 14:26, 22:19 1 Thessalonians 5:8 Hebrews 11:1	What is hope? What are the chief sources of hope? How is hope related to faith? What makes hope such a powerful motivator?
	Day 3	Three greatest motivators: Love Matthew 22:37–39 1 Corinthians 13 Romans 13:8–10 2 Corinthians 5:14, 8:8, 9:6–15 Ephesians 4:31–32 Colossians 3:12 1 John 4	What is love? Is love the same as kindness and compassion? What makes love such a powerful motivator?
	Day 4	Other motivators Deuteronomy 25:3 Exodus 20:11–12, 22:26 Leviticus 19:3, 19:20, 21:9 Proverbs 10:3, 10:7, 10:15, 10:21, 13:25, 15:15 1 Samuel 10:6, 10:10 Judges 3:10, 11:29 2 Kings 24:3	Of the ones referred to within these verses, which is the greatest motivator?
	Day 5	Incentives in the Bible Genesis Proverbs	Read the book of Genesis and note how many different incentives are referred to or inferred. Read the book of Proverbs and note how many different incentives are referred to or inferred. Which incentives are the best ones for a Christian to employ? Why?
	Day 6	Intrinsic rewards vs. extrinsic rewards Leviticus 26:3–4 Deuteronomy 7:12–15 2 Samuel 18:22 1 Kings 13:7 Psalm 17:14–15, 19:11, 65:4, 73:25 Proverbs 5:1–2, 17:2, 19:23 Ecclesiastes 2:10, 3:22, 5:18–19, 9:9 Jeremiah 31:14 Matthew 5:6 Luke 10:7	Compared with other types of rewards, how powerful are intrinsic rewards? Who has the responsibility of developing intrinsic rewards that are meaningful to employees: the manager or the subordinate? When is it appropriate for a Christian to use extrinsic rewards to motivate employees? Evaluate the Bible verses for this segment. What, if any, rewards are intrinsic and extrinsic?
	Day 7	What can you do differently at work to motivate workers in a way that brings glory to God? As a group, write a prayer about motivation that encompasses some of the deepest heart desires of group members. Include each group member's thoughts. Save this written prayer for review and discussion at the end of the series.	
	For further reading	See: Chapter 11 of this book. Faw, H. W. (1995). *Psychology in Christian perspective: An analysis of key issues*. Grand Rapids, MI: Baker Books. Miller, W. R., & Delaney, H. D. (Eds.). *Judeo-Christian perspectives on psychology: Human nature, motivation and change*. Washington, DC: American Psychological Association.	

Module 11	Theme: Power and Influence	Topics and Bible Verses to Read	Discussion Questions
	Day 1	Reward power Deuteronomy 5:16 Psalms 81:13–16 Proverbs 3:27, 18:21, 22:1, 27:2 Ecclesiastes 7:1	Is it appropriate for a Christian to give rewards for high performance at work? If Jesus were in charge of a pay for performance system in your organization, what would such a system be like?
	Day 2	Coercion power Exodus 5:9–11, 20:2–6 Leviticus 25:43–53 Deuteronomy 15:6 Judges 8:22 1 Samuel 9:17 Ephesians 6:9	Is it ever appropriate to compel workers? If a Christian manager uses the power of coercion, should that manager ask forgiveness from God?
	Day 3	Legitimate power from position Genesis 1:26–28; Exodus 20:12 Psalm 8:6 Proverbs 1:8–9, 23:22–25 Romans 13:1–8 Ephesians 6:1–3 Colossians 3:20 1 Timothy 5:17	Does the Bible support the use of power that comes from an appointed position? How can a Christian prevent misusing legitimate power that comes from position?
	Day 4	Expert power Genesis 41–47 Leviticus 19:32 Proverbs 12:24, 24:5 Ecclesiastes 7:19 Acts 7:22	How can a Christian use expert power without becoming proud? Will Christians wait for others to request their expertise or will Christians offer expertise?
	Day 5	Referent power Genesis 24:12–14, 39:21, 40:14, 47:29 Joshua 2:12–14 Mark 1:7, 6:22–23, 10:35 John 6:68–69, 21:15–19 Acts 9:26–30 Philippians 3:10 2 Timothy 1:7–9	Under what circumstances is it appropriate to use referent power to influence the organization? Describe how referent power can be misused.
	Day 6	Ecological power (power to restructure jobs, the work environment, the organization, the culture) Exodus 5, 18	What things will a Christian manager consider when restructuring jobs, the organization, or the organization's culture?
	Day 7	See 1 Thessalonians 4:11–12. What are the fundamental Christian traits and behaviors that command respect of nonbelievers? Review the passage that discusses limiting a king's power: Deuteronomy 17:14–20. Why was the king's power to be limited? Which type of power is best for a Christian manager to use? What can you do differently to influence others at work in a way that brings glory to God? As a group, write a prayer about power and influence that encompasses some of the deepest heart desires of group members. Include each group member's thoughts. Save this written prayer for review and discussion at the end of the series.	
	For further reading	See: Chapters 5, 13, and 16 of this book. Walsh, J. P. M. (1987). *Mighty from their thrones: Power in the biblical tradition*. Augsburg Fortress Press. Grottanelli, C. (1999). *Kings and prophets: Monarchic power, inspired leadership, and sacred text in biblical narrative*. New York: Oxford University Press.	

Module 12	Theme: Efficiency and Wealth Building	Topics and Bible Verses to Read	Discussion Questions
	Day 1	God enjoys our prosperity Joshua 1:8 Psalm 1:1–6, 34:6–10, 37:3–4, 84:11, 92:12	If God enjoys our prosperity, then why do we feel uneasy about money?
	Day 2	God gives the power to build wealth Deuteronomy 8:17–18	Notice the covenantal terms with which the power for building wealth is given. How is the human part of the equation for building wealth a covenantal activity?
	Day 3	God values efficiency and practical utility Leviticus 25:3–4 Proverbs 1:17, 24:27 Ecclesiastes 3:2, 10:9–10 Matthew 13:8, 13:23 Mark 4:8, 20 John 15:1–2 2 Corinthians 9:6 1 Thessalonians 4:11–12	How can the believer be encouraged to build wealth (God looks favorably on this) and at the same time avoid loving money (which is the root of evil)?
	Day 4	The purposes of wealth Leviticus 25:25–39 Deuteronomy 6:5, 10:12, 26:2 Psalm 17:14 Proverbs 3:9, 13:22, 31:26–27 Matthew 6:1–4, 2:37 Mark 12:30–33 2 Corinthians 9:13 Philippians 4:14–19 1 Timothy 5:8–13 Titus 3:14 James 2	How is using wealth a means of loving God with our might?
	Day 5	Generosity for the poor Deuteronomy 15:4–11, 24:12–15 Proverbs 14:21, 17:5 Romans 15:26–27 Ephesians 4:28 James 2:2–6, 2:15–16	What resources does a manager have discretionary control over that can be used to help the disadvantaged in the organization? Under what circumstances is it ever appropriate for a manager to use company resources to help someone outside the organization who is economically disadvantaged?
	Day 6	Building wealth using moral means Psalm 37:16, 49:5–6, 52:7, 73:3, 73:12, 92:7, 109:8, 123:4 Matthew 5:44–45	Notice the disapproving tone of the Bible when it talks about building wealth. Why does God give both the faithful believers and unbelievers the power to build wealth?

(Continued)

Module 12	Theme: Efficiency and Wealth Building	Topics and Bible Verses to Read	Discussion Questions
	Day 7	See Ecclesiastes 3:2; Matthew 3:10; Luke 3:9, 13:6–7. What does Solomon mean that there is a time to plant and a time to uproot that which is planted? How can a Christian pursue economic success and at the same time be a faithful witness for God? Why is the goal of maintaining a balance between pursuit of economic success and developing personal family relationships so elusive? What can you do differently to be a responsible steward of finances at work in a way that brings glory to God? As a group, write a prayer about efficiency and building wealth that encompasses some of the deepest heart desires of group members. Include each group member's thoughts. Save this written prayer for review and discussion at the end of the series. As a group, write another prayer that expresses your heart's deepest desires for being with family. Include each group member's thoughts. Save this written prayer for review and discussion at the end of the series.	
	For further reading	See: Chapters 5 and 17 of this book. Griffiths, B. (1984). *The creation of wealth: A Christian's case for capitalism*. Downers Grove, IL: InterVarsity Press. Henderson, J. W., & Pisciotta, J. (Eds.) (2005). *Faithful economics: the moral worlds of a neutral science*. Waco, TX: Baylor University Press. Grudem, W. (2003). *Business and the glory of God*. Wheaton, IL: Crossway Books.	

Module 13	Theme: Calling	Topics and Bible Verses to Read	Discussion Questions
	Day 1	Calling in the Old Testament Exodus 28:3, 31:1, 35:30 Numbers 11:17–29, 27:15–19 Deuteronomy 34:9 Judges 3:9, 6:34, 11:29 1 Samuel 10:6–10, 11:6, 16:13–14, 19:20 2 Kings 2:15 Psalm 51:11 Isaiah 42:1, 44:3	If the Holy Spirit comes upon a manager, does the manager know when this is occurring? How can managers know that what they feel is actually the Holy Spirit? If you do not have a feeling that you have the Holy Spirit, does this mean that you do not have a calling?
	Day 2	Jesus' calling Matthew 3:16 Mark 1:10, 1:38–39 Luke 4:43–50 John 6:38–40, 12:27 Philippians 2:1–11 1 Timothy 1:15 Hebrews 2:14	How clearly did Jesus understand his purpose? How clear is your purpose to you? How can Christians bring more clarity to the sense of purpose in their vocation?
	Day 3	Calling in the New Testament Mark 3:14 Acts 1:8 Romans 1:6, 9:24, 11:29 1 Corinthians 1:1, 1:9, 7:20 2 Corinthians 5:18–19 Colossians 3:12 2 Thessalonians 2:13–14 1 Peter 5:10 2 Peter 1:10	How would you describe calling from the perspective of the New Testament? Is calling the same as your occupation? Why?

Module 13	**Theme: Calling**	**Topics and Bible Verses to Read**	**Discussion Questions**
	Day 4	Calling and salvation Romans 8:28–30 Ephesians 1:18, 4:1–4 Philippians 3:14 2 Thessalonians 1:11 2 Timothy 1:9 Hebrews 3:1	Why do you think the Bible writers discuss calling primarily in terms of salvation rather than occupation? What has your awareness of your own relationship with God contributed to your awareness of your purpose in life?
	Day 5	Calling and spiritual gifts Romans 12 1 Corinthians 12	What are your spiritual gifts? How are you using your spiritual gifts to fulfill your purpose in life?
	Day 6	Calling and love 1 Corinthians 13	Which phrases that describe love seem the most applicable to you and your work? What are the ways that love can be expressed through a calling like yours? What barriers exist for you to express love to God and love to others through your calling?
	Day 7	What is a calling? Is your calling something you can pursue and obtain or is it something that you have and need to find? Can a calling change during one's lifetime? Of all the concepts relevant to a Christian manager that we have considered during our discussions, which one is the most important? What qualities of a Christian manager set this person apart from others? As a group, write a prayer about calling that encompasses some of the deepest heart desires of group members. Include each group member's thoughts. Save this written prayer for review and discussion at the end of the series.	
	For further reading	See: Chapter 15 of this book. Stevens, R. P. (2006). *Doing God's business: Meaning and motivation for the marketplace.* Grand Rapids, MI: William B. Eerdmans Publishing Company.	

Bonus Module	**Theme: Spirituality**	**Discussion Questions**
	Day 1	In your experience, how can you develop spirituality *within* managerial work activities? How can a manager develop spirituality *between* managerial work activities?
	Day 2	What is the difference between religion and spirituality in your experience?
	Day 3	What spiritual exercises or disciplines help you the most in terms of feeling close to God? What dimensions of your personality might influence your choice of spiritual exercises?
	Day 4	Describe a situation at work in which you sensed God's presence. Describe a situation at work in which you felt that God was far away. What accounts for the differences in your feelings?
	Day 5	In what way is your work as a manager also worship to God?
	Day 6	Is it appropriate to talk about managerial work in terms of sustaining, redeeming, and consummating God's plan for this earth? If so, in what ways do you participate with God in creating, sustaining, redeeming, and consummating God's plan for this earth?
	Day 7	What is the difference between getting meaning from our work and putting meaning into our work? What paradoxes of spirituality have you experienced in your own life?
	For further reading	See: Chapter 15 of this book.

Bonus Module	Theme: Sharing Faith	Discussion Questions
	Day 1	At your workplace what individual activities are considered appropriate in terms of sharing religious faith? Think of an example of a time when a Christian tried to share his or her faith at work. What was the reaction of others around that person? What is inappropriate at your workplace in terms of sharing religious faith?
	Day 2	In what ways, if any, is it appropriate to share your faith at the organizational level? What must you consider when thinking about sharing religious faith at the organizational level?
	Day 3	In what ways, if any, is it appropriate to share your faith at the industry and professional association level or economic system level? What is inappropriate behavior when sharing your faith at the industry and professional association level or economic system level?
	Day 4	Review the religious belief factors at work in a Christian that shape beliefs regarding witnessing and evangelism (Chapter 16). What religious belief factors are most dominant in your experience?
	Day 5	Review the contextual factors at work in a Christian that influence the actions of witnessing and evangelism (Chapter 16). What contextual factors are most dominant in your experience?
	Day 6	What is more important: the message Christians want to share or the way in which the message is delivered?
	Day 7	Review the various models of faith integration in Chapter 16. Which model best describes what you aspire to? Which model best describes your actual approach? What barriers exist that prevent you from living your aspirations in terms of sharing your faith at work?
	For further reading	See: Chapter 16 of this book. Nash, L., & McLennan, S. (2001). *Church on Sunday, work on Monday*. San Francisco, CA: Jossey-Bass. Solomon, L. D. (2004). *Evangelical Christian executives: A new model for business corporations*. New Brunswick, NJ: Transaction Publishers. Miller, D. W. (2007). *God at work: The history and promise of the faith at work movement*. New York: Oxford University Press. Hicks, D. A. (2003). *Religion and the workplace: Pluralism, spirituality, leadership*. Cambridge: Cambridge University Press.

Case 1
The J.M. Smucker Company Culture

To understand the organizational culture of the J.M. Smucker Company, we need to understand some of the history of this family business.

Jerome M. Smucker grew up in agricultural Wayne County, Ohio, as a member of the Oak Grove Amish Mennonite congregation.[1] Before he turned 18 years of age Jerome's mother died. He was the oldest child in the family. To help support the family's 120-acre, heavily mortgaged farm, Jerome worked side by side with his father learning the details of farm economics from growing to harvesting to marketing. When he was 33 years old Jerome attended the high school in Smithville, Ohio, for 2 years, studying business.

Mennonite families are deeply religious (Protestant Christian) and practical. Traditionally they have shunned the amassing of great wealth. Known worldwide for their religious beliefs regarding peace, Mennonites typically are conscientious objectors to war and as a result refuse to bear arms. Jerome's great-grandfather Christian Smucker had refused to bear arms during the American Revolution—an action that resulted in his imprisonment in Reading, Pennsylvania. Jerome became an active leader in the Mennonite congregation teaching Sunday School class, working in the church library, and becoming a regional advocate for church Sunday Schools. He remained a congregational leader until his death. Soon after 1900, the Jerome Smucker family along with two other Mennonite families moved from the Oak Grove congregation and settled in Orrville, Ohio, to help plant the Orrville Mission Church.

The Smucker commitment to family and community values is evident in several ways throughout the life and work of Jerome Smucker. Jerome became a member of the board of trustees for the Mennonite Mutual association that offered assistance to Mennonites if their property was damaged from fire, wind storms, or earthquakes. The Mutual association was one way that the Golden Rule, "do unto others as you would have them do unto you," was expressed at the community level. After one of the banks of Orrville failed, Jerome was appointed vice president of the Orrville National Bank. In spite of the many hours of work devoted to caring for and growing his farm, Jerome contributed many hours of volunteer service to help the Orrville community. One of his favorite Bible verses comes from Galatians 6:7, "Be not deceived. God is not mocked. Whatsoever a man sows that shall he also reap." For Smucker, this verse applied at both the personal, family, and community level. How you treat people speaks louder than your words about your religious beliefs. Following the Golden Rule in business, he believed, would bring good economic results.

Smucker had moved to Orrville to begin working a farm. While most Mennonite farm families were content to live and work just one farm, Jerome had an unsurpassed drive to grow his family business beyond the confines of a single farm. Gradually he expanded one farm into four. Then he began operating a commercial creamery making homemade dairy products available to cities such as Cleveland and even New York. An abundant supply of apple trees in the Orrville area provided Jerome with an additional entrepreneurial idea: Pressing apple cider for his neighbors and using the surplus cider given to him by his customers to produce apple butter. Jerome personally signed the sealing paper on crocks of apple butter. His son Willard took a wagonful of products into town and sold them door to door.[2]

As more American families moved from the farms to the cities to work in factories, their lifestyles became increasingly hectic. Smucker realized that families needed food they could "eat on the run." To help fill this need, Jerome began experimenting with a recipe for apple butter that his grandfather had used in Pennsylvania. He experimented with various processes and new technologies for producing products most efficiently. For example, he began using a steam engine to run the cider mill. And he found that he could boil cider in wooden tanks by using a coil of copper piping in the tank. While he had a gift for developing an efficient production process, Jerome's true gift seems to have been for marketing the Smucker products in Orrville and surrounding communities in northeastern Ohio. It was the Smucker Apple Butter that made Smucker's a nationally recognized household name by 1945. But apple butter was not the only product Smucker made. After World War I, Jerome diversified his product line to include the well-known line of jams, jellies, and preserves.

In 1959, the J.M. Smucker Company made two key decisions that positioned the firm for rapid expansion. A new processing plant was built in Salinas, California. Key leaders from the Smucker Orrville facility were transferred to California to oversee operations. In October of that year, the company announced that it was going public with the initial public offering of 165,000 shares sold at $20 per share. A few years later Smucker entered the New York Stock Exchange.

One marketing strategy that fueled the long-term growth of the firm was the choice to enter the "eat away from home" market by selling Smucker's products to schools, hospitals, restaurants, employee cafeterias, and other institutions. In recent years the company's strategy has included expansion into industrial fruit fillings and new product development to extend product lines. It has also included acquisitions of leading brands that have the potential of adding to the company's strength as a leader in North American family foods among product categories that are similar to manage: jams, peanut butter, and home baking products.[3]

While Smucker became a household name in America, the Smucker entrepreneurial drive also gradually took the Smucker family away from the Mennonite church. Jerome Smucker maintained his loyal participation in the congregation until his death. The next and succeeding generations did not follow the Mennonite tradition in the same way, although many of the basic beliefs of their tradition continued to influence their work. Jerome's four children became Presbyterian.

In the life of Jerome Smucker we see an interesting blend of two driving forces: religion and entrepreneurship. We see a deeply spiritual man who loved God and knew what the claims of Holy Scripture meant for his family's life. We also see a whole family steeped in the drive to innovate, take and manage risks, and grow a business far beyond where many in the Mennonite tradition were taking their businesses. Although Jerome was raised to believe (and act) in the community sharing of wealth, and while he supported his church's mission with financial support, he also knew the importance of building capital that could be leveraged for growing future free cash flows. This placed him in potential conflict with the Mennonite traditional skepticism regarding personal wealth.

Company Culture

The family work-related values espoused and lived by Jerome Smucker were passed to his son Willard, to his grandson Paul, and to Paul's two sons, Tim and Richard, who were raised as Christian Scientists. It was under Paul's leadership that the company expanded rapidly. Paul's simple code of conduct has remained steadfast with company leaders long after his passing: Listen with your full attention, look for the good in others, have a sense of humor, and say thank you for a job well done.[4] The passage in Galatians 6:7 is connected not only with the Golden Rule but also with the need for treating everyone with respect. One of the ways this translates down to the level of the individual worker is a prohibition against open expressions of power and anger toward others.[5] It also means being careful how you interact with customers. For example, the company believes advertising to children is manipulative, so it directs its promotional messages toward adults. Its marketing policy is to avoid advertising on television programs that do not match closely with family values.

The interaction of top company leaders that allows for consensus building and addressing other perspectives is passed down the chain of command. This basic, small-town approach to taking care of reputation, theirs and yours, has translated into straightforward, gimmick-free management that pervades company culture. Even though maintaining a consistent company culture has not always been easy, especially when the company was experiencing high growth, the company consistently ranks in the top ten of *Fortune's 100 Best Companies* to work for. In 2004 it won the top prize.

Smucker family members have learned how to translate the deeply held fundamental values from one generation to another. Even though the company does not offer stock options or expensive perks, morale is high and the company belief system based on commitments to each other rings true with employees.

The company continues to focus on values of product quality (using only the best ingredients inspected by their suppliers before shipping to Smucker's processing facilities), openness and honesty (overfilling jars to give customers more than is indicated on the label), and personal attention to employees. Paul became an expression of the cautious financing philosophy that characterized most of Smucker's growth: avoid borrowing money, own everything you can, and pay for it out of retained earnings. During Paul Smucker's leadership, the fundamental value of truth-telling was used as the company began advertising its products. When company leaders needed to deal with employees who were not performing well or who were found not to be a good match for the company culture, employees were sometimes given time to find another job more suitable for them inside the company or a job outside the company using the company resources.[6] The company was not out to gain maximum profits if that meant hurting people.

Key owners and officers of the company have been Smucker family members since 1921 when Jerome made his four children shareholders and directors. This tradition has continued. The Smucker aversion to long-term debt means that to grow the business company officers must continually plow retained earnings back into the company. With each newly acquired brand controlled by J.M. Smucker, company leaders impose company values and management styles.

The fundamental values on which employee behavior is based have been codified into the company statement of Basic Beliefs, which focuses on five key ideas: quality, people, ethics, growth, and independence.

In its annual report to shareholders and employees, the company openly states the points of emphasis in its corporate culture. These include things like attention to detail and the importance of doing the right things and doing things right.[7] Company officials also believe that the company culture is built on the Basic Beliefs, the commitments that individual employees make to each other and to customers, clear communication and collaboration, and appreciation served up family-style.

Another way the company culture is strengthened and transmitted to new employees is through its emphasis on ethics during and after the hiring process. For its efforts on ethics, Smucker's won the *Optimas Award* for Ethical Practice in 2006 by stressing the values of honesty and integrity. All company employees attend a day-long training session on moral awareness, moral courage, and values.[8] During the hiring process when managers talk with prospective employees they emphasize the company values that are related to the particular job the applicant is seeking. The decision makers rely on information gleaned from rigorous reference checks on applicants to determine the fit with ethical standards. One training session concentrates on three ways a decision can be reached when faced with a dilemma: (1) attempting to do the greatest good for the greatest number of people; (2) using a rules-based method in which the employee's action sets a standard that everyone else follows; (3) using the Golden Rule. Some dilemmas that an employee may face require the employee to make a choice between two good things such as loyalty and truth-telling, the individual versus the community, or the short-term versus the long-term. For these examples, company trainers emphasize the importance of siding with community, truth-telling, and the long-run impact of the decision. At the conclusion of the ethics training session, employees sign a nine-page ethics statement. Ethics training is repeated every 3 to 5 years. Signing the ethics statement is repeated annually. Managers can refer to the ethics statement during performance evaluations of employees.

Case Study Discussion Questions

1. How can a company like Smuckers that emphasizes fundamental family values create the culture of family commitments and respect without making the pressure to conform so strong that it undermines motivation for excellence?
2. How do the fundamental values maintained by Smuckers contribute to preventing an excessive focus on profits while at the same time encouraging innovation, growth, and economic success?

Endnotes

1. Smucker, D. E. (1996). *Jerome M. Smucker: Pioneer Ohio Mennonite entrepreneur*. Lima, OH: Fairway Press.
2. Livezey, E. T. (1965). When you make better preserves . . . *Christian Science Monitor*. February 27, p. 11.
3. Anonymous (2004). Online extra: How the Smuckers stick together. *BusinessWeek*. October 4; Weber, J. (2004). Keeping out of a jam. *BusinessWeek*. October 4, p. 104.
4. Levering, R., Moskowitz, M., Boorstin, J., & Tkaczyk, C. (2004, January 12). The best companies to work for. 149(1), 56.
5. Feldman, S. P. (2006). Moral memory: Why and how moral companies manage tradition. *Journal of Business Ethics*. 72, 395–409.
6. Grosecloses, E. (1975). The Scions: Paul H. Smucker takes great pains to preserve his products' quality. *The Wall Street Journal*. February 3, p. 1.
7. Smucker, T., & Smucker R. (2007). Dear shareholders and friends. *Annual Report*. J. M. Smucker Company.
8. Schoeff Jr., M. (2006). J. M. Smucker Co: Optimas award winner for ethical practice. *Workforce Management*. http://www.workforce.com/section/09/feature/24/30/34/index.html. Accessed December 23, 2007.

Case 2
The Burger War: In-N-Out Burger[1]

It is late afternoon in early May 1948 somewhere near Baldwin Park, California, a suburb of Los Angeles. The school year is almost over and you can't wait for summer. Your high school principal has just done something that "sticks in your craw" (makes you angry). One of your friends "got the shaft" (received severe and unfair treatment) after a "punk" (rebellious person) opened his "big yap" (mouth) about something that happened in the locker room after gym class. But what can you do about it except study for those final tests coming up in a few days?

In L.A. County in 1948 there's a lot to do. First, you need to get with your friends to talk about old principal "What's His Name" and that punk who should have been minding his own business. You could hang out with the "cool cats" who are walking around downtown—hipsters who "dig" (enjoy) jazz music. Or, because you "got your boots on" (know what is happening), and want to "make the scene" (show up at the popular place), you put on your cool "threads" (popular clothes) that everyone will be wearing, comb your hair into a ducktail (for guys) or a pageboy (for girls), borrow your parents' car, and tell them that you need some "bread" (money). If they give you money and the car, you can "fade" (leave home for a while), pick up your friends, and drive them down to the Snack Shack "hop" or "joint" (fast-food restaurant) for some good food.

At the drive-in hop you crank up the volume on the car radio to hear the new musical sensations that later would come to be known as Rock 'n Roll. Songs such as "Guitar Boogie" by Arthur Smith and the Crackerjacks and "We're Gonna Rock. We're Gonna Roll" by Bill Moore entertain your friends. Hop servers wheel around your car on roller skates carrying car window trays as they fill orders for customers seated in their cars.

History and Strategy

In 1948, times are changing but the owners of drive-*in* hop restaurants across the country don't realize it yet. In southern California, the soon-to-be-epicenter for the fast-food industry, consumers are becoming increasingly dependent on cars to commute farther and farther away from home to work. Down the street in the city of Baldwin Park, Harry and Esther Snyder are opening what may be the nation's first drive-*through* fast-food restaurant, which they name In-N-Out Burger.® That same year, not too many miles away in San Bernardino, another entrepreneur is experimenting with a similar idea at a restaurant he calls McDonald's.

Customers order at a menu board and a two-way speaker system and then drive to the pick-up window to pay and receive their food. The In-N-Out menu offers only a few choices—a tradition that continues for decades. Its menu is still the narrowest of all its competitors. The atmosphere is clean and bright. The food is clean, fresh, and tasty. Each burger is made to order with 100% fresh ground beef—no freezers, no microwave ovens. Lettuce and vine-ripened tomatoes are delivered fresh daily, washed, and prepared by employees. Burger buns are baked fresh daily. Potatoes are shipped to each In-N-Out facility in burlap bags. Employees manually clean and slice the potatoes, which are then fried in vegetable oil. Preparing fresh food takes a little extra time but customers don't seem to mind waiting in line a couple of extra minutes.

Harry and Esther do not rush to open more stores immediately even though the idea of drive-throughs was catching on not only in the fast-food business but in other types of retail stores, too. Three years pass before the Snyders decide to open a second In-N-Out Burger. They decide to maintain private ownership of their company instead of forming a franchise organization—the opposite strategy compared to the strategy pursued by the McDonald's chain. It is not that they didn't have opportunities for franchising. It's that they turned down all the requests. They maintained their staunch resistance to franchising to control product quality. The practical reality of this meant that at first they could expand only in southern California, managing the growth slowly enough to maintain the level of quality that drive-through customers came to expect. This philosophy rubbed off on the mindset of the Snyder's two sons Guy and Rich, who were also involved with the family business.

But grow they did. By 1976 the family owned 18 drive-throughs. In that year Harry Snyder passes away from cancer. Their son Rich, only 24 years old, assumes the role of president, and his older brother, Guy, becomes vice president. Esther continues as the accountant.

The In-N-Out menu consists of just three types of burgers: the traditional hamburger, the cheeseburger, and the Double-Double, which is essentially a double cheeseburger. They also sell French fries and three flavors of milkshakes—made with real ice cream. Other beverages sold include milk, coffee, lemonade, and flavored sodas. A few years after the company was established the only change to the menu is the addition of "The Animal"—a Double-Double with grilled onions and extra sauce.

While most fast-food restaurants change their menu options to attract customers away from competitors, In-N-Out keeps its menu simple and relatively unchanged. During the early years of its history, McDonald's also maintained a simple menu but that changed in the 1990s when the burger wars broke out. Since 1955, McDonald's has added over 30 new menu items. In the late 1990s, McDonald's experimented with making custom orders, but this proved to be very difficult to accomplish across more than 13,000 facilities nationwide for a franchise that is built on speed and pre-made food.

In-N-Out stays with its simple-menu, fresh ingredients, and cooked-to-order strategy. In essence, it trades off menu choices for consistency of quality and inventory control, not to mention complete control over the entire business. This reliability became something that its customer base could count on. Over the years In-N-Out Burger has developed what some call a "cult following." This has helped it avoid several temptations that other fast-food chains have caved in to: price wars, trying to be all things to all people, and, consequently, menu development wars. As a result, In-N-Out's customer loyalty has remained strong (or increased) and its profits have grown. It doesn't have a kid's menu; its products are as unhealthy (in terms of saturated fats) as the next burger joint. But it sells tasty burgers with the freshest ingredients.

The simple menu doesn't mean that customers have only three choices of burgers, though. In-N-Out Burger managers became trained to offer customers customized versions of the standard menu—a responsiveness that has contributed to customer loyalty. A secret code or hidden menu has developed between In-N-Out facilities and their customers that, in essence, expanded the menu options for sandwiches several times without changing the basic ingredients needed. Knowledge about these hidden menu items are passed through word of mouth. For example, carbohydrate-conscious customers can order the "Flying Dutchman," which is two 100% ground beef patties and two slices of cheese but no bun. Customers also can order the "Veggie Burger" (a.k.a., "The Wish Burger"), which is just lettuce, tomato, and spread on a burger bun but no burger. If you want two beef patties and four pieces of cheese and the rest of the fixings, then just order the "2 by 4." A grilled-cheese sandwich is not on the menu, but you can order that, too.

In-N-Out Burger developed a reputation for treating its employees with respect and dignity. Most jobs are entry level, but in spite of this the company pays above minimum wages. The fast-food industry is known for its high turnover rates, and while In-N-Out faces this same challenge, some employees have remained with the company for as long as 20 years, and some entry-level employees stay on and work their way up to managerial positions.

With the expansion of stores and the growth in popularity of the fast-food market among consumers, Rich and Guy needed to make some changes that would contribute to better efficiency. Soon after becoming the new leaders after their father's death, they established a fresh-food receiving and distribution facility ("commissary") located in Baldwin Park that serviced all of their retail locations. In 1983 they created the In-N-Out University, an intensive training program for employees.

Better trained employees and its own distribution facility for food products enabled In-N-Out Burger to serve more customers faster. But the increased volume of customers served at each facility had an unintended consequence: The line of traffic could get so long that in some locations it created traffic jams that became a problem for city officials. As word got around from city to city about the success of In-N-Out Burger, city officials became more hesitant to issue building permits for new In-N-Out stores. One result of this, other than keeping the growth curve slow, was that Rich and Guy decided to build facilities with small parking lots and offer inside and outside seating for customers who did not want to wait in line in their cars.

These efforts paid off. By 1990, the family owned and operated 55 facilities in Los Angeles and the surrounding counties. Between 1990 and December 1993, 38 more facilities were added in other parts of California. In December of that same year, Rich Snyder and several other high-ranking company leaders died when their private plane crashed at John Wayne Airport in Orange County. After his brother's death, Guy Snyder took over the leadership of the company and moved the corporate headquarters to Irvine, California, a move that had already been planned. Guy headed the company until his death in 1999. By 2003, the chain had grown to over 170 locations in a few Western states and was still growing. In 2003, average annual gross revenue per facility was $1.6 million dollars, which is twice as great as other similar fast-food chain stores generate. Total annual gross revenue is over $200 million dollars. McDonald's earned $40 billion dollars the same year.

In the mid-1980s Rich Snyder, who was deeply religious, instituted the practice of printing Bible verses on product packaging. There are four different verses printed in different places:

- Soda cups: John 3:16 "For God so loved the world, that he gave his only begotten Son, that whosoever believeth in him should not perish, but have everlasting life."
- Burger and cheeseburger wrappers: Revelation 3:20 "Behold, I stand at the door, and knock: if any man hear my voice, and open the door, I will come in to him, and will sup with him, and he with me."
- Milkshake cups: Proverbs 3:5 "Trust in the Lord with all thine heart; and lean not unto thine own understanding."
- Double-Double wrapper: Nahum 1:7 "The Lord is good, a strong hold in the day of trouble; and he knoweth them that trust in him."

After Rich died in 1993 the company continued the practice out of respect for him.

Other traditions have continued, too. Most In-N-Out Burger facilities present two crossed palm trees on the property. Employees use large safety pins to hold their aprons in place. This is a holdover from the early days when Harry Snyder ran the restaurant and used large safety pins on his apron. They are used today to remind employees of the heritage and the values that Harry stood for.

By 2006 In-N-Out Burger owned and operated 202 restaurants. But in January that year, Richard Boyd, vice president of real estate and one of the members of the Snyder family trust, filed suit against Lynsi Martinez, the 23-year-old granddaughter of Esther Snyder and sole surviving descendant of Harry Snyder. Boyd had been asked to resign in 2005, but he refused. Then in September 2005 he was given written notice that his employment agreement would not be renewed.

Boyd claimed in his lawsuit that Martinez was trying to remove him to gain control of the family business. Allegedly, one reason Martinez wants to gain control of the firm is so she can take the iconic brand national. If she did this, then she would be taking the company in a direction that was directly against the wishes of the Snyder family and in particular Esther Snyder, who by now was in her 80s. When Lynsi Martinez turns 35, she stands to gain control of the family trust valued at over $450 million.

Among other things, Boyd claimed that In-N-Out Burger leaders told company employees that Boyd was "a thief and unethical." Further, he alleged that they had excluded him from management meetings and denied him access to company security clearances and company documents. Company officials allegedly hired an outside accounting firm to investigate the finances of Boyd's department.

In his lawsuit Boyd sought monetary damages, reinstatement of his employment agreement, renewal of security clearances, and access to company documents. He also sought an injunction prohibiting company executives from excluding him from trustee meetings and from paying company vendors discount prices for personal projects.

In a countersuit, In-N-Out Burger executives charged Boyd with fraud, embezzlement of company funds, and disclosing confidential company information in his lawsuit. On April 5, 2006, a Los Angeles court judge ruled that two of the In-N-Out countersuit claims—breach of contract and breach of fiduciary duty—violated Boyd's free speech rights.

In May 2006, both parties came to a secret settlement over the dispute. Whether the allegations are true will never be known because both parties agreed not to talk about the details to the public. Under the terms of the settlement, Boyd will no longer be involved in the company or the Snyder family trusts.

Vice President Mark Taylor (also one of the Synder family trustees and Lynsi Martinez's brother-in-law) stated after the settlement was reached that the company's strategy is to continue its slow growth by adding 10 to 12 new stores each year for the next 5 years.

Industry experts believe that the lawsuit will not have a lasting effect on the company's future. They cite the company's strong cult-like customer loyalty as one of the reasons for this.

Case Study Discussion Questions

1. Comparing McDonald's and In-N-Out Burger, which company is likely to have the fewest supply-chain management headaches to deal with? Why?
2. Evaluate In-N-Out's long-term strategy. Should it develop a franchise program to expand nationally?
3. What are some of the trade-offs In-N-Out is making with its strategy?
4. Evaluate the company's strategy to express the faith of Rich Snyder. How effective is it? What alternatives exist for expressing faith at work at the corporate level?
5. After the death of the founder and his sons, how likely is it that the corporate culture that supports Rich Snyder's religious values will continue?
6. Why is it that customers don't seem to be offended by the openly religious theme used on product packaging?
7. After the death of a key family member and leader of a private company, what do company leaders need to do to continue the company culture?
8. Under what circumstances would company disunity harm the firm's ability to pursue its economic strategy?
9. Under what circumstances would company disunity weaken the firm's ability to pursue its religious faith strategy?

More information regarding In-N-Out Burger can be obtained at the company website, http://www.in-n-out.com.

Endnotes

1. (2007). In-N-Out Burger Strategy. http://www.fundinguniverse.com/company-histories/InNOut-Burger-Company-History.html. Accessed May 2007; Green, F. (2003). In-N-Out Burger carves niche in the fast-food market. *Quick Service Restaurant*. http://qsrweb.com/article.php?id=493. July 27; Hawn, C. (2003). The In-N-Out Burger is giving McDonald's a run for its money. *Fast Company*. http://www.fastcompany.com/magazine/74/burgers.html. September 1; Savio, K. (2006). The Ins and Outs of In-N-Out. *Gilroy Dispatch Newspaper*. March 6; McNichol, T. (2002). The secret behind a burger cult. *New York Times*, August 14; Luna, N. (2006). In-N-Out ordered to alter some claims in law suit. *Orange County Register*. April 6; Bronstad, A. (2005). In-N-Out Burger burned by exec's lawsuit. *Los Angeles Business Journal*. December 19; In-N-Out, former VP reach secretive settlement. *The Orange County Register*. May 11.

Case 3
eHarmony.com

It might be said that in some ways the Internet is a mirror of culture. It is also changing culture. Nowhere is this more applicable than with romance. Technology is changing how we find and share our love.[1] These changes have spawned the online relationship industry, which now is one of the more successful e-commerce industries.

When this industry got started in the mid-1990s, skeptics and cynics thought that users essentially were social losers, socially inept, or worse than that, social predators. But online dating services worked vigorously to clarify the image through product development that resulted in discouraging predators. Plus, with thousands of seemingly successful marriages under the online bridge, it appears that online dating and romance is here to stay.

The good news about online dating is that it is anonymous. Under the cover of anonymity, a person can display all sorts of charm, caring, and emotional connection that he or she might not otherwise be capable of in person. The bad news, if there is any, is that anonymity is a huge buffer between you and the truth about a person. That can be a recipe for a disaster.

This good news/bad news, trust/deceit situation for dating in the virtual world of the Web is not too different from relationships in the rest of life. Our romantic relationships typically are more than meets the eye. Truth and openness open the door to secrecy and deceit. The more committed to the other person we become in a relationship the more restrictive the relationship becomes and the greater the chances that the one we place the most trust in is the one who will deceive us.[2]

The Consumers and Their Behaviors

Traditional matchmaking processes work well for many singles. But waiting for the next church social event can take months. In some congregations it can seem like years. Even when there are plenty of aboveboard, safe social events to go around, for millions of other people the traditional approaches of finding potential matches for dates don't work like they used to. For some it is because they are isolated geographically. For others it is the pressures of their long-day work life that keeps them out of the dating arena. Brick-and-mortar dating services have been around for years, but for many consumers, these matchmaking programs have problems, too. They can be expensive. The sales-service personnel may have financial incentives to make a match even when such a match is based on fallacious assumptions about compatibility. The dating service can feel more like a sales job than a matchmaking service.

Consumers try online matchmaking services for several reasons. Some feel they are unsuccessful at the traditional approach. Others do not have the time or prefer not to take the time to visit nightclubs and bars where singles hang out. Others want to save time because of their busy schedules.

Although customers sign up all year long, the peak enrollment season begins the day after Christmas and runs through Valentine's Day. The importance of this season is attributed to singles who vow not to spend the holidays alone.[3]

Online dating users who are more serious about finding a meaningful long-term relationship are 63 percent more likely to pay for subscriptions than other users—a finding that eHarmony pioneered and that some other online dating services began to copy.

Even with all the things that online dating services do to minimize the chances of a less-than-satisfying experience, there is still the possibility that individuals responding to profiles will not be a good match. One of the central issues for this type of product is that of safety and trust.[4]

Fear that intrusive crackpots will respond to a personal profile still concerns many users. They fear that giving personal information might unleash a cyberstalker who might turn a good-faith effort at finding a relationship into a nightmare. Thus, the safety and confidentiality of personal, private information is one of the central issues in this industry. Online dating companies try to educate subscribers that there are limitations to what the company can do in terms of managing the risk. Most firms require customers to click acknowledgement that they understand that once the customer selects an individual for personal follow-up contact the responsibility of the online company ends.[5]

Information privacy policies of the various companies differ. Some websites are linked with other co-branded companies who may share the information. Some companies may use private information to advertise other products not requested by subscribers. This tends to make the online relationship service more like a spam-request service.[6]

Enter eHarmony

Located in Pasadena, California, eHarmony was founded by Dr. Neil Clark Warren in 1999 with the help of an angel investor Greg Waldorf. Warren, a practicing counseling psychologist with 35 years of professional experience, is fascinated by what holds relationships together. He is the author of several books including the best seller *Finding the Love of Your Life*.

eHarmony uses a research-based approach to finding matches for individuals interested in developing a long-term relationship with someone. For many, this means the hope of finding a marriage partner and life's soul mate. The research slant used in starting the company is one of the elements of company culture that continues.

Market Segments

While each dating company can finely tune the broad market based on customer-supplied information, it is recognized that several segments exist:

- 20-somethings young adults. Compared with the older subscribers, younger users are more likely to be interested in getting together, hanging out, and "hooking up." This age group may be more willing to try free dating services.
- Middle-aged divorced-with-children. This customer segment has particular relationship needs that because of the presence of children in the household make the relationship potentially more complicated.
- Over-50 baby boomers, some who are divorced or who are widowed. This is the fastest growing segment in the online relationship industry. Older daters have different needs than younger members. But they are more likely to be willing to pay subscription fees. Older users are less skilled in using websites, but in general, boomers are tech-savvy and know what they want in a relationship.[7]
- 55% of subscribers are at least 35 years old. When you add to this the fact that many of these are interested in a meaningful, serious relationship and are willing to pay for access to other like-minded individuals who might be a good match, you have the recipe for a successful business model.

Marketing Mix

Product

The backbone of the eHarmony product starts with a 436-item questionnaire that requires applicants 45 minutes or more to complete at no charge. Items on the questionnaire provide information that is computer analyzed along 29 different personality characteristics. These factors include things such as traits of adaptability, curiosity, and intellect; family background and values; spirituality; feelings about children; temperament; and skills. eHarmony tests (and rejects) applicants for probable insincerity and dishonesty. Applicants who claim to be less than 21 years of age are rejected. Women are not matched with men who are shorter than they are.[8] eHarmony rejects individuals who have been married three or more times, who are attempting to contact someone of the same sex, or who appear to be unstable. The end result of this comparably high selectivity is that about 16 percent of applicants are rejected.[9]

Promotion

eHarmony uses a variety of promotional efforts, some paid and others free. Its advertising budgets have been in the range of \$50 to \$80 million dollars annually for creative portrayal of the website. This includes television and radio ads that feature Dr. Warren. Dr. Warren, the author and speaker, is another way in which eHarmony is promoted. Also, he has been interviewed by many freelance writers and journalists who have included his perspective on relationships in their articles. eHarmony has used Commission Junction, an online marketing firm, to drive Internet users to the eHarmony website. It also must pay for online advertising at other websites and for prominent listings on Internet search engines such as Google and Excite. It partnered with Gannett Co., Inc., to launch branded online personal advertisements in *USA Today* and Gannett's daily newspapers.

Pricing

A potential user can log on to eHarmony and get essentially a free "peek" after completing the questionnaire. To gain access to individuals who are potential matches, you must subscribe. eHarmony is the highest priced online dating service with its \$59 per month subscription fee. The fact that millions of individuals continue to subscribe suggests that eHarmony has sufficiently differentiated itself from rivals to charge what amounts to a premium. Applicants have a 7-day trial period during which time they can cancel the subscription.[10]

Distribution

The heart of distribution is access to the value that is offered by the company on the Internet. Like other online businesses, distribution for eHarmony is centered on the Internet community to which it is connected. Its presence on World Wide Web search engines such as Google® create access. Advertising on other websites that potential users visit also creates access when click-through buttons are strategically placed for users to connect directly with eHarmony.

Strategy

Dr. Warren obtained from the U.S. Patent and Trademark Office a patent for the company's computerized compatibility matching system developed from the results of researching 5,000 couples.[11] Other websites, including its archrival Match.com, use computer analysis of personality characteristics for matching.

Rather than let people browse profiles, eHarmony controls the matching process by sending customers information on individuals who are believed to be compatible. On the one hand, this can save an applicant time spent in scanning profiles of people who are not a good match. On the other hand, some customers can see the tight control as a negative feature.

Another point of difference from the competition is that eHarmony has focused solely on the American market while some competitors have gone international.

Company Performance

For its own performance, eHarmony has grown to 17 million registered users. Emphasizing the success of the organization's mission to help people find satisfying long-term relationships, company leaders claim that 16,000 marriages occurred among subscribers in 2005 alone. That's about 90 eHarmony subscribers getting married every day—an impressive number that alone speaks directly to the mission of long-term relationships.

Even though it is ranked behind Match.com and Yahoo Personals in terms of subscribers, eHarmony's annual revenues have built up to over $150 million dollars. And it may be number one in terms of the amount of time its members spend on its website.[12]

A Rapidly Maturing Industry

There are an estimated 89 million Americans who are single. Many of them are seeking short- or long-term relationships.[13] In 2002, just within a few years of the online relationship industry beginning in the mid-1990s, there were 16 million users registered to online dating services. 45 million American Internet users visited online dating web sites during 2005.[14] In 2001, the online dating industry earned $72 million. During the next year, the growth rate reached 400 percent as revenues shot up to over $300 million. By 2006, industry sales totaled more than $550 million.

This rapid growth made online relationship services one of the largest categories of online paid content. Today, thousands of online relationship websites compete for attention around the world. Following the rapid growth in the late 1990s and early 2000s in the double digits and over 70 percent growth rate in 2003, the peak year, growth rates plummeted. Growth is now in single digits, between 6 and 9 percent per year. In 2005, online dating services started losing more users than they were attracting.

Increased competition and the flattened growth curve also have sparked a wave of new product development to strengthen ties with the market segments that at the same time develops new revenue streams. For example, eHarmony launched a new product designed to keep couples together. Newlyweds can pay a different subscription fee of $239 for a 12-session marriage wellness program designed to explore the relationship's weaknesses and strengths.[15]

Competitors

There are thousands of competitors in the online relationship industry, many of which are adult websites that are pornographic and explicit sex-oriented sites rather than meaningful relationship sites.[16] But eHarmony's chief competitor is Match.com with more than 15 million subscribers. Match.com is attempting to attract the same market segments as eHarmony. It offers personalized advice from Dr. Phil.[17] Match.com ran into legal trouble when it was accused of *date-bate*—sending emails to subscribers to keep them renewing their membership. The trouble is that some customers alleged that Match.com had sent flirtatious, bogus emails from fictitious persons.[18]

Other competitors include Yahoo Personals, another market leader with nearly 15 million subscribers. Yahoo Personals partnered with beliefnet.com in an arrangement that connected both user groups, allowing access to a larger database for Christians who want to find a soul mate based in part on spirituality.[19]

Chemistry.com (a subsidiary of Match.com) is another rival of eHarmony. It has attempted to exploit the trade-off inherent in eHarmony's strategy. Chemistry.com promotes the concept that eHarmony is so selective that many potential users are rejected before they get a chance to find a potential match.[20]

Cut the market another way along the lines of religious beliefs and you have opportunities for online services such as ChristianSingles.com, EquallyMatched.com, ChristianCafe.com, SinglesofFaith.com, CatholicSingles.com, and Christian SoulMates.com.

Finding Meaning by Serving the Greater Good

Warren's Christian faith is intertwined with the business model of eHarmony. He says that his religious beliefs are founded in humanism and psychology. And, given that his mission is to serve the world, not just Christians, the bonding of psychology to the human fundamentals of faith make for finding meaning in helping people get married well.[21] It is no surprise then that eHarmony employees find meaning in their work as they consider the greater good of helping individuals develop meaningful long-term relationships: If you can lower the divorce rate by just 1 percent, then you are contributing to the greater good.[22]

Although Warren is a Christian, he insists that the site serves a wider market. Even so, in the early years eHarmony developed the reputation that it was primarily for Christians. Warren advertised eHarmony on the *Focus on the Family* radio show and on Christian websites. Word got around that eHarmony was based on Christian principles. In 2005, eHarmony stopped advertising on the show, believing that the radio program had become too political. eHarmony has targeted Christians who are looking for a long-term relationship with someone who shares their spiritual values.[23] Partially because of this, the company has been accused of attempting to use its website to promote evangelical Christianity. Critics accused Warren of favoring evangelicals in the matchmaking process, an allegation that he categorically denies.[24]

All this does not come without problems. In May 2007, Linda Carlson sued eHarmony alleging that the website blocked her from using the site to meet another woman.[25] eHarmony's position is that its patented algorithm is based on years of research on couples based on the patterns of heterosexual marriages. While nothing would prevent the company from offering a same-sex matching service in the future, it is something that the company has not researched.

Case Study Discussion Questions

1. Evaluate and comment on Dr. Warren's approach to integrating his religious faith in his company.
2. What is eHarmony trading off with its strategy? Do these trade-offs suggest any long-term disadvantages the company might face in the future?
3. What are the strengths and weaknesses of focusing on a particular narrow segment of the online relationship market, for example, evangelical Christian singles?
4. In an industry where truth-telling is so foundational, to what lengths should the Christian online dating service go to ensure truth telling?
5. Is it wrong for Christians to use their religious affiliation(s) to promote the business they own? Give reasons for your answer.

Safety Tips

eHarmony provides several safe online dating safety tips that are similar to safety suggestions provided by other online companies:[26]

- Always use your best judgment. Truthfulness and honesty is difficult to verify and an online dating service will not be able to do for you what you must do for yourself. Be wary if an online potential date:
    - Asks for money
    - Asks inappropriate questions
    - Wants to speed up the relationship beyond your comfort level
    - Is inconsistent in telling stories about her past
    - Gives vague answers to specific questions
    - Urges you to compromise your principles
    - Blames others for troubles in his life
    - Insists on getting overly close too fast
    - Asks for your login or password
- Be cautious about sharing personal information that could reveal your identity. Before you give your phone number, come to agreement that if either of you decides to end the communication in the future, neither of you will use the phone number as a means of pursuing an unwanted relationship.
- Do your own research on the other person's background. Many online dating services do not perform background checks with the state police. These formal background checks are not free.
- Plan the first date carefully so that it is safe and successful.
    - Choose a time and place wisely. Meet in a public place at an hour when people will be around.
    - Use your own transportation. Drive yourself or take a taxi. It is never a good idea to get into someone else's vehicle on a first date.
    - Carry a fully-charged cell phone.
    - Don't leave personal belongings and beverages unattended if you leave the room.
    - Do not meet at your house or your place of employment.
    - Don't go home with someone on the first date even if it seems like everything is going great.
- Take your time. Meaningful, fulfilling relationships do not blossom overnight.
- Be respectful and kind. Treat the other person as you would want to be treated regardless of how the date works out.
- Report concerns to the online dating service.

Endnotes

1. Anderson, A. L. (2001). Surf here often? *Christianity Today*. 45(8), 38–40.
2. Cole, T. (2006). Intimacy, deception, truth and lies: The paradox of being close. *Entelechy*. Spring/Summer, 7. http://www.entelechyjournal.com/timcole.htm. Accessed November 16, 2007.
3. Chaffin, J. (2006). Matchmakers fight for the hearts of the world's singles. *Financial Times*. December 22. p. 16.
4. Epstein, R. (2007). The truth about online dating. *Scientific American Mind*. 18(1), 8–35; Parker, E. (2007). The weekend interview with Greg Waldorf: The matchmaker. *Wall Street Journal* (Eastern Edition). February 10, p. A-9; Silver, S. (2007). Internet romance: How Match.com found love among boomers. *Wall Street Journal* (Eastern Edition). January 27, p. A-1; Anonymous. (2006). Romance.com. *Consumer Reports*. 71(12), 43–45; Smith, A. D. (2005). Exploring online dating and customer relationship management. *Online Information Review*. 29(1), 18–33.
5. Smith, A. D. (2005). Exploring online dating and customer relationship management. *Online Information Review*. 29(1), 18–33.
6. Mangis, C. A. (2003). Love at first site. *PC Magazine*. 22(3), 124–125.
7. Juarez, V. (2006). In the internet dating world, boomers are a hot commodity. *Newsweek*. 147(8), 60; Silver, S. (2007). Internet romance: How Match.com found love among boomers. *Wall Street Journal* (Eastern Edition). January 27, p. A-1.
8. Palmeri, C. (2006). Dr. Warren's lonely hearts club. *BusinessWeek*. 3972, February 20, 82.
9. Anonymous. (2006). Romance.com. *Consumer Reports*. 71(12), 43–45.
10. Anonymous. (2006). Romance.com. *Consumer Reports*. 71(12), 43–45.
11. Chaffin, J. (2006). Matchmakers fight for the hearts of the world's singles. *Financial Times*. December 22, p. 16;

Information also found at the eHarmony website: http://www.eHarmony.com.
12. Gomes, L. (2007). PlentyofFish owner has the perfect bait for a huge success. *Wall Street Journal* (Eastern Edition). May 23, p. B-1.
13. Stanley, T. L. (2006). Online-dating sites get stood up by consumers. *Advertising Age*. 77(16), 10.
14. Smith, A. D. (2005). Exploring online dating and customer relationship management. *Online Information Review*. 29(1), 18–33.
15. Gamerman, E. (2006). Pursuits; relationships; mism@tched.com. *Wall Street Journal* (Eastern Edition). April 1, p. 1; Stanley, T. L. (2006). Online-dating sites get stood up by consumers. *Advertising Age*. 77(16), 10.
16. Chaffin, J. (2006). Matchmakers fight for the hearts of the world's singles. *Financial Times*. December 22, p. 16.
17. Ballal, S. (2006). Who says e-romance is dead? *BusinessWeek*. 3993, July 17, 12.
18. Gamerman, E. (2006). Pursuits; relationships; mism@tched.com. *Wall Street Journal* (Eastern Edition). April 1, p. 1.
19. Religion News Service. (2006). Beliefnet, Yahoo! Add spiritual chemistry to cyber soul mate searches. *National Catholic Reporter*. 43(6), 3.
20. Hein, K. (2004). Matchmaker eHarmony makes notes of successes. *Brandweek*. 45(43), 13; Hein, K. (2007). Chemistry.com paints rival as "Heartbreak Hotel." *Brandweek*. 48(18), 9.
21. Kornblum, J. (2005). EHarmony: Heart and soul. *USA Today*. May 19.
22. Gamerman, E. (2006). Pursuits; relationships; mism@tched.com. *Wall Street Journal* (Eastern Edition). April 1, p. 1.
23. Smith, A. D. (2005). Exploring online dating and customer relationship management. *Online Information Review*. 29(1), 18–33.
24. Palmeri, C. (2006). Dr. Warren's lonely hearts club. *BusinessWeek*. February 20, 82.
25. Mangu-Ward, K. (2007). Dating discord. *Reason*. 39(6), 7-8; Parker, E. (2007). The weekend interview with Greg Waldorf: The matchmaker. *Wall Street Journal* (Eastern Edition). February 10, p. A-9.
26. Information found at the eHarmony website: http://www.eHarmony.com.

Case 4
The New Fitness Club

A small, private, nonprofit organization built a new wellness/fitness center for its clients, employees, staff, and their family members, all of whom the organization collectively called its "family." The fundraising program included the attempt to raise $1 million for an endowment fund that the employees came to believe, rightly or wrongly, would be used to cover the expenses of operating the new facilities. During the fundraising and construction phases, employees were encouraged to donate their personal funds toward the cost of construction and the endowment.

After constructing the new facility the organization's leaders announced that there had been cost overruns of approximately $1 million during the construction. Partly because of this, the endowment fund was not developed. A few weeks before the opening of the new facility administrators announced that it would charge an annual membership fee to employees and their family members to use the new facility. At about the same time the leaders announced that because of the downturn in the economy there would be no cost-of-living pay raises for employees for the coming year. To encourage employee use of the organization's food services, administration announced that employees would receive a 25 percent discount on all food purchased. During the annual fall festival weekend, leaders proudly showed the new fitness facilities to the community. New client recruitment began highlighting the organization's unique advantages by showcasing the new fitness facilities.

In spite of protests by some employees over the fitness facility membership fees that were assessed, the organization started charging employees a fee for using the old swimming pool and the old racquetball courts. Prior to this, all fitness-related facilities were free to employees. However, at the end of the year after these decisions had been made, the organization's financial officer announced that the organization had achieved a better than expected positive net gain after expenses.

The succession of events triggered a flurry of discussions and some emails among employees. Employees began to ask each other sarcastically what would be next on the administration's "revenue enhancement" checklist—revenue that the employees would have to carry: use of the softball fields, parking lots, and sidewalks? They asked the administration for an explanation of why they would now have to pay to use the old pool. Some voiced a decline in trust of the administration.

Two perspectives emerged from the informal debates that occurred among employees: those who favored the administration's decision and those opposed it. A summary of some of the arguments put forward follows.

Those in favor of the administration's decision argued that if employees and their families wanted to obtain access to fitness and swimming facilities elsewhere, they would have to pay membership or use fees. Having these facilities right at the organization makes it very convenient for employees and their family members. There should be a fair price for this. An employer should not be expected to give everything away for free to employees. It is not the employer's responsibility to provide "welfare" to employees and their families. One reason people work for pay is so they have the financial resources to enjoy leisure time activities such as what can be found at a fitness club. If clients pay their fair share, then employees should pay their fair share, too.

The Bible does not define specifically how much or to what extent an employer must provide for the needs of employees. The employees' desires for more benefits are not a valid biblical standard of justice because employees will naturally be self-interested. Organizational administrators, however, are interested in the common good of the entire organization. Net positive gains after expenses are vital if the organization expects to be able to replace aging facilities or expand in the future to support continued growth in economies of scale. If employees do not like the benefits and if employees do not like their workloads, then they should look for employment somewhere that their specific needs can be met. The biblical principle here is that the organization's administration should continue to fulfill its duties as good stewards of the organization's assets with a look to the long-term financial health of the institution. See Proverbs 27:23–27. Also consider that the organization is doing an inherently good thing by offering employment in a faith community that supports the institution. See Galatians 6:10.

Those opposed to the administration's decision argued that because of the convenient location, an employer should not take advantage of a lower than normal price sensitivity of employees for using the organization's fitness facilities. Further, when the fitness facility project was announced before construction began, nothing was said to employees regarding the charging of fees. Employees gave voluntarily toward the construction costs. Now they are required to pay to use the facilities that the endowment pays for. This is unjust and simply a modern form of oppression and subtle robbery under the false guise of caring for the needs of the organization—the endowment fund was believed to be established to pay for the operation of the new facilities. See Leviticus 19:3, 19:11, 25:43; Deuteronomy 23:24–25, 24:14; Psalm 62:10; Proverbs 22:22–23; Isaiah 61:8; and Malachi 3:5. Instead of trying to find ways to take from employees the organization should be looking for ways to do good to employees where they can. See Deuteronomy 15:7–11; Proverbs 3:27, 19:17; Isaiah 1:17–19; and Galatians 6:10. The biblical principle is that employers should allow employees to benefit from organizational assets as long as the employee does not take advantage of the employer by attempting to extend this benefit to other people outside the organization. Employees should not have to pay for mistakes in the construction decisions that led to cost overruns. Further, because the organization actually made a positive gain in net income in spite of the weakened economy, and given that employees would not receive cost-of-living pay raises for the coming year, employees should not be burdened with paying fees for using the organization's facilities. Employees at small, private, religious-affiliated nonprofit organizations already sacrifice a large disparity in salary compared with what they could earn in for-profit organizations. In addition, employees of such institutions typically have heavier workloads than their counterparts in for-profits. To require employees to pay for the use of fitness facilities that they believe the endowment pays for is like asking the ancient Hebrew workers to continue making the same quota of bricks only now they have to gather their own straw. The administrators' desire to improve the bottom line (and thereby make themselves look good to the board of trustees) also is based in part on their own self-interests. Because of this the administrators' desires are not the biblical standard of justice. If this organization continues to *take* from employees, employees will start to leave for better jobs elsewhere. This will place a huge burden on the organization to recruit replacements that are willing to work under such conditions.

What do you think? Is the action of the organization's administration with respect to employees and their family members a valid expression of biblical justice in the employer–employee relationship?

If we can assume that there will be a difference of opinion on how much or to what extent the organization should provide for the needs of its employees (employees desiring to receive more; employers choosing to give less), on what basis can we say that an employer is doing less (or more) than what the Bible expects?

Case 5
R. W. Beckett Corporation: Corporate Culture

Timothy A. O. Redmer
Regent University
timored@regent.edu

Case Synopsis

Kevin Beckett has recently become president and CEO of R. W. Beckett Corporation, a company started by his grandfather almost 70 years ago and effectively and efficiently run by his father, John, for close to 40 years.[1] Kevin will be leading the company into the 21st century with many changes and challenges on the horizon. One of the most immediate dilemmas was a decision to outsource some of the manufacturing activities to China.

The company had never outsourced labor activities to a foreign country before. However, increased competition and decreasing product margins necessitated that all feasible options be considered. Company employees had remained extremely loyal to R. W. Beckett over the years, even preferring to remain non-union in a highly unionized area and industry.

Greatly complicating the decision process was an underlying corporate culture of the organization. John, a devout Christian, had spent years perfecting a biblically based corporate culture that was foundational to all aspects of the business's activities. The thought of transferring some business to China, an atheist nation with questionable labor practices, seemed to go counter to much of the values that the company stood for.

Source: Christian Business Faculty Association, Christian Business Academy Review

There were other corporate culture–related issues that Kevin would soon have to confront, including new senior leadership, acquisitions, changes in society, and new entrants in the workforce, along with governmental nondiscriminatory regulations and intervention. Could or should the current corporate culture withstand these changes over time?

Kevin was also aware that a large percentage of family-owned businesses do not survive through the third generation. This added pressure made Kevin realize that decisions he made could be even more critical. Would the company corporate culture help or hinder Kevin's ability to operate effectively in the years ahead?

Introduction

In the fall of 2004, Kevin Beckett, 37, became President and CEO of R. W. Beckett Corporation, succeeding his father, John Beckett. John Beckett had been president from 1965 through 2003. As the third generation of the company's leadership, Kevin soon realized he would need to make some major decisions. To remain competitive, the company needed to reduce costs. The most feasible option appeared to be outsourcing some of the manufacturing functions to a foreign country—most likely China. Because of R. W. Beckett Corporation's values-based corporate culture, this outsourcing decision was even more complex for Kevin than for many manufacturing executives throughout the United States.

R. W. Beckett Corporation's values-based corporate culture, shaped by R. W. (Reg) from the company's inception almost 70 years earlier, was foundational to everything it did. John added a biblical dimension to this values-based approach after becoming a Christian. Kevin and his five siblings grew up knowing how important this concept was to their dad and how key it was to the company's success.

Now, with the company under his watch, Kevin realized cultural considerations would have to either be set aside or sustained across multiple "thresholds" as the company brought in new senior leadership, established facilities in other locations (including globally), made acquisitions, wrestled with changes occurring in society, and adjusted to the uniqueness of new entrants into the workforce. Decisions and actions in all of these areas would impact or be impacted by the R. W. Beckett corporate culture.

The most immediate dilemma was outsourcing. It would test the corporate culture in ways not previously considered. Kevin wondered how, if at all, Beckett's values-based corporate culture, which incorporated biblical principles like an absolute truthfulness and accountability to a divine authority, could be incorporated into foreign operations. In a country such as China with the government's promotion of atheism and where most of the population followed decidedly different standards and norms, the challenge was even greater.

Kevin questioned whether the company's culture needed to extend globally or if it was sufficient to accept the corporate culture primarily for domestic decisions. However, if R. W. Beckett assumed an international or more global mission, regardless of the countries involved, any venture into foreign operations added new complexity to its corporate culture. Furthermore, was it a deal-breaker if the R. W. Beckett corporate culture didn't fit the norms and practices of an international community or society? Kevin knew that to keep jobs in-house and to serve the best interests of relevant stakeholders, changes such as these, at the very least, had to be seriously considered.

Succession

The succession of Kevin to CEO in 2003 had gone smoothly. John had focused for years on the character development of all six of his children along with instilling an appreciation for the family business. He often thought that eventually one or more of his children might join or even lead the business. However, for John there were some critical aspects to succession. Chief among these was his desire to preserve a values-based corporate culture rooted in the Bible, for this was indeed foundational to every aspect of his business and his life. Principles such as honesty, integrity, service, and quality were just a few of the concepts practiced under the Beckett corporate culture.

When the time was right, John had handed the company over with no strings attached. He did not set any conditions but had expectations. John realized that Kevin would go through unforeseen challenges. He had high hopes but was also realistic.

As he became the third CEO in the company's history, Kevin was keenly aware of the uniqueness of the company's culture. But practically speaking he had to ask: How much of the culture was "John Beckett"? How much was "R. W. Beckett Corporation"? How much needed to be "Kevin Beckett"? What aspects would be new and different under his leadership? What would be continued from previous generations?

John had led the company for four decades. Times had changed, society had changed, and the business had changed. Now the company was contemplating doing business abroad and it had to grapple with vastly different cultures, religions, and values. Kevin knew it was a basic fact of business success that change must occur as conditions changed, but he needed discernment on the extent to which such changes applied to the corporate culture.

Issues were pressing in, including customer pricing expectations, and the organization needed to respond. Kevin was certain that his next steps would be carefully watched, not just by customers, but by employees, other family members, and the company's board of directors. This was an inflection point. Key decisions now would set the tone for whether the legacy of John Beckett would be honored or dismissed as dated and decreasingly relevant.

Company History

R. W. Beckett Corporation was founded in 1937 by Reg Beckett just as the conversion from coal furnaces to oil heat was heating up—literally (Leggatt & Beckett, 1987). Cottage industries in basements and garages in the oil heat market had sprung up by the hundreds and almost as many failed for lack of quality products or sustainable cash flow. Reg's commitment to hard work, product excellence, and customer service helped his fledgling company survive those early years.

Reg gained experience in the oil heat industry working at other companies before he ventured out on his own. His first product, the "Model OB" oil burner, was of high quality and superior workmanship—of utmost importance where safety and reliability for the homeowner through the harsh cold of winter were at stake.

The advantages of cleaner burning and fully automatic oil heat over dirtier, more labor-intensive and less efficient coal became readily apparent in the 1920s and the industry prospered, especially after the end of World War II. The company built its first permanent facilities in 1952 in North Ridgeville, Ohio, some 25 miles west of Cleveland.

The introduction of natural gas as an alternative fuel source in the 1950s made a rapid and indelible impact on the oil heating market, causing the first downturn in demand in almost 30 years. Reg Beckett, discouraged by this looming competition, became distracted and let the company fall behind in product innovation. Sales slumped. Reg eventually realized that since he could not change the market, he would have to change. With fresh energy, he developed new, more efficient and smaller oil-burning products. The "Model S" oil burner was created, and slowly but steadily sales began to improve in the early 1960s.

John, who had studied economics and engineering at M.I.T., began his work career in the aerospace industry. In a surprise invitation, his father asked him to join the family business. John made the change in late 1963. After just one year of their working together, John's father suddenly died of a heart attack. At age 26, John was thrust into the leadership of R. W. Beckett Corp. Trying to guide the company under such stressful circumstances caused John to reach out for help in ways that were new to him.

> Perhaps for the first time in my life, I really seriously prayed. After a period of searching, the answer began to emerge in a clear way. I came out of that time with the strong conviction that I was to run the company and that I was to do everything I could to make it succeed.

John realized he needed to add capable people in leadership, especially to market more broadly the company's strong product offerings. He hired Bob Cook in marketing and Paul Deuble in sales. Both individuals were knowledgeable about the industry and began opening doors to new sales. But after only five months in leadership, John was awakened in the middle of the night to learn of a major fire engulfing the company's manufacturing plant. John led a small band of volunteer firefighters through the pitch black in an all-night battle. Fortunately, the fire was brought under control, and total destruction of the facility was averted.

These challenges—first his father's death, then the fire—had a huge impact on John. He said, "I had always been able to rally my own strength and abilities, but now my confidence was deeply shaken." As a result, he sought spiritual reality as he never had before. "For the first time in my life I let go, yielding to God as fully as I knew how." John's conversion then began to influence his approach to business. He became deeply convinced he could no longer live in two separate worlds but rather would need to integrate the two in every way possible (www.lifesgreatestquestion.com).

Through the late 1960s and into the early 1970s, the company experienced steady growth. The marketing-focused strategy was paying off. Yet challenges were never far from the company's doorstep. Beckett faced a union organization attempt (unsuccessful) in 1972, followed by major disruptions in the oil markets sparked by the Arab oil embargo of 1973.

In the late 1970s, just as a major facility expansion was completed and with the prospect of strong sales growth, a pivotal event happened thousands of miles away: the Shah of Iran was overthrown. This precipitated further oil supply problems—fuel prices skyrocketed, and burner sales for the entire industry plummeted. As a result, a major consolidation of companies in the oil heating business began, with many burner manufacturers going out of business.

John took a different tack than most of his competitors; he stepped up the promotion of oil heating, convinced the oil crisis would be relatively short-term. Beckett continued to improve product quality and capture market share, even though the overall market was dwindling. John's long-term strategic outlook proved successful, and Beckett became the undisputed market leader among just a handful of surviving companies.

Through this challenging time, John leaned heavily on his growing faith. He concluded that "God was bigger than the Middle East crisis, and that we should take each day one at a time, with our trust in him."

From the early 1980s, and with the industry consolidated, Beckett benefited from continued expansion and growth. Their focus was on operational efficiency, product quality, and customer service. They brought enhanced product technology and innovation into the oil heat industry. The company had also diversified their product lines and ventured into related industries. Morrison, a son-in-law, and Jonathan, Kevin's younger brother, joined the company during this period, bringing solid experience from other businesses.

Corporate Culture

In his best-selling book, *Loving Monday* (1998), John Beckett described how he integrated a biblically based philosophy into the workplace. John was convinced there should be integrity and ethical practices in every phase of the operation and when dealing with all stakeholders. He expected nothing less than excellent products and encouraged every employee to treat others—inside and outside the company—with dignity and respect.

The lifelong principles John believed in were first taught to him by his father. John fine-tuned these basic values through his many years in business, bolstering them with a biblical perspective as he grew in his Christian faith. He concluded that using the Bible in business and business success could complement each other. In his book, he documented how a person can succeed in business "without selling his soul."

Featured at the beginning of the book was the story of how ABC's *World News Tonight with Peter Jennings* did a feature story on Beckett Corporation. The story focused on ways the company related faith to their business practices. Jennings noted that the leaders of Beckett Corporation "are using the Bible as a guide to business." There was ample evidence in the nationally televised story of a servant leadership management style where others were put first, both by John and other members of top management. Employee loyalty and devotion to the highest standards of excellence were the norm in company operations. John commented in the television interview, "My main mission in life is to know the will of God and to do it."

John always felt called to business. As he explained in his book, being called to minister through business can be just as high a calling as a call to the "ministry." As long as a person was in harmony—and not in conflict—with God's will, any calling—be it the church, entertainment, business—was equal in the eyes of God. John's call into business gave him the opportunity to create an operation and corporate culture that was consistent with the teachings of the Bible.

From studying the Bible, John saw a strong emphasis on both absolutes and character. Moral boundaries were unambiguous. Character qualities of integrity, humility, and justice were dominant themes in the Scriptures. He realized that vital aspects of one's faith can be transported to the workplace, and the Bible can serve as a dependable and unfailing guide in making that connection. The corporate value statement for R. W. Beckett best illustrated its corporate culture:

> R. W. Beckett is built on a platform of three core values: integrity, excellence, and profound respect for the individual. Beckett works to nurture relationships daily: with employees by creating a work environment that fosters growth and well being; with customers by providing a product that is well-made and priced as a cost-value; and with suppliers and others with whom we conduct business, by treating them with respect and fairness. We strive to serve others, helping meet human needs in the community and beyond.
>
> The character of a company is determined by those in leadership—their values, their competence, their commitment, their ability to work well together, and the example they set. We aspire to the finest possible management at all levels, seeking long-term relationships, internal and external, based on respect and trust.
>
> Our company endeavors to apply a biblically based philosophy throughout every phase of its operations. We've created a corporate atmosphere that is not in opposition to family life, but rather, supports and encourages it through maternity leave and other family centered programs.
>
> Finally, we aspire to be THE company our industry turns to for excellent equipment and technical support.

While Kevin was clear in what the corporate culture should be for R. W. Beckett, he questioned how the specifics would or would not apply in everyday situations. He realized corporate culture was not fully expressed by mere words, however carefully crafted, but were etched over time into an organization's very fabric by people, history, products, services, practices, and even problems.

In fact, he realized there was no guarantee that sustaining the existing corporate culture was a given. This point was driven home by the fall of Enron, which occurred shortly before Kevin became CEO. He had reviewed the Enron Statement of Values (2000) in their annual report and was amazed at how similar their values were to those of Beckett. Both companies focused on the importance of integrity, excellence, and respect as key aspects of corporate culture. The Enron Statement of Values highlighted four areas: communication, respect, integrity, and excellence.

> Communication: We have an obligation to communicate. Here we take time to talk with one another . . . and to listen. We believe that information is meant to move and that information moves people.
>
> Respect: We treat others as we would like to be treated ourselves. We do not tolerate abusive or disrespectful treatment.
>
> Integrity: We work with customers and prospects openly, honestly, and sincerely. When we say we will do something, we will do it; when we say we cannot or will not do something, then we won't do it.
>
> Excellence: We are satisfied with nothing less than the very best in everything we do. We will continue to raise the bar for everyone. The great fun here will be for all of us to discover just how good we can really be.

R. W. Beckett Corporation Today

The issue Kevin kept coming back to was how, and to what extent, the company should build and/or retain its distinctive corporate culture as it dealt with critical issues. Within the next five to 10 years, the company expected to make decisions regarding:

- Growth in employment—With an ever-widening mix of personal backgrounds and expectations in new hires, how deliberately and proactively should the company pursue "diversity"?
- Development of people—What was the best way to embed cultural norms as a sustained aspect of that development?
- New business acquisitions and mergers—How would they handle acquisitions and mergers with the reality that merging cultures from different organizations can often become an insurmountable Achilles' heel to successful integration?
- International expansion—How would they work through wide, deep, and long-standing cultural differences?
- Hiring senior leadership—How would they ensure that senior leadership would have full "buy-in" to sustain cultural continuity?

Kevin also recognized that profound cultural changes were taking place in society, affecting employment and business relationships. The historic moral foundation of society enjoyed by our nation was eroding in many ways, and there was increased government regulation supporting many of those changes. There was also a general recognition and acceptance of other forms of religious faith along with government regulations preventing religious discrimination. Even basics such as the work ethic and professionalism seemed to be changing. Would the existing corporate culture remain harmonious with these cultural changes, or would Beckett have to adjust to prevailing culture to remain operationally effective and relevant?

Every entrepreneur understands that companies must change to remain viable. R. W. Beckett had a history of changing when conditions warranted in response to, or even in anticipation of, events. The company remained dynamic and would increasingly need to be adaptable in the future. But the question remained: Do reactive and/or proactive changes apply to the area of corporate culture?

Outsourcing Manufacturing Functions

As noted earlier, Kevin had recognized the increased pressures on product margins to remain competitive. The oil heating business was a mature industry with other substitute products, such as natural gas, impacting demand levels. The industry was also subject to the political uncertainties of the supply and demand of foreign oil.

Beckett was the market leader with an established history of quality products and unquestioned integrity. The company took great pride in the workmanship of its products and was very sensitive to the needs of its employees. Employees, in turn, were generally satisfied working at Beckett even at often routine, repetitive jobs. They appreciated the efforts of top management and were highly loyal to the company, choosing to remain non-union, even though many manufacturers in the surrounding area were unionized.

Kevin was limited in his ability to raise prices so product margin improvements had to come through cost reductions, productivity improvements, or increases in volume. The company was constantly working to eliminate waste in terms of the product development process, manufacturing, and assembly. However, eventually incremental improvements reach a point of diminishing returns. Kevin wrestled with the realization that in order to secure domestic jobs, he had to consider outsourcing some jobs to foreign countries.

Once processes are sent to geographically diverse locations, the issue of maintaining intellectual property and quality standards becomes more challenging. Product quality and reliability are essential, and Kevin was aware that the potential for compromise existed.

Kevin also would be dealing with potential employee-relations issues. How might the current workforce respond to certain jobs being performed outside the Untied States? Would Beckett now be considered just like every other manufacturing company—that when costs had to be reduced the simple solution was to search for less expensive foreign labor? What would happen to the morale of loyal company employees? Again, how was the decision process influenced by the consideration of corporate culture?

Case Conclusion

Kevin felt mounting pressure to do the right thing—both by customers, employees, suppliers, and the community. He also sensed a special responsibility as the third generation of Becketts in the business, especially as he read the findings of Ernesto Poza (2003), that over 85 percent of family businesses don't survive to the third generation.[2]

Was business failure a result of too rigid a corporate culture, or in spite of corporate culture, or the failure to define and defend corporate culture? Was the fall of Enron due to a breach in corporate culture or something completely unrelated? Could an Enron situation even occur at Beckett? Was the corporate culture outdated? Can or should practices first established by his grandfather be passed on to the son and grandsons? Kevin felt the business was on solid footing, but what about 5 to 10 years from now?

How would outsourcing to China impact the corporate culture of R. W. Beckett Corporation? Were concerns regarding corporate culture important enough to influence the decision? Kevin pondered his new responsibilities and decisions.

References

Beckett, J. D. (1998). *Loving Monday.* Downers Grove, Illinois: InterVarsity Press.

Enron Statement of Values in Annual Report (2000). Retrieved, April 5, 2007 from http://picker.uchicago.edu/Enron/EnronAnnualReport2000.pdf.

Leggatt, D. & Beckett, J. D. (1987). *Beckett: the First Fifty Years.* Elyria, Ohio: R. W. Beckett Corporation.

Poza, E. J. (2003, August 11). "Heirs and Graces in a Family Business," by Ernesto J. Poza, *Business Week On-line.*

R. W. Beckett Corporation Web site (2007). Retrieved, April 5, 2007, from http://www.beckettcorp.com.

Endnotes

1. R. W. Beckett Corporation of Elyria, Ohio, is one of the leading privately owned companies in the world in the production of oil burners for residential and commercial heating systems. Affiliates supply air-moving and gas combustion components for heating, cooking, and related application heat products, supplying critical parts from blower motors to fuel economizer components.
2. Ernesto J. Poza is an internationally recognized, top-rated speaker and consultant to family-owned businesses. He is professor for the Practice of Family Business at Case Western Reserve University. His work has been featured by CNN, NBC, NPR, *Business Week, Family Business Magazine, Inc., Industry Week, El Norte, El Pais, Expansion, Excelsior, Forbes,* and *Fortune.* He is a founding member and fellow of the Family Firm Institute, serves on the editorial review board of *Family Business Review,* and is the 1996 recipient of the prestigious Richard Beckhard Award for contributions to the practice of family business advising. He is the author of *Family Business* (Thomson, 2004) and *Empresas Familiares* (Thomson, 2005).

Case 6
Cardone Industries: *Chaplain Program*

Timothy A. O. Redmer
Regent University
timored@regent.edu

Introduction

Cardone Industries, a remanufacturer of auto parts, hired a major consulting firm about 18 months ago with expertise in supply chain management to review their supply chain operations, find bottlenecks, and identify other areas of concern. The consultants became very familiar with every operation. Their report recommended improvements to company operations and overall activities.

One of their first recommendations to improve profitability was to eliminate the company chaplain program. Several top managers were somewhat surprised by this. The chaplain program represented the very fiber of the organization and reflected its corporate culture. To some, it was untouchable. Others in top management were more concerned about costs, profitability, and building a "new" Cardone model, and generally accepted this recommendation.

Opposing sides formed within management. How far did corporate culture go when measured against costs and profitability to the organization? Should functions like a chaplaincy program, which could have been considered as nice to have, been subject to the same scrutiny or an even higher level of accountability than an operational activity that directly contributes to the bottom line? What decision criteria, if any, should have been applied to a function that could be claimed as part of a corporate culture?

With seven chaplains, support staff, and several outreach ministries, Cardone Industries had an extensive chaplain program. Company founder, Michael Cardone—respectfully referred to as Mr. Cardone—had called his employees "the Cardone Factory Family" and implemented a chaplain program in 1979 with founding leader and now Chief Spiritual Officer Mark Spuler. But "that was then, and this is now." In 1988, Michael Jr. became president, and in 1994, Mr. Cardone passed away. Even so, Michael Jr. had fully embraced the Cardone Factory Family concept and even increased the role and influence of the chaplain program. Mark and Michael, who had worked so closely together for years, saw the value of chaplains. These two founding culture bearers of the integration of faith and work at Cardone Industries viewed chaplains not only as a vital part of their heritage but also good for business and the bottom line. But financial pressures had been mounting and margins declining, which led to the decision in 2001 to hire a consulting firm to provide an objective analysis from outside experts.

Some executives wanted to fight the recommendation. At the same time, Michael, with his more participative style of management, recognized others who viewed spiritual life while at work, and more specifically the chaplaincy program, as not relevant to business. Eliminating the chaplain program with its annual overhead of $600,000 could increase profits. Perhaps the company could still preserve its corporate culture and Factory Family image—just not to its current degree. Furthermore, to gain the maximum efficiencies in overall operational improvements wasn't it necessary to accept the consultants' recommendations in total?

When considered from a cost benefit perspective, it was easy to identify the cost; there was $600,000 of overhead burden that the company was dealing with. However, it was virtually impossible to determine the benefits of the chaplaincy program. When questioned, the chaplain staff could not really put a price tag on the perceived benefits of their program. There were no specific measurements—either financial or otherwise—of the impact of this program on either the company or the corporate culture.

Cardone management had to decide whether or not to accept the recommendation to eliminate the chaplaincy program. Whatever its decision, the strong emotions that quickly developed on both sides were making the process that much more difficult.

History

Mr. Cardone had started a business in 1935 remanufacturing vacuum windshield wipers. When they finished high school, his three younger brothers joined the business then named Automotive Unit Exchange (AUE), and they expanded their operations to include the remanufacture of fuel pumps. After World War II, the demand for remanufactured automobile parts increased and included remanufactured foreign-car parts. In the 1950s, the company name was changed to Cardo, and the company prospered.

When Mr. Cardone was 55, he could have easily retired. Although he wanted his son, Michael Jr., to come into the business, a provision in the company bylaws forbade any of its partners' children from assuming company leadership.[1] Consequently, Mr. Cardone decided to resign from the presidency of Cardo and start over with a new company with Michael Jr. who had just graduated from Oral Roberts University.

Cardone Industries began as A-1 Remanufacturing in 1970 remanufacturing electric windshield wiper motors. A-1 had six employees: Mr. Cardone; his wife, Frances; his daughter, Ruth; Ruth's husband, Ruben; his son, Michael; and Michael's wife Jacquie. They worked out of a rented row house in a terribly run down section of Philadelphia—their home town. Rats the size of house cats were unwanted occupants of the basement of the three-story structure.[2]

Since his childhood, Mr. Cardone had been a very religious man. He believed that the corporate culture of his business must reflect his strong Christian principles. From the very start, his vision was to have a triple bottom line reflecting financial,

Source: Christian Business Faculty Association, Christian Business Academy Review

social, and spiritual returns. This was the company's "ministry of business." One of their goals was to provide jobs and create a unique working environment that would produce better financial results and satisfied customers, while making a difference in peoples' lives. The company had four corporate objectives.[3]

- Honor God in all we do
- Help people develop
- Pursue excellence
- Grow profitability

Early on, Mr. Cardone made a deal with Chrysler for 20,000 surplus windshield wiper motor cores retuned under warranty for $9,052. The company only had $9,500 in its checking account and no customers looking to buy remanufactured motors. While rebuilts had been successful for vacuum wipers, it seemed there was no market for the newer electric motors. Mr. Cardone took a big risk and offered his remanufactured wiper motors to customers at no cost and no obligation on a consignment basis. He also agreed to advertise the products in automotive journals. Customers would only have to pay for motors sold. Mr. Cardone would have to convince customers that the remanufactured wiper motors were as good as or better than the original equipment at a significantly lower price. His willingness to take a risk proved successful and profitable.[4]

Disaster struck 9 months after starting A-1 Remanufacturing when a fire destroyed the entire inventory, equipment, and records. However, within 3 days, they found new facilities that were better suited to their operation. Both Mr. Cardone and Michael believed that God was watching out for them and that the business would be successful. It was through trials like these that the company's most valuable resource—people—really came to the rescue and the concept of the Factory Family was born.

Cardone Inc., a global business, had seven major product divisions consisting of 43 product lines and offered a full line of brakes, drive trains, electronics, motors, pumps, and steering. In Philadelphia alone, they had over two million square feet of manufacturing and distribution functions under roof in 12 different factories encompassing eight buildings. The company also had distribution centers in Los Angeles and Canada with additional operations in Chicago, Europe, and Mexico. Cases of raw material and finished goods were stacked up to 20 feet high in some spots. The company had over 22,000 catalogued part numbers with core components servicing cars as far back as the 1960s, as well as the current models.

Remanufacturing

The basic idea of the remanufacturing (RM) process was to rebuild the old car part, thus creating an exact replica of the original equipment (OEM), while repairing the original failure mode. When an automobile part failed to function properly, it needed to be replaced with a similar part in fit and function. The RM business developed to meet that need. Businesses like Cardone take the core (old defective automobile part), disassemble it, clean components (including an anti-corrosion treatment), test components, replace worn parts, perform final testing, and provide accessories.[6]

Generally, new parts from an automobile manufacturer are quite expensive. They would be even more expensive if the RM industry did not exist. The automobile manufacturer's prime focus was to make new cars; they were not in the primary business of producing and stocking old automobile replacement parts. RM companies evolved to give consumers a choice and filled a market void left by automobile companies more focused on original equipment.

Remanufactured parts at Cardone were guaranteed to meet or exceed original equipment specifications, which gave consumers a high-quality alternative at a much lower price. Additionally, Cardone provided an environmental alternative to the disposal of extremely corrosive core products in landfills. The RM process saved 80% of the energy and material cost it took to manufacture new parts which was equivalent to 16 million barrels of crude oil.[7]

As the industry leader, Cardone's philosophy of remanufacturing emphasized the highest levels of quality and service. Even before parts were remanufactured, the company engineers examined original equipment parts, looked for potential defects and weakness, and corrected flaws in the OEM process which made the remanufactured products as good as or better than new.[8]

The Factory Family

Philadelphia was a melting pot. With the factory located in an economically disadvantaged area and with jobs available to the less-skilled worker, Cardone Industries was a very attractive opportunity to a large labor pool. The cultural diversity of it 4,000+ employees was evident—there were 32 nationalities speaking 24 different languages. The term "family" was a natural classification of the employee population as multiple family members and extended family were often recommended by fellow employees and hired by Cardone.[9] To get the best results from his people, Mr. Cardone believed that he must demonstrate that each employee was a highly valued part of a family. Early on, the words "employees" and "workers" changed to "Factory Family Members."

Cardone executives practiced a "servant-leadership model" of management patterned after the teachings of Jesus before such a concept was generally recognized in business school theoretical discussions. Servant-leadership encourages people to serve others first—be it employees, customers, suppliers, or the community. Cardone believed servant-leadership should apply not only in the workplace, but in every aspect of life. Much like the golden rule—"do on to others as you would have them do on to you"—the model builds trust and loyalty.[10]

Factory Family Members were very dedicated to the company, even though the hourly work force was completely union, as would be expected in an industrialized city like Philadelphia. Employee turnover was far below average when compared to other competitors, and most new jobs were filled either by internal promotions or referrals from employees. The company provided ample training and opportunities for job advancement. They started every day with a 5-minute session called "Take 5" where section leaders offered a voluntary time of devotion and prayer and looked to serve their employees' needs. This was a part of the corporate culture in Cardone, and it developed both a working and personal relationship between leaders and team members.[11]

Chaplain Program

In 1979, to further strengthen the corporate culture and support the needs of the rapidly growing Factory Family, Mr. Cardone hired the first chaplain. The purpose of the program was to impact the world for Christ. Many of the employees were immigrants from various nations. This was their first job in the United States, and they needed personal help in various areas of their new lives in this country. The chaplain could help. Top management and the chaplains understood that it was important to recognize the whole man—body, mind, and spirit—and strived to meet their physical, emotional, and spiritual needs. Their philosophy was that in meeting all the needs of their employers, these people would be even more dedicated and productive for the company.

To meet the diverse and numerous needs of the staff, additional chaplains were hired who initiated various programs and services. The chaplains:

- established ethnic churches using company facilities on weekends so that various nationalities could develop a sense of community;
- assisted with doctor needs, government registrations, social service support, financial dilemmas, city services, and domestic issues;
- instituted a voluntary chapel, Bible studies, a benevolence fund, musical groups, cultural nights, sporting activities, and recognition programs and awards; and
- served as a confidential source of encouragement and support when an employee felt uncomfortable discussing an issue with his team leader or immediate supervisor.

In addition, the Cardone Foundation was established to use a portion of the corporate profits for specific needs of the Factory Family community. The Foundation primarily supported local social, medical, and educational organizations for the needs of the Philadelphia area community.[12]

At the same time, Cardone was aware of "Title VII" government regulations regarding activities considered legal in the workplace. While employers and employees had the right to religious freedom and practiced their Christian beliefs in the workplace, they knew they could not enforce their beliefs or discriminate against those who chose not to support similar religious practices. Chaplains also had to recognize that activities were voluntary and should not be practiced on company time. While a Christian-based company, Cardone's employees were allowed to practice different religious faiths at different levels of commitment.

There was also tolerance for those who did not have or support a particular religious belief.[13]

Transition

After Michael Jr. become president of Cardone in 1988, he continued to practice the same values established by his father. Eventually, Michael assumed full control and responsibility for the organization's success. Times changed. Running the business was increasingly complex. As profit margins diminished from increased competitive pressures, the number of competitors actually declined. Some public companies wanted to purchase Cardone; however, Michael decided to keep it a private company. Surviving it all, Cardone became the market leader of remanufactured automotive parts and experienced significant growth.

Michael and Chief Spiritual Officer Mark Spuler often worked in tandem and completely supported the corporate culture at Cardone and the Factory Family mindset. This was the culture they fortified together for over 25 years of their career by their example, continued support, and by the congruent decisions they made. They strengthened programs to enhance cooperation within the company and between suppliers and customers including the establishment of a CARE fund to help employees in financial and personal crisis. Creative new approaches to meet Factory Family Member's needs were adopted into the chaplain program.

Michael believed that Factory Family Members should be allowed to share in the company's growth and profits, so he introduced an employee stock ownership plan. He also established a matching 401(k) program. These incentives were an outcome of the servant-leadership model and provided the best service and product to all interested parties.[14]

There was also a transition in many upper management positions as a new generation assumed leadership; many were promoted from within the company along with those hired from the outside as the company continued to grow and prosper. There was a good mixture of book knowledge and on-the-job experience and these people were familiar with faith at work concepts and the use of chaplains in the workplace; however, the consultants were not as aware of this practice.

Consultants

In light of the increased dynamics of running a business, Cardone management hired outside experts to assess the company's operations. They were especially interested in supply chain activities and any recommendations to make operations more efficient and improve company performance and profitability.

In its basic supply chain activities, Cardone annually received millions of used automobile cores from all over the world representing more than 20,000 different sku classifications in various states of disrepair. The cores were quickly identified by sku part number so that customers were properly credited and paid for the returned cores. Cardone stored the parts for future use. Some part numbers from late-model popular cars tended to be in large quantities and in high demand. At the other extreme, there were parts that could only be used for antique or classic cars that might never be made again. To meet the various levels of customer demand, Cardone carried a huge core inventory.

The work in process function followed both a job order and continuous process approach. Parts in high demand were constantly remanufactured. At the same time, there were many parts that might be ordered in small quantities. Some batch processing could be completed with products in less demand, but that might require more finished goods inventory.

In finished goods, many of the final products were boxed under the Cardone name, as well as other company names such as NAPA, Carquest, Autozone, and Advanced Auto. Given the large variety of products and the commitment to rapid customer service, the company maintained a fairly substantial stock of finished goods.

Cardone had a fleet of trucks and employed drivers to cover their biggest customers and routes, which provided the fastest possible delivery and superior customer service. Cardone also supplemented their own transportation service with independent carriers and professional delivery like Federal Express and UPS. Some of these carriers left a truck on site and made Cardone the last pick-up of the afternoon so that goods reached customers in the shortest time.

The consulting firm spent 18 months reviewing Cardone's various activities to look for ways to improve the process, cut costs, and increase margins. During these last few years, economic and competitive conditions made it almost impossible to use price as a tool for improved profitability. At the same time, increased labor, energy, and material costs, which could not be totally passed on to the customer, had reduced the profit margin. Foreign competition with its lower labor costs had impacted the domestic market, especially on new products. Also, the price of many original equipment items had gone down with production efficiencies. Since Cardone priced their RM products significantly below the OEM market, they faced an ever-decreasing ceiling price.

As the number of remanufacturers declined, so did the number of auto parts customers. Gone were the days of the mom-and-pop auto parts companies. The "Walmart model" had overtaken the retail auto parts industry with only a few major companies like Advance Auto, AutoZone, CARQUEST, O'Reilly, Pep Boys, and NAPA remaining. These customers needed larger and more capable suppliers in more of a one-stop shop arrangement. Like Walmart, since these companies tended to order parts in large quantities, they had a greater say on price. If suppliers did not comply, these large retailers looked elsewhere.

Given the challenges of the industry and company, the consultants reviewed the entire operation, not just supply chain activities, when they made their recommendations. With the overall survival of Cardone possibly in the balance if profit margins could not be improved, all factors needed to be considered.

Eliminating the chaplain program was actually an obvious recommendation for the consulting firm. This program, although nice to have, seemed to be growing without any level of accountability. Some services could easily be incorporated under the human resources department. Additionally, terminating the chaplaincy program would remove many of the potential legal problems when dealing with Title VII issues of religious freedom. The company could still maintain its corporate culture of a "ministry of business" and the "Factory Family" and honor God in all they did even without the chaplain program. In the minds of many, providing a job in a cooperative work environment should be all that was expected or required by a company without these additional "soft services."

The Dilemma

In spite of the corporate culture issue, top management was weighing both sides of the consulting firm's recommendations. Some of their comments were:[15]

> Why couldn't others in the organization be responsible for the activities the chaplains were doing?
>
> Why were other businesses, which do not have chaplaincy programs, successful?
>
> Why did Cardone do the work of the church?

They understood the numbers and realized that the company had to be profitable. Cardone had an obligation to all of its stakeholders. If they could not be profitable, what impact might that have on employees and many others? Any reduction of unnecessary overhead burden that would not compromise the operational mission and core business seemed advantageous to the company.

However, other executives wanted to continue the chaplain program. Their comments included:[16]

> This company was founded on biblical truths; if we eliminated this program from the company, it could fail.
>
> We promoted a triple bottom line, focusing on spiritual, financial and social returns. It was not just about the money.
>
> The corporate culture, as reflected in the chaplain program, had benefits far beyond what was typically measured in terms of costs and actually improved the profitability of the company in many ways.

The chaplain department had numerous stories of how they had helped employees. They were often the only hope and only people to come to the aid of employees. In their mind, nothing in the company better represented the Factory Family than the chaplain service. Additionally, having the chaplain program was in full compliance with at least two of the four corporate objectives: (1) honor God in all we do, and (2) help people develop.

Some in leadership believed that the chaplain ministry had a direct and positive impact on at least eight employee issues. The chaplains' work had:

- improved quality
- increased productivity
- enhanced employee morale
- reduced absenteeism and tardiness
- decreased voluntary and involuntary terminations
- reduced workplace injuries
- decreased the need for discipline
- reduced conflicts on the job.

The costs of chaplaincy services could easily be documented; however, it was virtually impossible to determine the value of their benefits in the way of cost reductions, increased efficiencies, or revenue enhancements. The chaplains knew in their hearts what they were doing was right; they just could not quantify their impact and influence on the organization. This failure to report the numbers seemed to really hurt their legitimacy in the eyes of some.

Case Conclusion

When Mr. Cardone was alive, there would be no question about continuing the chaplain program. However, times had changed and the current challenges seemed much more complicated than when Mr. Cardone was running the company. Michael also recognized the importance of the chaplain program but his management style was more participative; he worked for a consensus on some issues even if it might not be entirely consistent with his own viewpoint. While total agreement might not be possible on the consultant's recommendation, a decision had to be made.

Endnotes

1. Cardone Sr., M. (1988). *Never too late for a new beginning.* Old Tappan, NJ: Fleming H. Revell. pp. 84–96.
2. Cardone, pp. 84–96.
3. Scout, E. (Ed.). (2005). *Cardone: A heritage.* Philadelphia, PA: Cardone Industries. p. 1.
4. Cardone, pp. 97–112.
5. Scout, p. 2.
6. Scout, p. 2.
7. Scout, p. 29.
8. Scout, p. 2.
9. Scout, p. 13.
10. Scout, p. 6.
11. Scout, p. 6.
12. Scout, p. 7.
13. American Center for Law and Justice (1977). Sekulow, J. A. Christian rights in the workplace. pp. 1–2.
14. Scout, p. 21.
15. Cardone Management Meetings, Cardone Inc., 2003.
16. Cardone Management Meetings, Cardone Inc., 2003.

Case 7
Ethics, Decision-Making, and Responsibility: Tough Call Knowing Someone Loses

Donald V. Drew
Oklahoma Christian University

Scene 1: Welcome Aboard!

Thomas held out his hand and welcomed Mike "aboard." After a 3-month search, Thomas was certain he had found the right man for the job. He was impressed with Mike's credentials and felt good to be able to deliver such good news to a man he knew had been out of work for 6 months. Although Thomas would never have placed Mike's credentials as a committed Christian over the basic skills and experience the candidate would need to be successful in this job, Thomas was pleased to hire a man who made it clear he, too, possessed Christian values. Thomas was especially impressed with the manner in which Mike spoke openly in the interview about his love for his family and his active work as a Christian. He felt pleased that Mike felt comfortable enough to volunteer this information in the interview. Thomas already felt an affinity for Mike. Sometimes the business of defense contracting could be harsh, and it felt good to have a new employee to whom he could relate in more personal terms. No sooner had Thomas delivered the good news than he felt the façade of playing "interviewer" start to drop.

"So, tell me more about yourself since we'll be working together," Thomas queried. They spoke casually for about 20 minutes before John Spencer stuck his head in Thomas' office and asked Thomas if he wanted to go to lunch. Replying affirmatively to John, Thomas turned to Mike and asked him to join them. Several others joined the group, and they all enjoyed getting to know one another better at lunch. Afterward, as they queued up to pay their lunch bill, Mike, standing in line in front of Thomas, appeared shocked that his credit card was rejected. Without missing a beat, Thomas said, "Allow me to get this," and paid for his and Mike's lunch. As they walked to the car, Thomas remembered that Mike had been out of work for 6 months, and he imagined that things might have gotten very tight financially for Mike and his family. He thought nothing else of the incident for some time.

As they approached their work site, Thomas felt more positive about the future than he had in a while. He was responsible for Alsom Defense Technologies' (ADT's) support operations at the federal government's system program office, and all of his crew worked within the government's organization on site. His government client could be a tough taskmaster, but he had developed an unusually good relationship with his government bosses/customers, and the rules for working with government employees were well-known and documented. He knew Mike would not have any trouble adjusting since Mike had more than 20 years experience in this business. Thomas felt that one of his highest responsibilities was to always conduct himself, his employees, and his business in a manner beyond reproach.

Source: Christian Business Faculty Association, Journal of Biblical Integration in Business—Case Edition

When he hired, he always included this as one of his chief considerations. Thomas had spent 27 years creating a reputation as both caring and competent, and he was determined to keep it.

Scene 2: Two Months Later

Cindy Johnson looked serious when she approached Thomas. It turned out she was serious.

"I don't know if this is a real problem or not, but Mike just tried to sell me an insurance policy," Cindy blurted. She didn't sound angry, just concerned.

"What do you mean by 'an insurance policy'?" Thomas responded. "Was he telling you about some good insurance product he's found?"

"I don't think so," Cindy replied. "I got the impression he's got a business of some sort."

Thomas was really too busy to worry about this right at the minute. He would look into it later. In the meantime, he thanked Cindy, telling her it was probably just a misunderstanding, but he would look into it.

Thomas was irritated because he knew Mike should know better than to sell anything on company time. All of the ADT crew were on billable hours to the government, and conducting personal business on government time would be the worst kind of offense, but the issue would have to wait. By the end of the day, Thomas had convinced himself that it was probably an isolated incident and that it was not likely to happen again. He had not had time to say anything to Mike that afternoon, and by the next morning the issue was forgotten. That is, until 2 days later.

Sara Marker had been with Thomas since they started ADT's work with this government customer. She was reliable and well respected, so this time, when he heard the same story Cindy had told 2 days earlier, he had to listen. Sara added one more item.

"I also think Mike's hitting up some of our customers to buy his product as well," she said. "I overheard him talking to Julie Langston about insurance."

Thomas could tell by Sara's tone of voice that Sara was more certain of her convictions than her words allowed. He didn't want to believe it, but it was becoming clear that Mike was placing all their jobs in jeopardy by his misconduct. As far as Thomas could tell, Mike was a very competent worker; however, carrying on personal business while being paid to perform work for his government customer and, even worse, attempting to sell his personal insurance product to that very same customer were extremely serious breaches of ethics. Furthermore, Mike, like all ADT employees, had received initial training regarding both ADT policies and U.S. law governing contractor/government employee relations. He had signed a statement declaring he understood what was required and what was forbidden.

Thomas returned to his office to consider what needed to be done next. He thought about how Mike had been unemployed for so long and how Mike had probably turned to his "business" to make ends meet between jobs; however, his overwhelming thought was anger that Mike would do such a thing—that he would endanger his own job and those of his ADT co-workers. Most of all, Thomas was upset because he thought Mike should know better, because he expected Mike to conform to a higher standard than his actions were betraying.

That night Thomas found time to think over both Mike's behavior and his own reaction to it. He opened his Bible to search for an answer. The first verse he thought of came from Romans 3:23—" . . . for all have sinned and fall short of the glory of God . . . ". Thomas remembered his own past and the many opportunities God and others had given him when he made errors in judgment. As he read on in Romans, he was struck by the sheer number of calls for Christians to love and care for one another. Thomas felt convicted of a need to respond to Mike on a higher level than simply as his boss. Still, Thomas had to reconcile a deeply felt responsibility to care for everyone under his leadership, regardless of his or her religious beliefs. He reminded himself that Sara and several others were Christians as well. The same passages that admonished Thomas to care for Mike directed him to care for the others, too. Just before closing his Bible for the evening, Thomas' eyes fell upon one last passage: Romans 12:8–10—"If God has given you leadership ability, take the responsibility seriously. And if you have a gift for showing kindness to others, do it gladly. Don't just pretend that you love others. Really love them. Hate what is wrong. Stand on the side of the good. Love each other with genuine affection, and take delight in honoring each other." He bowed his head to pray.

First thing in the morning, Thomas decided that it would be best to call a meeting for 3 p.m. that afternoon to discuss proper protocol and ethics with all his ADT employees. That way, it would be clear to all what the rules were, and Mike would immediately see his error and take corrective action.

The meeting that afternoon was very short. Thomas explained company policy and U.S. law regarding the conduct of personal business and emphasized that conducting personal business on company time would result in immediate termination. He emphasized that if the government managers found out this was happening, they could throw all of ADT's employees out of the building, resulting in all of them losing their jobs.

That afternoon, as Thomas walked through the parking lot to his car, he heard Mike call his name from behind. Thomas stopped and waited for Mike to catch up.

"Thomas," Mike apologized, "I'm really sorry about that. I didn't mean to cause any trouble. I started this business when I was out of work, and it's a really good product. It saves folks a lot of money. But I promise I won't sell my product at work again."

Thomas listened quietly as Mike spoke. Mike explained more about his business, but Thomas was no longer listening. He was searching for the right response.

He replied, "I understand your need to take care of your family, Mike, but you've placed us all at risk and, frankly, I expected more of you. As Christians, you and I need to be above reproach. We need to look out for one another and not just ourselves. I need you to understand that what you were doing was unethical." Mike didn't respond.

"Look," said Thomas, "I know we can get past this and I won't hold this over you, but this cannot happen again." Mike confirmed that he understood, and they parted ways, each heading to his own car.

Over the next month, Mike appeared to be a model employee. Thomas, feeling his confidence in Mike being restored, looked toward the future and decided he needed to acquire additional training for himself and Mike. The customer was willing to send Thomas and Mike to Boston for a week to receive training in new project management software their customer had purchased. Thomas made travel arrangements and, to ensure nothing fell through the cracks, he scheduled Mike to attend first and scheduled himself for two weeks later. Thomas was pleased that he and Mike would be first to receive the training, as it would further secure ADT's position with this customer.

The time came for Mike to leave for Boston, and Thomas went over the details of what Mike must be sure to learn. So it was with great disappointment that Thomas found out upon Mike's return that he had been unable to learn what was needed. Mike explained that the computer training system had "crashed" during the week, and they had only been able to complete about 2 days of training out of the 4 days allotted. Thomas didn't say anything to Mike, but he determined that he would take this failing up with the contracted training organization when he traveled to Boston himself.

Scene 3: Not Again!

Boston was cool that November, but not cold. The training facility sat on the northeast corner of an intersection of two highways and was plain but quite functional. The staff seemed professional enough, and the first day was filled with about 6 hours of basic software instruction. During a break on Tuesday, Thomas mentioned to the instructor that he had sent Mike up for training 3 weeks earlier and was disappointed that they had had so much computer trouble that week. The instructor gave Thomas a quizzical look.

"Who was this you sent here, and what company do you guys work for?" he asked.

"Mike Carlin, and we work for ADT out of Dayton, Ohio," Thomas responded.

"I'll tell you what," the instructor stated, "I think there's someone you need to speak with. I'll make arrangements for Nancy Quinlan to meet with you on our next break. She's our director of training."

Clearly, there was something wrong, but Thomas knew he would have to wait for the lunch break to learn what Ms. Quinlan had to say. It was only an hour, but Thomas found himself struggling to concentrate.

Nancy was waiting for Thomas just outside the training room door as he exited. "I understand Mike Carlin works for you," she said. "I would like to talk with you in private. Can we go to my office?"

This didn't sound good, but Thomas was compelled to answer Nancy affirmatively. He followed her through a maze of cubicles to arrive at the double cubicle she used as an office.

"Look," she started, "maybe this isn't my business, but I think you should know this. Mr. Carlin spent at least half his training time on the phone in the break room. Your instructor said you were under the impression that our system was down for 2 days. That is untrue. Also, one of our employees whose cubicle is next to the break area complained that it sounded as though he were conducting business over the phone and selling something. He was speaking on the phone so much that it became disruptive to her work. I know our companies both work for the government, and I know that if I were you, I would be very concerned about this."

Thomas was speechless. He sat in the chair as if the air had been sucked from his body. Gathering his thoughts, he thanked Nancy for her concern and assured her that he would take action. He then asked to use the phone himself.

Thomas placed a call to his vice president of operations in Dayton. The two of them had come far since their early days of establishing ADT's operations with their Dayton clients, and the VP trusted Thomas. That made Thomas feel all the more guilty that he hadn't informed the VP of Mike Carlin's earlier mistakes, but he had thought he could handle it himself. After what seemed an eternity of explanations, the VP simply said, "What do you want to do?"

"I don't know," Thomas said, sounding defeated.

"I'll call the human resource manager in California and get her feedback," the VP responded. "Don't do anything for now, and I'll call you at your hotel room tonight."

Thomas felt very small as he waited in his room for the call that night. The decision was tougher than he expected. He was torn between his convictions to reach out and help a fellow Christian in trouble and his duty to protect others for whom he was equally responsible. He wished that the answer would be as simple as finding the right Bible passage that would tell him what to do, but he sensed that the answer wouldn't come that easy.

The phone call came two hours later. He had clearance to terminate Mike, but the decision would ultimately be his.

Scene 4: Decision Time

Thomas' flight arrived in Dayton just before noon. He went over again and again what he would say to Mike and how he would say it. As soon as Thomas could get to his office and return a few phone calls, he summoned Mike.

Thomas stated, "Mike, I have discovered that you were conducting personal business on company time, that you did not attend much of the training the government purchased for you, and that you lied to me about the training system being 'down.' I warned you about such behavior previously, and I'm truly sorry you didn't take me seriously." Mike looked shocked. There was no more time for Thomas to mull this over; a decision had to be made.

Case 8
Coping with Scandal: Individual Redemption and Organizational Recovery

Janis Balda
George Fox University

When Harry called, Heather was glad to hear from him. Harry, the vice president for human resources at CareED, Inc., was a longtime acquaintance. They had worked together at another nonprofit organization earlier in their careers, and Harry left to join CareED when it was a fairly young and small educational organization providing training and technical support in targeted areas of the world. At the time of the phone call, Harry had been with CareED for more than 15 years and had been instrumental in increasing the size of the staff and improving its professionalism.

CareED in the United States was primarily responsible for recruiting, preparing, and placing trainers in the developing world and newly industrialized countries. The organization viewed itself as a Christian entity and adopted an evangelical statement of faith. It did not call a great deal of attention to its evangelical orientation, however, believing that it could be more effective in its mission throughout the world without doing so.

In 2003, CareED had revenues of just under $14.5 million. The organization received no government grants or funding, and since 1989 it had been a member of the Evangelical Council for Financial Accountability (ECFA). CareED had approximately 83 administrative employees in its main office in the United States, with small teams in seven satellite offices within the United States and Canada. The staff had supported the work of between 500 and 700 trainers a year, as well as some smaller and newly created initiatives, for the last several years.

Heather was an attorney and sole practitioner. Her client load consisted primarily of nonprofit religious organizations with a few business start-ups and a real estate development company thrown in. Having provided legal counsel to CareED for almost 13 years, she knew most of the board members and the senior staff. While there had been occasional issues causing consternation for the professional, especially with regard to some employee concerns and with the international nature of the organization and the accompanying risk, its legal exposure had not been high. The most significant issue confronting the organization in recent history had been its involvement in the New Era Foundation debacle in the early 1990s.[1] Unlike some who faced possible collapse because of their participation, CareED had had relatively limited financial involvement, and management was able to "rescue" the organization with effective outside legal assistance and involvement of their key donors. On the whole, Heather felt comfortable with the mission and management of the organization and believed that it was stable, responsible, and accountable to the appropriate constituencies.

CareED was founded by a former missionary who had a "heart" for countries where missionaries were forbidden and was visionary enough to recognize the advantages of having well-qualified trainers willing to spend time in difficult locations. Being astute enough to see that their training would be a tool that even the most inward-looking country would probably recognize as needed by some part of the population, he exerted his own persuasive gifts, passion, and finances to push the enterprise. He had the good fortune to enlist the support, financial and otherwise, of some significant Christians in the United States. He personally conducted tours for supporters, resided part-time with his family overseas to promote the work of the organization, devoted his own resources extensively to furthering its work, and currently served as CareED's president.

His commitment and ability to attract capable and loyal staff made the organization fairly stable, although, like all nonprofit organizations, it struggled to match resources with vision. Not surprisingly, trainer turnover was high since most volunteers viewed their time overseas as a "short-term" missions experience—an opportunity to see a foreign country while "sharing" their gifts and their faith. Very few trainers stayed for a term of 4 years, and even fewer renewed for 8 years. That meant that there was always pressure on the recruiters to meet the quota of trainers needed.

The president's friendship with wealthy individuals meant that there was a fair representation of them on the board of directors, and they served without term limits. They made up the majority of the board with the remainder of the positions held by representatives of the church and the professions. The bylaws provided that the president and executive vice president were *ex officio* members of the board, although it was not clear whether they counted toward the total number of directors comprising a variable board of between 9 and 15.

When Harry called, Heather was expecting to respond to one of the more usual issues affecting the organization. Instead, Harry invited her to have lunch with him and Keith, the organization's independent accountant and auditor, the next day if at all possible. From the tone in his voice, Heather suspected that something serious was afoot but could sense that Harry did not want to discuss it on the phone. She attended the meeting the next day, though with more curiosity than concern.

Shortly after the opening pleasantries, Harry got right to the point. "Heather," he said, "we believe that Dave has embezzled money from the organization, and we are attempting to substantiate it and determine how much he took." Heather was dumbfounded. She had worked more with Dave than anyone else in management. He was the COO, and like most in that position, was overworked, overweight, and stressed, but he always had a kind word for his staff and demonstrated a humorous streak and

Source: Christian Business Faculty Association, Journal of Biblical Integration in Business—Case Edition

a genuine interest in others. She liked his direct but kind manner and the way he was considerate of those with whom he worked. She could be equally direct with him and not have to worry about how her advice would be received. So it was a shock on several different levels to hear the charges. She responded with a series of questions for both Harry and Keith (Keith was already working on reviewing receipts, expense reports, and financial records).

Surprisingly, the discovery had been made by an outside party. Dave had paid his son's college tuition for the semester with a check written on the organization's account rather than on his own. An alert bookkeeper at the university found this puzzling, called the CareED human resource department, and asked to speak to Harry. The organization made regular payments to the university for the use of training facilities and other services, and so it was not uncommon to have a check from CareEd, but she was curious why a check from the organization would be used to make tuition payments.

Once Harry had absorbed the information, he and Keith went to work. It seemed that the bookkeeper's concern was merited, and Harry prepared to confront Dave that evening. Harry spoke with the board chair and the president (who was traveling) that afternoon, and they left the task to Harry and Keith to gather the information and then to confront Dave. The chairman of the board would join them in this task if necessary. Harry now looked to Heather for suggestions on what he should say in confronting Dave and also sought general advice on the next steps. Heather raised concerns about accountability, privacy, and proof and noted that further research would be necessary over the next several days, depending on what they would learn from Dave. All agreed that they needed to get at the truth, but they wanted to do this without assumptions and in Christian love. Heather and Harry both hoped that it was an "oversight" and that Dave had perhaps "borrowed" the amount because of an emergency, had forgotten to alert anyone, and then neglected to repay it as he should have.

These hopes turned out to be an exercise in denial. By the next day, Dave had confessed to stealing funds which went well beyond the single payment discovered by the university. When confronted, he confessed, was remorseful, expressed deep regret, and communicated a desire to make restitution. He had been unable to support the lifestyle that he and his family had become accustomed to and used the organization's money to support these wants. He admitted to obtaining other items such as household furnishings, jewelry for his wife, and additional "minor" purchases. He thought the total was between $35,000 and $40,000. He told his wife of the theft, and she accompanied him to the meeting with Harry and Keith. Harry called Heather to let her know the details and explained that the president was on his way home and the board chairman was coming that day to have a follow-up meeting with the couple. Harry asked Heather to join them. Heather agreed and continued researching the legal issues facing the organization.

It was a difficult meeting that involved coming face-to-face with a broken and desperate man who had abused his position and been caught. Heather had mixed feelings. She was angry that he would abuse the trust of those who worked for him and their beneficiaries and use donated funds to maintain his own standard of living. But she also knew how hard he had worked, and after listening to him began to see how desperate he had become. His morals were obviously clouded by his desire to act out a role he thought society demanded of someone in his position, and now he knew that the shame and public ridicule he would be facing would only demean him more in the view of others. He was apologetic and stated at the outset that he would make full restitution—"no matter what it took." At the same time, he was unrealistic. Dave thought he ought to be able to stay in his position, after full confession to his staff, and that greater controls and accountability to the board would continue to make his role tenable. Heather and Harry both knew that this would probably not be possible. Dave agreed to provide a list of amounts stolen, to let the board decide his fate, and to do whatever else was asked of him. That was a relief to Heather, although she knew that what people sometimes said when they were emotionally distraught often changed in the light of day and after speaking to their own attorney.

Together they explored the following items and reached agreement on them:

1. Dave would not return to the office.
2. All files, keys, and other company property would be handed over to Harry that day.
3. Dave would acknowledge that the wording of the letter to be shared with the staff was accurate and fair.
4. Dave would meet with a financial counselor within 2 days to explore a strategy and methods for repayment and provide a rough plan within 48 hours of that meeting.

Heather explained to Dave the importance of demonstrating an immediate good-faith effort, the need to make restitution, and that concrete steps would need to be taken.

It was agreed that the CFO would coordinate all organizational communication with Dave, including conversations the auditor or other professionals might want to have with him. Harry was assigned to handle internal questions related to the matter and to inform the staff that they should not directly contact Dave or his family at this time.

Heather told the board's executive committee that it was the board's responsibility to act in the best interests of the corporation. This included exercising the appropriate level of care and making the necessary inquiries before taking action.

The next day a "crisis" team was formed to discuss how to inform the staff, trainers, and donors about the criminal implications of Dave's behavior; his future; and the legal and financial issues for the organization. Many different approaches and possible scenarios were discussed. Some immediate steps were taken. The executive committee of the board met and decided that Dave must resign or be fired. The total for actual amounts stolen grew daily as the accountant and finance vice president investigated further. They discovered that not only had Dave used CareED's checks, but he had also paid for personal items on the corporate credit card and had forged receipts. When confronted, Dave admitted to the additional thefts, though it was growing difficult to believe his initial remorse was genuine when he had not been forthcoming about the amounts he stole. He belatedly agreed to go through receipts and credit card statements and indicate what was for personal use.

Prior to the meeting at which Dave's resignation was accepted, the leadership team, Heather, and a public relations/crisis management expert met to prepare responses to the various interested parties that would be seeking answers—donors, staff, and media, among others—and to outline the information that would need to be communicated. The senior managers were briefed and prepared to respond to issues as they arose, including the wide range of emotions the staff would feel and the frustration and criticisms that key donors might express upon hearing the news. They were charged with working to protect the organization legally and responding fully so that it was clear that the organization was taking decisive action.

By the end of the next week, a board representative, the president, and Heather met with Dave and his wife to discuss the decision reached by the board and to answer questions they might have about the actions of the organization. Heather explained that the board did not intend to pursue criminal charges against him at that particular point in time but that a final decision would not be made immediately. The organization was still gathering additional information which the board would need to discuss. She stated that the integrity of the organization and the board's responsibility to retrieve any amounts stolen were the most important issues and that his ability to make restitution would be a significant factor in any decision made. She suggested that Dave retain his own legal counsel not only to understand the issues related to his termination, but also to explore his tax implications and potential criminal liability. She had learned from a criminal defense attorney that where funds are available for restitution by the embezzler or his family, it was possible to make a case to reduce the charges significantly and perhaps resolve the matter.

The board wrestled with whether it was appropriate to file criminal charges against Dave. The statute of limitations for grand larceny was 4 years, and it was important that the board take the time to gather the facts before determining whether to pursue criminal charges or even to file a civil action. The board learned that if they reported the crime, the investigation and handling of the matter would be taken out of their hands and controlled by law enforcement and the district attorney. They also learned that a prison term for Dave was probable and that while restitution might help reduce his sentence, it would not affect the criminal charge itself. Finally they discovered that criminal charges are rarely pursued by nonprofit organizations against such individuals.[2]

The board was unwilling to concede that additional action, including the bringing of criminal charges, would not occur. It was further possible that a third party, such as the Attorney General, the Internal Revenue Service, or others, might independently decide to bring action against Dave, as well as against the organization itself. Although it was unlikely, the possibility reinforced the need for the organization to recover the stolen funds, to put in place safeguards against other potential abuses, and to overhaul the system of checks and balances within the organization.

References

Gibelman, M., & Gelman, S. (2004). A loss of credibility: Patterns of wrongdoing among nongovernmental organizations. *VOLUNTAS. 15*(4), 355–381.

Gibelman, M., & Gelman, S. (2002). Should we have faith in faith-based organizations. *Nonprofit Management and Leadership, 13*(1), 49–65.

Gibelman, M., & Gelman, S. (2001). Very public scandals: Nongovernmental organizations in trouble, *VOLUNTAS, 12*(1), 49–66.

Endnotes

1. As reported in *The Wall Street Journal* and *Christianity Today*, John G. Bennett Jr., head of the Foundation for New Era Philanthropy, defrauded donors, including Laurence S. Rockefeller, William E. Simon, and charities, of $135 million by means of a pyramid scheme, promising to double the amount of a donor's gift in 6 months with funds from anonymous wealthy benefactors. In reality, he used incoming donations to pay off his outstanding double-your-money pledges and diverted substantial amounts to personal use and his for-profit companies. He was sentenced to 12 years in federal prison for carrying out what many believe to be the biggest charity fraud case in American history. A charismatic individual, he was described by acquaintances as a religious man committed to the Lord and his church. Considering he owed Rockefeller and Simon $11.4 million and $6.5 million, respectively, the loss by CareED was not monumental.
2. For a discussion of the types of scandals and the repercussions upon the individuals committing them, see a series of articles by Gibelman and Gelman:
   Gibelman, M., & Gelman, S. (2004). A loss of credibility: Patterns of wrongdoing among nongovernmental organizations. *VOLUNTAS*, 15(4), 355–381.
   Gibelman, M., & Gelman, S. (2002). Should we have faith in faith-based organizations. *Nonprofit Management and Leadership*, 13(1), 49–65.
   Gilbelman, M., & Gelman, S. (2001). Very public-scandals: Nongovernmental organizations in trouble, *VOLUNTAS*, 12(1), 49–66.

Case 9
Choice of an Executive Assistant

Tom Whetstone
Montreat College

Jack Brown, an active member of his local church, genuinely desired to serve as a Christian businessperson. At the age of 42, he was hired as the CEO of ZYX Corporation. The previous CEO's executive assistant, Miss Emma Cummings, who had served 30 years as personal secretary/executive assistant to the last six CEOs, decided that it was a good time for her to retire. This would allow Mr. Brown the opportunity to select her successor as he began his tenure.

The executive assistant to the CEO serves a strategic role. In larger organizations that have a team of executive officers, there may be a group of personal secretaries or executive assistants who jointly as well as separately exercise great influence. Whereas the executive officers generally have only a few years' tenure, especially in any one position, the executive assistants often make a career of their roles, typically having proven their company loyalty, skill, and intelligence by moving up from other secretarial positions in the organization. They do not make policy decisions but are most influential regarding access to policy makers. They value the public reputation and integrity of the organization and are gatekeepers between the CEO and its stakeholders, including owners, managers, employees, customers, suppliers, and the public at large.

CEO Brown, recognizing the critical importance of the position, asked human resources to set up interviews with the three most technically qualified candidates. The manager of human resources suggested the following three applicants:

1. **Cynthia Whyte**, 30, a college-educated teacher with excellent computer skills. Two years ago she married the vice president of human resources for ZYX Corporation. They have had no children, and she says she wishes to assume a full-time position for her personal career development. She emphasizes that she already knows the company well because of her husband.
2. **Edgar Greene**, 33, an employee of ZYX's engineering department. Since joining the company 3 years ago, he has risen rapidly due to outstanding performance reviews and a track record of productive suggestions. He has completed 2 years of college and is unmarried. He says that he is seeking the position as a way to broaden his business experience.
3. **Amanda Blue**, 56, a widow, is a recent early retiree who served 20 years as an executive assistant in ABC Corporation, a firm in ZYX's industry with headquarters in another state. She says that she seeks the executive assistant position because she misses her work, having realized she is a long way from needing to retire. In addition, whereas she recently moved to the community in order to be close to her grandchildren, she now realizes that she should work so as not to interfere too much with the child-raising efforts of her son and daughter-in-law.

After interviewing each of the candidates, Jack Brown is convinced that each is well-qualified in terms of the technical skills listed in the job specifications and that each, based on reference checks and interview discussions, appears to be a person of good Christian character. Moreover, each candidate appears to understand the requirements in the formal job description and has confirmed that he or she will accept the job, if offered. Jack faces a difficult choice and wants to make the right choice with godly wisdom.

Jack wonders if he needs to consider anything else—any special circumstances or relationship factors that will help him to determine the most appropriate choice. He wonders whether it would be culturally appropriate to hire a male as his personal executive assistant. He is unsure how he would relate to a significantly older personal assistant. He and his wife already have a close acquaintance with Cynthia and her husband, Bernard Whyte, not only because of company gatherings but also because they attend the same church and belong to the same neighborhood ministry group. Edgar Greene and Amanda Blue regularly attend other churches whose pastors have supplied good character references.

Jack has been very impressed with Bernard Whyte as a capable and innovative executive, one who is enthusiastic about some major strategic changes. Jack Brown thinks ZYX Corporation needs to meet its strategic objectives. In particular, Bernard has proposed hiring a small computer consulting firm with expertise in ZYX's industry. Jack knows this firm very well, having worked with it during college. He worked directly for its founder, who also is Bernard's uncle. Jack sees Bernard Whyte as someone with whom he needs to work closely in building the company, but wonders whether the other employees would see his hiring of Bernard's wife in the strategic gatekeeper role of executive assistant as an appropriate choice.

References

Butler, J. (1726/2001). Upon self-deceit. Fifteen sermons upon human nature. In Sommers, C., & Sommers, F. (Eds.). *Vice and virtue in everyday life: Introductory readings in ethics* (5th ed.) (pp. 397–403). Fort Worth, TX: Harcourt College Publishers.

Carroll, A. B., & Scherer, R. W. (2003/2005). Vital speeches of the day. In J.E. Richardson (Ed.), *Annual editions: Business ethics* (17th ed.), *59*(17) (pp. 529–533). Dubuque, IA: McGraw-Hill/Duskin.

Source: Christian Business Faculty Association, Journal of Biblical Integration in Business—Case Edition

Chewning, R. C., Eby, J. W., & Roels, S. J. (1990). *Business through the eyes of faith.* San Francisco, CA: Harper San Francisco.

DeGeorge, R. T. (2006). *Business ethics* (6th ed.). Upper Saddle River, NJ: Pearson Prentice Hall.

Derry, R. (1991). Institutionalizing ethical motivation: Reflections on Goodpaster's agenda. In Freeman, R. E. (Ed.). *Business ethics: The state of the art.* New York: Oxford University Press.

Holy Bible (New International Version). (1978). Grand Rapids, MI: Zondervan Publishing.

Jennings, M. M. (2003). *Business ethics: Case studies and selected readings* (4th ed.). Mason, OH: Thomson South-Western.

Jennings, M. M. (1999). *Business ethics: Case studies and selected readings* (3rd ed.). Eagan, MN: West Legal Studies in Business.

Sanders, J. O. (1980). *Spiritual leadership.* Chicago, IL: Moody Press.

Shaw, W. H. (2005). *Business ethics* (5th ed.). Belmont, CA: Thomson Wadsworth.

Case 10
How Gay-Friendly Should Your Workplace Be?

Michael Zigarelli
Regent University

Scott pulled into the parking lot, found a spot, and then pointed the rearview mirror toward his tie. Not perfect, but it never would be. IT guys don't do ties that often. "No matter," he thought as he gathered his interview materials. "These guys aren't going to judge me on my tie anyway."

Inside the building, the corporate headquarters of Master's Software Solutions, the group preparing to interview Scott for the software engineer position assembled in the conference room. Adorning the walls was an assortment of industry awards and Christian artwork. The photo of Jesus at a computer terminal was particularly intriguing and usually provided a nice icebreaker for the interviews.

Master's is a company of 53 employees, proudly run on Judeo-Christian values. It had always been run this way, ever since its founding 20 years ago by Walt DeVries, a seminarian turned entrepreneur and self-described "geek for God." And although the company's commitment to those values had never wavered, today's events would test something even deeper than the commitment—they would test what the company values actually mean.

Walt had been part of every interview since establishing the firm. From vice president to office clerk positions, Walt was central to the hiring process. He even insisted on having input into which interns Master's would accept from the local university. But otherwise, Walt was no micromanager and certainly no autocrat. Rather, he saw himself as a shepherd, caring for his employee flock, wanting to know each "sheep" personally. He also wanted to ensure the quality of the flock, so to speak, and the corporate culture of Master's; hence the meticulous attention to the staffing process.

As Walt walked into the conference room, there sat the three other members of the selection committee: two software engineers in their late 20s, Dave Anderson and Jeanie Thompson, and the firm's chief operating officer, Bill Maxwell. Self-effacing but brilliant, Bill was Walt's first employee and the only M.B.A. in the firm. In fact, Walt credited Bill with having saved Master's on a number of occasions from making unwise business decisions, some of which could have sunk the once-fledgling firm.

Walt closed the door and smiled at his team. "Thanks for coming, everyone," he began with customary genuineness. "And a special thank you to Jeanie for boiling down the resumes to these five candidates. As you know, we're going to do a group interview with each one this morning and then do individual interviews later today. Anything you want to discuss before Theresa shows in the first guy?"

Dave spoke right up. "Well, his resume shows he's qualified for the job—he practically got a 4.0 in college and he's worked three years for Microsoft. But what's with all this gay stuff at the bottom of the resume? President of the Gay-Lesbian-Bisexual Club in college? Member of GLEAM: the Gay and Lesbian Employees at Microsoft? Member of Digital Queers? *Digital Queers*? I don't understand why we're wasting our time. This is a company run on Christian values. It's in our mission statement. It's how we operate. It's even in the artwork on the walls. This seems like a no-brainer to me that we shouldn't even be interviewing this guy."

Dave was not one to mince words. But neither was Jeanie. "You can't be serious," she replied with a set of nonverbals that punctuated her irritation. "That's the same as saying that we think it's acceptable to discriminate against African-Americans or women!"

"Excuse me, but it's not even *close* to the same thing," Dave shot back. This was getting uncharacteristically emotional for a Master's discussion, but Jeanie had touched a sensitive chord. "You didn't choose to be female, and I didn't choose to be black!"

"And they don't choose to be gay," Jeanie returned calmly, considering it checkmate.

Gloves off, Dave raised his voice a half-notch. "No way. *No way.* You can't compare their struggle for acceptance with ours. And regardless of the choice issue, there's nothing in the Bible that says it's a sin to be black or a sin to be a woman. But there's plenty in there that says the practice of homosexuality is a sin."

Source: Christian Business Faculty Association, Journal of Biblical Integration in Business—Case Edition

Bill interjected in the interest of focus. "Look, we're getting a little off track here. This is just about whether we should be hiring this one guy."

"But actually, Bill, it's not," explained Dave. "It's about what inevitably follows when we compromise our principles. If we don't take a Christian stand on this, then we're letting a secular society drive our decision-making and ultimately our corporate policies. And when we do that, we lose our distinctives."

"Oh, so now bias is a Christian distinctive?" winced Jeanie. "I swear, Dave, you've gotta listen to yourself sometimes. This is why people stereotype us Christians the way they do."

Walt finally reeled them in. "Folks, I understand that you have some strong opinions about this, but we should have a more reasoned discussion here. Now, Jeanie, I've always admired the depth of your faith. So help me to understand why you *don't* think this guy is a problem for us."

"Sure, Walt," Jeanie answered, regaining her composure. "Here's how I see it. This company operates on Christian values, right? We consider God in every decision we make. And that's as it should be. So we need to do that here as well. My read of the Bible tells me that God doesn't play favorites—that non-discrimination is a Christian value. Everyone's created in the image of God, and so everyone's entitled to be treated with love, respect, and fairness. In business, then, I think we just need to consider people on their merits. We have absolutely no place judging people the way Dave is judging them."

Despite the insult, Dave gently offered his best rejoinder. "Can I interject something here? I'd be the last person to advocate arbitrary discrimination. It's ugly, and I know firsthand how much it hurts. But there is such a thing as *legitimate* discrimination. We do it all the time if an applicant or employee doesn't embrace our corporate values. And there's real urgency to do it here, too. If we follow the path that Jeanie's suggesting, we're helping normalize a lifestyle that God condemns. In my mind, that's more wrong than 'discriminating' against this applicant."

With a slight raise of his hand, soft-spoken Bill came at it from another angle. "Can I jump in here really quick? I don't know about the Bible issues and all that, but what I can tell you is this. Although it's technically not illegal in this state to consider sexual preference in personnel decisions,[1] it would be pretty unwise in our industry to maintain a hiring policy that intentionally screens out gays and lesbians. There are a lot of homosexuals in the IT industry. *A lot.* And if word gets around that we discriminate, we could lose some of our top commercial customers. What I'm saying," he clarified, "is that gay-friendly has become an industry norm. Just look at the gay affinity groups in IT companies and how pervasive domestic partner benefits have become. Like it or not, we have to recognize that if we don't become gay-friendly too, over time we're going to be at a competitive disadvantage. So maybe we should just hire the best and brightest we can find."

"That a good point, my friend," Walt said with a smile. "But I have to admit, I think I'm with Dave on this one. And if our business has to take a hit to do what's right in God's eyes, well, that's a cost of doing business God's way."

Jeanie was incredulous. "So that's it?!" she asked rhetorically. "We tell Mr. Superstar Applicant—a guy with unbelievable potential to move this company forward—to take a hike because we don't like who he sleeps with? And on top of that we risk losing some of our B-to-B customers? That makes no sense at all to me."

"Look, Jeanie," Walt responded, now provoked by her tone, "non-discrimination might sound innocuous—even godly to some—but the bottom line is that a 'neutral' non-discrimination stance on the issue is not really neutral at all. It implicitly validates the lifestyle. And if homosexuality is a lifestyle that's equally valid, then as a company and as a society we proceed down a very slippery slope."

Walt continued, but now in a more didactic tone. This was turning into a quintessential shepherding moment for him. "What I mean is this: non-discrimination implies there's nothing wrong with the lifestyle. That leads to demands for equal treatment, which in turn leads to insistence on things like domestic partner benefits and sensitivity training for employees. It's how gay marriage and gay adoption are becoming 'civil rights' in parts of this country. Ultimately, we end up with a culture that condones what God condemns. As Christians and a Christian company, I don't think it's wise to take even one step down that road, whatever the cost to our business."

As she saw it, much was at stake here. So Jeanie made one last attempt. "Quite frankly, Walt, I don't understand your theology on this at all. Or yours, Dave. What about the Christian calling to be witnesses, to actually introduce people to God? If we Christians are so exclusive that we never come into contact with people who are alienated from God, how will we ever bring more people into God's family? We just isolate ourselves in this little Christian bubble: we go to a Christian church, we send our kids to Christian schools, we run Christian companies dealing with a lot of Christian clients, all of our friends are Christians, we read Christian books and magazines. We're becoming separatists. We've developed our own comfortable subculture that insulates us from engaging people God might want us to reach."

"That's not what Jesus did," Jeanie continued, now as confident as she was entrenched. "In fact, he did just the opposite. He associated freely with all people, regardless of their lifestyle or their past, and through those relationships, he pointed people to God. What I think is that we should open our doors—and our minds—and do the same."

Walt was thoughtful, his eyes reflecting the conflict in his heart. "That's a valid point, too, Jeanie," he conceded. "I'm left wondering, though, where Jesus would draw the line in business. At nondiscrimination? At equivalent benefits? And what about the customer side of things? What happens if a gay rights group wants us to develop some software for them? Do we just do it? Wouldn't we be advancing their movement by creating something for them?"

Nobody spoke for a several seconds. Finally, Walt broke the silence, framing the challenge ahead. "This is a hard issue," he said with a slow shake of his head. "From a Christian perspective, just how gay-friendly should a company be?"

A knock at the door interrupted their deliberations. Theresa stuck her head in. "Scott Mitchell's here for his 9 a.m. interview. Are you ready for him?" she asked.

"That's a good question," Walt replied, chuckling at the timing of her query. "I'm not sure . . . but show him in anyway."

A few moments later, Scott walked in. Clean cut. Professional. Smartly dressed (except for his crooked tie). He extended a cheerful "Good morning!" to the group. Walt stood, smiled, and shook Scott's hand. The group then proceeded to interview Scott, offering no hint of the seeming dilemma that his presence created for the company.

Endnote

1. As of the writing of this case, there is no federal law in the United States that prohibits companies from considering sexual preference when making personnel decisions. However, 13 states and the District of Columbia, as well as approximately 200 U.S. cities, have enacted workplace anti-discrimination laws that apply within their jurisdiction. This case is set in a state and city where the employment-at-will doctrine prevails on such matters; that is, Master's Software would not be violating any federal, state, or local law by refusing to interview Scott on the basis of his sexual preference.

Glindex

D

Q

R

S

U

V

W

X

Y

Z